ORGANISING HISTORY

A Centenary of SIPTU, 1909–2009

ORGANISING HISTORY

A Centenary of SIPTU, 1909–2009

FRANCIS DEVINE ∿

for Declan Clancy
with fraternal best wishes,

francy Dwine

Gill & Macmillan

Gill & Macmillan Ltd
Hume Avenue, Park West, Dublin 12
with associated companies throughout the world
www.gillmacmillan.ie

© Francis Devine 2009
978 07171 4535 5

Index compiled by Verba Editing House
Typography design by Make Communication
Print origination by Carole Lynch
Printed by ColourBooks Ltd, Dublin

This book is typeset in Linotype Minion and
Neue Helvetica.

The paper used in this book comes from the wood
pulp of managed forests. For every tree felled,
at least one tree is planted, thereby renewing
natural resources.

A CIP catalogue record for this book is available
from the British Library.

5 4 3 2 1

CONTENTS

FOREWORD

Sisters and Brothers,

It is a great honour to write this foreword to SIPTU's *Organising History* written by Francis Devine. In many ways it is a history of the modern Irish State, from the early years of the struggle for independence, through the difficult formative decades, the equally difficult period of post-war adjustment and the gradual evolution of policies that would finally ensure the belated modernisation of our economy and society. Throughout the past century, our Union has always been a champion of social justice and the concept that the economy must serve the people rather than allow the people to be slaves to the rich and powerful in our society. That was the guiding principle of our founding fathers, most memorably articulated by Jim Larkin and James Connolly. Unfortunately, there are still 'wage slaves' in Ireland, especially among vulnerable groups, and during this current recession we are witnessing a sustained attack on the minimum wage and social welfare rates from those whose greed knows no bounds.

Larkin and Connolly saw the trade union movement as being about much more than simply securing better pay and conditions for members, important as these objectives were. The movement they helped found, with thousands of other pioneers, was fundamentally about transforming society and about securing control of the commanding heights of the economy to serve the interests of those who had created the wealth in the first place—ordinary working people. It was for that reason they were among the primary movers of the proposal to establish the Irish Labour Party in 1912. That party started its life as an integral part of the Irish Trade Union Congress and SIPTU continues the long association with it today, conscious of our need to engage in the political process at all levels.

The development of Social Partnership over the past twenty-two years adds another dimension to the political process in its broadest sense. SIPTU and its founding affiliates played a leading role in the debate within the trade union movement—as well as with the Government and the employers—to transform the old-style National Wage Agreements into something more substantial that gave us a real say in wider social and economic policy formation. Needless to say, it is far from perfect and it has not prevented us campaigning through other means on important issues such as tax reform, education, protecting our health services and defending employment standards.

Organising History assesses the role of SIPTU and its constituent unions over the past century. As such, it will be an invaluable resource for labour and social historians who want to understand the problems, the aspirations and the role played by ordinary working people in forging modern Ireland. In many ways our role has been unique. Few other trade union movements in Europe during the early twentieth century played such an important part in the struggle for national independence of the country in which they were based.

It can be argued that the Easter Rising might never have occurred without the involvement of James Connolly and the Irish Citizen Army. Certainly the political programme outlined in the 1916 Proclamation, printed in the basement of Liberty Hall, the Union's Headquarters, would have been far less radical and democratic in its content. After Connolly's death the Labour Movement may not have played such a central role in the strategic direction of events, but major elements of the struggle, such as the adoption of the Democratic Programme of the First Dáil, the General Strike against Conscription, and the ban on the movement of troops and munitions during the War of Independence, would not have occurred without our involvement.

Organising History gives a detailed account of how the Union continued to develop and adapt to new challenges that confronted organised workers in the subsequent decades. Perhaps the most important lesson to draw from it is the way that, despite disagreements about strategy and tactics that were vehement at times, the various unions that eventually came together to form and expand SIPTU all recognised the value of unity and that we are all stronger working together rather than pursuing what were usually the same agendas separately. In doing so we were doing no more than recognising a fundamental trade union principle that in unity is strength.

While some of the challenges we face today are new, and we must adopt new means to meet them, others have not changed at all. After one hundred years we are still fighting for recognition, for the right to organise and represent workers in the workplace. If we played a uniquely important role in securing the independence of this State we received little thanks for it from the powerful political and business elites that continue to dominate it. Indeed, we are almost unique in Europe in that workers in Ireland do not have a right to union representation and collective bargaining as a legal entitlement. It is, we suppose, a back-handed compliment to our effectiveness in representing workers' interests that employers want to keep us out of as many workplaces as possible. But if we are to keep faith with those who went before us we must ensure that workers do not have to wait another 100 years to secure the basic civil right to organise and bargain with their employers.

Finally, we wish to wholeheartedly congratulate Francy on a magnificent job of work, painstakingly researched and written with conviction and passion. He has delivered what was asked of him and he has done himself proud, but more, he has done our Union proud as we mark our Centenary of organising for fairness at work and justice in society.

Jack O'Connor	Brendan Hayes	Joe O'Flynn
Jack O'Connor	**Brendan Hayes**	**Joe O'Flynn**
General President	**Vice-President**	**General Secretary**

PREFACE

In commissioning this history the General Secretary of SIPTU, Joe O'Flynn, gave three instructions: that it be accessible, that it consist of one volume, and that the 'union be let speak for itself.' I have endeavoured to honour those instructions.

'One volume' was most problematic: how to confine 100 years—166 years, given two unions from 1924 to 1990—within two covers? To facilitate access, each chapter follows a template, with sections on membership, organisation and finance, women, wages and disputes, economic and social policy, safety and health, education and training, solidarity, and politics. After 1924, dealing with two distinct organisations simultaneously was challenging. They are treated separately. From the late 1920s the ITGWU and WUI led parallel existences, which facilitated this approach. There is, necessarily, some repetition as events are looked at from the two viewpoints. To balance the sectionalised narrative, the book's five parts are prefaced by short contextual essays, and each chapter concludes with some reflections.

The union 'speaks for itself,' as the evidence is overwhelmingly drawn from its own records and publications.

Time was the constant curse, precluding an intended extensive use of oral history. I have drawn on Paddy Cardiff's and Michael Moynihan's memoirs, published by the Irish Labour History Society and SIPTU,[1] unpublished interviews with John F. Carroll, and observations from those reading drafts of the book, particularly Charles Callan, Barry Desmond, Tom Geraghty and Jack McGinley. The examination of SIPTU Executive Council minutes or of ICTU Reports was not possible. Norman Croke, Head of SIPTU College, facilitated the work, but from the commencement in September 2005 my teaching commitments were maintained for a year. In addition, the union requested two pamphlets, by-products of the main work.[2] From July 2006 research became virtually full-time, but—as with all Officials—other insistent demands had to be met.[3] To meet the deadline of publication for the union's Centenary, September 2008 was the cut-off date.

Trade unionism abounds with initials and acronyms. A table of those used in this book is given below. Depending on the context, 'Congress' may mean the ITUC, CIU or ICTU.

ACKNOWLEDGEMENTS

I am very grateful for the assistance and guidance of many institutions and individuals: the National Library of Ireland, especially Gerard Lyne, Tom Desmond and Gerry McLoughlin; Catriona Crowe, Brian Donnelly and staff, National Archives; Mary Clark, Máire Kennedy, Clodagh Kingston, Eithne Massey and staff, Dublin City Archive and Library; Ed Penrose and staff, Irish Labour History Society Archives; Howth Library; the Registrar of Friendly Societies; the Public Record Office of Northern Ireland; the Linen Hall Library, Belfast; the National Library of Scotland; Peter Rigney, Irish Congress of Trade Unions; John B. and Alice Smethurst, Ruth Frow, Royston Futter, Eric Taplin and the Working-Class Movement Library, Manchester, and North-West Labour History Society; and Mick Naughton (Troon). Union comrades, especially Bill Attley, Bernard Byrne, Breda Cardiff, John F. Carroll, Tom Dunne, John Fay, Tom Garry, Dympna Harper, Peter Keating, Martin Naughton, Manus O'Riordan, Deirdre Price, Jim Quinn, Anne Speed and Tony Walsh, have been of great assistance and encouragement. Patricia King first suggested that I take on the task; and Norman Croke, Jean Kennedy, Eileen Meier, Carol Murphy and SIPTU College workmates facilitated every request for information and provided tremendous support. Others who added weight to the wheel included Liam McBrinn, Belfast; Tom Morrissey, Donal Nevin and Pádraig Yeates, who trod inspirational paths before me; my fellow-editors of *Saothar*, John Horne, Bob Purdie and Emmet O'Connor, who taught me so much; all ILHS comrades over many years, especially Paddy Bergin, Brendan Byrne, Tom Neiland Crean, Paul Cullen, Ken Hannigan, Theresa Moriarty, Greagóir Ó Dúill, Niamh Puirséil, Fionnuala Richardson, Eddie Soye and Éamon Thornton; Eugene McCartan, Communist Party of Ireland; Séamus Scally, Labour Party; and, from Howth, Paddy Daly, Howard Davies and Diarmuid Ó Cathasaigh. With Hugh Geraghty's death in 2007 I lost a valued comrade and inspiration. I am indebted, over many years, to Christy Hammond, Richard Kelly and Mark Dennis, CRM Design and Print, for a general education in words.

Drafts were perused and improved by Norman Croke, Catriona Crowe, Brendan Hayes, Joe O'Flynn, Jack O'Connor, Manus O'Riordan, John P. Swift and Helga Woggon (Berlin). Charles Callan, Barry Desmond, Tom Geraghty and Jack McGinley offered constructive criticism and advice, not all of it taken, providing valuable insights and contexts from their collective experiences as activists within the union and the movement. Fergus D'Arcy acted as academic adviser throughout, providing meticulous assessments, detailed critiques and tremendous encouragement.

Fergal Tobin, Publishing Director, Deirdre Rennison Kunz, Managing Editor, and Neil Ryan, Photo Researcher, Gill & Macmillan, and Séamas Ó Brógáin provided professionalism and tolerance in bringing the manuscript to publication. Family members Ann Riordan, Caoimhe, Caoilfhionn and Odharnaith Ní Dhuibhinn, Fiachra Ó Duibhinn, Grace Devine and Posh the Dog endured my temperamental moments, apparent untidiness and long absences, mental and physical. As with any work, ultimately it is a collective effort, although only I can accept responsibility for inaccuracies, errors and limitations in writing.

Finally, I owe special acknowledgement to Joe O'Flynn, who has been boss, comrade and friend throughout, providing leadership and drive but great freedom for the process of research and writing.

If anyone is unintentionally excluded from the acknowledgements, forgive me. I owe much to so many comrades within the movement, particularly SIPTU and the ILHS. In the task of organising history, no more than in other organisational briefs, learning comes from all sources. I can only sincerely hope that I have not let too many down, not least past and future members of an indisputably great organisation—our union.

As to the title, *Organising History,* it was agreed upon to reflect the fact that no Labour history just happens, other than that of repression, which is a given constant. Organising activity, individually and collectively, accounted for all union achievements, its growth and impact on society. That same organisation will ensure that it is never 'confined to history,' the task for today's and tomorrow's members.

NOTE ON SOURCES

Within this history there are patent disparities in the length of treatment of the ITGWU and WUI. Apart from factors of size and geographical distribution, this reflects the relative strengths and weaknesses of source material. The ITGWU published an Annual Report from 1918, the WUI only from 1947. A full set of ITGWU Executive or National Executive Council minutes exists from 1918 and before that, within the O'Brien Papers in the National Library, the minutes of Dublin No. 1 Branch, which acted effectually as the Executive. For the WUI there are large gaps. Minutes of the General Executive Council exist only for February to July 1938, June 1946 to 3 June 1949 and 8 June 1956 to December 1989 (with the exception of a missing volume, 1972–79). The ITGWU produced a newspaper from 1911 to 1927 and from 1948 to 1989, and copies of virtually all issues survive.[4] ITGWU sources are held in the National Library of Ireland (William O'Brien Papers and O'Brien-Kennedy Papers, ITGWU Special List A8 and C. Desmond Greaves Papers).[5] In addition, Executive minutes and published papers are held in SIPTU College, Liberty Hall, and the Irish Labour History Society Archives.[6]

For the WUI, newspapers were less frequent and, in the case of *Bulletin,* largely untraceable. The exclusion of the WUI from the ITUC from 1924 to 1945 imposed another limitation. Larkin was a Delegate to Dublin Trades Union Council from 1936. The minutes of DTUC survive in the National Library and the Labour History Society Archives, but time precluded reference to them.

ABBREVIATIONS

AGEMOU	Automobile, General Engineering and Mechanical Operatives' Union
AHSU	Alliance of Health Service Unions
AOH	Ancient Order of Hibernians
ASE	Amalgamated Society of Engineers
ASLEF	Amalgamated Society of Locomotive Engineers and Firemen
ASRS	Amalgamated Society of Railway Servants
ASTMS	Association of Scientific, Technical and Managerial Staffs
ATGWU	Amalgamated Transport and General Workers' Union
AUEW	Amalgamated Union of Engineering Workers
AUEW-TASS	Amalgamated Union of Engineering Workers, Technical and Supervisory Section
B&I Line	British and Irish Steam Packet Company
BIM	An Bord Iascaigh Mhara
BTG	Building Trades Group (Dublin Trades Council)
CIF	Construction Industry Federation
CII	Confederation of Irish Industry
CIU	Congress of Irish Unions / Comhar Ceard Éireann
CPGB	Communist Party of Great Britain
CPI	Communist Party of Ireland
DCTU	Dublin Council of Trade Unions
DMP	Dublin Metropolitan Police
DTPS	Dublin Typographical Provident Society
DTUC	Dublin Trades Union Council ('Dublin Trades Council')
DUTC	Dublin United Tramways Company (later Dublin United Transport Company)
EC	Executive Council
EEC	European Economic Community
ESRI	Economic and Social Research Institute
ETUC	European Trade Union Confederation
FÁS	An Foras Áiseanna Saothair (the Training and Employment Authority)
FETAC	Further Education and Training Awards Council
FRW	Federation of Rural Workers
FUE	Federated Union of Employers
FWUI	Federated Workers' Union of Ireland

GEC	General Executive Committee (WUI and FWUI)
HETAC	Higher Education and Training Awards Council
HSA	Health and Safety Authority
IBEC	Irish Business and Employers' Confederation
ICTU	Irish Congress of Trade Unions
IDATU	Irish Distributive and Administrative Trade Union
IEIU	Irish Engineering and Industrial Union
IFA	Irish Farmers' Association
IFTU	International Federation of Trade Unions
ILHS	Irish Labour History Society
ILO	International Labour Organisation
ILP&TUC	Irish Labour Party and Trades Union Congress
IMETU	Irish Municipal Employees' Trade Union
IMHWU	Irish Mental Hospital Workers' Union
IRB	Irish Republican Brotherhood
IRU	Irish Railwaymen's Union
ISPWU	Irish Seamen's and Port Workers' Union
ITGWU	Irish Transport and General Workers' Union
ITUC	Irish Trades Union Congress
ITUC&LP	Irish Trades Union Congress and Labour Party
ITUT	Irish Trade Union Trust
IUDWC	Irish Union of Distributive Workers and Clerks
IWL	Irish Worker League
IWW	Industrial Workers of the World ('Wobblies')
IWWU	Irish Women Workers' Union
JIC	Joint Industrial Council
JLC	Joint Labour Committee
LGPSU	Local Government and Public Services Union
MPGWU	Marine, Port and General Workers' Union
MSF	Manufacturing, Science and Finance Union
NATE	National Association of Transport Employees
NCEA	National Council for Educational Awards
NEC	National Executive Council (ITGWU and SIPTU)
NILP	Northern Ireland Labour Party
NLP	National Labour Party
NSFU	National Sailors' and Firemen's Union
NUDL	National Union of Dock Labourers
NUR	National Union of Railwaymen
NVQ	National Vocational Qualification
OBU	'One Big Union'
PAYE	pay-as-you-earn (income tax)
PRSI	Pay-Related Social Insurance

PUOITUM	Provisional United Organisation of the Irish Trade Union Movement
RCA	Railway Clerks' Association
RIC	Royal Irish Constabulary
SIPTU	Services, Industrial and Professional Trade Union
SPI	Socialist Party of Ireland / Cumannacht na hÉireann (1910–21)
TUC	Trades Union Congress
UBLTU	United Builders' Labourers' Trade Union
UIL	United Irish League (Irish Party)
WU	Workers' Union (a British union formed in 1898 and amalgamated with the [British] TGWU in 1929)
WUI	Workers' Union of Ireland

A NOTE ON MONEY

Until February 1971 the Irish pound was divided into 20 shillings, each of 12 pence. The symbol *s* was used for shillings and *d* for pence (e.g. 10s 6d), but such sums were also written in the form 10/6 ('ten and six'), while amounts in shillings only were often written in the form 10/–. Relatively small amounts greater than £1 were sometimes given in shillings only: thus 50s might be written instead of £2 10s. From 1971 to 1990 the pound was divided into 100 pence, for which the symbol *p* was used.

Chapter 1 ~

BEFORE LARKIN: TRADE UNIONISM IN THE NEW CENTURY

CRAFT AND TRADE

By 1900, trade unionism was firmly established as a voice of working-class expression within work-places and in the public conscience. Organisation began among the trades, often confined to one town or District or, in Dublin, one locality within the city, as with bakers. Trade unions were defined and confined by craft and local economic considerations. They developed complex recognition arrangements for entry to their trade through apprenticeship, defended the trade's parameters from encroachment by competing crafts, and kept a close eye on technological developments that threatened the dilution of skill. Controlled entry limited the supply of labour and maintained wages. Often, close relations developed with the masters, upon whom work depended, although strikes took place in defence of wages, job content, dismissed members or working conditions.

AMALGAMATED SOCIETIES AND CONGRESS

From 1850 on, 'New Model' unions appeared in Britain. Organisations took on a 'national' character through amalgamation or the absorption of local societies, developing internal governance through Rules that provided for a Head Office, a National Executive and elected Officers, Branch or District Committees, and the centralisation of funds and dispensing of benefits. Before the provision of state welfare, these benefits—the 'Friendly Society' aspect of unions—provided for members in times of unemployment, sickness, death, emigration or dispute. The assertion of craft status and the provision of social insurance attracted members. Admission, however, was exclusive to 'time-served' craftsmen, excluding women and the unskilled. Indeed until the 1880s organisation among unskilled workers was rare and short-lived. For crafts there were regular attempts to federate or associate societies within towns, for the purposes of collective solidarity, lobbying municipal authorities and co-ordinating activities on campaigns in what would now be called Trades Councils.

The Amalgamated Society of Engineers, formed in 1851, typified 'New Model' organisation and quickly proved attractive to Irish members.[1] Irish societies were absorbed into these 'national' bodies, with their Head Office usually in London or Manchester. They allowed Irish workers to be part of a more solid, financially secure body. Should the need ever arise to travel to Britain for work they possessed a card that was instantly recognisable and acceptable, and a Lodge or Branch to provide assistance, work contacts and comradeship.

Attacks on trade unionism led to the Royal Commission on Labour in 1867 and threatened legislation to remove union freedoms. Workers united to form the Trades Union Congress in 1868 to petition against repression. The TUC Parliamentary Committee did good work, and the resultant Trade Union Act (1871), granting unions full legal status, remarkably still remains, in part, on the Irish statute book. It is partly under the 1871 Act that SIPTU is registered in the Republic.

Employers' concerns about picketing and strikes were assuaged by the enactment of the Criminal Law Amendment Act (1871) and the Conspiracy and Protection of Property Act (1875). These Acts allowed the criminal prosecution of strikers and introduced such concepts as 'watching and besetting,' which imposed limits on who might picket and where.

Britain's Great Depression, 1873–1896, a general slowdown of economic activity, and a tendency for craft unions to be deferential—summed up by a common slogan, 'Defence, not defiance'—meant that these legal restrictions were little handicap for a movement that concentrated on the pursuit of respectability, informed lobbying, and used such expressions as the 'working classes'. In contemporary parlance, this was 'tuppence ha'penny looking down on tuppence.' Political aspirations were few and, where they did exist, were expressed in support for Nationalist or Unionist politicians. There was little concept of independent labour representation.

Belfast and District Trades Union Council, established in 1881, and Dublin Trades Council, established in 1886, reflected gathering organisation. The TUC, however, was the 'Parliament of Labour'. It met in Dublin in 1880 and in Belfast in 1893. Increasing militancy and Socialist aspirations were brought in by Trades Council Delegates, drawn from the lower ranks of local leadership, rather than more conservative and cautious national officers. It led to the Trades Councils' exclusion from the Parliamentary Committee. This tipped Belfast Trades Council into agreeing, after years of debate, to the formation of an Irish Trades Union Congress in 1894. This was not a challenge to the British TUC, and many Irish unions remained active affiliates of the TUC. The ITUC dealt with Irish issues, often neglected by the TUC, and co-ordinated matters within Ireland. The nature and culture of trade unionism was, however, rapidly changing.

THE RISE OF THE UNSKILLED
As industrialisation advanced, more and more workers were employed in unskilled jobs: machine-minders, packers and sorters, transport and dock workers, railway

workers and seamen, service, sales and distribution staffs, entertainment, hotel and catering workers. They were beneath the organisational dignity of craft societies. They worked very long hours for extremely low wages, when lucky enough to gain employment. Many were employed casually, and only when work was available. Dockers were never permanently employed. In Dublin and Belfast a 'spellsman' was someone literally employed for a 'spell' of work—a few hours or the duration of a cargo's unloading or loading.

As urban populations grew and rural workers were driven off the land, attracted to the apparent opportunities of cities and towns, a 'reserve army of labour' was constantly available to employers. Attempts at organisation among the unskilled were met by mass dismissals and the recruitment of substitute workers.

In the late 1880s 'New Unions' extended organisation downward to the unskilled, including women. To combat Lock-Outs by employers and the use of scab labour, during disputes they used new tactics of mass picketing—'an injury to one is the concern of all'—'blacking' and lightning strikes. New Unions were formed among emigrant Irish dockers in Glasgow, Liverpool and London.

The Great London Dock Strike of 1889 epitomised the unskilled rebellion, with thousands marching for the 'full orb of the docker's tanner'—sixpence an hour. Unable to raise large reserves from poorly paid, casually employed members, the New Unions concentrated funds for dispute purposes, abandoning the elaborate range of benefits provided by the craft unions. They argued, Why should the state not provide from the wealth that, after all, workers produced? They demanded the provision of social welfare and the nationalisation of the means of production, distribution and exchange. Tuppence did not want to emulate tuppence ha'penny: it wanted a society in which workers had ownership and control of the wealth they produced to eliminate poverty, poor housing, illness and inequality of opportunity. In short, New Unionism brought a militant, Socialist vision.

In the countryside the Land Law (Ireland) Act (1881) had a positive impact on rural workers' families, and Charles Stewart Parnell restructured the Land League to demand improvements in workers' conditions. Michael Davitt formed the Irish Democratic Labour Federation, which led to the Irish Land and Labour Association, formed at Limerick Junction in 1894. It demanded land and houses for the people, work and wages, education, state pensions, and all local rents to be paid by ground landlords.

By 1900 the ITUC represented 67,000 workers, almost exclusively drawn from craft unions. New Unionism in Ireland had withered away. Congress was strongly influenced by the 'Amalgamated' (British) unions, which, consciously or unconsciously, 'colonised' the Irish movement, imposing a conservative and confining vision averse to Socialist aspirations. At best they were ambivalent on the National Question. The fence was the most convenient seat when the risk of dividing a movement for or against Home Rule threatened. Trades Councils displayed hostile attitudes to unskilled unions and reflected the dominant, local politics of their Unionist or Nationalist masters.

LABOUR POLITICS

Failing to physically repress the unskilled, employers turned to law. A series of limiting decisions culminated in the Taff Vale Case in 1901, which turned earlier legislation on its head. Allowing employers to sue for damages in the event of a strike, in effect it made union funds available to employers. Trade unionism's very existence was threatened. Those who had hitherto fought shy of abandoning Liberal politics or argued against independent working-class political expression recognised that the law could be reversed only in Parliament. The Labour Party emerged from the Labour Electoral Association in 1901. Forty-six Labour members entered the House of Commons after the General Election of 1906, and held the balance of power. They persuaded the Liberal Government to enact the Trade Disputes Act (1906). This introduced the concept of immunity from damages, provided that workers and their unions were engaged in a 'trade dispute'. This Act remained on the Irish statute book until the introduction of the Industrial Relations Act (1990).

In Ireland, Socialist politics had a tougher time. The Irish Socialist Republican Party, Ireland's first Marxist Party, employed James Connolly from 1896 to 1903; but after his emigration to the United States radical Socialist politics dimmed.[2] The Labour Electoral Association set up Irish Branches and succeeded in getting members elected to local authorities, but increasingly tensions arose around the national question. Labour quickly discovered that it had enemies in the Unionist and Nationalist camps, foreshadowing tensions that would be a central, virtually permanent divisive element.

The Dublin Labour Party held a celebration dinner after the 1906 General Election to fête Michael Davitt, who had campaigned tirelessly on labour's behalf throughout Britain's 'Irish' constituencies.

Before Larkin's arrival, Irish trade unionism could be characterised as cautious and conservative. Dominated by Branches of British 'Amalgamated' craft unions, it was content with respectability rather than hungry for revolution, social or national. On 26 January 1907 James Larkin, Liverpool Organiser for the National Union of Dock Labourers, arrived in Belfast. Trade unionism in Ireland was about to change, change utterly.

Chapter 2 ~

THE ARRIVAL OF LARKIN, 1907–8

James Larkin's arrival brought 'New Unionism' to Ireland, 'a generation late.' It had flared in the 1880s and 90s and has been underestimated, but it did not flourish. The unionising of coal porters was killed off by a prolonged slump from 1884 to 1887. After this, organisation was mainly through two British unions: in the south, east and west the National Union of Gasworkers and General Labourers (with Head Office in London) and in Ulster the National Amalgamated Union of Labour (with Head Office in Newcastle-upon-Tyne), a union started among unskilled shipbuilding and engineering workers. The United Labourers of Ireland Trade Union, formed in 1889, catered for builders' labourers, while the United Corporation Workmen of Dublin Trade Union—later the Irish Municipal Employees' Trade Union—formed in 1883, survived in Dublin.[1]

Michael Davitt's Democratic Labour League led to the Land and Labour Associations organising among rural workers, with political agitation for land reform and labourers' cottages. Belfast Trades Council set up the Textile Operatives' Society of Ireland and Flaxroughers' Union among unskilled textile workers.

The National Union of Dock Labourers had been founded in Glasgow in 1889, largely among emigrant Irish. Its three leading figures, Richard McGhee, Edward McHugh and Michael McKeown, 'the Three Macs', were Irish. The inevitable recognition dispute was mediated by Michael Davitt MP. The NUDL quickly spread to Liverpool and to Ireland, where McKeown built Branches in Belfast, Cork, Drogheda, Dublin, Galway, Limerick and Newry, often in parallel with the National Sailors' and Firemen's Union. In 1891, 2,009 of the NUDL's 14,552 members were in fourteen Irish Branches. The first Branch outside Glasgow was in Belfast, established in April 1889.

The fortunes of the NUDL fluctuated wildly. By 1895 it had only fifteen Branches, three of them in Ireland: in Derry, Drogheda and Cork. Cork was debarred after shenanigans with its Branch Secretary and funds. The difficulty of maintaining organisation among casually employed dockers in the face of economic misfortunes proved the stumbling block to a permanent waterfront presence. Although organising Irish workers, the NUDL did not consider them a priority and, given the

additional costs and the distance and logistics involved, did not show the same concern about reverses in membership as in their Merseyside and Scottish heartlands.
By 1900 the NUDL was virtually defunct in Ireland.[2] In 1907, now based in Liverpool,
with James Sexton as General Secretary, the NUDL despatched James Larkin as
Organiser to Ireland to revivify moribund Branches.

Larkin was born in 41 Combermere Street, Liverpool, on 4 February 1874, the
son of Irish immigrants, James Larkin and Mary Ann McNulty. After an apprenticeship in engineering, labouring and sporadic unemployment, a naturally adven-
turous character led Larkin to go to sea in 1893 before returning and seeking dock
work. He was active in the Independent Labour Party and a strong believer in
temperance if not a strong trade unionist. Until 1905 at least he held ambivalent
views on unions. Eventually he was spotted by T. and J. Harrison, a large firm at
South End Docks, Liverpool, having impressed them as a 'model employee'. Eric
Taplin reflected that 'temperance was a rare virtue' among dockers. Larkin was 'an
honest, diligent worker who had the added sterling quality of driving his men hard.'
He was not popular among dock porters: they saw him as a 'cod boss' and nick-
named him 'the Rusher' for the way he drove them. Nevertheless he was 'respected
for his honesty and fairness.' He took no part in the petty corruption that was most
foremen's stock in trade.[3]

Harrisons' long honoured an Agreement made in 1890 with the NUDL that
provided for recognition and negotiating machinery but that expressly excluded
foremen from joining the union. On 27 June 1905 eight hundred men 'marched out
on unofficial strike demanding that the foremen rejoin or be discharged.' Sexton
repudiated their actions, fearful perhaps that Harrisons would take this opportunity to reject the NUDL, whose membership base was in the firm. Blacklegs were
imported, and violence ensued. Sexton tried to settle matters by accepting that foremen need not join if old conditions could be returned to. Harrisons refused. Larkin
went out with his men.

While the dispute was a bad blow to Sexton, 'it was the making of Larkin. From
obscurity he became known throughout the Liverpool waterfront as a militant
Leader of men.' In 1906 the young firebrand was put on the NUDL payroll as
National Organiser, at a wage of £2 10s a week—his first job as a union Official.
Sexton later claimed that he had opposed the appointment, but Larkin was his
Election Agent when he was successfully returned to Liverpool Corporation in
1905 and in the 1906 General Election in the West Toxteth constituency. Sexton
acknowledged that he owed much to Larkin, who 'plunged recklessly into the fray,'
displaying 'an energy that was almost superhuman ... nothing could frighten Jim.'
He was 'convinced that it was largely owing to Larkin's overwhelming labour that
we reduced a Tory majority from 4,000 to 500, but I would rather not give an
opinion on some of the methods he adopted.'[4]

Sexton saw Larkin's worth and potential at first hand. He was impressed and
intimidated in equal measure. The two were very different. Sexton was cautious,
pragmatic and conciliatory. He believed that progress was best achieved through

moral argument, gentle persuasion and legal reform. He had no pressing ambition to overturn capitalism. Larkin, in contrast, was driven by a sense of mission. As National Organiser he breathed life into a fading organisation. In 1905 the NUDL had 13,485 members; by 1908 this had risen to 22,075 as a consequence of Larkin's vision, energy and barn-storming tour of Preston, Aberdeen, Glasgow and Govan. By May 1907 Derry was a 'vast improvement' and the Belfast Branch was revived, with virtually all 3,000 dockers catered for in two Branches. Sexton and his Executive in England had reservations about expansion in Ireland, not sharing Larkin's growing belief in the need for separate Irish organisation nor his horror at the conditions he found at the dockside and its adjacent tenements.

THE BELFAST DOCKERS' AND CARTERS' STRIKE

Larkin arrived in Belfast and lodged with his old Liverpool friend Thomas Johnson, then a member of Belfast Trades Council and later Leader of the Irish Labour Party. He sought out Michael McKeown, a Nationalist City Councillor and NUDL pioneer, and appointed him Branch Secretary. By April they had 4,000 members, with three offices in Belfast and Derry. Cross-channel dockers, mainly Protestant, had rooms at 11 Victoria Street, Belfast; deep-sea men, largely Catholic, at 41 Bridge End. The NUDL affiliated to Belfast and District Trades Union Council on 9 April.

Larkin had first arrived as an NUDL Delegate to the British Labour Party Conference on 20 January. John Gray observes that he 'came as no evangel' and that 'no-one foresaw the explosive consequences of his arrival.' The 'prevailing view of the British and Irish trade union leaderships was that the strike was an outmoded weapon, that a new age of arbitration and conciliation was dawning, helped by the election of a Liberal Government in 1906.'

The NUDL Executive saw the subsequent Belfast dockers' and carters' strike as the longest conflict they had endured. It cost the union more than £7,000, a tremendous sum in relation to its balance sheet. Sexton attempted to manipulate a settlement 'that left the striking dockers isolated.' In November he 'positively misled the carters and cranemen who struck a second time into believing that he had negotiated an honourable return to work when he had not done so.' Sexton was damned, while Larkin 'emerged a popular hero.'[5] The die of mutual animosity was cast.

This clash of visions, beliefs and styles led Larkin to be frustrated with Sexton. Eric Taplin sees Larkin's Liverpool years as 'the apprenticeship of a revolutionary.' His 'experience in Liverpool was critical,' giving him 'the opportunity to discover his powers of leadership and oratory, to harness his restless energy to a practical cause' and to 'use the trade union movement as a vehicle for the realisation of his vision of a new society of brotherhood and unity.' Larkin's trade unionism 'embraced the totality of people's lives not only for industrial change but also political and social revolution, to create a dignified life for all. To Sexton, this was "Larkinitis".'[6]

Belfast laid bare other, more fundamental truths. Viewed as a purely industrial dispute, the Belfast strike never involved more than 3,500 men. But the spontaneous, non-sectarian mobilisation was what caught the worried eye of authority and baffled British union leaders. Between five and 10,000 people attended strike meetings, and 100,000 marched on the Trades Council's demonstration on 26 July, heralding a marching season of potentially very different hue from the norm. John Gray suggests that it was in 'British' Belfast that it first became apparent that unskilled Irish workers, north and south, had no easy path. They were, as yet, unarmed with appropriate union organisation and tactics. There is no doubt that Belfast in 1907 set in train a series of events that culminated in the Dublin Lock-Out of 1913–14, perhaps beyond to the syndicalist agitation of 1917–1923. Either way, in the attempt to identify the root-stock of the Irish Transport and General Workers' Union its spores can be detected in Belfast's summer air in 1907. Perhaps none could see them, but they were to float far from the triumphant scenes of working-class unity on 26 July.

Gray further suggests that it was in the person of Larkin that forces and weaknesses that already existed and awaited exploitation found their focus. 'In so far as there is a heroic and revolutionary mythology associated with events of 1907, it quite legitimately revolves around him.' Larkin's 'revolutionary instinct, made all the more potent because it was combined with exceptional talents as a popular orator and enthuser of men, had an immediate and profound impact and ignited tinder where others had failed for years past.'[7]

Larkin's brief time in Belfast—he was never there again after the spring of 1909—made a huge impact. Today it is commemorated by John McLaughlin's vivid stained-glass window in City Hall, by Anto Brennan's sculpture of a Larkin, arms aloft, at the ICTU offices in Donegall Street Place; by Gareth Knowles's statue, *The Speaker,* at the Custom House steps, which, while not Larkin, was clearly inspired by his capacity to address crowds of more than 20,000 there; and by the Pilot Street Dockers' Club mural, close to the corner where generations of deep-sea dockers were 'schooled' each morning. These works are illustrated in SIPTU's republication of Gray's account of 1907, with many photographs from the celebrated Hogg Collection displayed in Belfast and Dublin City Halls as part of extensive Centenary celebrations.[8]

AN IRISH UNION?

At the Irish Trades Union Congress in Sligo in May, Larkin, an NUDL Delegate, was a conspicuous figure. He spoke to amend the Small Dwellings Acquisition Act (1899), against the importing of brushes, for compulsory insurance under the Workmen's Compensation Act (1907) and for improved sanitation and ventilation in factories and workshops. He championed the claims of Belfast carters. He was elected to the Parliamentary Committee, Irish Labour's governing body. His thirty-two votes confirmed support well beyond the NUDL, a stunning achievement for a man not in the country twelve months.[9]

By 1908 the NUDL Executive lacked enthusiasm for Larkin and its Irish membership. The ideological and personality clash between Sexton and Larkin over the nature of trade unionism and the suggestions for an Irish expression of general unionism propelled Larkin into a camp he once opposed, like the failed attempt to form an Irish National Workers' Union. His changing view was expressed thus:

> He has always believed in the solidarity of labour the world over, but it might be that the best way to bring Irish workers into line with the workers of the world was to organise them on Irish lines first. He could not say whether he would put his hand to the plough—but if he did he would not turn back. In any case, he meant to organise the Port and Docks Board men, the tramwaymen, the shop porters in the immediate future.

The plight of unskilled Irish workers and their chronic need for organisation convinced Larkin to take on the task. Whether it was to be through the NUDL or some new body was not yet certain in his mind. Sexton made it up for him by suspending him from office on 7 December and pointing out that further 'action by you will be on your own responsibility.' It was a strange decision, as the NUDL Executive neither withdrew him nor replaced him. Dublin dockers had found a Leader but were losing their union. Many believed, and Sexton probably foremost among them, that Larkin was perhaps more interested in the larger, British stage and in Sexton's job. But on 8 December, having had his boat 'cut adrift from the other side,' Larkin was now prepared to 'fight out an existence in Ireland . . . to start a new organisation of his own.'[10]

PART 1

Forming and storming, 1909–23

CONTEXTS

Political events

The Irish Transport and General Workers' Union was born in an Ireland in political flux. Agitation for self-determination resulted in Britain's concession of Home Rule but—indulging Unionist threats—with suggestions of Partition. The Great War 'swept aside impediments to Partition,' initially opposed by Nationalists and Unionists, and the Government of Ireland Bill (commonly called the 'Third Home Rule Bill') passed in September 1914.

Ireland seemed on the brink of civil war, until the majority, north and south, were swept up in the jingoism of an imperial conflict that 'would be over by Christmas.' Labour, and James Connolly in particular, were angered by international Socialism's betrayal of the anti-war position. The banner *We Serve Neither King Nor Kaiser but Ireland* hung from Liberty Hall. Liberty Hall and the ITGWU, through its Acting General Secretary, Connolly, were central to Easter Week, which changed things 'utterly'.

In the 1918 General Election Sinn Féin swept the Irish Party aside, while Unionist MPs increased in number from eighteen to twenty-six. The War of Independence engulfed the country. Exponential growth by the ITGWU fused radical republican sentiment with Labourite demands for the improvement of wages and conditions to match wartime inflation. It drew significant attention from the military and police. Union leaders and members were regularly arrested and property seized and vandalised. The ITGWU was closely identified with General Strikes against Conscription on 23 April 1918 and on May Day 1919 to secure the release of political prisoners.

The Civil War broke out in June 1922 when the first Dáil Éireann accepted the Treaty and de Valera and his followers repudiated it. The ITGWU attempted to act as broker, avoided taking sides and urged peace. It recognised the new state as a reality, especially across negotiating tables. The General Treasurer, William O'Brien, was elected Labour TD for Dublin South City, 1922–3. Thomas Johnson, Secretary of the ITUC, was elected for County Dublin and, as Leader of the Labour Party, led the opposition in the Dáil. Such attitudes jarred with Larkin, imprisoned in America, who took a strongly republican position on his return in April 1923.

The ITGWU's identification with the project that was, however defined, 'Ireland' was a significant element in its interweaving with the psyche of the nation, or at least what emerged in 1922 as Saorstát Éireann. It gave the public, the establishment and the union itself a sense of its rightful place as a founding component of the state—a peculiar legitimacy that was to be both strength and Achilles heel.

Events from 1916 to 1922 cemented the ITGWU into the very fabric of society, identifying it, crucially, with the independence struggle. The exception was within what became Northern Ireland. Here, otherwise unimpeded growth was hobbled by simultaneous tarrings with Fenian and Bolshevik brushes. The outcome was a rump organisation, essentially based around Belfast and Newry docks, an outpost that suffered, as outposts do, from neglect and siege mentality.

The Labour Party arose from a motion at the ITUC in Clonmel in 1912, proposed by Connolly and Larkin, as the movement readied itself for a Home-Rule Parliament, to secure the place of the working class at the new table. The Labour Party chose not to contest the 1918 election, the 'famous fudge' justified 'on the grounds of giving electors a free hand on what was presented as a referendum on the constitutional status of Ireland.' Whether its legacy can still be cited, as it often is, as an explanation of the Labour Party's continuing electoral failure is not the issue. for it marginalised and subordinated Labour within this period.

This was not immediately apparent as the Irish Trades Union Congress became the Irish Labour Party and Trades Union Congress in 1919 and 'adopted Labour's first Socialist programme, demanding collective ownership of wealth and democratic management of production.'[1] The Democratic Programme adopted by Dáil Éireann as its economic and social policy on 21 January 1921, though diluted from Thomas Johnson's original, gave false hope. Having assisted in constructing the table of state, Labour was kept from sitting at it. Those who ultimately inherited the Irish revolution were not the heirs of those who, in the main, had laid down their lives for it. It was far from the vision Connolly and the Citizen Army had when marching out from Liberty Hall in Easter Week. The ITGWU decried the Civil War and attempted to broker peace. It may have feared dividing the membership, but, as its core purpose was to represent them industrially, it dealt with the practical reality of new state-employer relations. The Government soon demanded severe wage cuts, and workers' interests were marginalised. The ITGWU's acceptance of the new order's legitimacy was a central Larkin criticism.

Economy and society

In economic terms, when the ITGWU was formed most workers saw the land as a source of employment or non-employment, migration or emigration. Agricultural labourers, with or without their own parcels of land, were for the most part without trade union experience and accepted their lot. In towns, employment was predominantly casual, poorly paid and unskilled in food-related, import-export, low-technology manufacture or service. Skilled trades were extensively unionised and used their power to restrict membership to the sons of existing members. Many craft unions were Branches of British societies.

In Ulster, matters were different, with textiles, engineering and shipbuilding offering greater employment if not, by British standards, high wages. This economic divide between agrarian south and industrial north tied into the British economy lay at the heart of Partition politics.

The first steps towards the 'Welfare State' came in 1909 with National Insurance providing Unemployment Benefits, sickness assistance and old-age pensions. Irish MPs in London showed little enthusiasm and blocked some provisions being extended to Ireland, fearing an inability to afford them under Home Rule—an indication of what was to come from the Free State Government.

The ITGWU's Socialist vision was that the state should provide for old age, sickness and unemployment. It offered members only Dispute and Mortality Benefit. It did, however, quickly register an ITGWU Approved National Insurance Society under the National Insurance Act (1911). The Cumann na nGaedheal Government was conservative, parsimonious and callous in its service to the narrow class interests of the large farmers, merchant princes, businessmen and property-owners who financed them and subservient to the partly departed imperial power. Labour's opposition was purposeful but largely impotent.

The population of Ireland decreased to 4.3 million in 1911, part of a continuous downward trend from 1841, when a population of 8.175 million was recorded. In an economy producing too few jobs, emigration was 30,573 in 1911, although this figure, naturally, fell to very little during the war (unless the 'emigration' of soldiers is included). From 1911 to 1926, 405,000 people left the country, an average of 27,000 per year.

Matters were not so bad in Northern Ireland.[2] Poor employment was allied to terrible housing conditions and low standards of public health. Rural poverty, especially along the western seaboard, was acute. Death rates remained stubbornly high: in 1900, 17.8 per 1,000 population; in 1910, 17.1; in 1920, 14.8; and in 1923, 14.0 in the south, 15.3 in the north.[3]

Prices and wage rates are more difficult to discern; suffice it to say that, even allowing for considerable wartime wage increases granted in order not to impede production, they fell short of price rises. The cost-of-living index rose, in urban areas, from 288 in 1909 to a height of 847 in 1920, falling back to 598 in 1923, and in rural areas from 352 in 1909 to 979 in 1920 and 558 in 1923.[4]

There was, in short, much raw material for social revolution, factors that accounted for the ITGWU's dramatic impact. The clouding cloak of national revolution obscured the target, however, and when it was lifted many of Labour's targets were lost from view, north and south.

Union contexts

Trade union contexts have been examined in the two previous chapters. The Irish movement was confined, numerically and geographically, mostly around Belfast and Dublin, with very few in rural areas. When the ITUC first met, in 1894, it represented merely 21,000 workers. By 1900 this number had reached 67,000 and in 1909—the year the ITGWU was formed—89,000. The trade cycle affected membership, however, with significant fluctuations taking place. In general, the underlying trend was upwards till a peak of 229,000 was reached in 1920.

While it was not appreciated at the time, the removal of wartime price controls and hardening attitudes by the Government and employers on wage concessions started a slow, steady decline from that point. Not all unions were affiliated to the ITUC, but its membership is a good indicator of trends. It showed what a hugely significant element the ITGWU almost instantly was: in 1913, 30,000; in 1918, 67,000; in 1920, 120,000; and in 1923, 89,000. The ITGWU often represented more than half of all affiliated members, an astonishing fact given that by 1923 it was only four-teen years old. The Trade Disputes Act (1906) provided immunity for unions engaged in trade disputes, while the Trade Union Act (1913) obliged unions to have a separate Political Fund in order to engage in political activity.

Table 1: Affiliated membership of ITUC, 1909–23

1909	89,000	1917	150,000
1910	n.a.	1918	250,000
1911	50,000	1919	270,000
1912	70,000	1920	229,000
1913	100,000	1921	196,000
1914	110,000	1922	189,000
1915	n.a.	1923	183,000
1916	120,000		

Source: Nevin, *Trade Union Century*, p. 433.

More significant for trade unions, however, was the politics of organisation. An examination of unionisation trends reveals three distinct phases: 1889–1907, the 'New Unionism'; 1907–1917, Larkinism; and 1917–1923, syndicalism. The 'New Unionism' brought unskilled organisation in an impermanent way, but after 1907 the ITGWU became its Irish expression, creating a permanent platform through the energy and imagination of its Leader, leading to the term 'Larkinism'.[5] From 1917 syndicalism expressed an ambition for all workers to be in 'One Big Union,' organ-ised on an industrial basis and that, through the General Strike, could assume power at the point of production.

Labour's failure, industrially and politically, to secure social change during the national revolution and its subsequent marginalisation, certainly politically, are seen as missed opportunities. To what extent that can be attributed to the ITGWU, to its leadership and, most crucially, to the internal conflict that came when it was under severe attack throughout the country and when unity, in all senses, was most needed, is debatable. Or was the ITGWU the victim of a broader submission of labour to Nationalist politics? Either way, it cannot be forgotten that the ITGWU, by Rule and objective, was a trade union. Within that brief it performed admirably, advancing and then defending members' living standards and rights. It acquired recognition not simply from employers but within the nation's conscience. Its identification with 'Ireland' raised fundamental questions about trade unionism's role, particularly in the absence of a strong left-wing party.

PERSONALITY

It is tempting but often misleading to read history in terms of personalities. Connolly's political thinking and the Larkin-O'Brien conflict certainly cannot be ignored. Connolly's preparation for insurrection, evident after he succeeded Larkin as Acting General Secretary in the autumn of 1914 and in the *Workers' Republic* from 1915, identified the ITGWU with the Rising. After the event at least, the ITGWU continuously drew on Connolly's sacrifice and claimed that 'Easter Week saved the union.'[6] Connolly became canonised within the ITGWU panoply, and Larkin demonised.

Even before Connolly's first reservations about Larkin and his decision to go to America, tensions existed between Larkin and the Executive. After 1916 the ITGWU grew dramatically, and new management structures were required. William O'Brien, a tailor and an officer of the Trades Council, was closely associated with the union though he joined it only in 1917, being elected General Treasurer almost immediately.

Rules had to be operated to secure democratic governance. By 1919 victims of O'Brien's intolerance of incompetence, and of opposition, created a rancorous resistance centred around the deposed P. T. Daly and Delia Larkin (Larkin's sister). Jim Larkin was imprisoned in the United States. When he returned, in April 1923, he found country and union transformed. Unable or unwilling to accept the new order that seemed at first more than prepared to accept him—he was unchallenged as General Secretary throughout his absence—resignations turned into opposition and, finally, expulsion. The ground was set for a split that reverberated for decades and reduced Labour, industrially and politically, to competing, antagonistic and fractious fractions. Service to the working class was abandoned.

In the social model of forming, storming, norming and performing, the period 1909–1923 saw the ITGWU indulge in forming, norming and some very spectacular performing. It was the unresolved storming that would be the immediate legacy of what was surely one of the most amazing fourteen-year introductions to any trade union anywhere.

Chapter 3 ～

| THE BIRTH OF A GIANT

THE FOUNDING OF THE ITGWU

On Tuesday 28 December 1908 Larkin called a meeting of the National Union of Dock Labourers 'Irish Executive'—an entirely unofficial body— in the Trades Hall, Capel Street, Dublin. Michael McKeown represented Belfast; Dobbins represented Dundalk; probably James Fearon represented Cork; and others came from Dublin and Waterford. They decided to form an Irish union—the Irish Transport and General Workers' Union. It was formally established on 4 January 1909.

Its arrival received scant public attention, and when notice did appear it was referred to as the Irish Transit Workers' Union or Irish Transport Workers' Union. It has been said that the latter was its original title and the words 'and General' were added later. Indeed the union's first quarterly-control badges were stamped 'I.T.W.U'. Throughout its existence, workers referred to it as the 'Transport Union'. However, William O'Brien, in his Eason's Penny Diary, recorded on 4 January, ' I.T.&G.W.U. Founded,' while the Registrar of Friendly Societies, D. O'Connell Miley, giving evidence in Cork on 4 September, testified that he registered the Irish Transport and General Workers' Union on 6 May 1909.[1]

The New Union's 'material assets consisted of a table, a couple of chairs, two empty bottles, and a candle.' Seán O'Casey, in *Drums Under the Windows*, adds a poet's imagination to the union's creation.

So Jim came out of jail, and in a room of a tenement in Townsend Street, with a candle in a bottle for a torch and a billycan of tea, with a few buns for a banquet, the Church militant here on earth of the Irish workers, called the Irish Transport and General Workers' Union, was founded, a tiny speck of flame now, but soon to become a pillar of fire into which a brand was flung by Yeats, the great poet, Orpen the painter, Æ, who saw gods in every bush and bramble, Corkery the story teller, James Stephens, the poet and graceful satirical jester, Dudley Fletcher, the Rector of Coolbanagher, and even Patrick Pearse, wandering softly under the Hermitage elms . . . even he was to lift a pensive head to the strange new shouting to be heard in Dublin's streets . . . to say 'No private right to property is good as against the public right of the people.'[2]

Both are exaggerations. The NUDL did not contest the take-over of its rooms, registers, petty cash and records. While the idea may have originated in Townsend Street, the formal meeting was in the Trades Hall. What is striking is that those involved immediately had a sense of the historic, that something of enormity was being born.

Recalling events more than half a century later, O'Brien suggested that he had a hand in choosing the union's title. In 1908 Joseph Harris tried to establish Branches of the Workers' Union, but 'everywhere he went' he 'met with opposition that it was an English body.' Harris told O'Brien that his project 'should be a great success if we could have an Irish body.' Agreeably surprised, O'Brien asked Harris what Larkin's view might be. 'He would be heart and soul with it,' was the reply; but when Larkin later saw O'Brien he allegedly expressed opposition, adding 'I might accept the view that there was a case for an Irish Socialist Party but I would never agree to divide the workers on the industrial field.' O'Brien recollected that in 'November or December' Larkin

> suddenly said at a meeting that he understood there was a movement afoot to form an Irish union and while he believed in the solidarity of the workers in every country, it might be that the best way to bring that about would be to organise them on an Irish basis first.

Harris met Larkin on 24 January and offered his Workers' Union membership in exchange for an ITGWU position. Larkin declined.[3] He did not ride tandem. In contradiction, at a meeting in the Trades Hall on 17 January 1909 Larkin said he 'never meant to form a New Union until forces over which he had no control forced him.' Conversely, it was suggested that James Sexton, General Secretary of the NUDL, might have approved of an Irish union had Larkin sought permission. He certainly allowed the ITGWU to retain the NUDL premises in Beresford Place without argument and might have allowed things take their course had rivalries in the north of Ireland not emerged.[4]

NEW UNION, NEW PERSPECTIVE

Whether Larkin was truly committed to an Irish project will never be known. The ITGWU's actions demonstrated from the beginning that four new propositions guided and inspired it and led to the movement's transformation: belief in the tactics of the militant 'New Unionism'; a Socialist philosophy; Irish unions for Irish workers; and strong independent Labour political action.

Larkin's already remarkable achievements in the last six months of 1908 should not be judged in terms of wage increases but of recognition. They have gone largely unnoticed in the retrospective shadow of the formation of the ITGWU. Emmet Larkin rightly praises advances won in the face of economic depression, serious unemployment and a hostile NUDL Executive as 'remarkable'. New, militant class-consciousness stirred in Dublin. The ITGWU was its organisational and

psychological expression. Larkin, shocked by the abject squalor of Dublin's tenement poor, developed a sense of mission. His commitment to Ireland, with or without his expulsion from the NUDL, seems, with hindsight, pre-ordained.[5]

Having laid the keel for his new, Irish vessel, Larkin made plain his commitment.

> He could not say whether he would put his hand to the plough—but if he did
> he would not turn back. In any case, he meant to organise the Port and Docks
> Board's men, the tramwaymen, and the shop porters in the immediate future.

Cathal O'Shannon, reviewing events in 1959, saw the union's birth as the 'outcome
of two converging but separate developments among trade unionists in the city.'[6]
First was the growing desire to establish an Irish union administered by an Irish
Executive, agitation largely carried on by those who had been associated with James
Connolly in the Irish Socialist Republican Party after 1903. Within this 'Irish-
Ireland' sentiment also fell those associated with the Gaelic League (Conradh na
Gaeilge), the GAA, Sinn Féin and associated cultural bodies. Second were the
'parallel' but 'independent' campaigns of militant women's suffrage and of Socialism,
the latter culminating in the formation of the Socialist Party of Ireland in 1904.

RULES

The ITGWU's Rules were not greatly different from standard union Rules. They
provided governance through a General Executive Council, three General
Officers—President, Secretary and Treasurer—and below that District and Branch
Committees. In an unusual, lengthy 'Preface', however, the union clearly set out a
novel stall, asking,

> Are we going to continue the policy of grafting ourselves on the English Trades
> Union movement, losing our own identity as a nation in the great world of
> organised labour? We say emphatically, No.

Workers had to realise that

> society is changing rapidly, the capitalist class in Ireland is being reinforced by
> the influx of foreign capitalists, with their soulless, sordid, money-grubbing
> propensities. It behoves the Irish workers to realise the power of the employing
> class, who are not only well organised industrially but practically monopolise
> the political power in this country as they do in all other countries at present.

This has been seen as a 'Nationalist' expression. Indeed it was, but it was first inter-
nationalist, as it asserted a right to self-determination and served an expectation of
Home Rule.

To achieve its aim the ITGWU did not believe in 'the old system of sectional
unionism' but appealed to 800,000 unorganised unskilled.

The Irish Transport and General Workers' Union offer to you a medium whereby you may combine with your fellows to adjust wages and regulate hours and conditions of labour, wherever and whenever possible and desirable by negotiation, arbitration, or, if the conditions demand it, by withholding our labour until amelioration is granted. Further, we demand political recognition for the enforcement of our demands. Our immediate programme being a legal eight hours' day; provision of work for all unemployed, and pensions for all workers at 60 years of age; adult suffrage; nationalisation of canals, railways and means of transport; the land of Ireland for the people of Ireland. Our ultimate ideal: the realisation of an Industrial Commonwealth.

Despite this, the Rules made no other provision for industrial unionism, and, although espousing the 'Industrial Commonwealth', Rule 12 provided for 'Financial Assistance to Labour Members' provided the 'said Labour member is not connected with any political party.' The Rules generally were prosaic, Rule 2, under 'Objects of the Union', stating that

the organisation is for the purpose of raising the standard of social life of the workers, and the raising of funds to provide for:—
(*a*) Dispute Pay in the case of Strike or Lock-out, or as the result of obeying the lawful demands of the Union at the rate of 10s. per week;
(*b*) Legal assistance for the purpose of enforcing the application of industrial laws and the recovery of wages;
(*c*) A Funeral Allowance for members;
And generally to regulate the relations between employers and employed, to encourage co-operation and enterprise amongst its members.

Membership was through an enrolment fee of 3 pence. The highest rate—4 pence a week and a quarterly levy of 4 pence—entitled benefit members to full Dispute Pay and funeral and Mortality Benefit.

One of the lengthiest Rules, Rule 9, dealt with Dispute Pay. This was clearly where most money would be dispensed on members called out or victimised. Dispute Pay was available as follows:

Every member of the Union paying full subscriptions, in benefit, who may be locked-out by an employer, or withdrawn from employment by the Union in consequence of any trade dispute, on satisfying the Branch and the General E.C., as to the bona fide nature of the dispute, shall receive the sum of 10s. per week for ten weeks, 6s. for ten weeks, 3s. for ten weeks. Any member claiming strike or Lock-Out pay must sign the Vacant Book each day. Members failing to sign shall forfeit benefit for such days.

There were controls for the GEC. 'Notices to cease work' were recognised only after the consent of the GEC had been obtained before any action and 'provided time for consideration has been given by the firm employing our members.' In 'sudden and unavoidable disputes' the GEC had 'discretionary power to grant or withhold Dispute Pay.' The General Secretary had 'power to negotiate when our members are in dispute.' The GEC could 'close any dispute when they consider it advisable in the interests of the Union.' In language peculiarly suggestive of the Industrial Relations Act (1990) the Rule also insisted that each Branch Secretary seeking sanction for strike 'must forward to Chief Office'

> The number of members who voted for and the number who voted against the dispute;
> The number of workmen directly affected by the dispute;
> The number of members entitled to benefit, with their Chief Office number;
> The number of members not entitled to benefit; and
> The number of non-members, if any, and the position of similar workmen in the District.

The 1912 Rules were signed by Thomas Foran, James Larkin, John Bohan, Stephen Clarke, Peter Ennis, Thomas Hewson, Joseph Kelly and John O'Neill.[7] Rule 35 provided for a National Convention to be held adjacent to the ITUC Congress. It was the union's supreme authority.

In practice, most Rules were never really operated in Larkin's time. Indeed, until reorganisation in 1917, Dublin No. 1 Branch acted as Executive, despite some attempts by Connolly from 1914 to implement internal structures.[8] Larkin made a huge issue of the Rules after 1923, but an examination of the 1912 Rules against the later, contested ones shows little change. But then it was practice rather than content that Larkin found objectionable.

BELFAST

James Connolly, observing events from New York, gave the ITGWU a front-page welcome in his paper, *The Harp*. Writing to O'Brien in July 1909, he said, 'If I were in Ireland now one of the first things I would do would be to start an Irish Workers' Union to combine all Irish unions gradually into one body.' He was 'glad to notice' that the 'Irish working class on the old sod are up and doing abreast of the times.' He published extracts from Irish papers to settle 'doubting ones' and 'telling of the formation of a great industrial union in Ireland at a time when American workers are still split up into warring crafts.'

The *Irish Nation* was cordial, noting a meeting of 'carters, dockers and other trades' from Dublin, Belfast, Dundalk, Cork and Waterford to create a new Irish union 'for those engaged in the distributive trades.'[9]

> The New Union is to be called the Irish Transport Workers' Union, and will adopt exactly that attitude of friendly co-operation toward the English unions that they extend to the unions of Germany and France; but it will not merge

itself in any English unions, as too many Irish workers have done. Mr. J. Larkin, late Organiser for the English Dockers' Union, will act as Organiser. It is to be hoped that this example of independence will be followed by the workers throughout Ireland.

The *Evening Telegraph* was close to the mark in its analysis of the split between Larkin and Sexton, claiming that the ITGWU appeared to have been 'brought into being mainly in consequence of the differences which arose' between them.

The union itself, reflecting in 1918 on its own formation, cited a 'lack of support from the Liverpool Executive' as the spur to form 'an Irish Union open to all grades of workers.' Those differences continued in Belfast, where, unlike Dublin, not all transferred from the NUDL. On 12 January in Victoria Hall, Alexander Boyd introduced Sexton to a 'stormy meeting'; on rising to speak he was 'received with loud boos' and 'repeated cries for Larkin.' Boyd, a central figure in 1907, now saw the ITGWU in black-and-white terms (or, perhaps more accurately, green-and-white). It was a 'Sinn Féin organisation that not even a decent Nationalist in Belfast would have anything to do with.' This was the first playing of a card that would be callously played over and over against the ITGWU in the North.

Sexton refused to directly engage with Larkin, because 'it was a waste of energy to deal with a man who was not even a good liar. A good liar lied scientifically so that he could not be discovered, but Larkin lied indiscriminately for the sake of lying. There was not even finality about Larkin's lies.[10]

The following night Larkin addressed a meeting 'under the auspices of the Irish Transit Workers' Union,' also in Victoria Hall. Sexton and Boyd were invited to attend but declined. Patrick Dobbins from Dundalk presided as Larkin, in stage-managed style, read out a telegram from a Father O'Leary in Cork, who said he would 'gladly bear testimony to your assistance in settling the strike here. Your prudence, firmness, tact at and before the Conference, secured a satisfactory settlement.'

On the third night Sexton addressed about a hundred dockers, who passed a resolution 'advocating allegiance to the N.U.D.L.' Larkin disparagingly claimed that the NUDL was left with only sixty men, of whom forty were registered with the Free Labour Bureau. Belfast dockers remain divided between two unions to the present.

There were disturbances, with ITGWU men showing 'increased activity'. Attempts to picket streets leading to York Dock were thwarted by 'strong bodies of harbour police and constabulary.' Steamers were discharged by Free Labour Bureau men, and several 'isolated members' of that organisation were 'waylaid and beaten.' An ITGWU member, Rice, was convicted of assault. Official reports suggest that about 250 men joined with Larkin but did not reckon that the ITGWU would survive long in Belfast.

None of these could get employment at the Docks as thc stevedores had instructions to employ only members of the National Union [of Dock Labourers] or Free Labour Bureau. Larkin's men committed a number of assaults on the men who were working, but arrests immediately followed. Larkin himself came to

Belfast, but he had no money, and the trouble soon ended. He then left Belfast and his organisation there collapsed.[11]

DUBLIN

The wages and hours of carters and maltsters, a cause of strikes the previous November, were referred to arbitration under P. J. O'Neill, Chairman of Dublin County Council, and Sir Andrew Porter. They reported on 16 February 1909 that a Saturday closing of work at three o'clock, 'while very desirable in itself,' was not possible by strict Rule, 'for the discharge of vessels . . . must go on.' Similarly, they considered that giving carters meal breaks was 'manifestly unworkable' but did 'recommend that if and when it can be done the men should be allowed a short Saturday and a meal hour'; but they did not formally include such comments in their award. They strongly rejected the practice of the 'back shilling' in malting, whereby money was retained by the employer until the end of the season and paid only if the men's conduct was satisfactory. This rendered it impossible for men to know exactly what they were earning and left them 'liable to an equal penalty in respect to trivial and important deviations from duty.' They recommended that the practice cease forthwith and that a shilling be added to the weekly wage.

On three other matters the arbitrators felt they had 'no authority to do more than to offer a recommendation to both parties.' It was 'highly unreasonable that it should be in the power of masters or men to determine a hiring without proper notice,' and 'both parties should agree, in writing, not to dismiss a man, or to throw up work, without a fortnight's notice, save in the case of breach of agreement or other misconduct.' A 'Court of Conciliation' was strongly advised; and it was 'our hope and expectation that nothing shall be done which would have the effect of punishing or injuriously affecting any of the men concerned in this arbitration, or their comrades, in relation to the recent strike.'

Increases for carters were recommended: overtime after 6:30 p.m. increased by 6 pence; additional rates for storing and loading different classes of vessel; and the rates for carting corn, flour, oats, barley and malt within and without the city boundary.

Larkin approved the settlement, particularly as it represented full recognition for the nascent ITGWU. In the Trades Hall on Thursday 18 February he pointed out that attempts had been made by the employers to exclude him and to deal directly with the men. This was resisted. He felt the award for maltsters 'was the worst thing he had ever known.' The better paid got more than the worst paid, but, 'taking all in all, outside the malthousemen, it had been a glorious victory.' He recommended that the men accept it for six months to 'see how it works and in the meantime keep their powder dry and have it ready for action. (Applause.)' He agreed to future conciliation and arbitration as long as proceedings were public. As to 'no victim-isation', he pointed out that 'it was for the men to see that that did not occur.'

By early March fifty men in Merchants' Carting stopped, again seeking a sup-plementary award. Porter and O'Neill explained that their settlement was not designed to interfere with any special rates. In fact some employers were attempting to renege on the agreement. The ITGWU insisted on full implementation. Thomas Greene, Branch Secretary, noted the expression 'Final Award' of 17 February, asking 'how, in the name of common sense, can a supplementary award be issued?' Eight days after their acceptance, said Greene, the manager in Merchants' Carting, McCullagh, told the men to accept the old prices or leave. 'This is what McCullagh calls a strike . . . Let the blame rest on the right shoulders . . . It was the employers who refused to accept the awards.'

Employers were clearly uneasy with the new threat, but in Dublin their response was, as yet, disorganised.[12]

CONGRESS

By March 1909 the ITGWU was affiliated to Dublin Trades Council, and Larkin sat on its Executive. In May, having been recognised by Dublin employers, the union attempted to gain admission to the ITUC at its annual meeting in Limerick. P. T. Daly of the Trades Council moved the deletion of a chapter of the Executive's report, 'The Dock Labourers' Disputes', which had been compiled by the Secretary, E. L. Richardson. It traced the 'starting . . . of another union under the name of the "Irish Transport Workers' Union" with Mr. Larkin as Organiser, and which, your Committee are informed, was largely made up of former members of the National Union.'

McKeown requested a 'Sub-Committee to inquire into the merits of the dispute' and that matters be referred to Belfast Trades Council. It was decided, 'Mr. Larkin dissenting, that, pending a settlement of the dispute, no invitation to attend the Congress be sent to the Transport Workers' Union.' Sexton protested against 'Larkin voicing the opinions or representing in any way' the dockers, as he was elected to the Parliamentary Committee as an NUDL representative but 'has since broken away and formed an opposition union in Ireland.' Sexton insisted that 'by the decision of the Joint Board of the British Trades Union Congress, the Labour Party, and the Federation of Trades,' such new bodies 'shall not be recognised' by the ITUC.

Daly argued that both sides of the argument must be heard. Who had given the Parliamentary Committee the authority to expel Larkin the day before the Congress, one who had continued to attend since January, presumably representing the ITGWU? Greig (Belfast) urged support for the Parliamentary Committee, a position 'strongly' taken up by E. W. Stewart, who claimed it was a 'deliberate attempt by renegades who were lying low to smash up' Congress. He concluded in rousing, if questionable, style that it was

> only when dictation would not be allowed that Mr. Larkin fell into the arms of Mr. P. T. Daly and some Socialists and Sinn Feiners. This was a question of deliberately driving trades unionism in the interests of a political party. Mr. Daly and his political faction were attempting to smash the combination of trades unionism in Ireland, and if they succeeded in capturing that Congress they would eventually do so. (Applause.)

McCarron (Tailors, Derry) opposed, on the principle of resisting splits and saying that he bore 'no animus against Larkin.' Patrick Murphy (Cork Trades Council) supported, knowing the ITGWU as 'one of the strongest and best organised in Cork.' It was largely composed of the previously unorganised. John Murphy (Belfast) looked on the ITGWU 'as a private venture working against an established Amalgamated Union.' While he 'knew Larkin's ability as an Organiser' he also knew 'that unless he was boss he would always be an opponent.' D. R. Campbell (Belfast) moved that an Investigative Committee be appointed.[13]

Daly's motion was defeated, 49 to 39, thus excluding the ITGWU from Congress. Larkin, who intervened from the gallery, was refused the opportunity to speak. The union was kept at official trade unionism's door.

CORK EMPLOYERS ATTEMPT INFANTICIDE

Cork employers' opportunity to attack the ITGWU came in June after Joseph Harris (Workers' Union) organised coal porters on Morrison's Island. On 10 June the ITGWU demanded that Sutton's dismiss a stevedore, Rourke, and his men who had joined the Workers' Union. Instead of waiting for the management to arrive, the men walked off the job and were quickly joined by coal porters, carmen and store-men. Backed by Harris, Rourke said he would not join the ITGWU, as it was an 'unrecognised body'. Interestingly, the police described Rourke as a 'Free Labourer'. James Fearon led the ITGWU in Cork and drew police attention, because matters 'ended in a free fight, in which several men were injured.' Fearon and three others were arrested. Unused to such swiftness, the Dublin unions did 'not countenance hasty action' and regretted that 'the men did not take Counsel from their leaders.' They were to become used to fiery ITGWU tactics.

Larkin arrived in Cork and addressed a mass meeting in Parnell Place. He portrayed the dispute as centring on 'independence from Britain'. The men were more alarmed by the prospect of mechanisation and feared that Rourke would introduce steam winches. On 14 June two hundred men of an 'English dock union' worked the quay. Railway workers quickly took supporting action, despite attempts at restraint by their Officials. Shipping Federation scabs were soon required. Father O'Leary attempted mediation, but the employers' minds were elsewhere. On 16 June the Cork Employers' Federation was formed, and it enunciated a hard-line policy:

> That we, the employers of Cork, hereby bind ourselves and the firms we represent as follows:
> (1) To immediately dismiss any employee who shall wilfully disobey any order out of sympathy for any strike or trade dispute;
> (2) That the vacancy so caused shall be filled forthwith by local labour if procurable, failing this that the vacancy be filled from any available source;
> (3) That any such employee discharged shall not be employed by any members of the Federation.

A mass Lock-Out began. John Reardon, Secretary of the Federation, circulated members to the effect that in order to achieve point 3,

> each member shall now and in future notify to the Secretary the names, addresses and occupations of any employees dismissed; and of those that leave their employment in sympathy with any strike; and that a register of such names, addresses and occupations be kept for the guidance of the members of the Federation.

At a meeting in the Assembly Rooms on 6 July the Federation gave substance to the men's fears of mechanisation.

1. That in case of unskilled workers, employers shall be free to employ either the members of a union or non-Unionists; and members of a union shall make no objection to working either with the members of another union or non-Unionists;
2. That unskilled workmen desiring employment must make application direct to their late employers for such employment as it may be now possible to give.
3. That all such workmen applying for re-employment, and who may be re-instated, shall undertake to obey all lawful orders under all conditions in the future, and not to leave their employment again without giving legal notice.
4. That the employers may adopt any conditions necessary for the conduct of particular businesses (including the use of machinery), and that the work-men shall agree to same.

After sixteen days the dispute began to wither. The police reported that strikers' parades were diminishing in number, 950 marching on 23 June, 700 on the 24th and 550 on the 25th. The merchants had 'formed themselves into a Federation—their attitude is at present very firm and their intention is to fight the matter to a finish.' Chief Inspector M. W. Davies, reporting to Dublin, thought that 'want of funds' would see the men give way; that the strong, reinforced force was coping; magistrates were attending police Courts and handing out stiff penalties; and the Cork press 'both Nationalist and Conservative in their references to the strikes are adopting a very friendly tone towards the police.'

By July a 'portion of the extra force had been sent away' as the police relaxed. The employers were 'only taking back picked men on their own terms and some will not be taken back on any conditions.' The battle against steam winches was lost: 'Steam colliers now unloaded by their own steam winches, instead of by hand winches, resulting in a saving of labour by which the men suffer.'

Larkin, Fearon, Sullivan and Cooney, 'whose leadership has proved so dis-astrous for their followers,' were prosecuted and 'returned for trial on a charge of conspiracy to defraud' the NUDL. This action had consequences for Larkin later on, but to some extent it was not abnormal practice when organising dock workers.

Dermot Keogh observes that Fearon's methods 'were rough. Many Cork dockers were simply handed a Transport Union card when they went to pay their sub-scriptions at the Liverpool union's offices. Bullying, threatening and boycotting of recalcitrants was not uncommon.' Fearon's tactics were not 'uncommon or excessive. The rough and tumble of the docks necessitated a strong, physical approach.'[14] The Shipping Federation, apparently abetted by Harris, set about stamping out any vestiges of trade unionism on the Cork quays.

By 31 December the ITGWU had survived a tempestuous first year, an 'adequate though hardly spectacular' beginning.[15] It had 3,000 members, mostly in Dublin, with a presence in Belfast, Cork, Dundalk and Waterford, although things were much less secure outside the capital. Many dockside unions collapsed under the first employers' offensive or economic downturn. The reaction of the Cork employers showed that the New Union's potential was realised by them, if not by workers. That potential was the capacity to revolutionise trade unionism, to enthuse it with a new militancy in pursuit of an agenda that stretched well beyond wages and conditions to question the validity of capitalism itself.

Chapter 4 ⌇

LARKINISM, 'ONE BIG UNION', AND EMPLOYERS IN THE LONG GRASS, 1910–13

MEMBERSHIP, ORGANISATION AND FINANCE

Consolidation was the objective of the ITGWU in its second year: maintaining and developing membership, overcoming obstacles thrown in its path by employers and cementing recognition from Dublin Trades Council and the ITUC. By December 1910 membership was roughly 5,000, with 2,700 in Dublin No. 1 Branch. Other Branches were James's Street, High Street, Belfast, and Cork. Painters and lamplighters were recruited, but casual dockers were the mainstay, in the Burns and Laird Line, City of Dublin Steam Packet Company, T. and C. Martin, Brooks Thomas, Tedcastle, and Dublin and Wicklow Manure Company.

By 1911 Dublin was solid. Expansion continued in August, with active Branches established in Cos. Kilkenny, Waterford and Wexford. Gathering in confidence, Larkin turned his attention to organisational black spots: the Guinness Brewery and the Dublin United Tramways Company. Two years before William Martin Murphy issued his odious 'Document' demanding that employees renounce the ITGWU, the union published a form on which tramway workers could indicate their 'desire to become a member.'

> Sign the form, send on your entrance fee, enrol in the workers' army. We are marching on to liberty. We are marching on to the tune of universal brotherhood and peace in every clime.

A newsboys' strike, attributed by the *Irish Times* and *Evening Herald* to Larkin's inspiration, was denied as part of union action, although the boys certainly took example. Larkin said he 'had never spoken' to newsboys and urged them to 'keep order, tabulate your grievances and keep the public on your side.' The *Irish Worker* championed their cause, casting them in a heroic light. They repaid the support in 1913, as the paper forecast: 'It is against these boys that the whole force of the authorities of Dublin has been hurled.' The DMP had 'kicked and batoned' them. One, aged nine, was 'crippled by the blow of a baton'; another, aged eight, 'had his head cut open.' Larkin concluded: 'Let us hope to Heaven that it is these boys, who ten years hence (or sooner), when the time comes, will remember to-day, and remind the brutes of the D.M.P. and R.I.C. what vengeance and retribution is.'[1]

The scale of the industrial whirlwind was demonstrated by 'One week's work accomplished by the I.T.&G.W.U.' It listed twenty advances: sandwich-men, increase of 3d a day; 5s increase for draymen; 2s for workers in soap, milling, wines, ink and mineral water. Even the Guinness Brewery was not immune, as 'new arrangements of work equal to three shillings per week for contractors' men' were announced.

Organisation advanced in Belfast, Bray, Cork and Sligo. Significant increases were won for thousands of workers in local authorities, docking and shipping, transport, distilling, brewing, and manufacture. Strategic alliances developed with sailors, firemen and railwaymen. Thoughts turned to more long-term policies and the value of 'One Big Union'. All was not rosy, however. Employers learnt lessons from Cork, and the formation of the Dublin Employers' Federation saw trenches being dug.

A union excursion to Cork on Whit Sunday, 4 June 1911, was new and exciting. The ITGWU Fife and Drum Band and O'Connell Pipe Band marched members to Kingsbridge (Heuston) Station. Larkin spoke at rallies in Cork and Queenstown (Cóbh). Members were advised to uphold the 'reputation and dignity of the Dublin workers' and urged to 'take no strong drink for this one day in the year—be an example and a light unto others.' As the ITGWU organised breweries and distilleries, Larkin (although reminding all that he did not himself drink) suggested that for 'men foolish enough to consume strong drink, it would be better that they should drink the liquor, stout or beer made by such firms as Watkins, Jameson, Pim and Co. who not only employ Irishmen in every Department, but who, I am informed, use practically all Irish-grown grain.'

P. T. Daly remained in Cork as Southern Organiser, reviving Waterford and opening Branches in New Ross and Kilkenny. McKeown claimed 1,000 members in Dundalk by Christmas, having organised two breweries, timber and coal merchants, brickworks and merchants. A series of bloody strikes involved clashes with the police, arrests and imprisonments. The Bray Branch was founded on 10 September, with George Burke as Secretary, and Sligo Branch on 17 September, with John Lynch as Secretary. By December, membership was 18,089, with 13,009 having joined since January.

The ITGWU banner and Band attended the unveiling of the Parnell Monument in O'Connell Street, Dublin, on 1 October and a temperance demonstration on 4 October. In the same month the founder-Secretary of No. 1 Branch, Thomas Greene, resigned, shaken by the Socialist line adopted. He was replaced by John O'Neill, a central but undervalued figure until his retirement in 1923.

The ITGWU was no longer a toddler but a strapping youth. To the employers' gathering alarm, its growth showed no signs of stopping.[2]

In 1912 R. J. P. Mortished contributed statistical articles on poverty to the *Irish Worker* as 'justification for the agitator.' Larkin secured the distribution of bread to

Enniscorthy during a bakery strike to feed the people. In Dublin, cinema and theatre workers struck. McKeown led the women workers of P. J. Carroll and Company, cigarette manufacturers, in a bitter strike for basic improvements. On Friday 9 February they marched to the Market Square in Dundalk, holding a banner, *Tobacco smokers note—The Blackman's workers on strike for a living wage* (a reference to Carroll's device, a plantation slave sporting a long pipe and informing the public that 'My Mamma sells de best tobacco'). Stephen Carroll relied on intransigence and starvation to break the women.

Advances were won in Waterford Gasworks and Belfast docks. George Burke was appointed District Secretary in Bray, and premises were opened in Kingstown (Dún Laoghaire). By April 1912 the ITGWU boasted sixteen Branches. An Approved Society under the National Insurance Act was founded. Recruitment in Thomas Healy's and Eason's created the first section for engineering machinemen. (A section is an industrial unit within a Branch, with its own Committee.) The Inchicore Branch met at Emmet Temperance Hall, and William Partridge was installed there.

Table 2: ITGWU Branches, April 1912

No. 1: Dublin (Liberty Hall)
No. 2: Dublin (James's Street)
No. 3: Dublin (17 High Street)
No. 4: Belfast (12 Corporation Street)
No. 5: Dundalk (Labourers' Hall, Quay Street)
No. 6: Newry (Foresters' Hall)
No. 7: Sligo (Labour Hall)
No. 8: Kingstown [Dún Laoghaire]
No. 9: Bray (The Castle)
No. 10: Kill of the Grange, Co. Dublin
No. 11: Wexford (Charlotte Street)
No. 12: Waterford (Ballybricken)
No. 13: Cork, Storemen and Carmen's Union (George's Street)
No. 14: New Ross
No. 15: Enniscorthy
No. 16: Dublin (York Street and Jacob's)

Source: *Irish Worker*, 22 April 1912.

Organisation was so rapid that as soon as a new delivery of badges was received a 'Badge and Card Inspection' was ordered for Monday 26 August to see who was and who was not in compliance. More than seven hundred attended a meeting with P. T. Daly and Thomas Foran in Sligo in late August, and by October a new word had entered the dictionary: 'Larkinism'.

By December 1912 recession slowed the pace of increase, but membership had reached 22,935 by the end of the year.[3]

Table 3: ITGWU membership, 1909–13

	ITGWU figure [1]	Registrar's figure [2]
1909	1,200	2,500
1910	5,000	5,000
1911	18,089	18,000
1912	22,935	24,135
1913	30,000 (August)	26,135

Sources: *Irish Worker* [1]; National Archives, Registrar of Friendly Societies, file 275T [2].

New Rules were registered on 10 October, to comply with the National Insurance Act. (See appendix 1.) There was little difference from the original Rules, although the reference to compulsory arbitration was removed. They provided for a General Executive Committee with one Delegate from Munster and Connacht, two from Ulster and four from Leinster. McKeown was the Ulster member, Connolly presumably the second and Lynch the representative for Connacht. Elected in November to serve from the following 1 January, the Executive seldom if ever met.

Boom conditions returned in 1913, but the ITGWU chose to consolidate rather than mount new offensives. During the ITUC Congress in Cork in May, Larkin addressed more than 2,000 people in Grand Parade, and Nellie Gordon and Connolly organised women in Cork and Queenstown (Cóbh).

In Dublin the union called meetings of Guinness workers, 'all iron workers and railway employees' and, most tellingly, 'tramway employees, all grades,' under the heading 'Organise! Organise! Organise!' Meetings were held at midnight on Saturday 1 June at the Transport Union Hall, 35 George's Street, Kingstown, with Thomas Lawlor, and Emmet Hall, Inchicore, with Partridge. A warning came with the notice:

> No John J's, Government Murphy's or any other job seeker allowed at these meetings. Every man who works on the tram system is invited—remember, MEN! Any scab or pimp, or other vermin, caught within the precincts of the above Halls will be dealt with!

A tramway demonstration was held on Sunday 27 July. The ITGWU demanded a minimum wage of £1 for a 54-hour week, overtime at time and a quarter between six and eight, time and a half for eight to twelve and double time for twelve to six and all Sunday work. The company responded with a mass dismissal of union members, an action immediately condemned by Dublin Trades Council. By August the union's membership had reached 30,000, an extraordinary achievement in less than five years. It is even more remarkable given the total Congress affiliation of 100,000. ITUC figures for 1911 and 1912 were 50,000 and 70,000, respectively, demonstrating the ITGWU's numerical impact.[4]

LARKIN AND CONNOLLY

Arising from events in Cork in 1909, Larkin appeared before a County Dublin Common Jury on 17 June 1910. He was sentenced to twelve months' imprisonment with hard labour, although his plea for his fellow-defendant, Daniel Coveney, was successful. The prize was Larkin. Who now was to lead the ITGWU?

At a meeting in Beresford Place to protest against Larkin's conviction, Councillor Lorcan Sherlock suggested that P. T. Daly take over *pro tem*. Daly accepted 'but stipulated that the position should be a purely honorary one.' William O'Brien later suggested that 'it would have been much less expensive to have paid him a wage as his expenses were most extravagant.' Daly spent most of his time in Belfast, with little or no organisational return.

Larkin was released on 1 October, and the union's fortunes instantly rose. But Daly's anointment had planted a seed of dissension that later bloomed in an ugly fashion. Daly was a member of the Supreme Council of the Irish Republican Brotherhood but disgraced himself in 1908 by not accounting for £300 he had collected for the organisation in America. There were suggestions of drink. The IRB chose simply to expel him. It was an act of folly that haunted Daly and created a suspicion of him within Nationalist circles. O'Brien was certainly an enemy. Larkin's gift of the ITGWU was a godsend for Daly and cemented his devotion to the Chief.

A memorial for Larkin's release, signed by distinguished names, was submitted, claiming that there was no evidence that he used NUDL funds for his own purposes. A martyr in prison, he became a hero on his release. A torchlight parade and mass meeting in Beresford Place excited the whole city. O'Brien saw Larkin's imprisonment as a 'considerable fillip'. The ITGWU 'was stronger on his release than prior to his conviction.'[5]

In January 1910 James Connolly invited Larkin to become sub-editor of his paper, *The Harp*, which was transferred from New York to Dublin. Connolly hoped to return to Ireland. In correspondence with O'Brien he agreed to a speaking tour for the Socialist Party of Ireland, which might lead to more permanent employment. He returned on 26 July. O'Brien was 'anxious to see him appointed to some position in the Union,' not least because he knew the SPI would not provide a living for Connolly's family. He recognised the contribution Connolly could make to the ITGWU. Connolly declined, for, as Greaves has suggested, 'he had come home for the purpose of producing and disseminating Socialist propaganda.'

He soon discovered that this ambition and employment in the ITGWU were not mutually exclusive. He spoke in Dublin, Belfast and Cork, establishing or energising SPI Branches and drawing considerable reaction from thinking trade unionists. P. T. Daly joined the SPI on 16 September, and Connolly enrolled in Dublin No. 1 Branch of the ITGWU at the end of the month. Dies were being cast.[6]

CONGRESS

On 5 March 1910 E. L. Richardson, long-standing Secretary of the ITUC, announced that he would not continue. E. W. Stewart was appointed by the Parliamentary Committee—not a move welcomed by Larkin and the ITGWU, of which Stewart was an opponent. Dublin Trades Council had its misgivings about Stewart.

The Dundalk Congress proved to be a turning-point for the ITGWU in its relations with the movement. It sent five Delegates: Thomas Foran (General President), John Bohan, James Halligan, William Hopkins and John O'Neill. Larkin was a Delegate from the Trades Council, which ensured his right to attend. The ITGWU's attendance depended on a ruling by the floor on the NUDL dispute. After much discord the ITGWU was admitted, and Daly succeeded Richardson as Secretary.

The dominance of traditional craft unions, divided between those that saw the United Kingdom as one country and those that, while Nationalist, saw independent Labour development as a threat to their position, was swept aside. Those who believed in independent Labour expression in an independent Ireland won the day. The way was clear for the ITGWU's separatist Socialist politics. At Galway in 1911 the ITGWU Delegation was the largest, paying £5 8s 8d in fees. It was an uneventful affair but confirmed trends set in 1910.

In Clonmel in 1912 Larkin gave notice of 'One Big Union'. 'We are going to advocate one society for Ireland for skilled and unskilled workers, so that when a skilled man is struck at, out comes every unskilled man, and when an unskilled man is struck at, he will be supported by the skilled tradesmen.' He moved the formation of an 'Irish Federation of Trades', but this was rejected, by 28 to 23.

It was Connolly's motion that 'the independent representation of Labour upon all public boards be, and is hereby, included amongst the objects of this Congress' that was historic. It effectually created the Labour Party. Independent working-class expression would be necessary in the Home-Rule parliament. The ITGWU wanted the 'abolition of the capitalist system'—the motion that most disturbed watching employers. Larkin was elected Chairman of the Parliamentary Committee, a remarkable acknowledgement for the four-year-old ITGWU. With O'Brien as Vice-Chairman and Daly and D. R. Campbell as Secretary and Treasurer, respectively, Socialists controlled Congress.

At the Cork Congress in 1913 the ITGWU sent thirteen Delegates, from Belfast, Dublin No. 1 Branch, Dublin No. 3, Dublin No. 16, Kingstown, and Sligo. In addition, Delia Larkin and Ellen Gordon represented the Irish Women Workers' Union, Richard Corish the Wexford Foundrymen's Union, and Daniel Lynch the Cork Carmen and Storemen. Larkin, presiding, called for the extension to Ireland of medical benefits under the National Insurance Act.[7]

IRISH WOMEN WORKERS' UNION

In August 1911 Delia Larkin appealed to women in the *Irish Worker*:

> Sisters—we appeal to you, whether you work in the mill, the factory, biscuits or jam, sack or packing—whether you are a weaver, spinner, washer, ironer, labeller, box-maker, sack-mender, jam packer, biscuit packer—whatever you do, or wherever you work, enrol now in the new Irish Women Workers' Trades Union, entrance fee 6d; weekly contribution 3d. Your brothers of the ITWU are prepared to render moral and financial assistance.

The Irish Women Workers' Union—in effect an ITGWU Branch—was launched in the Antient Concert Rooms, Great Brunswick Street (Pearse Street), on Tuesday 5 September 1911, with Jim Larkin as President and Delia Larkin as Secretary. William O'Brien claimed that Larkin interpreted 'persons' eligible to join the ITGWU under Rule 5 as meaning 'male persons' and hence the need for a separate women's union. He added that 'many people (including myself)' saw no necessity for it, and opposed organisation 'on a sex basis.' But Larkin 'had his own reasons (or prejudices) and had his way.' Whether this was so is unclear. To adopt a sectional attitude seems at odds with ITGWU philosophy. It may have been a case of providing 'jobs for the girls,' namely Delia.

Within days of the appeal three hundred women in Jacob's biscuit factory were on strike. The IWWU took rooms in Liberty Hall; its staff were paid by the ITGWU; its Trustees were ITGWU people; and, although it affiliated independently to Congress in 1912, it was not formally registered as an independent union. Its weekly column in the *Irish Worker* dealt with women workers' issues, exposed sweated conditions, promoted Delia's choir and drama group and also carried tips for housekeeping and dress. It had Branches in Belfast, Cork and Dundalk.[8]

DUBLIN

A general Lock-Out in the Dublin coal trade was supported by a mass meeting in Beresford Place on Sunday 16 July 1911, addressed by Connolly (Northern Organiser), P. T. Daly (Southern Organiser) and Harry Hopkins (Govan Trades Council, Scotland), one of many regular British speakers who spoke on union platforms. Connolly spoke in class terms of what the issues were likely to be:

> Whatever else may be said about Dublin people, there is one thing they are prepared to do and that is to stand straight and true to the working class . . . Yet there was never a war in which there was more heroism, more self-sacrifice, more humanity, more intense love of fellows, and more capacity for sacrifice shown than is shown by the working class during strikes. (Cheers.)

He spoke of the inter-relationship between sailors and dockers. The ITGWU would act in this international struggle of the working classes . . . We appeal to you to recognise what it is we are fighting for. We are fighting primarily for the right to organise. Our point is that Labour should have the same right to organise as the other class. After that we place our rights in regard to wages, hours, conditions of work. But we place this question of the right to organise first and also that the union most be recognised. By proceeding on these lines we will build up our organisation, getting higher wages and better conditions of employment in the future. In building up the unions we are raising Ireland up.

Connolly's message, so prophetic of the coming crisis, was echoed in a displayed notice:

WORKERS!—Fall into Line! Join the Transport Workers' Union—not an English Branch affair, but Union of Irishmen, governed by Irishmen—and doing good work for the workers! Remember, to be free, yourselves must strike the first blow!

The dispute arose from an Agreement of 1908 'signed by Sexton.' This was 'repudiated' because it was 'made against their interests,' causing the men to 'throw over the National Union.' The *Irish Worker* continued, somewhat erroneously, that 'there has been no members of the N.U.D.L. in Dublin—nay, in Ireland except Derry—since November, 1908.' It listed blackleg firms, advising readers that 'if you want coals or salt get them from the following trade union firms who can supply all classes of coal and who pay the union rate of wages.' Similar notices appeared regarding general cargo and cattle, with potential users invited to ring up for advice.

The principle of 'an injury to one is an injury to all' and 'all for each and each for all' stalked the Dublin quays. The firms worst affected were the Burns Line, 'struggling along' with scabs, the Laird Line, 'practically all tied up,' the City of Dublin Line, 'all tied up, no cargo moving,' and Tedcastle McCormick, 'cargo and coal tied up.' Edward Watson of the City of Dublin Line led the employers' resistance, refusing to recognise the union or to employ union labour. It was a 'Jekyll and Hyde' situation, though, as in other companies of which Watson was an agent or shareholder the union rates were paid and badges worn.

The *Irish Worker* asked—not for the first or the last time—'why is the Irish Party silent?' If trade was badly affected, 'why not charter boats?' Irish firms, such as Palgrave Murphy, paid the going rates; so Watson and Samuel McCormick were challenged to attend a public debate in the Antient Concert Rooms. Larkin would even 'stand aside,' so confident was the union in the virtue of its case.[9]

On Sunday 23 July in Beresford Place, Larkin rallied his forces. He had no quarrel with the Amalgamated unions but believed it would be 'better for Ireland if the men of Ireland were organised in a national union first, and then lined up with the International Trade Union movement.' He continued, in bread-and-roses style:

We are going to rouse the workers out of their slough of despond—out of the mire of poverty and misery—and lift them to a higher plane. If it is good for the employers to have clean clothing and good food, and books and music and pictures, so it is good that the people should have these things also . . . Don't bother cheering Larkin—he is but one of ourselves. It is you that want the cheers and it is you that deserve them. It is you, the class from which I came—the down-trodden class—that should get the cheers and all the good things that follow the cheers. I don't regard myself—a mere soul like myself in a mean body—as being the movement. You are the movement and for the time being I have been elected as your spokesman. I die tomorrow or the day afterwards but you have to live on.

Larkin and McKeown met Sir James Dougherty in an attempt at a settlement. They 'secured that every man who worked on the quays of Dublin goes back as a union man with the right to wear his badge.' This was a little premature. At a further meeting in Dublin Castle, Larkin, accompanied by P. Doyle and D. McKenna, met the Assistant Under-Secretary, O'Farrell, under the Chairmanship of Lord Aberdeen, to broker final terms.

What emerged was a Conciliation Board. Larkin was favourably disposed to conciliation and arbitration, despite his militant image. In the early, uncertain days such mechanisms created problems for the ITGWU and, at times, unnecessary or unfortunate compromise but offered recognition from employers and authorities. The principle of arbitration was written in to the ITGWU Rules. Larkin urged:

Now, drop the word 'conciliation'. It is not a Conciliation Board we are asking for. What we are asking for is a Board representing the men and the employers, both sides to have full powers to settle any matters pertaining to certain industries. Therefore, it is not a Conciliation Board we are to have.

Such explanation may have been mere hair-splitting, but it was sound, pragmatic trade unionism. In the settling of one dispute the settlement is incomplete without agreement to create a mechanism for preventing, mediating or settling further disputes. The *Irish Worker* noted that the employers' actions brought 'no howling from the unscrupulous, lying press; no appeals from the pulpits to these Christian gentlemen.'

A railway dispute lingered and caused William Martin Murphy to demand that the Government run the system while the dispute lasted, a view echoed in the press. The union observed: 'It's a strange world, my masters! The *Irish Times* and *Independent* turned Socialists. Ye Gods!'[10]

THE WEXFORD LOCK-OUT

In July 1911 McKeown recruited Wexford sailors and quaymen. Pierce's iron foundry locked out their men for joining, and Star Engineering, New Ross and Selskar Iron Works quickly followed suit. *Sinn Féin,* never a paper particularly on the workers' side, accused Larkin of 'dictating to the workers.' The ITGWU repudiated this: 'Jim Larkin never desired to boss any man or men; Jim Larkin on the contrary believes in democratic control.' Seán Etchingham of Gorey moved that the entire gate receipts of the Leinster hurling final between Dublin and Kilkenny at Maryborough (Port Laoise) 'be presented to the locked-out men in the Wexford foundries.' This was a 'true demonstration of the organisation and shows that a bond of brotherhood exists.' In Wexford, frustrated employers found that 'the weapon of starvation was insufficient' and brought in 'hired bullies' and additional police to protect imported scabs and to control pickets.

A local motor manufacturer, Belton, and the editor of the *Wexford Record*, English, lay in wait for P. T. Daly in an alley near the quays. When he bent to lift his fallen hat, 'Belton, with a heavy stick, beat Daly into a senseless condition.' Two passers-by came on the scene, otherwise Daly might well have been found 'floating in the river.' The RIC refused to take action, even though Daly 'was bleeding profusely from a severe cut on the head.' More scandalously, when he was brought to the Infirmary 'the authorities there refused to dress or even look at the wound.' Belton was 'guarded by a special force of police,' while English 'took the first train to Dublin.' This blatant violence showed how corrupt but determined the union's class enemies were. The men remained solid, despite the 'wire-pulling, the clerical influence and back-sliding.' Belton was fined £1. At the same sitting John Mullaly was given a month's imprisonment with hard labour for a 'trivial assault'; others were bound over for twelve months, some for 'singing songs' or 'playing an instrument accompanied by men carrying small flags.' There was no pretence at impartiality.[11]

In November, sixteen-year-old Rosanna Sinnott was given a month's imprisonment for failing to keep the peace for twelve months. This 'hardened criminal' was convicted for laughing at Pierce's manager, Salmon. The *Irish Worker* speculated that had she 'laughed very loud she'd have been sent to penal servitude for life.'

Encouragingly, suggested terms for a settlement emerged: all labourers to be paid 14s per week; the ITGWU to withdraw but the employers to recognise a local union of men working in the factories; an Arbitration Committee, with two from each side and an agreed Chairman to be established, with the possibility that the 'final and binding' award be brought to another Committee after six months; and workers to be given back their positions. In a secret ballot, however, only eight voted in favour: after fourteen bitter weeks of 'a strenuous fight the men are just as determined' in the face of 'great coercion.' In early December, Wexford was utterly divided: employers, large farmers, priests and press, supported by the police, on one side, and ordinary townsfolk and many shopkeepers on the other. The *Owain Tudor* left with no cargo, as dockers refused to load it. Suppliers pressured shopkeepers to stop advancing credit to the strikers. Praise was heaped on the women, 'whose sufferings God alone knows,' and children, 'whose merry prattle in the face of privation is heard at every street corner, cheering their heroic fathers in the fight.'

As Christmas approached, the deadlock seemed impossible to breach. Matters worsened when Daly was sentenced to two months' imprisonment in Waterford

Jail. Two local leaders, Richard Corish and Furlong, received shorter sentences. The employers thought they had severed the head from the beast. It proved to be a hydra.

The Lock-Out concluded in triumph, even if the vehicle was the Irish Foundry Workers' Union, a supposedly local union that the employers would recognise. Connolly, who brokered the final Agreement in Daly's enforced absence, reported that there was to be 'no restriction' on the IFWU. It could be directly affiliated to the ITGWU. All married men were to be taken back immediately, and others within thirty days. The officers of the IFWU had to be 'bona fide workers resident in the District.' Its Secretary was Corish, 'a willing lad, made of the best of metal.' So the men got recognition, the right to be in the union of their choice, no victimisation, control of the order of readmission, and the removal of all scabs. The only drawback was that Daly, 'the man who won the strike,' languished in jail, refusing to accept bail so that 'he might be at liberty to rejoice with the soldiers of the industrial army who he so ably led.' The ITUC complained to the authorities, while the *Irish Worker* noted that 'Daly has vindicated himself, and again proved, whatever his faults, he is still one of the workers, tried and true to his class.'

More than 3,000 people marched down Main Street, Wexford, on Thursday 8 February 'to do honour to the plucky Leeds fitters, who refused every inducement to scab' and who had been 'brought to Wexford under false pretences.' There were one or two 'after-shocks' after the men men resumed work as the employers attempted to retain scabs, were chary of dealing with IFWU Officials, or objected to men wearing their union badge. The solution to this last problem was Connolly's promise that 'we will have another button.' There was a euphoric atmosphere after what was now openly described as the second Wexford Rising, 'a rising of the manhood and womanhood of Wexford to the recognition of their power and dignity.' The IFWU won a special place in the 'inmost sanctuary in the hearts of their Transport brothers.' Five thousand people gathered at the Faythe in a torchlight demonstration of victory. Corish sang 'Freedom's Pioneers', Connolly's newly composed song to the air of 'The Boys of Wexford'. A thousand copies were printed, to be sold for the benefit of the Lock-Out's victims. 'The chorus was taken up by the vast audience and sung in most impressive fashion.'

> O, slaves may beg and cowards whine!
> We scorn their foolish tears,
> Be this our plan to lead the van
> As Freedom's Pioneers.

In his address Connolly showed the same pragmatism and concerns as he had in the all-night negotiations that produced the settlement.

> We will say, in order to avoid hurting any poor man's feelings, that it is a drawn battle, but we may think something different . . . You know that this Union is made to carve out its own destiny, wherever it pleases, however it pleases, and with whomsoever it pleases.[12]

Daly was still in prison, words that brought 'joy to the capitalists of not alone Wexford but Ireland.' Congress supported his release. On Monday 26 February, Connolly and Peter O'Connor of Waterford urged the Government to release Daly and other prisoners, as 'settlement has now been effected.' In Wexford a gold watch was on view in Sinnott's jewellery shop, together with an illuminated address in Daly's honour. His eventual return drew vast rejoicing crowds, first in Waterford, where a reception gathered, and then at the scene of his triumph. His wife was among those who marched with the Foresters' Brass and Reed Band and St Brigid's Fife and Drum Band to hear Daly, Corish and Larkin. The illuminated address was presented, expressing gratitude for all Daly's 'services, sacrifices and leadership.' It emerged that £100 had been sent to Wexford by the ITGWU for six months. Francis Sheehy Skeffington wrote of the 'heroic staunchness of the Wexford men' and their resistance, over months, to 'threats, cajoleries and violence.' He saw the Lock-Out as 'historic in the records of the Irish struggle for economic freedom.' The significance of events was on a 'National plane.'

Waterford saw 'one of the finest labour meetings ever held' in the Theatre Royal on Sunday 11 February. Greaves called the 'Workers' Police' who spontaneously defended strikers and pickets the 'first proletarian defence force recorded in Ireland.' It is a claim made also for a similar force created by James Fearon in Cork in 1909. Not organically linked to the Irish Citizen Army, Wexford and, before it, Cork undoubtedly planted the seed of a workers' defence force. In all three instances it was a reaction to employers' brutality and physical repression and their allies in the Courts, police and military.[13] Wexford demonstrated Connolly's skill and intelligence as industrial negotiator.

BELFAST AND DUNDALK

At a mass meeting in Beresford Place on Friday 21 July 1911 Michael McKeown recalled the struggle for 'social emancipation' in Belfast in 1907. The failure that followed was because the 'movement was not started in the right place.' Sectarianism divided the city. Since the 'general exodus from the Union' after Larkin left, 'the exploitation of labour had piled outrage upon outrage, iniquity upon iniquity,' until anyone with a 'spark of manhood left was ripe for rebellion.'

Connolly provided fresh leadership. Together with J. H. Bennett of the National Sailors' and Firemen's Union, six hundred men in the Head Line joined and struck. They received 4s Strike Pay the first week and 4s 6d the next. More than half the money came from Dublin, the remainder collected in city streets 'among the loyal-hearted workers.' With typical flourish, Connolly enthused:

We are proud of having taken part in the recent wonderful revolt in the world of Labour and look forward, with pleasure, to future activities in the same cause and to future successes under the banner of the Irish Branch of that great onward-moving, conquering army of toil, which is destined, I believe, in our time, to conquer and own the world.

The ITGWU was 'in the vanguard of that Irish Branch of the Army of Labour, and we are honoured when we carry its banner.' His direct-action tactics did not please 'lawyers, politicians or employers': it kept 'the two former out of a job and after leaves the latter out of pocket.' The union repudiated claims that a docker, Keenan, was killed because he was a non-Unionist. He was a needless victim of a rushing job when a bag shot down a chute.

Offices were opened at 6 Dalton Street in the Ballymacarett District of Belfast for quay and chemical workers. A railway strike saw the city streets again packed with the RIC, eager to use their batons. A peaceful unarmed demonstration on 13 August resulted in two deaths and a complete transport closure. Soldiers shot dead two more on 15 August. The only positive result was that members flocked to join the union. On Tuesday 11 September a large demonstration chaired by D. R. Campbell, President of Belfast Trades Council, and addressed by Connolly and Father Hopkins of the NSFU supported Wexford and called for a boycott of 'all the bicycles and other products manufactured' in the town.[14]

In October a thousand women enrolled after walk-outs from the York Street and Milewater Mills. Connolly saw them return without gaining concessions, but they 'had won the admiration of all who watched their conduct.' They were 'assuredly the stuff that will make a strong union.' They returned 'doubly strong in self-respect, with the spirit of revolt in their hearts.' But the dispute caused bitterness, especially with Mary Galway's Textile Operatives' Society of Ireland, which considered textiles its preserve. Women had joined the ITGWU at 'their request', however, despite Galway and Greig of the National Amalgamated Union of Labour appearing at factory gates and advising them not to. More than 3,000 attended a meeting in St Mary's Hall addressed by Marie Johnson, 'who has worked herself nearly to death in the struggle.' Connolly created the Irish Textile Workers' Union, an ITGWU section, and thanked the thousand strikers.

At the heart of the dispute, in addition to poor wages, were petty rules that resulted in constant fines and penalties. Connolly came up with a novel solution.

> If a girl is checked for singing, let the whole room start singing at once; if you are checked for laughing, let you all laugh; and if anyone is dismissed, all put on your shawls and come out as a body. And when you are returning, do not return as you usually do, but gather in a body outside the gate and march in singing and cheering.

The tactic was successful. Larkin ordered the women to transfer to the IWWU. The ITWU kept 'forging ahead' and acquired premises at 50 York Street, with a Committee of two representatives for each room of the York Street and Milewater Mills.

Labourers in Mulligan's and Antrim Iron Ore dithered over joining: 'There are no worse treated labourers in the city but the fatal sectarian and political divisions which are the curse of Belfast have hitherto conspired to keep them unorganised and at the mercy of their employers.' Slaters' assistants similarly could 'not summon up courage enough.' Connolly suggested the answer:

> Instead of divisions along the lines of creed we will see a union along the lines of industry, and instead of all the petty unions we will see the I.T.&G.W.U. gathering all into ONE BIG UNION of Irish workers against the united front of the employers. That, at least, is the hope and aim of Séamus.

This was one of the union's first direct references to the concept of the 'One Big Union', although it was still a cloudy vision, not yet well articulated. The sheer range and pace of activity left precious little time for strategic reflection. In November, Connolly issued an address 'To the Linen Slaves of Belfast,' with Winifred Carney and Ellen Gordon assisting in a vigorous campaign. It was the high point of Connolly's time in the city. Sectarian violence flared in July 1912. Many Protestant trade unionists were victims of their co-religionists. In Dundalk, McKeown made advances for distillery, local authority and general workers and pushed for improvements in housing. Members praised the management of Dundalk Distillery for its concessions, and labourers in the Great Northern Railway won advances. McKeown was an able Leader, in some respects much in Larkin's mould. 'Now, I am myself a teetotaller, a non-smoker, and I never lay a bob on the winner or the loser, and I am always delighted to see my fellow workers practise these virtues.'[15]

CORK, SLIGO AND GALWAY

In 1912 matters disimproved in Cork. Daly found disorganisation but men 'clamouring for a visit from Jim Larkin.' He reflected on earlier successes 'when the I.T.W.U. was in full swing' and labour conditions on Cork docks were 'the best in Great Britain and Ireland.' Stevedores had been 'representatives of the men elected by members of the Union'; wages were considerably increased; men got the best legal advice in cases of compensation; and 'victimisation was absolutely wiped out.'

Attempts at revival were made after the 1913 Congress, with Larkin, Connolly, Thomas Lawlor, O'Brien, Partridge and Ellen Gordon addressing meetings in Cork and Queenstown (Cóbh). Partridge reopened the Branch at Liberty Hall, 4 Merchants' Quay. Peter Larkin (James's brother) replaced Partridge and was assisted by Daly, Con O'Lyhane and John Dowling. By mid-June 900 members were enrolled. When Ben Tillett attended the Conference of the General Federation of Trade Unions in the city in July 1913 he urged all to join the ITGWU. The Storemen and Carmen's union became No. 20 Branch and were rewarded with unsought increases of 2s a week. This ITGWU was worth joining.[16]

The Sligo Branch was denounced from the pulpit by Bishop Clancy in March 1912, when Larkin visited the town. Clancy spoke 'lest silence on my part in such an emergency might be interpreted . . . as a tacit approval.' He condemned Larkin's 'Socialist tendency' and 'pretended sympathy with the poor,' suggesting that 'no faithful member of the Church' would attend any meetings. The clergy were, apparently, 'only too glad to help workingmen remedy grievances.' Should they instead turn to Larkin they would earn 'not only the condemnation of the Church but God's displeasure.' He prayed that God would 'preserve us, both now and for all future time, from the enemy.'

Whether or not encouraged by the bishop, violence dogged the union. Larry Garvey and his son savagely assaulted a docker called Rorke. George Burke was despatched from Dublin. McKeown extended membership to storemen, ware-housemen, Corporation workers and the Liverpool ships. When Martin Moffat, a seaman, looked for 'stock money' on 8 March 1913 the striking crew were arrested for disobeying orders. The Secretary of the Sligo Branch, John Lynch, blacked the ship, now crewed with Shipping Federation scabs. Blacklegs arrived from Liverpool and Daly from Liberty Hall with an Official of the NSFU, J. H. Bennett. The number of police and soldiers increased over the next three weeks as the strike was stepped up. Violence broke out and a blackleg, Garvey, murdered a union member, Dunbar, by hitting him over the head with a shovel. Connolly insisted, 'Remember Sligo.' Employers were playing a 'desperate game,' and Dunbar was 'a good lad. May his soul rest in peace and may the hellhound who murdered him—may he get his reward!'

The 'largest meeting seen in Sligo in the past fifty years' took place in the Town Hall on 20 April, addressed by two local Councillors, Lynch and Daly. The Foresters' Brass and Reed Band and the Transport Union Band paraded. The town's 'inhabitants and ratepayers' offered their 'entire support to the workers in their fight against the tyranny of the employers' and demanded that they 'at once give way to the voice of the people of the town and county.' From what they had seen and heard there was 'justice in their demands.' The Sligo Branch sent 'hearty congratulations' to their Dublin comrades 'on their magnificent victory over the City of Dublin Steam Packet Company' and acknowledged the efforts of Larkin and George Burke (NSFU). Grateful members urged workers to 'purchase the necessaries of their households' from local employers and traders who had supported them.

In May some members made public repentance for their 'recent acts' and accepted any penalties that 'may be inflicted within the Rules.' On 20 June a Stevedores' Association was founded, under ITGWU control, to secure the dockers' independence from unscrupulous employers. The employers 'completely caved in.' The union's position 'was secured.'[17]

Galway became an exception to the ITGWU rule. After Larkin addressed what was until then a compliant local work force after the 1911 Congress, the response was not to join the ranks of the ITGWU but to create a local body, the Galway Workers' and General Labourers' Union. By 1912 this had grown large enough to advertise for a full-time Secretary, 'preferably an Irish one.' A more obvious move would have been to throw in their lot with Larkin. It became clear, however, that 'the militant reputation of Larkin's union . . . made some people apprehensive.' In early December 'an arrangement was concluded with the N.U.D.L.' The only Irish NUDL Branches left were Belfast, Derry and Drogheda. James O'Connor Kessack, Larkin's successor as Organiser, must have been mightily persuasive. Galway's resistance to the ITGWU became a continuing problem.[18]

INTERNATIONALISM: THE SEAMEN AND RAILWAYMEN'S STRIKE, 1911

The National Transport Workers' Federation was established in Britain in 1908. In June 1911 it co-ordinated an international attempt to break the control of seamen by employers through the Shipping Federation. Not losing sight of its international outlook, the ITGWU championed the cause in Dublin, where the NSFU had 400 members. The General Secretary of the NSFU, J. Havelock Wilson, appointed the ITGWU as its agents, and its members were paid Strike Pay from ITGWU funds. In July £1,520 was spent in the first three weeks of the strike, and the men voted a levy of 6d a man. On 12 June, Larkin asked William O'Brien for Connolly's address. On 14 June he was appointed Northern Organiser, initially at least to act for seamen. It was a historic moment. Putting Connolly on the ITGWU payroll gave him a reliable income and committed him to industrial as well as political labour in Ireland.

The much-feared Shipping Federation controlled access by crews to British ships. Larkin attacked to belittle it, reduce fear and make previously unbeatable opponents seem fragile targets.

> My friends, there is no fairy story about the Shipping Federation. The devil himself is a decent chap in comparison with the soulless creatures who organised and who control that industrial octopus—the men who carry out the functions of that Black Hand organisation.

The seamen's strike warranted a special number of the *Irish Worker,* with a notice for a 'Mass Meeting of All Workers' to be held in Beresford Place on Sunday 18 June. It was 'our duty in this fix' to support the sailors: Irishmen were urged to stay away from shipping lines in dispute, with the exhortation 'Don't act the scab.' Larkin talked of the 'momentous event' and how it affected them all: 'old-style' union leaders were the 'real enemy to advance and progress.' The union 'had no difficulty with organised employers. These men could be beaten to a "frazzle" if it was not for the fact that besides defeating the employers, they had to defeat the old-time conservative trade unionists.' The 'old system' of unions had to go. A new spirit, 'based on a scientific knowledge would enable them to contend with the employing classes.'

News of the seamen's ultimate success was carried over the next few weeks. The role of the ITGWU attracted interest in many Irish ports. Buoyed with success, and noting that membership of the NUDL had fallen to 7,000 through its opposition to the seamen, Larkin trumpeted his new vision.

> The time is rotten ripe for one union, for one union only, a Trade Union, not a local transport federation but a real federation. A local federation—will result in that Union having a number of small-minded men with their narrow, limited outlook, quarrelling and snarling at one another to see who will boss the show. We have had this exhibition before, and I plead with those who lead, and with those who are willing to drop their sectionalism, to form up in one solid phalanx. Let your cry be, 'One union of all men engaged in the transport of goods—one

Trade Union' . . . Be true to your class—no dissension, no bickering, speak like one man—act like one man.

Some amongst you will say why should a paper catering for the Irish worker appeal to us in Liverpool. Seven out of ten of those who toil in or about the quays of that great port are Irish, either by birth or blood. Again, I speak on behalf of the first and only Trade Union in existence—a union which embraces all classes of the workers—the Irish Transport Union. National in name; international in aim and object. A union which stands for the overthrow of the present brutal system of master and slave, and because, last but not least, when you in Great Britain were attacked—when the Shipping Federation imported scabs to load and reload boats on our side—we, of the Irish Transport Union, took our fate in both hands, and refused to load or unload boats sailed or loaded by scabs.[19]

The message, however, was unclear. Did Larkin still harbour ambitions to take 'his union' back to Liverpool? Was this part of a persistent attempt to amalgamate and merge British transport workers' unions into one giant body? How did such motives square with a commitment to Irish self-determination?

Not for the first or the last time, horns were locked with the Burns Line. Larkin charged that the men were poorly paid and 'compelled' to pay into an 'alleged Benefit Society, managed by a clique in Glasgow,' and that no Irishmen were allowed any involvement. Correspondence from the 'Silent Slaves of the Channel' suggested that the men were the worst paid, at 28s a week. The Liverpool seamen achieved victory, while matters in Dublin remained unresolved.

Almost lost sight of was the settlement in Brooks Thomas, where an increase was won, recognition gained, blacklegs ejected and no victimisation guaranteed. Belief in Larkin was growing. Seamen's settlements quickly followed in the Dublin Scottish Line, Burns and Lairds, Liverpool, City of Dublin Line and Tedcastle's. In Palgrave Murphy all union conditions were granted, while the Dublin General Steamship Company was praised for having 'granted union conditions' and as 'the only firm sailing out of Ireland who always recognise union Rules and rates.' Stirring the pot further, the question was asked why 'they don't sail to Liverpool or take livestock . . . instead of allowing them to starve to death around the bare fields of Cabra.' The seamen's triumph reminded members that they were part of an international brotherhood and sisterhood.

We have something at stake . . . [that] Irish workers took our share in the struggle of the working class, and that we have in the past brought no blush of shame to the cheek of any Irishman, either at home or abroad. We close, wishing our brothers of all nations—an maith duith [sic]—good luck with you.

Internationalism motivated the ITGWU's support for a railway strike in August. Joint notice was published by Larkin and Walter Halls of the Amalgamated Society of Railway Servants.

Owing to the bloodthirsty and callous manner in which the Government are supporting the irreconcilable attitude of the railway magnates in declining to meet the just claim of the Railway Workers, we, Irish workers, have been appealed to by our fellow-workers in Great Britain to stand by them in their heroic struggle. Their fight is our fight, therefore we, the undersigned, acting on behalf of the Committee in charge of the strike, declare that no traffic must be handled in, about, or on the Irish rail system until the members' grievances are remedied.

On Sunday 20 August a mass meeting 'of immense proportions' took place in the Phoenix Park to celebrate the railwaymen's victory. William Partridge chaired, attacking John Saturnus Kelly of the scab Irish Railway Workers' Union. Bob Grier (ASRS, Portadown) emphasised that no victimisation would be tolerated. Halls said it was 'the proudest day of my life. I feel more pleased than if I had been a millionaire.' Larkin, who, as ever, drew the loudest cheers, picked out the 'heroic' women of Inchicore for special praise. They 'faced starvation rather than do work for those men who remained in,' and that 'should not be forgotten, and it will not be forgotten. We will not forget those brave women.' He wanted to 'see you fighting in Ireland for a Federation of Transport Workers. Don't forget that transport workers won you your fight.' This echoed ideas for a grand transport workers' union in Britain. It is not clear whether Larkin was echoing this idea for Ireland or attempting to maximise the potential negotiating power of the ITGWU in federal talks.

Another general railway strike took place throughout Ireland from mid-September. Despite solidarity with the earlier British strike, there was to be no return support from across the channel. Larkin threatened to pull out any workers even remotely connected with railways, and railway directors took back nine-tenths of their employees. The ITGWU, for all its infancy—it was still not three years in existence—was expending huge energy and resources on other unions' strikes. It would be rewarded for such endeavours in its own imminent hour of need.[20]

DUBLIN EMPLOYERS' FEDERATION

The Dublin Employers' Federation was founded on 30 June 1911. It was set up to 'prevent strikes' and oppose 'intimidation and violence.' In classic 'free labour' parlance, men 'desirous of retaining or returning to their employment, are prevented from doing so.' The situation was 'very grave.' There was 'an urgent necessity for co-operation to protect the interests of employers.'

The objects of the Federation were 'mutual protection and indemnity of all employers of labour' and 'to promote freedom of contract between employers and employees.' The Dublin employers had learnt well from their Cork counterparts. Two years previously the situation there was bad; it was now 'entirely satisfactory and they have experienced little or no labour trouble since the Federation was founded.' William Martin Murphy was conspicuous within the Provisional Committee of the Federation.[21] Employers were going to deny the principle of combination to the workers by themselves combining.

CITY OF DUBLIN STEAM PACKET COMPANY

Were it not for the events later in the year, the dispute with the City of Dublin Steam Packet Company would be regarded as the major event of 1913. It arose from attempts by the union to recruit foremen. Men apparently agreed to join, but the manager of the line, Edward Watson, would 'not allow them.' The ITGWU felt that Watson 'must, therefore, accept the responsibility for the stoppage.' In addition to the direct grievance, Watson's veto on the creation of a Wages Board for seamen also rankled.

The strike began among quay porters on the morning of Tuesday 30 January, without, as far as the City of Dublin Line was concerned, 'any notice, previous complaint, or even any request.' Whereas the company previously obtained substitute workers, 'organised terrorism and intimidation' prevented that on this occasion. Sailings were suspended until further notice. Naturally, the company felt in no way 'responsible for any loss, damage or delay to goods.'

The ITGWU forthrightly answered the charges. 'We print below a circular published by the Company in which they state they have had no complaints, no notice, no request. That is a lie!' The company alleged 'organised terrorism'. Larkin challenged 'Mr. O'Callaghan or Mr. Edward Watson' to join him at a public meeting of company employees, where each would state their case. He was 'prepared to abide by the result. Now, what say the two gentlemen? Where is your intelligence?' Conversely, Larkin was happy to attend a shareholders' meeting, and 'if we cannot convince them that the men's claim is justified, we call off the strike.' Watson was 'using other people's property to vent his spleen on the workers.'

Emmet Larkin thought the City of Dublin Line was a 'good choice for a stand up fight,' but Greaves asked, Why would they wish for such a fight? They were not fighting elsewhere. He suggested that, even almost a century later, propaganda by employers about a belligerent ITGWU obscured the facts. William Martin Murphy's support for the City of Dublin Line, directly and indirectly through the *Irish Independent,* incurred Larkin's wrath. Larkin dismissed Murphy as the 'most foul and vicious blackguard that ever polluted any country—whose career has been one long series of degrading and destroying the characters of men.' Murphy employed 'a group of journalistic renegades, whose bodies and souls he controls. They write and publish the most foul, vicious and lying tirades against the working class at so much a column.'

Mass meetings began, although the Lord Mayor, Lorcan Sherlock, refused the use of the Mansion House, offering instead to 'get the facts published.' More than 6,000 people attended in Smithfield on Sunday 16 March, proceeding to Liberty Hall with Bands. The ITGWU's close relationship with the Irish Stationary Engine Drivers' and Firemen's Trade Union saw them place themselves 'morally and financially' at Liberty Hall's disposal 'in their heroic fight' with the shipping line. The ITGWU's 'fight is our fight, and our fight theirs.' It was a message of solidarity that would be tested to the limit.

Larkin, however, was 'anxious and depressed.' The campaign of vilification took its toll, together with his non-stop activity of the previous six years. Surprising everyone, he resigned as Chairman of the Parliamentary Committee of the ITUC in March, flatly declining to reconsider and insisting that he would not even be a Congress Delegate. Was this the first sign of Larkin's mental exhaustion, not usually observed until after the 1913 Lock-Out? Or was it some more sinister streak in his character of irrational behaviour, a proneness to depression?

O'Brien, writing to Connolly, was worried.

Larkin is looking and feeling bad lately and if the strain is not eased soon I fear he will break down mentally and physically.

O'Brien still admired him:

He must be made of iron to stand it so long. He is despondent too, which is most unusual with him, and he told me a week ago, and a number of us last night, that if the fight with the City of Dublin was over, he would resign and leave the country altogether.

That he should have said this seems extraordinary, almost incredible. O'Brien finally persuaded Larkin to see a doctor. Not surprisingly, 'nervous debility caused by overwork' was diagnosed. In early April the union complained that the City of Dublin Line was 'subsidised by the Government, practically a State concern,' and yet it denied their workmen 'the elementary rights of a free citizen.' Entering its employment, a worker lost his 'invaluable right of a human being to associate with his fellows.'[22]

In mid-April, Larkin told a rally in Beresford Place that the employers had spent more than £20,000 to break the union. They had failed. Richardson, Sheridan and, sadly, Thomas Greene, former Secretary of No. 1 Branch, were 'guaranteed £1,000' if they could break the ITGWU. In March they set up a yellow union, the Dublin Transport Workers' Union, and took strikers' places in the City of Dublin Line.

Larkin outlined the quay labourers' demands: essentially 30s (£1 10s) for a nine-hour day, a 56-hour week, with corresponding rises for casual men, checkers, sailors and firemen. Reflecting on the settlement terms, Larkin said he was, 'of course, aware that the ultimate solution is the ownership and control of the means of life' by the workers, 'but we are not at that stage of development as yet.' He outlined a structure of control based on shipbuilding and engineering, construction, transport and distribution, and suggested that three workers and three employers meet regularly as a Wages Board at the trade level with, above it, a City Wages Board and a Controlling or Appeals Board above that, with a Chief Commissioner and five employers and five workers nominated by Dublin Trades Council.

At the successful conclusion of the strike Thomas MacPartlin, Chairman of Dublin Trades Council, reflected that twelve or so weeks previously 'the Dublin press came out very bad against the workers. They stated that they were out of funds, had no money and were "eating one another to get back to work". The strike would 'fall through,' and only 'Larkin was keeping them out.' But there had 'not been a single scab,' and 'not a single man weakened.' MacPartlin did 'not believe another city could carry out a fight for so long without having a traitor in the ranks.'

Larkin published an open letter in the *Irish Worker*, headed 'How to stop strikes', repeating his conciliation ideas. It seemed an unlikely message from Larkin, but there was method in his madness. Conciliation extended unions' authority, prestige and membership, allowed funds to build and extended union rates in all industries, organised or unorganised. It gave the lie to the suggestion in the employers' press that Larkin was simply interested in strife.[23]

CO. DUBLIN

An ITGWU campaign in Co. Dublin began in earnest in June 1913. Meetings from Balbriggan to Kingstown demanded 'better housing, more land with cottages, and a half-holiday on Saturday.' Labourers were advised: 'Bear in mind, workers, this is no political agitation, but an agitation in which you should all join if you wish to improve the position of yourselves, your wives and children.' In Baldoyle, Partridge was said to have the 'finest and most powerful voice for outdoor meetings.' No matter 'how big the meeting or how strong the wind' his voice penetrated 'to the outer limits.'

On Sunday 8 June, Peter Larkin addressed crowds who flocked to join. 'Ireland's Eye' told the *Irish Worker's* readers that

> the remedy is in your own hands to improve your present unenviable lot. Strike out for yourselves, locking together the different Districts in one solid organisation, and I promise you that if you do so then before the next harvest moon appears you will be in receipt of better wages, you will have received your half holiday on Saturday, and . . . be on the right road to better housing accommodation and more land for yourselves, your wives and families in the future.

Crumlin on 22 June maintained the momentum. Farmers were not passive and met to confront 'Larkin and the Union', opened a subscription list, appointed a drill sergeant and decided that 'guns were to be ordered.' Undeterred, hundreds joined the union. On Sunday 13 July a meeting was arranged for Clondalkin at one o'clock 'to forward the campaign on behalf of the slaves of the countryside.' A Farm Labourers' Section was formed, holding meetings at Crumlin Forge and Baldoyle on Saturday evenings and in Lucan Band Room and Swords on Sundays after last Mass.

On 30 July the County Dublin Farmers' Association said they would have 'nothing to do with Larkin as our men are well satisfied with their lot and have no grievances whatsoever.' The Association opened premises at 23 Bachelor's Walk and exchanged correspondence with the union in August, stressing that there should be no stoppage while matters were under discussion. By October an inquiry was held by Dublin Castle, but on the ground, employers like Andrew Kettle imported blacklegs to St Margaret's. Against 'tremendous odds and unprecedented difficulties,' labourers 'displayed a heroism and self sacrifice which must ever resound to their credit.' Their struggle, however, was increasingly falling within the shadow of the Lock-Out. In January 1914, Co. Dublin labourers had been 'five months fighting and fighting still. Think of it! . . . Today they are of its very salt.'

Greaves regarded the Co. Dublin strikes as 'of great historical importance.' The ITGWU reclaimed most of the ground once occupied by the Gasworkers' Union after 1890. City workers supported their rural comrades and applied blacking action when contested products entered the capital's markets.[24] The strike also demonstrated the ITGWU's attractiveness for rural labourers, presaging its huge geographical and numerical growth after the Rising.

THE *IRISH WORKER*

The first edition of the *Irish Worker and People's Advocate* appeared on Saturday 27 May 1911, edited by James Larkin. It made its 'bow—not in any humble manner' but came as 'one who desires to speak to you . . . with honour and pride.' It concluded: 'Too long, aye! Far too long, have we, the Irish working people, been humble and inarticulate.' It quickly rid workers of humility and brought hope where once there reigned despair. Larkin noted that the 'Irish Working Class (capital letters good Mr. Printer)' was beginning to awaken and 'realise the truth of the old saying, "He who would be free himself must strike the blow."'

On Tuesday 24 October the Irish Co-operative Labour Press was founded to secure the *Irish Worker*. Shares to the value of £1,000 were issued, the usual suspects investing. The paper told its ever-growing readership:

> We want the *Worker* to be your paper. It was started without capital—it has already proven its usefulness. It can be made a powerful weapon in the hands of men who are imbued with principles that animate us all, namely, that the Government of Ireland should be in the hands of the people.

On 30 December the ITGWU reflected on the year, recording that 600 children attended Dublin No. 3 Branch Christmas Party. The Secretary, John Bohan, was Father Christmas, and Delia Larkin was among the Organisers. 1911 had witnessed 'two epoch-making events': the launch of the Irish Labour Party and the 'birth of the *Irish Worker,* the only independent paper in the country, started for the express purpose of advocating the principles of the common people, articulating their grievances, and voicing their demands.'

The circulation of the *Irish Worker* was 26,000 in June, rising to 66,500 in July, 74,750 in August and a staggering 94,994 in September. 'Out of the depths' it had 'arisen to articulate the cause of your miseries.' The circulation of *Sinn Féin* never rose above 5,000 and averaged about 2,000, making these remarkable figures.

The degree to which the *Irish Worker* 'conditioned' workers can only be surmised. Greaves saw it as 'Larkin's oratory congealed in print.' Dermot Keogh thought it 'contained no original labour philosophy,' was 'vitriolic and scurrilous,' with many issues containing a 'libel a line,' and yet this 'confused and palpitating sense of grievance and unrequited appeals for redress became known pejoratively as Larkinism.' Emmet O'Connor saw Larkinism as giving workers 'an ethical vision' and forging an 'alternative morality by the patient construction of a workers' counter-culture,' while for John Newsinger 'the scabrous attacks on slum landlords, sweat-shop employers, lying journalists, various scabs, corrupt politicians [and] bullying policemen served a definite and calculated purpose.' Larkin was 'out to diminish them by ridicule, to cut them down to size and show them up as moral pygmies.' The paper was distinguished by cartoons, songs, poetry, short stories, even one and two-act plays—all manner of literary material, best exemplified by the special Christmas edition of 1912. The *Irish Worker* was undoubtedly one of Larkin's great achievements—and one of his neglected legacies.

By 1913 the *Irish Worker* was referring to Larkin as 'the Chief', 'the one and only Jim Larkin' and similar titles. Connolly hated 'all this playing to one man' and complained to O'Brien about Larkin's thirst for admiration.[25] There was an element of chicken-and-egg about this sycophantic praise. On the one hand Larkin undoubtedly courted it, while on the other it was a genuine outpouring of affection and belief in the man. Without such adulation and respect the morale of workers and their families would have been unable to withstand the onslaught that awaited them after August, or indeed to have incurred that onslaught in the first place in defence of the principle of trade unionism.

LIBERTY HALL AND CROYDON PARK
On 24 February 1912 it was announced that the ITGWU had

> re-opened the old Northumberland Hotel, 18 Beresford Place, as the Head Office. In future the above building will be known as Liberty Hall.

It crystallised growing self-confidence in brick and stone. Both the IWWU and NSFU had offices, with rooms for the Band, weekly Irish classes, a choir and a drama group. 'Shellback' [Richard Braithwaite or Branagan] suggested a holiday camp, an idea taken up by Delia and Jim Larkin, initially in the form of a summer camp. In August 1913 it was announced that the ITGWU had taken control of Croydon Park in Clontarf, described as a 'Jovial Revolution'.[26] A social centre now accompanied a new Head Office.

THE *TITANIC*
The ITGWU recorded its shock at the loss of the *Titanic*. George Burke was elected Secretary of the NSFU at a large meeting in Liberty Hall addressed by James Larkin. Under the heading 'Titanic horror', improved safety regulations were demanded. 'We tender to the relatives of those who went down on the coffin ship, *Titanic*, our sincere condolences.' It was hoped that 'the sacrifice of their valuable lives will be the means of doing away with the soulless creatures who control the Board of Trade allowing a vessel to go to sea carrying over 2,000 passengers with only sufficient

life-boats to carry 900.' If it was not murder, 'what is murder?' Perhaps now 'a demand will be made for the proper authority to supervise all vessels, passenger and cargo; and the question of ship-owners' profits, dividends or shareholders will not stand in the way of the preservation of human life.'[27]

POLITICS

Freedom was not considered possible by many struggling in urban slums or on rural wastes. Sinn Féin, Nationalists, even Unionists had their own versions of 'freedom' but generally excluded the common people. Larkinism brought new concepts and, more importantly, new possibilities. The *Irish Worker* vented these ideas. 'Freedom', expressed in straightforward, class terms not previously used, was

> a land where the farmer or gombeen man having, with the money or pledging the credit of the Irish people, been enabled to buy from the Kenmares, the Barrymores, and the other parasites—formerly known as the landlords—the land of the Irish people, the people will be allowed by the grace of, and with the permission of, the new landocracy to exist on the soil of Ireland, always keeping in mind, however, this fact: that permission to exist will only be continued so long as the people are willing to work for this new gang of parasites long hours for low wages, and under the most degrading conditions.

Industrial struggle would not be successful without the indivisible struggle for self-determination. Unionists were attacked as 'sycophants, privilege-mongers, place-hunters, nation-levellers, blood-suckers, carrion-crows.' Sinn Féin was dismissed for its 'imported economics based on false principles,' which would 'encourage foreign capitalists to exploit cheap Irish labour.' Nationalists did not believe in political freedom and 'knew nothing of economic freedom.' Larkin insisted that the ITGWU, on behalf of workers, wanted 'neither imported economics nor imported capitalists': 'By freedom, we mean that we, Irishmen in Ireland, shall be free to govern this land called Ireland by Irish people in the interests of all the Irish people.'

Jobbery, corruption and double standards among the members of Dublin Corporation (City Council) were exposed. Among the 'questions we would like answered,' Alderman Cotton MP was asked 'how many trade union workers' he employed in his gasworks, and how many imports.

In nominating Thomas Greene, Secretary of Dublin No. 1 Branch, for the South Dock Ward the union unequivocally identified with Labour. Greene had 'known what poverty meant' and was 'always accessible,' having 'no axe to grind' and being 'under the control of the Union which employs him.' The paper advertised a meeting to be held in Albert Place, off Grand Canal Street, on the following Sunday in his support and in protest at 'gross police interference' on the previous Sunday. The authorities, if not the masses, understood well what message the new paper was preaching.

In 1911 Greene was successful, as were Lorcan O'Toole (Trinity Ward), Thomas Lawlor (Wood Quay) and Richard O'Carroll (Mansion House). Foran chaired a celebration meeting with Bands and procession to Albert Place. In January 1912 three ITGWU Labour candidates fought the Dublin Municipal Elections: Larkin (North Dock), Foran (South Dock) and William Hopkins (Trinity). They held torchlight rallies in Beresford Place; but Labour had mixed fortunes. O'Carroll, a bricklayer, was returned for Mansion House; Lawlor, a tailor, won in Wood Quay. Larkin and Hopkins were returned but were disqualified through having criminal convictions. In Belfast, Connolly contested the Dock Ward and McKeown switched from the United Irish League (Irish Party), for which he held a seat, to fight Smithfield for Labour. Union candidates were returned in Sligo and Wexford. Michael Mullen (Mícheál Ó Maoláin) contested Inn's Quay, Dublin, on a programme of night sittings for the Corporation, baths and wash-houses, better accommodation and tighter control of the Public Health Acts and those who 'adulterated' food.

In January 1913, however, ITGWU candidates had disappointing fortunes in local elections. McKeown and Connolly lost in Belfast. Partridge claimed, rightly, that Larkin brought hope. He also threatened those holding the power to sweat, rackrent, profiteer and generally exploit. These pulled out all the stops of bribery, personation, character assassination and negative press campaigning.[28] Liberty Hall's disappointment was palpable. Its expectations had been high.

CONSOLIDATION

In 1911 the ITGWU's membership advanced in Dublin, Belfast, Bray, Cork, Waterford and Wexford. Significant increases were won for thousands. With expansion, strategic alliances developed with sailors and railwaymen. Thoughts began to turn to longer-term policies and to 'One Big Union' for Ireland. All was not rosy, however. Employers learnt lessons from Cork, and the formation of the Dublin Employers' Federation saw preparations for a counter-offensive. The *Irish Worker* concluded that 1912 had not been a 'bad sort of fellow'. It saw improvements in wages and conditions, the introduction of the State Insurance Scheme and of the Government of Ireland Bill. Six Labour Councillors were elected in Dublin. 'We had the satis-fac-tion of proving in a concrete manner the spirit of divine discontent amongst the intelligent section of the working class, by the return of the six tried and true representatives to our local Administrative Chamber, Cork Hill.' As for 1913, it

> seems to presage a more hopeful outlook for Labour, but as we believe God helps those who help themselves, keeping in mind that success means further success let nothing dispirit you, good Reader. Up, take your place in the ranks, and play the man, make the year proud of you and your efforts. Let it be a long pull and a strong pull, but all pull together. Our watchword—the World for Labour. Equal Opportunity for All.'[29]

Chapter 5 ⌒

WHO DARED TO WEAR THE RED-HAND BADGE?: THE DUBLIN LOCK-OUT, 1913–14

The Dublin Lock-Out is extensively recorded, particularly in Pádraig Yeates's monumental account.[1] This chapter merely examines some iconic moments and assesses their significance.

The central issue was the right of workers to join the union of their choice. The Lock-Out lives large in the imagination of the public, writers and historians. The issues, however, are not just 'history'. After two decades of Social Partnership, union recognition still tops the agenda, despite an illusory 'right' to trade union membership enshrined in the Constitution of Ireland.[2] The right of a privileged, powerful few to control wealth and its distribution and to deny the right of those who produce that wealth to gain access to its control remains the central issue.[3]

ECONOMY AND SOCIETY

In 1911 more than 400,000 people lived in Dublin, a city then bounded by Clontarf, Drumcondra, Clonliffe, Glasnevin and Kilmainham. The main employments were Guinness's brewery and Jacob's biscuit factory, administrative and civil service positions, carters, dockers and transport workers. Most jobs were unskilled and casual. There were 17,223 general labourers, 3,081 carters and draymen and 4,604 messengers and porters. Competition for employment was exacerbated by the continuous influx of those coming off the land. Persistent large-scale unemployment depressed wages. An average labourer's wage was about £1 a week, assuming he got a full week's work. For women, wages were as low as 7s. These rates were low by comparison with Belfast or large British cities. There were 13,551 domestic servants, 4,294 dressmakers and milliners, 2,296 tailoresses, seamstresses and shirt-makers and 1,246 charwomen.

Trade unionism was well established among craftsmen, but the unskilled were largely unorganised. Industrial relations were autocratic and paternal, with employers holding the whip hand over a supine work force. When the Lock-Out began the ITGWU had 24,000 members, half of them in Dublin.

Low incomes were reflected in terrible living conditions and poor diet. A Committee of Inquiry into the housing question reported in 1914. It found that 87,305 people lived in appalling squalor in city-centre tenements, with 80% of families occupying only one room. 22,701 lived in 'third-class' housing, officially termed 'unfit for human habitation'. Overcrowding and insanitary conditions meant that disease was rife. The Public Health Report for 1913 showed that of 8,639 deaths 1,444 were from tuberculosis and 4,642 from 'nervous, circulatory, respiratory and digestive diseases,' such as pneumonia and diarrhoea. There were 1,808 deaths of infants under one year of age. Alcohol and crime added to the desperate conditions. Grinding poverty and degradation bred despair. It was this crippling quality that Larkinism was to get rid of. Once given hope, a tattered multitude became a ragged army.[4]

WILLIAM MARTIN MURPHY

There were several attempts to organise Dublin's tramway workers. The Dublin and District Tramwaymen's Trade Union, formed in 1890, had petered out by 1897. Revived in 1901 with the support of Dublin Trades Council, it enlisted the assistance of city Officials to gain recognition and respectfully forward its memorials. Lacking self-confidence, it was easily thwarted by Murphy, who, while tolerating representation, insisted that it be docile.

In 1908 a 'house union' was set up, but its leaders were intimidated, bought off or, in one case, banished to Murphy's bus company in Paisley, Scotland. This sorrowful tale was told in the *Irish Worker* in December 1913 to stiffen the spine of those who joined the ITGWU after the great transport battles of August 1911.[5]

Murphy kept his men in check through autocratic management, providing little or no time off and maintaining a reserve system so that 'trouble-makers' always knew there were men ready and willing to replace them in a city where any permanent job was a godsend. With a yellow union planned to block the ITGWU, tramwaymen were called to Liberty Hall on 28 June 1913. Larkin identified the powerhouse workers for their strategic importance. If they came out, the power went off and the trams stopped.

By 12 July 800 men had joined. Murphy tried to dissuade them but would not enter a public debate: 'We cannot disguise ourselves from the fact that an attempt is being made by an Organiser outside the Company to seduce the men.' The directors had 'not the smallest objection to the men forming a legitimate Union. (Applause.)' The matter became personal. The *Irish Worker* branded Murphy a 'damned liar' who had been 'driven from public life as a toady, renegade, an untruthful and dishonest politician, a false friend, a sweating employer, a weak-kneed tyrant.' Larkin would meet him on any platform to prove that Murphy was a 'poltroon, liar and sweater' and 'that your only god is profit.'[6] Such language induced nothing but the hardest attitude from Murphy.

William Martin Murphy was born in Bantry, Co. Cork, in 1844 and educated in Belvedere College, Dublin, before taking over the family building business at nineteen after his father's death. He rapidly expanded it, constructing public buildings and railways in Ireland, Britain, Africa and South America. He was elected Nationalist MP for St Patrick's Division, Dublin, in 1885 and refused a knighthood in 1905, the year he amalgamated his three Dublin newspapers into the *Irish Independent*. He owned Dublin United Tramways Company and Clery's Department store, among many concerns. He wrote *The Home Rule Act, 1914, Exposed* but never lived to see an independent Ireland, dying on 25 June 1919 in Dublin.[7] Used to his own way, he feared that the ITGWU threatened the social system he had utilised so well. He was a bitter, unremitting enemy.

While it is tempting to portray 1913 purely in terms of Murphy and Larkin—and they were certainly central figures—forces beyond them, to which they gave leadership and personality, provided the preconditions and substance for its occurrence and duration. But it must never be forgotten that, inspired by Larkin's public speeches and apparently superhuman gifts, the ultimate heroes and heroines were thousands of faceless men, women and children. Whether ITGWU or trade union members or not, they stoically resisted physical, nutritional and spiritual suppression in support of the principle of organisation. They took hope from Larkin and abandoned their passivity, believing in a future that was worth the fight. It is in the photographs and memories of grandparents and great-grandparents of contemporary Dubliners that 1913's true heroism can be found.

BLOODY SUNDAY

On Friday 15 August, Murphy ordered the despatch staff of the *Irish Independent* to leave the union or be fired. 'As the Directors understand that you are a member of the Irish Transport Union whose methods are disorganising the trade and business of the city, they do not further require your services.'[8] Forty were immediately paid off, and battle began.

Newsboys, who had idolised Larkin since 1911, refused to sell the *Evening Herald*, and Eason's vanmen blacked the papers. Scab drivers were brought in, and scuffles broke out. On Sunday 17 August 200 tramwaymen were sacked for not repudiating the ITGWU.

Murphy personally visited Dublin Castle. The fruits of his call were immediately evident in the reinforcement of the DMP by the RIC. The authorities abandoned any pretence at impartiality from the beginning.

On Tuesday 26 August at about 10 a.m. large numbers of tramwaymen left their cars where they stood. At a mass rally in Beresford Place on 27 August, Larkin wanted to know why Edward Carson and his Ulster Volunteers could arm, parade and urge civil disobedience, even resistance by force, and be untouched while ITGWU members, who had infringed no laws, were subject to physical harassment. This was the employers' first card: physical intimidation in a brutish display of power. The second weapon would be the law. On Thursday 28 August Larkin, P. T. Daly, William Partridge, Thomas Lawlor and William O'Brien were arrested in their homes and deposited in Mountjoy Prison. Connolly was fetched from Belfast, and the five were released on promise of good behaviour.

A demonstration planned for O'Connell Street on Sunday 31 August was proscribed by the Chief Magistrate, E. G. Swifte; that he was a shareholder in the tramway company gave further evidence of the 'impartiality' of the law. Larkin, speaking from a window in Liberty Hall, set fire to the proclamation and said he would attend on Sunday, 'dead or alive.'

Connolly and Partridge were arrested on Saturday 30 August and sentenced to three months' imprisonment by a Special Court. Larkin evaded arrest and was hidden by Constance Markievicz. O'Brien reached Liberty Hall as baton-charging police killed James Nolan. Another victim, James Byrne, died later in hospital.

It was agreed to transfer the proposed meeting to the ITGWU premises at Croydon Park. A crowd assembled at Liberty Hall on the Sunday morning and marched off to Clontarf.[9] The police were stationed in large numbers in every side street adjacent to O'Connell Street. It was later revealed that all soldiers were confined to barracks in full gear throughout Saturday and Sunday. Had the demonstration not been transferred, the consequences might have been significantly more horrendous than they were, as the colluding authorities were clearly prepared to wreak mayhem on any assembly.

Rooms were booked in the Imperial Hotel, owned by Murphy (on the present site of Clery's) in the names of Mr Donnelly and niece, Miss Gifford. They arrived at ten o'clock and were shown to rooms 13 and 24. At midday, Donnelly—in fact Larkin disguised as a clergyman, wearing Kazimierz Markiewicz's frock coat—came into the smoking-room, stepped onto the balcony overlooking the street and shouted, 'I'm Larkin!' He was instantly arrested, while the DMP poured out of their hiding-places and mercilessly set about those around them. Most were neither ITGWU members nor trade unionists but merely strolling the city's main thoroughfare. The *Daily Sketch* reported 460 injured and 210 arrested and the *Saturday Post* that more than 600 people were admitted to hospital, from infants to old folk.

The official inquiry was universally dismissed as a whitewash. Partridge, addressing the British TUC, said that many policemen were the worse for drink, a fact reported throughout Europe. The public outcry, at home and abroad, was intense.

The event gave the union massive moral strength. The *Daily Mirror* on Thursday 4 September had a graphic front page showing wounded victims, broken tenement homes vandalised by the police, and Liberty Hall with its black drape, *In Memory of Our Murdered Brothers*. It shocked a public unused to wanton violence from their police, even if the DMP and RIC were not 'their police'. The TUC added its voice to those demanding an inquiry and set up a Food Fund.

'Bloody Sunday' remains Labour's most enduring image. It presented the ITGWU with international attention and sympathy. The Larkin Monument in O'Connell Street today surveys scenes that thousands of people have digitally stored from school texts, reading *Strumpet City* or watching RTÉ's serialisation. It is why trade unionism remains an essential part of the fabric of society, identified with the creation of the modern Irish state, integral to our culture.

THE DUBLIN EMPLOYERS' FEDERATION

On 3 September, with employer after employer locking out their workers, the Dublin Employers' Federation determined on general action. Murphy's request was supported by 404 others. They issued the famous 'Document':

> I hereby undertake to carry out all instructions given to me by or on behalf of my employers and further I agree to immediately resign my membership of the Irish Transport and General Workers Union (if a member) and I further undertake that I will not join or in any way support this union.

It was blatant hypocrisy that 400 employers themselves combined to deny the same right to tens of thousands of workers.

Even those unconnected with the ITGWU were cast out of work. Here was the third weapon in the employers' armoury: starvation. By 22 September more than 20,000 were locked out in city and county. From October evictions began of those not paying rent. In addition to constant press misrepresentation, the ITGWU was scurrilously attacked in the yellow press. Bernard Doyle's *Liberator* was Redmondite, reflecting that element of nationalism that feared for its usurpation by Labour. First appearing on 28 August, it was anti-Socialist in content and spoke well of the Labour renegades William Richardson and John Saturnus Kelly. P. J. McIntyre edited the *Toiler* from 13 September, a more threatening publication whose stock in trade was slander and character assassination, the most infamous being that Larkin was simultaneously an Orangeman and the son of Carey the informer, with side-by-side pictures appearing as weekly 'proof'. The 'short and spiteful' lives of these papers were a peculiar compliment to the ITGWU. The 'sustained attack on the honesty of its leader' failed: by their own admission, workers 'remained loyal.'[10]

TUC FUNDING

The Trades Union Congress granted £5,000 for immediate food aid, and a national collection in Britain was sustained until Christmas. The first food ship, the *Hare,* with the emblem of the National Transport Workers' Federation fluttering aloft, docked in Dublin on 27 September. To have heard Larkin say that he would bring in shiploads of food, then to stand on a cold quayside and watch a ship actually arrive must have been an incredible experience. It goes far to explain the faith in Larkin long held in thousands of Dubliners' hearts. It was a defining moment and encapsulated the working class's will and force to withstand, whatever the odds. It is the 'Heroic Dublin' of today's banner of Dublin Trades Council, through which the supplies were distributed.

There was criticism that the TUC sent food but denied industrial support. Larkin was accused of antagonising Delegates when they met in a Special Congress to discuss Dublin—the first single-strike Special Congress since 1868. British leaders were disinclined to sanction support for strikes, irrespective of Larkin. Dublin was not Derby or Dundee. Even if it had been, Rule Books would have been cited as to why supporting action was impossible. In addition, there was no precedent for a General Strike led by the TUC. Its Parliamentary Committee was instinctively hostile to the idea. Greaves suggested that had the British leaders merely sanctioned the 'blacking of tainted goods', 'not only would Dublin employers have been defeated, but they themselves would have been immeasurably strengthened. They lacked the vision.' It would still be lacking in 1926 and in 1984–85.

Dublin workers had asked for action akin to that they had unstintingly given to British transport workers in 1911. They received charity. But, oh, what charity! To examine the list of recorded donations in the TUC Dublin Food Fund accounts is to witness the spontaneous solidarity of miller and miner, docker and engineer, labourer and clerk, Temperance Leaguer and co-operator, women's activist and Christian Socialist. It was a historic debt that Irish workers attempted to repay in cash, food and holidays for children during the British miners' strike of 1984–85.

TUC funding for Dublin workers was crucial. On 13 October the ITGWU sought a 'temporary loan of £1,000 in cash to tide us over the present deadlock.' Food supplies had 'given us great strength but the long drag without money was very hard.' A Delegate meeting of the Trades Council on 22 October showed the breadth of the disruption and the financial burden on the unions concerned. Worst affected were the United Builders' Labourers and General Workers of Dublin Trade Union, with 1,250 full-benefit members out against an income of £8 per week. The Sawyers, Stationary Engine Drivers and Slaters had significant numbers out, but others were in work or had enough reserves to meet their obligations 'for some time.' In addition to providing meals and essentials for strikers' children and families the ITGWU paid Strike Pay, largely from the money raised in TUC collections. The amounts between 8 December and 20 January are documented in correspondence between the General Secretary of the TUC, C. W. Bowerman, and the Treasurer of Dublin Trades Council, William O'Brien. The ITGWU claimed for 10,650 men at 5s a week, 970 at 4s a week and 840 women at 2s 6d. On 8 December the Secretary of Dublin No. 1 Branch, John O'Neill, received £2,961 10s from the TUC Fund. Numbers fell to 9,800 men at the higher rate by 6 January. ITGWU cash in hand was as low as £144 by 6 January 1914. The ITGWU was not the only beneficiary of the TUC Fund: the UBLTU claimed for more than 1,000 men at 5s and 4s a week.[11]

The Dublin No. 1 Branch Strike Committee determined the method and means of distributing Strike Pay and food aid to members' families. By 29 January the TUC was not 'holding out any hopes that the food supply can be continued after this week.' Daily receipts declined, and there was 'not sufficient money in hand to pay for the provisions ordered for this week.' Amounts fell from more than £2,800 a week in January to £800 in late March and £400 on 8 April. (The ITGWU accounts for November to January are shown in table 4.)

Eight other unions received TUC money on a much smaller scale. The TUC accounts show that £28,975 16s was dispensed to Dublin, of which the ITGWU received £23,456, or 88%. A further £62,889 6s 6d was paid to the Co-operative Wholesale Society for food. Dublin Trades Council's accounts for 1913, audited by D. O'Connor and published on 25 November 1914, show that the TUC donated £38,976, with an additional £13,379 forwarded from the public in Ireland and Britain, a total of £43,314. Of this the ITGWU received the lion's share, £35,794 14s, or 82%. Whatever else they show, the figures demonstrate the unflinching solidarity of thousands of men and women, or, seen from another viewpoint, the iron hand of Murphy in starving workers.

Table 4: ITGWU Strike Pay from Dublin Trades Council TUC Fund (£), 1913–14

Week	Men 5s		Men 4s		Women 2s 6d		Total on hand	Cash	Other demand	Net
1 Nov.	10,017	2,504	1,000	200	840	105	2,909	406	300	2,203
8 Nov.	10,019	2,505	1,000	200	840	105	2,810	463	320	2,027
15 Nov.	10,134	2,533	982	196	840	105	2,835	324	300	2,211
22 Nov.	10,894	2,723	982	196	840	105	3,025	406	—	2,619
29 Nov.	11,007	2,752	982	196	840	105	3,053	198	200	2,655
6 Dec.	10,847	2,712	970	194	840	105	3,011	—	500	2,511
13 Dec.	10,650	2,662	970	194	840	105	2,961	—	670	2,291
20 Dec.	10,100	2,525	970	194	840	105	2,824	600	200	2,024
3 Jan.	9,980	2,495	970	194	840	105	2,794	84	200	2,510
10 Jan.	9,800	2,450	970	194	840	105	2,749	144	200	2,405

Source: National Library of Ireland, ITGWU, Special List A8, ms. 13,913 (1). All amounts have been rounded up to the nearest 10s.

It was later admitted that as the Lock-Out developed, 'income was considerably higher than the demand for actual Strike Pay.' John O'Neill and Tom Foran put surplus amounts in a safe in Liberty Hall until around Christmas, 'when there was something in the neighbourhood of £7,500.' Larkin was not told of this nest egg.

The basement of Liberty Hall became a soup kitchen, each day distributing thousands of meals to starving women and children, as well as clothing. In the evening, concerts and dramatic works entertained and generated much-needed income. Workers were drawn to the Hall, whether ITGWU members or not, identifying with the cause and seeing the union as an expression of their whole being, industrially, politically, socially and culturally. The ITGWU was more than a 'mere trade union'.[12]

THE LOCK-OUT MARTYRS

On 2 September a tenement house at 66 Church Street collapsed. Five of its twenty-six inhabitants were killed and more injured. Eugene Salmon died heroically trying to rescue his siblings. Partridge praised 'Young Salmon, the hero,' who was a 'member of the Union led by the hero Larkin.' Salmon was sacked by Jacob's, 'who paid such miserable wages as compelled the poor lad to reside in the pile that was not a home but a tomb.' He concluded: 'Before God, Jacob had killed this lad.' Salmon was a fine 'sample' of a Transport Union member.[13]

Alice Brady was shot by a scab, Traynor, on 18 December 1913 and died in hospital on 2 January. She was sixteen. Traynor's charge was murder, reduced to manslaughter; he was acquitted and walked free. The magistrate held that he carried the weapon with police permission. An absence of permission to fire it, from the police or any other source, was apparently irrelevant.

In 1988, on the seventy-fifth anniversary of the Lock-Out, the ITGWU and FWUI erected headstones over the martyrs' graves in Glasnevin Cemetery. A plaque was placed in Liberty Hall commemorating John Byrne and James Nolan, *victims of a baton charge in Lower Abbey Street and Beresford Place by members of the DMP on August 30, 1913*, and Alice Brady. More than 10,000 people attended their funerals.

A forgotten martyr was James Byrne, born and reared at 5 Clarence Street, Kingstown [Dún Laoghaire]. Inspired by Larkin, he became Secretary of the Kingstown Branch and of Bray and Kingstown Trades Council. He was arrested and charged with intimidating and 'jostling' a tram worker on 20 October and was incarcerated in Mountjoy Prison. In protest at the refusal to grant him bail he embarked on a hunger and thirst strike. After a number of days the authorities relented and he was given bail, pending trial. He had contracted pneumonia, however, and he died in Monkstown Hospital on 1 November, two weeks after his arrest. Pádraig Yeates observed that Byrne's heroism 'unfortunately . . . went unnoticed.' His death also coincided with press hysteria over Dora Montefiore's plan to take children to England. Connolly delivered Byrne's funeral oration from the roof of a cab, saying that 'their comrade had been murdered as surely as any martyr in the long line list of those who had suffered for the sacred cause of liberty.' On 13 November 1996 union activists in Dún Laoghaire-Rathdown County Council laid a wreath on Byrne's grave, and on Saturday 1 November 2003 a memorial was unveiled by Jack O'Connor, President of SIPTU. Byrne's details were also added to the Liberty Hall plaque.

SENDING CHILDREN TO GODLESS HOMES

As the Lock-Out stagnated in cruel stalemate in October, Dora Montefiore, an English suffragist and Communist, suggested that some children be taken to sympathisers' homes in England to be fed and cared for. Larkin agreed—either for what today would be called a 'publicity stunt' or from genuine concern for their plight. On 21 October, Archbishop William Walsh condemned the move as 'proselytising'. Alarm spread that children were being taken to 'godless homes in England'. Wild scenes developed as Dora Montefiore, Grace Neal and Delia Larkin assembled their small charges at Tara Street Baths for washing and re-clothing pending departure.

Montefiore was arrested and charged with abduction, and the children returned to their homes. Delia Larkin was tried on 27 October for incitement and sedition and given seven months' imprisonment. Connolly became Acting General Secretary of the union. He opposed sending the children away but demanded that those who stopped them going now feed them. He suspended Liberty Hall's food kitchens for a week, and charitable organisations were overwhelmed. He invited Walsh to show as much interest in the children's stomachs as he had in their souls. Walsh joined those clamouring for a settlement.

The episode was something of a diversion. Employers brought in blacklegs under cover of the frenzy. Connolly appealed to British workers to oppose their Government. Liberal candidates were defeated in two by-elections in England and Scotland on 10 November, and Labour's vote increased substantially in Keighley, Yorkshire. Encouraged, Connolly called for a total blacking of all goods bound for Dublin and closed the port 'as tight as a drum.' He was demonstrating his acumen for industrial leadership and moved the dispute forward by pressuring Government, merchants and employers. Workers had strong weapons of their own.

BRITISH LABOUR

After Larkin's release, on 28 October, he was in poor shape. He went to England, and expectant eyes turned to the TUC, which met in a Special Congress on 9 December. Those attending, however, would be Officials, not rank-and-file Delegates. The coming fudge was visible from a distance. The deadlock was broken by the TUC's refusal to act industrially. To objective eyes, like Connolly's, with this reverse went any chance of outright victory.

The ITGWU Executive met on 14 December and decided that any who could return without signing the 'Document' should do so. Larkin either did not know of this decision for an orderly retreat or would not identify with it. The British Joint Labour Boards, TUC and Labour Party came together for the last time on 18 December and brokered terms of truce, if not settlement. The Document would be withdrawn, sympathetic action stopped, and a Wages Board set up in March. Victimisation appeals would be heard in February. Larkin never made an issue of any of these events in later attacks on the ITGWU and so presumably accepted their inevitability and common sense in the context of an exhausted organisation.

Some British Labour leaders were antagonistic to Dublin. By November the General Secretary of the National Sailors' and Firemen's Union, J. Havelock Wilson, had made a *volte-face*. ITGWU solidarity in 1911 was conveniently forgotten. Liberty Hall expressed shock and annoyance, recalling that 'when the seamen and dockers of every other port were hesitating or gibing at the call of the Sailors' Union, every ship that touched the port of Dublin was immediately held up by Larkin and his dockers until the crew joined the Union' and 'signed under Union conditions.' The cost of 'saving the Sailors' and Firemen's Union' had plunged the three-year-old ITGWU 'into a long and deadly struggle on the quays of Dublin, cost it thousands of pounds, and left behind a trail of bitterness . . . of which the present conflict is one of the results.' In short, part of the employers' rancour in 1913 arose in 1911.

Richard McGhee, Nationalist MP and joint founder of the NUDL, simultaneously slandered Labour candidates in the South Lanarkshire election. In December the Leader of the British Labour Party, Arthur Henderson, drafted settlement proposals, accepted by the Joint Labour Board and the Lock-Out Committee, that 'the employers undertake that there will be no victimisation and that employment will be found for all workers within a period of one month from the date of settlement.'

Connolly revealed the ITGWU's suspicions. 'There may be somewhere trade union leaders who can regard with calmness the certain victimisation of a number of their rank-and-file, but, thank God, we are not of their number.' For Connolly, 'rank-and-file fighters' were 'the real heroes of this struggle,' and the union would 'never consent to their being sacrificed, not while there is a shot in our locker or a shred of our organisation together.'

Throughout their various engagements in the dispute, British labour leaders displayed different ambitions to their Irish counterparts. The 'British wanted to settle, the Irish wanted to win.' The arch-opponent of extending action to Britain was the Railwaymen's Leader, J. H. Thomas. Faced with spontaneous action among his members, he snuffed it out. He was not alone in displaying an absence of vision or courage and was well practised in such arts when the opportunity came again in 1926.

In December 1913 the employers agreed 'to withdraw the circulars, posters and forms' presented to their workers, provided that the unions abstain from 'any form of sympathetic action' pending the setting up of a Board of Wages and Conditions of Employment on 17 March 1914. No union member was to be refused employment 'on the grounds of his or her association with the dispute,' and no new workers would be engaged 'until all the old workers have been re-instated.' Disputes about re-employment would be dealt with at a Conference no later than 15 February.[14]

The conflict was petering out, with exhausted workers and their unions accepting these mediated terms. The refusal of the British TUC to sanction supporting industrial action ultimately determined the outcome, while its consolation prize of money and food had prolonged the agony.

Larkin attempted to go for broke, a policy assisted by Connolly's temporary incapacitation in Belfast. On 18 January, in Croydon Park, the ITGWU invited all in dispute to 'consider the present situation' and 'such actions as may be . . . necessary.' Partridge advised all who could go back without signing the Document to do so. Larkin, arriving later, vehemently disagreed, saying they could hold out for another year if need be. He was 'received in silence.' Two hours later the press was informed. The dispute was effectually over.

Larkin and Connolly were refused a hearing at the British Labour Party Conference in Glasgow the following week, and on 1 February the UBLTU signed the Document. On 15 February there were still 4,000 men and more than 1,000 women locked out, but there was no more Strike Pay. The TUC Relief Fund closed on 10 February. The ITGWU's solicitor, William Smyth, presented a legal bill for

£1,422 3s 10d—a massive sum. The union had fought more than 4,000 cases for members accused of intimidation, riot, resisting arrest, illegal picketing, assaulting policemen, and disorder. There were many evictions, including Larkin's family, who, after their second eviction, went to live in Croydon Park in January.

This role of a union, especially a general workers' union, as its members' defender in law was novel. It added significantly to the appreciation of its worth among members and the wider society. Greaves argued that this was a new outlook, that saw workers as citizens, not criminals, something of 'incalculable importance' and foreshadowing 'the great change in the status of the worker.'[15]

THE IRISH CITIZEN ARMY

Following Larkin's release from Mountjoy Prison on 13 November 1913, a torchlight rally was held outside Liberty Hall in Beresford Place. The huge attendance heard Connolly demand:

> The next time we go out for a march I want to be accompanied by four battalions of our own men. I want them to have their own corporals and sergeants and men who will be able to 'form fours.' Why should we not drill men in Dublin as well as in Ulster?

He wanted 'every man who is willing to enlist as a soldier to give his name and address,' and stated that he had 'been promised the assistance of competent chief officers, who will lead us anywhere.' He knew 'nothing about arms at present. When we want them, we know where we will find them. (Laughter).' The laughter was a mixture of black humour and incredulity at the suggestion that beleaguered workers, severely punished by police and soldiers at picket lines, should organise their own defence force.

The following day Captain J. R. 'Jack' White, who had been involved in a Citizens' Committee that unsuccessfully attempted mediation, went to Croydon Park and offered his expertise. The Irish Citizen Army (first called the Transport Union Citizen Army) at once organised physical protection for strikers and their meetings.

A notice appeared in the *Irish Worker* calling on 'all men willing to join for progress of training' to attend Croydon Park, where 'Captain White will take charge.' By 13 December, attitudes had changed from initial amusement and dismissal. 'At first looked upon as a mere piece of Liberty Hall heroics, it assumed a different aspect when it was discovered that regiments had actually been organised and drilling under the command of an experienced officer and competent N.C.O.s was in progress nightly.' White, 'late Captain, Gordon Highlanders,' was impressed by his charges: 'the material is as good as could be wished,' a large proportion being 'old soldiers'.

White explained his involvement. 'The supreme object of Larkin at the present day I take to be emancipation from wage slavery and organisation into co-operative industries owned and managed by the workers.' Such a task required 'discipline and the simplest teacher of discipline is drill.' He pondered: 'Whether the first fruit of our labours is the freeing of ourselves or the freeing of your country, time will show, but ultimately Ireland cannot be free without you nor you without Ireland. Strengthen your hand for the double task.'[16]

The seeds of the Citizen Army can be detected along the Cork quays in 1909 or during the Wexford Lock-Out; it was not a new idea that workers should defend themselves. The Citizen Army made an immediate difference at meetings and demonstrations. It was not yet apparent that it would have ambitions beyond protective, industrial duties.

CONCLUSION: WON, LOST OR DRAWN?
The Lock-Out was a defeat for the workers. The ITGWU was left with little option but to ask members to seek to return individually and, if possible, not to sign the Document. The working population were starving, mentally and physically spent, and external assistance had dried up. The union was heavily in debt and had lost thousands of members. A depression hung, like a miasma, over Liberty Hall for months.[17] However, in defeat the ITGWU gained many adherents and international prestige.

Connolly concluded that it was a 'drawn battle' from which 'both sides are still bearing heavy scars.' Reviewing Arnold Wright's *Disturbed Dublin*, an employers' view that portrayed the 'ignominious defeat of the attempt to establish a peculiarly pernicious form of syndicalism on Irish soil,' Connolly wrote:

> The employers, despite their Napoleonic plan of campaign and their more than Napoleonic ruthlessness and unscrupulous use of foul means were unable to enforce their Document, unable to carry on their business without men and women who remained loyal to their Unions. The workers were unable to force the employers to a formal recognition of the Union, and to give preference to organised men.[18]

The working class had

> lost none of its aggressiveness, none of its confidence, none of its hope in the ultimate triumph. No traitor amongst the ranks of that class has permanently gained, even materially, by his or her treachery.

The flag of the Irish Transport and General Workers' Union still flew

> proudly in the van of the Irish working class and that working class still marches proudly and defiantly at the head of the gathering hosts who stand for a regenerated nation, resting upon a people industrially free.

1913 thus became a celebrated victory wrung from the jaws of a defeat that the employers were too exhausted to enforce. Workers gained a new sense of their own power. The trade union and labour movement became important elements in society, which had to deal with the broad tenets of social democracy, if not Socialism, reflecting the need to extend care to the underprivileged.

The battle was not won in 1913, however. Progress since has been uneven. Would a social audit in 2009 compared with 1913 show workers to be in credit? Extreme, widespread poverty has gone, but things are relative. Contemporary society has a shortage of social housing, a permanent health crisis, educational disadvantage and problems of drug abuse, vandalism and crime. There is a constant attack on trade unionism and its collective values, to which society owes many of its freedoms. The new 'Documents' are the tenets of privatisation, deregulation, cuts in public spending, increasing appeals to individualism and an ostrich-like approach to global problems of climate change, hunger, Third World debt and exploitation. Union values are dismissed as 'old-fashioned' or 'belonging to the nineteenth century.'

SIPTU feels that it was 'never more necessary if we are to win the struggle for control of our destinies and management of our own economic, social and political affairs.' It concludes:

> Lessons must be drawn from 1913's solidarity between trade unions, national and international. The trade union movement fought for the whole of the working class not just the organised sectors. The *Irish Worker* through its mass readership countered the employers' message from the bosses' servant press. The trade unions provided social and cultural activities for its members as well as industrial and political leadership. The Lock-Out tried to outlaw a culture counter to capitalism. It failed partly because it was so crude and ham-fisted. Today's attack is more subtle and all the more dangerous because of it. To honour the memory of 1913 we must begin, on an individual basis, to commit ourselves to trade union activity not just trade union membership. We must once again set out the task of regenerating a nation on 'the shoulders of a people industrially free.'[19]

Larkin, in his Presidential Address to the 1914 ITUC, thought the 'workers emerged from the struggle purified and strengthened.' The outcome was the

> initiating of a new principle of solidarity inside the unions, and for the first time in the history of the world of labour . . . the principle had received universal recognition; viz. 'An injury to one is the concern of all.'[20]

Partridge, rallying the Inchicore Branch, cited the London *Times,* which 'declared, and the Employers realised,' that 'you cannot smash the I.T.&G.W.U.'[21] That the union survived the Lock-Out was a great victory.

It has been said that 1913 paved the way for 1916. Certainly, had the ITGWU not survived, the role of Connolly, the Citizen Army and Liberty Hall would have been absent, perhaps crucially so. The working class learnt much in 1913, not least that it stood alone. Any who might have wavered on the question of Irish independence now appreciated its value. Perhaps the behaviour of the TUC leadership and the British authorities, urged on by Dublin's employers and merchants, persuaded Connolly that self-determination was vital if the working class was to free itself.

A final legacy of 1913 is the union's red-hand badge. The ITGWU issued annual badges, making use of elements from the arms of the four provinces. In 1913 it was the red hand of Ulster. In 1918, when the ITGWU was reorganised, the Executive adopted the red hand as its permanent emblem to honour the men, women and children of 1913. It caught the imagination. In 1924 the Workers' Union of Ireland also chose it. In 1990 SIPTU maintained the tradition of the ITGWU and FWUI and proudly adopted the red-hand badge.

Chapter 6 ～

FROM LOCK-OUT TO RISING

ORGANISATION, MEMBERSHIP AND FINANCE

As the Lock-Out began, in August 1913, the ITGWU claimed 30,000 members, its highest total. After the Lock-Out many members were unemployed or could not pay their subscription. Finances fell alarmingly, while debts were massive. Economies were called for.

In February 1914 the General President, Thomas Foran, asked that the union 'devise some means of curtailing' expense. Many members applied for assistance or the fare of the emigrant ship. Most were refused, through lack of money, although victimised men were supported as far as possible.

On Tuesday 24 March a break from the gloom was made when Foran presented Constance Markievicz with an illuminated address. It recorded the union's 'high esteem and affection' and recognised her 'unselfish and earnest labours on their behalf during the Great Dublin Lock Out.' It concluded: 'Enthused by your example, we were proud to have you amongst us, and now that the fight is over, we desire that you remain one of us, and to that end we unanimously elect you Countess as an Honorary Member of our fighting Irish Union.'

Markievicz was sent to Dixon's Scrap Works after the men had applied for and were granted assistance, lifting their morale.

Tightness in waterfront employment was evidenced by disputes with the O'Connell Band after they canvassed for a Shipping Federation stevedore, M. Long. Action was proposed against ITGWU members 'who accompanied the O'Connell Band on parade under the leadership of J. Toole, the Free Labour Organiser.'[1]

James Connolly, Acting General Secretary, imposed financial and industrial discipline. It was dictated by necessity but also reflected his eye for orderly organisation as essential to any 'fighting union'. In correspondence with John Lynch of the Sligo Branch between October 1914 and August 1915 Connolly continuously demanded payments to Head Office and quibbled over claims for dispute and other benefits while demonstrating comradeship and support for Lynch and local industrial activity. It was Connolly and Foran, rather than O'Brien, who first imprinted the authority of Head Office, laying the foundations of the internal financial rigour that came to typify the union. Practical measures to raise funds and morale included a boxing tournament featuring famous pugilists, most noticeably the

Welshman 'Jimmy Wylde, Tylerstown, the unbeatable'. In contrast, members of the DMP were awarded an extra month's pay for their troubles.

Cash flow occasioned tightness, necessitating the General Fund calling in money from the High Street and Dublin No. 3 Branches. This offended Branches that under Larkin—as was the union itself—were run as individual fiefdoms, with little central control. John Bohan, Secretary of No. 3 Branch, was particular recalcitrant. Money had to be begged from Dublin Trades Council. There was virtually no return from Larkin's American activities.[2]

At the Annual General Meeting of Dublin No. 1 Branch on 13 December, Foran and Larkin were confirmed as President and General Secretary, respectively, and John O'Neill and Joseph Metcalfe as Branch Secretary and Assistant Secretary. The Treasurer was Patrick Smith and the Trustees Michael Cunningham, William Fairtlough, Joseph Kelly and Joseph Metcalfe. The Committee represented coal-porters, the City of Dublin Line, cross-channel dockers, general carriers, Morgan Mooney's, Ballybough Manure, the Midland Railway and other dockland employments. The 'outside Delegates' were Laurence Redmond and Patrick Nolan.

The ITGWU was presented in terms that could not be denied. It 'aided the organisation of all Trades Unions in Dublin, raised the wages of the Irish working classes, and improved the condition of the toiling masses—yes, even of some who foolishly fought against its efforts.' It had 'fed the Dublin workers in 1913, when the employers and the English Liberal Government sought to starve them into submission' and 'thereby defeated that dastardly attempt.' With that sense of its historic importance the ITGWU said it had 'fought the greatest Labour struggle for the right of combination ever waged in these Islands, involving huge expenditure— and would have fought it successfully had not our friends failed.' Now, it 'frustrated the attempt of our false political leaders to stampede the Irish workers into the British Army—and faced the fight when others "funked" it.' It had 'prevented Conscription, thereby saving the Irish father for his family, the Irish son for his home, and both for Ireland.'

The final question was fair enough: 'Are you a member of this Union? If not, why not?'[3]

In the early summer of 1915 the business of Dublin No. 1 Branch was routine: applications for selection for employment and benefits, relief of distress and questions of membership status and arrears. A barber's shop and billiard room were opened in old Shipping Federation premises in Eden Quay to provide facilities and to generate income. On 28 July a loan of £40 from the Bricklayers' Society was acknowledged, an indication of parlous finances. At the same meeting, however, small amounts were given to the O'Donovan Rossa Committee.

In August the ITGWU campaigned for the amalgamation of all labourers' unions as the idea of 'One Big Union' emerged. All unions were invited to communicate their views to Liberty Hall or to Dublin Trades Council, 'letting us know whether they would be prepared to send Delegates to a Conference to discuss this question, and frame a scheme to be submitted to the various bodies.' There was no rush to respond.

Transfers between the ITGWU and the National Sailors' and Firemen's Union were discussed between Connolly, Laurence Redmond and J. H. Bennett of the NSFU. The relationship between the two unions, especially in Dublin, continued. Liberty Hall apparently surrendered seamen back to the NSFU.

Connolly visited Belfast and Sligo to assist with organisation and to appoint Officials. Croydon Park raised income through hosting special events and hiring out playing-fields to Strandville Football Club. Such events could be counter-productive, however. Committee members were expected to attend and perform duties, their absence being minuted. The Baldoyle Branch complained on 25 August that scabs were pulling in the tug o' war and resigned their membership of both the union and the Citizen Army. Discipline was toughened and card inspections made of officers and Committee members.

A public meeting on Monday 30 August in Beresford Place commemorated James Byrne and James Nolan, 'murdered on August 30 1913, by the Uniformed Servants of the British Government, for asserting their rights as Workers.' Members of the Citizen Army 'of all ranks' attended in 'full equipment'. The procession was led by the Band of Dublin No. 1 Branch, and there were 'spontaneous bursts of cheers' from spectators. The march visited the spot in College Street where Alice Brady was shot.[4]

Aungier Street Branch caused financial problems and, while the shop did well, the work room was closed pending a review of its operations. In the barber's shop it was decided 'to get a boy and then dispense of the regular man.' The need to 'cur-tail expenses in every way they possibly could' was heightened in January 1916, the union 'having lost a big source of income by the suppression of the game of House [lotto].' Matters looked grim. The AGM of No. 1 Branch adopted a new Committee structure, with market, Corporation and gas workers, engineers, railwaymen and chemical workers broadening the Branch from its traditional boatmen, carters, dockers and general labourers.[5] Membership fell rapidly.

Table 5: ITGWU membership, 1913–16

1913 (Jan.)	22,935	1914 (Dec.)	15,000
1913 (Aug.)	30,000	1915 (Dec.)	10,000
1913 (Dec.)	26,135	1916 (Apr.)	5,000

Source: National Archives, Registrar of Friendly Societies, file 275T.

Volatile swings in membership in dockers' unions were not unfamiliar. For some, downward swings became irreversible. It is quite possible that, given Larkin's departure and the deepening gloom following the Lock-Out, extinction might have been the ITGWU's fate—or, if not extinction, an existence confined to east-coast waterfronts. The union's sense of its historic purpose may have been undiminished, but the credibility of its achievement was severely challenged by the events of April 1916.

LIBERTY HALL AND CROYDON PARK

In March 1914 Thomas Foran and the Secretary of Dublin No. 1 Branch, John O'Neill, took £3,500 from funds 'that had accumulated and put it into a mortgage in part payment' for Liberty Hall 'when they discovered that influential opponents were on the point of buying it, a transaction that would have been disastrous for the Union.' Had Liberty Hall been lost it might have struck a body blow to the reeling ITGWU. The accumulation of these funds, in effect unpaid Strike Pay provided by the TUC, was a bone of contention in the coming row with Larkin. He was not told of its existence. Had he been told, the money would probably have been dispensed.

Foran and O'Neill's 'secret fund' was eventually well spent. The urgent need to reduce expenditure led to a significant decision on Wednesday 24 November 1915, when 'instruction was given to surrender Croydon Park as soon as possible.' The 'disposal of stock and fittings' was 'left with the Officials.' Delia Larkin's refusal to supply accounts for Croydon Park and her occupation of Liberty Hall's largest room irked Connolly and the Committee. It led to the closure of the Women's Co-operative Society in July and her resignation from the IWWU.[6] The rent for Croydon Park was £250 a year. In addition, money was spent on furnishings and on a cow, so that the Larkin family, living there rent-free after twice being evicted from their home, 'might have a plentiful supply of milk.' Its sale became a thorn in Larkin's side, the abandoning of the cultural, artistic and athletic dimension. But financial needs dictated.

LARKIN'S DEPARTURE

A Special General Meeting was held in the Antient Concert Rooms on Monday 22 June 1914. Long 'before the meeting commenced the building was filled to its utmost capacity.' Hundreds were unable to gain entry. When Larkin took the platform he was accorded 'a remarkable ovation, the audience rising to its feet and cheering lustily. The scene was one of extraordinary enthusiasm, spontaneous and prolonged.' Foran said that after such a reception 'he did not think Jim Larkin would find it in his heart to leave them.' The meeting continued from the previous day in Croydon Park, when Larkin resigned, convulsing the union. To a 'veritable hurricane of cheering' and greetings shouted from all quarters, Larkin referred to the root of his concern, without naming names.

> The Great Omnipotent chose twelve men and one of those twelve betrayed Him. It would be too much to expect that a humble man like himself should not find a Judas in the ranks because of the loyal members' attitude towards one another. Dissensions had been going on amongst themselves which he could not put up with. The Committee of the Union had not been doing their duty as they ought.

Even 'without his guidance,' Larkin felt the ITGWU 'would still be impregnable and unbeatable.' Irish history taught him that men were placed on pinnacles merely to be dragged down. He was speaking 'under strong emotion and physical disabilities,' but some men seemed 'to be apathetic and lackadaisical.' In the hall that night Larkin thought the members were 'inspired with a new hope.' He implied criticism of Connolly's management of the union during his period of imprisonment before ranging into a discussion of Croydon Park and its role in the union's plans. He talked of education 'for defective children' and a general medical clinic and dental facility but complained of a lack of co-operation with such proposals 'from those from whom he expected much.' The Committee 'were actually interfering with him and preventing his proposals from being carried out. (Shame.) The Committee were penny wise in regard to funds.' Larkin complained of being verbally abused and the subject of malicious gossip. His sister, Delia, had been attacked, insulted and threatened.

Foran said he was proud to have been Larkin's 'servant and apprentice' during the previous seven years. He had never betrayed him. Committee differences were not personal but in his and the union's interests. He burned Larkin's letter of resignation 'amidst an incredible scene of enthusiasm.'

Connolly moved a motion of support and fidelity to Larkin, seconded by Daly and Partridge. The motion was adopted with three cheers. Many then marched back to Liberty Hall, headed by the Citizen Army, 'Jem Larkin in command,' having resolved not to accept his resignation. 'Shellback' in the *Irish Worker* argued that the 'Red Hand needed to be built up' and suggested that every member try to enrol ten others within three months, when each would be promoted to junior Delegate 'with a distinguishing button to show his rank.' More than a hundred would make the person a Delegate and more than 1,000 a paid Official.[7]

Larkin attended an 'Amalgamation Conference' in London on Thursday 9 July, representative of 400,000 workers, part of a process that would eventually create the Transport and General Workers' Union. Larkin regarded the event as a success. His reading of events was that most were 'conscious that they must accept the new idea or get run over.' It was

stimulating to hear the 'dumb dogs' voicing the new cry of One Big Union— creatures who, even six months ago, were doing their utmost against the move- ment for solidarity. Aye, even rare, if not fishy brooks have been compelled to sing the New Evangel, 'An injury to one is the concern of all.' A change my countrymen!

Dublin's 'misery, suffering and class-conscious solidarity was the industrial Archimedes; One Big Union the lever, class-solidarity the fulcrum.'

Twenty-seven unions considered amalgamation. It is not clear what the strate- gic interest of either Larkin or the ITGWU was. What would emerge would be a British union. Perhaps they hoped to pick up Irish members. A sceptical view might be that Larkin simply could not resist an audience and the opportunity to 'have a cut' off the British leadership. He did not resist the opportunity to show disrespect for Havelock Wilson. It may have been that it was best to keep an eye on the Irish aspect of the potential new body at the same time as expressing ideological approval.

On 28 October, Larkin announced that he was leaving for America to advance the ITGWU's interests, explaining his reasons in an open letter. He damned the Irish political leadership and the failure of the European and British working class to resist the war, again condemning the latter for their role during the Lock-Out. He felt that the ITGWU and Citizen Army were ringing alarm bells 'to awaken the country to the betrayal—to the foul compact of the traitor, Redmond—to hand over the keys of the Citadel of Irish Nationhood.' He then laid a demanding challenge before the membership.

> As bravely as ye bore yourselves in the past, you are now called upon to do even greater deeds for Ireland and its people in the future. You must live up to your greater responsibility; all selfishness must be got rid of; you must bear yourselves in public life that you will be an honour to your country and yourselves. No meanness, no narrow view can you allow to obscure the purpose of your work. Ours is not an ordinary trade union—our Union is a world movement.

He condemned the old, 'fossilised trades unionism' and outlined the structure he was to leave behind him.

> Jim Connolly is in command of the Union, Citizen Army, *Irish Worker* and general propaganda work; P. T. Daly is taking over the work of the Insurance. Foran will take charge of Croydon Park and its activities. Each Secretary and Official must be unwearied. Bohan and Partridge have each their appointed task. The daily paper I spoke of is now under discussion—a Committee is in being to go into the matter of its publication.

He asked members to subscribe sixpence or a shilling a week towards his expenses, reminding them that his tour of Britain brought in £1,900 for the union.

> All monies accruing from my tour goes to re-build Liberty Hall and start productive works. I want every member of the Union who has not already joined the Co-operative Movement to do so at once.

He concluded by reiterating his wishes regarding his successors and appealing for unity, reflecting tensions concerning his departure.

> The election for office-bearers and National Executive will take place next month. I desire that no prejudice will exist in the mind of any member about any

individuals in the past. I go away having full confidence in every man and boy in the Union.

To the 'Old Guard' he said:

I depend on you not only to carry on but to encourage and help the Young Guard. Remember—Jim Connolly is in charge until I return. Thomas Foran, the President, acts for me in all things.

At this point it is hard to know who 'Old Guard' and 'Young Guard' were. Presumably the former were original docker and carter members. After Larkin's return the term 'Old Guard', apart from indicating Larkinites, referred to pre-1916 members and especially to 1913 veterans.

He recalled that

when I went into Mountjoy Gaol things looked gloomy. I came out finding the membership doubled and 100% increase in income. I expect even better results on my return home.

He sent messages to the Citizen Army and the Women Workers' Union.

Dublin Trades Council paid its respects to Larkin on his imminent departure. It acknowledged his 'tireless and self-sacrificing manner' over the previous seven years. It 'earnestly hoped' he would return 'restored in health and with renewed vigour' to continue his mission.

On Sunday 18 October a 'Grand Carnival' in Croydon Park heard Larkin's farewell address and witnessed 'an attack on an emigrant caravan by Indians and rescue by American Army' enacted by the Citizen Army, fireworks, a céilí, and a 200-yard rifle range, all for 6d or 2d. Despite such 'high admission being charged,' a large gathering assembled, along with many prominent union leaders.

On the Wednesday before his departure from Queenstown (Cóbh) on Friday 30 October, Larkin bade farewell in City Hall, Cork, accompanied on the platform by Partridge and John Good, Secretary of Cork United Trades and Labour Council.

In the rows after Larkin's return in 1923 he was accused of leaving the union 'broken in funds, in numbers and in prestige.' Once gone, he was almost immediately 'out of sight, out of mind,' certainly as regards references in ITGWU publications. In September 1915 the *Workers' Republic* carried the front-page news that 'Jim Larkin Astonishes the Americans'—rare coverage of his activities. He appealed for the organising of the unskilled and opposed the capitalist war, suggesting that 'it is a pity that the workers fighting in the trenches do not remember and heed the advice of George Bernard Shaw, "Shoot your officers and come home". A letter from Larkin was published on 30 October, only the second 'received since his departure,' although the union felt that 'that is not to say that no more were sent by the Chief, but our Government is at present not very scrupulous about other people's letters.' Larkin's attendance at the funeral of Joe Hill in Chicago was reported in November 1915.[8]

DISPUTES

In May 1914 Dublin farmers reneged on the Agreement of 11 August 1913 that had granted 17s a week and a half day on Saturday. The employers' attacks encouraged scab unions, such as those of Thomas Greene, 'the drunken wastrel and renegade,' and Father Flavin's 'Yellow Scab Union' in Kingstown.

In January 1915 advances were gained for casual boatmen, constant cross-channel ships and general carters of between 1s and 4s, despite the fact that carters were considered to be 'badly organised'. In May the *Workers' Republic* announced wage increases for Stevedores' Association men, deep-sea ships, casual cross-channel docks, Dublin Dockyard, Ross and Walpole, Dublin and General Company, and General Carriers. The union was recovering.

Larkin remained in all minds. Connolly, in a strangely prophetic article, wrote: 'And the day will come when we, or such of us as the enemy leaves alive and at liberty, will welcome Jim back to the scene of his former battles and victories—and welcome him in triumph.' In July, Connolly asked all Branches for assistance during a railway strike, 'but No. 16 Branch refused to send any money,' so the Committee 'instructed Mr. Connolly to demand what money they had in hand.' Urgency was emphasised by the fact that, on 21 July, Connolly saw 'no prospect of settlement' and 'did not see any possibility of paying the men on Saturday.'

In Fingal the memory of past victories faded as employers clawed back their grip. With an eye on the employers' desire to maintain their hold, Connolly observed: 'So, whilst so many of our brothers are out fighting for freedom abroad, the master class are, as usual, busy forging fresh fetters with which to bind the sur-vivors when they reach home.' 'Fingal Notes' observed that, 'previous to the great Lock Out and for some time afterwards things hummed' in the area.

> Organisation had practically won for us the right to think, the first, most neces-sary stage in the growth of human liberty. Unity and brotherhood existed among us, and the forces that held us down for years drew in their horns and claws. We won some victories but the end came.

The Dublin Farmers' Association was regaining its old dominance. As to the Citizen Army, it had 'disappeared' in Fingal.[9]

CITY OF DUBLIN STEAM PACKET DISPUTE

In October 1915 a quay dispute resulted in Connolly calling a meeting of all cross-channel men to 'ask them to pay a levy to assist the men out.' They were 'fighting the cause of all cross channel workers,' although victory had been gained for boatmen. Under the headline 'To Hell with contracts,' the *Workers' Republic* saw 'another Labour War' as 'forced upon us as needlessly and as calculatingly as ever was conflict.'

The central issue was the defence of members' living standards in the face of ever-rising prices. Increases were gained in February, and talks for further increases expired on 1 October. By 10 October the employers withdrew their offers and took back increases granted for casual men. Connolly observed that 'these are the gentry who howl loudest about breach of contract, and yet are first to go back upon their solemnly pledged word whenever they imagine they can profit by doing so.' The men closed ranks. Connolly stated that 'the Transport Union knows how to fight, and has a rank-and-file that any union might be proud to have.' He linked the employers' conspiracy to the war.

Trouble worsened, and the City of Dublin Steam Packet Company became the fulcrum. The Master Carriers' Association granted an increase of 2s a week in November, which was 'accepted on condition that no man be put off for refusing to go to the City of Dublin while the strike is on there.' Mick McCarthy complained that City of Dublin men were not doing their share of picketing, suggesting tensions within the ITGWU membership. The union was willing to contain the dispute but, equally, could not 'allow its toleration to be taken advantage of by unscrupulous employers.'

Advances were simultaneously gained for gas workers. On Saturday 23 October terms were agreed on cross-channel ships, with significant increases won. Connolly thought, 'Thus the Cause of Civilisation is maintained by the forces of Organised Labour.' The Master Carriers' Association drew in its horns in November and, instead of a Lock-Out, granted an increase of 2s instead.

It was a different story with the City of Dublin Line. The dispute involved about 150 men. The company stated that its quay porters were 'compelled' by the ITGWU to tear up their Agreement on 13 November 1913. After direct contact with the company they were allowed to resume on the old terms on 17 January 1914. They reneged on this arrangement on Thursday 4 November 1915; and, as far as the company was concerned, until the men complied with the conditions of the Munitions of War Act and referred matters to arbitration, the company's services were suspended.

Connolly offered a reward of 5s if anyone could comprehend the employers' letter to the press. He corrected matters with his own letter, stating that all shipping companies were asked for an increase and all, bar the City of Dublin, granted between 1s and 3s a week. He added that the employers were providing opportunities for drilling men at Liberty Hall.

> Thus the whole quay is getting drilled, and the Irish Citizen Army has a larger reserve of drilled fighting men than any force in Dublin. It is a great game! And all these men are ready to fight—in Ireland.

The 'great danger', from Connolly's point of view, was that the 'dispute may be over before the men are thoroughly drilled.' But they would go back only on the same terms as every other company.

William Martin Murphy, on behalf of the Dublin Employers' Federation, met the Master Carriers' Association on Monday 8 November and urged 'drastic action' against the ITGWU. He 'pleaded for a general Lock-Out of all of its members.' The military situation gave employers 'an unexampled opportunity.' Murphy's 'fierce tirade' was, however, 'received in silence,' and fears were expressed that the Defence of the Realm Act (which gave the Government wide-ranging powers, including the requisitioning of buildings, land or other property needed for the war effort) might be used against employers in the event of a Lock-Out, however unlikely that was. After a long discussion, the Master Carriers 'did not consider it wise at present to take the extreme step' of a general Lock-Out.

The strike in the City of Dublin Line raged on in December. Foran expected trouble with the men and appealed for 'instructions as to how they were to act when the occasion arose.' Some suggested that any who 'had got four weeks regular work' since the strike began be debarred from Strike Pay, while Connolly, disgusted by the actions of NSFU men on City of Dublin ships, 'considered the mistake made was in the handing over of the Dublin men to the London union.'

An Irish Party MP, Esmonde, visited Liberty Hall in mid-November and threatened to 'wage war' upon the union if it did not settle with the City of Dublin Line. Suggestions that the Admiralty would seize and operate its ships would 'mean war.' Connolly insisted: 'We are going to win this fight. We are not going to allow Sir William Watson, William Martin Murphy, nor the British Government to single out any body of workers for attack and destruction.'

He soon found that the NSFU was willing to scab, encouraged by their General Secretary, Havelock Wilson. The ITGWU asked why 'our brothers' in Dublin remained in the NSFU. Having been ordered to scab, they refused, and 'the Liverpool men who were on the boats were refused their fares home.' The ITGWU 'had to pay their way, which it gladly did in recognition of their splendid stand for Trade Union principles.' Eighty NSFU men were idle but got no Strike Pay from their union. Connolly referred to the age-old interdependence of dockers and seamen and the debt the NSFU owed the ITGWU, but it seemed

to be the policy of the N.S.F.U. to play a lone hand in Ireland against every Irish organisation, and be prepared at all times to sacrifice shore workers everywhere in order to serve its own interests . . . in order to vent their spite upon what ought to be a friendly organisation to which they owe their very existence in Dublin, Sligo, Belfast and Waterford.

Liberty Hall was

always inclined to be patient and fore-bearing. But there are limits. Our answer to this latest attempt to compel Trade Unionists to scab upon us may be of such a character that our 'friends' in Maritime Hall may long remember.[10]

The ITGWU concluded: 'If they cannot get recognition from their Union when they are fighting for a Trade Union principle, what were they paying in for?'

The *Workers' Republic* proudly published lengthy lists of individuals and organisations contributing to the City of Dublin Men's Christmas Fund. Dublin Trades Council opened a Support Fund.

Meanwhile, run-of-the-mill issues were dealt with. The practice of 'Sunday reeds' (gatherings of men at which work was awarded) was 'again creeping in along the docks.' Stevedores were warned that this 'detestable practice' would not be tolerated. The union would 'hold up any vessel for which the men were taken on at a Sunday Reed.'[11] Connolly thanked the Trades Council for its 'excellent effort' but reported that there was 'not much change in the situation.' He thanked NSFU members who, 'when ordered to take the boats to sea after they had been loaded by clerks and scabs, had heroically refused to blackleg.'

He was less pleased with the NSFU itself, which 'refused to pay them Strike Pay, but had voted instead £11,000 as a War Loan to the Government. The Transport Union now paid the Strike Pay of these men as well as their own. (Applause.)'

The City of Dublin strike was a severe strain, raising serious questions. They had 'the spectacle of one man [Watson] being able to upset the business and destroy the happiness of a whole community, in order to gratify his personal spleen against men who refused to be lowered beneath the level of their fellows.'

On 2 February 1916 the President of Dublin Chamber of Commerce rang Connolly to attempt a settlement. A deputation of the Irish Industrial Development Association met the ITGWU, to no avail. An intervention by the Citizens' Association was also fruitless. Dublin Port and Docks Board asked the Government to take 'such steps as are necessary' for the purpose of compelling the City of Dublin Line to resume its cross-channel business, and urged that the Admiralty not requisition ships of the Laird Line or any other vessels 'while a fleet of idle steamers are tied up in Liverpool.' It was felt that if the City of Dublin Line could not pay the same rates as its competitors it was 'a confession of bungling incompetence.'

In late March the City of Dublin men 'agreed unanimously not to go to work until they got the same money as the other firms are paying.' There was some fragmentation of union solidarity, but this was dealt with in quite brutal fashion in the *Workers' Republic*, under the heading 'SALE OF SCABS: TAKE NOTICE.'

It is my intention to sell by public auction on the 1st day of April, 1916, twenty-six well-bred scabs the property of George Fredrick Marshall, Superintendent of the City of Dublin Steam Packet Company, North Wall.

They were of the 'finest quality, well trained, well cared for,' and bidding would be 'very brisk, as Sergeant Storey, of the ill-famed Scottish Borderers, will attend and make a choice selection of the animals.' A song concluded the notice:

Oh, scabs are the names of those knaves the most obnoxious of weeds,
Whose talents are rare and famed for the worst class of deeds.
Their names to a period to send the end of times will be known

Like the bloodhounds who chased to the grave, Sheares, Sheehy and Tone.
'The names of this choice lot will appear on my next poster.'

On 1 April, under the heading 'A Cheap Bargain', the *Workers' Republic* reported
that the capitalist press had 'announced with great exultation' a settlement in the
City of Dublin Line. The facts published were, needless to say, inaccurate. Sailors
and firemen had come out because they refused to act as scabs. 'That was all. There
was no question of money, or of a demand for an increase in wages involved in
the matter. It was simply a strike upon a point of honour.' The press claimed
they had returned to work on the promise of an increase of 5s a week, accepted
'as a satisfactory settlement' upon the advice of their Officials. But still the ITGWU
was vexed.

> Do you understand that? Do you understand how the payment of five shillings
> per week can buy men to do a thing that they had declared was a dishonourable,
> unclean thing to do? They did not come out for an increase, they came out upon
> a point of honour. But for the payment of five shillings per week per man they
> have sold their honour, and betrayed their comrades in the hour of victory. In
> the hour of victory, for negotiations for an all-round satisfactory settlement were
> in progress when the seamen and firemen, prompted by their English Officials,
> sold the pass upon their Irish brethren. It is not hard to understand that. We
> see it every day. But it is hard to write temperately about it. So we will stop
> writing—and go on thinking.

A demonstration in Beresford Place on Sunday 2 April laid 'before the Public the
facts of the case' and the course of action now that a 'Bribe of Five Shillings' had
persuaded NSFU men to desert 'their Transport Union Comrades.' On 15 April it
was reported that the men agreed to return to work pending arbitration. All scabs
would be 'discharged immediately and no new hands employed' until old hands
were re-engaged.

Connolly could not resist a final swipe. 'We venture to prophesy that the
Arbitrators' Award will compel the firm to pay the Port rate, and thus prove that the
struggle of the Company against it was a vain and malicious piece of stupidity.'[12]

THE IRISH WOMEN WORKERS' UNION
On 28 July 1915 Delia Larkin's resignation allowed Connolly to suggest that 'the
Women Workers' Union be reorganised,' or the ITGWU would control the IWWU 'in
the same way that it controls the Branches of the Union.' While the *Workers'
Republic* announced that 'we regret to be compelled to announce that Miss Delia
Larkin has resigned her position in the I.W.W.U. and Women's Co-operative, and left
Ireland,' privately few tears were shed.

A 're-organising meeting' was held on 10 August.

Special Invitation is given to all Past Members. All girls who suffered Imprisonment for the Union during the Great Lockout are Entitled to Enrol themselves free as Honorary Members for Life.

Partridge and Connolly asked them to 'rally to the old flag.' On 27 October, Helena Molony was appointed by Connolly to act as Secretary. She attended a meeting of No. 1 Branch Committee to report progress and to pay rent owed. The names of some IWWU Committee members were challenged, as 'they do not work for wages'; 'any person not working for wages not be eligible for the Committee.'

The IWWU ran the Workers' Co-operative Stores at 31 Eden Quay, manufacturing a variety of men's, women's and children's clothing. On 30 October it urged women to

unite to fight against Low Wages, long hours, bad conditions, and unemployment. A Strong Union could get a Minimum Wage fixed for every girl in Dublin!

The union provided 'clean amusements for young people,' and attendance at dances and concerts was encouraged. Living wages, it claimed, had been fixed for cardboard box making, tailoring (bespoke), confectionery and shirt-making. 'Why work for 3/6 a week when a little agitation would get you 10/–?' Women were urged not to scab and married women 'to fight for increased Maternity Benefits, Pensions for Widows, etc.' New Branches opened in Crumlin and Dolphin's Barn, and officers and Committee were elected: Larkin as President, Connolly and Markievicz as Vice-Presidents, Molony as General Secretary, and Miss Mulhall, Treasurer.[13]

BELFAST AND KERRY
In January 1915 the Belfast Branch moved an increase in contributions, beginning on the first Saturday in April, to meet the 'very large amounts payable in benefits' and 'in order that the funds available for trade union purposes may be kept secure.'

In July a strike of more than 6,00 men in the Head Line proved difficult. There were no funds, and Head Office donations and street collections were necessary. An increase of 7s a day was finally agreed for hours worked between six in the morning and nine at night. In the autumn a strike in Munster Warehouse, Tralee, heralded the serious arrival of the ITGWU in Co. Kerry. In October, Connolly visited Tralee to investigate the 'possibility of getting the members of the Workers' Union to transfer.' 160 transferred under the guidance of M. J. O'Connor, who was victimised by his employers for his troubles. Connolly, 'on behalf of all our members,' extended a 'hearty greeting to the Tralee Branch.'

January 1916 brought mixed news. The Waterford Branch was lost but three opened in Co. Kerry: Dingle, Fenit and Tralee. M. J. O'Connor forwarded a cheque for £7 14 11d from Tralee. Partridge won an increase of 1s a day for Fenit dockers, with membership 'increasing day by day.' Partridge and O'Connor founded the Listowel Branch on 1 February.[14]

NATIONAL HEALTH INSURANCE SOCIETY

On 17 July 1915 a notice in the name of the ITGWU National Health Insurance Approved Society stated: 'This Concerns Your Interests, Insurance Cards and Books, Advice and Warning,' giving an insight into the administration of the scheme.

> Unless your Insurance Card for the last half Year is given up at once to the Irish Transport Workers' Society, if you are a Member, you will suffer reduced Benefits if you should fall sick during the year beginning November next (the Penalty Year). Bring or send in your Insurance Card and Book to-day. Don't wait until to-morrow. Have you got your Insurance Card for the Half-year beginning now (4th July, 1915)? If you have not, ask for it. Have you found any Stamped Cards belonging to you which you thought were lost? If you have, send them at once to Liberty Hall. Is anyone trying to make you join another Society? Ask him or her if he or she will give you more Benefit, or give the Benefit half as quickly as your Society—***The Workers' Society***—gives it when you are sick. Workers should stick to the Workers' Society because it is the best Society for the Worker.
>
> If your **husband or son** has joined the Army let the Society know, and send the Society any of his stamped Cards.

Matters for the society reached crisis point in September. Connolly told the No. 1 Branch Committee that in order to save costs a reduction in staff was necessary. Repercussions for the union were grave. 'One of the oldest hands had been the first to get notice of one week to terminate his term.' He surmised that the 'General President would be one of the first to go' and 'suggested to Mr. Foran that he should give notice of his resignation in order to avoid being dismissed and considered it would be well to give the President some position to look after the working of the Hall in general.'[15] Foran was forthwith appointed to 'a position at a weekly wage' within the union.

WAR

On 15 August 1914 the *Irish Worker* urged workers not to join the British war effort, 'not to become hired assassins.' Another agenda loomed.

> Conserve your energies; preserve your strong men and beautiful women. Remember your country needs you. You know no King. Let the political compromisers and hireling press sell themselves for thirty pieces of silver. They are but things of the hour. It is for you to remember the great Queen who drank the waters of bitterness for 800 years! Surely you will not disgrace the fathers that bore you! They suffered and died that she, 'Our Dark Rosaleen', might enter into her inheritance.

In 1918 the ITGWU would recall that 'Connolly stepped into the "bearna baoghail"' after Larkin, but 'the reaction from the great Lock Out was still strong.'

Victimisation was rife, and members fell away. 'With a shrunken membership, an empty treasury, and a load of £3,000 debts, the prospects before the Union were anything but bright. All through 1915, despite rigid economy and Connolly's genius, the financial millstone continued to drag the Union down.

Connolly, Acting General Secretary, produced the *Worker* after the suppression of the *Irish Worker* in December 1914, loyally stating that it was 'edited by Jim Larkin.' The issue made great play of the authorities' efforts to remove the streamer from Liberty Hall declaring: 'WE SERVE NEITHER KING NOR KAISER BUT IRELAND.' At 2 a.m. on Sunday 19 December 'a force of about sixty police, accompanied, we are told, by military officers, marched round to Liberty Hall' and leaned a sixty-foot ladder 'against the parapet of the building.' They swarmed up, 'tore down the sign and carried it off in triumph to Dublin Castle,' on the orders of Brigadier-General Hill. In satirical vein the paper added:

> We understand that a medal has been struck to commemorate this great victory. It will have upon the one side a Red Hand, and on the other a Policeman Rampant, with the motto, 'Thank God I have a country to sell.'

Photographs of the streamer were available, and its significance was patent.

> This sign was the first thing that caught the eye of poor recruits landing from boats at the North Wall or being brought around from the Great Northern Railway. But it is gone! Captured by the Allies! Alas!

The union increased its opposition to the British war effort, publishing 'slightly altered' versions of the recruiting posters festooning the country. 'What will you say to your children when they ask you what you did *with your arms and legs* in the Great War?' was among them. British Labour disappointed, as it failed to resist the employers' attack and surrendered the 'position they ought to have given their lives to hold.'[16]

THE *WORKERS' REPUBLIC*

An 'enslaved press' maintained anti-union propaganda. Through the *Workers' Republic*, Connolly put plain facts before the public. Irish employers paid their workers less than English employers, even where there was no competition; and Irish employers were 'shining examples of obstinacy and pig-headedness.' British-controlled firms in Ireland were quicker to settle than Irish ones. Workers had learnt 'self-imposed discipline'—not to strike if such action endangered all. 'What or who will teach the Irish Employer that his power is a trust to be administered for the good of all, not a whip to be used like a child to gratify his foolish whims?'

The paper wanted to wish readers a happy new year but concluded that 'such a wish rings better when it is accompanied by a belief that the wish may be realised, and at the present moment the signs of a Happy New Year are none too plentiful.' Connolly concluded in a prophetic manner, whether intentionally or not:

> A happy New Year! Ah, well! Our readers are, we hope, rebels in heart, and hence may rebel even at our own picture of the future. If that is so let us remind them that opportunities are for those who seize them, and that the coming year may be as bright as we choose to make it. We have sketched out the future as it awaits the slave who fears death more than slavery. For those who choose to advance to meet Fate determined to mould it to their purpose that future may be as bright as our picture is dark.

On 25 February 1915 claims for Mortality Benefit for ITGWU members killed in the British army were raised. The union insisted that the benefit 'only covers cases in civil life, therefore the answer is in the negative.'[17]

TOWARDS EASTER WEEK

Connolly and Foran managed the union's recovery from the Lock-Out and Larkin's departure. Membership fell continuously, however, as economic conditions deteriorated and men left for the war. The union's opposition to war was absolute; but it is not clear how many shared or were privy to Connolly's developing agenda. Disillusioned by international Socialist compliance with the war, Connolly began to shape the capacity to take advantage of what he increasingly saw as an opportunity. The union operated industrially as normal, and Connolly's energy and leadership, as exemplified by the dispute in the City of Dublin Line, was remarkable. Normal union activities were being maintained in increasingly abnormal circumstances.

Chapter 7 ~

THE ITGWU AND THE 1916 RISING

For Dubliners, a conspicuous part of the ninetieth anniversary of the 1916 Rising was the enormous scarlet banner draped on Liberty Hall. Below the plough and the stars—emblem of the Irish Citizen Army—were the words

Liberty 1916–2006: The Republic guarantees religious and civil liberty, equal rights and equal opportunities to all its citizens, and declares its resolve to pursue the happiness and prosperity of the whole nation and all of its parts, cherishing all the children of the nation equally . . .

Ninety years and a day after its bombardment by gunship, on 27 April 2006 a commemorative plaque was unveiled in Liberty Hall by the General President of SIPTU, Jack O'Connor, reading:

The Cause of Labour is the Cause of Ireland . . . The original Liberty Hall served as the base of operations of the Military Council of the Irish Republican Brotherhood in making the final preparations for the Easter Rising of 1916. The Proclamation of the Irish Republic was printed here by Christy Brady, Michael Molloy and Liam Ó Briain on the night of Easter Sunday, April 23, 1916. In this document the Provisional Government of the Irish Republic declared: 'the right of the people of Ireland to the ownership of Ireland', guaranteed 'religious and civil liberty, equal rights and equal opportunities to all its citizens' and resolved 'to pursue the happiness and prosperity of the whole nation and of all its parts, cherishing all the children of the nation equally . . .' On this site on Easter Monday, April 24, 1916, members of the Irish Citizen Army assembled under the command of the Union's Acting General Secretary, James Connolly, to take part in the struggle for Irish independence along with members of the Irish Volunteers. The Irish Citizen Army—which had been created as a workers' militia during the 1913 Lock-out—was deployed with Connolly at the General Post Office, at St. Stephen's Green led by Michael Mallin and at the City Hall under Seán Connolly . . . The Cause of Ireland is the Cause of Labour.'

In 1966 the ITGWU thought that 'the promises and undertakings' of 1916 had 'not yet been won.' It reminded members:

> This is now our heritage and our responsibility—the heritage and the responsibility of Liberty Hall and what it stands for. Let us, therefore, re-dedicate ourselves to strive for the achievements of what Connolly and his colleagues fought for—'equal rights and equal opportunities to all citizens . . . cherishing the children of the nation equally.' Let us determine to absolutely refuse to accept the position of second-class citizens for the working class. Let us re-dedicate ourselves and our comrades, citizens of Ireland, inferior in no way to any other class, and resolve to pursue the happiness and the prosperity of the whole nation of all its people. That is Liberty Hall and that is its objective.

Rosie Hackett, recalling her involvement, observed: 'Historically, Liberty Hall is the most important building that we have in the city. Yet, it is not thought of at all by most people. More things happened there, in connection with the Rising, than in any other place. It really started from there.'[1] 1916 became central to the union's self-perception.

Literature on the 1916 Rising is extensive.[2] In it the ITGWU and Liberty Hall get short shrift. Perhaps this is how it should be, as, formally, the ITGWU might be said to have had little to do with it. Indeed there are suggestions that significant elements within the union opposed involvement and distanced themselves from events afterwards.

Conversely, it can be argued that without the determination of James Connolly, Acting General Secretary of the ITGWU, and the strategic value of Liberty Hall as military headquarters, the Rising might not have taken place at all, or could have done so only with far greater difficulty. As early as 1918 the union proudly claimed that 'the Rising made the Union.' Its subsequent identification with the independence movement, particularly in the eyes of the British military and police, added to its attraction and was central to its extraordinary growth until 1922. From the outbreak of hostilities in 1914, the ITGWU opposed the British war effort.

On 22 January 1916 the *Workers' Republic* on its front page published Maeve Cavanagh's poem 'Straining at the Leash', together with an article, in the section 'Notes on the Front', headed 'What Is Our Programme?' Here Connolly argued that the strength of the labour movement derived from the fact of 'being like no other movement. It is never so strong as when it stands alone.' In peace time the ITGWU strove to gather all workers into the union, to 'control the forces of production and distribution.' Connolly hoped that, 'should it come to a test' between 'those who stood for the Irish nation and those who stood for foreign rule, the greatest civil asset in the hand of the Irish nation for use in the struggle would be the control of Irish docks, shipping, railways and production by Unions who gave sole allegiance to Ireland.' In times of war the ITGWU believed 'we should act as in war' and that 'while the war lasts and Ireland still is a subject nation we shall continue to urge her to fight for her freedom.'

Séamus McGowan went further, asking, 'When?'

Must we wait until the arms we have are taken from us? Until English dungeons are again filled with our chosen leaders? Men of Ireland wait no longer! Remember now is always the acceptable time. NOW is always the time to strike. Waiting for the day to come is but waiting for the mirage that will lure us on to despair and destruction.

The union's mechanism for any fight was the Irish Citizen Army.

THE IRISH CITIZEN ARMY

By March 1914, the Lock-Out done, morale low, and its immediate purpose apparently gone, only about fifty remained in the Citizen Army. In addition, on 25 October the Irish Volunteers were launched at the Rotunda Rink, providing an alternative for those who, in Seán O'Casey's eyes, 'preferred Caithlín Ní Houlihan in a respectable dress than a Caithlín in the garb of a working woman.' O'Casey opposed the Volunteers on class lines and was dismayed that the 'old lingering tradition of the social inferiority of what were called the unskilled workers, prompted the socially superior tradesmen to shy at an organisation which was entirely officered by men whom they thought to be socially inferior to themselves.'

On 13 March between two and three hundred demonstrators at Liberty Hall were attacked by the police and Captain White arrested. The union was determined to reorganise the Citizen Army, and on 22 March in Liberty Hall a new constitution was adopted and an Army Council elected. The constitution had five points:

1. That the first and last principle of the Irish Citizen Army is the avowal that the ownership of Ireland, moral and material, is vested of right in the people of Ireland;
2. That the Irish Citizen Army shall stand for the absolute unity of Irish nationhood, and shall support the rights and liberties of the democracies of all nations;
3. That one of its objects shall be to sink all differences of birth, property and creed under the common name of the Irish People;
4. That the Citizen Army shall be open to all who accept the principle of equal rights and opportunities of the Irish People;
5. Before being enrolled, every applicant must, if eligible, be a member of his Trades Union, such Union to be recognised by the Irish Trades Union Congress.

White was elected Chairman; James Larkin was among five Vice-Chairmen, with Thomas Foran, P. T. Daly and William Partridge (all ITGWU Officials), and Seán Ó Cathasaigh (O'Casey), Secretary. A Committee of fifteen was appointed. It did not include Connolly, who was away on union business in Belfast, or Michael Mallin, two leaders of the army in 1916.

Only five of the twenty-four elected were 'out' in Easter Week. Frank Robbins, long-time Secretary of No. 7 (Theatre and Cinema) Branch and a member of the Citizen Army, reflected on the 'Socialist ideals' expressed in the new constitution; but others have concluded that, 'like the ITGWU, the ICA was a labour body, an organisation of workers rather than Socialists. Its ranks included many quite sophisticated Socialists, but its training was military, not political.' There was, however, a clear influence by the Citizen Army in the Proclamation of the Republic.

The response to the revivified Citizen Army, despite appeals in the *Irish Worker,* was poor. This led White to seek to merge the Citizen Army with the Volunteers. He resigned after the Citizen Army challenged the Volunteers to publicly debate their class base.

Larkin succeeded White and was considered 'the most committed' of the Citizen Army's first three leaders. He led it at the Bodenstown Wolfe Tone Commemoration in June and by August claimed 1,000 members. Growing strength made affiliation with the Volunteers unlikely, although the two bodies engaged in some joint activities, most significantly the Howth gun-running, which brought the Citizen Army some weaponry. O'Casey sought to have Constance Markievicz expelled, as she was a member of Cumann na mBan, a sister organisation of the Volunteers. He bungled his case and resigned.

In September, John Redmond pledged the Irish Volunteers to the British war effort. All but some 10,000 members followed him, a further limitation on the potential for collaboration. In October, Larkin sailed for the United States.

Connolly now assumed the leadership of the Citizen Army. In O'Casey's view, in doing so he abandoned the Socialist path for the 'crowded highway of Irish Nationalism.' This view can be rejected, as Connolly's commitment was to international Socialism, against the imperialist war. He increasingly saw the necessity of striking; and 'starting thus, Ireland may yet set the torch to a European conflagration that will not burn out until the last throne and the last capitalist bond and debenture will be shrivelled on the funeral pyre of the last war-lord.' It proved a vain hope, as most European Socialists abandoned internationalism and supported the conflict.

Connolly saw the ITGWU as a fighting union, infused with a Socialist vision as central to the project of achieving the Workers' Republic. In October 1914 he outlined his position.

If it requires insurrection in Ireland through all the British dominions to teach the English working class that they cannot hope to prosper permanently by arresting the industrial development of others, then insurrection must come, and barricades will spring up as readily in our streets as public meetings do today.

Any conflict would depend on the working class.

Equally true is it that Ireland cannot rise to Freedom except from the shoulders of a working class knowing its rights and daring to take them. That class of that character we are creating in Ireland. Wherever then in Ireland flies the banner of the Irish Transport and General Workers' Union there flies also to the heavens the flag of the Irish working class, alert, disciplined, intelligent, determined to be free.[3]

Liberty Hall became central to the achievement of these ambitions.

Connolly

Connolly's 'disappearance' in January 1916 has been interpreted by historians as either 'kidnap' or participation in a voluntary debate. Either way, the editorial in the *Workers' Republic* of 29 January was unequivocal.

The issue is clear and we have done our part to clear it. Nothing we can now say can add point to the arguments we have put before our readers in the past few months; nor shall we continue to labour the point. In solemn acceptance of our duty and the great responsibilities attached thereto, we have planted the seed in the hope and belief that ere many of us are much older it will ripen and blossom into action. For the moment and hour of that ripening, that fruitful and blessed Day of Days, we are ready. Will it find you ready?

The die was cast.

Industrially, the ITGWU gained strength. Cos. Cork, Kerry, Wexford and Sligo all progressed, and Belfast's AGM was 'the best in our history.' Growth was based on the ITGWU's capacity to deliver wage increases and improve conditions.

Connolly maintained the anti-war propaganda, emphasising the fact that 'the Dublin slums were more unhealthy than the trenches in Flanders.' Those in the vanguard of Dublin's recruiting drive were 'the men who locked us out in 1913, the men who solemnly swore that they would starve three-fourths of the workers in Dublin to compel them to give up their civil rights—the right to organise.' Recruiters generally were 'the men who pledged themselves together in an unholy alliance to smash trade unionism, by bringing hunger, destitution, and misery in fiercest guise into the homes of Dublin's poor.'

Details of raids on Liberty Hall on Friday 24 March were given in the *Workers' Republic,* under the provocative heading 'The Call to Arms'. The British authorities, for some 'occult and inexplicable reason,' determined to suppress the Nationalist journal *Gael.* Having raided the printers and dismantled machinery, soldiers and police were ordered to seize all copies of the paper. They raided the shop of the Workers' Co-operative Society at 31 Eden Quay. 'The little girl in charge was not at all daunted by the bullying of the daylight burglars and coolly answered that she had no authority to give up the property placed in her charge.'

The 'little girl' was Rosie Hackett, and she notified Connolly, upstairs in the adjoining Hall. He arrived just as the police got in behind the counter and asked if they had a warrant, which they had not.

On hearing this, Mr. Connolly turning to the policeman behind the counter as he had lifted up a bundle of papers, covered him with an automatic pistol and quietly said, 'Then drop those papers, or I'll drop you.' He dropped the papers. Then he was ordered out from behind the counter, and he cleared. His fellow burglar tried to be insolent and was quickly told that as they had no search warrant they were doing an illegal act, and the first one who ventured to touch a paper would be shot like a dog.

The Citizen Army was mobilised in anticipation of more comprehensive raids. When a DMP sergeant returned, armed men were already in position. One hundred and fifty men answered the Citizen Army muster within an hour, prompting concerned calls to Dublin Castle.

Staid middle-class men in the streets, aristocratic old ladies out shopping, well-fed Government Officials returning from lunch were transfixed with horror when they beheld the spectacle of working men with grimy faces and dirty working clothes rushing excitedly through the streets with rifle in hand and bandolier across the shoulders on the way to Liberty Hall.

Connolly reported that men came from railways, factories, dockyard, from the 'holds of coal boats, in stables, on carts, lorries and yokes of every description, in buildings in process of erection.' When the call reached them, 'on the instant tools were dropped.'

Liberty Hall remained guarded, day and night, until the Rising. The *Northern Whig* on Tuesday 28 March suggested that a military attack on Liberty Hall was considered but abandoned at the last moment. Such a raid could have had calamitous consequences, both for the ITGWU and for the planned Rising.

Connolly's editorial concluded with a mixture of realism and prophecy.

The British Government thought to make a coup that would demoralise the National forces, and suppress all their papers, but they reckoned without the splendid discipline of the armed manhood of Ireland. So endeth the First Chapter. Who will write the next?[4]

THE ITGWU AND THE RISING

The *Workers' Republic* appeared on 29 May 1915, replacing the suppressed *Irish Worker*. It consistently criticised the war, urged men not to enlist, raised such issues as the maintenance of the food supply, and publicised Citizen Army activities. Everything fitted a wider plan: the Rising. Even the ITGWU's organisational efforts in Co. Kerry were linked to plans to land arms. This would be 'facilitated if I.T.&G.W.U. Branches were established at the ports of Fenit and Dingle and railway towns of Tralee, Killarney and Listowel.' All towns established Branches in the period 1915–16.

Normal 'day-to-day' organisational activity continued in 1916. Membership was extended, and increases were gained for dockers, seamen and factory workers. The lengthy strike in the City of Dublin Steam Packet Company was settled only on 17 April.[5]

From January, it seems that rebellion was determined upon, and Liberty Hall henceforth operated at two levels: normal union work above; preparations for insurrection below. Members of Dublin No. 1 Branch Committee, the nearest there was to an Executive, were well aware of this duality, but the degree of their support or opposition is not simply gauged. When Connolly suggested 'hoisting the Green Flag' over the Hall there was open dissent. It was announced on 8 April, and on 12 April the Branch Committee met, with William Fairtlough and William O'Toole moving that no such decision be made without consulting the general body. Foran secured adjournment for a day so that Connolly could attend. John Farrell again moved for delay, supported by William Early. Connolly said he 'would hand in his resignation rather than fall out with them or give it to anyone to say there was disunity in the ranks.' He asked to speak privately with Farrell, after which Farrell withdrew his motion. It is likely that Connolly told him that the flag heralded the Citizen Army's withdrawal from the Hall. The flag was duly hoisted—not, as intended, by the absent Constance Markievicz but by fourteen-year-old Mollie O'Reilly, a member of the IWWU.

It seemed a foolhardy act of provocation so close to the secretly planned Rising, and revealed clear tensions within the union about Connolly's determined path. What would have happened had the military intervened?

Greaves argued that 'without the resources' of the ITGWU the 1916 Rising 'would have been a very limited effort.'[6] From Tuesday 18 April, Liberty Hall became 'the essential headquarters without which a rising would have been impossible'; and, as is well known, the Proclamation of the Republic was printed on ITGWU presses.

Events crowded in on those planning the Rising. Bulmer Hobson and MacNeill, President of the Volunteers, discovered Pearse's intention on Monday 17 April, ruling out the use of the Volunteers' premises; the attempt to land arms in Co. Kerry failed and Roger Casement was arrested; and, finally, MacNeill issued a counter-manding order, cancelling any action on Easter Sunday. Undaunted, the Citizen Army appears to have been willing to have fought alone, without the Volunteers. Fewer than a thousand ultimately fought, 250 of them Citizen Army men—a turn-out of 80%. The Citizen Army suffered fifteen fatalities and many casualties. On the front page of the *Irish Worker* of Saturday 3 May 1924 Larkin published a 'Roll of Honour' of Citizen Army dead, with twelve portraits, under the heading 'In Memoriam—Comrades All! Men—Union men—Who Went Out to Die for Liberty and a Workers' Republic, Easter Week, 1916.'[7]

Liberty Hall, regularly raided by the police in the weeks leading to the Rising, was shelled by the gunship *Helga* on Wednesday 26 April, reducing the empty build-ing, which no longer served any military purpose, to a ruin. It was then occupied by soldiers. Only the caretaker, Peter Ennis, was inside when the bombardment began.[8]

By the end of the Rising the ITGWU had lost Connolly and Mallin through execution. Three other Officials, Thomas Foran, John O'Neill and William Partridge, were imprisoned or interned, as were P. T. Daly and William O'Brien, soon to become the union's dominant personality; Liberty Hall and its contents were destroyed; and there was only £96 left in the kitty. The union survived 1913 but stood to be obliterated by Easter Week.

'EASTER WEEK SAVED THE UNION'

The ITGWU quickly tried to pick up the shattered pieces, the 'work of repair', as Greaves observed, being 'undertaken by the unpretentious men who had manned the engine-room while Larkin and Connolly strode the bridge.'[9] Thomas Foran acted as General Secretary as well as President and slowly led the union back to the business of serving claims and defending members. By January 1917 it was claimed that 'never in the whole history of the union was the organisation in a better position, both numerically and financially.'[10]

In the union's first published Annual Report, for 1918, the impact of the Rising was analysed. Connolly 'and his companions had no illusions' about what they did. 'Connolly did not deal in illusions': 'His clear and analytical mind had reached the conclusion that the political circumstances of the day rendered it imperative that Ireland's right to Independence should be asserted by force of arms regardless of the consequences.' There were now no dissenters. The ITGWU acknowledged that it had been a 'military failure . . . replete with tragic suffering and cruel losses.' But the 'wonderful renaissance of national sentiment which followed more than justified the prescience of the dead leaders.'

> From the Union point of view, the immediate losses have been more than offset by the ultimate gain. Easter Week saved the Union. It cancelled out the reaction from 1913, and removed the bitter prejudices which had blocked its progress. It linked up the Labour Movement with the age-long aspirations of the Irish people for emancipation from political and social thraldom, and formed a national moratorium under cover of which it was able to make a fresh start on better terms with increased membership.[11]

Suggestions that Connolly was expelled from the union after the Rising are not supported by documentary evidence, and it is surely inconceivable that, had such an expulsion occurred, Larkin would not have used it as a mighty weapon against the ITGWU leadership when he returned.

By December 1917 membership had risen to 14,290 and by December 1918 to 67,827. An unprecedented organisational tide carried the ITGWU into every corner of the country. Liberty Hall was quickly restored. As successful wage improvements were won in 1917–18, the ITGWU adopted the policy of 'levying the first week's payment of any increase off each Dublin member, the proceeds being applied to rebuilding' Liberty Hall. It was observed that 'in this way, [the] Liberty Hall frontage has actually been rebuilt by the employers of Dublin!'

In the mind of members and the public, both the ITGWU and Liberty Hall were central to the Rising. Connolly and the Citizen Army fought for a Workers' Republic—yet to be achieved. They did not fight for a Partitioned Ireland, Connolly having correctly foreseen a 'carnival of reaction' when the possibility of parts of Ulster being allowed to opt out of Home Rule was first mooted.[12] Conscious of sectarian dangers, he gave instructions that during the Rising 'not a shot was to be fired in Ulster.'

In the standard histories of 1916 the Socialist aspect, through the ITGWU and the Citizen Army, is seldom acknowledged. William O'Brien, addressing the ILP&TUC Congress of 1918, stated that he believed that when Connolly 'laid down his life for the Irish working class he laid it down for the working class in all countries, for he believed that an example of action ought to be given to the workers to spur them to resistance to the powers of imperialism and capitalism which have plunged Europe in the war of empire and conquest.' Nor was his sacrifice in vain, 'for we know the influence it exercised among those great men and women who have given us the great Russian Revolution.'[13]

In 1924 Seán McLoughlin, writing in Larkin's *Irish Worker*, recalled his own part in Easter Week, concluding with a criticism of the abandonment of the memory of Connolly and the Citizen Army.

> What followed is known to the world. Imperialism found its victims and struck home. The men who were chosen will live in the memory of every revolutionary as men who knew how to die. These men died for complete freedom, for full Liberty for all the people. In these days men have fallen away from their principles and purposes, and betray the heritage that was given.[14]

McLoughlin excoriated 'one renegade' who had the 'dastardly cheek to assert' that Connolly, 'had he lived, would have accepted the Free State . . . What a base lie. We of the Irish working class know different. These men have left us a heritage and we must make ourselves worthy to enter it.' The Free State was not what Connolly and the Citizen Army believed they were fighting for. The significance of the Rising as far as the Dublin Employers' Federation was concerned 'was unquestionably industrial as well as political, as the practical side of the movement was undoubtedly supported by a body which had its origins in the strike of 1913–1914.'

Even during the dock strike of 1915 'this armed force paraded the quays.' Dublin employers 'made no mistake when they declared the Irish Transport Union to be an anarchistic organisation' and were 'determined not to tolerate its dictation in the industrial life of the city.'[15]

For the union, 1916 ultimately represented a beginning, a spark that lit a wilder fire, rather than a final accomplishment. SIPTU's contemporary role remains similar: to organise the Irish working class, throughout Ireland, and to resist the powers of capitalism and imperialism.

In that sense, 1916 remains of the present and not the past.

Chapter 8 ❧

'ONE BIG UNION': THE ITGWU, 1916–22

T he years 1916–1922 were among the most exhilarating in union history. From Rising to War of Independence and Civil War, the ITGWU played a prominent part in the emergence of a partially independent Irish state. Only fourteen years old in 1922, it had transformed the labour movement and, to a considerable extent, the fortunes of Irish people generally.

In membership, 1921 proved the high point until 1951. The union's historic sense of itself seemed assured, the future for the Workers' Republic bright. An alternative view saw missed opportunity, the end of the ITGWU as a syndicalist agent for Socialist revolution.

MEMBERSHIP, ORGANISATION AND FINANCE, 1916–19

The ITGWU lay shattered when the dust of Easter Week settled. By 1918, however, the Executive observed the 'wonderful renaissance of national sentiment' that 'more than justified the prescience of the dead leaders': 'Easter Week saved the Union.' By December 1916 membership had reached 14,000. Assumptions by the press that the union was extinct were challenged.

On 4 June 1916 there was a fully attended meeting of Dublin No. 1 Branch in the Trades Hall in Capel Street. Joseph Metcalfe and Patrick Stafford proposed that a deputation under the City Engineer examine Liberty Hall to see what repairs could be effected. Office hours were fixed at 10 to 8 and at 10 to 9 on Friday and Saturday, with a 'day book for Officials to sign in.' Michael Cunningham and Michael Brohoon were appointed Delegates to Dublin Trades Council, to replace Connolly and Partridge. On 8 June 'Thomas Johnson' of the ITUC was authorised 'to rescue on our behalf the books and papers' in the 'possession of the military authorities.'

A financial statement of 10 June recorded a balance of £1 14s 2d, handed to the Treasurer, Joseph Kelly. The union's funds after the Rising were £96. By 18 June, meeting again in Liberty Hall, correspondence was received from the Belfast, Cork and Killarney Branches. Any Officials who had 'returned from deportation' took up 'their duties at once.'[1]

The authorities would have preferred the ITGWU to have met its demise. The police assumed that 'a very large proportion of members' were 'in sympathy with the Sinn Fein movement.' The Government had 'no objection to the Trades Union or Industrial side.' Foran, once released from prison in England, acted as General Secretary and suggested 'a small Committee to get finances in order.'

Disputes in the Gas Company and City of Dublin Steam Packet Company brought a welcome normality, although Patrick Stafford complained of poor attendances. Bizarre attempts were made by J. Dillon Nugent MP to control the union in June when he 'negotiated with the Castle to buy it.' He dealt with a Major Price when the ITGWU seemed 'broken and bankrupt.' Quite how any 'sale' would have been concluded is unclear.[2]

Miss O'Reilly claimed Mortality Benefit for her brother John, 'killed in the late Insurrection.' All such claims were agreed. A very different attitude was expressed to those seeking benefit for men killed in the trenches.

Affiliation to the ITUC on the basis of 20,000 members was agreed. Whether the union had 20,000 members is contestable. Ten Delegates attended the Sligo Congress, representing Dublin No. 1, Dublin No. 3, Belfast, Cork, Kingstown and Sligo. In Cork, Tadhg Barry, Bob Day, William Kinneally and Éamon Lynch were all 'either in gaol or on the run, severely disrupting' organisation. When the men of the Burns and Laird Line wanted a rise, Foran advised 'not to rush it,' parlous union finances worrying him.

A flicker of internal conflict arose on 2 August to mar the growing optimism. A Committee member, Mills, 'raised the question of who was the head of the Union now.' Foran was 'the Responsible Official,' but the 'very bad conduct of the High Street Society' needed control. On 24 October Foran wrote to M. O'Connell, Tralee, saying he 'would be grateful of any information.' 'Almost all' Branch Officers were 'out of action' and Head Office had 'no one available to send.' They hoped M. J. O'Connor 'would have been with us before now.' The disappearance of Tralee 'would be a deplorable thing' and would give 'great satisfaction' to their enemies. Denis Houston, the Organiser, soon sent heartening reports.

In Sligo there were continuing tensions with John Lynch. Foran queried a weekly claim of £1 9s 10d for 'firing and cleaning' and, as ever with Sligo, appealed for cash to be forwarded to Head Office.[3]

In September a wage increase for 'Inside Officials' was denied, although the 'staff needed a living wage.' Foran feared friction, he met the staff, and 3s was agreed. The finances eased slightly, and £350, 'got from some friends,' was lodged in a Building Fund to start the repairs on Liberty Hall. A decision to 'revert back to the old 10% to all Shop Stewards' was agreed to get 'better results'. Johnson was asked to 'look after Tralee, Cork and Killarney Branches' while the imprisonment of Officials continued. The *Dublin Saturday Post* broadcast union news 'until we can start our own again.' Foran queried the number of recent death claims. 'I hope you are not paying for those killed in the War as we never had three Death claims in any one week since we started!' In late November 2,000 badges were ordered for 1917.

Table 6: ITGWU membership, 1916–22

1916 (May)	5,000	1918 (Dec.)	67,827
1916 (Dec.)	14,000	1919 (Sep.)	110,752
1917 (Jan.)	14,920	1919 (Dec.)	102,419†
1917 (Dec.)	25,000	1920 (Sep.)	102,823
1918 (Mar.)	40,000	1920 (Dec.)	120,000‡
1918 (June)	43,788	1921 (Dec.)	69,560
1918 (June)	100,000*	1922 (Dec.)	82,243

*Figure claimed in *Voice of Labour* but dismissed by J. J. Hughes as an over-estimate.
†The drop was most certainly in farm labourers falling out of benefit after harvests.
‡Sometimes this estimated figure is given as 130,000. It refers to 'book' membership.
Sources: ITGWU, Annual Reports, 1918–1922; National Archives, Registrar of Friendly Societies, file 275T.

As Organisers were appointed in the field, relations between them and Head Office created tensions. The balance of autonomous and self-starting Officials with the discipline of a national union structure created problems. They learnt as they went along. Foran fretted about industrial action but quickly recognised the value of good Organisers, feeling in April 1917 that 'it wouldn't be possible to have too many.' In May he suggested Cathal O'Shannon 'as a man who could be very useful.' His 'services could be dispensed with in Belfast,' as he 'could do more useful work elsewhere.' He went to Cork, allowing Denis Houston to 'break new ground.' M. J. O'Connor, Tralee, and John Dowling, Queenstown, were appointed Organisers in August.

The Branches listed on the Head Office letter-heading were: Dublin No. 1, High Street, Inchicore, Kingstown, Baldoyle, Rathcoole, Crumlin, Clondalkin, Belfast, Cork, Sligo, Wexford, Tralee, Killarney, Killorglin and Waterford—not greatly different from Easter 1916. By 6 November, Ballysadare, Blanchardstown, Collooney, Lucan, Maugherow, and Wexford were added, with Cork Branches for Carters, Storemen, Builders' Labourers and Tramwaymen and one in Douglas. By December there were 14,000 members in forty Branches.

On 9 September problems arose in the National Health Insurance Approved Society, particularly in Wexford, and Joseph McGrath was appointed manager. Foran wanted a 'good man as Chief Clerk' to manage the administrative load. The possibility of employing R. J. P. Mortished foundered, because there were 'too many and too stringent conditions laid down.'

Larkin's possible return from America was raised on 24 June. Foran wanted to 'have everything going on well and in proper working order should he return.' The approach to Mortished, whom Larkin did not like, may well have been ill-timed. On 14 October J. J. Hughes was appointed as Financial and Corresponding Secretary, at £2 10s a week.[4]

An audit gave opportunity for the financial relationship between the Executive and Branches to be defined. A 'regularly elected' Executive emerged. These elections were central to subsequent disputes with Larkin, but a management structure was essential for running a union with more than 15,000 members, a Head Office staff of two and five Organisers.

The union 'underwent a gradual change from a Transport Workers to a General Workers' Union.' Organisation fell on the General President and the 'staff of No. 1 Branch whose energies and accommodation were more and more needed for their own increased membership.' This presented a new, unplanned difficulty, the creation of a Head Office 'catering for every class of workers, of administering the finance and property' and 'handling the varied problems.' The ITGWU was now a National Organisation, geographically and politically. Progress in Cork enabled the purchase of premises.

An unsavoury reminder of 1913 was the refusal to accept transfers from the United Builders' Labourers' Union. For their actions during the Lock-Out the ITGWU 'did not recognise' it as a trade union. UBLU members were welcome on payment of an entrance fee of 10s.

In late 1917, Dublin members of the National Association of Theatrical and Kinematograph Employees 'organised themselves as a Branch of the Transport Union' and sought a general increase. The transfer of Branches of other, particularly British unions, often with little formality or paperwork, became commonplace. By December, membership exceeded 25,000.

William O'Brien applied for membership on 30 December and was elected Vice-President of Dublin No. 1 Branch at its AGM in January 1917. O'Brien's admission and his immediate elevation to office had a profound impact. Until his retirement in 1946 he was the dominant personality of the ITGWU. The death of Partridge on 26 July 1917 was marked in 'silence all members standing.' At the Congress, O'Brien said said Partridge 'died a martyr to the principles he held and believed in just as assuredly as those who died with their backs to the wall.' In May 1918 Foran surprisingly 'raised the question of having the weekly grant to Mrs. Partridge brought to a conclusion on account of the very generous settlement the National Aid had given her.' No decision is recorded; but Foran's requests were rarely rejected.[5]

1918–19: 100,000 MEMBERS

On 6 January 1918 Foran thanked everyone for their work. He thought it 'might be the last chance he would have of doing so as after the General Meeting' it was 'intended to make a clean sweep of existing Officials.'

At the AGM in the Mansion House on 13 January he clearly felt under threat as internal tensions rose. He hoped that 'members in general would in the future take more interest' in the union, to 'see that it was conducted properly and established in a proper business basis.' There were now Forty-Five Branches, from Antrim to Kerry. 'No friend of the Irish Transport Union could have come away from the A.G.M. of the parent Branch without a feeling of deep satisfaction.' There were more than 5,000 members in Cork, and it was 'already the biggest Union in Ireland [and] had still bigger prospects before it.' Its assets were more than £12,000. Praise was heaped on the Secretary of No. 1 Branch, John O'Neill, who was prevented by illness from attending, for his 'unflagging devotion and sterling honesty.'

By 3 February expansion was such that 'every other week and day, fresh demands were being made for Organisers.' Dublin No. 1 Branch gave £500 to the General Fund in mid-February, in addition to the £2,212 handed over for 1917. Advances were won in Tralee and Killarney for carters, storemen and employees of the urban District (town) council. M. J. O'Connor, Organiser for Limerick, gained £8,000 worth of increases in the year. 'A wave of organising' by March established Branches in Aghada, Athenry, Athy, Balbriggan, Ballincollig, Bishopstown, Clarecastle, Clones, Donabate, Dunlavin, Ennis, Eyrecourt, Killaloe, Kilrush, Naas, Newbridge (Droichead Nua), Oilgate, Pettigo, Riverstown, Sandyford, and Skerries. An exception to this inrush was the loss of the tramwaymen, who, having been absent from the union since 1913, joined the National Amalgamated Tramway and Vehicle Workers' Association.

By 9 March there were 40,000 members in seventy Branches. Farm labourers were a dynamic Section. Increasing strikes caused the Executive to suggest raising the contribution to 6d per week for 'building up a reserve fund.' Larkin, exiled in America, wrote to Foran congratulating him on the success. 'I see by the news reports that the old ship, I.T.W.U., seems to have been refitted. Keep her head to the wind, spokes hard down, steer a straight course, no matter what storms you may encounter don't veer a point.' He praised Foran: 'You don't know how I rejoice to hear good news . . . Man, I never doubted ye!' Larkin was cheered by the singing of 'The Red Flag' at the Mansion House and support for Soviet Russia.

An ever more confident ITGWU offered potential members 'free membership' in a novel recruiting campaign in May. 'The advanced wages gained by the Union for its Members exceeds by several hundred times, the amount of subscriptions paid by them. Don't worry about your dues—the boss will pay them for you!'

As Balbriggan reached 500 members, a new image was depicted. 'Throughout all Ireland, the Transport Workers' Union, the former dread of everyone who had 20/– in a stocking, is recognised as the peaceful but powerful agent of the new social order.' Wherever it 'set up' it gave 'new hope and spirit of initiative' to workers and the 'first taste of prosperity the toilers on the land have known since the plantation of feudalism.' By the end of June membership was a staggering 100,000. In Britain 'only the N.U.R., Weavers, Textile Workers, Miners and General Workers' Union exceed it.'

Such rapid growth 'severely taxed' the Head Office staff. All members were urged to clear their card by 30 June to enable a full census and financial assessment. J. J. Hughes cautioned that 100,000 was an over-estimate. The ITGWU was now 'too big to run on rule of thumb methods.' Accurate membership figures were required. In July the Kenmare and Blanchardstown Branches opened, praise being given to an Organiser, Máire Mullen.

In a *Voice of Labour* Congress Special a full-page notice by the ITGWU asked readers, 'What is it?' and answered: 'It is an Irish Trade Union run by Irish Workers in the interest of all who labour by hand or brain in Ireland.' It then asked, 'What does it Want?' and answered in unequivocally Socialist terms: 'The right to live and enjoy life. The right to the full product of our toil. The right to evict the drones from control of the social hive. A better, freer, fuller, happier life for all who labour.' Under the slogan 'Each for All and All for Each' the union had 'survived the combined attacks' of employers and the British Government. It was 'still inspired by the teachings of Larkin and Connolly' and was the biggest union in Ireland, 'with over 120 Branches and still growing.' In August, Ballina, Carlow and Nenagh experienced large expansion. The Organisers Rooney and Dowling founded Branches at Kells, Oldcastle and Virginia, while South Kildare Labour Union, 'a vigorous organisation', amalgamated. Newtown Drogheda Land and Labour Association came in September, followed by W. J. O'Reilly bringing in a Ballinasloe society. Branches also opened in Ballaghaderreen, Elphin, Listowel, Newtownsandes, Castlepollard and Enfield. The June census showed 43,788 members, the highest ever and a more accurate figure than the 100,000 claimed. But it was quickly dwarfed: by December there were 67,827 members in 210 Branches, a Head Office staff of twelve and seventeen Organisers.

Table 7: ITGWU membership by industry, June 1918

Transport, including docks, railways, tramways, canals, carters and porters:	7,059
Fuel, coal and turf workers:	1,694
Food, including agriculture (9,634), creameries, eggs and poultry, bacon factories, butchers, bakers, corn and flour mills, groceries, hotels, breweries:	16,888
Industries, including building trade, timber mills, brickyards, textile mills, woollen mills, laundries, munitions, gas, chemicals, and general labourers:	15,399
Public services and others, including public board employees, theatres, clerks, shop assistants and trade agents:	2,808
Total:	43,788

Source: ITGWU, Annual Report, 1918.

The Rules 'were re-written almost entirely' and published. Branch bookkeeping and stationery were remodelled and provision made for local funds, whereby Branches kept 25% of contributions to meet all non-benefit expenses, remitting the remainder to Head Office. No attempt was 'made to keep a Head Office record, as in other Unions, of the financial status of each member.' The inspection of Branch accounts was thrown on Committees and Officials. The ITGWU nevertheless confidently claimed that the 'book-keeping system at Head Office will be found to correspond exactly to the needs of the Union' and to 'provide complete security for the finances.' An increasing administrative apparatus was central to Larkin's

subsequent criticism. But how else could the expanding ITGWU maximise its efficiency and industrial strength? The Rules put the union on a more democratic
basis. From foundation to October 1914, Larkin 'controlled absolutely' all union
affairs. 'No proper Executive' was 'elected or functioned as required by the Rules
then in existence.' The 'only authority, other than Larkin, was that of Dublin No. 1
Branch Committee.' The first Executive minutes book 'apart from that of No. 1
Branch' was for 1918. In 1913 Larkin had instructed John O'Neill, Secretary of Dublin
No. 1 Branch, 'to burn all records of the Union then in existence,' which presumably
accounts for the absence of earlier records. A Delegate meeting on 24 May 1915
elected the 'first Executive'. The first Annual Report was for 1918.[6]

In 1919 the ITGWU expected 'real progress towards the goal of our social emancipation.' It 'profited to the full by the boom,' gaining enormously in 'membership,
prestige and driving-power.' Birr Land and Labour Association joined. More than
1,000 attended the Lucan AGM, and Branches were started in Cloncurry, Drangan,
Granard, Horse and Jockey, Mulinahone and Ratoath. Máire Mullen and Nora
Connolly (daughter of James Connolly) did good work in Cork. Thomas Farren
persuaded the Maryborough [Port Laoise] Land and Labour Association, with its
2,500 members, to transfer. In Tralee premises were opened in the Tan Yard.

Rapid advances, particularly among previously unorganised workers, created
problems. On 15 February the *Voice of Labour* published 'Three Don'ts for New
Branches', a gentle touch on the brakes.

> Don't expect the millennium after a month's affiliation. Don't make demands for
> increases until the job or the District is well organised. Don't press the farmers
> just yet, unless where conditions are favourable—work is slack and they can
> mostly dispense with labour for a little while. Collect the arrears under the
> Agricultural Wages Board regulations and wait for the Spring offensive.

In March, Constance Markievicz added her shoulder to the ever-speeding wheel.
Her rallying cry was:

> Comrades, the best and the last of the long fight is before us, the watchword is
> 'Organise.' Every man, woman and child must be ready to take their stand for
> Connolly's Commonwealth. Organise Politically and Economically. Put your
> trust in God and the spirit of Republican Ireland, and full steam ahead.

Admission to the AGM of Dublin No. 1 Branch, held in the Round Room of the
Mansion House on Sunday 12 January, was 'by card only.' This was evidence of
increasing administrative organisation and a realisation that, even in such a vast
auditorium, places were at a premium. The *Voice of Labour* for May Day cited No.
1 as the 'Union's Pioneer Branch', claiming more than 11,000 members, 'organised
like an army', the members 'grouped scientifically in their industrial sectors,' able to
'plan their own campaigns' and 'choose their own officers.' It was a 'union of small
unions.' It had absorbed local bodies that were powerless on their own. However,

'behind the banner of Number One' they 'preserved all that was vital in their old traditions, retained full freedom of action' and raised their members' living stan-dards. A further invitation was issued:

> If your Union remains isolated, weak and helpless, confronting hopelessly the well-knit organisation of the master class, don't let the interests of persons, the bondage of alien and narrow craft-unionism, or the fetish of the funeral benefits, keep you apart from us. Act now. Lead your fellow-workers to see their future assuredly in the One Big Union.

No. 1 Branch comprised forty Sections, encompassing waterfront occupations, stonecutters, account-collectors, bank porters, brewers and Corporation staffs. In addition to industrial activity it provided a co-operative grocery, provision and bakery shop, café and restaurant, tontine society, concerts and dramatic classes, athletic club, and Brass and Reed Band. In June and July the Dublin Operative Farriers, Dublin Carpet Planners and Dublin Saddlers and Harness Makers were absorbed.[7]

On 1 March the new Executive Council was announced: Joseph Kelly, Patrick Stafford, Michael McCarthy and Thomas Kennedy (Dublin), Patrick Kelly (Belfast), James Connor (Tullamore) and William Kenneally (Cork), with a ballot for the remaining position. William O'Brien was elected General Treasurer after Michael Feeney and Michael Gallagher (Collooney) withdrew, both encouraged by John Lynch of Sligo.

O'Brien immediately instituted new financial procedures, arranging that an EC sub-Committee meet every Wednesday evening to consider payments. All appli-cations received after Wednesday morning had to await the next EC meeting for sanction, except for Mortality Benefits, 'which will be paid by return of post.' O'Brien advised: 'Your strict attention to this instruction will obviate disappoint-ment to your members, and will facilitate the efficient working of the Union.' All 'circulars and instructions to Branch Secretaries' appeared in the *Voice of Labour,* 'distinguished by a sub-heading, thus:— (Official).'

Articles by J. J. Hughes, a central energy at the organising core, began on 24 May, addressing 'Union Problems'. His 'Branch Management' is still recognisable. 'No one seems to know his or anybody else's place or duties, and the carrying out of the work is left by everybody to a vague somebody who often turns out to be nobody.' There was need for 'an enlightened and democratic rank-and-file.'

> Without a membership that studies the Union's doings, without intelligent Committee men to advise and control their paid servants, the Officials, without Branches that can think nationally as well as parochially, without the moral courage in all to insist on their rights and perform their duties as defined in the Rules and regulations made by themselves, we are only flying from evils we know—to evils we don't know, but soon will, out of the frying pan into the fire.

Unless we can have democracy in the I.T.&.G.W.U., we cannot have it at all. When we have democracy we won't need leaders.

The Branch Committee was the key. In some places it did not meet, in others it met but discussed nothing worth while, while some were one-horse affairs dominated by a strong personality.

Next was 'Democratic Management'. Hughes condemned the 'one man show' as leading to inadequate supervision, corruption and, if it collapsed, a setback. He wanted more democracy, acknowledging that 'educational work was slowly under way.' The editor of *Voice of Labour*, J. M. MacDonnell, addressed a Shop Stewards' Council on 'The Rise of the Shop Stewards' Movement'.

An underlying theme in Hughes's articles was caution. Many farm labourers joined up, secured an increase, then promptly left. The only way to achieve anything in the long run was hard work. It was 'impossible to clear away the ills that have accumulated through years, aye generations, of carelessness in a week or a month.' Hughes advocated One Big Union—

> not a big incoherent mass but scientifically organised and efficiently worked, thoroughly enlightened and democratic. That is why we must build up the Union and not exploit it; cultivate the verb 'to do' and put the verb 'to say' in its own place.

A bitter dispute arose between O'Brien and Hughes early in 1921. O'Brien alleged that Hughes did not comply with instructions. Hughes suggested that O'Brien wanted to oust him and install Éamon Lynch in his place. Lynch moved from Cork in November to become 'Organiser of Organisers'. Matters descended into the choice of office and other petty disagreements. Hughes finally resigned on 2 July.[8]

By 17 May there were 340 Branches, compared with 209 on 1 January; 'and still they come.' Swaggering growth brought determined opposition by employers. The Irish Unionist Alliance was formed to split the ITGWU, give 'financial support for wreckers,' disrupt the ILP&TUC and broadcast 'foreign propaganda'. Among its officers were Mrs Fane Vernon, wife of the Governor of the Bank of Ireland; Mrs Craig Davidson; and C. A. Scannell and Cecil Fforde of the Incorporated Law Society. Such 'attempts to defame and divide the Union' were countered by Dublin No. 1 Branch instituting fortnightly meetings of the Shop Stewards' Movement. The first, on Tuesday 21 May, was 'confined to 76 Delegates.'

By September, Head Office again tried to assess the basic who, where and how-many questions. Branches supplied details of classes of work, numbers employed, weekly wages, kind and quality of any allowances, bonuses such as war, harvest, etc., piece-work rates and times, hours worked per day and per week, overtime rates, and whether there was a half day on Saturday and from what time. On 13 September the 'First Hundred Thousand' was trumpeted when the census revealed 110,752 members. These included transport, land and fuel, 17,198; industries, 28,911; food, 58,940; and miscellaneous, 5,703. Farm labourers, with 40,016, were the biggest group, while dockers were now a mere 3,750. An obvious conclusion was drawn. 'If unity is strength, then this combination of 110,000 workers, organised as workers, without distinction as to occupation, represents strength of a degree and of a kind hitherto unknown in the annals of Irish Labour.' OBU was 'in the making.'

By December there were 433 Branches and a net financial membership of 102,419, covering the country 'with [the] exception of Fermanagh and Armagh.' The 'most gratifying feature' was growth in Belfast from 500 to 3,000. In many towns the ITGWU 'was the only Trade Union' and its Committee effectually served as 'a Trades Council for the town ... The Branch in such cases acquires a degree of influence and a strength which no other system of organisation could give,' reflected in 'town movements, particularly in the West and Midlands.'

Significant numbers of craftsmen joined. Rationalisation efforts did not always succeed, 'partly owing to the apathy of the workers concerned.' Such was the bubbling enthusiasm that apathy hardly seemed possible. The ITGWU pursued national wage movements to break the endless round of often unrelated local endeavours. This welded it into a more disciplined, manageable unit. A fundamental complaint has echoed throughout union history: 'The tendency of the Sections is to expect the Branch Officers and Committees to carry out the work that should properly be done at Sectional meetings,' and Branch Officers and Committees were 'too frequently' inclined to seek the intervention of Organisers 'in matters that could with equal advantage be decided locally.' (Twenty-one Organisers were employed.) Conversely, inexperience led new Branches to act without consulting Head Office. Failure damaged prestige. There was a simple remedy: 'It cannot be too frequently or too strongly emphasised' that the union's 'whole stability and health' depended 'upon the quality of its Committee members' and the 'regularity of their meetings.' The problem was a lack of education. Too many regarded the union as a 'mere protection and Benefit Society'—Connolly's 'pure and simple' trade unionism— and 'for want of wider vision' such a member failed to see in it 'the instrument of his advancement to a higher level of life and comfort.'

Branch libraries were recommended so that members could gain access to Connolly's works and those of 'other great social thinkers.' Members' 'varied talents' were expressed in social activities of music and study. Co-operative societies were to create jobs and bring consumer benefits. 'Were this done on a sufficiently wide scale, a Workers' Food Committee' would 'grapple successfully with the food problem on democratic lines.'

Despite reservations about membership claims, financial returns confirmed staggering growth. Total receipts for 1918 of £27,699 grew by 170% to £74,475 in 1919. That new Branches, most with no previous organisational experience, should willingly and conscientiously return large sums to Dublin was testimony to their belief in and identification with the union, creating a fundamental solidarity. Unquantifiable on any balance sheet, trust and commitment were the ITGWU's greatest assets.

Expenses grew as prices rose, and more staff and part-time Officials were employed. This had a double effect. Many Branches lacked experience in dealing with arrears and benefits, which older Branches and unions found so valuable in conserving and maintaining their funds. Inexperienced employers 'did not hesitate to enter into disputes . . . which would easily have been avoided had these employers been accustomed to dealing with organised labour.'

Mortality Benefit rose from £321 to £3,282 as the influenza epidemic wrought 'dreadful havoc'. There were few liabilities, however. Even the lingering 1913 legal bills of £850 were settled. The union proudly boasted that it was 'practically clear of all debt,' owned 'considerable property' and was 'firmly established in all parts of Ireland.' Foran could scarcely have believed it, two-and-a-half years after Easter 1916.

Table 8: ITGWU income, expenditure, surplus and credit balance (£), 1918–22

	Income	Expenditure	Surplus	Credit balance
1918	27,699	18,986	8,713	17,929
1919	74,726	63,379	11,346	29,038
1920	100,011	62,848	37,163	66,202
1921	81,584	45,596	35,997	102,199
1922	96,007	64,506	31,501	133,700

Source: ITGWU, Annual Reports, 1918–22.

Size bred self-confidence. The union was a 'tree whose roots are so widespread and grip every variety of soil that it cannot be uprooted by force or outward attack.' Industrial Councils, like that for Munster creameries, formulated joint action at the national, industrial, regional or town level. The union brought trade unionism from town to country. Land workers were given leadership and inspiration. This induced a very optimistic inference: 'The national significance' of 'land workers' rally to the Red Flag is that the last subject class, the rural proletariat, has awakened to the failure of its sacrifices in past generations.' Years of political progress, in which Catholic lawyers, doctors and professional men advanced and farmers became 'owners of the soil', brought labourers 'as a class' nothing. Emerging independence was delusive unless the class war was won.

> Looking back on the years of struggle, the debt of Ireland to the pioneers becomes clear. To Larkin, the founder; to Connolly, the architect; to the faithful dockers of Dublin, Belfast, Wexford and Sligo, who bore the brunt of the battle from 1909 to 1916, the Union in its fuller development owes its growth and very existence.

In August came a powerful statement of the case for One Big Union. It was not uncommon to find four or five organisations in one job. The largest union usually did best, to the detriment of others. This was 'the apex of absurdity', and the ITGWU 'proved it.'

> All employees should be in the One Big Union so that One Big Demand can be served on the employers, and One Big Settlement reached, satisfactory to the needs and requirements of all, or, failing that, One Big Strike. These are the aims and objects of the I.T.&.G.W.U. Which shall it be? Craft Unionism and class progress backward, or Class Unionism and class progress forward?[9]

1920–22: THE CALM BEFORE THE STORM

Expansion continued in 1920. Denis Houston broke new soil in Broughshane and Glenravel, while saddlers—recent affiliates—improved conditions until their craft was 'blackleg-proof'. The *Watchword of Labour* suggested that 'this proud position is but another example' of the 'practicability and desirability' of OBU. Membership on 31 January 1920 was 102,823; by December it had reached 'at least 120,000.' The 'truest index' was the income recorded, comparative figures being: 1919, £74,475; 1920, £104,088. Weekly comparisons were: 1919, £1,432; 1920, £2,002. This was an annual increase of 40%. Although expenditure rose, the excess of income over expenditure was £35,941, bringing a credit balance of £55,539—a staggering figure, given the kitty of £96 after Easter 1916. Total assets were valued at £66,202, with all debts paid.

There were still concerns about participation. In April the *Watchword of Labour* listed 'Ten Ways to Kill a Union'. Contemporary members might consider that history constantly repeats itself.

1. Don't come to the meetings.
2. But if you do come—come late.
3. If the weather doesn't suit you—don't come.
4. If you do attend a meeting, find fault with the work of the officers and other members.
5. Never accept an office; it's easier to criticise than to do things.
6. Nevertheless, get sore if you are not appointed on a Committee; but, if you are appointed, do not attend the Committee meetings.
7. If asked by the President to give your opinion on an important matter, tell him you have nothing to say. After the meeting tell everyone how things should be done.
8. Do nothing more than absolutely necessary when other members roll up their sleeves and willingly and unselfishly use their ability to help matters along; howl that the Union is run by a clique.
9. Hold back your dues as long as possible, or don't pay them at all.
10. Don't bother about getting new members—let George do it!

The British 'Terrorist Campaign' after September 'chose out the Union as a special object for its malignancy [malignity].' The ITGWU 'rose superior to it,' but it halted wage movements and Branch activity. The attainment of 'our great objective—Economic Liberty' depended on 'how we are organised.' Ironically, a slowed pace of growth afforded an opportunity to strengthen internal structures.

The 'ugly spectre of unemployment' raised its head and ate 'into the vitals of the Organised.' The response was to consolidate vulnerable smaller units within a radius of eight or ten miles around a town Branch. National industrial Sections provided 'the foundation and framework on which the whole superstructure' would rest. The 'driving force' derived from the 'workshop—from whence emanates all economic power.' The union's 'achievements have naturally been the wonder of the workers of other countries, while the malignant vituperation of its enemies testifies splendidly to its efficiency and power.'

The Irish Clerical Workers' Union, a breakaway from the National Union of Clerks, was invited to amalgamate. Conversely, the National Union of Dock Labourers was dismissed as a 'sanctuary for scabs' after a dispute in Galway. ITGWU strikers in Galway Flour Mills were replaced by NUDL men, making them the 'buttress for bullying bosses and offal heap for the outcasts of other unions.' In the Chemical Works a 77-hour week was challenged by the ITGWU, which sought a reduction to 48 hours, only for NUDL men to again renege. In Clonmel Brewery there were similar problems.

An unexpected enquiry about amalgamation came from the Flax Dressers' Trade Union in May. Was it 'a sign of a coming revolt'?—for such an enquiry must have 'upset the Counsels of a Tory Executive Committee.' Nothing came of it. Dublin Portmanteau Makers' and Leather Workers' Trade Union did join.

There was growing criticism of Sectional trade unionism, and moves towards Irish industrial unions in engineering and the distributive trades. In June, John Hill, 'late employee of Messrs. Guinness,' dismissed for union activities, acted as Secretary of the Brewery Section 'without remuneration.'

By August, Lucan looked 'much livelier' since Jim McDermott 'took up the captaincy,' with 'scores of workers,' hitherto non-union men, 'carded and badged by him,' so that 'non-Unionists' were a 'memory of the past.' Hill's Woollen Mills tried to break the union through starvation tactics, but strikers stood firm 'with praiseworthy grit' until 'Hill was humbled.' A football match with a 'good gate' and a parade 'a couple of thousand strong' through Lucan supported them.

'Comrades Houston and O'Donnell' succeeded in Derry, with 'dozens of workers of every calling' joining and new premises opened in William Street. Shipyard, mill and factory hands enrolled. It was 'only a matter of time' before the ITGWU became the 'largest and most influential combination in the city.' But recognition by Derry Trades Council was not forthcoming.

In Dublin a Mansion House arbitration award produced a significant increase in the newspaper, hotel and restaurant trades. But expansion did not please everyone. J. J. Farrelly of Dublin Trades Council condemned poaching without 'taking a plebiscite of the full Union to see whether or not' it 'would go over to the One Big Union in a body.'

At the annual Delegate Conference, held after the Cork ILP&TUC, Foran congratulated Delegates, and O'Brien took satisfaction in the fact that all big fights were met without a necessity to levy members. He emphasised internal discipline: the union's good name was 'more important than funds, and for this reason ill-considered action should be avoided lest the prestige of the Union should suffer.' They had 'to bring the reserve funds up to a point that would render the organisation secure from any attack.' A War Chest was created.

In October the United Builders' Labourers' Union fell victim to a Dublin building strike. They voted by 714 to 12 to transfer, giving Liberty Hall, with 'this new accession of strength,' virtually a 'monopoly of the work for builders' labourers.' In spite of old differences, 'the Transport came to its aid when struck.' They were welcome, 'if latecomers,' into the fold, 'provided they maintain the fighting traditions, discipline and spirit of comradeship of our Union.' Members were urged to 'cling to them as comrades in evil as well as bright days in the OBU.'

The ITGWU Builders' Labourers' Section, operating from 17 High Street, was small, but in 1921 the UBLU's existing members in builders' providers, marble-polishers and stonecutters came together as Dublin No. 5 Branch. In August the Cork Brewery Workers, Vintners' Assistants' Association, Gas Workers and, in Passage West, Dock, Wharf, Riverside and General Labourers' Union all came over.

A census of 25 September showed a membership of 102,823. This was 'exclusive of all lapsed members and members in arrears . . . about 20,000 farm labourers who are not in employment during the winter months but have since renewed'; thousands of seasonal timber and dock workers who could not complete twelve months' membership; and those transferred from smaller unions. Book membership was over 130,000. The ITGWU heralded its achievements as the 'greatest, most militant and most successful of Irish Unions' and 'one of the pioneers of revolutionary Unionism in Europe,' all achieved in its first ten years. The Annual Report for 1919, available to everyone, 'even the enemy in Dublin Castle, the Kildare Street Club and the Employers' Associations,' at 2d a copy, published the data.

From 21 August the EC closed any Branch more than eight weeks in arrears, charged Branches for stationery (although first supplied on credit), and for Dispute Pay did not regard itself as 'liable in the case of members who are thrown idle through the shortage of supplies, etc., owing to a strike or Lock-Out.' Branch Secretaries were notified that 'rates, hours and conditions in various occupations' could be obtained from Head Office, particulars that would 'be found most useful in local negotiations.' There was a caveat: 'In many instances, information is incomplete.' This fault was 'attributable alone to Branch Officials who will not deliver the goods.'

In 1921, as the War of Independence intensified, Officials were subject to harassment and imprisonment. O'Brien embarked on an eight-day hunger strike after Andrew Bonar Law, a member of the British Government, made the 'most abominable and most terrible of charges' against the General Treasurer. On his release he was moved to a nursing-home before arriving in triumph at Kingstown. He was met by Thomas Foran, Tom Kennedy, Thomas O'Reilly and a large demonstration bearing red flags. Cathal O'Shannon was arrested in London for alleged seditious remarks made in Kells; his release came after the hunger strike. He was still in the Mater Hospital in mid-May, 'making fair progress' but not 'yet fit to leave.' Edward Nunan, a Head Office clerk, was arrested by soldiers at his home and incarcerated in Mountjoy Prison.

On 2 November, County Inspector R. D. Morrison, Lisburn, revealed the authorities' attitude. Reports had to state 'any tendency towards Bolshevism, e.g. the making of revolutionary speeches or circulation of revolutionary literature,' any connection between Irish and British labour agitation, and 'the relations between the I.T.&G.W.U. and Sinn Fein.' In Galway two Organisers, Gilbert Lynch and Denis Houston, fled the town under threat from Black and Tans.

The impracticality of doing normal business necessitated circumvention by the Executive of breaches of Rule and the maintenance of benefit for those imprisoned. The dominant feature of the period was the 'intensification of the onslaught of the British Forces on the Irish Nation' and the 'Black and Tan arm' of the 'Greenwood régime hardened in vengeful rigour.' The union saw Labour's response in magnificent terms: 'The only result was the welding of the Irish Forces, of which Labour formed an honourable portion, into a still more cohesive and a still more vigorous resistance.' Any internal discord was resisted, and 'Labour unhesitatingly responded to the call for unity in the face of the common enemy.'

Liberty Hall proudly claimed that the union came 'through the stress and storm' with 'flying colours, its organisation intact, and strengthened by the contest.' Despite the 'never-sleeping opposition' of employers and continuous 'fierce hostility' from British forces, the balance sheet showed that income fell by only 18½%, to £81,593, which 'in the circumstances' was 'eminently satisfactory.' The 'mere existence of the Union' was nigh impossible 'over wide stretches.' Increasing unemployment resulting from the 'world-wide slump in industry and agriculture' might have 'bankrupted very many other Unions.' Expenditure fell to £45,596, representing £876 a week, compared with £1,208 per week in 1920. The amount added to the union's reserve was £35,997, a remarkable figure and one that brought cash funds to £90,789 and total assets to £103,473.[10]

The ITGWU reflected on its relative success, certainly compared with the crushing defeats for British miners, transport workers and railwaymen on Black Friday and subsequently of the engineers and seamen. It was due to the union's 'scheme of organisation'. Had 'British workers been possessed of the same fighting spirit' as the Irish 'we would doubtless have been spared the spectacle of humiliating defeats,' and Irish employers could not have constantly cited lower British rates when demanding cuts. British unions were condemned for their passivity and Irish members encouraged into the OBU. The 'sins of slackers' remained an issue, for where 'organisation was good, wages were not impaired.'

Despite the fact that the great majority of members were only four years, at most, in a union, a 'glowing tribute' could be paid to their 'morale . . . manliness and . . .

class-consciousness.' Despite violent intimidation, threatened unemployment and 'intolerable privations,' 'scarcely a single man' was found with the 'slightest inclination to scab.' This spirit mocked 'virtual starvation' and laughed 'in the teeth of famine.' It was 'one of the most inspiring evidences of the glorious possibilities which the Ireland of the future holds for us.'

On 11 July, when the Truce was declared, Head Office barely coped with demands for reorganisation. Under the Chief Organiser, Éamon Lynch, nine Organisers were on the road. After the union had been criticised at the ITUC for poaching, some wondered whether, if the expansion of the ITGWU continued, there would be any need for Congress.

The outbreak of the Civil War on 22 June 1922 rendered ordinary union activity virtually impossible. Communication between Head Office and Branches and Organisers became a problem. Railway, road and postal services collapsed. In addition, unemployment and depression occasioned continuous demands for wage cuts. Despite all this the EC appointed more full-time Branch Secretaries and Delegates and maintained ten Organisers. William Vennard, a railway worker from Portadown, joined Head Office, and Patrick O'Doherty was appointed to Tipperary.

Some Organisers in this period who had a British background were alleged to be spies. Michael Collins warned O'Brien on 6 July, 'from a reliable source,' that men were being planted, 'supplied with faked union badges and forged instructions.' Collins was not sure 'how far this thing has gone' but suggested that a 'couple of reliable Branch Secretaries should be informed' about how 'the Enemy regards the Unions.' He was 'sure that the Transport would be the first body to be dealt with.'

Income rose by 17 % in 1922 to £96,007, only 4% less than the boom year of 1920. Conversely, expenditure was £18,909 more than 1921, at £64,506, 'the highest in the history of the Union since it became a nationwide organisation.' A working surplus of £31,500 was recorded, bringing cash reserves to £109,430 and total assets to £134,824. There was a glaring lesson to be learnt from the blizzard of wage cuts: 'the necessity for the One Big Union.'

The ITGWU's standards were undermined by weaker organisation, particularly in British unions. The battle was for the new 'Social Order', not just to resist wage cuts—a society in which

> none shall batten in idleness on the brains and brawn of his fellow-men, where the self-seeker, the exploiter, the parasite, of whatever class, shall perish, where all shall give work and service in the interests of the community at large, where the weak shall be protected, and the tyrannous humbled, and where all shall have justice and equality of opportunity.

Greater education was needed to strengthen and inform organisation. On 31 December 1921 the newly created Irish Engineering and Industrial Union adopted a motion that, as 'a new era is about to dawn . . . every Irish working man should be a member of one of the Irish unions catering for their particular industries.' It approached the ITGWU to consider a joint Executive as 'Industrial Unionists'. Two meetings were held early in 1922, with the IEIU suggesting co-operation where membership overlapped or was complementary and the development of long-term joint industrial strategies. Foran and O'Brien, however, would only countenance the IEIU's admission as a Craft Section. This was a bridge too far for the IEIU, and the talks petered out. (The mutual relationship sought by the IEIU was in fact not too unlike that developed in the Trade Union Federation begun in May 2003 between SIPTU and the Technical, Engineering and Electrical Union.) Strong rumours of financial difficulties in the IEIU may have prompted its action. Liberty Hall perhaps hoped to engulf it.

An opportunity to take in the Irish National Assurance Company Super-intendents was not followed, as, having previously taken in agents, 'we had found them a difficult body to deal with, and we were not enamoured of extending our operations in that direction.'

Table 9: ITGWU membership by Branch or county, December 1921

Dublin No. 1	12,560	Dublin County	4,437
Dublin No. 2	1,174	Kildare	1,589
Dublin No. 3	8,993	Kilkenny	894
Dublin No. 4	1,800	King's County [Offaly]	930
Dublin No. 5	1,170	Longford	82
Cork City	9,022	Louth	909
Cork County	2,003	Meath	1,270
Clare	629	Queen's County [Laois]	837
Kerry	635	Westmeath	1,298
Limerick	4,529	Wexford	2,089
Tipperary	2,459	Wicklow	2,231
Waterford	2,984	Connacht	1,645
Carlow	1,358	Ulster	2,011

Source: ITGWU, minutes of Resident Executive Committee, 18 December 1921.

In December 1921 financial membership was 69,560. This figure had leapt to 82,243 by 31 December 1922. The AGM of Dublin No. 1 Branch in the Mansion House on Sunday 15 January reported 16,833 members, a slight increase on the 16,642 of 1920. The balance sheet similarly showed a rise from £21,538 to £22,409. Dispute Pay totalled £15,073 in 1921, 73% of the national total of £20,409, an indication of where the cockpit of struggle had been. The Branch represented builders' labourers and providers, saw millers and stonecutters, marble-polishers, sculptors and stone-masons, tile and mosaic fixers and steel erectors, many from previously independent unions.

In Cork an 'over-flowing' AGM of Connolly Memorial Branch heard that remittances to Head Office totalled £5,255 13s 5d, with £1,712 15s 9d retained locally. In September the Irish Automobile Drivers' and Automobile Mechanics' Union completed lengthy, and at times rancorous, transfer. It was admitted as a Section, '100 on full benefit with clear cards and 50 on half-benefit.' The remainder came as new members on an entrance fee of 2s 7d if done within two weeks. Its Secretary, Ciarán J. King, joined Head Office.[11]

With peace announced on 3 May 1923, the ITGWU could concentrate on further growth. Its rising membership and credit balance of £133,700 were impressive.

THE IMPRISONMENT OF C. F. RIDGWAY

Charles F. Ridgway was detained without charge by the RIC in Monaghan in 1922. His captors ran down the labour movement and the 'Irish Transport Workers' Union in particular,' accusing him of being the Organiser for a 'murder gang'. His Protestantism was demeaned. He was threatened with being summarily shot. Brigadier Terry Magee abused him when he was held in Dundalk, which led Ridgway to demand an end to all militarism. He escaped when the wall of Dundalk Jail was blown open.

Senator Thomas Farren moved a motion in 1923 condemning the 'continued imprisonment without trial of thousands of citizens' as 'unjust, tyrannical and detrimental to the true interests of the country' and demanded their trial or release. Archie Heron drew attention to the plight of those interned aboard the *Argenta* in Larne Harbour, a ship 'infested with rats' while the prisoners were 'rotting to death.' Frank McGrath (Belfast) suggested that a 'general stoppage might bring about the release of all the prisoners.'

Congress had done it before, but the mood on this occasion went little beyond adopting the motion.[12] Ridgway would become Branch Secretary of Dublin No. 4 (Hotels) and an extremely influential figure within the ITGWU.

WOMEN

In July 1916 Foran reported requests from 'a lady' to relaunch the Irish Women Workers' Union. They were found a room in Liberty Hall 'while they got organised,' on the understanding that they would move out 'when they got settled up.' In 1917 the ITGWU recognised the IWWU as a fully independent body, and it remained so until amalgamation with the FWUI in 1984. It had two rooms in which to start a co-operative factory, in which Dr Kathleen Lynn and Madeleine Ffrench-Mullen took a 'great interest'. Lynn offered her medical services 'to attend to our people that are sick.'

In December 1920 an ITGWU Organiser, Helen Hoyne, claimed that 'owing to the curfew she was unable to carry out duties,' and requested clerical work in Head Office instead. She was dispensed with, having already blotted her copybook in September. A request by the Waterford Branch to admit women was sanctioned in December 1921.[13] In general, women joined the ITGWU in greater and greater numbers, although there was no 'gender agenda' at that time.

ULSTER

Harry Midgley, Secretary of the Linen Lappers and Warehouse Workers' Trade Union, sought a job with the ITGWU in October 1920. He was invited to an interview in Dublin, 'his expenses to be paid,' but he 'yielded to pressure' and remained with his own union. In a city 'racked, torn and shot-up with dissensions—ostensibly based on political and religious differences but in reality having their source and objectives in the furtherance of the interests of Big Business' and 'malevolent designs of the shattering' of workers' solidarity, the Belfast Branch maintained rates for deep-sea dockers and flour-millers. Other unions' 'weak-kneed' attitude in 'servilely submitting to wholesale wage-clips' notwithstanding, the Branch proudly announced that 'in the history of the Union' there were 'few episodes more gallant than the stand made by our members and Officials in this Northern outpost of the O.B.U. in the teeth of foes and difficulties innumerable.'

In June 1921 Councillor James 'Dungaree' Baird enquired about 'getting employment with the union.' Nothing was immediately available but he was invited to Dublin for an interview, expenses paid, and was employed as an Organiser from 1922.[14]

THE ATGWU

As moves towards the creation in Britain of the Transport and General Workers' Union advanced, the Secretary of the National Transport Workers' Federation, Robert Williams, suggested that 'Irish members of the Dockers' Union be transferred to' the ITGWU, and a Delegation was invited to talks 'here or there.'[15]

LINES OF PROGRESS

Promoting workers' education, the ITGWU launched a series of pamphlets called the Liberty Hall Library in July 1918. The first, *The Lines of Progress,* was 'written out of the necessities of the case,' was a 'veritable Red Republican Manifesto and will make history.' It was written 'primarily for the guidance of the Officials and members of the Union,' and the union hoped 'it will be available for the members of other Unions.' It was 'a successful attempt to apply that thought and intelligence to Labour problems which we have pleaded for in *The Voice*.' It took 'the big and broad view' of the union 'as the germ of the new social order which will take the place of the present inhuman system.' It outlined the 'ideal of the One Big Union' and 'encouraged [the] Sectional classification' of members in 'Big Branches'. Others would 'follow this excellent lead.' *The Lines of Progress* was presented as 'a simple outline' of the ITGWU's organisation and its place in the movement. Attributed to Foran, it was more probably written by J. J. Hughes. He addressed similar issues in the *Voice*.

A second pamphlet, *Trade Unionism,* explained the 'Rules and working methods of the Union that gives benefits every pay day.'[16]

WAGES AND DISPUTES

In July 1916 a dispute among coal porters occasioned the intervention of the Lord Mayor of Dublin. A Delegate, Laurence Redmond, attended the Mansion House for discussions but was accused of 'working a boat' while employed by the union. Foran thought some penalty on Redmond appropriate. Internal discipline demanded the safeguarding of Delegates' status and independence—in effect that of full-time Shop Steward. A dispute in the Gas Company involved the ITGWU and the Gasworkers' Union. Jack Jones came over from London and, with Foran and Redmond, negotiated a settlement without a strike. Foran thought 'they got out if it very lucky.'

November saw activity and confidence grow. Increases were won in Ross and Walpole's, Dolan's, Leask's, Bristol Shipping, City of Dublin Steam Packet Company and Gillen's. Deported men were given membership credit for the 'eight months that they were away.' The Acting Secretary of Dublin No. 1 Branch, J. J. Nolan, was given a week's notice of the 'termination of his temporary employment' as John O'Neill became free to resume his duties.

The clouds, while parting, were still leaden. Increases for casual dockers having been gained without a fight, a claim for labourers in Inchicore Railway Works, 'as they find it almost impossible to exist owing to the great increase in the cost of living,' was sanctioned. Foran Counselled that 'if it came to a fight' the union was 'not in a position to support them.'[17]

In Cos. Cork and Kerry more than £400,000 was won in increased wages from January 1917. Bitter conflict raged in Castlecomer coalmines, Co. Kilkenny, where the local manager complained that the ITGWU would 'smash capitalism, then all is lost.' The union replied:

> *All* is the chance of having three bond slaves for Forty-Five bob [45s] a week! *All* is giving a man, his wife and two children fifteen bob to live on. *All* is feeding the worker, housing and clothing the brute, his squaw and their spawn at a cost of four and three sevenths pence per head per day.

Throughout 1918, when the cost of living was officially reckoned to be 125% higher than before the war, the ITGWU advanced wages throughout the economy, 'greatly helped by facilities offered by such Government bodies as the Ministry of Labour for arbitration cases.' 'Almost every Section' gained improved conditions. It was a wonderful organisational message. A dispute in the Gas Company demonstrated the union's strength and confidence. The company attempted to dismiss Shop Stewards, but men stopped all work until they were reinstated. It proved to the management that it 'cannot ride roughshod over the men now that they are organised.' Gas Company employees were 'treated not as men but as slaves' through non-organisation. By mid-April, Foran feared that 'he would have to extend it to end it,' as the company dug in. Work resumed in late April, pending arbitration. Success followed.

There were 'satisfactory' settlements for grain porters, while Denis Houston won concessions for Cork building workers. Foran had reservations about Houston's work, however, preferring that he 'kept more in touch with Head Office.' Houston was inclined to 'work more or less off his own bat.'

The authorities clearly viewed the expansion of the ITGWU with alarm. District Inspector V. Gregory, Lisburn, was instructed, along with all RIC officers, to note 'strikes and labour unrest,' while the formation of Branches 'should be reported at once' to Crime Ordinary Branch. Congress lobbied all County, Urban and District Councils, Boards of Guardians and Government Departments regarding the adoption of a Fair Wages Clause. Much progress was reported.[18]

The biggest outlay in 1919, £41,806, was on Dispute Pay, 57% of total income. There was always concern that size would affect militancy, and opponents were quick to suggest that growth would inhibit fighting qualities; but such expenditure demonstrates that such fears were ill-founded, and in any case the EC was sensitive to the possibility of loss of drive and purpose and was committed to resist it. 'The figures are a complete refutation of the suggestion sometimes made that the Union in acquiring size, had lost its fighting spirit.'[19]

Agricultural workers had received £15,015, road workers £2,228, dockers £2,212, town movements £3,786, flour and grist mills, creameries and bakeries £2,076, and others, including motormen, £5,627. Yet the great majority of disputes were settled without a strike, such now was the union's reputation. To the charge that it exploited rural workers to the benefit of townsfolk, or handled some Sections to the detriment of others, the union simply pointed to the facts that demonstrated action and achievement in all areas, geographical, structural and industrial.

Table 10: ITGWU total income and Dispute Pay, 1918–22

	Total income (£)	Dispute Pay (£)	Dispute Pay as proportion of income (%)
1918	27,699	8,407	30.4
1919	74,726	40,571	54.3
1920	100,011	36,847	37.1
1921	81,593	20,409	44.1
1922	96,007	33,139	32.8

Source: ITGWU, Annual Reports, 1918–22.

In the autumn of 1919 progress on the wages front was substantial, with settlements throughout the country in a wide variety of trades and industries. Shop Stewards, meeting in Liberty Hall on Wednesday 26 November, heard that the response to establishing a 'strong War Chest' to 'meet all emergencies' had 'been magnificent.' Yet there were 'instances where the spirit of generosity has been sadly lacking,' and 'such a state of affairs' was, 'to say the least, disappointing.'[20] The war-chest idea never seemed to be hugely effective, raising relatively small amounts, both in money terms and as a proportion of general income (which would include the War Chest) and of Dispute Pay dispensed. The cataclysmic events of 1923 appear to have put paid to the concept and its practice.

Table 11: ITGWU War Chest, Dispute Pay and total income, 1919–24

	War Chest (£)	Dispute Pay (£)	Total income (£)	Dispute Pay as proportion of income (%)
1919	1,322	40,571	74,726	54.3
1920	6,884	36,847	100,011	37.1
1921	433	20,409	81,593	44.1
1922	39	33,139	96,007	32.8
1923	6	128,724	84,122	153.0
1924	—	10,906	50,137	21.8

Source: ITGWU, Annual Reports, 1919–24.

The union appealed to members to support the 'War Chest' by suggesting that it was the bosses who were really paying. Such arguments did not seem to convince the troops!

> What are you doing with the first week's increase you are getting? Are you giving it to the profiteer or are you going to give it to yourself? Do you know that it was with their first week's increase after the troubled times in 1916 that the Dublin members began the renovation of the shattered Liberty Hall, and made possible the extension of the Union throughout Ireland, paid for organising you and your mates, and got you most of what you got since you joined the Union! They made the employers pay for all of this. Will you make your employers pay your Strike Pay the next time you have to down tools? You can do it by giving your first week's increase to the special fighting fund of the Union. Do It Now! You won't be a ha'penny the poorer. The boss will. Make the boss beat himself by paying your Strike Pay.[21]

In January 1920 readers of the *Watchword of Labour* were reminded again of the practice, but some Branches were 'lacking in this respect and require gingering up from Secretaries or Organisers.'[22] Frustration with the response to the 'War Chest'

ITGWU GENERAL OFFICERS, 1909–1989

Thomas Foran, General President, 1909–1939

James Larkin, General Secretary, 1909–1924

P. T. Daly, Acting General Secretary, 1910

James Connolly, Acting General Secretary, 1914–1916

William O'Brien, General Treasurer, 1918–1924, General Secretary, 1924–1946

Thomas Kennedy, Vice-President, 1924–1939 General President, 1939–1946, General Secretary, 1946–1948

William McMullen, Vice-President, 1940- 1946, General President, 1946–1953

John Conroy, Vice-President, 1946–1953, General President, 1953–1969

Frank Purcell, General Secretary, 1948–1959

Edward Browne, Vice-
President, 1953–1969

Fintan Kennedy, General
Secretary, 1959–1969, General
President, 1969–1981

John F. Carroll, Vice-
President, 1969–1981, General
President, 1981–1989

Michael Mullen, General
Secretary, 1969–1982

Thomas O'Brien, Vice-
President, 1981

Christopher Kirwan, Vice-
President, 1982–1983

Edmund Browne, Vice-
President, 1983–1989

THERE ARE MEN IN WEXFORD YET !

'There are men in Wexford yet!' *Irish Worker*, 2 March 1913. (Reproduced by kind permission of Dublin City Library and Archive)

The odious 'Document' issued by the Dublin Employers' Federation to trade unionists in 1913 asking them to renounce the ITGWU on pain of lock-out or dismissal. (From *Fifty Years of Liberty Hall*, 1959)

𝕴 hereby undertake to carry out all instructions given to me by or on behalf of my employers, and further I agree to immediately resign my membership of the Irish Transport and General Workers' Union (if a member) and I further undertake that I will not join or in any way support this Union.

Signed

Address

Witness

Date

[THE DOCUMENT BY WHICH THE EMPLOYERS SOUGHT TO ENFORCE REPUDIATION OF MEMBERSHIP OF THE UNION]

Pity the Poor "Blind" Employers.

Pity the Poor 'Blind' Employers: William Martin Murphy's appeal for funds, cartoon by Ernest Kavanagh, *Irish Worker*, 4 October 1913. Note worker's Red Hand badge. (Reproduced by kind permission of Dublin City Library and Archive)

The unloading of the 'food pucks' from the first food ship, the *Hare*, in 1913. (WUI, *Jim Larkin Anniversary Programme*, 1 February 1953)

The Irish Citizen Army at Liberty Hall with the celebrated banner 'WE SERVE NEITHER KING NOR KAISER BUT IRELAND!' 1914. (From *Fifty Years of Liberty Hall*, 1959)

JIM LARKIN'S MESSAGE.

To the Members of the Irish Transport and General Workers' Union.

GREETING to all the Old Guard. To the New, I leave this thought : The men of this Union saved the nation in 1914, when all other forces—Political, Economic, Ecclesiastical—in the nation failed to sense the perils confronting the nation. The Union you are honoured by holding Membership in spoke out with Clarion Voice. We stopped the Stampede of the men of this nation, others took to themselves all the credit of that achievement, assumed responsibilities of which they have proved unworthy. Now in the crisis confronting the nation we again speak and with no uncertain voice.

"PEACE, Reconstruction, Charity to all," is the demand we make and to you this charge is given, unto each and every man, member of Rank and File or Officer entrusted with duties, perfect your organisation. Solidarity the Keynote. Get Ready, be prepared to enforce Peace, to carry out construction measures, and live true to the Motto of this Pioneer Union. "Each for all, and all for Each," steady, and be ready! I again give GREETING, to you and your care.

"A nation one and indivisable."

Your Comrade,

JIM LARKIN.

Larkin's message to ITGWU members after his return from America. (*Voice of Labour*, 5 May 1923, ILHS Archives)

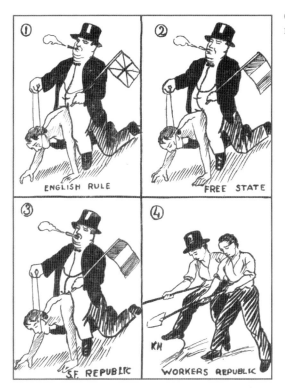

(*Voice of Labour*, 24 September 1923, ILHS Archives)

OUR WORKERS AND FIGHTERS—III.
SKETCHED BY K. N.

'Our workers and fighters
sketched by KN', Archie Heron.
(*Voice of Labour*, 9 February
1924, ILHS Archives)

Richard Dunne's wuɪ Freedom Fund certificate, 1 September 1924. (sɪptu Archive)

Liberty Hall after the eviction of occupying Larkinites, June 1924, with streamer 'WHAT WE HAVE WE HOLD'. (*Voice of Labour*, 7 June 1924, ɪlʜs Archives)

was expressed again in February 1920. 'Our Fighting Fund is still open. Those having received more cash from the bosses might kindly note.'[23]

Dispute Pay fell in 1921 to £20,409, although there was plenty of action. In the face of calls for unity against the British, how did employers respond? The ITGWU observed that while 'it would be ungenerous' and 'untrue' to deny that 'some had sufficient patriotism' to refrain from wage reductions, 'truth compels the remark that, if the Irish employers in general did not provoke industrial strife during the January–July period' their 'abstention' was not 'the promptings of patriotism' or absence of 'the will' but was because the way was blocked 'by weapons which had been steeled in shape and in effectiveness, in the grim forge of experience, and which would be wielded with all the more fierceness on anyone menacing the essential unity of the Nation. When the 'way was open' most employers 'seized the advantage of the state of things in the country to attack.'

'Unorganised Districts' emerged from the Anglo-Irish conflict with 'their wage standards badly battered' and 'lines pushed back even behind the pre-War position.' In contrast, in ITGWU Districts 'men's wages were on the whole maintained intact.'

The class concerns of Irish employers dominated 'national' thinking and should have set alarm bells ringing in an emerging Irish state. Wage 'clips' were resisted in all towns but one. Living costs, while higher than in Britain, abated slightly as the year ended, relieving pressure on both sides of the negotiating table.

In May the ILP&TUC issued a circular on wage reductions. It called for generalised opposition to cuts, a 30% improvement in pre-war standards to be fought for and defended, 25s to become a *de facto* minimum weekly wage and with rents, directors' fees, expenses and salaries to fall before wages, industrial or joint councils of unions to be formed to co-ordinate opposition within industries, counter-offensives made, information gathered and sent to the Executive, and a Wage Defence Fund created. Dublin engineering unions, including the ITGWU, federated and prevented British cuts being applied in Ireland.[24] Congress supplied detailed information on cost-of-living increases.

Dispute Pay in 1922 was £33,139. The ITGWU saw itself as having 'led the world, or at least that part of it still subject to the Capitalist system.' It was a bold claim. The reality was more one of defence than attack. By December more than half the members 'were still in possession of their peak rates,' while those who 'had to give ground . . . gave as little as possible.' A return to peace would open the way for more aggressive demands by employers. The maintenance of union solidarity would be vital. Town movements continued, mostly to resist reductions. Linen workers in Munster gave 12½% already conceded in Ulster, and flour and grist millers, railway workers and engineers were on the cusp of concessions by December. Using the military language of the times, the Executive felt that 'every Branch area had at least its baptism of fire and its reductions' engagements, though usually it was a case of individual sniping.' Where this 'was promptly tackled and the sniper silenced, the ardour of his fellow-supporters was cooled.'[25]

On 18 January 1922 the EC circulated Branches regarding the 'advisability of forming a Workers' Army' in the light of the changes in the 'political life of the country.' In the event of this army being formed it asked, 'What support do you think it would meet with in your area?' Was there any 'tendency on the part of any of the working class members of the IRA to leave the force, and if so on what grounds?' If a Workers' Army was formed, were there any 'who would be competent to act or be trained as officers?' Replies were to be marked 'Personal'; but the circular seems remarkably trusting, or foolhardy.

The restoration of Mallow Flour Mills to its owners by the IRA was an example of why a Workers' Army was considered. Mallow Strikers' Council suggested that the IRA did not initially interfere. The EC refused Lock-Out pay, and after twelve days, 'during which not a single penny entered one of our members' homes,' the workers decided to work the mill 'for the public good.' The IRA stated it would not interfere if there was no looting. In fact it forced the workers out, and Mallow men felt 'stabbed in the back.' T. Walsh (Chairman) and M. P. Linehan (Secretary) blamed the leadership. 'Our H.Q. may deny it officially—that is a way trade unions have, but we will want convincing proof to the contrary.' They 'readily understood' the IRA position, and members 'had better see to it at once that our Dublin leaders are no longer tolerated—but treated as traitors to our cause ought to be.'

The occupation began on 26 January, and £700 worth of produce was sold. On 3 March, Walsh and Linehan signed a statement that their names had been appended to the original without their consent. It was 'not written by us, or with our knowledge or consent, and we are satisfied that the allegation was utterly unfounded.' They 'deeply deprecate' its publication, 'which might have had serious consequences' for the whole union. 'We would have made this denial at an earlier date but thought that the party responsible' would 'have accepted responsibility.'[26]

The union's expenditure on Strike Pay was significant, £139,373 in Dispute Pay being paid out in five years, or 37% of total income.

AGRICULTURAL LABOURERS

'Immediate steps' were decided upon in support of Co. Dublin farm labourers in September 1917. J. J. Mallon, Secretary of Workers' Representatives on the Trade Board, criticised an award for labourers. Under the heading 'Labourers Arise', he urged them to campaign for improvements. 'The moral of the award of the Board is only too plain! The farm worker during the war has seen everybody connected with farming making money but himself.' He worked harder but reaped no gain for work crucial to the nation. Labourers' families were 'offered a half-life—a life of want, pain and hopelessness. A life in which there is neither a basis of happiness for himself nor gain for his nation.' He urged labourers to 'refuse this life' through 'resolution, courage, intelligence and class loyalty which feed and are fed by Trade Unionism.' The ITGWU would fight for them.

A rate of 32s to 35s from 1 May was won in Co. Dublin, an excess of 7s over the minimum wage established by the Agricultural Wages Board. 30s (£1 10s) was then won in Co. Kildare, triggering widespread local movements elsewhere. Agricultural labourers flocked to the union in their thousands. Castle Dermott Land and Labour Association transferred. Addressing the Congress in 1918, William O'Brien said that labourers were 'too long neglected and despised, wretchedly paid, miserably housed, badly educated.' The 'stress of war and menace of famine through submarine activities' awoke them. In May the Achill Branch disputed with Scottish farmers about arrangements for potato-pickers and harvesters. John Lynch of Sligo and Masterson of Blacksod Bay travelled to Glasgow for unsuccessful negotiations with the Glasgow and West of Scotland Potato Merchants' Association. The merchants sent a train to Westport to collect the workers in mid-July, but no-one boarded it.[27]

The abolition of the Agricultural Wages Board on 1 October 1920 exposed farm labourers and freed farmers to attack weak organisation. The ITGWU held the line or else kept cuts to a minimum only where fully organised. The country 'was flooded with Union pamphlets calling on such men to organise.' The response was 'not altogether gratifying,' but the union was firmly committed. In 1921 Foran pointed out that labourers were not fighting a foreign but a 'local enemy'. The Corn Production Act had provided a minimum wage. The union fought hard even to enforce this, but through its efforts in the Agricultural Wages Board tens of thousands in arrears of wages were wrung from farmers. With the board scrapped, labourers were thrown 'back to the hospitality of the generous employer.' Tillage showed a 'big decline, even outside the war zones,' the beginnings of a long slump. Closely allied roadmen suffered as roads were mined or blocked, bridges wrecked, and contests for funding between the Irish and British Local Government Boards denied resources. By April half the 8,000 ITGWU roadmen were unemployed and many on short hours. The union 'induced the Local Government Department of An Dáil' to operate the principle of 'Equality of Sacrifice' as between 'Officials (Surveyors, Secretaries, etc.) and employees,' but, not surprisingly, most county councils 'made little attempt to carry out the Department's injunctions.' In contrast to more privileged employees, the union congratulated its members on enduring 'their desperate hardships with thorough grit and with little complaint, rather than hamper the work and objectives of the Dáil.' Their sacrifices received little recognition, and no reward. At the end of the year, as conditions eased, union pressure gained much relief for the men.

What attracted thousands of farm labourers went beyond the defence of wages. At Easter 1921 the ILP&TUC issued a Manifesto on unemployment, calling for compulsory tillage and the development of agricultural industries. *The Land for Men—Not for Bullocks* demanded the maintenance of tillage levels. If farmers would not work their land it should be worked at union rates or, 'in the alternative, they must resign the occupation of that part of their holding which is beyond their capacity to work, to those who are willing to work it.' The section concluded:

> Let it be remembered that the land is held in trust for the Nation; it must be made the most of in maintaining the largest possible number of persons. If a genuine effort is not made to effect this result, the trust is forfeit.

Such sentiments encouraged labourers to see the ITGWU as their path to land ownership and unquestionably persuaded farmers to fear the hand of Bolshevism. M. P. Linehan (Mallow), Charles Gaule (Arklow) and William Kinneally (Cork) argued that landowners were not patriots, or they would work the land themselves. Knocklong and Arigna pointed the way. Philip O'Neill (Birr) called for a 'constructive agricultural policy' as essential 'to make possible an easy transition from capitalism to the new social order under a Gaelic State,' a new system of ownership to 'supplant the present one based on confiscation.' ITGWU policy called for co-operative farming and an Agricultural Guild. It mortified graziers and ranchers.[28]

At Limerick Junction on 22 December 1921 all members in the Condensed Milk Company emphatically protested against wage cuts. A Committee of Action was put together by the local Organisers, McGrath and Jack Dowling, with 'Comrade Leo' as Chairman. A Conference was organised with the Dáil Ministry of Labour to arrive at a just scale, taking into account the costs of living and of production, volume and market, and deciding upon a base year. A permanent Tribunal to facilitate industrial peace was created. The ITGWU objected to clause 8, which spoke of a 'community of interest' between worker and employer: there was 'no such community of interest.' 'White Guardism' on the part of farmers resulted in some union men being burned out in Old Parish and elsewhere in Co. Waterford. Farmers were defeated in Cos. Dublin and Meath 'after a comparatively short, but sharp, fight,' even though the IRA protected scabs. Most settled for 43s per week, the previous year's rate but a significant advance on farmers' demands for cuts. The 'famous victory of 1920' was not repeated. Men, in Co. Meath especially, 'found ordinary strike tactics insufficient' and adopted 'more modern methods of class warfare.' They felled trees, blocked roads and bridges, drove cattle and sheep, and gave 'joy-rides for the bosses' flunkies and toadies.'

The opening campaigns in Cos. Dublin and Meath in March 1922 were 'brilliantly successful'. Unemployed Meath men demanded 'work on the ranches on the basis of one man, at least, to fifty acres,' a strategy 'vigorously pressed'. Disputes followed in Cos. Cork, Laois, Limerick, Tipperary, Westmeath and Wicklow, 'from all of which the labourers emerged victorious.' Co. Louth was especially rewarding, as the British union to which the men had belonged conceded 8s from the 1921 rate. The ITGWU regained 5s at harvest time. Increases were won in Co. Carlow, but in November the 'historic Lock-Out' at nearby Athy began when labourers refused to accept the 'inhuman proposals' of local farmers.

Despite the union's brave face and the courage of the south Kildare men, Athy was where the tide sharply turned. This was not known when the union wrote: 'In its duration, its important bearing on the wage-rates of farm labourers elsewhere' and the 'gritty manner' in which the men fought, 'this was, perhaps, the most remarkable agricultural fight in which the Union had engaged in recent times.' Athy was 'destined to extend far' into 1923.

The Government refused Labour demands for compulsory tillage orders. James Mallon (Edgeworthstown) insisted that labourers' voices be heard at the Congress.

The agricultural system had to be changed, 're-establishing the workers on the lands now enjoyed by the bullocks. (Hear, hear.)' Michael Duffy (Meath) opposed breaking up large holdings, as 'the moment men got possession of small holdings they became alienated' from unions. M. P. Linehan (Mallow) agreed, demanding that 'when the Government will not clear the ranches and demesnes we should see to it ourselves and have them worked by workers for the workers. Let us open co-operative stores in the towns and sell the produce.' Road workers 'experienced a bad time,' with only the counties with significant Labour representation keeping men fully employed. Shortage of funds was the cry, and yet, 'strange to say, most of them kept on their highly-paid Officials, though the surface-men were let go.' Organised wage reductions were in evidence, however, with non-Socialist and farmer Councillors content to go along.

In August 1922 the Meath Herds' Union transferred 'as a section on payment of 2/6 entrance fee and a half year's contributions for each member, and on payment of same they be admitted to full benefit.'[29]

HOTEL WORKERS

More than 500 hotel and club workers formed a Branch in May 1918. The Secretary, Thomas Gordon, urged members to purchase the *Voice of Labour,* and a Hotel Workers' Club operated at 29 Eden Quay, Dublin. Gordon wanted to 'abolish the blood-sucking employment agent,' who 'kept his unfortunate victim out of employment until that victim is compelled to beg for a job at whatever price the agent wishes to name.'

A strike in hotels, restaurants and cafés began in September. It was successful, pending an arbitration award, if only in exposing hotels' profits. The Hanna Award was accepted. Gordon made the claim for the 1,800 workers organised; 'not one worker does not benefit.' It was not all it might have been, but for the first time there were 'minimum wages for all grades from Chefs to Charwomen.' The employers' refusal to recognise minimum rates precipitated the strike. Within six months of the Branch's formation, all grades received an increase, ranging from $33^{1}/_{3}$ to 60%. Accommodation had to be found for those striking workers who normally lived in. The 'swagger hotels' sweated and defrauded workers by reneging on the Agreement.[30] The Hotels and Restaurants Branch became the flagship.

ANTI-CONSCRIPTION STRIKE, 1918

Rapid, unplanned expansion caused concern about policy and direction. *Irish Opinion* felt that Connolly's loss was 'irreparable', and 'we suffer to-day, as all Ireland suffers, from the absence of our clearest thinker, greatest mind and ablest Leader.' There was certainly a need for leadership.

On 20 April 1918 a Conference in the Mansion House declared: 'We Will Not Have Conscription.' English Labour would be treated 'with that indifference you have always exhibited towards Irish Labour, whose very existence you have ignored.' Reference was made to workers killed in Belfast, Llanelli, Tonypandy and Liverpool and to the Government, which included Labour men, that 'sent James Connolly to his death.' There was a final denunciation.

> Before the International we denounce you, traitors to our common class, false to your own people, accomplices in the oppression of the Irish race. Your ranks are not redeemed by one honest figure. No voice of sincerity and truth speaks from your midst.

The Conference—'the greatest and most important' Labour event ever held—sent out a 'clarion call'. 'In numbers, in spirit, in determination, in resolve and in decision, Labour in Ireland has done nothing in its history to equal this.' In 'many respects' it 'had no parallel outside Russia since the All-Russian Congress of Soviets.' The ITGWU mused: 'If only Saturday's had been a Congress of Soviets and not of Unions! But as it is, the Unions have done the next best thing.'

Foran lodged £1,000 'with a trusted person ... in case of any trouble arising out of the enforcing of Conscription.' He further advised that 'as many of the Committee who could, should attend at the Hall every night in order so they might be prepared for any emergency that might arise.

O'Brien praised the 'great success of our General Strike against Conscription,' thanking the 'hundreds of thousands of workers who, at the call of Labour, ceased their work' and 'shook these islands with their unique demonstration of opposition to compulsory military service. It was magnificent, and it was war.'

The *Irish Times* thought that 23 April would 'be chiefly remembered as the day on which Irish Labour realised its strength.' They were a 'subject but unconquered people.' But dangers were far from over, and O'Brien warned of greater repression yet to come.

In October the union felt obliged to state its policy regarding the granting of permission for meetings. It refused 'to apply for permits, and its Officials will not take part in permitted assemblies.' Perfectly legal union activities were badly affected by the restrictions of the Defence of the Realm Act (commonly called DORA). Expressing open contempt for the blatant class bias in its application, the union stated: 'If a burglar enters your house and steals your goods, you can have him arrested; but if a burglar comes around and steals the products of your labour— hush, here comes DORA!'[31]

The geographical organisation of the ITGWU made the Anti-Conscription Strike both possible and successful. Irrespective of the spontaneity of protests, except in the north-east, without the union's active Branch network and Committees some organisation would have been essential for the strike's success. That organisation was already in place. The strike's excitement and victory further boosted the dynamic of union expansion.

DOCKERS AND SEAMEN

ITGWU dockers suffered from the quiescence with which British port workers accepted wage reductions. In the last months of 1921 'OBU' dockers assented to a small reduction, 'after resisting every inch of the way.' At the AGM of the Cork Branch in January the Secretary, Alderman Tadhg Barry, referred to the Commission established by the late Lord Mayor, Tomás Mac Curtáin, which determined that a living wage should be £3 10s a week. Few members enjoyed this rate, and yet employers demanded cuts. On 16 February a claim for £3 10s was served on Cork Harbour Commissioners. They wrote holding letters to Laurence Prior, Secretary of the ITGWU. Matters dragged on while the union sorted out arrears in antici-pation of conflict. Bob Day assured the men in April that matters were progressing. Himself a member of the Harbour Commissioners, he raised it at every meeting. Barry was arrested after the AGM and interned in Ballykinler Internment Camp, Co. Down, where he was killed in November.

Black propaganda was started with rumours that members objected to the first week's increase being paid into union funds, the common practice at the time. On 5 June the anticipated rejection of the claim finally came, and matters moved quickly towards strike. On 12 August the Harbour Commissioners again refused the claim, and strike notice took effect on the 26th. It was 'marked as read' by recalcitrant Harbour Commissioners. Cork Traders' Council appealed for peace on 24 August, again suggesting arbitration. The men accepted Beamish, McDonnell and Father Cahalane, but the Harbour Commissioners rejected them. Notice expired on Friday 2 September. The Red Flag was hoisted over the harbour, irking local Republican authorities, who thought the 'tricolour had been dishonoured.' There were rumours that the IRA would execute the Branch Chairman, William Kinneally.

The strike began on 5 September, and men blockaded the port. On 6 September the Harbour Commissioners reported that 'it was the intention of the Transport Workers' Union to take over the work and business of the port.' Day assured them that if the £3 10s claim was conceded the men would return to work under the Commissioners' authority; however, 'the time for talking was gone.' If the Harbour Commissioners could 'not run this Port and pay . . . a living wage' the men would run it themselves.

The ever-antagonistic local newspapers described Day's comments as an 'Amazing Statement'. Day and Kinneally occupied the offices of the Secretary of the Harbour Commissioners, Sir James Long, in order to 'get the port working,' issuing permits. Thomas Coyle, General Steward, and Murphy, Delegate, went to Queenstown (Cóbh) with 'instructions from Commissioner Day' to assume full control of Cork Harbour.

In response to press attacks, Day's address to the men used irony as a weapon of rebuttal. 'Fellow Workers, Comrades, Fellow Bolshevists. (Laughter.)' There was no 'better title than Bolshevists, because that meant that the bottom dog would go up and the top dog would come down. (Cheers.)' The meeting concluded with 'The Red Flag'.

Settlement terms emerged on 14 September, with each man receiving 10 guineas (£10 10s) 'to cover all claims' from 14 February to 10 September and a further £1 per month for three months or until a Commission of Cork Corporation (City Council) deliberated on the basic claim. The Agreement was signed by Proinsias Ó Dálaigh, Chairman, Cork Harbour Commissioners, Robert Day, ITGWU, and W. B. McAuliffe, Dáil Éireann, Conference Chairman. The Branch wrote to the Secretary of Sinn Féin on Cork Corporation repudiating all Republican charges against Day and Kinneally and expressing full confidence in them.[32]

In 1922 dockers were the union's 'bridgehead', 'engaged in close, but emphatically unloving embrace with the Shipping Ring and its allies.' The union recognised that 'a serious defeat here would probably have been the prelude to an All-Ireland assault on wages.' The Carrigan Award of 15 January imposed longer hours on railwaymen, while dockers' wage cuts were briefly postponed. These were 'victories of sorts' but 'only little ones', which would be temporary.

Victories were won against a united front of employers and press, which mounted a 'campaign of lies, slanders, vituperation and misrepresentation.' Edward Hart of the NUDL ('Éamonn Mac Airt when the patriotic fervour is upon him') made separate arrangements, agreeing to cuts from 1 January. Intervention by the ITGWU managed to secure a postponement of all cuts, thus benefiting NUDL members who had shown no willingness for struggle (and provoking the wry comment 'And there are those revolutionists who still suffer from the delusion that the social revolution in Ireland will come from the Orange proletariat of Belfast!'). At least in the railways there was trade union unity.

By 14 January the ITGWU felt it was in a crisis of the 'first magnitude'. Bosses were 'professing their patriotism and their loyalty,' but they could prove their professions though averting the industrial upheaval by withdrawing their notices. The ITGWU rallied its members.

> Dockers, Railwaymen, Workers! Get ready to fall into line. Prepare to quit your jobs if need be . . . Steady, Boys, Step Together!

NUR dockers at the North Wall depot of the London and North-Western Railway transferred and struck for increases to bring them level with other Dublin dockers who were bitterly resisting cuts.

Relations between the ITGWU and the National Sailors' and Firemen's Union were fraught since the war. The jingoism and open pact of the General Secretary of the NSFU, J. Havelock Wilson, with the Shipping Federation was a far cry from Liberty Hall's gallantry of 1911 and the payment of Strike Pay to NSFU members in 1913. The NSFU was seen as the 'prey of the most unscrupulous and corrupt set of Trade Union Officials that the whole working-class movement has produced.' The decision to enrol seamen was 'responded to with alacrity,' and 'in a very short period most' Irish seamen transferred. In June 1921 Archie Heron called for a Marine Transport Workers' Union. In September a Delegation of the British Seafarers'

Union agreed that the ITGWU should 'immediately admit such seafarers as resided in Ireland . . . carry on propaganda with seafarers calling at Irish Ports in favour of closer unity among seafarers,' join a 'Conference of all parties interested at an early date in Liverpool' and 'act as agents in all Irish Ports for the B.S.U.' By October the Marine Section of the ITGWU had large numbers in Belfast and Dublin.

The BSU liaison came to naught after Mick McCarthy travelled to the National Transport Workers' Federation in London to meet their officers. He withdrew after being kept waiting, protesting about 'the manner in which our Delegates were treated.' John Lynch of the Sligo Branch, long a thorn in Liberty Hall's side, complicated matters by insisting that local seamen pay into the NSFU, holding up the discharge of ships in May 1922.[33]

OPEN LETTER TO BRITISH LABOUR AND PROPOSALS FOR A TRUCE

The ILP&TUC issued an open letter to British Labour on 8 January 1921. It argued that whatever future Ireland was to have was for Ireland's people, and Ireland's people only, to decide.[34] It put forward proposals for a truce, to include a 'complete armistice', approaches made to potential intermediaries, and an indication of how far the British would respect such a a truce. The Irish, under this proposal, would cease all armed attacks on British forces and barracks and stop all raids, arrests and other provocative acts. The British in turn would cease attacks on Irish Volunteers, Sinn Féin and Labour, no longer arrest but release members of Dáil Éireann and stop raids, searches, burnings and other provocative acts.

The British Labour Party accepted these terms. They were rejected, however, by the Prime Minister, and military repression intensified.[35]

PARTITION

While welcoming the prospect of peace, Thomas Foran, addressing the 1921 Congress of the ITUC&LP, set his face firmly against Partition. As a trade unionist he failed to comprehend the demand from workers, as wages and conditions in what was to become Northern Ireland stood very poor comparison with wages and conditions elsewhere in Ireland, something that went 'some way to explain the interest of the employing classes in doping and fooling the workers in these parts.' He concluded:

> They have never come into our movement as they ought to; they have never taken their share in the struggle for the emancipation and uplifting of the workers of this country, and perhaps they are blind to their interests in this connection . . . Perhaps if these people could realise that their enemy is neither in Rome nor in Dublin but in Belfast they would join with their fellows in Ireland come forward and work for the great ideal that Connolly preached, wrote about and died for. (Applause.)[36]

Cathal O'Shannon moved Congress's 'resolute opposition' to Partition, demanding one legislature for the country.[37] William McMullen qualified matters by outlining Protestant workers' opposition and asking how that resistance could be accommodated.

CONGRESS

The ITUC&LP held a Special Conference on 16 December 1916 to consider the food crisis but still 'waited on' the Irish Food Control Committee on 29 October 1917. Shortages, prices and profiteering concerned the movement greatly. It wanted an Irish Food Control body, independent of London, a census and control of production, better management on internal transport to avert local shortage or glut, municipal authorities to manage milk supply, wide advertisement of agreed maximum prices, local Food Committees representative of 'working class consumers' and, given an 'abnormal harvest of potatoes,' the immediate installation of machinery for drying and preserving potatoes or manufacturing potato flour. On the ground the ITGWU intervened directly in some places, freeing supply or pressuring merchants.[38]

At the 1917 Congress in Derry nine ITGWU Delegates were from Belfast, Cork (Connolly Memorial), Dublin and Sligo Branches. William O'Brien gave the Presidential Address, deploring the 'awful carnage' and seeing as the 'one bright spot' the 'organised working class of Russia.' He hoped events there would spread 'to the other belligerents' and thus end the war. The 'silver lining' for Ireland was that each country 'engaged in slaughter' professed that it was 'on behalf of the freedom of small nations,' and therefore Ireland's claim to nationhood would be readily accepted. Tellingly, he concluded that 'it is almost impossible to organise on a class-conscious basis until the question of the Government of Ireland, which has so long divided us into different political sections, is finally settled.' That said, O'Brien was not abandoning Labour's position. 'Sinn Féiners, Redmondites, Carsonites, Catholics and Protestants all join together with the one common object, and that is to grind down the organised workers—all of which points to the necessity of a strong, virile Labour organisation keeping itself independent and always ready to grapple with any tyranny no matter what flag it sails under. (Applause.)' He condemned Partition, arguing that no-one wanted it, even in Ulster. Ulster Delegates had voted against it at the 1914 Congress, even those who were opposed to Home Rule. He moved that Congress resist any attempt at Partition, 'temporary or permanent', as being 'destructive of the Unity and Solidarity of the movement.' Rather wishfully, he thought the motion superfluous, as 'Partition was a dead horse.'

O'Brien also moved the establishment of a Federation of Labour, urging Congress to develop an appropriate scheme, binding together Irish and British organisations. Rimmer (NUR) said they wanted 'less trade unions and more trades Unionists,' although pointing out some inherent dangers in the plan. Foran argued that before they could be 'good internationalists they must be good Nationalists'— the standard ITGWU line since its foundation. The federation would maximise Labour influence in the expected Irish parliament. Denis Houston thought federation would standardise wage rates and encourage the further rationalisation of local societies. The motion was carried.

After the Congress an Organising Committee investigated union organisation. Suggestions emerged for the development of local Trades Councils as organising units with autonomous Sections catering for, say, distributive trades, building, transport, engineering, general workers and domestic service—with, interestingly, no specific mention of agricultural labourers (although they were mentioned elsewhere in the report). Meetings were held in Cork, Limerick, Bruff, Sligo, Waterford and Wexford, 'with very good results,' but, to a considerable extent, the flood of members into the burgeoning ITGWU overtook Congress's plans, presented as Congress proposals being 'taken in hand' by Liberty Hall.[39]

William O'Brien's Presidential Address to the 1918 Congress in Waterford talked of the 'stripling' Irish Labour movement attaining manhood and taking its place 'by the side of its elder brothers' in the international rank. It was time it progressed further, to 'be the peer in power and influence of any Labour movement in any country' and central to the reconstruction that would follow the 'barbarism of this War.' Three factors accounted for Labour's growth: 'hard work, the untiring sacrifice and the unbroken perseverance and determination of the few, but heroic, men and women' who had fought against mighty odds to unite Irish workers; the international awakening of class consciousness to 'industrial serfdom' and 'subjection at the hands of powerful, unscrupulous and dehumanised' capitalists; and 'bold leadership'.

In this last category he picked out two men, citing the 'able and courageous propaganda of action, the unending toil, the revolutionary teaching, the high and splendid thinking, the great and noble vision, the magnificent example, the sacrifice and heroism in death as in life which have been contributed by James Connolly and Jim Larkin. (Prolonged cheers.)'[40] He eulogised Connolly at length, asserting that when he 'laid down his life for the Irish working class he laid it down for the working class in all countries,' in leading resistance to imperialism and capitalism, which had plunged Europe into war. His example had inspired the Russian Revolution, which was 'still battling for its existence against both internal and external foes.' The real aims of the war—complete exploitation by the capitalist class—were revealed by these assaults on Russia by a combination of forces that were locked in conflict just a short time before.

At a Special Congress on 1 November 1918, Thomas Foran, President of the ITGWU, rose to move the expulsion of NSFU Delegates, on the grounds that they supported capitalist attempts to prevent workers meeting at the International. P. Coates (ITGWU) seconded, as 'Havelock Wilson's gang' were preventing the International Conference taking place and receiving 'cheques galore from stockbrokers and manufacturers who wanted the war to continue on account of the money they were making out of it.' J. H. Bennett (NSFU) admitted the charges but explained that it was as much to do with anti-German sentiment and their war crimes, on land and sea, as any other matter. William O'Brien insisted that the NSFU were 'scabs in the movement.' The motion was carried, 99 to 10. As Bennett and his Delegation left the hall he defiantly cried, 'We will continue to stop carrying them!'[41]

Thomas Foran presided over the 1921 Congress in Dublin. The last time it had assembled in Dublin, in 1914, Larkin had presided, and Foran reflected that 'he is now suffering for his labours on behalf of the workers of the world as a prisoner in the land of the free—America. (Laughter.)' Affiliated membership had risen from 110,000 to 300,000.[42]

DUBLIN TRADES COUNCIL

Following the establishment of a 'Dublin Workers' Council' as a rival to Dublin Trades Council, Congress would not at first formally intervene in the matter, though it took the view that 'there cannot be two Councils for the same city.'[43] After the Dublin Workers' Council showed that it represented the majority of Dublin workers, however, it accepted its affiliation and urged those still outside its ranks to join it. J. J. Farrelly complained that this was 'sending the old Council . . . into oblivion.' The proposal was carried, 165 to 12.[44]

RAILWAYMEN

The North Wall Branch of the National Union of Railwaymen proposed a motion at the 1922 ITUC&LP Congress protesting against the ITGWU preventing locked-out NUR members from gaining employment. It was 'highly provocative and calculated to provoke dissension and disunion and personal recrimination,' and the motion condemned the 'spirit of compulsion and coercion.' The matter involved the employment of a man called Noone in the railway agents Wordie's and one Murphy in Goulding's Manures. Both were dismissed, as the ITGWU insisted that their idle members be given preference. Ward (NUR) instanced members in arrears being accepted into the ITGWU. Foran was eventually moved to respond. NUR members at the LNWR North Wall depot worked at rates much lower than the accepted standard in Dublin Port. Men sought to join the ITGWU and struck for the port rate. The NUR stood with the employers. If the LNWR men were still in the NUR they would be earning '45s per week for a week of 48 hours, night or day, no overtime.' After a six months' strike they now earned 84s for a week of Forty-Five hours, with overtime for any hours before 8 a.m. and after 5 p.m. The General Secretary of the NUR, Cramp, suggested that as the LNWR was a British company it should be subject to British conditions. The NUR motion was withdrawn. The case came before a Congress sub-Committee in March 1923, which upheld the ITGWU's actions.[45]

UNEMPLOYMENT

At Easter 1921 the ITUC&LP issued a lengthy manifesto on 'Unemployment and the National Crisis'. It cited the Democratic Programme adopted by Dáil Éireann on 21 January 1919 in relation to the ownership of Ireland's wealth and made proposals for defending living standards, the development of indigenous natural resources, non-payment of annuities, and market controls 'for the duration of the war' to maintain supplies at appropriate prices. It also sought the repatriation and investment of Irish finance, compulsory tillage and workers' control as part of the continuing task of building a nation of free men. The manifesto, signed by Thomas Foran and Thomas Johnson as Chairman and Secretary, respectively, of the ITUC&LP, concluded:

> For our part, we insist that while Ireland's industries must be encouraged, protected and developed, the purpose of it all must be kept clearly in mind, dominating all our thoughts on the subject, inspiring all our activities, that purpose being to build a nation which shall be the master, not the slave, of its material wealth—a nation of free and fearless, healthy, happy and noble men and women.[46]

It was a policy statement at one with ITGWU aspirations.

JIM LARKIN

Emmet O'Reilly of the Larkin Defence Committee, New York, sent Larkin's view of the Treaty for publication in the *Voice of Labour,* although, 'while agreeing heartily with the anti-Imperial and anti-Monarchical position,' both paper and union 'dissociate themselves from much that is in the document,' particularly 'the personal charges of cowardice, treachery and aggrandisement.' Larkin, writing from Comstock Gaol, New York, opposed the Treaty, still standing for the Workers' Republic.

Attitudes to Larkin and his possible release and return to Ireland were developing. The *Voice of Labour,* in March, reprinted Connolly's views on 'Hero Worship' from the *Workers' Republic,* 7 October 1899. This may have been timely, although the canonisation of Connolly himself might well have been the object.

> The belief that great political principles can never move the masses unless such principles are symbolised in the personality of a great Leader is, in our opinion, one of the great flaws in the teaching to which the Irish people have been accustomed by our middle-class agitators. One result of this theory has been the total suspension of all intelligent discussion and free expression of opinion . . . and the substitution of cut and dried resolutions by carefully-selected speakers, whose word it was rank heresy to question, for thoughtful consideration by all interested, and the growth of a hero-worship which always ended by over-shadowing alike the party and the principle.[47]

THE *VOICE OF LABOUR*

The *Watchword of Labour* was suppressed following raids on Liberty Hall in November 1920. No ITGWU journal was published until 22 October 1921, when it took over *Irish Opinion* as the *Voice of Labour.* Members were reminded that the ITGWU was not a 'mere wage-raising machine'. As an agitational paper the *Voice of Labour* would inculcate in them Socialist ideas. At the 1921 Congress there were calls for a weekly Labour paper, but the ITGWU Delegates remained silent.[48]

On 14 February 1921 O'Brien, writing to Foran in London, said that 'the only startling information' was that 'Delia is married to a young Citizen Army member named Colgan. I take it he has your sincere sympathy. I daresay he needs it.'[49]

LIBERTY HALL
After the Rising an immediate problem was regaining access to Liberty Hall. A 'policy was adopted of levying the first week's payment of any increase off each Dublin member,' the proceeds being applied to rebuilding the Hall. Congress took up the ITGWU case and wrote to the Secretary of the British Labour Party, Arthur Henderson, on 20 February 1917, pointing out that once the Citizen Army had left the Hall 'not one shot was fired from it.' The military, however, not content with bombarding it, ransacked it, and much property 'was taken away by souvenir hunters,' including a cottage piano and a baby grand.

A second letter, on 10 March, pointed out that 5,000 ITGWU members had enlisted and more than 2,000 were killed. These men would think ill of a Government that would 'compensate capitalists but not workers' organisations.' Henderson's reply of 12 March 'frankly' saw 'no possibility of obtaining any Government assistance.' The matter was taken up with the Lord Lieutenant of Ireland, with no success.

By December the restoration of Liberty Hall was complete and the building reoccupied. The mortgage was 'entirely cleared' and the 'extensive premises partly rebuilt, renovated and suitably equipped.' The only financial liability carried into 1919 was a 'debt for legal expenses incurred during the great Lock-out of 1913.'

Late in 1921 the ITGWU premises at Camden Quay in Cork were burned to the ground by the Black and Tans. The union purchased the Soldiers' Home adjacent to St Patrick's Church and, probably with a sense of ironic satisfaction, held the first meeting in the new Connolly Hall on 18 May 1922. Michael Hill, NEC, presided over thirty-eight Delegates. An insurance agent, Hill used the occasion to call for independent working-class education 'as the first essential step towards industrial democracy.'[50]

RUSSIA
Cathal O'Shannon moved an Emergency Motion at the 1921 ITUC&LP Congress calling for support to alleviate the effect of famine in Russia. He blamed the international blockade and the attempted invasions by western powers. William O'Brien suggested that a food ship be sent, and the motion was adopted unanimously.[51] An appeal was made to all unions on 9 March 1922, to which £258 was subscribed.[52]

POLITICS
In 1918 Congress lobbied the Government over the Representation of the People Act, entering lengthy correspondence with the British Labour Party to seek support for complete adult suffrage with full proportional representation, the redistribution

of seats and the publication of electoral registers. They were not successful on all counts. William O'Brien, at the 1917 Congress, saw electoral reform as crucial to working-class interests within the anticipated Irish Parliament.

In June the ITUC&LP established an Organisation and Labour Representation Fund to provide resources in areas where the movement, industrially and politically, was weak. Labour was emerging politically in America, Australia, Canada, China, Japan and South Africa, and it suggested 3d per month from each subscribing member, stamps being acknowledged on OLRF cards.

A manifesto 'To the Workingmen and Women of Ireland', November 1916, was debated at the 1917 Congress. It urged all workers to join Labour and build the new nation. Foran, O'Brien and Farren were signatories. A 'heated discussion' took place on the motion to send Delegates to the Socialist Conference in Stockholm. Northern Delegates particularly opposed, on the grounds that 'to avert war in the future the German military machine should be smashed' and supporting the annexations and indemnities. Foran asked, 'Were they going to destroy the German war machine and keep the British one intact?' When the motion was finally carried, 68 to 24, it was 'received with loud and prolonged applause,' the 'most enthusiastic that was witnessed during the Congress.' J. H. Bennett (NSFU) commented: 'I am glad there are twenty-four Britishers in the room anyway.'[53]

A Special Congress on 1 November 1918 declared that should Sinn Féin become the 'dominant power they would have to fight them as they had to fight the rotten and corrupt party in 1914. They would be another political mouthpiece of the capitalist class.' Labour should fight its political battles alone.

Civil war, ironically, mitigated the worst excesses of wage cuts. Labour and the ITGWU 'deplored and strenuously attempted' to 'avert the fratricidal strife.' A Congress motion in 1922 called for peace by Sunday 26 August or all Labour TDs would resign. Some saw little purpose in any resignations, but the motion was passed unanimously.

Congress was the biggest organisation in the country, geographically and numerically, yet had stood aside politically. Its non-contesting of the 1918 General Election was perceived as having allowed Republicans a clear run and paved the way for partial independence. The split within republicanism over the Treaty terms of 1921 strengthened Labour's hand, but at a Special Congress in February 1922 it became clear that the party had no real position. Thomas Johnson did not even see the Treaty as necessarily a central issue. He proposed that Labour participate but was opposed by two ITGWU speakers.

The union Delegation, like the country, was divided. They argued for abstention, as Labour had no position. Thomas Kennedy said that it was 'all right talking about the Workers' Republic, but when they went before the working-class electors, the question they would have to decide was whether you are for peace or war, and put up with the consequences.' Under proportional representation Johnson argued that voters could vote Labour and then transfer to whichever side of the Treaty question they wished. It hardly answered Kennedy's question but carried the day, 109 to 49. O'Brien was among those voting yes. He feared that Labour would be sidelined if it did not participate.

In a manifesto issued by the ITUC&LP five days after Dáil Éireann accepted the Treaty by seven votes it was felt that the matter was settled. Energy could be devoted to the pursuit of economic and social issues. But matters had not reached that far, and Labour was more involved in trying to prevent civil war and end militarism than focusing minds on the horrendous unemployment crisis. On 24 April a one-day strike against all forms of militarism and a drift to civil war brought 75,000 workers onto the streets. On 30 April de Valera, Brugha, Collins and Griffith sat down with Labour mediators, but matters descended into personalised arguments.

The ITGWU attempted to create a Workers' Army by bringing the Irish Citizen Army under Labour control. It was unsuccessful, and the Citizen Army, now totally separate from the ITGWU, participated on the anti-Treaty side in the Civil War. The commander of the Citizen Army, John Hanratty, told Johnson that workers were not going to be fooled 'politically or industrially' by him and his 'renegade colleagues.'

In 1922 the Labour Party obtained 17 TDs from its 18 candidates, thirteen being ITGWU members. They outpolled de Valera's anti-Treaty Sinn Féin, which won 35 seats, 16 uncontested. Pro-Treaty Sinn Féin obtained 58 seats. The union boasted: 'Our members everywhere took a leading part in the electoral battle, and helped materially in the victory.' They had demonstrated 'their determination to be predominant on the political as well as the industrial field.'

Honouring its pre-election pledge, the Labour Party accepted Free State struc-tures and participated in Dáil Éireann. Johnson claimed they would use 'whatever political instruments' were at hand to pursue their main objective, the 'Workers' Republic.' Less than a fortnight after the election, civil war broke out on 16 June when Free State forces attacked the Four Courts. The Dáil was suspended. The Executive Committee of Congress and the Labour TDs invited all Deputies to meet on 30 July to consider how peace could be achieved. Only Labour TDs turned up. It was a second setback after Labour had brokered talks on 1 July with the help of Archbishop Byrne and the Lord Mayor of Dublin, O'Neill. At the Congress the Executive reported having 'practically exhausted all the avenues' in an attempt to prevent or stop war. The Delegates instructed all TDs to resign if the Dáil was not convened by 26 August, simultaneously condemning the 'Republican Party' for their 'irrational' stance and 'their method of warfare.' The sudden death of Arthur Griffith on 12 August and the killing of Michael Collins on 22 August provided an incentive for W. T. Cosgrave, the new head of the Free State Government, to progress matters, with promises that the Dáil would convene on 9 September.

On 2 September Johnson and O'Brien had a meeting with Cosgrave and the Free State Chief of Staff, Richard Mulcahy, at which Republican forces were offered a ceasefire that would enable them to retain their weaponry. This was rejected, after which military victory was to be the only solution.

Labour's participation in the Dáil was seen by Republicans as the 'ultimate betrayal'. Some argue that it still has echoes in a reluctance among workers to vote Labour. But what else could it have done? O'Brien in particular wanted to end the waste and suffering and to attempt to rebuild a shattered society and country. Cumann na nGaedheal welcomed Labour's active participation as legitimising the whole process, but generosity was not in its nature or that of the class forces that drove it.

For Larkin, witnessing events from his prison cell in America, it was a betrayal of the Workers' Republic. Worse, most vestiges of the Democratic Programme vanished into the ether. The Minister for Justice, Kevin O'Higgins, dismissed the document as 'poetry'. Labour's influence was minimal. The one thing the Labour Party could claim was that it moderated the Free State's actions in the war and probably saved many prisoners from the firing squad, even though military Courts and the infamous Public Safety (Emergency Powers) Act (1923) were pushed through.

In August 1923 the Labour Party fielded 41 candidates, of whom only 14 were elected, losing in all its urban constituencies. It fell from being the second-largest Party to the fourth, having fallen between two stools. Cumann na nGaedheal was the Party of the centre and stability and de Valera the focus of opposition. Labour politicians, especially Johnson and O'Brien, received great credit from mainstream historians for their contribution to facilitating the foundation of democratic politics in the Free State, but for workers the price paid was high and long-lasting.[54]

Chapter 9 ～

1923: THE WORST YEAR IN UNION HISTORY?

MEMBERSHIP, ORGANISATION AND FINANCE

Faced with agricultural and industrial depression, unemployment and a 'general onslaught by employers' and the Free State authorities, the ITGWU suffered badly. The Executive Council blandly reported that 'in most respects' 1923 would 'bear comparison with any year since its establishment.' Though not realised at the time, however, it was a decisive, downward turning-point, not to be reversed for a decade.

Branch income fell by 12%, to £80,268. Expenditure exceeded income by £76,305, the first loss since 1916. The explanation lay in the staggering amount of Dispute Pay. Miraculously, a credit balance of £58,462 was maintained. At the Congress the Irish Mental Hospital Workers' Union complained that members had been poached in Grangegorman and Portrane Asylums. M. J. O'Connor, previously ITGWU Organiser in Limerick-Kerry and General Secretary of the Irish Automobile Drivers' and Mechanics' Union during the Motor Permits Strike of 1919–1920, was now General Secretary of the IMHWU. In 1921 members of the IMHWU in Cork transferred *en bloc,* and no objection was made. Now O'Connor argued that only a minority transferred, although they included the National Treasurer of the union. Transfers were approved, subject to arrears being cleared.[1]

WAGES AND DISPUTES

Dispute Pay of £128,724 represented 153% of income. From 1919 to 1923 more than £260,000 was expended on disputes, a remarkable average of £1,000 a week continuously for five years. It was an 'indication of the fight put up by our members.' That the ITGWU survived without levying members spoke 'eloquently for its strength and power of resistance.' The EC considered imposing a levy on all members in September, 'owing to the heavy drain' on funds. It was rejected by Dublin No. 1 Branch and a voluntary levy suggested instead.

In January at least half the members were 'still on their peak rates,' but by December 'scarcely a Section' escaped a 'more or less severe reduction.' The ITGWU saw things in stark terms:

In no year since 1913 was the Union so severely engaged; nor did the Union ever fight with so much grit and determination as in 1923. The blows struck at the Union were tremendous; the employers of the whole country federated; the Government lent them every assistance.

In some weeks £6,000 more than income received was expended. Internal troubles provided opportunity and encouragement for an inevitable attack that had been hanging fire. Encouraged by defeats for dockers and seamen, heavy demands were enforced on Dublin carters and chemical workers and in all Cork employments. The three-month docks stoppage closed down bacon factories in Limerick, Cork, Tralee and Waterford, and employers coldly enforced cuts of £1 a week. Lunham's Bacon Factory in Dundalk, like those in Munster, closed because of bad trade and lost export markets.

Cork, Dublin and Wicklow chemical workers endured a five-month Lock-Out from the first week in August. A reduction of 6s per week, half the original demand, was first agreed in Dublin, with stabilisation until June 1924. A minor victimisation case blew up after the occupation of Liberty Hall by Larkinites when the Druggists' Association locked out all Dublin employees. The presentation of their 'tainted goods' at Grand Canal stores completely shut the canal system. Earlier a six-week stoppage halted all Irish flour mills, their plight exacerbated by foreign dumping. Given that wages were more than £1 above British rates, the ITGWU advised the acceptance of reductions of 12s. The men believed they could retain more and opted to strike. Cork and Limerick men 'put a tax on foreign flour,' and Dublin rationed bakeries from day to day.

Such workers' control, while gallant, had to be mindful of public opinion and working-class need. Imports 'could not be stopped altogether, or all Irish workers would have been left immediately without bread.' The Government and the middle class 'protested against our regulations, but they could do nothing, as the alternative was a complete stoppage of flour.' Despite such power, the final outcome was a spreading out of reductions over a longer period. Following settlement, a Joint Council was established.

Town movements generally held wages, but a Lock-Out in Cork 'involving dockers, chemical workers, bacon curers, grist mills, shops and stores, hotels and undertakers' forced a retreat. Tralee resisted reductions from April to December, while there were 'minor engagements' in Ballymahon, Clonmel, Cóbh, Dundalk, Eniscorthy, Mallow and Newry. A two-week Lock-Out to enforce substantial reductions took place in Dublin theatres and cinemas, ending in a favourable settlement. Serious disputes occurred in Longford and Waterford gas works. All this paled in comparison with seamen's, dockers' and farm labourers' strikes.

In reviewing the year the EC optimistically thought it had seen 'the rock-bottom of wages depression.' It proved a forlorn hope. It thought that 'the violent campaign of 1923 tore itself out with noise and fury' and would be followed by calm. The only silver lining was that 'shorter hours won in the war period are retained intact.'

At the ITUC Congress, Frank McGrath (Belfast) said that a 'big industrial war' had begun. He was right. He assured Delegates that there was no split in the ITGWU, although 'there may be a difference of opinion between some of their members.' Those who demonstrated outside the Mansion House, venue of the Congress, played into the hands of those attacking Labour.

Seán Byrne (Swords) said that the main battle on Dublin's quays was on working hours, not wages. If dockers were forced to go back to a ten-hour day, builders and others would follow. Unions were 'not revolutionary enough.' Bosses took advantage of any difference. He condemned those fomenting trouble.[2]

LARKIN'S RETURN

James Larkin left Ireland in October 1914, with the ITGWU 'broken and bankrupt,' to raise much-needed funds in America. He remained unchallenged as General Secretary during his absence, although Annual Reports, published from 1918, rarely mentioned him. Larkin's 'wages in full were paid to his wife' throughout his absence, but the ITGWU claimed that only £100 was received from him, against £2,000 paid to her. Larkin was £11 10s in arrears on his return but cleared his card in two lump sums in May. 'Very few communications' were received, and during his 8½-year absence the ITGWU had expanded from eastern seaboard waterfronts to become a National Organisation representing virtually every industry.

Larkin was released from imprisonment in January 1923. The EC cabled congratulations and asked when it could expect him back. No reply came for six weeks; then, on 24 March, an unsigned telegram was received by Foran requesting £5,000 to purchase a 'food ship'. The EC replied asking for confirmation that the telegram was Larkin's and seeking greater detail. Larkin cabled back to Foran, addressing him as 'Acting Secretary', demanding that the money be sent and accusing the General President and others of withholding funds from him in 1913 without his knowledge. He did not indicate when he would return. The EC turned down the application for £5,000 and again asked when he would return. At the Delegate Conference on 24–25 April 1923 these telegrams were read out and the EC's actions endorsed.

Larkin was deported from the United States on 30 April 1923. An EC meeting was arranged for 4 May to greet him. He 'complained bitterly' of the refusal of the money, queried the EC's status, announced that he was proceeding on a mission to Russia and 'tendered his resignation as General Secretary. He was urged to reconsider, to postpone his trip and instead to tour the Branches, where there was excited anticipation. 'At Larkin's request' it was agreed that no public mention of differences be made.

An Adjourned Delegate Conference on 14 May heard Larkin 'make a long statement as to his alleged national and revolutionary activities' in America before he indicated, 'with the exception of one or two,' that he accepted the new Rules. When it was pointed out that they had to be accepted or rejected as a whole his only objection remained that the Political Secretary not be an EC member. He appeared satisfied.

A tour of Branches followed but was terminated by Larkin before its con-clusion. Among the excited crowds he addressed was one in Cork, where he spoke from a second-floor window in Connolly Hall. At a meeting of Dublin No. 1 Branch held in the La Scala Theatre in Prince's Street on Sunday 3 June, Larkin 'opened his campaign of disruption,' challenging the legality of the EC and 'vilifying and slandering' Foran, O'Brien and others. At an EC meeting on 5 June he insisted that the new Rules were invalid.

At a meeting of Dublin No. 3 Branch on Sunday 10 June in the Olympia Theatre and later that day at 'an illegally summoned meeting of Dublin No. 1 Branch called by himself' Larkin repeated his charges and accusations. The ITGWU said that 'con-tinuously since then, at public meetings and in the columns of his own weekly paper [the *Irish Worker*]' he conducted his campaign.

On 11 June, Larkin and supporters occupied Liberty Hall, preventing members of the EC from entering and discommoding business. The EC suspended him from office. Repossession was achieved on 21 June, 'but only when legal proceedings compelled their surrender.' The EC was encouraged by the 'support of the Branches throughout the country.'

At the Congress in August the ITGWU Delegates 'met on their own initiative' in an endeavour to halt legal proceedings begun by the EC and Larkin and to 'have the dispute settled within the Union.' They were given 'every facility' by the EC to call a Delegate Conference. This rank-and-file Conference met on 31 August and elected an Investigation Committee. Members of the EC, who were not present, attended at the Conference's request to state their position. Larkin declined the same oppor-tunity, although he addressed some Delegates in the Mansion House. The EC pledged in writing to the Investigation Committee that they would abide by the decisions of the Delegate Conference, provided that Larkin similarly agreed. He declined, and the EC felt it had no alternative but to resort to the Courts.

Matters dragged along unsatisfactorily for the remainder of 1923. The process eventually concluded in February 1924 in favour of the EC, and by unanimous vote 'James Larkin was expelled from membership of the Union on 14 March, 1924.' The EC offered what it thought was a conclusion to the matter in the Annual Report when it declared that

> these proceedings have involved the Union in serious trouble and heavy expense which a sense of more loyalty to the working-class on the part of a would-be dictator would have prevented. Yet in the long run this trouble and expense may have been well worthwhile. The members must now realise that in one form or another they must buy their experience at a dear price.[3]

That 'dear price' was to rise even higher.

New Rules

The 1918 Rules were 'revised and recast,' a process begun through notification to Branches in December 1921. A Special Delegate Conference on 24–25 April 1923 gave

approval, 97 Branches to 7 favouring their adoption. The Rules were 'duly registered on 2 June.' Larkin questioned their validity at the meeting of the EC on 5 June,
'alleging that they were not passed by the Branches' and 'registered without proper
authority.' The EC suggested, in order to assuage Larkin, that their application be
suspended pending a ballot of the members. Larkin rejected this proposal and also
a proposal that a Delegate Conference consider his objections. The legitimacy of the
Rules was central to Larkin's case.

After legal actions, the Courts upheld the validity of the Rules. They were confirmed in February 1924. The National Executive Council argued that 'one of the
most important and salutary changes within the Rules was that "an Annual
Conference of Delegates, representing the members, shall exercise authority in the
Union, electing the National Executive Officers"' to control the financial, industrial
and general working of the union. 'This is an absolute innovation in the organisation,
long desired, and will, we believe, permit a great advance in democratic management.'[4] It was difficult to argue against such standard union governance.

DISSENSION

The 'grave internal crisis' occurred when tens of thousands of members were
engaged in protracted strikes that 'threatened the very existence of the Union.' For
those who, like Foran, saw the ITGWU struggle for its life after 1913 and 1916 it was
a terrible blow.

By January 1924 a 'firm stand made against the wrecker' saw the ITGWU apparently safe but with 'somewhat diminished power and prestige.' At a Special Meeting
of No. 1 Branch on Tuesday 6 February, Foran stated how he saw the union,
'compared with the position after the 1916 Rising.' Members and Officials had 'good
reason to congratulate themselves on the progress they had made within the past
year.' But 'he was sorry to have to say that some members instead of assisting in the
good work had allied themselves with a few would-be wreckers.' He 'felt that kind
of business more than anyone could understand it did more to tire him of his position than all the hard work he ever had to contend with in helping to build up the
Union to its present sound position, both financially and numerically.' His was a
constant, stalwart presence. The strain on him was enormous.

Within the Building Section a 'certain number' started 'a union of their own
again.' Foran intended to 'crush this so-called union out of existence at the very
beginning.' This was a reference not to Larkin but to the re-emerging United
Builders' Labourers. In contrast, Rosie Hackett's Women's Section and the Stationary
Engine Drivers' Section seemed stable. In March alleged scabbing by members of
No. 1 Branch at Michael Murphy Ltd caused a row. Work was 'tabooed' because of
a continuing dispute with Dublin Dockyard. At a Special Meeting Foran, in fighting language, declared that 'no employer had money enough to bribe members' to
'deliberately scab,' as was 'done on the occasion in question.' Members were too
'proud of the prestige and good name of the Union' to 'in any way lower the prestige or besmirch' its good name. Those concerned were suspended for one month.

On Thursday 10 May, Larkin made his first reappearance at a meeting of No. 1 Branch. The Vice-President, Thomas Butler, 'extended a hearty welcome to the General Secretary,' who thanked them for 'their expression of welcome.' On 31 May, W. Stone and P. Osbourne moved that 'new Draft Rules as submitted to the members be ratified and recommended for adoption.' W. Mitchell 'did not think the Committee had any power to receive these Rules and he for one would oppose.' They were carried with 'one dissentient.' The Branch Secretary, John O'Neill, said he had been 'called upon to go see the General Secretary.' They talked of 'many things that had taken place during his absence.' Larkin wanted a General Meeting the following Sunday in the Mansion House. It was agreed that posters and leaflets could not be got out in time, and the meeting was arranged for Sunday 17 June at 12:30.

Disruption was such that at a Special Meeting on 26 June complaints were made that normal Branch business was nigh impossible. On Sunday 19 August a circular was issued by Séamus Byrne, Secretary of the Select Committee of Five appointed by the unofficial Delegate Conference that met at 35 Parnell Square after the ITUC Congress. Branch Secretaries were asked to summon General Meetings to appoint Delegates for the 'All Ireland Conference of the Union', to be held at 35 Parnell Square on Friday 31 August 'to consider the present internal dispute' and 'try to find some solution.' To a question from A. Doyle (Harness Makers) why the Special General Meeting did not take place on Sunday 5 August the Chairman, Thomas Butler, explained that the EC had 'intervened and cancelled the order as they did not consider the meeting would be in the interests of the members in any way.'

Foran said that funds had fallen from £120,000 to £91,000. Dispute Pay ran at 'about £6,000 per week,' and 'unless some change took place within the next two months or so the funds of the Union would be almost depleted.' He appealed to 'members present to put their heads together and endeavour to carry on the business of the Union the same as heretofore.'

A Special General Meeting of Dublin No. 1 Branch was held on Sunday 26 August to select Delegates for the All-Ireland Delegate Conference the following Friday. As the Secretary, John O'Neill, rose to speak, P. Murray intervened and moved a vote of no confidence in the Chairman, Thomas Butler. After 'some commotion and disorder' P. Doran took the chair and the house was divided: all in favour moved to the right, all against to the left. The motion was carried, and P. Grogan was elected to chair the proceedings.

Larkin arrived and said that 'parts of the circular contained statements that was not correct.' He was allowed to speak, although the minutes record that he 'dealt with matters mostly which had no bearing on or in no way had anything to do with the object for which the meeting was called.' Having 'detained the members for about an hour,' he withdrew. On Thursday 30 August, No. 1 Branch met and unanimously instructed the Secretary to 'send a written statement' to the All-Ireland Conference to be held in the morning 'explaining the reasons why No. 1 Branch are not represented.'

When the Secretary of the Select Investigation Committee wrote calling for Delegates for the next All-Ireland meeting in December, No. 1 Branch Committee decided—once bitten twice shy—that 'they did not think it would be advisable to call a further meeting of the Branch for the purpose specified on account of what took place when the previous ballot was being held.'[5] Intimidation and disorder accompanied the attempt.

DOCKERS' AND SEAMEN'S STRIKE

In April, newly recruited seamen in Belfast, Cork, Dublin, Dundalk, Newry, Limerick and Waterford struck against a reduction of 6s 6d 'arranged by the Maritime Board (London).' British sailors accepted the reduction with murmurs of protest but no stoppage. With cuts enforced throughout the British mercantile marine and a 'large proportion' of Irish sailors inexplicably loyal to the National Sailors' and Firemen's Union, 'the position of our seamen members was untenable.' After a Conferences with the Ministry of Industry and Commerce, and to avoid involving dockers, the reduction was accepted after a week's stoppage, on condition that a Committee be set up, made up of equal numbers of Irish shippers and ITGWU marine members, to decide whether the British reductions should apply to Ireland. The Chairman, however, decided he could only rule on notice of cuts, and the 6s 6d was lost.

Registered dock labour employers then sought a cut of 1s a day. Notwithstanding other significant disputes and internal conflict, a 'strong front was displayed' to employers, who were forced to postpone the cut for two or three months. The ITGWU showed that it would not compromise, but at this point matters unravelled. 'Unfortunately, a Section of the Dublin seamen were used in precipitating a national Lock-Out' of dockers. Towards the end of June the crew of a B&I Line vessel 'unofficially gave twenty-four hours' notice on account of alleged discrimination in the selection of ratings for another vessel. The EC was not informed. After a number of Conferences with the Shipping Federation, when many vessels were tied up, a breakthrough appeared likely when 'one of the seamen participating introduced a document' stating the only terms upon which men would settle, namely the restoration of 6s 6d. Larkin's hand was clearly seen by Liberty Hall. The 'document was not framed' by seamen but by 'parties behind the scenes who knew that its terms would never be accepted' by the employers. Seamen's representatives had not disclosed their intention to cast this bombshell either to their Officials or to the dockers' representatives negotiating with them. As they would not withdraw it, negotiations broke down.

Thus the 'object desired by the sinister advisers of the seamen was achieved.' An offer of a reduction of 1s a day and an inquiry was put to ballot and rejected, whereupon the EC ceased to pay Strike Pay.

On 12 July, Michael McCarthy (NEC) announced that, 'owing to the action of their representatives,' the EC 'had decided not to support the sailors and firemen.' It would, however, support dockers' resistance to proposed reductions and worsening of conditions 'to the last shilling in the funds.' Larkin accused the ITGWU leadership of openly supporting the men but covertly 'intriguing to compel' them 'to accept reductions.'

On 16 July, in reprisal, Barry (Dublin Employers' Federation) locked out all cross-channel men and Cork employers sought 25% reductions. Limerick, Sligo, Waterford and Wexford were also affected. On 28 July a Conference arranged with Officials of the Ministry of Industry and Commerce suggested that the Lock-Out be withdrawn, cuts suspended until 2 January 1926 and an inquiry established. The employers rejected this and on 4 August refused to meet the Government or the men.

Matters were compounded when coal porters came out against a cut of 1s a day. After a three-month stoppage the Government set up a Court of Inquiry, although 1s a day was conceded forthwith. A large majority accepted these terms through ballot.

A dockers' deputation demanded a General Meeting in the Mansion House. No. 1 Branch Committee said 'they would like to hear what the meeting was intended for' and asked 'if there was any genuine grounds' for it. The minutes record that 'discussion became very heated as it developed and a regular cross fire of words ensued'; yet the outcome was unanimous. At the meeting in the Mansion House on Sunday 14 October ostensibly called to elect Delegates to the All-Ireland Delegate Conference to enquire into the internal troubles the EC recommended the reduction proposed by the President of the Executive Council (Head of Government), W. T. Cosgrave. Larkin, betraying his now considerable antipathy to the leadership, observed: 'We tried to move a motion that the ballot be postponed for a week.' Foran refused 'our motion on the grounds [that] we were not a Docker. This creature whom we made sensible of the benefits of unionism.' The motion was moved but attracted only one vote. The *Irish Worker* reported to counter the 'mischievous lying report of the proceedings' supplied by Foran to the *Independent*. The ballot was not proceeded with and the cut not imposed.

More than 8,000 men and ninety women were on strike for 'Death or Liberty', but docks, ships, factories and shops were still working. Under the heading 'Free State Strike-Breakers' Larkin complained that 'every force of the Government is used to assist' employers to 'force conditions on a body of men who gave unlimited and unpaid service to the revolutionary movement that resulted in placing the same Government Officials in places of power and high emolument.' When 'Black and Tans were masquerading as a Government force in this area, no men dared as much as the dockers, carters, sailors and firemen . . . Much of the ammunition and machinery of warfare was conveyed and handled by these workers in defiance of the then hired assassins.' In contrast, Barry and the Shipping Federation were 'assisting to the limit of their power' the British side. The dockers' reward was to have police and army 'ordered out to overawe, and if necessary by force of gun and bayonet, protect the hired gunmen to ship cattle.' The NSFU was slated for its betrayal; so too were the ITGWU's 'loyal (?) honest (?) intelligent red flag leaders,' who had 'at the psychological moment, as they thought, heard their master's voice and declared the dispute settled.' Emphasising his criticism of the Government's class nature, Larkin concluded that workers could now understand the meaning of the word Freedom—and its connotations. It means, brother, Freedom for the Barrys, Hewats, etc., to force you to work at the wages they fix and under the conditions they lay down—and if you don't agree to accept them, Mr. Barry's-Hewat's Government will bring in the hired patriots to compel you to submit, and these two forces, plus the gaol and the bayonet, not sufficing, Mr. Barry has still the same honest Union Leaders to fall back on.

Evidence of the ITGWU's abandonment of principle was complete.

We are glad this manifestation of open, naked, unashamed treachery of Union leaders (moryah!) has been made plain to all workers affected. Every Union man or woman who associates with these gentlemen of the Transport Executive (by injunction) label themselves—they are in the same category—Strike Breakers. So we have three in one—one in three—Employers' Federation—Labour Leaders—Government Officials—the organised Strike Breakers!

Cosgrave wrote to Larkin on 29 October, saying he was 'not satisfied either as to your wish or your power to promote industrial or political peace in Ireland . . . The language used in your paper does not encourage me to credit you with either, or to accept as serious the suggestion in your letter of today.' Larkin's

attempt to complicate a dispute about wages with a large political issue affecting the safety and stability of the whole country, if honest, would be another example of that lack of a sense of proportion which has been so largely responsible for recent troubles. Your suggestion offers no security for a real settlement either of industrial or political questions.

Larkin had written to Cosgrave, 'in the first place in my capacity as Secretary of the Irish Transport Union' and secondly 'as a citizen,' with a suggestion that, 'in my opinion, will bring political and industrial peace,' namely that a Conference be called at which workers might accept the proposed wage reduction if the Government released all political prisoners. Larkin undertook to facilitate a return to work in all areas except on the land in Co. Waterford. A Council of Action circular simultaneously sought a national strike for the release of political prisoners, signed by Larkin and P. T. Daly, Dublin Trades Council.

Larkin was baffled by Cosgrave's reference to 'language used', stressing that workers' willingness to accept lower wages marked their sincerity on political questions. The support of the ITGWU for the 'infernal' National Loan merely confirmed the unholy alliance confronting workers. Larkin dismissed the loan as a 'national betrayal'. Capitalists, 'not satisfied with their 5% blood profit,' demanded 'as an inducement, that the workers' miserable wages must be reduced. Thus is the unholy compact—lower wages and we will support the Loan.'

In November the ITGWU abandoned its dock members in Belfast, provoking the Branch Secretary, William McMullen, to decry those who took 'advantage of their position to promise them great things' and arguing that it was better to 'face the position.' If men were prepared to stay in the ITGWU they would get more support than in any other union, but the 'E.C. is not prepared to allow them to pursue what is a forlorn hope.'

Larkin was quick to attack this apparent weakness, but economic circumstances permitted little alternative action. In Dundalk dissatisfied members of the ATGWU considered transferring to the ITGWU after their own union accepted wage cuts, but they wanted Larkin to address them.[6]

Larkin attempted to organise an alternative shipping company to break the 'foreign shipping combine'. A 'Workers' Co-operative Shipping Company' was planned, and 'every citizen interested' was invited to attend a meeting in the Mansion House on Sunday 7 October. 'For the ships are on the sea, says the Shan Van Vocht' was the headline of the *Irish Worker*. Larkin was to deal with 'Foreign Combines that control the economic arteries of the Nation's Life.' There could be

> no liberty of body or mind within the nation except we win Economic Liberty. A start must be made somewhere, somehow. We are on the way. Are you with us or against us?

Larkin was 'surfeited with suggestions and plans from disinterested persons' for settling the dock strike, which 'dislocates trade and embitters life.' It was, however, the 'best educating medium' for workers and citizens about the oligarchy that controlled their lives and defied 'all laws and regulations' and 'outrages every clause and section' of 'Port Charters, all in and to their own selfish betterment.' He attacked Cuthbert Laws of the Shipping Federation, stressing that it operated from outside the state. He

> made it manifest that that super-Government in London can order men out built in the image of God, born in this country, to burn the homes of workers and terrorise their wives and children, threaten the worker with death, if they will not submit to the midnight assassins—as in County Waterford—no condemnation is expressed by Church or Press and no action taken to protect these unarmed workers against these criminals, guilty of arson and attempted murder.

E. Dowling and R. Tancred raised the dismissal of the ITGWU Sailors' and Firemen's Delegate, P. McGuiness, on 15 November. If he was not reinstated 'dockers would cease work again.' The EC was given a week's grace. Dowling explained that a dockers' deputation called on Foran to question why a week's Dispute Pay had been withheld and were told that 'if they returned to work on Monday' the EC 'would consider the question.' Foran wrote to the Secretary of No. 1 Branch, John O'Neill, to say that the EC considered that 'the conduct of McGuinness during the Seamen's dispute was such as to convince' them that 'it was not desirable that he should be retained' in the union's employment. Action would have been taken earlier, but they 'deferred doing so as his dismissal during the course of the dispute might have injured the position of the men.'[7]

The long-held resentment among sailors and dockers against the ITGWU ultimately crystallised in the formation of the Irish Seamen's and Port Workers' Union in 1933.

FARM LABOURERS

On the land, 'struggles against the enforcement of heavy wages reductions on our agricultural members were unequalled.' A false impression was created when Dublin and Meath maintained their rates early in the year without much effort. But in Athy, Ballingarry and Waterford, 'conflicts surpassed in intensity and duration, if not in magnitude the National Lock-out in ten Saorstát Ports.' They were 'unparalleled by anything' in ITGWU history 'except the memorable Lock-Out of 1913.' Armed scabs operated by day and hooded terrorists by night, actively assisted and protected by military, police and bench, all met by farm workers, who 'fought with unyielding courage.' In Athy the ITGWU resisted a cut of 5s on 'their already miserable standard of thirty shillings per week.'

Unabated class war ended in defeat in November. However, the 'men's sacrifices' had 'an undoubtedly restraining effect' on farmers elsewhere, and thousands indirectly benefited from their resistance. Ballyline and Kilmanagh Sections, Ballingarry, struck for an increase on their average wage of 28s. On 24 April a District Lock-Out was imposed after the men rejected reductions of 8s on their 34s rate. For seven months Ballingarry 'was in the throes of a bitter and uncompromising struggle' on farm and in creamery, where 'men, women, boys and girls participated with relentless determination,' again unsuccessfully.

It was Waterford, however, that became the rallying cry. More than 2,000 were locked out at the end of May for refusing to take a cut of 6s on their rate of 36s and work an extra day. The 'ring' was kept exclusively for employers by the heavy military and police presence, which protected 'their armed scabs, by bullying, beating and even firing on strike pickets, and by allowing farmers' scab goods to be removed during curfew hours, and their masked "torch-brandishers" to stalk forth during the same hours to burn out and brutally ill-treat Officials and other members.' Waterford Farmers' Association resisted all negotiation and arbitration, and was as aggressive with any of its own who dared settle as it was with the labourers.

By winter, crops were irretrievably lost, but the landlords' real harvest fruit was crippling the union. Winter brought mass unemployment. The ITGWU has been accused of abandoning its Waterford members. This is a harsh assessment. It dispensed £41,522 on Strike Pay and, in response to a plea from the Organiser, Jimmy Baird, at Christmas forwarded another £300 to alleviate suffering among unemployed labourers. The union fought nobly and courageously but, from a fairly early stage, pointlessly, as victory was clearly beyond it. It paid a high price financially and never again embraced farm workers in membership. Geographically, the triangle formed by Carrick-on-Suir, Dungarvan and Waterford remains to the present a weak area for union membership.

At the Congress, Thomas Johnson and E. Mansfield (Irish National Teachers' Organisation, Tipperary) reported on the Commission on Agriculture. They sent a questionnaire to all rural ITGWU Branches. More than a hundred replies indicated the need to substantially increase the size of labourers' plots and extend unemployed insurance to agriculture. In Congress's view, however, they did not reveal any 'agricultural policy based on a study of what was practicable as well as desirable.' Future agricultural prosperity lay in the 'co-operative administration and development of small holdings' and 'planting of the larger farms and untenanted lands with the property-less workers, on the basis of common ownership.'[8] Such policy passed without debate. Roadmen, who suffered badly in 1922, fared worse in 1923. Local Government tactics were to offer unemployment relief schemes at the lowest local agricultural wages, often to their farmer cronies rather than to labourers. In all cases, 'lower wages, longer hours and a greater output' were demanded. The Free State was much freer for some than for others.

CORK

Practically the entire Cork labour force was engaged in a General Strike to resist wage cuts, with 'huge parades' and 'gigantic meetings at the National Monument.' The ITGWU was led by Bob Day, elected Labour TD during the strike; Dominick O'Sullivan, prominent in both the Tan War and the Civil War; Larry Prior, long associated with Connolly; Éamonn Lynch, Southern Organiser and later Secretary of the ITUC; and Jim Hickey, who transferred from the Dockers' Union. Hickey's 'ability, steadfastness and integrity helped to build up and mould the character' of the union in Cork.[9] The outcome was a drawn contest. Cork remained an ITGWU stronghold.

UNEMPLOYMENT

When the Congress debated unemployment, Frank McGrath (Belfast) argued that it was 'not by passing pious resolutions' that 'the evil could be got rid of.' They were 'rather weak on the subject.' The social order needed to be entirely changed. Thomas Ryan (Waterford) complained that an 'enormous number' were 'improperly disqualified' from benefit because of their involvement in farm strikes. This view was echoed by Michael Nolan of Belfast, where locked-out seamen were disqualified from benefit. The scheme would not operate effectively until workers administered it.[10] Denial of welfare benefits was an important weapon for the Government and employers.

LABOUR

Owing to the 'internal crisis,' the ITGWU was 'unable to shoulder its accustomed responsibility' in the General Election in August. Eleven of the fourteen Labour TDS returned were ITGWU members. Political action remained a priority, as 'the present stage of class-consciousness reached by Irish workers leaves much to be desired.' Many fighting 'hardest to maintain control of wages' willingly handed over 'complete political control to the employing class' at elections. Connolly had warned them 'against scabbing at the ballot box,' an 'admonition . . . largely disregarded today.'[11]

CONCLUSION

With the ITGWU under constant attack from external forces of employer and state, Larkin's return in April fuelled internal disruption. The union struggled to hold wages and conditions in every industry and every quarter of the country. 1923 was the worst year in the union's history, threatening its very foundations. The height of the storm, however, had not been reached.

The psychological and physical scars of 1923 were long-lasting. Never again would the ITGWU organise farm labourers. It was their loss, above all others, that accounted for the huge decline from more than 120,000 members to 14,000 in 1932. 1923 induced caution, pragmatism in organisation and reduced ambitions for OBU and Workers' Republic to the less glamorous imperatives of survival and holding hard-fought lines of minimal wages and conditions. Overtly revolutionary ambitions died.

PART 2

Splitting and splintering, 1924–45

CONTEXTS

Economy and society

From 1925 until 1931 the economy slumped through global depression and, as the ITGWU insisted, the hopeless, conservative policies of Free State Governments. It hardly inspired confidence in the nation's capacity for independence.

From 1932 until the Second World War matters slowly improved. The index of industrial production (using 1953 as 100) was 35.2 in 1925 and 37.6 in 1931 and by 1939 had climbed to 56.0. A trade deficit was shown every year from 1925, with the exception of 1943 and 1944, when trade virtually stood still. Imports declined from £56.7 million in 1930 to £37.3 million in 1935, recovering to £43.4 million as war broke out, reflecting expanding personal and industrial consumption. Exports fell alarmingly: from £44.9 million in 1930 to £17.9 million in 1934. International trade was crippled by protectionist policies. With farsightedness, the ITGWU blamed poor management, the absence of marketing and imaginative innovation, and high borrowing costs. By 1939 exports had recovered to £26.8 million.

Persistent underemployment disproportionately affected the working class. Emigration was not always an available 'safety valve'. Hourly wages were fairly static, rising from 44.5 in 1930 (using 1953 as 100) to 47.9 in 1939. Union demands were handicapped by the electorate's refusal to reject Governments that favoured the wealthy minority and marginalised labour. Industrial concerns centred on defending jobs and their content: there were repeated complaints about juvenile labour and replacement by machinery. In the debate on the Conditions of Employment Act (1936) there were concerns about standards of health and safety and restricting hours in line with ILO conventions. Sexism and sectionalism were rife. The ITGWU, in common with other unions, had little to be proud of in not challenging women's further exclusion from economic activity. Contemporary values placed male 'breadwinners' first. Even the IWWU displayed ambivalence towards the employment of married women.

Table 12: Unemployment and emigration (26 Counties), 1925–45

1925	36,400	1936	99,300
1926	25,300	1937	81,700
1927	21,100	1938	88,700
1928	22,700	1939	93,100
1929	20,700	1940	84,100
1930	20,400	1941	74,700
1931	25,200	1942	76,900
1932	62,800	1943	67,600
1933	72,400	1944	60,300
1934	103,700	1945	59,700
1935	119,500		

Total and annual average emigration, by census period

	Total	Annual average
1926	166,751	16,675
1936–1946	187,111	18,711

Source: Fleming and O'Day, *Longman Handbook of Modern Irish History,* p. 503, 620–21.

War

The de Valera Government's policy of neutrality was overwhelmingly supported by the people. As the period of 'National Emergency' unfolded, 26-County nationalism intensified, facilitating William O'Brien's desire to eliminate British unions and encouraging what many saw as a compact between Fianna Fáil Governments and the ITGWU. If needs be, O'Brien was even prepared to consider the Labour Party entering a 'National' (all-Party) Government.

Preparations for the Trade Union Act (1941) included private meetings between Department Officials, O'Brien and Thomas Kennedy. By May 1941, 426 cases of profiteering were investigated, but the fines on 72 guilty companies were extremely light, hardly evidencing even-handedness as increasing wage controls were exercised through Wages Standstill Orders.

The social consequences of declining living standards were manifest in 'disturbing levels of malnutrition, infant mortality and tuberculosis.'[1] The ITGWU opposed the Standstill Orders—some thought ritualistically. Unemployment fell from 93,100 in 1939 in the South to 60,700 in 1945, the bulk of the decline after 1943. In Northern Ireland, where industrial and agricultural economies benefited from the war effort, unemployment fell from 76,300 in 1939 to 20,300 and to a mere 15,100 by 1944. Annual emigration from the South averaged 18,711 in the period 1939–1946, with many more migrating north or enlisting.[2]

Union contexts

Not surprisingly, union membership mirrored the poor employment figures and fell until there was a slow recovery, although the numbers for 1925 were not surpassed until 1938. The collapse of the ITGWU was fastest: more than 100,000 from 1920 to 1930. It led the revival, however. In 1943, slow-burning tensions between Irish and British organisations reached a climax with a secession from the ITUC, led by the ITGWU, and the formation of the Congress of Irish Unions.

Tensions between the ITGWU and WUI persisted. The WUI was denied affiliation to the ITUC but secured affiliation to Dublin Trades Union Council in 1929, allowing Larkin personal access to Congress. Muted opposition by the ITGWU to the Trade Union Act (1941) and the Wages Standstill Orders allowed Larkin an Indian summer as Leader of street-based protests by the 'Council of Action'. While vigorous and contributing to a surge in support for the Labour Party in Dublin, it could not prevent either measure. The ITGWU opposed the orders but simultaneously used them to secure the maximum possible returns for members. So, while the WUI's membership fell to 8,093 in 1944 from 16,208 in 1939, the ITGWU's membership recovered to 37,970 in 1945, from a low point of 30,615 in 1943. The successful use of Tribunals and intelligent presentation of cases supported by fact, data and reasoned argument provided a base of skills for the post-war industrial relations infrastructure of Labour Court and Wage Rounds.

The ITGWU consciously organised to avoid losing its 1939 position when it felt it was back to where it was in 1924, 'except for the farm labourers.' Badly burned in 1923, it eschewed all opportunities to organise labourers.

Table 13: ITUC affiliated membership, 1925–44

1925	149,000	1935	125,000
1926	123,000	1936	134,000
1927	113,000	1937	146,000
1928	103,000	1938	161,000
1929	92,000	1939	162,000
1930	102,000	1940	163,000
1931	102,000	1941	173,000
1932	95,000	1942	164,000
1933	95,000	1943	183,000
1934	115,000	1944	187,000

Source: Nevin, *Trade Union Century,* p. 433.

The ITGWU 's nadir was 1932, with a mere 14,123 members. From then it grew solidly, more than doubling by 1939, reflecting diligent organisation and regular transfers from British unions, particularly the ATGWU. Indeed if the ITGWU had an 'enemy' it was not the WUI but the ATGWU, whatever about the feelings among leading

Officials. From the bloody fight on Dublin's coal quays in the autumn of 1925, the violence was over. The ITGWU and WUI settled into co-existence, inhabiting parallel universes. Conversely, the ITGWU and ATGWU had significant battles on trams and docks, mostly won by the ITGWU. The notable exception was Galway, where, led by a former O'Brien lieutenant, Gilbert Lynch, the Branch defected to the ATGWU.

In 1945 the CIU broke away, ostensibly over the ITUC's affiliation to the World Federation of Trade Unions. The split persisted until 1959. At last the WUI could affiliate to the ITUC. The Congress split was a book-end to ITGWU Divisions and the formation of the WUI in 1924.

Given the adverse economic circumstances, disputes fell in parallel with bargaining fortunes until 1932. Recovery brought greater conflict, especially in 1937, the year of a major building dispute. That year brought the decade's average of days lost from 228,285 to 335,300. Although the Standstill Orders removed legal immunity during trade disputes, the number of strikes and working days lost during the war was surprisingly high. That said, the impact of the Orders was evident, as the average for strikes in the five years immediately before and after the war was much higher: 1934–1938, 117.4, 523,600; 1946–1950, 150.6, 149,719.

Hourly wages in industrial occupations (using 1953 as 100) rose from 47.9 in 1939 to 55.3 in 1945. This showed that while the Government certainly exercised control, the unions squeezed something from the complex Tribunals, the ITGWU especially. Even in agriculture, forever cited as the lowest-paid and most exploited sector, average weekly wages rose from 33.7 in 1939 to 49.4 in 1945. These increases, painstakingly won and grudgingly conceded, must be seen in the context of a cost of living that rose from 579 in 1939 to 959 in 1945 in urban areas and from 539 to 894 in rural areas. The net effect was a considerable fall in workers' real wages to below 1939 levels.[3]

Table 14: Industrial disputes (26 Counties), 1923–45

	Disputes	Working days lost		Disputes	Working days lost
1923	131	1,209,000	1935	99	288,000
1924	104	302,000	1936	107	186,000
1925	86	294,000	1937	145	1,755,000
1926	57	85,000	1938	137	209,000
1927	53	64,000	1939	99	106,000
1928	52	54,000	1940	89	152,000
1929	53	101,000	1941	71	77,000
1930	83	77,000	1942	69	115,000
1931	60	310,000	1943	81	62,000
1932	70	42,000	1944	84	38,000
1933	88	200,000	1945	87	244,000
1934	99	180,000			

Average number of days lost

	Disputes	Working days lost
1923–1929	76.5	301,285
1930–1939	106.3	335,300
1939–1945	82.5	113,428

Source: Fleming and O'Day, *Longman Handbook of Modern Irish History since* 1800, p. 535.

Politics

Both Larkin and the ITGWU claimed credit for persuading de Valera and Fianna Fáil to enter Dáil Éireann in 1927. Celebrations at the change of Government in 1932 were quickly dispelled, as Fianna Fáil proved little better than its Cumann na nGaedheal predecessors. It did, however, purloin some of Labour's clothing. There was a feeling that Congress, the ITGWU and the Labour Party were happier dealing with Fianna Fáil than with Cosgrave. There were developments in state enterprise and the creation of employment, rural housing and social welfare. Many workers voted for Fianna Fáil.

In 1932 only seven TDs were returned for the Labour Party, its worst performance ever. Recovery was slow and uneven—in 1933, 8; in 1937, 13; in 1938, 9—until 1943, when the winning of 17 seats heralded a possible breakthrough on the strength of agitations against Standstill Orders and the Trade Union Act. The decision of the Party Leader, William Norton, to admit the Larkins, father and son, angered O'Brien intensely.

The secession of the ITGWU saw the Labour Party's performance reverse in 1944, with a mere eight seats, although four more were won by the National Labour Party. O'Brien covered his anti-Larkin tracks by alleging Communist infiltration.

On his retirement in 1946 O'Brien surveyed a movement whose wings, industrial and political, were rendered in two. Even he can hardly have regarded this as an achievement. Post-war reconstruction had to start within the movement itself.

Chapter 10 ⌒

AND THEN THERE WERE TWO: THE BIRTH OF THE WUI

LARKIN'S CASE AGAINST LIBERTY HALL

After Larkin's return from the United States in April 1923, rancorous differences arose between him and the ITGWU Executive. He resigned at his first EC meeting in May but was persuaded by Thomas Foran to retract and to tour the expectant Branches instead. Having spoken in Wexford, New Ross, Waterford, Dungarvan, Clonmel, Mallow and Cork, he was to travel through Charleville and Tipperary to Thurles.

Without explanation, he terminated a triumphant tour in Limerick and returned to Dublin, addressing Dublin No. 1 Branch in the La Scala Theatre on Sunday 3 June and starting what Liberty Hall called his 'disruption'. Emmet Larkin has observed that 'within the week, there was a civil war raging in the Irish Labour Movement.' Larkin was determined to drive O'Brien out of the ITGWU, but Emmet Larkin felt he may have overestimated O'Brien's position, sensing that he was heavily dependent on Foran's prestige and industrial presence.

The Irish Worker League, founded by Larkin, produced a new edition of the *Irish Worker* on 16 June 1923, interestingly suggesting that 'freedom is based on principles. Principles are greater than personalities'—a tenet that would soon be severely tested. A front-page notice got straight to the point. 'The Position' that 'we have been forced into, in connection with the Government' of the ITGWU is 'one to be regretted, but responsibility must be accepted, and what we have done has been done out of a sense of duty to the Members of the Union and no personal or vulgar libels will cause us to diverge from the line which we intend to pursue.' As matters were 'before the Courts,' Larkin—using the royal 'we' and signing himself General Secretary of the ITGWU—would 'refrain from any reference to the case further than this.' Members 'and public will know in good time all the facts at issue.' He concluded: 'We await, calmly and confidently, the justification of our action. Right and justice must prevail.' He sent greetings to the 'working class of Ireland'.

We have returned to the scene of our former labours after eight and a half years, to the work to which we put our hand sixteen years ago, and which initial labour brought into being two organisations which we fervently hoped would be the means of educating the workers, and helping forward the emancipation of the Irish working-class.

The first was the ITGWU, which 'never paused or hesitated to do righteous battle' on behalf of the workers, until 1917, when 'certain individuals assumed control' and 'used the organisation to their own aggrandisement' and the 'enslavement' of members.

Herein lay the kernel of the volcanic schism that rent apart the tectonic plates of Labour. Larkin claimed that when he left 'to carry forward the work of this Union' the ITGWU had 14,000 members, a cash balance of £2,381 6s 9d and 'a man—James Connolly—in full control.' On his return he claimed during his barnstorming tour that the ITGWU was dead in spirit and the Labour Party full of 'self-seekers' and a 'feeble imitation' of its English counterpart. Freedom, in a horribly Partitioned Ireland, was for the privileged few. The toiling masses remained downtrodden. His objective remained the Workers' Republic.

Larkin's mission was then a noble one against class enemies within and beyond the movement. In an open letter to members he said he had 'done all that was possible to do to keep this trouble . . . within the Union.' He appealed to members to stand by each other and have patience; but 'desperate diseases require desperate remedies.' The 'surgeon's knife' was 'going to be applied until this cancerous growth is cut out of the body of the union, a cancerous growth which has been eating at the very vitals of the Irish Labour Movement.' After 1916 Foran and O'Brien (in Larkin's view suspiciously released from prison before most Citizen Army men) did not wait to take organisational advantage of the revolutionary mood created by 1913 and 1916. 'It is common knowledge that the re-organisation of the Union dates from 1918—two years after 1916.' To anyone knowing the present General Officers a 'lapse of two years between planning a campaign and carrying it out is a brief interim—but the twinkle of an eyelid.' He suggested that the ITGWU's growth 'went hand in hand with the Republican movement, or to be more correct, it followed it at a respectable distance.' They fatally stood aside to let the 'Collins's, the Griffiths and the Cosgraves, the O'Higgins's and the Blythes get away with it' and had 'since bent themselves to the task of "implementing" the treachery.'

Industrially, the failings of the ITGWU were worse, as, in addition to standing idly by during wage cuts, they did not 'own a single factory, not one creamery, not even one ice-cream emporium; their sole adventure into business is a retail newsagent and tobacconist's which bids fair to come down into the street if some dare-devil of a newsboy pulls the sustaining placard from the outer wall.' Larkin felt they had sufficient funds in local Branches for 'capitalising industry on a large basis. But it will not be.'

Central to Larkin's case was the leadership's alleged denial of Mortality Benefit. The *Irish Worker* brought relief.

NOTICE! All members of the Union who were denied Mortality 'Benefit' during my absence, are requested to send in a statement of their case, together with card of Members and Death Certificate. They must be sent in a registered envelope, addressed to Jim Larkin, 17 Gardiner's Place, Dublin.

Larkin published emotive examples of denied mortality claims, based on contesting various levies imposed by the ITGWU but seen as invalid by Larkin. Levies should not have been considered as disqualifying arrears for claimants. Heartless denials for alleged arrears as low as 1d were made by Liberty Hall clerks. The charge was 'illegally withholding Mortality Benefit from relatives of deceased members.' The *Irish Worker* established a fund and published both donations received and mortality cases dealt with, issue by issue. The 'unctuous, legalistic phraseology' of the refusals added tinder to the fire. By October, £206 was donated to an 'ITGWU Relief Fund', £271 to 'ITGWU Dependants' Fund', all expended in relieving cases.

A second plank of the *Irish Worker's* policy was to demand the release of republican prisoners in Irish and British jails. A Prisoners' Defence Fund was created, and 'our Comrade John Bohan' forwarded £62 from No. 3 Branch for 'wives and children of interned' members. The Irish Worker League Christmas Draw allowed readers to turn a 'bitter Christmas, an inhuman Christmas, an unchristian Christmas' into a 'human Christmas' for prisoners' dependants. 'All men and women' of the ITGWU were urged to attend at City Hall on Sunday 18 November to sign a petition demanding the release of hunger-strikers. Larkin addressed a crowd from Liberty Hall's windows before a one-day strike demanding the release of three hundred prisoners. He dismissed the Government as a 'tyrannical oligarchy'; but while 'they hold the bodies of their opponents, they cannot imprison the soul.' Although he attracted a large audience, the strike was ineffective.

Larkin made much of the alleged ITGWU income. Anything, for example, O'Brien 'ever did for the Union, before and after entering the Dáil, he was well paid for.' In addition, O'Brien and Senator Michael Duffy, a Meath member of the EC, were accused of claiming exaggerated expenses. Cathal O'Shannon's income was heavily criticised, together with that of Joseph and Patrick O'Kelly, Head Office staff and O'Brien and Foran's 'right hand men.'

Such information created two impressions: that Larkin had insiders supplying details they found distasteful, not to say immoral, and that the ITGWU was corrupt. Of particular annoyance to Larkin were the 'boastful outpourings of the superhuman controllers' of the 'ONE BIG UNION', all supported by 'pseudo scientific interpretations of the philosophy and practicality' of the theory and repeated '*ad nauseam.*' Larkin insisted that 'we are always fearful of the abuse of power,' and he lampooned Liberty Hall's Officials.

These supermen only had to give voice and even the earth stood still; the sun and the stars moved not in space. Joshua, himself, was a piker in comparison to them. And when they opened their mouths there were loud tremblings heard, and the trumpet sounds that caused the fall of the walls of Jericho were but sweet sounding reeds in comparison to the loud cymbals that heralded the fall of the walls of Capitalism. This was, of course, according to the V(o)ice of Labour and the repeated statements of the super-leaders of the ONE BIG UNION.

Larkin surveyed the two Trades Councils, divided by mischievous personality; two Transport Unions, one foreign-controlled; 'Each For All and All For Each' more commonly interpreted as 'All For Me and Me For Myself;' individual disputes resulting in wage cuts and the manning of ships by non-Irish crews; the passing of pickets and general reverses—all cited as examples of neglect and loss of principle by 'self-elected' ITGWU leaders. Putting Larkin back in his rightful authority was the only solution.[1]

TWO TRANSPORT UNIONS?

Larkin accused the ITGWU leadership of operating illegally under 'fraudulent Rules'. He had 'fought single-handedly against this oligarchy.' He submitted a statement to the High Court in June 1923, alleging that the 1918 Rules were invalid, as under Rule 33 of the Rules registered on 8 June 1915 no amendments were sought from Branches, nor had the proposed Rules been properly voted on. Even if such Rules were valid, Foran and O'Brien had not since been properly elected as General President and General Treasurer, respectively. (As Larkin was simultaneously elected with them, by this logic his position as General Secretary was also invalidly held.) The Delegate Conference of 24–25 April 1923 was challenged as having been improperly convened, even within the terms of the contested Rules.

New Rules were registered on 2 June, and these too were challenged. At an EC meeting on 4 June, which Larkin attended, Foran and Thomas Kennedy acknowledged that the Rules of 2 June had been 'illegally' implemented and worried that it could be a 'case of perjury' and that they should be withdrawn. Larkin objected to the presence of O'Brien, Kennedy and Michael McCarthy and sought their suspension. A three-hour discussion had no 'practical result.' Larkin finally withdrew when the EC seemed determined to call a Delegate Conference to ratify the contested Rules. In addition, he raised the issue of money withheld from his knowledge by Foran and John O'Neill, Secretary of No. 1 Branch, surrounding the purchase of Liberty Hall in 1914.

At a meeting of Dublin No. 3 Branch held in the La Scala Theatre on 3 June and reconvened in the Olympia Theatre on 10 June, by a show of hands of the 1,200 men and 200 women present Foran, O'Brien, Kennedy, McCarthy and O'Neill were suspended from office. This was reported as the 'Swan Song of the Three Virtues'. They were accused of 'conspiracy, fraud and corruption,' of 'enriching themselves while robbing the widows and orphans,' and misusing a Political Levy—something else to which Larkin took exception. The meeting elected a Committee of Investigation to inquire into all matters.

On Monday 11 June, Larkin went to Head Office, 35 Parnell Square, with Thomas

Healy, Michael Lyons and Patrick Colgan, instructing them to wait at the door for the arrival of Foran, O'Brien, McCarthy or Kennedy. When the 'suspended' men arrived, Larkin informed them that they had no right of entry. In the ensuing discussion O'Brien called out all the clerical staff; with the exception of O'Shea and Ciarán J. King, all left the building. On 11 June the EC, in turn, suspended Larkin, a suspension he considered unlawful.

After this, Larkin, through representatives from Newbridge (Droichead Nua), Waterford and Limerick, attempted to get rank-and-file Executive members to return to work and handed over the key to Liberty Hall. Larkin now began to arrange for Shop Stewards to hand contributions in to offices in Luke Street rather than to 'Head Office'.

Roddy Connolly (James Connolly's son) endorsed Larkin's mission, for he 'is the militant Irish Worker—he is more, he is the incarnation of the great revolutionary up-swelling of the Irish masses.' He asked whether Larkin could 'reorganise the Irish unions, solidify their fighting machinery, perfect their solidarity, and revive their sinking enthusiasm—can this be done before the storm breaks upon us?' He was referring to the storm of wage cuts imposed by the Free State Government and the gathering global recession.[2]

On 15 July, George Nathan and J. Campion moved at the Inchicore Branch that 'the funds of this Union should not be utilised by either Party in legal matters now pending.' Larkin maintained the title of General Secretary, and the Irish Worker published notices of ITGWU meetings as if the status quo existed. All 'official' ITGWU activity Larkin dismissed as illegitimate, including the selection of Congress Delegates.

The Irish Worker took pleasure in asking embarrassing questions of Liberty Hall. In September it asked whether 'Nob Connor paid back £400 taken from Union funds'; why the Organiser Patrick Coates was sacked; whether £600 of Dublin No. 1 Branch's stake in Marlborough Co-op had gone; what became of James Grimley, 'the 1913 scab who got a job in the Union,' and why he was sacked; what were the exact amounts from Assurance Society offices of cheques cashed in pubs, and what was the connection between football coupons and a betting book; what amounts were to be invested in a Co. Dublin sewerage scheme; and what was the connection between the ITGWU and Malcolm Lyon.

Conversely, James J. Hughes, recently purged from employment in the ITGWU by O'Brien, wrote a conciliatory letter to the Irish Independent, republished, perhaps surprisingly, in the Irish Worker.

> Look here, Jim, you're a Big Man. For God's sake and the sake of our class do the Big Thing. State publicly that there is no division in the ranks of the Irish Transport.

Presciently, he asked Larkin to state

that there is no intention of having another Union. That the differences among certain Officials is a matter that has been referred to the members.

He concluded:

Go over to 35 [Parnell Square], take up your duties, let the errors of the past be buried. Give to the rank-and-file the knowledge that the leaders are a united body, and inside of a month we shall have regained all the ground we have lost. What does it matter, in a few years we shall have all passed but the cause shall still live.

This was generous and astute comment from Hughes.

Larkin argued that legal actions prevented the rank-and-file from settling matters. The Rank-and-File Investigation Committee echoed Hughes's sentiments.

We must not be guilty of any action that would injure the Union. We must stand united. Remember the forces of capitalism are united against us; we must face them with a solid front. In our own interests we must not allow our ranks to be broken, our solidarity shaken, or our progress impeded by this dispute.

An All-Ireland Delegate Conference held on 31 August elected an Investigation Committee, consisting of Michael Usher (Chairman), James Flanagan, George Nathan, Thomas H. Redmond and Patrick Brophy (Secretary). As Court actions proceeded,the Committee urged that the 'Union must not be disrupted or stampeded into two factions.' It had sought 'a written undertaking from both parties' to 'abide by the considered findings of Conference.' Larkin would give no such undertaking but would 'submit his charges in writing for investigation without prejudice to any legal status he possessed.' The EC was willing but pointed out that without a 'similar undertaking' from Larkin the Conference would, in effect, be powerless.

The Committee gathered all materials and set up structures; but without Larkin's ultimate acceptance of the authority of the Conference as binding, the Committee felt that 'any further expenditure would be but a waste of money.' The majority of the Committee subsequently became members of the WUI. The EC preferred to submit matters to a Delegate Conference.

Maurice O'Regan, Secretary of the Galway Branch, appealed to the 'rank-and-file throughout Ireland' to 'step in now, even at the eleventh hour and rescue the Union from the disgrace and shame' that legal proceedings would bring. Galway suggested a 'ballot vote' to elect officers to 'carry on the work of the Union and that an entirely new set of Rules be drafted.' This seemed to underline the mixture of bewilderment, disappointment and frustration felt among members, expressed in a desire for settlement of the row as soon as possible and tinged, perhaps, with a growing sense of 'a plague on all their houses.'

Larkin, continuing to act as if he were the ITGWU, suggested a voluntary levy to aid the dockers' strike fund—an irony, given his objection to existing levies that he considered illegal. By December he was still asking questions about the union's financial management, such as how much the levies had raised, how much was spent on Dispute Pay and given to Collectors, how much on union cars and property. Particular objection was raised to the £10,000 National Loan payment made from the Budget of the ITGWU National Health Insurance Society. This provoked a typical attack by the *Irish Worker*.

> We wonder who instructed the Hon. Bill—and the other members of the inner shrine—to take up £10,000 of the 'Infernal Loan.' Is this the price we pay as members of the ITGWU—National Insurance Section—for the deep silence and denial of a complete investigation into the accounts.

A clerk, John Johnston, was given two years' imprisonment for the larceny of £3,000, prompting the comment:

> Whew! How some one must have smiled. Johnston in quod could not squeak— maybe not! Wait and see!

In January 1924 the *Irish Worker* announced its resolution for what would prove an eventful new year: 'No Compromise!' Workers had been misled by a 'compromising, self-seeking group of place and fortune hunters masquerading as Labour Leaders,' causing a 'slough of despair'; but 'Truth, Moral Honesty and Class Solidarity will win and the Irish Working Class, so often misled and betrayed, will again realise their responsibility and close their ranks and march breast forward, an Intelligent and Disciplined Army of Workers.'

The ITGWU 1924 Almanac was derided: they should be sent to the 'Blind Asylum', as they would 'make excellent insoles.' Head Office staff were attacked for allegedly refusing to contribute to strike funds, as their wages were 'barely sufficient to maintain their social status,' so that they sometimes found it 'difficult to save the price of admission to the Abbey Theatre.' The EC was allegedly to unveil a 'mural tablet' of Head Office members who fought in the Civil War, their names to be inscribed at the EC's expense 'on receipt of death certificate and contribution card showing member to be not more than eight weeks in arrears one clear week before death!'

In March, Martin Cunningham, Roscrea Branch, wrote to the *Irish Worker* complaining that road workers in Co. Tipperary, out since 5 January, were reliant on a levy of 2s per member and a hurling match played between Laois and Offaly on 13 April, while the EC could make a £10,000 loan to the Free State. Two Organisers, Lynch and O'Doherty, were criticised, and Larkin was requested to go and settle matters.

An Irish Worker League excursion was organised for Sunday 13 April. 'UP TIPP! All the way to Roscrea and back for seven shillings.' The trip, organised jointly by the IWL and Dublin Trades Council, attracted large crowds and 'contingents' from twelve ITGWU Branches. Matters were becoming irreversible.[3]

COURT CASES

Actions arising from the 'occupation' of Liberty Hall and 35 Parnell Square on 11 June came before Mr Justice Charles O'Connor, Master of the Rolls, in the High Court, Chancery Division, on 14 February 1924. Larkin conducted his own case. The *Irish Worker* published full transcripts.

The judge determined that the 1918 Rules were valid and granted an injunction against Larkin for interference with the EC but ruled that Kennedy and McCarthy were illegal EC members, being paid ITGWU employees. Larkin failed to sustain his charges in the Courtroom but repeated allegations and questions every week in the *Irish Worker*. His argument remained that those who established the ITGWU 'set out to remedy the grievances of the Working Class, to help the down-trodden and oppressed, and to bring into existence a new social order.' Members were now

> oppressed by these Defrauders who have by intrigue and illegal methods seized the Executive offices, the property and money of the Union, and organised a corrupt machine of paid Officials, usurped and abused power, and have taken the money of the members under Rules drafted and registered by themselves for a purpose that was never approved of by the members and used the money, not in the interests of the members, but to their political and social aggrandisement.

As he published verbatim Court reports, Larkin presumably thought he had done a good job. He would have been better served by employing Counsel. He continuously annoyed the judge by introducing irrelevancies, using intemperate or offensive language to those he examined, and generally tested the Court's patience. Guidance from the judge was interpreted as interference, part of the general conspiracy by Court, state and employers to deny the absolute validity of his case. Larkin published an 'In memoriam' notice for Kennedy and McCarthy, 'who were cut off from a good job in the height of their affluence.' Despite such black humour, their removal was poor compensation for the loss of his central argument.

As soon as the verdict was declared, the ITGWU acted and Larkin 'was thereupon expelled from membership of this organisation on March 14th by unanimous vote of the EC.'

Liberty Hall saw sinister motives behind the lengthy Court process. They were 'very protracted and expensive,' and it 'was apparently Larkin's object to hold up the machinery of the Union and to compel the spending of large sums of Union money in the Courts and embarrass the organisation.' Legal expenses indeed rose from £269 in 1922 to £1,207 in 1923, £866 in 1924 and a peak of £2,056 in 1925. (Not all legal costs referred to Larkin actions, as members' compensation and other cases were pursued.) Increased legal costs were not of a scale to embarrass the ITGWU. Larkin gave notice of appeal but withdrew in June 1924. Costs were awarded against him. He did not pay, and on the application of the ITGWU for them he was adjudicated bankrupt.

On one issue Larkin felt he had a strong case: the £7,500 that Foran and O'Neill 'saved' from the 1913 TUC Strike Payments. A contrast was drawn between sums spent on the election expenses of O'Brien, Foran and others and the denial of Mortality Benefit to John Christian's widow because her husband was 'one penny in arrears' at his death. Such financial details were designed to cause suspicion and resentment among impoverished members and probably had far greater impact than the nuances of legal argument.

Messages of solidarity with Larkin came from Sections and Branches, typically pledging themselves to 'sustain him in his fight for the uplifting and betterment of the workers.' The AGM of Dublin No. 3 Branch in the Mansion House on Sunday 11 May—'admission by card (1924) only'—was to deal with 'circular letters from Head Office and delinquent Officials' as Dublin opposition to the EC mounted.

On 16 July 1924, after the creation of the Workers' Union of Ireland, three ITGWU members—Michael Connolly (father of Seán Connolly, Citizen Army member shot dead in 1916), Richard Lynch and Patrick Brady—took an action against the EC, repeating Larkin's challenge to the validity of the Rules of 20 December 1918 and 2 June 1923, as they were registered through 'false and fraudulent statements.' Further, they sought a declaration that the EC had been misapplying union funds since 1 January 1913 'by expending same upon political and other unauthorised purposes' and 'not accounting for same.' Finally, they sought an injunction restraining the EC from acting and the application of a receiver to the union.[4] All actions failed.

THE FORTY-FIVE

On 20 May, Larkin addressed a mass meeting in the Mansion House, at which he appealed for members to withhold their contributions and hand them over to a gas workers' 'Unofficial Committee'. Pickets attended Liberty Hall to enforce this diversion of funds. On the morning of Sunday 25 May Forty-Five members of the ITGWU Port Committee, led by Barney Conway, met in Liberty Hall and refused to leave. In the early morning, under the controversial Public Safety Act, police and soldiers arrived to evict them, take them to Store Street Barracks, and thence to the Bridewell. Here they were asked to pledge that they would not go near Liberty Hall or otherwise they would remain incarcerated. They gave no pledge. The 'lick-spittlers' of Parnell Square, O'Brien in particular, were accused of inviting the military to rid the Hall of 'intruders'. The wives and children of 'the 45' were assembled on the steps of Liberty Hall. A Dependants' Fund, operated from 45 Luke Street and 17 Gardiner Place, generated support, with the imprisoned men serving as a tremendous rallying-point against the ITGWU. The *Irish Worker* observed that the Forty-Five 'were jailed by the Free State Government at O'Brien's request.'

Although they were 'discharged as being completely innocent,' the magistrate 'demanded that they give bail for future behaviour.' Refusing to do so, they 'were immediately jailed again. What a farce.' O'Brien's 'influence (or rather partnership)' with the Government was derided. The plight of the Forty-Five was contrasted with that of two Free State soldiers who committed armed burglary and, rather than being hanged, were let off with a caution.

A 'Monster Concert' to 'help the women and children of the 45' was held in the Mansion House on Monday 30 June. Protest meetings assembled outside Mountjoy Prison, with Edward Tucker, President of Dublin Trades Council, Councillor John Lawlor and P. T. Daly speaking. On Thursday 3 July the Forty-Five were released at eight o'clock in the morning, in batches of fifteen at a time, and were met at the gate by 'fellow working class men and women' and a Band. 'The walls of the Mountjoy Bastille re-echoed the wild cheers and hearty shouts of welcome to those victims of class hatred.'

The imprisonments were a serious miscalculation by those accused of engineering it. They provided a focus and impetus for what was to become the WUI and apparently confirmed a central plank of Larkin's case: the ITGWU was in league with Cosgrave's Government.

The ITGWU version of events was that the EC closed Liberty Hall on Sunday 25 May, transferring operations to offices in York Street. When this was notified in the press 'a number of Larkin's gang—some of whom had never been members of the Union—took possession of the Hall and refused to leave it at the usual closing hour on Saturday night.' The police ejected them early on Sunday morning but then withdrew, 'without notifying the caretaker' or 'any person of authority,' the ITGWU knowing nothing of police intentions. The 'disrupters re-entered immediately, but were summarily ejected on the Wednesday night by a number of our Dublin members, who organised unofficially and kept guards in occupation of the Hall until all likelihood of a re-entry by the Larkinites had passed.'⁵ Although handed back to the control of the EC on 28 May, Liberty Hall remained closed for business until 1927.

FORMATION OF THE WUI

Whereas the ITGWU was 'brought to birth by James Larkin quietly enough in a back street room,' by contrast the WUI 'was born in the stress of industrial struggle on the quays of Dublin.' On 5 June 1924 Larkin went to Moscow to attend the 5th Congress of the Communist International. Three days later, on 8 June, his brother Peter issued a 'Notice' to all ITGWU members to pay their subscriptions to a Port, Gas and General Workers' Provisional Committee. They 'would receive *All Monies* until further notice and issue receipts for same.' The rank-and-file had taken matters into their own hands, as 'all buildings which are the property of the Members of the ITGWU are now under *Armed Guard,* placed there by the *Junta* calling themselves the Executive Committee,' who 'have repeatedly proven themselves to be the Tools of the Employers and Agents of the Government.'

At the Inchicore Branch of the ITGWU, Peter Larkin asked all to follow the Provisional Committee, which—bar the Branch Secretary, Michael Kavanagh, and Chairman, Michael Cunningham—they did. On the following Tuesday, accompanied by CID men, Kavanagh left work to collect all ITGWU books from Emmet Hall. The *Irish Worker's* headline read: 'Is the Government a Tool of the Transport Union Executive?'

The Provisional Committee enforced its authority among B&I men, forcing them to appear before it on charges. On 14 June the *Irish Worker* declared that an ITGWU card was tantamount to 'scabbery': 'Our advice to those who have no cards—or wrong cards—is: "Act quickly" and join the right body of men because if you don't join willingly, perhaps you may join unwillingly.'

Before his departure, Larkin had expressly told Peter 'under no circumstances to allow the members of the Union to break away from the I.T.&G.W.U.' It is not clear from this what he intended. He had eschewed internal mechanisms when offered to him and had lost in the Courts. Jack Carney concluded: 'When Jim returned from Russia he was faced with a *fait accompli*. He could do no other but accept it.'

On Sunday 15 June, 'at the old spot by the riverside . . . announcements of an important nature would be made.' Workers were advised to 'watch our smoke!' The 'smoke' was the announcement of the formation of the Workers' Union of Ireland. The first members were reported in Dún Laoghaire Gas Workers, Baldoyle, Dublin No. 1, Dundalk and Inchicore Branches, Coal, Markets, Butchers and Municipal Employees' Sections and Marino Builders. By 21 June new cards were issued, and 'badges will be available.'

The *Irish Worker* was full of notices for meetings of ITGWU Branches, where the clear intention was that such meetings would swap allegiance. Dublin No. 3 Branch, including the Secretary, John Bohan, transferred. Only three—Hardiman, McGrath and Keavy, all paid Officials—stayed loyal.

The ITGWU condemned the 'most lying propaganda and vituperation' being 'spread amongst the members in Dublin city and county.' It succeeded but, in ITGWU eyes, only among the weak.

Reflecting on events in 1949, James Larkin Junior, General Secretary of the WUI, stated:

> There were no cards for the members, no premises, no staff, no money; nothing except thousands of men and women revolting against injustice to fellow-members. Within a week of the Union being organised it was fighting, not merely a New Union had to fight to establish itself, but it was fighting also for the life and welfare of those who supported it.

When Larkin returned from Moscow the immediate problem was to find pay for 3,000 men out in six major disputes. The WUI was under 'relentless attack', because it was 'based on progressive thought and militant action' and was 'not prepared to sell itself to anybody in this country.' To the ITGWU it was 'the alleged "Workers' Union of Ireland," a body 'completely under the control of the Larkin family, a violent rival and supplanter.'

> The most strenuous efforts were made to cajole or drive our members away from our Union. Bullying, terrorism, physical violence, lying, libelling and intimidation

by large bodies of men were the methods adopted. In several instances Shop Stewards transferred our members and their contributions to the new body without the knowledge or consent of the members concerned.

There is more than a grain of truth in these remarks; but neither side was innocent, both indulging in rough-house tactics. For dockers, 'rough justice' was integral to their culture and must be viewed in that context.

The ITGWU Conference drew derision from the WUI, which dismissed its record in 1923 as one of 'losses in the industrial field with consequent diminution in the receipts of Branches,' a state 'verging on bankruptcy,' resulting from the 'jobbery' that had been 'found out.' The programme had been one of wage reductions abetted by 'the Senator' (Michael Duffy or Thomas Farren) and 'cheap labour Government,' supported by the ITGWU leadership.

Published ITGWU accounts led to strong criticism. Expenditure 'for the year 1923–1924 exceeded income by about 100%.' This 'unusual lavishness' was because the Executive feared that 'their gains in the preceding years would be lost owing to the existence in the country of a critical opinion not existing before.' It tried to convince the workers that the Executive was the workers' friend, but 'the hoarding instinct could not stand the strain.' The 'scheme broke down long before the critical period in the Union's finances was reached.' The

> history of the year 1923–1924 will make interesting reading when written. The political and industrial union of 'Executivism' and Capitalism is the outstanding feature of the period and at the proper time the tale will be told.

No mention was made of £128,724 spent on Dispute Benefit, 153% of the union's income in 1923.

Industrial battles immediately broke out between the WUI and ITGWU. The *Irish Worker* suggested that 'every man and woman in Ireland must take sides in this fight. There can be no neutrals.' It was a fight of 'rank-and-file and gentlemen of no property' against the 'armed forces of the State, Courts and press . . . hellish secret societies' and the 'power of the banks.'

By 1 July the WUI claimed 17,000 members. It complained of 'armed thugs' occupying—or, indeed, re-occupying—premises in High Street, Inchicore and elsewhere. The WUI operated from Unity Hall, Marlborough Street. Among its members were builders' labourers who, angered by ITGWU decisions, had attempted to re-establish the United Builders' Labourers' Union in February 1922 with two hundred members. Seán McLoughlin, an enthusiast for a New Union driven by a Socialist commitment, saw the 'rise of the W.U.' as proclaiming 'the determination of the conscious workers to forge a new weapon of industrial unionism—All for One and One for All; no divisions, no sectoral weaknesses, and an end to Fakirs and organised treachery.' The WUI would 'build a pure labour movement' and 'cleanse the movement.' The rank-and-file had 'cleared the decks for action. Never again must the workers of this country permit themselves to be fooled and sold.' It is not clear how many WUI members ultimately shared McLoughlin's visionary Socialism.

Some order had to be put on the chaos of ITGWU fragmentation. On 12 July a notice was published in the *Irish Worker* from the 'Provisional Executive Committee'.

> No support, financial or otherwise, will be given by the Workers' Union of Ireland to any Union that does not withdraw its representatives from the 'Workers' Council' by the 31 July, 1924 . . . No transfers to the WUI will be accepted on or after the 31 July, 1924. Entrance fee on or after that date will be £1.

Similar notices appeared for 'cinema and theatrical workers and management.' If any worker was not a member of the WUI by 31 July 'none of our members or public sympathisers shall contribute to the support of any houses where our members are not employed.' Such intimidation was commonplace. The belief was that the power of numbers was sufficient to guarantee success and that the ITGWU must be driven out.[6]

The WUI Rules were registered and on sale by 19 July. It was a proud boast that, whereas ITGWU Secretaries were paid £3 10s a week, they received only £2 10s in the WUI. A meeting in the Mansion House on Sunday 30 August welcomed Larkin back from Russia and launched a £1 levy from all members to sustain 'the re-birth of unionism in Ireland . . . All comrades, tendering such an amount, would receive a certificate of payment from the Union, this certificate being a testimonial to the donor's unionism and comradeship.' This was the Freedom Fund, and 'the old Transport membership under a new name' distributed the bonds 'payable on demand five years from the date of issue.' Although Ireland was 'a poor country', by October it was 'hard to believe the amount of money rolling into the Freedom Fund.'

By 13 September the WUI referred to its opponents as the 'defunct Transport Union', claiming Branches in Baldoyle, Balgriffin, Blanchardstown, the Boot, Clondalkin, Coolock, Drumcondra, Finglas, Howth, Lusk, Sandyford, Santry, Swords and Tallaght. In a sinister and threatening declaration the WUI saw itself (with an interesting retrospective use of the term 'this Union') as 'the old guard of the I.T.G.W.U. combined with younger comrades who, determined they would not be disgraced, exploited or robbed by the Junta and their corrupt machine.' The WUI had 'stripped them naked of the robes of unionism,' exposing them 'as naked scabs and strike-breakers.' It would next

> strip them of the properties and monies they have withheld, and compel them to repay the thousands of pounds they have robbed from the members of this Union during the time they were enrolled in the Transport Union. Sufficient men have been left in the dens to clear up the job.

This suggested that some members had stayed 'loyal' only to be ready to act as double agents.

Complete triumph was apparently at hand. Vigilance was required, however, and rigid card checks enforced transfers to combat the 'depths to which the so-called Executive of the almost defunct I.T.G.W.U. and their dupes' were sinking. Larkin made much of the ITGWU's indifference to the plight of members, particularly the denial of Mortality Benefit; but in October the WUI Provisional Executive announced that any members experiencing work-place accidents must 'report same within twenty four hours,' directly or through relatives or representatives, or be denied benefit. Similarly, 'any member who accepts compensation under the Workmen's Compensation Act, Employers' Liability Act or Common Law without first acquainting this Union, will be dealt with.' Hurling from the ditch was not the same as being on the park.

In November it was announced that 'the remains of the Transport Union in Dublin are being cleaned up.' An 'Open Letter to Transport members' asked them to 'consider your attitude. You are an ever-diminishing number—dupes of a corrupt, ambitious, money-seeking, porter-swilling group.' Larkin personally suggested that 'they have your properties lying idle, such as Liberty Hall and Emmet Hall, which I bought for your use and enjoyment.' Larkin reckoned that £54,000 was owed to the WUI. 'One of your oldest comrades', William Fairtlough, was now a convert, and Larkin urged:

> Fire the bunch; take charge; open up your halls; join with your old comrades and get together, boys . . . No soreness, no recrimination: come along to Unity Hall, same old pals, same old spirit. Get busy together. Each for All and All for Each as in the old days. Solidarity, Humanism, Honesty and No Scabbery. Your old-time comrade, Jim Larkin.

Some workers opted out of both unions, indeed all unions. They 'lost all interest in unions and what they stand for.' Such attitudes were hardly surprising, given the vituperative and personally bitter nature of the split. The WUI lampooned the ITGWU staff by nicknames that represented their alleged weaknesses or betrayals, such as Gilbert Lynch, 'the White Hope,' William Vennard, 'Portadown boy with the Orange flavour,' 'Snuffy' Foran, and 'Hoofy' O'Brien. Some jibes have lost their meaning with time, but all contributed to an atmosphere of personal animus.

The competition for members, or perhaps more accurately for the control of members, resulted in violence, with frequent incidents, arrests and charges. Jack Dempsey and James Bond were convicted of savagely beating John Burke, ITGWU Delegate, Fish Markets, and Dempsey and Costelloe for hospitalising Vennard for five weeks. A WUI rally in the Mansion House on Sunday 23 November—'admission by card only, wear your badge'—heard that not since 1912–13 had there been such a combination of the forces of reaction, an 'Unholy Trinity' of Government, employers and ITGWU. Tough times meant that a levy of 6d a week was imposed on

WUI members for four weeks to give 'unemployed members and children a Christmas.' A libel action by Thomas Johnson against James Larkin and Gaelic Press, publishers of the *Irish Worker,* resulted in damages for both defendants of £1,000.

By March 1925 the WUI claimed 25,000 members and Branches in Dublin, Dundalk, Dún Laoghaire, Clondalkin, Sandyford and Lusk. The *Irish Worker* published a swingeing criticism by Patrick Nolan, former ITGWU Delegate, of his old comrades. Earnán Ua Núnáin objected to Nolan calling the Liberty Hall staff 'swanks', pointing out that some had been farm labourers, shipyard workers, or steeplejacks. These 'swanks' had even gone on strike in February 1922, five never to return to work, but Nolan never offered 'support or sympathy.' He concluded: 'Is binn béal ina thost, a Phádraig!'

A WUI Hospital Levy of 6d per quarter was imposed, together with a 1d weekly *Irish Worker* levy, both from 1 May 1925.[7] Members not paying such levies quickly found themselves in arrears. Anyone more than eight weeks in arrears forfeited all benefits; anyone twenty-six weeks in arrears ceased to be a member. What went around rapidly came around.

THE GAS COMPANY

Central to the formation of the WUI were events in the Alliance and Dublin Consumers' Gas Company. In May 1924 ITGWU members struck 'in defence of a vital principle of trade unionism.' The EC felt it 'had an excellent case' and was officially supported. At a meeting addressed by the Officials, some workers called for Larkin to represent them, though he was no longer an ITGWU Official or indeed member. Liberty Hall felt that most 'did not approve of this' but 'allowed themselves to be stampeded,' became 'his unconscious tools' and 'repudiated the authority of the Union.' The ITGWU representative, George Spain, was regarded as having 'no position.' When the EC decided to withdraw Dispute Pay, Martin Magennis 'took charge of the Strike Pay which had been borrowed on behalf of the strikers' after 'he and some of his fellow-strikers removed the money from Liberty Hall.' ITGWU men 'organised unofficially and kept guards in occupation . . . until all likelihood of re-entry by the Larkinites had passed.'

A settlement emerged that was a victory for the men. Two dismissed members, Dunne and Ward, were reinstated, with Ward given a boy helper and Dunne an increase retrospective to July 1923; wages were raised to £3 14s, retrospective to July 1923; and no victimisation. The terms were accepted unanimously, with the men declaring thanks for Larkin's 'able advice and leadership.' The lesson for the 'unhappily-terminated' gas workers was clear: 'United they have won against a combination of all the forces of reaction—the Government, capitalistic institutions and traitor labour "leaders".' Dies were being decidedly cast. 'Victory for the Gas Workers' was declared on 28 May, a 'signal victory' against the 'forces of the "Government", ITGWU "Executive" and employers.' Work resumed on Thursday 29 May, with differences raised at the Ministry of Labour Conference of 27 December

1923 to be 'settled amicably' and, 'failing agreement,' resubmitted to 'Mr. Ferguson whose decision shall be final and binding on both sides.' The Agreement, signed between the company and P. Forde and B. Finnegan, representing the men, 'was accepted unanimously.'

The lesson was clear: new organisation was required to oppose new enemies. For the ITGWU the gas workers were 'very badly beaten in a short time and forced to surrender the great principle that a worker has a right to join and remain a member of a Trade Union.'[8]

THE MARINO, CORPORATION AND THEATRE STRIKES

After June 'turf wars' erupted between the ITGWU and WUI. The Government supported the Marino Housing Scheme to create employment and provide accommodation, but the wages offered—50s (£2 10s) a week—were below union rates and were rejected by workers. Larkin saw Government tactics as an attempt to put ex-servicemen and trade unionists at each others' throats and a conspiracy to 'bolster up the shaking oligarchy entrenched in Parnell Square.' The WUI claimed 260 members in Marino to the ITGWU's dozen; and yet, thanks to a compact between O'Brien and the Builders' Employers' Federation, they got no recognition.

Marino has been cited as the fulcrum of the internecine battle. The men at Marino were 'fighting in the front-line trenches,' and 'the whole Irish working class' stood or fell by the result. 'O'Brien and his clique, with their armed guards, must go, even though all the Freemasons' Lodges, Rotary Clubs, Chambers of Commerce, and the Government say, "Nay"!' Why were the employers so determined to settle with the ITGWU? It was because they would 'knuckle down to the low wage campaign of the Government.'

On 21 August the WUI notified 'our members and the public generally that all outdoor collections for the financial support of those on strike have ceased.' After twelve weeks, any further collections were thus 'unauthorised'; but the notice did 'not apply to the Special Levy on members,' which was still in force. The 6d per week levy was imposed from 15 July to 31 October. Non-payment was counted as arrears.

The ITGWU insisted that its Marino members were 'coerced' into the WUI. The 'strike' was to compel WUI membership rather than against employers for improved wages or conditions. Similar tactics were tried in the Fish Markets—where the Secretary of No. 1 Branch of the ITGWU, John O'Neill, was much vilified—but 'this policy of attacking our members resulted in a series of complete failures which have become memorable in labour history . . . In every case' Larkin's 'strikes' had 'left men of the working-class idle and penniless.'

In July, Dublin Corporation tried to reduce the wages of cleansing, sanitary and public-health workers. Not only would this action result in a strike but it would mean 'an increase in disease and death.' This did not 'disturb the Government,' as, since it assumed power, 'disease and death have walked this land. Privation and hunger have been the nightly bedfellows of the working class . . . And still the terrible inhuman campaign goes on.' The wui urged all to come out and that 'the old slogan must rule again—"Each for All and All for Each".'

In August the strike drew the criticism of the itgwu. Rather than have the *Irish Worker* 'printed by scab electricity' after a strike in the Pigeon House Power Station, a duplicated sheet was produced to carry the attack, unlike 'our esteemed contemporary the *Voice of Labour.*' The issue was, once again, wage cuts, and the wui claimed that the 'Transport Union has ceased to exist—except as a scab herding organisation.' Its card was 'nothing but a pass to scab.' Cosgrave talked of being 'blackmailed' by workers who would not simply roll over and accept cuts, prompting the observation that 'talk of blackmail comes well from this political harlequin, whose public record has been one of bluff, intimidation, sophistry—and personal ambition.' There was no sign of a reduction in Cosgrave's salary. What had he 'done for the nation in return for the princely remuneration he receives?'

The wui attacked the Irish Municipal Employees' Trade Union, as its Officials attended the il&tuc in Cork, seen as a Liberty Hall prop and led by the hated 'Felix' Johnson.

The wui held meetings for flour mills, Corporation, theatre and cinema Sections—all previous itgwu strongholds. Not all was plain sailing, and the financial demands of so many disputes meant that Shop Stewards were called to Unity Hall to agree that their 10% commission would be deferred until January 1925 to keep the union afloat. A dispute broke out in Inchicore Running Sheds. The itgwu let an old grievance among helpers lie while engineers received a 3s increase. The wui quickly accused them of 'scabbery'. Members crossed not only from the itgwu and imetu but from the 'yellow' Association of Ex-Officers and Men of the National Army Trade Union.

Dublin cinemas and theatres were the battleground in November, a 'culminating point' in the struggle. Larkin persuaded a minority of workers in the Carlton and Corinthian cinemas to withdraw their labour so as to coerce the itgwu majority into the wui. In compliance with the Agreement with the Theatrical and Cinema Owners' Association, Liberty Hall simply filled the vacancies, an action interpreted by Larkin as scabbing. The itgwu argued that no trade dispute existed. wui pickets were arrested outside the Queen's Theatre, and cid men shot into the air to disperse workers demonstrating outside the Seanad.

The strikes spread in December, and Court actions found picketing to be lawful at the Carlton and Queen's, although as far as the itgwu was concerned they were placed there to 'coerce our members, the majority in both houses,' to join the wui. Battles followed in Morgan Mooney's and on the docks but 'met with ignominious failure,' and when 'faced with a stand-up fight' Larkin retreated and could not stop itgwu men working there.

The itgwu issued a public notice in November. On the docks and in the city members would 'remain at work unless involved in a genuine trade dispute, and they will fill the place of Larkinite workers who are foolish enough to quit their employment at the behest of Larkin's agents.' Liberty Hall was 'determined that in each case that arises' workers would 'have an opportunity of choosing between their jobs and Larkin's interests.' This had a 'sobering effect,' and by December, Liberty Hall claimed a substantial return to the fold.

Larkin, conversely, felt that 'every strike' involving the WUI 'during the last eight months has, without exception, been caused or prolonged by the actions of the Transport Union officers.' Further, and rather less credibly, the WUI felt it had 'never vented feelings against the I.T.G.W.U. rank-and-file—except the scabs and agents provacatuer.' Under the heading 'An Injury to One is the Concern of All', Larkin protested that the conspiracy of Government, employers and ITGWU forced the WUI into strikes 'in the hope that the financial strain will break the new organisation.'

Discipline and finance were required, and on 30 August an order was issued to all members: 'All cards must be cleared up to date, contributions, levies, fines, entrance fees, regardless of the amount. You must support your comrades.' By October the WUI claimed that the ITGWU 'weekly income barely reaches £100,' which, on an average weekly contribution of 9d, would mean 'a financial membership of roughly 2,500 members.' If that were true the union would have been in irreversible difficulty. The ITGWU thought it 'notorious that in no single instance' did Larkin 'call a strike against employers . . . all his strikes were directed against this or other unions.' This 'wrecking policy' generated ill feeling not just from the ITGWU but from 'the Labour movement as a whole.'[9] With jobs scarce, many simply wanted to be on the 'right side' to secure their job.

OUTSIDE DUBLIN

Although Dublin ITGWU members substantially transferred to the WUI, it was a very different picture outside the capital. Most country members joined during Larkin's time in America. They did not have the same identification with him as Dubliners, particularly those who lived through 1913, and stayed true to Liberty Hall. Unsuccessful attempts to set up WUI Branches took place in Belfast, Limerick, Nenagh, Sligo, Tullamore and Wexford but lacked any critical mass. By July the WUI claimed Branches in Baldoyle, Duleek, Dundalk, Dún Laoghaire, Dunlavin, Nenagh, Roscrea, Swords, and Tullow. Few were maintained. Barney Conway was despatched to Nenagh and Limerick to follow up requests for WUI speakers. On Sunday 24 August an excursion was planned to Athlone to cement organisation in the Region, but this was abandoned.

In the fifth week of a strike in Tullamore, and despite boasts of large reserves, the ITGWU sent its Band down to play at a special football match to raise funds, as only 35 out of the 120 men were in benefit. The *Irish Worker* claimed 'The Scab Band Takes Its Expenses', that 'gate receipts' were about £15 but the Band's expenses £32, 'including £17 for dinners.' Strikers 'found that no money was left to aid them.'

On 18 August an organising drive in Limerick was announced. Con Ryan, P. T. Daly, Jack Flood, John Crotty and Denis O'Loughlin addressed meetings. A 'military guard' was placed on the 'OBU Hall'. Limerick dockers ceased to pay into the ITGWU. Greenore heard the Secretary of the ITGWU Dundalk Branch, M. P. Whittle, and

Peter Larkin address a rally on 7 September. In December, Larkin visited Sligo and his old friend John Lynch. He accused the ITGWU Organiser 'Shamus [*sic*] O'Brien' and the Branch Secretary, Maurice O'Regan, of corrupt dealing with Laurence Garvey, stevedore, to destroy the hard-won system of direct labour on the quays. Despite much commotion and interest in the town, the WUI could not establish a foothold. Outside Dublin the ITGWU 'was solid against disruption and stood loyally to its allegiance to the democratic principles of our organisation.' After 'the Daly libel action' the NEC 'expelled the leading disrupter in Sligo,' John Lynch. Sligo became 'one of the most loyal Branches.'[10]

THE ITGWU AFTER THE SPLIT

The ITGWU published details of Larkin's expulsion and a transcript of various legal actions, all essentially concluded in favour of the EC, as *The Attempt to Smash the Irish Transport and General Workers' Union* and, briefly, in the Annual Report. The attempt was 'so treacherous a blow' that a 'public exposure of its causes' was the 'least service' that could be done. Larkin adopted delaying tactics, possibly to put the ITGWU to expense and hold up its activities. In June 1924, possibly believing that the creation of the WUI represented victory, he abandoned his actions. They were revivified 'in the names of three of Larkin's dupes.' But all actions were lost and costs awarded against Larkin.

   The ITGWU felt a mixture of justification and frustration. The WUI, a heroic and revolutionary rejection of Liberty Hall's reactionary junta in Larkin-speak, was viewed very differently by the ITGWU.

> The most lying propaganda and vituperation of the Executive Committee were spread amongst the members in Dublin city and county. Sustentation funds, stamps, and many other devices were adopted to raise money to smash up the Union, and in certain jobs in the city, these efforts met with some success, especially amongst lapsed members and men and women suffering from personal grudges against the Union and its Officials.

The 'severe struggle' nevertheless had a 'very bad effect' on organisation generally.

> Workers became reluctant to join up while disruption was rampant, and the less class conscious sections got an opportunity of shirking their responsibilities.

On 21 August, the split still raw, P. Doran called for weekly reports to Dublin No. 1 Branch 'in order to nullify the lying propaganda' around the docks about 'the men who had remained loyal to the Union.' In September a clearly anxious Doran asked to 'inspect the roll books' to 'find out roughly the number of members at present paying on their cards,' even though there was some evidence of men returning from the WUI. John O'Neill, Branch Secretary, bemoaned the 'leakage of the business discussed' being 'carried to outside sources.' A letter from the three Delegates—O'Brien, Patrick Nolan and Lar Redmond—to Dublin No. 1 Branch Committee in

September was regarded as 'scurrilous and altogether unworthy of the men who signed it.'

A sign of tough times on the docks was that William Fairtlough, a founding member, could not get work in his normal spot on the grain wharves. Branch criticism carried in the October *Voice of Labour* was considered 'most unfair.' The paper's articles on Soviet Russia also drew reservations, as Doran reported that 'members took exception to them,' and 'under the circumstances' it might be better 'if those articles were curtailed for the present at any rate.' Russia became a Larkinite preserve.

P. Spain reported that two men in his job were WUI members, and he asked 'would he be within his rights to refuse to work' with them. No. 1 Branch Committee 'decided he could refuse.' Matters became rough, and WUI members were charged with assaults on three ITGWU Officials, John Burke, William Vennard and Frank Robbins.

Thomas Kennedy announced a reorganisation scheme, so scattered was the Dublin membership. John O'Neill raised the matter of the three members who brought legal proceedings against the EC 'at the dictation of J. Larkin' and suggested their expulsion. The three had 'done their utmost to help to break up the Union and had miserably failed to do so' and 'should not be permitted to retain their membership,' whether 'inclined to do so or not.' Michael Connolly, Richard Lynch and Patrick Brady were duly expelled. Spain resigned after the motion was carried.

A Special General Meeting of No. 1 Branch on Monday 8 December devised a Branch reorganisation 'rendered necessary owing to the action of the late General Secretary and his Band of disruptive followers,' matters being handled by Vennard. By January 1925 the Committee felt it had 'no alternative under the circumstances but to give a week's notice to all the members of the staff' and 'terminate their present working conditions.' An alternative was that staff members agreed to 'work week about [alternating weeks].' J. Manweiler complained that having Delegates working week about was detrimental to organisation. Vennard suspended the services of Patrick Nolan as Delegate before his full dismissal, despite pleas on his behalf by Joseph O'Neill. Joseph McCabe succeeded John O'Neill as Secretary of No. 1 Branch in March.[11]

The ITGWU's income fell from £84,122 in 1923 to £50,137, a drop of £33,985 or 40%, the lowest figure since 1918. In addition to the split, unemployment, agricultural depression and the defeats and reverses of 1923 told heavily. Concomitant with falling income, expenditure fell dramatically. Surprisingly, the union declared a surplus of £9,720, raising the credit balance from £58,462 to £68,183. Some rural Branches had 'fallen away . . . very considerably and in some cases had disappeared altogether.'

O'Brien put the union's losses into a broader context when claiming that all unions suffered diminished membership. By December the ITGWU felt it had 'certainly broken' the back of 'disruption.' It was confident that lost ground could be recovered.

In January 1925, with no little sense of relief, the ITGWU felt it could 'congratu-late itself that in the Old Year just passed it was able to withstand all the forces of corruption and treachery which perverted members of the working class itself had let loose.' It had been a 'dismal' year for people, 'made so by the capitalist system and those in political power who buttressed it up with all the armoury of the State.' It was optimistic, however, that '1925 should see steady and solid progress' and 'a complete recovery from the treachery and distractions of Larkinite disruption.' It hoped to regain the 'proud position we occupied in 1922 when the Irish working class almost held the future destiny of Ireland in their grasp.'

As soon as legal proceedings permitted, the annual Delegate Conference was held in Dublin in June and a National Executive Council elected. A Special Delegate Conference in Connolly Hall, Cork, in August amended the Rules and introduced standing orders for Conferences, confirming the NEC's authority and completing the reform process begun before Larkin's return. The Conference approved a polit-ical fund, decided 'by a large majority' early in 1925. Cathal O'Shannon was appointed full-time Political Secretary. From this point the ITGWU was governed by the annual Delegate Conference, at which the General Officers and NEC were elected.[12]

ITGWU DISPUTES AND CAMPAIGNS

Fights against wage and job cuts continued throughout 1924, despite distracting internal conflict. A wounded ITGWU noted that workers 'became reluctant to join up while disruption was rampant' and 'less class conscious sections got an oppor-tunity of shirking their responsibilities.' Against these badly stacked odds the ITGWU managed in most cases to mitigate cuts. £10,906 was dispensed in Dispute Pay, the lowest amount since 1918 and £117,724 less than 1923. The most notable strikes were those of road workers in Co. Westmeath, town workers in Ballinrobe, Birr, Mountmellick, Portarlington and Tullamore and woodworkers in Edenderry and Navan. A projected cut in flour mills was held off, and successes came early in the year for agricultural workers in Cos. Dublin, Meath and Wicklow. A reviving spirit among members saw increased claims late in the year, but employers must have rejoiced at seeing the apparently ever-growing monster writhing and grievously wounded from a blow struck by one of its own. Had strikes followed a similar pattern to 1923, O'Brien revealed that a national levy would have been necessary. But despite being badly holed the ITGWU stayed afloat and proved capable of resisting employers' cuts, fighting effectively when called upon.

Given Larkin's tirades against it, the ITGWU felt that 'one of the most pressing problems' was that of working-class education. Its ultimate goal could not be attained 'without well-trained workers, educated on the most up-to-date princi-ples and methods of trade unionism.' It was hoped that 'sufficient provision' would be made in this regard 'in the near future'—a reference to proposals by the ITUC&LP for a Workers' Educational Institute. In the meantime the *Voice of Labour* was seen as the mechanism for educating members.

Towards the end of the year, and in response to increased advertising demand and troubles with Larkin, it was decided to permanently enlarge the *Voice of Labour*. P. T. Daly, 'Larkin's right-hand man and chief adviser', took a libel action against the paper. The matter first appeared in June 1923 but did not reach final trial until December 1924. The case related to Daly's 'expulsion from the national movement', his neglect of duty while in charge of the ITGWU Approved Insurance Society and the 'lack of trust both Separatists and Labour men had in Daly.' The jury found against Daly, and costs went against him. He had burned all his ITGWU boats, and after briefly appearing to be a WUI member and acting as an Official he soon relied solely on his poorly paid position as Secretary of the Trades Council.

The ITGWU maintained pressure on the Government on economic and social questions. After the virtual collapse of unemployment insurance, Frank McGrath (Belfast) thought it a 'very bad inducement' for Northern workers to link up with the Free State. The division of Ireland on economic and social lines was quickly becoming real. James Larkin (this one from Newcastle, Co. Limerick) complained that unemployed workers had to travel long distances to Courts of Referees without expenses. The Unemployment Insurance Act (1924) proved wholly inadequate. O'Brien called for the creation of jobs at 'trade union rates' or for 'full maintenance for all unemployed men and women' to be paid. This could be done by works of national reconstruction and by amendments to the Unemployment Insurance Act. He decried the abolition of local authorities, which denied both the rights of local democracy and an opportunity for maintaining employment.

Congress produced a pamphlet, *Unemployment, 1922–1924: The Record of the Government's Failure,* but it made little impact on policy. It called for more Factory Inspectors, male and female, and the immediate appointment of a 'Lady Inspector' for Cork. Jim Hickey (Cork) demanded that Inspectors have a 'technical knowledge' of the work. Foran was appointed to a Congress Committee to examine Workmen's Compensation and to work with the ILO in seeking improvements in Irish statutory provision. A memo on the provisions of the Factory and Workshops Acts and Shops Acts was circulated, emphasising the need for enforcement. Only two replies were received: from the IWWU and Ballinasloe Trades Council. The silence of the ITGWU reflected less a lack of interest than a preoccupation with internal problems.[13] In the face of the split it was attempting to demonstrate the strategic value of normality.

CONGRESS AND DISUNITY

There was reaction in the broader labour movement. Congress viewed 'with alarm the growing tendency of opportunists, etc. to form local Associations purporting to be trade unions,' and refused to affiliate any such 'flapper' unions. In the midlands former ITGWU members set up an organisation to 'reconcile the interests of employers and employed' as a further alternative to Liberty Hall. The ITUC&LP 'publicly warned the organised workers of the dangers to trade unionism' threatened by such activities.

At the Congress in August the split agitated Delegates. J. T. O'Farrell (Railway Clerks' Association) said that there was a reverberating effect throughout the movement. He alleged, presumably with an eye on Moscow, that 'those concerned in the present dissension had set out to destroy the Labour Movement.' They had 'set up in its place some sort of nebulous institution, whose only object was to create widespread chaos and exploit the families of the workers, as well as the workers themselves, for purposes outside their shores.' People should not be led by the 'personal vilification' and turmoil, as its object was 'only designed to gratify the over-weening ambition of a number of disgruntled politicians and demagogues.' In a racist flourish he concluded that he would not accept a policy 'set up by Russian Jews and calculated to suit half-civilised Asiatics.'

Dan Morrissey TD (ITGWU, Nenagh) said it was not purely an internal problem. His union had been attacked for the purpose of smashing the whole movement. Miss O'Connor (IWWU) suggested a Committee to investigate and settle matters, as men were walking the Dublin streets, out of work over the row. Patrick Doran (ITGWU, Dublin) assured the Congress that 'everything had been done within the Union' to settle things, but 'the rank-and-file of the organisation would not allow its democratic principles to be trampled under the feet of any dictator.' The Secretary of Congress, Thomas Johnson, thought it was not purely a matter for the ITGWU: it was 'much deeper than personal antipathies or quarrels.' Trouble was not being fomented by revolutionaries outside Ireland, but such figures were ready to take advantage of revolutionary opportunities should they arise.

O'Brien concluded matters by pointing to the widespread tendency 'to have a rap at what was called the O.B.U. It was a very hurriedly mobilised army and had many defects.' He was hopeful that 'if any workers had been led astray by vilification and abuse, they would have to be given their head, but by sufferings and education they would learn their mistake and would come back to the true fold again.' He felt that 'the worst was over' and was encouraged by the general support given to the ITGWU.

Congress was in a difficult position. It was not practice to interfere in individual affiliates' internal affairs. Consequently it rejected an Emergency Motion from the IWWU that sought to 'set aside one day' for a private session on ways of developing greater unity and 'to consider the possibility of a settlement of the sharpest points of difference between the I.T.G.W.U. and their opponents.' Helena Molony (IWWU) suggested it 'be the first business' of Congress to end the 'internal disputes at present disrupting the Labour Movement,' the 'cause of great scandal, growing weakness, and a loss of confidence.' This was withdrawn, given the im-practicality of adequately debating matters in the time available.

Congress, however, was unequivocal in its view of events, referring to them under the heading 'The Attempt to Disrupt the Irish Labour Movement.' At the meeting of its Executive in September it fully considered the 'attack on the I.T.G.W.U. led by Mr. James Larkin' and 'other minor, irresponsible attempts to form New Unions.' Five of the Executive's seventeen members were members of the ITGWU:

O'Brien (Treasurer), Senator Thomas Foran, Archie Heron, William McMullen MP and Thomas Ryan (Waterford). On 26 September it issued a manifesto, *A Call for Unity,* decrying the 'ruinous disputes in Dublin, which have caused grievous loss and distress' both to those directly involved and to 'many others who had no direct part in the conflict.' (See p. 172.) Congress believed that the manifesto had a 'steadying effect', together with the ITGWU's 'firm stand'. The evidence would suggest that the conflict had blown itself out quite naturally and that the actions of Congress, while understandable, probably had little impact generally and none on those who joined the WUI.[14]

CONCLUSION

For the ITGWU the 'not very edifying' events of 1923–24 ought to 'convey to the working class a salutary lesson upon the control, management and leadership of a great trade union.' It was hoped that *The Attempt to Smash the Irish Transport and General Workers' Union* would help workers to 'eject this Larkinite poison from their system.' Were this so, the 'publication of this painful chapter in their history will be work well done.'

Until Connolly became Acting General Secretary, Larkin had not applied the Rules and ran union affairs in his own fashion. It is an inescapable conclusion that, however else it is dressed up, the challenge to his absolute authority by the application of standard trade union governance was central to the row. His subsequent control of the WUI adds weight to the argument. In April 1923, when Larkin returned to Ireland, the ITGWU was 'no longer his personal property' and 'he could not rule as a dictator.' This was 'more than Larkin could stomach.' In Court he was exposed as being economical with the truth, reduced to personal vilification and abuse and unable to sustain a consistent case. One particularly sad aspect was summed up by an observation by the judge as Larkin hectored Michael McCarthy in the witness box. He asked McCarthy to confirm that 'I' established the union. The reply did not please him. 'Oh, Jim, no. Yourself, myself and a few others who sat in a room in 10 Beresford Place.' Endeavouring to constrain Larkin, the judge observed: 'I can see that though there is this public contest you are very good friends. (Laughter.)' The futility and waste of personality-driven conflict between former comrades and friends was tragic.[15]

Just as Larkin's actions are to be condemned, the ITGWU was equally vituperative, with horrible cartoons in the *Voice of Labour* and constant personal insult. It saw itself as right, moral indignation fuelling its outrage. For Foran, having seen the ITGWU survive 1913 and 1916 and grow to an enormous National Organisation by 1923, it was a particularly bitter pill. The split triggered a decade of decline by the ITGWU, although direct conflict with the WUI was over by 1925. The ITGWU's fault rests on O'Brien's shoulders and his apparent inability to make use of the high moral ground to exercise a generous authority. His hatred for Larkin remained obsessive. The ultimate outcome by the time he retired in 1946 was a sundered movement. Larkin's actions were those of an erratic, spontaneous individualist;

O'Brien's were meticulous in intent and preparation and therefore possibly more unforgivable.

All that said, the split was not alone inevitable, it was necessary. Larkin would not have survived within the ITGWU that he discovered on his return. Its revival after 1932 was in marked contrast to the stasis of the WUI. The effect, however, was that a great organisational river was split in two. It became weaker, vulnerable and diminished in its individual and combined parts. It would not be reunited until 1990. The loss to the working class of the energy, focus and resources of a united union was incalculable and unforgivable.

A CALL FOR UNITY
Issued by the National Executive of the ITUC&LP, 26 September 1924.

The National Executive of the Labour Party and Trades Union Congress, elected at the Annual Congress in August, views with anxiety recent developments in the Labour ranks, more especially in respect of the ruinous disputes in Dublin, which have caused grievous loss and distress, not only to the workers directly concerned, but to many others who had no direct part in the conflict.

Strikes such as those at Marino and Inchicore, even if successful, could not have brought any benefit to the workers, either materially or morally. Workmen lost wages, businesses were dislocated; the erection of houses, for which the workers have such crying need, was held up; tradesmen not connected with the dispute were disemployed, and no material advantage was even hoped for— certainly was not attained—while the moral damage to trade unionism in loss of strength and prestige is incalculable. No good cause was served by these disastrous strikes, their only use seems to have been to pander to the vainglory of individuals desirous of making a show of power.

Being anxious for the welfare of the organised Labour movement, upon which we believe depends to a high degree the salvation of the country as a whole, we feel compelled to issue this warning to trade unionists generally against being led into a course of action which, if followed, will certainly lead to disaster to their unions and cause irremediable damage to the country.

WRECKING TACTICS
In the work of reconstruction of the national life the trade unions, if they are to rise to their responsibilities, ought to take a dominating part. This cannot be done if unions are to be weakened by internal dissension, where jealousy and envy take the place of good-will and helpful criticism. Nor can it be accomplished by organisations which emanate from a craving for notoriety in any individual, whether he has attained international renown as a disruptionist, or merely enjoys local fame as a shallow but shrewd 'chancer,' lacking any knowledge of what is meant by trade unionism.

The history and achievements of the Irish Labour movement in the last ten years should be sufficient guarantee that the interests of the workers and the country will be safeguarded by the unions, whose members and leaders have borne the burden of that trying, but in many respects inspiring, decade.

Rates of wages and conditions of labour have been improved and the improvements maintained, in face of a general failure to do the same in other countries; the unions, if wisely led, can hold that advantageous position if the members stand firm to their unions and refuse to adopt the tactics of the wrecker.

In the bitter struggle for national independence the generous enthusiasm, unbreakable determination and self-imposed discipline of the organised workers were admittedly of the greatest value in the struggle. In the awful orgy of civil strife which followed the operating of the Treaty, organised labour preserved its sanity in an atmosphere of hate and alarm.

TRADE UNIONS' PURPOSE

When the storm clouds are gathered once more on the political horizon it would be calamitous if the steadying influence of organised trade unionism were weakened or destroyed by suicidal tendencies on the part of even a small proportion of its membership. We do not pretend that our unions are faultless in construction or that the Officials have always been sound in their judgements; but we claim that in general they have served well and successfully the interests of their members, and deservedly won a commanding influence in the sphere of negotiation with employers or in the wide life of the community.

The primary purpose of trade unions is to protect the workers by collective action from the ever-present downward pressure upon wages which employers in a competitive world are driven to exert. If there were no trade unions each workman would have to make a separate bargain with his employer, and the man out of work would compete with the man in work for his job by offering to work for lower wages. Trade Unions have introduced the system of collective bargaining, and have thereby averted many of the evils of unmitigated competition in the labour market.

NEED FOR UNITY

But the trade unions, having established their position as protectors of the workers' wages and conditions by collective bargaining have developed their powers, evolved new functions and assumed greater responsibilities. It is not enough in these days for trade unions simply to resist reductions in wages or fight for higher rates for their own members. Solidarity and loyalty are essential, even if those primary purposes are to be fulfilled; but when organised Labour essays to play its greater part in the general social, economic and political life of the community, there is even greater need for unity of purpose and responsible leadership.

These considerations apply with double force in Ireland to-day, when we are faced with problems which, if they are to be solved, will require that all the powers—moral, intellectual, economic—which make for a healthy national life shall be utilised and directed to the task of finding and working out their solution. There are the problems especially affecting the workers, and there are, in addition, the problems affecting the nation as a whole.

It is the task of the trade unions to protect the standard of life of the workers, and at the same time to have regard to the well-being of their fellow-workmen and the prosperity of the nation. We hold that these objects are not incompatible, but rather that the true prosperity of the nation will be achieved through the practical recognition of the truth that the workers, by hand and brain, constitute the only vital factors in the nation, and, therefore, the well-being of the workers means the prosperity of the nation.

If we allow personal jealousies, Sectional envy, partisan hatreds to inspire our actions, leading to dissensions and rupture in the ranks, then the power of the unions, either to protect their members or to influence beneficially the national life, will be utterly dispelled.

We ask the workers to recognise that at the present time there are many powerful factors operating which tend towards the disintegration of the nation.

DECLINE OF PRODUCTION
Chief amongst these is the serious decline in wealth production, in what is almost our only source of wealth—viz., agriculture. Arising partly through political troubles, partly through the fall in prices in England, partly through bad weather conditions, the total wealth production, upon which practically all our industrial operations ultimately depend, has seriously declined in the past two or three years. This is a fact of gravest import which organised labour is bound to take into account.

One of its consequences is that enterprise is limited; new projects are held up, and commercial depression is prevalent. To adopt tactics of a kind which merely deepen and extend the area of depression is to deprive the workers of employment and weaken their powers of resistance against the day when all their strength will be needed to resist an attack on wages. The resources of the country are ample to provide health-giving sustenance and comfort for all our people. It is imperative that the country shall apply itself earnestly to the work of supplying these needs and stimulating economic activities, especially those which are directly productive, so as to add to the nation's strength.

MORE WORK WANTED
More employment is necessary, but more employment at directly productive work is required if the country is to grow strong.

The times demand immediate attention to the crying evils of unemployment and the poverty resulting therefrom. These evils are deep-rooted and are not to be easily eradicated. The ultimate solution, we believe, will not be found without a radical change in social relations and a new spirit and purpose to direct the economic activities of our people.

But these changes are not to be wrought without long-sustained endeavour in the fields of education and public discussion. In the meantime some temporary remedies must be applied to save the present generation, and make possible the enjoyment of a better life by the next. All genuine efforts to promote employment and increase production under fair conditions ought to receive the support of organised labour. But it should be apparent that spasmodic strikes and stoppages of work without valid reasons (i.e. reasons which will stand the test of trade union scrutiny) will only result in retarding, perhaps utterly destroying, industrial development or prospect of increased employment.

Trade unions will need to be stronger, not weaker, in the future if a fair standard of living is to be maintained; they will need to be directed with foresight and discretion, and a lively regard for the common welfare if they are to retain any power of influencing beneficially, the current of the nation's life.

THE VOLUNTEER SPIRIT

A voice has been heard from one of the political camps calling for a revival of the spirit which inspired the Volunteers. We would most heartily endorse that appeal in its application to social and economic endeavour. The Volunteer spirit, as we understand it, led to the subordination of the individual to the nation; the acceptance of a strict discipline; enthusiastic work for an unselfish purpose, devotion of personal energies and material resources to the common weal.

If this true Volunteer spirit could be revived, and find expression in the field of industry, the salvation of the country would be assured. We feel that the dangerous state of the country, owing to the failure of agricultural production and other causes, will only be overcome when a new spirit takes possession of our people, inspiring us all to active work for the common good.

Political change of whatsoever character is of small account in comparison with the necessity for saving the economic life of the nation, and setting the men who comprise the nation at useful work. Is it too great a thing to ask that the forces which, however divergent they may be as to means, all aim at re-building the nation on a secure foundation, shall seek to find agreement as to the best means of reaching economic safety?

We deplore the disunity in the ranks of Labour, and warn the workers of the danger; we do so the more earnestly because we are convinced that it is but a symptom of a disorder that is permeating all phases of the national life. It can be overcome by a united expression of the 'will-to-live' and the revival of the 'spirit of the Volunteers.'

THOMAS JOHNSON, Secretary

Source: ITUC&LP, 31st Annual Report, 1924–5, p. 33–6.

Chapter 11 ~

YEARS OF DECLINE: THE
ITGWU IN THE 1920s

MEMBERSHIP, FINANCE AND ORGANISATION

In 1925 the ITGWU returned to 'normal activities' and a 'marked increase' in 'prestige and influence'. The NEC insisted that 'at the moment its power and reputation are greater and higher than at any period for some years.'

Archie Heron, General Treasurer, chaired the annual Delegate Conference in August in the absence of Foran, 'recalled to Dublin on urgent Union business.' This business was the 'last and eminently successful steps to give the knock-out blow' to 'disruption.' A 'counter-offensive' re-established the ITGWU's presence on the 'coal quays, among carters, in the bakery trades, etc.' A triumphant picture was drawn as battle apparently ended. 'On occasions since, puny efforts' were made 'to attack the Union or its members,' but 'in no instance' did 'they threaten any serious consequences,' being 'confined to mere wordy abuse, which signifies nothing, but reveals the disappointment and powerlessness of our enemies . . . Large numbers' who 'left the Union or were bullied out of it' returned. Loyalty, comradeship and 'business-like earnestness' characterised matters. The 'danger was completely disposed of'; Larkin's 'last strong-hold . . . carried triumphantly.'

There was some truth in these statements, not least that open conflict abated. But the financial returns of the Dublin Branches tell a different tale. Branches remitted 75% of subscription income to Head Office; in the absence of membership figures, these are therefore the best indication of membership trends. No. 1 Branch returns almost halved between 1923 and 1924. Membership continued to fall until 1928, when the practice of publishing figures ceased. All Branches showed similar trends.

Although 'quite free from all traces of the disruptionist campaign,' membership still fell. The explanation was less Larkin and more the 'extremely bad industrial and trade situation.' All unions suffered decline. Membership of the ITUC fell from 149,000 in 1925 to 92,000 in 1929. ITGWU affiliation fell from 100,000 in 1922 to 20,000 after 1925. The ITGWU observed: 'One of the most reactionary consequences of Larkin's activity has been the re-establishment of a few of the smaller unions.' But it confidently expected its return, as the 'helplessness of these bodies in times of need' meant it could 'only be a temporary phase.' In 'due time this position, too, will right itself.' The United Builders' Labourers' Trade Union re-established its independence.

The claim that the ITGWU had high 'prestige', a regular boast, was at odds with the discredited view many people had of trade unionism as a result of the 'bickering and dissension.' The ITGWU claimed that 'big rallies of the Dublin membership at general and aggregate meetings this year have had no parallel in the history of the Union.' Such comments smacked of 'putting a brave face on it.' The data shows that, if not holed below the waterline, the schism severely damaged the ITGWU vessel. Unemployment and depression made seas even choppier.

Table 15: Dublin Branches' financial remittances (£), 1918–28

	1918	1919	1920	1921	1922	1923	1924	1925	1926	1927	1928
Dublin No. 1	6,835	12,579	16,865	16,752	16,454	14,530	7,813	4,790	4,836	4,153	2,948
Dublin No. 2	706	1,159	1,387	1,420	1,453	1,406	680	246	171	97	71
Dublin No. 3	2,925	6,859	8,997	8,695	8,138	7,743	3,909	1,694	1,610	1,230	986
Dublin No. 4	297	399	1,593	1,108	1,496	1,520	1,084	891	722	787	728
Dublin No. 5	—	—	—	—	64	392	290	—	—	—	—
Dublin No. 6	—	—	—	—	—	—	142	368	293	263	310
Total	10,763	22,226	28,970	29,704	31,050	28,496	14,983	8,844	8,143	6,924	5,356

Source: ITGWU, Annual Reports, 1918–28.

New Rules enabled the ITGWU to run with a 'smoothness which could not have been anticipated some years ago.' It was 'now quite clear that with whatever slight amendments changing circumstances may compel from time to time,' members had 'a code of Rules and a machine which they can understand work without more friction than is inevitable in an organisation of men and women drawn from so many different kinds of employment.' Despite this claim, inordinate time at annual Delegate Conferences in the 1920s was absorbed in debating Rule changes, often without result, as motions were withdrawn or defeated.

In January 1925 the Tea and Wine Section was one of a number returning from the WUI. The Secretary of No. 1 Branch, Jack McCabe, was made Organising Secretary although at 'the disposal' of the Branch, an indication of how problematic things were. To make use of every penny, the union's bankers were instructed at the end of each quarter that all interest accrued on deposit receipts was to be credited to the union's current account. Court actions cost £1,600, a sum that stretched resources. Rules relating to the reinstatement of lapsed members were regularly tinkered with to facilitate those who wished to return and were financially able to do so.[1]

In 1926 improvements were made to Mortality Benefit, providing for payments of between £4 and £9. A Provident Fund for paying Mortality Benefit was established in 1929.

There was still lingering violence. Such violence was by no means one way. Those convicted did primarily come from the WUI, although this could be the evidence the authorities favoured. Galway dockers rejoined in May, and 'although the spirit is not ripe for a popular feast of rejoicing on the first of May, the ancient festival will not go un-honoured.' In Herbert Park, Ballsbridge, the 'famous Transport Union No. 1 Band' provided 'a feast of music from 7–9 p.m.' Earlier at the Olympia Theatre a concert for the staff of the *Freeman's Journal* was held, and 'every working-class family in Dublin' was 'expected to grace the celebration.'

In short, the ITGWU kept its best side conspicuously out. In July the Cork Branch nominated Éamon Lynch for General President, but when informed 'he laconically replied, "Messmates before shipmates".' Foran was unopposed.[2] Michael Deegan, Secretary of Dublin Shop Stewards' Committee, complained that the NEC was cutting its funding; 'but surely comrades a healthy SSC ought not to die.' It could 'be a tremendous factor on the side of the rank-and-file.' The Committee survived.

The Irish Mental Hospital Workers' Union formally merged with the Amalgamated Transport and General Workers' Union—no surprise, given that its General Secretary was M. J. O'Connor. In practice, most Branches transferred to the ITGWU, however, as did ATGWU dockers in Newry and Galway. Nearly all dockers were now 'under one single, united control.'

A Mental Hospital Staffs Conference, held at 35 Parnell Square, Dublin, on Thursday 22 April 1926 called on union members on Asylum Boards to defend or improve conditions. Best conditions existed where Labour was in the majority. The meeting heard that 'another Union had made an attempt to take over some Irish mental hospital workers,' but it was handicapped, as it had no representatives on boards. The question was asked: 'Since Ireland had cut the English connection politically,' was it 'anomalous that Irish workers should seek to maintain English control industrially?'

Unemployment among motormen brought suggestions of a breakaway union. The failure of the motor permits strike, 1919–20, was recalled to 'set the men thinking.' They were advised to stay put, as the Labour Party opposed the increase in the charge for a driving licence to £1. A loan of £175 to the Irish Clerical Workers' Union was written off as a bad debt.

More than 4,000 attended a General Meeting of Dublin Branches at the La Scala Theatre on Sunday 28 March, an event opened by the 'splendid Brass and Reed Band.' It was Thomas Kennedy's coming of age. He rounded off the meeting 'in the way that it should go. Unsuspected fires blazed in his deep, impassioned appeal for a reawakening of working class consciousness, for the exercise by the workers of the intelligence and the acquisition of the stores of knowledge that lay at their doors.' He 'surprised many by his force of expression, by the far-seeing idealism, the bigger and broader issues he impressed on the minds of his hearers.' From 'the point of view of force' his 'speech was the most successful and most popular; and he richly deserved the deafening round of applause that acclaimed his tour de force.'[3]

1927 began with a flourish. Members marched behind the Band to rally in the La Scala, women conspicuous in the throng. The reopened Liberty Hall was to be 'the centre of social and educational work.' It was 'not enough that members should simply pay their Trade Union subscriptions': they had to 'take an active interest in the political work of the Labour movement if progress was to be made.' Foran told the annual Delegate Conference that the year 'was not a very satisfactory one': an 'industrial stalemate' had been reached. Unemployment was stultifying, with 'little hope' of immediate improvement. Any work was of a casual nature, making organisation a problem. Membership continued to decline. Agricultural workers, 'at one time such a strong force,' became 'almost entirely unorganised.' It was 'impossible' to hold their wages and conditions. They drifted from organisation.

The 1926 balance sheet was 'not very inspiring' and reflected a defensive posture. Staff numbers were a concern as income fell again. Heron introduced a more optimistic view. The hotel workers' victory and an influx of dockers and mental hospital nurses were evidence of an underlying confidence. A presence was re-established on the Dublin coal quays and in the new Carlow sugar factory. The ITGWU observed that, because it charged low subscriptions, it could not pay 'unemployment and other friendly benefits' as craft unions did. This removed a motive for members to retain membership. The Cork Branch persuaded the 1928 annual Delegate Conference that quarterly finance and organisation reports should be issued to Branches, reflecting concerns about diminishing incomes. Matters disimproved further, although among unemployed former members the 'old spirit of unionism' was 'far from dead.' It was heartening that after months, even years, of unemployment they were 'prepared to carry out their responsibilities as Union men' and 'join the ranks of their organised comrades again.'

Three Dublin Branches reverted from Class D to Class C membership, or 9d to 6d per week, a reflection of week-to-week hardships, even for those employed. Branches formed or re-formed included Ardglass, Ballinacurra, Birr, Blarney, Camolin, Tullamore and Urlingford. Despite the gloom, the ITGWU invested £15,000 in Housing or Corporation Stock.[4]

Membership fell again in 1929. As motor traction more and more displaced horse traction, jobs were lost. Minor gains were made in Dublin, Limerick, Tralee and Waterford among hotel, flour and bacon workers. Membership, which reached a peak in 1920, fell throughout the decade. Income followed a similar pattern. With the exception of 1923 and 1925, however, surpluses were returned, indicating sound financial management. O'Brien, the tailor, knew how to cut his cloth according to his means.

With the impact of global recession, those closest to the union must have harboured fears about the future, drawing comfort only from members' continued loyalty and union solvency. In 1925 Heron said: 'This Union is not merely a wage-raising organisation.' The aim was 'to create a new system of society and secure control' and to 'attain supreme power, both economic and political, so that the workers should share the wealth their labour produces.' Such ambitions were grand, but by 1930 the union's very survival was at risk. There was a desire to see light at the end of what was proving a very dark tunnel.

Table 16: ITGWU membership, 1920–29

	ITGWU figure	*ITUC figure*	*Registrar's figure [2]*
1920	120,000	100,000	101,970
1921	100,000	100,000	100,000
1922	82,243	100,000	100,000
1923	89,000	100,000	89,000
1924	67,000	89,000	67,000
1925	50,984	61,000	42,000
1926	40,000	40,000	42,000
1927	22,000	35,000	37,500
1928	18,857	30,000	35,000
1929	15,453	20,000	35,000

Source: ITGWU, Annual Reports, 1920–29; National Archives, Registrar of Friendly Societies, file 275T [2]. In December 1924 ITGWU membership was 61,000, ATGWU 8,000, IWWU 3,000 (*Voice of Labour*, 16 January 1926).

In 1925 five Organisers—Houston, McCarthy, Metcalfe, O'Doherty and Vennard—addressed the Conference. By 1930 no Organisers were employed among a greatly diminished staff. In November 1927 staff wages were cut by 10s and some Officials, including Frank Robbins and Thomas O'Reilly, put under notice. Vennard complained that a meeting of all full-time Officials and Delegates should have been called before any NEC decisions.

George Spain, long-serving Secretary of Dublin No. 3 Branch, was suspended over financial irregularities. The Branch Secretary, J. C. Flanagan, was dealt 'drastically with' in April 1928 for persistently defying Branch and NEC authority.

Archie Heron's resignation from 1 December 1928 was 'accepted with regret.' He became General Secretary of the Civil Service Clerical Association. His position as Financial Secretary was abolished. In January 1929 ITGWU clerks in Cork were put on week-about work, and the Senior Clerk, Prior, was 'offered one year's wages to retire.'5

Membership fell from 50,984 in 1925 to 14,608 1930. In Dublin city and county it collapsed from 18,538, 36% of the total membership, to 6,074, 42%. The WUI in 1930 claimed 16,909 members, which, if taken at face value, made it nearly three times bigger than the ITGWU in Dublin.

The ITGWU was increasingly desperate for members. Not all were worth having, however. In October 1925 'Two Classes' were identified in every union: 'the useful and the useless.' ITGWU members were asked, 'To which class do you belong?' This was an invitation to stand up and be counted. The questions have never lost their relevance.

> The useful class consists of those members who know what they ought to do and do it.
>
> The useless class consists of drones and those who do nothing at all to advance the interest of the organisation, but whine spitefully against those who do something.
>
> The useless class claims that it alone is right—all others are dishonest, selfish, obstinate or blind. To meet the arguments of the useless class the union is fortunate that there is a useful class—the pushers—that army of conscientious, patient, unknown, practically unrewarded persons whose best years and strength, intelligence and knowledge have been devoted to perfecting their organisation and bringing about the solidarity of the organised workers.
>
> Moral—'Be a pusher in place of a do-nothing, fault-finder and knocker. Assist to organise, federate and educate the workers.'

Table 17: ITGWU income, expenditure and surplus (£), 1918–29

	Income	Expenditure	Surplus (deficit)
1918	27,699	18,986	8,713
1919	74,726	63,379	11,346
1920	100,011	62,848	37,163
1921	81,584	45,596	35,997
1922	96,007	64,506	31,501
1923	84,122	160,427	(76,305)
1924	50,137	40,417	9,270
1925	32,880	36,883	(4,003)
1926	27,182	24,617	2,565
1927	21,292	19,231	2,062
1928	17,866	14,783	3,083
1929	17,368	14,506	2,862

Source: ITGWU, Annual Reports, 1918–29.

The ITGWU required not just new members but useful ones. In May 1926, feeling confident that Larkin's threat was diminishing, the *Voice of Labour* published a 'Conversation between two "Old Reliables"'.

> Mick was standing with his back to Liberty Hall door, and Bill came along.
>
> Bill—Good evening, Mike.

Mike—Good evening, Bill.

Bill—This is like the old times (referring to the Union) being back in Liberty Hall.

Mike—Yes, only a hundred times better. All the bosses are gone. It is a pleasure to come here now—civility and business is the motto.

Bill—Yes, its great alright. It is worth the trouble in that respect. Men have started to think for themselves, and are finding out it's to their own interests to be civil and courteous. It gets them further in the end.[6]

It concluded:

This is the spirit. We want a Union of thinkers and workers working for their own and their comrades' benefit. No bitterness. No hate. Every man with his shoulder to the wheel. Get it back to 1923, with the memory of what we have learned for the past three years always before us.

Numerically, the ITGWU suffered badly, but the quality of those remaining was unquestionable.

Table 18: ITGWU membership, May 1925 and May 1930

1925		1930	
Antrim, Cavan, Down, Longford	2,105	Belfast	996
Carlow-Kilkenny	1,018	Carlow, Kilkenny, Wexford, Wicklow	522
Connacht and Clare	2,013	Clare, Galway, Kerry, Roscommon	459
Cork city	6,070	Cork city	2,345
Cork county	3,082	Cork county	415
Dublin No. 1	8,082	Dublin No. 1 (2,809) and 5 (250)	3,059
Dublin No. 2	1,010	Dublin No. 2 (48) and 3 (911)	959
Dublin No. 3 and 7	4,121	Dublin No. 4	1,010
Dublin No. 4	1,254	Dublin No. 7	411
Dublin No. 5	1,013	Dublin county	635
Dublin county	3,058	Kildare, Laois, Meath, Offaly	503
Kerry	1,069	Limerick city	1,136
Kildare	2,359	Limerick county, Tipperary, Waterford	500
Laois-Offaly	2,008	Louth (266), Westmeath (302)	568
Limerick city and county	4,020	Mayo (268), Sligo (295)	563
Louth	1,002	Newry 527	

Meath	1,315		
Tipperary	1,074		
Waterford and Wexford	2,004		
Westmeath	1,071		
Wexford	2,031		
Total	50,984	Total	14,608
Delegates	49	Delegates	29

Source: ITGWU, minutes of National Executive Council, 22 May 1925 and 9 May 1930. These figures were those used to allocate Delegates to the annual Delegate Conference.

1930 figures: Carlow 56, Kilkenny 233, Wexford 117, Wicklow 116, Clare 74, Galway 23, Kerry 357, Roscommon 5, Limerick county 106, Tipperary 194, Waterford 200.

FORAN AND FATHER ALBERT

Foran was absent from work on a number of occasions in 1925 and 1926. O'Brien explained that the unostentatious 'father' of the union seldom spoke 'about himself.' From the union's foundation, through the traumas of 1913 and 1916 and 'internal troubles . . . the strain had been very great on his health. He might not be able to work as much as he had in the past.' He recovered but was weary.

Father Albert, former Church Street Capuchin, died 'in exile' in February 1925. He was remembered by the ITGWU 'with an especial gratitude for the interest he took in its progress and the help he gave in his own quiet way when help was needed.' When 'Conscription menaced' in 1918 he was the Catholic clergyman with whom Foran secreted £1,000 in cash of 'our fighting funds.' It 'could not have been put in safer hands' and 'was a measure of their confidence in him.' He assisted the ITGWU and Labour Party in mobilising for peace after 1916, and 'when the Four Courts went up in flames and the great tragedy of the Civil War' opened, he 'worked with indefatigable zeal and heroic courage to stop the strife and effect a settlement.'

The sudden death of the stalwart Charles Gaule, Arklow, in December 1925 shocked all. He was the 'very soul of humour and geniality' and 'a favourite amongst all the workers who knew him.' His funeral was massive. The death of the Liberty Hall caretaker, Peter Ennis, in St Vincent's Hospital in January 1927 came 'after an illness of some months.' Only with great reluctance had he gone to York Street after the closure of the Hall. More than 3,000 people, including members of the 'Old Guard', attended his funeral, led by the union Band.[7]

WOMEN

There were 5,000 women members out of a total of 100,000 in 1920. By 1930 women accounted for 1,100 out of 14,680. After 1925 women were a conspicuous presence at union rallies; at annual Delegate Conferences they were virtually invisible. Tom Kennedy thought there was a 'need for a Woman Organiser' in May 1929. Margaret O'Donnell, 'who had been employed for some time as a part-time Official' in Dublin No. 4 Branch, was suggested. As organising staffs were cut and financial crisis deepened, she was never appointed.[8] There was no suggestion of equal pay or equality.

BATTLES WITH THE WUI

In January 1925 the *Voice of Labour* delighted in Larkin's bankruptcy proceedings. He admitted giving no money to the ITGWU from the $2,000 he had on his return from America. He sent £200 for prisoners' relief to Belfast and 'lived off the rest.' It was suggested that he earned income from Dublin Rapid Transit Company and from dealing in soap, sardines and coal, as there was 'no I.W.L. co-op.' A further £200 came from the WUI Sustentation Fund and Freedom Fund. £1,000 was spent on the *Irish Worker,* which ceased publication. It was an Irish Worker League publication rather than one of the WUI.

Apart from discrediting Larkin, the ITGWU intended WUI readers to see themselves as dupes. Material from this and Daly's failed action were published in pamphlet form. In reply to Larkin's coal importing, a 'hotch-potch trio of Civic Guards, Larkinism and Coal Ring' attempted to prevent ITGWU imports 'direct from our mining comrades.' As the *Deansgate* berthed in Wicklow Harbour, 'cheers of welcome drowned the rattling of the chains and the noise of the engines.' There 'opened up for the workers of Ireland much more than a defeat of the Disruptionist element in Wicklow, much more than the fulfilling of a promise that the Transport Union would deliver the goods.'

James Everett and John Conroy were arrested, while Joe Metcalfe was knocked unconscious. WUI coal was allegedly dearer than that in the 'Transport Union Store.' Accounts show that the ITGWU 'Wicklow Coal Depot' ran at a loss of £311 18s 3d.[9]

On Wednesday 19 August came the decisive battle. Transport Union men in coal yards 'took steps to end the tyranny of the Larkin Family Organisation in the coal trade by presenting themselves for work in the ordinary course' after a Lock-Out by the Coal Merchants' Association, which decided that it would work with one union but not with both. Larkin ordered WUI men not to work with ITGWU men. Newman's sacked ITGWU men if they refused to join the WUI. This was followed in Robinson's and tried in Sheridan's. When ITGWU men refused, Larkin pulled out all his men, and the Coal Merchants' Association responded with a general Lock-Out. The ITGWU stressed that at no time were wages or working conditions an issue. In 'the ordinary course of affairs there was, and is, no trade dispute.' The 'only issue was, and is,' whether WUI members 'are to refuse at Larkin's dictation' to work with ITGWU members. No other question was raised.

When ITGWU men turned up for work they were subject to 'bitter and violent attacks.' Gangs visited homes, 'smashing up furniture.' Liberty Hall appealed to old emotions: 'What the employers failed to do in 1913 Larkin and his bullies will fail to do in 1923. The I.T.G.W.U. will go on.' Accused of scabbery by Larkin, ITGWU men cleared twenty backlogged boats. WUI men visited the homes of those working and offered Strike Pay from Unity Hall. Liberty Hall congratulated those who resisted 'on their courage and determination—and above all on their own good sense.'

As to the Unity Coal Company, 31 Marlborough Street and 17 High Street, coal workers were asked, 'Is the Russian Army behind you? You were told it is. Is it true? Nonsense! Wake up and see who and what is behind you, and unmask the ghoul.'

When Larkin gained support from British unions the ITGWU placed notices in the *Daily Herald* and *Sunday Worker*.

WARNING TO UNIONS
Working-class organisations are warned that there is no trade dispute in the coal trade in Dublin, and that no question of wages or conditions is at issue.

No collections in furtherance of any alleged strike or Lock-Out is authorised by any recognised Trade Union affiliated to the Irish Labour Party and Trades Union Congress, and our comrades in Great Britain are requested not to supply funds to any individual or body attempting to disrupt working-class solidarity in Ireland.

It was signed by Foran, Kennedy, O'Brien and Heron on behalf of the NEC. The *Daily Herald* published the notice, but the *Sunday Worker*, 'which claims to be a Left Wing organ and has from time to time printed misleading statements about the movement in Ireland, refused.' The ITGWU complained that it 'did not fail to participate in the campaign of disruption which the Larkin gang conducted under the auspices of the Workers International Relief (W.I.R.). But it won't publish the truth when sent by the I.T.G.W.U.' It would 'do nothing to save British working-class money from being wasted in a futile attempt to smash the I.T.G.W.U.' and Irish Labour movement solidarity. Under the heading 'The Tin Cans Go Round Again', the President of the WUI, John Lawlor, claimed the WIR paid 5s to locked-out WUI men, angering the ITGWU.

The locked-out dupes and victims of Larkinism are not fighting for better wages or conditions. They are not fighting the employers. They are fighting James Larkin's lost battle for control of the I.T.G.W.U. and for his personal dictatorship over the masses of Irish workers.

The ITGWU won the day. Men desperate for work tired of inter-union bickering, and 'quite a collection of cards, badges and other emblems of the W.U.I.' accumulated 'at York Street and other Branches of the O.B.U.' By November it was claimed that the 'high priest of the disruptionists' had 'failed in his "mission" to smash' the ITGWU. He had 'now gone into business as a coal merchant,' trading as 'Unity Coal Company—some unity! Some coal company!'

The Agreement between the ITGWU and the Coal Merchants' Association was for 1s 5¼d per ton, with a winchman at 17s a day, two singers-out at 15s and a guy-hauler at 15s. However, 'Big Noise's outfit pays the tonnage rate alone, which means that four extra men have got to share in the divide,' and the WUI breached the Port Agreement on hours. When men complain of being diddled in this shameless manner the mighty ruler of the earth answers with a flourish, 'h'it's orlright boys, you just carry on and remember h'it's your own coal.' Needless to say, the unfortunate slaves keep scabbing it for the would-be coal king, as the only alternative to starvation.

In Carter's and Goulding's wuɪ men were replaced by ɪᴛɢwu men. Sensing a decisive moment in the battle, the ɪᴛɢwu adopted the slogan 'Back to Liberty Hall.'

> The old building whose name has been the very symbol of the ɪ.ᴛ.ɢ.w.u. since Connolly's days—is a hive of Union activity. It has become the centre and rallying-ground for the Union forces which are defeating Larkin at every point and on every front.

Members were in possession of the Hall, and Dock and Coal Sections carried on 'as vigorously as in the old days.' John O'Neill, Secretary of No. 1 Branch, was on duty. There was 'no need to tell the dockers, carters and coalmen about John. He is almost an institution in the Branch.' This contrasted with 'Disunity Hall', where 'well they know where Liberty Hall is. They know what it stands for. They know it was their bulwark and their defence in the years that are gone.' Then, most tellingly, workers were reminded, 'through it they can find work, and wages and food.' On Thursday 5 November the wuɪ sought work and pledged it would do so alongside ɪᴛɢwu men. But it was not to be that simple.

> Perhaps they were of the opinion that they only had to walk in at the front door to witness the men who replaced them in consequence of their own folly retreating at the back, but not so. Much as we regret that any Section of the Dublin workers would suffer, even when their sufferings are the result of their own foolishness and disloyalty to the Labour movement, we must insist that these men who have borne the brunt of the battle for the past few months and stood loyally by their organisation, will not be victimised in the interests of those who permitted themselves to be used in an attempt to smash Trade Union organisation on the quays of Dublin. We bear no grudge or ill-will towards our misguided fellow-workers and we sincerely hope that they will be shortly working side by side with our members, but our first duty is to secure the position of those who have, by their loyalty and good sense, saved the docks of Dublin for trade unionism.

Lawlor spoke instead of Larkin at the weekly Beresford Place meeting. It was rumoured that the Unity Coal Company was collapsing. The ɪᴛɢwu said that applications for 're-entry would be sympathetically heard.' McGettrick and Son, South Quay, threatened to cut their rates by engaging wuɪ men according to an Agreement of 1925 between the Stevedores' Association and the wuɪ for lower rates. The 'Old Reliables Section' (Carters) met in Liberty Hall, regretted any disloyalty and decided on minimum entrance fees.

In February 1927 Dublin carters asked for wage cuts of 3s, reductions in overtime rates and longer hours. The ITGWU boasted, 'From the early days' in 'every city in Ireland the carters were one of the best fighting Sections of the Union. Whoever thinks they will lie down now under the blow of this, is under-rating the spirit of the carters and laying a heap of troubles for his business.' The 'Old Reliables' were urged:

> Carters! Get Ready! Strengthen anybody in your ranks who may not realise everything this could mean! Workers of Dublin! Rally to the Carters! They are again in the vanguard of Dublin's fighters!

It would be difficult, as 3s was lost in 1926 through disorganisation and disunity.

John Lynch, former Secretary of the Sligo Branch, Gleeson, an ITGWU dissident from Nenagh and James Mitchell, former President of the Irish Automobile Drivers' Union and an ITGWU Section member were members of the General Executive Council of the WUI in May 1925, along with Ciarán J. King, Treasurer, a former Liberty Hall employee.[10] Few of these figures remained long in office. By 1930 the two unions co-existed, if not happily. On the ground, members, Shop Stewards and Officials got on with practicalities.

CONGRESS AND TRADES COUNCIL

In Newry in 1925 William O'Brien chaired the Congress. He recalled the 'lessons and effects of the War,' rising prices and economic pressures that brought 'thousands of new members, many never previously organised, on land as well as in factory.' From 1916, 'whilst there was no "organic connection," there was a "mutual association" of labour and national movements.' After 1921, however, working people were

> neither invited nor allowed to share in the gathering of the fruits . . . By that time, while Labour had been recognised as a very useful ally by both sections of the Irish negotiators, it was made plain that it was not entitled to independent judgement or action.

Labour played no part in the Treaty negotiations, 'discreditable' or 'creditable.' In the Civil War 'we did not throw our Unions into the vortex.' He spoke proudly of Labour unity and indivisibility but, as if he were in no way connected with events, bemoaned the 'campaign of disruption which for the past two years has been waged against the largest of our affiliated organisations.' He railed against unemployment, inadequate housing, emigration, and the effectiveness of tariff protection. There could be no solution under capitalism.

The ITGWU presence at the Congress was a declining one. Managing retreat is always difficult. With few signs of improvement, the Congress created a gloomy image. The ITGWU felt it a 'pity' that P. T. Daly was elected Secretary of the reunited Dublin Trades Council in 1928. It briefly withdrew but came back into the fold and remained an affiliate, if not a very active one. Daly was free to rebuild his reputation as a diligent and effective Secretary.[11]

DISPUTES

In 1925 economic circumstances 'prevented anything in the nature of a general offensive on wages.' Effort was confined to a 'defence of conditions and Agreements already won.' Many cuts were resisted or mitigated as 'employers were quick to realise that the Union was again in a position to pull its weight' and did not tempt a strike. Nearly all engagements were defensive. The ITGWU had sufficient financial resources to sustain action, and compromises were quickly struck. A mere £7,117 was spent on Dispute Pay. 'Economy' measures adopted by local authorities had an effect on road workers. A twin defence was mounted by the ITGWU and Labour Party Councillors, but 'unfortunately, too many road workers were indifferent to their own interests,' so weakening the strategy.

In Hobb's of Trim a strike was broken when 'scabs were all given w.u.i. cards.' In May the ITGWU thought 'there are good signs, eagerly watched for, as it has been a perpetual and painful struggle against reductions since the end of 1920 . . . But, looking back, we can truly say this pride is ours—we fought every inch of ground yielded, and retained most of what our attackers sought.' The 'intensity of the struggle' was gauged by the fact that finances were 'wracked off at a rate of £1,000 per week' in Strike Pay alone. 'Tot it up and you will see that the total works out at the enormous sum of £260,000. And still we have shekels galore for our members, and kicks *quantum sufficio* for our enemies.'

Table 19: ITGWU Dispute Pay, 1918–29

	Income (£)	Dispute Benefit (£)	As proportion of income (%)
1918	27,699	8,407	30.4
1919	74,726	40,571	54.3
1920	100,011	36,847	37.1
1921	81,593	20,409	44.1
1922	96,007	33,139	32.8
1923	84,122	128,724	153.0
1924	50,137	10,906	21.8
1925	32,880	7,117	21.7
1926	27,182	3,042	12.3
1927	21,292	2,445	11.5
1928	17,866	989	5.5
1929	17,386	1,276	7.3

Source: ITGWU, Annual Reports, 1918–29.

Agriculture suffered badly. The ITGWU rallied its diminishing troops by reminding them that 'even in these days of the most acute agricultural depression, good organisation and thorough preparedness, if they cannot wring new gains from the farmers, they can compel the signing again of the wage and hour Agreements of the previous year.' Attempts to reduce membership contributions for farm workers were defeated at the 1926 Annual Delegate Conference. Different classes of membership existed within the Rules. The agricultural disputes of 1923 left the ITGWU badly bitten. Farm workers would have to take their chances. Economising in local authorities resulted in a nationwide attack on road workers' terms.

A 'very unwelcome' feature was the 'hostile attention' to pickets and Organisers from the police, especially in the Metropole Cinema dispute and in Tralee during Urban Council and mineral water strikes. Organisers, thought to be acting within their legal rights, were arrested. This demonstrated that 'in this country, as elsewhere, the legal rights for which Trade Union pioneers fought so hard are in constant danger from attack by the employing class and the forces of the State.' A strenuous fight would be needed 'lest the rights won in the past be filched from us.' J. P. Hughes (Kilrush) condemned 'in the strongest and most emphatic manner' attempts by 'law officers of the Irish Free State to assist employers in forcing employees to accept reductions . . . by directing illegal prosecutions' against trade unionists 'engaged in peaceful picketing.'   Magistrates and judges simply ignored the Trade Disputes Act (1906). At a strike in Sutton Sandpit, Dublin, the Association of Ex-Officers and Men of the National Army Trade Union supplied scabs. This Association had been formed at the Shannon Hydro-electric Scheme as a strikebreaking body. Ultimately, the WUI accepted the reduced rates.

There was a 'great fight in Tralee' after the sacking of the Branch President, McCrohan, from the Urban District Council's gas works. Despite his long service and an Agreement that 'McCrohan is a master of his craft, and cannot be excelled by any other smith in the District,' he was dismissed. It was an attempt to break the union and facilitate cuts. A fudged settlement emerged in August, with McCrohan back on the payroll but not before an Organiser, Séamus O'Brien, and McCrohan were detained in Limerick Jail.

A strike among Galway builders' labourers began on 20 November. Employers tried to enlist an 'English Union', but matters were settled. In the Carlow sugar plant a question was raised about the union 'entering into a bond providing against a stoppage of work without notice,' a suggestion apparently agreed to by Kennedy.[12]

In 1927 demands for cuts were felt among road, building and creamery workers, carters and dockers, flour-mill workers and maltsters, woollen mills, bacon and egg stores and groceries. A lengthy strike took place at Blarney and Navan Woollen Mills; Co. Meath road workers resisted cuts; and Cork dock employers were prevented from breaching the national Agreement. The ITGWU pledged not to support those striking contrary to the Agreement with the Flour Milling Association.

A marked success was the National Roads Scheme, which raised wages and improved conditions. Closed-shop Agreements were enforced by strikes. Some

Officials were 'prosecuted for dealing effectively with slackers,' actions successfully defended in the Courts.

In 1928 the ITGWU slogan was 'Standard wages and conditions and nothing less.' Defence dominated over offence. Praise was given to Kilrush and Limerick flour millers, who held on to hard-won holidays and other benefits, renewing old Agreements after a struggle. This led to the sector's national reorganisation. In bacon-curing a Council for Munster Factories was re-established in 1929.

In April 1929 Glynn's of Kilrush, flour merchants, would not honour the National Flour Mill Agreement. They made men work on Good Friday, and there was a strike. When Glynn's ship arrived in Limerick on Wednesday 3 March, dockers 'promptly refused to handle the stuff.' The vessel was unloaded by Glynn's own men, brought from Kilrush. Limerick merchants said they would continue to supply Glynn's. Men in Banntyne's struck, and all three Limerick flour mills lay idle, with the men out. Kennedy addressed men in the ITGWU Hall. The Mayor, Michael Keyes, secured agreement that on their return the men would not handle Glynn's materials. Foran addressed Dublin's flour mill Section, which pledged 'moral and financial support' to Limerick.

A Ministry of Labour Conference, attended by Foran, Kennedy and Frank Robbins, agreed to maintain twelve days' holidays. The employment of non-union men would be followed by an immediate stoppage. At Easter, dissatisfied with the ATGWU's refusal 'to take any action' for restoration of the town wage, members in Killarney 'transferred . . . en masse.' All firms complied with the new demand from Monday 8 April. On Monday 15 April the 'largest Labour demonstration held in Killarney for several years' supported the men, addressed by John Murphy, former MP, and Cathal O'Shannon. The Killarney Workingmen's Band, 'which has not attended any public meeting since 1922,' paraded the town. Five shillings was secured for Hilliard's boot factory.[13]

THE SHANNON SCHEME

The 'unromantic title' of the Shannon Scheme—the building of a large hydro-electric station on the River Shannon at Ardnacrusha, Co. Clare—was welcomed by the ITGWU. It would 'revolutionise economic and social conditions throughout Ireland.' This 'bold and audacious scheme,' were it 'in the hands of a working-class Government,' would benefit the 'whole State in such a manner as to create a new and more wholesome social order.' But it was controlled by a 'non-Labour Ministry,' deriving 'power and support from capitalist sources,' which was 'inclined to infect this measure with germs of great danger to a working-class Ireland.

Labour on the scheme was employed on conditions 'contrary to practice in all Government contracts, and in direct breach of promises made before work.' All union Rules, conditions and wage rates were ignored. 'Every attempt' was made by the ITGWU and Limerick Trades Council to force compliance, 'but without success.' Contractors were backed by the Government. A Special Congress for general, transport and engineering unions decided upon a boycott. It signally failed and was abandoned. Unorganised, unemployed and desperate men were recruited to work, despite big demonstrations held throughout the country and ITGWU newspaper advertisements castigating the wages offered. An entrenched Government was happy to 'enforce starvation wages.'

The dispute lingered into 1926, with no success. The ITGWU thought this due to the 'type of worker employed on the Scheme,' the huge army of unemployed and the strong position of the Government in the Oireachtas. There was an obvious conclusion: 'Wages and conditions on this great undertaking still remain the blackest feature in the recent industrial history of this country', which is 'not likely to be removed until Labour has become much stronger, both on the political and industrial fields.' A big meeting at Parteen on Sunday 18 April 'bitterly expressed' discontent against poor wages, food, hours and conditions. The 'bullying' by many German gaffers, employed directly by Siemens-Schuckert, and their 'sucks' among the higher-paid Irish workers extended as far as physical 'persuasion to sweat more by working harder.' Large numbers tried to join the ITGWU. The employer confused matters by dealing with the yellow Association of Ex-Officers and Men and other 'cod' organisations. The Secretary of the ITGWU Limerick Branch, Seán Connolly, the Organiser Séamus O'Brien, Clare Labour TD Pádraig Hogan and Cathal O'Shannon all undertook organising duties. In July, 300 to 400 men were sacked every week without notice and ordered to clear their huts at once.

In 1927 'huge numbers of men, forced by hunger,' were still 'willing to take up work on any terms.' After the German management increased wages to 8½d an hour, enabling workers to earn 'nearly £2 after fifty-five hours,' the ITGWU called off its boycott. There 'was little else it could do, so many thousands being idle.' Many arrived in Ardnacrusha and Clonlara with 'scarcely a boot on their foot and not a penny in their pocket.'

In the early summer of 1926 Dan Morrissey, Labour TD, addressed huge meetings. A 2,2000-strong Branch was founded, and 'soon the familiar Union badge with the Red Hand was to be seen everywhere.' Conditions improved, but not wages. At the 1927 ITUC the ITGWU called for the withdrawal of a 'regulation enforcing a maximum wage in connection with road construction financed by Government grants.' It removed an 'anomaly of using the authority of the State to compel' local authorities and contractors 'to pay starvation wages in contravention of the spirit of the Fair Wages Clause.' The effects of the Shannon Scheme were felt throughout the country.[14]

THE METROPOLE

The Metropole Restaurant in O'Connell Street, Dublin, opened in 1921. There was constant friction with an oft-changing management. In July 1925 an unofficial strike was supported by casuals. Although the ITGWU 'took disciplinary action . . . none of the unofficial strikers were allowed back.' The restaurant closed, determined to become a 'black shop'. Pressure was applied to the Hotel, Restaurant and Catering Association to break its Agreement with the ITGWU. The Metropole reopened with a smaller staff, some non-union but none employed through the union, a 'direct breach of the regulations' made in 1918. Those attending a union meeting were threatened with dismissal. The *Voice of Labour* observed that 'this is the wisdom and strength of a petty little imitator of Queen Elizabeth who is masquerading as manageress—a dictator who has caused more trouble in the Metropole than all the Dublin managers combined.'

A Lock-Out began on 7 July at one o'clock, and pickets were placed. It was alleged that only 'members of Larkin's so-called Workers' Union' defied the pickets. Edward Foley, a 'well-known Unity Hall supporter', helped unload a mineral-water lorry. He had been an operator in the Carlton Cinema and tried to get the staff there to secede to the wui. The itgwu Organisers Ridgway and O'Shannon were arrested and were charged with intimidation. The union published details of the Metropole directors and a 'Black List' of scabs, their names and addresses providing few hiding places.[15]

Ridgway was arrested again on 10 July by police who were 'ignorant of the law affecting trade disputes, or else they are trying deliberately to override it.' Union humour was unabated. 'Last week the picture at the Metropole Cinema was *The Broken Law*. This week it is *The Silent Watcher*. Coincidences are interesting.' The union was derisive of the scabs.

> Little boys and women employed in this palatial restaurant at work formerly carried out by men. Dressmakers, laundry workers, married women with husbands working are the material which at present comprise the Blackleg Staff. Yet withal, not half a dozen genuine customers have entered the place this past week. The Dublin public and Dublin's visitors are wholeheartedly supporting those on strike, and the method employed is to refuse to enter the scab-controlled premises.

There was 'sour milk by the gallon, cream gone wrong and eggs getting fusty' while No. 4 Branch's marquee at Portmarnock, the Silver Strand, was going strong. It offered weekend visitors 'a good tea, and a good cause, killing two birds with one stone.'

On Friday 24 July 700 hotel and restaurant workers met in the Rotunda. A majority of fifty-six were against extending the strike throughout the city. Apart from the cost, it was probably felt that such action would not sufficiently affect the Metropole management. Worse, it might encourage others to follow suit. Apologies were offered to Letitia O'Brien, 'mentioned last week.' She was 'not a scab,' and 'we desire to apologise for any trouble caused her or her family by reason of the publication of above, and we are glad to be able to state that the family is opposed to scabbery.'

By September a weekly collection was taken up for the Metropole fighters. In October an attack on a worker presented the itgwu with great moral ammunition. The assault stemmed from bad meat being used and resulted in a prosecution under hygiene regulations. The *Voice of Labour* warned clergy and 'members of the Jewish community' about crossing the picket lines. They stressed that there was neither anti-clericalism nor racism in their appeal. Undeterred, the management remained bloody-minded and insistent on giving not an inch until the end of the year.

Christmas 'stirred many to contribute to the Fighting Fund,' with John Conroy heading the list. 'In his card are the names of many saints and also that of the aristocracy. This is not due to his wandering into strange realms but to the response which the dockers employed on the boats named made.' More than £355 was raised.

Cryptic messages suggested a possible breakthrough in January 1926; but it was to 'be War to the end,' as the directors overruled the business managers. Members were urged:

> Never mind their big pictures and their foreign Bands, imported to help fill an empty ballroom; the fight has to go on; that is the directors' decision; and as far as possible every worker and every lover of justice has a part to play in seeing that the fight goes on, until victory is won.

Some dances were held, and foreign musicians took the places of local ones. The directors tried bringing in big names: Charlie Chaplin's *Gold Rush* and the celebrated Jack Hylton Band. The ITGWU observed that Chaplin 'in his sympathy with the workers never thought that his work might be used to attempt to break a strike; it is not the sort of compliment he would seek.' The public stayed away, despite slashed admission prices. It was clear that 'men will be prepared to lose money rather than do the right thing.' Bective Rangers, Palmerston, Monkstown, Clontarf and Catholic University School rugby clubs had no qualms about strike-breaking, although 'decent clubs have refrained' or went elsewhere. Lennox Robinson (dramatist and Abbey Theatre producer) and W. B. Yeats found Chaplin irresistible. 'They didn't see or hear the pickets. How could they, poor dears? It's enough to drive one to write a play or a poem. Perhaps next week we will.'

A sensation was caused when two members of the Jack Hylton Metro-Gnomes Band were mysteriously kidnapped and abandoned in the Wicklow Mountains. It discouraged other British Bands, whoever was responsible. The Ireland-France rugby international teams ignored the post-match dinner in the Metropole and attended an event at Clery's instead, a coup for the ITGWU. Suggestions that charges against Ridgway might be dropped if pickets were removed merely underlined their usefulness.

In May the employers played their last card: a yellow union, the Hotel Employees' Association, 'organised and controlled by employers for the maintenance of a Free Labour Bureau.' It was bedevilled by internal strife and failed miserably in what became known as the Five Houses dispute.

At the 1926 ITUC Foran registered 'emphatic protest against the repeated interference of the responsible authorities with the right to picket.' Seventeen members had been arrested. On one occasion the State Prosecutor approached the picketers' defence solicitors and told them that the prosecution would be dropped if pickets were lifted.

In June the Metropole battle had waged for a year. The manager, Madame Delasur, had gone, but there were suggestions of more vigorous management tactics. Defiantly, the *Voice of Labour* stated:

> The fight is still on and we face the second year confident of a settlement which will prove creditable to the men and women whose sacrifice has set an example which, if copied by the workers generally, would make the Labour movement irresistible.

In August, Jack Payne's Band, 'under a very considerable escort,' came to play. The ITGWU remarked that the 'fee may be a fat one, but it takes a lot to compensate a man for allowing a policeman to sleep upon his doorstep.' They felt 'sure the ratepayers will be delighted to know their money is going to uphold the stubbornness of the directors.'

Not for the first time, Horse Show Week was a flash-point. A 'long line of police, plain-clothes men, Superintendents, Inspectors, sergeants and cycle scouts' stretched from the ITGWU offices to the Metropole. Many pickets were arrested. Some sinister boards reading 'La Grève au Metropole' ('Strike at the Metropole') were confiscated; those hurling stones, pennies and abuse at pickets were not interfered with.

Victory finally came just before Christmas 1926. Kennedy told a rally in the La Scala that the fight 'had shown employers what their members could do, and how this Union could maintain a dispute no matter for what period it was prolonged.' Great pride was taken in an important victory that defeated a yellow union and maintained recognition. It drew a line in the sand and cast the Hotel and Restaurant Branch as the union's flagship. It would lead the fleet in a yet-unseen revival.

Ironically, the NEC, concerned about the costs of what was seemingly an unwinnable contest, had decided that the dispute 'be closed before the end of the current year.' It was well that it did not. Ridgway's Branch Annual Report declared:

> We started the year 1926 with the Branch a rather weak, some thought, dying patient. We finished, I am glad to say, stronger and better than even the most optimistic thought possible, and that was achieved by the staunch loyalty and united effort of the men and women, young and old, who not only believed in the right, but were prepared to make sacrifices for it . . . The Metropole strike, after an eighteen months' struggle, finished up just prior to Christmas. Looking back over this struggle, one can admire the endurance of those who for long weary days maintained the picketing in all weathers, and appreciate the generous actions of the workers who contributed to the Metropole and Unemployed Fund, the totals received during the year amounting to over £200. That in the second year of a dispute is something of a record. And those who contributed even a little will, we feel, have not contributed in vain.

Morale was boosted by the hotly contested Cinema and Hotels Football League, with many League of Ireland players showing their midweek paces.[16]

THE FIVE HOUSES DISPUTE

In 1926 Dublin hotel employers established a new union and employment bureau, the Hotel Employees' Association, 'for the purpose of superseding this Union.' The ITGWU felt that strikes were 'not desirable at the moment.' Depression bred scabs, and the ten-week dispute with the Hotel Employees' Association was a crucial test.

At 6 p.m. on Saturday 26 June staff in the Moira, Wicklow, Dolphin, Central and Grosvenor Hotels came out. The press said it was business as usual, and replacement staffs were found. Of 166 ITGWU members, 166 came out, although 'tears were shed as the staffs passed out, and sincerely shed, for there is between Hotel staffs and their management a link which does not exist in other commercial undertakings.' It said 'much for the staffs in such circumstances that their loyalty to their Union stood the test.' Strikers paraded outside the hotels and the Employees' Association offices at 18 Duke Street. Members included 'Swiss, German and French comrades.'

> Seldom will one find a more perfect international comradeship than that of the Hotel workers these days. Here you clasp the hand of men from other countries, strangers in our land, but ready to share in the risks of the fight and risk their all in a cause they believe in. There is in these things an inspiration to go on and take more and more of their share of the responsibility in the progressive movement of this country.

Agreements of eight or nine years' standing were revoked and union recognition withdrawn; but 'within three days the employers had capitulated.' The settlement was 'better in several respects' than the old one. The dispute reverberated favourably for the ITGWU for decades. It was a credit to the 'value of skilful and well-directed organisation.' Committees were established in the Five Houses, as the Branch determined never again to be outflanked.

In January 1929 hotel workers got a two-week temporary contract for Horse Show Week through an employment agency and paid a fee of 5s. Work lasted twelve weeks, and the agency tried to charge an additional 1s per week and would not hand over the workers' references, preventing them getting other jobs. A civil Bill was issued against the agency for damages. It was lost, as the agency showed a clause referring to the 5s and 'any further charges that may be made.' Dublin No. 4 Branch suggested that hotel and restaurant workers throughout Ireland should be organised, with a General Officer in charge. All Branches were 'instructed to do their part,' and legislation was drafted to cover conditions in the catering trade. The 1926 Agreement was enforced and in 1929 was improved. Organisation extended beyond Dublin.

The 'outstanding success in 1929' was in the Savoy Cinema, Dublin, where, although non-union applicants were 'so many that the police had to regulate the queues,' the ITGWU compelled the employer to pay the highest cinema rates in the country and 'employ none but Union labour through the Union.' This was 'one of the most successful trade union victories in recent years.'[17] Hotel and cinema workers were unexpected shock troops for union recovery.

AGRICULTURAL WORKERS

At Oola, Co. Limerick, on Sunday 14 December 1924 some 'cycled over twenty-five miles' to meet the Organiser Paddy O'Doherty. Creamery workers were at the 'limit of human endurance.' They 'carried on essential services in the worst days of the Tan terror' but were 'now slowly starving—aye, in the festive season of Christmas.' They demanded, 'on behalf of all unemployed,' work 'at living rates of pay for all, irrespective of their political creed or partisan services.'

In 1925 Sligo Trades Council suggested that steps be taken to embrace 'those hard-working and badly-paid individuals, the small farmers with uneconomic holdings.' The 'undemocratic and reactionary' policy of the Free State and Northern Ireland Governments in replacing local authorities with paid Commissioners was condemned. Jim Hickey pointed out that Commissioners on a salary of £20 a week were declaring that £2 14s was enough for any man to live on. Archie Heron saw it as replacement of democracy by dictatorship.

Road workers in Co. Meath would not join the union. They felt that 'nine Labour Councillors will look after them.' The ITGWU's response was one that many frustrated Officials can identify with. 'They think of the Union as a glorified sausage machine. They drop their tanner [6d] in at one end, and expect a substantial and immediate return in a material form to drop out at the other end.'

The 'Knocklong Treaty' was broken when the rate guaranteed to 1 March 1926, after a dispute in August 1925, was cut in February by Cleeve's, owned by an English firm, Lovell and Christmas. The Managing Director—a Cumann na nGaedheal TD—dismissed union men and replaced them with non-union workers, resulting in a lightning strike. In an amazing development 'he had Barry ready—Tom Barry, the famous militarist patriot (Republican) who began his martial career as a British Tommy, and now purposes to finish it as a White Guard in the service of the English capitalists and under the supervision of a Free State T.D.' Barry was commissioned to organise 500 scabs and 'brags he will vanquish all the Reds in Knocklong.' This 'latest campaign of Commandant Tom Barry' the union thought 'unfitting of a soldier of his reputation.' He was, after all, 'waging war' against the miserably paid employees of the Condensed Milk Company. Barry, 'this gallant' soldier,' was 'not averse to making himself very offensive towards any worker who refuses to desert his comrades.'

By August 1927 Foran reported that farm labourers, only four years earlier the largest proportion of members, were 'almost entirely unorganised.' It 'was impossible to hold their wages and conditions at anything like what they had.' Any work being done was now of a casual nature, making organisation difficult. The pain of 1923–24 made the NEC chary about attempting reorganisation.[18] The loss of farm labourers, rather than the split with Larkin, was the most significant element in the ITGWU's decline to 1930.

BELFAST AND NEWRY

Newry carters defected from the ATGWU in February 1925. William McMullen wrote a weekly column in the *Voice of Labour*, 'Under the Wee Parliament', providing news and views of Ulster happenings. He was elected MP for Belfast West for the Northern Ireland Labour Party on 3 April 1925, one of the first three NILP members. He was unable to devote sufficient time to the Branch after his election and became Organiser, with C. F. Ridgway succeeding him as Secretary in January 1926.

In October, Newry dockers transferred from the ATGWU with their own Official, although seamen were declined. Ridgway visited Russia 'under circumstances which the Officers considered warranted refusal of Head Office consent' and appears to have been dismissed in November 1927. He had been a courageous, inventive and dedicated Official. McMullen was re-elected Branch Secretary in March 1928.[19] ITGWU membership held well.

SLIGO AND GALWAY

In February 1925 the NEC 'unanimously decided to expel John Lynch, Sligo,' for 'attempted disruption.' He was given his 'walking papers' for disruption and corruption by the Organiser, Séamus O'Brien, who attacked Larkin and Lynch. 'In the enthusiasm no one noticed how Johnny Lynch managed to get away and desert his chief, whom he had introduced and then deserted when he saw how the wind was blowing.' McMullen saw Lynch as an old friend who 'had taken the wrong turn.' At the AGM in the Town Hall 'thunderous applause' greeted O'Brien, leaving 'no room for doubt as to the esteem in which . . . he is held.' It was approval of Lynch's expulsion. The Branch Hall was purchased by Head Office and the dock surface concreted to improve conditions. Reorganisation followed.

A successful Court case established the right to picket in a one-person dispute at a Sligo drapery. On May Day a

> great procession marched from Ballysodare with a new banner by Tom Kain and Sligo Town Band leading 2,500 . . . Its size astonished the boss class . . . It was the envy of the half-dozen Larkinites who took no part in it . . . It took Sligo's breath away.

This was in contrast to John Lynch's 'miserable little Larkinite fiasco in Dublin,' when 'twenty-three dupes followed the Larkinite Band' and Larkin himself sang 'The Rising of the Moon'.

Members in Galway, especially dockers, had an inconsistent relationship with the ITGWU, repeatedly departing for the ATGWU and then coming back again. On Sunday 20 January 1929 Foran defended 'our Union' when transfer to the ATGWU was proposed. It had a 'reputation and a record second to none, and when it goes abroad that an English union is going to look after the affairs of Irish workers, our union cannot, and will not, allow misrepresentation.' It was 'incomprehensible' that Irish workers should invite an English union to look after their affairs. Rule-book benefits looked better, 'but they were hedged round with traps and difficulties so that very few people could claim them.' William O'Brien said that only 140 took part in the ballot to transfer, of whom 91 'were in favour of the change.' Gilbert Lynch, a stalwart Organiser, went with his members.

The ITGWU catered for dockers more efficiently in Belfast than the ATGWU. Some ATGWU members and Lynch were present, and Foran said he had 'never yet known an instance where boats were held up in England in the interests of Irish workers.' O'Brien said that 'for every pound contributed' to the ITGWU by Galway workers 'thirty shillings had been expended.'[20] The ATGWU, rather than the WUI, was the ITGWU's main competitor and opponent.

THE BRITISH GENERAL STRIKE
In July 1925 the ITGWU read 'with envy' plans for a British 'Industrial Alliance' of mining, railway, transport, engineering and shipbuilding unions. Celebrating Red Friday, Charles Ridgway said:

> It is hardly necessary to point out the moral of the victory to Irish workers. We have seen disruption and defeat at our doors, we have seen unity and victory across the Channel—it is for us to choose which we prefer, whether the path that leads downwards or that which leads to the heights.

Unity retained its power, and 'the old maxim still holds true, "United we stand, divided we fall".' Delighted with the miners' apparent success and the 'abuse which their victory has called forth,' he said that even greater satisfaction would be gained if 'the workers of Ireland imbued with the old spirit' cast aside disruption and got 'back to the unity and solidarity of 1918–1923—a unity and solidarity which made history and meant progress to the 100,000 members of the O.B.U.'

The ITGWU was 'not called upon to take a direct part' in the 'great struggle of the British Miners' in May 1926. But matters were 'closely watched,' not least for the 'effect on our membership,' by a specially convened NEC meeting. They were 'prepared to co-operate in any way that would serve the common interests of the working-class in both islands.' It suggested to the ITUC&LP that the British TUC should Delegate control of the strike in Ireland 'so far as it might be necessary to supplement action in Great Britain.' Were this done the ITGWU 'would be prepared to respond to any instructions given.' A 'small token of recognition' was made, with £100 sent to the Miners' Lock-Out Fund, not least in 'recognition of help received from the Miners by this Union in past years—a reference to 1913. Branches assisted visiting miners' Delegations 'during their long and heroic struggle.'[21]

UNEMPLOYMENT

By 1925 unemployment was the 'outstanding problem'. 'Real relief' would come only 'when the working class can take into its own hands the control of industry and the conduct and administration' of all state affairs. Members continued to 'scab in the ballot box', however, marginalising Labour's Socialist solutions to economic ills. The ITGWU was concerned that a 'Religious Institution . . . spent recently £200 on German Rosary Beads . . . What do the Workers think of that?' An Irish horn rosary would 'last you a lifetime and give work to Irish Girls.' Members were reminded: 'It is the Buyer, not the Trader, who creates the demand for Foreign Rosaries.' The ITGWU constantly urged people to 'buy Irish.' In Dublin an independent unemployed workers' organisation carried on agitation, supported by Dublin Workers' Council. Congress urged all unions to organise the unemployed or to involve themselves in unemployed organisations, thus securing them from being taken over by 'irresponsible leaders'. The Free State Government 'obstinately refused' to extend or improve unemployed insurance benefit.

At the 1925 Congress Heron called upon the 'two Governments functioning in Ireland' to introduce legislation to provide 'either work under Trade Union conditions or maintenance at full Trade Union rates.' More than 257,000 people were unemployed in the country as a whole. How long would they have to wait for the Shannon Scheme to begin? J. P. Hughes drew attention to the plight of women, 'who might be driven to far greater degradation than was possible in the case of men.' He suggested that a General Strike might make the point plain. John F. Gill (Laois-Offaly), 'from a rural area ruled by a paid Commissioner,' complained of ex-soldiers' desperation driving them to work at low rates. J. H. Bennett (NSFU) observed that a 'hungry belly would make a man do many things.' Hickey (Cork) complained that motions were fine but he had heard no definite plan of action from the NEC. Foran emphasised hopes for the Shannon Scheme and the political realities delaying its commencement. It was the 'only decent scheme formulated in recent times to do any good for the people.' Senator John Keane 'admitted that the opposition to the scheme was based solely on the fact that it was now to be a national scheme, not financed by private capital.' He threatened 'to withhold the money necessary to carry out the scheme.'

Senator Thomas Farren (ITGWU) moved that 'Unemployment Benefit be paid to all insured contributors' who, through long-term unemployment of two years or more, had exhausted their entitlements. He wanted the school leaving age raised to sixteen. C. Matthews (Trim) wanted waiting periods for benefit of five or six weeks removed and Courts of Referees more accessible. Some had to walk twenty miles to attend Courts, and expenses should be provided.[22] At ITGWU Conferences, economic policy was little discussed.

EDUCATION AND TRAINING

The Workers' Educational Institute was created at the 1925 Congress after an ITGWU motion on political education. The ITGWU contributed financially and in personnel.

Although the first session was 'largely experimental', from the beginning there were complaints that members made insufficient use of the Institute's facilities. It had arisen from a Congress Committee that included Archie Heron, Cathal O'Shannon and D. J. O'Leary (ITGWU). In its first winter, activities were confined to Dublin. In both 1925 and 1927 ITGWU Officials attended the Summer Schools of the National Council of Labour Colleges in England, 'with great beneficial effect.' The Workers' Educational Institute quickly withered away.[23]

THE *VOICE OF LABOUR*

In June 1925 the *Voice of Labour* was enlarged but still cost only 1d. It was a public indication that the ITGWU was emerging from the mire. Privately, Branches received free copies, with the proceeds of sales to members supplementing local funds.

In May 1927 a libel action by a Newry employer culminated in a judgement and costs against the paper, the 'only instance of a successful action against the *Voice* since its establishment.' Control of the paper was transferred to the ITUC&LP to provide 'a weekly organ for the whole movement.' The *Irishman*, incorporating the *Voice of Labour*, appeared before the June elections.

Even before its transfer the *Voice of Labour* published an increasing quantity of Labour Party and non-union material, reflecting the ITGWU's decline. Decreased income dictated that economies be made in the union. Shedding its newspaper was an obvious one. It would be twenty years before the ITGWU again published its own journal.[24] The paper ended:

In taking farewell of our readers, we may be allowed to express our gratitude to them for such support as they have given the paper in the last nine years; to the correspondents and contributors from far and near, at home and abroad—and a mixed and gallant Band they were—who responded to its call.

LIBERTY HALL

On 31 July 1927 the ITGWU leased premises at the Murrough on the outskirts of Wicklow for a 'Holiday Hostel for workers.' Extensive repairs were undertaken and preparations made for the 1928 season. It was hoped that members would take the opportunity of 'an inexpensive holiday amongst some of the most beautiful scenery in Ireland,' an ideal spot for 'Comradeship on Holiday' at 'inconsiderable expense.'

At a time of depression and decline this was an extraordinary decision. Was it a hope for the future or a return to earlier values that sought to provide for all members' industrial, economic, political and social needs, as Croydon Park once attempted? It proved a millstone. It opened in June 1928, 'at considerable expense,' but support was 'far from satisfactory, notwithstanding . . . that special rates' were allowed to members' families.' In July and August there were full bookings, mainly through cross-channel visitors. The Cork Branch held a draw, with a week in Wicklow, including train fare, as the prize.

By 1929 the NEC feared that the centre's 'object will have been defeated' if more support was not forthcoming. In 1930 only 34 members attended out of the 141 guests, down by 80 from 1929. A loss of £247 17s 3d was recorded, and it was 'obvious from these figures' that union support was absent.

In 1925 premises were bought in Kilrush for £650; in September 1927 compensation was sought for damage to Liberty Hall in 1916; and in 1929 many properties were let or sold. In August 1928, with membership plummeting, Dunlop Rubber Company sought to buy Liberty Hall. The NEC was 'not prepared to entertain an offer of purchase at the present time'—a little short of an emphatic no. Compensation for damage to Liberty Hall in 1916 was again raised in Dáil Éireann on 6 November 1929. The Minister for Finance, Ernest Blythe, said that if it was the only building for which the Government paid compensation it would open the door to a great variety of claims, imposing a heavy burden on the exchequer. Investigation would be difficult, given the lapse of time. Hugh Colohan (Labour Party, Kildare) said that 'this is really a debt of honour on the part of the State, considering the part that the Union took in the Rebellion'; but de Valera wondered, 'How many other cases of a similar character are there?'

Some members of the ITGWU Brass and Reed Band defected to the WUI in 1924. The Band survived. Reports of the 1927 All-Ireland football final noted the 'presence of three pipers' Bands and the I.T.G.W.U. Brass and Reed Band,' which 'gave us an impressive rendering.' At the hurling final the 'music started suddenly and caught the crowd unawares, and one person in last Sunday's crowd was glad that the Band struck up at the right moment—for when that mighty audience trickled back to its homesteads again it is well that they bring back with them the memory of a day that was national in all its phases.'[25]

The Band long graced All-Ireland finals.

Politics

In 1925 the ITGWU saw the political field 'as ever' as 'the spear-point of the working-class movement.' Union candidates contested local and Seanad elections, making gains throughout the country, fighting on 'bread and butter questions.' On local councils they were 'lined up in a solid and disciplined phalanx on the class issue.' Foran was re-elected to the Seanad 'by the solid and loyal support of the Union membership.' William McMullen, Belfast Branch Secretary, was returned at Stormont for the NILP. All this was possible because the membership had voted (5,658 to 1,108) to set up a Political Fund, though almost immediately some Branches sought exemption.

The ITGWU was prominent in protest meetings held on the Boundary Agreement. The position of Political Secretary was abolished in July 1925 when Cathal O'Shannon resigned, having allowed himself get into arrears. He was transferred to the *Voice of Labour* on reduced wages. Archie Heron became Political Organiser of the ITUC&LP in March 1926. In Dublin by-elections in March 1925 the ITGWU message was:

Cut the Government that Cuts You; the Government has CUT Teachers' Pay;
CUT Nurses' Pay; CUT O.A.P.s; CUT Workers' Pay. To Workers the Government
takes a cut off their Income. But to the Rich the Government hopes to give a cut
off their Income TAX. It is time for the Workers to give the Government a CUT
in return.

Few listened. Denis Cullen (Bakers' Union) and Thomas Lawlor trailed in last
behind Government candidates. Cuts apparently met with workers' approval. If
unemployment and other social evils were to be combated, a strong Labour Party
was necessary. To that end, and in preparation for the General Election, the *Voice
of Labour* could 'perform an important function, and for that reason the increased
support and distribution of the paper amongst our members and the workers
generally is urgently and earnestly called for.' The paper strongly condemned the
military tactics 'adopted by the Govt., the bankers and employers . . . in their
attempts to stereotype and strengthen their existing social and economic power
over the Irish working class.' There was a

> general denunciation of the 'uneconomic' demands of Irish Labour for a main-
> tenance of existing wage rates. They drilled their Press, their marionettes in the
> Dáil and Senate, their servants and hirelings in trade, industry and commerce to
> attack Trade Union rates as the source of all our economic and financial weak-
> ness. The Irish worker has been painted as a vampire sucking the vitality and
> health of the State—a sponge soaking the spring of wealth and prosperity dry at
> their sources in the farms and factories of the nation.[26]

1925 was a 'year of hardship and economic distress' for workers and 'brought disillusionment to every decent-minded Irishman or woman.' Month by month the
country's industrial and agricultural wealth declined under rank Government mismanagement. One solution was to end the futility of Republicans 'disenfranchising
forty-seven seats and giving Cumann na nGaedheal a dictatorship.' That said, 'the
cause of Labour is still the cause of Ireland.' In 1926 the Labour Party set up 'Local
Labour Parties'. The ITGWU was active in the endeavour. Heron argued that joining
the Labour Party should be easier for those who were not trade union members, for
'business people, small farmers and others' who were then excluded. Two elections
in 1927 strained the union's resources. Undaunted by losses in the second election,
the ITGWU still saw in the 'progress of Labour' a 'better and more conscious organisation of the working-class.' Education and propaganda work would 'repay the
effort expended on it tenfold'; but there were limits.

   On a motion of Thomas Ryan and William O'Brien, the NEC made a very
honest decision in April 1927. It accepted the reality of the union's position on the
ground and advised its members 'to support all the Labour Party candidates.' It
had 'regard to the views held by leading members of other unions' that 'close association with the I.T.G.W.U. would not be to the benefit of the Labour candidates,' so

'no use should be made of our Union's halls or other Union machinery as far as Dublin city is concerned.' At the annual Delegate Conference members complained about the dominance of politics over industrial matters. Those supported financially by the ITGWU in elections did not keep close touch afterwards. The British General Strike resulted in changes to the Political Fund in Northern Ireland: workers now had to 'contract in' rather than 'contract out,' necessitating a change in the ITGWU Rules.

In September 1927 the union pledged considerable financial support to candidates who were members. An election victim was Denis Houston, a long-standing union Organiser. He wrote letters to the *Derry Journal* critical of the Labour Party candidate A. J. Cassidy. Houston, from Ballybofey, fought the 1923 General Election, polling 2,456, but was joined by Cassidy in June 1927, when they polled 2,005 and 2,491, respectively. Houston was dropped in September and Cassidy took the only Donegal Labour Party seat ever, polling 3,675. Cassidy lost the seat in 1932 and by 1933 was standing for Fianna Fáil, perhaps confirming Houston's reservations. Houston's service was rewarded with a week's wages—a sad departure.

In 1929 the annual Delegate Conference instructed all TDs who received financial assistance to present a written report of their activities to the NEC. Suspicions of their lack of 'value for money' persisted.

A Labour Government in Britain encouraged the ITGWU's hopes, despite 1927's reverses and the loss of McMullen's Stormont seat in 1929. It supported the separation of the Labour Party and ITUC into separate bodies, seeing developments on 'broader and better lines.' In 1930 Charles Ridgway and John Manweiler moved that the NEC prepare a 'political programme in keeping with the history of the Union, to which all members seeking public office must subscribe,' maintaining pressure on sponsored politicians.[27]

After Thomas Johnson, Leader of the Labour Party, lost his Dáil seat in 1927 the Executive of the ITUC&LP nominated him to the Seanad, not least to secure his income as Secretary. Thomas Kennedy topped the internal poll, and O'Brien suggested that ten votes be cast for Johnson and eight for Kennedy, so running the risk of electing neither. Johnson resigned as Secretary of the ITUC&LP and canvassed the Parliamentary Labour Party, which opted to give eleven votes to Johnson and seven to Kennedy, thus securing Johnson's election.

From December until the Seanad was abolished in 1936 the ITGWU Senators, Foran, Michael Duffy and Thomas Farren, sat as independents, occasionally voting against the Labour Party, as in their failure to support J. T. O'Farrell as Vice-Chairman. O'Brien is assumed to have led this spiteful antagonism to the Labour Party's decisions and the ITGWU's rejection of the Labour Party whip.[28]

Chapter 12

BAPTISM OF FIRE: THE
WUI IN THE 1920s

Larkin's homecoming on 30 April 1923 was 'solid proof of the love and loyalty' of Dublin workers, who 'thronged the streets to welcome their hero.' Although he was undisputed General Secretary of the ITGWU, Liberty Hall was 'now in the hands of different men.' In Christy Ferguson's view they 'had built the Union on a basis of quiet unspectacular bargaining' and feared the 'eruption of "Larkinism". It couldn't work, they could not become fighters, nor could Jim Larkin become tame.'

Conversely, Larkin had maintained little contact with the union and 'did not seem to realise the implications, or the extent, of the changes in the union's membership, organisation and leadership that had taken place' since he left for America in 1914. From 1917 his sister Delia, P. T. Daly, Barney Conway, Michael Mullen (Mícheál Ó Maoláin) and others had been at loggerheads with Liberty Hall, especially the General Treasurer, William O'Brien.

O'Brien's opponents made great play of the fact that he joined the union only in January 1917. While this is true, it ignores his closeness to the ITGWU from its foundation. He was a central figure in 1913, confidant and adviser of both Larkin and Connolly, although clearly favouring the latter. By 1924 Larkin was fifty and had spent less than eight years of his adult life in Ireland. He had been absent nearly nine years. His behaviour was 'highly erratic, to say the least,' explained by his allies as due to years of overwork, frantic organisational activity and, particularly, his American prison experiences. Much of this could be said of other leading figures, especially Connolly and the indefatigable Foran, but their behaviour was more constrained and rational. Larkin's capacity to make personal attacks on virtually everyone left him few allies. If the ITGWU were as bad as he claimed, proof would come now that he again had total control of his own union, the Workers' Union of Ireland.[1]

ORGANISATION, MEMBERSHIP AND FINANCE
On Sunday 15 June 1924 at a meeting in Beresford Place, significantly outside Liberty Hall, Peter Larkin launched the Workers' Union of Ireland. It was registered on

behalf of a Provisional Committee, its foundation date given as 1 June. Its Rule Book was uncontroversial: it 'existed to organise the workers of Ireland for the attainment of full economic freedom.' The name is in many respects obvious, echoing that of the Workers' Union (the Dock, Wharf, Riverside and General Workers' Union of Great Britain and Ireland), led by Tom Mann from 1889.

Rooms were secured at Luke Street on the south quays. Members included 'dockers, coal, carters, builders, bakeries, public services, distributive and productive, and miscellaneous.' It is estimated that 16,000 members transferred from the ITGWU. Few of the names appended to the Rules or the Provisional Committee were familiar from ITGWU records, suggesting new faces and voices. Among well-known ones, however, were Michael S. Sheppard, former Head Office clerk who had been dismissed; Barney Conway, member of No. 1 Branch Committee and the 1918 Executive; Henry Fitzsimons, No. 1 Branch Committee; Patrick Forde, prominent in the Gas Workers' Section; and James Mitchell, former President of the Irish Automobile Drivers' and Automobile Mechanics' Union, a bitter opponent of Liberty Hall since the Motor Permits Strike of 1919.

Weekly contributions were 6d, the same as the ITGWU, with Dispute Pay at 15s for men and 10s for women for the first ten weeks, with 10s and 7s, respectively, for a further ten weeks. Head Office moved to 31 Marlborough Street, named Unity Hall, which James Larkin occupied on his return from Moscow on 25 August. John Lawlor was first President; Peter Larkin, National Organiser; and Ciarán J. King (former General Secretary of the Automobile Drivers' and Automobile Mechanics' Union who had joined the ITGWU Head Office), General Treasurer.[2]

Membership for 1924 was 15,754, in twenty-seven Branches, all in Dublin except for Abbeyfeale, Bray, Dundalk, Nenagh and Roscrea. Membership did not grow much in the 1920s, but stability was no mean achievement, given the general collapse of union membership and spectacular decline of the ITGWU from 67,000 to 14,608. That said, financial records tell a slightly different tale. Income reached a peak in 1927 at £12,540 yet fell to a meagre £4,337 the following year. In no year were surpluses declared. Total losses amounted to £25,182, one-and-a-half times 1929's annual income. Finances rather than membership claims demonstrated the WUI's parlous condition.

Table 20: WUI membership, 1924–9

	Membership	Women	Branches
1924	15,754	—	27
1925	16,741	—	28
1926	17,231	—	11
1927	14,531	1,071	18
1928	15,095	945	17
1929	16,159	1,480	16

Source: National Archives, Registrar of Friendly Societies, file 369T.

On Sunday 1 March 1925 the No. 1 Branch held its AGM in the Mansion House, chaired by Patrick Murray. The Acting Branch Secretary, Michael Sutton, conducted financial and other matters, while the speakers included Larkin and Bob Stewart (Communist Party of Great Britain). Larkin recounted victories at Marino, in theatres and cinemas and, most recently, David Allen's (advertising hoardings). In Inchicore there had been what some regarded as a retreat, due 'in the first instance, to the manoeuvring and dishonesty of a man in whom the workers . . . put their trust,' a reference to Seán McLoughlin. The meeting took nominations for positions and approved a levy of 1d per week for the *Irish Worker* and an annual levy of 2s for the Hospital Fund.

Patrick Nolan, a dismissed ITGWU Delegate, provided the *Irish Worker* with ammunition. He submitted lengthy correspondence regarding his case. He was suspended on 20 January and dismissed the following day. The ITGWU argued that it no longer had the membership to pay his wages. Although happy to publish Nolan's criticisms of ITGWU leaders, the WUI was anxious to hold out a fraternal hand to 'our workmates—Unionmen not scabs,' from a position of perceived strength.

For May Day the *Irish Worker* issued a rallying cry.

Comrades, what of the morn—the new May morn? Why stand ye despairing and despised? Even though you have been misled and betrayed by self-seeking sycophantic place-hunters, masquerading as Labour Leaders, is it too late to seek Heart Grace; reform your ranks and seek inspiration for the future from the sacrifices and service of the men 'like you men' who have passed from our ranks having given all that men can give to the Cause of Labour? Men like Byrne, Nolan, Mallin, O'Carroll, Riley, Partridge, and the teacher and exemplar—Connolly, and many others too numerous to name whose memories abide with us in all our work and harassment of mind and body.

The 'disgraced' Labour movement should return to the principles of Connolly. Workers were at a crossroads. Connolly's death was commemorated by having him speak from the dead. He addressed not just the members but, implicitly, the ITGWU and Labour leaderships.

Comrades! For why and what are you waiting? Many who failed me in life, now exploit my work and memory in death. Surely you will not forsake me or fail to carry on the task?

The WUI May Day rally was reported in the *Voice of Labour* as a 'miserable little Larkinite fiasco.' WUI forays outside Dublin were unsuccessful. On Sunday 28 June, Larkin ran an excursion to Limerick 'accompanied by his alleged Bands' and 'attempted a meeting at the O'Connell monument.' The *Voice of Labour* observed that 'it was a good job he brought his audience with him as he was completely frozen out by the natives.' They 'thought it wiser to keep a safe distance between themselves and the thugs and "nice ladies" who had invaded their city.' Limerick's 'impression of their visitors was something bordering between amusement and disgust.' A 'number of the excursionists were arrested and detained for being drunk and disorderly'—something that would have angered Larkin if it is true.

Whatever about the ITGWU's partial reporting, the WUI's efforts in Limerick fell on barren ground. In Nenagh, Martin Morgan and Bill Gleeson formed a Branch, and Gleeson served on the General Executive Committee. In Sligo, John Lynch, long-time ITGWU stalwart, was defeated in an attempt to form a Branch. He paid a high price: expulsion from the ITGWU and marginalisation in the town. James Mitchell campaigned, without success, to establish a presence in Dundalk.[3]

Allegations that the ITGWU cheated members of benefits were central to Larkin's complaints. Scores of ITGWU mortality claims were settled without investigation by the WUI and publicised in the *Irish Worker*. The financial realities of the new union quickly reversed this policy, however. The *Voice of Labour* publicised the case of John Guilfoyle, a member of the WUI, whose widow was denied his mortality pay as he was in arrears.

In 1929 the WUI was brought before Dublin District Court, prosecuted by the Department of Industry and Commerce 'for failing to lodge Annual Returns' for 1926–28 'as required by law.' On their undertaking that returns would be made 'within a reasonable time,' Larkin and the union were each fined £1 with costs. The Labour Party paper took great pleasure in this embarrassment, which reflected Larkin's lackadaisical approach to administration. An examination of the WUI's financial record shows that it was fighting for its existence. Returning form AR21 to the Registrar of Friendly Societies was not a priority.

Similar pleasure was taken in the come-uppance of the maverick John Bohan, who deserted the ITGWU No. 3 Branch for the WUI. Judge Shannon in the Circuit Court on 28 January 1930 heard his appeal against dismissal and eviction by Larkin. When asked under which Rule the WUI was taking action, Larkin could not say. He did, however, read the decision suspending Bohan from the minutes book. The judge asked for the minutes. 'Witness (after looking through the Minute Book) stated these Minutes must be in another book.' The judge sent him to the WUI offices to fetch the records. Larkin explained that the 'staff had gone to lunch and the place was locked up.' An adjournment was granted at the WUI's cost. On 2 May the story was the same, with the 'Branch account still not furnished.' Despite this, Bohan was dismissed and removed from union premises.

What emerged was a somewhat chaotic image of the WUI. Bohan showed that no elections for any position had been held since 1927. Although Larkin was General Secretary, he could not produce a membership card. Bohan, expelled from the ITGWU in July 1924, sought and was granted readmission in March 1931, 'as a new member.'[4]

Table 21: WUI income and expenditure (selected items) (£), 1924–9

	Total receipts	Members' receipts	Total expenditure	Dispute pay	Legal benefit	Funeral benefit	Staff salaries	Balance
1924	9,479	9,267	9,006	5,220	252	333	1,759	(9,007)
1925	11,942	9,366	11,204	9,345	225	806	2,519	(4,790)
1926	6,051	5,946	5,288	46	337	366	2,799	(4,491)
1927	12,540	7,194	7,063	132	347	506	4,172	(4,027)
1928	4,337	4,337	6,807	1,160	338	250	2,584	(1,019)
1929	6,335	5,885	7,164	1,459	76	233	2,008	(1,019)

Source: National Archives, Registrar of Friendly Societies, file 369T.

WAGES AND DISPUTES

No sooner was the Gas Company dispute over than 800 railwaymen, 400 building workers and 300 in the Fish Markets came out. All were paid Strike Pay. Emmet Larkin noted that 'there began a whole series of disputes that had nothing to do with either wages or hours' but rather 'which union was to have control over a particular job.' In common parlance, it was a 'turf war'. Typical was the row in the Marino housing project. With the exception of five men, all 300 labourers on the job defected to the WUI. They demanded that the five ITGWU men be sacked, but the contractor refused. The needs of 5,000 homeless families on Dublin's housing list were forgotten as the dispute dragged on for months. There were similar, sometimes violent, confrontations in the Fish Markets, cinemas and theatres. Donal Nevin observed that 'passions ran high and physical contact was not rare.' Worse, 'strong loyalties developed in the course of these disputes,' leaving 'bitter legacies, persisting for two decades.'

Jobs were a scarce and diminishing commodity in 1920s Dublin, and a high price was paid by families cast adrift because of the wrong allegiance. Given that the bulk of Dublin members went to the WUI, it was among ITGWU loyalists that the highest price was sometimes extracted. Credit is hard to find on either side. Both, nonetheless, claimed the moral high ground.

The ITGWU issued a manifesto, *To the Workers of Dublin,* in November 1924. The whirlwind having calmed a little, men were drifting back to the fold. It said that in future, on docks and elsewhere, ITGWU men 'will remain at work unless involved in a genuine trade dispute.' It would 'fill the places of Larkinite workers who are foolish enough to quit their employment at the behest of any of Larkin's agents.' The union's 'full support' was behind this, and it was 'determined that in each case . . . workers will have an opportunity of choosing between their jobs and Larkin's interest.'

The WUI 'principle' was 'plain and definite' and stated on the front page of the *Irish Worker.* It had 'no enmity against the rank-and-file, however small, of that organisation,' and 'in all jobs where the two Unions have members, the w.u.i. is prepared and is actually working with the Transport men, and no dispute has arisen anywhere.' Where the wui had 'complete control of a job, as in the North Wall Extension, where out of 500 men not one is a Transport man,' it refused 'to have any dealings with Transport men.' Any carters or their workers sent to such jobs had to be wui members. But

> in jobs where there is a division, then the Transport card is recognised; in jobs where only w.u.i. men are, then only w.u.i. cards and no others, will be recognised. This is our position. It is neither over-bearing nor provocative. It need cause no divisions or turmoil, and if employers will recognise and abide by it, no disputes will arise.

This was a retreat from August 1924, when the *Irish Worker* insisted that

> the Transport Union had ceased to exist—except as a scab-herding organisation. The Transport Union card is nothing but a pass to scab. There is only going to be one labourers' union in Ireland: that will be the Workers' Union, which has earned its place by right of conquest.

The word 'conquest' was an interesting choice.

The reality was of two competing organisations. In 1929 Larkin led the fight against redundancies and wage cuts on the railways. In 1930 the 'Big Fight' was for state recognition that 'men were unemployed not because they would not work, but because there was no work for them.'[5] The wui's expenditure on Dispute Pay reached a peak in 1925 at £9,345 but was a mere £46 in 1926. On average, £2,449 was spent per year. This seems quite small until it is set against average total income of £8,356. By this calculation, Dispute Pay averaged 29% of income, an indication of a fighting union.

COAL

The climax of internecine conflict came in July 1925. The Coal Merchants' Association announced a Lock-Out of all workers 'until a satisfactory guarantee is obtained that the men employed there will work amicably together.' Looking back, and consistent with the wui's view of itself as a victim, Christy Ferguson saw it as 'all the forces of the State and employers' combining to crush it—with, of course, O'Brien's conniving hand everywhere.

> Tragically, the full weight of the itgwu was thrown not on the side of Larkin and his workers, but on to the side of the State and the Bosses. Liberty Hall was used as a recruiting station for blacklegs while the State provided arms to safeguard the Officials of the Transport Union.

The ITGWU quickly disclaimed all responsibility and insisted it had no connection with the Coal Merchants' Association. The Dublin Employers' Federation—Larkin's enemies from 1913—promised the Association 'organised support' and 'constitutional labour, so that the liberty of action should be secured for employers and labour, irrespective of the union to which any worker may belong.' David Barry, Managing Director of the B&I Line, said the employers merely wanted the same rights as workers to organise 'protection against tyranny and Bolshevism.' Larkin was opposed lest he 'become the sole dictator of the wage-earners of Dublin.'

The *Irish Times* gave a plainer view of establishment thinking.

> Mr. Larkin, who does not conceal his association with a malignant and alien power, has chosen his time cunningly. He has precipitated this crisis at a moment when the national mind is beginning to recover from the confusion of the last few years, when new works of construction are being taken in hand, and vital matters of economic development are in the balance. His triumph would be the triumph of anarchy in the Free State.

The WUI's 'intimidatory tactics' thwarted the plans of the Coal Merchants' Association and Dublin Employers' Federation. Workers refused to unload their coal. On 12 August men holding ITGWU cards worked under police protection. Violence ensued. Drivers remained loyal to Larkin, but the ITGWU offered men there too. Larkin said that trade unionists would walk out anywhere that 'black' coal was delivered, but it happened only in the Gas Company, and even there men went back after a day, on 27 August, agreeing to 'obey orders.'

On 3 September WUI loyalists made a last savage attack on ITGWU men working at Alexandra Basin, throwing stones, coal nuggets and 'anything they could get their hands on.' By 8 September, however, the Coal Merchants' Association, with ITGWU help, held its ground. WUI resistance petered out.

A unique aspect of the strike was the establishment of the Unity Coal Company. The WUI had only £130 in the bank, and yet every one of the several hundred men received Strike Pay throughout. This was done 'by making the employer pay strike money.' The £130 was 'invested in the purchase of cargoes of coal consigned to the Union, officially distributed and bought by Union men and women.' The profit paid Strike Pay and brought in further coal.

> Sixteen colliers carrying cargoes of coal to this Union in one week alone was a new feature in an industrial struggle—but the men who went through the strike know that it broke a coal ring in this city and brought down the price of coal by 10/– per ton.

By 29 July coal was 'being sold at cost to the poor and needy.' It was a victory for Larkin on a par with the 1913 food ships in subsequent public conscience. Although it was July, many families relied on coal for heating water, washing and cooking.

In November a WUI clerk, Michael Sheppard, was fined under the Weights and Measures Act in connection with the coal distribution. This was interpreted by Larkin as harassment of his fuel venture. Larkinite support for Gray, a stevedore and employer, in Dock Ward in January 1927 was cited by the ITGWU as an indication of the depths sunk to in order to preserve territory. Stones were being thrown from glasshouses.

In 1926, during the British General Strike and miners' Lock-Out, the Unity Coal Company brought coal from Arigna, Co. Roscommon, to supply the Dublin market. This demonstrated the commercial viability of domestic coal, a discovery that would later carry Irish industry through the years of the Second World War, when Irish coal augmented rationed British supplies. Earlier, in January 1925, the ITGWU alleged that Larkin's men violently assaulted ITGWU dockers bringing cheaper coal through Wicklow.[6]

INCHICORE

Two simultaneous disputes erupted in Inchicore Railway Works in August 1924. Millwrights' helpers in the running shed wanted an increase, and vicemen had a demarcation quarrel with craftsmen. Seán McLoughlin, unanimously elected Secretary of No. 2 Branch, tried to dissuade men from taking action: they were not well enough organised, had only £30 in local funds and no strike fund at Head Office, and were inviting the management to take the side of the Irish Engineering and Industrial Union against them.

At a mass meeting Peter Larkin 'dominated' proceedings, holding the union 'in trust for his brother,' who was in Moscow. James Mitchell assisted in persuading the men to strike. McLoughlin 'pleaded for wider powers with a view to staying action in the event of a compromise being arrived at, but it was useless.' At 4:15 the next day, talks having broken down, hundreds walked out, and the strike, 'for good or ill,' started. Pickets were quickly extended to Kingsbridge (Heuston) Station. They were initially resented by carters.

Peter Larkin did 'everything in his power to make our position impossible,' with 'all of our Strike Committee . . . complaining about his attitude and his actions.' Matters progressed, with Matt Kavanagh of the ITGWU lending support and brokering negotiations that failed. A shock occurred when a lorry from the Dublin Rapid Transit Company, 'known by every worker in Dublin to be the property of the Larkin family, broke the picket line' at Kingsbridge. From then on 'nearly all who were stopped invariably said, "Why don't you hold up Larkin's yokes?"' When Jim Larkin returned he declared, 'There should never have been a strike in Inchicore.'

McLoughlin found the management's tolerance turning to intransigence. He felt the only solution was to bring out WUI coal porters to deny the company fuel. Larkin refused. He denied any knowledge of Dublin Rapid Transit Company (though it was owned by his sister and her husband, Patrick Colgan, and operated out of the house Larkin lived in).

Jack Carney expressed a view of Delia in a letter to Seán O'Casey in 1948, claiming that she had vetoed a proposed authorised biography of Larkin, as she 'wanted to be played up in the book.' As far as Carney was concerned,

> Delia ought not to be mentioned at all ... She did more harm to the Big Fellow than any of the employers ... She and Pat Colgan, during the carters' strike, organised the Rapid Transport Company. They made lots of money because all the other carters were out. From that day to the hour of his death, Jim never spoke to Delia. They lived in the same house and sat at the same table but no word passed between them.

In Larkin's bankruptcy proceedings on 16 January 1925, reported in the *Voice of Labour*, it was claimed that he made about £200 from the Sustentation Fund. He admitted that he sent no money to the ITGWU and had arrived in Ireland with $2,000. He sent £200 to Belfast and lived off the rest. The ITGWU lampooned the WUI as 'L.F.U.'—Larkin Family Union. Such revelations were extremely damaging, bewildering Larkin's followers.

At Inchicore, Larkin met the General Manager of the Great Southern and Western Railway, Neale, and McLoughlin drafted settlement terms that provided for no victimisation on return but little movement on the claims. At a mass meeting in Inchicore Picture House on 4 October, Larkin said that those who were not allowed to return would 'be supported by those at work' through a weekly levy. Some volunteered to fill redundant positions. When McLoughlin raised objections, Larkin threw himself to the floor, insisting that McLoughlin had gunmen planted in the room. The meeting broke up in pandemonium. The strike collapsed.

McLoughlin resigned, his belief in Larkin, until then unquestioning, shattered.[7] He emigrated to Britain shortly afterwards, disillusioned and tired of constant police harassment of himself and his family.

NENAGH

After Larkin's action against Liberty Hall in June 1923 the Secretary of the ITGWU Nenagh Branch, William Gleeson, forwarded no more contributions to Head Office. Secretary since the Branch's formation in 1918, Gleeson led a faction known as the Town Hall Group. Those remaining loyal, led by the Labour TD Dan Morrissey, were known as the Shamrock Club Group. In a Court action in July the ITGWU attempted to recover its books from Gleeson. Morrissey, involved in conciliation efforts at the national level, outlined the view of the loyalists after Larkin laid down 'conditions and reservations' so that 'no one with any sense of honour or decency could accept.'

The dispute dragged on, and Larkin

> threatened to burst up [the union] unless he is allowed to rule and put us at one another's throats unless we accept his dictatorship. There is no doubt he's a great

personality, but it is equally certain that the men who built up the labour movement in his absence are also entitled to consideration.

Gleeson opposed both Morrissey and Patrick O'Doherty, ITGWU Organiser, in the General Election of August 1923. His 655 votes possibly cost O'Doherty a second Labour seat. Morrissey complained that Gleeson 'unfurled the Larkinite banner' but his 'clumsy defence and flimsy excuses would not impose on even the greatest fool in the community.' Gleeson was suspended, not by Liberty Hall but by Nenagh Branch Committee. It was Gleeson's non-selection as a candidate, after originally being selected with Morrissey and Doherty, that possibly provoked his actions. Larkin sent supporters to canvass with Gleeson.

In September fifty ITGWU members 'marched in military formation from street to street endeavouring to persuade employers from continuing to employ' Gleeson's followers. Employers 'in most cases stood neutral.' There were some fisticuffs, and 'shots were fired into two houses of the disputants but fortunately none of the occupants was injured.' The following week ITGWU men left the Shamrock Club and posted themselves outside jobs where Gleeson's men worked. Eventually Rev. Patrick O'Halloran mediated and a joint meeting was agreed. It never took place. Larkin encouraged Gleeson.

> You are Secretary, Nenagh. Don't give up the books, documents, to any alleged representatives of the Union. Proceedings against you never legally authorised. Have wired the Court.

He signed himself General Secretary, ITGWU.

In May 1924 trouble flared again at Grange quarry, where both factions claimed membership. O'Halloran attempted further conciliation; but on 17 May the *Nenagh Guardian* published the following advertisement:

IMPORTANT NOTICE
Notice is hereby given to Employers and the General Public THAT FROM MONDAY NEXT 19TH MAY, DRASTIC ACTION will be taken against all NON-MEMBERS of the above Branch, I.T.G.W.U., the properly constituted and Officially recognised Organisation of the Irish Workers. This notice is issued in order that Employers and the General Public will not be taken unawares, and to give them an opportunity to deal with any situation that may arise out of this action, which we are compelled to take.
By Order, I.T.G.W.U., M. O'REGAN, SEC.

The gloves were off.

Matters rumbled on until 9 August, when a WUI Branch was founded. P. T. Daly addressed a meeting that elected Gleeson as Branch Secretary. Only five WUI Branches were outside Dublin, two in Co. Tipperary—Nenagh and Roscrea. In

Nenagh the ITGWU had 380 members, the WUI 40. Strikes in the Gas Company—a WUI stronghold—and the Urban District Council set a pattern of internecine conflict. In the 1925 local elections Labour (ITGWU) candidates polled 478 (30%) of the vote and the WUI 224 (18%)—a remarkably strong performance by Socialist candidates and an indication of the two camps' relative strengths.

The ITGWU and WUI co-existed for the rest of the decade, but trade unionism went into serious decline, struggling against continuous wage cuts and rising unemployment. On 16 February 1928 2,000 men marched through Nenagh to protest against local authority cuts. Dan Morrissey's stature was at its height: he polled 10,307 in the June 1927 election, bringing in his running-mate, William O'Brien, General Secretary of the ITGWU. In September his vote fell to 8,344 and O'Brien lost his seat.

By 1932 Morrissey was Independent Labour and by 1933 Cumann na nGaedheal, his defection beginning with his support for the Constitution (Amendment No. 19) Bill after the shooting of Superintendent Seán Curtin.[8] By 1930 both ITGWU and WUI Branches had disappeared. Gleeson formed a United General Workers' Union to keep a union flag flying. In the 1940s an ITGWU Branch fully revivified trade unionism in Nenagh, and all previous factions were forgotten.

MALLIN HALL

In 1929 the WUI took over 'an almost derelict yard at 9 Fishamble Street, with a well-built office adjoining.' It was turned into 'one of the finest and most commodious halls in the city' and named Michael Mallin Hall after a 'skilled artisan (silk worker), a Unionman, a good citizen, a good Irishman . . . Staff captain in the Citizen Army in the Revolution,' and 'one of the Immortal Twelve.' In addition to 'comfortable rooms' there was a wireless and billiards. In the early days Jim and Peter Larkin, 'with their driving restless energy,' and many volunteers cleared 'hundreds of tons of rubbish out of the big hall,' laid floors and completed general renovations. Mallin Hall became a 'centre for all workers of the Old City' and much loved by members.[9]

DUBLIN TRADES COUNCIL

In June 1925 the WUI sought affiliation to Dublin Trades Council. The ITGWU was part of the rival Dublin Workers' Council, so there was no impediment to affiliation 'on behalf of 1,000 craftsmen members.' The rest would follow when the WUI was 'in a position to afford it.' No. 1 Branch already owed money for the hire of rooms in the Trades Hall. Larkin and Conway, however, attacked Trades Council Delegates at a Conference of the National Minority Movement in September, and matters were held over until February 1926.

In September 1925 an Irish Minority Movement was launched, with Brushmakers, Musicians' Union, Ballinasloe Workers' League and Garment Workers involved. By March 1926 the *Voice of Labour* observed that 'it seems to have been a premature birth.' A Minority Movement Conference was due to be held on 14 February, with Tom Mann, the grand old man of British labour, as the main attraction, along with

Larkin. Larkin declined at the last minute. An exasperated trades council expelled the WUI and tried, unsuccessfully, to reclaim the money owed.

Dublin Trades Council were not the only ones despairing of Larkin. Bob Stewart of the Communist Party of Great Britain also recognised that eggs should not be placed in the Larkin basket if there were to be a Communist Party of Ireland.

After Larkin's intervention in the General Election of September 1927 there was a realisation that division worked against Labour. In February 1928 all unions were invited to attend a Conference, whether affiliated to Dublin Trades Council or Dublin Workers' Council. The ITGWU did not attend. Progress was impeded in May when the ITGWU served bankruptcy proceedings on P. T. Daly, Secretary of the Trades Council. He was sentenced to three months' imprisonment. Talks on Trades Council unity were broken off.

Daly was determined on unity, however, and on his release in October he persuaded both councils to adopt a unity motion. The Workers' Council did so without division, but it took a little longer within Dublin Trades Council. Both groups held their final meetings on 18 November, with Dublin Trades Council writing off the £200 loan to Larkin as a bad debt. The new, united Dublin Trades Union and Labour Council was established on 19 November 1927, with Daly elected full-time Secretary. The slogan adopted on unity was 'Back to the Unions.' The ITGWU had stood aside, no longer the dominant force it once was, and could do little to prevent Daly's election, although it felt it 'a pity that Mr. Daly should have been elected ... We think the post requires to be filled by a young man, not only free from Associations with the past, but filled with the enthusiasm that is the blessed gift of youth.' It added, rather strangely, that those who condemned Daly 'do him too much honour.' It was because he was the wrong choice that the 'Council must be condemned and extinguished.' But Secretaries do not hold position for ever, the 'movement is bigger and longer-lived than any individual' and mistakes can be got over 'by the exercise of a little patience and good will.'[10]

The ITGWU withdrew from the Trades Council in early 1929 but re-affiliated in October. Once again the question presented itself: Given the new spirit of unity, would the WUI apply, and would it be accepted?

THE RED INTERNATIONAL OF LABOUR UNIONS
Workers' International Relief rented offices from Dublin Trades Council with the ostensible purpose of relieving chronic food shortages in the west of Ireland. It was part of the CPGB's assistance in the hope of re-establishing the CPI. Congress, under ITGWU influence, dismissed it as 'souperism' and 'Communist propaganda.'

WIR was a fund-raising front for Larkin.

The locked-out dupes and victims of Larkinism are not fighting for better wages or conditions. They are not fighting the employers. They are fighting James Larkin's lost battle for control of the I.T.G.W.U. and for his personal dictatorship over the masses of Irish workers.

The ITGWU demanded published accounts for WIR, asking, 'Of the 'over £1,000 sent from abroad to the Larkin-Daly Committee, how much was spent on Bob Stewart?' The Communist International established the Red International of Labour Unions as an alternative to the International Trade Union Centre (Amsterdam). The WUI and Nicholas (Nixie) Boran's Castlecomer Miners' and Quarrymen's Union were Ireland's only affiliates.[11]

LIBEL ACTIONS
Whatever about his rows with Liberty Hall, Larkin managed to create enemies in many quarters, increasing his siege mentality and doing himself no favours. At a support meeting for Denis Cullen (Bakers) in Phibsborough, Dublin, Barney Colgan and James Ralph led heckling that concentrated on Thomas Johnson's Englishness. Johnson's rejoinder was complete.

> I had the honour to be born in Liverpool within 500 yards of the very same house in which Jim Larkin was born (laughter and cheers) and I have lived in Ireland three times as many years as Larkin has lived in this country.

Larkin referred to Johnson as 'Felix' (after the cartoon cat who appeared and disappeared) and attacked him regularly in the *Irish Worker*. Johnson was eventually goaded into a reaction and sued Larkin and the paper, successfully, in November 1924, winning £500 damages against each in April 1925. A leaflet accused Cullen of having voted for wage cuts in Grangegorman. Cullen won £1,000 in his libel action.[12] Larkin's animus proved costly.

POLITICS
Larkin formed the Irish Worker League in September 1923, centred on the *Irish Worker*. At a meeting in the Mansion House, with Bob Stewart (CPGB) among the speakers, more than 500 people signed up. Larkin never wanted a political party, in which he would have to share authority. The IWL never really functioned as a party, but as occasion required, Larkin utilised it. It had initially been a purely social body but adopted a political constitution on 27 April 1924. When Larkin was elected to the Communist International the paper declared him 'one of the twenty-four rulers of the world.' The *Voice of Labour* took great delight in satirising this.

John Lawlor of the WUI approached Dublin Trades Council in early 1925 when the CPGB tried to transform the IWL into a fully fledged party, but the council—still Dublin Trades Council and Labour Party—decided against involvement. It held suspicions about a party driven in effect from outside the country. Larkin, in any case, scuppered the plans. The CPGB sent Stewart to facilitate matters but abandoned the project.

In February 1925 Larkin addressed a meeting in the Mansion House to commemorate Lenin. The ITGWU dismissed the occasion as 'Big Noise' and a 'convention of the red, rebel, revolutionary minority, the Communist elements.'

The *Voice of Labour* seized on every opportunity to cast Larkin in a poor light, taking particular pleasure when criticism came from Communist sources. Tom O'Flaherty, editor of the *Irish People,* who had been Secretary of the Larkin Release Committee, wrote in the *Daily Worker* of Chicago about 'an incurable egomaniac.' He thought that while there was 'considerable left wing sentiment' within Irish unions 'it had no leadership.' Larkin's return put him in a 'powerful strategic position,' but he, 'as usual, muffed the ball.' O'Flaherty was particularly critical of Larkin's 'resort to a capitalist Court,' seeing his action against the ITGWU as 'extremely stupid'. 'Even if he could get his hands on the $180,000 which he accused the Officers of misappropriating for political purposes, putting up Labour candidates, he would have nevertheless suffered a moral defeat before the masses in playing the role of law enforcement agent.' Larkin's bankruptcy was no surprise: 'he should know by now that capitalist Courts are dangerous playthings for workers.' Damningly, O'Flaherty concluded that 'Larkin has a reputation of being a revolutionist but that reputation is not founded on any basis more substantial than a loud voice.' That he had 'liquidated the Communist Party to hold centre stage' was a cardinal sin, allowing the conclusion that 'he does not believe in organisation, unless it takes orders from him. An incurable egomaniac, he refuses to accept advice from anybody.'

This last point was one of the most vexing for those who wished to be Larkin's allies. For O'Flaherty, and increasing numbers of others, Larkin 'had no programme,' and Irish workers remained leaderless.

O'Flaherty concluded: 'By splitting the Union, taking the Officers into a capitalist Court on the sordid charge that they had used Union funds for political purposes, calling strikes of members of his dual Union against members of the Transport Workers' and 'engaging in business ventures' Larkin had laid 'himself open to suspicion.' In general, 'his all-round buffoonery is a splendid lesson in the wrong way to fight revolutionaries in the trade unions.'

There were clashes between Roddy Connolly's emergent Workers' Party of Ireland and Larkin, who still held the Communist International's trust. By the General Election of June 1927 the Workers' Party of Ireland dismissed Larkin as someone who had failed to organise a proper party. His method of debate consisted of 'threats, attacks and allegations,' and 'his tactics have completely smashed whatever there was of a left-wing movement . . . Now like an infuriated animal he is stamping on the wreckage lest anyone make order from the chaos.'[13] The Labour Party strengthened its position in the election.

Emmet Larkin felt that with trade unionism generally in decline, for Larkin 'the pendulum began to swing to the great alternative—political action.' It was hard to see where industrial and political activity began and ended with Larkin. The *Irish Worker* was always the Irish Worker League's paper, not the WUI's. It is a scant source for union activities.

When Kevin O'Higgins, the Minister for Justice, was assassinated on 10 July 1927 the Cumann na nGaedheal Government enacted the Public Safety Act (1927), suspending civil liberties. Larkin held a protest meeting in College Green against such

'Czarist Methods', but the police refused to allow him speak. He spoke instead from a window in Unity Hall, Marlborough Street. He suggested a Conference of all those who opposed the Government to 'find a common denominator in defence of their lives, liberties and the rights of the common people.' He brought the idea to Éamon de Valera, Leader of the newly created Fianna Fáil. De Valera responded by inviting two members each from the Labour Party, Farmers' Party, National League, Sinn Féin, 'Transport Workers' Union', 'Irish Workers' Union' and Fianna Fáil 'to consider the present position' and determine 'joint national action which will save the country from the consequences of the legislation.' Only Larkin and de Valera met in Wynn's Hotel, Lower Abbey Street, on 4 August and then for 'less than ten minutes.' Thomas Johnson (Labour Party) urged that Fianna Fáil take its Dáil seats as a more constructive gesture.

At Unity Hall on 6 August, Larkin told his supporters that there 'were only two ways' to proceed: 'one was by passive resistance' and 'the other way was by revolution.' He doubted that the 'country was ready for revolution at present, either mentally or physically,' and the only two lines were within the Dáil or passive resistance. The upshot was that de Valera announced that Fianna Fáil would take its seats if elected in the General Election in September. Larkin, who realised that this was 'the only hope of providing an alternative Government,' claimed credit for persuading de Valera of this course: 'Into this job he put his gift of oratory, his sense of political tactics and his own transparent sincerity.' When Fianna Fáil entered Dáil Éireann, 'both friends and foes alike admitted that Jim Larkin was the man who bore the greatest responsibility for this historical step.'

Larkin contested North Dublin for the IWL, while his son, 'Young Jim', fought County Dublin and John Lawlor, General President of the WUI, South Dublin after Larkin decided that 'immediate action' was needed in September 1927. The economic crisis was not all the Free State Government's fault. He blamed the 'alleged Official Labour Party and many of the trade union leaders that represented British Unions in Ireland.' His appeal was 'over the heads of those so-called leaders' to the rank-and-file.

Despite being described in the press as a Communist, Larkin won a seat; Young Jim split the Labour vote and deprived Johnson of his seat; while Lawlor equally prevented any Labour gain in South Dublin. The IWL vote totalled 12,500, to the Labour Party's 10,000—testimony to Larkin's continued pulling power.

The *Irishman* 'confessed ourselves perturbed' by Larkin's election in Dublin North City. It pulled no punches in its assessment of his character and politics, as he

for years past has shown himself to have no other principle than to get himself into the limelight, who is a convicted libeller, whose campaign was one long stream of personal and lying abuse of men who owe their positions to the confidence they have earned from thousands of decent Trade Unionists, who has spent years in trying to wreck the Trade Union movement in this country, and who professed to stand as representative of the most anti-national force in the world, the Communist movement—and yet over 7,000 electors of Dublin gave him their first preferences!

Consolation was found in transfers from Alfie Byrne and 'less intelligent supporters of Fianna Fáil.' It demonstrated the size of the educational task confronting Labour. Later the *Irishman* qualified its attitude.

> We are not Communists, but we can appreciate the case that can be made for Communism, and it would be quite right and proper for a party to be formed to advocate Communism openly in this country. Such a party would, we think, meet with very little success.

Communists were not just 'non-sectarian and anti-clerical; they are definitely anti-religious.' They were 'not international, but definitely anti-national.' Thus, the 'strongest sentiments' among Irish people, religion and nationality, were a 'formidable obstacle' to any would-be Communist Party. Communists expressed concerns for wage-earners and small farmers but acted 'under orders of a cosmopolitan Executive which has no belief in either nationalism or democracy.' Interest in Irish people would only be 'insofar as they can be utilised to further grandiose schemes of world-revolution.' And the 'greatest difficulty the Communist International' had in Ireland was 'the instrument it has selected and apparently takes seriously'—James Larkin.

Larkin could not take his Dáil seat as an undischarged bankrupt arising out of his lost action against the ITGWU Executive. He refused 'on principle' to pay the costs. He naturally claimed that the Labour Party was part of a conspiracy to keep him out of the Dáil. This was denied.

> There is not the slightest truth in this. The Labour Party would be glad to see him in the Dáil; it would be the quickest way of exposing his flamboyant futility.

He stood knowing that he was disqualified 'under the ordinary law' and

> since the election . . . made no attempt whatever to claim his seat . . . Mr. Larkin does not want to make speeches or give votes inside the Dáil. He prefers to strut the stage outside.

In the by-election of April 1928 Larkin increased his vote to 8,232 but lost in a three-way fight with Vincent Rice (Cumann na nGaedheal) and Kathleen Clarke, Tom Clarke's widow (Fianna Fáil). Larkin was embittered by Fianna Fáil's actions but equally was 'glad', as it 'showed that the workers had to have their own party and their own movement.'

Through the IWL, Larkin was Ireland's representative in the Communist International. He made his last visit to Moscow in February 1928, declining to offer an opinion on the internal wrangling then current within the Soviet leadership. He agreed, however, with the line that Communists should oppose rather than ally with Labour Party candidates, thus gaining vindication for his actions in 1927. He called for a 'real fighting party' and a daily political paper.

Surely Larkin would return to lead an invigorated Communist Party in Ireland? He was approached by many to find ways of ending the civil war within the labour movement but stated that 'political power can only arise out of and express itself in a class sense and with full effect and purpose, if it is based on industrial solidarity.' Emmet Larkin has concluded: 'To Larkin, then, political unity was impossible without some agreement between the Transport and Workers' Unions, which, as far as both he and O'Brien were concerned, was out of the question.'14 Consequently, after 1928 Larkin's 'popular fortunes went into a decline from which they never really recovered,' and he ceased also to have an international significance.

Chapter 13 ∽

CONCLUSIONS

WHICH WAS THE BIGGER UNION?

A comparison of ITGWU and WUI membership shows that by 1930 the WUI was the larger organisation. The ITGWU claimed 14,608 members, and the WUI declared 16,909 to the Registrar of Friendly Societies. The ITGWU figures were All-Ireland, the WUI essentially Dublin, making it far bigger in the capital. WUI membership remained fairly static, an achievement in the context of collapsing employment. ITUC affiliation figures demonstrate a general collapse, from 175,000 to about 100,000, much of it resulting from the ITGWU's melt-down.

The ITGWU's decline is not simply explained by the development of the WUI. If 15,000 or 16,000 went to the WUI, where did another 35,000 go? Some re-established their former unions—Builders' Labourers, Stationary Engine Drivers, and Automobile Drivers—although only the first did so immediately. Local unions re-emerged; but this did not account for the missing thousands. Most were agricultural labourers who fell out of membership after the defeats of 1923–25. It was difficult enough to find employment, never mind joining a union. By 1930 these were the depression's hardest-pressed victims. Badly defeated, the ITGWU never again organised farm labourers. But despite a spectacular decline, the ITGWU maintained a National Organisation.

Table 22: Comparative membership of ITGWU, WUI and ITUC, 1925–30

	ITGWU	*WUI*	*ITUC*
1924	67,000	15,754	175,000
1925	51,000	16,741	149,000
1926	40,000	17,231	123,000
1927	30,000	14,531	113,000
1928	18,857	15,095	103,000
1929	15,453	16,159	92,000
1930	14,608	16,909	102,000

Sources: ITGWU, Annual Reports, 1924–1930; National Archives, Registrar of Friendly Societies, files 275T and 324T; Nevin, *Trade Union Century,* p. 433.

Union membership presents problems of both over-declaration and under-declaration or, more often, miscalculation. There are various methods of arriving at figures: 'book membership' (those 'on the books'), 'financial membership' (those actually paid up, benefit members) and Congress affiliation (reflecting what unions could afford, financially and politically). More accurate and revealing comparison can be gleaned from the financial records. The collapse of ITGWU membership is mirrored in the decline in its income. Conversely, declared WUI membership is not reflected in a stable income. Its income was erratic; 1928 was near disaster. Both unions' standard weekly contribution was 6d, although the ITGWU had other, lower rates that many opted for.

In general, however, similar rates allow for reasonable comparison. In 1930, when the WUI was supposedly the bigger organisation by 2,300 members, the ITGWU's income was more than twice as high, £16,901 to £7,811. The WUI undoubtedly counted all 'on the books' and, with no Head Office or disciplined financial administration, had a cavalier approach, certainly with regard to whether members were entitled to benefit or not. This was one of Larkin's central arguments against Liberty Hall's 'cold-hearted bureaucracy': in the ITGWU you either were or were not a 'benefit member'. In addition, it was in the WUI's interests to exaggerate, or at least not to understate, its strength. The ITGWU did likewise, certainly in over-declaring for the purpose of Congress affiliation, although financial realities caused it to reduce its affiliation figure from 67,000 to 20,000. Published ITGWU audited accounts were accurate. It made no attempt to hide its position.

Table 23: Comparative income, expenditure and balance (£), ITGWU and WUI, 1924–30

	ITGWU			WUI		
	Income	*Expenditure*	*Balance*	*Income*	*Expenditure*	*Balance*
1924	50,137	40,417	9,270	9,479	9,006	(9,007)
1925	32,880	36,883	(4,003)	11,942	11,204	(4,790)
1926	27,182	24,617	2,565	6,051	5,28	(4,491)
1927	21,292	19,231	2,062	12,540	7,063	(4,027)
1928	17,866	14,783	3,083	4,337	6,807	(1,019)
1929	17,368	14,506	2,862	6,335	7,164	(1,019)
1930	16,901	12,505	4,396	7,811	6,167	(829)

Sources: ITGWU, Annual Reports, 1924–30; National Archives, Registrar of Friendly Societies, file 324T.

Finally, the ITGWU showed a deficit only in 1925, cutting its cloth according to its measure and demonstrating good housekeeping. The WUI, however, experienced continuous losses, not at all consistent with its declared membership but owing much to slapdash administration and endless loans to members, most of which were never repaid. Loans reached a peak at £1,566 in 1930 (20% of income), rising generally in the period.

The ITGWU Dublin No. 1 Branch operated in this fashion in its early days, paying for unemployed members' ship and train tickets to seek work in England, granting funeral expenses, or simply lending to those particularly stuck. Larkin operated the WUI as a personal fiefdom. Each week, Delegations of disgruntled members appeared before him to argue their case, complain about others or of their treatment within the union, state their grievance or plead for alms. From 1917 the ITGWU ceased such practices and operated strictly by Rule. Larkin had little time for the fine detail of union management, and in any case the WUI's continuously parlous state suited Larkin's portrayal of it as the 'ordinary man's union'.

Table 24: WUI loans to members, 1924–30

Year	Loans (£)	As proportion of income (%)	Repaid (£)	Written off (£)
1924	183	2	39	—
1925	790	7	—	—
1926	533	9	324	152
1927	709	6	584	240
1928	861	20	11	940
1929	496	8	200	804
1930	1,566	20	728	459

Source: National Library of Ireland, ms. 13,958, William O'Brien Papers, WUI finances.

MILITANCY

A comparison of Dispute Pay for the two unions—and they provided similar payments—reveals that the WUI endured the rougher period. Amounts were similar but, as a proportion of total income, higher in the WUI. This did not, however, tell the whole tale. ITGWU disputes fell as the union contracted and members displayed increasing reluctance to strike. Some significant battles were fought, particularly in hotels and flour milling. The WUI fought for its very existence and demonstrated its worth as a 'different', 'fighting' union. It sanctioned virtually every dispute, although many were of an inter-union character rather than against employers.

A lull came after the initial storm, but a second wave of disputes erupted as the decade closed. Financial data shows that the WUI led a hand-to-mouth existence. It owned no property and had precious few reserves or assets. Levies on members and financial appeals were commonplace. The ITGWU books were balanced by offloading investments, property and staff. Remarkably, prudent management meant that the ITGWU never had to resort to levies. Its credit balance grew from

£68,183 in 1924 to £71,997 in 1929, an astonishing tribute to O'Brien's ability to keep the ship afloat, whatever the tide or storm.

Absolute conclusions from the data are difficult. Neither union ever shirked a fight. Both asserted that financial considerations were secondary to any industrial demands.

Table 25: Comparison of Dispute Pay, ITGWU and WUI, 1924–9

	ITGWU			WUI		
	Total income (£)	Dispute pay (£)	As proportion of total income (%)	Total income (£)	Dispute pay(£)	As proportion of total income (%)
1924	50,137	10,906	21.8	9,006	5,220	57.9
1925	32,880	7,117	21.7	11,204	9,345	83.3
1926	27,182	3,042	12.3	5,288	46	0.8
1927	21,292	2,445	11.5	7,063	132	1.8
1928	17,866	989	5.5	6,807	1,160	17.0
1929	17,386	1,276	7.3	7,164	1,459	20.3

Sources: ITGWU, Annual Reports, 1924–9; National Archives, Registrar of Friendly Societies, file 324T.

PARALLEL UNIVERSES

From 1925, conflict along Dublin's waterfront ceased. On the ground, and certainly between Branch Officers, the two unions learnt to live with each other. In large measure they inhabited parallel universes. They rarely contested memberships within the same employments. Where they did, and neither was averse to stealing a march on the other, negotiating-table realities, not least in severe recessionary times, dictated a practical tolerance, even unspoken collaboration. Undoubtedly the union leaderships saw themselves as enemies, but outside Dublin most ITGWU members never encountered the WUI. The WUI's ostracism from Congress and Trades Councils meant there were few formal occasions when the two met. Indeed for the WUI, always prominent in Dublin Corporation, the Irish Municipal Employees' Trade Union, which insisted on its primary bargaining position with the management, was a more 'natural' day-to-day adversary. By 1930 Larkin had given personal offence to virtually every Leader and organisation possible, so the WUI had many enemies and few friends.

For the ITGWU, its opponent was more often the ATGWU. Regular clashes arose over poaching but more fundamentally over whether British unions should even operate in Ireland. Proof of Larkin's criticism of O'Brien's 'style of trade unionism' could be read in what became the WUI. Here Larkin had complete, unchallenged control. He could shape the union how he liked, albeit in terrible economic times. By 1930 the WUI did not, on the ground, appear greatly different from the ITGWU.

Chapter 14 ❧

MARCHING BACK UP THE HILL: THE ITGWU IN THE 1930s

LOWEST EBB AND RECOVERY

The ITGWU reflected on its unique history when coming of age in 1930: 'strife and struggle and conflict' marked its every year. Always based on 'an injury to one is the concern of all', the first period culminated in the 'great struggle' of 1913 that 'literally attracted to Dublin the attention of the whole world.' No mention was made of Larkin. The union was no longer 'a one-man show' but democratic, run by the 'will of the members.' Foran, at a Conference in Head Office, 35 Parnell Square, rallied the troops: 'They had the money, the men, the organisation and the spirit to fight' and would show 'they were as determined to stand up for the workers' rights' as in the 'most historic period' for labour.

All was not rosy, however. In 1932 membership reached its lowest point since 1917, at 14,123. Branch remittances were a mere £12,809, although this was a slight improvement on 1931, at £12,678. They would prove to be the lowest levels ever. Recovery, slow at first, gathered pace to 1939.

In 1930, economic depression affected morale and belief. The 'unappreciative attitude' of younger workers, who took for granted wages and conditions they inherited without struggle, was a concern. Since the union's formation 'nothing less than a revolution' had taken place. 'Unfortunately,' this was 'lost upon too many,' who 'became trade unionists at a time when readily recognised material results were easily obtained.' They had 'little or no knowledge of the old, bad conditions, or of the early and heroic struggles.' Membership nevertheless had 'not merely been maintained' but 'actually increased.' A surplus of £4,395 brought the credit balance to £76,393. Many staff members were dispensed with, however, including the stalwarts Joe Metcalfe, David O'Leary and Rosie Hackett. A 'record' meeting in the Mansion House on Sunday 23 February, as 'Liberty Hall comes of age,' was the 'best and biggest meeting in the last seven or eight years.' It 'was quite inspiring to note how the audience were moved' by the strains of Connolly's 'Watchword of Labour'.

Table 26: ITGWU membership, June 1932

Dublin No. 1	2,581	Leinster No. 2	491
Cork city and county	2,492	Dublin county	474
Belfast and Newry	1,189	Leinster No. 3	472
Dublin No. 3	1,165	Leinster No. 1	468
Limerick city	1,125	Munster No. 1	458
Dublin No. 4	961	Dublin No. 2/7	451
Dublin No. 5	692	Munster No. 2	445
Connacht	659	Total	14,123

Source: ITGWU, minutes of National Executive Council, 24–25 June 1932. Figures are as grouped for Annual Conference: Connacht: Ballina, Ballysadare, Belmullet, Sligo, Westport; Cork: Bandon, Buttevant, Cóbh, Dunmanway, Mallow; Dublin county: Balbriggan, Blanchardstown, Clondalkin, Dean's Grange, Dún Laoghaire, Lucan, Rathfarnham, Skerries; Leinster No. 1: Arklow, Athy, Carlow, Kilkenny, mid-Kilkenny, Naas, Wexford; Leinster No. 2: Laois-Offaly, Mountmellick, Navan; Leinster No. 3: Athlone, Drogheda, Mullingar Mental Hospital; Munster No. 1: Fenit, Kilrush, Tralee; Munster No. 2: Cahir, Foynes, Waterford.

Remittances of Dublin No. 1 Branch to Head Office were £2,670, from a total of £5,703, down on 1928, at £2,948. There were no 'sensational victories,' and members 'suffered victimisation, unemployment and imprisonment in defence of their right to combine . . . Defeat after defeat' was followed by a 'new gathering together . . . in preparation for the next battle with the exploiters.'

'Out of this sacrifice' grew the 'contemporary movement with its proud new status in the community,' and 'in these sacrifices, as in the new liberty, our Union has had its place, and that place is in the vanguard.' Given the long decline, this was a defiant, confident declaration.

The annual Delegate Conference in Killarney was delayed by half a day while the membership of the General President, Foran, apparently mislaid, was found and verified. Neither Standing Orders Committee nor Delegates allowed matters to proceed until 'everything was in order.'

The ITGWU's presence on that year's May Day march numbered 4,000. 'Every Section had its banner,' with 'a special pictorial banner' carried by Hotel and Restaurant Workers 'stressing the importance of tourist development' and the 'still greater importance of seeing that the workers are properly remunerated.' The were banners for Nos. 1, 2, 3, 4, 5, and 7 Branches; in addition, 'slogans from Connolly's writings were carried.' Virtually every occupation was represented, the 'most striking group' being the 'mounted horsemen' of the Undertakers' Section, No. 3 Branch.

There were great celebrations in Sligo. Frank Robbins thought the best thing was that it 'it gave the appearance' of 'one huge, happy family. The dominant spirit might be expressed by saying "Now that we have unity let us have still greater unity.

Let us consolidate our ranks so that the past can never be repeated."' At the May Day dance a relaxed Bill O'Brien was 'regaling an audience on the side-lines with anecdotes,' revealing the engaging and amusing side of his personality.[1]

In Waterford in 1931 Foran urged 'The Union first and all the time.' O'Brien reported that the 'falling off' in membership had 'been stopped.' Recovery was marked in towns, but decline in rural areas continued. A proposed Staff Superannuation Scheme awaited an actuarial report, but a similar scheme for members was considered impractical. Economic prospects were bleak, and the 'best that can be hoped for is that the rock-bottom' of agricultural depression had been reached. Indeed, 'no part of the country is free from the grave consequences of lack of work.' It was clear that throughout the world 'the present social system is breaking up' and 'must be replaced by a new social order more in consonance with the needs and demands of the working class.'

Income actually rose, but this, ironically, was due to returns from securities that had 'considerably augmented' union funds. The ITGWU 'tightened up' on those who fell 'heavily into arrears without reasonable cause.' Small, ineffective Branches were closed. Assistance from and to other unions was sought and given, but while this was a 'commendable practice' the NEC recognised that 'great care must be exercised in the use of our organisation and members for this purpose.' There were strategic and logistical limitations to solidarity. Despite the admission of Limerick Dock Labourers' Society, membership, at 14,123, was the lowest since 1916.[2]

Continuing unemployment provoked a reconsideration of organising strategy in 1932. Previously the union 'had endeavoured to take in all wage earners,' but 'this was no longer possible.' It was 'their desire to build' on the 'basis of industries, local or national' and in 'larger towns where a good membership was likely to be maintained.' Was this a casual obituary for OBU? Certainly, although the motto remained on ITGWU badges it was no longer a policy ambition. The ITGWU openly admitted it was 'compelled to discourage organisation' of farm workers and pushed instead for an Agricultural Wages Board to fix minimum wages. While the year was 'one of the most critical and trying in the country's history,' it was, 'without exaggeration,' one of the 'most successful and active periods in the last decade.' Worldwide depression persisted, but 'again and again' the ITGWU successfully demanded wage increases and defended existing rates. It was 'doubted whether any other organisation in these islands can make a similar claim.'

The Conference called for a 'Union Monthly News Sheet' to be freely distributed, but this was defeated. There were demands to reopen Branches, many from previous members or officers returning to the fold as they regained employment.

The problem of lapsed members required neat NEC footwork. It gave grace to members to reduce arrears within their first six months back in employment. After nine years 'of almost unprecedented depression' the credit balance increased by £29,534. The union's income and investments, which contributed so much to its assets, were 'spent or invested in Ireland, and in Ireland only.' 'Primarily,' the funds 'were for fighting purposes, but such funds as they were free to invest were put into such socially productive and beneficial things as house-building in Ireland instead of being sent across the water to do no good to anybody in Ireland.'[3]

1932 was the lowest point in union history in income and membership. There were only forty-nine Branches, many struggling. Yet 1933 was regarded as 'the most important' for almost a decade. There was a 'very gratifying and continuous increase' in membership.

Table 27: ITGWU Branches and Branch Secretaries, 27 June 1932

Arklow	Thomas Weadick	Fenit	Patrick O'Donnell
Athlone	Peter Mulvihill	Foynes	P. Jackson
Balbriggan	Michael Brady	Kilkenny*	J. P. Pattison
Ballina	Patrick Gallagher	Kilkenny (Mid)	M. Kelly
Ballysadare	Maurice O'Regan	Kilrush	M. Reidy
Bandon	James O'Donovan	Laois-Offaly*	John F. Gill
Belfast*	William McMullen	Limerick*	John Conroy
Belmullet	John Fallon	Longford	Joseph McKenzie
Blanchardstown*	George O'Driscoll	Lucan	Michael Gannon
Bray*	John Dunne	Mallow	P. J. Mullane
Buttevant	A. Powell	Monaghan MH	William Farrell
Cahir	Patrick Lonergan	Mountmellick	John Troy
Carlow	John F. Gill	Mullingar	Thomas Egerton
Clondalkin	M. Fagan	Mullingar MH	James Mellen
Cóbh	Seán O'Connor	Naas	Peter Geraghty
Cork*	Dominick Sullivan	Navan	James Bain
Dean's Grange	James O'Neill	Newry*	Dan McAllister
Drogheda*	Michael Connor	Rathfarnham	Christopher Mulvey
Dublin No. 1*	John (Jack) McCabe	Skerries	P. J. Curran
Dublin No. 3*	Thomas O'Reilly	Sligo*	Maurice O'Regan
Dublin No. 4*	Frank Purcell	Tralee*	Jeremiah Murphy
Dublin No. 5*	Patrick Moran	Waterford*	Thomas Dunne
Dublin No. 7*	Frank Robbins	Westport	Thomas Bourke
Dún Laoghaire	Joseph O'Neill	Wexford	Patrick Hayes
Dunmanway	Jeremiah Coughlan		

* Full-time Branch.
Source: National Archives, Registrar of Friendly Societies, file 275T.

Branch remittances rose by £1,885; and the credit balance, in real terms, impressively touched £100,000. The tide had turned. On a 'necessarily smaller scale' it was seen as 'a parallel' to 'the great days' of 1917–18. This overstated things. Whereas previously anyone and everyone was taken in, now where 'local circumstances' did not warrant organisation, it was not pursued. Increases were the product of 'campaigns of intensive organisation conducted by Branches.'

A press advertisement looked for a National Organiser, 'without mentioning the name of the Union,' demonstrating a gathering confidence that increased membership was possible and a willingness to appoint the best candidate from within or without the union.

Applications from members of the National Union of Railwaymen in Cork were accepted when they were from 'any Section of the road workers,' but all railwaymen had to come over as a unit.

An interesting development was the creation of the Irish Seamen's and Port Workers' Union in July 1933. Despite competing in the ITGWU's core area, the docks, it does not appear to have been resisted, as might have been expected. Instead it was encouraged and eventually became at ally. The new union emerged from longstanding animus among Irish seamen to the National Union of Seamen, a British union. As Larkin's hand appeared to be if not on the tiller then offering pilotage to the new craft, the ITGWU's passivity was a little puzzling. Liberty Hall had abandoned seamen but was sympathetic to Irish efforts to get rid of the corrupt NUS.

Hundreds of disillusioned and unaffiliated port workers, weary of ITGWU-WUI rancour, founded a short-lived Dockers' and Carters' Union. It merged with seamen to form the Irish Seamen's and Port Workers' Union. It was this element that the ITGWU might have opposed.[4]

SILVER JUBILEE

Addressing the Silver Jubilee [twenty-fifth anniversary] Conference in May 1934, Foran felt 'justifiable pride' that 'for a full quarter of a century' he had led 'the greatest organisation in the history of trade unionism in Ireland.' Comparison between wages and conditions for workers in 1909 and 1934 said it all. The 'terrific onslaught' of 1913, war, Rising, 'disruption of 1923' were all recalled, as well as the union's 'guiding star and ablest Leader,' Connolly. Larkin was studiously ignored. Foran concluded: 'We haven't had a better or more successful year for ten years.' The Conference expanded from a two-day adjunct to Congress to a separate three-day affair.

More than sixty requests for new Branches were received in 1933. Senator Michael Duffy (NEC) challenged the caution of the Vice-President, Thomas Kennedy, in ignoring rural workers.

> Money would have to be spent on organisation. The slump had now passed and the need for a conservative policy no longer obtained . . . Had the Union not been so generous in the past to rural workers they would not now have five members in the Dáil.

Country members, whatever about Head Office, had a deep concern for the plight of rural workers. An Agricultural Wages Board was finally conceded in 1936. Branch remittances rose by £4,645 to £19,339, the highest since 1926.

What had occasioned the growth in membership? The ITGWU's explanation was threefold: 'prestige of the Union'; 'planned' organisation of developing, new industries and establishment of industrial Branches; and the capacity to win significant disputes. Foran thought 1934 'equalled anything done by the Union at any period in its fighting history.' Thousands benefited from its militancy and efficiency. It had a '£100,000 fighting fund', designed, if need be, for 'big, long and strenuous struggles.'

Disappointment with Seán MacEntee's Budget, when workers were asked to pay disproportionately for social legislation, meant the ITGWU would be forced to make employers pay their rightful share 'in the shape of wages, shorter hours and better conditions.' Workers responded to this 'fighting talk.' O'Brien reported that by December 1935 income would have risen by 100% in three years.

Kennedy wanted industrial Branches catering for whole sectors. Dublin Clothing Trades Branch acquired 2,000 members in a year. Kennedy talked again of 'One Big Union,' but this was a very different-coloured fish from the original. Murtagh Morgan (Belfast) thought 'O.B.U. should be built on scientific lines,' and the 'finest tribute' to Connolly was to 'go forward with a definite scheme of industrial unionism.' Dominick Sullivan (NEC) called for Industrial Councils, provided for by the Rules but not acted upon. Contributions should be increased, as 'there was only a surplus of 4s 1½d in every £1 to cover emergencies.' Kennedy felt that organisation was handicapped by the difficulty of recruiting specialist staff, although he ruled out 'competitive examination.'

1935 saw growth 'on a scale comparable to the most strenuous' in the union's history: 'not for many years' had there been 'such intense and continuous activity.' This placed a strain on the organisation, but it was handled successfully. Growth was 'most gratifying' to 'members and friends' and 'most disconcerting' to 'enemies and opponents.' In a demonstration of growing self-confidence Foran warned it would 'be unwise for any body of people, employers or otherwise, to attempt to trip up or hamper' them. There was a swipe at 'some of the recently converted would-be leaders' outside the movement who had 'been telling them how to fight . . . but these gentry had nothing they could teach the front line fighters of trade unionism.' They had 'neither responsibility nor a working-class industrial and political tradition behind them,' and their 'attempts to gain a rank-and-file following amongst the working masses had been inevitably vain and futile.'

Fragmentation into smaller organisations was opposed. J. P. Hughes (Kilrush) again raised the neglect of rural workers. Duffy (NEC) disagreed, as there were great difficulties in keeping in touch even with county council roadmen, and those in private employment were nigh impossible to organise.

There were demands for greater publicity for wage advances won, such as the increase of £1,300 a year for a hundred members of the Dublin Carpet Section, increases of 5s to 25s for workers in Dunlop in Cork, and an increase of £2,000 to £3,000 a year for fertiliser workers.

Membership reached 20,951. The biggest Branches were Dublin No. 1 (3,265), Cork (2,738), Dublin No. 3 (1,519), Limerick (1,419), Dublin No. 4 (1,250), Belfast

(970), Dublin No. 6 (854) and Dublin No. 8 (512). Ten Branches had between 250 and 500 members, fourteen between 100 and 250, another fourteen between 50 and 100 and twenty-three fewer than 50. Geographically the ITGWU was in all counties except Longford, Armagh, Derry, Fermanagh, Monaghan and Tyrone.

Congress asked the ITGWU to consider 'undertaking the organisation of agricultural workers,' but it declined. It was not prepared to 'undertake this task as, in our opinion, the organisation of agricultural workers on trade union lines, under existing conditions, was not possible.' In January 1936 the growing Cork Branch was divided in two.[5]

Table 28: ITGWU membership, 1930–39

	Union figure	RFS figure
1930	14,608	33,400
1931	14,500	32,580
1932	14,123	32,400
1933	14,660	35,000
1934	16,670	30,000
1935	20,951	30,000
1936	24,810	36,000
1937	28,514	36,000
1938	33,095	36,000
1939	36,444	36,000

Sources: ITGWU, minutes of National Executive Council, 1930–40; National Archives, Registrar of Friendly Societies, file 275T.

Substantial progress was maintained in 1936. In four years membership 'actually doubled': 'whenever new industries were established, our Organisation and machinery have been put at the service of the workers concerned.' Even so, 'requests for organisation had to be refused in many rural areas.' National Conferences were held for flour-milling, woollen manufacture and sugar-beet, with Joint Industrial Councils established. In 1937 J. P. Hughes (Kilrush) wanted specialised Organisers appointed to take in all wage-earners in creameries, turf works and fisheries 'until those industries are 100% organised.' Con Desmond (Cork No. 1) said that workers in these industries were a 'menace' to the organised. Duffy predicted difficulties: in turf, wages were low and yet turf was 'dearer than coal in most towns.' M. Kelly (Bennettsbridge) thought County Secretaries were the solution. Kennedy 'regretted having to damp the enthusiasm,' but, taking into consideration the subsidising of turf and concessions to farmers to grind their own wheat, he thought the prospects in those areas poor. The Agricultural Wages Board, once established, had 'many defects' and was a 'tardy acknowledgement' of ITGWU representations.

Table 29: ITGWU Branch remittances to Head Office (£), 1930–39

1930	13,291	1935	23,531
1931	12,678	1936	26,654
1932	12,809	1937	30,228
1933	14,694	1938	32,887
1934	19,340	1939	32,831

Source: ITGWU, Annual Reports, 1930–39.

Income in 1937 showed a 100% increase over 1932 but only a narrow surplus of £857, as Dispute Pay was £18,948. Surpluses were invested in Trustee stocks of local authorities 'for erection of working class housing.' A Prices Commission heralded the possibility of problems when more than 100,000 people were already un-employed and with young workers 'crossing in thousands every week' to England and Scotland. Foran told the 1938 Conference: 'If that Prices Commission was going to check profiteering, prevent dumping and stop the new capitalists from exploit-ing the community and the consumers, well and good.' But if it 'were to be used in favour of foreign capitalists' he could foresee 'plenty of industrial trouble.' Industrialisation brought mechanisation, and mechanisation brought job losses.

Membership rose by 4,000 in 1938. Both organising and negotiating staffs 'had to be increased.' The immediate task was shortening the working week and gaining paid holidays. James Gilhooly (Galway No. 1) asked the Labour Party 'to have legis-lation introduced to prevent the employment of persons who do not possess a trade union card in any industry which has a monopolistic control.' P. Macken (Mullingar) committed the ITGWU to seeking superannuation and pension provision for men-tal hospital nurses, but calls for a Special Conference were rejected.[6]

Table 30: ITGWU income, expenditure and surplus (£), 1930–39

	Income	Expenditure	Surplus
1930	16,901	12,505	4,396
1931	16,994	14,653	2,341
1932	17,380	10,158	7,222
1933	19,340	11,891	7,449
1934	24,389	19,377	5,012
1935	27,482	26,590	892
1936	30,471	19,962	10,509
1937	35,081	34,224	857
1938	37,340	19,956	17,384
1939	37,494	16,974	20,520

Source: ITGWU, Annual Reports, 1930–39.

It was claimed that, 'leaving out farm labourers, the numerical strength of the Union is probably as great as in its peak period.' For Foran, on the point of retirement, this must have been highly satisfactory. He had steered the ship back to enticing open waters from the menacing rocks of 1923–5. The ITGWU was represented in thirty-seven of the thirty-eight Department of Industry and Commerce employment categories. Still primarily a transport and general workers' union, it had thousands in manufacturing, and a quarter were women and girls. Membership was 160% higher than in 1931 and the union 'financially stronger than it had ever been at any time in its history.'

Interestingly, Head Office kept no record of membership. The only way of calculating it was by financial returns. A membership census was conducted in July 1938. William McMullen was National Organiser.

At Congress, affiliations from the Irish Automobile Drivers' and Automobile Mechanics' Union, Limerick City Workers' Union, the United Builders' Labourers' Union and the United Stationary Engine Drivers' Trade Union—all formerly part of the ITGWU or breakaways—were opposed. In addition, the application of the WUI was denied, as it would not undertake to confine activities to Dublin city and county.

Table 31: ITGWU Branches, July 1938

Ardfinnan	Fermoy
Arigna	Ferns
Arklow	Fethard (Co. Tipperary)
Athenry	Foynes
Athlone	Galway No. 1*
Athy	Galway No. 2
Balbriggan	Gorey No. 1
Ballina	Gorey No. 2
Ballinasloe	Graigue
Ballymore Eustace	Kildare
Banagher	Kilkenny*
Bandon	Killarney No. 1
Belfast*	Killarney No. 2
Bennettsbridge	Killarney Mental Hospital
Birr	Kilrush
Blanchardstown*	Kingscourt
Blarney	Laois-Offaly*
Bray*	Limerick*
Cahir	Lisnaboe
Carlow*	Longford

Carrick-on-Shannon	Lucan
Carrick-on-Suir	Macroom
Castlebar	Mallow
Castlerea	Midleton
Cavan	Mitchelstown
Clondalkin	Monaghan Mental Hospital
Clonmel Mental Hospital	Moneenroe
Cóbh Mullingar	Mountmellick
Convoy	Mullingar Mental Hospital
Cork No. 1*	Naas
Cork No. 2*	Navan
Cork Mental Hospital	Newry*
Dripsey	Port Laoise Mental Hospital
Drogheda*	Rathdowney
Droichead Nua	Rathfarnham
Dublin No. 1*	Sligo No. 1*
Dublin No. 2	Sligo No. 2
Dublin No. 3*	Thomastown
Dublin No. 4*	Thurles
Dublin No. 5*	Tralee*
Dublin No. 6*	Trim
Dublin No. 7*	Tuam
Dublin No. 9*	Tullamore
Dublin No. 10*	Valleymount
Dún Laoghaire	Waterford*
Dunmanway	Westport
Enniscorthy	Wexford
Fenit	Wicklow

* Full-time Branch.
Source: National Archives, Registrar of Friendly Societies, file 275T.

A further £250,000 advance in wages was won with national Agreements being struck in bacon-curing, cement manufacture ('a quite new industry in Ireland'), flour milling, hosiery, paint, sugar-beet and woollens. Weekly hours were widely reduced below forty-eight. This was a 'magnificent thing' for a union with a 6d a week contribution. Wages 'were not everything,' however. The ITGWU was more than a 'mere wage-raising machine.' Under capitalism, increased wages were often offset by higher prices of commodities, goods and services and 'greater accumulation of wealth in the hands of manufacturers.' The only remedy for the new President, Thomas Kennedy, was 'putting into full political power' the Workers' Representatives.

Kennedy's speech was a radical statement of the Socialist agenda. He concluded that members should 'give a little of their time to thinking of the unemployed,' because unless they could do something for their plight 'we will have to write ourselves down as failures.' To do anything, workers, indeed society as a whole, 'would have to give up their selfish attitude of the past.'

The union received a scare on 13 October 1939 when William McMullen was injured in the Bletchley train crash in Buckinghamshire, in which four people lost their lives.[7]

Table 32: ITGWU, credit balance (£), 1930–39

1930	76,393	1935	101,297
1931	78,734	1936	111,807
1932	87,956	1937	113,845
1933	95,405	1938	131,229
1934	100,405	1939	151,874

Source: ITGWU, Annual Reports, 1930–39.

THOMAS FORAN

At the end of 1938 Thomas Foran indicated his intention to retire. He had been General President of the ITGWU from its formation in 1909. He had 'contemplated resigning' in June 1932, as the 'state of his health would not permit of his resuming active work.' Although he recovered, 'his old drive and energy were diminished.' The NEC learnt this news 'with regret' and 'tendered to him its appreciation of his work' before granting him a 'retiring allowance.' At the 1939 Conference his successor, Thomas Kennedy, 'paid warm tribute' to Foran, who simply slipped quietly from the bridge.

The solid position of 1938 almost matched the high point of 1923. The sheer volume of work undertaken by Foran was incredible. He attended countless negotiations, settled innumerable disputes and maintained a dignified, solid presence, around which the ITGWU could rally. He remains *the* unheralded ITGWU hero.[8]

WOMEN

In 1935 Louie Bennett (Irish Women Workers' Union) asked Congress to reaffirm 'its allegiance to the fundamental principle of equal rights and equal democratic opportunities for all citizens and equal pay for equal work.' William O'Brien seconded, supporting the motion but not Bennett's speech. The 'whole tendency' was to 'substitute cheap, low-paid women's labour for men's.' Organising women workers was difficult. He welcomed the Minister's action in embodying Section 12 of the Conditions of Employment Bill (which provided for the 'restriction of employment of female workers') at Congress's request. Bennett spoke alarmingly about women being driven out of employment; but the reverse was often the case. O'Brien concluded that 'the occasions upon which Miss Bennett and himself agreed were rare,' and he thought he 'should seize any opportunity in supporting anything she put forward. (Laughter).'

Women queued up to attack O'Brien and Section 12. Thomas Birch (Dublin No. 3) said that 3,000 women in his Branch worked in tobacco, where some work was definitely unsuitable for them. He 'thought it was a very wrong thing that young girls should be sent to factories and young men kept out.' Bennett thought it disappointing that 'an independent body of labour men should be willing to give the Minister such power.' Men should stand with women in opposing Section 12.[9]

The ITGWU's female membership rose from 1,000 in 1930 to 6,000 in 1939, an increase from 7 to 15% of total membership. Union attitudes did not reflect this. Women's issues were not mentioned, and traditional hostile attitudes to women in the work-place persisted.

NORTHERN IRELAND

At the 1932 Congress McMullen called for the abolition of the Means Test and Anomalies Regulations as applied in Northern Ireland under the Unemployment Insurance Acts (1931). Supposedly operated in the 'spirit of equality of sacrifice,' practice was far from that. Representations made to the Unionist Government met the common cry of hands being tied by the British exchequer. McMullen observed that 'unfortunately, we in Northern Ireland, are in the subordinate and humiliating position' of 'following whatever legislation is introduced in Great Britain.' The Labour Party would contest every ward in the 1933 Poor Law Guardian elections, and 'if we get a majority we will feed the poor at all costs.' They did not.

In 1938 McMullen asked that organisation be extended in the North of Ireland if the ITGWU 'intended to remain a National Organisation.' The Conference concurred, but there was little evidence that much was done. O'Brien saw only problems: 'competing unions, very low wages, prejudice of employers and the Northern Government.' It might be argued that similar problems existed in the Free State. Head Office attitudes to activity in the North were ambivalent.[10]

ITUC SPECIAL COMMISSION

On 1 November 1930 the ITUC paper, the *Irishman*, was retitled *Watchword*. The 'greatest possible economies' were necessary, and Cathal O'Shannon's editorial services were dispensed with. A former Organiser, Éamon Lynch, was appointed Secretary of Congress on 30 August and took over, supported by a Watchword Development Committee, which O'Brien briefly attended, expressing pessimistic views of the paper's future.

After a number of inter-union disputes, notably between the ITGWU and ATGWU, Congress moved the 'co-ordination of union activity,' as 'disintegration must lead to demoralisation and invite an attack by employers.' A Special Congress, held on 25 April 1936, considered the amalgamation or grouping of unions; setting up machinery to co-ordinate trade disputes and settle inter-union issues of demarcation; conditions upon which unions could affiliate; establishing all legal matters relating to unions; and making recommendations for general organisation. It set up a Commission of Inquiry, of which O'Brien was a member, which began lengthy deliberations. It divided by seven to five in favour of Irish organisations, together with the Secretary, Lynch. The ITGWU, from its creation, had organised 'on principles and methods . . . designed to remove the very difficulties' being discussed. In many towns there was only the ITGWU. This 'had proven by far the most efficient and most profitable' organising model. They hoped workers in other unions would learn this lesson and act accordingly. The ITGWU's successes led to enquiries from unions in Britain, and exchanges of experience and advice proved 'of service.' The union nevertheless had reservations about the Commission's work. The proposal to reduce the number of unions to ten, each catering for a specific industry, led William Murphy (NEC), a bus worker, to raise objections, as 'we would lose some of our members.' The Commission of Inquiry published an interim report in 1937. 'OBU' was in sight but would not necessarily have been recognised by Connolly.

A Special Congress early in 1939 considered the proposals of the Commission of Inquiry. The ITGWU favoured a model of industrial unionism that would put all workers into one of ten unions. It would have meant the union's 'dissolution' in its then form and the transfer of members to new organisations. The NEC saw this is as huge sacrifice. 'For the I.T.G.W.U., the biggest and leading Union in Ireland, with its long, honourable and glorious record, and proud and unequalled achievement in the working-class movement, this was no mean gesture. Unfortunately the proposals we were prepared to accept were not adopted by the majority at the Special Conference.' Reorganisation would have to wait.

Congress had set up the Commission partly under pressure from Seán Lemass, Minister for Industry and Commerce, who suggested that if unions did not rationalise themselves it would be done for them. At the 1939 Congress, however, the divisive nature of the process was revealed in complaints that the National Executive's report was disingenuous. The ITGWU made no comment.[11]

DUBLIN TRADES COUNCIL

James Larkin's petition to discharge himself from bankruptcy in late 1931 was opposed by the ITGWU. It continued to ostracise him from the movement. His wife was finally removed from ITGWU property at Beechwood Avenue on 14 November 1932, where she had lived since 1922. Foran was protective of her interests at the NEC. Much union property was being disposed of, and the decision was purely economic.

Dublin Trades Union Council accepted the affiliation of the WUI in 1936. It angered the NEC, but it felt that the 'decision was with Dublin membership.' It consulted 'other unions who opposed and who would probably be influenced by the decision of this Union as to whether or not we would remain in affiliation.'

Foran and Kennedy wanted to withdraw, but O'Brien was in the majority of 8 to 4 who 'favoured our remaining in affiliation for the present.' All unions consulted 'favoured our remaining in affiliation.' This was accepted, although Daniel Clancy wanted a Special Conference. Dublin Shop Stewards and Branches welcomed the decision.[12]

DISPUTES

At the 1930 ITUC Congress McMullen seconded a motion calling for a Charter of Industrial Demands, including statutory rights and the defence of public-sector wages. 'The sooner we stiffen our backs to prevent reductions in wages, and the lowering of the standard of living . . . the sooner we enter the high way which will bring us to success.' O'Brien was morbidly realistic. It was difficult to co-ordinate actions among competing unions: the floor was 'doomed to disappointment.'

Despite widespread cuts, the ITGWU won 'notable victories' for Limerick pork butchers through the Bacon Workers' Council, gained paid holidays in sweet factories, and achieved 100% membership in Dublin cinemas. Resisting cuts dominated industrial activity in 1931, successful in flour mills, Dublin cinemas and theatres, Belfast and Newry seed merchants, Belfast and Sligo docks, creameries, shirt-making and bacon factories, and 'in a great many miscellaneous jobs.' The reorganised Bacon Factory Workers' Council was a future model. The turning tide was indicated by the 'remarkable success of our pickets at a new Dublin cinema' in enforcing unionisation.

A few wage increases were gained, and employers' favourite new tactic, replacing adults with boy labour, resisted. In Mullingar the long-ignored town rate was regained. The Hotel and Restaurant Branch renewed its three-year Agreement with employers in 1932, retaining 1919 rates and improved conditions. By 1934 'all hotels and restaurants in Dublin' were organised and 'employment could only be obtained through the Union.'[13]

In 1932 Foran called for a National Minimum Wage. The local agricultural wage was generally taken by industrial employers as the norm. Fair-wages clauses, although adopted by public authorities, were ignored. All this raised spectres of the Shannon Scheme; but, with acute depression, questions of consumption and demand were also relevant. Foran spoke of the success of the Labour Party in securing a guarantee that all future public housing schemes would be operated at union rates.

A dispute in the Dublin printing trade involved the ITGWU and Dublin Typographical Provident Society. It centred on wage claims at a time when, behind tariff protection, employers made significant profits while 'some of the unskilled workers from 21 to 25 years of age' received only 'from 21s to 25s a week.' Printers in the *Evening Herald* refused to print a management statement on the eve of the strike, which outraged the employers, who blithely ignored an agreement to provide a fortnight's notice to cast men out overnight. Foran particularly praised IWWU members, but Congress gave primary support to the ITGWU.

By 1933 wage increases were being won again. A six-month recognition strike among Benduff and Madranna quarrymen, Dunmanway, was 'fought stoutly and determinedly,' even though the men were 'isolated.' They were 'fully worthy' of their victory. The union recorded a 'general revival of spirit and of militancy' and regularly struck to enforce closed shops. Dispute Pay rose from £425 to £1,394. Historically this was tiny, but the strength of the ITGWU meant that threatened action was often enough. The 'greatest victory' was in Dublin cinemas, where, after five years' fruitless picketing, a three-week strike finally broke the employers' resolve. Their 'scab labour' and strike-breakers were fired and full union rates and conditions achieved. Dominick Sullivan (NEC) called for a national cinemas Agreement. In Cork alone £5,000 was spent on cinemas and the theatre, much of it by the working class, but 'very little of this' went to pay wages. O'Brien noted that Dublin No. 3 Branch gravediggers, who had earned 16s for a seven-day week, now earned 55s for a six-day week, 'because of organisation.'

New protected industries employed child and female labour and needed organising as a matter of urgency. Congress submitted a 'Fair Wages Clause' to the Government for insertion in all public works, later changed to a 'Fair Labour Clause', covering conditions and remuneration. Contractors had to compel subcontractors, transferees or assignees to accept the same conditions, enforceable if necessary through machinery 'such as the Industrial Courts Acts, 1919.'

The ITGWU complained about a form that anyone promoted from temporary to permanent positions in the Electricity Supply Board had to sign, stating that they were satisfied with their conditions. Complaints about pay or conditions had to go 'directly through the District Engineer.' Congress agreed that this was an inducement for workers to secede from their unions. The ESB replied that it was standard procedure. A Conference of ESB unions made representations to the Government on 26 March 1934, pointing out that the document would not be tolerated. No reply was received by July 1935.[14]

Table 33: ITGWU Dispute Pay, 1930–39

	Income	Dispute Pay (£)	As proportion of income (%)
1930	16,901	983	5.8
1931	16,994	4,450	26.2
1932	17,380	425	2.5
1933	19,340	1,394	7.2
1934	24,389	7,000	28.7
1935	27,482	13,509	49.2
1936	30,471	6,871	22.6
1937	35,081	18,948	54.0
1938	37,340	5,234	14.2
1939	37,494	2,652	7.1

Source: ITGWU, Annual Reports, 1930–39.

In 1934 there were strikes in Dublin jobbing printers and newspapers, the Waterford building trade, Blarney woollen mills and Arigna mines. Workers' self-confidence was returning. The managers of three Dublin daily newspapers refused to meet the ITGWU to discuss improved wages and conditions. Support was given by Dublin Typographical Provident Society, which took sympathetic action 'as a matter of principle.' After a 'stubborn struggle' victory was achieved, with increases, weekly hours reduced from forty-eight to forty-five, compulsory union membership and the establishment of a conciliation board. Neither the three morning nor two evening papers appeared for nearly ten weeks, 'a record unequalled anywhere.' Of particular pleasure was the fact that ITGWU membership was now compulsory in 'concerns owned by employers who led the war' on the union in 1913. The union was 'right to be proud' of its 'triumph twenty-one years after the tremendous effort to wipe' the ITGWU 'out of existence.' In the separate book and jobbing houses dispute, increases of up to 30s doubled wages after a three-week strike.

A four-day stoppage in Carlow sugar factory reversed cuts previously agreed by an English union, benefiting 3,000 workers. Later, the wages of 1,500 men building factories at Mallow, Thurles and Tuam were raised without industrial action. J. F. Gill 'paid tribute to the Czechoslovak workers' in Carlow, who refused to scab 'even when threatened with cancellation of their passports.'

A new Clothing and Cap Branch, started in 1933, won significant advances in February. In construction the ITGWU busily enforced the wage and conditions clauses of the Housing Act (1933). In Waterford, employers refused to reverse cuts, but 'after a hard-fought strike' an increase of 1½d an hour was won. The union brought out men in Bray, Carrick-on-Suir and Kilkenny in support. More than 700 workers in Blarney Woollen Mills eventually persuaded a recalcitrant employer to grant increases of 4s 6d. The ITGWU's prestige, in ordinary workers' eyes at least, was immeasurably advanced.

In 1935 Dispute Pay rose to £13,509, the highest since the record-breaking year of 1923. Far more claims were settled without action.[15] The elimination of non-union labour was widely achieved, and 'certain legal rights of members and Branch Officials' in dealing with non-Unionists were 'reaffirmed on appeal' in the Courts. The ITGWU established that it had a 'legal right to call out members to compel the dismissal of non-Unionists.' A building worker, Cranny, sued Alderman J. P. Pattison TD, Secretary of the Kilkenny Branch, for inducing his employer to break his contract, dismiss him and not re-employ him without joining the union. Judge Seely in the Circuit Court found for Cranny and awarded damages, but on appeal Mr Justice Hanna said it seemed clear to him that if Seely's decision stood 'it would virtually mean the repeal of the Trade Disputes Act, as far as it gave protection to the Secretary of a trade union with regard to the employment of certain of their members.' Pattison had 'called to the works' and 'intimated to the employer that if Cranny was not dismissed' other members 'would be called out.' Hanna's opinion was 'that this intimation' was 'made in furtherance of a trade dispute in existence at the time he made it, and that Judge Seely was wrong.'

A large Dublin hotel strike was averted at the eleventh hour. Big increases and reductions in hours were achieved and the 'last big house outside the union' organised. Some unions, having neglected organisation, would demand, after Liberty Hall stepped in and won advances, that they return to their original union. The ITGWU had no problem in giving assistance where 'consultation or co-operation' had been sought but complained that too often 'we were called upon to bear the burden of the fight.' Internal discipline was demanded, as some members allowed themselves to get involved in situations that courted disaster.[16]

In 1936, 'at a moderate estimate,' £250,000 was gained for members, with improved holidays and conditions and shortened hours. Unofficial strikes occurred 'without the knowledge or against the advice' of the NEC and 'occasioned some difficulty.' Strikes centred on non-unionisation or were 'against the employment of non-local labour.' More than £3,500 was won for mental hospital workers in Carlow, Killarney and Monaghan, but, on the debit side, progress stalled in sugar-beet and bacon-curing. Comhlucht Siúicre Éireann 'strongly resisted' demands for a Conference. When the season opened in Mallow a strike ensued, 'fought with great vigour.' Unfortunately in Thurles, 'seduced by local pressure,' workers were 'persuaded to establish a blackleg and strike-breaking organisation.' Ultimately both sides referred matters under the Industrial Courts Act. By a majority, the Court agreed to hear evidence from the 'Thurles blackleg organisation,' whereupon the ITGWU withdrew and the ITUC representative resigned.

In Waterford a strike for recognition in bacon firms was 'eventually conceded after a fight lasting thirteen weeks.' A significant strike in Tralee was settled as the Congress opened in August 1936, Delegates congratulating the men 'on the magnificent fight they had put up in the cause of trade unionism.' Building strikes took place in Cork and Dublin in the summer of 1937. Foran invited the Conference to wish 'these front trench fighters—many of them women and girls'—a victorious outcome.

Dispute Pay ran at about £1,500 a week in June, a position O'Brien assured Delegates they could sustain indefinitely. The ITGWU had never 'imposed a levy to pay Dispute Pay, although practically all other Unions had done so.'

In Convoy, Co. Donegal, 400 woollen mill workers transferred from a British union to firmly establish the ITGWU in the county. Expansion was difficult, however, an eleven-month strike being necessary in the bacon factory in Ballybofey. It was a 'vicious strike,' with 'many violent clashes and clashes with the Gardaí.' Blacklegs were brought from all over the country. The Branch Secretary, J. A. McElhinney, and Carlow Branch Secretary, Stephen Carroll, were 'hustled from the factory by the employer wielding a pitchfork.' Scabs were finally paid off, but the factory shut rather than concede. Local relief schemes were a 'big scandal.' 24s a week was 'bad enough,' but the rotational system was worse. Many became poorer working than if unemployed for the whole week. The ITGWU saw the establishment of Joint Industrial Councils as generally advancing its members, establishing new ones for hosiery, linen and cotton, and sugar-beet.

The number of disputes fell in 1938. The 'most difficult fights' were the result of 'anti-trade union attacks by employers on, or opposition by, other organisations.' At the Congress Murtagh Morgan called for 'statutory recognition' of JICs, but Lynch was 'chary': the flexibility of voluntarism was superior to the rigidity of law.

James Larkin, a DTUC Delegate, asked what there was to fear in JICs unless their representatives were not competent. Kennedy pointed out that JICs, unlike the old Wages Boards, provided for direct negotiation between worker and employer, with no independent, Government-nominated presence. The problem was that employers reneged on Agreements. He demanded legal enforcement. JICs facilitated organisation, although unions did not broadcast this.

In 1939 Kennedy complained that the Government was not operating sections of the Conditions of Employment Acts to enable the registration and, therefore, enforcement of Agreements. The required six months frequently elapsed before any response was made when attempts were made to register Agreements, thereby nullifying them. Such Agreements in any case applied only to wages. Kennedy wanted hours and conditions included; the 'legal enforcement of trade union Wage Agreements would do a good deal to help the movement generally.' Constant recourse to legal protection could, of course, be interpreted as reflecting a lack of industrial muscle and an incapacity to enforce matters directly with employers.[17] The 1930s did not suggest that the ITGWU suffered any such lack.

DUBLIN BUILDING LOCK-OUT, 1931, AND STRIKE, 1937

In the autumn of 1930, 'recognising that division in the ranks of the builders' labourers had led to considerable disorganisation and weakness,' the Dublin Master Builders' Association demanded wage reductions. The ITGWU met this challenge by carrying out a 'vigorous and intensive campaign of reorganisation.' Labourers 'responded well' and 'finally decided not to agree to any reduction.'

As the time for the proposed reductions neared, the employers announced that individual contractors would take men on at any rates they could agree, 'tantamount to repudiating the old Agreement.' The ITGWU informed the employers that men would not work for less than the old rates. It sought to compel the employers to sign Agreements to pay these rates, a campaign 'that was eminently successful.' The union was strongly supported by the craft unions in the Building Trades Group of the Trades Council, to which it authorised, 'if necessary,' a loan of up to £1,000. Resistance was 'an example and an inspiration' to other building unions and 'to all Sections of workers, organised and unorganised, throughout the whole country.' With the ITGWU membership, and unions generally, at their lowest ebb, the outcome was crucial and timely.

A small number of contractors 'stubbornly resisted' the unions' demands. Towards the end of the year they changed tactics, terminated all Agreements and demanded big reductions. This led to the Lock-Out of all building workers in the spring of 1931.

ITGWU Dispute Pay was £4,450 that year, mostly spent on the building strike, which lasted from January until April. It was 'fought stubbornly . . . on all sides,' as it was 'recognised that its outcome would determine the attitude of the general body of employees outside, as well as inside, the building industry,' making it 'essential that the most strenuous resistance should be put up.' The ITGWU claimed a leading role. It was 'in large measure' the ITGWU's 'energy, initiative and resources' that 'brought it to a satisfactory conclusion,' despite 'exceptional obstacles.'

Craft unions were divided and 'did not always act in harmony.' 'Amalgamated or English' unions 'refused to accept the terms which the great majority of the strikers of all unions had agreed upon' before they too made an agreement 'substantially the same as the others,' in which 'wages were slightly reduced.' The ITGWU led 'flying columns' of the Building Trades Group to 'enforce the observance of the Agreement, including the employment of none but union labour.' It 'regretted that Amalgamated craft unions subsequently withdrew' from the Trades Council, 'but, for this our Union was in no way responsible.' In March the NEC was 'authorised if necessary' to lend up to £1,000 to the Operative Plasterers and Bricklayers, should they require it, a quiet, unpublicised gesture of solidarity.

In December 1936 the Building Trades Group resisted attempts by employers to take advantage of the Conditions of Employment Act to change contracts. The group countered by demanding increases, reduced hours and a guaranteed working week—'a new step in the movement towards a better life for the building worker.' Compromise was offered on 30 December, but the Master Builders' Association asked that matters be delayed until 31 January 1938. There had been no improvements since 1931, so a thirteen-month delay was unacceptable.

Talks dragged on until March, when the Minister for Industry and Commerce intervened. The Employers' Association offered a 47-hour week (40 had been sought) and an increase of ½d an hour from 10 August 1937, to 'obtain for five years, fluctuating with the cost of living.' The Building Trades Group rejected this paltry offer and demanded 3d an hour from 1 January 1937, a 40-hour week from 31 March, improvements in country allowances, height money, better apprentices' rates and a guaranteed working day. A further Government-brokered Conference followed, but an inevitable strike began on 13 April in Dublin, closely followed by Cork, lasting seven months.

Advances of 2d an hour were ultimately made, together with a pledge by the Government to introduce 'Wet Time' measures. Differences between the many unions involved, particularly with plumbers, 'introduced complications which were not easily disposed of.' Heavy financial burdens were placed, but the ITGWU 'came through them all triumphantly.' Most unions heavily levied their members, 'in some cases even for regular Dispute Benefit,' but there was no such need for the ITGWU: 'we were able to finance the whole struggle without as much as a penny piece being levied off any member.' Building workers in Cos. Galway, Kildare, Sligo and Waterford gained increases without a strike.[18]

Thomas McCarthy recalled the impact of the strike twenty-five years later as 'emphatic': 'Workers had suffered great hardships, reflected automatically on their dependants. But in ratio to their sufferings their loyalty to the Union increased and much of the bitterness, mistrust and suspicion had gone.' He was referring in particular, of course, to relations on the ground with WUI members. A signal victory lifted morale within the movement.

FLOUR-MILLING

By 1932 many flour mills had ceased to operate, put out of business by dumping. The remaining mills, all fully unionised, met and proposed that the Government take the industry into public control. This was not achieved, but the Agricultural Produce (Cereals) Act (1933) did make the observance of union rates and conditions compulsory for any miller seeking an operating licence. Workers won representation on a Milling Advisory Committee. Similar conditions operated under the Housing Act. In 1933 Kennedy called for controls over the introduction of machinery. He wanted the Minister to 'fix a definite ratio between output and the labour employed,' concerned to establish a 'fair balance between' inland port mills, which captured trade to the detriment of inland business. Joe McCabe (Dublin No. 1) added concerns about the replacement of adults with boy labour.

In 1934 the benefits of the Agricultural Produce Act saw many rejoin the union. The Flour Milling JIC was re-established and immediately dealt with demands for a national increase of 10%. Kennedy cautioned about 'over-milling' and complained that union proposals were rejected by the Milling Council: workers had only one member, compared with six employers. If matters were not improved the Conference instructed Kennedy to resign. Despite lobbying by the Labour Party, parity was not achieved.

In 1935, after a nine-week strike to enforce ITGWU membership in Clara flour mills, J. F. Gill reported that 500 workers in the local jute factory joined: success bred success. The owners' 'profitable monopoly' was not shared. The union's fears of 'over-production' and a fall in workers' incomes were realised. It wanted no further mill licences granted: 'state control was the only solution.'

National strike notice was served in 1936 before 'substantial all-round increases' were accepted by ballot. The national Agreement contained 'two special features': standard rates for boy labour, with the restriction of boys to specified jobs and extra payments for night shifts. Increases in the boy rate were retrospective over twelve months.

The ITGWU continued to warn of the dangers of over-production, as it did for the boot and shoe trade. Further motions in 1937 and 1938 called for a restriction on licences for wheaten flour mills, the establishment of a Maize Milling JIC, the nationalisation of flour mills, a reduction in hours to forty-four a week, with two weeks' paid holiday, and the employment of union labour only.[19] Flour was an important industry for the ITGWU, building membership and attracting others.

DUBLIN TRAMWAYS

In 1932 Foran forecast the 'possible break-up of foreign trade unions in this country.' Bus workers transferred from a British union in Cork, as did general workers in Tuam. After an Agreement on wages and conditions with the Irish Omnibus Company and Great Southern Railway, 'whole Sections and Branches' transferred from the ATGWU, 'numbering hundreds.' In some instances applications were held at bay, as 'times and circumstances were not favourable.'

In 1934 the formation of an ITGWU Tramways Branch was discussed, and the ATGWU made efforts to 'deprive of their employment those who had taken a prominent part' in setting it up. The ATGWU forced a strike; it was won after three days by the 'men who came over.' Daniel O'Hanlon (ITGWU) criticised the Minister for Industry and Commerce, Seán Lemass, as having acted against the 'interests of Irish Trade Unionism.' Had he not taken the action he did all 'Dublin Tramway men would now be in an Irish union,' their money retained in the country 'instead of being transferred to England.'

The ITGWU's actions were the subject of a formal censure by Congress. 'To describe as "poaching" the revolt' of Dublin Tramwaymen was 'a wanton misuse of a well-understood term; in fact, it is a claim that Irishmen shall not be permitted to manage their own affairs.' The ITGWU denied that its actions violated the constitution of the ITUC, as there was 'nothing in [it] which would prevent Irish workers from severing their relations with foreign Unions whenever they desired to give their allegiance to an Irish Union.' When a 'large body of Tramwaymen assured us that they had definitely decided to become members of an Irish Union, we conceived it our duty to accept them as members of the ITGWU.' Congress accepted that the men were indeed 'determined' to change allegiance. Lemass set up a Conciliation Board, representing unions and company.

At the 1934 Congress O'Hanlon (a leading ATGWU defector) protested about the composition of the Road Traffic Act (1933) Advisory Council: rank-and-file busmen should have been selected. Gilbert Lynch (ATGWU and a recent defector from the ITGWU) and his colleague E. P. Hart suggested that this was a personal attack. O'Hanlon insisted that his criticism was purely of the board and its actions. Sensitivities were raw and were to become more so in the debate on the tramways dispute. Kyle 'merely looked for fair play': 'no union had a right to win cheap popularity at the expense of another . . . Spurious patriotism' caused the problem, and he thought the Executive's actions 'Hitlerite.' Helena Molony (IWWU) paid tribute to the contribution of British unions in Ireland but did 'expect from them a certain breadth of vision.' Tempers were high, and rising.

An attempt in 1935 to 'smash' the Tramways Branch was resisted. O'Hanlon thanked DTUC for its support. The year opened with a minor skirmish over timetables and the failure of the Conciliation Board to settle matters. More than 1,000 ITGWU members officially came out for eleven weeks after the dismissal of an ATGWU man. The ITGWU seemed to be opposed by company, Minister and state but gained a victory with the restoration of old wage rates and improvements in conditions. It concluded that 'our success' was 'all the more noteworthy and satisfactory because it was clear from the outset that the old feeling of bitterness engendered in 1913 still affected the Company in its attitude to this Union.' It also thought it 'had the added difficulty and complexity of temporary alliance with an English Union.'

Lemass suggested that 'legislative action will be necessary to prevent [the] recurrence of a similar emergency.' The NEC 'expressed satisfaction at the result' and entertained the DTUC Executive and the Branch Strike Committee to dinner.

The ITGWU instituted proceedings against the ATGWU in 1935 to 'restrain them from carrying on business in Ireland' as 'Transport and General Workers' Union' or 'any other name so nearly resembling the name of this Union as would be likely to deceive the public.' It wanted the name ATGWU declared 'illegal and invalid' and damages arising from a decision of the Dáil Éireann (Republican) Courts in 1922 preventing the use of 'TGWU.' Justice Meredith declared on 30 October in favour of the ITGWU and awarded full costs. The ITGWU decided that the 'report of this case should be printed' but the journalist employed to 'furnish a full report' did a 'very incomplete' job. It was 'doubted if it would be wise under the circumstances to publish.' In 1936 Dublin No. 9 (Tramways) Branch signed an Agreement with the ATGWU regarding organisation and joint action.

Another fall-out of the dispute was the approach by the Irish Road and Rail Federation, virtually broken by strikes and caught between the two bigger unions, to merge. The NEC decided it 'would not accept this Union as a whole but that we would be willing to accept those of the membership employed in road services.' This maintained an understanding with the NUR that it would not take railway workers.[20] Skirmishes with the ATGWU suggested that it, rather than the WUI, was still the more constant threat to the ITGWU.

In 1937 Kyle and Lynch regretted the 'action of an affiliated union through the Courts of law on a constitutional issue.' The National Executive of the ITUC had 'considered this question in 1927.' It did little for working-class unity. Kyle took the moral high ground: the ATGWU 'were prepared, and are still prepared to work in harmony' with others 'as far as humanly possible,' wanting and being prepared to give a 'fair deal'. Lynch suggested that if the ITGWU 'turned their attentions to organising the working class rather than having disputes in open Courts' they 'would be achieving something worth while.'

O'Brien replied in imperious manner. The legal action arose from the creation of the Transport and General Workers' Union in 1922 and the attendant confusion with the ITGWU. In February 1922 O'Brien had written to the General Secretary of the TGWU, Ernest Bevin, as the 'names of your Union and ours are practically similar' and the ITGWU 'was known widely as the 'Transport Union.' Both unions had offices in Parnell Square, making confusion even greater; and the press regularly mixed up the two bodies. O'Brien found it hard to believe that the Registrar of Friendly Societies had allowed two such similar names. He asked Bevin what action he was prepared to take to clear matters up.

Bevin's reply of 28 March was cleverly dismissive before pulling numerical rank.

Surely the word 'Irish' has some value in indicating the different society, at any rate if I were to say it hadn't you, I think, would be the first to remonstrate with me. I cannot think of any other name which would more adequately represent the half-million members for whom we cater.[21]

And there matters lay, as, according to O'Brien, 'Bevin refused to discuss the matter further.' There could be no agreement between the two until this confusion was sorted out. Congress moved to next business.

COALMINING

James Gilhooly (Arigna) thanked the 1934 Conference for its support during Leyden's strike and wanted a statutory 'legal minimum rate of wages and fair conditions' for all underground workers, with a pension at sixty. It won compulsory membership and an increase of 1s 8d in the pound, while at Lynn's 3d a ton was secured without a strike. Nixie Boran (Moneenroe) expressed disappointment that the Conditions of Employment Act did not apply to coalmining. Miners had 'harsher conditions than other workers,' but nothing was done for them, and they 'were not considered worthy of a week's holidays.' In 1936 he wanted the Government to establish the principle that all workers on attaining the age of twenty-one be entitled to 'the full adult rate,' irrespective of their job. Oliver McMorrow (Arigna) 'emphatically' protested against the failure to set up a Court of Inquiry, 'as requested,' into miners' conditions. He urged a 'legal minimum', 'fair conditions' for all underground workers and a pension scheme providing for retirement at fifty-five. Boran cited a Medical Officer's examination of men over fifty in Castlecomer. He found the majority unfit for work, because they were 'physical wrecks from diseases contracted.' 87% were unfit for underground work.[22]

SUGAR COMPANY

On 18 October 1934, two weeks before the new 'Sugar Campaign', the ITGWU wrote to Comhlucht Siúicre Éireann in Carlow demanding that all employed should be members of unions affiliated to the ITUC. The factory was already pulping, and any action would delay the campaign.

Congress brought the eight unions involved together and met Lemass. By Saturday 20 October the ITGWU's demands were not conceded, and it struck the following day. The understanding was that the Irish Engineering Industrial Union would come out with it, but Congress 'were very much surprised' to learn that they remained at work. This was 'considered serious', as it involved the 'prestige' of Congress. The stoppage was now partial, with obvious consequences for industrial relations. The ITGWU was 'grievously disappointed.' The IEIU had attended all Conferences and negotiations and never indicated any change of intention.

On 24 October the IEIU Executive said it 'had no option other than to endorse the decision of our Carlow Branch' to work as normal. This was regarded as abandonment of the principle of employing union labour. Congress sought to 'severely censure' the IEIU.

The dispute ended in victory on 25 October, at least as far as permanent positions were concerned. As for casuals, union membership would be necessary 'at the next campaign, provided the Union [ITGWU] could show a representative percentage of organisation amongst' such workers. The ITGWU complained to Congress that the IEIU was taking in unskilled workers, 'whose conditions have been improved' during their ITGWU membership. It denied all charges. Better communication within Carlow would have solved everything: 'it was not their ambition to fight with anybody of their own class and they were not doing so.' Inter-union tensions in Carlow long persisted.[23]

AGRICULTURAL LABOURERS

The ITGWU resisted regular calls to organise rural labourers, demanding instead an Agricultural Wages Board to 'fix minimum rates of wages and conditions for agricultural workers.'

Michael Duffy thought this should have happened long ago in what was in effect a 'sweated industry', employing 'pariahs of the community.' Improvement in the workers' lot generally was a function of the betterment of those at the bottom of the pile. From 1922 the labourers' position had worsened. Cheap produce from abroad—'mainly the colonies'—which was largely 'State-aided or State-organised,' flooded the market. Wages of 35s to 55s per week in 1923 had declined to barely more than 20s. Farmers had all sorts of grants and bounties to improve husbandry, introduce new crops, extend land utilisation and more; labourers had nothing. The Land Commission and the Department of Agriculture were 'run at considerable expense,' but only in farmers' interests. They even got concessions in not having to pay full land annuities, but still nothing for labourers. In Britain an Agricultural Wages Regulation Act operated since 1924, with tripartite Committees determining wages regionally. John Gill (Laois-Offaly) cited a man getting a day's work to thin beet from 7:30 a.m. to 9:30 p.m. for 2s.

In 1935 it was suggested that either affiliates organise agricultural workers or a New Union be formed. Duffy agreed about the need but insisted that an Agricultural Wages Board, rather than union organisation, was best. It was difficult to organise those 'brought into close contact with their employers, who were often relatives and school chums, and attended the same church, who in extremities helped each other, and were closely associated in their everyday life on and off the farm.' T. J. Murphy TD (Dunmanway) did not entirely agree, as 'it was a remarkable fact that the agricultural areas were almost entirely responsible for the existence of a Labour Party in the Dáil.' The ATGWU agreed to undertake the task. The ITGWU agreed it would not compete in the area, other than to retain county council road-workers.

In 1936 Kyle (ATGWU) complained that 'it was an exceedingly difficult job.' Many labourers were 'prospective owners of their land,' and the seasonality of employment complicated matters. He requested help; but there was no stampede from the floor.[24]

NURSES

At Congress the ATGWU regularly sought improved pay, conditions and pensions for nurses, general and psychiatric. On 6 December 1935 a mental hospital attendants' Conference was held in Dublin. Kennedy, S. McMorrow and A. Doyle represented the ITGWU. They appeared to have held fire at joint gatherings, holding ammunition for more direct approaches. The ITGWU was the biggest nursing union, despite a presence by the ATGWU and IWWU. It did participate in a joint meeting on 6 December 1936, which led to a campaign for improvements, particularly in Grangegorman Hospital, Dublin. James Everett TD was part of the Congress Delegations but the Minister saw 'little useful purpose' in all the approaches.

Attempts to change the local authority managerial system failed. All power in mental health was held by County Managers, which made industrial relations extremely difficult. In 1938 further joint union meetings took place, with matters referred to the Joint Committee of the ITUC and Labour Party to add political clout to demands for improved pay, hours and conditions.[25] The ITGWU would emerge as the psychiatric nursing union in the next decade.

EMPLOYMENT

In 1932 the ITGWU argued that 'no permanent cure for unemployment' could be provided 'by the existing social organisation of society.' It demanded 'a National Scheme of social reconstruction and economic planning' through a National Economic Council.' The state should assume control of 'all unoccupied or unused land' for afforestation and housing, nationalise all public utilities, provide for workers' representation throughout industrial management, improve social insurance, control mechanisation to minimise disemployment, encourage rural enterprise, ensure that juvenile employment did not exceed an agreed proportion of adult employment, and restrict hours to create jobs. McMullen worried about de-industrialisation and urged the lesson of the Russian Five-Year Plan. The ITGWU supported tariff barriers as part, rather than the totality, of a package of job creation. Employment rose in protected industries, but the ITGWU complained that 'in too many cases—indeed in the majority of cases—such increased employment as was given by tariffs was confined to women and young girls and generally at low wages and under bad working conditions.' The state should compel manufacturers who benefited from tariffs to 'employ trade union labour at trade union rates.' Tariffs had the negative effect of reducing work for dockers. The ITGWU demanded alternative employment.

In 1933 McMullen criticised the 'continued inactivity' of the Free State and Northern Ireland Governments. 'If private enterprise cannot provide work' then surely it became a state responsibility. He wanted adequate monetary provision for the unemployed by an amendment of the Unemployed Insurance Acts, 'with the democratic organisation and reconstruction of industry, so that the right to work shall be guaranteed.' The Free State, in McMullen's view, was worse than Northern Ireland. Had the Government possessed a 'spark of humanitarian impulse . . . we would be spared the spectacle of people suffering in the midst of plenty.'

Senator Michael Duffy's Presidential Address to the 1934 Congress reflected his visit to the ILO in Geneva and his insight into worldwide economic problems. He cautioned the Government and employers.

> When unemployment has continued for winter after winter without any ade-quate relief and without any sign of early alleviation; when farmer and peasant are reduced to penury by inability to sell the fruit of their labour at a reasonable price, when the flow of capital and credit is reduced to a precarious trickle, the bounds of psychological endurance are eventually reached. In the end a tidal wave is generated which is apt to sweep away not only Governments but consti-tutions; not only economic policies but even economic creeds which have long been worshipped with religious devotion.

Contemporary 'catastrophic political upheavals' in Europe gave substance to these remarks. The World Economic Conference 'failed to establish stable monetary con-ditions,' leaving 'embittered economic warfare', in which wages were a major victim. Duffy saw 'national tempers more dangerously aroused than in any period since 1914,' the international market breaking up, 'to be supplanted by mediaeval-like nationalism.' The 'New Deal' in the United States offered some hope, but this was balanced by Hitler's rise to power in Germany. Duffy was prescient in his view that

> the rosy promises of improvement held out to the German people remain unful-filled. Today they are governed by a gang of praetorian guardsmen, the well-paid Pinkertons of the capitalist class, and freedom has been banished from the land of a freedom-loving people.

He warned of terrible calamity for Europe. He cited Australia, Canada, Poland and the United States to support his claim that reduced hours benefited economic performance, created more jobs and generated demand. The Government claimed 'to be representative of all the people,' a democratic Government;

> let them put this claim into effect economically . . . If Government is in earnest about the political status of this island, we say as a condition precedent to the suc-cessful prosecution of political freedom that they free the Irish Workers from eco-nomic servitude and the foreign ideas of the Manchester School of Economics.

In 1935 Duffy moved the annual motion demanding economic planning. The unemployed could be applied to 'industrial and agricultural works,' such as afforestation, main drainage and road reconstruction in 'self-sustaining groups' managed by an Economic Planning Commission after consultation with the national education authorities and Congress. Bog and moorland should be com-pulsorily purchased for forestry.

It was McMullen's turn in 1936 to castigate 'futile Governmental efforts to stabilise private ownership in the vital industries … by bounties, tariffs and quotas.' There 'was no reason why there should be hardship in this or any other country.' Frank Robbins put his finger on the key. The DTUC gave great assistance to the unemployed, but in the last Municipal Elections not many of the 30,000 unemployed voted Labour.

On 11 November, Congress issued a 'Memorandum from the National Executive on the Subject of Unemployment and Proposals as to How the Condition of the Unemployed may be Alleviated and Abolished.' It led to a flurry of relatively meaningless correspondence and an equally fruitless meeting with the head of the Government, de Valera, and Ministers in June 1937. The unlikely prospect of significant Labour gains allowed politicians to keep their arms firmly folded.

On 29 March 1939 Lemass angered Congress by his speech in the Dáil. 'I think it is not unfair to our Trade Union Movement as a whole to say they have been indifferent to the problem of the unemployed.' This triggered a lengthy, highly detailed refutation. Since 1931 Congress and the ITGWU had made the same demands for greater planning, increased state control and involvement, and worker democracy. Lemass was being mischievous, the unions predictable.[26]

PENSIONS, SOCIAL WELFARE AND SAFETY

In the 1930s the ITGWU called for pension schemes for public servants and reform of the Unemployment Assistance Act. In 1934 the union was asked to introduce a members' sickness benefit scheme. It was dismissed as impracticable. McMullen voiced the principle of a non-contributory scheme, as the 'unemployed are not responsible for their plight.' A 'National Scheme of Social Insurance, embracing all wage-earners, and administered directly by the State,' should provide adequately against 'sickness, invalidity, unemployment, accident, widowhood, orphanhood, old age and mortality.'

In 1932 an amendment to the Workmen's Compensation Act was sought to provide for the compulsory insurance of all workers, either through a state scheme or insurance companies. This would compensate for fatal injury and define a 'schedule of Industrial Diseases'. There was no action on the Commission on Workmen's Compensation, which was 'now long overdue.' Kennedy wanted the ratification of numerous ILO conventions, namely Hours of Work in Industry (1919), Hours of Work in Commerce and Offices (1930), Childbirth (1919), Employment of Seamen (1920), White Lead (1921), Workmen's Compensation for Industrial accidents (1925), Night Work in Bakeries (1925) and Sickness Insurance in Industry and Agriculture (1927), and the implementation of the Merchant Shipping (International Labour Conventions) Act (1925).

Congress took its role in the ILO very seriously and with pride. The ILO was the first international arena in which an Irish state participated. The ITUC was sensitive to the honour and responsibility. Kennedy pointed out that there was 'nothing revolutionary' about the conventions. Some dated from 1919. With much delight, Congress reported the ratification of many of them by 1934.

The ITGWU National Health Insurance Approved Society, subject to annual scrutiny at the Delegate Conference, was absorbed into a Unified Society on 15 December 1934 under the National Health Insurance Act, ending the union's involvement in this area since 1911. The manager and four members of the ITGWU Society's staff were employed in the Unified Society, with compensation offered to the remainder.

On 17 July 1935 the Minister for Industry and Commerce informed Congress that workers on strike would be debarred from receiving Unemployment Benefit as long as the stoppage of work continued. This refined an existing interpretation, extending debarment to those who might be made idle even if not directly in dispute. A Labour Party amendment to the Unemployment Assistance Bill (1933) failed to rectify matters. Little progress was made, despite persistent lobbying.

In 1938 Kennedy demanded that Congress reiterate 'its demand for the compulsory insurance by employers of all workers against the risks inherent in the workers' occupations.' James Hickey TD (Cork) decried employers who did not stamp cards and the negligence and lack of vigilance by National Health Insurance Officials. James Larkin (DTUC) called for the restoration of all benefits lost after the amalgamation of the approved societies. Hickey supported him and demanded a detailed inquiry into the whole system. In 1939 T. J. Murphy TD (Cork) pointed out that under the Unified Society benefits had fallen back to 1912 levels, yet there was £4¼ million in the Reserve Fund. Kennedy did not want a return to the old Approved-Society system but equity and value for money. He wanted to see that 'some form of insurance was introduced by legislation which would guarantee to every insured person not only what was owed to him, but what would enable him to get back to work with renewed health.'[27] The Government continued to resist this reasonable demand.

CONDITIONS OF EMPLOYMENT ACT (1936)

Congress felt that the Conditions of Employment Act (1934) fell behind its British equivalent. Its 'outstanding weakness' was that it did 'not make insurance compulsory' and required many additions before there were 'satisfactory provision for the casualties of our industrial system.' De Valera was asked to make May Day a public holiday. He replied that 'there was no sufficient reason for such a course.' Labour Party amendments to the Conditions of Employment Bill were defeated.

In 1935 Foran said he could see some of the bad points of the Conditions of Employment Bill but he 'could not see in it the roots of all evil which some of those in the movement saw in it.' Trade Unionists would 'never surrender their last weapon, the right to strike,' but the Bill 'would do something to check the abuses' of the exploitation of women and juveniles in tariff-protected industries. He outlined ITGWU thinking: 'The man was generally the breadwinner and he was being driven out of employment. If the Bill helped to keep adult male labour at work it would serve a useful purpose.' Contrary to what others thought, he did not think the Bill would 'abrogate or repeal the Trade Union Acts.'

Kennedy 'heartily approved' of Section 12 as the first real effort to give male labour its rightful place in the new industries. Frank Robbins expressed 'utmost dissatisfaction' that Lemass had failed to apply the forty-hour maximum. He thought that for women and juveniles it should be thirty hours, 'without reduction of wages', and that twelve working days' paid holidays should be provided for. Section 12 prohibited the employment of children under fourteen.

When the Act came into operation it merely gave legislative effect to provisions previously enforced by the union through industrial action. It did not touch wages—an ITGWU priority—particularly for child labour.

Robbins pointed out that 'in Russia the school leaving age was eighteen.' Kennedy answered criticisms by pointing out that unions 'had taken very little interest' in the Bill: 'not a single suggestion' was received from unions by the Labour Party. There were 'no grounds for the fears' that the Act would lead to the displacement of adult male labour. D. O'Hanlon (Tramways Branch) suggested that the union produce an explanatory booklet.

At the 1937 Conference legal entitlement for paid holidays and public holidays was raised and criticism made of the Minister for exempting creameries and the Condensed Milk Company. Frank Purcell (Dublin No. 4) protested that the Shop Assistants (Conditions of Employment) Bill (1938) allowed for the increase of hotel workers' hours to fifty-six per week and the compulsory introduction of two hours' Sunday duty without compensation. The Employers' Federation was playing the ITGWU at its own game by introducing conditions by legislation that it would not have succeeded in enforcing industrially. Employers who did not like the outcome of JIC negotiations could renege by simply withdrawing, thus avoiding 'obligations honourably entered into.' Protests to the Minister simply drew the suggestion that JIC Agreements should be registered under the Conditions of Employment Act. This would not provide a full remedy, however, as registration was a long 'and by no means simple' process and covered only wages, not hours and conditions. On non-wage matters 'offending employers could still go scot free so far as the law was concerned.' Only the Hosiery JIC Agreement was registered. Industrial legislation consumed union resources. In 'too many instances' employers found 'ready means of defeating the legislature's intentions without incurring legal penalty,' and 'only by vigilance' did ITGWU members enjoy legal benefits. Such legislation, while important and necessary, was not the panacea and was no substitute for alert organisation.

In 1936 Jack McCabe (Dublin No. 1) spoke against the Special Powers Act, complaining that 'any prominent Trade Unionist might be thrown into prison' because of their normal activities. Kennedy complained that the enforcement of wage rates under the Conditions of Employment Acts did not operate, instancing the Pigs and Bacon Act as an example.

In 1938, for the first time, a review of the Factories Acts and factory inspection was sought, particularly in clothing, with its 'one-room workshops where workers are herded together under conditions that are a menace to health and future well-being.' The Shops (Conditions of Employment) Act (1938) and Holidays

(Employees) Act (1939) added to social legislation, even if the 'machinery of inspection' and prosecution 'were woefully defective and inadequate.' Cathal O'Shannon supported calls for paid holidays. He suggested a 'slow-down—to show not only the boss class, but Mr. Lemass and the Government that working people were as anxious for more leisure and a better time as for an odd half-crown.' Kennedy called for the more effective enforcement of statutory rights. The only ones doing any enforcing were trade unionists.[28]

LIBERTY HALL

The union's holiday hostel at Wicklow continued to struggle. Receipts dropped to £207 in 1931. The NEC, 'having reviewed all the circumstances,' decided there was no alternative but to dispose of it at the first available opportunity, although the Marine remained open for business, and 'a greater measure of support' was hoped for. It was put up for sale in 1932—an inauspicious time for property. A small profit was shown in 1933, but still members neglected a venture 'being conducted for their benefit.' It housed a 'large number of people' whose homes were endangered by flooding in the spring of 1933. In both 1934 and 1935 it was the venue of the Annual Conference, demonstrating its attractions so as to generate more business. Losses were incurred in 1936, despite the Labour Party's Summer School being held there. A 'substantial loss' in 1938 was, 'no doubt, due to the bad summer.' It was an albatross around the ITGWU's neck.

The premises of Newbridge [Droichead Nua] Branch were closed in 1930, and the sale of the Cork offices to the Salvation Army considered. In 1932 £2,000 was received as compensation for damage done to Liberty Hall in 1916. The original claim, made under the Insurrection Act, was rejected 'on the grounds that the Union was implicated in the Insurrection.' O'Brien, while a TD, resurrected the claim in the Dáil in 1927, and the Minister for Finance promised that the matter would be considered. The claim was refused, because 'no money was available out of which it could be met.' Foran took the matter up in February 1932. 'The Government intimated its willingness to settle the sum', and £2,000 was paid in July.

In 1935, on Foran's suggestion, J. McCabe (Dublin No. 1) and J. Clarke (Dublin No. 3) moved that a fund 'be devoted to the re-building of Liberty Hall as an object worthy of the associations and traditions of the Union.' O'Brien poured cold water: there were 'many difficulties', not least the estimated cost of '£100,000 to erect a suitable building.' Kennedy thought it 'not feasible.' Foran betrayed a rare public disunity among General Officers. He wanted an 'edifice worthy of the Union.' J. Barry (Cork) asked that a levy be struck. The motion was adopted.

In 1936 the union sold premises in Kilrush and Banagher. Dublin Corporation closed union premises at 74 Thomas Street as unfit, and No. 3 Branch moved into Liberty Hall. In 1936 O'Brien told Jack McCabe that 'the profits of the Shop had been set apart' for the purpose of rebuilding Liberty Hall—an unusual explanation for a long finger. McCabe and Barry were back in 1937 asking what happened to their 1935 resolution and that at least £1,000 be set aside each year from the General Fund for Liberty Hall. An Emergency Motion in 1938, moved by Frank Robbins and Frank Purcell, attempted to address the 'absolute need' for 'equipment, accommodation and assistance' for Dublin Branches—in other words, the renovation at least of Liberty Hall. The motion was withdrawn once O'Brien agreed to meet a Delegation of Dublin District Council.[29]

EDUCATION AND TRAINING

In 1933 the ITGWU was concerned that young workers had no knowledge of past struggles, took conditions and wage levels for granted, and needed 'to learn the basic principles of the working-class movement.' Labour study classes, Summer Schools and the Labour press all had a part to play, but education was the movement's 'greatest weakness'. The 'want of a weekly journal' was 'a most serious loss.'

Murtagh Morgan (Belfast) demanded an Educational Department that would 'embrace all social and economic matters.' O'Brien expressed sympathy but contented himself with announcing that they had 'acquired the rights to publish James Connolly's works' and bemoaning the absence of a Labour paper. Kennedy saw education as 'one for the Political Party.' There was no clear thinking on education and nothing on skills training for industrial staff and Shop Stewards.

At the 1934 Conference senior figures and Labour Party TDs presented papers on housing, employment, mechanisation, dockers, pensions and the 'political situation', a novel use of the Conference for educational purposes.

In 1935 Dan McAllister (Belfast) suggested spending on 'working-class education.' The response was a joint ITUC and Labour Party Summer School. The ITGWU guaranteed a number of students; but this was hardly the answer to workers' education. Twelve were sent in 1936.

Members wanted a monthly newspaper. *Labour News,* a weekly, was published, but was not focused on the ITGWU.

In 1937 Robbins suggested that Dublin District Council might subscribe 'towards sending children of members to the Gaeltacht.' McMullen and McAllister (Belfast) asked that a 'monthly journal' be produced 'free of cost' to Branches. McAllister raised the union paper again in 1938, but O'Brien said the NEC understood that *Labour News* 'met the case.' The General Election prevented the attendance of the ITGWU at the Labour Party's Summer School. Morgan called for winter classes as well. Robbins thought it 'the most important' motion under debate, for the need for working-class education was immense, as the 'Connolly Labour Colleges established in 1920, considering the hours spent in them, produced very effective workers in the Labour movement.'[30]

FASCISM

In 1934 Senator Michael Duffy warned of the dangers of fascism. In Ireland the Blueshirts were engaging in 'the same blustering, saluting and parading' as in Nazi Germany, with behind it all 'the hope of the reactionary politicians that they can successfully exploit economic distress and ride to power in the storm.' The Labour

Party and ITUC held meetings to expose the danger. Fascism could not be allowed to succeed, in whatever guise, as it put trade unionism in dreadful jeopardy. Employers wanted an abundance of cheap labour, 'which, dragooned beneath the Blueshirt Fascists, would be voiceless, impotent and incapable of resistance.'

In 1934, alarmed by Fine Gael's announcement of a desire to inaugurate the 'Corporate State', which would 'organise all the workers and all the employers in a federation,' the ITUC and Labour Party issued a 'Manifesto to the Workers of Ireland on the Fascist Danger'. The threat was '"Corporate State" or "Corporate Slavery"?' Forced labour gangs were a feature of fascism. Workers were urged to oppose the Blueshirts. Public meetings were organised in a call to action by 'not alone the working-class, but every hater of arrogance and lover of liberty.' An appeal raised £133 14s 5d.

With an eye on Europe, workers were warned on Connolly Day, 6 May, that 'similar treatment will be meted out' in Ireland 'if ever the self-styled "Corporate State" advocates of Blueshirt Fascism should succeed in securing political power.' The irony of choosing Connolly Day, rather than May Day, was that opponents of the international and Socialist significance of May Day were accommodated before more radical and outward-looking elements. Congress justified this as an appreciation of Connolly and the 'great principles of social and national freedom he yielded up his life to establish.' Connolly would no doubt have preferred May Day, especially when confronting fascism.

At the 1934 Congress Roddy Connolly (Bray Trades Council) called for support for the Republican Congress 'as the expression of the revolt of the young workers and small farmers against reactionary Imperialist tendencies in Ireland, North and South, and for the advancement of the struggle for an Irish Workers' Republic as conceived by James Connolly.' McMullen seconded, 'on his own responsibility.' Tardiness among Continental trade unionists cost them dear.

O'Shannon opposed an 'ingenuously drafted' motion. He cautioned: 'In the IRA those people found that the narrow path of nationalism was not enough. They had got a new slogan and they said they got it from Connolly. He 'knew them for many years, and he knew 'perfectly well that with most of them the new movement was only varnish for Socialism and Communism . . . All sorts of efforts' were being made to organise a Communist Party, and this was one of them. Every effort in the previous seventeen years 'had been a miserable failure,' as workers were 'not such mugs' as to support Communists. The Republican Congress gave them another name. 'Was there any reason in the wide world why any of those people who said they were anxious to organise the working class and small farmers should not join the Irish Labour Party?' Murtagh Morgan (Belfast) spoke for the motion, regretting that divisions had appeared in the ITGWU. The motion was defeated.

In 1935 McMullen opposed any 'Corporate State' attempts to restrict union freedoms, as this was 'merely the Fascist State under which all liberties of the working-class will be suppressed and must disappear.' He warned of Mosleyism and Blueshirtism, although in the North 'they had a remarkably good substitute for the

Fascist movement in the Government of Northern Ireland.' Fascism must be destroyed in Ireland 'before it becomes too formidable.' Thomas Farren warned that Lemass's threatened legislation to curtail strikes was an example of Southern fascist tendencies.

In 1938 the Congress again condemned fascism. James Larkin (DTUC) warned that the Southern Government was trying to deny Freedom of Association.

In 1939 Dawson Gordon (Belfast Trades Council) saluted 'the heroic Chinese people in their glorious struggle against Japanese imperialist aggression' and called for a boycott of Japanese goods and all possible assistance to China. O'Brien sarcastically criticised the 'rather high-falutin' language,' expressed surprise that there was a boycott, and wanted to know who the China Campaign Committee in London were.

Richard Anthony (Typographical Association) demanded that Communism be equally condemned. O'Brien rose to attack those who raised the 'bogey of Communism': 'These "friends" give ammunition to the Blueshirts and the wreckers of the trade unions by references that give people an opportunity to say we did not condemn Communism.' He opposed any 'opportunity being given to wreckers to attack us.'[31]

INTERNATIONAL SOLIDARITY

McMullen attended the TUC Tolpuddle Martyrs Centenary Commemoration in Dorset in September 1934—an 'honour' at 'so unique and so historic a function.' Kennedy reported as ITUC Delegate to the meeting of the International Federation of Trade Unions in Weymouth on 27–28 August, presided over by Walter Citrine of the TUC. Twenty countries were represented, although only Canada and Palestine from outside Europe. Action against any future war was discussed, with the League of Nations being asked to take preventive action. The fascist menace was again raised.

At the ITUC Congress in Derry, Sam Kyle (ATGWU) moved that Congress affiliate to the International Federation of Trade Unions. What seemed a non-contentious motion, not least given an absence of speakers, appeared to be adopted until one Delegate demanded a card vote. The result was rejection, 42,925 to 76,197. If affiliation were to be considered, Congress decided that its affiliation fees would need to be increased.

In 1936 Louie Bennett (IWWU) again moved affiliation to the IFTU. It was not a straightforward decision. O'Brien was among those who argued that 'they should first have their own movement organised and controlled as a national entity in Ireland,' although 'there was much to be gained by association with the workers of other countries.' A decision was deferred.[32]

THE LABOUR PARTY

The ITGWU remained affiliated to the Labour Party after its division from Congress in March 1930. J. C. Flanagan (Dublin No. 3) was clearly concerned about the new independent Labour Party: it was 'too much towards "the Right".' The NEC drafted a 'political programme in keeping with the history of the Union,' to which members seeking public office should subscribe.' Shamefully, some Labour Party TDs fell out of benefit, and it was agreed that any 'Oireachtas member who lapsed a second time' would not be re-admitted.

When the former Organiser Éamon Lynch became editor of *Watchword* in 1931, Larkin's *Irish Worker* commented—probably to Lynch's surprise—that he was a 'noted Bolshevik.' Paddy Hogan TD was reinstated after lapsing and regarded as a new member from December 1930. In 1932 the Conference kept its eye on Labour Party activity, or inactivity. The 'state of the law' prevented union affiliation to the Northern Ireland Labour Party. The ITGWU was never an affiliate. In the General Election the ITGWU supported the largest number of candidates on the Labour Party list, five of the seven elected being union men.

Although small in numbers, the Labour Party was powerful, as it held the balance of power and helped bring Fianna Fáil into Government for the first time. While 'under no illusions as to Fianna Fáil,' the Labour Party, 'in view of Cumann na nGaedheal's record,' had no difficulty in supporting it. It 'brought to an end the ten years' Rule that had failed to serve working-class interests.' There were constituency problems, most notably in Carlow-Kilkenny, where Ned Doyle's alleged ineptitude 'prejudiced . . . our candidate, J. P. Pattison.'[33]

One regret was the loss of the movement's paper, *Watchword*, published under various titles since 1917. For ten years it was the ITGWU paper. Lack of finance caused its closure. 'We cannot conceive of an alert, active and well-informed movement without at least one weekly paper to express its views and demands, to educate its members and the general public, and to rally support to its side.' A General Election in 1933—the second in twelve months—severely taxed the finances of the Labour Party and the ITGWU. McMullen and O'Shannon undertook national speaking tours in support of union-sponsored candidates, all of whom pledged to uphold union policy in the Dáil. Of the eight Labour Party TDs returned, five were ITGWU men: Corish, Everett, Hogan, Murphy and Pattison. The 'fusion of reactionary parties' to create Fine Gael determined the Labour Party, with some reluctance, to continue support for Fianna Fáil as the lesser of two evils. The ITGWU thought the decision 'wise in the circumstances.'

The Labour Party claimed 'its share of credit' for the Unemployment Assistance and Workmen's Compensation Acts. At the 1934 ITGWU Conference a notable feature was the contribution of Labour Party TDs. Richard Corish read a paper on housing, describing direct-labour housing schemes successfully completed in Wexford. Fianna Fáil depended on Labour Party support in 1934, but the Party insisted on 'its freedom of action', despite de Valera's invitation of 'closer co-operation.' Fianna Fáil took 'many planks' from the Labour Party's programme, but, as Connolly had insisted, 'Labour was never so strong as when it stood alone.'

Internationally, capitalism was in collapse. It was time for new systems to be tried if Governments were to fulfil their primary obligation to 'feed, clothe, house and educate' their people. The ITGWU supported Labour Party demands for joint councils to control industry, raising the school leaving age to sixteen with continued, vocational training to eighteen, fair rents and more houses. Since 1922 the ITGWU had spent £15,000 in the 'political field', more than all other unions put together. Robbins argued that the Labour Party should 'advocate clearly a Workers' Republic,' while the Vice-President, Kennedy, said the 'working class would not be organised on a programme of reform of the capitalist system.' The Labour Party 'needed a clear-cut policy of advocating the complete abolition of capitalism.'

Such fighting Socialist language proved short-lived, but its sincerity in 1934 cannot be doubted. Demands for 'loyalty' to the Labour Party resulted in the Secretary of the Belfast Branch, William McMullen, being reprimanded for attending the Republican Congress in 1934. A number of other charges were made against McMullen's leftist activities. The NEC issued an edict that no member or Official 'had authority to associate with' the Republican Congress or any organisation other than the 'Irish Labour Party to which this Union is affiliated.'[34]

T. J. Murphy TD was praised for his part in the Widows' and Orphans' Pensions Bill and agitation led by the Labour Party for protective legislation for agricultural workers. The Leader of the Labour Party, William Norton, addressed the 1935 ITGWU Conference, thanking the union for its assistance and outlining the Party's achievements. Using its political power, the Labour Party got wages clauses into the Pigs and Bacon Act (1935).

In November 1935 the Labour Party wanted £2,000 to launch a weekly newspaper. The ITGWU granted £500, 'provided the full amount of £2,000 was made available, and subject to the Union being satisfied with regard to its control and management.' In May, Connolly Commemorations, organised jointly by Congress and the Labour Party, were held throughout the country.[35] All agreed to commemorate Connolly by 'steadfastly' pursuing the 'twin ideals of Irish Independence and Social Emancipation.' The ITGWU's attendance was prominent throughout.

The 1937 General Election gave 'wage-earners another opportunity of electing representatives of their class,' a chance to show they 'considered factories and fields and workshops, and the conditions prevailing in them, of far more importance than Constitutions, thrones, commonwealths and politicians' quarrels.' 'Union loyalty' should be carried into the ballot box. The 'finest jubilee of Connolly's creation' of the Labour Party would be 'to increase its representation.' Robbins thought they needed to reappoint a Political Secretary. The creation of the Agricultural Wages Board demonstrated the 'usefulness of political action' where 'industrial action might not be effective.'

At the 1937 General Election the Labour Party was considered 'well on the way to becoming a big force in politics with every prospect of attaining power.' O'Brien won back a seat in Tipperary. On the re-establishment of the Seanad in 1938 Foran complained that Congress's 250,000 members 'had been put on a level with a ghost body, representing at most only a handful of people.'

The Labour Party suffered General Election reverses. The *Irish Times* ('organ of the de Valera-Chamberlain Agreement and advocate of an Anglo-Irish military and naval pact to defend Britain's interests') boasted that 'Mr. de Valera set out to rid himself' of Labour. O'Brien and Hogan (Clare) lost, but Labour 'would never be got rid of': the 'workers' economic war—the war against poverty, slums, starvation and unemployment—would not end until it ended in victory for Labour.'

Electoral defeat turned workers' minds to the industrial battlefront. The ITGWU would provide 'very stiff and stubborn militant shock troops in the front line trenches.' The Lord Mayor of Cork, Jim Hickey, ITGWU Official and member of the Labour Party, addressed the Conference, condemning attacks on the Labour Party and employers' encouragement to workers not to pay the Political Levy. John F. Gill (Laois-Offaly) noted a 'peculiar feature,' namely that where the largest union membership existed 'the percentage of Labour votes was very small,' despite the ITGWU having 'left nothing undone to stimulate political organisation.'

In 1939 P. J. O'Brien moved that a successor to the defunct Labour paper, the *Torch*, be produced.[36]

The ITGWU was close to the Labour Party throughout the 1930s. Many Labour TDS were simultaneously union Officials. The NEC clearly felt it had controlling rights over 'its TDS' but fell short of an absolute commitment to members' political education. Hopes for a Labour Government seemed genuinely high, even if they ignored the harsh electoral facts.

Chapter 15 ～

TREADING WATER: THE
WUI IN THE 1930s

MEMBERSHIP, ORGANISATION AND FINANCE

Poetry was a regular feature of the third series of Larkin's *Irish Worker*. In inspirational style, the following, published in October 1931, set a tone.

> For I dipt into the Future, far as human eye could see,
> Saw the Vision of the World and all the wonder that would be;
> Saw the heavens fill with commerce, argosies of magic sails,
> Pilots of the purple twilight, dropping down with costly bales;
> Till the war-drum throbbed no longer, and the battle-flags were furled,
> In the Parliament of Man, the Federation of the World.

Larkin asked his readers, 'What a beautiful dream! Can it be realised in our day of surety if and when the peoples of the world determine it?' It could not 'be achieved under a Capitalist form of society; that surely must be patent to all men and women who possess intelligence.'

On 9 October 1930, in more mundane fashion, the WUI concluded an Agreement with the Irish Maltsters' Association, granting 66s for a seven-day week, signed for the union by Peter Larkin, J. Connolly and Edward Ormonde.

Competitive attitudes prevailed. It was emphasised that all members 'must insist on the men engaged in this industry holding Union cards, and, further, each man is individually and collectively bound by this Agreement during the lifetime of the Agreement.' The card would, of course, be a WUI card. No. 1 Branch reported activities with Dublin Corporation (City Council), milling, Grangegorman (psychiatric hospital), docks, bread-van delivery, railways, and Williams and Woods (confectionery manufacture). Requests for organisation came from Bagenalstown (Muine Bheag), Castlecomer, Derry, Kilrush 'and other places' and were considered by the GEC without action being taken.

In January 1931 a full-page poster in the *Irish Worker* urged all workers to join a trade union, with a sturdy working man demanding:

Say Fellers!
The Bosses are Organised—Are You?
The Bosses are on the Attack—Are You?
The Bosses are Unionised—Are You?
In Union there is Strength.
Outside the Trade Union—means inside the Poor Law Union.

Homage to Jim Larkin was a regular feature of the paper, causing no embarrassment to the editor. Typical was a poem by a 'recently deceased Glasgow Comrade',
Barney Havilan, published in December 1930.

Jim Larkin
Justice is the freedom of those who are equal. Jacobi
A day, an hour of virtuous liberty. Addison
Mammon led them on. Milton
Even Malice to my grave with tears shall come. Elliot
Strong reason makes strong actions. Shakespeare

Labourin' men an' labourin' women her one glory an' one shame. Lowell
A mighty name, for evil or for good. Arnold
Rage is the shortest passion of our souls. Rowe
Keep thy chains burst, and boldly say thou art free. Keats
In true men, like you men, their spirit's still at home. Ingram
No dread of man from duty shall me stay. Neilson

With mass unemployment, low wages, terrible housing and hunger, such a stark
exhortation had much sense about it. Dockers answered the call, 150 returning to
the WUI fold in February 1931. 'Practically every firm' was represented at a Carters'
Section meeting as the WUI's dockland presence grew. Marble-polishers were in the
Building Branch.
    On 15 May 1931 the 'Founder and Organiser' Peter Larkin died in Baggot Street
Hospital. The *Irish Worker* published 'The Story of a Man by His Brother' over a
number of issues. Peter Larkin was a firebrand who engaged in militant syndicalist activity in Britain, Ireland, America and Australia, regularly suffering imprisonment. He was at the heart of ITGWU opposition. It is still not certain whether he
founded the WUI with or without the sanction of his brother. His death was a blow,
as was that of the President, John Lawlor, who died on 26 June.[1]

Table 34: WUI membership, 1930–39

Year	Membership	Women	Branches
1930	16,909	1,115	10
1931	17,117	1,245	11
1932	16,781	1,005	12
1933	17,363	925	11
1934	16,693	*n.a.*	11
1935	15,763	*n.a.*	13
1936	14,776	1,898	16
1937	16,997	2,028	21
1938	16,720	1,993	21
1939	16,408	2,104	13

Source: National Archives, Registrar of Friendly Societies, file 369T.

Throughout the 1930s membership remained steady, reaching a peak in 1933 at 17,363. In the teeth of international recession these figures, at first sight, seem satisfactory; but the ITGWU's membership rose from 14,608 in 1930—301 lower than the WUI—to 36,444 in 1939, more than 20,000 higher. The WUI trod water.

Income returns show a somewhat different picture, income rising from £7,811 in 1930 to £10,996 in 1939, reaching a peak at £15,541 in 1937. Given that the subscription did not change, these figures either show a rising membership not recorded or, far more likely, a far higher proportion in benefit. Either way, virtually 100% of income came from contributions. 1930 was the last year in which a deficit was recorded. From 1931 on, surpluses were returned, slowly securing a more stable footing.

An aspect of WUI finances was the amount given in loans to members. This had typified the ITGWU's early days. Larkin clearly thought such practices appropriate, and he was admired for his largesse. There are many tales of him walking from home to office or elsewhere and being regularly stopped by people seeking assistance, which he very often gave. Evidence of WUI loans comes from a document drawn up for William O'Brien, General Secretary of the ITGWU. It clearly concerned him more than it did Larkin. The loans were not insignificant, however. In 1931, for example, £2,924 was handed out from an income of £7,957, more than 36% of the total. From 1924 to 1936, £12,616 was given, out of which only £4,258 was repaid and £5,945 written off, equal to 48% of income. Such generosity perhaps goes far to explain why poverty-stricken workers loved Larkin's union; but it raises a series of never-asked questions about Rule Books, benefit status and equity of application and reward.

A contradictory example of WUI logic was a notice from the Operative Butchers' Section in December 1931, warning that in the new year no-one would be employed unless they were a union member, and that 'all in arrears' would be 'removed from their job and idle members substituted.'

Table 35: WUI income, expenditure, Dispute Pay and surplus (£), 1930–39

	Income	Expenditure	Dispute Pay	Surplus (deficit)
1930	7,811	6,167	787	(829)
1931	7,957	7,538	1,489	1,236
1932	6,303	4,714	982	2,825
1933	7,482	6,598	1,597	3,709
1934	7,892	7,947	2,469	3,634
1935	8,678	8,701	2,587	3,630
1936	8,098	6,916	697	4,811
1937	15,541	15,088	6,088	5,268
1938	12,710	12,499	2,733	5,476
1939	10,996	10,894	1,850	5,578

Source: National Archives, Registrar of Friendly Societies, file 369T.

On 6 May 1935 Dan Byrne, Secretary of Dún Laoghaire Branch, started a Bray Branch among butchers' porters. Jimmy Byrne became part-time Branch Secretary, assisted by Bill Forde. In 1937 gas workers, dockers, coalmen, sandpit and general workers were organised. There were many debts resulting from the building strike in 1937, but they were 'gradually being cleared off,' and 'income was very good and holding steady.' A General Meeting, addressed by Larkin, announced that, the Solus lamp factory having been taken in, a full-time Secretary was possible, and Seán Dunne was appointed. After being interned in the Curragh in 1940, Dunne was soon transferred to Head Office.

Table 36: WUI loans to members (£), 1924–36

	Loans	Repaid	Written off
1924	183	39	—
1925	790	—	—
1926	533	324	152
1927	709	584	240
1928	861	11	940
1929	496	200	804
1930	1,566	728	459
1931	2,924	1,004	1,975

1932	906	906	122
1933	1,225	191	175
1934	520	136	476
1935	686	266	327
1936	917	308	327
Total	12,616	4,258	5,945

Source: National Library of Ireland, ms. 13,958, William O'Brien Papers, WUI Finances.

By March 1938 'newly established Branches were not doing well.' The GEC wanted a 'more strict check to be exercised over petty cash, fares and Conference expenses.' George Nathan expressed concern over the 'very heavy item of staff wages', asking if it was 'justified in relation to the membership.' Larkin thought they had the 'smallest staff of any of the leading Unions in the Free State and in not one instance did the wages they paid equal the wages paid to Officials of other unions.' In addition, because of the union's 'character' it 'interested itself in many questions other than actual industrial ones . . . housing, unemployment, accidents, etc., all of the staff were called upon to do far more work than was usual.' In all unions, 'much was done without recognition by the members or their families who benefited by it.' If anything, he felt that the union was 'actually shorthanded,' but 'they found difficulty in getting suitable and capable people.' Larkin exaggerated the degree to which the demands on WUI personnel were unusual: what he described was standard. Nathan's eye was on staff costs in a more general way.

For 'some considerable time' there were requests from members for badges. Larkin 'had not been very enthusiastic about this' but 'finally decided that it might be best to comply with the requests' and ordered a supply of 'red hand' badges.[2] The first WUI badges were struck in 1938.

Table 37: WUI income, expenditure and staff salaries (£), 1924–39

	Income	Expenditure	Staff salaries	Salaries as proportion of income (%)	Salaries as proportion of expenditure (%)
1924	9,479	9,006	1,759	18.5	19.5
1925	11,942	11,204	2,519	21.0	22.4
1926	6,051	5,288	2,799	46.2	52.9
1927	12,540	7,063	4,172	33.2	59.0
1928	4,337	6,807	2,584	59.5	37.9
1929	6,335	7,164	2,008	31.6	28.0
1930	7,811	6,167	3,239	41.4	52.5
1931	7,957	7,538	2,253	28.3	29.8
1932	6,303	4,714	1,750	27.7	37.1

1933	7,482	6,598	3,060	40.8	46.3
1934	7,892	7,947	2,641	33.4	33.2
1935	8,678	8,701	2,731	31.4	31.3
1936	8,098	6,916	3,072	37.9	44.4
1937	15,541	15,088	3,049	19.6	20.2
1938	12,710	12,499	4,090	32.1	32.7
1939	10,996	10,894	4,210	38.3	38.6

Source: National Archives, Registrar of Friendly Societies, file 369T.

WOMEN

A noteworthy aspect of the WUI in the 1930s was the high proportion of women members, a figure that grew consistently. Little is known about who they were or where they worked, but in 1931 the union declared: 'There is no sex discrimination in the Workers' Union.' It added, 'let this be sufficient notice,' suggesting tensions on this issue. What is known is the mutual antagonism between the WUI and the Irish Women Workers' Union. In August 1931 Louie Bennett, General Secretary of the IWWU, was attacked.

> Keep on going, Louie, while the going is good. And when, in the cool of the evening, you stand on the hills of Killiney, on the doorstep of your lovely country home, viewing the poverty and the misery of Dublin, heave a sigh of thankfulness that the working class of Ireland, for a time, ceased fighting under the banner of Connolly, thus making possible your trips to Geneva, Amsterdam and your home in Killiney.

Such comments did not endear Larkin to anyone at a time when he needed friends. When Bennett was President-Elect of the ITUC, rather than rejoicing in the first woman President since Congress was founded in 1894 Larkin insisted that any movement that 'tolerates at its head any person of the calibre of Louie Bennett will never command the respect of its friends or its enemies.' It was evidence of how far the movement had sunk. For Larkin, Bennett was not a 'Labour Leader ... for any-one that perpetuates snobbishness in any form is but a tool of the employers.'[3]

Table 38: Women in the WUI (%), 1930–39

1930	6.6	1935	n.a.
1931	7.3	1936	12.8
1932	5.9	1937	11.9
1933	5.3	1938	11.9
1934	n.a.	1939	12.8

Source: National Archives, Registrar of Friendly Societies, file 369T.

DISPUTES

In October 1930 correspondence was exchanged between Larkin, R. C. Ferguson of the Department of Industry and Commerce and Ernest Thompson of the Master Builders' Association and was published in the *Irish Worker*. It arose when the WUI alleged that John Kenny and Sons were not paying the 'recognised rate of 1s 4d' on Dublin Corporation's Donnycarney Housing Scheme. Workers on site, members of the WUI, ITGWU and United Builders' Labourers' Union, all claimed to be earning at least that rate. Larkin hotly disputed this, dismissing the investigation as 'going to law with the Devil and holding the Court in Hades!' The defendants found themselves not guilty. Larkin insisted on a public inquiry. Builders' labourers were warned that a strike for the recognised rate at Wallace's, Mount Jerome Cemetery, had entered its twenty-first week. A foreman's letter complained about general conditions and disorganisation; it was interpreted as an invitation to extend membership and to attempt correction.

In the spring of 1931 a thirteen-week strike took place at the Greenmount Spinning Company's plants in Drogheda and Harold's Cross, Dublin. On 11 April the workers returned, 'not victorious, yet with gains.' The Drogheda workers were 'foolish enough to allow their living standards' to be decided by a British union. The agreed reductions were the stick used to attempt to beat WUI members in Dublin. The Greenmount employer, McElderry, evicted some from their homes, raised rents and refused to take back members of the Strike Committee.[4]

The WUI dispensed £21,279 in Dispute Pay from 1930 to 1939, and in virtually every year it was up to a fifth of total income, the average being 21%. This indicated a militant union that gave disputes a high priority. The virtually complete absence of WUI records for the period makes it difficult to know where disputes took place.

Table 39: WUI Dispute Pay, 1930–39

	Income (£)	Dispute Pay (£)	Dispute Pay as proportion of income (%)
1930	7,811	787	10.0
1931	7,957	1,489	18.7
1932	6,303	982	15.5
1933	7,482	1,597	21.3
1934	7,892	2,469	31.2
1935	8,678	2,587	29.8
1936	8,098	697	8.6
1937	15,541	6,088	39.2
1938	12,710	2,733	21.5
1939	10,996	1,850	16.8

Source: National Archives, Registrar of Friendly Societies, file 369T.

THE 1931 AND 1937 BUILDING DISPUTES

Skilled workers in Dublin's building trades came to the 'rescue of their weaker brethren' in 1931. The Building Trades Guild met the workers in a Conference under the auspices of the Department of Industry and Commerce. The Department's representative, R. C Ferguson, agreed that a rate of 1s 4d should be paid by all firms. The unions for their part undertook to make unscrupulous employers toe the line. The action was seen as a defence of an Agreement made in 1920. Although ostracised from both the ITUC and Dublin Trades Council, Larkin drafted a protocol that committed the three labourers' unions to the 1s 4d and to not permitting transfer between them except on production of a clear card. The ITGWU would not, apparently, even 'peruse it.'

At the beginning of the strike Larkin urged the creation of one union for building workers. The WUI clearly saw an opportunity, and published a rallying notice.

A TIME LIKE THIS CALLS FOR MEN. RALLY, GET A UNION CARD; STAND BY EACH OTHER; DEMAND THE STANDARD RATE (1 and 4d AN HOUR), NOT A FARTHING LESS, ON EVERY JOB. DON'T WAIT TO BE SAVED.

'GET AN OAR OUT & PULL YOUR WEIGHT IN THE BOAT'

A UNITED FRONT IS IMPREGNABLE. IF A COMRADE OFFERS YOU HIS HAND AS A COMRADE, BE A MAN—SHAKE. LET YOUR SLOGAN BE: 'EACH FOR ALL & ALL FOR EACH.' 100% UNIONISM IN THE BUILDING TRADE.

In January the WUI warned: the 'Building Bosses Declare War.' The 'game of settling with the individual Unions' was a 'dangerous move.' Strangely, commentary on the dispute disappeared from the *Irish Worker,* which contented itself with reminding 'every member of the Workers' Union' to do 'his duty in this crisis.'

By February the WUI was predicting defeat. It blamed the leadership and urged the men, 'Don't shirk the issue. You cannot leave it to the Officials.' It mysteriously kept suggesting that 'we refrain from commenting upon' the strike, 'for reasons which we will explain at a later date,' and announced its intention of publishing the minutes of the Buildings Trade Group. It never did either.

A settlement in April was severely criticised by the WUI. The men's solidarity had been 'above reproach.' The union alleged that notorious scabs had been taken into the ITGWU by Frank Robbins—worse, that Thomas Kennedy had flown the kite that some wage reduction would be acceptable, thus strengthening the employers' resolve. The WUI claimed that 'in this fight, as in all fights,' it was 'with the class in their struggle.' The Agreement with the Master Builders' Association was published in full, showing the increases gained.

Despite public criticism of the ITGWU, on the ground matters were not as clear-cut. The Building Trades Group of Dublin Trades Council was responsible for joint negotiations. While the WUI was not part of the group, 'the I.T.G.W.U. did not object to their participation, although when the W.U.I. applied to join the B.T.G. they were told they would first have to be Council affiliates.' More than 3,500 men were out. The vote among members of the BTG for the eventual settlement—a return to existing rates until 31 July 1931 and then a reduction of 1d from 1 August—was accepted, 1,747 to 603. ITGWU building Officials accepted the WUI presence on the ground, perhaps the first occasion since the split on which *realpolitik* played out, despite the *Irish Worker's* attacks on Liberty Hall. It declared in April: 'The Irish Workers' Union undertake to work amicably with the members of the I.T.G.W.U. and United Builders' Labourers' Union, and agree not to raise any objection to the employment of members of those unions.' There was an element that saw the WUI, and especially Larkin, as hurlers on the ditch. With no immediate responsibility or role in the dispute, it was easy to be constantly critical of others.[5]

After the 1937 strike the WUI was 'overwhelmed with new members,' and it was decided that, although the 'Old Strike Committee had worked very hard,' it was 'advisable to organise the Section into a separate Branch with its own Officials.' The membership of the Branch grew to more than 2,000.[6]

CINEMAS

A two-year dispute in the cinemas of the Irish Kinematograph Company (owned by Alderman J. J. Farrell) was a sore point between the WUI and ITGWU. The *Irish Worker* concentrated its attention on Farrell's businesses and the alleged poor behaviour of the ITGWU. The cinemas affected were the Grand Central and the Pillar (O'Connell Street), Plaza (Granby Row) and Electric (Talbot Street). Mary Street Cinema was closed but was still picketed. The WUI claimed that its dispute was effective by publishing the 1929 balance sheet for Farrell's company, showing a loss of more than £6,068. The 'slum proletariat' were condemned as 'ever the enemy of themselves and their class.' They 'allowed themselves to be used as strike-breakers by patronising and allowing their children to patronise' disputed houses. The O'Connell Street cinemas were patronised by a 'different type of worker,' products of the Free State who had 'lost all sense of principle and loyalty either to their country or their class.' They were 'political and social blacklegs.' The 'rottenness' of the 'Official-rigged United Dublin Trades Council' was excoriated, as 'painters and glaziers' worked in the Grand Central with 'the picket walking up and down underneath them.' Plasterers and carpenters renovated Mary Street Cinema; 'organised scabbing as well as unorganised, is now the order of the day. Cinema strikers, as well as other strikers, will welcome the re-appearance of the *Irish Worker*, knowing that it will expose such rottenness and corruptions.'

In December 1931 all cinemas showed 'scab shows for scabs by scabs.' When the Theatre Royal reverted to variety in 1932 the management, with the assistance of the Musicians' Union (a British union), imported a conductor and musicians from London. The Dublin Secretary of the Musicians' Union replaced three local musicians with himself and two Londoners.

This is what the Dublin musicians are getting for sending away some £30 a month contributions, while at the same time they cannot afford to pay their rent of their Dublin office . . . The slogan of the Dublin musicians should be:— IRISH MUSICIANS FOR IRISH THEATRES and CINEMAS.[7]

The Musicians' Union would not permit foreign musicians to enter Britain, and Larkin felt that Irish musicians' unions should play the same card.

THE *IRISH PRESS*

In late 1930 the *Irish Worker* learnt that Dublin newsboys were forming a union. Their appeal was published in poetic form. In 1932, 'goaded beyond the point of acceptance,' and as a union having loyally supported the paper, WUI members struck in the *Irish Press*. Newsvendors 'made common cause with the strikers' and refused to handle the papers. The workers produced their own crude duplicated paper, *The Truth That Is News* (a play on the *Irish Press* slogan, 'The truth in the news'). It urged ITGWU men and others who stayed in:

> This is a fight for Trade Union principles. Just because a trade union, ever loyal to its scab record, brings disgrace on the proud record of the Irish labour movement, don't you join in with them. Be true to your class!

It called for a boycott of British goods and thought it odd that a former Free State Army officer, McGrath, was now managing the *Press* while putting republicans on the street. A second edition asked readers to 'pay what you can. All proceeds go to the newsboys' who had joined the union.

The central argument was that the ITGWU had accepted a 48-hour week in the *Press*, whereas only 40 hours were worked in the *Irish Independent*. The WUI had no desire to handicap the *Irish Press*, as it had raised £500 to purchase shares when it first appeared, on 5 September 1931. *Truth* assuaged fears that there was any political aspect to the strike.

> IMPORTANT. We have learned that attempts are being made to spread rumours that the strike is a political provocation. We would only point out that the men on the picket line are ALL Republicans, most of them have long records of service to the National Movement, and have been repeatedly jailed. While the individual mainly responsible for the dispute is Mr. McGrath, ex-Captain in the Free State Army under Cosgrave and Mulcahy.

Larkin personally instructed 'every member' to attend the Rotunda Picture House on Sunday 27 October 1932, 'on penalty of fine'; 'admission by card.' Robert Briscoe TD and James B. Lynch TD were offered as mediators. Oscar Traynor TD and M. J. Whelan, Secretary of Dublin Typographical Provident Society, asked pickets to return on the 'verbal promise of no victimisation.' The ITGWU would 'stand by them.' The offer was rejected, as coming from the 'very Union that is responsible for the prolongation of the dispute and is now scabbing on the strikers.' Traynor was warned that he would 'be remembered in the next election.' The *Truth That Is News* published cartoons—limited in quality by the technology—and squibs such as 'McGrath the Czar', satirising opponents. There was friendly tension between strikers and Head Office, the latter disclaiming all responsibility 'for what might appear on this page. It was written at one in the morning while members of the rank-and-file were giving of their best.' All agreed that it was a lie to say they were trying to get better conditions than the *Irish Independent.*

The end came as 'alone' the WUI had 'fought for the common people.' It was betrayed by the ITGWU, in 'organised conspiracy' with the *Irish Press* management. The last *Truth That Is News* defiantly stated that WUI members 'pledged to levy themselves during the course of the dispute' and 'will not scab on the working class.' It seems the ITGWU was not the only offender.

Seán MacBride recalled Larkin as being 'inclined to look upon all Republicans as drawing-room Republicans who preached certain principles, but never put them into practice . . . Strangely enough,' some of his worst criticism was saved for those 'whom he considered to have strong left-wing views,' such as Peadar O'Donnell. MacBride, however, became 'solid close friends' with Larkin, largely as a result of the *Irish Press* newsboys' strike. R. M. Fox and Geoffrey Coulter, both *Press* journalists with leftish views, opposed the idea of members of the National Union of Journalists 'downing tools' and joining the newsboys. MacBride, however, took to the picket line and joined the WUI for the duration of the strike, addressing a meeting in the WUI's Marlborough Street premises. MacBride, by now working for the bar, ended his association with the *Press.*[8]

IRISH HOSPITALS TRUST

The newly established Irish Hospitals Trust occasioned open letters to the principal owner, Joseph McGrath, strongly criticising its recruitment, employment and wage policies. The WUI felt that 'if this Sweep business is to be allowed, decent conditions of labour, Trades Union pay, Trades Union hours and no sex discrimination, must apply.' It was not envisaged that the battle to win such demands would be so long-drawn and fraught.

In rather contradictory fashion, 'any reader' or WUI member who 'desires to purchase a ticket or a half-ticket' in the Sweep could do so 'at Unity Hall up to Sunday morning. We have a few reserved tickets and will be glad to assist any reader wanting a ticket.' The Sweep made £20,000 a day and yet 'discriminated against competent men.' The WUI found it incredible that no clerical unions complained about conditions in the Sweep offices, a 'sanatorium for bourgeois parasites.' There was double-jobbing, 'married women with husbands receiving good salaries' and other abuses 'under sweating conditions.' McGrath replied to P. T. Daly, Secretary of Dublin Trades Council, regretting that the company 'cannot comply with your request to employ only Trade Union workers.' It recruited the unemployed and paid a 'very reasonable wage.' Women predominated because of their suitability, 'not for economic reasons.' Preference in selection was always 'to cases that appear to us to be the hardest.' Larkin thundered: 'They can carry out the same blackleg system as was carried out' on the Shannon Scheme (on which McGrath was 'labour adviser') but 'they will not be able to hornswoggle those who have the power, not only to create a sensation, but who also cannot be outwitted.' Unfortunately, militant members were first required to create sensations.

The Hospitals Trust's accounts were published in the *Irish Worker* of 7 February 1931 under the heading 'Hospitals' Sweep or Bookmakers' Trust.' The amounts officially retained by the company were criticised. Charges of labour exploitation were repeated and Trades Council Officials dismissed as naïve in their belief that McGrath would allow unionisation. 'Sweep Racketeers' were unnecessary. The WUI believed hospitals should be 'adequately maintained by public funds,' and any trust should be a Government one. 'The Hospital Sweep is organised for the benefit of the Hospitals, and not to provide lip-stick decoration and face-lifting treatment for the petted dolls of the bourgeoisie nor cushy jobs for the friends of the corpse.'

Camac Press held a competition for five sweepstake tickets for the Derby by asking readers of the *Irish Worker* to spot word differences in the paper. This reflected a fascination with the Sweep and inevitable dreams of winning. 'Amazing disclosures of Sweep conditions' were made in December, as 'needy working class girls' were 'discharged while nieces of aristocrats' remained. The positions of various women's husband's were publicised. Helena Molony and the IWWU were lampooned, as they accepted that their 'claim was not sustainable.' McGrath was asked to recall his own 'hungry days' and to have sympathy with those he dismissed. His one-time position as Head of the ITGWU National Insurance Society was surprisingly overlooked. The ITUC published full-page advertisements for the Sweep in its Annual Report, surely sending mixed messages.[9]

IRISH SEAMEN'S AND PORT WORKERS' UNION

Immediately after the signing of an Agreement between the National Union of Seamen and the shipowners on 23 May 1933 Irish seamen gathered to reject it and their union. This had happened in 1913 and again in 1922, when most Irish seamen transferred to an ITGWU Marine Section. After strikes in 1923, and partly as a result of the 1924 split, seamen drifted away from the ITGWU. In any case, no Irish sailor could obtain a berth on British merchant ships without the infamous form PC5, signed by the NUS and the Shipping Federation.

Joe Ellis and Seán O'Moore created the Seamen's and Firemen's Union of Ireland (simultaneously known as the Irish Seamen's and Firemen's Union). It was instantly attacked by Captain Tupper of the NUS as 'Communist agitation', an utterly untrue allegation.

Pickets were placed on Dublin port, and both ITGWU and WUI dockers honoured them. The ITGWU Dublin No. 1 Branch held a Special Meeting, addressed by Tom Foran and Jack McCabe; but as Derry, Glasgow and Liverpool dockers were already out in defence of the new Irish union, Liberty Hall's hand was decided.

Walk-outs followed in Belfast and Cork, both supported by the ITGWU. Regular meetings were held at the ISFU rooms at 1A Commons Street, Dublin, and the adjacent Oriel Hall, but after a week there was a stalemate.

On Friday 7 July eight hundred men marched into Dublin carrying the banner *Strike of Sailors and Firemen against slave conditions—All ports closed today—Dublin leads.* The WUI officially supported them, and Larkin wrote a long letter to the Taoiseach, Éamon de Valera, concerned that a lengthy seamen's dispute would affect the whole economy. He urged support for the new body.

Three general unions operated in Free State ports: the ATGWU, which Larkin considered had 'no right to be here,' the ITGWU and the WUI. Larkin submitted that 'no country in the world is in such a paradoxical position as this Free State. In no country in the world is any alien industrial and economic organisation permitted to function.' He cited France, Belgium, the Netherlands, Poland and Italy to support his case, even the Dominions of Australia, New Zealand and South Africa. Why should the Shipping Federation and NUS control Irish ports?

On the same day William Davin TD, an employee of the London, Midland and Scottish Railway, worried about the 'disastrous' consequences of the unofficial action and lack of procedure. Rather cryptically, he spoke of 'paid agitators' who were 'helping to create industrial trouble,' advising the Government to 'watch the activities of certain gentlemen, some of whom were not citizens of the Free State.' This was a reference to supposed Communist involvement, although none could be traced

Séamus Redmond, later General Secretary of the Marine, Port and General Workers' Union, in his study of the ISFU, stated of Larkin: 'To what extent he was involved and whether he had any influence on the direction of the dispute has never been fully determined.' Frank and Joe Ellis certainly consulted him on setting up a union, and 'there is no doubt they had his support.' Indeed Larkin issued a circular to WUI members on 6 August 1933, saying that he advised seamen

> to revolt, advised them during the negotiations, afforded them accommodation for their meetings, paid for the halls they used and drafted and printed their posters. We were the only Union that stood by them officially and paid out Dispute Pay to our own men who stood by them in their struggle.

A mass meeting was held in the Mansion House on Monday 10 July, after a march of 1,000 men and women headed by the St Laurence O'Toole Pipe Band and WUI Brass and Reed Band. By Friday 14 July 2,500 men were directly involved. Seán Lemass picked up mediation efforts, and agreement was reached on Saturday 15 July between the B&I Line, Palgrave Murphy, Dublin and Silloth Steamship Company, the NUS and what was now described as the Irish Seamen's Union.

As the seamen's strike unfolded, a second union emerged, the Dockers' and Carters' Union. It shared the ISFU's premises in Commons Street and was organised among hundreds of 'hitherto casual and unorganised' port workers, alienated and disillusioned by the fratricidal strife between the ITGWU and WUI strife. On Sunday

23 July both ISFU and DCU members attended the Rotunda Picture House 'to form
a new union with the ultimate object of forming One Big Union of all Irish transport workers'—familiar language. James Murphy, presiding, said that 'Communism
or Bolshevism would not be tolerated.' The only 'ism' they would have anything to
do with was trade unionism. The new union would not have any allegiance with any
political party.

Joe Ellis said that 'not alone the men on the quays, but the mass of workers of
Dublin were looking for a Union to start afresh.' Although there were three or four
unions already on the quays, 'during the strike there was only the one union—the
union and brotherhood of men.' They wanted the Shipping Federation out of
Ireland. One speaker said that 'about 40% of the men in the room would not touch
any of the existing unions.'

John Kelly was elected General Secretary and Joe Ellis General Organiser, and
the title Irish Seamen's and Port Workers' Union was adopted. A further strike took
place in October by 200 ISPWU dockers. At a meeting in Cathal Brugha Street on
Friday 3 November 1933 Andy 'Block' Byrne invited Larkin to join the platform.
Both the ITGWU and ATGWU were invited up, but there was no-one to take up the
invitation. Larkin said the WUI was in the 'fight officially' and supported 'those of
our men' who were out, 'whether in benefit or non-benefit.' He suggested a Strike
Committee representative of the ISPWU, WUI, ATGWU and ITGWU. Lemass brokered
a settlement that was mediated by Judge Shannon and effective from January 1934,
by which time the ISPWU was an established and recognised part of Dublin port
trade unionism.[10] The ISPWU's birth was an indirect product of the 1924 split
between the ITGWU and WUI. Dockers and seamen lost faith in both and wanted
their own organisation.

RELATIONS WITH THE ITGWU

By 1930 work-place conflict with the ITGWU had abated. The two unions occupied
parallel worlds. Larkin continued to accuse Liberty Hall of 'scabbery'. A dispute on
Dublin trawlers dragged through the autumn, centring on landing times for
catches. WUI members in Carroll's, coal merchants, were dismissed for refusing to
bunker trawlers, leading to wider action among carters and trimmers. The WUI
was 'pleased to add that representatives of the I.T.G.W.U.' instructed their members
to follow suit on the coal wharves. Simultaneously a receiver's conditions for
reopening the Irish Glass Bottle Company were balloted on by the WUI, which
demanded a tariff to protect the industry from foreign imports. In December, however, Carroll's ITGWU men were accused of breaking the strike.

> The Shipping Federation in its worst days could never command such a well-
> disciplined supply of scabs as can be supplied by the Scab Bureau in Beresford
> Place. All day, and every day, these creatures hang around the Scab Bureau
> hoping and sighing.

The WUI had been 'living on false hopes' and now vented its spleen against the enemy.

> The No. 1 Gang, A Company, of the best-trained scabs in the English-speaking world, the pride of Liberty Hall, and the sure stay and support of the Coal Importers' Association, O'Brien's Life Guards, marched down to their appointed places. What a pity Bill did not order the Union Band to attend them to the stations!

Court action came as a result of the dispute. The ITGWU allegedly objected to the employment of non-union labour and struck, but Robert Mooney, Secretary of the WUI No. 1 Branch, gave cards to non-Unionists while denying 'that it was the policy of his Union to admit members who were involved in a dispute with another union.' Of course he did not recognise the ITGWU as a legitimate Union. The employer discussed matters with the ITGWU but 'would not coerce their employees to join any union.'

Jack McCabe, Secretary of the ITGWU Dublin No. 1 Branch, complained that women were being paid only 14s to 17s a week, while the minimum union rate was 27s, which the WUI appeared satisfied with. ITGWU pickets remained. The employer obtained an injunction and a ruling that, as it had no members in Carroll's, there was no trade dispute. Membership and the control of employments was still more important than workers' circumstances.

The Irish Glass Bottle crisis continued into 1931, with 'an Englishman, Schofield,' stating that investment would be made to reopen if the work force abandoned the WUI in favour of the ITGWU. A meeting in the Mansion House on Monday 26 January opened a debate on the Glass Bottle Company but was not attended by any Labour Party Councillors. A public enquiry was demanded. The WUI led a Delegation to Dáil Éireann on 19 February, meeting both Labour Party and Government Deputies.

In November 1930 Larkin published his views on a 'Unity Committee.' Nearly one hundred unions were too many: 'each Union has a policy of its own. Consequently, we are not moving in line. We are not keeping in step, as it were.' He agreed that 'we are undisciplined,' a comment that probably raised smiles in union offices throughout Dublin. But he had a point. Unions were 'almost powerless' in the face of wage cuts and job losses. The article suggested that 'we prepare ground for the One Big Union,' in which 'every Irish worker would be enrolled. Carpenter, plasterer, fitter, docker, clerk, railway man, shop assistant and agricultural labourer, all in one big Union,' each supporting the others. The problem had to be solved, 'or else misery and starvation will overtake us as a class.'

Not surprisingly, Larkin did 'not accept the deduction' of the Unity Committee, although its 'argument is well-taken' and 'we appreciate the spirit,' which proved that 'the militant and progressive spirit is not dead.' The columns of the *Irish Worker* were 'open to full and free discussion,' but 'O.B.U. is not the way out.' He concluded

by effectually recommending what he had rejected: 'apply your mentality to organise on correct lines, organisation by industry with a centralised staff.'

John Sunderland's article in July 1931 drew attention to the 'Need for Industrial
Unionism' and the creation of 'OBU': organisation on industrial lines; the needs of
craft and technical requirements met by the organisation of Branches; all Branches
to be represented on one Executive; 'all be members of one industrial union, which
should embrace all Branches of the industry'; and 'all industrial unions be joined
into ONE BIG UNION—with one card for the whole O.B.U.' This was a surprisingly
positive view on 'OBU' to be found in a Larkinite paper, but little happened.

In the same issue, attacks were made on Johnny Dunne and Joseph Metcalfe for
betraying Bray building workers and leaving a similar 'slimy trail' in Ballina. Bray
men defected to the WUI, despite agreeing wage cuts.

Anger at Liberty Hall's apparent control of the movement mounted during the
1931 Congress. Foran, O'Brien and Johnson were accused of sapping the movement's strength and presiding over a 'spineless thing.' P. T. Daly was again 'permitted to play in the garden that once was barred to him.' Larkin was not best pleased
as 'the very men who dragged his name through the mire and dirt of Dublin permitted him to speak on their platform at Waterford. We trust his digestive organs
were equal to the task of swallowing the anchor.'[11] The labour movement needed
remoulding, but not by the ITGWU.

CONGRESS

Larkin attacked the ITUC paper, the *Irishman*. It was the target of regular abuse in
the *Irish Worker*.

> We understand Mortished's organ yclept *The Irishman*, the alleged Labour paper
> published weekly and given away gratis to anyone unacquainted with its
> purpose, is to change its name title. Someone has said the leopard cannot change
> its spots; neither can the skunk change its odour. A skunk by any other name is
> still a skunk.

Even the name vexed Larkin. 'Mortished's organ is still carrying the name title of
Pigott's patriotic paper.' Richard Pigott was the 'agent provocateur for the "Bloody"
Old Times and the Castle against Parnell . . . So you see there were Malcolm Lyons's
abroad even in the thirties.'

Larkin did not endear himself to the ITUC. The WUI's application for affiliation
was rejected in 1936. It was the first episode of what would be a long-running saga.
Plasterers and Woodworkers attempted to refer the rejection back to the Executive.
In 1937 the application moved to the 'pending' tray. Larkin, attending as DTUC
Delegate, made his presence felt when asking what progress was made. The
Secretary of the ITUC, a former ITGWU Organiser, Éamon Lynch, replied that
matters were 'still under consideration.' Larkin complained that the WUI had
'applied and re-applied' and that he had met the Congress officers—Helena

Molony, Seán P. Campbell and Lynch himself—to answer their questions. Lynch insisted there was no undue delay. Other unions were waiting longer.

Larkin, by refusing a certain proposal, could have obviated the obstacles but had refused to give any understanding. He then wanted standing orders suspended, being supported by the Irish National Union of Woodworkers but opposed by his one-time ally P. T. Daly (DTUC), who supported Lynch. The sole authority in affiliation matters lay with the National Executive.

The first application by the WUI, on 26 July 1935, was rejected. A second came on 25 February 1937. After a full investigation the Congress officers asked the WUI to restrict its activities to its 'de facto position,' Dublin city and county. Congress could see 'no good reason' for geographical expansion, but Larkin declined this limitation. Both the Irish National Union of Woodworkers and ISPWU were cited as precedents for delay and conditional terms. Larkin complained; they had to 'spend seven years in the wilderness because some other Union did so.' Lynch cited a Congress resolution of 1935 that viewed with 'concern the increase in number of rival unions' and called on the National Executive to 'restrain this tendency.' Larkin persisted: 'We are making no compromise' but are 'giving you our word of honour that we will never break the Rules' of Congress if admitted.

The discussion took more than forty-five minutes. Larkin talked of his battle to get the ITGWU recognised by Congress, only to have it thrown at him that he had subsequently split that union. 'Next business' was eventually carried, by 85 to 79, a close vote that encouraged Larkin in his quest. ITGWU Delegates were conspicuous by their absence in the debate.

In 1938 the WUI application was merely marked as refused. Congress could argue that it was not singularly hostile to the WUI, however. It rejected the Irish Automobile Drivers' and Mechanics' Union and the United Stationary Engine Drivers' Trade Union because existing unions catered for the memberships. Mergers were suggested to the applicants. Both unions had at one time been part of the ITGWU, which still retained some organisation in the industries concerned, although some drivers, mechanics and stationary engine drivers went to the WUI after 1924.

Reincarnations of earlier bodies were more likely to have sprung from contemporary WUI memberships than the ITGWU. Although Larkin was present as a Dublin Trades Council Delegate, the matter of the WUI's affiliation passed without comment. He did speak against proposed amendments to standing orders that would have meant that Trades Council Delegates, like himself, could come only from affiliated unions. If this was adopted he would be disqualified as a Delegate.

J. J. Farelly (Irish National Union of Woodworkers and Dublin Trades Council) thought 'they should bury the hatchet of discord,' and all unions should be accepted. P. T. Daly, Secretary of DUTC, would vote against, as Trades Councils had to have the authority to select their own Delegates. Larkin saw the amendment as 'personal: the same machine was moving all the time.' He had DTUC's confidence and 'a record that could not be equalled by any man on this side of the water.' Despite Lynch's elaborate explanation and an assurance that this was a matter

unrelated to Larkin or the wuɪ, the proposal was defeated, 52 to 78. The tide was
again moving in Larkin's direction.

In 1939 Larkin asked why the application was 'not mentioned' and what action
was being taken. Lynch explained that they had only received the application a
fortnight before. P. T. Daly, president, reiterated that it was entirely a matter for the
incoming National Executive.[12] The wuɪ was kept outside.

THE *IRISH WORKER*

Larkin used the original title-piece for his 1930 *Irish Worker*. The wuɪ's hand-to-
mouth existence made publication difficult and dependent on the acknowledged
support of stalwarts: Frank Cluskey Senior, Richard Dalton, William Griffin, John
Martin Kavanagh, Maurice Kavanagh, John Lawless, Seán Nugent and Charlie
Totten. The paper was printed at James Ardiff's Camac Printing Works in
Mount Brown, Dublin, and subscriptions were 6s 6d for a year, 3s 3d for a half
year. Advertisements appeared from no. 1, reflecting trades in which the wuɪ
was organised. An 'Eat More Meat' page contained advertisements from different
butchers.

While publishing wuɪ news, the *Irish Worker* did not purport to be the union's
official publication. In addition to domestic matters, international analysis was
published, particularly about the Soviet Union. The 'Adventurer Hitler', 'eulogised
by all the Capitalist Press,' was strongly attacked. The paper emphasised that 'Unity'
is the 'slogan of the hour' and urged new strings to be added to the 'Old Harp':

> To the task. Into the Unions. A more active interest in your Unions. Make your
> Unions weapons of advance as well as means of defence. Get the disgruntled
> ones to understand; enrol him or her. The tired ones—give them a shoulder. The
> apathetic ones must be aroused. This move forward must not be confined to
> Divisions or Sections. No compromise. No evasion. No excuses. No selfishness.
> All for one and one for all.

The paper's fragile existence led to appeals to 'every reader who desires the paper
to continue' to attend a meeting at the *Irish Worker* office in Kilmainham: 'enter
through the wicket gate opposite Kearns' Place.' By November readers were asked
to give a Saturday afternoon's work, where 'one volunteer [was] worth ten pressed
workers.' Voluntary labour and sales for 1d would keep 'seven men and two women
directly employed.'

Larkin was the selling-point, and readers were invited, along with the Irish
Worker League, wuɪ and 'any other militant members of any other unions' to a
meeting in the Mansion House on Sunday 23 November 1930, where 'Jim Larkin will
address himself to topics of the hour.'

The issues of late 1931 were extremely scrappy and printed on various coloured
papers. In February 1932 police raids and confiscations of the paper were reported
as the parlous production system came close to collapse. It remained defiant: 'The

Irish Worker has no apologies to offer. It may go down in the struggle, but it will rise again.' Readers should

> remember that Governments are only strong in proportion to the weakness of the organisation of the working class. A united working class commands respect; a disunited working class gets what it is getting today. Be wise, men and women of Ireland!

Voluntary labour drew on the WUI's siege mentality—'us against the world.'

> Comrade Reader, if you feel this, your paper, is needed, why not participate actively in the work of getting it out, distributing it? Every reader can be found work according to his or her capacity. If you can write, get busy. If you can talk, get busy. If you can sketch, get busy. If you can do anything, tell us what you can do, and we will find you a niche. Work, for the Day is coming, Reader. You pay one penny for a copy of this paper. Do you know what that means? Your penny joins the pennies of other readers, finds employment for seven men and two women directly; indirectly gives other workers employment. They would miss a week's work and a week's wages. This is better than organised charity. This is better than signing on at the Shame Exchange. All of you interested in *The Worker* willing to work, present yourself for work at The *Worker* Works Saturday afternoon. All kinds of jobs for willing workers. One volunteer worth ten pressed workers. This is your work.

By March 1932 the paper's end was in sight. Readers were asked to pledge 1s per week. Matters were critical: 'If by Monday morning there is a sufficient response, *we continue*. If not, *it must be au revoir.*'13 It was au revoir.

EDUCATION

There was no formal WUI education activity in the 1930s. The *Irish Worker* regularly published analysis of political, economic and social matters; a letters column occasionally provoked good debates; and extracts from Connolly's *Labour in Irish History,* other Socialist writings and the serialisation of Tressell's *Ragged-Trousered Philanthropists.*

At the 1938 Congress Larkin spoke in favour of the improvement of school buildings, criticising the Minister for Education and 'the general apathy of the people themselves as regards education.' He was appalled that money allocated for schools had been returned because of a lack of plans submitted. He wanted greater involvement by parents in school management. In Dublin, sites for new schools were available and school buses overcrowded. Two of his niece's children died from diphtheria, examples of overcrowding and neglect that allowed epidemics to ravage school populations. No doubt annoying Delegates of the teachers' unions, who were a little precious about non-teachers contributing to such debates, he concluded: 'To my mind, a great deal of this wretchedness and suffering is due to the teachers, who have shown neither independence of character nor any democratic feeling for themselves or their pupils.' As teachers were lacking 'in dignity and self-respect' it 'must have its repercussions upon the development, or want of development, of character in their pupils.'

He spoke again in 1939, identifying sites for schools in Crumlin and the North Strand, while children survived on fish and chips and received their 'Christian culture' in appalling circumstances. Parents, he alleged, did 'not take the slightest interest . . . As long as the children are taken away from them in the morning and kept away for a certain number of hours, they are apparently satisfied.'[14]

SOCIAL ACTIVITY

In October 1930 morale was lifted by the WUI Brass and Reed Band winning the Treaty Stone Cup in Limerick under its conductor, T. A. Devlin. The Band did great work 'during the recent election campaign,' attracting crowds to rallies and adding glamour. Applications for membership of the Band could be made at Unity Hall, 31 Marlborough Street. The Band's winter season could be attended on 'moderate terms.'

Regular socials and dances were held at various venues, such as the Halloween dance at Rathmines Town Hall on 31 October, or the Grand Cinderella Ball at Johnston, Mooney and O'Brien's Café on 27 November, providing important funds for the cash-strapped union.

When the Band folded is not clear. In 1938 George Nathan raised the question of a union Band. Larkin was 'very dissatisfied with the whole thing,' but little appears to have been done to remedy matters.

Under the heading *Mens sana in corpore sano* ('a sound mind in a sound body') the Unity Boxing and Physical Culture Club asked workers:

> Say Fellows! Why hang around the street corners at night smoking cigarettes? Why not come around and join with the boys and learn something about the noble art of self-defence under the able tuition of Jim Young and Instructor Crookshanks?

In October 1931 Mallin Hall hosted a professional boxing tournament, with the Irish Heavyweight Champion, Tom Toner, topping the bill against Louis Casimir, 'the French Carnera'. Larkin was a strong believer in physical culture and the discipline that boxing provided.

In November 1930 Frank Cluskey Senior championed the achievements of Dolphin Football Club. Originating in the Pork Butchers' Social Club, they carried all before them in the Leinster League and Metropolitan Cup. They entered the Free State League in 1930, playing games at Dolphin Park, Iveagh Grounds, Harold's Cross and Shelbourne Park. They were defeated in two Cup finals by Shamrock Rovers, in 1932 and 1933, but were League champions in 1934 and 1935. They dramatically resigned from the League in 1937 and were replaced by Limerick. Larkin was not too pleased. Dolphin's manager, Dixon from Glasgow Rangers, brought in many 'Cross-Channel players,' to the detriment of the all-conquering butchers. Larkin strongly urged Irish footballers to follow the lead of the emerging Professional Footballers' Association in England and to form an Irish Players' Union.[15]

POLITICS

The *Irish Worker* attacked every political faction, with special contempt reserved for the Labour Party. In November 1930 a headline ran: 'Lemass Obliterates the Irish Working Class,' but the point of attack was still the Labour Party. 'Comrade Lemass, the High Jack and the King of Fianna Fáil . . . almost converted to Socialism—Tom Johnson's Socialism.' At the Ard-Fheis of Fianna Fáil, Lemass moved the nationalisation of road, rail, canal and road transport. Larkin's solution was a 'Unified Irish Workers' Party.' Working-class Fianna Fáil supporters were urged to see the light: 'Organise! Unite! Back to Connolly and the men of 1907 to 1916.'

An Irish Worker League 'Manifesto to the Workers of County Dublin', issued in December, dismissed the Labour Party as the 'seven-headed oracle', taking 'Malcolm Lyons's golden sovereigns.' Readers were urged to vote against the anti-national Finlay, as he represented a Government that closed Clondalkin Paper Mills and the Irish Glass Bottle Company and repressed workers.

Larkin Senior and Larkin Junior both sat on Dublin Corporation (City Council), where they raised issues of poverty, welfare and WUI industrial disputes. A circular issued by the 'Election Committee', ITGWU, 71 Dame Street (William J. Norman, Agent), while Larkin was in prison in the United States was reproduced in the *Irish Worker* in December 1931 under the heading 'They Wanted Jim Larkin Home. Moryah!' The leaflet stated:

DO
you realise that in 1909, as workers of Dublin, you were merely slaves, and that the conditions under which
YOU
then laboured were directly the results of your own apathy. Though your working conditions have since been much bettered, there is still many a
WANT
to be supplied before YOUR FIGHT for industrial freedom is won. The man who made the workers of Dublin THINK was
JIM LARKIN
and it now behoves you TO ACT up to the lessons of democracy which he taught. BY registering your No. 1 VOTE in his favour you will be driving
HOME
to the employing class the fact that although he lingers in an American gaol, you do not forget the man who first taught you how to win 'your place in the sun.'

Larkin harked back to his 'food ship' idea of 1923. He was offered a 10,000-ton ship 'refitted with new Scotch boilers' that could be had for the 'ridiculous sum of £5,000.' Exiles could come to the ship in New York with 'gifts for their people at home.' The ITGWU Executive, 'with as much vision as could be expected from that piratical gang,' had turned down his request for funds. 'What did it matter that 14,000 of the rank-and-file were in jail,' or that wages were being reduced 'without protest'? The ITGWU had more than £100,000 in the bank, but it would not give it to Larkin. The idea 'fell through. It was a great idea—unfortunately, great ideas cannot be converted into inspiring realities with men such as O'Brien, Foran and the rest of that gang.' The 'rank-and-file wanted Larkin home,' but the 'Transport Executive never did.'

In October 1931, when Larkin urged every worker and political group to oppose the Constitution (Amendment No. 17) Bill—often called the Public Safety Bill—he went back to other glory days. 'Your lives are at stake—defend them! In 1913 we smashed them and by solidarity we will smash them again!'

The *Irish Worker* thought it significant that Lemass ceased his attacks on the Labour Party in January 1932. No votes, 'not even a No. 2,' were to be given to the Labour Party. The Party was on the run, and the advice was to 'keep it going until it joins R. J. P. Mortished in Geneva.'

'Political wedding bells' were heard in February as the Labour Party confidently expected to be in Coalition with or close support of Fianna Fáil. The Labour Party's attacks on Larkin were rebuffed in February, with the paper calling for support for IWL candidates. 'Join the Irish Worker League' was the cry after 3,890 voted for Jim Larkin Junior in the February General Election. An 'Appeal to the Men and Women of the Irish Working-class' was published on 12 March. No advertising was carried as a result of a boycott—not surprising, as the paper had 'aroused the inveterate hatred of every scab employer, every corrupt politician, every profiteering shopkeeper, every labour fakir, and the enmity of Garda Síochána in such places as Bray and elsewhere.'

Anti-Soviet fears drove more hatred and suspicion. Police repression was followed by a campaign of 'terrorism and intimidation' against those who sold the *Irish Worker*. Sixty shops ceased carrying it, and the fathers of newsboys in Bray were put out of their jobs until their sons stopped selling it. Under such circumstances the production of the paper was 'almost impossible.' Its offices had helped hundreds of workers, taking up their cases, writing letters, making representations. It would be a tragedy, therefore, if it closed. The *Irish Worker* was the 'newspaper that neither Governments, nor the forces of the employers could crush.'

The IWL enjoyed little success. In February 1932 Larkin Senior polled 3,386 in Dublin North, the fifth-highest first-preference vote, but failed to take one of the seven seats. Larkin Junior polled 917 in Dublin South. In January 1933 Larkin Senior polled 2,792 in Dublin North, the tenth-highest. These interventions probably cost the Labour Party seats on each occasion. In July 1937, however, Larkin Senior was elected in Dublin North-East with 5,970 votes. Victory was short-lived, however, as he lost the seat in June 1938, polling 4,859. His thoughts began to turn to joining the Labour Party.

At the 1938 ITUC Congress Larkin chivvied the Labour Party for participating in the new Seanad. Its attitude 'surprised him . . . more particularly when they took exception to the organisation which, they claimed, was a bogus organisation, while within shot of their own headquarters they favoured an organisation that was contrary to the principles of the trade union movement.' The Labour Party had 'never made the slightest protest against this institution, known as the Mount Street Club.' Michael Colgan, Irish Bookbinders, said that 'Mr. Larkin believed he was always right and everybody else was always wrong,' and there was 'nothing to keep' him from joining the Labour Party 'but he preferred to remain outside, so that he could criticise without offering any practical suggestions.' Congress was accused of a *volte-face* when nominating candidates to the Labour panel for the Seanad. Larkin seconded a motion that condemned fascism and the loss of trade union liberties, warning that the Government was trying to deny Freedom of Association. It urged united action by workers.

In 1939 Larkin moved the suspension of standing orders to demand the release of Frank Ryan, 'a citizen of Éire and a trade unionist.' He praised Ryan's scholarship as 'second to none,' his intellect and physical courage. Jim Hickey, ITGWU and Lord Mayor of Cork, supported Larkin's call.[16]

When Larkin decided to join the Labour Party it was to cause a dramatic re-action. Those who criticised him for remaining on the outside did not necessarily want him inside.

Chapter 16 ∿

| CONCLUSIONS

MEMBERSHIP AND INCOME

The ITGWU's nadir was 1932, with a mere 14,123 members. By 1939 it had recovered to 36,444, bringing it back to where it was in 1923, 'without the farm labourers.' Recovery was part of a general resurgence as employment picked up. WUI membership remained static and confined to Dublin. The ITGWU's income rose from £16,901 to £37,494, annual surpluses enabling the credit balance to virtually double, from £76,393 to £151,874. The ITGWU reasserted itself as the largest union, within the Free State at least. The WUI's finances displayed an upward trend, a picture rather different from its sluggish membership returns, most probably explained by more 'book' members becoming 'benefit' ones. More importantly, the first surplus was declared in 1931 and thence annually. No figures for credit balance are available. The WUI could not be compared with the ITGWU, as it owned little property and had minimal investments. While it was now healthier, its existence was still from hand to mouth.

Table 40: **Comparative membership, ITGWU, WUI and ITUC, 1930–39**

	ITGWU	*WUI*	*ITUC*
1930	14,608	16,909	102,000
1931	14,500	17,117	102,000
1932	14,123	16,781	95,000
1933	14,460	17,363	95,000
1934	16,670	16,693	115,000
1935	20,951	15,763	125,000
1936	24,810	14,776	134,000
1937	28,514	16,997	146,000
1938	33,095	16,720	161,000
1939	36,444	16,408	162,000

Sources: ITGWU, Annual Reports, 1930–39; National Archives, Registrar of Friendly Societies, files 275T and 324T; Nevin, *Trade Union Century,* p. 433.

Table 41: Comparative income, expenditure and balance (£), ITGWU and WUI, 1924–30

| | ITGWU | | | WUI | | |
Year	Income	Expenditure	Balance	Income	Expenditure	Balance
1930	16,901	12,505	4,396	7,811	6,167	(829)
1931	16,994	14,653	2,341	7,957	7,538	1,236
1932	17,380	10,158	7,222	6,303	4,714	2,825
1933	19,340	11,891	7,499	7,482	6,598	3,709
1934	24,389	19,377	5,012	7,892	7,947	3,634
1935	27,482	26,590	892	8,678	8,701	3,630
1936	30,471	19,377	10,509	8,098	6,916	4,811
1937	35,081	34,224	857	15,541	6,088	5,268
1938	37,340	19,956	17,384	12,710	12,499	5,476
1939	37,494	16,974	20,520	10,996	10,894	5,578

Sources: ITGWU, Annual Reports, 1930–39; National Archives, Registrar of Friendly Societies, file 324T.

Table 42: ITGWU credit balance (£), 1930–39

1930	76,393	1935	101,297
1931	78,734	1936	111,807
1932	87,956	1937	113,845
1933	95,405	1938	131,229
1934	100,405	1939	151,874

Source: ITGWU, Annual Reports, 1930–39.

DISPUTES AND BENEFITS

A comparison of Dispute Pay reveals that militant traditions were maintained, the building strikes of 1931 and 1937 being evident strains on resources. In aggregate the WUI spent £21,279 on strikes, the ITGWU £61,466. As a percentage, the WUI spent an average of 21% of its income each year, the ITGWU 22%. The two unions had similar records, neither of them afraid to finance members' industrial struggles, irrespective of cost.

Table 43: Comparison of Dispute Pay, ITGWU and WUI, 1930–39

	ITGWU			*WUI*		
	Total income (£)	*Dispute pay (£)*	*As proportion of total income (%)*	*Total income (£)*	*Dispute pay(£)*	*As proportion of total income (%)*
1930	16,901	983	5.8	7,811	787	10.0
1931	16,994	4,450	26.2	7,957	1,489	18.7
1932	17,380	425	2.5	6,303	982	15.5
1933	19,340	1,394	7.2	7,482	1,597	21.3
1934	24,389	7,000	28.7	7,892	2,469	32.2
1935	27,482	13,509	49.2	8,678	2,587	29.8
1936	30,471	6,871	22.6	8,098	697	8.6
1937	35,081	18,948	54.0	15,541	6,088	39.1
1938	37,340	5,234	14.2	12,710	2,733	21.5
1939	37,494	2,652	7.1	10,996	1,850	16.8

Sources: ITGWU, Annual Reports, 1930–39; National Archives, Registrar of Friendly Societies, file 324T.

The only other benefit offered was Mortality Benefit. Larkin made a great issue of this in his opposition to Liberty Hall, accusing the ITGWU of defrauding members' relatives of mortality payments—a hugely emotional issue. The benefit allowed burial with decency and provided much-needed cash at a significant moment. The two unions in fact dispensed similar relative amounts to bereaved claimants.

Table 44: Mortality payments, ITGWU and WUI (£), 1930–39

	ITGWU	*WUI*		*GWU*	*WUI*
1930	1,199	246	1936	1,487	476
1931	1,030	233	1937	1,441	505
1932	979	315	1938	1,550	476
1933	979	305	1939	1,554	649
1934	1,021	387	Total	12,445	4,419
1935	1,205	557			

Sources: ITGWU, Annual Reports, 1930–39; National Archives, Registrar of Friendly Societies, file 324T.

STAFF

A comparison of staff costs reveals—perhaps surprisingly—that the two unions spent almost identical amounts: WUI £30,185, ITGWU £30,355. As a proportion of total expenditure the WUI's outlay was twice as high: 37%, compared with 17%; but these figures are misleading, as the ITGWU Branch Secretaries' and clerks' wages were paid from local funds and did not feature in national accounts. Nevertheless the WUI's outlay is surprising, in absolute amount and relatively. Its wages were regarded as inferior to Liberty Hall's, further distorting the picture. For a union that was supposedly very much led by the rank-and-file the WUI was perhaps more Official-oriented than has been imagined. Conversely, the ITGWU was perhaps not as bureaucratic or Official-controlled as is often suggested. Until the post-1932 revival the ITGWU cut staff numbers extensively.

Table 45: Staff costs, ITGWU and WUI, 1930–39

	ITGWU		WUI	
	Staff costs (£)	As proportion of expenditure (%)	Staff costs (£)	As proportion of expenditure (%)
1930	2,771	22.1	3,329	53.9
1931	2,020	13.7	2,253	29.8
1932	2,006	19.7	1,750	37.1
1933	2,300	19.3	3,060	46.3
1934	3,381	17.4	2,641	33.2
1935	3,303	12.4	2,731	31.3
1936	3,480	17.4	3,072	44.4
1937	3,656	10.6	3,049	20.2
1938	3,573	17.9	4,090	32.7
1939	3,845	22.6	4,210	38.6

Sources: ITGWU, Annual Reports, 1930–39; National Archives, Registrar of Friendly Societies, file 324T.

CONGRESS AND POLITICS

Having gained affiliation to Dublin Trades Council, Larkin had access to ITUC Conferences as its Delegate. This led to lively exchanges as he demanded explanations for the refusal of Congress to accept the WUI's affiliation. O'Brien's hostility was unswerving; the WUI was kept at the gate. Within Congress the Council of Irish Unions, set up within the ITUC in 1939 'to look after the interests of Irish unions,' ratcheted up pressure to rationalise the movement by reducing the number of wastefully competing unions and, simultaneously, raising serious questions about British unions' Irish presence.

The seeds of disunity were sown after 1936 with Congress's failure to agree on self-rationalisation. Rivalry between the ITGWU and ATGWU continued, particularly within Dublin trams. The entry of Fianna Fáil to Dáil Éireann (for which both Larkin and Congress claimed credit) and its rapid accession to power apparently gave O'Brien an inside track to Lemass for promoting his ideas on rationalisation and the elimination of British unions, despite the ITGWU's continued support for the Labour Party.

The Labour Party's electoral performance disappointed, with seven seats in 1932 and only nine in 1938, despite a false leap forward to thirteen in 1937. In 1932 and 1933 Larkin Senior and Larkin Junior ran in Dublin, polled well and probably cost the Labour Party seats. In 1937 Larkin was elected in Dublin North-East but in 1938 lost the seat, finally abandoning his independent line and seeking to join the Labour Party.

The 1930s began with severe depression and difficult times for workers and their unions in which to survive, resist wage cuts and retain employment. After 1932 things slowly improved, and the ITGWU—which never lost its nationwide presence—grew by organising emerging industries and reorganising those previously lost. When Foran retired in 1939, after thirty years as President, he could look back with considerable satisfaction. The ITGWU survived the 1913 Lock-Out, the 1916 Rising and the Larkin split to re-establish itself as the leading union. In the WUI, although records are scarce, Larkin's diminishing energy was balanced by James Junior's increasing contribution, organisationally, intellectually and strategically. Seeds for division and self-destruction were being sown, however. The imminence of global conflict fundamentally altered the industrial relations infrastructure. There was little talk of revolution or Workers' Republics but attempts to find bargaining mechanisms for more equitably distributing wealth and opportunity in what remained a very poor society.

Chapter 17

GOVERNMENT LOAN, SPLITS, AND ADVANCE BY TRIBUNAL: THE ITGWU, 1939–45

WAR

In 1940 the General President of the ITGWU, Thomas Kennedy, reflected that little more than three months after he warned of a world political and industrial crisis 'the dreaded war for supremacy among the capitalist Great Powers of Europe had broken out on the helpless people.'

There was no mention of Hitler or of resistance to fascism. Those who lived through the last war 'never wanted to see another holocaust in our lifetime . . . Tremendous advances in science and invention' meant that war of the 'most terrible mechanised kind' would 'bring literal destruction on millions of innocent people, suspend hard-won rights and liberties, and stop the social and economic progress the working class had been making.' Workers were the 'first victims of this devilish onslaught.'

In sentiments reminiscent of Connolly in 1914, although uttered in very different circumstances for international Socialists, Kennedy continued: 'I am sorry to say that too many of the workers' in Europe 'failed to recognise that their first duty and allegiance' should have been 'to their own working-class.' It was a 'mad world' that could spend millions on war and not provide for employment.

For the 'neutrality of the greater part of Ireland' thanks were given to those whose past sacrifice purchased that right 'we now enjoy.' The ITGWU was 'in firm and determined agreement on this neutrality' and would 'do all in our power in maintaining it.'

In 1941 Kennedy complained that, amid widespread shortages, wealthy people stockpiled food and coal, having been encouraged to do so by the Government, supporting calls for rationing.[1] Continued gratitude for non-participation was expressed as the war proceeded.

MEMBERSHIP, ORGANISATION AND FINANCE

War halted the ITGWU's forward march. Depressed trade resulted in unemployment, but this 'in no wise impaired the efficiency, or slackened the activity,' of the union. Income and membership were maintained. Many 'were unable to understand how' the ITGWU 'could spend money freely, and even lavishly' and 'keep a nation-wide network of Branches and Officials, and have in reserve a fund large enough to guarantee benefits,' all 'on weekly rates of contributions ranging from three-pence to sixpence.' O'Brien could not resist a cut at absent friends. The ITGWU was a 'working democracy, controlled by its members . . . They had no use for one man rule.' The union was, 'in the fullest sense, the property of the members, and every Official and employee was subject to their will.'

The NEC insisted that organisational strategies be better informed, while others worried about the impact of army recruitment. In 1940 Branch remittances fell by only £545, a 'source of great satisfaction.' Bus and road freight men transferred in the Great Southern Railway, Waterford, and Dublin United Tramways Company, while in Drogheda large numbers of clothing workers were organised.

Decreasing imports of raw materials, transport and shipping problems began to bite in the autumn. More than £300,000 was gained for members in wage increases. In March unpublicised financial support was given to the Irish Seamen's and Port Workers' Union and the Irish National Union of Woodworkers to prevent their collapse. In April membership stood at 36,825, distributed among seventy-eight Branches, varying from 3,627 in Cork No. 1 Branch to 14 in Carrick-on-Shannon. In 1941 O'Brien declared: 'It would take more than a war to wipe out their Union.'

Although falling slightly, membership, remarkably after two years of 'war reaction,' was higher than in 1936. This required committed organising. In Branches where 'through indifference or unemployment' members had left, 'they were pursued.' New Branches opened for coal and turf workers as import substitution or replacement took place. 'Despite transport and other difficulties,' every effort was made to maintain contact with Branches.[2]

Table 46: ITGWU membership, 1939–45

	Union figure	RFS figure
1939	36,444	36,000
1940	36,825	36,000
1941	35,271	36,000
1942	31,228	36,000
1943	30,615	36,000
1944	34,853	51,874
1945	37,970	53,185

Sources: ITGWU, minutes of National Executive Council, 1939–1946; National Archives, Registrar of Friendly Societies, file 275T.

Table 47: ITGWU membership by Branch, April 1940

Ardfinnan	98	Foynes	117
Arklow	465	Galway No. 1	444
Athlone	232	Galway No. 2	285
Athy	204	Gorey	111
Balbriggan	195	Graigue	36
Ballina	38	Kildare	162
Ballymore Eustace	253	Kilkenny	243
Bandon	64	Killarney	121
Belfast	580	Killarney Mental Hospital	85
Bennettsbridge	31	Kilrush	259
Birr	36	Laois-Offaly	1,001
Blanchardstown	118	Limerick	2,726
Bray	186	Lucan	217
Cahir	91	Macroom	124
Carlow	373	Mallow	111
Carrick-on-Shannon	14	Midleton	147
Castlebar	18	Mitchelstown	86
Cavan	119	Moneenroe	289
Clonmel Mental Hospital	48	Mountmellick	73
Cóbh	244	Mullingar	42
Convoy	325	Naas	39
Cork No. 1	3,627	Navan	135
Cork No. 2	2,977	New Ross	160
Dripsey	90	Newry	403
Drogheda	683	Port Laoise Mental Hospital	55
Droichead Nua	166	Rathdowney	28
Dublin No. 1	2,551	Rathfarnham	461
Dublin No. 2	2,463	Sligo No. 1	268
Dublin No. 3	2,013	Sligo No. 2	335
Dublin No. 4	1,800	Thomastown	39
Dublin No. 5	1,491	Tralee	365
Dublin No. 6	1,099	Trim	301
Dublin No. 7	1,047	Tuam	106
Dublin No. 8	640	Tullamore	32
Dublin No. 9	1,071	Valleymount	21
Dún Laoghaire	168	Waterford	562

Dunmanway	169	Westport	54
Enniscorthy	209	Wexford	178
Fenit	131	Wicklow	14

Source: ITGWU, minutes of National Executive Council, 18–20 April 1940.

There were acute shortages, even the complete disappearance of some goods. Members required all their moral courage. They were asked to 'acquit themselves with the firmness and bearing worthy' of the union.

1941 was a trying year. Loss of income, however, was offset by the tiny amount of Dispute Benefit—£745—even if Mortality Benefit, at £1,922, was the highest since 1925. The credit balance rose, reassuring members that there was 'no cause for anxiety.' McMullen thought a 'new departure' in strategy was needed. An Organiser was sent to Kildare turf works, without much success.

D. McGuigan (Convoy) thought more could be achieved in Co. Donegal, and Pádraig Mac Gamhna (Carlow) moved that recruitment be aimed at 'all road and bog workers.' McMullen cast members' minds back to Waterford in 1923. Apart from the cost, it greatly damaged the union's reputation. It 'did not want to repeat that experience.' There was a lively concern for organisation.

Membership rose slightly in 1942, generating a surplus of £14,862. The organisation drive kicked in. The 'usual pacific measures' were used against non-Unionists, but in some cases it was necessary 'to refuse to continue at work alongside' them. 'Dire forebodings' of a severe decline in membership were not realised, initial losses being more than recovered. An additional Organiser was appointed. Confidence grew to the extent that talk of OBU emerged again.

A 'substantial increase' in membership occurred in 1943, with income up 25%. Mortality Benefit was high, at £2,117, but the surplus was £19,710. Membership was 'remarkable' in view of the 'further big decrease' in employment and rising emigration. It was a tribute to the ITGWU's 'prestige', an awareness of its benefits and services, the 'democratic, equitable and proficient manner' of the conduct of its business and a 'splendid system of organisation.' A number of small unions that could not afford Negotiating Licences under the Trade Union Act (1941) transferred, Ardagh Trades and Labour Union and Cork Coopers' Society in 1942 and Ennis United Labourers and Protective Benefit Society, Limerick Operative Plasterers', Slaters' and Tilers' Society, Tipperary Workingmen's Protective and Benefit Society and Waterford Operative Coopers' Society in 1943.[3]

Table 48: ITGWU income, expenditure, selected benefits, surplus and credit balance (£), 1939–45

	Income	Branch remittances	Dispute benefit	Mortality benefit	Total expenditure	Surplus	Credit balance
1939	37,494	32,831	2,652	1,554	16,974	20,520	160,916
1940	37,969	32,398	5,054	1,812	21,304	16,665	181,470
1941	33,533	27,387	745	1,923	17,342	16,191	199,691
1942	33,649	27,475	288	2,117	18,787	14,862	216,874
1943	37,137	31,652	430	1,898	17,427	19,710	237,058
1944	39,960	34,011	252	1,898	16,245	23,715	261,694
1945	41,072	35,212	4,581	1,871	21,806	19,266	285,592

Source: ITGWU, Annual Reports, 1939–45.

In 1944 membership stood 'at its highest figure for many years,' despite employment in transportable goods, the union's traditional base, falling by 15,000. The organisation campaign begun in 1940 paid dividends: rural areas were opened up, urban Branches strengthened and non-unionism widely eradicated. Income was the highest for twenty years.

By December 1945 book membership was 60,000, a fifth of it women. Organisation aimed at 'establishing the Union in those villages or small towns in which trade unionism was more or less unknown or had not operated for many years.' By 1943 this campaign had spent itself, not because of lack of effort but because few unorganised places remained. In any post-war recovery the ITGWU was well placed to take every advantage. Hard times, however, were reflected in Branches trying to avoid paying the Brass and Reed Band levy or in shifting members to lower contribution scales. John Conway was seconded from the NEC as temporary Organiser after roadmen in the Great Northern Railway were actively pursued. In March 1945 membership was 37,970. The ITGWU affiliated to the Congress of Irish Unions for 51,874 members in July.[4]

WOMEN

As employment fell sharply in 1940, some unions sought to have women excluded from certain occupations under Section 16 of the Conditions of Employment Act (1936). The ITGWU did not oppose such moves. Louie Bennett (IWWU) fought the suggestion to exclude women at the 1941 Congress, demanding 'equal pay for equal work.'[5] The number of women members in the ITGWU increased from 6,000 in 1939 to 10,634 in 1945, an increase from 17 to 28% of the total. This was a substantial numerical increase and accounted for a significant part of the wartime rise in membership. After the war, women would become an ever more significant component of the union and of its policy.

NORTHERN IRELAND .

In February 1940 Belfast was in an 'extremely critical position' because of the 'decline of grain work due to erection of silos.' Head Office returns almost halved in four years: 1936, £923 18s 11d; 1937, £874 17s 5d; 1938, £678 4s; 1939, £580 6s 9d. Remarkably, given McMullen's position as Vice-President, the NEC decided that in the 'best interest of our Belfast members an effort ought be made to obtain favourable terms of transfer to the A.T.G.W.U. as the only means of preserving employment for them.' John McLarnon asked that members be given the opportunity to decide. Meanwhile negotiations were opened with the ATGWU to see what terms could be got.

From long before—and, it must be accepted, long afterwards—the ITGWU had an ambivalent attitude to its Northern members. While it was proud to be a 32-County organisation, little effort was made to expand membership, geographically or industrially. There was little or no engagement in Belfast Trades Council. Nothing came of the suggested transfer to the ATGWU. 'Considerable increases' in wages were gained in Belfast, Newry, Portadown and Warrenpoint in 1941. The Stormont Government made strikes illegal, and all disputes had to be submitted to an Arbitration Tribunal. Belfast and Newry dockers got wages 'equivalent to the highest rates paid in the last war when the cost of living was 100 points higher.' Flour and grist millers, seedsmen and chemical and distillery workers won advances. By 1945, Northern membership was maintained.[6]

WAGES AND STANDSTILL ORDERS

Rapid increases in the cost of living caused living standards to fall. The ITGWU thought long about its reaction. The 'fruits of this attention' did not 'appear until the close of the year,' but the NEC thought them 'so important and widespread that the time spent on sowing the seeds' resulted in one of 'the best periods of the Union's usefulness to its members.' This considered approach marked all union wartime endeavours.

The NEC decided it was 'not opposed to a wage settlement on a cost-of-living basis for particular Sections' but was against this as general policy. More than £200,000 was gained in wage increases. From September a 'bonus on a sliding scale arrangement, or a fixed sum for which an additional demand could be later made,' was agreed as a war bonus.[7] In the first twelve months of the war 35,000 members gained increases in money terms, even if real wages fell. The Government induced employers to concede nothing, and the Prices Commission accepted that increases could not go on wages. Unemployment was untouched, save that thousands went to Britain to find work in war production, with no 'guarantee that the men who have gone will not be compelled to share in the imperialist blood-lust.' The Minister for Industry and Commerce, Seán MacEntee, threatened that the 'occurrence of serious strikes in basic industries' might compel the Government 'to restrict them by law' for the 'duration of the war.' He made a 'patriotic' appeal, asking industry to come together and solve its own problems. The Government investigated 426 cases of profiteering by May 1941, but fines on 72 companies found guilty were 'absurdly light,' hardly an example of even-handedness.

Kennedy put down a marker for the Minister. 'Now I needn't assure you that in this union we stand for peace in industry and peaceful negotiation, but the other side forces conflict.' Industrial peace was not acceptable if it meant 'a substantial reduction' in workers' living standards. Before considering 'any peace pact', the Government 'would have to devise machinery that would effectively prevent any increase in the already heavy war burdens carried by our class.'

The war 'did not catch us unawares,' Kennedy continued. As to 'hints of legislation to restrict trade union activities,' the ITGWU was 'not going to surrender, without a fight, the rights the pioneers . . . won for us and those rights include the right to withdraw our labour, the right to strike when we have just cause or no other remedy.' Mechanisms for avoiding conflict, such as Joint Industrial Councils, gave rise to 'strong dissatisfaction,' as employers 'ask us for peaceful negotiations' and then 'deliberately refuse to register' standard negotiated Agreements.

Kennedy recognised that things 'may worsen' but demanded that the Government tackle unemployment with 'as much attention and mobilising as much financial and other forces for its solution as they would for a war measure,' or they would 'be heading straight for a situation as desperate as war itself.' Were 'they big enough for that?'

The ITGWU would 'weather the present hurricane no less successfully' than previous storms. McMullen argued that 'employers on the whole had readily recognised' workers' right 'to extra remuneration to offset the increased cost of living.' By June 1942 living standards were halved amid growing misery. After fighting for freedom and twenty years of 'native Government' it was a scandal that 'no better use' could be found for thousands of young people than being forced to emigrate and risk their lives in British war manufacture. Emigrants' remittances were a 'strange remedy for poverty.' Kennedy refrained from totally blaming the Government: after all, 'people get the Government they deserve.'[8]

In February 1940 the ITGWU and Irish Seamen's and Port Workers' Union were informed by the Department of Supplies that, in order to maintain the prices of essential commodities, neither wage nor price increases could be granted for fertilisers or flour. The unions sought the assistance of the ITUC, but the Government insisted that wage increases must be met from profits or by reducing staff. These were opening shots in moves to curtail wages. The Minister for Finance, Seán T. O'Kelly, threatened wage controls in his Budget speech on 8 November 1939, arguing against an 'artificial price structure' like that of the First World War. The Government 'set its face against the efforts of any class to obtain compensation for the rise in prices at the expense of the community.'

Congress responded against this 'thinly veiled threat' and asked workers to close ranks. Congress and the Labour Party issued a pamphlet, *Planning for the Crisis*. The Government lagged well behind in its plans for avoiding shortages, managing production and restricting profiteering. A National Council for the Building

Industry was established, Kennedy being an ITUC nominee. Frank Robbins demanded an 'emphatic protest' against Government attempts 'with the aid of the employers to cripple' the movement.

In moving a supplementary Budget O'Kelly made it clear that the Government opposed wage increases. Robbins recalled the anti-combination laws that drove the movement underground, forcing it 'to adopt methods which we did not wish to see repeated.' John Conroy (Limerick) warned that a lack of self-discipline would attract repressive reaction. They 'should make it clear' that the ITGWU 'does not stand for unofficial strikes' and must 'have some respect for Rules and the general public.' O'Brien recognised that war 'called for extra restraint.' J. Conway (Dublin No. 9) remembered the Tolpuddle martyrs; 'slaves had to be fed, clothed and housed, but if wage-earners did not work they were neither fed, clothed nor housed.' Jim Hickey TD, Lord Mayor of Cork, thought that, whatever happened, war would 'occasion a change in the social system.' Ireland should 'set an example' and build up a 'new social system which would correspond with this [coming] age of plenty.' The Government's and employers' cards were well marked.

Richard Corish TD promised vigorous defence by the Labour Party of union rights in the Dáil, but 'very little of what Labour Deputies' said 'got into the newspapers.'

Ministerial orders prevented increases sanctioned by public authorities—in one case approved by a Commissioner—depriving thousands of legitimate increases. JICS, Conciliation Boards and Trade Boards continued to be employed, but approved increases for aerated water, handkerchief and household piece goods, tobacco and sugar confectionery were blocked. The ITGWU's 'power, however, was such that arrangements' were made directly with employers to achieve equivalent rates. It fought hard to mitigate the impact of rising prices, but Emergency Order No. 83 prohibited wages rising above the level of 7 May 1941. Kennedy saw the Order as neither constraining prices nor preventing better-paid workers doing better than lower-paid ones. Even with, say, a 10% increase in wages, workers still suffered a 17% loss. No industrialists or farmers suffered similar losses. What the order would do was what it was designed to do: 'if it is not withdrawn or defeated by workers and their unions, it will hamstring the unions' and 'create a slave mind and an anti-trade union feeling among some workers.' The 'Trade Disputes Act, wrung from a Conservative Government in Britain, went overboard.' Trade Boards also went 'into oblivion,' and the Agricultural Wages Board ceased to function.

An immovable Government responded that the order had 'been very much mis-understood.' It was 'not an attack upon the standard of the workers' but an attempt to share out limited resources more equally.[9] But the ITGWU felt it would 'breed discontent, disillusionment and indifference at the very moment the Government declares that national unity on neutrality is a vital necessity.' Whatever could be done to oppose the Emergency Order should be done. Cork No. 1 Branch wanted a 'one-day campaign of public protestation,' led by Congress and the Labour Party.

By December 1941 the Order had reduced living standards by at least 8%. Workers had no illusions: the Order had little to do with controlling inflation, as profiteering was 'still rampant.' Throughout the country, Branches protested and called for its annulment. All fell on deaf Government ears. It was an attack on workers 'made under the flimsy excuse of national emergency.'[10]

The Government was 'compelled' by 'continued protest' to revoke the obnoxious Order on 8 April 1942 but promulgated a new Order (No. 166). A slight improvement, it still contained 'many objectionable features' and covered every worker save state, local Government, agricultural workers, turf workers and seamen. Workers could seek increases not exceeding 2s for every ten-point rise in the cost-of-living index above 225 points. Before this a declaration from the National Advisory Tribunal about the standard wage on 8 April 1942 in the industry concerned had to be obtained. Consent from either employer or Minister was then required before a claim could proceed. Even then, if it was successful, Ministerial approval was necessary for any increase to actually be paid. There was no compulsion on employers to pay, only union pressure—provided, of course, that the union held a Negotiating Licence under the Trade Union Act (1941). Kennedy thought it was 'so designed as to make it almost impossible for workers to gain increases.' It was 'an insult to the intelligence.' Hickey was 'quite satisfied that there are men and women in Congress who helped put this Government into power.' He might have added that, given the choice in the morning, they would do so again.

The ITGWU actively pursued increases, and by December more than 150 bonus orders were made in the union's name. Pressure from the ITGWU also brought some amending orders. Members gained 'over £240,000.'

Table 49: Cost-of-living index, 1939–45

1939 (August)	179	1942 (December)	275
1940 (January)	192	1943 (March)	284
1940 (April)	197	1943 (November)	294
1940 (August)	204	1944 (February)	296
1940 (December)	214	1944 (May)	292
1941 (March)	218	1944 (August)	296
1941 (May)	220	1944 (November)	296
1941 (August)	228	1945 (February)	295
1941 (December)	237	1945 (May)	292
1942 (March)	240	1945 (August)	293
1942 (June)	250	1945 (November)	298
1942 (August)	273		

Source: ITGWU, Annual Reports, 1939–45.

McMullen thought that no Government in Europe had done more to depress workers' living standards than the Irish Government. This sprang less from anti-working-class bias—workers voted them in—and more from dependence on 'worn-out and discredited' economic theory, 'in comparison with which' the 'Manchester School of Economics would seem almost Utopian.' Workers' patience ran very thin. The orders were 'nothing but a declaration of war' on workers.

P. J. O'Brien (Cork No. 2) thought they had no alternative but to use the order to gain whatever increases they could. Hickey thought a strong Section should be chosen to fight the order through a strike. How this could be done with immunities removed and a legal bar on paying Strike Pay was not explained.

McMullen observed that many who criticised the Orders had no problem giving their services to the Local Defence Force or Local Security Force, which 'might be utilised if they were to have drastic action in the public street.' If Government policy were 'not a shroud for Fascism he did not know what the term meant.'

Conway said they 'might talk until they were blue in the face' about drastic action, 'but the fact remained that the general body of workers were not backing such action.' Kennedy defended the ITGWU's use of the Orders, as it sought 'even the miserable pittance' they provided to improve matters. He suggested stopping supplies of bread or flour to pressure the Government and called for price controls to prevent profiteering and to improve distribution.

In 1943 the ITGWU's use of JICs and Trade Boards brought gains for boot and shoe repairers, waste reclamation, sugar and confectionery, food-preserving, women's clothing, millinery, shirt-making, tobacco, packing, handkerchief and aerated waters. The Emergency Powers (No. 260) Order (1943) was condemned for fixing the ceiling for increases 'below the actual cost of living of mid-August, 1939.' However, the ITUC's opposition diminished, as 'virtually all licensed' unions 'nominated members to the Workmen's Panels,' and Congress itself participated. More than 800 awards were recorded, mostly after Tribunal hearings.

The ITGWU assiduously sought the maximum benefits permitted in a two-pronged strategy: in rural areas to bring rates to the permitted maximum plus bonus, and in urban areas to obtain bonus orders. This involved the staff in negotiations with employers, the preparation of briefs, investigations into wages and conditions, gathering statistics on prices, profits, output and consumption, and keeping abreast of national economic developments. Hundreds of advances were won, totalling more than £250,000. The cumulative aggregate since war began was a staggering £3 million. That said, by December 1943 it took 34s to 'equal the purchasing value of the pre-war pound sterling.' In other words, the pound fell in value to 11s 8d.

For state employees the ITGWU adopted a 'roundabout and tedious method' of increasing local rates first and then appealing for relativities. It had members in all Departments, but the biggest increases were won in military barracks in Athlone, Gormanston, Longford, Mullingar and the Curragh. A similar strategy was used for local authority workers, backed by Dáil agitation. Success within Trade Boards induced some workers to ask what was the need to be unionised when increases came without their involvement. They missed the point. It was union representation that won the awards.

Psychiatric nurses met in Conference in the Mansion House, Dublin, in November, with men and women from Ballinasloe, Carlow, Castlebar, Clonmel, Cork, Enniscorthy, Grangegorman, Killarney, Kilkenny, Mullingar, Portrane, and Sligo. The presence of General Officers and TDs showed the assembly's significance. Many matters were presented to Dr Con Ward TD, Parliamentary Secretary to the Minister for Local Government and Public Health, including a revised scale and reduced hours.

On 3 January 1945 a second Conference considered the Mental Treatment Act (1944). A deputation met Ward on 16 January, and submissions were made through the National Labour Party. Wage scales, reluctantly agreed to in discussions with Ward, were finally implemented after October. Employers in rural areas met the ITGWU with 'indifference, if not hostility,' and mechanisms for protecting the lower pay were sought.

The Emergency Powers (No. 260) Order (1943) governed wages in 1944, with a limit of 60s (£3) a week applied to Cork, Dublin, Dún Laoghaire, Limerick and Waterford, 50s (£2 10s) in towns with a population of more than 7,000, and correspondingly lower amounts for smaller towns. Maximum bonuses did not rise above 11s. All this notwithstanding, members gained another £200,000. A Ministerial Memorandum on Bonus for Overtime in August confirmed the calculation of overtime rates. Trade Board increases were gained in tobacco, shirt-making, aerated water, millinery and clothing, packing, sugar and confectionery, tailoring, and paper box making. JICs were largely inactive. A crash in the pig population caused the Munster Bacon Council to suggest a Committee of Inquiry on Post-Emergency Agricultural Policy. A body representing employers, workers and the State should control production, processing and marketing; all producers and curers should be licensed; landowners over a certain acreage should be compelled to fatten a quota of pigs; and producers should be guaranteed an economic price. The Department of Agriculture should establish pig farms to improve stock, and all bacon pigs should be slaughtered on licensed curers' premises. The number of slaughterings fell from 1,039,261 in 1939 to 221,125 in 1944.

Reflecting on wartime experience, McMullen suggested that 'the time had arrived when Labour Courts should be established.' Questions of Workmen's Compensation and other matters could be referred there instead of to ordinary civil Courts. D. J. Galavan (Dublin No. 8) wanted workers' standard of living as in August 1939 re-established by removing all bargaining restrictions. Belief in Trade Boards was reiterated, with demands for a new board for hotel and catering. The splendid job done for more than 3,000 mental hospital employees was acknowledged, while amendments to the Mental Treatment Bill (1944) were sought. Similar work was done for transport workers through the Transport Act (1944). Hundreds of railway workers wanted to join, even though Conway (NEC) thought that 'outside the main lines there was no future for the railways': road traffic was the 'transport of the future.' McMullen felt that railwaymen 'for the present' should 'not be encouraged.'

Wages Standstill Orders were expected to cease before December 1946. By the end of 1944 the ITGWU had gained practically every increase and bonus available under such orders. In many instances, permitted maximums were exceeded. In 1945 attention turned to bonus orders. Most of the 3,000 submissions made were for ITGWU members. The total of extra wages paid to members in the period 1939–45 was estimated at approximately £4 million. An Advisory Tribunal occasioned considerable additional clerical work, as oral and written submissions had to be made; but the union enjoyed much success.

In 1946 the revoking of Emergency Wage Regulations 'ended a period of unparalleled activity' and 'phenomenal success.' More than 60% of all Wage Orders issued were on behalf of the ITGWU, and extra remuneration gained was 'not less than £10,000,000'—a significant achievement.[11]

Was the ITGWU's opposition to the Standstill Orders a 'phoney war', as opponents suggested? O'Brien's closeness to the Government painted him as the architect, but this was more likely in the case of the Trade Union Act. While others shouted at street corners about Standstill Orders, the ITGWU got on with the business of securing every increase available. Its success undoubtedly attracted new members.

DISPUTES

In 1940 the ITGWU established a Provident Fund from which to dispense Dispute Benefit and significantly raised amounts to 11s 3d, 18s 9d and 30s per week. The 'big increase in the cost of living' vied with the 'national unity brought about by the war emergency' as workers considered their actions. Employers forced the 'withdrawal of labour.' The ITGWU never accepted the cost of living index, but it did indicate the 'tendency of prices.' With few exceptions, wage-earners' living standards declined from September 1939. The purchasing power of the pound fell to 15s 3d. In 1941 the ITGWU sought to 'determine a standard of human needs . . . preliminary' to legislation establishing an 'annual living wage.' Significant stoppages were in Sixmilebridge Woollen Mill, Grand Canal Company and Dublin United Transport Company, only the first being official. It ran from November 1940 to March 1941, when the company finally paid national rates. On the canals few workers were organised, whereas in the DUTC some ATGWU members 'endeavoured to stipulate special terms as a condition of entry' into the ITGWU. This was refused. All other ATGWU men transferred unconditionally. The men were thus dismissed in accordance with the 'Union clause' in the Agreement. Action on their behalf collapsed after a few days, 'with all sympathising strikers returning' as ITGWU members.

In 1942 Dispute Pay was only £288. Advances were won through Conciliation and Trade Boards. Despite repressive legislation, twenty-five minor strikes took place in a 'quiet and unspectacular' year. In 1943 Dispute Pay was £430. The number of disputes increased as a result of the 'ever-increasing weariness and mental strain suffered' by workers endeavouring to 'make ends meet.' An unofficial strike in

Mallow sugar factory affected the national economy. Head Office responded by removing the Branch Secretary. In 1944 disputes were rare, short and local in nature.

There were more in 1945 than in the previous six years. About 3,000 members were involved in Athy, Ballyshannon, Castlecomer, Cork, Dublin, Enniscorthy, Galway, Kingscourt, Limerick, Lucan, New Ross, Newry, Tipperary, Tralee, Tuam and Wexford, mostly in sharp actions for wages, hours, dismissals or holidays. Dispute Pay was £4,581, the highest since 1940.[12]

BUS AND TRAM WORKERS

The ITGWU and ATGWU signed an Agreement with Dublin United Tramways Company in 1937. A joint claim for improved wages was served on 30 April 1940. The ITGWU, however, refused to support or take joint action, claiming it would breach the company-union Agreement. The ATGWU took no action, only to discover that the ITGWU served an individual claim, securing retrospective increases up to 30 October 1940. The Branch Secretary, William (Old Bill) Murphy, postered garages, asking 'all applicants for retrospective pay' to contact him by that date. The ATGWU complained to Congress that this notice, displayed 'with the consent of the Company,' was 'an inducement' to ATGWU men to transfer in order to obtain increases. In November the Congress Executive decided, by eight votes to seven, not to concede the ATGWU's requests for a Disputes Committee, as Dublin Trades Council was dealing with things. Kyle touched the nub: the ITGWU action was 'a wanton and deliberate betrayal of all Trade Union practice (an injury to one is the concern of all).' A 'Disputes Committee should report to the next Congress.' McMullen emphasised that Kyle's statement was 'entirely *ex parte*' (partisan). No-one would 'be so foolish as to assume that there was not another side to the story.'

In March 1940 the ITGWU tried to broker a 'general settlement for the whole country.' O'Hanlon, Leader of the ATGWU defectors, left the ITGWU to join the company management. At the AGM of Dublin No. 9 Branch no business could be done, 'owing to continued disorder which appeared to be deliberately organised.' Tempers were high as transport workers were let go because of fuel shortages. Their selection was complicated by lapsed memberships. In August six 'disrupters' were expelled from the ITGWU. Matters were complex.

In 1942 peace broke out between the ITGWU and ATGWU with an Agreement drawn up by Congress. Signed 'in a spirit and form which ought to give satisfaction,' it contained eight points, including the stipulation that prior Agreement would be obtained before 'an exchange of members in any areas, service or job,' transfers would be subject to members clearing arrears, there would be no recruiting or canvassing in each other's areas, and a Disputes Committee, appointed from the ITUC Executive, would resolve any contentious issues. This Committee gave each union a questionnaire and held ten meetings in its first year. Taking the moral high ground, the ITGWU quickly agreed and made a similar Agreement with the Amalgamated Union of Upholsterers. A strike in the Great Southern Railway's bus service resulted in the termination of the Agreement with the NUR.

Proposals for the reorganisation of transport services in 1943 brought the ITGWU and ATGWU into close alliance. They represented most workers in the Great Southern Railway and DUTC. Railway unions expressed immediate hostility to the Transport Bill (1944). The ITGWU made application to the Trade Union Tribunal under the acts of 1941–2 'for the sole right to organise in respect to the Road Traffic services' of the newly established CIÉ, engendering opposition from competing unions.

In 1945 the ITGWU raised the issue of dock workers' registration. Section 16 of the Harbours Bill (1945) allowed each harbour authority to 'take such steps as they think proper to improve conditions' of casual workers and to 'institute a system of registration.' Agreement was also reached with CIÉ for national scales for road passenger and freight, railway, and mechanical. Negotiations were conducted solely by the ITGWU.

Rows between the ITGWU and ATGWU were commonplace, while disputes with the WUI were almost unheard of, as the two unions seldom competed directly.[13]

COAL

McMullen sat on a Committee of Inquiry to determine whether Emergency Order No. 83 (1941) should be relaxed for coalminers. Many 'never received payment' for holidays or public holidays. Government 'laxity' was 'very much to be deplored.' In 1942 Pádraig Mac Gamhna, lifelong advocate of the development of natural resources, moved that immediate steps be taken to develop the country's coal reserves, fire and brick clay, graphite, iron ore and asbestos. Carlow produced infinitesimal amounts of coal but had reserves of 199 million tons. The inquiry produced majority and minority reports in 1942. The former, signed by the Government and mine-owners, opposed the exclusion of coal from the list of scheduled occupations. McMullen's lobbying finally achieved a 10% increase, and an attendance bonus of 1s a day. Nixie Boran called for an investigation into miners' 'terrible conditions.'[14] By December 1944, miners' wages had increased nearly 100% since 1939.

EMPLOYMENT AND ECONOMIC POLICY

McMullen condemned Government inaction on employment in 1940. With more than 140,000 in the country as a whole out of work, a Commission to seek solutions was warranted. James Hickey (Cork) gave 'marvellous illustrations' of what the unemployed could do if given access to land. The Government organised a Construction Corps as part of the army, Unemployment Assistance being refused to those nominated to participate, so contradicting its supposedly voluntary character. The Government insisted it would save young men from the 'disastrous consequences of chronic unemployment.' It would consist of eight hundred men, aged 18 to 25, and would undertake road-building and construction.

The attitudes of Congress were ambiguous. Kennedy suggested that unemployment might have to be dealt with on the 'basis of camp life.' Robbins opposed: it was economic Conscription and a breach of constitutional rights.

In 1942 Hickey wanted a Congress pamphlet with 'six or seven points' regarding economic development. Self-sufficiency had developed strongly and enabled £2 million worth of goods to be sent to Britain. William Kenneally was '100% proud of the achievements of Russia since 1917' and thought its society a possible model for post-war development. T. Horan (Mallow) suggested that ITGWU funds be invested to create employment. It was shot down as being hare-brained. Many thought funds only barely adequate if a major conflict arose, while others felt that large reserves intimidated employers. The ITGWU sought 'to pool all the resources of the nation' in order to achieve equal distribution, condemned the Government for failure to make proper provision for safeguarding necessary imports, and called for an Economic Advisory Body and a comprehensive scheme of post-war reconstruction. Demobilisation and returning emigrants would cause dislocation. Now was the time to plan education, social services, local Government and finance and to bring coal, transport, power and milling into public ownership. Such forward thinking elicited no Government response.

Fianna Fáil returned to power in 1943. Kennedy suggested that, as the electorate had decided, the Government was 'justly entitled' to assistance, co-operation and good will from the community and 'particularly' from members of 'this great Irish trade union.' After the ITGWU withdrew from the Labour Party in 1944, Kennedy reminded the Government of the expectations it carried. 'Having voted Fianna Fáil into power, the people now looked to the Government for a cure for their social ills.' The unemployed wanted work; 'slum dwellers decent housing; the young people of school-leaving age a chance in life; the victims of tuberculosis, sanatoria and treatment; and the community in general a just social order.' He trusted that 'the confidence placed in Mr. de Valera and his Party will not be abused.'

In June 1945, at the first ITGWU Conference after war ended, Kennedy said that, now 'the brutal system of Nazism' was crushed, the victorious powers should put aside 'all idea of hatred and instead of laying the foundations for another world war by starving, enslaving and exploiting the peoples of the conquered lands, with consequential disastrous effects on the economic life of the world,' should 'make a peace based on charity and mercy.' Such peace would 'have the qualities necessary to render it enduring.' He cited 'His Lordship Dr. Dignan, Bishop of Clonfert,' for focusing 'public attention on the misery caused by unemployment and disease.' Kennedy could see 'no reason' why social problems could not be solved 'by means of methods which are in harmony with national ideals and Christian principles', and he broadly welcomed the report of the Commission on Vocational Organisation. Some warned that this 'could only lead to Nazism or some other evil,' but there was some sympathy for its findings. Kennedy concluded by expressing sincere thanks to members, Shop Stewards and Branch Committees for their 'loyalty and service' in 'troublesome times.' In preparation for peace, motions were adopted on combating short time, on co-operative industry, on juvenile employment and on reafforestation.[15]

THE TRADE UNION ACT (1941)

At the 1939 ITUC Congress O'Brien opposed suggestions that Congress meet the British TUC to 'make clear' the movement's attitude to the impending war. In 1940 he suggested that it was 'generally agreed by all intelligent people in the movement' that union organisation was 'chaotic and hopeless.' It was four years since Lemass suggested that the movement put its own house in order. Failure to do so invited Government intervention, and yet the ITUC Special Commission's proposals to rationalise the movement into ten industrial unions, supported by the ITGWU, were rejected.

Robbins said that Congress's attitude had 'nullified the propaganda' about the ITGWU 'wanting to gobble everybody else up.' The WUI's application was declined in 1940, together with the Irish Automobile Drivers' and Automobile Mechanics' Union and the Irish Creamery Workers' Association. The ITGWU's opposition was at odds with its calls for unity.

The Trade Union Bill was published on 30 April 1941. It provided for a system of 'Negotiating Licences', which would be issued only to unions able to deposit with the High Court sums ranging from £2,000 for up to 2,000 members to £10,000 for 20,000 members or more. It was the death knell for many small societies, and made the establishment of breakaway organisations more difficult. A Trade Union Tribunal would adjudicate between unions organising in the same sectors.

A Special Congress was held on 16 May and registered its 'emphatic opposition.' The Labour Party spoke vigorously against the Bill, and voted against it. The ITGWU had been willing to change, 'perhaps even to the dissolution of our great and historic union.' It was 'willing to give all our resources, financial and material . . . our long experience, our skilled staffs, our prestige and power and unparalleled and honourable record.' The Bill was 'not of our making nor to our liking': its good points were outweighed by bad. No union more than the ITGWU had reason to 'complain of the nuisance' of 'small, unnecessary and undisciplined "unions" founded on mere selfishness and mere anti-social sentiment.'

Kennedy gave the obvious solution.

Nobody more than our Union has stood through many hard and bitter years for the remedy of all our organisational defects—the scientific organisation upon industrial lines of all wages earners in the united, militant One Big Union.

The Bill would not do away with 'unnecessary unofficial strikes . . . confine the organisation of Irish workers to Irish unions . . . bring industrial peace' or 'do away with . . . inter union rivalry,' no more than it would 'provide machinery for the settlement of industrial disputes . . . But it will through its Tribunal put the whole future development of trade unions . . . out of the hands of the workers . . . into the hands of people who have no knowledge of the movement and no interest in the uplifting of the working class and our emancipation from wage slavery.' Radical restructuring was the work of the movement, and no-one else. The Bill's only virtue was that 'it will open workers' eyes to the need for rationalisation.'

WUI AND FWUI GENERAL OFFICERS, 1924–1989

John Lawlor, General President, 1924–1929

James Larkin, General Secretary, 1924–1947

John Kenny, General President, 1929–1943

John Smithers, General President, 1943–1968

James Larkin Junior, General Secretary, 1946–1969

John Foster, General President, 1968–1982

Denis Larkin, General Secretary, 1969–1977

Patrick Cardiff, General Secretary, 1977–1983

Thomas Garry, General President, 1982–1989

William Attley, General Secretary, 1983–1989, Deputy General Secretary, 1978–1983

Patrick Murphy, Assistant General Secretary, 1979–1983

Tom Murphy, Deputy General Secretary, 1984–1989

'A pictorial history of the OBU'. (*Voice of Labour*, 1–15 March 1924)

(1) 1909—The Launching of the Ship.

Captain Larkin: ''Ere I am Captain of a real h-Irish ship at last. It's much more comfortable than working as Third Mate on a h-English ship.'

First Mate Foran: 'Aye, aye, sir.'

(2) 1913—The Storm

Captain Larkin: 'Keep at it lads and h'I'll stick with you for h-ever.'

Mate Foran: 'You'd better lend a hand yourself or the bloomin' ship may sink.'

(3) 1914—After the Storm

Captain Larkin (deserting the ship which he thinks is sinking): 'You all stick to the ship; I'll save my life and bring back 'elp some day.'

Mate Foran: 'We'll stick to the ship all right and keep her afloat.'

(4) 1915—Anxious Days

Acting Captain Jas. Connolly: 'It will take us all our time to keep the ship afloat. If that pirate attacks us we will have to fight to the death.'

The Crew: 'So we will.'

'A pictorial history of the OBU'. (*Voice of Labour*, 1–15 March 1924)

(5) 1916—The Ship Blown Up

Prisoner James Connolly: 'This looks like the end of the old ship, but if either of us escapes we will start on the fresh.'

Prisoner Tom Foran: 'You can rely on me.'

(6) 1916—Execution of Connolly

Connolly: 'Good-bye, boys. Don't forget your promise to restart the ship.'

Foran and O'Brien: 'We will do our best.'

(7) 1916—December. Wise counsels

Foran: 'I'm afraid it is all up with us.'

O'Brien: 'Not at all. You will be released soon, and you can start again. When I get away I will join you and help.'

(8) 1917—A New Ship

Foran: 'I think this will be a better ship than the old one. What will we call it?'

O'Brien: 'We will continue under the old name.'

'A pictorial history of the OBU'. (*Voice of Labour*, 1–15 March 1924)

(9) 1920—Steady Progress

Captain Foran: 'If this progress continues we ought to be able to reach our goal.'

Mate O'Brien: 'If the crew remain loyal nothing can stop us.'

(10) 1923—The 'Captain' Returns

'Captain' Larkin: 'h-I've returned, boys. I h-am the Captain, and h'I'll now take over command.'

Foran: 'No more self-appointed Captains for us, thanks. This ship is run by an Executive elected by the crew. If you wish you can take your place with us in the fight.'

Larkin: 'If h-I can't be Captain h'I'll sink the bloomin' ship!'

(11) 1923—Revenge!

Larkin: 'h-Open fire, boys. If they won't surrender the ship to me, we'll sink it.'

(12) 1924—The Boomerang

_____: _____ : _____ !'

Anti-Larkin cartoon, front page, *Voice of Labour*, 25 October 1924. (ILHS Archives)

'The state must control the banks', *Voice of Labour*, 18 April 1925. (ILHS Archives)

IRISH TRANSPORT & GENERAL WORKERS' UNION

HOTEL & RESTAURANT BRANCH.

The Hotel Association say;

"TO HELL WITH CONTRACTS."

Seven Years' Agreement broken without Notice
by Employers

STRIKE
AT THE
MOIRA, CENTRAL, DOLPHIN, WICKLOW, AND
GROSVENOR HOTELS.

A Fight for the Right of Hotel Men and Women
to remain Trade Unionists.

A Fight for the Right of Free Men and Women to
make their Own Choice.

☞ A FIGHT AGAINST SLAVERY ☜

VISITORS, WORKERS, AND THE PUBLIC, DO YOUR PART!

Out of a Combined Staff of 180, only 8 Scabs
remained at Work,

If this Solidarity makes an Appeal to you, Back up the
Workers in this Fight.

ISSUED BY STRIKE COMMITTEE.

COLUMBA PRESS, PRINTERS, AMIENS STREET, DUBLIN.

ITGWU Hotel and Restaurant Branch
'Five Houses Dispute' handbill, 1926.
(SIPTU Archive)

ELECTORAL AREA, No. 3.

Name _____ Your Number on Register is

Address _____ No. _____

YOUR CANDIDATES ARE:

We Stand for
Union Wages
Union Conditions
Security of Tenancy

Reduction of Municipal
House Rents
Continuance of Rent
Restriction Act

HILARY WILLIAMS
Bricklayer

Direct Labour on
all Municipal
Undertakings

FRANK CLUSKEY
Trade Union Secretary (Butchers)

HOUSES FOR THE POOR

JOHN SUNDERLAND
Railway Worker

PLUMP NUMBER 1, 2, 3 for the
Above Working-Class Candidates
According to your Preference
IRISH WORKER LEAGUE

Printed by John T. Drought, 6 Bachelor's Walk, Dublin, for The Irish Worker League.

Irish Worker League election
handbill, n.d. [1930s]. Note Frank
Cluskey Senior, WUI Butchers'
Branch Secretary. (SIPTU Archive)

ITGWU Shop, 33 Eden Quay.
L–r, Mick Kelly, winner of
the 'Sweet Afton banks'
competition prize of £50,
and Nellie McCarthy and
Jimmy Smith, who shared
the retailer's prize of £36.
(*Irishman*, 24 November
1932, ILHS Archives)

Chris Ferguson, WUI National
Organiser. (WUI Silver Jubilee
Souvenir, 1949)

McMullen's response was 'to get as fully organised as possible' so as 'to get Negotiating Licences for negotiating for 95% of the people.'

The ITGWU was seen as shedding crocodile tears. In preparing the Bill, Officials of the Department of Industry and Commerce met O'Brien and Kennedy privately. Some thought they succeeded in persuading MacEntee to shift from confrontation with the unions to accommodating the ITGWU's desires in exchange for its compliance. The proposed Trade Union Tribunal was seen 'as a means of consolidating and extending' the ITGWU's influence and control. British unions and others saw it as 'an O'Brien-inspired strategy aimed at realising' his 'long-held objective of "One Big Union".'

Foran nevertheless unsuccessfully moved the Bill's annulment in the Seanad, stating that 'the whole Labour movement throughout the country regard this order as the culmination of an apparently definite effort on the part of the Government to enslave the workers.' The movement gave 'its united opposition' but could not prevent its enactment.

At the 1941 Congress James Larkin (DTUC) suggested that MacEntee had told them that the Bill was not 'of his own initiative.' Certain unnamed trade unions and Officials were privy to its drafting. All Delegates had O'Brien and the ITGWU in mind. ITGWU speakers, pro or con, were conspicuous by their absence. When the WUI's affiliation to DTUC was accepted, the ITGWU decided that Branches should cease their affiliation from June 1941.

O'Brien linked the reception given to the Bill with the anger created by the Wages Standstill Orders. He retraced the history of attempts to self-rationalise: Agreement for change in Drogheda in 1919 and the ITUC Commission's 'complete and absolute failure' in 1936–39. The supreme irony was Congress's frequent calls for workers' control when it palpably could not manage its own affairs. The consequence was well-heralded Government interference.

There would, in any circumstances, have been opposition, not least from those who would be victims of the surgeon's knife. The only solution was to strengthen their ranks and then 'maybe the Trade Union Bill, 1941, and Emergency Order No. 83 may have the effect and the place in history of an Irish Taff Vale Decision.' His optimism was misplaced. He presided over one of the most divisive and cantankerous Congresses ever. Shrugging off virtually constant challenges to the chair, O'Brien closed the Congress by saying there was life in the event at least, and the 'most appalling thing' was 'apathy and indifference.' He acknowledged that strong criticism of the old Executive had some basis, but Delegates returned the same personnel; 'so the more we change, the more we stay the same.' He nevertheless hoped the incoming Executive would understand that they had 'received a very severe caution.' As to himself, he spoke of his memoirs, much of which would be kept until 'things quieten down,' and 'as the years pass by all my fights, faults and unpopular rulings will be forgotten, and my virtue will ascend and ascend.' For many Delegates O'Brien's virtue could only ascend, for it could get no lower.

The ITGWU decided to comply with the Trade Union Act and informed a Special ITUC Congress to that effect on 23 October 1941. Kennedy promised the full support of the ITGWU for a campaign seeking repeal, but it had 'no alternative' but to lodge £10,000 with the High Court to obtain a licence. It decided to support any Irish union 'which might require financial assistance in connection with their application,' actions at odds perhaps with its public opposition to the Act and pleas for rationalisation.

Most ITUC affiliates quickly sought licences. Limerick Pork Butchers considered taking out their own licence, but the NEC assured them that this was not necessary. With the collapse of the Federation of Irish Rail and Road Workers in 1942 the ITGWU supported a new Irish Railwaymen's Union, providing it with £250 for a Negotiating Licence.

A second Special Congress was held on 25 March as the national campaign against the Act closed. The Taoiseach refused to meet an ITUC Delegation or to alter the Act. Why would he? Most unions now held licences. The national campaign was a curate's egg, with ten demonstrations in large centres but none in Carlow, Cavan, Clonmel, Galway or Tralee, 'where local people found it impossible to arrange' anything, or in Waterford or Wexford, where 'transport difficulties led to abandonment of arrangements.' These were not all centres where the ITGWU was prominent, suggesting that ambivalence went beyond Liberty Hall.

Other than Richard Corish TD in Kilkenny and Cathal O'Shannon, no ITGWU personalities spoke at meetings. O'Shannon was now Secretary of the ITUC. With few exceptions, the speakers were from 'Amalgamated' unions.[16]

The 1942 ITGWU Delegate Conference demanded the act's 'immediate repeal' as 'a grave violation of the rights and liberties of the working class.' The NEC's 'lack of leadership' and its 'total disregard for the claims and rights of the rank-and-file to express their views' was deprecated—a rare display of criticism from the floor. The Conference claimed 'the right to direct the N.E.C. as to whether the Union should apply for a Negotiating Licence.' J. Duggan (Cork No. 1) said his Branch had requested a Special Conference. McMullen stressed ITGWU work with the ITUC campaign. The Conference could not direct the NEC 'to do an illegal act.' Without a licence, the union would be rendered impotent. At the Congress the NUR proposed a motion against the Act. No ITGWU Delegate spoke, their silence no doubt interpreted as compliance.

On 5 April 1943 the Tribunal set up under Part 3 of the Act was established to restructure the movement down to ten unions. The Congress position was that it alone had the authority to fashion structural change. Such thinking might have explained why a number of unions' applications for affiliation were held in abeyance. If the cake were to be divided, better that there were fewer knives.

McMullen seconded a motion by Seán P. Campbell (DTPS) that addressed the 'imperative need' to remove 'unnecessary and often fatal obstacles and difficulties presented by the continued operation' of competing unions. He called for the 'early unification' of many unions, for which there was 'no industrial justification.' The ITGWU had few fears of impending rationalisation. Congress asked that any unions intending to make submissions to the Tribunal first do so through it.

The ITGWU held a number of joint Conferences, with the clear intention of making submissions, the most intriguing being that between itself and the ATGWU. The ITUC Committee on Re-Organisation, upon which both McMullen and O'Brien sat, thought 'merger or unification and not simply absorption' the best course. Conferences were held for building, engineering, insurance, and printing, but with little progress.

A Northern Ireland Committee of the ITUC was established. The ITGWU's involvement was minimal. In 1944 McMullen explained the role and function of the Northern Ireland Committee and praised the ATGWU for limiting its huge numerical strength in the interests of broad democracy.

The Tribunal granted 'the sole right to organise' bricklayers and stonelayers to the Building Workers' Trade Union and binders, book-finishers, paper-rulers, guillotine operators and paper warehousemen to the Irish Bookbinders' and Allied Trades Union. The ITGWU's application in respect of the 'road passenger and tramway services of Córas Iompair Éireann' provoked a constitutional challenge by the NUR, which was initially rejected.[17]

THE CONGRESS SPLIT

In 1943 the British TUC issued an invitation to the ITUC to attend a 'purely consultative and exploratory' World Trade Union Conference to be held in London on 5 June 1944. In January 1944 a majority of the National Executive 'decided for obvious reasons' to decline.

At the Congress Sam Kyle (ATGWU) challenged this decision. O'Brien cautioned that, if accepted, it would be 'the first step in the break-up' of Congress. He did not object to supporting beleaguered unions in Europe—indeed the ITGWU made a 'substantial donation' for that purpose through the International Transport Workers' Federation. The problem was that the invitation was for 'Allied Nations' and underground movements. Ireland was neutral, yet 'belligerent in the Six Counties.' In the interests of harmony, Congress twice rejected the invitation. It was not an independent gathering but a Conference of unions in the Allied cause. Although not opposed to that, Ireland could not participate.

By 96 votes to 73, the Executive was supported. Those committed to participation ensured, after a 'heavy canvass', that a majority of the incoming Executive represented British unions, and the decision was reversed. Two Delegates from British unions were elected to attend as part of the 'so-called neutral Section.' Kennedy asked what the results were that so pleased those 'purporting to represent this neutral country.' Was it that 'Conference had agreed to the mutilation and Partition of many European nations, Poland, Latvia and others, a policy which would leave thirty million denationalised and without a home?' It was a last straw for those who felt it 'essential' that there should be an 'Irish body to speak for the Irish workers.'

On 10 January 1945 a meeting of the Council of Irish Unions expressed 'indignation' at the National Executive's action 'in misrepresenting the attitude' of Irish unions. At a Special Conference, 'with the exception of the Delegates of one Union all were in favour of having a Congress composed of Unions having their Executives in Ireland.' A Delegation met Lemass, who 'gave very satisfactory assurances as to what his attitude would be in the event of an Irish body being set up to supersede the present I.T.U.C.'

At a Conference on 21 March the ITGWU supported disaffiliation and the setting up of a 'purely Irish body', provided this was supported by the majority of members of the Council of Irish Unions. On Friday 20 April 1945 a Special Conference was held in Head Office, Parnell Square, to give members 'an opportunity of deciding a matter of the very greatest importance.' Kennedy moved the establishment of a Congress of Irish Unions.

Of the 186,000 members in unions affiliated to the ITUC, 81,000 were in Irish unions and 105,000 in British unions, 'controlled by Executives . . . not bound by the laws of this country and who had no interest in its development.' Kennedy hoped that the 29,000 members of British unions in the 26 Counties would now join Irish unions. Abuse hurled at the ITGWU and others for disaffiliating from Congress could be ignored: 'Only the slave mind could pretend to see any justification for a free people entrusting the welfare of its workers to organisations alien in origin and controlled by Executives resident in another country.' The CIU was not to be seen 'in any spirit of hostility to Britain.'

Kyle (ATGWU) protested at the ITUC Executive on 23 March, condemning the disruption. He did not believe rank-and-file members agreed, and worried at the impact on the border of further division. Members were called upon 'to stand fast' and 'repel this latest mischievous attempt at sabotage.' The next Congress should be a 'great demonstration of unity and progress, as against faction and reaction.'

Kennedy, President of the ITUC (and General President of the ITGWU), refused to accept the motion, and by eight votes to six he was removed from the chair. Ten unions withdrew between 15 April and 8 May, representing 52,974 affiliated members.

A Special Congress of the ITUC was held on 11 May to condemn the secessionists and publish a manifesto, 'Democracy or Dictatorship?: The ITUC Appeals to the Workers of Ireland.' The ITUC saw the 'dominant influence' as the ITGWU.

The ITGWU had broken from the National Union of Dock Labourers in 1908 not on grounds of nationalism but because it 'was not aggressive enough' for 'militant workers' on Dublin docks. The ITGWU's national viewpoint was cast in an inter-Nationalist, Socialist context.

> Irish workers suffered from a double subjugation: as Irishmen from the political subjugation of their country, as workers from their dependence, being men without property, upon capitalist employers for the means to live. Patriotic feeling was thus linked with the economic and social needs of the workers and the spiritual urge for human freedom.

The ITUC asked, could it be said that 'cross-channel' (British) unions were hampering their Irish members? Was this merely a further attempt by the ITGWU to achieve 'One Big Union'? The ITUC thought the attraction of OBU lay 'not in the doctrine but in the preachers.' It helpfully suggested that a reissue of *The Lines of Progress* (1918) and Connolly's pamphlet *The Axe to the Root* (1921 edition) would 'remove much misunderstanding.' In the latter pamphlet Connolly argued that 'the development of the fighting spirit is of more importance than the creation of a theoretically perfect organisation.' The 'most theoretically perfect organisation may, because of its very perfection and vastness, be of the greatest possible danger to the revolutionary movement if it tends, or is used to repress and curb the fighting spirit of comradeship in the rank-and-file.' Firmly on the moral high ground, the ITUC Executive concluded by reminding the ITGWU what it said of the ITUC&LP in 1921: 'As the central organ of the Trade Union movement it must transform itself and its constituent Unions into a perfected Industrial Union, and as the political party of the Irish working class carry on the struggle against capitalism in the governing bodies of the State.' If the ITGWU truly held such values, 'the present crisis may then indeed result in the reinvigoration of our movement and a renewal of the spirit which animated it in 1913 and during the period of its greatest power, 1918–1923.'

The ITGWU complained of the 'tirade of abuse, slander and vilification' heaped on Irish union leaders but pointed out that there was 'no suggestion that American, Canadian, Russian or other Associations' be 'allowed to establish and maintain Branches in Britain.' It was wrong to 'continue exporting money to Britain as Union subscriptions for the purpose of permitting the Executives of British Unions to dictate to and pretend to speak for Irish workers, as if this country were merely a British colony.' It was a 'humiliating position which no Irishman or woman should tolerate, especially after the recent display of Imperial arrogance by the bosses of the T.U.C. and their local admirers.'

Ten unions withdrew from the ITUC, while long-standing exclusions, the WUI and National Association of Operative Plasterers, as well as the newly formed Cork Grocers' and Allied Trades Assistants' Association, were admitted. Cathal O'Shannon resigned as Secretary of the ITUC to become Secretary of the CIU.[18] There were now two Congresses and two Labour Parties.

THE COMMISSION ON VOCATIONAL ORGANISATION

In March 1939 Senator Tom Foran was appointed to the Commission on Vocational Organisation. He resigned on 17 April 1939 and was replaced by Luke J. Duffy (Distributive Workers). Other ITUC nominees were Louie Bennett (IWWU), Seán P. Campbell (DTPS) and James Larkin (WUI). Larkin felt 'we are treading on rather dangerous ground.' Some were intent on enforcing corporatism, happily citing Portugal and Italy—not models Larkin felt trade unionists should welcome.

At the 1942 ITUC Congress Louie Bennett called for a full investigation of the 'possible reactions, economic and social,' of the Commission. O'Brien talked of the 'confusion regarding the meaning of Fascism, Vocationalism, Communism and Socialism.'

Kennedy said he 'did not give a brass farthing for what you call the system that will abolish that under which we are living today' if it 'ended poverty and unemployment.' This was both dangerous and untrue: dangerous, as it opened the door for fascism, even if Kennedy was not intending it to do so, and untrue, as the ITGWU had already, in defeating a motion condemning fascism, nailed its colours to the growing anti-Communist mast. Church influence was strong. The Commission, particularly in its early work, constantly cited the Papal encyclicals *Rerum Novarum* and *Quadragesimo Anno*. As war unfolded, the Commission's enthusiasm for corporatist values diminished.

The ITGWU was recorded as having 51,000 members in 1938 and such complete organisation of hotel and restaurant workers that, 'by agreement with the hotels, all labour is supplied through' the union, and a Joint Conciliation Board operated to regulate industrial relations. The Commission on Vocational Organisation thought 'it would be quite feasible' for the ITGWU 'to establish its Hotel Section as a distinct union and organise it throughout the country.' The Joint Conciliation Board could then operate on a national basis.' Nothing came of the report.[19]

INDUSTRIAL RELATIONS

On 13 March 1940 there were moves to establish a 'permanent Industrial Court' to examine industrial disputes and promulgate 'advisory judgements.' It was a demand consistent with ITGWU and ITUC policy. McMullen wanted the registration of Agreements and instanced boots and shoes, where Departmental Conciliation Officers would sanction a JIC Agreement only if it allowed for lower rural rates. T. D. Looney (Tipperary) cited the organising of workers by Co. Donegal employers to protest against betterments in their wages and conditions. Brain-washed low-paid workers maintained their bosses' ability to undercut Dublin and city employers. Thomas Ryan (Waterford) said that local employers' cant in Co. Mayo was that 'here is the Irish Transport Union coming in to break up the industry, as they want it for the big centres.' This was not true, but only the registration of Agreements would level the playing pitch. Lynch, Secretary of Congress, opposed any Labour Court, as it would interfere with voluntarist industrial relations. The ITGWU systematically used Trade Boards to pursue increases for the poorly paid.[20] It worked to great effect, facilitating organisation.

INTEREST-FREE LOAN TO THE GOVERNMENT

At the NEC in July 1940 there was a 'proposal to offer a loan of £50,000 (fifty thousand pounds) free of interest' to the Government 'for the term of the national emergency' (i.e. the duration of the war). In September, O'Brien reported that 'Government stocks valued for £40,000 had been transferred to the Minister,' and 'a cheque for £10,000 would be forwarded to complete the transaction.' The ITGWU received a 'Certificate of Indebtedness' in December. The loan was reported to the

1941 Conference. In 1940 the ITGWU credit balance was £182,000, Branch remittances £32,400 and total income £34,500. The loan thus represented nearly 25% of the credit balance and was considerably greater than an entire year's income. O'Brien explained, to 'those who had any experience on public boards,' how much 'the question of interest affected the machinery of Government.' After the 1914–18 conflict Britain faced interest payments of £350,000,000 per year on its war debt. In Dublin Corporation, of every £100 spent on financing the building of working-class housing, repayments of £313 accrued. The NEC 'therefore decided to set a head-line in this matter' by advancing the interest-free loan.

The Conference reacted negatively. D. Looney (Cork No. 1) objected that 'members had not been consulted' and thought it a 'violation of the Rules.' What was to stop the present capitalist Government buying 'weapons to be used against the workers'? What would happen if the ITGWU needed this money?

McMullen said the money was given to the state, not 'any particular Government.' They were trying to encourage 'wealthy capitalist organisations' to do the same and prevent the state 'having to borrow money at high rates of interest.' J. McCabe (Dublin No. 1) thought the NEC's actions had the support of 'at least 90%' of members, but J. Conway (Dublin No. 9) doubted that the capitalist class would take the example: 'one might as well expect a wolf to spare his prey as a capitalist to forgo his interest.'

Thomas Ryan (NEC, Waterford) referred to the union's 'magnificent gesture.' Cork No. 1 Branch sent letters of protest on 18 April and 5 June, but the NEC referred matters to the Delegate Conference. The Branch persisted and, in addition, wanted a Special Conference on the Trade Union Act (1941). The NEC merely said it had 'nothing to add' and ignored the requests.

With war in Europe over, Robbins returned to the loan and advocated that the Government grant 'loans free of interest' for building 'houses for persons of low income.' O'Brien, now a director of the Central Bank, stated that the 'date of the termination of the Emergency would be fixed by the Dáil,' and 'no doubt the stock would then be re-transferred' to the ITGWU's Trustees. He had 'informally discussed' repayment with the Secretary of the Department of Finance in October. The Department said that an application for repayment would be met, even though the union was 'not entitled to a refund until the end of the Emergency had been fixed by legislation.' This was arranged in December and effected in February 1946. The Minister conveyed 'his warm appreciation of the public spirit of the Union in assisting the State finances during a critical period by the making of the interest-free loan.' The 'cost of interest' on the loan was approximately £7,687 10s, although, allowing for income tax of £2,844 7s 6d, the net loss was £4,843 2s 6d.[21] It was an astounding gesture by the ITGWU, offered, in the continuing tradition of such payments, with 'no favours being sought or given.' In the context of the Trade Union Bill and the Wages Standstill Orders, suspicion about the true motives was inevitable. That said, while it was a considerable sum for the ITGWU the money was of less consequence for the Government. It made no effort to take the loan at face value and use it as a lead to encourage others to make similar gestures.

SOCIAL WELFARE

Congress lobbied the Government and National Health Insurance Commissioners for improved payments in 1940. The Minister conceded that a 'Department of Social Services might be necessary,' but progress was slow, with wartime shortages cited to explain delays. T. J. Murphy TD (Dunmanway) sought increases in old age, widow's, orphans' and blind pensions, not because of the emergency but because adjustments were long, long overdue. J. P. Pattison TD (Kilkenny) decried Government taunts in the Oireachtas, when the Labour Party raised such matters, that 'they did not represent the organised workers.' Sadly, it was true that '40,000 trade unionists in Dublin had failed to elect a Labour member.'

In 1941 McMullen pointed out that the Southern state operated a 1920 scale of payments and benefits and was hugely out of line with Northern Ireland. The ITGWU urged compensation for dockers for losses under National Health Insurance and Workmen's Compensation. Legislation should guarantee 80% of current wages to those incapacitated from work. The ITGWU took a legal test case on behalf of bread-servers in Drogheda in 1941 to prove that their vans were 'shops' within the meaning of the Shops (Conditions of Employment) Act (1938). Judgement in the Circuit Court favoured the vanmen, with a decree made against the employer in respect of overtime. On appeal to the Supreme Court it was decided that a bread van was not a shop within the meaning of the Act, but that some provisions did extend to the bread van. As the employers were the proprietors of the van, servers were employees of the 'shop', but their 'work was not done within the precincts' of that shop. Having lost this case, the ITGWU withdrew other civil Bills, as the proceedings were 'protracted and expensive'. The ITGWU had to pay the costs of both sides, close to £1,200.

Motions in 1942 sought amendment of the Unemployment Insurance Act to permit workers to draw benefit until 'their stamps are exhausted' and for sickness and disablement payments under the National Health Insurance Acts to be equal to those for unemployment, including allowances for wives, children and other dependants. The ITGWU wanted a 'liberal scheme' of Family Allowances, part of its 'grave concern' at the increased spread of tuberculosis among juveniles resulting from malnutrition.

The Insurance (Intermittent Unemployment) Act (1942) provided 'wet money' for building workers. Labourers contributed 10d weekly to the scheme and tradesmen 1s 4d, half paid by the employers. In 1943 a simplification of the Workmen's Compensation Act (1934) was sought, with more adequate compensation, fixed rates for casual workers and the elimination of delays on claims. Complaints that the Government would not alter the means test for old-age pensions were made, while the Children's Allowances Bill (1943) was greeted warmly. In 1944 the provision of a state pension for all workers at the age of sixty was sought and in 1945 a 100% increase in Children's Allowance up to sixteen. Bishop Dignan's proposals for a social insurance scheme were supported.[22]

PAID HOLIDAYS

Before the war the ITGWU initiated a campaign for a fortnight's paid holiday. Wartime pressures meant that holidays were largely neglected until 1945, when the union reactivated its campaign. A series of official strikes in Cork and Dublin ended in complete victories. On 24 October, James Pattison raised the matter in the Dáil. He told the Minister for Industry and Commerce that 'many thousands of workers' had or would soon have a fortnight's annual leave with pay, thanks to the ITGWU,' and asked when all workers, including agricultural workers, might expect the same. Lemass replied that it was not the Government's intention to amend either the Holidays (Employees) Act (1939) or the Shops (Conditions of Employment) Act (1938). More than 12,000 ITGWU members had a fortnight's paid leave by December.[23]

The ITGWU is not often credited with much involvement in the paid holidays campaign, but it is clear that, within work-places, it broke much new ground in many industries.

TUBERCULOSIS

Concerns about the TB epidemic triggered an Emergency Motion at the 1944 Conference. The Government was called upon to 'implement immediately a progressive scheme' to 'eliminate this dread disease from the life of the people.' Measures should include a system of industrial medical services and mass radiography, up-to-date sanatoriums for adults and children, the payment of wages for breadwinners during illness, the provision of after-care and the removal of restrictions on wages that depressed living standards. In 1945 George Gillis (Dublin No. 1) demanded the increase of Children's Allowance by 100%, 'convinced that by doing so, the necessity of spending large sums on the treatment of tuberculosis will be eliminated.'[24]

HEALTH AND SAFETY

In 1941 a compensation case for a seasonal worker in the Carlow sugar factory, Thomas Kelly, was appealed to the Supreme Court. Costs approached £1,000. The company, while acknowledging liability, argued over the amount of compensation, the practice being to total a year's earnings and divide by fifty-two, a system evidently handicapping the unemployed. The Supreme Court determined that 'potential earnings' had to be considered; and Kelly, who earned £2 16s in a 'campaign', was awarded 30s a week, a figure arrived at not by taking his earnings but the 'average wages paid to men in the same grade in the same employment.' John A. Costello SC acted for the ITGWU and produced a summarising memorandum of the issues.

At the 1943 Conference D. J. Galavan (Dublin No. 6) and William Kinneally (Cork No. 1) demanded a 'better system of factory inspection so that prevention against ill-health and accidents' could be made. The use of the word 'prevention' was ahead of its time. They quickly returned to 'prescription' by demanding 'drastic penalties' on employers. The reliance on statutory standards enforced by an external army of Inspectors was considered the only method for dealing with work-place health and safety. In 1945 Jim Hickey (Cork No. 1) demanded 'a more rigid inspection of factories' and attention to heating and the provision of canteens, equipment and proper cloakroom accommodation.[25]

EDUCATION AND TRAINING

In 1940 Frank Robbins (Dublin District Council) thought the Labour Party and ITUC Summer Schools were 'not getting as useful results' as when the ITGWU sent students to events organised by the National Council of Labour Colleges in Britain. It opened up debate about what was 'worker education.' Robbins called for facilities to realise Rule 3 (c): to 'provide facilities for the education of its members in social, industrial and political affairs.'

In 1941 a call for the 'establishment of a National Labour College' was ruled out of order. The ITGWU did set up a 'Study Circle for the purpose of propagating Trade Union and working-class principles.' Classes were a 'decided success', even if the numbers disappointed. Transport and other logistical problems confined the circle to Dublin. D. Cronin (Cork No. 1) and Thomas O'Reilly (Dublin No. 3) wanted university scholarships for members, and T. D. Looney praised the extension scheme of University College, Cork. Jim Hickey, noting that the present General Officers would soon retire, thought it 'essential to have men trained and ready to take their places.' They 'required Officials who had a high standard of education and some training in research work.' He noted that the Miners' Union in Britain trained its Officials through university extension; the ITGWU should do the same. Robbins protested at demands for a union journal being ruled out of order; he was reassured that they 'would have a journal when the N.E.C. felt it could be established and carried on with success.'[26]

STAFF

In 1940 the ITGWU inaugurated an Officials' and Employees' Superannuation Fund. A year later McMullen warned that the union 'might have too many Officials.' The Superannuation Fund opened in 1941, with more than £850 spent on providing staff pensions. The ITGWU was the only Irish union to have such a scheme, and it said much about the union's self-confidence that it began during the war.

Some stalwart figures passed on. Seán Rogan, Citizen Army veteran, long-serving Head Office Official and director of many Liberty Hall musical and dramatic shows, retired on 16 February 1942; Dominick Sullivan, NEC member and Liberty Hall Official, died in March 1942; Jeremiah Murphy, long-standing Secretary of the Tralee Branch, died on 9 September 1944; and Thomas Nagle, Organiser and Head Office man, died suddenly on 5 November 1944. Michael Mullen was appointed Branch Assistant in Dublin No. 1 Branch on 12 February 1945.[27]

LIBERTY HALL

In 1940 Jack McCabe and Seán Byrne moved the familiar motion on rebuilding Liberty Hall. O'Brien bluntly stated, after the adoption of the motion, that the NEC 'did not propose taking any action'—not surprising, perhaps, given wartime uncertainties. Calls for a special Liberty Hall fund were ruled out of order in 1944, but Tom McCarthy asked that Dublin District Council be given the opportunity to make proposals directly to the NEC.

In February 1941 Wicklow Urban District Council raised £2,482 to protect the promenade, charging local property-owners 5s in £2 on valuations, a further burden on the loss-making Marine. In August 1942 the Air Raid Precautions Section of the Department of Defence expressed its intention of taking over the Marine, paying £150 a year and 'all outgoings and taking over responsibility of caretaker.' It was a gift horse for the ITGWU, which sold underused premises in Birr, Wexford and wherever else it could. The Department terminated its tenancy of the Marine from 27 September 1945 and in August 1946 it was sold to Wicklow County Council for use as a fever hospital for £2,000.[28]

FASCISM

At the 1942 Congress Betty Sinclair (Belfast Trades Council) urged all to do their utmost to defeat fascism. John Swift (Bakers) suggested that there was 'no neutrality' as far as the Southern Government's 'fascist tendencies' were concerned. O'Brien taunted Swift for converting from opposition to an imperialist war to support for the same war now that it was against fascism. If Swift were in Russia, he alleged, he would not have such freedom to speak. Fascism in Italy had grown out of an 'irresponsible, ill-controlled, foolish and wild trade union movement' that was 'not able to control and discipline itself.' They should concentrate on Ireland before 'we start talking about the freedom of China and Timbuctoo.' Some recalled the leopard O'Brien championing the 1917 Revolution before he changed his spots.

Dan McAllister (Belfast) talked of 400 political prisoners in Northern Ireland who would be starving but for the Green Cross. J. Conway (Dublin) insisted it was an imperialist war, about markets and resources.

The motion was defeated, 47 to 43. ITGWU Delegates, silent during the debate on the Trade Union Act (1941), queued up to defeat this motion, expressing for the first time a clearly anti-Communist position.

In 1943 Kyle (ATGWU) made a humanitarian appeal on behalf of refugees. Hickey (Cork) opposed, feeling it should be left to the Government. Kyle's mention of refugees 'who have succeeded in getting away from the tyranny of invaders of their countries' provoked Conway (Dublin) to ask if they would 'receive refugees from the Six Counties who succeeded in getting away from the tyranny of Imperialist Britain?' It was carried.

Billy McCullough (Belfast Trades Council) tried again to express 'admiration' for those fighting fascism and proposed a pledge to 'eternal vigilance against this danger at home and abroad.' Seán Byrne (Dublin) opposed, as 'the supposed

democratic states' had fed the 'little pup—fascism' until 'it proved too big for them.'
He wanted a 'plague on all their houses.' Were workers being slaughtered so that
living standards could be increased? British bankers and bosses sent men to the
battlefields to defend their markets. The motion was carried.[29]

THE LABOUR PARTY

Labour Party Deputies were significant participants at ITGWU wartime Conferences.
Some were simultaneously Branch Secretaries. In 1941 the Party Organiser, Séamas
O'Farrell, addressed Delegates. In 1942 Kennedy welcomed new TDS: John O'Leary
(Wexford), Dan Spring (Kerry North), Paddy Hogan (Clare) and T. D. Looney
(Cork South-East).

The admission of James Larkin and James Larkin Junior to the Labour Party
angered O'Brien. All union Oireachtas members were summoned to a meeting on
16 April 1942 to ascertain their views. James Hickey felt that it was 'not desirable to
take any further action.' T. J. Murphy said he 'hadn't fully understood' but was 'now
satisfied that Larkin ought not to have been admitted.' Corish, Everett and Pattison
said they would carry out NEC instructions, though whether simply to appease
O'Brien or as an indication of the compliant nature of the ITGWU-sponsored
Deputies is not clear. The upshot was that ITGWU Deputies sought Larkin's removal.
The advice of Senior Counsel was sought about the powers of the Party's
Administrative Council.

A grant of £500 was agreed for the Labour Party in March 1943 but 'not acted
upon given our present relations.' Hickey refused to vote with Kennedy and other
ITGWU members of the Administrative Council on Larkin's expulsion. The NEC
'took a serious view of his conduct.' In Co. Clare, Senator Paddy Hogan 'undertook
to accept and act on the decisions of the Union on matters which the Union considers it necessary to decide and indicate a definite policy attitude.' And yet in the
election it was felt 'regrettable that there was not greater co-operation between the
two Union candidates,' Hogan and J. P. Hughes, Secretary of Kilrush Branch.
Among those refused financial support was R. M. 'Bobby' Burke, East Galway.

Reference was made to relations between the Labour Party and the ITGWU 'as
a result of certain developments which had taken place in Dublin City.' The
conference gave 'its unanimous approval' of the NEC's opposition to the two Larkins
as party members. 'Admission into its ranks of undesirable and disruptive elements'
and the ITGWU's efforts within the Administrative Council 'to induce the
majority ... to protect the Party from the activities of these sinister influences' were
the problem. 'Unless action was taken to purge' the Party the ITGWU felt 'compelled
to disaffiliate.' Efforts to have the Labour Party 'conducted on proper lines were
unsuccessful.' The NEC had 'no option but to sever our connection.' Disaffiliation
lasted until 1967.

Within the Administrative Council, Kennedy moved the Larkins' expulsion. It
was defeated, 9 votes to 8, the 'minority being composed entirely of our members.'
J. Conway and O'Brien moved for the ITGWU's disaffiliation and the setting up of

'a Political Department to cater for the needs of our members in the political field.' ITGWU Oireachtas members 'received the news without any enthusiasm' and asked the NEC to defer notice to the Party until the second Sunday in January in order to meet their supporters.

The Labour Party's election manifesto in 1943 argued for the removal of restrictions on trade union freedoms and an all-in social insurance scheme. Senator Kennedy made no reference to the affair in his Presidential Address in Bray in 1944. The Conference approved the NEC's decision and pledged its commitment to the newly created National Labour Party. M. Maloney (Waterford) and J. J. Sullivan (Dunmanway) suggested that the NLP was 'an unwarrantable step.' It would have 'nothing but calamitous consequences,' and 'every avenue' should be explored to create a 'united Labour Party.' They failed to defeat the NEC.

Michael Connor (Drogheda Branch Secretary) chaired a meeting in Co. Louth at which Councillor Larkin spoke, boasting of the high bonuses won by the WUI and 'poor work of the "Big Unions".' Connor was censured by the NEC.

On a motion of J. J. O'Leary and J. J. Cleary the National Labour Party was established in January 1944. The ITGWU was 'authorised to expend such funds as may be necessary.' By March, £150 had been given, and existing ITGWU Oireachtas members and P. Clarke, James Hickey, P. J. O'Brien and Frank Robbins acted as the Organising Committee. Support for the Labour Party's paper, the *Torch*, was dropped, and Frank Purcell 'was loaned' to act as Secretary of the NLP. Two thousand copies of Connolly's *Labour in Ireland* were ordered and each NLP candidate given £400 in June. The Lord Mayor of Cork and Secretary of Cork No. 1 Branch, James Hickey, declined an NLP nomination. Four of the five NLP candidates were successful: James Everett (Wicklow), J. P. Pattison (Kilkenny), Dan Spring (Kerry) and John O'Leary (Wexford). A further difficulty with Hickey was a wrangle over whether or not he received an income as a director of the *Catholic Standard*. If he did, would he pay any money over to the union? A veteran Waterford member, Thomas Ryan, was reprimanded for addressing a Labour Party meeting. Ryan resigned from the Labour Party, and Hickey paid over his fees.

In 1944 it was explained to Delegates that whenever an ITGWU officer was elected to Dáil Éireann or Seanad Éireann, their wages were given to a special fund. O'Brien partly covered his antagonism to Larkin by suggesting that the real enemy was Communism, publishing a pamphlet to justify this line.

The effect of the Labour Party split retarded political Labour at a point when a real advance seemed possible. Just as Larkin had split the union when it most needed unity, so O'Brien now surveyed a fractured Congress and Labour Party. He had 'defeated' Larkin at the cost of severely damaging the movement. If he had truly had a Socialist heart, could he have argued that it was worth it?[30]

Chapter 18 ⌒

LARKIN'S INDIAN SUMMER: THE WUI, 1939–45

MEMBERSHIP, ORGANISATION AND FINANCE

The wui's membership fell during the war. Larkin delegated more to his son, James Junior; whether this was by accident or design is unclear, as his attention was caught by campaigns against Wages Standstill Orders and trade union legislation and by serving as a Dublin City Councillor. There was an impression, however, that deference to his father stayed Young Jim's hand; essential reform of the wui had to await the unthinkable. In contrast, the wui's income showed an almost continuously upward trend, and a surplus was declared each year. Indeed, given a total wartime income of £81,129, a surplus of £39,329 was an impressive 48%. A prohibition of strikes facilitated the building of funds. Staff salaries remained static, at about £5,000, having dropped in 1940–42, suggesting general stability. In 1940 the Secretary of the Bray Branch, Seán Dunne, was interned. On his release he was transferred to Head Office.

Table 50: wui membership, 1939–45

	ITUC	Membership	Women	Branches
1939	—	16,408	2,104	13
1940	—	15,681	2,257	15
1941	—	12,542	1,870	12
1942	—	10,780	1,988	15
1943	—	9,451	1,774	14
1944	8,000	8,803	1,502	14
1945	8,000	9,129	1,464	15

Sources: National Archives, Registrar of Friendly Societies, file 369T; ITUC, Annual Reports, 1944–45.

Table 51: WUI income, expenditure, Dispute Pay and surplus (£), 1930–40

	Income	Expenditure	Dispute Pay	Surplus (deficit)
1939	10,996	10,894	1,850	5,578
1940	10,542	10,558	1,471	6,064
1941	9,145	9,255	112	5,413
1942	10,794	9,606	12	6,027
1943	11,127	10,686	0	6,468
1944	13,496	13,340	384	6,615
1945	15,029	18,480	7,196	3,164

Source: National Archives, Registrar of Friendly Societies, file 369T.

In 1942 the WUI moved from Marlborough Street to a new Head Office at 5A College Street, naming it Thomas Ashe Hall. (This is where Larkin was held after his arrest on Bloody Sunday, 31 August 1913, when it was a DMP barracks.) From 1943 the WUI began to organise farm labourers in Cos. Dublin, Meath, Kildare and Wicklow, hoping to break free of the capital and become a national body. With the ITGWU's secession from the ITUC in 1945, further barriers came down and the WUI was admitted to Congress. In contrast with the ITGWU's membership and income figures for 1945 of 37,970 and £41,072, the WUI had fallen far behind.[1]

WAGES AND DISPUTES

The Emergency Powers (No. 83) Order (1941)—commonly known as the Wages Standstill Order—came into force on 7 May. The Government's intention was to restrain wage increases so as to protect consumers from employers passing them on to consumers: 'And so the mad race goes on, higher wages followed by higher costs, higher prices and again higher wages—all in rapid movement.' Protections under the Conspiracy and Protection of Property Act (1875) and the Trade Disputes Act (1906) no longer applied to strikes taken in defiance of the order. They were not regarded as 'trade disputes' and so forfeited all legal immunity. The Labour Party unsuccessfully proposed a Seanad motion to annul the order, and a Special ITUC Congress, held on 16 May, protested 'in the strongest possible manner.' Meetings with the Government were fruitless. Congress thought 'the Order is perhaps unprecedented in the history of Trade Unionism, and the resolutions of protest' showed the 'profound depths' to which the movement 'had been disturbed.' The order was 'harsh and inequitable in character,' and hostility to it had to be 'sustained.'

Larkin's leadership of the opposition was his Indian summer as agitator. Christy Ferguson, reflecting in 1952, saw it as a 'losing battle' because of the attitude of the rest of the movement, especially the ITGWU. The 'largest and most powerful trade union stood aside' and made 'its attitude more obvious' by investing '£50,000 in Government securities—interest free.' Congress was 'hesitant and failed to lead.'

Larkin aroused Dublin Trades Council and Councils of Action; a stirring campaign developed and the Government was forced to amend its Wages Standstill Order and permit the bonuses obtained by workers during the Emergency.'

Attacking the order in Congress, Larkin (DTUC Delegate) alleged that 'they had been on the retreat for twenty years.' Certain union Officials had been seen to be 'working night and day against their own class' during elections. They had got a bit ashamed of using the word "class".' They had 'allowed themselves' to become 'respectable people,' and 'because they had fairly decent salaries as Officials that they had lost touch with the common rank-and-file . . . I thank the Government for introducing these measures,' as they had brought together 'elements that have been diverse and antagonistic into a common fold.' He was never as uplifted as at recent Dublin demonstrations. With more effort they could sweep out the Government. Optimistically he concluded: 'I feel that we have got the birth of a new movement.'

The DTUC set up a Council of Action and published a militant journal, *Workers' Action*. Under Young Jim Larkin's direction the campaign broadened to include unemployment, housing, food and fuel prices and supplies. In addition the Labour Party's paper, the *Torch*, devoted space to the campaign. Big Jim Larkin was back on street corners bellowing out the message. A leaflet was issued to show what had happened to prices and wages. The campaign may not have won its objectives but it reinvigorated the Labour Party, which took an unprecedented thirteen seats in 1942 Corporation elections. This success was echoed in 1943 Dáil elections, when seventeen TDs were returned.

If it was to prove to be 'Old Jim's' swan song it was 'Young Jim's' debut, bringing a 'dynamic approach to trade union politics' and extending campaigns directly into working-class communities. He sought to 'unify workers around such concrete issues as food shortages and prices,' with much success. Further, he brought the Labour Party to workers' minds as the political vehicle through which they could effect change.[2]

Emergency Powers Order No. 166 became effective from 8 April 1942, enabling workers to claim increases of up to 2s for ten-point rises above the cost-of-living index figure of 225. Congress presented a memorandum on the Standstill Order to the Minister on 15 January 1942, but to little avail.

The WUI continued its opposition through DTUC. Larkin spoke on an ITGWU motion condemning the order, asking, 'Could they think out some plan' that would influence the Government? He was 'an Ishmael: possibly making my swan-song today.' He suggested picking one industry and having a serious go at destroying the order. If his union, still unaffiliated, were chosen to lead, 'I would not hesitate for a moment to tell them that it was their duty to take the field.' He claimed the WUI set the highest rate for dockers in the 'English-speaking world' in Dublin, 1s 6d an hour, proving its capacity to lead.

By 1943 and the introduction of Order No. 260, the ITUC's opposition had withered, most 'licensed' unions and Congress itself participating in Tribunals that adjudicated in more than 800 cases.

In DTUC, matters were not so smooth. At a demonstration on 11 October 1942 Congress 'learned with great regret' that some of the DTUC contingent 'had broken away from the main body of the parade.' The Trades Council avoided direct reply to enquiries by Congress about the parade and the false suggestion by DTUC that Congress had appointed representatives to Tribunals to represent non-affiliated unions, including the WUI. A threat of exclusion produced a request for a deputation. A meeting took place in March, but Congress viewed DTUC as making no attempts to be anything other than evasive. On 26 May 1943 Congress wrote to the council, referring to its behaviour as 'reprehensible in the highest degree' and stating that a repetition would result in disaffiliation.

Leo Crawford thought Congress was 'trying to score a point over one of its affiliated units' and moved that the Section be referred back. WUI members who did not attend the demonstration were subject to a fine and, to determine who was present and who not, its contingent left the main body at College Green. He felt that some did not want to see DTUC affiliated to Congress.

> We want to get away from the quarrels that have obtained between individuals and personalities. We want unity: it will have to be achieved some time. Personalities did enter into the movement: you are asked which side you are on, and if you are not on one side or the other, you are in the wilderness.

Seán Byrne (ITGWU) found the explanation 'unsatisfactory', seeing the WUI's action as 'a deliberate attempt to sabotage' it. Matters continued, with charge and counter-charge. One speaker suggested that 'we commit many crimes in the name of unity.' This accurately summed up a certain disingenuousness on all sides. The call to refer back was defeated, 122 to 37.

At the 1945 ITUC Congress James Larkin Junior, speaking on price and wage control, complained that the cost of living had risen by 70% but wages by only 15%. War had ended in Europe, and it was reasonable to expect that gap to close, although 'if we think that gap is going to be closed by anybody except the Trade Union Movement we are making a very grievous mistake.' De Valera's appeal to maintain emergency powers took no account of the masses having to live on what purchased less than half what their pre-war wages would. For Larkin Junior the 'problem is not one of prices and wages' but 'the standard of life for our people.' The Prices Commission was a failure. The cost-of-living index did not accurately reflect workers' consumption.

In his first Congress presentation, Young Larkin set out what became a familiar vision. For him, trade unionism was 'not a movement merely engaged in the adjustment of industrial relations': it had a 'bigger and wider outlook. 'It is not a question of adjusting disputes but of having a greater share in the control and management of industry, having a hand in the control and ownership of industry.' He argued for the retention of the war bonus to boost consumption and revive an ailing economy. Wage restrictions should be loosened, especially for those on lowest rates.

He argued that organisation badly needed to be increased—there were 30,000 to 40,000 in the Dublin area alone who could be recruited. This appeal was to be regularly repeated: extensive organisation on a class basis.[3]

PAID HOLIDAYS

In 1945 Jim Larkin Senior was central to the successful strike for a fortnight's holiday with pay. Demands were made before the war but lost sight of during the conflict. In Congress, Larkin called for united, direct action, making a remarkable attack on women's shopping habits and the capacity to pass pickets as obstacles to success. The laundry workers' and butchers' strikes brought the issue to a head. Dublin Trades Council established a fund to assist the strikers. General agreement was secured at a joint Conference of the ITUC and Federated Union of Employers at the Department of Industry and Commerce on 22–23 October. Work resumed in laundries on 27 October, with the principle of a fortnight's paid holiday secured. In 1946 Larkin said that about 80% of Dublin workers had achieved the right through negotiation. More than a million workers throughout the country were giving 'the unemployed man and woman a chance, at least, to get a loaf of bread for a week or two.' His interest was primarily one of employment creation rather than workers' welfare. He concluded, however: 'Growing boys and girls, absolutely neglected by everybody, were entitled to holiday conditions just as everybody else.' In July 1946 Larkin Junior reported the ITUC's 'praise for the leading role it took on its industrial struggle to enforce the claim for extended holidays.'[4]

BUTCHERS' STRIKE

A long strike for a fortnight's paid holiday took place in the pork and beef trade in 1945. The trade's women workers already had the holiday, but they 'fought alongside the men, marched in the picket lines and resisted every attempt to divide them from the men and break their spirit.' Their victory 'placed all union members in their debt,' as it was a 'milestone' in workers' 'struggles for better conditions in this country as a whole.'

The butchers' strike had a tremendous effect, with half the shops shut and men locked out. A co-operative was formed and two workers' shops opened, a tactic the Master Butchers had not bargained for. Seán Dunne gave assistance, in direct and indirect ways, his six-foot stature proving very useful in the former capacity. He received one month in jail after an altercation with scabs. He was defended by Seán MacBride on appeal to Wicklow Circuit Court, and a deal was done involving suspension of the sentence in exchange for an apology, one that Dunne would not provide. In Congress, R. Stapleton (ATGWU) proposed a motion supporting the butchers' strike, as it had 'decisive significance' for all those 'seeking increased annual holidays.'

Only in 1947 could Larkin Junior announce that they had 'overcome the financial strain of the strike of 1945.' Breda Kearns's memory was that the butchers' Strike Pay 'emptied the reserves of the union and we had to start up again from scratch financially.' Larkin had refused to call off a hopeless strike but 'turned a blind eye' to Young Jim's intervention for a settlement.[5]

CONGRESS

Affiliation to the ITUC was refused to the WUI in 1940. Attempts to refer the Section of the Annual Report back, as it 'would be in the best interests of the movement as a whole,' failed to find a seconder. The tide, although turning, still did not flow fast enough for the WUI.

In 1941 the application was 'under consideration.' Gilbert Lynch (DTUC) suggested that, in view of the attacks on unions, the time had surely come 'to have a definite strengthening and cohesion,' and 'at no time should they have unions outside the movement.' He called upon Congress 'to direct' the National Executive. William O'Brien, General Secretary of the ITGWU and President of the ITUC, refused to accept the proposal, on the grounds that the matter was entirely one for the National Executive. A. Jackson (DTUC) asked O'Brien, 'Are you becoming the new dictator?' A. J. Ryan (ATGWU) thought they looked ridiculous when the constitution of Congress 'can be dominated by one man. I say it is all wrong.'

Pressure mounted on O'Brien. T. Waldron (National Union of Tailors and Garment Workers) suggested that his rulings were less than objective interpretation of the constitution and standing orders. 'Any motion that comes before Congress that is not acceptable to you and your colleagues will be ruled out of order.' Betty Sinclair (Belfast Trades Council) wanted to know why matters remained 'under consideration.' Why could the National Executive not reach a decision? What were the grounds for non-affiliation, as some applicants had big memberships and were happily affiliated with local Trades Councils?

Larkin, who was remarkably constrained, rose as the last speaker but merely added further confusion without getting to the substance. The first day of the Congress concluded with no business done.

O'Brien opened the second day's proceedings by quoting verbatim from earlier reports to substantiate his position that his rulings were bound by precedent. Larkin was quicker to his feet and declared that 'we have got the overwhelming opinion of the Delegates on our side.' However, he did not pursue matters further, 'because of the graver matters that confront workers at the present time.' Next business was quickly moved. The WUI, and other rejected applicants, no doubt felt that the gates would soon open to them. They were mistaken.

In 1942 the WUI's application was again rejected, 'because of its record as a cause of disruptive action' and 'promoter of libels against Officers of affiliated Unions and of Congress.' This reversed the apparent preparedness to accept it subject to certain geographical conditions. Admission now would apparently be 'a disintegrating instead of a harmonising element.' While the National League of the Blind and the Amalgamated Union of Upholsterers were admitted, the WUI was lost among six rejected bodies. E. J. Tucker asked that the section be referred back. All rejected unions were affiliates of DTUC, and the need for unity should be paramount.

Non-affiliation hampered the movement, and also prevented affiliation to the Labour Party. Some unions were in existence more than twenty years, and consideration should be given to their members. How did rejection square with calls for unity? As to the WUI, 'it might have trodden on the corns of certain persons [but] in the past two years its members and officers had shown an admirable restraint.' Larkin's role in the campaign against the Trade Union Act was praised. Between the 'two big Transport Unions . . . personal abuse and public abuse' had been 'overcome and forgotten'; why could the same not apply to the WUI?

Sam Kyle (ATGWU) changed tack and supported the National Executive. Unhelpfully, he suggested that 'further amalgamations' might be the preferred way forward.

Larkin was goaded to his feet. He recalled that the ITGWU was admitted to Congress in 1910 'over the ruling' of the National Executive. If unification was so advantageous, 'why did not the two large Transport Unions which embrace multifarious activities . . . agree to unification?' He spoke in favour of the applications of the Irish Engineering and Foundry Union, the Irish National Union of Vintners', Grocers' and Allied Trades Assistants and the Irish Automobile Drivers' and Mechanics' Union. The IADMU had broken away from the ITGWU and WUI, 'exercising the right that a man or woman has the right to choose the union with whom they may associate.' As to the 'lying, mischievous statement' in the ITUC report about the WUI, this was exactly what James Sexton said about the ITGWU in 1909. He admitted that he libelled one man on the platform, but never Congress itself.

He was reminded of the Thomas Johnson and Denis Cullen libel cases by T. J. Murphy TD (ITGWU). O'Brien jogged Larkin's absent memory that he had suggested that Cullen left Artane School as a blackleg during a strike. Cullen joined in, dragging Larkin from the safety he had originally found in the herd of other rejected applicants and into the mire that he should have strictly avoided. Larkin accused the ITGWU and ATGWU of having 'closed ranks,' providing further ammunition to his opponents. He concluded by claiming the WUI had 'the highest rate of wages in many of our Sections.' They would maintain and improve them, with or without Congress. He wanted the 'good sense of this body' to decide. He concluded with the 'prophesy' that 'before many years when some of you have passed out because of old age, I will be in' the movement.

Larkin angered the hall. Cullen asked him to withdraw his repeated libel. John Swift (Bakers) attempted to pour oil on pitching waters. The 'rank-and-file were sick and sore of this conflict.' He wanted the WUI and others in the fold. Unity was the only basis for much-needed political advance.

After virtually a full day's wrangling, referral back was defeated, and the Section stood. The WUI and others remained outside.

It got worse. P. J. Cairns moved a constitutional amendment that all Delegates had to be from unions affiliated to Congress. If it was adopted, Larkin would be prevented from attending as a DTUC Delegate. Sam Kyle (ATGWU) continued his conversion to O'Brien's reason by supporting this. Betty Sinclair opposed, repeating that unity should be the cornerstone. Waldron was to have voted against a 'means of purging Larkin' but abstained, to 'let the big battalions have their way.' The 'amendment was not to put out these disruptionists but to put out the town tenants and the unemployed.' Larkin insisted that unemployed organisations had every right to be at the Congress. They were 'always blatherskiting and talking about their love for the unemployed' but wanted to deny them representation. As to the platform, 'death is the only hope for some of those gentlemen,' and 'the execution of myself or my Union, through any choice of certain Delegates to this Congress, is not going to destroy the Union I belong to.' He became rambling and called O'Brien 'an unmitigated liar,' increasingly playing into the hands that he felt were being applied to his neck. The motion was carried on a show of hands, 107 to 60.

With the secession of ten unions from the ITUC in March 1945, the WUI finally came in from the cold. The first Congress attended by WUI Delegates was a Special Congress on 11 May. Larkin was accompanied by Alderman Barney Conway. He spoke, unusually perhaps, 'with some hesitation' in paying tribute to Congress for its 'appreciation of international leadership and solidarity.' He seconded the suggestion that the 1945 Congress be held in Dublin. At that Congress, on a motion suggesting that in future the National Executive would refer its decisions on affiliation to the full Congress, Larkin referred to 'abuses of power . . . over the past ten or twelve years.' The movement, however, had 'returned to the path of progress and unity.' In future, the 'High Court of this particular body should be Congress.'

In his first recorded contribution, James Larkin Junior TD spoke on price and wage control, referring to the possibilities offered by the 1941–2 campaigns. With 'determination in leadership' they might have brought radical change. His view of secession was plain: 'It is remarkable that one of the groups that was mainly responsible for hamstringing and destroying' possibilities in 1942 had 'now got the audacity, in its circular, to claim that its record entitles it to the support of Irish workers.' The ITUC had 'at last . . . got rid of the old men of the sea.'

It was a statement of political frustration, a kicking over of the nearest convenient obstacles. There may have been some truth in it, but the ITGWU had been successful in improving members' wages under the imposed wages system. The question on Young Larkin's and many others' lips was, however, To what extent had the ITGWU been complicit in the construction of that system? Had the price paid been worth their reward?[6]

THE TRADE UNION ACT (1941)

On 6 May 1941 Dublin Trades Council condemned the Trade Union Bill, a behind-the-door triumph for O'Brien's plans to rationalise the movement and, simultaneously, eliminate many of his opponents.

The ITUC's criticism of the Bill was muted. The Standstill Order triggered an avalanche of rank-and-file protests. Their living standards were being sharply eroded by inflation. O'Brien isolated Larkin from involvement by ensuring that Trades Councils were excluded from protests led by the Labour Party and the ITUC.

At a Special Meeting of DTUC on 20 May, however, Larkin proposed a Council of Action. Young Jim was appointed Secretary. About 20,000 marched to College Green on 22 June, and, although he was not listed as a speaker, the crowd demanded Larkin. He rose amid thunderous cheers, denounced the 'rotten fascist Government,' and, in the best traditions of Larkinite theatre, produced a copy of the infamous Bill from his pocket and set it alight. Owen Sheehy Skeffington afterwards wondered if this act of showmanship was not a risky ploy. Larkin replied, 'No fear of that, with ten matches tied together, sandpaper on the seat of the trousers, and the paper well soaked in paraffin.' For a man not listed to speak, these seemed elaborate preparations. He gave the crowd what they craved. He told the 1941 ITUC Congress, 'I never felt so uplifted as I was that day in Dublin.'

Congress was vexed by Larkin's triumph, more so when he stated what others suspected, that Seán MacEntee confirmed to him that the Trade Union Act had been initiated by 'certain' union leaders, who 'had fairly decent salaries' and 'had lost touch with the common rank-and-file.' Congress's revenge came the following year, rejecting the WUI's affiliation because of 'its record as a cause of disruptive action.' When the previously supportive Sam Kyle (ATGWU) took the National Executive line, the game was up. Worse, the ATGWU supported ITGWU proposals that Trades Council Delegates must be members of affiliated unions, thus making Larkin ineligible. He reclaimed the streets at the price of being cast from important chambers. His consolation prize was the continued support of DTUC, which elected him President in 1943.

A Special Congress on 16 May registered its 'emphatic opposition' to the Trade Union Bill. The Labour Party spoke vigorously against the Bill, to no avail. P. T. Daly, Secretary of the DUTC, wanted to move an Emergency Motion at the 1941 Congress expressing opposition and urging unions not to register under its terms. The Bill 'takes away every function a trade union has' and 'leaves us at the mercy of bureaucracy.' He accused the National Executive of giving no support. 'Every time' they had sought the President, either as Chairman or as William O'Brien—'and sometimes a good deal of William peeps out through the Chairman'—he 'never graced us with his presence.' The report on the Bill was 'absolutely bald, colourless and not of the slightest assistance' in the fight to oppose it, and 'no effective protest had been made.' They had not sought registration, because it would kill the Bill.

Robert Tynan (IMETU) suggested that were it not for DTUC the Bill would have passed without comment. They had kept Congress fully informed but had been let down when the campaign should have broadened into a national one.

Larkin praised Michael Keyes TD (NUR) and other Labour Party Deputies who resisted the Bill in the Dáil. De Valera acknowledged that they were entitled to know which unions were complicit but did not name them. Everyone in the hall thought of O'Brien and the ITGWU.

By the end of the second, rancorous day of the Congress Daly's motion was neither moved nor debated. Sam Kyle talked of ILO rights of Freedom of Association; but, no doubt from fatigue with the circular discussions and the belief that Congress would not provide leadership, the Section was referred back. ITGWU speakers, pro or con, were conspicuous by their absence. Gilbert Lynch (ATGWU) finally moved dismissal of the Bill as 'highly detrimental' and 'inimical' to workers' interests and demanding that it be 'immediately withdrawn.' The upshot of the persistent attacks on standing orders and the questioning of O'Brien's rulings was the resignation of the Standing Orders Committee.

A Special Congress on 23 October decided on a national campaign of opposition, with Labour Party support. The WUI, although excluded from Congress, expressed its opposition through DTUC. A second Special Congress was held on 25 March 1942 as the national campaign closed. The Taoiseach refused to meet an ITUC Delegation or to alter the Act. Congress's repeated opposition was weakened by the fact that some unions had taken out licences. The Trade Union Act (1942) introduced minor amendments, and by 1943 the 'majority' of Congress affiliates were in compliance. A Tribunal to implement part 3 of the Act was inaugurated on 5 April 1943, the intention being to radically restructure the movement.[7]

DUBLIN TRADES COUNCIL

The DTUC remained a loyal Larkin supporter. His maverick actions gave it status and limelight in opposition to Congress's gathering power. The 1942 row about May Day protocol was typical of tensions between them. The DTUC regarded the snubbing of Larkin as demeaning its independent status. He was selected democratically as its Delegate.

John Swift (Bakers) recalled sitting around the DTUC Executive table, where 'Larkin's usual sign to start the proceedings was the raising of his hooked stemmed pipe in the style of a conductor's baton.' The Secretary, Daly, 'passed his carefully prepared agenda' to him, but 'more often than not' Larkin 'swept it aside and began talking about himself.' Swift discovered that the best way to make progress was to 'keep always to the line of least persistence!'

P. T. Daly died on the steps of the DTUC premises in Lower Gardiner Street on 20 November 1943. Larkin paid tribute to him at a memorial meeting on 30 November.

Daly's career was chequered. Exposed by unsuccessful libel actions against the ITGWU, he could not deny his mismanagement of IRB funds, which cast doubts in the minds of O'Brien and Connolly. He was Acting General Secretary of the ITGWU in 1911 and was first chosen by Larkin to succeed him in 1914. After strong lobbying by Connolly and O'Brien, Daly was given the poor consolation prize of the ITGWU National Health Insurance Approved Society. Ejected from this position in 1919, he became central to opposition to Liberty Hall, contributing to the split in 1923–4. He was not rewarded by Larkin with any WUI position. He regained his position as Secretary of DTUC in 1920 after the ITGWU's withdrawal. Somewhat surprisingly, he survived opposition to become Secretary of the unified council from 1929. There is no evidence that he was a WUI member other than in its early days and was apparently an ATGWU member at his death. His long Trades Council service led to his gradual redemption. He 'provided an elaborate and effective service' that 'under-pinned the multifarious activities' and was 'always there when work needed doing.' The history of DTUC recognised that he was 'not a great or imaginative Leader . . . not a theoretician and produced no writings of any significance' but was 'the type of solid, committed and effective Official without whom the working class move-ment could not have developed.' Seventy-three when he died, he was an old man still giving all to the movement.[8]

COMMISSION ON VOCATIONAL ORGANISATION

Larkin was appointed a member of the Commission on Vocational Organisation. He once expressed an interest in guild Socialism and some elements of vocational-ism—elected councils within industries were akin to syndicalist ideas—and pro-moted vocationalism in his 1938 election campaign. Now he felt 'we are treading on rather dangerous ground.' He dismissed the Commission's academic members as 'dangerous' and intent on enforcing corporatism.

As war unfolded, the Commission's enthusiasm for corporatism diminished. Larkin 'put in only twenty attendances' and 'did not sign the report' but neither resigned nor provided a minority report. John Swift later recalled that, 'to my knowledge, Larkin regarded the Commission and its work with more or less silent contempt.' Luke Duffy, a more regular union participant, did not sign the report either 'but rather ridiculed the recommendations, in spoken and written comment.'

The WUI told the Commission that in 1938 it had 'over 17,000 members' in 'almost every Branch of industry and commerce as well as agriculture and fishing.' Written by Young Jim, the WUI's substantial submission confirmed a belief in vocationalism in the syndicalist mould of industrial unionism and OBU.[9] Nothing was done to implement the report.

POLITICS

Arising from the Council of Action's success, both Larkins were admitted to the Labour Party in December 1941, and with other ex-Communists they formed Dublin Central Branch in February 1942. In 1941 the Communist Party of Ireland had suspended its Dublin Branch and instructed members 'individually' to join the Labour Party and to campaign for a Coalition of Fianna Fáil and the Labour Party in the hope that Ireland might enter the war.

Larkin Senior was re-elected to Dublin Corporation in August 1942, when the Labour Party became the largest group, with thirteen out of thirty-five seats. In 1945 the ITGWU opposed Larkin's selection as a General Election candidate. Larkin assured the Party Leader, William Norton, that he would 'work in accord' with any-one, 'regardless of previous personal differences and antagonisms and put aside all divisions and conflicts.' He added, 'You may be assured that this declaration will be scrupulously observed by me and I shall at all times accept the judgement of the Administrative Council as to whether or not I have been faithful to that declaration.' O'Brien wanted expressions of regret from him. Larkin complied and wrote to

Norton on 22 May 1943, stating that he was 'deeply sensible' of the efforts being made to resolve matters and acknowledging that 'if in the heat of past conflicts statements were made by me, I regret having made such statements if those statements today appear as obstacles in the way of a united effort by all members of the Party at the present moment.'[10] He qualified this by saying that he was 'willing to do all possible . . . short of coming in conflict with my own self-respect and principles.'

O'Brien wanted more. The Administrative Council, on which the ITGWU had eight of the seventeen seats, rejected Larkin, by 8 to 7. Two members who would have voted for Larkin were absent. Norton persevered, however, sensing a Labour Party breakthrough electorally and that the ITGWU was isolated, certainly in Dublin. On 27 May, Norton announced that Larkin would be a candidate nominated by the Executive of the Dublin Labour Party, which had no authority to overrule the Administrative Council. Adding to O'Brien's annoyance, the Labour Party increased its vote from 10% in 1938 to 16% nationally and from 7% to 16% in Dublin, supporting Norton's political instincts. Larkin was returned in Dublin North-East, warmed by the fact that an old enemy but new friend, Thomas Johnson, spoke on his behalf. Young Jim was returned in South Dublin. Lemass appointed Larkin to the Commission on Youth Unemployment, and his lively Dáil contributions drew praise.

The ITGWU maintained its opposition, seeking to expel both Larkins, in Young Jim's case as Secretary of Dublin Labour Party, for breaching the Party's constitution. The Administrative Council, buoyed by the election, rejected the ITGWU's moves, 9 to 8, on 3 December 1943.

On 7 January 1944 the ITGWU disaffiliated. O'Brien cited Larkin's enmity towards the union and Communist 'manoeuvrings'. ITGWU Labour TDs resigned from the Parliamentary Party. Norton countered by suggesting that the roots of the split lay in secret ITGWU backing for the Trade Union Act (1941) and a 'thirst for revenge' against Larkin, 'without any reference to their own members.' These charges had credibility, and O'Brien was seen as being prepared to go to any lengths 'in his private war' against Larkin. Within the ITGWU, 'Officials shook their heads in disbelief at Labour being undermined because of an old man's spite.' The General President, Kennedy, 'Counselled restraint' to O'Brien, who altered his point of attack to insist that Communist 'infiltration' was the real problem. Five ITGWU TDs echoed this and formed the National Labour Party, on the union's direction.

Emmet O'Connor noted that O'Brien added a second coat of camouflage to his vindictiveness by conniving with Alfred O'Rahilly, correspondent of the *Catholic Standard*, in 'prosecuting an anti-Communist witch-hunt over the next five months.' Norton unavoidably swallowed some of the bait and expelled a number of alleged Communists. Both Larkins survived, but the Dublin Central Branch and Executive did not.

The real victors came when de Valera called an election in May 1944. The Labour Party's vote plummeted to 9%, and Larkin Senior lost his seat, although Young Jim held on. No more than with Larkin's actions in 1923–4, O'Brien's machinations were ill-timed, set the Labour Party back politically and played into de Valera's hands. Fianna Fáil increased from 66 to 75 seats; Fine Gael fell from 32 to 30 and the Labour Party from 17 to 8, albeit with 4 for the National Labour Party.

At the 1945 ITUC Congress Larkin's first motion was to call on 'all Irish workers in England, Scotland Wales, to vote Labour' in the British General Election. Northern Ireland workers, he thought, knew to do their duty well enough.[11]

A sense of class duty was shamefully absent in Ireland. O'Brien's actions in 1944 were deplorable and set the Labour Party back at a point when it was making significant advances.

Chapter 19 ~

| CONCLUSIONS

MEMBERSHIP AND WAGES

Union membership increased during the war, despite initially declining employment. The ITGWU and WUI had contrasting fortunes. After an initial loss of 6,000 the ITGWU's membership climbed to achieve a net gain of 1,526—a tribute to assiduous organising. The WUI experienced almost continuous decline, although signs of recovery were apparent in 1945.

Despite Wages Standstill Orders and the statutory removal of immunity during trade disputes, the number of strikes and working days lost was surprisingly high. The impact of the Standstill Orders is evidenced by contrasting average numbers of strikes in the five immediate pre-war and post-war years: 1934–8: 117 strikes, 523,600 days; 1946–50: 151 strikes, 149,719 days. The index of hourly wages in industrial occupations (using 1953 as 100) rose from 47.9 in 1939 to 55.3 in 1945. So, while the Government certainly exercised tight control, unions squeezed gains from the complex Tribunal system. The ITGWU made particularly successful use of them.

Even in agriculture, roads and local authorities, forever cited as the lowest-paid and most exploited sector, average weekly wages rose from 33.7 in 1939 to 49.4 in 1945. All theses increases, painstakingly won and grudgingly conceded, must be set against a cost of living that rose from 579 in 1939 to 959 in 1945 in urban areas and from 539 to 894 in rural areas. The net effect was a considerable fall in workers' real wages to below 1939 levels.[1] The ITGWU nevertheless claimed to have won more than £10 million for members. Whatever justification there was for criticism of the ITGWU's attitudes to the Trade Union Act and the Standstill Orders, behind the scenes or on the ground it organised to secure best wages. Success attracted members.

Table 52: ITGWU and WUI membership, 1939–45

	ITGWU	WUI	ITUC	Unions with head office in 26 Counties
1939	36,444	16,408	162,000	135,000
1940	36,825	15,681	163,000	128,000
1941	35,271	12,542	173,000	104,000

1942	31,228	10,780	164,000	113,000
1943	30,615	9,451	183,000	115,000
1944	34,853	8,803	187,000	134,000
1945	37,970	9,219	146,000*	143,000

*After the secession of CIU unions.

Sources: ITGWU, Annual Reports, 1939–1945; National Archives, Registrar of Friendly Societies, file 369T; Nevin, *Trade Union Century*, p. 433; Fleming and O'Day, *Longman Handbook of Modern Irish History since* 1800, p. 535.

Table 53: Industrial disputes (26 Counties), 1939–45

	Disputes begun in year	*Working days lost in year*
1939	99	106,000
1940	89	152,000
1941	71	77,000
1942	69	115,000
1943	81	62,000
1944	84	38,000
1945	87	244,000
Average:	82.5	113,428

Source: Fleming and O'Day, *Longman Handbook of Modern Irish History since* 1800, p. 535.

POLITICS AND PERSONALITY

The Larkin-O'Brien clash culminated in splits in Congress and the Labour Party, with the ITGWU seceding from both to create the National Labour Party in 1944 and the Congress of Irish Unions in 1945. O'Brien covered his anti-Larkin tracks by alleging Communist influence within the Labour Party, but his targets were Larkin Senior and Junior. The Labour Party's fortunes, particularly in Dublin, rose on the back of agitation by the Council of Action against the Standstill Orders, broadened to include prices, jobs and housing, bringing thousands onto the streets and raising workers' political consciousness. Both Larkins were returned to the Dáil.

The Labour Party's fortunes slid after the split, playing into Fianna Fáil's hands. The ITGWU's remarkable loan of £50,000 to the Government, its alleged complicity in the Trade Union Act—a possibility of winning OBU by legislative stealth, simultaneously banishing British unions—and its inconspicuousness in Congress and Trades Council campaigns against Act and orders created an impression of a compact with Fianna Fáil. The ITGWU seemed oblivious of the dangers of further Partition—even, shockingly, being prepared to surrender Northern members to the ATGWU.

Some suggested that the Congress split was less wrong than ill-timed. Perhaps it should have happened after 1922, or could have been entirely avoided if British unions had abandoned imperial attitudes and withdrawn from Ireland. Irish neutrality made support for the ITUC's participation in the World Congress genuinely problematic. British unions' attitudes could have been more understanding. Their Executives, of course, saw the world from London (or Belfast), not Dublin.

Partitionism was not solely the preserve of Free Staters. Engagement in the anti-fascist war had transformed Belfast Labour, binding it closer to British viewpoints.

O'Brien's behaviour was unforgivable, just as Larkin's had been in 1923–4. Had O'Brien taken the moral high ground and tolerated Larkin and the WUI within Congress, ironically, splits might have been avoided. WUI votes might have swung finely divided decisions in favour of Irish positions. Similarly, the Labour Party's advance might have continued. But dies were cast when O'Brien's eggs were placed in the basket of the 1941 Act at least.

Larkin was an old man. O'Brien would retire in 1946. One can speculate whether at any time, once Larkin was dead, in January 1947, O'Brien wondered where more forgiving paths might have led. As war ended, the Labour Party, in the South at least, lay sundered. British Labour's promise of a Welfare State cast Northern eyes east rather than south. Energy in the 1950s would be devoted to healing divisions rather than winning Socialist policies. Economic, political and social opportunity costs were high.

PART 3

Reunification, 1945–59

CONTEXTS

Economic and social contexts

While Britain and western Europe experienced a post-war boom, driven by reconstruction and the growth of international trade as consumer markets expanded, Ireland suffered mass unemployment and emigration. Unemployment fluctuated but averaged 60,500. Emigration totalled 528,334 in the period 1946–61, an average of 35,200 per year. Not surprisingly, employment was trade unionism's central concern. There were constant calls for planning, expansion of the public sector and the full development of agriculture and natural resources.

Only when the reunification of Congress was close did unions speak with one voice, through the Provisional United Organisation of the Irish Trade Union Movement and its pamphlet *Planning for Full Employment*. Its voice was largely ignored.

Table 54: Unemployment, Republic and Ireland Northern Ireland, 1946–59

	Republic	*Northern Ireland*	*Total*
1946	59,700	31,300	91,000
1947	55,600	29,900	85,500
1948	61,200	27,800	89,000
1949	60,600	30,000	90,600
1950	53,400	26,900	80,300
1951	50,500	28,500	79,000
1952	60,700	48,300	109,000
1953	70,600	38,000	108,600
1954	62,400	33,000	95,400
1955	55,200	32,800	88,000
1956	61,400	30,100	91,500
1957	69,700	34,700	104,400
1958	65,300	43,500	108,800
1959	61,700	36,900	98,600

Source: Fleming and O'Day, *Longman Handbook of Modern Irish History since* 1800, p. 620–23.

The cost of living rose consistently, depressing living standards. In 1946 the urban cost of living was measured as 946, rural areas 882. The corresponding figures in 1950, 1955 and 1959 were 1,047 (976), 1,327 (1,236) and 1,509 (1,406). There was constant pressure on unions to modify wage claims in order to put a brake on inflation, but few, if any, attempts were made to control professional fees, profits and dividends. The unions argued for an incomes and prices policy rather than narrow wage restraint.

Once the Wages Standstill Orders were revoked, tensions between the ITUC and CIU led to competing attitudes, both Congresses simultaneously claiming to have maximised income for affiliates while demonstrating the most informed restraint in the 'national interest.'

In 1946 the first Wage Formula was agreed with employers under the Government's watchful eye in its role as employer. This 'First Round' set a pattern of regular Wage Agreements, operated at the national or the local level, with the Labour Court policing their terms. The CIU's deliberations were led by the ITGWU and, increasingly, those of the ITUC were influenced by Larkin Junior and the WUI, each cutting off the other in claiming the most intelligent strategy. The unions offered voluntary wage restraint, in the national interest, in 1946–8 and 1952–5, eliciting no response from the Government or employers on incomes control or planned development. Supervision of Wage Rounds by the Labour Court encouraged the development of national bargaining units in creameries, flour-milling, bacon and construction, led by the ITGWU and formulated through Joint Industrial Councils in stronger industries and by Joint Labour Committees in weaker areas, such as hotels outside Dublin and clothing. Money wages consistently rose, although real wages were trammelled by constant inflation.

Table 55: Wage Rounds, 1946–59

1st	1946–7	Average wage rates rose about 25%.
2nd	1948	'Eleven-shilling formula': average increases of 8s to 10s for men, about half this for women.
3rd	1951	Increases between 10s and 19s for men, women about two-thirds this.
4th	1952	National Agreement from trade union side; 12s 6d for men, women two-thirds.
5th	1955	General increase of 11s to 17s; some groups came back for more.
6th	1957	National Agreement: 10s for men, 5s to 7s 6d for women.
7th	1959	General movement; men 10s to 15s, women 7s 6d to 10s. In 1960 there was a move to reduce hours and introduce a five-day week

Sources: Adapted from Kieran Jack McGinley, 'Neo-Corporatism, New Realism and Social Partnership in Ireland, 1970–1999,' PhD thesis, Trinity College, Dublin, 1999; Patrick Gunnigle, Gerard McMahon and Gerard Fitzgerald, *Industrial Relations in Ireland: Theory and Practice* (Dublin: Gill & Macmillan, 1999).

Table 56: Index of hourly wages in Republic (1953 = 100)

1946	57.0	1953	100.0
1947	68.3	1954	100.3
1948	74.5	1955	100.4
1949	81.1	1956	108.4
1950	81.3	1957	110.8
1951	81.7	1958	112.7
1952	91.7	1959	116.6

Source: Fleming and O'Day, *Longman Handbook of Modern Irish History since* 1800, p. 584–5.

The social wage improved after the Social Welfare Act (1952) but was poor by comparison with Britain, while limited opportunities in education, medical costs and poor housing exacerbated persistent poverty, adding to the attractions of emigration and strengthening the border. Unions consistently demanded improvements, but there was little imagination and no real attempt to trade industrial strength against these demands. The powerful Church influence suppressed matters. Bishop Dignan's social welfare plan was promoted, while the Catholic hierarchy torpedoed the Mother and Child Scheme. Larkin Junior began to seek solutions beyond wage bargaining. Endless circles saw wage increases chase prices and prices chase wages, *ad nauseam.*

Union contexts

Membership climbed from 250,000 to more than 411,000. Divided between two Congresses, the trade union movement seldom punched its weight. Much energy and time was necessarily expended in pursuing reunification. The WUI claimed a significant role in the creation of the Irish Congress of Trade Unions. There is no doubt, as an Irish union within the ITUC, it had a particular influence in persuading British unions to accept the principle that Irish union affairs should be governed by Irish structures, once the main barrier to unity and the key to rapprochement were accepted.

O'Brien's retirement in 1946 and Larkin's death in 1947 removed the two dominant actors from the stage. The WUI immediately talked of unity, and Young Jim's famous letter to the *Irish Times* after his father's death (see p. 372) displayed a generosity of spirit that was in sharp contrast with earlier animus. Once Conroy succeeded McMullen as General President of the ITGWU, progress to unity was rapid and inevitable.

The ITGWU doubled in size, from 61,260 to 125,571, leading Larkin to observe that, notwithstanding significant criticism by others, 'they were doing something right.' The WUI's membership trebled, from 10,080 to 29,631, the leading dynamic being the National Organiser, Christy Ferguson. His death in 1957 obliged Larkin to surrender his political career.

Table 57: Trade union membership, 1946–59

	ITUC	*CIU*	*Total*	*ITGWU*	*WUI*
1946	147,000	n.a.	147,000	61,260	10,080
1947	151,000	n.a.	151,000	78,380	13,225
1948	181,000	131,400	312,400	89,054	17,251
1949	196,000	143,600	339,600	101,609	21,427
1950	197,000	169,622	366,622	116,257	24,427
1951	210,000	170,601	380,601	128,191	24,217
1952	214,000	179,223	393,223	127,480	26,376
1953	209,000	183,385	392,385	119,377	27,469
1954	211,000	189,575	400,575	122,903	28,090
1955	218,000	193,479	411,479	126,180	28,320
1956	221,000	192,905	413,905	126,707	28,939
1957	222,000	199,991	421,991	124,183	28,745
1958	226,000	187,968	413,968	125,571	29,090
1959	224,000	187,340	411,840	125,571	29,631

Source: ITUC and CIU, Annual Reports, 1946–59.

In 1937, 1,755,000 days were lost through strikes—mainly the building workers' dispute—and the average number of days lost was 319,600, compared with 420,100 in the 1960s. Quiet advances were made in wages and conditions, but there were few dramatic national disputes. Inter-union conflict, beyond the ITUC-CIU division, centred on disputes in CIÉ involving the ITGWU against the ATGWU and NUR. The NUR withdrew altogether from Ireland, facilitating the formation of the National Association of Transport Employees; but the conflict between the ATGWU and ITGWU persisted. The Factories Act (1955) and amended Workmen's Compensation Act were the only advances in protective legislation. Unions' obsession with wages meant there were few demands to bring legislation into line with industrial practice or to set a floor of employment rights on notice, dismissal, leave or redundancy.

Equality began to be talked about and ILO Conventions cited; but Catholic social teaching placed greater emphasis on male breadwinners than on women's rights. Although a steadily increasing portion of the movement, women did not themselves lead any great challenge to patriarchy. Moulds were being broken, however. Elizabeth Harrison in 1951 and Betty Jevons and 'Nurse Hallinan' in 1953 were the first women elected to the General Executive Council of the WUI and Sheila Conroy in 1955 to the National Executive Council of the ITGWU.

Table 58: Strikes and days lost (Republic), 1946–59

1946	105	150,000	1953	75	82,000
1947	194	449,000	1954	81	67,000
1948	147	258,000	1955	96	236,000
1949	153	273,000	1956	67	48,000
1950	154	217,000	1957	45	92,000
1951	138	545,000	1958	51	126,000
1952	82	529,000	1959	58	124,000

Source: Fleming and O'Day, *Longman Handbook of Modern Irish History since* 1800, p. 533.

Political contexts

The participation of the National Labour Party in the first Inter-Party Government in 1948 angered the National Executive Council of the ITGWU. It was the death knell of the NLP, which quietly merged with the Labour Party.

Despite seeking improvements in social welfare, education, health, housing and, above all, planning, neither the ITGWU nor WUI affiliated to the Labour Party. Led by William Norton, the Party trod water electorally, with 19 seats in 1948, 16 in 1951, 18 in 1954 and 11 in 1957, twice participating in the Government, in 1948 and 1954. Three ITGWU members—Corish, Everett and T. J. Murphy—held Government posts. It was felt that industrial unity should precede political unity, although one was not necessarily dependent on the other. Indeed the Labour Party played honest broker in attempting to facilitate trade union dialogue.

Larkin led the Parliamentary Party and came agonisingly close to membership of the Government. That he did not says much for Fine Gael's prejudice and the Labour Party's lack of nerve. Within the ITGWU and CIU, Catholic social teaching was pre-eminent, circumscribing radical thinking and action. The Labour Party's accession to Government did not appear to greatly excite either movement or electorate to the prospect or desirability of a Socialist Government.

In Northern Ireland, Unionism held Labour at the margins, despite the post-war strengths of the Northern Ireland Labour Party and the Communist Party, politically and industrially. The National Question, obligingly, divided Labour's ranks.

Chapter 20 ~

DIVISION AND MULTIPLI-CATION AFTER O'BRIEN: THE ITGWU IN THE 1940s

The 1946 Annual Conference was the largest since 1921. William McMullen, General President, welcomed the end of Emergency Powers Orders. Never was anything more 'discriminatory' in 'depressing workers' standard of life.' From a 'more comprehensive and more objective view,' however, they brought some advantages. They forced unions to adopt a 'new technique where the force of argument counted for more than the efficacy of the strike.' Their passing was not regretted, but the ITGWU awaited 'with equanimity' the establishment of 'Labour Courts, conscious of the power of our own strong right arm' and the desire 'in the more judicial atmosphere of the Conference room to acquit ourselves competently where dialectical skill is the *sine qua non.*'

The ITGWU's policy was 'to act in a responsible way, as befitting an organisation with such wide-spread ramifications in the country,' and 'to exhaust every possibility of settlement before resorting to the strike.' The union 'had duties as well as rights' and 'could be all the more insistent upon our rights while conscious of our duties.' It was not in the ITGWU's 'nor the country's interest to have recourse to industrial disputes on the slightest provocation.' As to the war, what the workers' position would have been without the union it would be 'perhaps idle to enquire.' The ITGWU was 'and still is the most powerful and best organised weapon that the workers of this or any other country ever possessed.' Internationally, McMullen asserted that 'Communist imperialism vies with capitalist imperialism.' Ireland's neutrality provided the potential to assist in the rehabilitation process, and its exclusion from the United Nations was regrettable.

At home, unscrupulous traders readily exploited people, free from any Government interference. No group could criticise the working class 'unless it can do so with clean hands and clear consciences.' Indeed 'duty to the community is as conspicuous by its absence in other walks of life.' The cost of living would tumble if 'employers, traders, landlords and black market racketeers' demonstrated the same sacrifice as workers.

The theme of 'responsibility' was resumed in 1948. McMullen acknowledged that increased wages meant increased prices. This thinking was brought into a discussion with the Federated Union of Employers regarding wages, resulting in arrangements 'infinitely to be preferred' to Emergency Orders. The ITGWU strongly believed in the 'fitness' of workers to 'occupy their rightful place in the management of industry.' Worker's participation 'could be the most effective antidote to the 'Communist menace, which is at present striding the European Continent like a Colossus . . . threatening to undermine the fabric of our civilisation.'

In 1949 McMullen led the celebration of the union's fortieth anniversary. Had there been no ITGWU 'there would have been no Irish Citizen Army,' 'probably' no Insurrection, and 'without 1916 there could have been no Republic of Ireland,' recognised 'by every country in the world.' The 'hopes and aims and aspirations of the many gallant men and women who, feeling the weight of the oppressors' might, strove to rouse the drooping spirits of our countrymen, might have remained an empty dream.'[1] He dismissed newspaper comments that suggested that Larkin's death and O'Brien's retirement meant that problems caused by personal antagonisms could be resolved. 'Disagreements between leaders there undoubtedly were, but this was but a symptom of a much more deep-seated cause as to whether the Union was to be democratically managed or was to be a personal dictatorship.' 'Fortunately' those 'who stood for democratic management won.'

WILLIAM O'BRIEN AND THOMAS KENNEDY

O'Brien retired as General Secretary on 23 January 1946. Born in Ballygurteen, Clonakility, Co. Cork, in 1880, he was a member of Connolly's Irish Socialist Republican Party in 1897 with his brothers Dan and Tom and helped arrange Connolly's return from America in 1910. A tailor, he was active in the Amalgamated Society of Tailors from 1901, becoming Branch President at twenty-three and representing it on Dublin Trades Council. He was Treasurer of the Trades Council during the 1913 Lock-Out. After Easter Week he was deported to England and interned in Wales and England. He was Labour representative at the Mansion House Anti-Conscription Conference in 1918 and was again imprisoned in England but released after a hunger strike in 1920.

He joined the ITGWU in 1917 and became General Treasurer, 1918–23, and General Secretary, 1924–46; President of the ITUC, 1913, 1918, 1925 and 1941, Chairman of the Administrative Council of the Labour Party, 1933–9, and Labour TD for South Dublin and Tipperary, 1922, 1923, 1937 and 1938. He made and retained many contacts in British Labour, including Jim Connell, Jack Jones, Tom Mann and Ben Tillett, using those friendships if need arose on Irish Labour's behalf.

McMullen observed, with Larkin in his thoughts, that 'the historian of the future, seeing events in clearer perspective, would record as one of his outstanding triumphs his successful fight in keeping the movement on a democratic base against the subversive elements who wished to establish a personal dictatorship in the Union and working-class movement.' The 1946 Conference sent a telegram to

O'Brien in Seattle, where he was attending the International Labour Conference, expressing 'appreciation of your magnificent work' and wishing him 'long life and happiness.'

On 23 November 1946 in the Metropole Restaurant, Dublin, O'Brien was honoured with a presentation of his portrait in oils. McMullen praised him as 'a man of strong conviction, sound judgement and unvacillating in action.' Once the 'soundness of an opinion was determined upon, expression was fearlessly given to it, even if the originality of the view, or its heterodoxy, would flutter the dove-cotes of the pure-souled or orthodox.' It was 'this trait in his character, perhaps more than any other,' that saved the organisation 'when faced with treachery from within and hostility from without.'

O'Brien was not blessed with the 'arts of the spell-binder' but relied on 'irresistible logic, cogency of argument and pungency of humour.' The 'man in the street' considered him 'aloof or perhaps frigid,' but to those who knew him he was 'the embodiment of friendliness, without peer as raconteur, matchless in the scintillation of his wit and humour.'

McMullen thought he had 'disappointed some of his erstwhile admirers, as since youth he held out the promise of becoming the Robespierre or the Marat of the Labour Movement.' Now, 'he threatened to become its Thomas Carlyle.'

At the 1941 ITUC Congress, when opposition from the floor abounded, his final speech was 'so replete with gaiety and irony as to charm even his severest critic.' His international reputation was central to the recognition of the CIU beyond Ireland. He was close to a Government seat and had contributed much to Labour and the nation.

O'Brien was the dominant ITGWU personality, and yet in Official records— Conference reports, NEC minutes, publications—he is hardly apparent. His was the unseen hand, guiding—and, many suggest, manipulating—matters after his fashion. The 1924 division became personalised as the Larkin-O'Brien split, but it can be argued that it pre-dated O'Brien's involvement and was probably inevitable once rapid growth meant the ITGWU could no longer be treated as a personal fiefdom.

The ITGWU's financial rigour and bureaucracy are ascribed to O'Brien; but Connolly was the first to impose internal discipline and to activate democratic structures under the Rules. J. J. Hughes, a victim of O'Brien's purge, did much to shape administrative and industrial structures. O'Brien nevertheless held the ITGWU together through the desperate decade after 1924. He certainly personalised matters—though no more than Larkin himself—and used his influence within Congress, the Labour Party and, to a lesser extent, the Trades Council (O'Brien was never too interested in Dublin Trades Council) to exclude Larkin and the WUI. During the war O'Brien's Machiavellian manoeuvrings laid the ITGWU open to sus- picions that it was hand in glove with the Fianna Fáil Government. The Trade Union Act (1941) was perhaps, in O'Brien's eyes, an opportunity to achieve OBU through legislation and to kill off Larkin and British unions in one fell swoop. When this was frustrated, not least by the NUR case, and as Labour's fortunes rose with

Larkin's leadership in the Council of Action's protests against the Wages Standstill Orders, O'Brien was central to splits in Congress and the Labour Party. His final legacy was therefore one of division. Had he put personal animus aside, his legacy might have been greater. He would be judged more kindly for his many significant achievements in a career ultimately blighted by his actions in the years immediately before retirement.

The succeeding General Secretary, Thomas Kennedy, died on 18 September 1947. The union said that 'all his life' he was 'an upholder of the cause of the Common People, in whose memories and [the memory] of all who knew him he will live.'

Larkin displayed a particular antipathy to Kennedy. A close friend and foundation member, Mick McCarthy, died on 4 October 1948. He had fought 'with the Irish Citizen Army in 1916 with the famous "Shotgun" Division.' He served on the Executive Council, 1918–23, before becoming Secretary of Dublin No. 1 Branch. Three great stalwarts were gone.[2]

MEMBERSHIP AND ORGANISATION

In 1945 membership was higher than at any time since 1923, at 60,000. The credit balance reached £285,592, although arrears were a problem. An Agreement with the ATGWU was criticised by Delegates, but the ITGWU insisted that it gained much from it. Kennedy demanded a 'clear cut and planned policy' for organisation, as 'indiscriminate and irresponsible' campaigns were unwise. In 1946 a further increase 'was scarcely expected,' as 'our National Organisational drive had spent itself.' Remarkably, membership rose to 70,000. Almost 'complete organisation was won' in trades covered by Joint Labour Committees. The union received 'very many applications' from agricultural workers but, 'with great regret,' rejected them. National bargaining Committees were established in flour-milling, woollen and worsteds, creameries and bacon-curing, often involving Labour Party TDs, enabling national representation. The Movements Department of Head Office provided sophisticated statistical support for negotiators.

Table 59: ITGWU membership, 1945–9

	CIU affiliation	RFS	Women	Branches
1945	36,000	53,185	10,634	92
1946	80,000	61,260	12,000	100
1947	80,000	78,380	15,676	110
1948	95,000	89,054	17,811	130
1949	108,000	101,609	20,322	134

Source: ITGWU and CIU, Annual Reports, 1945–9; National Archives, Registrar of Friendly Societies, file 275T.

In 1947 membership was regarded as having hit a peak. Despite significantly increased Dispute Pay, finances grew, reflecting a growth in membership to 'not less than 100,000,' equalled only in 1920–22. This amounted to 'almost a quarter' of 'all persons employed,' excluding agricultural labourers. The union's 'outstanding influence' in national life explained the surge—together, of course, with the 'integrity and sagacious leadership of its Officers, Officials and NEC.' Where Branches were once opened in 'every town and village,' newcomers were referred to existing Branches in their locality. By December there were 110 Branches.

An unexpected approach came from the Ulster Transport and Allied Operatives' Union, created from a bitter feud with the ATGWU. McMullen was 'personally of [the] opinion that amalgamation with us would not be in the best interests of the Ulster Union.' It approached again in 1952, but the deputation that visited Liberty Hall was disciplined on returning to Belfast. Most went to the General Union of Municipal Workers. The CIÉ Clerical Association did transfer in 1947–8; the Secretary of the Convoy Branch, William Doherty, persuaded nurses in Letterkenny Mental Hospital to transfer from their British union, with John Nugent as Secretary; and Buncrana shirt and hosiery workers came from the National Union of Tailors and Garment Workers, establishing an ITGWU Branch. Conversely, a Killarney Section joined the National Union of Boot and Shoe Operatives.

In 1948, W. J. Keenan (National Trustee) warned those who thought the ITGWU 'a very wealthy organisation.' Assets per capita were 'only in the region of £3'; in other unions it was £5 to £25. The ITGWU was, 'therefore, a poor one financially.' Were there a 'national upheaval' or 'period of nationwide strikes or lockouts,' funds would be quickly exhausted. The NEC had 'to be very careful and sagacious' in deciding how 'funds should be invested.' Thomas O'Reilly (Dublin No. 3) felt that £3 million was needed before they could feel secure.

Frank Robbins moved that 'the time is opportune' to again organise 'agricultural and other rural workers.' Dan Spring TD warned of the dangers, not least the control of wages by County Managers. O'Reilly, who was heavily involved in the 1920s, cautioned that it could 'conceivably wreck or seriously damage trade unionism' if a campaign 'was launched without the essentials necessary for success.' They felt this had happened with the Federation of Rural Workers.

McMullen agreed that the time was not right. He took satisfaction from the fact that by forcing up rates for road and rural workers the Agricultural Wages Board was forced to raise farm labourers' rates. The ITGWU appealed for any who had 'retained their membership since the 1920s' to come forward to act on the Area Committees of the Agricultural Wages Board.

Table 60: ITGWU income and expenditure (£), 1945–9

	Income	Expenditure	Surplus (deficit)
1945	41,072	21,806	19,266
1946	49,720	21,868	27,852
1947	61,298	74,861	(13,563)
1948	74,074	35,427	39,277
1949	85,404	46,910	38,494

Source: ITGWU, Annual Reports, 1945–9.

Membership reached 120,000, an increase of 140% on 1938. More than 120,000 of the 160,000 who might be in were now in.[3] In 1949, 100,000 financial members were recorded—7,000 in hotels and restaurants, 4,000 psychiatric nurses, 5,000 creamery workers, 8,000 road workers, 3,000 flour-millers, 2,000 bacon-curers, 4,000 clothing trade workers, 2,500 hosiery workers and 2,000 coalminers. In contrast, the founding cornerstone, dockers, accounted for only 3,000. Servicing claims and drafting Agreements, administering benefits, maintaining meetings and organisation and dealing with individual queries and grievances was an immense task. The union fought a two-week strike for recognition in the Ford Motor Company in Cork, while the hurling champion Christy Ring, Oil Section, was praised as 'as fine a trade unionist as he is a hurler.' His 'presence' was 'felt at every meeting.'

In 1949, 130,000 members equalled if not exceeded the 'combined numerical strength of all other unions' in the Republic. From 1945 to 1949 the credit balance increased by £184,084, or 45%; in 1945 it was £285,592; in 1946, £320,559; in 1947, £313,420; in 1948, £355,965; and in 1949, £403,623. A decline in membership was expected as the pace of wage increases slowed. The most satisfying aspect, therefore, was the apparent recognition that the union was 'no mere wage fixing machine to be discarded' as soon as rises were secured but a 'tremendous force in the economic life of the nation.' The ITGWU remained the 'best and cheapest insurance against victimisation, low wages and poor conditions.' A bonus was the decision of 'thousands of members of British unions' to transfer as a result of the 'iniquitous Ireland Act.' To railway and clerical workers a 'hearty Céad Míle Fáilte' was extended. Most came from the ATGWU and NUR.[4]

WOMEN

In 1946, 14,000 members, or 20% of the total, were women. Increases larger than those for men were widely won, and 'their average rate' was brought up 'to a higher ratio of the men's than ever before.' No-one yet talked of 'equal pay.' Even this narrowing of the gap was in large measure an accidental and unintended side effect: 'the limits to which remuneration could be legally increased without the authority of a Bonus Order were the same for men and women.' The 'vast majority of males were already' paid maximum basic or standard rates. Most women were much below them. Consequently, 'more could be done for the women than for the men.'⁵ Despite this, women's rates were still 'substantially less' than men's.

In 1947 Robbins (Dublin No. 7) was disappointed to find no woman at the Annual Conference. He 'hoped something would be done' to get women 'to take a more lively interest.' M. Connor (Drogheda), reflecting confused and ambivalent attitudes, moved (supported by twelve other speakers) to 'impress on the Government, owing to the declining population, to institute a scheme of Marriage benefits which would enable our young people to face the responsibilities of married life.' In 1948 James Gilhooly (Dublin No. 6) called for a legal ban on women as pressers in the clothing trade, a motion adopted without comment. In 1947 so rare was a female presence that Mary Fitzgerald was personally welcomed from the platform as an ITGWU Delegate to the CIU, with the hope that 'there would be many more.'

In 1948, 30,000 of the 120,000 members were women, a number 'larger than the female membership of all other unions combined.' The estimated figures for women members given in Annual Reports are substantiated by the figures of the Registrar of Friendly Society, which show 10,634 (20%) of the total membership of 53,185 in 1945 to be women and 23,251 (20%) out of 116,257 in 1950.

THE 'OCCUPIED AREA'

Northern membership was healthy in 1946, with wage improvements won across the board. In Newry 'a great deal of progress was made' regarding dockers' decasualisation through a Court of Inquiry. On 22 October 1947 a long-standing NEC member, John McLarnon, a Belfast docker, died. He was Chairman and Assistant Secretary of the Belfast Branch.

In the ITGWU's Annual Reports 'Northern Ireland' had become 'the North', reflecting a hardening line on its legitimacy. In August five hundred dockers ceased work in protest at the Ministry of Food giving the discharge of ships to members of a British union, 'part of a deliberate policy to wipe us out at the docks.' McMullen's personal intervention with the Stormont Government secured a settlement, although there was further tension over the loading of potatoes. The ITGWU fought for its quarter of the work.

Joe Meehan (Belfast) commented on the 'nauseating attitude' of some British unions. In the South they played the 'Nationalist game', 'calling for unity,' while in the Six Counties they 'were co-operating with the Empire elements in an endeavour to smash the Irish Transport Union.' P. J. O'Brien observed, in an attack on Ernest Bevin, that 'Connolly did not die in order that the trade union dominated by His Britannic Majesty's Foreign Secretary should hold sway in Ireland.' Dan McAllister sought more Organisers.

In 1949 Meehan objected to the term 'Northern Ireland' and suggested 'Six Counties' or 'Six Occupied Counties' instead. It became 'the Occupied Area'.

In 1949, under the heading 'Anti-Irish Legislation', the ITGWU condemned the 'latest act of aggression of the British Government' in 'presuming to legislate for any portion of our national territory by the passing of the Ireland Act.' Robbins declared that 'Partition cannot be justified or maintained by a British Act of Parliament, nor even by a continued armed occupation.' The Labour Government had 'forsaken its teachings and lent its power' to preserving 'the vested interests of reactionary Tory elements' within the Northern 'statelet', built 'on a denial of ordinary democratic principles.'

The union gained 'substantial' members 'despite the opposition' of British unions, 'employing class and the totalitarianism operating there in the guise of democratic Government.' Tribute was paid to members who, 'in the face of bitter antagonism,' remained steadfast. They were 'an inspiration to all who believe in decency, democracy and freedom in human, national and international affairs.'[6]

The abandoning of members to the ATGWU was no longer mooted. Equally, expansion was never seriously attempted.

WAGES AND DISPUTES

At the first CIU Congress, in 1945, Kennedy wanted wage-fixing machinery introduced 'for the more expeditious making of collective Agreements' and the 'peaceful settlement' of disputes. He was particularly concerned about rural workers, shop assistants and others beyond unionisation, whose terms and conditions suffered accordingly. Naturally, he opposed any compulsory element. He drew on his experience of wage-fixing under Emergency Orders. Having won bonus payments when employers could not justify an inability to concede claims before a Tribunal, he suggested: 'I think most people will agree that the machinery set up under the E.P.O. was reasonably good.'

In 1946 McMullen emphasised that 'unofficial strikes are the negation' of collective bargaining principles and 'should not be countenanced by responsible' trade unionists. 'Adequate machinery' existed within 'democratically controlled' unions 'for the adjustment of all legitimate grievances.'

Dispute Pay in 1945 amounted to £4,581, the highest since 1940, with 4,000 members involved in twenty-three strikes. Jim Hickey (Cork No. 1) asked the Government to appoint a Committee representative of the medical profession and other experts to determine 'a weekly wage sufficient to maintain a standard of living based on human needs.' The ITGWU cleared up maximum Bonus Order settlements and, after 23 September, embarked on straightforward claims.

Cash returns were less than in previous years, 'but the total number to benefit was higher.' Dublin dockers, out for five weeks seeking extended annual leave, won decasualisation and twelve days' leave in 1947. Casual men, who hitherto had no holidays, got three days on completion of 1,000 hours worked.

The repeal of the Emergency Wage Regulations in 1946 'did not result in any slackening': there 'was no breathing spell.' McMullen considered that the responsibility for casting the post-war wage structure fell largely upon the ITGWU, requiring 'leadership of the highest quality' and 'not a little knowledge of economic science.' It tried to balance raising members' living standards with avoiding wage-led inflation. It was conscious that 'it was not the nominal wage that is important but the real wage translated in terms of purchasing power.' He felt they achieved their twin objectives.

In 1947 the ITGWU called for subsidies on essential items. Practically 100,000 members in 2,000 employments gained average increases of 10s, totalling 'not less that £3,000,000.' More than 10,000 were involved in seventy-two strikes, costing £55,992, the highest Dispute Pay since 1923. Road workers' pay was improved by inducing the Minister for Local Government to set 'equitable and legal minimum rates' and to sanction increases agreed with County Managers. The second strategy bore far more fruit than the former.

A stoppage by 3,000 members of Dublin No. 4 Branch, Hotels and Restaurants, was narrowly averted on the eve of the Horse Show through the intervention of J. P. O'Brien, Chairman of the Irish Tourist Board, and an offer close to their demand. In Cork, hotel workers won 'substantial increases' through the Labour Court. Hotel workers around the country joined up.

After five months a national flour-milling dispute came to a head in November. De Valera suggested emergency legislation to make any strike illegal and to 'ensure an adequate supply of bread.' The CIU met de Valera as the men rejected a Court recommendation and improved JIC offer. The NEC protested strongly, as it had 'pursued every possible method with a view to settlement' to 'ensure some fair measure of compensation to meet the increased cost of living.' The Government's gratitude for the £50,000 loan had not lasted long. The NEC recognised that if legislation were passed it 'would have no alternative but to comply' but insisted that no steps be taken 'to prevent the members from withdrawing their labour if they decided in accordance with the Rules.' A stoppage was averted by an acceptable offer in June 1948.

In Carlow, Paddy Bergin, Irish Electrical and Industrial Union, accused the ITGWU Branch Secretary, Stephen Carroll, of canvassing workers to replace IEIU members on strike in Messrs Thompson's. A legal action was supported against Bergin and his claim strenuously denied.

In 1948, 6,000 members were engaged in strikes, most lasting only hours or days. A dispute in Baxendale's of Capel Street, Dublin, lasted six months, but few members were involved. Dispute Pay was £9,813, bringing the total paid out since 1918 to £500,000, 'more than £300 every week continuously for thirty-one years.'

An unofficial stoppage at Foynes occurred when John Sisk erected an oil storage plant but would not accept seniority in laying off men. Two members were expelled for 'opposing the strike and attempting to organise a body of men from outside the area to break it.' Members would not accept their reinstatement, as they had 'attempted to organise strike-breaking.'

More than 20,000 members were involved in strikes in 1949: Cork pawnbrokers were out twenty-two weeks; Cashel building workers, thirteen; and Mallow chocolate crumb workers, nineteen. Castlecomer coalmines, out on 14 March, and Killorglin bakeries, on 5 September, were still out in the new year. Dispute Pay totalled £19,347. Issues involved non-unionism, unwarranted dismissals, annual leave, victimisation, recognition, hours of work and overtime.

There was 'no diminution' in the union's 'endeavour to improve the lot' of farm labourers. McMullen wrote to Michael Keyes, Labour Minister for Local Government, drawing attention to the 'palpable injustice' of poor rates paid to road, forestry and local authority workers. 'No heed' was paid. The Agricultural Workers (Holidays) Act (1949) provided statutory holiday entitlement to labourers. The ITGWU claimed a 'considerable share of the credit' for this 'belated measure.'[7]

Table 61: ITGWU Dispute Pay, 1946–9

	Income (£)	Dispute Pay (£)	Dispute Pay as proportion of income (%)
1945	41,072	4,581	11.2
1946	49,720	3,447	6.9
1947	61,289	54,992	89.7
1948	74,704	9,813	13.1
1949	85,404	19,347	22.7

Source: ITGWU, Annual Reports, 1945–9.

WAGE ROUNDS

In 1947, although the Wages Standstill Orders were rescinded, the Government still desired wage control, in contrast to the continued absence of price and profit control. In October discussions began between the CIU, ITUC and FUE, under the Labour Court, to agree 'the principles to be observed in future negotiations.' After 'an exhaustive examination' it was 'generally agreed that there was not much to choose between the sliding scale formula under consideration by Congress' and Ministerial proposals, the latter in fact 'more favourable to workers who had low basic rates.' The Minister broke off discussions because of pending Dáil elections. The CIU protested and suggested talks with the FUE 'to secure agreement on stabilisation' on the basis of the Minister's formula.

In 1948 the ITGWU Conference approved the emerging terms, praising the union as among their prime architects. The First Wage Round was guided by 'Principles to be Observed in Negotiations for the Adjustment in Wages': 'every effort must be made' to avoid any unjustifiable increases in prices; adjust wage increases within limits that gave reasonable assurance that they would not drive inflation; avoid losses in production caused by stoppages; and maintain increased output by greater efficiency and productivity. No increase, generally, would be over 11s, with the onus on employers to show 'exceptional circumstances' if they could not pay. All disputed matters were processed through the Labour Court.

The Industrial Efficiency and Prices Bill (1947) met Congress's wishes 'to a large extent' regarding 'more rigid price control.' Consultative Committees on price-fixing and Joint Development Councils for industry were to be set up. The Coalition Government did not, however, pursue the Bill, leading for demands for its enactment. The ITGWU immediately sought First-Round increases. In less than twelve months more than £2 million was won. The ITGWU spelt out the system's advantages: apart from the 'saving of time, energy and clerical work,' the results were 'usually much more satisfactory.' They 'invariably' led to a 'higher degree of uniformity in rates of pay for the same class of work in all Districts.'

Only in construction and council roadwork were difficulties faced. Immediately the 'Eleven-Shilling Formula' was agreed the ITGWU approached the Federation of Builders, Contractors and Allied Employers of Ireland. No national Agreement could be reached, and twenty-six separate county claims were made, gaining increases for most. The Wage Round was 'rightly regarded as a magnanimous gesture' by the CIU 'in the interest of the community.' The wage ceiling gave the national economy space to rehabilitate and stabilise prices, reducing inflationary pressure. The ITGWU praised some industrialists and employers while calling for sanctions against those who exploited war conditions. McMullen explained that the ITGWU had applied 'intelligence as well as power,' as a 'false step of ours' could endanger living standards. It had not called a wages truce but was 'thinking upon new lines of approach' to align future wage increases to increased production standards.' Increased production would benefit all.

In 1949 wage activity slowed. Some Sections that had gained 11s wanted the formula revoked. The ITGWU resisted these calls and maintained a three-point wage strategy: raise national wage levels by reducing the cost of living; maintain existing standards where they are considered comparable to those in general; and improve remuneration for the lower-paid. The wisdom of this strategy is demonstrated by the following graph. It shows that the upward trend in the cost of living almost halted, while earnings almost caught pace. The position was almost back to that of 1939, although this was not a satisfactory result. Evidence supported the union's view that the First Round should be followed by another. James Gilhooley (Dublin No. 6/8) complained that while 'captains of Irish industry had taken full advantage,' prices had not reduced, and profits rose considerably. Conroy said that a 'free for all sort of checkmate game of wages chasing prices every few months' would mean the 'whole community would suffer.' Serious harm would be done to recovery and development.[8] The ITGWU's eggs were firmly in the Wage-Round basket.

Comparison between earnings and cost of living (1939–48) (Base 1939 = 100)

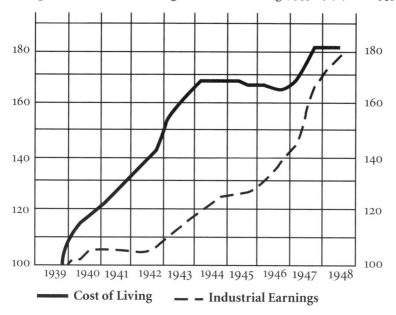

━━ **Cost of Living**   ▬ ▬ **Industrial Earnings**

Source: ITGWU, Annual Reports 1949, p. 11.

CIÉ

In 1945 the ITGWU negotiated national settlements for road passenger, freight and maintenance within the new national transport company, Córas Iompair Éireann, winning a maximum emergency bonus of 16s. After the repeal of the Emergency Wages Regulations in September 1946 the union made a claim for bus workers. It was the subject of a Labour Court recommendation on 16 December, accepted by both parties but not codified by written agreement.

In August 1947 the ITGWU sought an increase of 30s and a forty-hour week. A strike began on 3 September. Despite a recommendation on 18 September, members rejected the terms. After 'many prominent individuals and public bodies' inter-vened, direct negotiations with CIÉ were resumed in mid-October. A cost-of-living increase of 5s above the original Labour Court terms, to be readjusted after the publication of cost-of-living figures in February 1948, was accepted by four to one. Work resumed on 3 November. It was the first national strike of bus workers, involved 3,000 members for nine weeks and cost 'over £40,000.' P. J. O'Brien (Cork No. 2) asked whether it was justifiable. It was a 'second post-Emergency increase,' when the 'great majority' had 'not even got one advance.' Why did the NEC not insist that they await the outcome of the Labour Court, as it was directed to do? It was 'said that CIÉ workers were running the Union' and the NEC 'had no control over them.' Ballots were not conducted properly or in secret.

J. Brennan (Dublin No. 9) denied all charges and congratulated the NEC for its support—particularly McMullen's Labour Court presentation—and took a swipe at the compliant NUR. Comments about CIÉ members' influence persisted, however. They were the new dockers; and, of course, there was competition for their favour with the ATGWU and NUR.

In 1948 the Milne Report made recommendations on the running of CIÉ. The union saw them as 'impracticable, deficient or anti-social' and would resist 'any unwarranted attempt to reduce staff or wages.' In March the company employed 21,279 people, an increase of 17% since 1945. The ITGWU sought trade union representation in 'control and management' and legislation to provide for 'equality of privileges,' improved sickness and pension schemes and 'workmen's tickets' on bus and rail services. CIÉ should be subject to annual parliamentary review. Union representation on the Traffic Committee of Dublin Corporation, consisting of an Official, driver and conductor, was sought. The full nationalisation of public transport was also demanded. In the late autumn seven hundred members of the Irish Railwaymen's Union and NUR transferred, creating a Rail Branch. Limerick men threatened to join the WUI unless accepted. By July 1949, 1,579 had joined in Dublin, Cork and Limerick.

A dispute in CIÉ road freight resulted from the dismissal of a driver and helper on Saturday 13 August 1949. They had 'disregarded instructions' after being 'badgered and abused by a certain Inspector.' They got 'no notice or opportunity of defence.' The ITGWU did 'everything possible to avert it,' the company nothing. Lengthy Labour Court procedures followed, much delayed by the company. The final hearing, over six days in September, witnessed evidence given under oath and Counsel representing CIÉ. Amazingly, the company never produced any written statement or evidence, nor was it asked to do so.

The recommendation contained thirteen pages of an 'unwarranted attack' on the ITGWU. The union was not best pleased. R. J. P. Mortished's Labour Court recommended a return to work without the two dismissed men. Included was 'a lecture on how, in the opinion of the author or authors, the affairs of the Union should be conducted.' CIÉ 'emerged practically unscathed . . . notwithstanding the damaging admissions they were forced to make under oath.' Their 'case was so weak' and 'actions and attitude so deplorable' that they 'feared to put anything in writing no doubt feeling that if they did so it would constitute an actual signed confession of guilt.'

Within forty-eight hours, however, the union obtained a direct settlement, 'under which all the members resumed work together, undaunted, undivided and victorious,' 'a complete triumph' and defeat for CIÉ and an 'indictment' of the Labour Court.

The ITGWU drafted numerous amendments to the Transport Bill (1949), endeavouring to protect 10,000 members in CIÉ.[9]

PSYCHIATRIC NURSES

A Conference of psychiatric employees held in Dublin on 1–2 October 1946 sought national scales of £96 to £209 for male nurses through twelve annual increments of

£9 8s, £71 to £156 for female nurses through twelve increments of £7 1s 8d and an extra allowance of £40 a year for a charge attendant and £20 for a Deputy. The importance of nursing members was affirmed by McMullen chairing the meeting and the attendance of Frank Purcell (Head Office), S. O'Farrell (Secretary of the National Labour Party) and three TDS, James Everett, J. P. Pattison and John O'Leary. Dáil pressure enabled the ITGWU to favourably amend the Mental Treatment Bill (1944) with regard to pensions. McMullen sought a Mental Hospitals Advisory Council to improve nurses' and patients' lot and circumvent the hated County Managers.

The union lobbied for conciliation and arbitration machinery for nurses, as 2,000 members 'feel so humiliated and exasperated' by the denial of the right to directly bargain with County Managers. They felt 'compelled to take strike action to enforce the elementary right to have a voice in the determination of wages and conditions of service.' They were reluctant to strike, however, given the humanitarian nature of their work, but 'should it have to happen, responsibility would be clearly on the shoulders of the Government.'

In 1947 the ITGWU called upon the Minister to provide extended sickness leave. M. Ryan (Clonmel) expressed 'sincere thanks' for the 'splendid improvements in wages and conditions secured.' In July new scales, effective from 1 November 1946, were accepted, giving male nurses an increase of £120 and female nurses £110. Relaxation of the 56-hour week meant that the 'advent of the forty-eight hour week was definitely in sight.' In 1948 the ITGWU increased pressure to secure the 48-hour week through a national Delegate Conference in May.[10]

The NUR case

In March 1945 the ITGWU applied to the Trade Union Tribunal under the Trade Union Act (1941) to act as sole representative in respect of CIÉ employees. The National Union of Railwaymen sought adjournment pending a High Court decision on its claim that Part 3 of the Act was repugnant to the Constitution. It was awarded an injunction on 24 May. Mr Justice Gavan Duffy heard the case on 3–4 July 1945 and dismissed it, stating that the 'Tribunal had express authority from an Act of Parliament,' and allowed costs to the Tribunal and the ITGWU. The NUR appealed to the Supreme Court in July 1946, and part 3 of the Act was struck out. The ITGWU's disappointment was manifest. McMullen thought that agitation against the 1941 Act was 'palpably dishonest' and 'sustained in the interest' of British unions. In retrospect, much of it was a 'sham and humbug devoid of any sincerity or merit.'[11]

The Trade Union Acts (1947 and 1948) continued the practice of allowing smaller, Irish unions to obtain Negotiating Licences while not able to lodge the full deposit required. They had to do so by 8 July 1949.

COALMINERS

In 1948 agitation by the CIU led to an order reducing the hours required by miners to qualify for paid annual holidays from 1,800 to 1,600, part of an ITGWU offensive to improve miners' conditions.

On 14 March 1949 a strike began among 488 Castlecomer miners over the revocation of an Agreement 'which had prevailed in one form or another since 1881.' The Agreement, originally introduced against the men's wishes, provided for a sliding scale linking wages to coal prices. A strike against the scale in 1926 was defeated and the men compelled by economic necessity to return on the employers' terms. The scale was enforced but worsened and, 'as in 1881, so in 1926 the workers had no hand, act or part in the drawing up of the contract': 'Take it or starve was the ultimatum.'

Another strike occurred in 1940 as prices rocketed. The men were 'compelled to work like the beasts of the field' to provide 'even the barest necessities of life.' The employers thundered, 'There must not—there cannot be—any departure' from the Agreement. The 'face of the earth was being changed, the world was in flames, the greatest war in history' being fought but what happened in 'Castlecomer in 1881 was not to be altered in 1940.' Work resumed after a lengthy strike through Government appeals as coal shortages affected industry. Workers returned in the community interest but met only intransigence by the employers and the old contract. There was one concession: 'they agreed to pay percentage compensation on breakages' under a Soft Coal Agreement.

Between 1940 and 1947 the ITGWU secured various increases under the Emergency Powers Wages Orders, 'but the principle of the sliding scale contract continued.'

In 1948 the employers hinted at cancelling the contract. In March 1949, in a 'complete volte face,' they revoked it. Why? Was it

> because they suddenly became repentant of the injustice they had meted out to the workers for six decades? Did they now, filled with Christian charity and conscious of their past inhumanity, want to atone for their wrongs and present the workers with a new improved contract? Or were they trying to put a quick one over?

They maintained the contract because it was profitable; workers resisted because it was unfair. As the Government held down prices during the war, the contract remained, but from July the company significantly increased coal prices. It forgot the contract, because new prices entitled miners to an advance of 8s a ton, plus 5% under the Soft Coal Agreement. A further increase was due from a price increase of 5s in July 1949. The employers' refusal to honour their own Agreement was 'shameful.' They were 'not content' to receive substantial windfall profits 'from fortuitous circumstances beyond their control,' which they 'could not have expected': they wanted 'the whole hog', proposing static rates not based on selling prices. Existing wage rates were not satisfactory, as they fell below local skilled rates—yet mining was a skilled, dangerous job. The 1942 Committee of Inquiry into coal described conditions as 'notoriously hard.' Labour shortage was a problem, and it took four years to train a miner.

The Labour Court investigated the dispute on 17 May. Its recommendation of 13 August was rejected by the men, who remained out for eleven months. In January 1950 W. J. Keenan (NEC) thought the dispute 'appeared to be interminable and in his opinion should not be continued indefinitely,' but Conroy said it was necessary to continue support. The strike ended in July 1950 with 100% victory 'over a tyrannical employer' after 'terrific sacrifice by the men, women and children in their District.' Some men got twice what the Labour Court recommended. Nixie Boran acknowledged that the Castlecomer miners won only because the rest of the union stood by them.[12]

RURAL WORKERS

The ITGWU refused to organise agricultural workers after 1923, despite numerous requests to do so. The formation of the Federation of Rural Workers in 1946 did not involve the ITGWU, which showed no desire to either block or organise against it. In 1949 Conroy called for Government action against the 'grave social injustice' that was 'incompatible with the social precepts of Christian teaching and a serious menace to the nation,' namely the low wages and poor conditions of land, forestry, county council and road workers. The ITGWU had thousands in these sectors. Wages were low by comparison with JLC rates and barely constituted a living wage. The NEC expressed concerns about burgeoning membership of the FRW in Cos. Dublin, Wicklow and Kildare, which 'might constitute a potential danger': 'later on they might seek to organise industrial workers or induce them to join some other Union.'[13]

CONGRESS OF IRISH UNIONS

At the first Congress of Comhar Ceard Éireann (Congress of Irish Unions) in July 1945 a lengthy explanation, or perhaps justification, of its creation was given. In 1934 it had been proposed that the British TUC withdraw from Ireland, not in any antagonistic spirit but as a natural consequence of the emerging Irish state. The TUC agreed but then stalled, allegedly because of misrepresentation of the motive of those who called for Irish unions for Irish workers. The Government continuously threatened legislation, especially to deal with demarcation disputes. An ITUC Special Congress in April 1938 set up a Commission, which reported in November, and the report was debated on 9 February 1939. The day before, the Council of Irish Unions, a meeting of Irish unions within the ITUC, considered their view. Proposals to amalgamate or group unions in specific industries or occupations were rejected when three Irish unions supported British unions. The ITGWU led a withdrawal from the Conference. In March 1939 those who withdrew appointed a Provisional Committee to 'devise a national economic policy for Irish Unions.' There matters rested until 1944.

At the 1944 ITUC Congress a previous decision not to 'participate in a World Congress of Trade Unions' was reversed after British unions secured a majority in the Executive. As Ireland was a neutral state, the ITGWU and its allies believed they could not participate. It was, in effect, a Conference of Allied states, not a World Congress.

On 21 March 1945 the ITGWU led a withdrawal from the ITUC, and on 25 April the Congress of Irish Unions was established. McMullen denied that the genesis of the problem lay in differences between the ATGWU and the ITGWU in 1934. The break was the 'completion of the national work begun twenty-five years ago.' In fact 'it was a disgrace' that Irish trade unionists had not put their house in order before.

Fourteen unions founded the CIU, many of them castigated as ITGWU 'satellites'. This was unfair to those who believed in the validity and necessity of their actions. Whether they would have acted without the ITGWU could be questioned, however. No differently, British unions could stand firm because of the support of significant Irish unions, such as the Bakers, National Teachers and Post Office Workers. The ITUC issued an appeal, 'To the Trade Unionists of Ireland', naturally finding a suitable Connolly quotation: while 'the interests of Labour all over the world are identical it is true, it also true that each country had better work out its own salvation on the lines most congenial to itself.' The CIU was at least to be congenial. Cathal O'Shannon resigned as Secretary of the ITUC to become Secretary of the CIU.

Table 62: Affiliates to the CIU

Founding members
Ancient Guild of Incorporated Brick and Stone Layers
Dublin Typographical Provident Society
Electrical Trades Union
Electrotypers' and Stereo-typers' Society
Irish Bookbinders' and Allied Trades Union
Irish Engineering Industrial Union
Irish National Painters' and Decorators' Trade Union
Irish National Union of Woodworkers
Irish Seamen's and Port Workers' Union
Irish Transport and General Workers' Union
Irish Union of Distributive Workers and Clerks
National Union of Sheet Metal Workers
Operative Plasterers' Trade Society of Ireland
United House and Ship Painters' Trade Union

Later affiliates

Irish Automobile Drivers' and Automobile Mechanics' Union
Irish Engineering and Foundry Union
Irish National Union of Vintners', Grocers' and Allied Trades Assistants
Irish Railwaymen's Union
Irish Society of Woodcutting Machinists

The CIU urged Irish workers to abandon 'Foreign Unions' and sought legislation that 'will give no less advantageous terms to workers transferring to or establishing non-profit making Trade Unions,' citing legislation for merging approved National Health Insurance societies. This would allow those leaving British bodies to preserve their benefits and entitlements.

Many suspected that private nods were given equally private winks by a complicit Government. Perhaps there was an expectation of floods of transfers, or the formation of new Irish unions, as after 1922. The difference, which few mentioned, was the consequence of adding industrial Partition to political Partition, which, presumably, CIU members wanted to end. By accident or design, ITGWU personalities and speakers were largely absent from debates.

The first President of the CIU was Gerard Owens (Electrical Trades Union). Evidence of Government connivance was seen by the ITUC to be most patent in the selection of the CIU as sole Irish representative in the International Labour Organisation. The ITUC protested vigorously, but to no avail. O'Brien and O'Shannon travelled to Seattle in April 1946, making a 'good case with dexterity and forensic skill.' The whole affair was greeted triumphantly by CIU Delegates. Cries that the ITGWU was Partitionist McMullen thought rich, coming from 'people who have never been known to make as much as one speech in the past twenty-five years against the unnatural division of the country.' He asked, 'Was there anything more ludicrous than the spectacle of Officials of British Unions in Ireland commemorating the name of James Connolly, whose life's work was dedicated to undoing the conquest?'

Negotiations aimed at 'healing the breach' began almost immediately, but 'no serious intention' existed within 'the old Congress' of reconsidering its attitude. The ITGWU Delegates welcomed 'unity talks', and Jim Hickey trusted that the 'basis for the building of one united and progressive political Party, pledged to work for the Co-operative Ownership and Control of all wealth-producing resources by the people,' would emerge. The ITUC refused 'even as a long-term policy' to consent to the 'liquidation of the English form' of union in Ireland.

Much was made of the General Secretary of the British TGWU, Arthur Deakin, claiming that Ireland was 'part and parcel of Britain.' It fuelled an already blazing fire. That Deakin was a 'Commander of the Order of the British Empire' seemed appropriate. The CIU resented the fact that British unions had to consult their Executives, which could veto their moves (although in any union this was standard procedure). McMullen made the ITGWU's position clear: 'Oneness of aim, method and purpose is the *sine qua non* of unity, with the acceptance of sovereignty' of the Irish movement as 'the essential pre-requisite.' It was an 'anachronism of the first magnitude to have foreign-controlled Unions operating in a politically independent state.' This, of course, ignored Northern Ireland, which was not 'politically independent'.

Nixie Boran (Moneenroe) suggested that a more inclusive 'basis of unity' was in the 'promotion of close fraternal relations' between English and Irish movements 'based on the recognition of their respective independences.'

Discussions with the ITUC were organised by the Tánaiste, Lemass, from July 1946 and inched agonisingly forward. The CIU accused the ITUC of refusing to commit itself to anything more than a Joint Consultative Committee, while it insisted on prior commitment to the principle of Irish control of all union affairs. In March 1947 approaches led by James Larkin Junior were rebuffed, as all discussions 'must be official' and 'in writing.'

A letter from Roddy Connolly, Wicklow Unity Committee, got similar short shrift. At the 1947 CIU Congress Dan McAllister saw Belfast ITGWU members as 'holding a bridgehead' for Irish trade unionism. He believed that the 'unity of our country' could be achieved on the same principles as Congress: 'the recognition of the sovereign status of our country and the sovereign status' of the movement. Senator Foran, encouraged by younger Delegates, believed that 'as long as there were British unions here we could not have a free country or a united country.'

The CIU spent huge amounts of time justifying its position under the heading 'Support for Congress', the same speech being made over and over, the same windmills tilted at. Who were they trying to convince? Minds were focused when Lemass suggested a new Trade Union Act to replace those Sections struck out by the NUR case. Unions would have to have a Head Office within the state. The Government might enforce what union division could not, but probably at the price of industrial Partition. McMullen welcomed the Minister's initiative. He blamed those Irish unions still associating with British unions, remarks aimed particularly at William Norton, Leader of the Labour Party and General Secretary of the Post Office Workers' Union. He reminded Norton that 'political unity would not come without industrial unity.' Division seemed as deep as it could be. Irish unions still affiliated to the ITUC were urged to switch allegiance to the CIU. Norton and the IWWU were accused of traitorous behaviour for supporting the NUR's constitutional action.

In 1949 McMullen called for a re-examination of the Report of the Trade Union Commission (1939) to attempt rationalisation. It opposed legislative remedies. Great annoyance was expressed in 1948 at the refusal of the Coalition Government to send an ILO Delegation to San Francisco. All manner of ulterior motives explained the decision, particularly that the Minister for Industry and Commerce, Dan Morrissey, an ancient enemy, had acceded to ITUC pressure. James Everett, Minister for Posts and Telegraphs, provided a simpler explanation: 'shortage of dollars.'

Ideological differences between the CIU and ITUC were an added obstacle. The ITUC's affiliation to the 'Communistically dominated' World Federation of Trade Unions, albeit then suspended, contrasted with the CIU's desire to link with the International Federation of Christian Trade Unions. The ITGWU had no sympathy with the 'pernicious creed of Communism.' It felt 'the deepest abhorrence concerning the cruelties and indignities . . . inflicted on the leaders of all the Christian Churches in those Soviet satellite states' and joined protests 'of the civilised world against these barbarities.'

In 1949 Seán Dunne TD took part in a demonstration against the Ireland Act at the British Labour Party Conference in Blackpool. James Gilhooley (Dublin No. 6/8) asked how anyone could 'take seriously' his actions 'when at least four of his colleagues in the Dáil were members of British unions.' Dunne's union, the WUI, was 'affiliated with and sponsored by the British-dominated' ITUC. The British Government, 'taking a line from the actions and utterances' of the ITUC and Irish Labour Party, might well have felt 'they were acting in accordance with the wishes' of both. McMullen rejected the notion that the CIU were 'Partitionists,' pursuing OBU by stealth. The ITGWU was proud to be a 32-County organisation and would do nothing to sever Northern workers from their Southern comrades. OBU proposals in 1939 for ten or twelve industrial organisations were supported even though they 'would have shed half of their members' to them.

The British Labour Party's support for the Ireland Act (1949) was a 'gross betrayal' and 'display of bigotry and hypocrisy.' The ITGWU was unequivocal: 'Let there be no mincing of words, no Irish man with any manhood' or 'any pride in his nationality would remain a member of a British union when he could join' an Irish one. Unity seemed far distant.

At Christmas 1949 *Liberty* took issue with those who thought

> there is no reason for supposing that the existence of these unions in Ireland is in any way a threat to the independence of either industry or labour in the country . . . No reason! Aren't the British unions backing the British Government up to the hilt in its campaign to flood Ireland with British goods? Weren't many hundreds of Irish clothing workers thrown out of employment last year because of the importation of British goods?

British trade unionism in Ireland was 'a menace to the best interests of Ireland and her people.'[14]

RELATIONS WITH OTHER UNIONS

In 1946 an indication of increased hostility came with considerations of republishing *The Attempt to Smash the Irish Transport and General Workers' Union*. Conversely, the Irish National Teachers' Organisation was privately granted a loan of £10,000 during a major strike, its affiliation to the ITUC no impediment.

In 1949 there was a lengthy dispute with the Irish Automobile Drivers' and Automobile Mechanics' Union over its organising outside Dublin, though the terms of its affiliation to the CIU confined its activity to the capital. Although the ITGWU supported the affiliation of the Guild of Irish Journalists to the CIU, the union recruited forty-two journalists to Dublin No. 1 Branch in May. When 120 members of the Association of Shipbuilding and Engineering Draughtsmen sought transfer they were 'not encouraged.' They were 'more appropriate to an Engineering Union'—a reflection of the ITGWU's reluctance to embrace technical, professional or white-collar workers.

An Inter-Relations Committee with the ATGWU was established on 30 October 1947. The ITGWU was favoured in a dispute in which ATGWU cranemen prevented dockers gaining access to port facilities and granted them transfers in Dublin, Drogheda, Dungarvan and Portlaw. The ATGWU's refusal to acknowledge them was clearly contrary to the spirit of the Agreement. The matter was discussed by the Inter-Relations Committee on 25 July, but the fragility of relations was clear when the NEC determined that if the ATGWU continued opposition 'it might be necessary for us to declare our intention to take over the members in question with or without the consent of that Union.'[15]

EMPLOYMENT

At the 1946 Congress of the CIU Kennedy expressed concerns about army demobilisation. He pledged to protect and maintain trade unionists' positions while offering assistance in accommodating those re-entering civilian life. There were not enough jobs to go around. Persistent unemployment led to calls for the prevention of juveniles working overtime and the introduction of a five-day, forty-hour week.

The Industrial Research and Standards Act (1946) was welcomed, as 'scientific research nowadays plays an increasing part in the economic utilisation of natural resources,' and 'no progressive country can afford to neglect making the fullest use of scientific methods.' McMullen was a member of the Institute of Industrial Research and Standards. In 1947 the removal of protective tariffs and moves towards European free trade were recommended, a brave call given the slowness of economic recovery. The ITGWU wanted improvements in marketing agricultural produce, worker-representatives on the Irish Tourist Board, the inspection of hotels and restaurants and measures to guarantee fuel supplies.

In 1949 the ITGWU used economic arguments in its campaign against British unions. Britain was accused of dumping cheap goods in Ireland. The ITGWU reconsidered protection and condemned the import of foreign fertiliser. It wanted a 'policy of decentralisation' to help balance rural populations and slow emigration. The first 'Support Irish Industry Campaign' was mounted, with posters and an advertising slogan, 'BE IRISH and BUY IRISH.' The ITGWU cited Connolly:

> We affirm it is our belief that the working-class of Ireland should prevent, by united action, the conquest of the Irish market by any capitalist or merchant whose factories or workshops are not manned by members of their organisation, by all foreign manufacturers and all Irish employers of scab or blackleg labour.

Government purchasing policy should be 'Buy Irish.' The ITGWU attacked the Industrial Development Authority, created in May without consulting the CIU. Éamon Wall (Cork) thought it was set up 'under the shadow of failure.'[16]

INDUSTRIAL RELATIONS

At the 1945 CIU Congress McMullen called for the 'establishment of competent Industrial Courts or Labour Courts,' spelling out the model of independent Chairman, workers' and employers' representatives. The Industrial Relations Act (1946) marked the end of emergency regulation and established the Labour Court. It was welcomed, though much depended on the personnel appointed. There was delight when Cathal O'Shannon became the Workers' Representative. Employers thought it should have compulsory powers, with binding effect on workers, an opinion necessarily opposed by the unions. Problems soon arose. In April 1947, 'in order to expedite settlements on behalf of our members,' it was 'necessary to place one of the Union's cars at the disposal of the Conciliation Officers' to enable them to reach their cases. In June, McMullen thought 'hasty judgement' on the Labour Court should be stayed, as 'it was launched upon an uncharted sea of wage-fixing without a compass to guide it.' In the circumstances, 'it had done reasonably well.' A weakness was that after a recommendation was rejected and a strike ensued, no further involvement by the Department of Industry and Commerce was possible. 'This *ex cathedra* attitude must be changed.' Some employers perceived recommendations as binding, thus subtly introducing 'the thin edge of the wedge of compulsory arbitration.' While reluctant to strike, and then only as a last resort, the ITGWU would 'never under any conceivable set of circumstances' agree to abandon that right. The CIU made it clear that suggested legislation to prohibit strikes in essential services would be bitterly opposed. Against disputes settled peaceably, strikes were 'negligible in the extreme.'

The ITGWU made great use of Joint Industrial Councils and Joint Labour Committees to improve wages and conditions and as organising tools. Fifteen JLCs were created from old Trade Boards in 1946. Wage increases and a fortnight's holiday were sought from all JLCs, where virtually 100% ITGWU membership existed.

In 1947 Hickey (Cork No. 1) felt it was 'time they realised that much of the existing economic system required ending.' The proportion of national income going to wages was very small. Was it 'too much to hope' that the Labour Court 'would fix a basic income for every worker?' J. Doolan (Cork No. 1) thought that the Court appeared to be holding the 1939 rate plus 50%, an attitude that 'required little imagination.' The Government's 'low-wage policy' lay at the heart of things, inevitably raising questions about the independence of the Labour Court. As far as Ministers and others responsible for setting 'scandalous and unjust' rates were concerned, 'the best we can hope' is 'when they spend a few moments at night communing with their God before retiring that they will examine their consciences and ask themselves if they are doing to others as they would have done to them.'

The Conference placed its faith in third-party intervention, however, calling for conciliation machinery for local authority workers. In the Labour Court's first full year the ITGWU featured in more than 100 of its 125 recommendations, although the 'vast majority' of claims were 'adjusted without reference to the Court.' In 1948, while not indulging in 'any trenchant or censorious admonitions or reproaches,' and 'appreciating the difficulties' under which the Court operated, the ITGWU placed on record 'its protests against some of the decisions made . . . against the weight of the evidence,' which were 'stamped with the hallmark of expediency rather than of justice.' 'Compromise, not equity' was the key. Where decisions were considered unfair or unsatisfactory the union struck 'superior settlements by subsequent direct negotiations with employers.' The Court accepted some criticism. It would be more circumspect in future and not investigate every single case. It reiterated that the purpose of the Act was 'to assist the organisations to discharge their responsibilities, but not to relieve them of responsibility.' Neither employer nor union could automatically assume the Court's intervention. It had no intention of doing their work for them.

By 1949 J. McElhinney (Galway) thought the Labour Court had 'not lived up to expectations.' It was 'merely a part of the bureaucratic machine,' more concerned with 'preserving its dignity' than 'endeavouring to effect a satisfactory settlement.' Workers 'had lost faith' in it. It had 'out-lived its usefulness—if it ever had any— and should be abolished.' Given the 'unsatisfactory nature' of decisions in 1947 and 1948, the union was 'reluctant to make use of it' and referred fewer than a hundred cases. Conciliation was 'far more successful,' and the great majority of referrals were settled.

The union reminded the Labour Court of its duty under Section 68 (1) of the Act.

The Court, having investigated a trade dispute, shall make a Recommendation setting forth its opinion on the merits of the dispute and the terms on which, in the public interest and with a view to promoting industrial peace, it should be settled, due regard being had to the fairness of the said terms to parties concerned, and the prospects of said terms being acceptable to them.

It then asked, 'Now, can it be said with truth that the Recommendations of the Court invariably, or even in the majority of cases, indicate the implementation of this duty? Unfortunately, it can not.' The union cited the Dublin freight strike. Common sense was absent, and the recommendation couched in 'insulting terms.' Its rejection was self-evident. Few of the 350 recommendations issued granted workers' claims in full, and the Court had often recommended that the Eleven-Shilling Formula not be paid. 'Is it any wonder that workers in general firmly believe that the Court's approach to wage matters is based not on equity, not on fairness, but on the "split the difference" procedure?' The Court seldom challenged employers' pleas of inability to pay, thereby encouraging the 'exploitation of the workers by racketeers and budding capitalists, native and foreign.'

Allowing CIÉ to employ legal Counsel was heavily criticised. It led to legal wrangling and encouraged employers' fudge and filibuster. Whereas unions provided all data required in writing, employers often did not. Such 'discrimination' was keenly felt. Finally, the Labour Court's 'dilatoriness' was a major complaint. An application by the ITGWU for a JLC for messengers in Dublin and Dún Laoghaire waited nineteen months for a decision. The Court on occasion refused to endorse JLC outcomes, which could become legally binding only after its sanction. This was considered 'an extraordinary attitude', given the prior agreement of the employers and workers concerned.

In addressing the Court's personalities the ITGWU regarded their attitude as 'not conducive to pacific and satisfactory hearings' or of 'creating confidence.' Members inclined to be 'rather superior and at times contemptuous' towards workers and were 'more judicial than judicious in their approach.' The Court's attitude in refusing to investigate a blatant case for building workers in Peamount Sanatorium, Co. Dublin, without a full written statement in advance from the union was an example of uneven-handedness: the employers were asked for nothing! The ITGWU took matters to the Minister, as it cost £25,000 to maintain the Court.

It concluded: 'No individual or body regrets or deplores the failings of the Court more than this Union.' Officers, Officials and members were 'most anxious' for its success and were 'prepared at all times to do everything possible to assist towards that end.' Criticism was 'entirely without personal motive' but an 'endeavour to make the Court more effective in settling disputes and preventing industrial unrest.'

In 1947 McMullen called for Works Councils on the Swedish model to advance industrial management. Hickey (Cork No. 1) thought workers had a right to 'have a voice in the control and regulation of industry.' It would make it possible for their 'skill, experience and co-operation' to be fully drawn upon. A start should be made in 'State-financed industries' with profit-sharing schemes. Conroy wanted conciliation machinery for local Government workers to rid County and City Managers of absolute power. John F. Gill said that since the County Management Act elected Councillors had about as much say in local affairs as 'people in the Fiji Islands.'[17]

HOLIDAYS

In 1946 the ITGWU initiated a campaign for a fortnight's paid holiday. T. O'Reilly (Dublin No. 3) thanked the union for its support of Dublin laundry workers, 'without which the strike might have had a very different ending.' Dublin dockers won twelve days' leave as part of decasualisation arrangements. By the end of the year 40,000 members were 'assured' of a fortnight's annual leave, although attempts to amend the Holidays (Employees) Act (1939) were unsuccessful. In 1949 it was suggested that legislation be brought into line with industrial practice. P. J. O'Brien wanted Good Friday to be declared a public holiday.[18]

Although scarcely mentioned in the history of the fortnight's paid holiday campaign, on the ground and across negotiating tables the ITGWU was a formidable force. Most members enjoyed paid holidays before others.

HOUSING

In 1948 the ITGWU asked the Government to introduce a scheme for building working-class housing with direct labour, similar to those of Flint Borough Council in Wales and started in Strokestown, Co. Roscommon. It was suggested that the CIU set up a building society.

McMullen wondered about the legalities and referred to the ITGWU's policy of investment in local authority stock, while supporting the idea. Congress decided that it was impracticable, as liquid funds were needed for dispute eventualities. Pressure was instead applied to the Minister to 'produce houses by direct labour' and to follow central purchasing policy for materials.

In 1949 it was again asked, Why not build directly? Housing was a national emergency, the 'appalling' shortage estimated to be 44,511 in urban areas and 16,337 in rural areas. Problems with 'non-Federated contractors' resulted in the union referring the matter under the Housing (Amendment) Act (1948), which contained a 'fair employment' condition compelling employers to pay union rates or above on pain of having grants withheld. Some 20,000 workers were employed in construction, 'the vast majority' ITGWU members.

Poor housing was linked to the high incidence of TB. In 1946 the union wanted it to be made 'imperative that essential food, such as meat and bread, be sufficiently protected against contamination, exposure and mishandling.' In 1947 it looked for the provision of 'adequate weekly payments, not less than their normal weekly wages,' for the upkeep of TB patients during illness and convalescence. It was thought that this would encourage earlier diagnosis and treatment.[19] Poor housing and inadequate household incomes were well understood to significantly contribute to TB.

TAX AND SOCIAL WELFARE

In 1947 the ITGWU demanded increased personal allowances to compensate for a decline in real wages: £374 for married men, £204 for single men and parallel rises in exemptions from compulsory national health and widows' and orphans' insurance as well as 'substantial increases' in benefits. Amendment was sought to the Unemployment Insurance Act (1920) by providing that 'in the case of a stoppage of work due to a trade dispute, only such employees of the firm with which the dispute exists, as are immediately implicated in the matters in dispute, shall be disqualified from receiving Unemployment Benefit.' Substantial increases in old-age pensions and the abolition of the means test were sought, with the re-implementation of the Dental Treatment Scheme.

In 1948 the 'overdue implementation of a Social Security Scheme' based on that 'advocated by His Lordship, the Most Reverend Dr. Dignan' was demanded. Dan Spring TD took issue with known Fianna Fáil speakers supporting it, given that the Fianna Fáil Government defeated the proposal in the Dáil.

In 1949 a series of motions called for a 'national scheme of Social Insurance.' In October the long-awaited Social Security Scheme was announced by William

Norton, Leader of the Labour Party and Minister for Social Welfare. The various national health, unemployment and widows' and orphans' pension schemes were replaced by one contributory scheme, providing compulsory coverage of every employed person over the age of sixteen. The ITGWU welcomed the proposals.[20]

SAFETY AND HEALTH

In 1946 the ITGWU called for a forty-hour week and the appointment of additional Factory Inspectors. The answer to improving safety and health was prescriptive legislation, enforced by an army of Inspectors. Factory Acts should compel employers to 'provide more suitable accommodation, ventilation, floor space and cubic space,' canteens and cloak room accommodation. Pneumoconiosis should be certified as an industrial disease under the Workmen's Compensation Acts.

In 1947 increases in 'Wet Time' payments for construction workers were sought. Purcell wanted 'more adequate payments' under new compensation schemes, detailing costs, delays and inadequacies of common law actions for workers.

In 1949 the ITGWU sought a coal industry Advisory Committee, with miners' pensions a priority. A significant novel idea was moved by Dublin No. 9 (Bus) Branch, which urged that 'legislative provision be made for the setting up of Health Committees' in major industries. They would have equal numbers of management and Workers' Representatives, with a 'Medical representative nominated and remunerated by the Department of Health' as neutral Chairman, to 'consider how the improved health and well-being of workers' would increase production, 'implement measures for the safeguarding and improving' of workers' health and 'make suitable arrangements for rehabilitation' after sickness or accident. This was the first occasion on which joint structures were proposed. It cleverly emphasised the incentive of 'increased production,' introducing the then far from widespread understanding that safer, healthier working environments were more productive, profitable ones.

Concern for workers' occupational health partly emanated from national anxiety about TB. D. Gaffney (Dublin No. 1) deplored the fact that after more than a quarter of a century of native Government 'more effective legislation for the safeguarding of all workers against injury and disease' was not instituted. The Government, in consultation with a joint council of union and employers' representatives, should draft legislation, with 'effective enforcement of its provisions by Inspectors having special training and experience.' This was very far-sighted, coming nearly forty years before the Barrington Commission undertook the investigation requested.[21]

Conor O'Brien (Dublin No. 3) wanted 'snap inspections' of factories, reflecting the widely held belief that employers received notice and prepared their premises accordingly.

LIBERTY HALL

Motions by Dublin District Council on the 'rebuilding of Liberty Hall and Branch Premises' were ruled out of order in 1946. Concerns about the building's condition were raised at the NEC. Total income from rent paid by Branches and tenants was £1,028 9s 6d, less outgoings of £426 13s 5d, giving a net annual income of £601 16s 1d. The average annual repair bill since 1940 was £115. A new roof was required.

Premises in Parnell Square and Inchicore, Dublin, in Cork, Drogheda, Limerick, Sligo, Tralee and Blanchardstown generated an annual income of £1,115 18s 5d. There was a suggestion that, as part of a Town Planning Scheme, Liberty Hall could be rebuilt. Enquiries were made to the City Manager, but Liberty Hall was 'not affected by any Town Planning proposals,' leaving the ITGWU dependent on its own resources.

In 1947 Robbins (Dublin No. 7) sought the 'rebuilding of Liberty Hall as a National memorial to Connolly and his comrades, our tribute for their heroic sacrifice.' McMullen acknowledged that the 'building was unsatisfactory,' but there were problems. Tenants had to be 'heavily compensated,' and the costs of the project would be 'formidable.' The NEC had 'no definite policy.'

Tom McCarthy and Bill Murphy, Liberty Hall Branch Secretaries, demanded a 'statement of policy' in 1948. The NEC now 'favoured reconstruction.' The large Dublin membership made matters acute: either it would be rebuilt or new premises acquired 'elsewhere in the city.' Construction costs were estimated at £250,000.[22] Prospect Hill, Galway, was purchased for £2,500 and Mainguard Street sold for £16,000 in November 1949.

LIBERTY

The union's experience of publishing a paper had not been a 'happy one.' There was 'no demand' and 'no use publishing' it 'if the members would not read it.' Even when given out free it was not circulated. An NEC Sub-Committee costed a monthly print run of 2,000 and suggested Desmond Ryan as editor. It would cost £500 to £1,000 a year for 5,000 copies a month. Selling at 1d a copy, a 'certain loss would be inevitable.' Delegates were enthusiastic and wanted subjects beyond industrial relations: economics, art, and foreign affairs, an attractive design, with competitions and advertising to defray costs. The impact on morale justified any loss.

Kevin Aspell became manager of *Liberty: Official Organ of the ITGWU*. In 'deference to strong demands' the NEC hoped it would get the support it deserved. Purcell was surprised at the lack of criticism, as the General Officers 'were not altogether satisfied.' Massive union activity was quite impossible to encapsulate in an Annual Report. Members were recommended to keep abreast by reading *Liberty*, which first appeared in June 1948, containing 'most of the ingredients necessary for success,' produced in an attractive form and printed 'on good quality paper.' Articles on 'political, trade union, industrial and general affairs' supplemented union news, film reviews and matters of 'special interest to women,' GAA followers and gardeners.

At a price of 4d, 'it did not receive the support expected.' It was kept going only at 'considerable expense, time and trouble,' despite repeated appeals to Branches. 'Even more deplorable' was the Officials' lack of response. The NEC expressed 'grave dissatisfaction,' not just with the financial return 'but also with the matter published.' It was 'deemed unsuitable for an organ of the Union.' Writing in November,

McMullen said the best medium for studying working-class problems and becoming acquainted with union 'affairs, difficulties and activities' was 'your own paper.' 'It is yours. Buy it, read it, write for it, and endeavour to get your comrades and friends to do likewise. The success or otherwise of *Liberty* depends on you. I know you will not let it down.'[23]

STAFF

Frank Robbins (Dublin No. 7) complained in 1947 that 'many Officials were completely worn out,' working eleven hours a day, seven days a week. He did not seek 'exceptional treatment' but was 'asking—nay, demanding—that they be given fair play.' M. Ryan (Clonmel) said the union's prestige would suffer, as 'employers could not be expected to take the Union's demands seriously' if 'their wages and conditions were far superior' to those given to the staff. Conroy accepted that staff pressures were great. Extra personnel were appointed to Cork, Dublin and Limerick.

Acquiring staff was no simple matter. Education was not enough: 'personality counted for a lot.' An Official 'must possess more than mere physical or mental qualifications. He must be willing to make sacrifices.' Low wages would not attract 'young intelligent men,' who would be 'badly needed.' P. McNamara (Limerick) thought Officials were 'over-worked and under-paid.' McMullen resisted staff claims, although 'fully convinced that it was in the Union's best interests' to break the policy of relating Officials' wages 'to those of the members.' Their pay should accord with their duties and responsibilities.

A staff representative, P. J. O'Brien, complained that they had no voice in fixing their wages, that they wanted negotiated scales, their managerial duties recognised, personal financial worries eased, and a recognition that the job was becoming more complex. With 130,000 members, Thomas O'Reilly (Dublin No. 3) worried that expansion would be hampered by insufficient staff. 'An army without officers would become indisciplined. They needed more—a great many more Organisers.'[24]

EDUCATION

In 1947 Jim Hickey (Cork No. 1) looked for a statistical Department to assist Officials. In Cork a two-year diploma course in social and economic science was introduced with assistance from Dr Alfred O'Rahilly and Rev. Jerome O'Leary. Eight ITGWU students graduated. Éamonn Wall (Acting Secretary, Cork No. 1) gained first-class honours. In 1948 the scheme was extended to Limerick and Waterford. Rev. E. J. Coyne established a two-year diploma in association with the CIU and University College, Dublin, with twenty-two ITGWU students. C. Moore (Dublin No. 6/8) thanked the NEC for the opportunity given to him 'to further his education'— a typical reaction from participants.

Delegates seemed content that education should be conducted externally. P. J. O'Brien suggested that all Vocational Education Committees implement schemes. In 1949 Bill Murphy (Dublin No. 9) moved the publication of Connolly's works 'at a popular price.' A Section in Irish in Annual Reports was welcomed, and the union's title was printed in English and Irish on membership cards. In 1948 a report on 'Comóradh 1798' featured a floodlit Liberty Hall with the streamer 'We Serve Neither King Nor Kaiser But Ireland.'[25]

ANTI-COMMUNISM

At the 1946 Congress of the CIU the Bishop of Galway set a tone, focusing on Catholic social teaching. He was clearly well pleased that his audience were 'unmistakably Irish and not subject to any alliances or extraneous influences.' In 1947 Congress sought the implementation of the report of the Commission on Vocational Organisation to achieve the 'Christian way of life.'

In 1949 P. J. O'Brien (Cork No. 2) condemned alleged 'religious persecution in eastern Europe' and the 'brutal treatment' of Church dignitaries. There was an 'ever-widening attempt' to 'uproot the Christian way of life.' Professor Alfred O'Rahilly warned that ridding the movement of Communism was no easy task. 'Today, Communism is crypto-Communism. If you put the Communist out one door in the clothes of Stalin, he will come back dressed as Wolfe Tone through the back door.' Workers needed training as 'brothers in Christ with a spiritual destination' that would reject Communism. He had 'opened the gates' of UCC for that purpose. O'Brien wanted Good Friday as a public holiday so that 'Ireland, a pioneer State in the endeavour to uphold Christian values,' could make a gesture against the 'wave of religious hatred that was sweeping the world.' The International Federation of Christian Trade Unions 'wished God's blessing on your proceedings.' Delegates considered affiliation as an important bulwark against Communism.[26]

POLITICS

At the 1947 Congress of the CIU, with confidence that it was now firmly rooted, the Central Council was asked to explore the feasibility of a political arm. No mention was made of the National Labour Party. The mover's union was affiliated to the Labour Party and expressed dissatisfaction, particularly with William Norton's attitude on remaining within the ITUC. The NLP was seen only as a basis for a solution.

In 1948 Herbert Devoy (Thomastown) moved that 'no national or political purpose can now be served' by further discussion with the ITUC or the Labour Party unless the 'fundamental principles of complete sovereignty' for Irish Labour were recognised. It was a hard line that distanced the ITGWU from unity proposals. It seemed that Party divisions were irreversible.

Eleven ITGWU members contested the 1948 General Election for the NLP. The CIU concluded a pact with the NLP. The Labour Party polled 115,074 first-preference votes and won fourteen seats, while the NLP polled 34,015 for its five. J. A. Costello of Fine Gael (31 seats) led an Inter-Party Government with support from the Labour Party, National Labour Party, Clann na Talmhan (7), Clann na Poblachta (10) and independents (12). Norton became Tánaiste and Minister for Social Welfare, while T. J. Murphy held Local Government, James Everett (NLP) Posts and Telegraphs, Seán MacBride and Noël Browne (Clann na Poblachta) External Affairs and Health.

The NEC circulated Branches regarding the NLP's decision to enter Coalition. Anxious to avoid 'internal dissension,' their intention was 'a dispassionate condensation of the facts.'

On 11 February the NEC felt the NLP 'should preserve their independence': 'no approach should be made to Fianna Fáil' or any other party. If Fianna Fáil approached the NLP it would have to commit itself to a 'national scheme of social security,' abandon its low-wage policy for road and rural workers, abolish the means test for old-age pensions and increase pensions for the aged, blind, widows and orphans, enact conciliation machinery for county councils, eliminate 'alien control' in Irish unions, reduce the cost of living by price control and production efficiency, advance housing construction to eliminate slums and tuberculosis, cancel increased duties on beer, tobacco and cinemas introduced in the supplementary Budget, arrest emigration by providing employment and guarantee that there would be no future General Election unless on a major issue. The NEC 'advised against participation' in Inter-Party Government.

On 17 February five NLP TDs met the ITGWU General Officers and informed them that they were entering the Government. Canvassing experience taught them that working-class voters were embittered against Fianna Fáil because of emergency wage restrictions, the low-wage policy and the suppression of agricultural wages and pegging of county council workers to those rates. There was a desire for change. De Valera's refusal to enter an arrangement with any other party meant that they could only support a Fianna Fáil minority Government. This would almost certainly bring another election, in which they felt their support would be punished. If Inter-Party Government proved 'hostile to the efforts to rid' the movement of outside control they would withdraw.

At the 1948 Congress of the CIU McMullen defended the NLP Deputies. They acted against the NEC's wishes but were not 'guilty of betraying' the movement. James Hickey TD felt that events proved the wisdom of their actions. P. J. O'Brien insisted that they had broken the pledge they had signed. John O'Leary TD interjected: 'Are we going to listen to this, lads?' Tom Foran said that he 'could have had privilege and profit but I lost them through principle.' His contempt for Fine Gael could not have been plainer: 'We have thrown in our lot with Fascists.' Perhaps in retirement Foran could be more forthright than McMullen, who had initiated an increasingly acrimonious debate by holding out an olive branch. The NEC decided it did 'not serve the best interests' of the union to 'adopt any drastic action which might lead to a severance of relations with the Deputies or the precipitation of a General Election.'[27]

Chapter 21 ∽

IN THE SHADOW OF LARKIN'S DEATH: THE WUI IN THE 1940s

LARKIN'S DEATH

Concerns about James Larkin's declining health deepened in late 1946. On 29 November the GEC decided that a 'deputation [should] wait upon the General Secretary next Sunday morning at 10.30 a.m. to urge upon him the unanimous desire' that 'in the interest of the Union and his own health he would take a holiday of not less than two or three weeks as soon as he found it practicable, but not later than Christmas.' A cheque for £50 was drawn for his 'holiday expenses.' By 24 January 1947 an anxious GEC wanted the 'holiday money' to defray 'medical expenses' instead. A shocked GEC on 6 February moved a 'vote of condolence' with 'Mr. James Larkin, T.D., and relatives on his recent sad bereavement.'

Public acknowledgement was placed in the press 'in reply to the messages of condolence received officially by' the WUI. The GEC then 'adjourned as a mark of respect.' Emmet O'Connor insightfully notes: 'It says a lot about Jim's continuing attachment to Elizabeth [his estranged wife] that his own health deteriorated not long after her death on 2 December, 1945 at Young Jim's home in Bray.'

Larkin died on 30 January, leaving £4 10s in cash and a personal estate valued at £16 12s 6d. William Martin Murphy, who died in 1919, left a personal estate of £264,000, of which £2,000 was left for charitable purposes. In 1998 Donal Nevin estimated this fortune to be worth more than £9 million at that time.

The WUI bore Larkin's funeral expenses. A General Meeting in the Mansion House gave members the 'opportunity of paying their own particular tribute.' There was immediate talk of a Memorial Fund, the collection of material for a biography and exhibition, and calls for a James Larkin Branch of the Labour Party. James Junior was appointed Acting General Secretary until the Annual Delegate Conference. Surprisingly, the attendance at the Mansion House on 17 February was 'poor', blamed partly on bad weather and inadequate notice, although the GEC regarded these as feeble excuses from a membership of 12,000.

John Smithers, General President, addressed the union's Conference in June, four months after the loss of the 'dynamic presence of our beloved Leader.' Larkin had 'disdained to accept as the criterion for successful Trade Unionism, the possession of a large bank balance' but ever sought to 'raise the living standards of the toiling people as the only capital worth accumulating, as the only justification for the existence of a Trade Union.' The WUI had to 'sustain the loss of a courageous Leader,' one 'always at hand to provide us with inspiration' at a time when members were 'clamouring for substantial wage adjustments,' 'every Section demanding an impossible priority.'

Larkin Junior chose his father's death to appeal for unity. Smithers echoed his sentiment. 'We wholeheartedly welcome the measure of success that appeal has already had and we shall do our utmost to assist in helping him and his colleagues to realise a strong, united industrial and political movement of the Irish Working Class.'

The WUI was consciously proud of what, in its view, made it different. 'Comrades, we have splendid traditions.' The WUI was 'unique' and 'consciously based on the philosophy of Larkin and Connolly, refusing to submit to the narrow confines of mere economism.' Its broad outlook associated it 'with the manifold struggle of all Sections of our class, realising that every fight on whatever field, brings nearer the day when the dreams of countless Larkins and Connollys may be realised in a full and happy life for all.'

Young Jim, in his opening words as Acting General Secretary, felt that a 'fundamental change must take place in this Union.' His father was irreplaceable. He hoped, for his own part, 'to act as part of a team, not only of the Officials but every member.' They all had duties in the vanguard of industrial and political movements. In addition, he acknowledged the demise of Jack Connolly, a Delegate and a founder-member.

The WUI was in a parlous state. In 1959 Young Jim reflected that 'those of us who know the full story were doubtful that the union would last another twelve months. We had less than £5,000 and of that we owed at least half.'[1]

Congress began its Annual Report with the 'Death of Jim Larkin', reproducing the graveside oration of William Norton, Leader of the Labour Party, together with the remarkable letter to the *Irish Times* by Larkin Junior on 3 February 1947 in his personal capacity. The letter, reproduced here in full, held out olive Branches for any doves that might fly from Labour ships then battling rough seas of division, disunity, personal animus and no little despair.

Dear Sir,

   It is necessary for me to seek the courtesy of your columns because in the first place this letter is not and cannot, by its very purpose, be addressed directly to any person or organisation, and in the second place it is of concern to so many who can only become aware of it through the medium of the Press.

   Tonight I am writing letters to many persons and organisations to thank them for their expressions of sympathy on a loss, which by family name, is personal to me, but which is equally or even in greater degree, the loss of many thousands. But before doing so I feel that there is one letter which must be written by someone, and could be written even more forcibly by so many, yet, lest it be overlooked, I am writing it.

This day a man was laid to rest with the great dead of our race. Of his claim to that resting place many tongues have spoken during these past few days and a deep and wide-flung emotional wave has swept over great numbers of people. That common emotion, that appreciation of loss, has been keenest among working men and women and the organisations, political and industrial, in which they associate. Whatever be the measure of his claim to their thoughts and feelings, Jim Larkin has been mourned and his passing deeply regretted by persons and organisations in every Section and Division of the Irish Labour Movement.

Stirred by a common emotion, these diverse groups and persons have found that they hold in common certain simple, yet great, beliefs, which have been brought sharply to the surface by the death of this man. They have found that they possessed a common bond, because being of the Labour Movement they found their common heritage added to by the unique service of the dead man and the essential unity of labour has been indicated by the value placed by them on his life work in the broad stream of Irish Labour.

If it be true that Irish workers have suffered a great loss, and if in that loss something common to all in the working-class movement has been manifest, surely now at this moment that which is most essential to Irish Labour can be given to Irish working men and women—a Labour Movement, united in purpose, in struggle, and in its objectives. Unity is not such a great benefit that it may be purchased at any price, but today unity of labour, industrial and political, is so urgently required that the price, even if it be costly, can and should be paid by those who are in a position to make sacrifices.

The great mass of working men and women who constitute the Irish Labour Movement must ardently desire that their strength and purpose should be added to a thousand-fold by all that flows from unity, and those in whose hands lies the giving or the withholding of that unity should not deny the living, vibrant mass of labour, made up of the bodies, minds and spirits of living men, that which they need so urgently.

Irish people are emotional, and perhaps our common emotion this day may give us that unity we need, where reason and argument has failed in the past.

I have no doubt of the truth of my statement when I declare that unity is the single quality sought for by the working men and women who constitute and who are the Irish Labour Movement and why, therefore, when so little stands between them and the unity they desire should they be denied it?

With this great man's death, the last of the great figures of Irish Labour has passed, and we who remain are little people. If among those of us who occupy leading positions in the Labour movement there be individuals who, for one reason or another, represent obstacles or barriers to unity, let us grow in stature by stepping aside so that unity may be realised; if there are difficulties of policy standing in the way, let us, as we did this day, find the simplest common denominator in policy and agree upon that as an immediate objective; if there are difficulties of organisation to be overcome, let us overcome them in the understanding that our organisations were built to serve Labour, not to shackle it.

Who shall make the first step? Naturally those whose devotion to Labour is greatest. If the greater measure of devotion is not expressed by those of us who by chance are playing leading roles, then let the real and living body of Labour—the rank-and-file—show us and compel us to do our duty, but let it be quick and decisive whoever takes the first step.

I have, as I stated above, written this letter because I feel it should be written now on this day of mourning and deep and common emotion. I have consulted no person. I speak for no organisation, neither the Union of which I am a member nor the political Party I support. Neither do I write it because of the name I bear, which is mine by accident of birth, but being the only possession this dead man had to leave me, an obligation devolves on me of putting in words that which tens of thousands of working men and women felt this day—their common emotion spreading from their common needs and striving in this life and united in that which is known as 'Irish Labour.'

—Yours faithfully,

James Larkin.

Larkin's death was studiously avoided by the ITGWU and the Congress of Irish Unions. Larkin Junior's patent commitment to the fundamental principle of unity in workers' class interest, the timing and language he chose, marked him out as a great man. He was not one of the 'little people' and would make a huge contribution to Irish Labour and society over the next two decades. John Swift, President of the ITUC in 1947, took Young Larkin's message to heart, suggesting that there could be 'no fitting honour' if 'we cannot find unity again in our movement.'

Sadly, J. T. O'Farrell (Railway Clerks' Association), recalling Larkin's 'very patriotic and unselfish appeal,' reported that two National Executive members were detailed to sound out the 'other side' to renew the broken talks. 'Their response was quite abrupt and hostile. In these circumstances it is quite useless to indulge in a lot of sloppy sentiment.'[2]

THE LARKIN MEMORIAL

Dublin Trades Union Council started off with grand plans for a Larkin Memorial Hall and a stone in Glasnevin. Its ambitious target was a fund of £50,000, to be managed by 'representative people' and a full-time Secretary, launched in the Mansion House. Unions were asked to subscribe, with £1 certificates of receipt issued, draft sketches of the hall made for publicity purposes, and Committees to be set up in Britain and the United States.

At the Conference Larkin welcomed DTUC's launch of the fund. He suggested £1 from each WUI member, to help 'provide a suitable memorial.' Ambitions were quickly trimmed in the wake of a disappointing response. It proved hard to get 'prominent people' to act as sponsors. The target was cut to £5,000, but it was 'hoped to get more.'

In January 1948 the first annual Larkin commemoration event was held in the Olympia Theatre, chaired by Councillor O'Keeffe. The speakers included the Labour Party Leader William Norton, Louie Bennett (IWWU) and the British Labour MP Will Lawther. A Brass Band with Peter O'Flanagan (Bakers' Union) as MC provided entertainment, with Harry Craig (London) doing recitations, Irish dancers, and Pipe Band and a souvenir programme for one shilling. In November 20,000 appeal forms were distributed with a plea to the GEC for a secretariat, an office and an advance of £500.

At the 1948 ITUC Congress J. Collins (DTUC) moved support for the Larkin Memorial Fund, the ambitious aim now £100,000. Thomas Kavanagh (WUI) spoke of Larkin's 'unquenchable' memory. Indifference to the fund quickly quenched expectations.

In 1949 John Smithers expressed disappointment at the 'little response to date.' Although the WUI had 25,000 members in Dublin, less than £1,000 was collected, and 'outside our Union, the lack of response is even more deeply marked.' There should be 'deep shame, even a sense of personal humiliation.' In 1949, Larkin in Belfast in 1907 and in Dublin in 1913 was recalled to stir emotions. There were no contributions from the floor, and precious few afterwards.[3]

MEMBERSHIP AND ORGANISATION

In June 1946 a Branch of the Irish Engineering and Foundry Union transferred to create No. 6 Branch for boiler-men, fitters' helpers and semi-skilled engineering workers. It was part of general expansion. The ATGWU invited the WUI onto the Committee of the ESB Group; William Jones, Carlow Mental Hospital, wrote asking to start a Branch; and 'Mr. Digby, Manager Pye Radio, opening in Waterford,' asked if the WUI would organise there, as he wanted all workers in one union. Larkin Junior cautioned about stretching the organisation beyond Dublin. The Clondalkin Branch, reporting 1,000 members, was, by WUI standards, a 'country Branch.' J. Kavanagh was despatched to Carlow and the mental hospital staff enrolled.

Anthony Brack, a controversial figure often at odds with the GEC, investigated a request from Arklow Pottery to transfer from the ITGWU, one of many similar invitations around the country the WUI was reluctant to pursue. The reasons varied. Foremen and chargehands in Kilkenny Boot Factory were turned down 'in view of the good relationship which existed between the Boot and Shoe Union and our own,' while loading agents in Tuam Sugar Factory were refused because they were seasonally employed. Potential members kept knocking on the door, including teachers in Artane Industrial School and Gas Company slot Collectors attempting to transfer from the Irish Seamen's and Port Workers' Union. Both were declined, on the grounds of unsuitability and no wish to offend another union. This latter camaraderie was shaken when it became known that the ISPWU had no compunction about taking in lapsed WUI men.

In November the GEC considered the staff situation. Eight Officials were interviewed before conclusions were reached: the staff was adequate relative to numbers, although numbers were rapidly expanding; there was no 'proper distribution of staff or powers,' and 'pressure on Head Office' was 'too great'; Head Office too often dealt 'with matters more relevant to Delegates or Branch Secretaries'; Delegates' responsibilities needed to be 'better defined,' and they should 'attend certain hours each week'; and all Section Committees must report to Branch Secretaries. Staff wages were increased, with the exception of the 'full-time carpenter', who was let go.

Table 63: WUI income, expenditure, Dispute Pay and surplus (£), 1945–9

Year	Income	Expenditure	Dispute Pay	Surplus
1945	15,029	18,480	7,196	3,164
1946	18,080	14,599	664	6,644
1947	25,358	18,540	1,261	13,462
1948	32,017	21,899	483	23,952
1949	31,637	25,751	4,061	29,837

Source: National Archives, Registrar of Friendly Societies, file 369T.

In January 1947 between seven and eight hundred employees in solicitors' offices wanted to enrol, but as the Irish Union of Distributive Workers and Clerks had already attempted the task, permission to proceed was requested. On 1 March, Christy Ferguson was employed as 'Negotiator and National Organiser'. His work 'commended itself.' Denis Larkin, Larkin Senior's other son, was appointed Assistant Branch Secretary, and the General President, Smithers, made full-time at £8 a week, although the 'Bakery Section would lose by his appointment.'

After Larkin's death the GEC reorganised Head Office staff as 'an urgent and pressing task.' A Finance Committee was set up to 'inquire into and supervise all payments over £5,' and staff wages were again raised to 50% above 1939 rates.

Young Larkin wasted little time in restructuring. Addressing the union's Conference, Smithers reported that wages improved by 40 to 70% in all major sections above the figures prevailing in 1939. Most members 'now enjoy extended annual holidays with pay.' He concluded: 'The Workers' Union of Ireland, ever in the Vanguard, yields to no one in its claim to be the foremost militant body of organised industrial workers.' In Dublin new Sections catered for dental mechanics, law clerks, legal typists and telephone mechanics and 'the very newest form of industrial activity, Civil Aviation.' Branches opened in Kinsale, Portarlington and Trim, with the promise of one in Dundalk. Smithers felt they could 'only absorb that which we can successfully digest.'

As membership increased, attention was paid to structures. Active Branch Committees, which clearly had not operated in the past, were called for.

The contribution was still 6d, but Larkin Junior suggested that it be raised to 1s for men, 8d for women, and 6d for boys and girls. Tony Quinn (Building Section) supported the increase but expressed general concern, as competing unions charged less. The increases were carried unanimously, although there were complaints from some members and 'arrangements made.' Dispute Benefit was raised to 30s a week, Marriage Benefit for women introduced, and increases in Funeral Benefits considered. Death Benefit gave a member's representative four to six times their contribution, but the WUI was 'not an Insurance Company.' In 1949 Larkin enunciated a fundamental tenet of policy: 'we never allow a member of this Union to be buried by charity.'

James Condron (Clondalkin), paper-mill worker and foundation member, headed the poll for election to the General Executive Committee. By Rule, six GEC members resigned each year. Ferguson, addressing the Delegates as 'Comrades,' spoke of the new General Secretary being 'particularly fortunate in his name.' He qualified this view: 'Actually, in one sense this has been a disadvantage, inasmuch as it has tended to obscure the man's own inherent qualities.' If they visualised 'other Trade Union leaders and compare their qualifications with those of the man we have chosen, we will realise he towers above them all on the basis of his personal merit.' Predictably, Young Larkin thought such praise 'unworthy'.

T. J. Murphy and Paddy McAuliffe, Labour Party Deputies, suggested starting Branches in Bantry, Charleville, Kinsale, Kanturk and Millstreet. They would assist, and Larkin agreed to visit Cork to investigate the scheme's viability. Patrick Agnew, former Stormont MP, was suggested as Northern Ireland Organiser. Charles Hopkins, Arigna, asked if miners could transfer from the ITGWU, as they 'felt that they were not receiving sufficient attention.' Many were 'in arrears and not seeking transfer' but could 'come in as new members.' The GEC would take no-one 'unless they had clear cards.' It was proposed that they be accepted together with forty more in Limerick, but Larkin insisted that it was 'not fair to take country members unless we can service them properly.'

After the 1947 ITUC Congress approaches were made suggesting that a Waterford Branch of 300–400 members be established. The GEC sought to appoint a Country Organiser to look after Cos. Carlow, Kildare, Limerick and Offaly. Seventeen applicants proved unsuitable, and Seán Nugent was asked to spend time in Tullamore. C. Byrne, Secretary of the Limerick Branch of the Federation of Rural Workers, offered to open a WUI Branch and 'do it for nothing.' T. J. Murphy suggested Crotty as the man to organise west Cork. He was given a three-month trial, opening Branches in Buttevant and Charleville.

In September, Frank Cluskey reported moves, apparently initiated by Belfast Butchers, for one 'National Union' and an All-Ireland meeting to discuss matters. The North of Ireland Operative Butchers' and Allied Workers' Association invited Cork, Limerick and Dublin butchers and porters to a meeting, but nothing was concluded.[4]

Membership grew, but fortunes were mixed. More than 1,000 ITGWU men employed in Ballyshannon on the Erne Scheme supposedly wanted to transfer, but although 200 men met in the Market Square, 'only two names were left in.' Limerick Law Clerks approached the WUI but joined the IUDWC.

Consideration of the transfer of the entire Grocers' Branch of the IUDWC illustrates WUI policy. Two conditions were needed: 'only benefit members would be accepted and no industrial claims would be made for six months after any transfer.' When 600 men in CIÉ Freight—ITGWU and NUR members—applied, forms were issued, but a 'clear majority' was needed before any deal.

By February 1948, Crotty suggested that 'his employment be terminated because of slow progress made,' although Branches existed in Buttevant, Charleville, Kanturk, Kinsale and perhaps Mitchelstown. Fifty-one National Health Insurance agents wished to join, spread over Cos. Donegal, Kilkenny, Leitrim, Mayo, Offaly, Roscommon and Waterford, and in Carlow, John King, Secretary, wanted the Mental Hospital Branch to become a general Branch, with sugar factory workers transferring. Larkin was doubtful: 'We would want to be very cautious regarding accepting sugar beet workers.'

Growth in Dublin necessitated the division of No. 1 Branch into five new Branches: No. 1 for dockers and miscellaneous firms, with 1,600 members; No. 2, public boards (1,500); No. 4, bakery, sugar, confectionery (1,200); No. 7, brewery, distillery, mineral water and tobacco (1,500); and No. 8, building trade (1,700). Each would have its own Committee and officers, but contributions and the marking of cards would 'still be done by staff of No. 1.'

In April the total membership was 15,481, with 11,593 in benefit. There had been no returns from Butchers, Butchers' Porters, Dún Laoghaire or Aer Lingus, so estimated membership was higher, at 17,280, with 12,800 in benefit. Affiliation to the ITUC was made for 17,000. By May, Denis Larkin was appointed Dublin District Secretary and the reorganisation completed. With part-time Branches operating in Buttevant, Charleville, Mitchelstown, Doneraile, Kanturk, Limerick, Waterford, Clondalkin and Howth, the Branches were:

No. 1	Dockers, carters, miscellaneous
No. 2	Public service
No. 3	Fuel, miscellaneous
No. 4	Sugar, confectionery, bakery
No. 5	Butchers' porters
No. 6	Engineering, railway
No. 7	Tobacco
No. 8	Building
No. 9	Mineral waters, brewing, wine trade, miscellaneous
No. 10	Fish and poultry
No. 12	Civil aviation
No. 13	Gas
No. 14	Operative butchers

In June the Waterford Branch closed. It never had more than twenty-five members, and total income received was a mere £14 18s. Larkin observed that other unions in the town 'gave fairly satisfactory service.' Members were encouraged to transfer to the ATGWU. There were similar problems in Limerick, where only 60 of 500 members were in benefit, although Newcastle retained its Branch.

In July the Irish Woodcutting Machinists' Union applied to affiliate, with 200 members in Cos. Cork, Limerick and Waterford. This never materialised. By August Branches were established in Banagher and Nenagh (the James Larkin Branch), with agitation for organisation in Kilkenny. The Secretary of the Nenagh Branch was soon serving three months in prison for the misappropriation of funds.

Crotty's work in Co. Cork continued. The Cóbh Branch opened in November, but 'our members here seem to want the Union to work wonders, although they have only been associated with it for a matter of some weeks,' raising questions about what promises were made to induce them to join. The Cóbh Branch dissolved in April 1949, as 'since its formation the position has been most unsatis-factory'—grist to the mill for those cautious about expanding beyond Leinster. The Limerick Branch also closed. The Nenagh Branch struggled on, organising a quarry and two factories. Seán Nugent thought there were opportunities in CIÉ, where 'hundreds' of ATGWU men were likely to resign over Partition.

By May 1949 the WUI had 21,800 members, 12,400 in benefit. The union had more than doubled in size since 1945, even if arrears were still a serious problem.

Table 64: WUI membership, 1945–9

	ITUC affiliation	RFS figure	Women	Branches
1945	8,000	9,129	1,464	15
1946	8,000	10,080	—	16
1947	9,500	13,225	2,686	20
1948	15,000	17,251	3,836	39
1949	15,000	21,427	5,044	34

Sources: ITUC, Annual Reports, 1945–49; National Archives, Registrar of Friendly Societies, file 369T.

In 1949 continued, if slower, growth was reported. Workers in Guinness's Brewery and the Hospitals Trust consulted various unions and, 'after careful and critical examination' of what was offered, chose the WUI. Others tried to influence their decision; 'but lies, slander, bribery, intimidation, corruption—all failed!'

In celebrating the union's twenty-fifth anniversary it annoyed Smithers that some still thought it was of 'foreign origin'. It was Irish, founded among and by Irish people who had served the 'Irish Republic as courageously as any.' It had at 'all times qualified our conception of Irish freedom' and 'loathe the Gaelic-speaking exploiters of the poor, no less than their alien proto-type . . . Ireland without her people is nothing to us.' Those 'who merely see in Irish freedom the possibility for an even greater exploitation of our class, hate us, and at all times lose no opportunity to blacken our name.' The anniversary was marked by a special badge and 'Grand Sports Day' held at Shamrock Rovers' Glenmalure Park on 26 June.[5]

Larkin Junior reflected that the union had long had to live 'not only on borrowed money but borrowed time, the leisure time of each and every one of the men who served this Union.' It had survived continuous financial embarrassment but had a reputation of never backing out of a struggle and achieved wages and conditions as good as if not better than most. He felt that 'we have got as far as a Trade Union can reasonably go, becoming the second largest Irish' union.

Reorganisation was vital. Up to 1947 everyone, at every level, had 'laid his burden on one pair of shoulders.' Those shoulders were now, of necessity, many shoulders. Larkin cited 'Jim Connolly', who had cautioned that 'when a Union begins to accumulate big bank balances you would want to regard it with suspicion.' It was service, not shillings in the bank, that were, and should be, the test. Management expenses crept up to 60% of income; it was intended to reduce this below 50% by improved organisation.

The closure of Fuel Importers lost the union 2,000 members. A financial report was not made, mainly through the illness of 'Mr. O'Brien-Hishon,' a 'good and faithful friend.' One of Larkin's first acts as General Secretary was 'to write a Rule Book' and, having written it, to see that it was implemented.

THE FEDERATION OF RURAL WORKERS

In 1943 the Report of the Commission on Vocational Organisation stated that 'at present farm workers appear to be completely unorganised,' save for 1,000 in the WUI and 375 in the ATGWU. The Irish Farmers' Federation, registered as a trade union, claimed another 1,000. In 1920 the ITGWU had 40,000 of the estimated 100,000 labourers, encouraged by the 'fixation of wages under the Corn Production Acts.' The repeal of the Act and post-war agricultural depression meant that the ITGWU 'ceased to cater for them,' no longer had members and had 'no disposition to resume' organisation. The report noted that organisation was problematic: labourers were found in ones and twos scattered across wide areas; it was difficult to draw the line between labourer and small farmer; union discipline was difficult to impose and maintain, especially during strikes; many farmers employed relatives or neighbours; workers who were not related often lived in, increasing dependence on the employer or developing a 'family atmosphere'; and, as labourers were poorly paid, paid in kind or only 'settled up' at the end of harvest or season, paying regular union contributions was difficult.

The 1945 ITUC Congress identified a significant problem. 'When the agricultural labourer was unorganised he was a more dreadful menace than the unemployed man who has a background and would not sabotage or injure his fellow man.' The unorganised agricultural labourer 'had nothing in common with the workers' and 'would send his son or daughter to work at any price, under any conditions.' Skilled industrial workers should assist in organising them, 'because if they were left unorganised they would bring down wage rates and conditions.' At a meeting in the Trades Hall on 17 March 1946 Congress adopted a policy that 'rural workers on farms, bogs, roads, forestry, etc.' be organised by county in a national federation, charging low subscription rates, avoiding strikes if at all possible and, if they did occur, raising levies to support those out. The wui decided that the task was beyond it but co-operated 'to our utmost ability.' It transferred 2,000 members, a quarter of its total, to the newly created Federation of Rural Workers, a wonderfully generous gesture of solidarity. It made sense to Larkin Junior, as the union that 'goes out and organises rural workers is doing a job for us here in the city.' Organisation would protect the city's flank.

There were reservations, the associated costs nigh prohibitive, as new structures had to be considered. Larkin suggested that up to 120,000 rural workers awaited organisation and anticipated a membership of the FRW of 20,000–25,000. Larkin Senior claimed that the union was born after the Minister for Agriculture, Dr James Ryan, sneered and laughed when discussing the Agricultural Wages Board with him in the Dáil. 'I told him that within a year I would make him swallow his words.' Wages in Dublin were up by 14s. He did not want the FRW confined to the Republic, although this probably depended on the ATGWU taking the same beneficent attitude as the WUI.

Congress praised the WUI's role, qualified by an appeal for assistance, as, 'in the early stages it was understood that this Union would assist financially . . . by way of loan, the amount to be considered in relation to the purpose for which they would require the money.' The WUI's coffers were bare, and this request surprised the GEC.

In December the FRW requested the WUI to accept it as 'an autonomous affiliated Section,' which was acceded to. In parallel, requests for membership from Leitrim, Limerick, Kenmare and elsewhere were simply 'referred to the FRW.' The FRW operated as an autonomous unit of the WUI until its own Negotiating licence was approved.

In 1947, after an unofficial stoppage in Bord na Móna, the management stated that it would no longer recognise or deal with the FRW. Intervention by Congress persuaded the General Secretary, Seán Dunne, to commit the union to existing Agreements, and members in Cos. Kildare and Offaly resumed work on 7 June. The union emerged from its fiery baptism a little scorched but inured by the roasting.[6]

WOMEN

Speaking at the 1945 ITUC Congress to a motion demanding paid holidays, Larkin Senior complained that many workers, especially in agriculture and distribution, worked long hours and weekends without adequate overtime or plus rates. Part of the problem was the education of women. Until they 'educated' women 'they would always have these hardships and grievances about long hours.' 'They' were presumably men.

Larkin admitted that there were still men who took 'a delight in working long hours.' Employers would be glad to close shops at earlier times; but 'a great deal of the worries and hardships and irritation are due to the women.' He said this 'with all respect' but, displaying his acute knowledge of household management, thought 'they ought to arrange things so that they could go and buy the needs of the family in decent hours.' Worse, 'we find that our real enemies in this dispute, today, are the women. There is not one man who will break the picket line, but the women will break it—women married to trade unionists will deliberately go past the picket.' If women got 'into the firing line with us we would not only get this extension of holidays but we would get them something in return.' Surprisingly, none of the few women Delegates challenged him.

The WUI had one woman, Miss Nash, in its first ITUC Delegation. Remarkably, at the 1946 WUI Conference the GEC was 'authorised to co-opt two women members.' It 'investigated' the possibility but did not act upon it. Either way, the idea was far ahead of its time.

The number of women in the WUI rose from 1,464 in 1945 (16% of the membership) to 5,044 in 1949 (24%). A proposal for 'equal pay for equal work' or the 'rate for the job' was 'under consideration' by the ITUC in 1947, the first shoots of what proved a tender plant.[7]

WAGES

In 1947 wage increases were won for building, gas, Corporation, leather, butchery, sugar, fish, tobacco, health service, bakery, printing, fuel, brewery, confectionery and shipbuilding workers. Larkin Junior warned that if these increases were to be kept, political power had to be realised. Everyone agreed that production and productivity needed to be raised, but Smithers warned that employers alone seemed to want to reap the benefits that would accrue. Production Committees served the British war effort well, and the Irish Government could give leadership by pursuing similar policies. The WUI was part of the ITUC's acceptance of the 'Eleven-Shilling Formula' worked out with the Government and FUE, mediated through the Labour Court. Larkin saw it as a 'loose agreement' but felt that future dissatisfaction should be reported back thorough a consultative Conference.[8] The formula was won for most members in 1948–9, with some increases above that gained.

DISPUTES

Larkin Senior proposed an Emergency Motion at the 1946 ITUC Congress congratulating Dublin dockers 'on their struggle to enforce their long delayed claim for extended holidays,' the qualifying period reduced from 2,000 hours per year to 1,800. Dockers were excluded from the Conditions of Employment Act (1936), and 'a certain Union' had 'got nowhere, as usual,' with a legal challenge. Four unions collaborated to improve matters.

In 1947 Ferguson seconded a motion on price controls recognising DTUC as the only body 'alive to the situation' of rising prices, profiteering and the failure of the

Prices Commission. 'Never before' had any campaign like DTUC's Lower Prices Council 'received such support.' He paid tribute to the *Irish Times,* which 'despite its history' took the 'part of the common people.' Alas, 'despite the terrific publicity, unsought publicity, we failed to take advantage of it to drive home the campaign.'

In February 1948 the GEC suggested that the union sever connections with the Irish Municipal Employees' Trade Union and DTUC over negotiating rights in the Corporation. The WUI had five hundred members but was confined to negotiating through the agency of the IMETU, an unsatisfactory and at times hindering mechanism. Larkin felt that unofficial strikes were 'not good business' but that there were situations when workers would take 'justifiable action' on their own. He repeated his condemnation in 1949, even though the WUI made a strike in Clondalkin Paper Mills Official.[9]

TRADE UNION UNITY

At the 1945 ITUC Congress Larkin Senior called for more resources for Congress, warning that the FUE 'had a very fine staff' and 'could afford to fight not only with the knowledge gleaned but also had a lawyer to support them.' The FUE was 'very dangerous,' and unions needed to 'fit themselves to meet that body.' Compounding the movement's split, the Minister for Industry and Commerce, Seán Lemass, selected CIU rather than ITUC Delegates as Worker Representatives for the 1946 Congress of the International Labour Organisation in Seattle. The ITUC represented larger numbers, was the older body, and regarded the CIU as secessionists. Anger was compounded when William O'Brien (ITGWU) and Cathal O'Shannon were selected. It confirmed suspicions of complicity between the CIU and the Government, conferring unmerited legitimacy on the CIU.

On 13 September 1946 Larkin Junior reported that at a joint ITUC-CIU meeting chaired by Lemass the CIU had insisted that the ITUC 'should make a declaration of principle' that the movement 'should only consist of Irish Unions having their Headquarters and their economic and financial control in Ireland.' He saw little hope of immediate return to negotiations. The ITUC felt that the CIU's insistence on this 'formula', unsurprisingly enunciated by Lemass, left matters deadlocked. Lemass wrote that he could not 'conceive any British interest which would be served by the insistence of the right of British Unions to operate here.' He assumed that British leaders would do all they could to promote Irish trade union unity, the absence of which he considered a potential serious threat to stability. He urged the withdrawal of British unions. He did not contemplate any immediate action against 'Amalgamated Unions' but offered the stick that unity might be met by a statutory obligation on workers to be members of 'appropriate' unions.

Lemass took little cognisance of Northern Ireland. Equally, some unions most trenchant in their commitment to remaining in Ireland regularly adopted policies favouring Irish unity and independence. Affiliation to the World Federation of Trade Unions, an issue supposedly central to the breach, was made by the ITUC at specially reduced rates. Addressing Congress on 'Trade Union Disunity', Larkin

Junior paid homage to the objective and non-partisan presentation by the Secretary of the ITUC, Thomas Johnson, at the London WFTU Conference. He drew everyone's attention to the problem of Irish nationalism that neither Irish nor Amalgamated unions could ignore. The CIU had, he felt, broken away 'on what is recognised and accepted as a purely artificial excuse,' but it had 'received the support of many people in the country.' This could not be ignored. Unity in itself was not sufficient and not worth any price. Policy was the prerequisite and must drive unity.

He invited the Amalgamated unions to sit down and study the problem, working out their role, free from coercion, to lead a policy that would drive unity. It was a typically thoughtful and provocative address and marked Larkin and the WUI as leaders of moves towards unity.

Larkin Senior's last speech to Congress in 1946 was to praise its Secretary, 'one of my old colleagues, Comrade Johnson.' He felt there was a 'new life, new spirit and new atmosphere,' and he hoped Johnson, then seventy-four, 'will live long to assist you.' In the light of Larkin's vituperative attacks on 'Felix' Johnson and the libel action between them, his final comments were a testimony to that 'new spirit', a public burying of rusting hatchets. None were to know, but it was a final gesture, which rightly drew applause.

> We will always be glad to co-operate with him and to ask him to be still one of the apostles of Labour in this country. There has been no time in all the years that I ever thought of doubting his honesty of purpose and his great gift of conciliation. He was able at all times to deal with hotheads, like myself, who were young and enthusiastic and who were running, possibly, out of line. I say this and I hope he will appreciate it in the spirit in which it is offered.[10]

Both Congresses met Lemass on 10 September 1946. The ITUC accepted a formula 'without reservation' that could provide a basis for reunification: a joint Committee to discuss matters of mutual interest, discussions with the British TUC and individual Amalgamated unions over questions of separate Irish structures, and an availability to discuss matters of workers' interest with the Government. No further Conferences took place by July 1947, when Congress met in Waterford. Here Larkin suggested that the ITUC had 'made many concessions' before talks broke down.

A dispute in the ESB demonstrated what he always believed, that rank-and-file unity could accomplish and force what leaderships could not. They presented a 'solid and united front' to the employer. He emphasised that 'our Movement is not made up of Officials'; but in reality, despite his appeals to the rank-and-file, Officials made the decisions. Either because he felt it unworkable or because he was constrained by Congress's collective leadership, he did not suggest that workers demonstrate their feelings on the streets. Successful marches, at that point, might have placed the leaders in an awkward position. In any case, who would lead such marches?

On Friday 19 September the GEC stood as a mark of respect for the late Senator Thomas Kennedy, General Secretary of the ITGWU. It was agreed that the President of the WUI, Smithers, would formally attend the funeral, a gesture of friendship and solidarity with Liberty Hall.

Smithers addressed the issue of most 'deep concern' in 1949. 'The subject is too delicate a one for much comment from me at this stage. Clearly each side has been guilty of mistakes, unpardonable mistakes.' It was 'well recognised' that factors operated that were 'not immediately related to the problem' but that were 'probably more real and constitute the greatest obstacles to the unity we desire.' He hoped 'men of good will in both camps' would create unity.

Larkin Junior's desire was 'to see the movement united.' On 27 May, as President of the ITUC, he wrote to the Executive of both Congresses, the Labour Party and National Labour Party, suggesting that the National Executive would 'be very glad to enter at once' into discussions to remove 'all existing obstacles to unity.'

The CIU and NLP replied by reiterating that all unions operating in Ireland must be 'Irish-based' and Irish-controlled. The ITUC asked what 'Irish-based' meant—perhaps a reference to growing 26-County nationalism. Firmly anti-Partitionist views were held by leading ITUC figures, although in British unions and from backgrounds in the Unionist community. Leo Crawford, Secretary of the CIU, suggested that a movement based on the 'Irish-based' principle would advance the 'unity of our country.' The ITUC pointed out that many Northern workers would be reluctant to surrender membership of their existing unions. 'Confusion' and the 'absence of clarification' would be better dealt with in a meeting before any 'proposed unity Conference.' The temperature, while still chilly, was rising.

Meanwhile the Northern Ireland Committee of the ITUC was established. It was not intended to divide the movement on a North-South basis. Ferguson attacked the General President of the ITGWU, McMullen, as having appointed himself as the man who would decide which unions qualified under the principles. The ITGWU tail was seen to wag the CIU dog. Barney Conway spelt such feelings out more directly and would 'not be brow-beaten by Mr. William McMullen . . . We want control of our own movement in our own country,' but this had to come through 'co-operation with British Unions.'

The ITUC suspended association with the WFTU and proposed affiliation to the International Confederation of Free Trade Unions. Ferguson, considering the domestic split, argued against any affiliation. The WUI was fighting the 'rearguard battle on the part of the Irish Unions within the ITUC' and feared further obstacles to unity. 'Our first allegiance is to the working classes of Ireland.' Nothing should be done to 'hand them [the CIU] over to an organisation pursuing the most reactionary ideology in Europe.'

In 1949 Larkin referred to the ITGWU in tantalising terms. The 'two Unions attract attention today.' He did not 'want to go back over past history, but I do want to say this, if during the years that have gone by, the leadership of this Union had the resources, men and material given them that the Irish Transport Union had, this country would be a different country.' He lauded the 'loyalty and co-operation' received 'from our members' and felt that with better resources 'this Union can go places.' Was this a veiled suggestion of unity, a further criticism of the ITGWU's method and culture, or a challenge as the WUI's organisation, structure and operation improved?

At Congress, Larkin's Presidential Address was a 'courageous, wide-ranging and penetrating analysis.' It was published as *A Common Loyalty: The Bridge to Unity*. It stressed unity, reconciliation and constructive suggestions for progress, becoming regarded as a triumph of statesmanlike sense and sensibility. Larkin echoed the role of Belfast in 1798 in the 'struggles for civil and religious liberty' and the 'effort to bury the animosities and enmities dividing Irishmen and women and bring them together in a common bond of citizenship.' He spoke of the loyalty of working people, especially in 1907, to the cause of 'protection against economic and social injustices and in winning for the common people of a full and rightful share of the earth's abundance.' Losing sight of such common purpose would serve only the interests of their class enemies.

Larkin analysed the 'European Recovery Program' or Marshall Aid, drawing attention to its achievements and to its inherent weakness. It could not cure capitalism's ills of 'slump', 'crisis', 'recession' or 'cyclical adjustment of production.' In all such crises, workers ultimately paid the price. Courageously, given the worsening post-war political climate and the emergence of Cold War, Larkin suggested that 'capitalism, as an economic system, no longer serves the requirements of society.' Production held the key, but private ownership had proved itself a failure. It was 'essential that the onslaught by conservative elements be defeated' and progress 'towards more collective, social forms of ownership retained and made secure.'

In Ireland, while there were clear signs of recovery and shortages were abating, unemployment remained doggedly persistent. Increased production employing technical advances generated by the war did not necessarily decrease unemployment—indeed in some industries the reverse was true. Workers' only safeguard was access to industrial decision-making, starting in the boardroom and reaching down to the shop floor. In addition, greater equity in income distribution could be attained with the introduction of a comprehensive social security scheme.

He applied the same analysis to Northern Ireland, calling for greater cross-border co-operation and joint hydro-electric, railway and transport, shipbuilding and manufacturing projects. He appealed for national unity through a unified trade union movement demanding a united 'political, economic and social system.' He acknowledged that he was on dangerous ground. 'I know this is political dynamite, but dynamite is not only a destructive agent, it also has its positive use in clearing away obstacles so that the builder may create a new edifice.' Much old ground needed clearing. The Ireland Act could not be ignored, but common council in common cause was the way forward. A first and essential step was unity with the CIU.

He addressed practical problems in straightforward terms, not least the relatively insignificant presence of Irish unions in Northern Ireland. If those not in

Irish unions—140,000, compared with 10,000—were to be excluded from an Irish trade union centre, was this not an extension of Partition 'where it has not hitherto existed'? Would the CIU 'accept clear and full responsibility for such a purpose?'

This was a tough but central question. He accepted that he could be regarded by some as offering 'carping and biased criticism,' but such partisanship was proof of the ultimately destructive nature of division. He appealed for an end to gunboat diplomacy and a gathering of all parties around the same table.

Sam Kyle (ATGWU) articuláted what many felt having heard the address: 'great father, greater son.' Larkin Junior was anointed as a powerhouse figure within the movement. Jack Macgougan (National Union of Tailors and Garment Workers) had never heard 'such a brilliant analysis' and 'clarity of vision'—high praise from one renowned for his own insightful mind and political acumen; it was 'one of the greatest speeches Congress ever listened to.' Larkin was to be President again in 1952, but his speech then made less impact, although typically reflective and well argued.

In 1977 John Foster, President of the WUI, reflecting on the Northern Ireland conflict, cited Larkin's speech at length.

> Let us urge upon the Governments in both areas the need for utilising every opportunity for mutual exchange of views and where possible, joint endeavours in dealing with problems of economic development, trade, transport and cultural extensions, so that our people may come to learn in a practical manner of the possibilities and advantages of co-operation. Above all, let us not feel that any effort to find a bridge, however slender, across the gulf dividing the ordinary people, North and South, is a betrayal of principle or a compromise of positions.

He reflected 'how different things might have been' had Larkin had the 'power and authority' to 'translate his words into meaningful national policies' or had those with the power 'only listened a little more attentively to what he had to say.' The speech added greatly to the standing of Larkin and the WUI within movement and wider society.

At the 1949 WUI Conference Liam Ó Buacháin (No. 7) asked the union to 'secede from the ITUC and seek affiliation to the CIU.' He reasoned that 'if the Englishman has a right to rule trade unionism in Ireland we cannot deny his right to rule the country.' He felt that affiliation to the CIU would assist the 'unity which is so much desired.' He had voted against the Political Levy, as 'spiritual and national values' had to have 'pre-eminence' in building the nation. J. Moran (No. 8) summed up many Delegates' response when he simply stated, 'I would like to oppose everything the last speaker has said.' Christy Troy (Operative Butchers) thought the 'best day's work to be done' would be 'when the CIU seeks affiliation to the TUC.' Replying, Larkin said the WUI was wholly Irish and acted as a bridge between Irish and Amalgamated unions. Ó Buacháin revealed that his real motive, having entered the CIU, was 'to attack it.' His proposal that all WUI documents be printed in Irish and English passed with only five dissenting.

The CIU closed the correspondence initiated by Larkin. The ITUC set out conditions for a unity Conference: that there should be a 'National Trade Union Centre for the whole of Ireland . . . under Irish control,' necessitating changes in the structures of some existing affiliates. No reply was received, but the CIU indicated through the press that matters were closed. The ITUC persisted, and on 17 November a unity meeting was suggested to the Labour Party and National Labour Party. This took place on 2 February 1950 and suggested a unity Conference between the ITUC and CIU Executives. On 7 June a joint statement was made calling for 'unity in the Labour movement' in a 'united Party with a political programme in accordance with Christian principles and national ideals,' accepting the 'principle of Irish-based and Irish-controlled unions,' that was willing to arrange a Conference between the two Congresses.[11]

INDUSTRIAL RELATIONS

At the 1947 Congress Larkin cautioned Delegates about Lemass's intention to rectify the NUR's successful constitutional challenge to part 3 of the Trade Union Act (1941). The movement's voluntarist principles must be accepted and any legislation be an agreed measure. Lack of unity meant that any 'agreed measure' would be difficult. Larkin Senior viewed the Industrial Relations Bill with suspicion, although, once there was no compulsory element and it 'suited our purposes,' it could be usefully employed. The ending of the national emergency and the Industrial Relations Act (1946) necessitated different tactics: 'no longer would the merely sentimental appeal or the blunt threat to private employers suffice.' Negotiators now 'had not alone to express the traditional militancy of our class, but they had to employ both the science and art of logic and the cunning of the Lawyer.' It was a formula 'propounded by this Union' that provided the 'basis for argument at the now classic session of the Labour Court' in the ESB case, which the Court 'adopted as the pattern for subsequent settlements.'

Larkin Junior gave the Labour Court qualified welcome. It had 'limited power,' as unions were 'not forced to consult it or even to accept its decisions.' The right to strike was secure, although 'at the same time we will use every other form of machinery available to us before contemplating strike action.' The Court had, on occasion, taken it upon itself to 'speak sharply' of unofficial strikes, but 'we do not take dictation from the Court.' The right to strike was solely the movement's 'property'.

The appointment of Worker Representatives was one of the first battles between the ITUC and CIU. Without agreement, Lemass used his own powers to appoint Thomas Johnson and Cathal O'Shannon, coincidentally the Secretaries of the Congresses. They might well have been nominated in any case.[12]

GUINNESS

In May 1947 Larkin became 'aware that certain employees in Messrs. Guinness would like to become members,' but there were 'many difficulties to be overcome.' They concentrated on building up their Staff Association, the Guinness Employees'

Organisation—a company strategy to keep trade unionism proper out—although craft unions, such as the Coopers' Society, were recognised. It backfired, as the Association recommended to its members that it dissolve and affiliate to the WUI. At a meeting in the Mansion House a proposal was made to join the ITGWU instead. Press reports lit on this apparent disunity, but Ferguson assured Delegates at the 1949 Conference that the opposite was the case. A plebiscite was conducted in the brewery, apparently by the men themselves; 800 of the 2,000 voted and decided on the WUI. Organisational work remained. The ITGWU view was that the house union wanted 'to join a recognised trade union,' and 'information was supplied by us to the Secretary of the House Union' in support of the claim that the ITGWU was 'willing and able to cater successfully for those workers.' It 'had been withheld from a General Meeting' in the Mansion House. As the workers had joined the WUI, the ITGWU was 'obliged to take steps to have the facts communicated to them by literature distributed at their place of employment'; but the plan was 'abandoned for the time being.'[13]

THE GAS COMPANY

In November 1947 members took unofficial action in Dublin Gas Company in association with the Irish Seamen's and Port Workers' Union. The GEC took a dim view and decided that 'where members of the Union take part in unofficial strikes and . . . when instructed by a competent Union Official to return to work, refuse to do so, [they should] be subject to disciplinary action to the extent of suspending or withdrawing their cards.' Militant reputation or not, Young Jim Larkin insisted on discipline.

In March 1949 Patrick Forde was to retire after 'lifelong service' to the union. The Section asked that he be appointed Delegate before retirement The GEC reacted in stony fashion. While 'appreciating the long, loyal and very valuable service given by Mr. P. Forde to the Union since its inception,' and 'aware that there is hardly another member' to 'whom is owed an equal debt of appreciation as falls rightfully due to Mr. P. Forde,' it was 'with very considerable regret' that it found it 'impossible' to appoint him Delegate in 'view of the possible consequences which would follow, should they do so.' A deputation pleaded Forde's case at the next meeting of the GEC. He was unanimously nominated as Delegate in March. The Section was told that it was 'against the Union principle of not employing a man already on pension.' On 29 April principle bowed to pressure, and Forde began a six-month trial as Delegate. He remained in service until his death on 9 October 1959 in his mid-seventies.[14]

IRISH HOSPITALS TRUST

As the WUI battled for recognition in the Hospitals Trust, the ITUC Annual Report still printed a full-page advertisement for the Irish Hospitals Sweepstakes. By 1949 the WUI had organised 'some hundreds of the 1,400 employees.' The Staff Manager said that the 'majority of the employees do not wish to be represented' and had 'formed a separate Association, with which the company intend to deal with in future'—a common tactic among anti-union employers. More than 400 enrolled in the wui, but gaining recognition was not straightforward. The first of many references to the Labour Court followed in April.[15]

MUINTIR NA MARA

In July 1947 a group of Howth fishermen formed Muintir na Mara after an argument with buyers over catch prices. A Delegation visited Head Office to request that fish not be handled in the Fish Market while members' boats were tied up. O'Hagan's and Nolan's herring boats stayed berthed north of Wexford. Only a month in existence, Muintir na Mara expressed a desire to affiliate its 500 members in Arklow, Balbriggan, Clogherhead, Howth, Loughshinny and Skerries. The union's Fish and Poultry Section agreed not to handle imported fish while Howth boats lay idle, and the affiliation of Muintir na Mara was accepted.

Matters quickly turned sour. While wui members were being laid off because of an 'insufficient supply of fish,' Howth boats landed catches in the Isle of Man at good prices. Muintir na Mara, which had at first seemed a good catch, was quickly tossed overboard. It sought affiliation to the ciu, but this came to nothing.[16]

INDUSTRIAL DEVELOPMENT

In 1946 Larkin Senior addressed unemployment in shipyards, alleging that cross-channel shipping policy was that 'they would not buy eggs and bacon here if they could get them across the water.' He wanted Irish ships to be built in Belfast, Cork or Dublin. The country's belief in the 32 Counties could be demonstrated by having Irish merchant ships built in Belfast.

In 1947 the wui wanted co-operative enterprise to be encouraged. J. Dalton (Furnishing Trade) outlined his work in the Co-operative Society in Drimnagh and Crumlin, Dublin, which the wui had subvented for a year at £30 a month. It dealt in essential commodities, employing union labour.

In 1947–8 Larkin moved the development of turf, agricultural machinery and tractor manufacture, engineering, merchant shipping, forestry and electricity industries as part of a 'plan for economic development.' He asked Congress to publish its economic survey. He cited successful Government involvement in turf, electricity and beet sugar as examples of sound intervention. He wanted an 'independent Irish economy,' to be protected by tariff barriers, and demanded a National Economic Council. His motives were to generate economic activity, raise workers' incomes and avoid the terrible isolation and shortages they had just witnessed during the war. A declaration of neutrality was not sufficient: it had to supported by planned economic, communication, energy and transport structures. He wondered at Fine Gael's capacity, given its past hostility to state involvement and slavish commitment to failed private enterprise. He attacked the Federation of Irish Manufacturers for its opposition to any measure of workers' involvement through Development Councils proposed under the Industrial Efficiency and Prices Bill (1947). Unions should stake their claim 'in a very forcible manner to direct representation.'

In 1949 Ferguson dismissed Billy McCullough (National Association of Theatrical and Kine Employees) as making a 'nonsense' speech when talking of the crisis in capitalism, suggesting that minds should concentrate on how any crisis 'will affect us here'—a surprisingly narrow view. McCullough called for a survey of industrial and natural resources and their fullest development, essentially WUI policy.[17]

HOUSING AND SOCIAL WELFARE

The 1945 Congress demanded the construction of 350,000 houses throughout Ireland, to be available at reasonable rents to workers. Larkin Senior wanted a Special Conference to debate housing initiatives and the abolition of ground rents. He alleged that matters had not improved much since 1913, any Dublin Corporation building programme being outdone by the 60,000 families that had since entered the city. In 1946 he wanted social service reciprocity, suggesting that, although the inactive Irish Government expressed its sympathy on the matter, an appeal should be made through the British TUC to the Labour Government's 'common sense and decency' to at least repay money deducted from Irish workers in Britain. In 1949 Smithers called for a major housing programme, appealing to the building unions to remove their objections to prefabricated dwellings. Barney Conway talked of the 'rotten slums of Dublin.'[18]

HEALTH AND SAFETY

In 1946 Larkin Junior sought improvements in the Workmen's Compensation Act (1934) in the Dáil, pursing the ITUC's demands for parity with the Industrial Injuries Act in Britain. The Republic told the world that 'our Constitution is based upon the highest concepts of Christian morality,' but Government inaction showed the 'sham and hypocrisy' of this. The family of a man killed through his employer's negligence would receive £199 and an incapacitated man £110 with which 'to maintain himself and dependants for the rest of his life.' Ferguson said that 146 workers had been 'murdered' in the previous four years and yet 'claims in the Courts were rejected and their dependants did not receive anything.'[19]

EDUCATION AND TRAINING

Examinations for six Gaeltacht scholarships for members' children were held in 1946. Larkin Junior wanted joint education activities by the ITUC and Labour Party to continue, not least in the context of the Industrial Relations Act (1946). Appearance in the Labour Court required a knowledge of economics and commerce. Jim Dalton (Engineering Branch) suggested that 'Research and Enquiry Bureaux be set up,' while Seán Burke (Fire Brigade) argued that better-educated men were required as Delegates. J. Byrne (Corporation) cited British workers' colleges and looked for the 'education of workers from the working class point of view.' The ITUC should be asked to set up such classes in Dublin at least. Cobbe (Mental Hospitals) recalled his experience in National University courses arranged through the Labour Party, although badly attended.

The WUI and IWWU strongly supported the formation of the People's College Adult Education Association in October 1948. The WUI provided premises free of charge and lecturers. The idea was drawn from the ITUC's relationship with the Workers' Educational Association in Britain. In 1949 the WUI assisted members in undertaking courses provided by the People's College and University College, Dublin.[20] For all courses the WUI paid two-thirds of members' fees.

JOURNAL

In November 1946 the GEC considered the publication of a union paper. Larkin Junior cautioned that, despite 'restrictions on paper being lifted,' there would still be 'difficulty in securing an income to cover the expense of publishing.' In any case, who would edit it? The union's staff was small, and stretched.

In November 1947 Ardiff Printers gave an estimate of £48 per issue. The normally parsimonious Finance Committee said yes. Staff pressure was such that Larkin still 'did not think it feasible.'

In July 1948 the Tobacco Workers' Section wanted a monthly grant of £20 to publish twelve issues of a journal. The GEC decided that, 'in view of the possible precedent this would create,' the General Secretary and General President 'would meet the Editor and have further talks with him,' pointing out the difficulties and seeking alternative ideas. *Tobacco Workers' Review,* on sale from September, was assisted by a £25 guarantee for six months, although the Finance Committee opposed a levy of 1d a week. In November it was agreed that the union would meet the expense of two issues, provided that Bennett and Browne (GEC) sat on the Committee and a notice was inserted in each issue 'indicating that the views contained . . . did not represent the Official views of the Union.'

There were calls for a publication to mark the twenty-fifth anniversary of the union in 1949. Larkin began this task for *Tobacco Workers' Review* but quickly went far over his allotted five hundred words. He was writing a history not of the WUI but of the 'industrial and political development of this country' over forty years. The ITUC and Labour Party were hoping to produce jointly a sixteen-page illustrated weekly paper and circulated affiliates to raise the £4,000 to £5,000 working capital required, ultimately £10,000. Congress and Party each gave £500, and the WUI provided £100.[21]

STAFF

In 1947 staff salaries were improved, but so too were the GEC's expectations of performance. Staff problems occasionally arose, as when Anthony Brack was brought before the GEC following an incident in the ESB, when it was alleged that he 'entered District Engineer Harkin's room' and, 'although there was a lady present,' did 'not remove his hat or remove his cigarette from his mouth whilst speaking.' Such 'ungentlemanly conduct' was not untypical of Brack's rumbustious character.

In October, £1,000 started a Staff Superannuation Scheme. A Staff Section was created to facilitate the consideration of pay, conditions and performance between

the GEC and full-time employees. An insight into considerations for staff appointments is gleaned from the fate of an unsuccessful candidate in August 1948. He was
'very capable, with a good appearance and good business experience,' but he struck
Larkin as 'being far too go-ahead and of a type that would probably not confine
himself to his work but would be inclined to rush helter-skelter.' The veteran Ralph
James retired. Negotiations with the staff brought opposition from the GEC to a
Staff Association.

Despite pay increases, staff wages were 33% of income in 1945, 28% in 1946 and
29% in 1947, although total management expenses had risen to 70% of income.
Some GEC members thought the Staff Superannuation Scheme too generous when
it was approved in January 1949.[22]

Table 65: WUI, wages of staff and total income, 1945–9

	Number	Total maximum weekly wage (£)	Total annual wages (£)	Total annual income (£)	Wages as proportion of income (%)	Increase in staff over 1945 (%)	Increase in wage bill over 1945 (%)
1945	22	91	5,004	15,029	33	—	—
1946	22	94	5,007	18,079	27	—	1
1947	28	154	7,563	25,358	29	28	48
1948	30	193	9,545	32,000	29	37	90
1949	31	204	10,097	32,000	31	40	100

Source: WUI, minutes of General Executive Council, 14 January 1949.

POLITICS

In 1947 the WUI had no Political Fund. Ferguson said that 'we are fighting with one
arm behind our back.' Workers received the same share of national income as in
1914. The WUI started the Jim Larkin Branch of the Labour Party. In 1949 Larkin was
simultaneously elected President of the ITUC and Leader of the Parliamentary
Labour Party. The Labour Party entered Government to prevent the re-enactment
of another Standstill Order, preserve proportional representation and introduce a
comprehensive social security system.

In addition to Larkin's position as TD the WUI had four members in Dublin
Corporation and members on other authorities. Yet among members there was a
reluctance to fund political activity. In 1948 'very few members voted' in a ballot on
the Political Fund: 589 to 841, with sixteen spoiled votes. Within weeks, one Branch
that opposed the Political Fund sought every form of political representation possible to support an employment, without acknowledging the blatant contradiction
in its behaviour. Larkin thought it 'neither fair nor honest' to seek political improvements without contribution. Seán Dunne, Labour TD, looked for a personal loan to

pay off election debts. He owed £800, most pressingly £200 to £300. The WUI had already given him a £50 loan and granted £500 to the ITUC Legislation Fund. Larkin opposed, as 'we might need the money for industrial battles,' but the GEC, on Smithers's casting vote, granted £100, to be paid back at £10 a month.

In 1949 James Kelly, Secretary of the Gas Workers' Branch, visited the Soviet Union with a group of writers and artists. The Branch Committee approached the General Secretary, demanding that Kelly be dismissed, a request adamantly rejected. An invitation from the Catholic Women's Federation for the WUI to participate in public protests on 1 May against the imprisonment of Cardinal Mindszenty was rejected by the GEC: 'as the time was short it is doubtful whether it would be possible to carry out the necessary arrangements to permit the members to participate as an organised body.'

Conversely, full attendance was planned for the Connolly Commemoration on 11 May and the parade and concert on Sunday 15 May. The Labour Party sent Larkin to London to address the Conference of the Anti-Partition League in May, the WUI placing an advertisement in the League's journal.

On 6 May 1949 James Larkin divulged to the GEC that the Taoiseach, John A. Costello, had suggested that he be appointed Minister for Local Government. His instinct was that 'the Union came first.' The *Irish Times* suggested that he would have been given Education but that Fine Gael vetoed the appointment. His consolation prize was to be asked to be Leader of the Parliamentary Labour Party while Norton was preoccupied with Government office. While 'understandably sore about the episode,' Larkin never spoke of it.

Despite complaints at the GEC about Denis Larkin's work in the Gas Company, he was appointed Acting General Secretary should his brother become a Minister, 'particularly from the point of view of the name he bears.' The denial of Government office to Young Larkin raised unanswerable questions about missed opportunities, politically and industrially.[23]

Chapter 22 ∾

| CONCLUSIONS

Both the ITGWU and WUI experienced rapid post-war growth. The ITGWU passed the figure of 100,000 financial members by 1949, with Branches in almost every county in the Republic as well as Belfast and Newry. The WUI's membership doubled to 21,427, enthused by reorganisation under Young Jim Larkin, the appointment of Christy Ferguson as Organiser and the breaking of new ground at Dublin Airport and Guinness and among engineering and health-service workers.

The Congress split allowed the WUI access to the ITUC. Larkin Junior immediately sought to broker unity after his father's death. Although O'Brien retired in 1946, the ITGWU and CIU had the bit between their teeth and insisted that the principle of Irish control of Irish trade union affairs be accepted before reunification could be considered. Rapid expansion of the ITGWU and CIU undoubtedly strengthened their hand. As Larkin observed, whatever reservations ITUC member-unions, British or Irish, had, thousands supported CIU unions, many transferring from British unions in protest against the Ireland Act.

Table 66: Membership of ITGWU, WUI, ITUC and CIU and total trade union membership, 1946–9

	ITGWU	WUI	ITUC	CIU	Total
1946	61,260	10,080	147,000	n.a.	147,000
1947	78,380	13,225	151,000	n.a.	151,000
1948	89,054	17,251	181,000	131,400	312,400
1949	101,609	21,427	196,000	143,600	339,600

Source: National Archives, Registrar of Friendly Societies, files 275T and 369T; ITUC and CIU, Annual Reports, 1946–9.

The ITGWU's growth left the WUI far behind, numerically and geographically. Financially the differential was even more acute and ever-widening. The ITGWU credit balance in 1949 was more than £400,000, ten times larger than that of the

WUI. This bred self-confidence and created a public impression of solidity and strength. The ITGWU continuously offered new services, and its staff increased to meet the changing industrial relations scene: the creation of national industrial bargaining units, the emergence of Wage Rounds and the impact of the Labour Court. *Liberty* depicted a union sure of its step, highly socialised and surprisingly compact for such a large body.

A comparison of Dispute Pay shows the ITGWU as more militant, spending £108,469, compared with £8,037 for the WUI. Despite criticism of the ITGWU and CIU's wage policy, especially during negotiations for the Eleven-Shilling Formula in 1948, the ITGWU provided significant advances to members, reinforcing its attractiveness.

Table 67: Credit balance, ITGWU and WUI (£), 1946–9

	ITGWU	WUI		ITGWU	WUI
1946	320,559	6,644	1948	355,965	23,952
1947	313,559	13,462	1949	403,623	29,837

Source: ITGWU and WUI, Annual Reports, 1946–9

Table 68: Income and Dispute Pay, ITGWU and WUI (£), 1945–9

	ITGWU			WUI		
	Income (£)	Dispute pay (£)	As proportion of income (%)	Income (£)	Dispute pay(£)	As proportion of income (%)
1945	41,072	4,581	11.1	15,029	7,196	47.8
1946	49,720	3,447	6.9	18,080	664	3.6
1947	61,289	54,992	89.7	25,358	1,261	4.9
1948	74,704	9,813	13.1	32,017	483	1.5
1949	85,404	19,347	22.7	31,637	4,061	12.8

Source: ITGWU and WUI, Annual Reports, 1946–59.

Politically, the National Labour Party, created by the ITGWU, withered away after joining the Labour Party in the first Inter-Party Government in 1948. The ITGWU remained unaffiliated, although giving unofficial support to the Labour Party. Surprisingly, WUI members defeated attempts to establish a Political Fund, despite the GEC's support for the Labour Party and Larkin Junior becoming Leader of the Parliamentary Labour Party.

The tantalising prospect of Larkin becoming a Minister was denied, suggestions being that his former Communist Associations were too much for Fine Gael backwoodsmen. The ITGWU, still suspected of being happier to deal with Fianna Fáil, embraced Catholic social teaching. Speeches and Conferences were replete with reference to Papal encyclicals and appeals to employers' Christian values.

By 1949 continuing unemployment and emigration concentrated new leaders and new minds on the need for unity to remove wasteful duplication and to develop single policies to be implemented through one voice if workers were to be free of poverty and despair. Larkin Junior's letter to the *Irish Times* after his father's death was a beacon light, suggesting that the bitterness and animosity that followed the 1924 split could be overcome.

Chapter 23 ⌒

'THE EVER-FAITHFUL FEW': THE ITGWU AND MOVES TOWARDS UNITY, 1950s

In 1950 the General President, William McMullen, reflected that the union, with 120,000 members, was bigger than ever. Recruits came from previously unorganised workers or transfers from British unions, notably in Ford of Cork and among railwaymen and transport clerks. Workers' desire to seek periodic wage increases to keep pace with the cost of living was their prime motive. The ITGWU was highly effective; but 'with power has come responsibility.' McMullen insisted that 'neither the passage of time nor the altered social and economic circumstances' had 'caused us to depart from our main purpose or abandon a tithe of the idealism in which it was conceived.' Yet, in serving workers' interests, it must 'at the same time integrate our actions to harmonise with . . . the nation's interests.'[1]

In 1956 John Conroy, General President, claimed that, including members' dependants, the union represented a 'substantial portion of the people of Ireland, about 350,000, or one in twelve of the total population.' It had a 'duty and a right' to use its power and influence to 'endeavour to arouse our people from their growing despondency.' All progressive countries planned for development; Ireland merely drifted. Unions must lead in 'calling the Nation to action.' People must be mobilised to drag society 'out of the deep muddy rut.'

In 1958, hoping that the 'sun would shine on us' in Ballybunnion, Conroy felt that there 'was little hope of the sun breaking through the deep shadows that overcast' Ireland from nuclear proliferation and weapons testing. Reflecting predominant Catholic values, he commented that 'this earth created by the Almighty to provide man with all the things he needs to live a full Christian life is torn asunder by the actions of highly placed selfish men who desire and strive for still greater power.' They wished 'to retain for themselves and their class the personal wealth they enjoy today and the greater wealth and power they hope to have tomorrow when they slaughter a few more millions of their fellow human beings . . . In this little country' there was nothing much that could be done 'except to pray and hope.' A 'full life in their own country' was 'every Irish person's birthright,' but 'self and selfishness predominated.' All that was heard was 'increase interest rates,' 'restrict credit,' 'slow down development works,' make the unemployed, sick and aged 'do with less,' 'remove the food subsidies' and increase workers' taxes.' The 'haves' had triumphed over the 'have-nots.' The attainment of '£500 a year for every family man in the country' was the priority.[2]

THOMAS FORAN, WILLIAM MCMULLEN AND FRANK PURCELL

McMullen retired, under the age limit, after the 1953 Conference. The movement he served for forty years was transformed from one that was 'misunderstood' and 'whose objects were maligned' into one that had won 'universal respect,' with a 'special place in the councils of the nation.' He invoked 'God's blessing' on his successor.

Born in Belfast in 1897, McMullen, a Presbyterian, worked in Harland and Wolff and was inspired by Larkin during the 1907 dockers' and carters' strike. He served with Connolly and was Secretary of the Belfast Branch, 1920–37, National Organiser, 1937–9, Vice-President, 1939–46, General President, 1946–53, and President of the CIU, 1953–4. He was a member of Belfast Corporation (City Council) and an MP for the NILP. A confidant of Lemass, he was given directorships and regularly addressed Fianna Fáil meetings. He died in December 1982, aged ninety-five. A brilliant, analytical speaker, McMullen was a significant figure in ITGWU history.

The founding President, Tom Foran, died on 18 March 1951. Born in 1883, he was a docker and NUDL activist. He was General President from the foundation of the ITGWU until his retirement in 1939. He was a Senator, 1923–36 and 1936–48, and a member of the Council of State. The CIU stated that 'with his passing the workers have lost one of their greatest champions, a man whose unselfish devotion to duty and whose high ideals will be an inspiration to all who serve the Cause of Labour and the Cause of Ireland.'[3]

James Gilhooly, Secretary of Nos. 6 and 8 (Clothing and Hosiery) Branches died unexpectedly in 1951. An Arigna miner, he was Galway Organiser, doing sterling work throughout Connacht, before his appointment in Dublin, where he was viewed as a potential General Officer. He was a tough, intelligent negotiator, had a keen sense of justice and was well versed in labour law. He contested Leitrim for the Labour Party in 1945 but generally shunned the limelight. He was a member of the Hosiery JIC and Tailoring JLC and gave evidence to the Inquiry into the Irish Coal Mining Industry in 1942, extensively visiting British coalfields to complete his submission.

Frank Purcell, a native of Co. Kildare, retired as General Secretary in August 1959, not a well man. The stalwart Purcell served from 1920, suffered imprisonment during the War of Independence and led the flagship Hotels and Restaurants Branch, 1931–43, before elevation to the post of General Secretary in 1948. Talented, he was a shrewd tactician, personable, engaging, popular and revered in equal measure.[4]

FINANCE, MEMBERSHIP AND ORGANISATION

Almost every item of expenditure increased in 1950, yet the credit balance rose to £451,794, a huge increase from £181,470 in 1940. Membership was approximately

130,000, with virtually 100% organisation claimed for many industries. Expenditure increased in 1951, largely through increasing Dispute Pay. Increases in outlay panicked the union slightly and it appealed for a 'determined effort . . . by all concerned' to increase income. The reserve funds certainly needed strengthening. The credit balance fell slightly to £448,645, the first fall since 1927.

The Limerick Pork Butchers' Society, founded in 1890 but now a Section of the Limerick Branch, celebrated its seventy-fifth anniversary in 1965. They had 'never lost their identity or ceased to function as a craft Society, and we believe it never will.' They had their own Executive, premises, craft regulations and procedure. George Judge, their Treasurer, sat on the NEC. They honoured eight surviving founders and gave the Bishop of Limerick a 'Badge of Honour of the Society, investing him as Vice President.'[5]

There was no organisation campaign in 1951, mainly because industrial action was so widespread. The NEC imposed no logistical or financial restrictions—'on the contrary, our organisational policy has all along been inspired by a desire to improve the lot of the workers as a whole, no matter where or at what they are employed.' The union's 'service to the employees in the rural Districts is no whit less than that given to those in the cities and towns.' Organisers travelled 250,000 miles, and 'the standard of life in rural Ireland [had] improved enormously.'

Huge Dispute Pay was dispensed without touching reserves, but the underlying inadequacy of contributions and Strike Pay were emphasised. Members had a choice of contribution rates and attendant benefit scales. There were considerations beyond their immediate membership: 'We are rightly regarded by the enemies of labour as the bulwark of defence' of the entire movement, and 'if we could be rendered impotent, the remainder of the trade union movement would be less capable to resist.' It was its duty to put the ITGWU beyond the power of any group to injure it.

W. Davis (Dublin No. 1) suggested a central organising body and a National Organiser, with clerical workers the obvious recruitment targets. It was not acted upon. In July the ITGWU expressed 'our regrets to those members of the Gardaí who asked us to organise them,' but 'they are precluded from trade union Association.'[6]

Fintan Kennedy addressed a constant problem in verse, noting a 'big falling off in attendance at Branch meetings—so much so that it has become very difficult to obtain decisions, even on matters of vital importance.' He urged: 'Don't leave it all to the other fellows—the Ever Faithful Few'.

When the meeting's called to order
And you look around the room,
You're sure to see a chap or two
From out the shadow's gloom,
Who are always at the meeting
And who stay to see it through,
Whom you can always count on:
The Ever Faithful Few.

They fill the thankless office,
They're always on the spot,
No matter what the evening's like,
Be the weather fine or not;
They're not fair-weather members,
They're tried and they are true,
The chaps we can rely on:
The Ever Faithful Few.

There's a lot of other fellows
Who come when in the mood,
When everything's convenient
And if they're feeling good;
They're a factor in the Union,
And necessary too,
But the ones who never fail us
Are the Ever Faithful Few.[7]

By 1952 the membership had reached 'approximately 148,000,' and yet 'recalcitrance'
and 'non-Unionism' persisted. Given its services and the 'reasonableness' of contributions, the ITGWU was surprised at the extent of non-compliance. It intended 'to
take very strong measures in future against any worker proper to this organisation
who is not a member or who fails to keep his card in order.' In 'addition to the
benefits and services,' average wage increases 'equalling up to fifty times the
contribution payable' had been won. For benefits received, membership costs were
cheap. Rewards were 'paid for by the good members.' Any worker who accepted
them 'without having the decency' to maintain membership was 'guilty of disloyalty' to his fellow-workers. Branch Committees were invited to review matters every
month.

The General Secretary, Purcell, outlined the core features of ITGWU investment
policy in 1953. It was confined to Trustee stock in Corporation or state securities,
actuated by 'compliance with the law governing the investment' of union funds,
'absolute securing of the members' money' and the desire that 'investments would
serve the best interests of their own people in their own country.' It 'always subordinated the question of interest to those three considerations.' Current market
prices meant that investments would sell at a loss, but there was no intention or
pressure to sell.

More demands for Organisers led Conroy to ask 'what exactly it was intended
that they would do.' Extra Officials were appointed in Athlone, Dublin, Limerick
and Midleton, but if the existing staff could not maintain organisation, new
appointees would fare no better.

In 1954 the credit balance had increased to £614,286, with £40,000 transferred
to a special fund for the reconstruction of Liberty Hall. An Cumann Teicneoirí

Innealtóireachta (Engineering Technicians' Society) was incorporated on 9 August 1949 'to enable them to overcome the problem of a Negotiating Licence,' on condition that they donate 7d out of the contribution of 3s per week. They quickly drifted from membership.

Concerns were expressed over the decline of the Galway Branch. Only 356 members were in benefit, 458 out of benefit and 666 lapsed. Financial membership was 79,951 in 130 Branches.[8] Waterford Glass members transferred to the ATGWU; no-one was 'able to offer any explanation for what had happened.' It proved an expensive loss. An organisational drive was announced in 1955, although it was hampered by large numbers 'who did not have sufficient knowledge of Union Rules.'

Table 69: ITGWU membership by Branch, 1953

Ardee Mental Hospital	74	Ennis	170
Ardfinnan	167	Ennis Mental Hospital	72
Arigna	145	Enniscorthy	337
Arklow	978	Enniscorthy Mental Hospital	104
Askeaton	61	Fenit	34
Athlone	514	Fermoy	96
Avoca	67	Foxford	246
Bailieborough	99	Foynes	117
Balbriggan	91	Galway	1,000
Ballaghaderreen	70	Gorey	239
Ballina No. 1	107	Graigue	186
Ballina No. 2	58	Kanturk	60
Ballinasloe	40	Kilcar	63
Ballinasloe Mental Hospital	400	Kilkenny	894
Ballysadare	118	Killarney	89
Ballyshannon	28	Killarney Mental Hospital	112
Baltinglass	25	Killorglin	33
Bandon	142	Kilrush	134
Bantry	67	Kingscourt	274
Belfast	1,004	Laois-Offaly	1,020
Belturbet	103	Letterkenny	295
Bennettsbridge	44	Limerick	4,786
Birr	122	Longford	89
Blanchardstown	97	Lucan	1,056
Blarney	585	Macroom	184
Bray	146	Mallow	1,118

Buncrana	492	Manorhamilton	150
Cahir	141	Midleton	511
Carlow	1,045	Mitchelstown	177
Carndonagh	97	Mohill	24
Cashel	40	Monaghan Mental Hospital	163
Castlebar Mental Hospital	166	Moneenroe	430
Castlebar No. 1	144	Mullingar	202
Castlebar No. 2	74	Mullingar Mental Hospital	189
Castleblayney	88	Mullingar Rail	139
Castlerea	62	Naas	174
Cavan	186	Navan	229
Clara	612	Nenagh	342
Claremorris	63	New Ross	232
Clonakility	67	Newry	572
Clonmel	401	Rathdowney	45
Cóbh	374	Rathdrum	57
Convoy	358	Rathfarnham	80
Cootehill	74	Rathmore	158
Cork No. 1	5,271	Roscrea	368
Cork No. 2/3	6,530	Slieveardagh	119
Derry	2,619	Sligo	549
Dingle	43	Sligo Mental Hospital	185
Dripsey	60	Templecrone	27
Drogheda	1,859	Templemore	20
Droichead Nua	519	Thomastown	190
Dublin No. 1	9,144	Thurles	177
Dublin No. 3	4,313	Tinahely	90
Dublin No. 4	3,083	Tipperary	303
Dublin No. 5	1,560	Tralee	1,089
Dublin No. 6	1,621	Tuam	298
Dublin No. 7	1,577	Tullamore No. 1	55
Dublin No. 8	1,881	Tullamore No. 2	468
Dublin No. 9/10	3,058	Tullow	11
Dublin No. 11	1,050	Waterford	2,978
Dún Laoghaire	125	Westport	124
Dundalk	504	Wexford	1,048
Dunglow	44	Wicklow	233
Dunmanway	61	Youghal	154

Source: ITGWU, minutes of National Executive Council, 26–28 April 1954.

A 'sincere hand of friendship' was extended to 'loyal members', but the union 'does not want within it the wilfully disloyal member.' Union democracy was supreme and unalienable. The slogan 'Onwards to the half-million Mark' Purcell turned into 'A credit balance of £1,000,000.' At £679,286 there was far to go. He recalled that since the war 'the magnitude of our financial progress has been astounding.' A Craft Section was demanded.

In Tralee a 'Borough Rule' that enforced a closed shop within the town by employing only townspeople was lifted. It was introduced to combat employers' preference, if let, to employ rural workers nominated by big farmers who were merchants' customers. Tralee Branch Committee vetted applications, many a ruse being used to prove *bona fide* town credentials. This led to 'exploitation and undesirable practices.' At its removal 'no one was sorry.'[9]

Table 70: ITGWU income, expenditure and surplus (£), 1950–59

	Membership	Income	Expenditure	Surplus (deficit)
1950	130,000	97,686	55,532	42,154
1951	130,000	106,799	108,742	(1,943)
1952	148,000	109,533	103,897	5,656
1953	148,000	153,979	55,876	98,103
1954	150,000	159,907	64,970	94,937
1955	150,000	166,129	96,179	69,950
1956	150,000	166,469	84,203	82,266
1957	150,000	166,564	104,656	61,908
1958	150,000	166,177	93,194	72,983
1959	150,000	170,407	121,355	49,052

Source: ITGWU, Annual Reports, 1950–59.

Membership rose in 1955 but dissatisfaction was expressed, as, if all who could be organised were organised, it would be 200,000. There was a 'moral obligation' on men and women to 'become and remain' members to advance their class.

Size brought its own problems. External critics were quick to suggest that the ITGWU's numbers denied internal democracy, a criticism to which the union was highly sensitive. 'It is a gross slander to say the Union is not run on democratic lines or that the members have not a free choice to decide its policy and to absolutely control its management.' It was 'each member's duty to himself or herself' to 'use his or her influence and vote in the elections of officers and Committees, and to make sure that men and women of integrity and sound judgement, only those having all the necessary qualifications, are elected to such responsible positions.'[10] Ballots for Branch Officers and on all industrial decisions were central to the union's business.

Membership in 1956 was satisfactory, but a 'disproportionate part' of Officials' time was spent chasing arrears and pursing non-Unionists. Branch Secretaries were encouraged to call Special Meetings of Sub-Committees to address organisation locally, examine registers and then follow through, with Officials and Collectors concentrating on arrears. Cards were paid weekly to Collectors or Shop Stewards or directly into Branch offices. Members could fall into arrears through their own or the Collector's negligence, being absent through illness or leave, by withholding contributions to draw attention to a complaint, or because that week they were a 'little short'. The goal was to maximise benefit membership, 'reducing the rather high average of arrears.' Proposals to appoint four Regional Officers in 1957 were withdrawn.[11]

The General Fund passed £900,000 in 1957, with investments valued at £473,232. Membership fell by about 2,500, setting alarm bells ringing, given organising endeavours. With rising unemployment and emigration it was not surprising. Kennedy reminded the 1958 Delegates that 'from time to time' the union gave 'considerable sums of money' to 'help the country's economy.' At a time of low investment and lack of confidence it had 'investments in and loans outstanding with the State, Semi-State [state-sponsored] bodies and Local Authorities totalling £631,415.' In addition it commissioned building works worth £375,000. 'When our present building programme is completed' the union would 'have injected over £1,000,000 into the country's economy.' For thirty-five years the ITGWU's investments had assisted with hospitals, docks, electricity, sewerage and water services, much of it at very low-interest loans of between 2½ and 3½%, all this 'notwithstanding the fact that as a militant trade union we have expended huge sums of money on Dispute Benefits.'

The union's significance as an employer and as a generator of economic activity is rarely acknowledged. During economic crises the union showed faith, putting its money where its mouth was.

Overtures were made by the Clerical Officers' Section of the Irish Local Government Officials' Union in Wexford for a transfer. The ITGWU was 'prepared to accept . . . only on a friendly and national basis and provided a substantial majority' were willing. It never proceeded.[12]

Ground lost was regained in 1958. Total assets reached a staggering £1,049,128. 'Leadership' shown during negotiations for the Sixth Round significantly assisted. With the fiftieth anniversary pending, every possible member was sought: what better reward for 'those who took it through its difficult days than by making greater strides towards their objective of the O.B.U.' Kennedy cautioned those who thought they were in an 'impregnable position'. About two-thirds of normal income was disbursed in benefits and services, and the tendency was for the gap between income and expenditure to close. They must always be ready for a large industrial battle.

George Corrigan (Dublin No. 1) saw the £1 million mark as a 'deterrent to employers.' The ITGWU certainly exuded strength and well-being. In 1959 investments totalled £864,315 18s 1d, although their market value was £25,842 less than cost. Membership rose by 2,179.[13]

A worrying trend was rising Branch subsidies. Contributions, raised in 1953, increased local funds, but many Branches abolished local levies, so offsetting gains. Branch incomes remained static as expenses rose. Branches were encouraged to reconsider levies. Only half the membership paid the full rate of 1s 6d, the rest paying 9d or less. It would only be a matter of time before it would be 'necessary to examine the whole question' of contributions 'to bring our rates more in line with present day values.' It was still possible to conduct a strike to 'force the careless to clear cards,' as in National Board and Paper Mills, Waterford. It was 'regrettable' mainly because 'one would imagine that in this day of enlightenment, workers would of their own volition take pride' in a clear card.[14]

Full-page advertisements in *CIU Reports* boasted 150,000 members, a Reserve Fund of £750,000 and benefits paid out exceeding £1,250,000.

Workers of Ireland
You can most effectively manage your own affairs without alien control and alien interference.
Keep your trade union subscriptions inside your own country.
Don't let a foreign Executive try to manage your trade union problems.
Join an Irish Union
The Irish Transport and General Workers' Union is the most powerful Irish Union.
It is, in fact, the greatest organisation in the country—a Trade Union without parallel in its national record, unrivalled in its service to the workers of Ireland. It has ever been—and always will be—first in the battle for the uplift of the wage-earner.
There are Branches of the Union in all principal towns throughout Ireland.

Others emphasised their 'Irish' character, but this trumpeting of the ITGWU's achievement undoubtedly annoyed some. Although boastful in tone, the advertisement was quite truthful.

GOLDEN JUBILEE

The fiftieth anniversary was 4 January 1959. The ITGWU had grown from an 'infant' to 'a mature and powerful militant organisation' that 'dominated the scene of industrial relations' and 'brought ever nearer the goals enshrined by the founders.'

Conroy's presidential 'personal greeting' summarised all the union felt about itself: 'To all the members of the Union from the caves of Antrim to the shores of Cork and from the rugged hills of Connemara to the plains of Leinster, I extend greetings and felicitations.' He paid homage to the 'foresight', work and 'sacrifice of the founders,' who 'moulded the greatest and most militant working-class organisation Ireland or the world has ever known.'

Two additional benefits were offered: exemption from the payment of contributions during illness for up to three months in any year, and a Marriage Gratuity for women members up to a maximum of £10. There were 121 Officials, 98 part-time Officials and 2,550 Collectors. The ITGWU played 'its part in the country's internal economy,' contributing 'substantially by way of taxes, rates [and] telephonic communications' to the order of '£4,000 per annum.' £155,000 was spent on capital expenditure and investment in 'Government, Local Authority and Public Utility Funds,' totalling £706,622. The union faced the future with confidence, secure in the knowledge that there was 'acceptance of faith in the cause of Irish workers and in the cause of Ireland.'

Larkin was not mentioned in salutes to 'the founders.' Conroy thought the Golden Jubilee was the 'greatest single tribute' to them.

> Sacrifices, hardship, privations—these were the rewards of their solidarity. Pickets, parades, disputes, beatings, physical injury to themselves and their families, imprisonment—these were the hallmarks of their Union membership. But these were indelible marks that will never be effaced as long as a worker seeks justice from his employer.

He called for rededication 'to the Christian and noble work for which the Union was founded,' repeating demands for a minimum family income of £500 a year. He welcomed the formation of the Irish Congress of Trade Unions and asked that its combined power be used to create employment and economic growth.

The Jubilee Conference platform was crowded with old members. A sum of £16,734 was spent on the Jubilee, £7,547 on the souvenir publication, *Fifty Years of Liberty Hall*. It sold at 3s 6d to the public and 2s 6d to members but was 'value for four times its price.' Many congratulatory letters were received from 'historians, leading citizens, newspapers and journals.'

The celebrations began with a march from the site of the demolished Liberty Hall to the National Ballroom in Parnell Square. A dinner for more than 500 people was held in the Metropole Restaurant, and other events were organised in Mullingar, Castleblayney, Monaghan (mistakenly described as the 'birthplace of James Connolly'), Limerick, Waterford (where new premises were opened at Summerhill), Sligo, Buncrana, Enniscorthy and Wexford. Purcell retired as General Secretary in August, being succeeded by Fintan Kennedy.

WOMEN

In 1951 the President of the CIU, John Conroy, extended a 'special welcome' to 'some ladies,' with the hope that 'many more ladies would be present' in future. The ITGWU Delegation contained no women.

In 1952 Sheila Williams (Dublin No. 4) argued that women bore far more of the brunt of rising prices than men. Women lucky enough to be employed earned 'much less than males doing comparable work,' while 'those who were housekeepers had received little or no part of the various increases granted to their husbands, brothers or children,' as 'by far the greater portion of these increases' was 'spent in the pubs, race tracks and other forms of entertainment.' Men were fond of talking about the cost of living but 'had no appreciation of the extreme difficulties of their womenfolk in endeavouring to make ends meet.' It was their 'Christian duty' to make sure every penny of any increase entered the family Budget. She then asked when the ILO recommendation of equal pay for equal work for women would be implemented by the Government. She assumed 'the Union fully supported that recommendation.' With the exception of Patrick Lally (Galway No. 1), who thought Williams's contribution 'outstanding' and 'very sound', no-one responded. Conroy, when summing up, studiously avoided her direct question. Shoots of equal pay were meeting frosted ground.

In 1954 Sheila Williams said that 30,000 female members endorsed the ITGWU's incomes policy but were not satisfied with prevailing wages. She acknowledged the psychological value of wage increases, an obvious gain, as opposed to the more abstract benefit of a fall in the cost-of-living index. She again berated 'excessive drinking, smoking, gambling [and] cinema-going' as 'contrary to the Christian concept of society.' The principle of equal pay was 'fully endorsed by the Church.' The Pope himself said 'the Church has always held that women should receive the same rate of pay as men for equal work and output.' The exploitation of female labour injured women 'but also the working man, who would then be at risk of being out of work.' She instanced the Chancellor of the Exchequer (minister for finance) in Britain, R. A. B. Butler, gradually implementing equal pay in the civil service during the next financial year, at a cost of £32 million. 'Surely what a British Tory Government can do, an Irish Government with Labour representation would do also?'

Six women Delegates out of 168 constituted a record. If union women were organised in a separate organisation they would 'constitute a Union second in size only to that of the I.T.G.W.U. itself.' E. Carey (Dublin No. 6) moved that 'all Hoffman or similar steam pressing machines' be 'reserved for male labour,' a motion adopted without debate, giving Williams part of her answer.

Surprisingly little fuss was made of Williams's election to the NEC in 1955, the first woman to achieve this position. She was re-elected in 1958. A native of Bantry, Co. Cork, she worked as a waiter in the Capitol Cinema, Dublin, and was active on Dublin No. 4 Branch Committee.[15]

Williams called for a National Planning Council in 1956, drawing attention to thousands of unmarried women forced to emigrate and 'grass widows' left behind by emigrating husbands. She challenged suggestions that male unemployment was a product of female displacement. The female population had declined by 21,271, or 1½%, since 1951 and was 'the lowest ever recorded.' She predicted the 'impending extinction of the Irish race.' A declining population was nothing to do with a 'falling birth rate' or a 'failure or refusal of our young men and women to accept the responsibility of marriage'—that was 'utter nonsense.' The natural increase since 1951 was

134,623, yet the population declined by 65,771. Many emigrants married in Britain or the United States.

In 1957 she condemned cuts in food subsidies, as 'mothers of the working class homes are fighting the battle for existence for too long.' Women, according to the returns of the Registrar of Friendly Societies, constituted a solid 20% of the union's membership throughout the 1950s, an average of approximately 25,000.

Table 71: ITGWU, women membership, 1950–59

	Total	Women	As proportion of total (%)
1950	116,257	23,251	19.9
1951	128,191	25,638	19.9
1952	127,480	25,496	20.0
1953	119,377	23,875	19.9
1954	122,903	24,581	20.0
1955	126,180	25,346	20.0
1956	126,707	25,342	20.0
1957	124,183	24,837	20.0
1958	125,571	25,314	20.1
1959	127,571	25,830	20.2

Source: National Archives, Registrar of Friendly Societies, file 275T.

Marriage Benefit was paid for the first time in 1959, a payment 'wholeheartedly welcomed by our female members,' even if, with the existence of the Marriage Bar in the public service and some other employments, it was merely a repayment of contributions to members never again expected to return to work: their future would be as homemakers and mothers. Sheila Williams no doubt claimed her Marriage Benefit somewhat ruefully: she married John Conroy and, as a consequence, surrendered her employment and her membership of the NEC from 21 July 1959, occasioning what was described as a 'casual vacancy.'[16]

'NA SÉ CHONTAE'

Membership in the 'Occupied Area' remained static until an organisational drive in 1953. Seán Moroney accompanied Head Office Officials in this work. Workers knew 'they were being used' as 'pawns in a game to keep them in economic and industrial subjection.' Membership in the Region rose by 3,000, largely after Stephen McGonagle's Garment Workers' Union in Derry transferred. They were afforded a hearty 'Céad míle fáilte' and 'received with acclaim.'

It was not plain sailing. While 'agitation against the Union in Derry had subsided ... opposition was still strong.' Disruptive propaganda in factories continued, and more serious attacks 'could not be ruled out.' The *Derry Journal* reported that 3,316 voted for amalgamation, 212 against. More than 1,000 attended the Guildhall on 27 October to hear Purcell and McGonagle. The ITUC condemned the break-away and called on all Derry workers 'to work for the restoration of trade union solidarity and unity.' Clothing workers met in the Guildhall on 5 January 1953, addressed by ITUC speakers. It made no difference to McGonagle. His presence was a loss at ITUC gatherings.[17]

Citing *Plebs,* the journal of the National Council of Labour Colleges, *Liberty* damned the Stormont Government's boast of a 'substantial reserve of male labour.' The National Assistance Board bragged of saving £400,000, a 'theft from the mouths of children and a breaker up of families.' The North's 'Tory Government' proudly proclaimed that 'it has kept the workers without work.'

In 1956 the ITGWU was prominent in the campaign for parity with British Family Allowances and the National Insurance Act, the lower provisions by Stormont 'clearly constituting gross discrimination against the parents of large families—composed in the main of the working class.' Stormont was motivated 'by reasons other than equity,' namely by 'class interest.'

As the IRA border campaign began, the NEC condemned the 'malicious destruc-tion' of the sea-going locks on the Newry Canal on 13 May 1957 as 'completely irresponsible,' costing many members 'loss of their entire means of livelihood.' It 'most earnestly' urged 'all sincere Irishmen to refrain from such wanton destruction of property resulting in loss of employment and distress to our people.'

Not all concurred. A Waterford Official, Michael O'Brien, was charged under the Offences Against the State Act with membership of an unlawful organisation.

In 1958 the reports of the Newry and Belfast Branch AGMs showed active if static Branches. Unemployment and recession perturbed the NEC, and yet no drive attempted to reverse decline.[18]

WAGES AND DISPUTES

In 1950, £20,870 was spent on Dispute Pay for 107 strikes. In Larkin's Bakery in Killorglin a recognition battle was fought from August 1949, with flour-millers refusing to handle goods for the town. A three-month strike against merchants in Galway produced satisfactory adjustments.

Dispute Pay was £70,322 in 1951, with 101 strikes involving 16,000 members, most of short duration. Exceptions were railway, bus, hotel and restaurant strikes.

In 1952 the NEC stated that no CIU-affiliated union could embark on industrial action 'until all the available machinery of Congress was first utilised.' The Central Council would nominate a panel to investigate matters. Any union not doing so would not be accorded the support of Congress or any other union. This sounded like a forerunner of the All-Out Picket policy that emerged after the 1969 main-tenance workers' dispute. The issues were wages, dismissals, seniority, redundancy, hours, conditions and non-unionism. The ITGWU regretted unofficial action and issued a scalding circular, condemning it as 'the complete antithesis of trade union-ism' and 'worse still . . . extremely foolish,' invariably to workers' disadvantage. It knew of 'no case or complaint which could not better be handled by official than unofficial action.' Stressing the need for discipline, it said that 'any direction from a superior' considered unjust or not right should nevertheless be carried out and then reported to the Branch Committee. It could not, 'of course, accept responsibility for anything that befalls a member as a result of unofficial action.'

McMullen interpreted the £300,000 expended on Dispute Pay since 1945 not as a debit in the accounts but 'more accurately as a credit.' It showed the union's support for members. 'We recognise the justice of a claim of any Section' as being more important 'than any question of the preservation of its funds.'[19]

There were fewer strikes in 1953 than for a decade, and only £6,682 in Dispute Pay, indicating 'a general improvement in industrial relations' and a 'greater realisation' of the 'desirability of settling disputes by pacific means.' From July to December there was a strike in Ceimicí Teoranta alcohol factories. In February a dispute in the Theatre Royal, Dublin, begun in December 1952 with the Irish Federation of Musicians over rights to organise all theatre and cinema employees, including musicians, came to a head; and in September unofficial action in Denny's spread from Waterford to Cork, Mountmellick, Sligo and Tralee. The NEC declared the action 'not alone contrary' to the Rules 'but entirely without justification' other than on Suirside. Even here there was 'no justification for lightning and unofficial action' that brought hardship on a thousand members and their families.

In 1954 it was estimated that in the previous thirty years the union had spent £1½ million on Strike Pay. Great attention was given to the Consumer Price Index and household Budget survey to focus on the impact of prices on real wages. Concerns were expressed for rural workers' incomes, campaigns being based on 'moral, social and economic grounds.' Unless wages and living standards were brought up to 'Christian levels', national prosperity and well-being would prove impossible. The Agricultural Wages Board was 'shamed' into granting an increase of 4s.

Despite this and other advances, 300,000 workers received wages of 90s (£4 10s) a week or less. For the average family of father, mother and four children, if every penny of this income were devoted to food 'no more than sixpence per meal could be allotted.' Reflecting an apparent belief that the solution lay in theology rather than Socialism, the union urged: 'We shall continue to exert every effort, in both the industrial and political spheres,' to have rural workers' wages 'brought up to decent levels.' In 'this noble task we request and expect the full support and co-operation of all true Christians.'

Purcell sent out a stiff circular in which he was 'compelled to reiterate' previous warnings and to 're-emphasise the serious consequences of irresponsible and undisciplined action' for all. In taking unofficial action, members 'abandon their Union and forfeit all the rights and advantages of membership.' They risked being prosecuted by employers for loss or damage to goods, machinery or other property. In bold type he warned: 'No Officer or Official of the Union can be associated with an unofficial stoppage or render any encouragement or assistance to those concerned in it—morally, physically or financially—without exposing the Union to legal liability.'[20]

Employers would think twice about suing workers—damages might be unrecoverable—but they would 'have no hesitation' in suing the union. The ITGWU had not lost an official dispute in more than twenty-five years, whereas many unofficial actions were unsuccessful. Individual actions were 'absolutely indefensible.'

In December 1952 *Liberty* published an article headed 'Plain Speaking about Strikes' (republished in March 1954) that 'should be read,' which fulminated against unofficial action. Clearly irritated, in 1956 Conroy issued a 'final warning' to unruly members, their 'grave misconduct' to 'incur the severest penalties.'

Advances were not confined to urban areas. 2d an hour was gained on basic rates for Co. Donegal building workers, together with two weeks' annual leave. Increases were won for sugar and confectionery workers, turf-cutters, woollen and worsted workers, oil workers, Dundalk brewery workers, bank porters in Cork and Dublin, Cork building workers, and drivers in New Ross.[21] In addition, 'as a result of our nationwide campaign for extra pay for industrial workers,' the Agricultural Wages Board made upward adjustments.

Table 72: ITGWU Dispute Pay, 1950–59

	Income (£)	Dispute Pay (£)	As proportion of income (%)
1950	97,686	20,870	21.4
1951	106,799	70,322	65.8
1952	109,553	57,298	52.3
1953	153,979	6,682	4.3
1954	159,907	6,100	3.8
1955	166,129	22,789	13.7
1956	166,469	1,971	1.2
1957	166,564	22,719	13.6
1958	166,177	9,631	5.8
1959	170,407	16,993	9.9

Source: ITGWU, Annual Reports, 1950–59.

The ITGWU was preoccupied with 'the obligations of the worker.' In an unsigned article (although a clerical hand was not too far away) in October 1955 *Liberty* reminded members of their responsibilities 'to their employers, their families and their country.' The article said much for the psyche of the times, the summary of the worker's obligations being 'to carry out all lawful instructions given by those in authority over him and be a good time-keeper,' to 'do a fair day's work' to the 'highest standard he is capable of,' to 'respect his employer's property,' to provide 'adequately in accordance with his income for his family' and 'in all things treat them justly' and to 'conduct himself as a good citizen,' carrying out his obligations and giving 'good example to his neighbour.'[22] In addition, the trade unionist was obliged to 'honour all Agreements entered into by his Union on his behalf,' observe union Rules and 'give fair consideration to Union advice and respect its Officials.' An afterthought added: 'All of the foregoing, where applicable, applied equally to men and women.'

Dispute Pay in 1956 was a paltry £1,917. The CIU felt obliged to respond to the Minister's anxiety over unofficial strikes, urging 'strong disciplinary action' against those involved and that 'unofficial pickets be ignored.'

In 1957 the number of unofficial strikes was the lowest for fourteen years. The Minister for Industry and Commerce set up a Working Party, whose views the ITGWU was to 'endorse and implement' so as to eliminate unofficial action. Wage rates contributed less than working conditions, supervision and worker-management relations; the competence of supervisory personnel could be improved; machinery for handling grievances needed wider usage to give 'early ventilation and examination' of problems (although this was best left to employers and unions to work out); the management should give 'reasonable notice' and an 'explanation' of all changes being considered; disciplinary action by supervisors or junior management should be subject to 'early review'; no negotiations should take place while unofficial action persisted (although this should not prevent a union ascertaining the facts of the case); intervention by third parties should not undermine the management or unions; and all unions should have an agreed common policy and not accept members from another union involved in unofficial action within six months of such action. The Working Party acknowledged that its suggestions would not have 'unanimous support.' But Conroy said 'this means unofficial strikes are outlawed and ended so far as this Union is concerned.'[23]

Following Conroy's call in 1958 for an annual family income of £500, the ITGWU demanded that the Government introduce legislation 'to determine and fix a just family wage.' Brendan Corish TD thought it 'handed over the right' to fix wages, so long cherished by unions in direct contest with employers, to the Government, and he urged referral back. Conroy accepted that determining a 'just income' was difficult. It was carried 'by an overwhelming majority.' An intensive wage campaign resulted in nineteen stoppages, the shortest lasting one hour and the longest, at Hollypark Coalmine, Co. Carlow, begun on 30 May, unresolved. A recognition dispute in the Landscape Cinema, Churchtown, Co. Dublin, fought from 28 April 1957 to 27 October 1958, ended 'with complete victory.'

An increasing feature was productivity-related payments and the introduction of work study. An inter-union dispute took place at Whitegate Oil Refinery, Co. Cork, after the Electrical Trades Union (Ireland) gave insufficient strike notice, placed pickets and slandered other unions' Officials. It was a rare example of investigation by the CIU of such a dispute, although the ITGWU, representing general rather than craft workers, was essentially an onlooker.

Jubilee year was quiet. The Hollypark strike was won on 8 February. Others concerned non-union labour, unfair dismissals, working conditions and recognition, with only ten relating to the campaign for the Seventh Round, begun in June.[24] The 1950s were relatively peaceful, especially after 1952, with the Wage-Round system and poor economic performance contributing in equal measure.

WAGE ROUNDS

Problems with the 'Eleven-Shilling Formula' in 1950 led to discussions between the CIU and FUE under the Labour Court. Unions pointed out that the cost of living had risen substantially, much of it in items not included in official indexes; wages had not kept pace; profits and national income had increased; there were strong demands for wage increases; an agreed formula was better than industrial strife; three years of virtual freedom from strikes had given the Government and business adequate time to respond, and national output had increased significantly; too many workers suffered low pay; Irish industry could afford to improve living standards; and unless workers obtained relief, 'industrial strife is inevitable.' The employers declined to budge. Concerned not to create 'any undue upset in the economic life of the nation,' the CIU decided 'to confine claims to increases of 12s per week 'unless exceptional circumstances prevailed.'

In September the ITGWU announced: 'We are ready for a showdown if necessary,' as the employers' policy could 'be summed up as: "Not an inch",' although 'unable to refute irrefutable arguments.' The union wanted to restore purchasing power to 1939 values, as price increases had 'neutralised the 11/– rise.' Employers were apparently 'resolved to cast aside the opportunity of prolonged industrial peace,' instead inviting a showdown. 'Why? Has the spirit of the parent organisation, the Employers' Federation of 1913, re-entered the body of the FUE?'[25]

In 1951 there was a big push to improve rural workers' conditions. Michael Moynihan (Killarney) stated that current rates were 'scandalously low,' a 'disgrace to a Christian country.' John Nugent (Letterkenny) said the country was 'being stripped of its manpower and its womanpower,' as 'emigration was necessary to earn a livelihood.' In January McMullen noted with 'what smug satisfaction' some of 'our politicians arrogate to themselves credit for the degree of stability' enjoyed since the end of the war. While he was 'anxious not to withhold credit from anyone entitled to it,' the 'great stabilising force in modern society' was the trade union movement, a fact 'amply demonstrated in the voluntary wages control.'

The voluntary Twelve-Shilling Formula operated throughout 1951, members gaining more than £1 million. By December, however, workers strongly lobbied for a new Congress policy. They met the stone wall of 'selfish sectional' employers who merely wished to keep wages as low as possible but recommended a Twelve-Shilling Formula, concern for national economic welfare determining that figure. The Labour Court, under whose auspices negotiation took place, made no 'useful or acceptable contribution.' The state, which the ITGWU thought should be a model employer, to its shame still employed tens of thousands at rates below a living wage. The Secretary of the CIU, Leo Crawford, was a member of the Prices Advisory Committee, but it was considered inadequate and ineffective. McMullen thought another formula would best serve national interests and equity. The 'stronger battalions' got up to 16s, while weaker groups struggled to get anything above 8s 6d.[26]

The Twelve-Shilling Formula operated until December 1951, by which time the cost-of-living index had risen to 113 points (using February 1950 as 100). A new formula was agreed with the employers in May 1952, addressing the desire to maintain and expand trade and employment and the need to stabilise prices. A 'properly balanced relationship between wages and prices' was desirable, and the 'Subscribing Organisations' agreed to strive to maintain employment, 'avoid any unjustifiable' price increases, avoid stoppages of work, increase output and productivity and 'discourage by every means restrictive practices.' Wage increases would be paid only where 'economically justifiable,' with a consideration of prevailing rates, of the earning capacity of the jobs concerned and comparative rates in the locality, and of the recessionary impact. No stoppage could occur unless and until all available machinery for settlement was used, including the Labour Court. Either party could terminate the Agreement with three months' notice. Increases would not exceed 12s 6d a week.

From May to December the ITGWU negotiated increases for more than 100,000 members. Those who had 'rejected the Formula'—agricultural workers, civil servants and postal workers—secured little if any increase by the end of the year. No days were lost in major industries, something McMullen regarded as of 'utmost importance to the welfare of the community,' claiming the ITGWU-led constraint had been rewarded with obvious signs of economic recovery.[27]

He criticised the ATGWU. 'Do not let anybody confuse it with the Irish Transport and General Workers' Union because we would be insulted in the process if you did.' He accused the ATGWU of a 'great deal of dishonesty,' as it opposed CIU policy and argued for an unfettered 'free-for-all'. Its General Secretary, Arthur Deakin, President of the TUC, had visited a miners' Conference and argued for wage restraint, as, if prices were forced up, the main sufferers would be workers. In addition, no Government could effectively plan without price stability.

McMullen asked the pertinent question: 'Is Mr Deakin to have one policy for England and a different policy for Ireland?' English unions had done that in 'this country from time immemorial.' Anything was good enough for Ireland. They were happy to 'disturb the economy of the country' while 'trying to stabilise it in Britain.' It would not be the only occasion on which the ATGWU's Irish wages policy was diametrically opposite to that adopted in Britain. McMullen cited a railway strike in the 1930s 'when Northern Ireland was made the cock-pit for a wages movement for the whole of Ireland and Great Britain.' The ITGWU was 'thrown behind the fight' and stopped Belfast port. Leakage took place through Larne, but the NUR refused to close Stranraer. 'They allowed the railwaymen of the North of Ireland to be beaten sooner than let Britain be involved.' He asked that Larkin and Gilbert Lynch show more honesty. The 12s 6d was not the absolute answer: he had argued for 15s, but it was in the whole community's best interests.

McMullen repudiated charges that the ITGWU was too moderate. 'I have spent

£300,000 of the Union's money since 1947 battling to raise the standard of life of the people. I am supposed to be a moderate. Why, everybody outside the Movement regards me as a Communist, and when they are not telling me I am a Communist, they say I am an Orangeman from Northern Ireland who has come down to disturb the peace of the State.' Comparative figures for the ATGWU would be interesting but would undoubtedly be nothing like £300,000.

The ITGWU considered the '12s 6d formula' a success. Although it was initially rejected by the ITUC, many of its affiliates had not achieved the rate by April 1953. The ITGWU boasted that 'we got 12/6' while the 'Bakers' Union got 7/6 in flour-milling,' in cement 'the F.R.W. got only a few shillings' and in malting, brewing and distilling the WUI 'got only three-quarters in Guinness,' before concluding: 'Over the whole field of industry the story is the same: the I.T.U.C. selling out without a single struggle and the C.I.U. operating a planned, forceful and successful campaign.'

Prices continued to rise. All those who gained 12s 6d suffered a decline in living standards. The ITGWU concluded that prevailing wages were 'inadequate'.

In 1954 Conroy described 'as extremely false and misconceived the doctrine that improved wages must necessarily result in increased prices.' Unions exercised con-siderable restraint, yet still prices soared. The ITGWU 'did not contemplate the initiation of another round of demands just now' but instead sought to have the cost of living reduced. It felt that the 'circumstances that gave rise' to the Wage Rounds had 'gradually evaporated and stability has been restored.' Such 'normal-ity' nevertheless 'still condemns many thousands of our people to unemployment and distress'.[28]

In 1955 Conroy declared 'general levels of wages' to be too low. They could be raised 'without injury to the country's economy.' Edward Browne, Vice-President, launched a campaign for 'higher minimum wage rates' and 'improved social welfare benefits.' He reckoned that a third of the Southern population of 3 million lived at or below the poverty line. *Liberty* complained in February that 'it is now approaching three years since the trade unions took this reasonable and responsi-ble action' of moderating wages. There were no corresponding price reductions.

The Government returned on 3 June 1954 recognised that prices were a main election issues but did little. If prices could not be controlled, people should be told and the unions' wage policy adjusted accordingly.

Much 'to-ing and fro-ing' took place once the CIU gave three months' notice of terminating the 1952 formula in February. The FUE proved stubborn and accused the ITGWU of breaking the Agreement in an ironmongery strike in October 1954, although the strike was under way five weeks before the revelation dawned upon the employers. In May 1955 a 'free-for-all' seemed likely.[29]

The Fifth Wage Round was 'outstandingly successful', and when it was complete it increased members' wages by more than £5 million per year. Strike Pay of £25,000 was trifling in comparison. The ITGWU had 'some reluctance' in embarking on the Round, 'fully conscious that it could well prove catastrophic' because of the 'ineptitude of the authorities' and the possibility of large-scale actions. For workers, a 'falling cost of living' was preferable to a 'rising level of wages'. If the Government did its duty 'both objectives would be obtained simultaneously.' Average wage increases gained over the first five Rounds were £3. The union demonstrated that between 1938 and 1955 wages were slightly above increases in the cost of living. The fuller picture revealed that industrial workers did better than rural workers. The termination of the Fifth Round illustrated this, as difficulties were encountered in 'mopping up' small rural employers.

The Agricultural Wages Board was 'obliged' to make further advances on 28 May 1956, although, 'needless to say,' these were 'inadequate and insufficient to enable these workers to maintain themselves and their dependants in any degree of Christian comfort.' In August 1955 the cost of living was 134% higher than in August 1939. It took 'about 46/10d to purchase goods available at 20/– at that time'; conversely, what could 'now be bought for 20/– was obtained for 8/6.' Employers and politicians blamed wages, but there were periodic wage lulls since 1939, some led by the unions. It all added steam to the boiler of discontent.

Supporting the arguments for higher wages, the ITGWU called for putting 'intelligence to work' through better organisation, more efficient plant and machines, improved training of workers and supervisors, better time-keeping and 'a sense of pride in all concerned to turn out the best possible product.'

By October more than half the 150,000 members attained wage increases of between 10s and 15s per week, with Athlone, Drogheda, Dublin and CIÉ road and railway nationally at the fore.[30] By the end of the year more than 110,000 members had received an increase.

The Fifth Round concluded in 1956. Had it contributed to a rising cost of living? The ITGWU argued that Wage Rounds concluded 'without mutual agreement' with employers significantly raised prices but that where an Agreement existed prices were more constrained. All this, of course, assumed the acceptance of a direct relationship between wages and prices. Even if the Fifth Round did account for much of the parallel 5½% increase in prices, the union campaign was justified, as wages rose higher than this and prevented any fall in living standards.

In 1957 basic rates came under scrutiny. As Fifth-Round increases were accompanied by a halt in increases in the cost of living, most wage-earners 'would have been content to maintain the new standards.' Instead they called for further increases.

The Provisional United Organisation of the Irish Trade Union Movement met the FUE and ultimately, on 5 September 1957, an Agreement emerged. Both parties accepted the principle of collective bargaining and efforts 'to adjust and determine wage claims through the normal negotiating machinery.' There would be 'an avoidance of unnecessary friction and disturbance' by using 'every available means of peaceful settlement'; wage increases should not be followed by price rises; the Government, employers and workers should begin 'an immediate drive for tangible improvement in efficiency and production'; unions should moderate claims and employers 'should consider wage claims in an atmosphere of good will and understanding'; and awards should not exceed 10s. Where circumstances demanded, lesser amounts could be agreed. No stoppage should occur until the Labour Court or other machinery concluded its investigations.

In the circumstances, 10s was considered a 'fine achievement', built on the resistance and fight of manual workers. Some, according to Conroy, were now, on platforms and in the press, crying, 'We never accepted a 10/– ceiling' and 'We are not of the unclean.' He advised them to 'look back to the stony, rigid silence of all such self-advertising heroes in the Spring of 1957.' No professional body then took action. They cried that they were 'salaried' and required greater increases than mere manuals. It was easy enough from the ditch.

By December the union recorded 'outstanding progress in the wages campaign which we initiated less than four months' ago under the joint Agreement with the FUE. Complaint was made of the 'State's un-Christian attitude,' as resistance was greatest in the public sector. *Liberty* reminded employers and politicians that the 'Church's teachings' imposed 'moral obligations' on them to pay wages 'sufficient to enable a workingman comfortably to support himself, his wife and his children.'[31]

Advances under the Sixth Round gained momentum in 1958. By autumn most male members gained 10s, women 'an average of 6/6,' with *pro rata* adjustments for juveniles. Such pay differences raised few eyebrows. By August, however, a 10.6% increase in the cost of living nullified any advantage. The PUOITUM terminated the Sixth-Round Agreement in October.

The Sixth Round was based on the consumer price index for February–March 1957 of 132 points. By August 1958 this was 146, an increase of 10.6%. The ITGWU felt that this 'clears the way' for future wage policy calculated to increase purchasing power substantially, for 'we cannot have an expanding and sound economy unless the people's consumption of goods and services (and hence their purchasing power) is very much greater than it is or has been since the war.' It would be the first task of the united Congress.

In 1959 Mattie O'Neill (NEC) thought the union should 'select the most suitable industry' in which to initiate a movement to bring wages into line with the cost of living. Thomas Mannion (Ballinasloe Mental Hospital Branch) urged pursuit of the £10 policy but asked whether this was intended only for married men. 'Surely the Union subscribed to . . . equal pay for equal work, married or single?' He made no mention of women. Conroy cast a dampener on the enthusiasm of the floor by concluding that 'fair wage rates demanded fair output of work and good quality workmanship.'

The PUOITUM conducted an economic survey after the Sixth Round and entered talks with the Government and employers in the hope of 'finding common ground' for recognition 'that increased purchasing power coupled with a policy of increasing employment' would 'equate to an expanding and sound' national economy. The response, not for the first time, was discouraging.

A Seventh-Round campaign began in the summer of 1959, despite unsuccessful attempts by employers to 'thwart' union efforts. Many FUE firms happily negotiated settlements. Increases by December averaged between 10s and 15s for men, between

6s and 8s 6d for women. The Labour Court was little referred to, suggesting either
that employers were 'doing rather well and could negotiate wage settlements without economic upset' or that they 'accepted the argument that improved workers'
purchasing power was a necessary condition for economic expansion.' The absence
of significant increases in the cost of living in 1959 greatly assisted.

The ITGWU allowed itself a little prophesying along with self-congratulation.
'There can be no doubt that organised labour has again won the day.' The 1960s
would 'see our Union and the Irish trade union movement bring the working-class
of Ireland a steadily improving standard of living and a greater share in the wealth
which their labour produces'.[32]

Productivity was a major consideration. The ITGWU accepted that 'efficient and
economic' production led to 'reduced prices, greater consumption, industrial
expansion, increased employment and higher living standards.' The Irish National
Productivity Centre played a significant part in underlining the competitive challenge of the European Common Market and free trade. Workers needed to share in
the fruits of improved productivity. It was not to be a 'gimmick of capital to create
redundancy, job insecurity or sweated labour.' Higher productivity was linked to
national polices to raise living standards and create full employment. This was no
'new' concept but 'a more emphatic application of an idea obtaining since the
Industrial Revolution.'

Movement on the Seventh Round began in July 1959, 'notwithstanding the fact
that there has been no prior "Wages Formula" agreed.' Conroy reissued his demand
for a basic wage of £500 a year. By December more than 120,000 workers gained
increases ranging from 10s to 15s per week.[33]

CIU AND ITUC

James Larkin TD made approaches to bring about Congress unity in the spring of
1949. The CIU spurned the move, suggesting disingenuousness on the part of the
ITUC. While Northern trade unionists supposedly favoured an All-Ireland Congress,
the ATGWU, NUR, Amalgamated Engineering Union and Railway Clerks' Association
voted within the Northern Ireland Labour Party to ensure a pro-Partition line. On
17 November, Jim Hickey TD and Brendan Corish TD offered to act as intermediaries. A joint Conference with the ITUC took place on 2 February 1950 under
Hickey's Chairmanship, followed by another on 2 March. Much posturing and sniping took place, mostly occasioned by the Clontarf bus strike and animosities
between the ATGWU and ITGWU. Things petered out. The ITGWU insisted that any
united trade union movement should have no affiliated unions with Head Office
outside Ireland. It wanted an 'intensified campaign to eliminate alien control and
influence,' and it invited Irish affiliates of the ITUC to transfer to the CIU.

McMullen criticised the ITUC's 'impudent challenge' to be the country's
representative in the ILO. To suggestions that the Delegation be shared, he said if any
Government took that line 'you can give the T.U.C. the whole of it.' All Labour Party
TDs signed a document supporting the principle of Irish-controlled unions. Dan

McAllister (Belfast) said the split should have happened in 1921: that was their mistake. P. J. O'Brien (Cork) cautioned that unity would re-create conditions where British unions would exercise undue influence over Irish affairs. The CIU was not for turning.

An acceptance of affiliation to the International Federation of Christian Trade Unions was announced, but the fee of £600 scattered Delegates. The ITUC's acceptance, 'without reservation', of the 'principle of Irish-Based and Irish-Controlled Unions' enabled the Leader of the Labour Party, William Norton, to bring the factions together once more.[34]

In 1951 McMullen reported that efforts towards a United Labour Party were edging matters forward. The National Union of Boot and Shoe Operatives and the NUR planned to withdraw, creating two new Irish organisations, the Irish Shoe and Leather Workers' Union and the National Association of Transport Employees. To charges that the ITGWU was trying to grab any member it could he suggested that 'we probably have too many grades of workers'—an interesting limitation of the OBU concept.

In October 1950 the CIU agreed to affiliate 'fourteen or eighteen' Irish ITUC unions if they applied *en bloc*, but 'since then nothing.' McMullen assured everyone that the union considered matters not from the standpoint of what would increase its membership 'but from the standpoint of what is best calculated to promote the interests' of workers who wished to transfer from British to Irish organisations.

In 1952 the CIU considered Lemass's draft Trade Union Bill. It referred back to the Commission on Vocational Organisation, sought British funding to compensate workers withdrawing from British unions, and wanted all unions to have an Irish Head Office. It wanted to achieve this preferably by agreement rather than compulsory legislation.[35]

In 1953 opponents cited attempts by British unions to break ITGWU members in cinemas, theatres, the ESB and CIÉ, with the apparent compliance of the ITUC.

With the encouragment of Lemass and Hickey, letters were exchanged between Congresses. Private suggestions that fourteen ITUC affiliates, including the WUI and Post Office Workers' Union, were again willing to join the CIU gave the ITGWU a stronger sense of its bargaining power. McMullen, in his Presidential Address to the CIU, pointed out the contradiction within the position of those who argued that All-Ireland trade union unity was important as a path towards political unity when British unions, 'both politically and industrially, repeatedly declared in favour of their maintenance of the present territorial status' of Northern Ireland. Regarding unity, 'there is nothing further from their innermost thoughts than to abandon an atom of their present Partitionist attitude.' He was not offering these comments in a hostile fashion but to debunk the debate.

In 1955 Nixie Boran (Castlecomer) recognised the Border as a reality, cautioning, 'Who wants to have the trade union movement unified in the Twenty Six Counties at the expense of having another Congress in the Six Counties?' Demanding that Southern unions transfer to the CIU would achieve that. He

concluded wisely: 'I suggest that even a couple of years spent in negotiations would
be well worth the time if you succeed in getting genuine unity . . . north and south.'
Unity would 'break down the bigotry and prejudice' in the North and the South. It
'must be broken down on both sides' before national unity was possible.[36]

Discussions in earnest were held in 1954, chaired by Professor John Busteed of
University College, Cork. There was a 'friendly atmosphere', and 'some progress'
was made. The unions' 'cold war' was thawing. The ITGWU expressed 'its approval
of the unity talks.'

The Irish Unity Committee met the British TUC at the TGWU's Head Office in
London on 1 December. The TUC proved most reluctant to convene a meeting of
affiliates with Irish members, and the ITUC refused to call British unions together.
This was regarded as reneging upon the unity document and deadlocked matters
well into 1955. Robbins complained at the 'scurrilous' way the TUC behaved, only the
Assistant Secretary condescending to meet the joint ITUC-CIU Delegation.

An ITGWU Special Delegate Conference on 29 December 1955 considered the
report of the Joint Unity Committee, which proposed a Provisional United
Organisation of the Irish Trade Union Movement to draft a new constitution.
'Without a single dissenting vote,' the ITGWU approved. Simultaneous but separate
ITUC and CIU Conferences were held on 5 January 1956 and accepted the same pro-
posals. The cardinal principle that 'the Irish Trade Union Movement should be
Irish-based and Irish-controlled' was copperfastened. A constitution for the unified
body could be drafted. Conroy was a member of the PUOITUM Committee.[37]

On 27 January 1956, with unity talks advancing smoothly, the Northern Ireland
Minister of Education, Harry Midgley, one-time NILP but now Unionist MP, said
that thousands of Ulster workers in British unions were 'apprehensive'. His real fear
was the challenge that a united movement could offer a Government that boasted
in a booklet for potential investors that workers had their 'energies sharpened by
generations of competition for an insufficient number of jobs.'

Despite the establishment of the Provisional United Organisation, the two sides
still argued over representation in the ILO. Delegates of the CIU rather than of
the new united body were selected in 1956. Boran suggested some 'advisory
representation' for the ITUC, as 'we don't represent all the workers in this country.'
This conciliatory gesture raised hackles, as it would give British unions 'dual representation'. Everything should wait until united structures were completed. The
rancour emphasised how fragile matters were.

In September 1957 a draft constitution was issued for a trade union centre
domiciled and controlled in Ireland, governing affairs throughout the 32 Counties.
The ITGWU felt 'frankly' that 'recent activities in relation to Partition'—a reference
to the IRA border campaign—'made the situation even more difficult.' It 'greatly
intensified' problems arising 'from divergent political and religious views.'[38]

Achieving unity was complex and time-consuming. The PUOITUM considered
unemployment, European free trade, unofficial strikes, PAYE, wages, prices, the cost
of living, internal transport, and containerisation. On 19 February 1958 the ITGWU

considered the draft constitution for the Irish Congress of Trade Unions. Delegates expressed reservations about the composition of the Northern Ireland Committee, Resident Committee and Executive Council. While the position of British unions was questioned, the constitution was accepted.

A second Conference followed on 5 January 1959, at which Joe Meehan (NEC, Belfast) moved the constitution of the ICTU as a 'progressive step'. The motion was carried 'with but one dissentient vote.' Jack Macgougan addressed the 1958 CIU Congress, hoping he would be the first and last ITUC President to do so. He pointed to the 'new services, new forms of activity and new spheres of operation' the united Congress would bring. Kennedy spoke 'with emotion,' feeling that the 1945 decision 'had been perfectly justified.' With satisfaction, justification and pride, the CIU embraced the establishment of the ICTU.[39]

THE WUI AND OTHERS

In January 1950 the Irish Automobile Drivers' and Automobile Mechanics' Union looked for assistance in its dispute in Clonmel. The ITGWU referred it to the CIU, reminding it that its action in organising workers in Co. Tipperary was 'completely contrary to the terms under which they were affiliated.' The *Clonmel Nationalist* said the IADAMU were the 'only people entitled to speak for automobile workers,' which the ITGWU did not regard as being 'conducive to help being given.' The Irish Motor Trade Association locked out IADAMU members, but in Dublin its members were working, a factor in limiting the ITGWU's response.

At the 1951 CIU Congress the merger of unions 'catering for the same class of workers in industry' was agreed, a harking back to earlier ITUC proposals and elements of the ill-fated Trade Union Act (1941). In 1953 the ITGWU met building craft unions to submit a co-ordinated national wage claim and held regular meetings in the CIU offices. Employers resisted a national settlement, but the Wage Formula was achieved in twenty counties, an increase of 3½d per hour.

The launch of the National Association of Transport Employees on 14 December 1952, created by withdrawal from the NUR, was by way of an invitation 'to all transport workers in the city of Dublin' by Figgins, General Secretary of the NUR. The ITGWU said there were 'only 100 there, mostly N.U.R. diehards.' The NUR was losing £8,000 a year in Ireland but left a 'gift of £45,000' to NATE. The ITGWU clearly thought there was no need for NATE and that NUR men should surrender to it.[40]

An Agreement between the ITGWU and WUI, signed by the General Secretaries, Purcell and Larkin, was made on 12 March 1956, which provided that neither union would accept transfers from the other without clear cards or from members in dispute or within six months of a dispute. Difficulties would be dealt with through direct meetings between General Officers. Groups of workers expressing, by a clear majority, the will to transfer could do so. This was an 'anti-poaching Agreement'; no other significance was paid to the announcement.[41]

The ICTU

The Irish Congress of Trade Unions was established on 11 February 1959 in the Mansion House, Dublin. Conroy (ITGWU) was appointed President; Larkin Junior (WUI), Secretary; and Ruaidhrí Roberts and Leo Crawford, Administrative Officers. *Liberty* in March printed a front-page cartoon of two workmen in dungarees, labelled TUC and CIU, carrying a girder labelled *Unity*. The ICTU acknowledged that the fourteen-year division 'weakened all unions' and that 'one voice' would have greater strength and purpose. Congress supported democracy within the movement and society in its pursuit of an end to unemployment and emigration, north and south.

At the first ICTU Congress, held in the Mansion House in September, Fintan Kennedy was elected to the Executive Council. Following the death of the Treasurer, Walter Beirne, Conroy was appointed Treasurer.

There was a great sense of a new era. Conroy told union Delegates in 1960 that the ITGWU 'played a leading part in this achievement.' He hoped the ICTU would attain its goal of the 'maximum possible national economic achievement and the highest obtainable standard of living for our working people' and that it would work 'assiduously to achieve a full measure of understanding and unity amongst all the citizens of the nation, North and South.' In his Presidential Address Conroy talked at length about the needs of a 'Christian society' in condemning unemployment, mass emigration, poverty and underdevelopment. Additional objectives were to raise the school leaving age, improve vocational and technical training, secure adequate pensions for all, and increase social welfare payments. ITGWU speakers were inconspicuous: the largest Delegation was virtually silent.[42]

THE LABOUR COURT

The Labour Court's handling of the Clontarf Bus Depot and railway cases earned the ITGWU approval, as 'proceedings were quite informal.' After 'a friendly but painstaking examination' a recommendation was issued, but it did not settle matters. It did 'not reflect badly on the Court' but on the 'English Executive sitting in London,' which rejected a recommendation that was 'practical, constructive and statesmenlike in its approach and essence.' The CIU strongly attacked the Labour Court in 1950. By 1951 McMullen thought it was 'in the melting pot'. It 'failed to settle big disputes or maintain industrial peace. Workers had 'lost confidence in it.' It had a poor sense of intervention and a lack of a 'realistic and commonsense approach,' delivered ineffectual decisions that made settlements more difficult, created unnecessary delays and allowed employers to bring legal Counsel, and its Conciliation Service, while better than the Court, was not as good as the old Departmental system.

Mick Dunbar (Dublin No. 1), in contrast, thought the Court 'one of the finest instruments set up in this country.' He opposed a CIU motion from 1951 that it be remodelled 'on a basis similar to the Wage Tribunals that operated during the Emergency.' Labour Court personnel were the problem. A CIU Delegation met the Court in January 1952, putting forward criticisms and drawing tetchy correspondence from Lemass.

McMullen felt that in its prime duty of preventing industrial disputes the Labour Court, despite some good work, had 'signally failed.' Strikes were 'more costly and of longer duration' since its establishment, as it refused to intervene where a recommendation was rejected or, under Ministerial pressure, in some state sectors or enterprises. He deplored the low rates paid to forestry and rural workers, and stated that the Labour Court was asked to investigate and 'make it compulsory on all employers to pay the local wages applicable' and the Government to amend the Unemployment Insurance Acts (1920 to 1948) to include such workers. The CIU suggested that it was no longer independent of the Government.

There was annoyance with 'inability to pay' procedures and what was seen as the Labour Court's lack of evenhandedness and the increasingly judicial nature of proceedings. They wanted to tweak the system rather than abolish it.[43] R. J. P. Mortished's retirement as Chairman of the Labour Court in 1952 smoothed relations.

In 1953, in addition to untold numbers of day-to-day problems within Branches, more than 6,000 cases required formal negotiations with the FUE, Irish Motor Traders' Association, Irish Flour Millers' Union, Bacon Curers' Association and Federation of Builders, Contractors and Allied Employers of Ireland. Less than 5% of cases were referred to the Labour Court, with satisfactory outcomes gained in almost all. An exception was Ceimicí Teoranta, where the Government and company proved most intransigent. After many weeks the Court suggested a settlement of 4s a week on the claim of 9s 6d, itself the balance of the 12s 6d formula still owed. Reluctantly, the workers agreed, but the employers demanded a formal recommendation, which the Court would then not issue. The Minister declined to intervene and, after almost six months, direct negotiations produced a settlement giving the workers a bonus of 40s at the conclusion of each season. The ITGWU felt the Court might have effected a much earlier settlement.[44]

Niggardly recommendations drew criticism in 1955, with the Labour Court appearing to support the employers' line that no change in circumstances justified increases, despite sharp price rises. 'With regret' the ITGWU felt that the Court's 'stock or standing is below par.' Recommendations fell far short of a 'living wage'. It was recommended that staff be recruited from outside the civil service.

Fifth-Round wage increases quickly appeased complainants, and the Court was congratulated for 'fostering good industrial relations during the extremely difficult' times. Indeed Conroy thought 1955 'the most satisfactory year' yet for the Labour Court. Its standing was 'higher than at any period.'

Union pressure secured a wider interpretation of the word 'worker' under the Industrial Relations Act (1946), giving access for the first time to some local authority workers. Thomas Johnson's retirement occasioned best wishes from the ITGWU and gratitude for 'his lifetime of service' to 'Irish workers and the Irish people.'

Of 1,000 Labour Court recommendations issued in 1956 more than 700 concerned ITGWU members. In response to an invitation from the Minister for Industry and Commerce, William Norton, the CIU submitted a memorandum on the Labour

Court in November 1953. It criticised the Court's lack of initiative in not brokering national pay talks and its refusal to differentiate between high and low-paid workers in its awards, thus increasing rather than narrowing gaps between them. It wanted Conciliation Officers' reports published where conciliation failed; wanted craft union representatives within the Worker Representatives panel; bemoaned inconsistencies between recommendations and acceptance by the Court of *ex-parte* evidence, particularly after a hearing; complained about restrictions on Officials' capacity to ask employers questions at hearings; and expressed dissatisfaction at the non-enforcement of JICS and JLCS.

Few Seventh-Round claims required intervention by the Labour Court. The ITGWU now firmly believed in the Court and in 1959 noted that the 'high standard of submission, argument and negotiation' displayed by Officials required 'statistical data and reasoned arguments that are logical, sustained and convincing.' It recorded 'our appreciation of the prompt and satisfactory manner in which our research and statistical queries and questionnaires are responded to.'[45]

CIÉ

In January 1950 the Railway Clerks' Association attacked the ITGWU in its *Railway Service Journal* over the road freight dispute, claiming it was 'ready on the least excuse to down tools,' took 'irregular . . . hasty and ill-conceived action' with 'utter disregard for the repercussions,' acting in 'violation of Agreements' according to 'the rule of the jungle.' The ITGWU accused the Association of supporting the Labour Court's 'inequitable' recommendation. It asked why if the Association was 'unhappy we have won another victory for CIÉ workers.' It was because clerks in the North Wall had transferred, 'despairing of ever securing a standard of life compatible with present-day needs from the tepid, semi-professional British trade unions to which they belonged.' They found 'economic salvation in association with manual workers' in the ITGWU. McMullen said they joined for 'economic and patriotic reasons' and were 'outraged by the action of the British Labour Government in attempting to perpetuate the unnatural division of our country.'

In Clontarf Garage two members transferred to the NUR. The other 350 men refused to work with them. After a strike of several weeks, work was resumed 'without the two recalcitrants.' The Labour Court recommendation 'resuscitated the principle' embodied in part 3 of the Trade Union Act (1941), which had been declared repugnant to the Constitution. The Labour Court gave sole negotiating rights to the majority union in each CIÉ centre while conceding Freedom of Association to individuals. The ITGWU, while recognising individual rights, firmly believed in majority rule. It could not and would not 'confer such a right on an individual to smash at his whim the trade union solidarity so essential for the safeguarding of the rights of its members, and in this attitude it should have the support of every right-thinking person.' Only such 'a well-ordered trade union movement, capable of adequate control of its members and in a position to enforce discipline upon them,' could prevent 'the irresponsible action of a few' that 'rendered hundreds of workers idle' and 'inflicted much-resented hardship on the community.'[46]

The ITGWU felt that an amendment to trade union law was necessary to rectify matters. Linking the stoppage to the Ireland Act and Partition, McMullen asked, 'We wonder what other Government in the world would allow a foreign trade union, sitting outside its jurisdiction, to recklessly penetrate a stronghold of a native trade union and throw the transport of . . . its capital city into chaos, without feeling called upon to take some action.' It enlisted the executed 1916 Leader Tom Clarke, citing his speech to the North Dock Cumann of Sinn Féin in April 1909, when he said, 'We heartily approve of the movement now on foot amongst trades bodies in Ireland to break all connections with English trade unions.' It was 'our duty' to be 'absolutely independent of English control . . . On principle we refuse to admit England's right to govern Ireland.' It was an 'English union's attempt' to 'obstruct the will of the Irish workers' that had 'CIÉ buses standing idle in their Clontarf sheds today.'

Victory was welcomed in April. The ITGWU complained that a 'pro-British and anti-Trade Union' press had 'whipped itself into frenzy over freedom of association.' It asked—somewhat unfairly—'what ever did the N.U.R. accomplish for either its rail or road members in this country? It is not an exaggeration to state that its name stinks amongst those who have been engaged in transport in this country' and stated that it stood for low wages and casual work. The ITGWU was 'genuinely sorry' for Clontarf residents but reminded everyone that 'we favoured the Trade Union Acts, 1941–1942,' which the NUR killed.

The men returned on Sunday 26 March, after five weeks. The two who tried to join the NUR 'did not go back . . . Nor shall they return' to 'CIÉ city service depots without the consent' of the ITGWU. The trumpet sounded as the ITGWU declared that despite the 'ancient and universally exploited Saxon device of divide and conquer' the 'disruptionists in London and here have been beaten.' Anonymous letters in the *Evening Mail* 'worked overtime in misrepresenting the union.' The stoppage cost £10,454.[47]

A railway workers' strike began on 16 December 1950. McMullen wrote to the employers on 28 November, giving two weeks' notice, frustrated by the management's refusal to negotiate a claim submitted on 28 July. The management replied that three other unions—the NUR, Irish Railwaymen's Union and Amalgamated Society of Locomotive Engineers and Firemen—after a meeting with the management and the ITGWU had agreed to refer matters to the JIC, to be heard on 6–7 December. This correspondence was sent simultaneously to the Labour Court to allow for its possible intervention. The Board of CIÉ thought it inconsistent of the ITGWU to refer a busmen's dispute to the Labour Court and to serve strike notice on the railway. It should operate through the 'properly constituted negotiating bodies.' McMullen replied on 2 December to what he saw as 'such a misconceived and inadequate document.' In August 1949 the ITGWU was told that negotiating machinery would operate 'as a separate entity between us and you.' This worked for a while, but subsequently the management 'refused to implement your own authorised representative's proposal.' If the company was 'truly perturbed about the transport and economy of the country' it had had since July to respond to the claim. He concluded: 'In effect, your attitude is that you won't negotiate with us and you won't make use of the machinery of the Labour Court.' As to the notion that meeting the union before the expiry of strike notice 'would only serve to encourage' such action, he derisively observed: 'That statement is without parallel in the history of industrial relations.' Strike notice was 'a last resort because you would not do what every other employer of labour in the country does—negotiate on the just demands of workers. You—contrary to the expressed opinions of the Labour Court, the Government, the community and all reasonable beings— consider that strike action should precede negotiation.'

This letter went to the Labour Court and the press. On 3 December the Chairman of CIÉ, T. C. Courtney, replied to the Sunday newspapers. Given that the 1948 National Wage Agreement was subject to review by the FUE, CIU and ITUC under the Labour Court, it was unreasonable to expect CIÉ to unilaterally set a higher rate. The ITGWU was told, however, that the Board would be amenable to any new arrangement arising from joint discussions. Could the ITGWU not ask the Labour Court, which was 'dealing with the case of bus-workers tomorrow,' to deal with railway workers also?

McMullen continued the gunboat diplomacy on 5 December. There was no Agreement for railway workers, unlike bus workers. The cases were not comparable. There was nothing stopping the company referring the railway claim to the Labour Court back in July, although it would most probably have referred the parties back to direct local negotiation.

On 6 December, Courtney accused the ITGWU of clouding the issue. It represented only a small minority of railway operative grades, and discussions with JIC unions could not be ignored for the sake of direct talks with the ITGWU or the whole industrial relations machinery would be in ruin.

McMullen, on 8 December, noted Courtney's 'pathetic effort to try to excuse the Company's failure to discharge its function' and the Labour Court's refusal to intervene. The company should deal directly with the union. He challenged the suggestion that the ITGWU represented only a minority.

A direct Conference took place on 9 December, the ITGWU pointing out that the terms that emerged from the JIC might be acceptable to the NUR, ASLEF, IRU and RCA but not to it. It found itself against the company and four other unions. Without pressure from the ITGWU and the threat of strike notice the JIC offer would not have been made.

Strike notice was deferred for a week and a ballot held, in which the members rejected the offer by three to one. The strike began on 16 December.

Archbishop McQuaid intervened, organising a settlement that concluded the strike on 29 January 1951. All the men returned without victimisation, and negotiations on modifying existing negotiating machinery and wages began on their resumption. In October, McMullen regretted the Board's 'negative and deplorable approach.' The union's motives were 'considerations of principle not finance,' given Government promises. He advised McQuaid that his services might be required again.

On 19 November a final outcome, negotiated through the JIC, delivered an increase of 8s a week followed by further increases within the four groups of workers ranging from 12s to 19s. An ITGWU circular declared: 'Taking everything into consideration, especially the past history of wages movements on behalf of Railway workers, this is a good result and one for which full credit must go to this Union and its members.' The 'increases in December, 1950, inadequate as they were,' would have been 'far less were it not for the agitation conducted by this Union and the gallant strike of its members . . . THAT STRIKE WAS NOT IN VAIN; IT HAS NOW BORNE FRUIT.' All gains came only after the ITGWU began to organise railway workers. Bill Murphy Senior, Secretary of Dublin No. 9 Branch, was a member of the CIÉ Board, where his 'extensive knowledge,' long experience and 'sound, sensible and equitable approach' rendered his appointment 'most fitting.' The union alleged that 'in collaboration with the British-based N.U.R. and A.S.L.E.F' the company 'planned to defeat' a strike that ITGWU men 'did not want' before it began. The strike cost the union £40,000. The Dublin Rail Branch was established in April 1952.[48] Animosity with NATE persisted for years afterwards.

In 1955 a claim for the Road Passenger and Maintenance Departments, covering 4,700 workers, 3,712 in the ITGWU, won a Labour Court recommendation of 12s 6d for men and 8s for women and juveniles, doubling the company's offer. In February 1956 a 10% increase for 3,500 railwaymen was announced.

In 1957 millions spent on modernising the railways were wiped out by proposals by the Transport Committee for lines to be closed. Buses were to be imported in a double whammy that rid the country of railway jobs and displaced more by importing vehicles. The ITGWU condemned the plans. On the bright side, the Minister issued an order for a 'new, improved' CIÉ pension scheme for waged grades, the ITGWU national campaigning being 'a big part' in finalising it.

A Labour Court submission for CIÉ road passenger staff was published in *Liberty* in February 1958, including the claim that overtime and weekend bonuses be reflected in holiday pay. Dublin No. 9 Branch was extremely active, generating increased attendances and interest for meetings. The appointment of C. S. Andrews as Chairman of CIÉ led the union to hope he could 'overcome political pressure.' The company was 'hampered in every way' and 'prevented from operating efficiently and economically at every turn in the special interest of the wealthy and the "rake-off" Collectors and political expediency.'[49]

THE HEALTH SERVICE

Motions calling for improved National Health Insurance, external medical and surgical treatment and pensionable service for mental hospital employees were adopted in 1950. Such demands were not made for others, but there was little begrudgery. P. J. O'Brien (Cork No. 2) sought a 48-hour week without reduction in pay for all hospital employees 'who have direct contact with patients.' In 1955 a 'Nurses' Charter' was adopted after negotiations with the County and City Managers' Association. On 9 February 1956, 2,600 psychiatric nurses were due to strike over their year-long claim for improved basic salary scales. The union traced the claim from 1890 up to the 1920 Agreement and more recent claims for reduced hours and improved pay. The achievement of a unified national scale was seen as crucial. Stoppage was averted after intervention by the Labour Court resulted in the setting up of a JIC providing improved scales.[50]

TOURISM AND HOTELS

Worker representation was sought on the Irish Tourist Board and the Advisory Committee for Catering in 1950, together with a 'Hotel School' to train staff and to reduce the need for non-nationals. On 6 October 1951 a minority of Dublin and Dún Laoghaire employers refused a claim for the 'introduction of a 10% service charge, without wage increases, in the tipping zone' and increases of 8s to 12s for men and women in the non-tipping zone. More than 1,000 were involved in the ensuing strike, although more than 1,400 members had already gained the increases sought.

The Labour Court heard the claim on 10 October, the General Secretary, Purcell, making the submission. It recommended the introduction of a service charge, the abolition of tipping and immediate negotiations on wage increases in non-tipping zones, dates of implementation, and the identification of establishments where a service charge was 'undesirable or impracticable'. The employers accepted in toto, but the workers declined to resume work pending negotiations, 'governed by pre-vious experience of the lack of good will' on the employers' side. The employers did indeed repudiate their earlier acceptance. The Lord Mayor of Dublin, Senator Andrew Clarkin, intervened, although it was clear that the employers wanted no settlement and 'were prepared to stoop to any and every duplicity to prevent it.' Agreement, under Clarkin's guidance, on 14–15 December 1951 was first accepted and then rejected by the employers. Clarkin observed that the employers' reasons 'do not justify them in repudiating the Agreement' before, 'in this holy season of peace and good will', making an appeal to their better nature. The strike dragged into the new year. Privately the union thought the final award by Justice Shannon worsened that given by F. Vaughan Buckley in December 1951, although 22s 6d was won for men, 12s for women.

The Hotels Branch recognised the strike's lasting value, observing that the settlement 'formed the basis of the exclusive ownership of the service charge by workers,' which formed a 'substantive element of pay and conditions' for decades.[51]

In 1952 Purcell pointed out that tourism depended on quality service. The ITGWU should 'organise all hotel and catering staffs' throughout the country and establish bargaining structures, minimum conditions and proper training. Michael Moynihan (NEC, Killarney) said that the 'hotel workers by their great strike' had 'written a glorious chapter' in union history. Michael Mullen (Dublin No. 4) called for a National Catering Training College and union representation on Bord Fáilte. An editorial in *Liberty* in August 1955 addressed 'Our Guests' and championed tourism, urging members to provide a 'Céad Míle Fáilte' to visitors: 'a kindly thought would be to record their names' and send 'each an Irish Christmas card', a practical extension of the 'Buy Irish' message.

Dublin No. 4 Branch reported 'outstanding progress' in 1957, with more than 4,000 members, winning increases and improved conditions. It 'pioneered in Europe' the organisation of hotel and catering workers, the 'provision of a free employment bureau' and the 'fixing of minimum wage rates and fair conditions of employment.'

In October 1958 the ITGWU's prestige was greatly enhanced by the Catering Exhibition, the 'most successful ever held' in Dublin, reflecting the union's concerns for improved standards and training opportunities.[52]

DOCKERS AND MINERS

Dockers, once the union's core, disappeared as 'decasualisation and registration' and new technology wiped out dockside labour. Paddy Brogan (Dublin No. 1) 'did not want decasualisation,' nor did Dan McAllister (Belfast), who thought workers would lose control. The Panlibhonco Shipping case had 'significance to the trade union movement in the free world.' It was a 'rare case' in which workers around the globe, 'with different cultures, different backgrounds, different political, social and religious beliefs, different languages [and] different concepts were united in one common body to defend' union 'recognition, trade union rates of wages and conditions of employment.' Co-ordinated by the International Transport Workers' Federation from 30 November to 4 December 1958, a four-day ban was placed on Panlibhonco's 'runaway-flag fleet,' as its 'activities were endangering the whole maritime industry of the free world.' It was one of the first flag-of-convenience battles, and ITGWU 'docker members played their part.'

Castlecomer miners, 'who fought so heroically for hearth and native land in 1798' and who played a vital part 'in saving [the] country from economic disaster during war,' ended a twelve-month strike on 14 February 1950, gaining acceptable terms.[53]

EMPLOYMENT AND EMIGRATION

In 1950 the ITGWU held firmly to protection for Irish industry from 'unfair outside competition and dumping' while calling for improved domestic efficiency. It objected to preference being given to ex-army men in employment and demanded that any job be 'open to all Irishmen on an equal footing.' In the St Patrick's Day issue of *Liberty* it insisted:

BE IRISH—that doesn't of necessity involve what some might term fanaticism. It just means that in a world whose national boundaries are instantaneously overleaped by wireless and by cheap mass-produced reading matter, we maintain that Irish way of looking at things with which we were reared and take our views neither from Kremlin nor from Times Square New York;

BUY IRISH—if it sometimes means buying a little dearer, it almost always means buying better quality. If every family acted on that slogan it would do more to end emigration's blood toll of our youth and strength and to call home the exiles than a thousand Government edicts.

'BELONG' IRISH—by this slogan we mean that everyone should see that he or she is a member of an Irish organisation with headquarters here and not in London whether in our recreations (such as athletics), in our businesses or professions, or in our trade unions.

W. H. Taft of the Marshall Plan office addressed the 1951 Conference, asserting that wage increases required 'added production and productivity.' Taft was the first outside speaker to address the Conference, demonstrating the ITGWU's desire to engage in thinking through all options for national economic development. At the CIU Congress Conroy reflected that real fears for a new war had stimulated employment, a sad commentary on international economics. Countries never had any financial or production impediments when seeking to construct weapons for 'exterminating and maiming millions of human beings.'

The national disgrace of 470,000 people emigrating in the previous twenty-five years received little adverse press commentary. Conroy advocated rural housing and infrastructural schemes to reduce emigration, increase domestic demand, improve transport and communications and maintain diminishing rural communities.

In 1954 Ned Browne called for a National Planning Authority, 'to bring about the highest degree of efficiency in production and distribution and the maximum expansion of trade.' This was the first time the concept of 'planning' was raised. An OECD survey condemned Ireland's economic performance, suggesting there was potential for substantial rises in productivity and living standards and an attack on emigration.

On 5 October the Government finally announced a development programme, to be based on favouring agriculture, encouraging private investment to supplement public investment, home rather than foreign investment, encouraging exports, and achieving this through co-operation rather than compulsion. An Industrial Advisory Council was established to examine automation, design, packaging and marketing.

The ITGWU was not hugely impressed. The concern was the balance of payments crisis. The ITGWU constantly offered the same, neglected solutions of proper economic planning, financial controls, more equitable personal taxes and state investment.[54]

Concern with unemployment grew. A forty-hour week was demanded in 1953, with the banning of certain imports threatening Irish jobs, such as lager beer. Were this done 'there would be no need for unemployment doles . . . Unemployment Associations in Dublin, Cork or Limerick' or 'for people to lie down in the road to hold up traffic. (Applause.)' The applause showed the suspicion and antagonism of CIU Delegates for unemployed agitation.

In 1954 Conroy drew attention to human stories behind the statistics, 'the father of the family' unable to meet house charges or rent, school fees or weekly bills, a man obliged to take a child out of school to work as a messenger boy to bring in essential income, parents obliged to encourage a son or daughter to emigrate, the young couple having to postpone a marriage.' Human stories were largely unreported behind cold unemployment statistics.

Conroy had a tough, brusque exterior, but this speech revealed his fundamental humanity and his anger at injustice. The possibility of 'exempting unemployed members from paying contributions' was considered. Loss of job inevitably led to loss of membership. In March the ITGWU observed that 'we are not importing shamrocks into Ireland yet' but that many imports were of goods that were or could be made at home; such imports meant 'exporting Irishmen.'

In 1952 Éamon Wall (Cork No. 1) suggested that the co-operative movement was the only effective weapon whereby 'workers can shake off the shackles of capitalism.' An editorial in *Liberty* in March 1955 claimed that 100,000 people could be put to work if shoppers bought Irish. Speakers from the National Co-operative Council addressed the Conference, and in 1955 a Co-operative Development Society was set up in Dublin. Purcell wanted 'widespread' distribution co-ops to combat cost-of-living increases and profiteering. Hickey cited effective examples from Belfast, Castlecomer and Cork.

In 1956 concerns abounded for rural dwellers. 200,394 people had emigrated between 1951 and 1956, moving Browne to declare that 'never before in our history, even in the dark days of the Famine' or the Second World War, was there 'such a sustained and heavy exodus.' In no other country had 'such a high proportion of the population been driven away for economic reasons over a protracted period.' Equitable wage standards could unlock the stagnant economy. Hickey cited the first Dáil's Democratic Programme. Moynihan (NEC) called for a National Planning Council with the Government, local authorities, employers and unions to plan for full employment. In February 1957 Conroy attacked Fine Gael and Fianna Fáil as guardians of the 'moneyed classes'. All members of any Government 'must BELIEVE in a policy of full employment,' and to implement any such policy 'control over policy direction in all matters relating to money and credit MUST be in the hands of the elected representatives of the people.'

Details were given of the emphasis placed by the Provisional United Organisation on increasing capital programmes, building more housing and roads, relaxing the credit squeeze and reviewing special import levies. Conroy complained that rich citizens would not invest at home. It was to be remembered that a 'prosperous Ireland will lead to a United Ireland.' The Provisional United Organisation's pamphlet *Planning Full Employment* was largely ignored beyond the movement, despite the Government having no plan of its own. Conroy argued:

We live in an under-developed but potentially wealthy State with golden opportunities for the building of a rich economy, higher living standards for the
people and greater opportunities for health and happiness for all. But alas! The
practical application of Christian teaching is put aside when selfish personal
interests are involved.

Whatever about Sundays, on the rest of the week 'the Philistine pagan philosophy
of the jungle—might is right' is 'practised and glorified . . . I often wonder if there
is any country in the world other than Ireland where so much Christianity is taught
but so little practised.'

Table 73: Unemployment (26 Counties), 1950–59

1950	61,534	1955	55,185
1951	68,228	1956	73,786
1952	71,844	1957	84,093
1953	66,542	1958	70,300
1954	61,792	1959	83,300

Source: ITGWU, Annual Reports, 1950–59.

Some argued that people emigrated voluntarily in pursuit of better options elsewhere. The ITGWU thought this 'nonsensical'. 'How nice for them to know they
should have remained here as corner-boy bums and charity cadgers!' Mullen
(Dublin No. 4) called for full implementation of the Provisional United
Organisation's plan and its circulation and discussion within the union. No real
progress was made since its publication in January 1957.

On a micro-scale, Conor O'Brien sought the protection of the Conditions of
Employment Act (1936) to prevent machinery replacing labour. Wages were a lower
fraction of national income in 1956 than in 1938, an indictment of successive
Governments, despite the fact that productivity per worker had risen by more than
30%. Emigration ran at 40,000 a year, a national scandal that robbed the economy
of able and talented people.

Joe Meehan and Stephen McGonagle raised the question of emigration from
the North, describing potential employment prospects and seeing hope for united
action with Congress unity. In 1958 Conroy quoted article 45 of the Constitution of
Ireland, whereby the state 'shall strive to promote the welfare of the whole people'
and shall 'direct its policy towards securing that the citizens (all of whom, men and
women equally, have the right to a means of livelihood) may through their occupations find the means of making reasonable provision for their domestic needs'.
The Government and employers were guilty of unconstitutional practices!

The Special Delegate Conference of the Provisional United Organisation of the
Irish Trade Union Movement on 24 April 1958 exerted pressure on the Government.

The Taoiseach was asked, 'on behalf of the 80,000 unemployed,' to 'use the full resources of the state and semi-state [state-sponsored] bodies and substantially expand the state capital programme,' to build more 'urgently needed' schools and houses and to 'reverse the policy of exporting capital' and prepare projects that private and public capital could invest in. It welcomed the White Paper *Programme for Economic Expansion,* sounded cautions about the proposed European Free Trade Area and supported economic planning. A notice in *Liberty* declared: 'Shame on all of us!' It asked, 'Are you amongst the guilty? Did you personally purchase the imported article instead of the equal or better home-produced article?' What amount of members' income was 'needlessly spent on the purchase of imported goods?' The 'unemployed and the emigrants' called on members to do their duty: 'Purchase Irish produce yourself and see that preference is given in your home to goods produced in Ireland.'

Co-operation, seen as 'an outlet for true patriotism,' was promoted, but not in any passionate way. Co-operative production remained as one of the ITGWU's objects but was a seldom-visited aspiration. In 1959 Michael McLoughlin (Limerick) asked that a weekly levy of 6d be imposed to establish a 'fund for the establishment of a new industry' in each Branch area. Conroy shot down the idea, asking how it would work, 'particularly having regard to the Truck Acts.' It fore-shadowed Workers' Unity Trust of the 1980s. Conroy observed that the population of the 26 Counties had declined from 2,971,992 in 1926 to 2,898,264, 1956, a drop of 73,728 despite high fertility and natural increase.

Unemployment and emigration seemed acceptable to politicians, who did little to attack their causes. Governments predominantly represented employers' and landowners' interests.

> Political squabbling with a fringe aesthetic, inhuman, capitalistic system of exploitation and the greed of the few, together with the selfish and unworthy motives of others who are well entrenched and sheltered, has over the last thirty odd years, done grievous injury, if not irreparable harm, to our people and our country. If we are to pull out of the economic morass into which we have sunk the time for action towards this end is now.

Conroy accepted that unions were not blameless, given internal wrangling and lack of political education. He felt most strongly for young workers, thousands of whom left school with an inadequate level of education.

The 'so-called balance of payments crisis' had not cost bankers a 'five pound note' nor the 'loss of even one meal.' Any losses incurred were suffered by low-income manual workers' families. The cry was always to curtail wages. This was not the solution to unemployment. Ireland was a 'paradise for the man with £1,000 a year and upwards . . . a tolerable land' for those on over £600 but 'just hell on earth' for thousands on less than £500. All this pertinent analysis nevertheless fell shy of demanding clear-cut Socialist policies. Catholic social teaching opposed Socialism and preached the status quo.

Conroy's fight for social justice concluded: 'In this noble work we will have the blessing of God, our Creator, and, I hope, ultimately the satisfaction of bringing peace, happiness and complete unity to the working-class movement throughout the whole of Ireland.'[55] Employers and capitalists stopped shaking in their boots and gave thanks at their next church attendance.

TAX, SOCIAL WELFARE AND HEALTH

Taxation concerned ITGWU members more and more in the 1950s. In 1957 the Government announced a Commission on Income Taxation, an opportunity for unions to state their case for a fair and equitable PAYE system. In November 1959 the Government produced a White Paper. Initially PAYE was perceived as complex and confusing, although the unions approved it.

In 1956 the ITGWU decried excessive taxes on imported fruit. It declared: 'Yes! We can't have bananas' and worried about jobs in fruit importers, the effects on tourism and the threat to Christmas puddings! It was regarded as a typical Government measure, concerned to do everything except the necessary.[56]

In 1951 the ITGWU wanted the means test for old-age pensions abolished as an 'unchristian practice'. Purcell welcomed the projected legislation for 'Social Insurance and Mother and Child Welfare'. Labour TDs were exhorted 'to resist any attempt to worsen or curtail' proposed benefits. There was regret that the Government made no provision for workers injured at work or victims of industrial disease. Purcell's closing remarks, however, told the true story; for 'no matter how much' the NEC and members 'might want a satisfactory Mother and Child Scheme he felt sure they could not welcome any provision or development repugnant to the Catholic Hierarchy.' He worried that the union would be 'misinterpreted as hostile' to the hierarchy.

Addressing the CIU, Conroy demanded a comprehensive social welfare system, stating that the 'time is at hand to insist on the elimination of pauperism, red ticket systems, workhouses and all the other trappings and trimmings' they had to 'tolerate for so long.' The 'speedy introduction' of social insurance legislation, including the Mother and Child Scheme, was demanded, 'provided that, at all times, such schemes' were 'in accordance with Catholic Social and Moral teachings.'

Purcell denied taking sides in the 'controversy that arose in connection with Dr. Browne's Scheme. Nothing could be further from the truth'. It was 'only right that every possible measure consistent with Christian social and moral teaching should be introduced.' Without debate, the motion was adopted.

The Social Welfare Act (1952) extended and improved matters, but there were concerns about delays in processing payments and calls for increases in the cost of living. Conroy referred members to Bishop Dignan's proposals in 1944, *The Outlines of a Scheme of Social Security*, as a template for improvement. The Health Act (1953) was greeted favourably, and Kennedy, Mick Moynihan and W. J. Keenan (NEC) became members of the National Health Council. A national nutrition survey in 1954 showed that thousands lived 'on the borderline of extreme poverty.' Brendan

Corish, Minister for Social Welfare, addressed conferences, outlining statutory social welfare position. A call for 'free hospitalisation' for all was made in 1955, and Purcell sat on the advisory body investigating the provision nationally of voluntary health insurance.

Conroy considered that two items needed urgent repair: 'an increase in Children's Allowance' and a 'national scheme of retirement pensions on a contributory basis.' Children's Allowances was £52, compared with £124 in Britain, and yet it was Irish society that supposedly regarded the 'family as the fundamental unit,' which was 'very proper.' Article 4 of the Constitution of Ireland emphasised this. 'We must hang our heads in shame and admit that Christian Ireland treats its children with cold indifference and with a callous disregard for their needs and their suffering.'

Equally shameful was the treatment of 'wage toilers in their old age.' Many had to 'exist on charitable cadgings' or would end in workhouse wards. 'We should remember that they too are all God's children.' Denis Murray of the Irish Society for the Prevention of Cruelty to Children addressed the Conference, designating 26 October as 'Trade Union Day', when all members would give to the ISPCC. Corish was congratulated for 'his own personal efforts,' but the Government 'must share responsibility for the unjust treatment meted out to the unemployed, the sick and the aged.'

In 1957 Conroy said: 'Take a walk through Dublin's Grafton Street, Cork's Patrick Street, Limerick's O'Connell Street' and

> other fashionable and wealthy streets . . . see the idle rich parade . . . the expensive imported luxury wearing apparel, the decorative jewellery, the expensive knick-knacks and the lavish home furnishing they insist on . . . then ask yourself if Ireland is so poor than an extra 6d or 1/– a week to the aged pensioners would bankrupt the State.

Liberty contained an open letter from 'A Friend' to the Minister for Social Welfare in February, reminding him of Dignan's proposals in 1944 and Norton's White Paper of 1949, *The Welfare Plan*. On 31 May 1954 item 7 of the Inter-Party Programme for Government provided retirement pensions at sixty-five for men and sixty for women, Mortality Benefit and other benefits recommended by Dignan and Norton. The letter, published in a full-page block, argued:

> It would be shocking if after Six Years of Office, Labour Ministers had to again return to their constituencies to seek a renewal of their votes . . . not be in a position to say there is EVEN ONE PIECE OF NEW SOCIAL LEGISLATION that they can claim credit for. The only last forlorn hope in this respect lies with you as Minister for Social Welfare. Therefore, please Minister do bring in the necessary legislation immediately to provide—CONTRIBUTORY RETIREMENT PENSIONS and DEATH GRANTS.

In 1959 Patrick Sheedy (Limerick) sought statutory redundancy payments 'of at least one month's salary' for each year of service. Other demands were for free hospital treatment, the termination of three-day waiting periods for benefits, polio and tuberculosis testing, and the delivery of free turf.

A largely unseen aspect of union activity, within Branch and work-place, was the endless members' questions relating to their own or dependants' social welfare or health entitlements. A complete synopsis of entitlements was provided in the 1959 Annual Report. The Minister for Finance was asked, 'Could you live on 25/– a week, Dr. Ryan?' Conroy bemoaned the inadequacy of social services that would 'make any decent man blush with shame,' producing figures to 'show the wide disparity between sickness, unemployment and old-age pension benefits in the Republic and Britain for a man, wife and three children from five to eleven years of age.'

	Ireland	Britain
Sickness	6s per week	Scale geared to allow £6 7s plus rent
Unemployment	£3 1s, with maximum possible public assistance of £2 3s 6d in urban areas, £1 13s 6d in rural areas	Scale geared to allow £6 7s plus rent
Old-age pension	£1 5s (£1 7s 6d from August 1959)	£4 (£2 10s for man, £1 10s for wife)

There was still no state Retirement Benefit for dockers, building workers, general industrial workers or agricultural workers, who had to depend on their families, 'enter a Poor Law institution or spend their last days in some charitable cubicle. And this is Christian Ireland too!'[57]

HOUSING

In 1953 the ITGWU thought it a 'shocking commentary on the present economic system' that, while thousands urgently needed housing, unemployment in construction was rife. 'Private capitalists' could not or would not do anything about it, 'indeed they were the people who had brought it about.' W. O'Brien (Cork No. 1) suggested a National Housing Board, representing all interests, and condemned the 'restriction of credit, high interests and exorbitant legal and other charges.' Jim Hickey said they had 'cement, bricks, sand, slates and other materials in abundance.' Thousands of building workers stood idle but were willing to work, 'yet because of the restriction on financial credit by a small group of individuals who had no responsibility to the community they appeared helpless.' In 1954 Purcell noted 'with concern' the reduction in affordable houses built, demanding a 'revival' of the building programme to the most modern standards of 'accommodation, water, sewerage and artificial lighting'; rent or other charges to be kept at a minimum. More than 20,000 urgently required accommodation in Dublin alone.[58]

EMPLOYMENT LAW

At the 1950 CIU Congress Purcell demanded statutory entitlement to two weeks' paid annual leave. The law lagged behind established industrial practice, to the detriment of casual and unorganised workers. J. McElhinney (Galway) in 1951 wanted Joint Advisory Councils appointed for each industry to allow workers to participate effectively in the management and profits of their companies. He linked this moral entitlement to Catholic social teaching.[59] In general, there were few calls for new employment legislation in the 1950s.

SAFETY AND HEALTH

Liberty published informative articles on safety and health in 1950. In December it provided 'hard facts for the scaremongers' who cautioned about cigarette smoking. The 'question of whether to smoke or not to smoke' was a 'matter of free choice for the individual. Scare-bearing zealots and alarmists to the contrary, it should be kept that way.' In 1952 P. J. O'Brien wanted access by workers to Factory Inspectors' reports and Inspectors to be made give evidence in accident cases. In two fatalities the Inspectors declined to give evidence, as their reports were 'confidential to the Minister.' In 1953 Nixie Boran (Moneenroe), concerned at the 'high incidence of mortality and disablement' among miners because of pneumoconiosis, called for benefits in line with the Workmen's Compensation Acts. He demanded increased payments in line with the cost of living, based on actual earnings at the date of accident, increased compensation in fatal cases, and that the acceptance of Workmen's Compensation not prejudice a subsequent common law action. Reductions in the working week and restrictions on Sunday work were sought—although the motive was job creation rather than safety—and the provision of protective clothing, 'free of cost to all industrial workers.' Legislation was sought to reduce the 'excessive weight of sacks' that workers could be legally expected to carry and to 'compel all traders needing sacks containing one hundredweight and over on any floor approached by a stair or ladder to install and use a hoist or lift.' The Factories Bill was judged a 'good Bill,' as the union had called for a 'new code of factory laws and regulations' since 1949. The Bill introduced 'no radical change of principle,' but unions had not sought any change.

The union still pinned its faith on tough prescriptive legislation monitored by external inspection. The major amendment sought was to extend the definition of 'factory' to include 'practically all other premises—workshops, general and commercial offices, betting shops, warehouses, etc.' It was not successful, and a narrow definition of 'factory' persisted until 1989.

A mixed welcome greeted the Workmen's Compensation (Amendment) Act (1953). Improvements for wives and children and the capacity to proceed to common law while receiving compensation were not balanced by the low amounts payable. Purcell said that the 'constant dropping of the water had worn the stone' of employers' and Government's resistance, but a complete overhaul of the system was necessary. As to accidents at work, the ITGWU claimed that 'our legal advisers are always available with expert advice based on the countless successes they have won for our members over the years,' although 'some pay dearly for advice and come only when victims of poor settlements.' Legal aid was a rarely acclaimed but substantial union benefit.

In 1954 Purcell demanded that pneumoconiosis, or anthracosis, be classified as an industrial disease. Brendan Corish, Minister for Social Welfare, undertook to designate pneumoconiosis a Prescribed Occupational Disease in March 1955. In 1951 the Department of Social Welfare asked the Medical Research Council to investigate. The X-ray screening of Kilkenny anthracite miners concluded that problems were rife.

There were hopes of significant increases in the maximum payments under Workmen's Compensation to £1,800. *Liberty* praised Nixie Boran for his indefatigable campaigning: 'The victory is yours, Nick.' The Factories Act (1955) was welcomed, although the Government was asked to 'speed up implementation,' which Corish said was due on 1 October 1956. The Conference called for the nationalisation of 'both industrial Life and Workmen's Compensation insurance.' Conroy spoke against a motion calling for more Inspectors. Unions received few if any complaints, and he thought the Factories Advisory Council should be let evaluate matters. The few complaints reflected a lack of safety-consciousness, but this occurred to no-one.

The Factories Act (1955) codified all legislation applicable to Ireland from 1901. Two innovations were not found either in British or Northern Ireland legislation: an Advisory Council, to which both Purcell and Kennedy were appointed, and provision for Safety Committees. Safety Committees were voluntary, had no specified structure and could assist the occupier in securing compliance with the Act. 'Factory' was a place where people were 'employed in manual labour . . . making any article . . . the altering, repairing, finishing, cleaning, washing or demolition of any article . . . adapting for sale of any article.' This meant that only one in five workers was covered. Boran wanted a Coal Mining Regulation Act embodying all British regulations since 1922. The ITGWU believed that sixteen Safety Committees for the whole country was 'disappointing,' as they were a 'valuable means of raising the general standard of industrial safety and hygiene.' Lengthy extracts from Factory Inspectorate reports were republished in *Liberty*, but there was no mention of work-place, union-led activity, never mind Safety Committees. Officials tried to 'focus members' attention' on health and safety, and Congress gave it high prominence.

At last, work-place organisation was addressed. 'We cannot overstate the responsibility of our members in co-operating in the setting up of Safety Committees,' which could 'be of great value in conditioning workers and management to the precept that prevention is better than cure.' All Branch Secretaries were instructed to 'strive for the setting-up of Safety Committees.' Prevention was finally dislodging prescription as the central concept of how to deal with work-place hazards. An article on 'Diesels and dermatitis' concluded with the insight, 'an ounce of prevention is worth a pound of cure.'

The Workmen's Compensation Act (1955) was welcomed, members being advised that accident victims could pursue actions under common law, the Fatal Accidents Acts (1846 to 1908), the Employers' Liability Act (1880) or the Workmen's Compensation Acts (1934 to 1955).[60]

EDUCATION AND TRAINING

In 1950 Limerick wanted a Central Statistics Branch 'correlating data concerning wages, conditions of employment and all other relevant information' for negotiators, a response to demands for supporting evidence in Labour Court submissions. In 1953 J. McNulty (NEC) claimed that Head Office Movements already 'devoted considerable time and attention' to compiling industrial data.

In 1951 seventeen members were among the first recipients of the Diploma in Social and Economic Science from University College, Dublin. In 1953 Carrick-on-Shannon suggested that it would benefit the working class if the ITGWU sponsored university scholarships for the sons and daughters of members, a novel idea that would be introduced forty years later. Éamon Wall wanted the educational system 'remoulded' to provide 'equal opportunities for all,' and P. J. O'Brien urged that all VECs be asked to introduce 'Social and Economic' courses. The teaching of civics was demanded in 1955 to encourage more practical citizenship, as well as the reform of secondary and primary education to broaden opportunity of access and reduce class sizes. Consistent with its 'Irishness', the CIU set up Comhar Cultúra na gCeardchumann to foster spoken Irish, fully endorsed by the ITGWU.[61]

In 1956 Conroy recognised that a fundamental weakness was the lack of membership education. Existing efforts were 'half-hearted and unfinished.' Dan McAllister (Belfast) suggested a Summer School. Linking to the wider economic planning debate, Paddy Clancy (Dublin No. 2) called for greater attention to technical education through increased grants and opportunities. The Liberty Study Group was established in 1956, 'attached to Dublin No. 2 Branch.' Robbins praised the Catholic Workers' College but wanted additional, union-run schemes. In 1957 Kennedy attended Paris and Harvard Universities, sponsored by the European Productivity Agency and the Organisation for European Economic Co-operation for courses in industrial relations, economics and social studies.[62]

In 1959 the Director of the Catholic Workers' College, Father Edmond Kent, addressed Delegates. 'Trade Unionists could not serve God unless they are prepared to serve their fellow-men.' He paid tribute to Father Edward Coyne and Professor Alfred O'Rahilly before talking of the 'new workers' college' built in 1956, at a cost of £30,000. Brendan Corish moved a vote of thanks, saying that all should 'equip themselves in Christian and Catholic social teaching.' Wexford Trades Council had appointed a chaplain. There was no suggestion that the ITGWU should develop its own education and training programmes. It supported courses in the Catholic Workers' College, the NEC congratulating twenty-one graduates in 1955, including the future General Officers Edmund Browne (Dublin No. 7 Branch) and Christopher Kirwan (Dublin No. 11 Branch). The college trained workers 'in the principles of social science' and helped 'towards the establishment of a just social order.' Mattie O'Neill congratulated Comhar Cultúra na gCeardchumann on its seventeen-point submission to the Coimisiún um Athbheochan na Gaeilge, which sought comprehensive Irish, Irish-English and English-Irish dictionaries, a subsidy for *Inniu,* more Irish on radio and television and the translation of religious texts into Irish.[63]

Table 74: Catholic Workers' College, number of students, 1951–9

	Trade union students	Women students	Management students	Total
1951–2	44	—	59	103
1952–3	39	—	51	90
1953–4	45	—	44	89
1954–5	161	—	70	435
1955–6	152	—	84	559
1956–7	237	66	111	797
1957–8	309	107	172	990
1958–9	411	101	156	1,134

Source: 'Continued progress in Catholic Workers' College,' *Liberty,* June 1958. Note: The total includes supervisors and foremen, political science and 'pre-marriage' students.

After slow beginnings the Liberty Study Group became more prominent in 1958, with a symposium on 'Full employment and the Free Trade Area' held in December catching the imagination. In October 1959 educational pennies began to drop as the union recognised that if 'strong militant trade unions' were to win the battles on employment creation and economic planning, worker democracy and wage bargaining, it was 'more necessary now than ever before for greater education and greater knowledge.' Members demanded training in public speaking, meeting procedure and negotiation skills; but no commitment of union resources to this was yet made.[64]

LIBERTY HALL

In January 1950 McMullen thought the 'time had come when some step should be taken to provide for the rebuilding of Liberty Hall.' He promised £25,000 to open a fund and that members 'would be disposed to subscribe shares.' It might be possible 'to enlist support' in the United States. In 1951 Robbins wanted a Connolly Memorial Hall built on the Liberty Hall site. On 12 May 1954 new Head Office premises at 94 Merrion Square were blessed by Father Aloysius, who had attended James Connolly at his execution in 1916. The union had outgrown 35 Parnell Square, from which it had operated since 1921. Renovation work was carried out on premises in Athlone, Limerick and Midleton, while Corish Hall, Wexford, was purchased for £600.

Delay in any statement on Liberty Hall earned the NEC a rebuke at the 1954 Conference. A special fund for the reconstruction of Liberty Hall was created, however, with the first instalment of £40,000 transferred from the General Fund to supplement £25,000 already promised. Conroy said that Liberty Hall had 'through age become a very dangerous building.' Branches transferred to Parnell Square and Burgh Quay, as the NEC was 'very anxious' to evacuate Liberty Hall 'at the earliest possible date.' Purcell likened it to an old man whose 'ravages of age can only be combated by care and treatment, but he could not be restored to the health and vigour of his youth.' Any 'drastic operation would inevitably risk its collapse.' Public safety demanded evacuation. The new Liberty Hall would be 'a striking and beautiful example of modern architecture—worthy of the greatness and prestige of the ITGWU.' It was 'not a matter of choice, but of extreme and urgent necessity,' as the old hall was condemned by the municipal authority.

'Legal and technical difficulties ... considerably delayed' the project. Conroy said he would appeal to members 'for a substantial voluntary contribution' and expected a 'widespread and generous' response. Vacant possession was gained, and the building closed its doors for the last time on 12 December 1957. Demolition began. A brief history in Irish, 'Árus na Saoirse', was given in the 1957 Annual Report.

In 1958, union property was valued at £107,038 in sixteen towns. By 1959 the Liberty Hall Reconstruction Fund stood at £270,000.[65]

STAFF

Members of the staff complained about wages and conditions, especially those working in the dilapidated Liberty Hall. Staff numbers increased but not in proportion to membership, imposing greater demands. In 1956, however, Conroy warned any potential Officials: 'Be sure ... that your reason for doing so is that you are not looking for a soft job'. They did 'not want office or job seekers' but 'zealous young men and women with the vocation to serve mankind.' Anyone who thought of 'self and who is ever watching to see how much he can get for himself and in return give as little as he can get away with would be a burden ... not an asset.' Conroy was a hard taskmaster. Patrick Lally (Galway) in 1957 looked for better staff training and typing and shorthand for male Officials, 'as men should be employed in preference to women.' Sheila Williams (NEC) 'resented' his comments. Women in union service were a credit and 'contributing as much as the men.'[66] Staff morale was generally high, reflected in smiling faces and socials featured in *Liberty*.

LIBERTY

Frank Robbins said in 1950 that he 'couldn't congratulate the NEC on the paper.' It had been started 'not for the purpose of making money' but to provide members with a 'mouthpiece' and to 'disseminate Union propaganda.' One article in May was a 'discredit' to the NEC. Purcell acknowledged some problems but was 'doing his best.' If every Branch did what Mallow did—it disposed of 350 copies a month—the circulation would be more than 40,000. To complaints of lack of coverage *Liberty* answered: 'We cannot publish reports we haven't got.' Material received would be gladly printed, 'particularly from Branches in remote areas' or 'small young Branches.' It wanted news of 'presentations, outings, men on picket lines, births, deaths, marriages,' which 'needn't have the literary finish of a Shakespeare nor need the photography be up to highest press photograph standards, leave that end of it to *Liberty*.' Readers were urged: 'Pass This On: YOU are NOT through with this journal until you have recruited some other worker as a reader.'

Liberty was upgraded in January 1951, heralding 'an important and (need we say?) unexpectedly favourable turning-point in the career of the union journal.' It confirmed, 'too, that our declaration in the September issue that LIBERTY was here to stay was made without any attempt at bluff or wishful thinking.' It needed improvement to become 'attention-compelling reading matter that its readers will look forward eagerly to.' Better circulation was needed 'to make the magazine pay.' Among illustrious contributors was Thomas Carnduff, the Belfast shipyard poet and playwright.

Some complained that too much space was devoted to the 'activities and domestic affairs of film stars and other non-Union matters.' The tipster, 'Birdcatcher', was better suited to daily newspapers. Tom McCarthy (Dublin No. 1) disagreed: 'whether they liked it or not, a great many people backed horses . . . Birdcatcher's notes were most interesting and informative.' He himself had 'benefited from that gentleman's prognostications.' W. Connor (Dublin No. 4) suggested a weekly levy of 1d and free distribution. Accumulated losses for 1949–51 were £3,763. McMullen urged 'immediate close-down.' The blame was laid squarely on the 'lack of effort' by Branch Secretaries.[67]

In 1953 Purcell wanted *Liberty* 'universally read and supported.' The union wanted to avoid closing it down, with the attendant loss of prestige; but if members did not read it it was a 'sheer waste of time and money.' George Corrigan (Dublin No. 3) regretted that in an article by 'Kincora' a 'quotation from Karl Marx was used. That kind of thing should be avoided and the teachings of the Church quoted instead.' P. Dunne (Dublin No. 4) requested special women's features.

The journal was revamped and its editorial line used to 'promote a true social order based on Christian principles and the natural law.' Potential contributors could attend a 'Special Course of Lectures in Journalism and Public Relations by Basil Clancy.' Losses ran at £3,270. In 1956 Conroy bemoaned that 'in this age of propaganda when public opinion is considerably influenced by newspapers, radio and divers other publicity methods' the union had 'no trained staff.' They were needed if the union was going to be heard, never mind compete. The 'complete management' of the struggling magazine was handed to Richard Kinsella, who was appointed Publishing Comptroller. His impact 'amazed everybody.' 'No-one inside or outside the Union can deny, that as a trade union organ *Liberty* stands out away and above any other.' Its cost was now 2½d to 2¾d in the pound (i.e. 1%) of the

ITGWU's income—a 'remarkable improvement.'

In 1958 Delegates queried *Liberty's* rising cost, a grant of £3,948 being given. In 1959 P. J. O'Brien (Cork No. 2) thought the Golden Jubilee edition 'a magnificent production,' while Frank Murphy (Cork No. 2) complained that 'leading articles were too dictatorial.' Conroy dismissed the idea of an an editorial board as impractical. It was the age-old problem of too many Officials and members not giving the paper 'the support it merited,' and the 'highest tribute was due to those who did.'[68]

THE UNION BAND

Dublin Branches constantly complained about paying the ITGWU Brass and Reed Band levy. In 1954 the Band attended the world championships in Kerkrade, Netherlands, greatly enhancing its standing and boosting the union's morale. Funding problems were solved by diverting money from annual royalties from the International Federation of the Phonographic Industry to pay for uniforms, instruments and the Band Learners' Scheme.[69]

THE CHURCH AND ANTI-SOCIALISM

During the war, references to Catholic social teaching and Christian values emerged in ITGWU documents. After the war, anti-Communist rhetoric was added, particular horror being expressed at the alleged treatment of Catholic leaders in Soviet Bloc countries. On May Day 1949 Archbishop McQuaid 'convinced the Labour Party and trade unions to ally with Catholic lay organisations' to protest on behalf of Cardinal Mindszenty, 'martyr for the Faith,' arrested in Hungary. McQuaid described the ensuing scenes: 'Not only the Sodalities and Confraternities, but the political parties, in particular, the Labour Party, aligned themselves firmly on the side of loyalty to the Faith and to our Holy Father.' What he had 'never seen before' was the Papal flag flown, 'alone, on the headquarters' of the ITGWU, 'where the Citizen Army had flown its Plough and Five [actually seven] Stars in former times.' This 'manifestation' was

> but a continuation of the spirit that was rousing at the time of the Italian elections. And what is genuinely consoling, the result is a practical devotion to Mass and the Sacraments such as even the Eucharistic Congress of 1932 has not exceeded.

At the 1950 CIU Congress it was agreed that 'the blessing of Almighty God should be invoked on the proceedings at Divine Services to be held on the Opening Day.' P. J. O'Brien (Cork) suggested that two representatives be sent to Rome 'in this Holy Year' to 'convey to the Holy Father the loyalty and homage of the Irish Working Class.'

In January the *Evening Herald* denounced Communism as 'an insidious poison.' The ITGWU declared, 'We agree,' pointing out that not all Labour TDs would 'dis-associate themselves' and quoting James Larkin Junior as saying that the

Communist Party is a 'most immediate and vital need. Only a Communist Party can give a correct revolutionary lead to the workers.' (It did not date the quotation.) From 16 to 18 October 200 men and women with the leaders of the CIU flew to Rome as part of the Dublin Workers' Holy Year Pilgrimage 'under the banner of Matt Talbot.' Frank Purcell presented a 'Spiritual Treasury and Guard Book of the Dublin citizens' protest meeting' on May Day to the Pope.

Disciplinary action was taken against two bus men, Michael O'Riordan and Laurence Wright, who, although they opposed unofficial action on Dublin buses, were charged with statements 'in conflict' with union policy and Rules.' Their communism was reason enough.

Ballaghaderreen requested that the 'present salutation "Dear comrade" be 'discontinued and a more suitable term substituted.' 'A chara' replaced it in June 1958.

In 1951 McMullen could not allow 'this Conference of Catholic and other Christian workers' to pass without reference to the Diamond Jubilee (sixtieth anniversary) of the 'great Encyclical *Rerum Novarum.*' He recorded 'our appreciation of the thought and solicitude shown by His Holiness Pope Leo XIII for the welfare of the toiling masses.' The enunciation that employers should pay workers a living wage was one of 'courage, vision and sympathetic understanding.' The encyclical had 'stood the test of time,' and future generations would regard it as 'an outstanding contribution' to the masses' upliftment.'

Conroy referred to the expense of sending Delegates to Rome for the second national pilgrimage. 'In the circumstances no one will question the cost . . . nor will there be a single demur about it.' Congress, representing 181,040 workers, incurred a debt 'on account of its Holy Year expenditures.' The Vatican thanked the CIU for 'further proof of the devoted attachment' of Irish workers to the 'Vicar of Christ and of their fidelity to the Catholic faith which is their nation's most precious heritage,' complete with 'His paternal Apostolic Blessing.' The CIU Delegates attended the Diamond Jubilee of *Rerum Novarum* in Rome. £587 was spent on the Delegates' expenses and a 'spiritual bouquet' for the Pope out of a total expenditure of £2,594.

The 1953 Congress suspended business to hear an address by Monsignor Herlihy of the Irish College in Rome, who outlined *Quadragesimo Anno* and Pope Pius XI's denunciations of fascism and Nazism.

Despite widespread calls for economic development and the expansion of trade, the ITGWU drew the line when it came to 'trading with Communist-dominated countries while our fellow-Christians' are 'persecuted and denied freedom of conscience.' In Kilkee in 1954 the parish priest, Canon Grace, condemned the 'evil creed of Communism,' warning that the union was 'an automatic target for Communistic infiltration.' He was assured that union leaders were 'ever watchful' for this danger and concluded by drawing on his vast experience of industrial relations to caution delegates that unofficial action was the 'negation of trade unionism and played into the hands of the Communist enemies of the people.' While he felt that workers should be given a share in the 'control and profit of industry,' they must have 'full regard to the rights of Capital.'

Such tone-setting lectures from Catholic commissars were common at ITGWU and CIU Conferences. In 1956 Raymond Barrett from the American Embassy delivered an unobtrusive speech but made it clear that his approval might have been absent had the Conference displayed more radicalism. It was suggested that 'Annual Conference should be preceded by religious service' and 'all Union meetings . . . preceded by prayer.' The suppression of the Hungarian Rising was discussed, with the 'refusal of dockers at Belfast and Dublin to handle Russian cargo' cheered. It was decided that 'the Union would stand ready to take its full part in the action called for.' £500 for relief was given to the Irish Red Cross.

Thoughts of taking legal action against New Books, the Communist Party bookshop in Pearse Street, for republishing Connolly's works were abandoned in March 1956. The ITGWU thought it had sole rights and objected in particular to the Communist bookshop. In 1958 the US Ambassador, Scott McLeod, praised the 'well-disciplined and organised labour force' as the 'country's greatest asset.'

It was still common practice for Branches or employments to attend annual retreats organised by the union. At the Golden Jubilee Conference Monsignor O'Halloran, on behalf of Archbishop McQuaid, reminded Delegates of papal encyclicals. These 'great men' had defended workers' rights to a 'family living wage' and the organisation of 'free Trade Unions.' The Church taught that, 'in present circumstances,' unions were 'morally necessary,' without identifying circumstances where such moral need might cease. He was confident in his audience:

> You are mostly Catholic men. Hence you have need of leaders filled with an intelligent Catholic faith. This will not prevent you from claiming and fighting for your legitimate social and economic rights. We thank God your union has been fortunate in this respect.

He respectfully suggested that the leadership might 'seek ways and means of bringing the ordinary' members to a 'deeper understanding of their social responsibilities.' He hoped that the 'Holy Spirit of Truth and Love, may enlighten and direct each of you in your search for a Christian solution' to the 'many and serious problems.'

Canon Kerr, Rector of St George's Church (Church of Ireland), followed, explaining that he been a trade unionist before entering the ministry, since when he had not been able to find an appropriate union to join, supposing that the clergy were 'black-coated workers'. He described his disappointment that Connolly's 1916 ideals had not been achieved, that instead of 'cherishing all the children of the nation equally' there were the 'evils of unemployment, emigration, inadequate and insecure wages' and the 'miserable state of the old age pensioners,' widows and disabled. He asked not only what trade unionists' combined power should be doing but also the Church's. The Church could rejoice only when the state corrected social wrongs.

In August 1959 Limerick Pork Butchers' Society presented £100 to Bishop Murphy of Limerick for diocesan building funds, maintaining a strong relationship between the society and the Church.[70]

POLITICS

The National Labour Party's failure to endorse Foran's Seanad candidacy in 1950 was condemned by the NEC. The CIU considered a letter of 13 June, signed by thirteen Labour Party Deputies, suggesting that all wanted a united party based on 'Christian principles and national ideals.' 'Immediate' steps were being taken to 'bring about a formal unification.' Having achieved this, the united party appointed a Sub-Committee to pursue industrial unity. The NEC felt strongly that industrial unity should precede political unity. It was assured that the Party accepted the principle of Irish unions and 'would not have any English organisation represented on its Executive.'

James Everett insisted that the NLP had 'done their best by the union,' loyally supporting 'the Irish-based principle' despite 'abuse and misrepresentation.' In 1951 a Special Conference considered granting aid to 'certain members who had contested the recent General Election on behalf of the United Labour Party.'

The Labour Party gained votes but lost seats in the election caused by the row over the Mother and Child Scheme. Fianna Fáil resumed power. The NEC was criticised in 1952 for not calling a promised Special Conference to discuss the political situation. A 'protracted—and sometimes heated' discussion called for no support to be given to 'any political party' and that all candidates give an 'unqualified pledge of loyalty' to the union. Conroy said that any application for funding was 'considered on its merits.' Nixie Boran (Moneenroe), displaying his class politics, believed that 'unified political and industrial action is necessary.' The NEC should be instructed to 'take positive action' to heal the 'unfortunate split' and report to a Special Conference. Boran received no seconder, his belief in united action not shared by a narrow hall.

In 1951 McMullen was briefly debarred from the Seanad as a result of bankruptcy arising from a union debt. His return was unopposed once things cleared.

In 1954 there were calls for any member to receive support at elections, suggestions quickly rejected by speakers, among them John Howlin, proud that two Labour TDs represented Wexford. He recalled Connolly's dictum: 'Don't scab at the ballot box.' Purcell acknowledged that individual members might have their own political views, but the ITGWU 'stood for Labour in the broad sense.' Eight ITGWU members were elected and Brendan Corish (Social Welfare) and James Everett (Justice) became Ministers. The union nonetheless complained that, despite a change of Government, 'nothing was done' to 'enact urgently required working-class and social measures.'

Forty-four ITGWU-sponsored candidates were successful in the 1955 local elections. The NEC suggested that the 'time is now opportune' to 'again become an affiliate' of the Labour Party. Cork No. 2 said this should be done only by Special Conference, but the motion was withdrawn. The first of many invitations to re-affiliate was considered in June but rejected. Friendly relations were not dependent on formalising matters. The NEC complained of British unions represented on the Administrative Council. Herbert Devoy (Thomastown) was pressured to withdraw a motion on re-affiliation in 1956.

The NEC was divided. If it supported Devoy and it was defeated, affiliation would be 'rendered more remote and matters would be equally bad if the Council were forced to record their opposition to it.'

In 1957, through *Liberty,* the ITGWU engaged in debate with Dan Desmond TD about mounting criticism of the Labour Party in Government. Desmond demanded 'truthful and honourable' reporting of Labour Deputies. Under Fintan Kennedy's editorship a pro-Fianna Fáil line was discernible in *Liberty,* reflecting the politics of many NEC members and influential staff. Attacks on Fianna Fáil grew, however, especially after the Government's refusal to sanction public-sector wage increases due. These were the 'sort of tactics we condemn in non-democratic countries. Now, perforce, we must do the same at home.' In the teeth of economic crisis Conroy did 'solemnly protest against the conduct of our Dáil Deputies,' given their high levels of absenteeism. It said much of their indifference to social problems. Workers appeared to be equally indifferent, however, as 'Irish workers do not vote Labour.' This was always the political nub.

In October 1959 the ITGWU issued a 'Challenge to Labour', making 'some bald suggestions to put the Labour Party back on the political map.' The union was not affiliated but it suggested greater links between the Party and the ICTU. Re-affiliation was not specified but was implicit, as was a desire to build All-Ireland Party structures in Association with Congress.

In October 1958 the ITGWU pledged itself to fight de Valera's decision to abolish Proportional Representation. The move was regarded as part of a wider attempt to marginalise the Labour Party and weaken Irish democracy. It was only narrowly defended, by 51.7%. The ITGWU's intervention was therefore vital.[71]

Chapter 24 ∾

EXPANSION AND DIVERSIFICATION: THE WUI IN THE 1950s

LEADERSHIP

James Larkin Junior had a hard task in following his father as head of the WUI. His concepts of leadership and led were very different from his father's: 'Leadership cannot be regarded as consisting solely in the activities of one or two individuals.' It involved the 'active, intelligent participation of hundreds, nay thousands of conscious thinking members throughout the whole Union.' Members had to be aware of the union's operations and be taught a sense of loyalty and pride in their union, 'built and maintained by their own mental and physical efforts.'

In February 1953, in his thoughtful 'It Seems to Me . . .' column in *Report,* he expressed satisfaction at the manner in which unions serviced their 297,000 members in the Republic but wondered what else was possible. 'For example, and these are only hurried thoughts, we could have a countrywide medical system for members and their families giving them, for a minimum subscription, the most up-to-date and complete care and attention.' To this could be added 'our own insurance funds to supplement the social welfare payments from the State . . . our own rest homes and sanatoria,' building societies, schools, colleges and educational courses, travel agencies and holiday homes and camps in Ireland and abroad, social, recreational and sports clubs, with their own premises, theatres, cinemas and sports grounds, co-operative retail shops, wholesale organisations and 'even our own co-operative manufacturing concerns . . . We could do all this.' It seemed to Larkin that 'until we do make use of the full physical, mental, organisational and financial resources of this great movement of ours' they were 'only tinkering with the job of raising the living and cultural standards.'

The WUI had made a 'start in the sphere of recreational, social and sporting activities,' but united, national effort was required. Given the division between the ITUC and CIU, Larkin concluded, 'one immediate obstacle stands in the way—our failure to even act together as a single national movement.'

The President of the wui, John Smithers, addressing the 1953 Conference, described his position as 'mainly administrative'; others carried the industrial responsibility. The wui had the 'most capable and successful team of negotiators,' attracting members. It was stronger than ever before in membership, organisation, finance and (whether or not he was conscious of borrowing a very itgwu word) 'prestige.' Big Jim's loss was 'made good by the ordinary men and women'. They had grown in 'an atmosphere of mutual trust and co-operative endeavour.'

Larkin felt that a General Officer should not speak at the Conference, other than to provide explanation or detail. All matters should be in the hands of the gec and the members. The union's strength did 'not lie in its full-time staff but in the team of intelligent men and women throughout.'

He was concerned about apathy and non-participation. 'This problem must be faced up to, if this Union is to really serve the purpose for which it was established.' They had greater purpose than 'merely to act as a means for securing a few more shillings for members,' reducing working hours, gaining free supplies of protective clothing, improving overtime rates, or 'the keeping of one worker in a job as against another with a lesser claim.' They had to assist 'members to understand the conditions under which they live' and that determined 'their present and future living standards.' They had to become 'intelligent and conscious-thinking members of the community and nation.'

Such sentiments were well written; whether they were well read was another question.

In 1956 the Conference was proudly addressed by the Lord Mayor of Dublin, Councillor Denis Larkin, National Industrial Secretary of the wui, an occasion felt to bring much honour. Smithers quickly brought Delegates back to earth by asking, 'Is it worth it?' He reflected on the amount of organisational work that went into preparation for the Conference, the poor attendance at Branch meetings held to discuss motions, and the financial and opportunity costs. He answered his own question in the affirmative. The Conference was the cornerstone of the fundamental democracy that guided the wui's every move.

> So, if our Union is to serve the best interest of the members; if our Union is to be managed and controlled by the members; if the members are to gain experience and knowledge through running their Union; in short, if the members are to be the Union, and not just a series of names on cards, then the machinery of the Union must be democratic and this Delegate Conference must continue to be the final measure of control available to the elected representatives of the rank-and-file.

If the wui was not democratic, Smithers thought, 'we would be better without it'.

In 1959, with Smithers absent through illness, Larkin spoke of him. He was a part-time officer until 1947, when the union had fewer than 8,000 members and owed at least half its meagre cash assets. Smithers had a secure, pensionable job, working normal hours. He was asked to come into a job for which he had no special training and that required great personal sacrifice. He had been excellent, despite the fact that he was 'an ordinary kind of guy,' no 'spell-binding orator', 'flamboyant' Leader or 'great political figure.' He was 'one of yourselves, an ordinary Dublin worker,' a 'union man all his life, a foundation member.'[1]

CHRISTY FERGUSON AND FRANK CLUSKEY
The death on 4 February 1957 of the National Organiser, Christopher Ferguson, at the age of fifty-four, was a massive blow. A boilermaker in Inchicore Railway Shops, Ferguson came out in sympathy with WUI members in 1924, was arrested on the picket line and dismissed. In 1944, together with Peter Coates, a Citizen Army veteran, he brought the Boilermen's Section of the Irish Engineering and Foundry Union into the WUI. After Larkin's death in 1947 Ferguson was asked to give up his job in the Department of Defence and become full-time National Organiser. He did so at once, without knowing what impact Larkin's death would have. He made 'an outstanding contribution' to the union's 'numerical and industrial growth' and its 'ever-widening acceptance as an effective negotiating and militant trade union.' He was most closely associated with the Civil Aviation, Guinness, Papermaking and CIÉ Road Passenger Sections. The WUI measured its loss. 'Chris Ferguson died as he had lived—strong in his faith in working class and Republican principles—and his memory and his service will be cherished by the Union to which he gave such outstanding and selfless service.' The Conference stood in silent appreciation of a man 'available to the Union at all hours.' Ferguson wanted a united Ireland 'achieved by the free association of all shades of opinion.' He staunchly supported free speech. His trade unionism was a 'philosophy, a way of life.' His death left 'his friends a little bewildered.'

One immediate impact was that Jim Larkin Junior did not seek re-election to the Dáil, his right-hand man within the WUI gone.

On 21 June 1957 No. 8 Branch requested the GEC to 'erect a plaque or some other suitable form of a memorial in the Union's Head Office as a mark of appreciation and respect' for Ferguson. Surprisingly, 'the letter was noted,' with no action agreed. Perhaps Ferguson was still an outsider, much admired but nonetheless not absolutely regarded. This was unfortunate. Time has judged Ferguson's contribution as outstanding, in greatly enhancing the WUI but also in allowing Larkin Junior to combine politics with the union and contribute intellectually to the movement, secure in the knowledge that, industrially and organisationally, Ferguson's trusty hands were on the union tiller.

Frank Cluskey, Secretary of the Operative Butchers' Branch, had an unbroken period of thirty-eight years as official and was a 'close and intimate friend of Jim Larkin.' His death in 1955 was a loss, as he 'was everything a Branch Secretary should be, painstaking and careful, fully informed on his trade, courteous and patient, but determined and persistent.' His son, also Frank Cluskey, succeeded him, later becoming Leader of the Labour Party.[2]

MEMBERSHIP, FINANCE AND ORGANISATION

The proud boast in 1950 was that 'one member out of every thirty is actively engaged in some form with the day-to-day running' of the WUI. Many thought they should extend organisation throughout the country. By 1951 the WUI claimed to be the 'second largest Irish Trade Union' and 'third largest trade union organisation in Ireland.' The period of 'relatively easy expansion', beginning in 1946, was 'now past,' however. Further gains would result only from 'difficult, prolonged and costly organising activities,' which did 'not readily yield spectacular results.' The WUI's strength was in building, sugar and confectionery, meat, gas, brewing and distilling, docks, transport and civil aviation. More than fifty 'main Sections' were listed in an interesting mixture of public and private sectors, blue-collar and white. All Branches established 'financial autonomy' through local funds by retaining 25% of income, returning 75% to Head Office.

The reopening of Dublin shipyards, accredited to Larkin Senior's lobbying, provided an opportunity, and it was 'gratifying' that the Shipwrights decided to transfer their Dublin Branch in 1949. In April 1950 the Irish Airline Pilots' Association affiliated as a body, no doubt influenced by the existing organisation of supervisory, accountancy, traffic and operating staffs in the Civil Aviation Section. The Irish Pharmaceutical Employees' Association, formed out of the Chemists' Branch of the Irish Union of Distributive Workers and Clerks, sought affiliation and was told that 'we would only agree to establish a Chemists' Branch if a clear, substantial majority' so decided. More than 250 met on 12 February 1950 and, despite written objection from the IUDWC, were accepted as an independent body. Claims for recognition and improved pay and conditions were served on the Irish Drug Association and won at the eleventh hour after strike notice.

Expansion through the affiliation of semi-autonomous professional and trade groups became the stock in trade, a unique mechanism for growth and one largely eschewed by the ITGWU. Finances naturally improved, but arrears remained a problem.

In 1951 Con Rooney (No. 4) thought 're-entry a bad slogan. Re-joining should be stopped,' while William Hickey thought the 'main transgressor' of Agreements between unions not to accept those in arrears was the ITGWU.

Investments were tiny. Larkin explained in 1952 that the £100 'set out against Freeman's Publications' was probably 'worth nothing at all.' Investment in Inchicore Co-op was 'the same as when we made it.' 'Loans to Members' were 'part of a legacy left to us' and were 'bad debts.' The auditor wrote them off. The only loans given now were to accident victims struggling to meet legal Bills. As to the Freedom Fund, many looked for their £1 back and were accommodated, but most left their money lie.[3]

On 31 March 1952 the WUI had 27,000 members, 4,000 of them women. Full-time staff were appointed to No. 6 (Shipbuilding and Engineering), No. 8 (Building Trade) and No. 16 (Pharmaceutical Chemists). Jack Fitzgerald (No. 1) worried about the 'tremendous amount of apathy' within the rank-and-file and wanted this 'slackness' challenged to 'try and stop this rot.' New Rules allowed for the remission of

contributions and lower rates for unemployed and sick members. Weekly subscriptions were raised, with rates ranging from 2s for men earning over £10 a week
to 6d for juveniles. Dispute Pay rose to £3 and Funeral Benefit from £7 to £24,
depending on contribution scale.

In 1953 Larkin clearly distinguished the roles of Delegate and Shop Steward
(Collector). Only about 10% attended meetings. Members were warned by a 'Special
Notice of Stricter Enforcement of Rules on Claims to Union Benefits'. Past practice
had to change. The union never 'rigidly and harshly' applied the Rules 'in deciding
applications by members' for 'Strike Pay, Mortality Benefit or Legal Assistance.'
Members' explanations as to how arrears were accumulated were always considered and the benefit of the doubt given. But 'in future, there will no longer be any
reasonable excuse for falling into arrears.' It could 'not be pleaded' that arrears were
'due to sickness or unemployment.' New Rules provided for the remission of contributions in such situations. The Rules would be applied 'strictly' but 'not harshly.'
There would be 'improved benefits but equally members must now realise' that the
Rules 'must be more strictly enforced than has been the practice in the past.'[4]

Branches and Officials in October 1952 are listed in table 75. The Beef Section,
Pork Section, Hide and Skin Section and Offal Section were known as the
Meat Federation, a name given by Larkin Senior, 'who for years handled all negotiations . . . himself and knew practically every member by his first name or better
still by his nickname.'

Table 75: WUI Branches and staff, October 1952

No. 1 Branch: Dockers, Carters, Miscellaneous Groups. Secretary: Seán Burke, Thomas Ashe Hall, College Street, Dublin. Delegate: Bernard Conway TC.
No. 2 Branch: Public Services: Corporation, ESB, Port and Docks Board, etc. Secretary: Michael Byrne, Mallin Hall, 9 Fishamble Street, Dublin.
No. 3 Branch: Miscellaneous Group. Secretary: Seán Nugent.
No. 4 Branch: Sugar, Confectionery, Bakery. Secretary: John Bennett, Thomas Ashe Hall.
No. 5 Branch: Butchers' Porters. Secretary: Michael Greene, Thomas Ashe Hall. Delegate: Gerard Kennedy.
No. 6 Branch: Shipbuilding and Engineering Workers. Secretary: Thomas D. Watt, Ashe Hall.
No. 7 Branch: Tobacco Workers. Secretary: Thomas Doyle, Ashe Hall.
No. 8 Branch: Building Workers. Secretary: James Duffy, Ashe Hall. Delegates: D. Holmes and Michael Brennan.
No. 10 Branch: Retail and Wholesale Fish and Poultry. Secretary and Delegate: Patrick Moran, Mallin Hall.
No. 11 Branch: Pork Trade. Secretary and Delegate: Charles Phipps, Mallin Hall.

No. 12 Branch: Civil Aviation. Honorary Secretary: Captain S. F. Whelan, Ashe Hall.

No. 13 Branch: Gas Workers. Secretary: J. P. Kelly, Ashe Hall. Delegate: Patrick Forde.

No. 14 Branch: Operative Butchers. Secretary: Frank Cluskey, Ashe Hall.

No. 15 Branch: Clerical Workers. Secretary: Thomas Doyle, Ashe Hall.

No. 16 Branch: Chemists. Secretary: Seán Dempsey, Ashe Hall

Bray: Secretary: Samuel Hannon, 6 Ravenswell Row, Bray.

Carlow District Mental Hospital: Secretary: John King.

County Dublin: Secretary: Patrick Duff, Mallin Hall.

Dún Laoghaire: Secretary: Dan Byrne, 15 O'Donnell Gardens, Glasthule.

Enniscorthy: Secretary: G. Askins, 40 St John's Villas, Wexford.

Kildare: Secretary: James Byrne, 19 Fairview, Kildare.

Killybegs: Secretary: J. McGilloway, Conlon Road, Killybegs.

Kinsale: Secretary: Andrew Crowley, 24 St Eltin's Terrace, Kinsale.

Portarlington: Secretary: Arthur Dunne, 10 St Michael's Place, Portarlington.

Port Laoise: Secretary: John Ireland, Main Street, Port Laoise.

Portrane: Secretary: George Coleman, Portrane Mental Hospital.

Trim: Secretary: J. A. O'Dwyer, High Street, Trim.

Tullamore: Secretary: Michael Moore, Church Street, Tullamore..

Source: *Report*, December 1952. Note: There was no No. 9 Branch.

Membership reached 28,500 in 1953, with, most encouragingly, more than 18,000 in continuous benefit for more than one calendar year, 65% of the total and a crucial financial core. Members were acquired in Abbey Clothing Company by transfer from other unions and a Road Passenger Transport Section. A one-union Agreement in Dublin United Tramways Company squeezed out the WUI. After ten years refusing requests to organise, another union entered the area. The WUI recommended organisation in Ringsend Garage, Conyngham Road and Donnybrook.

In 1953 a surplus of almost a third of income was recorded, a very healthy return given the wage campaign. The WUI still complained that the 'cancer of our movement lies in the apathy' of members. Before the Conference Larkin reminded members that the WUI was 'founded and built up on faith in the Irish working class, faith in their courage and determination, faith in their intelligence to make the right decisions, to decide policy and tactics if they know the full facts and their significance in any given situation.' It was 'not run on the basis that the Officials know the answers to all questions, that they are always right and never make mistakes. Again, let me repeat, the members are the Union.'

Membership fell to 26,009 in March 1954, through slackness in building, sugar, confectionery and food-preserving. More than 73% were in benefit, 'a creditable position for a general union.' Tullamore Branch had many Sections that functioned as Branches, from as far apart as Mullingar, Roscrea, Monasterevin and Shannon

Harbour, members including 'navigating and engine room officers' on Gas Company boats who transferred 'from another professional trade union.'

The WUI prided itself on its internal democracy, but the members could not be the union if they chose not to participate. Management expenses held at around 57%. The WUI believed that 'the type of service expected by the members requires a relatively large staff,' but it was felt that the existing staff 'could cater for increased membership.' Jerry Fitzsimons (No. 3) felt that many thought unions were 'composed of Officials and Branch Committees,' an idea that 'must be got rid of.' A Committee to investigate participation was set up. T. A. Brown (Finance Committee) said the union maintained 'four motor cars, three motor cycles and one push cycle.' Most legal benefit went on a public enquiry at Portrane Mental Hospital.

The introduction of both Sickness and Unemployment Benefit was requested in 1954, subject to financial feasibility, together with a Tontine and Thrift Society. Despite doing well, the WUI was 'not a wealthy union.' Suggestions that the Conference be moved to midweek were opposed on cost grounds.

Celebrations of the thirtieth anniversary demonstrated a sense of triumph against adversity. The union had 'passed through great and epic struggles, overcome tremendous odds, beaten off attacks from many quarters, and, finally, growing from strength to strength,' had become established as 'a source of trade union inspiration and militancy'.[5]

Membership was 26,720 in 1955, including 6,000 women. Branches were established in Mullingar, for Co. Westmeath, and Longford. In Athlone a ballot of 'members of another union' resulted in 415 out of 500 voting to transfer, adding considerably to the Midlands presence. Ferguson was delighted that growth was horizontal as well as vertical.

Porters and attendants in Trinity College, Dublin, and Iveagh Trust joined, while outdoor Royal Liver Friendly Society agents 'transferred from a cross channel [British] organisation,' as did 'practically the whole membership of the National Society of Brushmakers.' Two Branches in Cork and Dublin did not transfer, and the Brushmakers appealed to an ITUC Disputes Committee. It found that the WUI had not notified it until matters were complete and criticised the absence of 'good trade union practice.' Conversely, some members in Williams and Woods, 'many in arrears, on quite unjustifiable grounds sought and were granted membership' of the Irish Bakers, Confectioners & Allied Workers Amalgamated Union. The Disputes Committee thought the Bakers' Union was about to instruct their return, but the workers joined the ITGWU, which insisted on holding them, 'as they had transferred from the Bakers' Union.' While 'what's sauce for the goose is sauce for the gander' may come to mind, the WUI saw this as an 'example of disorganising influences which flow from the absence of a united and disciplined movement.' Members in Batchelor's, Cabra, who transferred to the United Stationary Engine Drivers' Union, returned.

Financially, matters regressed. The ratio of assets to members represented £5 16s per head of full-benefit members, a figure that, while it did not 'provide adequate safeguards' against unusual demands, did provide 'reasonable assurance.' In a dispute between marble-polishers and the Stonecutters' Union of Ireland, Larkin proposed that a member of each Congress investigate matters. The dispute was contained and resolved.[6]

Table 76: WUI membership, 1950–59

	ITUC affiliation	RFS figures		
		Men	Women	Branches
1950	20,000	24,217	6,291	34
1951	25,000	26,376	7,053	29
1952	25,000	28,035	7,195	26
1953	25,000	27,469	7,118	27
1954	25,000	28,090	7,604	29
1955	25,000	28,320	7,600	35
1956	25,000	28,939	7,699	36
1957	25,000	28,745	7,539	35
1958	25,000	29,090	7,585	36
1959	30,000	29,631	7,715	36

Source: ITUC, Annual Reports, 1950–59; National Archives, Registrar of Friendly Societies, file 369T.

Rule changes in 1955 lowered the age of admission to fourteen and allowed 'a trade union or other Association of workers' to affiliate in exchange for an annual group subscription. Affiliates could not send Delegates to the Delegate Conference. Ferguson wanted the change to facilitate further expansion. Brendan Kavanagh (No. 6, Busworkers) pointed out that competitor unions offered better benefits. Ferguson pleaded that economic factors dictated increases in contributions. He disagreed that the Rules should be applied more rigidly as a contribution to good housekeeping. 'If there is one reason more than any other why we should not apply the Rules rigidly its is the fact that the late General Secretary, James Larkin, fought the Transport Union for applying their Rules rigidly.' He recalled that 'when an unfortunate woman claimed Mortality Benefit and it was discovered she was 3/– or 4/– over the amount of arrears permissible to allow the payment of Mortality Benefit he insisted that the Rules be waived. Let us keep that spirit. 'A vote against would deny strength to the union. The increases were approved.

Brendan Prone (No. 13) felt that Branches' autonomy was 'neither desirable nor feasible' and should be terminated. Ferguson pointed out that it was not merely a question of financial ability but giving workers control of their own affairs. The motion was rejected.

A call to make union membership a 'condition of employment' in all state and state-sponsored bodies was agreed. It was still non-recognition in the Hospitals Trust, where the WUI had only 400 out of 2,000 workers.

In 1956 Branches asked to retain 33^1/$_3$% of their income in local funds, a move opposed by the GEC. J. Kerrigan (No. 11) opposed making the General President and General Secretary permanent positions, as he was against the 'setting up of a boss class' as against their democratic principles. Smithers and Larkin expressed embarrassment and opposition. The proposal was rejected.

Membership rose to 27,263 but arrears remained high. Arrangements were made for the regular attendance of General Officers at Branch meetings to stimulate greater involvement. Increased contributions caused little friction and greatly improved finances. Members appreciated that higher income was necessary to improve such services as education, training, and research. New rates were put into a context that members could understand: 'It should not be overlooked that the price of two packets of twenty cigarettes is sufficient to pay union contributions for three weeks—and forty cigarettes are smoked in a couple of days!' The WUI won a significant reduction in Dublin firefighters' hours, supported a ban by dockers on handling container traffic and secured advances for mental hospital staffs, beef, pork and fish trades and the milk trade, where a 'considerable number' transferred.

Membership was static in 1957. Disappointment was expressed when the Irish Automobile Drivers' and Mechanics' Trade Union poached members in Dublin Gas Company garage, breaking 100% WUI membership. The IADMTU's action was 'contrary to good trade union practice' and might not have happened had there been a united Congress. Previously members of the Irish Local Government Officials' Union and the Irish Assistance Officers' and Superintendent Assistance Officers' Association affiliated. Since 1954 the staff of Dublin Royal Liver Assurance were members but could not secure recognition from the company, which dealt with a house union. So 100 Royal Liver members joined the Irish Liver Assurance Employees' Union, which in turn became an affiliate.

A Committee to investigate arrears was called for. Larkin asked, 'Why pass the buck to a special Committee?' It was a matter for Branch and work-place representatives. After an imaginative debate, the motion was defeated.[7]

No membership loss was recorded for 1958, despite dire economic conditions. Membership was claimed for all twenty-six counties, and members played an 'active and significant, if not leading role, in wage fixing.' Sections were created for physiotherapists and hospital pharmacists. It was a period 'between Wage Rounds,' and this often occasioned an increase in day-to-day activity, as individuals who withheld claims during wage bargaining peaks now brought cases forward. 'No fresh ground' was broken, although the National Hospitals Section gained greater recognition. Indeed the Section 'rapidly' became 'one of the largest and most influential.'

As to finance, it was a struggle to control costs. Officials were, however, subject to demands not uncommon throughout trade unionism, dealing with such problems as 'housing, social welfare benefits, sickness and hospitalisation . . . even the special family problems which arise over difficulties experienced with children of school age and over.' A surplus was generated, and financial security grew.

In January a former Official, M. F. O'Kelly, looked 'for the return of £80 he had loaned Peter Larkin in 1924.' The GEC asked him 'to submit the receipt for such loan.' Many members had made loans in the early days, loans that on occasion kept the union afloat. O'Kelly produced a receipt in March and was fully repaid in May; but his 'wallet and receipt were taken from his pocket on the way home.'

In 1959 E. Cassidy (GEC) cautioned that a survey showed 21,000 members and suggested the consideration of 'federation or merger with similar unions.' Séamus Bleakley (Athlone) qualified the usual comparison with the ITGWU's 100,000 by dismissing it as 'mostly made up on paper.' Gas Company members sought the extension of legal aid to those 'seeking redress for libels or slanders uttered against them by customers' or arising out of their employment. Denis Larkin (Industrial Secretary) reminded Delegates that legal aid was for those injured at work or affected by trade disputes. The motion opened potentially wide floodgates and was defeated. 'Nurse Mooney' (St Kevin's Hospital) called on the Dublin Board of Assistance to make it a condition of employment that all members of the staff be union members. It was compulsory in Dublin Corporation, why not in this sector?

In April the GEC conducted a full investigation into staffing and membership, concluding that the 'ratio existing between staff and membership at present appears to be unduly high.' The practice of 'floating clerical staff' meant that the collection of money needed a greater involvement by Branch Committees, and an officer or appointed auditor should carry out spot checks. A Central Cash Office would greatly facilitate the collection and recording of subscriptions. As for those making enquiries at Head Office, it was recommended that the 'nauseating sight of the grille' be done away with.' The union's membership now stood at 21,737.[8]

Table 77: WUI Branches and staff, April 1959

No. 1 (Miscellaneous)	2,534	Paddy Duff, Paddy Colgan, Barney Conway
No. 2 (Public Services)	1,377	Con Murphy, Anthony Brack
No. 3 (Miscellaneous)	1,500	Seán Nugent, William Eustace
No. 4 (Sugar, Confectionery and Food)	2,200	John Bennett
No. 5 (Butchers' Porters)	450	Michael Greene (part-time)
No. 6 (CIÉ, Engineering)	1,512	M. O'Brien (part-time), J. Hyland (part-time)
No. 7 (Tobacco)	770	Mick Canavan, Mick Cassidy
No. 8 (Building)	428	James Duffy, Mick Brennan

No. 9 (Guinness)	2,230	Jack Carruthers (part-time), Mick Kelly (part-time)
No. 10 (Fish and Poultry)	350	Paddy Moran
No. 11 (Pork Butchers)	528	Charlie Phipps
No. 12 (Aer Lingus)	904	J. C. Monks (part-time)
No. 13 (Gas Workers)	1,150	Hugh Montgomery, Patrick Forde
No. 14 (Operative Butchers)	550	Frank Cluskey
No. 15 (Clerical)	550	Joseph O'Connor
No. 16 (Chemists)	250	Paddy Moran
National Hospitals	1,100	John Foster (part-time)
Athlone	600	Barney Coffey (part-time)
Tullamore	100	Michael Moore, M. Flanagan
Kildare	224	James Byrne (part-time)
Thurles	585	John O'Reilly
Trim	141	J. A. O'Dwyer (part-time)
Brushmakers	180	A. Kelly (part-time)
Bray	494	Sam Hannon
Dún Laoghaire	530	Daniel Byrne
IALPA	100	James Larkin
Royal Liver Agents	300	Joseph O'Connor
Assistance Officers	300	J. Brophy (part-time)

RELATIONS WITH THE ITGWU

The Conference regularly heard criticism, direct and indirect, of the 'other union'. The ITGWU's activities were a benchmark against which to measure progress, or lack of it. In 1956 Mick Colleary (No. 6) congratulated the GEC on the Agreement with the ITGWU on recruiting, urging that similar Agreements be drawn up with others. Larkin spoke of its significance, going back to a 'breakaway which not only had its causes within the industrial struggle, but also within the political struggle and the Civil War.' The creation of the WUI 'was not something that merely took place by the issuance of some membership cards' but 'involved large bodies of workers in very severe industrial and physical struggles.' Men 'went to jail because they insisted on their right to form and be members of this Union, not only against the sneers and comments of opponents but in the face of guns carried and used against them.' Times had changed, and differences had 'existed for too many years.' Generally, ITGWU members wanted to transfer to the WUI only when in trouble or on unofficial strike.

An unofficial dispute in Irish Ropes saw an approach. It was rejected and the men told that, after a settlement, if a clear majority wished to transfer it would be considered. The ITGWU accused the WUI of fomenting trouble. Larkin replied seeking a bilateral Agreement similar to that which had existed for fifteen years between the ITGWU and ATGWU. From March a number of transfers, in both directions, were facilitated. The balance favoured the ITGWU.

Larkin's concluding remarks were redolent of possibilities. 'We have a common origin and were born in the inspiration and through the labours of the same man ... perhaps those of us in this generation may have the pleasant task of bringing back under a single banner the whole of the organised workers who owe their present position to the inspiration of a man who is no longer with us.'

The Agreement provided that transfers could take place without the prior written consent of the original union. Transfers could not occur if an unofficial strike happened or if disciplinary penalties were imposed. Where complete organisation existed, transfers required a clear and substantial majority. Neither union would actively seek to attract members from the other. The WUI thought the Agreement significant. It was between the two largest Irish unions, helped bury the past, and indirectly advanced talks between the ITUC and CIU.

It had not always been thus. In 1953 No. 8 Branch (Building) attempted to secure Agreement with the ITGWU No. 5 Branch, 'with a view to closing membership of both Branches.' Thomas McCarthy replied to James Duffy, WUI, on 15 April that 'no useful purpose at this juncture' would be served but promising to keep matters under review. It finally bore fruit with the establishment of a joint Committee governing transfers, thanks to the 'new and more co-operative atmosphere.' There was an air of disappointment, not least as unemployment led many new workers to seek building work, often at the expense of longer-established men.

Peter Purcell (No. 4) moved that the fiftieth anniversary of Larkin's arrival in Ireland be celebrated in 1957, possibly by opening a suitable hall. Tim Coffey (No. 8) suggested that they 'get in touch or try to get in touch with the Transport Union' to discuss possible joint commemorations. No mention was made of the Belfast dockers' and carters' strike.

In January 1954 the WUI noted that its own union, the ITGWU, IWWU and ISPWU all 'grew from that one seed—the seed of militant trade unionism sowed by Jim Larkin.' January 1909, the ITGWU's foundation date, gave all these unions a 'common heritage ... perhaps 1954 will yet bring to pass such changes in the Irish trade union movement as will make possible a unified acceptance of that common heritage which has changed the destiny of a people and above all the Irish working class.' It was an interesting challenge. For the immediate future it was a forlorn one.

In 1953 the Tobacco Workers' Branch struck up fraternal relations with the Tobacco Workers' Union in Britain, attending its Annual Conference at Weston-super-Mare and visiting the Wills factory in Bristol. At the 1955 ITUC Conference the WUI supported an Executive motion laying down procedures for transfer and resolving inter-union disputes. Richard Emoe's only concern was for the worker with a genuine grievance who, having been refused transfer, might drop out altogether. James Kelly pointed out that, in the absence of unity, any worker could simply swap to a CIU union. The WUI opposed 'poaching and sharp practice' but occasionally followed the law of the jungle, as others did, and welcomed proposals that would rationalise matters. The Provisional United Organisation of the Irish Trade Union Movement, established in June, adopted this Agreement with minor amendments.[9]

RURAL WORKERS

Larkin felt that 'tremendous valuable work' was done in Kinsale and in Portroe, Co. Tipperary, scene of a long and bitter dispute with quarry owners. The employer, never known to retreat, was defeated after four months and intervention by the Labour Court. Wage increases and complete organisation were gained. The quarries, however, had become flooded, and the men could not return after their victory. Advances were gained for Co. Kildare turf and briquette workers. The WUI was stretching well beyond its Dublin heartland.

The Tullamore Branch, established in 1950, welcomed as 'an outstanding achievement' the victory in raising the general town rate to £4. A full-time Secretary-Organiser was appointed to 'build up a large, effective, membership in the Midlands.' By 1952 the Branch had a thousand members. Many transferred from the ITGWU in Salt's spinning mill. Transfers were complicated and delayed by the temporary laying off of more than 200 workers, the company's objections to the WUI and discrimination against individuals.

The ITGWU believed it was assisting farm workers through the Agricultural Wages Board, the 1951 increases being a 'direct result of our campaign for extra remuneration for all workers.' While there was some truth in this, it ignored the activity of the Federation of Rural Workers and the ITUC. The WUI was urged to organise among mental hospital employees, as conditions were 'open to improvement.' Larkin pointed out that this could be done only by a full-time officer with the freedom to travel.

In 1957, with unemployment rising, the WUI 'admitted that no great progress' was made in 'building up strong and permanent organisation in the provincial areas,' despite 'many requests received.' Some who had come in, once their grievance or claim was settled, drifted away. It was apparently a 'common experience.' Provincial workers joined unions only when they had a problem and felt no obligation to remain once it was resolved.

In December the WUI supported Des Branigan, former General Secretary of the Marine, Port and General Workers' Union, who was found liable in a Court action for the purchase of new uniforms and instruments for the O'Connell Fife and Drum Band, a liability disclaimed by the MPGWU. The WUI paid the £20 instalment agreed on the amount of £639 4s one month and the ATGWU another to prevent Branigan's family losing their home.

In December 1958 the *Irish Independent, Irish Press* and *Irish Times* all wrote to the WUI asking if it wished to 'contribute to the supplement which the papers are carrying on the Golden Jubilee of the I.T.G.W.U.' No action was agreed.[10]

WOMEN

The ITUC Women's Advisory Committee met for the first time on 20 July 1950. In 1953 John Foster sought equal pay for nurses, a motion passed without comment. The question was how to move from easily agreed aspirations to practical achievement.

In 1954 Larkin asked that an IWWU motion asking the Government to accept the principle of equal pay for equal work and methods of implementing it be referred back. It was 'proceeding on two false assumptions': 'that all that is wanted is the practical implementation, and that the principle is accepted.' He moved a similar resolution in the Dáil, but there was a 'lack of support from women.' It was his experience that 'some of the best types of women trade unionists are not convinced of the correctness of the principle.' This somewhat confused contribution concluded with the advice that 'women have to propagate the idea . . . among their own sex and get acceptance for it.' Delegates disagreed and adopted the motion.

After an abortive dispute in the Tobacco Branch, Betty Jevons (No. 7) told the 1951 Conference that the majority, women, were 'not prepared to go out on strike in support of the male workers' claim.' Women accepted the company's offer, followed by the men, albeit under protest. The incident revealed tensions between male and female members and a growing appreciation of arguments for equal pay, at least among women. Men and women had been balloted separately, with majorities in favour of a strike in both.

Ambivalent attitudes to working women were reflected in the adoption of Marriage Benefit of up to £5 in 1952. This was payable to women on marriage, when the Marriage Bar meant they left their employment. It was a form of remittance of contributions.

In 1951 Elizabeth Harrison (Hospitals Trust) was elected to the GEC, followed in 1953 by Betty Jevons (No. 7, Tobacco) and B. Hallinan (Grangegorman), the first women to achieve national office in the WUI. Harrison's election was four years before Sheila Williams's election to the NEC of the ITGWU.

In 1952 it was estimated that 4,000 of the 27,000 WUI members were women. P. Brennan (No. 7) represented many women and suggested that if retiring for reasons other than marriage they should get some form of lump-sum benefit. Christy O'Rourke (No. 13) asked, given that the WUI was overdrawn, 'why should women get any more benefits than men?' They already paid lower contributions. It was referred back.

In August 1953 more than 6,000 women were 'loyal and conscientious members,' although 'not many' reached the 'long membership records of the men because the great majority leave employment' and the union on marriage. The union journal 'from time to time' published lists of the recipients of marriage benefit to 'extend congratulations and good wishes to them.'

Equal pay for equal work was covered in *Report*, citing a ruling by New York State Labor Department. The conclusion was that 'jazz and jeans are not the only things we might copy from the States.' In November, *Report* introduced a 'Woman's

Page'. Each month's centre pages featured an activist, starting with Bridie Stenson, Shop Steward in Fry-Cadbury's. Women's lack of participation was commented upon. 'We have come to the conclusion that women do not talk too much.' It was 'very evident' at Conferences, 'when all the discussion is monopolised by men.' To counter this 'Conference shyness' a discussion group was set up under the Social and Recreational Council. Although open to both sexes, it was hoped women would be the majority.

Margaret Cole's biography of Beatrice Webb was the Book Corner recommendation. It could be borrowed from Head Office. Larkin opposed the suggestion that the Woman's Page should be cut out. The union was 'especially anxious to cater for our women members.' The 'girls in the office, led by Miss McLoughlin,' undertook to supply material every month. He wanted to 'pay tribute to what they have done, and I intend to continue the page as long as I get the material.' McLoughlin gave a history of Dublin Trades Council, as she was a member of its Executive.

In April 1954 the WUI reflected that 'women are not given equal rewards' but noted that 'this inequality in pay is not general.' Women TDs, doctors, even a woman President of Ireland (possible under the Constitution if not then a reality)—all received equal reward. Yet 'even women themselves are not unanimous in their views on this question.' Women were invited to communicate their opinions.

In 1955 a Retirement Benefit for women who had to 'give up employment due to domestic circumstances,' for example looking after an elderly relative or sick child, was suggested. V. Lapslie (No. 4) sought to reduce the qualification period for this benefit from twelve years to eight in 1957. Larkin opposed. If it was carried, given existing female contribution rates, women would get eight years' full service for a mere £11.

In November 1957 No. 2 Branch suggested that 'all wage claims on behalf of women members should be made on an equal basis with men,' then a radical proposal. In 1959 Kay Fallon (GEC) found it 'disheartening' that only ten women were present to represent 6,000. Women recruits were particularly in need of education. She called for a Women's Advisory Council. The question of women in industry was a social problem, not least because they were 'second-class citizens' inside unions and seen as being 'subsidised by men.' Their lower contributions reflected their lower wages. Miss E. Hogan (No. 7) wondered whether a council would serve any purpose.[11]

WAGE ROUNDS

Satisfaction with the 1948 Eleven-Shilling Formula was expressed, but by 1950 it had served its purpose. Pressure mounted, through the ITUC, to open fresh wage talks after the required three months' notice. Real living standards, according to Larkin's analysis, were 13% behind 1939, and '1939 was no Utopia.' Workers' productive output was up by 48% and individual workers' productivity by 12%. Profits of sixty-one private companies in 1947–8 rose by £1.3 million to £1.6 million, 'free bonus shares were given to shareholders' and dividend rates maintained: 'times were good for many people.' Agriculture improved, and the 'National cake had got bigger . . . We were told that if we made the cake bigger we would get a larger slice. We made the cake bigger but we are not getting a larger slice.' In addition, prices continued to rise, hitting living standards.

Liam Ó Bucháin argued that unions had to act in national rather than sectional interests. Ferguson took him to task, pointing out that workers could have gained better increases purely from a share of profits. The ITUC sought price controls. For Ferguson 'we exist to advance the interest of the Irish working class. Let us be accused of being selfish. We are being accused that we are not paying enough for unity.' He cited Connolly: 'Unity. Yes Unity by any and every means, but not at any price.' Over and above unity stands the principle of democracy, 'the will of the majority. The majority of the people of this country are the producers.[12]

The WUI took credit for initiating the 1950 Wage Round, playing a central role in ITUC negotiations with employers and the Government. It added £750,000 to members' purses, contrasting significantly with £30,000 paid in union dues.

Most increases were gained without industrial action. Canal workers suffered by the amalgamation of the Grand Canal Company with CIÉ, as no comparative grades existed, and the railway strike of 1949–50 delayed progress. In tobacco, a strike ballot was controversially withdrawn at the Branch Committee's request. The GEC believed that once a democratic decision for strike was taken it 'should be loyally accepted by all.'

At the Congress Larkin moved the right to a 'living wage', decrying the fact that most workers earned less than £3 10s a week. Thomas Kavanagh and Ferguson challenged the basis of the cost-of-living index, suggesting that Congress compile its own index to more fairly reflect the impact of price increases on living standards. Larkin supported an Emergency Motion by Malachy Gray (ATGWU) that welcomed the termination of the 1948 Wage Agreement and called for a 'solid and united front' in new negotiations.

For Larkin, Congress's historic role 'first, last and all the time' was to address workers' living standards. They had shown patience and constraint. They were concerned not just with organised workers but with the broad working class, who needed increased purchasing power both for themselves and for their families and to boost national economic activity. Profiteering must be opposed, wage demands maximised.

Ferguson reasoned that increases in the cost of living were not the only criterion for increases. Productivity, work effort and demand could not be forgotten. WUI speakers were prominent in calls for price controls and union representation on the Prices Advisory Board. Larkin demanded that the results of higher productivity 'be shared by the workers.' Total income rose from £158 million in 1938 to £363 million in the South. Industrial output grew by more than 100% since 1944, yet workers' relative wages declined, increasing by 0.5% since 1938, from 43.4% to 43.9%. He gave many instances of hugely increased salaries for managerial grades, all of which dwarfed the shares going to wage-earners. Wage claims should be based not just on the cost of living but on 'the wealth of the community itself.' This was radical thinking, stretching Delegates' imaginations.

Ferguson criticised the CIU for imposing a new 'Standstill Order' with its Twelve-Shilling Formula, decided upon without consultation with the ITUC or before any real negotiations with the Government or employers. While unity was important, it should not come at any price. William McMullen and the CIU had 'far less excuse than even Mr. Lemass had.' They had 'no right whatever, in any conceivable circumstances, to impose a barrier to the forward march of the movement.'[13]

In April 1951 the WUI's preferred option was price reduction through the Prices Advisory Tribunal; but the 'Korean War and world re-armament' forced prices higher. Political action became as important as industrial action. Ferguson was credited with the establishment of a Lower Prices Council. John Byrne (No. 2) was a member.

On 1 May 1952 the ITUC recommended that unions proceed with wage claims. The WUI heard news of an Agreement by the CIU and FUE to a norm of 12s 6d. Ferguson strongly condemned it. 'We have an opportunity today, representing the rank-and-file as we do, to send a protest' to the leaders of the CIU 'that this time the working class is not going to stand for the same betrayal as they carried out in 1950. Thus far can the c.i.u. go and no further!' The ITUC was urged not to follow suit. Larkin, however, pointed out that the ITUC was made the same offer but had refused to recommend it. He had hoped the two Congresses would jointly reject it. The WUI had already begun 6% claims and, on that basis, 'increases should go up to 22/–.' The WUI rejected the '12/6 Formula' and did not feel bound by it. The CIU, however, accused the ITUC of carping against it in public but privately accepting it. It claimed that increases of 25s to 30s were feasible. Well, where were they? For the WUI, the CIU's comments were 'deliberate and calculated falsehoods.' Employers took the 12s 6d level as a ceiling and held the line there.

The ITGWU charged the WUI with a 'lack of militancy', a charge considered 'somewhat ludicrous in the face of the history of the two Unions.' It was 'even more baseless when it is realised that this Union of less than 30,000 members and no great financial resources is being charged with unwillingness to act as the advanced guard of the whole' movement by a union that 'claims 148,000 members and the greatest financial resources.'[14]

The ITGWU's charges were almost an honour. The clear implication was that 'on its record and by its policy and tactics' the WUI was 'regarded as the advanced Section.' Others expected it to set the pace.

The final outcome was not a happy one, revealing 'in its worst form the harmful effects of lack of unity.' Larkin concluded that the CIU 'would better serve the interests of their members by frankly admitting their mistake in ever having accepted the "12/6 ceiling".' The Agreement had been 'made farcical by life itself,' and a 'united effort' with the ITUC would have been better.

Larkin's frustration at disunity was palpable. Writing in *Report*, he said that 'many workers,' including 'even' WUI members, were 'confused over the figure of

12/6. They believe that the f.u.e. have offered a wage increase of 12/6 and it is only necessary for the Trade Unions to apply and it will be granted. This Is Not Correct.' He outlined his procedure for advancing claims. The amount was 'decided by the members concerned with the advice' of Officials. Negotiations were 'carried on by the union Officials accompanied by the direct representatives of the workers.' Where a claim was settled, any decision was 'made by the members themselves': 'That is trade unionism as we in the w.u.i. understand it.'

By December 1952 nearly £1 million extra was won for members. Larkin asked whether the previous four months' work could be considered successful. For the wui the answer was 'yes,' but for the movement the answer was 'no.'

In July and August they were 'shackled by the 12s 6d Agreement' but broke free with settlements in Jacob's and the mineral water trade. From then on, offers at or below 12s 6d were met with strike threats. Hurried Agreements were done with the itgwu by employers attempting to preserve the 'ceiling', but to no avail. Settlements in October and November reached 13s, 13 9d and 15s 6d. Even £1 million was 'too high a price' for Larkin: 'had there been no 12s. 6d. ceiling Agreement, no semi-secret rush by certain trade unions to clinch that figure by hurried settlements,' no disunity in the movement and 'above all the same degree of common policy, national leadership and unified action as that displayed by the employers, then the gains for the working class would have been greater.' Disunity cost workers 'an additional three to five million pounds.' But what it had cost 'in terms of wrong policy and tactics; ineffective leadership; weakness of organisation and the inadequate raising of workers' standards only the historian of the future can measure.' It was about time 'ordinary members . . . decided to stop footing a bill presented to them by incompetent and foolish leaders. The price is too high!'

Thomas Kavanagh pointed out that the cost-of-living had risen by 125% since 1939, with wages lagging behind at 93%, so 'it would take £2 5s. today to buy what a pound would have bought in 1939.' Irish industry had, significantly, stopped attacking William McMullen, now lauding him as a 'responsible' Leader. For Ferguson he was 'responsible' for curtailing workers' living standards.

In 1953 Larkin linked continuing falls in living standards with the absolute need for unification. Irish workers' 'right to live and work in their own country and to earn wages sufficient to ensure a reasonable standard of living' was being neglected. Real wages were below pre-war levels. Continued division meant that the movement fell down on its basic responsibility of improving living standards.[15]

In 1954 headway was made without having to engage in many disputes. Large disputes were 'spectacular', attracting 'widespread attention', but a general union's work never slackened and could be likened to building a wall. Brick by brick it rises; when the final wall is examined the 'small imperceptible gains are not noticed but the overall result is clear for all to see.'

The wui was certainly rising impressively. There were compelling arguments to justify wage increases. The retail price index was 232 in February 1955 (with August 1939 = 100), while Dublin wage rates were only 111. Real wages were therefore a tenth lower than before the war. This had occurred primarily since 1951, as the gap between prices and wages had largely been closed by then. In addition, workers considerably increased output since 1939, with no proper share coming back. Between 1938 and 1954 output per worker increased by nearly a third, while real wages actually decreased. Profits were rising.

The ITUC invited the CIU to joint discussions to avoid the differences of 1952. The FUE rejected invitations to talks. The WUI's solution was not that all workers should seek increases 'with machine-like repetition,' as there had to be consideration for national economic factors. Wage restraint had been given in 1946–8 and again in 1952–5 but had not won corresponding actions from employers or state. Since 1954 the WUI had served claims for increases and felt itself in the vanguard.

At the Congress James Kelly decried the fact that employers, apparently supported by the Labour Court, appeared to consider that the cost of living should be the only criterion for wage increases. They had fallen into the trap of feeling that 'if we simply restore 1939 standards . . . our job is done.' The employers had done this in their statement of 1 April, which Kelly felt was a 'significant date.' That there had been 'no marked increase in the cost of living since 1952' was apparently all that was needed to deny wage increases. The aim was to improve standards.

There was opposition from Senator D. F. Murphy (Transport Salaried Staffs' Association) and Billy McCullough (National Association of Theatrical and Kine Employees), claiming that costs could not be ignored, that the Labour Court, no more than the ITUC, was not to blame for the 12s 6d formula. A 'national wages policy' required a great deal more consideration and was the responsibility of all unions, not the incoming National Executive. Congress accepted the WUI's arguments and set the ground for a wider consideration of wages policy.

In 1957 Larkin stressed opposition to the mooted standstill. It was not a question of defending members' living standards but of improving them. He again attacked the increased profits and directors' dividends being enjoyed by those who lectured workers on restraint.[16]

The Fifth Round was, in its own eyes at least, 'led' by the WUI; but being early in the field was not always an advantage, as some later increases were greater, leading to many 'anomalies.' The Provisional United Organisation of the Irish Trade Union Movement sought a meeting with the FUE to discuss the next stage.

In 1957 Smithers pointed out that in 1947 and 1952, and now again, the Government attempted to cut consumption by indirect taxes, creating a vicious circle of economic depression, unemployment and emigration. Did this mean that unions should desist from seeking wage increases? The answer was 'emphatically NO!' What it did mean was that they should take a more active interest in national economics. The PUOITUM pamphlet *Planning Full Employment* offered solutions. Increased production was essential to boosting consumption and employment and generating wealth.

The years of wage increases were 1946, 1948, 1951, 1953, 1955, 1956 and 1957. A correlation between wage increases and rising prices can be drawn from table 78.

Whereas prices rose every year, wages moved only every two years. In addition, productivity rose consistently. Real wages were in fact lower in 1957 than in 1939.

Table 78: Cost-of-living index (August 1947 = 100)

1947	97	1953	125
1948	99	1954	126
1949	100	1955	131
1950	102	1956	134
1951	113	1957	143
1952	123		

Source: WUI, Report of General Executive Council, 1957–8, p. 1.

After the Budget the PUOITUM met and agreed criteria for new claims. The WUI led the field 'as fast as the democratic machinery' allowed. Criticism of wage tactics in 1958 provoked Larkin to suggest that they should not think 'along rigid lines.' Ireland was not a rich country. If workers wanted higher living standards they had to produce more wealth.

At the Congress, in a forensic analysis of the 1957 Agreement, not for the first time Larkin, noting uncontrolled prices and profits, asked whether wages and salaries were the only things to be controlled in the interests of combating recession. National wages policy could be recommended only if there were concomitant national price and economic policies. The alternative was to revert to Sectional claims. Should this happen, Larkin felt 'we should not be apologetic about it to anybody.' It would, after all, only be playing everyone else's game. But would it benefit the working class?

While the wage and salary-earning sections of the population had risen from 50 to 60% since 1946, their share of national income rose only from 49 to 50%. The number of farmers fell from 30 to 18%, yet their share of income rose by 26%. Real wages in 1958 were only 12% higher than in 1938, yet each worker's industrial output had risen by 30%.

Such figures justified wage militancy, but that would not achieve the broad objectives of national economic development and rising living standards. As the system really only allowed adjustments through the wage packet, Larkin concluded that 'we are going to see that they are going to be as good as we can make them.'[17]

The year concluded the 'ten-shillings Agreement'. The PUOITUM led negotiations, a practical indication of growing unity. Criticism of Wage Rounds was still rife. The WUI, while acknowledging that some stronger Sections were constrained, equally thought that poorly paid workers received increases they would not have gained without national Agreement. Whether such benefits for the lower-paid outweighed sacrifices made by the better organised was open to conjecture. Pressure from Sections wishing to make claims based on 'particular economic circumstances or problems within their own industry' had, partially at least, led to the Agreement's termination. This was especially true of clerical employees.

The Government was lobbied about updating and re-confirming its commitment to a Fair Wages Clause for all public contracts, something the wui campaigned for, given its extensive membership in the public sector. Increasing pressure for productivity saw speakers from the European Productivity Agency address the Congress. Calls for greater expertise in time-study techniques and their application were supported by Vincent O'Hara, expressing concerns over automation, for savings to be fully shared by workers and job losses minimised. Both Larkin and John Conroy (itgwu) were members of the Irish National Productivity Committee in 1958, designed to improve industrial efficiency.[18]

DISPUTES

The wui joined the general condemnation of unofficial strikes, believing that the Rules and machinery of the union were 'fully democratic and sufficiently responsive' to render unofficial action unnecessary, unjustifiable and 'against the interests' of the union. Unofficial action in June 1950 in Dublin Gas Company resulted in the Branch Committee being called before the gec to 'report on what measure they considered should be taken against the members responsible.' One member, 'whose appreciation of Union membership was such that his arrears were so heavy as to make him a lapsed member,' was expelled, two were suspended, and two fined. The stoppage 'arose from a selfish desire' on the part of members 'to place themselves in an advantageous position' compared with fellow-employees. This 'sectional wage claim' was 'ill-considered and thoughtless' and 'imperilled the welfare of hundreds of their fellow-members.' The wui's attitudes could not have been clearer, although 'at the same time' it did 'not desire to suppress the militancy and readiness of members ... to fight for their rights and defend themselves.'

In 1952 the wui served a claim for cié shopmen in an attempt to narrow the widening gap with craftsmen. An offer of 10% was rejected and referred to the Labour Court, where Ferguson made it clear that if a further increase was granted to electricians making a simultaneous claim, the closure of that new differential would be sought. The electricians took this as a prejudicial comment, and struck. On the second or third week they sought the wui's support and, despite their being in different Congresses, the wui agreed, suggesting that all railway shop workers, irrespective of union, should meet. Allegations were made that ciu members handled goods during the electricians' stoppage.

In 1952–3, despite a vigorous Round of wage claims, Dispute Pay was tiny. It had long been policy, 'while ready at any time to take action,' to win cases by 'proper preparation' and 'intelligent negotiation to secure the maximum possible gain for the members at the lowest possible cost.'

A third strike in five years took place in R. and W. Scott, jam manufacturers, in Artane, Dublin, the previous two having lasted sixteen and twelve weeks. Neither was over wages or conditions but the 'attitude of management,' the present strike being over seniority of service or 'last in, first out.' After five days victory was achieved, with 'last in, first out' conceded.[19]

A sixteen-day stoppage in 1954, involving the WUI and other unions, threatened cross-channel trade. More than 700 men in the B&I Line rejected a Labour Court recommendation. Eventually, six shillings a week was won. In 1956 Tim Coffey (No. 8), welcoming moves towards unity, called upon the PUOITUM to 'condemn unofficial strikes.' Larkin opposed, suggesting that when unofficial action occurred it was not the relationship between employer and worker that was at issue but that between worker and union. The motion was lost.

Small amounts paid in Dispute Pay might have led members to conclude that the union was inactive or sought to restrain strikes. Sanction had actually been given twenty times, but only four strikes occurred, as increases were won through effective negotiation. In 1957, after a tough Budget and with another Wage Round beginning, Ministerial intervention prevented Dublin City Manager negotiating with Corporation workers. By then most Dublin private-sector workers had won increases. It became a trial of strength, with other local authority and state employers watching keenly. The Labour Court recommended a 10s increase. The City Manager accepted the recommendation and the Minister sanctioned it. Dublin Corporation workers had won the fight for all public-sector workers, and the WUI had played the leading role.

Not all disputes were over money: employment was always high on the agenda. In June, Fry-Cadbury wanted to export Crunchies by container, but the WUI insisted that containers be packed by dockers.

In August the men voted by 375 to 68 to force 'seven or eight defaulters who refuse to fall in line' as part of a drive, with the ITGWU, to ensure full unionisation in Ringsend bus garage. The PUOITUM adopted the policy of a Working Party on Unofficial Strikes in August 1957 after suggestions from the Minister for Industry and Commerce. Larkin served on it, together with the FUE, construction and transport employers. It made general recommendations for avoiding unofficial action and laid down procedures for the transfer of members.

Unofficial action in Ballingarry Mines required the involvement of two local clergymen to effect a settlement. The Labour Court found the dismissal of a member, Delaney, to be justified, but the rest of the workers persisted in their action. After intervention by local politicians Delaney was taken back for three months, pending a final settlement. By November 1959, with work resumed, the strike had cost £5,939 9s 4d. A local dance raised £40, which the GEC made up to £100. Larkin criticised the Branch for its mishandling of the case.[20]

DUBLIN CORPORATION

Other than clerical workers, 60% of the employees of Dublin Corporation were members of the Irish Municipal Employees' Trade Union. In March 1952 a WUI claim for an increase of £1 was made to the City Manager. The practice in the ESB, Dublin building trade, Gas Company, Port and Docks Board, laundries and sugar confectionery was that where there was more than one union all were represented at wage negotiations. 'But the Corporation should be an exception, according to the I.M.E.T.U.,' which objected to the others' presence. The WUI refused to acquiesce in such an arrangement, as it represented eight hundred workers. The matter was referred to Dublin Trades Union Council, despite the objections of the IMETU. Both the WUI and IMETU were ITUC affiliates.

While the matter remained unresolved, the City Manager ignored the claim. He met the IMETU on 9 October and offered 12s 10d a week, backdated to 26 March. By the time the same offer was made to the WUI a day later, 'the morning papers already carried reports of the previous night's decision' by the IMETU, giving it the public relations advantage it sought. The WUI insisted that 'lack of unity' damaged all Corporation employees and felt that a larger increase could have been won, and for broader groups of members. It insisted that the 'WUI is not seeking to advance its position as an organisation at the expense of any other body,' and now that the wage issue was resolved it intended to pursue greater unity of action in future.[21] The WUI was in more regular conflict with the IMETU than with the ITGWU.

HOSPITALS TRUST

Organisation in Irish Hospitals Trust continuously met the management's 'anti-trade union attitude'. The WUI was reluctant to fight openly, lest it 'might adversely affect the finances available for hospitalisation,' but members could not accept matters indefinitely. In 1950 the union reflected ruefully that 'while it has been possible to establish normal industrial relations' with a private company, such as Guinness, and state-sponsored undertakings, such as Aer Lingus, 'a completely different experience' was 'met with when dealing with Hospitals' Trust.' Recognition was flatly denied, negotiations refused.

Members' determination was undimmed. In 1950 Ferguson welcomed 400 members. The management responded by forming a house union, granting an increase of 10s a week at its first meeting. Similar concessions were made on hours, after WUI members sought reductions.

At the Labour Court the management appeared to confuse the WUI and the ITGWU—not a mistake Ferguson could comprehend—before the Labour Court recommended that workers be free to join the union of their choice. The employer rejected the recommendation. Ferguson pointed out that £2 million had been distributed among the trust's five board members, the Managing Director receiving £600,000. These were astronomical figures, and yet 600 women were denied one of their basic rights. Only the *Irish Times* reported the case, the *Irish Press* and *Irish Independent* ignoring what was surely a newsworthy story.

This illustrated a peculiar difficulty in relation to the Hospitals Trust. As the company was one of the country's largest advertisers, getting publicity for the union's case was nigh impossible, as newspapers protected their own interests. One labour correspondent was 'called before the General Manager and severely reprimanded' and reminded that 'the truth for the paper is the truth conceived by our advertisers.' Even the income of £750,000 of the Hospitals Trust's General Manager was not apparently newsworthy.

Elizabeth Harrison complained in 1952 that they were 'still unrecognised,' with 'no hope for the future.' Ferguson offered a brighter aspect. Two women were off work, certified sick. They attended a wedding. Their car was involved in an accident, which was reported in the press, and they were fired. Ferguson wrote to the Managing Director seeking compassion and received a reply to say that the two women would be 'restored to their full employment.'

Much was made in 1955 of the Government's intention of ratifying ILO Convention 87, on Freedom of Association and protection of the right to organise. Larkin asked about the Hospitals Trust and whether the Government would ensure, once ratification took place, that its employees could join the WUI. The staff varied from 600 to 4,000. None were allowed join a union. Dues for the house union, controlled by the Personnel Manager, were deducted from workers' wages. Favourable Labour Court recommendations lay dead. The Government did nothing to seek the implementation of the convention in a state-sponsored body supposedly run in the public interest.

In June 1957 Thomas Doyle complained that No. 15 Branch's motion 'That the G.E.C. be directed to press the claim of the Union for recognition by Hospitals' Trust' was not reached. It was common enough for motions not to be reached, but this motion came behind far less important business. Doyle clearly felt that the omission said something about attitudes to the battle with Hospitals Trust. Strangely, the only suggestion that there be a 'public inquiry into the spending of Irish Hospital Sweepstakes money' came at the CIU in 1953, when a motion by J. Cheevers (Operative Plasterers) passed without debate.[22]

GUINNESS

Wage increases were won in Guinness in 1950 through the Labour Court, although the Court had controversially stated that because Guinness was 'making exceptional high profits' did not mean that workers 'should feel they were entitled to increases in wages.' For the WUI, this was an 'attitude we condemn.' The ITUC drove home to the Court that if it genuinely wanted 'peace and co-operation' in industry this would not do. Conversely, the Labour Court suggested to the Guinness Employees' Organisation that it consider joining a proper union. The organisation 'interviewed several trade unions' before deciding on the WUI. A Brewery Workers' Branch was formed, with 500 members, quickly rising to a thousand. J. Kinsella paid tribute to Ferguson's and Larkin's assistance, giving an insight into the direct involvement of WUI General Officers. They were 'justly entitled to feel proud' of having established union organisation in Guinness's, long regarded as 'almost impossible of organisation.'

Effective recognition was achieved by 1952, although access to the senior management was still denied. Guinness said that the ATGWU agreed to such an exclusion in London. The WUI insisted that this was a fundamental point, and finally won

Agreement. The Christmas bonus of 5% of annual wages realised 5s for the lowest-paid, 'a spectacular vindication' of the union's case for improved wages. A presentation was made to Jack Carruthers, Chief Shop Steward in the Cooperage Department, to show appreciation for the union's achievements. In 1954 the union co-operated with the company in the introduction of work-study methods; and yet 'when the Section sought an opportunity' to discuss 'overall improvements in wages scales' it was 'summarily rebuffed.' The union withdrew its co-operation before the management conceded a 'bonus related to the company's profits and the workers' annual wages.'

By 1 February 1958 the WUI had enforced a closed shop for all operative grades, and membership was 2,400. The Section established a voluntary fund of 1s a week to provide for employment for idle workers.[23]

AER LINGUS

In 1946 Dublin Airport fitters sought admission to No. 6 (Engineering) Branch, as no craft union would accept them. They had trained in the Irish or British army rather than through formal apprenticeships. Their acceptance was a gleeful one, as the WUI recognised the potential of the airline industry, and soon 'semi-skilled and unskilled manipulative grades' were organised. Clerical workers followed, and the construction of universal rates, reduction of scales and general improvements attracted more. The Senior Staffs' Association affiliated and immediately won increases of £100 to £250 a year. The affiliation of the Irish Airline Pilots' Association in April 1950 was the icing on the cake, bringing the WUI a prestige that echoed far beyond the airport.

By 1952 there were more than 1,000 members in Aer Lingus. Indeed the Assistant Airport Manager was a member. Some might have thought this would cause problems, but 'save for the inevitable one or two difficulties which were trivial, the whole staff have been moved forward without any dislocation whatsoever.'

In 1955 considerable increases were secured for pilots, stewardesses and clerical workers. The Minister for Industry and Commerce, William Norton, agreed that differences between pilots and the company on air regulations could be referred to the Department. At the end of the 'ten-shillings Agreement' in 1958 Aer Lingus clerical staff and pilots submitted claims for increases to re-establish what they saw as lost parities. Strike notice was eventually served against an obdurate company on 28 March but was averted at the eleventh hour by minor concessions and a request that matters be deferred until September 1959. The Labour Court rejected the claim, as it 'did not wish to create a precedent of giving a rise in a semi-state [state-sponsored] company' which would amount to an estimated loss of £350,000. The Airline Pilots' Association offered support. It was felt that the crisis cleared up 'much of the strained atmosphere existing in the company' and offered the possibility of satisfactory settlement in future. Stewardesses won a pay claim retrospective to May 1957.[24]

CLERICAL BRANCH

In 1952 No. 15 (Clerical Employees) Branch was created. All clerical workers transferred into it, with the exception of those in 'fully organised Sections' such as Aer
Lingus and the Gas Company. The Branch began with 600 members, which, 'in
view of the many approaches being made,' was expected to rise rapidly after recruitment in the Dublin Milk Board and Bord Iascaigh Mhara. In 1954 the Branch was
not considered to have 'been a success, although it is still maintained as a separate
unit.' A 'lack of interest and drive' meant it had 'not so far proved its worth.' This
seemed a harsh and premature judgement.

By January 1953 successful Fifth-Round awards had, by and large, not filtered
through to clerical workers in either the public or the private sector. Larkin's
explanation lay in the much lower rates of unionisation. It was the movement's
'over-all duty and responsibility' to rectify this and eliminate 'this dangerous
weakness.' Failure affected all members, manual and clerical. There were attempts
to put a standstill on clerical workers' wages, exploiting their timidity. A clerical
worker was 'Counselled to look after himself, keep his mouth shut, his nails clean,
and remember that Thomas Lipton [founder of the Lipton grocery chain] began as
a newsboy.'

In 1955 Gerry Bolger (No. 15) said that many members were 'white-livered' rather
than 'white-collar'. Ferguson questioned whether they were an 'economic asset' to the
union. They required more time. James Kelly (Staff) wanted to extend organisation.[25]

TULLAMORE AND TRIM

A petition by Tullamore workers was sent to Larkin in 1950, so poor were their
conditions. A Delegate was despatched and reported that 'worker feared worker,
unity of word or action was completely unknown and consequently wage rates and
general working conditions were deplorable.' On 28 January the WUI responded.
Seán Nugent addressed a mass meeting on 26 March, after which a Committee was
appointed. After two months there was still marked reluctance, ascertained to be
'due to mismanagement and downright neglect by other organisations,' creating
fear. After Ferguson addressed a public meeting on 5 June, confidence rose. The
first pay increase was won in December in B. Daly and Company, distillers, after
which 'all Tullamore and beyond rallied to the w.u.i.' Sub-Branches were set up in
Clara, Clonaslee and Kilcormac.

On 6 March 1952 a protest march of 500 to 600 people marched through
Tullamore, 'despite heavy rain,' in support of coerced workers in Salt's and demanding 'freedom of speech and right of association.' Membership rose rapidly afterwards, and ambitions developed for a hall and a social club.

In 1954 Michael Moore's energy resulted in organisation in Ballynacargy,
Banagher, Clara, Ferbane, Kilcormac, Lumcloon, Port Laoise and Turraun among
Bord na Móna and co-operative society workers, local authority roadmen, distillers,
power station construction labourers and maltmen. Branches opened in
Ballinagore, Boora and Kilbeggan. In Trim, Torc Manufacturing was organised in

1946 after work by Anderson and O'Dwyer, who then recruited Spicer's Envelopes, J. and E. Smith Mineral Waters and Spicer's Bakery.[26]

UNITY

The reunification of the Labour Party and National Labour Party in 1950 was seen as a 'helpful development'. Relations between the ITUC and CIU had 'not been quite as antagonistic or sharp as previously.'

Larkin regretted the limited progress. At the 1950 ITUC Congress he paid tribute to British unions for the 'unrepayable debt' owed them. They brought 'guidance and organisation' when 'we in this country were possibly not attuned to that particular need.' Now, however, circumstances had changed. British union leaders needed to sit down and examine the new situation, as 'what makes for progress at one stage can at a later stage become an obstacle.' If the Irish movement were to be international it first had to make clear its own identity. Congress now acknowledged the principle that the movement should be 'Irish-based and Irish-controlled.' He urged British unions to 'examine the possibilities for Irish autonomy.'

The WUI sought mechanisms whereby all unions operating in Ireland could be Irish-based and Irish-controlled. Some tension existed during the railway strike of 1949–50, but during the 1951 building strike CIU unions joined their ITUC brothers to effect a satisfactory settlement. Rank-and-file members had a greater grasp of the value of unity than those 'at the top.' The WUI was an Irish union, and it was 'quite absurd and unworthy of consideration' that Irish workers could not manage their own affairs. Some ITUC affiliates recognised this, and the National Union of Boot and Shoe Operatives and the NUR both allowed Irish members to set up their own organisation, providing them with capital sums.

Larkin reflected about the extent to which rank-and-file members were really interested in bringing about a united movement. Outside of Wage Agreements, when a united approach by the ITUC and CIU was welcomed, 'they lose their interest.' Yet 'every worker knows that he would be stronger' if there were unity. He concluded: 'It seems to me' that if unions could unite for wage purposes they could meet to talk about structures. 'What about a Constituent Assembly of Trade Unions to draft the constitution for a united Trades Union Congress for all Ireland?' Although it was only a suggestion, Larkin pleaded: 'At least let us think about unity with the intention and determination to not only think but act.' The price of disunity was too high. Unity would 'not come through wishful thinking, but only through action.'[27]

In 1952 peace began to break out, with a Joint Congress Conference Committee on 11 March to determine common policy on the cost of living and price control, safeguarding real wages, unemployment, and the co-ordination of activity in industrial disputes. The WUI called for all members in 'any defined industry' to be in one union. Denis Larkin, Industrial Secretary, sought the withdrawal of the motion, despite his sympathy with it, as it would 'in effect be instructing our G.E.C. to secede as a Union.' James Kelly (Staff) thought the motion was the 'attitude of the I.T.G.W.U.' It was withdrawn.

At the Congress Denis Larkin praised the NUR and NUBSO as the National Association of Transport Employees and Irish Shoe and Leather Workers' Union were created. He urged other British Executives to follow suit. For much of an Irish TUC debate 'one would imagine it was not taking place in Ireland at all but in the heart of London.' This in itself was 'one of the strongest arguments' in favour of a Congress serving Irish interests. Spokespersons of British unions queued up to oppose. Two votes both resulted in the WUI motion being lost, raising the question why it had been tabled and whether, had James Larkin not been President, its presentation might have been different.

Stalemate and pessimism marked unity talks in 1953, although ice began to thaw at the end of the year. At the Congress Larkin recognised that the WUI was sometimes guilty of putting its own interests before those of the movement. 'If we moved among the rank-and-file of trade unionists, we would find a greater appreciation of the principles put forward . . . than among full-time Officials.' A motion calling on ordinary workers 'to make their ardent desire for unity known and felt' came not from the WUI but from the Irish Union of Hairdressers and Allied Workers. Larkin undoubtedly supported this motion, but both he and, therefore, the WUI were too central to moves that edged towards direct discussions to be seen to make such an appeal.

In 1954 Smithers bemoaned the antagonism between the two Congresses while employers 'were able to pursue a unified course.' At the same time the WUI 'understood the practical difficulties' and opposed 'policies which resulted in keeping the movement divided.' The rigid enforcement of principles disregarded 'the whole historic development of the trade unions in this country, the loyalties of members of English based unions . . . and the practical problems arising in respect of any transfer.'

The WUI held the 'strongest hopes' for success. Ferguson opposed greater autonomy for the Northern Ireland Committee, accusing Billy McCullough of finding the solution to unity 'by drawing a 17th Parallel demarcation line across Ireland' (a reference to Korea and to McCullough's Communist politics). Any such formal split would be 'admitting intellectual bankruptcy.' Larkin explained that the peculiar problems of the 'north-east' were elaborately explained to the CIU officers, who were largely ignorant of them.

Talks with the British TUC proved 'fruitless', throwing the responsibility back on themselves. He felt the border was being too readily drawn by elements on both sides. The solution was not further Partition. The one positive feature of unity talks was that 'they had not broken down.' Perhaps, given that both Congresses seemed to agree on fundamental principles, they should simply unite and seek to 'induce' British unions to 'apply the already accepted principle by voluntary decision' rather than insisting on 'prior and rigid organisational and financial changes as a prerequisite.' The WUI was clearly getting impatient. Having Branches of shipwrights and brushmakers, both former British unions, Ferguson thought the WUI 'can justifiably say that we are effectively doing the job of building' an Irish movement.[28]

The Provisional United Organisation of the Irish Trade Union Movement was instituted on 2 July 1955. Larkin served as Treasurer and Secretary. In 1956 he thought that, as they were all around the same table, it was 'not easy to get up . . . and start quarrelling again.' Ferguson praised Larkin as the 'first to endeavour to find a formula' for reunification. The wui claimed a 'notable and leading contribution' towards unity.

Denis Larkin became the second wui members of the ituc National Executive in 1956. In 1958, as the puoitum shaped a united Congress, a dispute over organisation broke out in Ardmore Film Studios, Bray. Charlie Phipps, dtuc Delegate, called it a 'terrible reflection on disunity.' If the ciu had made the exclusive Agreement there was 'no sincerity in their efforts to make unity . . . We are not united nor are we in any form a movement, unless this kind of poaching, this separate and private Agreement . . . is put down underfoot. If it is not possible to settle this matter' with the Provisional United Organisation 'I fail to see where unity can prevail.' The absence of a puoitum Disputes Committee prevented further action but demonstrated that unity was still a fragile flower.

At the 1958 ituc Congress Denis Larkin urged that the 'final steps necessary to the formal inauguration' of a new, united trade union centre 'be taken with as little delay as possible.' While such a motion was ritual, it expressed the frustration of the wui. It had invested much effort, intellectual energy and political commitment and was anxious that last-minute hitches, delays or obstruction be avoided.

At the Special ituc Congress on 10 February 1959 Larkin was the last speaker. 'Plainly and forthrightly' he recalled that the wui had been defensive of its 'amalgamated brothers' in 1946–7 to ensure that there would be no coercion and to enable cross-channel industrial links to be maintained. In 1953 it accepted the principle that unions should be 'Irish-based and controlled.' He could not now understand the reservations and could 'not say what the consequences would be' if the draft constitution were rejected. The vote was 148 to 81 in favour, a significant but not unanimous endorsement that emphasised how problematic unity discussions had been and why leading figures, such as Larkin, a model of diplomacy and integrity, could feel proud of their achievement. Unity opened up all other possibilities.[29]

THE IRISH CONGRESS OF TRADE UNIONS

On 4 March 1959 the wui became the first affiliate of the Irish Congress of Trade Unions. Larkin was Secretary, and the General President of the itgwu, John Conroy, was President. The wui saw this as appropriate. In his 1959 Presidential Address (read by Michael Kiersey, gec, because of his illness) Smithers welcomed the ictu. 'We need better forms of organisation, more rational organisations, wider acceptance of common policy and leadership, and a higher standard of information, research, publication and educational services.' They needed clear and sharply defined policies and properly formulated tactics to tackle 'serious economic and social problems' and 'to win a way forward to a higher standard of security for our people.'

Richard Emoe wanted Congress's 'first endeavour' to be 'to secure the more effective and orderly development' of the organisation 'on lines adapted more closely to the development of modern industry and the industrial and economic problems of workers.' Without 'taking from the efforts of others' he thought it 'universally conceded' that the WUI's part in creating the ICTU 'was greater than any other.' Thomas Kavanagh (Trustee) felt that a united industrial arm should be accompanied by a Labour Party candidate in every constituency.[30]

EMPLOYMENT

In 1950 Ferguson welcomed the establishment of the Industrial Development Authority. He wanted union involvement in planning and decision processes for new industries.

In 1951 Larkin underlined the problems in gaining acceptance for WUI policy on economic planning.

Many people during recent years have become somewhat like Hitler—when he heard the word 'culture' he reached for his gun [a famous misattribution, actually a line from a play]. We have quite a number of people here, who, when they hear about planning, want to set up an Un-American Subversive Activities Committee.

An Agricultural Development Committee should work alongside the IDA to plan the fullest use of natural resources.

Richard Emoe repeated that private enterprise was 'completely outmoded' in 1953. He welcomed joint statements by the ITUC and Labour Party on employment, concluding that 'production should be geared to the wants of man and not the wants of war.' For Larkin, unemployment was a 'gangrene', growing and feeding on itself, 'an economic sickness in our nation, bringing privation, hopelessness, despair.' It could only be 'driven back by correct economic policies translated into resolute and determined action.' Nobody was better equipped to do this than the unions; but, if it was to be done, they 'must look beyond wage rates and working hours, and get down to basic economic facts . . . which determine jobs, wages and conditions in the existing economic system.' In facing the storm, however, unions had 'two coxswains, two crews, pulling against each other; cancelling each other's strength while the boat was swamped.'

Calls for profit-sharing and partnership were 'main planks' of WUI policy. It warned that deflation was the core economic ailment. Economic depression and unemployment led employers to cut wages and jobs, lengthen hours and worsen conditions. Worse, the creation of the Irish Management Institute provided employers with a think tank.[31]

In 1953 Larkin had three questions. Why are those people unemployed? How can we as trade unionists and citizens put it right? And what immediate, alleviating steps can be taken? The ITUC appealed for the release of members of Dublin

Unemployed Association arrested for obstruction. The wui supported their release and the provision, through Congress, of speakers for their meetings.

In 1954 the union called for control of the banks and insisted on investment in national economic development. G. Fitzsimons (No. 3), 'to dispel the idea that anyone who questions the financial system is a crank,' lengthily cited Pope Pius xi.

Ferguson objected to implied attacks on non-nationals while stressing that he had 'no sympathy with people who control our financial affairs whether they be Jews or Gentiles,' but they should 'not be condemned merely because they may be of a certain race, class, species or religion.' Larkin called for a survey of natural resources, their fullest, planned development, significant public investment, encouragement for agricultural co-operation and the alteration of financial structures to enable all this. If there were to be 'such an intelligent co-ordinated approach' it had to be underwritten by union involvement at all planning stages.

The wui was one of only three unions that attended a Co-operative Convention at Red Island, Skerries, in 1956, urging the establishment of new consumer and industrial co-operatives.[32]

The wui supported the puoitum's document *Planning for Full Employment*. J. Harris (No. 1) pointed out that his bus ticket was printed in England, in Irish, a sad commentary on domestic economic policy. The debate tailed off into opposition to automation, but the central thrust was that planning was needed. Larkin lampooned the Taoiseach, who had claimed that 'even yet nobody has given him and his Government a blueprint' of how to deal with economic problems. Had he never listened to Congress? Planning was the key, and yet

> to deal with emigration we decide to cut down on capital investment, so there will be less jobs and more people can go abroad. And so we keep hopping from one peculiar situation to another. Everything that we want is distorted in this peculiar economic looking-glass, and the very things we set out to do—to reduce unemployment, to reduce emigration, to give greater opportunities to our people at home—all of these things are twisted and become the opposite because we will not plan.

Too much Irish capital was invested abroad for personal gain against national interests. Larkin wanted a complete break from British Conservative Government policies, which were 'slowly, but surely, strangling our economy and continuing to intensify our present problems every week in every year that passes.' A national campaign of meetings and publicity was sought; but Betty Jevons asked, 'Is it to become a country of public meetings and blueprints and Commission reports which are published and nothing is ever done about?' Effort should be concentrated on unity talks.

The wui insisted that supports to agricultural be conditional assistance leading directly to increased production. M. Behan pointed out that since 1946 £70 million in state aid was given to farmers and nearly £13 million to reclaim 650,000 acres of land that lay idle.

Speakers from the Federation of Rural Workers wanted the motion referred back, but Larkin thought that 'hard neck'. If their objections were that they were better informed on agriculture, let them make the case against. They did not.[33]

In 1957 CIÉ wanted to abandon canal operations, with many job losses. The WUI, ITGWU, Inland Waterways Association and Maritime Institute formed a Trade Union Canal Protective Association to make detailed submissions to the Government. Seán MacBride was an active supporter. Larkin moved support for *Planning for Full Employment,* welcoming the opportunity to speak on a united, coherent strategy representing all organised workers.

PUOITUM Conferences were held in Belfast and Dublin in November and December 1956 to approve the policy, since when, not untypically, Larkin wondered whether it had 'become just another document.' Few Executives discussed it; almost none brought it down to the Branch level. They were transfixed by wages.

> The potential strength of our organisation is limited not merely by our fighting capacity, not even by our funds, not even by the willingness of our members to make sacrifices, but by the economic possibilities that exist in each industry and each job. If our people want, or are to get, a higher standard of living, then we have got to push back the economic limitations that are pressing in upon us.

His demand was an acid test for the PUOITUM. How would it translate endless aspiration into achievement?

In 1958 Michael Cassidy moved for participation in the European Free Trade Association. It offered greater market opportunities, provided the needs of the underdeveloped Irish economy could be protected. He wanted the 'levelling up' of currency values to facilitate trade throughout an expanded market. Frank Hickey thought 'we might also in future years see a European Government.' Answering opposition speakers, Cassidy concluded that there were 'no alternatives to joining free trade. If Europe does not associate in some community, the alternative may be big blocks and selfish isolationism, back again to the pre-1930s.' Free trade was coming.

In 1959 there were calls for a 'programme of protest meetings and public demonstrations' against the 'evils of unemployment and emigration.' The White Paper was 'wholly inadequate.' The exploitation of young workers was denounced. Entry to work should not be allowed before sixteen. The Irish Liver Assurance Employees' Union, a WUI affiliate, objected to 'fellow trade unionists who are in constant and well paid employment taking up jobs as part time Insurance Agents.' The GEC should 'have this matter raised at the highest trade union level.' It was defeated, because some insurance agents also had second incomes.[34]

INDUSTRIAL RELATIONS

Larkin queried what was meant by 'worker-employer co-operation'. Was the workers' role 'to be confined to discussing improved facilities such as canteens, cloakrooms, recreational and social facilities' or to the 'more efficient running of the enterprise'? Experience answered his own question. Co-operation had to be 'without qualifications or limits.' There was not much prospect of doors being immediately opened.

In 1959 C. Murray (No. 12) called for 'greater participation by employees in the decisions and policy-making of management.' Jack Harte (Guinness) cautioned enthusiasts by recalling their experience, where co-determinism was only allowed to a point. Dan Byrne (No. 7) wanted schemes of profit-sharing and workers' participation.[35]

In 1950 the wui sought conciliation machinery for local authority workers, not least to lessen control by County Managers. A more open, transparent system would not necessarily enable them to have their cases properly heard and adjudicated upon, but the public would be far better informed regarding public-service pay and conditions. Larkin pointed out that when the Labour Court was debated in the Dáil the Minister promised to act for public servants once it was operating. The ituc's criticism of the Labour Court was acute in 1951. It opposed attempts to make recommendations legally binding. Executive members met Court Officials in December to clear the air. The Chairman of the Court, R. J. P. Mortished, resigned on 31 May 1952 to work for the International Labour Organisation. Although he was a former Secretary of the ituc, few tears were shed.

In 1953 Betty Jevons (No. 7) moved that twenty members, workers and employers, be appointed to assist in judging Labour Court cases; that a Court of Appeal be established; that an annual gazette of the outcome of cases be published; and that a Commission to establish a national social minimum wage be set up. James Kelly (No. 7) opposed, fearing the prospect of even greater delays. There were attempts to look after 'the forgotten children, the messenger boys, the most exploited section of the working class,' even though the 'difficulties were always too great' and any organisational success quickly dissipated.

A Joint Labour Committee was achieved in 1953, although there were great difficulties regarding enforcement. In 1955 Larkin welcomed access to the Labour Court for 'servants' and some named 'officers', perhaps 50,000 workers. It ended direct, often unsuccessful talks with County or City Managers and unbreakable deadlocks. In 1958 No. 8 Branch called for the abolition of the Labour Court, a resolution lost on a show of hands. In 1959 the union insisted that the introduction of new machinery be allowed only where there would be 'no reduction of accustomed job rates' and that workers share in the results of increased productivity and be protected against redundancy.[36]

LABOUR LAW

At the 1951 ituc Congress J. Byrne called for Good Friday to be declared a statutory public holiday. The wui wanted union representatives appointed to a Committee examining company law. In January 1954 it was reported that the union's dispute with the Esplanade Pharmacy, Bray, over the fact that the company was opening for longer than the two hours agreed on Sundays had resulted in the Irish Drug Association gaining an injunction to prevent picketing. On 8 December 1953, in the High Court, Mr Justice Dixon concluded that while a dispute existed it was not a 'trade dispute' as defined by the Trade Disputes Act (1906) and, 'accordingly, the Union was not entitled to picket the premises.' This decision had a potential negative impact for the movement, and the WUI considered appealing.

On 24 March 1954 the WUI won a claim in the Labour Court regarding what should be paid on public holidays. Made for gas workers, the recommendation affected all workers, and the union published its submission.[37]

HEALTH AND SOCIAL WELFARE

In 1950 the WUI sought a National Health Service, one member, oddly, voting against. Michael Cassidy (Player's) objected to deductions for social welfare as he upheld the right of workers to the ownership of their wage packets. Ferguson took strong issue with him and suggested 'fifth-columnists' within the ranks attacking something so central to Labour policy. He was continuously interrupted before the motion was defeated.

In 1951 Larkin supported calls for a comprehensive social welfare scheme, defending William Norton and the Labour Party. Did the rejection of the Labour Party at the polls suggest that workers did not want social security? Unions did, and would have to more actively educate their members to push their demands. Richard Emoe said that they stood behind the Mother and Child Scheme without a means test.

In 1952 motions sought improvements in Unemployment Benefit, wet-time insurance, Workmen's Compensation and subsistence allowances to TB patients, as well as Retirement Benefits for men and women at sixty-five and sixty, respectively. The WUI had no Hospital Fund, despite efforts to establish one. Only 360 members out of 25,000 indicated a wish to join a scheme. Grangegorman and Portrane Branches ran highly successful schemes. The Social Welfare Act (1952), effective from 1 January 1953, was welcomed in principle but criticised in detail. In 1954 Ferguson cautioned that 'under this wonderful Act, the Means Test is more ghastly than under the old National Health Insurance Act.' J. Fitzsimons (No. 3) opposed the 'complete socialisation' of health, while Thomas Kavanagh (Portrane) concluded that 'a man must be almost destitute before he can qualify for maternity benefit.' J. O'Neill (Dublin No. 11) sought a WUI Hospital and Medical Fund to reserve hospital beds and obtain access to treatment for members.

In Congress the WUI called for better accommodation for hospital workers and after-care for mentally handicapped children and their carers, the reform of mental health provision and improvements in wages and conditions. Larkin opposed the proposal by Matt Merrigan (Dublin Trades Union Council) that the new Health Act be a charge on central funds and not local authorities. It was 'not quite as simple as that,' as central funding entailed central control, and 'what we regard as democratic local Government is completely pushed to one side.' Means

tests were not conducted by local authorities but by City and County Managers—
'exactly the thing we want to fight against—the bureaucratic control' by local
Officials under dictate from faceless Departments. As 60% of taxes came from
indirect tax, this led Larkin into a discussion of tax reform, its complexity being
sufficient to have the motion referred back.

In 1956 a speaker from the Irish Society for the Prevention of Cruelty to Children
addressed the Conference. Denis Larkin wanted reform of the Health Act, with 'the
provision of medical services being determined by need rather than means,'
increased levels of income for eligibility, confined hospital charges and clarification
regarding rates for specialist treatment. In 1957 a motion called for comprehensive
changes to the Mental Treatment Act to provide for the retirement of nurses after
twenty-five years' service, improvements in their pension scheme and Marriage
Gratuity, changes that did not meet with universal approval from manual Branches.
Modification of the means test for (blue) medical cards was sought.[38]

TAX

At the 1952 ITUC Congress James Kelly sought the introduction of 'pay-as-you-earn'
income tax, an attempt by the WUI to cushion demands on workers' incomes. There
was little debate. Richard Emoe looked for a Commission into income tax in 1955
to identify inequalities between different sections of the community and allow for
a code that would ensure fairness and equity. Farmers and industrialists would be
included in a widened tax base. Farmers who apparently never made a profit were
reassured that, in those circumstances, tax liability would not arise.

A Committee of Inquiry into Taxation in Industry, set up in October 1953,
reported in May 1956. It felt that tax policy discouraged investment, with suggestions
for various incentives and reliefs for enterprise. Leo Crawford, Secretary of the
CIU, signed the main report with some reservations, but Ferguson, representing the
ITUC, submitted a minority report, explaining that the Committee had decided it
could not

> consider the special case of the most important factor in production, the
> producer. I found myself in great embarrassment and difficulty. Representing
> the interests I do, it would be impossible for me to agree in a formal way to reliefs
> for other sections of personnel engaged in industry, if the actual producer,
> upon whom the whole process ultimately depends, should be excluded from
> consideration.

In addition, the Irish Management Institute was concentrating, 'by means of
work study methods, bonus incentive schemes, etc.,' on getting workers to increase
productivity *ad infinitum*. Perhaps relief for the real producers would be considered
in the Income Tax Commission announced by the Minister in answer to requests
by the WUI and ITUC for PAYE.

The PUOITUM made a submission on PAYE to the Commission on Income

Taxation in September 1957. Larkin and Fintan Kennedy were on the drafting Committee.[39]

THE LARKIN MEMORIAL FUND

In 1950 Smithers reported growth in the Larkin Memorial Fund. Thomas Kavanagh (Portrane) said that his Branch, through Charles Phipps's 'Non-Stop Draw', made considerable contributions. Repeated expressions of admiration for Larkin, from many quarters, were not replicated in donations; only £900 was received by May 1950. J. Collins sought the support of the ITUC, embarrassing Delegates with details of donations from Liverpool Trades Council and elsewhere in Britain.

In 1951 Seán Dunne TD (FRW) called for the erection of Larkin Memorial Hall, asking each affiliate to set up a Committee to work with the memorial fund. Barney Conway made an emotional appeal to 'erect this memorial to this great man.' In 1952 Charlie Phipps (Staff Section) thanked Portrane, Tullamore and Kildare, all new Branches, whose behaviour was in marked contrast to older, Dublin Branches. He thanked the Football Association of Ireland, which assisted with a fund-raising match played at Dalymount Park. He hoped that all would soon possess a 'Jim Larkin Memorial Certificate'. In fact the Larkin Memorial Fund was a 'wider fund under the auspices of the Dublin Trades Union Council.' Ferguson clearly still had high hopes. *Report* promoted the fund in its first edition, 'Lest we forget!' In truth, too many had forgotten.

Illuminated certificates, raffles, excursions, boxing tournaments, carnivals and football matches were organised, and the match between Drumcondra and Doncaster Rovers was 'fully enjoyed by the large attendance,' with the fund gaining 'to a considerable extent.' Sunday 1 February 1953 was declared 'Larkin Day'. The memorial fund stood at £1,936, only £500 having come from members, about 4d per member. It was only £1,995 a year later.

At the 1953 Congress J. Collins (DTUC) did 'not feel at all pleased' at having to make yet another appeal. It was his 'last appeal.' On a reading of the report more than half a century later the squirming silence of Delegates is palpable. The fund closed in 1955. Charlie Phipps rose 'not with pride' to urge that all members take out a Larkin Memorial Certificate. Michael Davitt (No. 8, Building) thought a man without a 'Memorial Certificate is not worthy to hold a w.u.i card.' Larkin, who generally did not comment, drew a distinction between the fund set up by Dublin Trades Council and whatever the WUI itself might do. Ferguson called for a second £1 from old veterans who had shamed the younger men, recognised by a second certificate.

In January 1954 the GEC 'decided to arrange for the early erection of a permanent and suitable type of headstone' over Larkin's grave in Glasnevin. It was 'expected that many members' would 'have ideas as to what they would regard as the most appropriate design,' and sketches were invited. By December the memorial fund stood at £2,259, with £284 coming in that year, although less than £20 came from members. The GEC concluded, with obvious disappointment, that 'no useful purpose will be served by keeping the Fund open any longer.' Since its inception, subscriptions in respect of 25,000 members represented 'a contribution per member of approximately 1s. 1d. over the eight years.' Appreciation was expressed to those who had contributed and to the Secretary of the fund, Charlie Phipps, Secretary and Delegate, Pork Branch, 'who spared neither time nor energy.' Dublin Trades Council had about £1,800 to £1,900 in its fund. The WUI thanked Dublin Corporation for its decision to name James Larkin Road in Clontarf and to facilitate the union in erecting name plaques.

In January 1955 a headstone was raised over Larkin's grave, the cost being borne by the union, not the memorial fund. The GEC considered 'some alternative form of annual commemoration' other than the church procession 'for the Memorial mass and the Commemoration Concert.' The Conference congratulated James Plunkett Kelly (James Plunkett) for his play *Big Jim,* which had 'gone out to the farthest quarters of the world.'

In 1956 Phipps suggested that the annual Jim Larkin Memorial Concert be given more attention and publicity. Theatre attendances had declined, and it was not held that year. Despite enthusiastic speeches in favour, the absence of a practical response left the future of the concert in doubt. Some members gave great commitment. John Ward (Gas Company) bequeathed £100 to the Larkin Memorial Fund. On 3 February 1957 copies of R. M. Fox's book *Jim Larkin: The Rise of the Underman* were made available at special rates. Sales proved slow, and the union was unable to avail of a generous offer from the publisher to purchase larger quantities at greatly reduced prices.

In 1957, with £2,300 collected, suggestions for spending the Larkin Memorial Fund included endowing hospital beds, providing scholarships and erecting a statue in Beresford Place. After discussions with DUTC, the fund was closed. There was not enough to build the intended Memorial Hall, and 'some less ambitious project' was needed. Séamus Bleakley (Athlone) wanted a condemnation of the ITGWU, which, during its fiftieth-anniversary celebrations, had not honoured Larkin. 'I level criticism against the old guard of the movement who did not, through the medium of the local Press, condemn the Irish Transport Union for not giving the proper honour to the late Jim Larkin.' The motion was defeated.[40]

SAFETY AND HEALTH

In 1952 the WUI addressed the problem of work-place accidents. The choice was an action at common law or taking a case under the Workmen's Compensation Act. Compensation at common law was possible only if a worker had not accepted Workmen's Compensation payments, although if a common-law case was lost resort could still be had to Workmen's Compensation. The reverse was not the case. *Macken v. Irish Shipping* altered this. If a worker, in ignorance of their legal rights, accepted weekly compensation payments they were debarred from taking common-law proceedings. Members were therefore advised that, 'in view of this Supreme Court decision and until such times as the law is amended, it is now vitally important that where a member meets with an accident a report should be made to the Union without delay and no monetary payment whatever should be accepted from the employer until the advice of the Union has been obtained.'

The Workmen's Compensation Act was regarded as 'an unsatisfactory stop-gap.' The WUI supported the Parliamentary Committee of Inquiry to examine the desirability of replacing 'the present unsatisfactory code' with 'a State system of compensation or insurance for industrial injuries.' In 1954 Ferguson suggested that the 'average worker was murdered in industry.' He said he chose the word carefully, as he felt that employers were 'guilty of criminal neglect.' He had researched fatality cases and found that the most the 'widow of the murdered man received for herself and her children' was the equivalent of one year's wages for an unskilled man. Uncontested cases were worse. William Norton would probably be Minister for Industry and Commerce 'within the next couple of days.' Ferguson placed the ball firmly at his feet, 'not because we like the Inter-Party Government—that is not our heart's desire—but purely on a material basis. By their deeds ye shall know them.'

At Congress, Thomas Duffy called for 'more up-to-date traffic regulations,' designed to secure greater protection, especially for children and pedestrians.

The WUI welcomed the Factories Act (1955), especially the provision for Safety Committees. More Factory Inspectors were demanded, faith being placed in prescriptive legislation, externally enforced. The GEC urged members to set up Safety Committees wherever possible. The Workmen's Compensation Act was an example of what could 'be achieved by Congress when we are able to approach Ministers who not only have got a general Labour outlook' but whose union background enabled them to understand what was required. The only improvements to the 1934 Act came from Labour Ministers. A full inquiry was promised into the whole compensation system.

In 1957 William O'Reilly (No. 7) asked Congress to 'collect available medical evidence' on the 'effects of dust on the health of factory workers.' Thomas Kavanagh (Portrane) said that medical evidence was scant and inclusive but it was an 'occupational hazard'. Tobacco workers pressed the issue, however, insisting that data was necessary. Larkin pointed out that the Gas Workers discussed safety at their AGM, and, despite Patrick Kearns's death the day before the Conference, there was still no Gas Company Safety Committee. It was the first occasion on which specific hazards were considered by the Conference.

In 1958 it was recognised that the sole responsibility for appointing Safety Committees and Safety Delegates lay with workers. 'If trade unionists fail to make use of the special legal powers now given to them it would make a mockery of our repeated outcries against lack of adequate protective measures for workers' health.' Each member was asked to examine the operation of the Safety Delegate and Safety Committees within their employment.

The Office (Conditions of Employment) Bill (1957) was welcomed, and clerical members were asked to achieve its fullest potential. A confused debate followed,

with one Delegate saying they declined to set up a Safety Committee to avoid taking disciplinary measures against their own members! The management had no
objection but could 'not see what useful purpose it would serve.' It had not occurred
to them, as Denis Larkin suggested, that it 'could be a stepping stone towards
participation in management.' A task of Congress was to significantly increase the
number of Safety Delegates and Safety Committees. Larkin accepted that, having
'had this Act placed on the Statute Book,' when it came to 'its implementation, we
have fallen down on the job.'

On Workmen's Compensation there was a growing feeling that money should
be paid to state insurance 'rather than to swell the profits' of the insurance industry. The Government appointed three new members of the Commission on
Workmen's Compensation representing that industry.[41]

EDUCATION AND TRAINING

Larkin reminded readers of *Report* in July 1952 of the slogan 'Agitate, Educate,
Organise!' While the first two elements were keenly implemented, 'the call to "educate" had not been listened to.' The 'tool of trade unionism' required instruction if
it were to be used to its full potential. 'It seems to me' that members must see the
union as a 'living organism of thinking men and women.' Members were encouraged
to engage in 'recreational activity, both sporting and cultural.' An Annual Excursion
and Sports Day was held, with drama, debate, dancing, music, art and literature,
involving members' wives and children. The response was immediate, with competitions in football, variety and drama, films, and table tennis. Smithers said 'we
have ambitious plans.' He hoped to see almost every form of sport, cultural, recreational and social activity 'among our members and their families ... all within the
framework of the Union.' Realising these plans required 'the help, the active,
willing, enthusiastic help of members, men and women, boys and girls, yes, even the
wives, sons and daughters of members.' In the WUI they could 'find industrial
leadership and organisational protection' but also a 'comradeship and social atmosphere which makes for common enjoyment and fellowship.' The Larkin Memorial
Fund would 'provide a social and recreational centre.' The GEC presented cups for
soccer and Gaelic football, 'together with sets of jerseys and togs' bearing the
red-hand badge. Hopes were high that an Inter-Branch League would result in
'representative Union teams playing in the senior Official Leagues' of both codes.
A Variety Group and Film Club became well established. Scholarships were
provided for the People's College Summer School in Drogheda on 'The Individual
and Society'.

In 1954, however, Smithers complained about the poor response to these
endeavours. It was 'disappointing' that they met with 'such little success.' The GEC
terminated matters in 1955.

The 1953 Conference wanted Shop Stewards' courses, but in February 1954 the
union complained that 'efforts to obtain names of Shop Stewards who would attend
such classes have not brought any significant response.' Calls by Congress for joint

Conferences with the Irish Management Institute got short shrift from Ferguson. There was 'too much mumbo-jumbo.' The Institute existed to 'extract more labour. Earlier, employers used threats, then stopwatches, and now this.' Instead, he suggested, 'let us match our science to theirs.'

Jack Harte (Guinness) suggested in 1955 that 'future staffing' should be made by 'suitable training.' Ferguson asked, 'not only as an Official but as President of the People's College,' 'what is suitable training?' He found that 'the results of training have been lamentable.' Courses for Officials, Shop Stewards and Branch Committees 'got little response.' An Official had to be a 'lawyer, doctor, adviser, etc., etc.,' and this 'cannot be achieved by lectures alone.' Lectures were of use only if people had 'gone through the Via Dolorosa of Shop Steward, Branch Committee member, and Branch Secretary in an honorary way.' Tim Coffey (No. 8, Building) said 'not to mind this resolution' but just put the best men in and 'surely they will be intelligent enough to know what is best for the Union.' Other Delegates sniped at Guinness members in a general anti-training tone. The motion was nevertheless adopted, the first commitment to union education.

The WUI paid fees to the People's College, University College, and Coiste na bPáistí for Gaeltacht scholarships.

Annual union sports were regarded as 'increasingly popular and successful each year.' In addition, a Jim Larkin Theatre Group presented O'Casey's *Juno and the Paycock* at the Gas Company Theatre. A training scheme for instructing members in the 'daily work of the Union such as negotiations, Conferences, organisation, etc.,' was called for to 'enable members to compete for vacancies in the Union on an equal basis with non-members.' In 1957 the WUI acknowledged that it 'must train and educate members.' There was a 'gap consisting in the failure' of the union to establish its own programmes. Conscious of this, the GEC planned evening classes and weekend schools, 'later developing into a continuous and standardised series of classes or study groups within the general Union machinery.'

Michael Cassidy (No. 7) was disappointed that courses in the Catholic Workers' College, the Institute of Catholic Sociology and Rathmines Technical School and extramural courses in University College were not mentioned, as these were 'based on sound, Christian social principles.' Monthly lectures on 'planning for full employment' were agreed, together with the establishment of a Research Department.

In February 1958 a weekend school held in Greystones, Co. Wicklow, attracted seventy participants. T. K. Whitaker, Secretary of the Department of Finance, addressed it, along with Rev. James Kavanagh, M. J. Costello, Dr Louden Ryan and Donal Nevin. The event was 'favourably commented upon' in the press. In the autumn a second seminar was held on productivity, with P. Fisher, a union expert from the European Productivity Agency.

At Congress, Michael Cassidy appealed for an education programme 'on a vaster scale than at present' to assist the union's leaders to force the Government 'to implement a decent financial and economic programme.' Frank Cluskey attended a

European Productivity Agency course at Harvard University, Massachusetts, from February to May 1959. J. Dalton (No. 1) suggested, through Congress, that a Trade Union and Labour Week be inaugurated to recruit new members, develop cultural activities and foster relations between unions through social activities. Farmers had their Rural Week, the RDS had the Spring Show and Horse Show Week, Muintir na Tíre had its week—what about Labour? In October a school was held on 'Job Evaluation', with Bert Gottlieb of the International Machinists' Union in the United States as the principal speaker.[42]

UNION PUBLICATIONS

In 1950 James Larkin praised *Trade Union Information,* Congress's monthly statistical and information digest. Its sales were a poor reflection of its quality. In 1951 Michael Cassidy and Michael Daly (Player's) sought a 'printed monthly bulletin, giving factual activities' of the union. Larkin was in 'complete agreement' but raised the question of cost.

In July 1952 *Report* was published. Smithers claimed it was 'the most obvious indication of the Union's growth.' It was 'attractive in both appearance and content,' was well received and highly commended by outsiders. 'Unfortunately,' it was not supported by Officials or members. Branches were encouraged to put *Report* as a standard agenda item to seek ways of improving matters. It was not intended to 'be merely a medium for airing the views of Head Office' but needed articles and Branch news. A sales table invited Conference Delegates to see if they could improve their own Branch's performance.

Table 79: Sales of *Report,* May 1953

No. 1 (Docks, Miscellaneous)	300
No. 2 (Public Services)	200
No. 3 (Miscellaneous)	300
No. 4 (Sugar, Confectionery, Food Preserving)	300
No. 5 (Butchers' Porters)	100
No. 6 (Shipbuilding and Engineering)	400
No. 7 (Tobacco)	250
No. 10 (Building Workers)	300
No. 11 (Fish and Poultry)	200
No. 12 (Civil Aviation)	300
No. 13 (Gas Workers)	300
No. 14 (Operative Butchers)	100
No. 16 (Chemists)	100
Bray	50
Carlow District Hospital	25

County Dublin	150
Dún Laoghaire	200
Enniscorthy	18
Kildare	100
Killybegs	6
Kinsale	50
Portarlington	20
Port Laoise	12
Portrane	100
Trim	60
Tullamore	200
Guinness Section	300
Grangegorman Section	60

Source: WUI, Report of General Executive Council, 1952–3, p. 16.

There were queries why the editor's name did not appear, and requests for obituaries. Larkin thought *Report* a 'genuine trade union journal', not like that of 'another well-known trade union journal,' which was more like a 'copy of *Home Chat*.' Larkin wanted 'ordinary members' to 'talk to each other through the journal.' What they really wanted to know was, was it a good read? Although reaching only one in six members, 'doubtless it is read by at least one out of every two members,' and many family members.

In 1954 it was 'only with considerable difficulty' that *Report* was maintained. Financial losses were heavy. Worse, it was suggested that 'there is no eagerness' among members to 'buy and read' it. The GEC decided to cease publication unless the Conference rallied around it. Ferguson thought *Report* had become largely the general officers' mouthpiece by default, as members were not offering material. There was no use in pious motions unless '(*a*) you are going to write for it, and (*b*) you are going to circulate it.' Vincent O'Hara (Guinness) cautioned against cutting off a 'vital stream of life.' *Liberty* (although not mentioned by name) was 'very hard to distinguish' from the 'organ of the Dublin Chamber of Commerce.'

Larkin said they would absorb losses of £200–300 a year. *Report* cost, on average, about £55 a month to produce, depending on photographs. Attempts to attract advertising income were 'not too successful.' He wrote about 60% of the material, and Ferguson was 'exceptionally active,' along with James Kelly (Gas Branch), Betty Jevons, Vincent O'Hara and W. Hickey. Five thousand copies were printed each month. Even at 1d they should have received £250 in return; they got about £100. Publication ceased in July 1954.

No sooner was *Report* gone than members wanted it back, its loss 'something of a catastrophic hit.' Tim Coffey (No. 8, Building) thought it 'healthy to see when we have the opposite crowd giving us a paper called *Liberty*,' but the movers did not tell the Conference how it would be financed. Christy Hand (No. 13, Gas) thought it should simply be given away. C. O'Brien wanted it because of the information it carried and because 'I made some money out of it.' He had a poem published that led to a Commission from a magazine in England! Tim Coffey (No. 8) wanted something akin to *Liberty*.

Larkin reported that no-one had asked about the Committee that was to be set up. 'Is it only at Conference that we are concerned about *Report*? Do we just enjoy talking for the sake of talking?' The GEC would bear a loss of £60 a month or £720 a year: journals were expensive items.

James Kelly made a mock-up of an edition; but the GEC felt there was a 'general air of pessimism cloaking' things. It was a 'problem to get workers interested,' as 'there is nothing but apathy prevailing at the moment.' Twenty-two volunteered to serve on a Committee and concluded that a journal was 'essential' to the union's 'proper working.' Arrangements were made with a commercial publisher, Irish and Overseas Publishing Company, for an elaborate 24-page magazine, but the 'project fell through.' The GEC fell back on a 'medium size newspaper type of paper of four pages.' Members were encouraged to see it as a 'matter of honour' to support it and read it. Difficulties in securing advertisements led to the publishing company pulling out. The union ploughed ahead, agonising over titles, such as *Union Record* and *News and Views.*

Unity was first distributed at the 1957 Conference. Peter Purcell (No. 4) urged every Shop Steward and member to ensure its 'continued circulation.' Enthusiasm brought Distribution and Editorial Committees, and the circulation settled down to a reasonably satisfactory level, but it had 'not yet become a channel of information' nor a 'medium through which individual members voiced their views or criticisms.' It was still 'in the main, an expression of official viewpoints set down by a small number of individuals.' The journal, actually called *Bulletin,* was edited by Kelly, and in 1958 it claimed a circulation of 3,500, although the GEC in August 1957 had cut this, complaining that sales were 'infinitesimal' and that they might 'have to give it away.'

By 1958 there was 'a growing surplus of unsold copies,' and suspension was considered. In 1957 the expenses were £380, while income was £84, a loss of £296. In 1958 expenses were £617, income £64 and loss £553. In the first five months of 1959 income was £7 17s 9d. The print run was cut to 2,500. Larkin thought they should 'stop a lot of codology.' A. McGrath (No. 3) did not think it 'very readable.' G. Russell (No. 13) found it 'uninteresting and unattractive' and said that it was a 'complete and unjustifiable loss.' *Liberty* had a full-time editor but lost 'more money than we do.'

Larkin was as much in the dark as ever as to whether members wanted *Bulletin* or not. In May 1959 the order was reduced to 1,000. By October, with losses up to £401 1s 4d, the GEC decided that the 'journal had got a fair chance and had failed.'

In 1959 Peter Purcell (No. 4) sought to 'intensify the programme of Educational Classes' and to increase *Bulletin* 'as part of this scheme.' Young people had no idea about the union's origins. J. O'Connor (Head Office) pooh-poohed the notion of expanding *Bulletin,* as who would provide its contents? He could 'not see the slightest chance of adding another page and filling it next month.' Fewer than twelve people in the hall had ever written anything, and more than 40% had never read the *Bulletin.*[43]

STAFF AND PREMISES

In 1953 the WUI had a full-time staff of thirty-two. Larkin offered the view that 'generally the only people I know . . . not paid the trade union rate are the people employed in trade unions.' Wages were poor: 'the less we say about the wages we pay in the Union . . . the better' for the union's good name.

In 1954, £13,248 was expended on wages, working out at between '£400 or £500 on an average annually.' Vaughan's Hotel, 29 Parnell Square, 'historic' for 'many associations with the struggle for national independence,' was purchased as the new Head Office. As news spread, 'there were numerous exclamations on the growth of the Union which made such large premises necessary.' Congestion in Thomas Ashe Hall in College Street, especially in the evenings and Sunday mornings, dictated matters: 'some nights . . . it is like Bedlam.' Not everyone was pleased. P. Kinsella (No. 13) said that gas workers found 'College Street more convenient' and objected to equipment being taken to Parnell Square. 'Thomas Ashe Hall is more historic to us than Vaughan's Hotel,' because of associations with Big Jim. Kinsella was assured that Ashe Hall would be kept. An overdraft of £13,000 was taken in order to secure the building and was paid off by 1956. Head Office moved in February 1954.

In 1955 there were calls for a superannuation scheme for old members: what was good for the staff should be good for the members. Ferguson took issue and asked, 'Are we to be like the doctor that cannot heal himself, or the barber who cannot cut his own hair?' A staff pay rise was granted in 1956. In 1957 it was asked that any vacancy be first notified to Shop Stewards and members. D. Byrne (No. 7) pointed out a weakness: the over-reliance on Larkin and the late Ferguson. There was 'too big a gap between the ability and competence of the General Secretary and his application to the job' and other Officials. What would happen if they lost Larkin? They would be 'to a very great extent an inferior organisation.' Right men cost right wages. Wages would need to be increased to attract and retain good Officials.

Larkin pointed out that it was often members who insisted on bypassing their Branch Secretary and coming straight to him. It might equally be said that he did little to refer them back.

Ferguson's loss was huge and was met by Larkin taking on his duties—hardly an ideal solution. In July, Thomas Doyle, a Branch Secretary, was interned in the Curragh under the Offences Against the State Act. While detained he was placed on half pay. He returned in April 1959.

In 1958 staff problems were caused by the 'high incidence of illness.' In 1959 the Commissioners for Public Works agreed to accept £3,350 for the purchase of the state's interest in Thomas Ashe Hall. It was held on a 999-year lease from 25 March

1827 at a rent of £20 per year. The GEC's intention was that 'the present building be demolished and a new building be erected,' in Larkin's name.[44]

TOTAL ABSTINENCE

The Larkin family were teetotal. The WUI seldom made public reference to drink, either as a problem or a source of recreation. Charlie Phipps recalled Father Cullen claiming that 'if Ireland had another Jim Larkin we would have a sober, industrious Ireland because the example shown by this great man should be an example to us all.' Larkin ended the practice of paying dockers in public houses.[45]

RELIGION AND THE COLD WAR

In 1950 the GEC arranged to represent the union in 'Holy Year' ceremonies and to 'convey to the Holy Father, the filial devotion' of members. 'Sets of sacred vessels for use in the Foreign Missions' were presented, resulting in a letter of thanks from the Pope with an 'Apostolic Blessing' of members. Thomas Butterly (No. 4) thought the Delegation 'enhanced our reputation considerably,' not least as it was entertained by the Irish Ambassador.

In 1955 the Guinness Branch deplored an 'Irish group visiting Russia' and 'accepting hospitality from a régime which is waging a relentless war against religion, particularly Catholicism.' As 'Irish Catholic Trade Unionists' they objected strongly. The motion was ruled out of order.

Delegates demanded that no WUI investment be made 'in any Society where members of the Communist Party are members,' a reference to £70 invested in the Ballyfermot and Inchicore Co-ops. Michael Davitt (No. 8) opposed, although not wanting anybody 'to go away with the idea that I am a Communist.' Who else were they to invest in? 'Not in private businesses run by Freemasons that did not benefit the working class.' Gerry Fitzsimons (No. 3) replied, 'One thing that makes the Communist Party distinct from the Freemasons is that they are making special efforts to get control of the trade union movement' and 'seeking to infiltrate by means of co-operative societies and Leagues . . . any thing that will find public support.' Communism was 'a vital threat, the biggest threat trade unionism has to face today. You cannot link it with any other enemy. It is enemy number 1.'

Ferguson declared that he was not a Communist Party member but thought the finest thing the WUI ever stood for was non-sectarianism. Malachi Phipps (No. 11, Pork) felt that a 'Communist element' had crept into the union. Gerry Bolger (No. 15, Clerical), attending his first Conference, asked, 'Who are Communists? I have never seen or heard any person who has admitted that he or she is such.' Larkin offered no comment. The WUI had moved a long way from the Red International.

On a motion calling for Good Friday to be declared a public holiday, Ferguson said it was

absurd to refer to Good Friday as a Public Holiday. Let us call it a Holy Day. For it is on that day we commemorate the Crucifixion. It we substitute the term Holy

Day, we should trust that the employers on that one day out of 365 will put into practice the principle of the Papal Encyclicals and give workers the opportunity to observe that day as it should be observed.

Quite how sincere he was being was not clear.

The 1956 ITUC Congress debated a decision to decline an invitation to visit the Soviet Union. Larkin placed the decision in the context of fragile unity talks. He also referred to James Kelly's visit to the Soviet Union, not as a union representative but under his non-de-plume as a writer (James Plunkett). 'If he had not taken very special precautions before he went, it was more than likely that his position as an Official of my union would have been terminated.'

In 1957 a motion suggesting that the Sunday session of the Conference should begin with Mass, 'with similar arrangements for other denominations,' was referred back, largely as it would 'look very bad if we had a poor attendance.' In 1958 Jack Harte (No. 9) moved that the 'appropriate Minister . . . stem the flood of evil literature into the country,' while P. Leonard (No. 8) wanted May Day declared a 'National Workers' Holiday.' Delegates quickly cited the Pope in their case for the 'Feast of St Joseph the Worker.'[46]

DISCIPLINE

In 1950 Larkin reported the Michael F. O'Kelly affair, which eventually resulted in the discipline of a number of those concerned. Delivering the verdict to the Annual Conference, he described it as an 'unpleasant duty' done. It occupied considerable time and twelve pages of the report—testimony to open union democracy. Larkin felt that there were many important issues they should have spent time discussing 'instead of wasting time as we have had to do on something that should not have taken place.' The affair showed that, while the union was open and democratic, indiscipline would not be tolerated. The GEC insisted that Branch and Section Committees assume responsibility for their own self-discipline.[47]

POLITICS

The ITUC recognised the 'benefits to the nation's health and the release from unnecessary suffering which the Mother and Child Scheme would promote' and on 30 March 1951 urged its early implementation. It asked the Irish Medical Association to accept the request of the Minister for Health, Noël Browne, for co-operation. It deeply regretted his resignation, and the scheme's loss. The WUI generally concurred.

Kevin Moore (No. 1) thought the 'best weapon we can fashion is a political arm.' Two ballots to establish a Political Fund, however, evoked poor responses and a negative outcome. The GEC balloted again in 1952, and a quarterly Political Levy was instituted from 1 July. Draft Political Rules were adopted, by 98 to 16.

In 1954 the Conference welcomed the election of James Larkin and Denis Larkin, Industrial Secretary, to Dáil Éireann. The Political Fund still gave rise to uncertainty in members' minds. No funds were given to political parties. 1,500 members, or 6%, sought exemption.[48]

Labour TDS were called upon to 'bring down the cost of living' and to 'adopt a more vigorous outspoken line' in the Dáil in 1955. John Foster (Grangegorman) rightly asked, as the WUI was not affiliated to the Labour Party, 'what right have we to call on the Labour Party more than any other?' A motion not debated in 1955, because time ran out, indicated alternative political views.

No. 2 and No. 8 Branches sought to endorse the 'actions of the Irish working class heroes who raided Armagh and Omagh Barracks' and struck the 'most definite blow against British Imperialism' since 1916, a reference to the IRA border campaign. The Conference sent 'cordial greetings' and pledged 'support to Irish Republican prisoners in British gaols.' Thomas Browne opposed the call of the Executive for the abolition of Seanad Éireann, as an unnecessary institution with an undemocratic election system. Larkin rose, 'with deep sorrow and regret,' to speak against Browne, who was 'guilty of a gross libel' against him. He was not in favour of reforming the Seanad: he wanted it abolished. A system of Committees, involving special-interest groups, would more effectively serve as a check on legislation, as with the recent Special Committee on the Factories Act.[49]

In 1956, P. Clarke (No. 4) deplored the 'treatment of Irish political prisoners in English jails.' He praised the Lord Mayor of Dublin, Denis Larkin, and the 'Town Council' for passing their own resolution on the subject. Prisoners had no heating in the cells and were 'denied Christmas mail.' Ferguson was among speakers who referred to their own 'active service during the Black and Tan War' and Civil War. He did 'not agree with the methods employed at present' but felt that 'these men have a right to do as they are doing. As long as any part of our country is held in subjection, it is our right to support the people who have the guts to fight against it.'[50]

Denis Larkin was re-elected to Dáil Éireann in 1957, his brother James not standing after Ferguson's death. In 1958, while 'not engaging directly in political activity,' the WUI, through the Provisional United Organisation of the Irish Trade Union Movement, protested at the proposed abolition of proportional representation, feeling it 'detrimental to National Unity' and urging all 'democratically minded trade unionists to unite in opposition.' The Conference agreed only after lengthy and heated debate.

Kay Fallon (GEC) said the abolition of PR was 'contrary to the basic principles of democratic parliamentary Government' and would lead to two-party representation. William O'Brien (Irish Liver Union) supported, on 'behalf of the little fellow and the little party.'

J. Dalton (No. 1) accused No. 7 Branch of supporting Fianna Fáil. It had voted the previous year against the release of its own Branch Secretary, interned in the Curragh. In September, after approaches from a financially struggling Labour Party, the GEC agreed to 'take over the debt due on the Head Office' in Earlsfort Terrace and to obtain a mortgage, 'up to the amount of £2,000, the money to be drawn from our Political Fund.' It advertised in a Labour paper 'in which Mr Donal Nevin is instrumental' and gave the Party a loan of £500 (interest-free for the first five years, thereafter repayable at 4%) to help clear the debt. In 1959 Hilda Larkin (sister of Young Jim and Denis) unsuccessfully contested the Dublin South-West by-election though receiving maximum union support.[51]

Chapter 25 ∽

CONCLUSIONS

MEMBERSHIP

Unemployment and emigration dominated union concerns. Despite sluggish economic development, total union membership grew from 366,622 in 1950 to 411,840 in 1959. The ITGWU's expansion slowed after 1951. Membership averaged 124,442, a reasonable achievement. The WUI displayed similar patterns, averaging 27,891. Both enjoyed a slightly upward trend, but the WUI grew geographically and sectorally, establishing firm footholds in the midlands and south Leinster, among white-collar and professional groups, often brought in through affiliations. The big prizes were Guinness, Dublin Airport and health service professionals.

The main dynamic was the National Organiser, Christy Ferguson, his energy allowing Jim Larkin Junior to operate within Dáil and union. Ferguson's death in 1957 necessitated Larkin's resignation from politics, placing a brake on the WUI's advance. The ITGWU's success stemmed from its national bargaining units, which advanced wages. As industry slowly grew, the ITGWU's nationwide structures took full advantage.

Table 80: ITGWU and WUI membership, 1950–59

	ITGWU	*WUI*		*ITGWU*	*WUI*
1950	116,257	24,217	1955	126,180	28,320
1951	128,191	26,376	1956	126,707	28,939
1952	127,480	28,035	1957	124,183	28,745
1953	119,377	27,469	1958	125,571	29,090
1954	122,903	28,090	1959	127,571	29,631

Source: National Archives, Registrar of Friendly Societies, files 275T and 369T.

Both unions enjoyed solid financial expansion. The WUI's breaching of the £100,000 balance in 1957 was dwarfed by the ITGWU's first million in 1958. For the WUI, however, it marked relatively permanent security. The dark days of living from hand to mouth and dependence on members' loans and others' good will were gone. For the

SIPTU Donegal and Leitrim Branch banners, the latter portraying Jim Gralton, at health protest in memory of Susie Long, 11 October 2008, passing Larkin Monument, O'Connell Street, Dublin. (Photograph Sasko Lazarov/Photocall Ireland, SIPTU Archive)

SIPTU Hotels, Restaurants and Catering Branch members support recognition dispute, Ballymun, 2008. (SIPTU Archive)

SIPTU banner on protest demonstration against Government handling of economic crisis, Saturday 21 February 2009. (SIPTU Archive)

SIPTU banners, including that of the Musicians' Union of Ireland, accompany tens of thousands of members on protest march of 21 February 2009 on economic crisis. (Photograph Laura Hutton/Photocall Ireland, SIPTU Archive)

SIPTU Centenary banner drapes Liberty Hall, 4 January 2009. (SIPTU Archive)

SIPTU poster against racism. (SIPTU *Report*, October 2000)

SIPTU poster, 2003. (SIPTU Archive)

SIPTU National Executive Council in deep consideration of national pay matters, 2008: *l–r*, Séamus Kelly (Monaghan 20/21), Martin Mealy (Kilkenny Industrial & Manufacturing), Tom Russell (Kildare/Leixlip), Brendan Hayes (Vice-President), Jack O'Connor (General President), Joe O'Flynn (General Secretary), Martin Naughton (Head, Administrative & Services Division), Barry Nevin (Civil Aviation), Danny Crowley (Cóbh), Paul Hansard (Construction), Mary O'Rourke (Cork 8), Margie McQuaid (Services), Paddy Cahill (Drinks, Tobacco & Wholesale Distribution), Peter O'Connor (Administrative, Supervisory & Sales Assistants), Brendan O'Donnell (Letterkenny), Jack McGinley (Education), David Johnston (Hotels, Restaurants & Catering), Noel Pocock (Health Service Professionals), Stephen Tobin (Tralee), Séamus Briscoe (North East), Noel Clune (Shannon Aviation). (SIPTU Archive)

MARCH, 1957   PRICE 6d.

ITGWU comments wryly on mass emigration and failure of Government economic policy. (*Liberty Magazine*, March 1957, SIPTU Archive)

SIPTU Dublin Regional Secretary
Patricia King, 2006. (SIPTU Archive)

SIPTU Centenary Badge

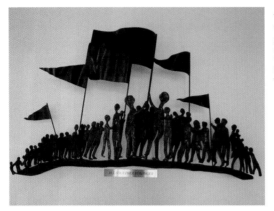

All Together Stronger, sculpture designed by Michael Wall and sculpted by former union activist Peter Hodnett and unveiled in new SIPTU premises at Coolcotts, Wexford, 2008.

SIPTU Centenary banner

ITGWU, solidity and strength were its by-words, cementing its reputation as the country's largest and most powerful organisation.

In 1956 the WUI and ITGWU arrived at an understanding regarding transfers, an indication of increasing maturity in their relationship. The spirit of unity grew, culminating in the foundation of the Irish Congress of Trade Unions in 1959. There were those in the WUI who, quietly and privately, thought that some future amalgamation strategy might have to be considered. This was consistent with the obvious needs for rationalisation that a united Congress would surely accelerate. There was a sense that the WUI was treading water and was not large enough to generate the resources to provide research, membership and staff training and the more sophisticated benefits and services being demanded. Amalgamation did not, of course, necessarily mean the ITGWU, but for the first time that possibility entered some minds, however obliquely.

Table 81: Credit balance, ITGWU and WUI, 1950–59

	ITGWU	WUI		ITGWU	WUI
1950	454,207	40,145	1955	760,598	78,003
1951	459,905	49,371	1956	858,700	91,587
1952	476,905	59,783	1957	639,741	101,252
1953	584,495	66,261	1958	1,048,128	109,252
1954	614,286	71,115	1959	1,123,284	111,895

Source: ITGWU and WUI, Annual Reports, 1946–59.

Industrial strengths

A common accusation against the ITGWU was that it 'didn't punch its weight.' The price for preoccupation with building its investment and property portfolios was alleged non-militancy. The decade did not witness major industrial dislocation.

The ITGWU and WUI had similar contribution rates and levels of Dispute Pay. A comparison of Strike Pay in fact suggests that the ITGWU was more militant. It spent £235,375, or £23,537 a year, an average of 19% of its income, while the WUI spent £16,566, equal to £1,656 a year or 4% of income. Allowing that the WUI was, roughly speaking, a fifth of the ITGWU's size, Liberty Hall's greater outlay was still pronounced. This attracted and held members, promoting the ITGWU as a dynamic, fighting organisation. Yet in 1952 Larkin attacked William McMullen for imposing unnecessary wage restraint on the movement and costing workers millions when the CIU allegedly imposed the 'Twelve-Shilling Formula' behind ITUC backs. Whenever Wage Rounds were led at the local rather than the national level the WUI saw itself as the vanguard, a position it was very proud of as a 'small, fighting union.'

The data suggests a somewhat different picture. Both unions continuously condemned unofficial strikes, not least for what they said about the failure of their Rules and procedures. The ITGWU sought to apply 'intelligence as well as power' to wage bargaining, with a continuous eye on the national interest and a desire to be seen to act 'responsibly'. It was a sentiment Larkin increasingly expressed as he sought to broaden bargaining beyond money wages to influence a fairer distribution of wealth and opportunity throughout society.

Table 82: Income and Dispute Pay, ITGWU and WUI, 1950–59

	ITGWU			WUI		
	Income (£)	Dispute pay (£)	As proportion of income (%)	Income (£)	Dispute pay(£)	As proportion of income (%)
1950	97,686	20,870	21.4	34,481	1,028	2.9
1951	106,799	70,322	65.8	37,597	2,027	5.3
1952	109,553	57,298	52.3	38,825	480	1.2
1953	153,979	6,682	4.3	35,859	987	2.7
1954	159,907	6,100	3.8	35,892	1,121	3.1
1955	166,129	22,789	13.7	39,791	876	2.2
1956	166,469	1,971	1.2	50,571	327	0.6
1957	166,564	22,719	13.6	49,900	192	0.3
1958	166,177	9,631	5.8	53,932	1,774	3.2
1959	170,407	16,993	9.9	58,345	7,754	13.2

Source: ITGWU and WUI, Annual Reports, 1946–59.

Politics

Neither union was affiliated to the Labour Party, although both clearly supported it. There were continued suggestions that elements of the ITGWU were happier dealing with Fianna Fáil, but this was less evident as the decade wore on. The NEC insisted that industrial unity come before political action. The influence of individual Labour TDs at Conferences and in corridors diminished, a certain distance emerging between union and Party. The closeness of the 1920s to 1940s was not repeated. In the WUI the relationship with the Labour Party was more personally expressed through James and Denis Larkin.

The 1950s were a decade of missed opportunity, economic stasis, continued poverty and limited social opportunity. Ireland was increasingly cut off from European economic growth. The reunification of Congress absorbed much time, with Conroy and Larkin central figures in the creation of the ICTU. The ITGWU's Northern presence was confined to the group of declining dock and port workers. With McMullen's retirement, Dublin's interest in Belfast waned.

By 1959, however, all seemed prepared and equipped, individually and collectively, to tackle the 1960s with a new vigour and purpose. There was a new hope.

PART 4

From Wage Rounds to Social Partnership, 1959–89

CONTEXTS

Economic and social contexts

Unemployment in the Republic and Northern Ireland fell to 47,700 and 31,200, respectively, in 1966 but then rose steadily. Membership of the EEC decimated traditional industries in the South, while the rise of low-cost Japanese, eastern European and Third World shipbuilding and textiles wiped out Northern staples. In the 1980s monetarist policies slashed public-sector employment, and demands for 'lean' production in increasingly competitive markets saw spectacular increases in unemployment. By 1986 more than 400,000 people were unemployed in an All-Ireland population of 5 million.

It might have been much worse but for renewed emigration: 134,511 in the period 1961–71, 104,000 in 1971–81 and 64,617 in 1981–91. From the Republic thousands went, many illegally, to the United States. Social welfare cuts made the lives of the unemployed pretty miserable, with constant inflation deepening their discomfort and distress.

Table 83: Unemployment, 1960–89

	Republic	Northern Ireland		Republic	Northern Ireland
1960	52,900	32,400	1975	103,200	43,900
1961	46,600	36,100	1976	112,800	55,900
1962	46,600	36,700	1977	111,000	63,300
1963	50,000	39,000	1978	102,900	66,300
1964	48,900	32,800	1979	92,900	65,700
1965	49,400	30,900	1980	100,000	79,600
1966	47,700	31,200	1981	127,100	92,000
1967	55,000	39,600	1982	154,800	103,000
1968	58,300	37,200	1983	180,800	113,000
1969	57,300	37,800	1984	204,300	112,000
1970	64,900	36,500	1985	219,600	115,000

1971	62,000	41,500	1986	225,500	125,000
1972	71,500	41,100	1987	226,000	121,000
1973	66,800	31,600	1988	217,000	114,000
1974	71,400	31,800	1989	196,800	106,000

Source: Fleming and O'Day, *Longman Handbook of Modern Irish History since* 1800, p. 621–3.

Table 84: Cost of living, 1960–89 (selected years)

	Urban	*Rural*		*Urban*	*Rural*
1960	1,515	1,412	1980	8,677	8,085
1965	1,863	1,736	1985	15,474	14,419
1970	2,410	2,246	1989	17,604	16,404
1975	4,491	4,185			

Source: Liam Kennedy, 'The cost of living in Ireland, 1698–1998,' in David Dickson and Cormac Ó Gráda (eds.), *Refiguring Ireland: Essays in Honour of L. M. Cullen* (Dublin: Lilliput Press, 2003), p. 249–76.

Wage Rounds shortened in duration as the unions attempted to keep pace with inflation. Conversely, employers and the Government, as employer, resisted all increases and cost-inducing concessions on hours and holidays, tightening National Wage Agreements with ever more restrictions. The index of hourly industrial wages showed a huge increase, from 124.4 in 1960 to more than 1,000 in 1980 (with 1953 as 100). New indexes demonstrated the unabated pace of increases: with 1980 as 100: 1986, 193.7; 1987, 204.9; 1988, 216.2; with 1985 as 100: 1989, 124.9.

James Larkin Junior questioned the point of endless catch-up bargaining as wages chased prices, prices led wages. By 1976 the ITGWU argued strongly for expanding bargaining to include social welfare, access to education, health and housing and, most central of all, genuine commitment to planning industrial development. What emerged was the first 'National Understanding', a template that suggested that significant advances on a broad spectrum of economic and social policy were possible.

Increases in money wages carried workers into higher income tax bands; and PAYE, originally welcomed by unions, was subject to mounting protests by 1979. The ITGWU was to the forefront, carefully making the point that tax reform, not tax cuts, was the target. It opposed increases in indirect taxes and cuts in public expenditure. Frustratingly, although thousands of PAYE workers took to the streets, their outrage did not translate into Labour votes. In contrast to farmers, who converted public protests into electoral change, working-class voices, while loud and articulate, could generally be ignored by Fianna Fáil, Fine Gael and Capital.

Table 85: Index of hourly wages in industrial occupations, 1960–80 (1953 = 100)

1960	124.4	1971	294.6
1961	126.4	1972	337.0
1962	145.3	1973	380.7
1963	147.5	1974	439.3
1964	166.8	1975	515.3
1965	169.9	1976	602.2
1966	173.3	1977	696.0
1967	191.0	1978	811.2
1968	197.2	1979	979.3
1969	221.1	1980	1,017.3
1970	252.9		

Source: Fleming and O'Day, *Longman Handbook of Modern Irish History since* 1800, p. 585.

Union contexts

Union membership showed a general upward trend. New members were recruited among white-collar, professional and public-service employees, and as new transnational plants were established they were generally unionised. In this regard the ITGWU's success in unionising EI at Shannon was a signal victory.

The ITGWU's membership doubled, from 83,256 in 1959 to 157,622 in 1989, although it fell back from 172,353 by 1980. The WUI's membership was 28,939 in 1959, rising to 41,939 in 1989, when it became the Federated Workers' Union of Ireland. Its highest membership was 45,939 in 1981.

From 1966 there was the tantalising prospect of a merger between the ITGWU and WUI, but the prospect faded after the deaths of Larkin and Conroy in 1969. The creation of six National Industrial Groups in 1964 and the Development Services Division in 1970 signalled the modernisation of the ITGWU. Its growth seemed unstoppable. Larkin feared stasis and lack of talent in the WUI, but under Denis Larkin and Paddy Cardiff it grew, concluding a series of strategic mergers.

Falling memberships after 1980, coupled with significantly rising costs and fears about employment after the Single European Act (1992), focused minds, and agreement to create SIPTU was reached.

Women were an increasing dynamic. Equality legislation enabled equal pay and equal treatment claims, but women demanded internal reforms to facilitate their involvement. They questioned all sources of discrimination in society, broadening perspectives and debate.

Table 86: Union membership, 1960–89 (selected years)

1960	432,000	1980	661,000
1965	465,000	1985	652,000
1970	510,000	1990	663,000
1975	576,000		

Source: Nevin, *Trade Union Century*, p. 435. Note: Membership is for ICTU affiliates only.

The end of National Understandings triggered an assault by employers, centred on the pursuit of 'lean' production and competitiveness. Public-sector wage deals maintained wages and jobs, but a New Right philosophy permeated politics, and by 1986 there were strident calls for massive public-sector cut-backs, privatisation and deregulation. With the country in deep crisis and pressure from international banks to trim the economy's sails, the Government surprised most commentators by agreeing the Programme for National Recovery in 1987, not then called ' social partnership'. Few were aware that the keel for a new 'Irish model' of national bargaining had been laid. Benefits were not immediately obvious, but circled union wagons at least noticed the attacking employers' reduced fire. Some elements in Congress resisted moves by the ITGWU and FWUI towards the Programme for National Recovery, feeling uncomfortable in their new role and joining those who saw a compact between the Government, employers and workers as threatening parliamentary democracy.

Table 87: Wage Rounds, 1946–87

7th (1959): General movement; men 10s to 15s, women 7s 6d to 10s. In 1960 there was a move to reduce hours and introduce a five-day week.
8th (1961): Increases up to 14s pushed up by electricians and building workers to between £1 and £1 5s for men, 10s to 15s for women.
9th (1964): National Agreement; 12%, with minimum of £1 for men.
10th (1966): No national Agreement; ICTU recommended £1 a week, supported by Labour Court and generally applied.
11th (1968): Practice of two-year comprehensive Agreements applied; men got £1 15s to £2 in two or three phases, women about 75% of this.
12th (1970): Electricians in November 1968 and maintenance craftsmen in April 1969 led the way for settlements in the region of £4 a week in two or three phases over eighteen months. Women got about 80% of this. There was a very wide spread of termination dates by this time.
13th (1971): National Wage Agreement concluded on 21 December 1970. Two phases over eighteen months: first, £2 a week, with women on minimum of £1.70, and second, 4%, with automatic adjustment for increase in the Consumer Price Index.

14th (1972): Second National Wage Agreement, concluded on 31 July for phased Agreement over seventeen months: first, 9% on basic pay up to £30, 7½% on next £10 and 4% on remainder; second, 4% after twelve months on basic pay with automatic adjustments for increases in the Consumer Price Index.

15th (1974): Third National Wage Agreement; 9% on first £30, 7% on next £10, 6% on next £10, minimum £2.40, and second phase of 4% plus 60p; cost-of-living escalator 10%.

16th (1975): Fourth National Wage Agreement; 8%, with minimum of 2% plus quarter of second phase of Fourteenth Round; second phase, 5%, minimum increase approximately £1; third, no increase except a quarter of second phase of Fourteenth Round; fourth, 2.8%.

17th (1976): Fifth National Wage Agreement; 3% of basic pay plus £2, subject to maximum of £5 a week or £3 if greater.

18th (1977): Sixth National Wage Agreement; first, 2½% plus £1, minimum increase £2 a week, maximum £5; second, 2½% plus £1, minimum increase £2 a week, maximum £4.23.

19th (1978): Seventh National Wage Agreement; first, 8%, minimum increase £3.50 a week; second, 2%.

20th (1979): National Understanding; first 9%, minimum increase £5.50; second, 2% plus amount relating to movement in the Consumer Price Index, minimum increase £3.50.

21st (1980): Second National Understanding; first, 8% plus £1 a week; second, 7%.

22nd (1981): 16.4% average cumulative increase over 14.9 months in the private sector.

23rd (1982): 10.9% average cumulative increase over 13½ months in the private sector.

24th (1983): 9.3% cumulative increase over 12¾ months in the private sector.

25th (1984): 6.8% cumulative increase over twelve months in the private sector.

26th (1985): 6% cumulative increase over twelve months in the private sector.

27th (1986): 6½% cumulative increase over 15.4 months in the private sector.

28th (1987): Programme for National Recovery; three-year Agreement: private sector, £4 minimum subject to local bargaining; no cost-inducing claims: public sector, six-month pay pause, then 3% on first £120 and 2% on balance, with a minimum increase of £4.

Sources: Adapted from Kieran Jack McGinly, 'Neo-Corporatism, New Realism and Social Partnership in Ireland, 1970–1999,' PhD thesis, Trinity College, Dublin, 1999; Patrick Gunnigle, Gerard McMahon and Gerard Fitzgerald, *Industrial Relations in Ireland: Theory and Practice* (Dublin: Gill & Macmillan, 1999).

One almost instant effect was the reduction in days lost through strikes. The 1960s were styled the 'decade of upheaval'. Tensions rose between crafts as technology blurred demarcation lines. Inter-union disputes were commonplace, with National Wage Agreements complicating matters by creating 'anomalies' and disturbed differentials. In 1964, 421,000 days were lost in a building strike; in 1965, 316,000 in printing; in 1966, 327,000 in banks and 154,000 in paper mills; in 1969, 629,000 in the Maintenance Strike; in 1970, 791,000 in banks and in 1976 another 482,000; in 1974, 247,000 in CIÉ buses and in 1979 a further 1,206,100.

The period just before the collapse of central bargaining, 1977–81, was worst, with 3,424,294 days lost. Strikes after 1981 were largely defensive, attempting to stop closures or to retrieve better redundancy terms. The number of days lost fell dramatically after the Programme for National Recovery.

Table 88: Working days lost through strikes, 1960–89

1960	80,000	1975	295,716
1961	377,000	1976	777,000
1962	104,000	1977	442,000
1963	234,000	1978	613,000
1964	545,000	1979	1,465,000
1965	552,000	1980	412,118
1966	783,635	1981	434,253
1967	183,000	1982	434,000
1968	406,000	1983	319,000
1969	936,000	1984	386,421
1970	1,007,714	1985	418,500
1971	274,000	1986	309,000
1972	207,000	1987	264,000
1973	207,000	1988	143,000
1974	552,000	1989	50,000

Source: Teresa Brannick, Francis Devine and Aidan Kelly, 'Social statistics for labour historians: Strike statistics, 1922–1999,' *Saothar*, 25 (2000), p. 114–20.

Neither the ITGWU nor WUI were particularly central to most strikes. Indeed they often had strong reservations about the tactics of those involved, generating much criticism of the inability of Congress to control affiliates. This was particularly so after the Maintenance Dispute. It cost the ITGWU £210,972, 39% of total income, and resulted in a deficit of £29,170. The WUI spent £67,000, or 49% of income, creating a deficit of £32,210 and large overdrafts. Neither had members directly involved.

The resultant ICTU All-Out Picket policy, however, was controversial and a cause of long-running differences. The WUI regularly accused the ITGWU of abusing the system.

Table 89: Industrial disputes by selected period, 1957–91

	Number	Days lost	Workers involved
1957–61	299	800,275	58,709
1962–6	418	2,219,011	141,664
1967–71	606	2,805,715	194,100
1971–6	817	2,038,178	168,899
1977–81	712	3,424,294	174,968
1982–6	686	1,951,079	306,388
1987–91	272	766,519	68,415

Source: Teresa Brannick, Francis Devine and Aidan Kelly, 'Social statistics for labour historians: Strike statistics, 1922–1999,' *Saothar*, 25 (2000), p. 114–20.

Political contexts

The Labour Party's fortunes gradually rose in the 1960s under Brendan Corish, with 15 seats in 1961, 21 in 1965 and 18 in 1969. The WUI affiliated for the first time in 1965 and the ITGWU re-affiliated in 1967, after twenty-two years unaligned. The '1970s were to be Socialist.' They were not.

The Labour Party participated in Coalition with Fine Gael from 1973 to 1977 but lost seats, from 19 to 16, part of a slow downward path, with outright union opposition to Coalition. Under Frank Cluskey another Fine Gael Coalition was entered in 1981 before Michael O'Leary's disastrous leadership. Dick Spring led a slow revival; but Coalition again from 1982 to 1987 brought rising protests that it breathed life into Fine Gael and emasculated Socialist policies. The emergence of the Workers' Party added left-wing pressure.

Electorally, the Labour Party stagnated: 15 seats in 1981, 15 in February 1982, 16 in November 1982, 12 in 1987 and 15 in 1989. The Workers' Party increased from 4 to 7 in the period 1987–9. Differences between the Workers' Party and the Labour Party featured among the ITGWU's staff and membership, indications of deep political frustrations after the failure to translate massive PAYE protests into Socialist votes.

Economic circumstances and constant public-sector cuts exacerbated matters. Michael Bell, an ITGWU Group Secretary, was an honourable Dáil exception, voting against the worst social welfare cuts. Continued political failure added emphasis to those arguing for the broadest possible national bargaining agenda. If advances could not be made electorally, then industrial strength could be exchanged for economic and social advance.

Northern Ireland troubles re-emerged in the 1960s. The ITGWU championed civil rights and pressured the British and Irish Governments and the TUC to deal with the fundamental problems, which it saw as stemming from Partition and the Unionist veto. The reform programmes of the ICTU Northern Ireland Committee, such as 'A Better Life for All', drew support and acclaim as sectarianism within the work-place was constrained. Some advances in social and economic policy were made until Thatcherite Tory Governments set everything back.

Chapter 26 ～

MODERNISATION AND THE MIRAGE OF UNITY: THE ITGWU IN THE 1960s

MEMBERSHIP, ORGANISATION AND FINANCE

In 1960 John Conroy, addressing the largest Conference ever, thought that they had 'witnessed an outstanding breakthrough in the field of economic development.' Hope was 'rekindled in the hearts of the people,' and 'depression and despondency' had 'given way to enthusiastic optimism.' It reflected a general sense of well-being within the newly united movement.

Fintan Kennedy was unanimously elected General Secretary to succeed Frank Purcell. An immediate concern was the increase in Branch subsidies, many Branches having abolished local levies when subscriptions were raised in 1953. About half the ITGWU members paid only 9d per week; only 15% paid the full rate of 1s 6d. Kennedy warned that it would be necessary to 'bring our rates more in line with present-day values'. Fursaí Breatnach (Galway) called for two National Organisers, 'top-class men' to build up the union.

Employment fell by 51,000 between 1956 and 1960, a bleak economic picture, underlining the need for organisation. Michael Neary (Castlebar) thought that with 'sufficient staff adequately paid' the membership could reach 200,000, a long-sought total that proved elusive. Between 1954 and 1959 expenditure rose from £54,000 to £103,000, with no concomitant increase in subscriptions. It 'could not go on.' The problem was not getting members in but servicing them. Although 250,000 out of 500,000 workers were organised, at least 100,000 more could be, a task that 'should be a labour of love' for Officials and Branch Committees.

Income rose to a record £280,228 in 1961, but, had subscriptions not been raised, losses would have been substantial. Éamonn Wall (Cork No. 1) wanted staff Conferences on organisation and an examination of structures.

In 1961 transfers to the Liberty Hall Reconstruction Fund diminished the General Fund. About 5,000 new members were enrolled from Cóbh, Castleblayney, Skibbereen and Manorhamilton. Winning Conroy's target of 50,000 new recruits demanded that every member be given a 'high standard of service.' To do this the ITGWU 'must have higher income and larger cash reserves.'

In 1962, members were in virtually every Branch of employment.[1] This created problems. The NEC reviewed 'vertical and horizontal' structures. The immediate results were the splitting of some Branches and the appointment of additional staff. Net membership increased by 6,000.

In 1963 there were calls for Regional Organisers. Members were 'more demanding in the service they expect.' The NEC established two sub-Committees, one to examine income and expenditure, trade union and specialised education, premises and the 'employment and direction of staff,' the other to examine industrial movements and policy, improvement to organisation, publicity and external relations. The primary outcome was that no Branch should exceed 3,000 members in size and that the 150,000 members be allocated to 'one of six National Industrial Groups.' The efficiency of part-time Branches was questioned.

Paddy Dooley (Dublin No. 9) questioned the legal problems that prevented CIÉ, and other employers, enforcing 100% closed shop Agreements. This had to be resolved if arrears were to be overcome. The Taoiseach, Seán Lemass, addressed the Annual Conference, stating that 'in any free democratic society a strong, well-organised and competently administered' union movement was 'essential for economic and social progress.' He praised the role of the ITGWU in fulfilling 'national development policies,' promised involvement in the Plan for Economic Expansion and expressed the opinion that Connolly 'would have been a very happy man if he could have foreseen the day when the head of an Irish Government would come to an ITGWU Conference.'

A Provident Fund was established to dispense benefits. Contributions were increased, but expenditure rose faster. The membership increase was not maintained. In years when Wage Rounds were not operating, membership income declined, causing the observation 'Undoubtedly, this is a human weakness which pinpoints the fact that some members' interests in trade unionism is at a peak during Wage Rounds but slackens off then.' Educational activity was a necessary but neglected antidote.

Increasing burdens were placed on Officials, and in October 1963 *Liberty* caught the growing pressures succinctly under the heading 'Your Union Official'.

If he speaks up, he is trying to run things.
If he does not, he has no interest in his job.
If he is seen at the office, why doesn't he get out around the jobs.
If he cannot be found, why doesn't he stay in the office.
If he doesn't stop to talk, his job has gone to his head.
If he does, that's all he has to do anyway.
If he can't fix up a wage increase, he is no—good.
If he does, that's what he's paid to do.
If he gives someone a short answer, WE'LL get him at the next meeting.
If he tries to explain something, who does he think he is?
If he is on the job a short time, he is inexperienced.

If he has been an Official for a long time, there should be a change.
If he takes a Holiday, he has had one all year, hasn't he?

New Branches were Cork No. 5 and (after dividing Dublin Nos. 1 to 3), Dublin Nos. 12, 13, 14 and 15. Before the establishment of National Industrial Groups a membership survey was conducted. Change had conflicting consequences: 'the more the infrastructure of the Union—horizontally at Branch level and vertically at national level—is strengthened and modernised, the more costly becomes the whole administration machine.' Contributions were the only source of income. More were encouraged to opt for higher subscription levels. Some members complained that 'voluntary' levels of membership contributions were 'absolute nonsense'.

By 1964, however, the union's assets were £1,500,000, a sum that allowed for the rebuilding of Liberty Hall.[2] In 1964 Cork had six Branches and the Limerick-Shannon District four. The emphasis was firmly on providing 'service', and 'organising', as concept and practice, slid from focus. Yet to service there could be 'no relenting from our organisational drive.'

The highest level of membership ever still did not please Conroy. 'All Officials and staff' were 'expected to devote the necessary attention and energy to a well-planned drive to recruit.' 'Leadership and service' were the selling points.

Subscriptions and benefits were raised in 1965. There was resistance. Jim Hickey (Cork No. 2 and 3) condemned the emerging 'business-organisation approach.' In contrast, Joe Meehan (Belfast) thought that 'you could not have trade unionism on the cheap.'

In 1965 organisation was 'somewhat inhibited' by an economic downturn. Membership was maintained, newcomers balancing those lost through closures and redundancies. It was, however, 'misleading' to 'say that all is well on the organisational front and that our job of work has been done. This is not so!' There were 'very many unorganised workers.' A growing concern was the rural siting of small-scale industry.

The Central Cash Office was established for 45,000 Dublin members. Membership and finances were better than ever, but Paddy Clancy (NEC) cautioned against the opinion that 'this was a rich union.' Assets of £1.7 million sounded great but when set against 150,000 members represented 'only a little over £10 per head.' Income had doubled, while expenses trebled.

A minor but well-appreciated organisational tool was the ITGWU Diary. In 1963 it was given to all members of Branch and Section Committees, Shop Stewards and Collectors, a 'token of appreciation for the valuable work they are doing.'

For Conroy, the three essential resolutions for the new year were, as they always were, 'organisation, education and better service.'

In 1966, 20,000 people emigrated. The membership reflected this, although Branches were opened in Ardee, Ballyjamesduff, Clones, Newtown Mount Kennedy and Roscommon for six hundred newcomers. Waterford was divided into two Branches, and new premises were opened in Belfast and Mallow.

In 1967 Conroy wondered about young members and Officials. Was the union's education and training programme adequate? Did youth receive sufficient encouragement and opportunity? Kennedy pointed out that the ITGWU 'returned over 33% to its members in cash benefits, surely a noteworthy feature.' Disappointingly, however, only 6½% of them contributed at the higher levels: Class 1 (3s 6d per week), (4½%; Class 2 (3s per week), 2%; Class 3 (2s 6d per week), 20.1%; Class 4 (2s per week), 34.1%; Class 5 (1s 6d per week), 11½%; Class 6 (1s per week), 25.4%; Class 7 (9d per week), 1.4%. For Class 1 members, 25% of their contribution was retained by the Branch, equal to £2 5s 6d per year; the remainder, £6 16s 6d, was sent to Head Office.

A male member could qualify for £50 Mortality Benefit for himself and £25 for his wife, and Retirement Benefit of £51. Kennedy asked, 'Would it be possible to get such a return anywhere else for the sum of £6 16s per annum? The answer is No.' Clancy was alarmed by Branch subsidies totalling £53,166, an indication of their inability to survive on the 25% retained. He wanted each Branch to determine its total membership, potential income, actual income and ratio of arrears and review their 25% retained ratio against potential income ratio—in short, to define Branch viability. He asked tough questions before concluding that current methods needed reform.

The introduction of National Group Secretaries, industrial Branches of 3,000 members and Central Cash Office had not brought the anticipated improvements but rather complaints of less and worse service. Members were lost to 'other less competent and less equipped' unions, 'not just in ones or twos, but in some instances in whole Sections of a hundred or more!' Had verticalisation worked, Clancy asked, and if not, why not? Was the Cash Office 'an obstructive luxury we can no longer afford?'

There was an urgent need for improved internal and external communications and better research, information and education—not least given the proposals for a national business and industrial organisation that would combine the Federated Union of Employers, the Construction Industry Federation and the Federation of Irish Industry. If reform was not addressed Clancy warned that 'the initiative for national development,' which appeared to rest between state and unions, would 'pass fairly and squarely to the management side.' His contribution was lengthy, detailed and shocking, even when read off the page half a century later. It clearly had an impact at the Conference. John Burke (Dublin No. 4) nonetheless complained of lengthy speeches, and few directly responded, probably having arrived with predetermined contributions. Clancy's comments, however, could be ignored only at the union's peril.

Conroy outlined a nine-point programme for 'Ireland's economic, social and cultural advancement' in a 'solemn declaration of intent.' The ITGWU would 'dedicate their every action towards these objectives.'

1.   positive and fruitful action to ensure post-primary education for every boy and girl;
2.   immediate steps to determine a legally enforceable living wage for all;

3. more frequent meetings and better communications within employments to improve human and industrial relations;
4. agreed improvements in efficiency and productivity in conformity with the Irish National Productivity Committee's Statement of Production Principles;
5. an incomes policy applicable to every citizen with effective manpower, training and re-training programmes to ensure full employment;
6. a planned, phased upward adjustment of social service benefits and services;
7. improved hygiene and cleanliness, supported by improved legislation, in handling food and public health;
8. provision of adequate housing, recreation, sporting and cultural facilities by local authorities;
9. all our people to resolve to be better neighbours and better citizens in 1966.

Progress on such a broad programme would attract members.

In 1967 membership increased by 6,000, a great success, as employment was static. In December the financial membership was 104,508, book membership 145,000. The country could be divided into three: south of a line from Dublin to Limerick, with strong organisation; south of a line from Dundalk to Galway, with reasonable organisation; north of this line, with poor organisation. These patterns long characterised ITGWU membership.

Table 90: ITGWU financial membership, December 1967

Dublin city	38,924	Derry	1,774
Cork city	14,616	Donegal	1,764
Cork county	6,469	Wicklow	1,752
Limerick	5,513	Offaly	1,725
Louth	3,626	Kildare	1,652
Antrim	3,519	Kilkenny	1,572
Waterford	3,367	Cavan	1,081
Tipperary	2,849	Westmeath	1,043
Clare	2,675	Laois	873
Dublin county	2,607	Down	490
Galway	2,566	Meath	366
Kerry	2,417	Monaghan	363
Wexford	2,176	Roscommon	219
Sligo	2,089	Longford	119
Mayo	1,781	Leitrim	97

Source: ITGWU, minutes of National Executive Council, December 1967.

In 1967 a lengthy dispute with the Revenue Commissioners over Provident Fund benefits was settled. The Commissioners objected to Dispute Grants to members who had not completed twenty-six weeks' membership but allowed previous claims of £52,000. The decision was appealed to Special Commissioners and the Circuit and District Courts before a 'reserved judgement' was given in the ITGWU's favour. Clancy suggested that 'if ever there was a machine constructed to mix-up or break-down communications then we have got it!'

Industrial groups extended an already lengthy chain. Considerable investment in education and training was his solution. In addition, he felt that fifteen people, twelve of them voluntary, meeting only once a month, could not manage an organisation with an income of £646,000 and a staff of more than 200. He argued for industrial, finance and service Divisions, the last-named including 'research and statistics, publicity and propaganda, education and training, premises and accommodation, and a political bureau. He outlined what became the Development Services Division.

Vincent Moran (Limerick No. 2) moved a significant motion calling for a 'nationwide campaign to have Union dues deducted at source.' At least 45,000 members were eight weeks in arrears. The problem was 'to achieve maximum revenue with the least financial and administrative effort.' What was the advantage of Deduction at Source (or 'check-off', as it came to be called)? It would ensure 100% income; Branches would be viable; administration could be streamlined; time would not be wasted in chasing arrears; bitterness and division would be eliminated from the shop floor; the union's control over its members would be strengthened and members would be less able to threaten to 'withhold dues'; and employers would be fully aware that the union operated from a position of strength. He could see no disadvantages, disagreeing with the argument that an important line of contact and communication with members would be broken. The NEC asked for referral back. It thought the motion infringed the movement's voluntary nature.

Table 91: ITGWU **membership, 1960–69**

	Union figure	RFS figure	Women	Women as proportion of total (%)
1960	150,000	136,179	27,236	20.0
1961	150,000	140,334	28,067	20.0
1962	150,000	146,339	29,268	20.0
1963	150,000	143,498	28,697	19.9
1964	150,000	149,915	29,983	20.0
1965	150,000	150,414	30,083	20.0
1966	150,000	148,804	29,760	19.9
1967	150,000	153,415	n.a.	—
1968	150,000	156,277	n.a.	—
1969	114,174	162,181	54,060	33.3

Source: ITGWU, Annual Reports, 1960–69; National Archives, Registrar of Friendly Societies, file 275T.

Membership rose to 108,270, including 14,583 new applicants. Michael O'Connor (Dublin No. 14) sought to organise the unorganised by appointing a 'sufficient number of Organisers.' He commented that £1,693 was spent on advertisements, *Liberty* was subsidised by £2,400 and educational courses cost £7,345. This £11,439 would be more effectively spent on organisation.

Tom Noone (Dublin No. 15) complained that they had handed members back to the Irish Union of Distributive Workers and Clerks, not an uncommon experience, and wondered when they would 'get tough.' Joe Meehan turned away nine hundred bus workers in Belfast wishing to transfer. Others wanted the word 'Craft' added to the union's title, both to satisfy increasing numbers of craftsmen already in and to attract more.

Clancy drew attention to the 'danger symptoms' of increasing expenditure and ever-rising Branch subsidies, chronic symptoms of malaise. New members were required, but where were they? Department of Labour figures showed that 9% of agricultural and forestry workers were organised; distribution, 30%; construction, 40%; and manufacturing, 75%. So why was the ITGWU's expansion rate a miserable 2½%? The answer was simple: 'our organisation, our methods, and our systems have not kept abreast of the changing times.' The ITGWU was 'trying to please everyone and offend none,' a policy perceived as softness. The example was the £270,000 the Maintenance Dispute cost; 'our members got absolutely nothing out of it,' although the ITGWU had more craft workers than the 'whole lot of other unions put together.' Moran again unsuccessfully sought Deduction at Source.

For Connolly's Centenary a campaign for the 'long overdue' goals of a living wage for all men and women was announced. Such ambitious thinking created a sense of purpose and momentum that urged 'Forward, ever forward, to the just society.'

Table 92: ITGWU income and expenditure (£), 1960–69

	Income	Expenditure	Surplus (deficit)
1960	183,031	101,617	81,414
1961	190,318	157,477	32,841
1962	223,392	125,776	97,616
1963	260,596	208,529	52,067
1964	292,852	197,438	94,414
1965	330,934	290,919	40,015
1966	433,160	344,532	88,628
1967	517,334	410,419	106,924
1968	501,527	390,632	110,895
1969	542,962	572,132	(29,170)

Source: ITGWU, Annual Reports, 1960–69.

A record loss of £98,005 was incurred in 1969 because of £255,280 Dispute Pay. Financial membership rose by 5,904 to 114,174, although a third of Branches showed a decline. New Officials were recruited for Donegal, Drogheda, Galway, Limerick No. 2, Shannon, Sligo, Westmeath-Roscommon and Wexford and premises opened or planned for Cork, Ardee, Clonmel, Kilkenny and Newry.

At the Annual Conference Kennedy was elected General President to replace Conroy; John F. Carroll was unopposed as Vice-President; and Alderman Michael Mullen TD defeated Séamus B. Kelly for General Secretary by 165 to 59.[3]

1968 was a 'Year of Agitation', ranging from the union's campaign for increased wages and better treatment for lower-income groups to global civil rights demonstrations. The press dismissed it all as the 'transient exuberance and liberalism of some young students' and the 'irresponsibility of a small number of professional activists.' This was 'dangerous thinking', as the masses' social consciousness was aroused, and 'incessant demands for social justice for all cannot long be denied.' The ITGWU felt it was 'always in the vanguard' of the 'struggle for that social justice' and 'welcomed the challenge of 1969 with its promise of further advances in the upliftment of the people of Ireland, North and South.'[4]

CONROY, O'BRIEN AND PURCELL

Frank Purcell, former General Secretary, died in 1960. A Kildare man, associated with the ITGWU from 1917, he fought in the War of Independence and was interned. Although 'neutral in the Civil War, in conformity with Union policy,' he was again imprisoned. He joined the Head Office Movements Department, developing into a 'very dependable, thoughtful, careful and conscientious Official.' In 1931 he was Secretary of the Hotel and Restaurant Branch and in 1948 was elected General Secretary, a position he held until ill health forced his retirement in 1959. A memorial to Purcell was unveiled in Mount Jerome Cemetery in April 1964. William O'Brien, the ITGWU's 'Grand Old Man', died on 30 October 1968, aged eighty-eight.

Fintan Kennedy, in his first Presidential Address in 1969, reflected on the loss of the 'service and guidance' of John Conroy, who died in the Adelaide Hospital on 13 February, aged only sixty-four. He was General President for sixteen years and was due to retire in 1970. Born in Wicklow, he was educated in the local National School and worked in a factory and coal yard before moving to Dublin as a building worker. He became Wicklow Organiser, fighting battles alongside James Everett, in the late 1920s Secretary of the Wicklow Branch and in 1926 of the Limerick Branch, where he also administered the local Labour Party. In 1942 he transferred to the Movements Department and was elected Vice-President in 1946 and General President in 1953. Conroy was 'a solid man of strong views, of forceful dedication, and absolute belief in the concept of social justice.' He 'brooked no opposition to this belief.' He was 'rough-hewn, down to earth, gruff at times' but highly respected within and beyond Liberty Hall, especially among the industrial staff. Jimmy Dunne (MPGWU and President of the ICTU) said that Conroy 'played a man's part in healing the divisions which divided our movement,' a fact reflected in his twice being President of the ICTU, from 1959 to 1960 and from 1967 to 1968. Conroy's speeches betrayed the influence of Catholic social teaching, and he was not counted on the left. He was, however, deeply sincere, very much in touch with ordinary members and their families and, no doubt under the influence of Sheila Williams, whom he married in 1959, increasingly committed to equality. He was open to new ideas and ready to consider what changes might be necessary to advance the movement. Said not to suffer fools gladly, rather like Foran before him, he came to personify the ITGWU. What drove him was a sense that whatever was achieved there was always more that could be done.[5]

Five days after the shock of Conroy's death James Larkin Junior lost his long battle against illness in St Luke's Hospital on 18 February. *Liberty* published a photograph of Conroy and Larkin shaking hands at the inaugural ICTU Congress in 1959 under the banner 'Unity'—with the caption 'United in Life and Death.' With their deaths, talks between the ITGWU and WUI and possible amalgamation withered. Drummers and buglers from the ITGWU Band sounded the Last Post and Reveille at Larkin's graveside, an appropriate note of unity.

WOMEN

Marriage Benefit, first paid in 1959, was 'wholeheartedly welcomed by our female members.' It was, in effect, a repayment of contributions for women, obliged by the Marriage Bar to surrender employment. Most had little expectation of re-entering the labour market after rearing a family; few questioned the benefit's discriminatory philosophy.

Women and gender issues were scarce at ITGWU Conferences. Esther Flynn (Dublin No. 3) sought a reduction in the qualification period for Marriage Benefit of fifteen years, as there were 'few female members who would reach the maximum.' The WUI gave the benefit after only seven years. In 1964 Paddy O'Brien (Tralee) moved that, 'in view of the large incidence of female labour in relation to male, steps be taken to ensure' that male workers 'should get adequate protection and priority.' Female labour tended to be 'a form of cheap and exploited labour.' While it was a 'rather controversial resolution' it was 'not an attack on female labour as such.' It was to 'prevent the exploitation of cheap female labour to the detriment of the natural breadwinner—the male.' Women were always cheap labour, even when they did the same jobs as men, who would be 'on the scrap heap' if employers could employ more women. Already in a hole, O'Brien kept digging. 'Therefore it behoves our Union to be on guard lest . . . we will find the natural breadwinner on the dole' and women at work.

Phil Darby (Dublin No. 2), one of only eight women among 200 Delegates, opposed. Ireland, as a member of the Council of Europe, had agreed to ratify the protocol and principle of 'equal pay for equal work.' The ITGWU should 'do all in its power' to seek its immediate implementation.

Esther Flynn said that the Tralee Branch were 'both selfish and insincere': 'female workers are not exploited by employers. They are exploited by the male members with whom they work.' If O'Brien were sincere he would fight for equal pay. This would 'not alone safeguard his own position' but would give employers the 'right to employ the better worker irrespective of sex.' The motion was defeated. The platform offered no view.

Phil Darby wrote of 'my first Annual Conference,' an interesting insight. She 'learned a lot,' heard much repetition and criticism—although 'some of those who criticised were, themselves, the worst offenders'—and 'was greatly struck by the small number of women.' Did eight Delegates really reflect 40,000? She wanted greater involvement. 'After all, our first Labour Minister was a woman!' (a reference to Constance Markievicz). The 'Late Late Show' on RTÉ television debated whether mothers should work, a question raised in *Liberty*. While accepting arguments against, the ITGWU pointed to necessity resulting from inadequate family income. Some women were 'just not domesticated' and wanted to work to 'get away from, what is to her, the monotony of daily household chores.'

This was controversial, but 'Oonagh' of 'Woman's Page' concluded: 'It is just nonsense to suggest that because a woman gets married and has a few children that her natural talents and intelligence must be shoved into the background.' This did 'not mean that such a woman cares less for her home and family.' The 'idea that a woman's place is in the home' was outdated. Oonagh was 'all in favour of her taking up a job if she so wishes and, of course, if her husband is agreeable,' and 'toddlers should not be left in the care of strangers.' She also reminded female readers that it was 'Spring-cleaning time', urged young women to wear 'softly feminine clothes' and provided two useful recipes for 'those working men'—curried fish and toad in the hole. Women had far to travel in 1965.

Frances Lambert said that a woman's place was in her union and championed the ICTU Women's Advisory Committee. Sheila Conroy wrote that women were 'in the background far too long,' her own isolation since marriage a case in point. She wanted female Labour Court Conciliation Officers. She pointed out that 'there is no Rule in the Rule Book' to say a woman had to resign from the NEC on marriage.

In 1965 Pearse O'Sullivan (Tralee) moved that the ITGWU 'help to implement equal pay for equal work for male and female labour.' Tralee had learnt its lesson. He praised women's role in the country's development, adding that 'we now recognise the right of women to work at our side in almost every Branch of labour, but we still do not recognise the right of women workers to share an equality of wage rates with us.'

Paddy O'Brien fell on his sword. The previous year's motion was 'badly put.' They were back to demand equal pay, realising that it was 'a revolutionary step for our Union.' Without further debate it was agreed.

The first specifically designed women's courses were held in 1966. Conor O'Brien (Dublin No. 3) called for the implementation of ILO Convention No. 100 on equal pay for work of equal value, reminding 1967 Delegates that membership of the Common Market necessitated ratification. In the Tenth Round his Branch Secured equal rises for men and women.

Carmel Harrington (Bantry) congratulated the union on having this principle enshrined in ICTU talks with the FUE, although little progress was made under the ITGWU Workers' Charter Action Programme. The union cited European equality experience, a novel element in Irish industrial relations and one that excited and bewildered in equal measure. No-one drew attention to the obvious contradiction between seeking an adult male minimum rate of £12 10s in the first point of the Workers' Charter, with 'related increases for adult females and juveniles,' and commitment to 'equal pay for work of equal value as between men and women,' which finally came at paragraph 4, sub-section (g).

At the Conference Conroy gave a 'very special welcome to the few of the gentler sex we have with us' but gave no indication of how the 'few' could become many. In 1968 there were fewer women working in Ireland than recorded in the 1901 census. This decline—from 356,000 to 281,000—was mainly accounted for by the decline in agriculture and domestic service. In the 1960s the number of working women slightly increased, from 278,000 to 280,800, mainly along the east coast. Women's equality had a mountain to climb.[6] The number of women members rose from 27,256 in 1960, or 20% of the total, to 54,060 in 1969, or 33%.

NORTHERN IRELAND

In 1960 the ITGWU 'flourished' in Northern Ireland, despite terrible economic depression. The ICTU did much to improve inter-union relations, and 750 Belfast dockers achieved 'the largest wage increase ever.' Stephen McGonagle (Derry) condemned the lack of democracy, the 'Government acting as despots,' a situation that would exist as long as political representation was 'determined by religious convictions.'

In 1961 the ITGWU fully supported Congress policy initiatives aimed at reducing unemployment, improving social services and regenerating the economy. This demanded more effective Labour representation in the British House of Commons on Irish questions, both from a better-informed British Labour Party and the Northern Ireland Labour Party.

In 1962 McGonagle called for Economic Planning Councils, while Ruby O'Reilly (Derry) complained that uncontrolled imports of shirts from Hong Kong had a fifth of the city's shirt workers idle.[7] McGonagle welcomed the final recognition by Stormont of the Northern Ireland Committee of the ICTU and membership of the Northern Ireland Economic Council. In July 1966 new premises were acquired on the Antrim Road in Belfast. Visits by the NEC and the Union Band were 'highly appreciated.'

In 1967 more than 1,000 deep-sea dockers won a pension scheme. In 1968 Joe McBrinn warned of containerisation. Continued mass unemployment dominated all action, putting workers on the back foot.

In 1969 Mick O'Brien (Waterford No. 2) supported the 'Civil Rights Committees', and Eddie Lawless (Dublin No. 14) demanded that Partition be raised at the United Nations. John McAleavey (Newry) said the only solution was a Socialist republic. Murtagh Morgan (Belfast) stressed how dependent they were on British subventions, while McGonagle (Chairman of the Northern Ireland Committee of the

ICTU) laid out Congress's economist reforms. There was a significant increase in civil disorder as Stormont failed to deal with the demands of the Northern Ireland Civil Rights Association or to control violent opposition. The ITGWU observed that 'Ulster Unionism with its hard core right wing extremists, pursued the defence of its ascendancy status to the point of no return.' The 'inevitable result was the overflowing of the boiling cauldron of hatred and suppression which had been stirring for so long.' Union members forwarded £6,500 in relief for displaced families.

The Northern Ireland Committee had the unenviable task of keeping sectarian violence from the work-place. Representing 215,000 trade unionists, it published a *Programme for Peace and Progress in Northern Ireland,* demanding action on civil rights, housing and employment and the reform of local Government and education. The overriding priority was maintaining 'calm, order and solidarity.' It felt that, 'in present circumstances,' unions had 'a very special opportunity of making an immense contribution to an improvement in community relations,' and that 'this opportunity should be taken.'[8]

The ITGWU was highly critical of the support of the British Labour Government for 'local Tory hardliners,' viewing 'with some derision' their taking 'full control of all security measures in the Six Occupied Counties . . . But surely we could have expected more than pious platitudes from the Right Honourable Harold Wilson, MP, that Socialist par excellence, that defender of the oppressed, that champion of the underdog and exemplar of social justice.' His 'recent meeting with a certain former member of the British armed forces who now heads up the Occupied Area's puppet Government [Terence O'Neill] was more glib politicalology [*sic*].' To hear him say he was satisfied with reform plans and the pace of progress was 'to hear the condescending tone of the ascendancy class to Irish second-class citizens that has echoed down the years. We have enough of it!' British troops were not welcome and not the solution. A 32-County state governed by social justice was the answer. Stormont should be abolished, the B Specials disbanded, all special powers scrapped, and 32-County free elections held.

The ITGWU concluded, after twenty years or more condemning Communism and fascism: 'Let us not talk any more about Czechoslovakia, Hungary, Spain or where-you-will as long as tyranny and oppression exist in our own green isle.' It was 'our opportunity to pursue the national aspirations . . . the heritage of all true Irishmen.' Working-class solidarity 'must be an invaluable means to this end. History will record how this means was employed.'

Acting independently of Congress, the ITGWU General Officers met the TUC in London. A statement said that the 'present trouble stems basically from the social and economic evils and injustices' imposed on Irish workers by Britain. The responsibility lay with the Labour Government and the TUC, who had failed to fulfil their moral obligations. The TUC was asked to support a Bill of Rights for Northern Ireland. The officers handed in a statement of protest at 10 Downing Street, and the General Secretary, Mullen, toured Belfast, Derry, Newry and elsewhere 'for the purpose of organising and assisting in measures to relieve distress' among members and their families. It was noted that 'all full-time Officials and staff of the Union are on constant stand-by in respect of this serious matter.'

The ITGWU sent a telegram to the Taoiseach, Jack Lynch, the Minister for External Affairs, Patrick Hillery, Harold Wilson and James Callaghan, calling on them to follow the union's lead and conduct an 'immediate and personal inspection' of matters 'to establish peace and social justice.'

Liberty published dramatic images of the 'destruction of Catholic homes and property in Belfast and Derry.' The Union Collection for the Relief was tabulated, reaching £6,471 0s 2d by December 1969.[9]

NATIONAL INDUSTRIAL GROUPS

In 1963 the ITGWU created six National Industrial Groups. Conroy warned that there were 'no glamour jobs and no easy pickings.' What was required was dedication, a capacity for hard work, and leadership. The ITGWU advertised for 'Industrial Group Administrators', listing the essential qualifications as 'practical experience', 'a high standard of education', 'outstanding ability' in 'organisation, leadership, adminis-tration and negotiations' and a 'marked dedication to duty and interest in the affairs of organised labour.' The six appointed were:

Group 1 (textiles, cleaning and dyeing, rubber and plastics): Michael Gannon, former Secretary of Lucan Branch and County Dublin Organiser.

Group 2 (theatres, cinema, radio and television; food, drink, tobacco, chemicals and drugs): Séamus B. Kelly, Secretary, Dublin No. 7 Branch.

Group 3 (building, public works, turf, glass and pottery, coalmining and quar-ries): Seán Ó Murchú, Secretary, Cork Branch, Irish Engineering, Industrial and Electrical Trade Union.

Group 4 (catering, personal services, entertainment, clerical and professional): Michael Mullen, Secretary, Dublin No. 4 Branch (hotels and catering).

Group 5 (transport, railway, air, docks and communications): Christopher Kirwan, Secretary, Dublin No. 11 Branch (Rail) and Head Office.

Group 6 (engineering, printing, paper and wood): Patrick Donegan, Assistant General Secretary, National Engineering Union.

Carroll, Chief Industrial Officer, addressed change, a concept and reality that 'scared' many. The reaction was often 'excessive caution, with an ultra-conservative eye or, for that matter, with deliberate opposition or open hostility.' Change had to be anticipated and embraced. New industrial structures were not 'forced on us' but 'planned' to provide 'optimum service.' Foresight was qualified by a residual tinc-ture of Catholic social teaching. Although an island, Ireland was not insulated 'against the happenings in the rest of the world.' The trend was 'towards free trade ... liberalisation and rationalisation of social and cultural standards ... national and international mobility of labour ... harmonisation of living standards' in the 'free world', a more rapid development of less advanced countries and 'fuller participation in a Christian world in which the prime motivation must be social justice.' Social advance was best achieved and served by communal effort and reward.

National Industrial Groups each marshalled 20,000 to 30,000 members, facilitating national support and co-ordination, negotiation and development through education. They were not to do the Branch Secretary's work but to 'help and advise.' They would make the ITGWU more attractive to young workers. The frequency, duration and means of communication of Branch Committees required examination. Change at the national level depended on action at the Branch level, which required revitalising. 'Let your Branch be as Connolly advocated—an instrument to a higher level of life and comfort and not just a mere protection and Benefit Society.'

With an eye on recalcitrant Dublin bus workers, Carroll said that a 'minority, vocal at times,' would 'derive pleasure, if not satisfaction, from unfairly criticising the Union.' He concluded: 'Let us show these few by good example how wrong they are and let us be united in fact and in deed.' His speech was a clarion call and a signpost to the future.

The National Group Secretaries addressed the Annual Conference. Mick O'Connor (Dublin No. 3) thought there was need for a 'course on how to condense a speech.' They had a 'long-winded President' and now 'long-winded Industrial Officers' leaving 'no time for Delegates to participate.' J. Caffrey (Dublin No. 3) continued the theme, suggesting that the NEC 'had a garden plot at the back of Head Office in which they buried all the resolutions passed.' A regular sentiment among Delegates was that the union 'did not punch its weight.' The motion was lost.

The reaction of members to the groups was 'very heartening.' The NEC felt the change 'more than justified itself.' From 1964, lengthy reports of the industrial groups described movements and disputes within individual employments, the activities of JLCs and JICs and significant precedents in wages and non-wage benefits. Huge detail about members and their industrial achievements is provided. There was no intention of concentrating affairs within national structures or Head Office. Carroll regularly addressed Branch seminars, reminding members of their role in the workplace and encouraging the maximum involvement of Shop Stewards. He placed his remarks in the context of national economic and social policy and introduced what were then relatively new ideas about work-place grievance-handling and negotiating procedures. Shop Stewards should deal with problems along defined paths: the individual worker discusses their problem with their foreman; failing agreement, the Shop Steward discusses matters with a higher level of management; failing agreement, the ITGWU Official is brought in and discusses the matter with the management; failing agreement, Head Office and the senior management discuss the problem; and failing agreement again, matters might then go to the JIC or the Labour Court.

The NEC's sanction for disputes was withheld unless procedures were followed. National Groups facilitated the introduction of grievance and disciplinary procedures within work-place collective bargaining Agreements. Carroll and the

Movements Department were central to creating national-level bargaining structures supported by work-place procedures—in short, the industrial relations infrastructure that existed until the employers' offensive of the 1980s. The emergence of
Shop Stewards indicated simultaneous development at the base and the top levels.
Shop Stewards' courses were provided and their role strenuously debated.

John Ryan answered the still often confusing question, 'A Shop Steward is . . .?'
They would be 'abused on occasion,' 'unappreciated on occasion' but gain tremendous satisfaction. He concluded:

A Shop Steward IS . . .
—chasing the foreman's job if he agrees the firm is right in the dispute;
—trying to create trouble if he agrees the men are right;
—accused of cowardice if he disagrees with the men;
—accused of being awkward if he agrees with the men.
A Shop Steward MUST HAVE . . .
—a hard neck and a soft heart;
—an open mouth and a closed mind and sometimes a closed mouth and an
open mind!
—a cynic's harshness and a child's gentleness;
—a good knowledge of everything and at the same time not considered to be too
smart![10]

For those new to work-place representation he concluded: 'Yes, indeed, a Shop
Steward is all that and then some! Simple, isn't it?'

CONGRESS

The ICTU began with 79 affiliates, embracing 429,000 members. The ITGWU felt
that 'already, the services and activities' of Congress had 'proved of immeasurable
value,' showing the 'fruits to be reached from the field of trade union unity.'
There was delight at reunification. Celebrations were held, all identifying high
expectations.

Kennedy saw 'danger symptoms' at the 1962 Congress, described as 'a most
undignified affair' but not 'altogether a dead loss.' There was a need for 'education
in Christian ethics,' especially among Officials and leaders. He praised the Catholic
Workers' College and Congress's own education programme; but 'there are spheres
in which no educational body can penetrate.' There 'disorder is preferred to order,
disunity to unity, disruption to decency, hate to love,' where 'the guiding forces
are personal vanity and power and greed rather than fraternity and humanity and
justice.' Some vilified the fragile Congress constitution and endeavoured to turn
worker against worker.

In 1963 a Committee on Trade Union Organisation, Demarcation Tribunal and
Appeals Board was created. The ITGWU talked proudly of its role within Congress.
Paddy Clancy (NEC) commented that press implications that the 'amalgamation of

general unions was just around the corner' were not 'just nonsense' but 'dangerously misleading' and potentially seriously damaging to talks. It would 'be a tragedy if, through ill-informed newspaper reports, participating unions were frightened off.'

In August 1966 the ITGWU welcomed *Trade Union Information,* Congress's digest. It regretted that 'even amongst trade union Officials' and those servicing and administering them 'there is a rather uninterested and casual approach to the matter of reading and studying.' *Liberty* was not universally read, but *Trade Union Information* was considered essential.

Dónal Lehane (Cork District Council) moved for disaffiliation from Congress in 1969. It had 'not provided a service to the Union commensurate with the cost of affiliation,' had 'failed to bring about the desired rationalisation' and was either unable or unwilling, or both, to 'exercise adequate control' over affiliates in disputes. The ITGWU 'and its membership very often suffer the consequences.' Affiliation fees, which were about to increase, could be put 'to far better benefit and advantage.' Since 1959 the ITGWU paid £60,000 in fees, donated £5,000 towards Congress premises, and provided a repayable loan of £23,000 at 3½% interest. Ned McNamara (Cork No. 1) insisted that the Maintenance Dispute had not influenced them, but it certainly made the case for disaffiliation stronger.

After a lengthy lunch break the Cork Delegates offered to defer for twelve months in a spirit of unity and in Conroy's memory. After a full debate Congress set up a Working Party 'designed to ensure' that they could 'speak for, act for and represent' the movement's 'collective will and purpose . . . including provision for the full acceptance of Congress decisions.' It reported in 1970. Nearly 300 attended a Conference on 'The Future Role of Congress' in Liberty Hall in January 1969. The President, Jimmy Dunne, said that Congress 'was not structured to implement political aims.' It 'did not stand for election and it could never be the Government in whose hands were the political decisions.' Referendums on PR in 1959 and 1968 nevertheless showed that Congress could sustain a political role. Union demands on national incomes, economic planning and employment creation, social welfare and education all necessitated political action.[11]

RELATIONS WITH THE WUI

Encouraged by Congress's drive for rationalisation, in 1964 the ITGWU began talks with the Federation of Rural Workers, the Irish Women Workers' Union, the Marine, Port and General Workers' Union, the United Stationary Engine Drivers' Union and the WUI to explore common ground. Paddy Clancy (NEC) reported to the 1967 Conference that these discussions were 'abortive' except in the case of the WUI. Discussions with it continued, albeit with the 'greatest care and caution . . . The split between the two unions more than a half century ago will not be cured in a day, a week or perhaps a year.' The NEC was 'proceeding accordingly—that amalgamation between the two unions is in the best interests of our members in particular and of workers generally.' Any amalgamation would be a catalyst for further, much-needed rationalisation.

Tom O'Brien (Dublin No. 5) commented on a wui proposal to the ictu that unions with more than 50,000 members be limited to one seat on the Executive Council. This could only affect the itgwu—although, despite its entitlement to elect more than one Executive member, it never had. 'Why then,' O'Brien asked, 'was this resolution put down?' The obvious answer was 'to clip the wings' of the itgwu.

Paddy Buttner (Dublin No. 5) warned Congress not to forget 'on which side its bread was buttered.' The itgwu paid £7,500 in affiliation fees, the atgwu £2,500 and the wui £1,500. 'We must guard against all efforts to reduce our power.' This 'applied equally' to amalgamating with the wui. 'We should retain our individualism.'

In 1967 talks with the wui proceeded, but 'no commitments of any kind' were made. Members were assured that 'no positive decisions' would be made 'without full consultation'. Having restructured itself, the itgwu met the wui on a 'mutual understanding of the other's position' and, 'most important of all, on a desire to build a movement that will give the best possible service.' In this 'the two unions' and the ictu Committee on Trade Union Reorganisation had 'the best wishes of all people of good will.' *Liberty* was silent on the talks.

In 1968 Kennedy reported progress. It was still 'in the best interests of all concerned' if 'amalgamation could be achieved.' The itgwu felt that Congress 'had more or less washed their hands' of rationalisation; but 'dialogue' with the wui continued.

In February a headline 'Larkin Remembered' in *Liberty* probably shocked readers. His name had been eradicated from all itgwu material. John Smithers, General President of the wui, was cited speaking at a Mass and Parade on Big Jim's twenty-first anniversary, arguing that 'tribute to the memory of Larkin could only be paid truly and conscientiously' by using the movement's strength 'for the purpose of raising the working class to the foremost pinnacle.' Instead, 'rent and weakened by our petty and selfish aims and conflicts,' they had 'lost the majesty of dedication and purpose which gave greatness to this man.' The itgwu Band joined the Emerald Girls' Pipe Band and St James's Brass and Reed Band to add pomp. If the itgwu Band played at a Larkin Commemoration, the permafrost was surely thawing.

However, in a hard-hitting speech in 1969 Clancy told Delegates to 'dismiss from your minds the word amalgamation where the Transport Union is concerned. We don't amalgamate. You don't amalgamate Williams and Power's [supermarket chains] with the corner grocery shop.' The wui would offer a 'fair and attractive basis' to 'any small union who wishes to come in from the cold,' a cold 'becoming extremely difficult, financially and physically.'[12] Shoots that appeared in the thaw were quickly burnt by this cold snap.

EMPLOYERS

As Congress pushed progressive economic and social policies, employers resisted through the fue. Conroy 'regretted that this powerful organisation' spent so much of 'its time and energy attacking' the unions. Its 'gospel' was the 'higher profit motive' and it dismissed workers' 'Christian and constructive' policies. In Dublin

Docks the FUE Shipping Group spent its time in a 'persistent attempt to pocket' men's wages instead of entering discussions that 'could be concluded in a matter of hours.' The Liffey quays 'could be lined with containers within a week.'

In 1965 Conroy condemned 'some major pockets of active antagonism to the wage-earning manual worker,' manifest often in 'violent and determined opposition' to any improvements sought. The 'speedy enlightenment' of employers would be welcomed by all.[13]

Outright hostility to the FUE was about to mellow. It promoted pre-emptive closed-shop Agreements with incoming transnationals, seeing its role as offering a countervailing power to the unions.

WAGES AND DISPUTES

The Seventh Round was a 'little drawn out' and 'not as fully successful' as the ITGWU would have wished. Conroy challenged those, like the Taoiseach, Lemass, who insisted on a low-wage economy. Why were wage increases to the low-paid so injurious while increases for higher-wage earners, dividend-receivers and profit-takers apparently did no damage at all? Conroy criticised gambling, whether conducted at races, dog track or stock exchange, again asking why spending in this area was never queried, while any proposed capital programmes were always closely questioned. He completed his moral exhortation by criticising excessive drinking.

At least 'real wages' improved, as the price index rose only one point. Dissatisfied, the ITGWU strove to attain the £10 a week standard. Low-paid road, forestry and agricultural workers and neglected groups in woollen and worsted had still not reached pre-war parity. The ITGWU insisted that 'we can never have economic expansion and a thriving community unless the scourge of emigration' was eliminated. While workers were 'paid a miserable pittance they cannot be blamed for leaving the land, flocking to England where they have the opportunity of living a fuller life which is denied them in their homeland.'

The Seventh Round, as with its predecessors, was uneven in application. Whereas industrial workers generally got 12s, roadmen, forestry workers and those in county homes and hospitals achieved only 7s 6d. That Labour Court recommendations did not grant parity was a source of frustrated anger.

In 1961 industrial peace was broken with strikes seriously discommoding the public and causing losses to thousands of workers not directly involved. The reasons lay in 'unnecessary delay and procrastination' in having claims completed; employers' negativity, almost regardless of the facts of a case; a lack of information from managements and the absence of appropriate training; and 'the past-century attitude' of some in their hostility to unions. The Eighth Round closed at the end of 1961, most members gaining between £1 for adult males and 11s 6d for adult females. Rises represented real wage increases.

Ministers and bank directors spoke of wage-led inflation. The ITGWU considered this 'ludicrous' as long as 'we still have thousands of male adult workers on £6 to £8 per week.' These workers, 'condemned to the meagre existence which such low wages enforce,' could not be faulted. It was estimated that about £3 million was gained for members. In many cases, working hours were reduced.[14]

Table 93: ITGWU Dispute Pay, 1960–69

	Income (£)	Dispute benefit (£)	Dispute grant (£)	Dispute Benefit and Dispute Grant as proportion of income (%)	
1960	183,031	7,904	—	—	4.3
1961	190,318	47,137	—	—	24.8
1962	223,392	9,692	—	—	4.4
1963	260,596	67,938	—	—	26.1
1964	291,852	33,814	—	—	11.6
1965	330,934	86,858	13,480	100,338	30.3
1966	433,160	85,553	27,133	112,686	26.0
1967	517,334	73,410	8,396	81,806	15.8
1968	501,527	63,617	21,975	85,592	17.0
1969	542,962	231,730	23,550	255,280	47.0

Source: ITGWU, Annual Reports, 1960–69.

Dispute Pay was £47,137, the highest since 1952. Critics saw strikes as 'anti-social and unpatriotic.' With the European Common Market looming, mutual trust was required. But the ITGWU recognised that 'as long as the profit motive remains the be-all and end-all,' the strike weapon must be jealously guarded.

In 1962 Liam Beecher (Cork No. 1) called for a 'Bridge the Gap' campaign to close differentials between craftsmen and labourers, while Michael Mullen (Dublin No. 4) sought rigid price controls. Strong and regular denunciations of unofficial action were made.

The Eighth Wage Round spilled into 1962. Union attitudes remained unaltered: 'we cannot accept an imposed pay pause' and 'insist on the right to continue free negotiations with employers.' The ITGWU subscribed to the principles of the National Productivity Committee but would 'remain free to evaluate and assess our obligations and responsibilities' to members in their best interests while having regard to 'community' needs. Dispute Pay fell to £9,692.[15]

Critics portrayed the Eighth Round as the 'death blow or almost so of the country's economy.' The ITGWU concluded that '1962 was easily the best year ever in Ireland' and expressed satisfaction that 'more people had more money to spend than ever before.' There were still 'pockets' of unemployment, low wages, poor social services and inadequate education and training. The responsibility for advances lay with unions. 'The efficient hard thinking, hard working trade union Official is the key to Ireland's progress in 1963.' Officials could 'advance Ireland to the same levels of production and productivity as obtains in progressive Europe.' Some thought themselves 'better qualified than the trade union Official' to lead against employers, but leadership 'at the Conference table is a task calling for experience, training and skill of a very high order.' Managements usually had better-quality information and more qualified teams, against which 'truth and justice', skilled advocacy and argument were the union's weapons.

In February the Government published the White Paper *Closing the Gap (Incomes and Output)*, drawing attention to the dangers of increases in income outstripping productivity. Congress was not consulted and criticised the attendant 'crisis of confidence' within the economy. The Government had to accept the 'consequences of its ill-conceived and unwarranted intervention' and 'for the partisan manner' in which it promoted incomes policy. Unions had, voluntarily, exercised wage restraint during the Eighth Round, and pre-war purchasing power was not regained until 1960. Irish wage rates were below most of Europe. Even from that low base, in percentage terms rates of increase were lower. The White Paper mentioned profits only in passing.

Matters were greatly aggravated by the Government's introduction of a 2½% turnover tax, directly affecting living standards. The ITGWU saw the White Paper as 'very black and dirty towards the wage earner . . . we cannot accept the pay pause proposed.'

Fifty strikes were officially sanctioned in 1963, involving 3,887 members and £67,938 in Dispute Benefit. In 1964 eighteen official disputes cost £38,103. In Cavan, Harton's workers were out the entire year.[16]

The ten-point Ninth Round Agreement from the Employer-Labour Conference, 'Recommendation on Wage and Salary Adjustments', emerged on 1 January 1964. It said nothing of statutory minimum rates, equal pay or incomes policy, all issues pushed by the ITGWU and Congress. Nevertheless the ITGWU approved it on 13 January 1964. On the wages front the Ninth Round, 'the first of its kind,' was not the perfect model but 'a major first step and as an intelligent and responsible experiment, it was highly successful.' The most obvious defect was the absence of price regulation. The goal was a more equitable distribution of national wealth, not just among wage-earners but among the young, aged, infirm and incapacitated. Within employment, eyes needed to be lifted beyond wages to improve 'hours of work, annual leave, protective clothing, congenial surroundings, satisfactory safety measures, adequate toilet and wash-room facilities'—all elements essential for a 'proper moral and social concept of work.' Carroll added 'pensions, sick-pay schemes, holiday funds, service pay, recreational facilities' to the wish-list.

In November the ITGWU complained about the 'spoliation of the National Wages Agreement.' Deliberately narrow interpretations by the FUE created resentment and were central to the building strike. The Labour Court 'fell from grace and, with a bang, barred and locked the door on any hope there was of successful mediation' without serious stoppages. The intervention of the Minister for Industry and Commerce, Jack Lynch, rescued the construction strike, showing that greater equity was possible. Bank managers' demands for an increase of £1,000 a year, a 50% increase on their existing salaries, raised not a squeak in the press or a question from the Government. 'Why is it always the manual worker who is pilloried and treated like an ill-bred mongrel to be chastised and whipped whenever the lords and masters of our society choose to do so in the belief that they could get away with such foul treatment of the working man?'[17] Inadequate Congress leadership was criticised.

In 1965 Carroll warned that talks for a new Wage Round would be difficult. Prices were 'soaring' and 'inequalities in living standards a constant source of just grievance.' The ITGWU demanded a National Minimum Wage of £10. Greater imagination was required on wages policy. On 2 March the NEC invited Branches to contribute to policy, reminding them of the contexts of free-trade competition, capital investment and employment, balance of payments problems, trends in imports and exports and projected growth in GNP and its distribution. In a comprehensive, sophisticated survey the NEC drew special attention to the existence of low-income groups and their families; equal pay for equal work; percentage adjustments as against flat-rate increases; the value of fringe benefits, such as reductions in hours, improved annual leave, sickness pay and pension schemes, and service pay and their impact on costs; and matching wage movements with productivity. The concluding response from the troops was that a 'national wages Agreement to replace the Ninth Round Agreement was desirable' but 'should legislate' for low-income groups; more should be given 'to those earning up to £800/£1,000 per year than those earning over that range'; any 'agreement must be accompanied by price control'; it should be 'for one year or eighteen months at the longest' and should 'provide a positive and planned approach to fringe benefits,' with an emphasis on the 'rationalisation and harmonisation of existing employment conditions by the rapid elimination of anomalies.'

The Annual Conference considered these responses. Government pronouncements against wage increases irked workers, against the 'backdrop of massive salary increases' to 'highly-paid civil servants' and 'members of the Establishment.' A Price Stabilisation Order in October lightened the mood slightly. In November the National Industrial and Economic Council warned that future development depended upon an incomes plan, effective action to contain aggregate demand and credit policy, all factors that unions both recognised and advanced. Members were reminded that Strike Pay exceeded 'the combined Strike Pay of all other unions.' £104,382 supported thirty official strikes in Dublin printing, cork, rubber and plastic, and confectionery. After twenty-two weeks a settlement was finally reached in Harton's of Cavan. The ITGWU had spent an average of £20,000 a year in each of its fifty-six years.

Conroy felt that history would view the period 1965–6 as years of strikes. If this were so, 'it is almost certain that future historians will not record the facts and will not truthfully explain' that the cause 'was and is the unjust and the scandalous treatment of working men and women by an affluent society in the autumn of the twentieth century.'

In 1963 the union had agreed a 12% deal with the FUE, with an upper bar of
£1,500. To his knowledge all salaries over £1,500 had in fact received increases
and since then additional rises of between 5 and 10%, affecting the cost of living. A
British surcharge of 15%, later reduced to 10%, on Irish manufactures resulted in a
credit squeeze on fat cats. The Establishment blamed the mistreated worker. 'What
a nonsense, what a colossal bluff the Establishment tried to put across the ordinary
Joe Soap.'

In December 1965 Congress agreed a £1 rise, but employers' shilly-shallying led
to strikes and unnecessary losses of production. Still the 'year of the strikes' propaganda persisted. 'No greater lie was invented, even during World War II, or so
slickly put over with such guile on the public at large.' Planners and economists
had 'not alone failed to lead the industrial worker into the Promised Land' but had
'failed to even give him hope that he will ever see it.'

Table 94: ITGWU Dispute Pay (£), 1909–70

1909–17	over 200,000	1941–54	255,000
1918–28	292,000	1955–65	300,000
1929–40	69,000	1966–70	611,487

Source: ITGWU, Annual Report for 1965, p. 64; Annual Reports, 1966–70.

In 1966 Conroy acknowledged that unions had to keep their own house in order. He
condemned the small number of Officials 'hell bent on seeking personal kudos out
of industrial strife.' He demanded discipline and rationalisation.

He talked of change. 'We accept space travel and moon shots without much
amazement any more. We accept mod clothes and the other visual examples of our
modern youth without too much concern. Again, a few years ago, a long-haired
titan would have been arrested for causing a breach of the peace. Now the only
question in our minds is to ask is it male or female?' Clancy (NEC) looked for greater
equity and a 'portion of successive national wage increases' to be devoted to
developing 'free post-primary education' and 'free full health and social welfare
benefits.' This strategy would be aided if either the ITGWU or Congress produced a
comprehensive economic plan. This would be a radical departure from existing
bargaining. Opposition from employers and their press allies could be guaranteed,
but the first task was to persuade members to adopt the new approach. Rarely in
history had a 'voluntary democratic society of such dimensions as the Irish Trade
Union Movement shown such care.' Not all were convinced. The change mooted
was accepted but not fully understood.[18]

At a Special Conference on 19 January 1966 Delegates were told of the FUE's
reluctance to talk. If it did agree it would be for twelve months only, with a moratorium on all non-wage claims and arbitration of disputes. Congress ended negotiations and issued a £1 recommendation to affiliates, approved on 20 January by

two to one. The Labour Court, finding sharp differences between the FUE and ICTU on the £1, issued guidelines on 21 April: £1 increases should be sought 'having due regard to the circumstances' of employments and the possibility of gaining increases in two instalments over two years; claims for service pay should be deferred or taken into account when determining basic wage increases; reduction in working hours was not appropriate, and claims for increased holidays should not be pressed; and pension and sickness schemes should be left for discussion between the parties. All this assumed some price control. The ICTU expected employers to now enter into negotiations 'in accordance with the spirit of the guidelines.' On 25 April the NEC urged Officials to immediately engage employers. From then on the Tenth Round 'was practically wrapped up within three months'—'one of the speediest Rounds' since 1946.

Although agreement was 'speedy and effective', some strikes were necessary. The two biggest, of bank workers and British seamen, did not directly involve the ITGWU. An eighteen-week strike in papermaking in Dublin and Waterford did. Class 1 members now received £7 10s in Strike Pay, and £116,659 was paid out. On occasion members tended to 'rush in,' perhaps because of inexperience or a false belief that serving strike notice caused the employer to cave in. The NEC insisted that appropriate conciliation machinery be used, decisions for industrial action be by ballot, in accordance with Rule, and that members 'must have a responsible appreciation of the impact and ramifications' of their actions.

The central issue in the paper mills was the introduction of four-shift working. It was resolved after interventions by the Labour Court and an independent Tribunal and a visit to Sweden and England sponsored by the Irish National Productivity Centre to examine production methods.

Despite Tenth-Round successes, Carroll stated that 37.4% of all male workers had less than £10 a week; more than 50% had less than £12. For women, 90% had less than £12; 80% had less than £8. A National Minimum Wage should be £12 10s per week. There was much to be done.[19] There was great resentment at additional benefits the FUE conceded to craftsmen.

The press blamed unions for constant disruption. The ITGWU invited it to 'start now to seek the truth' and 'set out clearly and fully the dividends paid, directors' fees, salaries, wages, hours of work, holidays, sickness payments and all other perquisites and privileges.' It should 'publish fully and truthfully all of the facts relating to the national income' and 'details of its distribution.' This would be a 'first essential to industrial peace and improved industrial relations.'

In April 1967 income *per capita* in the Republic was £279, as against £520 in Britain, an 86% difference. Why was the gap so large? With membership of the Common Market possible, what could be done to close it? The Scandinavian rather than British model was cited as a solution.

The co-operative nature of their society offered greater hope. On 25 November the NEC published a Workers' Charter and Action Plan for a Workers' Charter. The year closed 'with a major step by our Union, a step on the road to a planned and progressive improvement in the way of life and standard of living' of members. Conroy welcomed 1968 Delegates to 'Ireland's largest, most important and most militant Trade Union,' a claim borne out by the amounts dispensed on Dispute Pay in pursuit of the progressive Charter.[20]

Attention turned to poorly paid public-sector workers. Conroy saw 'no attempt' by state or local authorities to see that those 'not in a strong bargaining position' were 'justly paid and fairly treated.' Neither had they 'effective negotiating machinery.' Despite threats of impending restrictive legislation and the emotive EI strike in Shannon, the Conference agonised over the value of a strike. F. McLoughlin (Dublin No. 3) caught the mood in an almost heretical statement. 'Nowadays it seems that if anybody carries a placard outside a job the workers will stand across the road like sheep, afraid to go to work for fear of being called a scab. Surely there must be responsible people in these jobs who will say to the sheep, "Go to work and if you want industrial action then get the official action through your union."' Denis Carr (Dublin No. 8) said that, while it was right to criticise unofficial strikes, the question was, what motivated strikers? The Action Programme was welcomed, if not fully comprehended. Members primarily judged wage policy by their own purchasing power.

Éamonn Lawless (Dublin No. 14) again called for all future Agreements to be subject to membership ballot. He opposed the Action Programme as a 'petty and disgraceful defence of bureaucratic manoeuvring' by the NEC. It was an 'Inaction Programme'. The Conference should 'not be treated as a rubber stamp for NEC considerations.' Carroll acknowledged criticism but urged support. It got under way in 1968, and more than 90% of members achieved favourable returns.

Table 95: ITGWU Action Programme for a Workers' Charter, 1968

1.	A campaign be initiated to get acceptance by employers in the private and public sectors of our economy that all male workers in receipt of less than £12 10s a week basic should be brought up to that level with related increases for adult females and juveniles. It is recognised that having regard to present wage levels, productivity and viability, this target may require phasing.
2.	A campaign be initiated to have contract Agreements entered into to include an increase in wage rates of 25/– per week to compensate workers for the increase in the cost of living since the seeking of the £1 increase secured in early 1966. Again, in certain circumstances, a phasing of this amount over 1968 may be appropriate.
3.	That contractual Agreements be negotiated on a long-term basis, say three to five years, in which provision is made for—
	(*a*) retention of purchasing value by agreed periodic cost of living adjustments, plus
	(*b*) the improvement in living standards by the application of annual agreed increases in real wages.

4. These contractual Agreements to have regard also to the following targets:
    (a) a 40-hour week
    (b) an increase in the number of paid holidays
    (c) payment of wages during illness
    (d) the provision of retirement pensions, service pay, etc.
    (e) reduction of lengthy salary scale incremental periods
    (f) reduction in area wage differentials
    (g) equal pay for work of equal value as between men and women.

5. That such Agreements also make adequate provision for grievance, negotiation and conciliation procedures and machinery and that the concept of good industrial and human relations be promoted with particular reference to matters of discipline.

6. That pressure be continued on Government for the speedy revision of our social services and amenities and that recognition be given to the special importance of Children's Allowances in the case of large families and for the provision of financial sustenance to parents or guardians of children from 14 years of age upwards who are attending educational, vocational or training establishments on a full-time basis, i.e. five days a week.

7. That social justice be our motivating purpose.

The forty-hour week was widely gained; and so common was three weeks' annual holiday that the Government was pressed to amend the Holidays (Employees) Act (1961) accordingly. Progress was made on sickness pay, service pay and pensions. £85,592 was dispensed in Dispute Benefit, with all strikes of short duration. The Minister for Finance, Charles Haughey, declined to meet the NEC to discuss the Action Programme. The union was 'constrained' to write to him, including a Memorandum relating to wage increases, improved Children's Allowances and a 'just living wage for [public-sector] manual workers.' In the Department of Health more than 4,000 adult males were on gross wages of less than £10 a week; 4,000 in National Transport Services were paid £9 14s 2d to £11 3s per week; 12,000 county council men got £9 10s; in the Department of Defence about 1,000 earned a mere £9; while in the Department of Land more than 4,000 earned only £8 16s. The NEC hoped for an 'urgent and sympathetic response' from Haughey, who refused to meet a pre-Budget Delegation.

Eddie Lawless complained of Dáil Deputies' bad example in giving themselves £1,000-a-year increases 'while organised workers were required to be satisfied with an increase of £1 per week' and social welfare beneficiaries a 'mere pittance.' Forty-three Delegates contributed to a high-quality debate.

In 1969 Dispute Pay was £261,491. The Maintenance Strike involved 14,000 members, accounting for £210,972, or 81% of this. Major disputes were in Texaco (414 members, four weeks, £10,383), Goulding's (512 members, three weeks, £16,135) and Irish Glass Bottle (537 members, two weeks, £6,723).

The Eleventh Round concluded early in the year. Maintenance and building-sector settlements increased disquiet among others, including public servants, as inflation eroded the money value of awards. Within the Eleventh Round the ITGWU vainly tried to 'get a completely new concept accepted and applied': that wage adjustments would 'restore lost purchasing power plus agreed upward adjustments, over a predetermined period, that would have due regard to future price fluctuations, relativities where appropriate, skills, responsibilities, functions, and of course productivity.'[21] The Action Programme was an 'opportunity for a deeper and more active participation' within work-places, including access to financial and economic data. Commitment to industrial democracy remained a central element.

THE EDUCATIONAL COMPANY CASE

In 1959 the Irish Union of Distributive Workers and Clerks organised sixteen out of forty-nine clerical workers in the Educational Company of Ireland. On 29 February 1960 they placed pickets against nine colleagues who refused to join the union. The company obtained an injunction restraining them. Matters proceeded to the Supreme Court, where a majority of three to two decided that there was a trade dispute as defined by the Trade Disputes Act (1906) but that picketing to coerce workers to join a union was repugnant to the Constitution. This invalidated the trade dispute and made the picketing unlawful. The Taoiseach, Seán Lemass, set up a Working Party in 1963 to examine trade union law and to 'consider how, without conflicting with the Supreme Court, the right to picket can be safeguarded.'

In 1964 the ITGWU called for legislation to support the 'rights of association guaranteed under the Constitution.' In 1965 Paddy Armstrong (Dublin No. 13) wanted a Congress campaign 'to enable workers to take action against recalcitrants without leaving themselves open to legal action.' In 1966 Patrick Hillery, Minister for Labour, made comprehensive suggestions for alterations to trade union and industrial relations law. An ICTU Working Party reported on 16 December to codify a response. Carroll opposed legislation, on the argument that 'we will do it ourselves,' but they patently failed to do so. The Maintenance Dispute in 1969 brought matters to a head. Eddie Lawless wanted a campaign against the Criminal Justice Bill and 'any effort to introduce repressive trade union legislation.'[22]

THE EI DISPUTE

In 1967 Paddy Donegan, Group Secretary, noted that EI Shannon, a subsidiary of General Electric Company with more than 1,000 employees in Shannon Industrial Estate, had 'been non-union since it commenced operations five years ago.' In July the ITGWU secured a 'foothold' when some workers joined. Claims for 'a shorter working week, extra holidays, a revised wage structure and increased premium for shift workers' were served. The American company refused to negotiate or attend conciliation. It would not recognise the ITGWU, continuing 'to deal direct with their employees and not through a third party.' Strike notice, served in October, was withdrawn after intervention by the Labour Court. The company agreed to meet the union, 'with a view to drawing up an Agreement,' but little progress was made.

In May 1968 the ITGWU published its Labour Court submission of 18 April to broadcast the facts. A settlement was effected on 28 June by ballot of terms that gave 'to the Union and the members concerned practically everything for which the strike was fought.' That union recognition was ultimately won was highly significant, as subsequent transnational companies were less inclined to resist unionisation. Employers' bodies and state agencies accepted, indeed promoted, unionisation, setting the stage for pre-emptive closed-shop Agreements, Deduction at Source and the rapid expansion of union membership and income. This was sold on the servicing model and the belief that joint recognition more readily facilitated smooth industrial relations.

EI's recognition was heralded in *Liberty* in June 1969. During the strike 'tempers became frayed in the District' and 'resulted in the burning of a number of buses in Limerick and other areas.' None of this was published in *Liberty*. Indeed coverage was sparse during the strike.

The closure of Potez at Baldonnel, Co. Dublin, cost a hundred jobs 'without prior consultation with anybody and in indecent haste.' It illustrated 'the tremendous power which absentee landlords and foreign-based firms' wielded. Jobs were wanted, but not at any price. The ITGWU warned the Government: 'Take care, Mr. Minister, that the real cost of providing jobs only in the short-term, jobs which have a political rather than a social impetus, is a cost which the Irish nation will not bear in the long run.'[23] Selling 'cheap labour' was dangerous. Potez served as an example that a stronger economy would be built by fully developing natural resources and indigenous industry, improving education and training and creating higher added value or technically more advanced jobs.

THE MAINTENANCE DISPUTE

In 1968 Seán Ó Murchú, Group Secretary, raised eyebrows and hackles when condemning 'blackmail picketing' placed without warning or inter-union consultation. Such pickets were 'industrial cannibalism' and anathema to Socialist trade unionists. Passing pickets was still sacrosanct, and Ó Murchú shocked by advising: 'Yes, pass them! Until they learn how to conduct their trade unionism in an organised and self-disciplined trade union fashion.'

Events quickly defined things even more clearly than this attempt to preach new reason. In February 1969 the ITGWU complained about the 'dictatorship of the minority' and 'one of the most serious crises' in the movement's history. The threat could not be blamed on employers or the Government: 'on the contrary, this threat to the life and future of the movement' came 'from within its own ranks.' Carroll posed a question many asked: 'What in heaven's name went wrong with industrial relations, collective bargaining and wages policy?' Thousands were out because a minority, irrespective of their case, ignored procedures. This strengthened the hands of those wanting tighter controls over unions. He concluded: 'The picket has assumed such a hypnotic force' and has 'been so unwisely abused in recent times that even good ardent trade unionists are having second thoughts about the wisdom of industrial disputes brought about mainly by pickets, irrespective of the basis for mounting them.' Pickets must be respected, but respect had to be won. So indiscriminately was the strike weapon being used that there was 'little purpose in negotiating grievance procedures with employers.'

The strike became the object rather than a tactical weapon, blunting its effectiveness. There were fears that the Trade Disputes Act (1906) would be modified and that it would be illegal to strike during the lifetime of an Agreement. The movement had to have a long, hard look at itself.

The simple facts were that 3,000 craftsmen 'rendered approximately 35,000 industrial workers unemployed' in a strike from 24 January to 10 March. The ITGWU repeatedly asked, 'Why? Why did it have to happen?' Its Workers' Charter was underpinned by the values of social justice, the collective paramount over self or Section and the greatest concern for the lowest-paid. It was hoped that the 'present gloom' would not befog the Charter's validity.

Unions spent more than £400,000 on Dispute Pay. Little consideration for industry was given either by unions or the FUE should the negotiated 1966 Maintenance Agreement collapse. The Maintenance Group 'operated without a constitution or Rules' and entered no formal arrangement with Congress, which received notice of intention to strike only on 18 January, with no firms identified. No notification was given to other unions, and replies to Congress's requests for information, when they were received, were late and inadequate. Some craft unions took no strike ballot. All of this breached 1968 Congress policy, requiring inter-union notification and consultation.

The appeal of the Executive Council of Congress on 23 January for a delay and the suspension of pickets to enable talks to take place on 4 February went unheeded. While condemning the authority of the Strike Committee as 'unique', Congress was correct but also negligent in not recognising weaknesses in its own procedures and authority. The ITGWU held these criticisms but did not openly express them.[24] The eventual outcome was the ICTU All-Out Picket system.

BUS WORKERS AND THE NBU

Although bus workers obtained wage increases of 12s for men and 8s for women, cross-channel passes, travel privileges and better sickness benefits, they developed a strong sense of grievance. The policy of the Chairman of CIÉ, C. S. Andrews, was constantly questioned. A dispute in January 1961 was based on a claim served on 9 July 1960, the long delay speaking volumes about the company's obduracy and the ineffectiveness of third-party interventions. It was hoped that CIÉ 'would square up to its obligations' and grant increases in wages and a reduction in hours that were unchanged for more than twenty-five years. In 1962 official sanction was given to the Dublin Road Passenger Section in an action against one-man buses, but unofficial action broke out. The NEC 'disciplined some members', taking a tough line: it would 'never hand over to any self-appointed Leader or group the functions and responsibilities' of the Annual Conference and the Rules, 'nor permit any individual member or group to threaten the free, democratic process of the Union nor weaken its standing and status with the community.' Success had come from the 'loyalty, co-operation and solidarity' of members. Not every bus worker heeded these messages.

In 1963 Conroy revealed that since 1934 the ITGWU's outlay on busmen exceeded income by £80,000, all but £13,000 spent in Dublin. Most appreciated this, but 'a noisy minority' were never satisfied 'no matter what service or cash benefits' were provided. The union was concerned that change imposed 'too severe a mental or physical strain' on workers. This, however, could not be used to 'compel the Company to employ two men to perform a task' that could 'reasonably be undertaken by one.' It was clearly uneconomic. This was not a message busmen welcomed.

Conroy was adamant. 'No group of bus workers in Dublin, Cork, Limerick or elsewhere will be allowed to use the Union for any wrongful or unjust proposal such as the challenging of a Management decision in what is clearly a Management function and responsibility.' A five-week strike ended on Sunday 12 May, and press comment wondered why it had occurred. A minority did not want one-man buses under any circumstances. The ITGWU believed the majority were prepared to work the system in exchange for extended benefits. One-man buses operated widely elsewhere. Bad human relations underpinned the strike, not least growing tensions between the union and the men.

The Labour Court submission on the one-man-bus dispute was published in *Liberty*, the WUI and NATE being party to it. They would do their all to win improvements for busmen before an appointed Commission. Jimmy Cullen complained about the union's press advertisement during the strike as 'not helpful.' He could not understand why no pickets were placed, 'only observation groups.' P. Allen (Dublin No. 9) worried about 'a small number of Reds amongst busmen.' A Conference of ITGWU busmen was held in April 1963. It heard of alarm among rural bus workers as cuts in service were threatened, demands for the provision of early retirement, inadequate notice of transfers, poor disturbance allowances and sickness pay, and the fact that full fare had to be paid, even by men in uniform, when travelling home.

The Commission on Pensions and Sickness Benefit payments reported in March 1964, providing after forty years' service a pension, when combined with statutory social insurance benefit, of two-thirds of basic weekly wages, effective from 1 April 1963. The sickness pay scheme provided between 60 and 80% of wages over a 26-week period of certified sickness. This was accepted by ballot. *Liberty* gave details of all advances, but some busmen voted with their feet and formed the Dublin Busmen's Union (later the National Busmen's Union).

In 1965 Cullen moved that 'any union not affiliated to Congress should not be allowed to participate in any benefits negotiated' by ICTU-affiliated unions. This was aimed at the 'splinter-group amongst busmen.' Andrews wanted to break the NBU, although his actions had 'encouraged [its] setting-up.' An eleven-day stoppage affected all cié operations as unions pursued improved wages, hours, service pay and annual leave. The Labour Court recommended an increase of 12s 6d a week. In 1966 Conroy attacked the management for resisting justified claims and those who 'sow mistrust' among members of other unions to encourage transfer or foment trouble. They were 'small men with small minds.' If they had real commitment they would organise the 100,000 unorganised rather than indulging in the 'treacherous act of poaching.' Such 'breakaway, selfish trade unionists ... contribute nothing to working-class solidarity.' The target of his fire was clear.[25]

BUILDING WORKERS

In April 1963 Thomas McCarthy (Secretary, Dublin No. 5) addressed the 'organisation of the building worker,' concentrating on their deteriorating position relative to others, although emphasising the union's success in closing the gap with craftsmen. A nine-week strike by sixteen construction unions in 1964 involved ITGWU members in fourteen separate Branches.

Work resumed on Monday 19 October, reducing the working week by 1¼ hours in the of winter 1964/5 while a Commission was set up to recommend reductions for the summer of 1965, a 2½-hour reduction being agreed for the winter of 1965/6. Reductions entailed no loss of earnings. A non-contributory pension scheme was introduced, providing a death benefit of £500 for anyone twelve months in the scheme. Examination of the feasibility of a sickness pay scheme was promised. The dispute received little coverage in *Liberty*. A pension scheme was introduced on 1 March 1965, and Branches were advised to remind members to register in order to participate. A forty-hour week was achieved in Dublin in October and a National JIC established in May.[26]

Table 96: Building workers' wage rates, 1940–62

	Craft rate	*Labourers' rate*	*Labourers' rate as proportion of craft rate*
30 May 1940	2s 0½d	1s 6d	78%
1 January 1946	2s 4½d	1s 10d	77%
1 July 1948	3s 2½d	2s 7d	81%
6 April 1951	3s 7d	2s 11½d	83%
16 October 1952	3s 11d	3s 3d	83%
28 February 1958	4s 5¾d	3s 9¾d	85%
30 October 1959	4s 9d	4s 1d	86%
28 December 1960	4s 11d	4s 2¾d	86%
1 September 1961	5s 6d	4s 9¾d	88%
October 1962	5s 8d	4s 9¾d	85%

Source: Thomas McCarthy, 'Organising building workers,' *Liberty*, April 1963.

HOTELS AND CATERING

In 1960 hotel members demanded a 'fair employment' clause, improved training and better promotion of tourism. The ITGWU was prominent within Bord Fáilte. In 1961 Michael Mullen sought a Catering Workers' Wages and Conditions Act to pre-scribe minimum pay rates and working conditions as well as improved technical and professional education. In 1964 Agreements with Dublin and Cork hoteliers were registered and a JLC agreed elsewhere. In the North the implementation of the Industrial Training Act (Northern Ireland) (1964) met long-standing union demands. A 'major organisation drive' in 1965 was followed by a 'new charter' for hotel workers in 1967. Agreed between the ITGWU, FUE and Irish Hotels Federation, it applied whether workers were unionised or not and was formulated in an Employment Regulation Order.[27]

MINING AND WHITE-COLLAR WORKERS

Deerpark Colliery, Castlecomer, Co. Kilkenny, closed in August 1965 with the loss of three hundred jobs, despite Nixie Boran's valiant efforts. Union Delegations met the Minister, aided by a mining expert, P. C. M. Bathurst. An exploratory bore was sunk on 9 November by forty miners. A build-up to 200 men justified the union's persistence and optimism. Boran joined the Board of Directors.

For Arigna miners the news was less cheerful, as the ESB sited a generating station at Ringsend in Dublin rather than in Co. Leitrim. More than 350 metal mines at Tynagh (Co. Galway), Keel (Co. Longford) and Avoca (Co. Wicklow) were organ-ised. In 1968 Castlecomer, 'despite the presence of a seam of very high quality coal,' faced complete closure without Government assistance. Boran was virtually alone in believing the pit was viable. Closure was announced for 31 January 1969.[28]

In the early 1960s, led by Congress, an organisation drive began among clerical workers. Liberty Study Group, driven by Dublin No. 2 Branch, held a seminar on 24 March 1962 that identified targets. By 1963 the membership of the Branch had reached 5,500, a remarkable growth.[29] In contrast to the WUI, organisation was among private-sector employments, with no policy of absorbing Staff Associations or professional bodies.

By 1969, despite some resistance and misgivings among general members, administrative, clerical and supervisory grades were a central dynamic of union growth.

INDUSTRIAL RELATIONS

Constructive criticism was made of the Labour Court in 1961. The ITGWU was 'enthusiastically associated' with its creation, and when industrial action followed unfavourable recommendations 'no organisation in the State' regretted it more. The NEC wondered whether the Court's title should be changed to Industrial Mediation Board. Should it have technical and specialised Advisory Services? Would specially trained Conciliation Officers be better than civil servants? What was its relationship with publicly owned companies and state services? Was there undue

Ministerial influence? The Court's failure to persuade cross-channel shipping interests of valid union claims was the 'sole reason' containerisation was held up in Dublin.

A hotel and catering workers' JLC was agreed in 1957, but four years later nothing had happened. Congress asked the Minister 'not to create further confusion in an already difficult situation' nor to proceed 'with the self-contradictory, illogical, unworkable and ill-conceived' Trade Union Bill (1966). An Industrial Relations Bill was welcomed for the provision of conciliation and arbitration services in the public sector. The Trade Union Bill pressured the movement to address its own problems by a radical new approach to picketing and multi-union strike policy.

The Industrial Relations Act (1969) created the office of Rights Commissioner. Con Murphy was appointed. The Department of Labour was created in July 1966. The Redundancy Payments Act (1967) was first among proposed pieces of protective legislation. In 1969 the ITGWU asked why the Department should not secure, evaluate and disseminate information to both sides of industry. Should it not have a statistical and research centre on wage movements, conditions of employment, etc.? Prevention was always better than cure.

The Labour Court's Fair Employment Rules would be the death knell for 'unscrupulous and unchristian employers.' Surely the Department could persuade the Government to amend the Holidays and Conditions of Employment Acts to reflect prevailing industrial practice. 'So what about it, Minister?'[30]

Not all welcomed the Holidays (Employees) Act (1961), which granted six public holidays and two weeks' annual leave. Michael Neary (Castlebar) was a lone voice when suggesting 'there was too much concern in calling for legislation.' Unions would be better getting 'what they wanted by negotiations.' In 1963 the ITGWU sought the extension of the Conditions of Employment Act (1936) to agriculture, hotels, catering, transport and administration, to reduce hours in those industries. Eddie Lawless (Dublin No. 14) wanted at least a week's notice for any dismissed worker, and for a 'clear and positive statement' to be made to the union representative about why the dismissal notice was issued.

In 1968 unofficial action in the ESB brought howls of press protest. Legislation, the ITGWU argued, gave ESB workers little option. Effective industrial relations machinery was urgently required. 'Legal manoeuvring' tied the hands of those who acted officially, creating the 'apparently ludicrous situation' that all an employer faced with a strike had to do was 'go to the nearest dispenser of justice whether it be in his home or in the Courts,' and 'by *ex parte* application secure an Interim Injunction to immobilise official strikers.' It gave unfair advantage to employers and denied workers their 'moral, social and constitutional right to strike.'[31]

Interim injunctions were turned into interlocutory ones 'merely by the employer alleging that the picketing was either excessive, not peaceful, a façade for some other spurious purpose,' or citing 'some nebulous point of law.' It was a 'mockery of workers' rights.'

PLANNING AND EMPLOYMENT

In 1960 Conroy felt the country missed two 'glorious opportunities, one in the 1920s, when it was 'frittered away,' and the second after the war, when Ireland failed 'to win a place' in food or manufacture markets when Europe was 'devastated, sick and hungry.' If the latest opportunity was not availed of, many more than the million who were gone would be going. It was a stark choice.

The ITGWU did its bit by 'utilising nearly all of its liquid assets' and investing them in National Development Loan stock and Exchequer Bills. It demanded 'a planned economic programme.' Subsidising landlords and giving grants to capital had dismally failed: 'we have reaped the whirlwind' in 'shameful emigration', declining population and mass unemployment. Careful lest such talk reflect Soviet models, Conroy rooted his demands in 'Christian teaching' but with temporal consequences. To 'take any dividends or profit or unearned commission' before workers were paid a 'just wage' was 'a sin, but it should be more than a sin, it should be a criminal offence punishable by imprisonment.' Conroy had strayed beyond the bounds of Papal guidance.

The expansion of public enterprise—Comhlucht Siúicre Éireann, Aer Lingus, Bord na Móna, Gaeltarra Éireann and CIÉ—was welcomed with satisfaction, as was Shannon Industrial Estate and new town. Paddy Clancy (Dublin No. 2) challenged suggestions that 20,000 new jobs were required each year. It meant importing 'know-how', poor technology being the root of industrial problems.

Adrianus Vermeulen, Director of Social and Labour Affairs at the European Productivity Agency, addressed the Delegate Conference on the 'Moral Evaluation of Work in the New Europe', a contribution that indicated the raising of ITGWU eyes to a wider, future world. He argued for the 'administrative, economic and social mobility of labour' within Europe, a theme now familiar but then novel. It did not stir an audience only too familiar with labour mobility. Openness to new ideas was healthy. Father Liam McKenna of the Catholic Workers' College addressed 'Human Value' and 'Human Dignity.' There was little that could not be achieved when men were 'sufficiently prodded and directed by a Christian Conscience!'

In 1961 the ITGWU claimed that the Taoiseach and the *Sunday Independent* publicly endorsed 'trade union policies on full employment, emigration and higher wages.' The Committee on Industrial Organisation, established in 1962, detailed retraining schemes for redundant workers, half-funded by employers and state. The National Industrial Economic Council, created in 1963 and comprising civil servants, employers and unions, fulfilled long-standing demands for planning and programming.

Éamon Wall (Cork No. 1) approved the nationalisation of the B&I Line. The 'principle of public ownership' should be the 'basis of future Government policy.' He criticised all Governments since 1922. 'Every idea of planning, every idea of the common good, every idea of basic principles were cast to the winds,' while the 'owners of money and wealth were given a free hand to roam and rob.' Public ownership was seen 'as something dangerous, something contrary to our nature, something sinister to be avoided at all costs, even at the cost of unemployment, degradation and emigration.' State enterprise was set up only because the private sector was either unwilling to invest or had made a mess of the sector.

In 1965 seminars addressed economic planning. Professor Patrick Lynch (UCD), Donal Nevin and Ruaidhrí Roberts (ICTU) added expertise, and Stephen McGonagle provided an All-Ireland aspect.

In 1966 the ITGWU called for improved redundancy payments and retraining. All grants to foreign industry should be conditional on acceptance by investors of all union and labour law rights. Deflationary Government measures brought the economy to a standstill, nullifying the intention of the Second Programme for Economic Expansion.

In 1967 Carroll gave his attention to the NIEC paper 1980: *Work for All*. In 1968 the assassinations of John F. Kennedy and Robert Kennedy produced a hard-hitting editorial in *Liberty*, 'The Living Dead.' The 'almighty dollar' was 'king in the USA. The coloured people can return to their hovels and suffer on. The hungry millions must continue to go to bed hungry every night.' At home, had educational opportunity for working-class children died with Donough O'Malley? Both countries had their 'living dead', the unemployed and underprivileged. In 1969 Fintan Kennedy called for a system of public accountability in all publicly funded industry. Not all money was was wisely allocated, and political corruption was suspected in an unsupervised system.[32]

EUROPE

Ireland applied for membership of the European Economic Community in 1961. The Committee on Industrial Organisation critically appraised the ability of domestic industry to survive open competition. Britain's application gave Ireland 'no choice.' James Blake (Cork No. 2) wanted Schools of Technology to prepare for the 'major technological and structural alterations' that membership of the EEC would necessitate.

By 1963 membership was no longer a 'live issue' after France vetoed Britain's application. The ITGWU's relief was palpable, as 'certain industries could not survive.' The union nevertheless thought 'there is no future for our country as an isolationist.' There was no mention of European integration or political aspects of the EEC.

In 1967 Carroll observed that 'stripped of all the verbiage and high-faluting talk,' if Britain did not gain membership of the EEC, Ireland would not get in: there was 'no point in anybody trying to cod us otherwise.'[33] In 1969, tired of delays in application, the ITGWU urged an examination of the European Free Trade Association— anything that would lessen dependence on trade with Britain.

SOCIAL AND FISCAL POLICY

The ITGWU welcomed PAYE in 1960 as a 'substantial improvement on the old system.' A contributory pension scheme for wage-earners was now due. Conroy championed a minimum family income of £500 a year, embracing wages, tax and social welfare in combination. Lengthy discussions covered all aspects of health provision, demonstrating concerns for the social wage and an admiration for Britain's Welfare State.

In 1963 Conroy dismissed increases in health and social welfare benefits as so 'tiny weeny' as to be 'almost immeasurable.' The sick, aged and unemployed were not apparently looked upon as 'God's people.' A 'few flag days' and 'collection boxes here and there with a little Poor Law assistance' were evidence that the Government had forgotten the 1916 aspiration 'to cherish all the children of the nation equally.' Demands for welfare reform were annual mantras.

In 1966 there was hostile, disappointed reaction to the White Paper. The ITGWU wanted the system totally recast to provide for higher contributions by employers, improved benefits, the abolition of three-day waiting periods, the prompt and regular payment of benefits, and pensions at sixty for women and sixty-five for men. Officials spent much of their time dealing with queries from members and their dependants regarding welfare and health entitlements.

In 1968 the ITGWU campaigned for improved Children's Allowances, concerned that many families lived at or below the poverty line. Rates were 'hopelessly inadequate', providing 2s 4d per week for the first child, 3s 7d for the second and 6s 1d for the third or subsequent children. In comparison with Northern Ireland the position was 'most unjust' and would 'be shameful or worse' from the following April. The 'modest' proposal was that the rate for the third and subsequent children be raised to 3s 11d per week. More than 20,000 children left school each year at fourteen. Domestic economic pressure was a factor, so a subsistence allowance of £2 a week was sought to retain poor children in school.

In January 1969 the union welcomed the Ballymun housing development as a 'revolutionary departure' in the provision of housing. It fitted the bill perfectly.[34]

HEALTH AND SAFETY

In 1960 the ITGWU felt that Safety Committees were a 'very valuable way of encouraging workers' to take a 'keen interest' in health and safety. More Committees would be a 'major step forward,' but the union still sought more Inspectors and inspections, the potential of Safety Committees not fully appreciated. Fear of victimisation inhibited their creation, but once they were established significant safety improvement followed. Factory Inspectors reported growing 'safety-consciousness'. The National Industrial Safety Organisation in 1963 was welcomed, with Kennedy a member. Alcoholism, as a social, domestic and industrial problem, was frequently debated.[35]

In 1967, after a period when safety and health were not addressed, Vincent Moran (Limerick No. 2) moved that it be 'compulsory on employers to set up Safety Committees.' The 'number of accidents, fatal and non-fatal,' was unacceptable. A 'greater degree of vigilance, education and post-accident investigation' and measures to 'minimise, if not eliminate ... dangers to life and limb' were required. Moran broke new ground in moving from prescriptive concepts to a preventive approach. Employers viewed Safety Committees with suspicion. If implemented, Safety Committees, through 'patient examination and investigation,' would significantly reduce accident rates. Pa Dunne (Dublin No. 14) wanted booklets outlining statutory safety entitlements. The absence of clear information was a central element of non-implementation.

It was the most comprehensive Conference debate. The ITGWU talked of the 'need to develop Safety Consciousness' and did not simply call for greater enforcement, higher penalties and more Inspectors. After 1968 safety slogans and guidelines on safe practice appeared in union publications, such as the 'Ten Point Hand Safety Code' (below). The emphasis on education and training for Worker Representatives and Safety Representatives increased.

1. Keep hands away from moving machinery.
2. Never handle broken glass or swarf.
3. Watch out for hand traps.
4. Wear protective gloves in danger zones.
5. Look out for sharp edges and spiky objects.
6. Wash hands thoroughly to prevent skin diseases.
7. Use barrier creams regularly.
8. Keep machine guards in place.
9. Beware of hot liquids and surfaces.
10. First Aid fast for all hand injuries.

In March 1969 the ITGWU reprinted a *Sunday Times* article tracing the history of occupational cancer, from the first recorded death from scrotal cancer in a textile worker in 1875 and its legal notification after widespread problems among Lancashire mule-spinners and Scottish shale-oil workers to research in the 1960s on carcinomas related to petrol and oil. It was a breakthrough, encouraging workers to think of occupational disease as well as physical accidents.

In 1969 Tom O'Brien (Dublin No. 5) complained of insufficient construction Safety Officers. Of 25,776 recorded industrial accidents since 1957, 1,668 (6%) were in construction; of 177 fatalities, 72 (41%) were in building. This atrocious record warranted greater intervention. Effective Safety Representatives with statutory powers would have been far more effective.

Continuous lobbying resulted in the personnel of the Factory Inspectorate being increased from 28 to 46, a triumph for prescription. A safety campaign gave Branches 'sanction to institute dispute proceedings against any employer who was guilty of disservice in matters of industrial safety and health.' The NEC 'didn't get many takers.' Concerns about job security and a decent wage 'combined to minimise all our concern for the best possible code of safety measures.' 'Despite a number of circulars' and pressure from Group Secretaries to set up Safety Committees, the response was 'very, very discouraging.' Workers lacked understanding and motivation: 'indifference and unconcern' dominated.[36]

ANNIVERSARIES

Michael Mullen, Secretary of Dublin No. 4 (Hotel and Restaurant) Branch, and Patrick Donegan (President of Dublin Trades Council) jointly directed an exhibition at the RDS in Ballsbridge from 17 to 21 September 1963 to commemorate the 1913 Lock-Out. More than thirty companies took stands. A 'symbolic centre piece—a huge phoenix rising from the ashes'—was the main attraction. Donagh MacDonagh wrote a 'theatrical masque', devised by Vincent and Jack Dowling, *Dublin, One-Three-One-Six*. The exhibition was opened by President de Valera. A second event was held in Connolly Hall, Cork, on 6 October, with an exhibition in Cork School of Art. There was no joint ITGWU-WUI activity.

The fiftieth anniversary of 1916 was celebrated enthusiastically, because, while Easter Week clearly 'belongs to all Irish men and women and, indeed, to all peoples who strive and fight for independence and freedom,' the Irish working-class move-ment claimed it as 'our own because of the positive and direct role played by the Irish Citizen Army under the command of our executed Leader and General Secretary,' Connolly. He was more than 'just a name and a memory.' He and his comrades' dreams acted as 'beacon lights.' There was no mention of Socialism or the Workers' Republic.

It was an 'appropriate time' to 'take stock' and develop policies for a 'more rapid realisation of the ideals for which our early leaders fought and suffered.' Re-affiliation to the Labour Party was an appropriate commemorative gesture. The ITGWU warmly welcomed Gael-Linn's film *Mise Éire*, not least for previously unknown film of Connolly at O'Donovan Rossa's funeral. The film-maker, George Morrison, was congratulated and stills published in *Liberty*. Cathal O'Shannon regretted not having it available for *Fifty Years of Liberty Hall*. From April, *Liberty* serialised Ina Connolly-Heron's biography of her father. The Taoiseach, Seán Lemass, returned a Tricolour pennon and bandmaster's staff taken from Liberty Hall by the British. Tom Ryan was commissioned to paint a huge 1916 mural to adorn the fascia of the auditorium at Eden Quay. Among many nationwide union tributes a wreath was placed at the exact spot in Kilmainham Jail where Connolly was shot.

Thousands from all over Ireland attended the Connolly Centenary Commemorations on Sunday 12 May 1968, where John Conroy, President of the ICTU, took the salute and praised the EI strikers at Shannon. Wreaths were laid at Kilmainham and Arbour Hill and a plaque sculpted by Fergus O'Farrell unveiled at the ICTU Head Office in Raglan Road in the presence of Citizen Army survivors. A Connolly Library and Museum were opened in Liberty Hall, where prized items included the casing of the first shell fired from the *Helga*.

In Edinburgh a plaque was unveiled by Jimmy Dunne, President of the ICTU, in the presence of two of Connolly's daughters, Nora Connolly-O'Brien and Dr Fiona Edwards, and a large ITGWU contingent. Gerry Fitt, Republican Labour MP for West Belfast, although moved by the event, regretted that 'I am not optimistic that today's proceedings will bring about the support of the Scottish and British working-class for Connolly's ideal, and my ideal as his disciple, of a 32-county Irish Socialist

Republic.' On 5 June, Roddy Connolly unveiled a plaque at Glenalina Terrace, Belfast, where Connolly had lived, with the Republican Labour MPs Gerry Fitt and Harry Diamond. The ITGWU seems not to have been an official presence.[37]

EDUCATION AND TRAINING

In 1960 the ITGWU accepted the need for trade union education and training but made no commitment to providing it directly. Officials needed 'longer' and 'more specialised training,' which inculcated 'belief in the working class' and a knowledge of trade union law, work study, job evaluation, productivity and social sciences. The union 'could no longer afford the luxury of a gentleman Official.' Specialists would be required in public relations. In association with Gael-Linn the ITGWU announced a scheme of Gaeltacht scholarships for members' children. The Apprentices Act (1959) established An Cheard-Chomhairle (the Apprenticeship Council). Kennedy and Denis Larkin were among five Worker Representatives on its Board, charged with supervising technical craft training.

In 1961 the NEC allowed the Liberty Study Group to direct internal education. In conjunction with Dublin District Council, more than 600 attended weekend events. Symposiums on the European Economic Community were attended by more than 500 participants. The Committee of the Liberty Study Group was Paddy Clancy, Des Levins, D. Collins, J. Toner, C. French and P. Brannagan.[38]

'Better-informed Officials' did not mean 'academic qualifications', nor that the ITGWU would 'saddle ourselves with careerists and opportunists.' While the Liberty Study Group and People's College had done useful work, 'the time had come when the ITGWU should have its own training school.' In 1963 Kennedy announced that the union intended to invest 'at the rate of £10,000 per annum' for five years in promoting training. Dublin No. 3 Branch set up an Education Committee as an example to others.

Not all agreed. J. Lynam (Dublin No. 1) urged continued support for the Catholic Workers' College, 'this wonderful avenue for adult education,' though an eight-page Annual Report of the college in *Liberty* hardly suggested a lack of ITGWU support.

Regional seminars organised by the Liberty Study Group were held in Belfast, Carlow, Clonmel, Cork, Derry, Killarney, Limerick, Mullingar, Sligo and Waterford. *Liberty* published articles under the heading 'This Concerns You', describing Rules and procedures, hoping to 'energise' members. All union premises should 'be used to full capacity' for education: the 'age of scientific management and know-how is upon us.' Trade union education was in 'its infancy', but the union wanted the child to grow quickly.[39]

The Liberty Study Group's 'highlight' was a national seminar, 'A National Incomes Policy for Ireland', and pamphlets on *Structure and Administration of the Union* and *Tools and Techniques of Trade Union Education,* the 'products of much research' but 'not dogmatic in the views expressed and advice given.'

The union's position was unequivocal: 'there is no short-cut to efficient membership servicing.' The NEC did 'not want any corners cut.' A twelve-week course by the Liberty Study Group for senior and junior full-time staff members was run from the newly established Liberty Hall Training Centre. In 1967 education Committees were formed in Carlow, Cavan, Wexford and Youghal. The policy was 'Educate so that you may be free.' In Cork, seven Officials and members were awarded the UCC diploma in social and economic science. M. O'Connor (Dublin No. 14) criticised the 'slanted and biased' views of trade unionism as broadcast on RTÉ.

In 1968 the Liberty Study Group promoted events in Ardee, Ballina, Carlow, Castleblayney, Derry, Droichead Nua, Dublin, Kilkenny, Killarney, Limerick, Mallow, Monaghan, Shannon, Tullamore and Waterford on productivity bargaining, full employment, social and industrial benefits, industrial democracy and women's issues. However, O'Connor thought the Liberty Study Group seemed to 'reign for all eternity,' leading to stagnation. The group was a 'voluntary promotional organisation' and 'never intended and never will take on the role of training and education . . . on a full-time basis.' The NEC thought the group was 'singularly successful' in its objective; but the time was approaching when it had to 'consider establishing education and training on a permanent basis.'[40]

LIBERTY

Paddy Clancy wondered if members really appreciated *Liberty*. The sudden death of the Publishing Comptroller, Richard Kinsella, necessitated a complete review. In 1963 T. Farrell (Clonmel) wanted a levy of 1d per week so that it could be given away free. In February 1965 Cork No. 1 Branch sold 276 copies per month, Sligo 96, Ballina No. 1 72, Cahir 60 and Foxford 60. Conroy urged every Branch to try to increase sales by 25%.

J. Finn (Dublin No. 7) wanted a Public Relations Officer to deal with the 'half-truths, the distortions of facts, the omissions, the statements taken out of context and the downright untruths' that characterised the press. Both the Catholic Church and Fianna Fáil had PROs—why not the ITGWU? In November 1966 some wanted increased coverage of sports and social activities, with a 'situations vacant' column, more competitions and prizes, and a sales manager. In August readers were urged, as the *Irish Worker's* readers had been, 'when you have finished reading this . . . pass it on to a workmate or friend.'[41]

LIBERTY HALL

In 1960 the Liberty Hall Reconstruction Fund stood at £270,000. It was 'hoped that at least the foundation stone would have been laid in Jubilee Year.' Flush with a sense of strength and new beginnings after Congress reunification, *Liberty* suggested that the Powerscourt Demesne at Enniskerry, Co. Wicklow, be purchased as 'an ideal centre for Conferences and Summer Schools.' There were no takers.

An artist's impression of the new Liberty Hall received greater attention, the drawings being presented by Desmond Rea O'Kelly and R. J. Biggar. In 1961 the total cost was estimated at £800,000, of which £310,000 was set aside. The foundation stone was laid on 12 May 1962, Connolly's anniversary. In 1963 the union cashed in £100,000 in Exchequer Bills to meet the outlay, which reached £316,082. What was 'the message of the new Liberty Hall'? It was a memorial, not least to the men, women and children of 1913. Larkin got no mention, but Connolly's legacy was cited as inherent in the new structure. 'His dream was One Big Union, and today through the medium of one Central Trade Union Authority for the whole country, that dream is realised.' The new Liberty Hall stood 'as a monument to his work and ideals. As you gaze upon it, that is the message it must convey to you.' In 1964 the Waterford Branch wanted a 'room or plaque' installed in memory of John F. Kennedy. Conroy felt that the names of the 1909 founders were more appropriate.

Patrick Delany reflected on 'Dublin's first tall building' in October 1964 as the structure influenced the city skyline. Its 'glass wall' was 'over-simplification', ignoring 'time and place, scale and surroundings and above all, colour.' The 'general shape and proportions of the tower block' was 'reasonably elegant,' even with a 'somewhat eyebrow-less effect.' As to the 'folded-plate roof of the observation terrace' it was an 'elegant piece of concrete millinery' that 'successfully crowns what might otherwise be too austere a structure.' He sympathised with 'those who find it a bit too jazzy for comfort.'

It was formally opened on 1 May 1965. There was a sense of elation: 'Liberty Hall is not alone the Union's Head Office' and 'centre for the servicing of our large membership' but 'a very special part of the Union and national history.' It was a 'trade union and working-class symbol respected and admired throughout the world.' Jim Blake (NEC) saw it as a 'milestone', but 'this magnificent building' would 'mean nothing unless it symbolises the things, Gaelic and national, that are part of the history and tradition of this Union.' The Annual Report recorded in Irish the opening of 'Halla na Saoirse.' It 'made a tremendous impact' in the North.

The building was occupied by staff and members from January 1966. *Liberty* in May 1965 announced a 'red letter issue', as 'all members of the Union are thrilled by the magic and the music of the words "Liberty Hall".' Conroy took joy in the fact that the entire cost of £650,000 came from 'subscriptions paid to the Union by the members and no grant, loan or other contribution' was 'received nor solicited from any other source whatever.' This was a signal comment on the ITGWU's strength, confidence and solidarity.

Old times and old comrades were remembered. Among those present were Rosie Hackett, James Hickey, William McMullen, William O'Brien, Cathal O'Shannon and Frank Robbins. The Connolly and Larkin families were represented by Nora Connolly-O'Brien, Ina Connolly-Heron, Roddy Connolly, Denis and Hilda Larkin—a welcome acknowledgement of Big Jim's role in the original Liberty Hall. The building was blessed by Archbishop McQuaid in the presence of President de Valera and the Taoiseach, Seán Lemass. Greetings came from around the globe, including one from Ethiopia, a unique salute to an Irish union that stirred international interest and inspiration.

In welcoming Delegates to the 1966 Conference, Conroy hoped they found 'this building up to your expectations' and that the NEC 'has properly and wisely invested your money.' The building was 'one of the sights and tourist attractions of Dublin.'[42] With Liberty Hall operational, the ITGWU purchased a site in Cork on which to erect modern premises.

During its construction, Liberty Hall was the largest civil engineering project in the country, testimony to the union's confidence and forward thinking at a time of low national self-esteem, of emigration and unemployment. The ITGWU made a statement about the Ireland it had long fought for, albeit in concrete and glass.

STAFF AND BAND

In 1963 Conroy talked of the need for new, better-qualified staff members to meet the new technical demands. The union needed

> men and women who are capable of getting the job done and not those who will make excuses for their failure, spend their time providing alibis for themselves, or in passing the buck to colleagues. In short, we want only the best amongst the membership.[43]

He could have been speaking of himself.

At the International Musical Olympiad in Kerkrade, Netherlands, in 1966 the ITGWU Brass and Reed Band won two first prizes, bringing 'honour and glory.' More than 35,000 people attended parades in the stadium and 4,000 in the Municipal Concert Hall. In 1967 the Band won the Irish National Band Championship, the Smithwick Beer Perpetual Trophy in Monaghan and the Pangbourne Cup in Reading. The Liberty Choir was also highly praised. On 24 September 1969 nearly 800 packed Liberty Hall Auditorium to hear the Band's fiftieth-anniversary concert.[44] Dublin Branches paid a weekly levy to maintain the Band.

SOLIDARITY

In 1962 C. McDermott (Dublin No. 9) thought it an 'insult to the traditions of the Irish people' if an Emigration Bill 'complementary to that of Britain' was passed to 'restrict entry of coloured persons at Irish ports' so that they could not enter Britain. London pressured the Government to introduce this 'colour-bar legislation.' The Taoiseach ought to 'resist'. There had been previous demands to restrict foreign workers to protect Irish jobs.

In April 1960 the ITGWU republished *Apartheid and Trade Unionism in South Africa*. First appearing in *Free Labour World,* it contained shocking images of the violence, poverty and degradation suffered by blacks and called for a boycott of South African produce. Conor Cruise O'Brien defended the union's non-cooperation with the 1969 tour of the Springboks, an all-white South African rugby team. Such a team was not welcome, nor 'any other propagandists of racist oppression.'

In October 1964 tribute was paid to the Transport Workers' Union of America, which was celebrating its thirtieth anniversary. Its International President, Michael J. Quill, a native of Kilgarvan, Co. Kerry, paid homage to Connolly, Larkin and

O'Brien, clearly having derived inspiration from Liberty Hall in forming the TWUA. In July 1967 the ITGWU hosted the International Union of Food, Drink and Allied Workers. In April 1969 the union expressed concern about ILO reports of the exploitation of young people in developing countries. Such exploitation was not seen as a threat to employment in advanced economies but simply as capitalism exploiting youth in the absence of effective trade unionism.[45]

THE COLD WAR

At the 1960 Conference a mass was held for deceased members. The ITGWU was alarmed by the 'mad-dog scramble to see which of the world's powers can produce the greatest weapons of destruction.' This flagrantly ignored 'God's teaching.' In 'our little green isle we have no say in such matters' and 'our views are completely ignored,' but the message was that 'we will not have in Ireland Communism, Fascism or any other form of dictatorship, either of the left or of the right.' Conroy condemned all 'colour prejudices, religious bigotry and all types of racial segregation and differentiation and all impediments to individual freedom and restrictions of citizenship on racial, colour or religious grounds.' This must be 'made clear to the United States, Africa, Ireland, Britain, Germany, Russia, Israel or elsewhere.' Neutral Ireland could provide leadership to non-aligned nations, but this was not suggested.

The Conference's reflections on international relations were novel. In July 1961 the 'Dockers' Tribute to Our Lady', a monument at Bull Wall, Dublin, was erected from ITGWU collections totalling £20,000. The death of Pope John XXIII was a 'grievous loss,' and 'it was but proper that the Union should join in paying homage to a humble man.' Kennedy asked the Archbishop of Dublin to 'convey to the Hierarchy the Union's deep sympathy.' The Conference was Adjourned on the first day to allow 'Delegates to offer prayers for the repose of his Soul.'

In the debate on health and social welfare Conroy pointed out the contradictions so evident in an allegedly Christian society. 'Churches are filled on Sunday' but there was 'little thought of social justice and of Christian action towards needy citizens on the other six days of the week.'[46] The Conferences of Christus Rex featured in *Liberty,* its line being peaceful co-existence and compromise with management. Archbishop McQuaid participated in the opening of the new Liberty Hall and in 1966 his message was read to Delegates, appealing to their 'sense of justice and charity' in striving for industrial peace. He knew it was 'consolation' to members 'to know that you have the prayers of the Faithful of Dublin' and prayed that God, 'by the intercession of Our Blessed Lady, may grant you the grace of wisdom in your deliberations and justice in all your dealings.'

In June 1967 the ITGWU looked forward to 'marching into the 1970s' with 'hope and determination to see justice done to the working-class.' It urged that 'during the next decade Ireland will not alone be a religious country but also a practising Christian country.' The ITGWU's seventies would be Christian Socialist!

Frances Lambert visited the Soviet Union, her visit including International Women's Day, 8 March. She was particularly impressed with the absence of unemployment and the ability of women to freely work, 'doing all sorts of jobs which are usually reserved for men.' The provision of education and of health were superior. She stayed silent on the 'godlessness' of Soviet society, concluding, 'All I can say is the women seem to be quite happy.' Hers was the first endorsement of the Soviet Union since the heady days of the *Voice of Labour* in the early 1920s. Elsewhere in *Liberty*, Father Edmond Kent, Director of the Catholic Workers' College, expected directions to emerge from the Vatican Council that would oblige Catholics to think beyond worship to 'certain moral obligations.' In 1969 Father Murphy advised Delegates to study Pope John XXIII's pastoral letter *Mater et Magistra*.

The Conference was changing, however. Clerical speeches became a formal courtesy rather than obligations of faith.[47]

POLITICS

In 1960 the ITGWU's re-affiliation to the Labour Party was opposed by those who felt the union should be free to 'move around amongst all parties.' Affiliation might produce a 'split in the ranks.' A Working Party considered that the time was not ripe to bury the past, but members were nonetheless urged to elect Labour candidates in local Government elections. There were warnings 'against Communism and Materialism.' *Liberty* republished statements from American bishops; but slowly, anti-Communism abated. When Brendan Corish became Leader of the Labour Party it marked a 'new era': 'youth and vigour' had come to the top and the Labour Party was 'ripe for the enthusiasm and fire of animated leadership.' Corish's long union association was not mentioned.[48]

In 1961 it was agreed that any 'Union Official who secured an outside post carrying remuneration' should not 'benefit financially.' Payments went into a Special Fund. This applied to any officer who sat in the Seanad. Seven of the Labour Party's sixteen TS were union members. Kennedy thought the Labour Party's relative success owed more to personality than to policy. Demands for the ITGWU to build a 'strong effective Labour arm' were resisted. Members 'jealously guarded their right to belong to the political party of their choice.' Celebrating the fiftieth anniversary of 1913, the Annual Conference called for a stronger Labour presence in the Dáil.

In March, tribute was paid to James Everett, forty years a TD for Wicklow and 'one of their own.' Corish regularly addressed the Annual Conference, often receiving heavy criticism. In 1965 Michael O'Leary joined him, reminding Delegates that 'political action was an essential requirement for social justice.' They 'must accept that political Labour must supplement industrial Labour.'

In 1965 the Drogheda Branch again sought affiliation to the Labour Party. Pressure of work and the General Election prevented the NEC Working Party from concluding its investigation. In 1966 it was suggested that Connolly's fiftieth anniversary would best be commemorated by the union 'solemnly declaring' that it would 'pursue his ideals by the affiliation.' In two years, 91 out of 116 Conference motions required political action. In 1967 the Conference decided to re-affiliate.

Liaison with all elected members at the local and the national level would be maintained through written reports and safeguards to keep the Political Fund within Budget. Labour Party and union policies were synonymous, and there were hopes for a Labour Government.

Martin Curtis (Mallow) opposed, as its adoption would 'split the ITGWU from bow to stern.' Many members were not Labour Party supporters. He wanted the names of Branches voting for and against published. M. Forde (Cork No. 5) said it was 'obvious that the majority of our members do not support the Labour ticket,' so why affiliate? They would lose their independence and bargaining power vis-à-vis the Government. Many felt that the union 'should be independent of politics,' although few making this comment were themselves politically independent. Opposition came exclusively from country Branches. The motion was carried, 176 to 15. Corish looked forward to 'an early and effective association.' The affiliation debate was conducted in *Liberty,* with O'Leary acting as Liaison Officer, stating the case for.[49]

Affiliation of 100,000 members, for £1,642, was agreed from 1 January 1968. But what did it mean? Kennedy explained: 'It does not mean, as some people have said, that the Union is going to be run by the Labour Party or that our Political Fund is going to be handed over.' Affiliation would be reviewed in 1970 and every five years thereafter. Re-affiliation was 'most significant,' but in reality, although contributing to the Labour Party's sense of unity, it did not increase its finances sufficiently for it to compete with the capitalist parties. Nor did it guarantee that 150,000 members and their families would suddenly vote Labour.

The 1967 Labour Party Conference was held in Liberty Hall in October. Members were encouraged to attend any sessions that they could as observers. O'Leary assured them of 'an impressive expression of ordinary people participating in political decisions. Democracy in action in fact.' Delegates would be 'teachers, dockers, university professors, farmers, general workers—a vital cross-section of our community,' with fewer 'mohair suits' than at other ard-fheiseanna but 'more honest for the lack!'

In 1968 opposition to Fianna Fáil's attempt to abolish Proportional Representation and introduce single-seat constituencies dominated. Its rejection was a 'victory for democracy.' A chastened Government had to address unemployment, emigration, housing, low incomes and educational opportunity.

In 1969 Éamonn Lawless objected to Officials standing for political office. They probably did Labour Party work on union time. This was a common objection among members from differing political persuasions. Thirty-two ITGWU members contested the 1969 General Election for the Labour Party, twelve being elected.[50] The Party's hopeful slogan was that 'The seventies will be Socialist.' The ITGWU enthusiastically believed it.

Immediately after the election the question was, 'What went wrong?' Irish people were 'not ready' for 'advanced theories.' Socialism was 'still a dirty word.' The ITGWU thought the 'new constituencies were more cleverly arranged than even

Mr Boland had been given credit for.' With no sense of self-delusion, it concluded: 'Socialism is not a feared concept' by workers and trade unionists. Wage and other policies had been 'modelled' on 'Socialist tenets' for years, and Connolly was revered. What was 'feared' was the 'power of the whispered word, calculated to impugn their motives and to question their sincerity.' Only 'a small proportion of our people' believed in 1916, but 'now, very very few would have it otherwise. So will it be with Connolly's Socialism.'[51] For the ITGWU, the seventies would indeed be Socialist!

Chapter 27 ✨

UNITY AND DIVERSIFI-CATION: THE WUI IN THE 1960s

MEMBERSHIP, FINANCE AND ORGANISATION

The membership of the wui remained relatively static in the 1960s. Finances worsened slightly, owing to an increased outlay on strikes and inflation devaluing contributions. The report on internal organisation was acted upon, but the sheer volume of activity prevented its comprehensive application. Sea and river pilots in Dublin Port—who had transferred in, out and back again—gained considerable advances.

There was criticism that membership did not increase with the economic upturn. Servicing existing members was 'so all-demanding in attention and time' as 'to make it impossible for most Officials' to direct recruiting. The wui became more 'Official-oriented,' and members increasingly saw recruitment as the 'job of Officials,' not themselves. The union felt it was 'overall public activity' that attracted new members, directly or through transfers. Members were 'the main, and most effective, recruiting agents.' New employers never recommended the wui to their workers, and the union 'had never been gratuitously presented with a closed shop Agreement.' Maintaining existing membership was therefore an achievement, as there were constant losses through 'death, retirement, marriage, unemployment, and emigration.'

There was some expansion. Player's Clerical Staff Association entered as an 'autonomous Section', as did the Guinness Technical Assistants' Association and the Radio Éireann Staff Association—representing producers, Inspectors, balance and control officers, announcers, technical and stenographic staffs—once they were no longer civil servants. James P. Kelly, former Secretary of the Gas Workers' Branch, now a Radio Éireann employee, was the Secretary.

James Byrne, aged seventy-two, resigned as Secretary of the Kildare Branch, one of a number ageing Officials trapped by the absence of adequate pensions.[1]

There were concerns at the slowness in accumulating sufficient reserves, but increases in subscriptions were opposed. Opposition had to accept the constraints this imposed. Legal assistance was altered, qualifying the previous unlimited commitment to members taking legal actions. Two cases cost £1,400—an unbearable burden. New Rules provided 'fair and adequate legal assistance' but protected the WUI from 'unduly heavy' commitments. There were calls for a Special Arrears Committee.

The problem, while universal, was not constant. In Guinness only 120 out of 2,500 were in arrears. Few openly admitted the problem, even though the GEC expressed concern. A call for a Superannuation Fund, from which sickness benefits, hospital allowances, increased Mortality Benefits and pensions would be paid, excited Delegates. Thomas Kavanagh (Chairman of the Finance Committee) cautioned that it was 'completely unrealistic' and a levy of 6d utterly inadequate. It was rejected, and more modest proposals regarding sickness pay were referred back.[2]

In 1961 calls were made for a National Organiser, a position unfilled since Christy Ferguson's death. Larkin said that the 'least part' of Ferguson's work was organising. There were a 'tremendous number of unorganised workers waiting to join.' It was a 'hard, time-consuming job getting these people in.'

Mick Moore's Tullamore Branch mushroomed from Tipperary to Westmeath, Westport, Galway, Carlow and Kildare. Not all were good members. Discipline was badly required. As a result of increased contributions, income rose in 1961 by £4,110, although arrears ran as high as 20%. Out of every 8d of income, 7½d was spent. The Irish Liver Union was in such straits that it supplemented its Local Fund through raffles. The *Educational Company of Ireland v. Fitzpatrick* case changed the legal position whereby trade unionists could refuse to work alongside non-Unionists and strike to enforce a closed shop. Picketing in such actions was now unlawful. Members were cautioned accordingly. The Irish Pilots' and Marine Officers' Association integrated fully into the WUI. There was a long-standing relationship between pilots and the union, especially between their former General Secretary, Des Branigan, and Larkin.[3]

In 1962 M. Collins (No. 1) worried that the ITGWU would gain a 'competitive advantage' if contributions were again increased. He wanted Congress to set uniform rates for unions. P. Dignam (No. 4) suggested that the Conference move from the Mansion House, its permanent venue. Too many Delegates came and went from the centre-city venue, many seldom returning. The guarantee of a good Conference was not the venue but responsible Delegates. In 1963 a Central Cash Office was opened, 'a long-held dream' of Smithers. 29 Parnell Square was sold, at a small profit, and a tenancy agreed. Smithers wanted Head Office built in College Street and told members: 'Don't let the question of money—a mere detail of £120,000—daunt you!'

In 1964 subscriptions were raised to 3s 6d, top rate, with corresponding increases in benefits. The Thurles Branch, with more than 1,000 members on the books, had only four hundred active, mostly Ballingarry miners. It was closed in March 1963 and the Secretary, John O'Reilly, let go. In November No. 5, 11 and 14 Branches were merged as the Meat Federation, with Frank Cluskey as Secretary and Mick Greene Assistant.[4]

The WUI considered it had 'an obligation to spread trade union organisation' and assisted specialist groups. These accounted for more than 7,000 members. Not all agreed. Séamus Bleakley (GEC) said they should be full members, 'in it, not of it.' They wanted the benefits but were 'not prepared to accept full responsibility.' T. Duffy (No. 4) thought five years long enough for any affiliation. In March 1964 the fifteen Dublin Branches had 24,222 members.[5]

In 1965 a Biennial Conference was urged, held outside Dublin over midweek days, consultative Conferences being held in alternate years. Members objected: the Conference was for business, not socialising, and important issues would be neglected.

In January, Denis Larkin was appointed Assistant General Secretary, to relieve James Larkin. The appointment was not unanimous. One GEC member observed that 'Denis is not lazy but suffers from carelessness and a certain lack of responsibility.' Simultaneously Breda Kearns left the union in March on marrying Paddy Cardiff. Half a dozen married women were, ironically, among candidate replacements. Kearns was a loyal stalwart, trustworthy and deeply respected, acting as Personal Secretary to both James Larkins.

Table 97: WUI membership, 1960–69

	ICTU affiliation	RFS figure		ICTU affiliation	RFS figure
1960	30,000	28,904	1965	35,000	30,048
1961	30,000	29,230	1966	35,000	31,309
1962	30,000	29,329	1967	35,000	30,716
1963	30,000	29,833	1968	35,000	31,373
1964	35,000	29,361	1969	35,000	33,352

Source: ICTU, Annual Reports, 1960–69; National Archives, Registrar of Friendly Societies, file 369T.

A joint Agreement was made with the Merchant Navy and Airline Officers' Association in London. The WUI would organise and cater for officers on Irish vessels engaged in the home and coastal trade. The association in London continued 'to represent officers on Irish vessels sailing foreign.' A Mercantile Marine Officers' Section was created.

The Technical Officers' Staff Association of An Foras Talúntais affiliated in 1966. After eighteen months of negotiations the Voluntary Hospitals' Clerical and Administrative Staffs' Association, representing more than 600 members, won a complete national grading scheme and salary increases. It was welcomed by the staff, the Hospitals Commission and the Department of Health, as it 'brought order, guidance and security where previously there had been confusion, a jigsaw puzzle of grades and scales and a complete lack of any sense of security for staffs.' The WUI was now the largest and most broadly based health union. In addition to psychiatric and general nurses it represented ward attendants, domestic and maintenance staffs, voluntary hospitals' clerical and administrative staffs, the Medical Laboratory Technologists' Association, the Association of Irish Radiographers and the Irish Pharmaceutical and Medical Representatives' Association.

In 1967 Smithers thought it 'time to examine' trade unions' 'policies and tactics, their organisational structures, their methods of work, but above all their relationship to the world around us.' One change was the introduction of the 'check-off' or Deduction at Source of union subscriptions by employers. P. O'Brien (No. 12) wanted a 'system of paid representatives' to replace Shop Stewards' Commission. In Aer Lingus more than £26,000 had been collected since 1963, the company receiving £2,000 or 7%. The problem was attracting and retaining Shop Stewards. Jim Quinn (No. 2) thought check-off would distance members. It smacked 'too much of Franco's Spain, where there are bosses and workers together in Unions.' Larkin opposed, because it attacked the root of voluntary commitment, the union's lifeblood. It was lost.

In 1968 a working Committee investigated the apathy that existed. Seven working parties were set up in June, their report being discussed at two weekend seminars that reviewed their outcome and reported back. A parallel report on internal finance and structure was commissioned. Cyril Keogh assisted the Medical Laboratory Technologists' Association, radiographers and other health service professionals. 'Apathy Groups' generated discussion on how to improve communications, service and, most crucially, members' active engagement. For a union that prided itself on being compact, driven from the bottom up and member-focused, the term 'apathy group' was a startling public acceptance of problems. (The record of the 1968 Annual Conference proceedings is lost because of a malfunction in the tape-recording apparatus, not discovered until the tape was played back for transcription.)

In 1969 it was proposed that contributions become a percentage of members' wages. Much was made of the cost of the Maintenance Strike and the WUI's overdraft of £25,000. The proposal was referred back. The Bray and Dún Laoghaire Branches were merged to effect savings. The union 'was not growing very much,' but staff numbers increased. William Attley was appointed Secretary of the Bray and Dún Laoghaire Branch in January 1970.[6]

JAMES LARKIN JUNIOR AND JOHN SMITHERS

Members of the GEC became aware in December 1968 that the General Secretary, James Larkin Junior, was seriously ill. In January, up to their necks in the maintenance workers' dispute, they heard from Denis Larkin that his brother was 'very ill indeed and that there was no hope of his recovery.' His death came on 18 February 1969. He had been Assistant General Secretary from 1945 to 1947 and General Secretary from 1947; a City Councillor from 1930 to 1933 and a Labour Party TD from 1943 to 1957. He was a member of the Executive of the ITUC and ICTU, serving as President of the ITUC in 1949 and 1952 and of the ICTU in 1960. The WUI said:

> He was ever-available to members, never permitting personalities or prejudices to interfere with the quality of the service he rendered . . . It was said of his father that he found the workers on their knees and taught them to stand erect. It can be truly said of Jim Larkin that in every way he showed the value of thought, of training, of tolerance and of understanding.

In May 1968, while WUI Delegates attended the ICTU Conference in Killarney, John Smithers passed away. He became General President in 1943. His financial management helped secure the union. His successor, John Foster, paid homage to two lost leaders. The death of Young Jim Larkin, 'on whose shoulders the mantle of greatness had hung so lightly, and with such modesty and humility,' was not just an occasion for sadness or pointless speculation about what might have been. Rather, his life should serve as an inspiration. Foster urged:

> Let us above all, cast aside selfishness and self-interest, and let us be seen to have concern for the least better-off of our neighbours, the poor, the homeless, the itinerant, the lowly paid worker who lacks the economic strength to secure some small measure of social justice. In short, let us, as trade unionists, always have regard to our full social commitment, and let us begin by reminding ourselves from time to time that Dublin is not Ireland and that Ireland is not the world.

Denis Larkin reflected on the difference between his father, who made 95% of all decisions, and his brother, who had a 'different psychology' and 'believed fundamentally in involving the members.' Denis succeeded James as General Secretary, and at the Annual Conference Paddy Cardiff defeated Frank Cluskey and Tommy Watt to become Deputy General Secretary. Cardiff accepted office with tremendous optimism, while reminding Delegates of the 'nature of the beast': 'I will have my row and I will put it away when it is finished.'[7]

Smithers' steady and reassuring hand on the tiller represented a link with Big Jim while being a voice for change. Nine candidates contested the vacancy for President—Stephen Burke, Mick Canavan, Paddy Cardiff, John Dorgan, John Foster, Leo Gibson, Jack Harte, Liam O'Dea, Tommy Watt and Vincent Wynter—with Foster, surprisingly to some, defeating Cardiff on the eighth count, on 20 November, by 109 to 101.

WOMEN

T. O'Neill (Guinness) moved in 1960 that, 'because of the seriousness of redundancy, emigration and the low marriage rate,' the practice of replacing male labour by females be discontinued, especially in 'industries under semi-state control.' He drew a Doomsday picture: 'for the continuation of the race we must have marriages.' If men could not 'earn a decent wage you won't have many marriages.' Kay Fallon (No. 1) dismissed him as 'ridiculous'. Women wanted 'equal pay—the rate for the job—and equal rights.' She referred to ILO Convention 98, calling for 'equal pay for men and women for work of equal value,' which 'should be made the Government rule in Government employment,' as it had adopted the convention. The Conference 'should not argue against women replacing men' but 'see that the women get the same wages as the men.' When automation came about, women 'will be able to press a button as easily as a man.' She failed to convince a male-dominated Conference, which adopted the motion but saw men top the poll for election to the GEC.

In 1961 the Women's Advisory Committee of the ICTU held its first weekend school, though some unions that represented women sent no Delegates. The Committee resulted from a WUI motion, but Fallon criticised it in 1963 for having nothing done, 'except to hold two weekend schools.' They had not investigated women's problems, devised strategies for their greater involvement in trade unions, or furthered equal pay.

Table: 98: Women in the WUI, 1960–69

	Women	As proportion of total (%)		Women	As proportion of total (%)
1960	7,501	25.9	1965	7,963	26.5
1961	7,713	26.3	1966	8,284	26.4
1962	7,742	26.3	1967	8,090	26.3
1963	7,925	26.5	1968	11,981	38.1
1964	7,618	25.9	1969	10,907	32.7

Source: National Archives, Registrar of Friendly Societies, file 329T.

In 1964 Nora McSweeney (No. 12) wanted the ratification of Convention 98 as a 'basic principle.' Civil servants and teachers were now paid equally. Úna Doyle (No. 12) pointed out that women got greater increases under the Ninth Round than men in Aer Lingus to narrow the difference. W. Hammond (No. 12) thought that if women really wanted equal pay they would attend the Annual Conference, whereas only eleven women were selected.

In July 1965 the GEC considered a letter from Miss W. Hickson, who was getting married and wondered if she could resume work afterwards. They agonised. 'As this was the first time that a woman employee' had 'requested such permission a long discussion took place on the principle of whether women employees should be required to resign on marriage.' It was finally decided that a woman 'might continue in employment after marriage for a period of six months when the position would be further considered.' Kay Fallon became Kay Geraghty in August 1965 and resigned from the GEC in November. When Hilda Larkin married Seán Breslin in September she resigned as an Official but was asked to stay on.

In 1967 Nora McSweeney (No. 12) asked that similar contribution rates be adopted for men and women receiving the same basic wages. It was a logical suggestion if they were to truly champion women's equality.[8]

The number of women members increased from 7,501 to 10,907 in the 1960s, an increase from a quarter to a third of the total.

CONGRESS AND TRADES COUNCIL

The WUI was proud of its participation in the first ICTU from September 1959. In 1961 Congress was asked to study inter-union problems, set up better machinery, limit sectional actions and provide for the resolution of conflicts. Larkin talked of discipline, acknowledging that most wanted it for others but not for themselves. He cited examples of minorities holding up entire jobs. 'When a picket is on the job, you just don't automatically take instructions from the pickets and refuse to work, you get instructions from your own union.' This was well ahead of concepts of 'Two-Tier Picketing'. In 1963 Congress bought 19 Raglan Road, Dublin, as its Head Office. The WUI 'contributed a gift of £1,000' towards the cost. It initiated discussions among general unions to advance rationalisation. Many 'wild rumours' quickly circulated that there would be 'one large trade union' that 'will swallow every other union.' In 1965 Smithers did, however, 'boldly say the word "amalgamation"', reassuring Delegates that final decisions would be theirs. J. Casey (No. 7) moved 'confidence in the General Secretary in any action he may take towards the furtherance of trade union re-organisation,' a display of faith unanimously endorsed by the Conference.

In 1966 WUI Delegates, acting independently, particularly in Dublin Trades Council, were reigned in to 'protect Union policy and decision' and 'safeguard' its 'good name and prestige.' A dispute from late 1965 in Dublin port revolved around a claim by dockers for a forty-hour week. The Marine, Port and General Workers' Union was quickly tested by the strike. The WUI gave strong fraternal support, 'from close association with the MPGWU.' It knew 'the very heavy financial drain imposed upon them in recent years through stoppages of work (not all which were of their own making).' The GEC appreciated that its 'financial resources would be dangerously strained. A private offer of financial aid was made and accepted.' An interest-free loan of £5,000 was given, 'without publicity.' The MPGWU subsequently publicly acknowledged the assistance, and 'at later dates' offers were made by others. This solidarity influenced employers, who conceded the forty-hour week.

In 1967 the GEC quietly gave a loan to enable the newly established National Engineering and Electrical Trade Union to open a bank account.

In 1968 the WUI noted the 'diminished effectiveness' of the leadership and authority of Congress. Practically no progress was made on rationalisation—if anything, the trend appeared to be to increase rather than reduce the number of unions. The WUI felt this diluted democratic decision-making. The new policy was

'one of strength through separation, rather than the old slogan "unity is strength".'
In addition, rank-and-file Committees operated in Aer Lingus, Bord na Móna, the
ESB, paper mills and construction, their apparent objective being to 'criticise and
condemn' Executives and Officials but 'to refuse to stand for election' or 'accept any
responsibility' while seeking to commit their union to their own sectional interest.
'It is clear that the time is long overdue for some basic re-thinking by active trade
unionists before irreparable harm is done.'9

RELATIONS WITH THE ITGWU

A strike in the CIÉ Road Passenger Section in 1960 had a less than satisfactory outcome, but encouragement was taken from the co-operation between three unions;
there was 'no foundation for reports alleging inter-union rivalry.' At 'all times' the
WUI recognised the right of the ITGWU, 'representing the majority of busmen,' to
lead the negotiations. The cost of a statue of 'St Joseph the Worker', installed in the
Retreat House in Raheny, was borne by the WUI and the ITGWU, each also contributing statues of Larkin and Connolly.

   In 1961 Séamus Bleakley (Athlone) complained that he was unable to secure
transfers from the ITGWU in the building trades, Caltex and garages because of existing Agreements or ICTU regulations. In September 1963, concerned about spiralling
costs, inter-union rivalries and the waste of precious resources, and mindful of the
ICTU's rationalisation efforts, the GEC investigated. There was a 'wide divergence
in respect of attitudes to politics, policies, questions of service and benefits.' The
general union position was:

> Automobile Drivers' Union: 2,000 members; £5,000–£6,000 in funds; staff of
> 2 or 3.
> Stationary Engine Drivers: 700; funds unknown; 1 part-time.
> Marine, Port and General Workers' Union: 3,000; funds £5,000–£6,000; staff of
> 6–7.
> Irish Municipal Employees' Trade Union: 2,000; £40,000–50,000; staff of 5–6
> Federation of Rural Workers: 2,000; £2,000–3,000; staff of 5–6.
> Seamen's Union of Ireland: 1,000; funds unknown; staff of 2.
> ATGWU (in Republic): 12,000; funds and staff unknown.
> ITGWU: 150,000; £1¼ million; staff of 250.
> Irish Women Workers' Union: 6,000; £30,000–40,000; staff of 8.
> WUI: 30,000; £140,000; staff of 40.

Larkin thought there was an 'obligation on somebody' to suggest discussions
between them, 'without any prior commitment.' The WUI staff would 'not be a
problem,' as 'many were near retirement.' Discussion in the GEC was lively and not
at one with Larkin. Edward Cassidy and Paddy Cardiff favoured building up
'another big union which will act as a balance to the ITGWU.' Thomas Kavanagh
spoke of rank-and-file 'prejudices against the other union and long-standing

animosities.' Kay Fallon feared that if the movement did not rationalise itself the Government would impose change.

Larkin advised against any 'preconceived view,' especially towards what some thought of as the enemy.

> When it suits the Transport Union they are more militant than us. Their big difficulty is their size. With their background they have a closer relationship with employers than we would have, or would want to establish.

The WUI 'should not go into the discussions with "a holier than thou" attitude.' Times had changed. Members' only loyalty now was to service.

In October the GEC asked the General Officers to 'approach the various general unions' to initiate 'discussions on amalgamation.' It would be 'made privately and not released to the press.' Larkin circulated GEC members with an alarming if prophetic message. 'While not unduly valuing his own importance,' he said that 'within the next ten years there will be a crisis for this trade union. Certain things may happen to him and at that point there may be a crisis.' There were 'no insuperable obstacles to amalgamation,' and general unions 'should enter discussions.' The ITGWU, ATGWU, WUI, FRW, IWWU and MPGWU were peas in a pod. In many ways they had 'sprung from a common source' and pursued 'somewhat the same policies.' They overlapped in 'organisation, duplicate, triplicate and quadruplicate staff, premises, activities, wastefully and ineffectively.' Staffs were 'overworked, policies clash and are unclear and inadequate.' Research and communications were inadequate.

Larkin did 'not disguise the fact that in practice the question which may arise' for the WUI was 'some form of amalgamation with the ITGWU' and IWWU. Strategically the time was right. The WUI held a 'leading place in the movement,' exercised 'very considerable influence,' represented 'a militant outlook' but had 'not grown numerically during the past ten years,' despite considerable recruiting activity. It experienced difficulty in 'securing adequate, qualified staff, particularly at Head Office level.' It was 'no exaggeration to state that within the next ten years or so, due to the age of Officers, retiral, health, etc., we can find difficult problems arising within the Union insofar as leadership and Executive staff is concerned.' The WUI was 'not wealthy,' and 'any surplus could be wiped out by a dispute.'

Cassidy had a 'poor impression' of the ITGWU's service, and Kay Fallon regarded the IWWU, FRW and MPGWU as 'breakaways'. Larkin's circular shocked. A staff meeting was suggested to 'canvass views.'

Was Larkin's pessimistic view correct? In some respects it was. Membership grew from 24,217 in 1950, reaching a peak in 1963 at 29,833. It could not break the 30,000 barrier, creating a sense of stasis. The high prestige of the WUI within the movement and beyond was a product of Larkin's profile and the respect in which he was held, rather than the union's. Perhaps there was a combination of arrogance and ignorance in the view that his retirement or demise would leave the WUI bereft. It was arrogant because, as events proved after his death, others within the ranks provided informed and militant leadership; and ignorant because, if talent was underdeveloped or unapparent, where did the blame lie? Larkin was all-powerful. He never replaced Christy Ferguson and undertook far too much 'everyday work' that, in other unions, was rightly left to Branch Secretaries and activists.

There was an element of 'fiefdom' about the wui. Every Section, even member, felt they had a right of access to the 'Chief'. Endless, trivial Delegations before the GEC gave it the flavour of a mediaeval Court, where clan members appeared and the chief administered wisdom and justice. Just as the wui's modernisation had awaited his father's death, it might cruelly be argued that further modernisation had to await his own.

It was unfair to castigate those who were suspicious of merger, particularly with the ITGWU, as merely being hostile to change or reform. The views of Cardiff and others regarding the development of a 'second' or 'third force' within the movement had merit.

In January 1965 the *Irish Independent* asked the wui if it wanted to place an advertisement in a supplement for the opening of the new Liberty Hall. The invitation was tersely 'noted,' despite Larkin's ecumenism.

The Working Party on Trade Union Amalgamation met on 4 March, with Kevin Lynch expressing the view that the ITGWU should withdraw from proceedings, presumably on the grounds that it was large enough already. Larkin's attitude to its massive membership was somewhat different. 'If they have a membership of 150,000 then they must be conducting their business in a proper manner.'

In 1966 there were further discussions. G. Monks (No. 12) questioned what a union of 30,000 members had to gain from amalgamation with the ITGWU. Molloy (No. 13) asserted that 'the late General Secretary would turn in his grave if we ever became amalgamated with that Union.' P. Dunne and Tom Geraghty (No. 2) proposed that Congress facilitate rationalisation. The wui felt that much union activity was 'running fast to stay in one place.' A responsibility fell most heavily on the wui and the ITGWU. It was 'no exaggeration' to say that discussions initiated between the two could 'materially influence and determine the future capacity' of the movement to face and surmount the problems that lay ahead.

On 22 December 1966 the GEC received a letter from the NEC of the ITGWU regretting that discussions had proved 'abortive' and suggesting a bilateral meeting. The General President of the ITGWU, John Conroy, suffered a heart attack at Christmas 1966, leaving the General Secretary, Fintan Kennedy, as the main mover.

Séamus Bleakley thought Kennedy's letter 'one of the most important documents that the GEC had ever had to discuss.' It 'would be an achievement if we could come to a workable arrangement.' Smaller unions would then fall in. Jack Harte and Peter Purcell favoured amalgamation, 'in spite of the bitterness of the past.' Cassidy opposed. In abortive talks, the only union that had been prepared to amalgamate was the wui. Larkin advised, making an extraordinarily generous offer in so doing: 'The GEC should face the fact that if we go to these discussions and anything comes of them, it will not be federation. It will be a merging of some kind.' If he were in the ITGWU he would 'fight to keep the name of that union which is of great historical interest in this country. Ten years will make a change in the WUI and we should talk now when we are strong.'

Ironically, at the same meeting the Inter-Union Agreement on Transfers was discontinued. The ITGWU was blamed. Both unions fell back on Congress procedures.

In February a meeting with the ITGWU took place in the Marine Hotel, Dún Laoghaire. It covered an incredible amount of ground: constitution and Rules; machinery; whether there would be a new name or an old name would be retained; Executive authority; finance; rates of contributions and benefits; employment of staff; pension schemes; overall policy. W. Hammond thought the WUI was at a disadvantage: 'we are not financially sound and our only assets are our General Officers.' When they retired 'there will be nobody to lead the WUI and for the good of our members, we will have to amalgamate with the Transport Union.'

This essentially echoed Larkin's 1964 thinking. He now appeared to be having if not second thoughts then wit enough to see the need to strengthen his negotiating team's hand. The ITGWU had 'problems of organisation and service even if they have no financial problems.' Wherever you go, 'everybody is, at best, disappointed in the ITGWU.' It 'is not doing the job the way it should be done. Nobody considers the Transport Union to be a good union.'

If this was so, why amalgamate? Jack Harte said that in his opinion, 'we belonged to the ITGWU,' whereas Michael Collins, who had been in it, would not consider going back. William Gibson cautioned that 'by and large' members would 'not join the Transport Union.'

Vincent O'Hara returned to reality. Ten years previously the General Secretary carried the WUI and 'stopped it from collapse.' They had to look at ways of replacing the three General Officers, particularly if no merger happened. A memo, 'Amalgamation with the ITGWU', was circulated. B. Carney thought the moment opportune, as the ITGWU 'wanted merger at all costs' and were 'willing to "give" on everything.'

The GEC accepted the invitation, on the following considerations: The WUI and the ITGWU had a common origin and common inspiration through their joint founder, James Larkin; both were Irish general unions, broadly following similar objectives; they duplicated each other's activities industrially and geographically, which sometimes spread over into competition and friction, wasting time and resources; their combined membership of 180,000 represented 60% of all Irish trade unionists in the Republic (40% in the country as a whole), and their combined strength would have a profound impact beyond their own organisations. Caution was required, not just because such a project was best approached gingerly but in the light of statements made by Delegates in 1966 about the ITGWU.

The GEC assured members that a full report would be made. Any amalgamation proposals would be subject to a secret ballot of all members, which was 'a legal obligation imposed by law on each trades union.'[10]

In 1967 P. Garland (No. 6) moved 'not to consider amalgamation with the ITGWU': it would compromise the 'brand of militant trade unionism' that was the WUI's 'rich heritage'. W. Hammond (GEC) thought the motion 'does a discredit to those for and those against.' Amalgamation could be opposed 'because you believe it is wrong logically' or 'for emotional reasons.' If Delegates were over fifty, Hammond respected their emotional opposition, but others should be open to logical, factual discussion.

H. Cobb (National Hospitals Branch) thought they would give the ITGWU 'back the fire it lost.' There had not been unanimity in responding to the ITGWU's invitation, but the logic was strong.

On 27 October the GEC was 'awaiting word from ITGWU re further talks,' indicating that the initial, frantic pace had slowed. The two met on 20–21 January 1968 and discussed improved services, contribution rates, benefits, and members' living standards. The talks concluded that the best results would be reached either by amalgamation or by merging the two in a new organisation. A special study would be undertaken. It would take a considerable time, but in the interval both would 'endeavour in their day-to-day work to foster and strengthen co-operative relations.' A new organisation was considered the best option—as eventually happened in 1990—but members were reassured that 'no binding commitments will be made without full consultation' and full ballots. The full WUI and ITGWU Delegations were listed.

By May there was no further contact. Progress was nil. Kennedy wrote in October and November, but Larkin was seriously ill. In December the GEC was told that he might be back by May 1969. His illness took minds off everything.

Further meetings were held in the Montrose Hotel in January 1969, although Larkin was absent. L. Hardy (No. 9) wanted 'a greater sense of urgency.' The WUI and ITGWU were involved in claims for psychiatric nurses, 'dissipating our energies' and what had become 'slenderer resources.' Other areas of overlap were mentioned. Vincent O'Hara (No. 15) reported that things were 'going to be a terribly slow, laborious job.'

In August 1968 Larkin explained that his term of office expired in 1969. Another full term would take him past seventy years of age. Were he to run again he would serve only three years. Whether with any sense of imminence or not, Larkin was doing more than merely telling the union of his intentions: he was giving them an opportunity to prepare. In the context of talks with the ITGWU this could not be ignored and was a motive for either amalgamating speedily or holding firm.[11]

Nothing further happened until 1969, when, after a 'brief conversation' between Kennedy and Larkin, they met. Information regarding contribution rates was exchanged, and further meetings were expected. By December talks were cancelled. Denis Larkin told the GEC that 'it seemed unlikely that discussions would take place in the near future.' It 'was possible that the new officers were taking a different view of things.' With the deaths of Larkin and Conroy, the moment passed. New men sought smaller prizes.

In December, with talks stalled, Jimmy Dunne and the MPGWU re-entered the equation with an informal exchange of views with Denis Larkin and Kennedy; 'matters such as rationalisation of contributions and benefits might also be discussed.' Further meetings were arranged but postponed. Denis Larkin asked the GEC to 'keep this issue in confidence for the moment.'[12]

WAGE ROUNDS

The Seventh Round, begun in 1959, was the most successful yet, with increases rising from the initial 10s to between 12s and 16s 6d. Increases, won with few stoppages, were based not on cost-of-living considerations but on the economic performance of employments. In 1960 the WUI called for minimum rates of pay and the 'setting up of proper Price Control machinery.' As the Round drew to a close a campaign to reduce working time to between 42½ and 44 hours began. Saturday morning work was largely eliminated, outside retail distribution.

The Eighth Round brought the 'largest wage increases for the greatest number of workers in the shortest period of time.' Members gained more than £1 million. In 1963, however, the Government attempted 'in crab-like fashion' to impose a standstill on increases. Tax was increased through a turnover tax, increasing fiscal inequity. Inflation affected wage-earners and social welfare recipients, with no sign of countervailing Government response. The WUI saw this is a sly but largely unchallenged shift from direct to indirect taxation. It had to be challenged.

In its White Paper *Closing the Gap* the Government tried to demonstrate that Eighth-Round increases outran productivity, fuelled inflation and widened the trade gap and balance of payments. Congress showed that, while company profits rose by 21% in the period 1958–9, wages rose only 4%. Comparable figures for 1959–60 were 18% and 8% and for 1961, 10% and 7%. The White Paper mentioned 'profits' only once in its justification of an 'unfair and partisan wage policy.' Wages, it was argued, should be determined biannually at levels linked to percentage increase in national productivity. There was no indication of controls of any other incomes.

While rejecting the logic of differential rates of increase, the WUI nevertheless did not reject all the suggested policy changes. Unions 'naturally would wish to have a national system for dealing with wage increases' and 'bringing under review all relevant economic information.' Trade Unionists 'don't like strikes and don't wish to have recourse to strike action if they can be avoided,' but they were 'opposed to fake incomes policy which sets out to control and limit wages alone but leaves profits, professional earnings all uncontrolled, and even unmentioned.' Adding turnover tax to this inequity merely confirmed the Government's anti-working-class nature, and questioned the WUI's reluctance to commit itself to political affiliation.

Larkin thought the pay pause was ignored and designed to slow down the pace of increases rather than prevent them. He had argued for a wider approach. Writing in *Bulletin* in 1960, he drew attention to the Wage Rounds' ultimate pointlessness. 'What do we do about our backward national economy?—Get more wages! What do we do about the insecurity of jobs, and about unemployment and

under-employment?—Get more wages!' The same was true of improving education, health care, pensions and social welfare. It was always 'Get more wages!' He felt
'we can go on with Rounds of wages increases—the eighth—the ninth—the
tenth—the eleventh—the umpteenth'; but all the problems would remain. Surely
the movement could produce the 'correct policies, the right solutions?' It could,
once it accepted that 'these problems are our problems and not anyone else's, and
we are the people who have to do something about them.' To do that they had 'to
think beyond Wage Rounds' and 'make full and complete use' of their 'great power
and resources.' It was heady stuff, and twenty years before the first National
Understanding translated his ideas into practice.[13]

The notion of national Agreements between employers, the Government and
unions was mooted by T. K. Whitaker at a wui weekend school. It was attractive to
many. The wui would consider it only if there was control of prices and profits. It
rejected the White Paper. Government pessimism was potentially fatal, and unions,
in resisting deflationary policies, 'reaffirmed their conviction that the economy was
healthy' and would continue to expand. Congress had correctly read the economy:
growth continued; the alleged need to restrain wages and salaries proved mistaken;
and increased purchasing power helped to maintain home markets and expand
industry. Intelligent forecasting and planning was required. The establishment of
the National Industrial Economic Council, whatever its 'inadequacies', was a success accredited to the unions. The wui saw it as the 'embryonic form of the
Economic Council so long advocated.'

The Ninth Round reflected workers' growing determination to improve living
standards. Manoeuvrings between the Government, employers and unions ran over
months. The employers delayed or objected, but the Government invited unions to
discuss exchanging industrial peace for wage increases. It was a strategy of wage
restraint and voluntary surrender of industrial rights, not least as rents, profits and
the farming community were not part of any equation on offer. Wages policy had
to be superseded by an incomes policy.

Claims began in September 1963, culminating in a national recommendation on
wages and salaries, jointly issued by the ictu and employer bodies, of 12%.
Although they were not as high as some increases gained in 1961, two successive
substantial rises were 'exceptional' and 'elicited widespread favourable comment'
in union circles 'in Britain and Northern Ireland.' Two aspects were not so good: the
failure to achieve a minimum increase of £1 for women as well as men, and that
the minimum was not raised above £1 per week. Equal pay and low pay remained
rooted at the bottom of the agenda. There were fears that, in the absence of price
controls, 12% would be dissipated by inflation. There was little the unions could
do about it save to warn that significant price increases would be quickly followed
by additional demands.

The fue insisted that working hours and other conditions remain untouched
during the 2½-year Agreement. Congress challenged this. Many employers rejected
claims by citing this fue statement, even though it was merely a 'comment on and

not text of the Recommendation.' Price rises ate away at increases, but the WUI reminded members that prices could not be controlled by Agreements, only by legislation. What was the best way to respond, 'by "free-for-all" or by national Agreement'? There was no evidence that 'free-for-alls' secured higher increases, but national Agreements incontrovertibly benefited the lower paid. Lump-sum increases were not favoured by the WUI, which felt that percentage increases generally benefited more workers and reflected economic power.

In 1965 Larkin again argued for incomes policy. He asked, if there were a 'free-for-all' 'will we refuse to accept that wage increase if it is not tied up in price control?' They were not negotiating with the Government but with employers. Employers wanted to involve the Government in the hope of having wage control. Anything the employers wanted had 'to be viewed by us with a jaundiced eye . . . We have resisted it so far.' If the Government was to be tackled, 'let's tackle it on the political field, but let's not line up all of our opponents on the opposite side of the Conference table if we are going to discuss a National Agreement in the future.'

From May there were 'widespread industrial tensions and disputes.' The National Wage Agreement was terminated and a new wage campaign begun. Exporters encountered difficulties, foreign investment declined, and British import levies affected cattle exports. Productivity slackened, but imports rose. The WUI rejected the argument that it was Ninth-Round increases that caused the economic setback, pointing to the speed of recovery, guided by union efforts through the NIEC.

The WUI held a Special Conference in June 1965, which endorsed the view that, particularly in the interests of the low-paid, the concept of National Wage Agreements should be retained but there should be immediate interim adjustments to offset price rises. The ICTU adopted a similar view. Discussions with employers lasted from September to December before breaking down, resulting in Congress advising affiliates to look for increases not exceeding £1.

In 1967 E. Dillon (No. 6) argued that both the 1964 12% award and 1966 £1 Agreements were eroded through inflation. M. Collins (No. 1) thought the £1 increase a 'great victory over the FUE,' but the GEC 'did nothing about wages.' In 1968, with discussions for an Eleventh Round under way, the WUI thought it 'most unlikely that anything in the form of a nationally negotiated figure for a generally applicable wage increase will emerge.' Some would criticise the failure to obtain a national Agreement as letting down the poorer-paid and higher wage earners in the public sector, but any possible emergent figure would have been 'at such a low level' as to have made it 'unacceptable.' Commenting on productivity-related pressures, it concluded that 'an alternative policy of "little and often"' was 'better all round than big sums at infrequent intervals.'

In 1969 the WUI welcomed the Agreement for public-sector wages, negotiated by the ICTU Public Services Committee in direct discussions with the Ministers for Finance and Labour, as a first step towards an 'incomes policy' for the sector. Tom Geraghty (No. 2) saw the proposals as a 'confidence trick', arguing that 'it is not possible to run an incomes policy ... under a capitalist society.' Profits could not be curtailed under capitalism.[14]

DISPUTES

A dispute in Ballingarry coalmines in 1960 'should never have occurred.' Originating from an accident, it began as the employer considered the business's effectiveness. After fourteen weeks an unsatisfactory truce 'left the issue unsettled.' It proved a bitter experience, however, as 'the very heavy sacrifices' imposed on members and their families 'were excessive and possibly unjustified.' The 'financial drain' on the WUI was heavy for a 'stalemate rather than advance.'

The transfer of payment systems from book Commission to wage resulted in members of the Irish Liver Assurance Employees' Union, a WUI affiliate, withdrawing their labour from Tuesday to Thursday, picketing Head Office, transferring payments to Liverpool and not their local Branches, and working as normal from Friday to Monday. These novel tactics brought a Conference but did not resolve matters.

In April a strike at the International Meat Company cost more than £600 a week, money considered well spent, as members got an increase of 13s a week in May. After settlement, the plant did not immediately reopen, and lengthy negotiations were necessary before it did. It was a battle to move from casual, piece-related employment, which, with large cattle runs, could generate high wages but generally were felt unsatisfactory. Members wanted increased Dispute Pay, complaining that other unions paid more. There was no parallel motion to increase subscriptions. The GEC insisted on full compliance for any benefit, that members pay appropriate contributions (many paid at the lowest possible rate) and that no blind eyes be turned to arrears when benefits were being dispensed. Rules providing for the remission of contributions 'make it wholly indefensible for any member to be out of benefit except through actual neglect or refusal to pay.'[15]

In 1961 most disruption came from a strike by the Electrical Trades Union in the ESB. The WUI honoured pickets, but members were aggrieved, as they had received no increase since 1958. B. Murphy (No. 1) looked for a new position on 'lightning strikes', as existing policy was ineffective. Richard Emoe (GEC) distinguished between unofficial action and some lightning action that might be justified and sanctioned. Generally the view was, why have a union at all if the policy was lightning strikes?

Dispute Pay was increased to £2 4s a week and the Rules altered to allow the GEC to consider, after a strike ballot, not just the numbers voting but the numbers entitled to vote. On occasions very small minorities actually voted. The GEC wanted further protection.

In 1962 a historic first joint action with the ATGWU won increases in Jacob's. In Fleming's Fireclay, Athy, members were either unorganised or in a dormant ITGWU Branch. After transfer, the employer tried to break the WUI by taking vehicles off the road and not negotiating. All members were reinstated and increases secured, and

Fleming's became 'a strong union job.' The £14,000 Dispute Pay was divided between Gentex (£4,560), CIÉ (£2,270), Dublin Gas Company (£2,302), International Meat Company (£1,172) and Jacob's (£1,510). In Gentex, action had at first been unofficial. Members were severely rebuked, yet grants were paid to strikers.[16]

More than 500 bus workers struck over one-man operation in 1963. The WUI was in a minority but was ably represented by Tommy Watt, Kevin Lynch and Seán Breslin. Improvements were sought in psychiatric nurses' salary scales. Securing 12% was no great problem, but advancing beyond that met resistance from City and County Managers. Níall McCarthy SC was appointed arbitrator at the eleventh hour, and his award showed he 'had fully appreciated' the claim's 'genuine nature,' and, although binding, it was accepted by nurses 'with acclamation and appreciation.' Much credit was given to the 'able and indefatigable Secretary of the Nurses' Section, John Foster.

Conciliation machinery was set up in Radio Éireann; Dublin firefighters' hours were reduced from 72 to 56; compulsory membership was won in Bord na Móna; and a forty-hour week was secured in Dublin bakeries. Tom Geraghty (No. 2) congratulated Mick Canavan for his work in Dublin Fire Brigade. Sanction for its strike resulted in more than 100 new members, bringing the union's share of firemen above 80%.

In September 1964 a building strike alarmed the GEC, not least because of the manner in which the dispute was processed. There appeared to have been no ballot or access to ICTU services. The WUI asked Dublin Trades Council for a 'Campaign Fund' to support building workers' claims for a forty-hour week. The Irish National Painters and Decorators' Trade Union led the charge but could only operate as part of the Building Workers' Trade Union, of which it was an affiliate. The BWTU did not serve notice. There was chaos at Dublin Trades Council. The ESB Group of Unions then announced that if the strike was called off 'we'll submit a 40 hour claim.' The WUI resented the ESB Group decision, and criticised the ICTU's role, or absence of role. The INPDTU did not reply to the Trades Council's correspondence. If the strike spread to the Corporation, Port and Docks Board, ESB and County Council, more than 1,500 WUI members would be out.

Finally it was agreed, in somewhat contradictory fashion,

> that, in the event of the dispute spreading, our members be advised to carry on with their work until they get instructions to the contrary from the union. At the same time if they felt they cannot pass the pickets we will accept that position and support them financially.

To the ESB Group the WUI stated that it was 'not prepared to be party to a strike notice just to support the tactics of another union'; but an extra £1 was provided to strikers. In October the General Officers opposed calls for a levy on members, although funds were 'insufficient' and voluntary collections 'infinitesimal.' If a compulsory levy were imposed, would it count subsequently as arrears?

The strike was over by 23 October, when, despite tight finances, the GEC felt obliged to match ITGWU Strike Pay plus £1—such was the pressure of competitive trade unionism.

Dispute Pay rose to £19,000 in 1965/66. It mostly went on disputes involving other unions, the WUI nearly always settling its disputes 'without having to withdraw labour.' Employers were more stubborn, however, resulting in more conflict.

Strike Pay was more than £35,000 in the first six months of the year. A five-day week won in the bakery trade led to the entry of the non-union Brennan's and the demise of Boland's, Kennedy's, and Johnston, Mooney and O'Brien, drastically reducing Bakers' Union and WUI membership.

As the 1966 Conference approached more than 3,000 members were on strike in pursuit of the £1 increase. They were 'fighting directly the battle of all members,' who had to 'be ready and willing to share the burden, possibly contributing in greater measure' to sustain disputes. If 'increased aid' were sought it 'would be a lesser burden than direct involvement and participation in the direct industrial struggle with its consequent disruption of employment and withdrawal of labour.'

In April, Strike Pay exceeded £6,200 in the Sugar and Confectionery Branch. The GEC worried about bankruptcy, while Larkin, not for the first time, 'urged no panic.'

Not all strikes were over money. A two-week battle at Lullymore Bord na Móna Works in September and October concerned the deduction of union contributions.[17]

In CIÉ the 'unpredictable and divisionary role' of the National Busmen's Union was castigated. Self-cancelling and mutually conflicting claims from the company's four unions were counter-productive and harmful. The WUI noted: 'It is remarkable that busmen who left other trades unions' to form the NBU 'because they complained that they had no democratic rights' appeared 'to be quite amenable to being ordered to stop work or start work by individual Officials or Committee without any prior meetings or consultations whenever those Officials want some cheap publicity.' In promoting rationalisation, the WUI found the NBU irksome. The NBU policy of one-day stoppages was dismissed as having no effect on the company but involving all other bus workers in recurrent losses of pay and destroying public sympathy. The WUI, ITGWU and NATE eventually went on all-out strike for garage maintenance men, causing the NBU to abolish its policy. They won their demands. The WUI concluded: 'If at any earlier period decisive and definite lines of action had been jointly and unitedly pursued' by Congress busmen's unions there would have been 'no effort to form a breakaway union.'

Dispute Pay in 1966 was £42,907, an increase of 130% over 1965. It sent shivers down WUI financial spines. Members were reminded that such payments could come only out of accumulated reserves. From 1962 to 1965 total surpluses were £33,238, an annual average of £8,300. In 1966 the Revenue Account deficit was £6,361, leaving a net sum of £25,877 for five years, or £5,170 per year. Dispute Pay in 1966 'absorbed eight times that amount.' There was an urgent need to control expenditure. Contributions had not risen proportionately with costs. Competing smaller unions made it difficult to raise subscriptions. One week's Strike Pay was equivalent to almost a year's contributions.

Table 99: WUI contributions and Dispute Pay

Weekly contributions	Weekly Strike Pay	Total contribution for one year
9d	£1 10s 0d	£1 19s
1s	£2	£2 12s
1s 6d	£3 5s	£3 18s
2s	£4	£5 4s
2s 6d	£5	£6 10s
3s 6d	£6 10s	£9 2s

Source: WUI, Report of General Executive Council, 1966–7, p. 10.

Many saw their union card as a 'licence to work', but the WUI thought it 'more correct to state that it is an "IOU" on the Union for an unstated and unlimited amount.' Lost time and subsistence expenses rose to £9,184, a cause of concern but a natural product of a year of intense industrial activity. The Tavistock Institute's inquiry into Dublin busmen's grievances was partly financed by the Irish National Productivity Centre; the rest came from CIÉ and the unions, the WUI contributing £432.

A long strike in Clondalkin Paper Mills began in May. Negotiations for a three-year comprehensive Agreement met the stumbling-block of the employer's insistence that both sides agree either to binding arbitration or to acceptance of any Labour Court recommendation. Members sought to break off negotiations, but the GEC wanted to obtain the best possible draft terms. The ultimate offer, in which the management dropped the objectionable clause, was accepted by only two mills of the three, leading to 'an unhappy situation'. There were challenges to the Section Committee's authority, underlining developing tensions between rank-and-file and leadership. The WUI observed that the case 'indicated weaknesses in the trade union Group,' lack of understanding between Officials and active members and 'an unwholesome form of activity by a rank-and-file Committee which sought to dictate policy.' Individual rank-and-file 'representatives' refused to stand for or accept responsibility by election to the Section Committee.[18]

Table 100: WUI Dispute Pay (£), 1960–69

1960	3,933	1965	18,361
1961	14,929	1966	42,907
1962	3,383	1967	6,074
1963	13,795	1968	36,972
1964	12,113	1969	68,797

Source: WUI, reports of General Executive Council, 1960–69.

Dublin and Dún Laoghaire firefighters struck in 1968. After settlement was reached with the City Manager through the Labour Court, a strike was unnecessary and was forced purely by the management's intransigence. A pay link with gardaí was created following a Commission established by the Minister for Justice. Tom Geraghty lambasted the 'yellow press' for attacking the firemen. He canvassed support for District officers who had lost their service in Dublin Corporation. It was a scandal, and Geraghty wanted a resumption of the strike until their service was returned.

Bad blood with the Irish Municipal Employees' Trade Union surfaced again after a strike in the Corporation in September, with the WUI complaining to Congress about the behaviour of both the IMETU and the Irish Local Government Officials' Union. The President of Congress met the City Manager, purporting to represent all unions, but the WUI was not consulted. The GEC thought it 'bad policy to object,' underlining the seriousness of the situation that led it to breach its own practice.[19]

A call to increase Dispute Pay to £6 10s for the highest contributors was made in 1969 but, given the Maintenance Dispute, was not well timed. Dispute Pay was well behind that of the ITGWU. The WUI had a current account overdraft of £25,000, and interest payments were high. In April many members were 'under the impression that Mr Merrigan [ATGWU] was responsible for the recent lump sum payments' in sugar and confectionery. Denis Larkin thought 'Mr Merrigan acts in an irresponsible manner when his Union is in the minority'—a common complaint of those who hurled from the comfort of the ditch. Most WUI members were not anxious to push the claim but were forced to act as Merrigan's shock troops.[20]

DUBLIN GAS COMPANY

In 1960 Dublin Gas Company terminated the arbitration Tribunal under Professor Wheeler that had 'contributed significantly' to settling disputes. Demands for reduced hours required industrial relations machinery, and the management accepted the idea of a Joint Industrial Council. Proposals for a 44-hour week were rejected in an overall ballot, although only shift workers had real problems. They won a 42-hour week after intervention by the Labour Court, 'a significant victory.' A strike among clerical grades resulted in improved wages.

In 1965 service pay was won for manual workers and new scales for clerical staff, together with improvements in pensions, giving, with social welfare payments, a pension of about two-thirds of basic rates (but only 55% for single men). Gas fitters were locked in dispute over new productivity proposals, the only fly in an otherwise increasingly smooth ointment.[21]

THE FIRST STRIKE IN GUINNESS'S HISTORY!

Job evaluation caused difficulties in Guinness, absorbing the Branch's whole attention. In January 1961 Agreement resulted in wage increases throughout the brewery. The Technical Assistants' Association, representing laboratory workers, affiliated. The Senior Foremen's Association, a house union, was bypassed when the WUI won the right to speak and negotiate for all foremen and supervisory grades in 1964, extending its influence 'slowly but surely' into 'all parts and Regions of this giant enterprise.'

A 'most extensive and significant' productivity Agreement was concluded in 1965 through a joint job evaluation panel, resulting in restructuring, regrading and large pay increases. Check-off was introduced but caused problems for Shop Stewards and representative structures. 'Wide concern and speculation' accompanied the final job evaluation proposals, exacerbated by their technical impact on traditional work methods.

In late 1966 large increases were sought, to offset expected losses of overtime. The Board made only a limited offer, and a strike ballot was held. Just before Christmas the intervention of the Labour Court effected a settlement, providing an immediate increase, conditional on negotiations on revised Agreements on grade pay and productivity. It was the first known strike notice in the brewery's 200-year history, attracting widespread press interest at home and abroad. 'The fact that Guinness's employees would even think of strike action, never mind resort to it, was so unexpected as to be unbelievable.' There 'was widespread doubt as to whether or not the workers would go through with their threat or whether the Board of Directors would permit such a stoppage to take place.' The impact on the national economy was speculated on.

The WUI was 'not overawed by the size and resources of its opponent.' More than 1,400 men gathered in the Metropolitan Hall to hear Larkin and to ballot on the final offer. The climax came and passed, with both sides learning valuable lessons. The WUI, although keen to settle all matters through industrial relations channels, was seen not to be bluffing and to have faced and accepted 'the full consequences of its actions.' By May 1967 peace had returned, with solid progress made in negotiations.

In August 1969 Jack Carruthers retired as Branch Secretary, having 'done an excellent job for sixteen years.' He was a 'very capable negotiator' and 'excellent strategist.'[22]

AER LINGUS

The Irish Airline Pilots' Association struck in 1960. A Labour Court investigation resulted in a 'better atmosphere and more effective machinery.' From late winter the company wanted a night shift for maintenance workers, especially on trans-atlantic routes. Matters were referred to Father M. Moloney for mediation, resulting in terms virtually identical to those achieved through direct bargaining. The WUI bemoaned the failure of group union activity.

In February 1961, 350 of the 1,700 members in Aer Lingus attended a Special General Meeting to consider what to do in the event of an electricians' strike. It was agreed to observe pickets, although IALPA members would 'take all steps possible' to ensure that their members were not involved. The GEC instructed all members to observe pickets. The matter revealed tensions between airline grades.

The WUI instigated the concept of incremental pay scales for Aer Lingus employees, including skilled workers, but divisions emerged within the Union Group, resulting in unofficial actions. In May 1966, a vote of 638 to 277 for strike supported a wage claim. The company offered £1 a week and some additional payments, bringing clerical staff above the ESB for the first time. The report of the Quinn Tribunal placed a Government bar on increases being paid for those earning above £1,200, but in June a three-year deal emerged, and the strike was averted.

In 1967 the retirement of Gerry Monks, a long-serving part-time Official, led to a debate about whether a full-time replacement should be made. Members threatened to revert to 'affiliate status' if no full-time Official was appointed. They were rewarded with the appointment of Joe McGrane in August and the establishment of an Airport Office in November.[23]

IRISH HOSPITALS TRUST AND RTÉ

One hundred and fifty members stubbornly stayed solid in Irish Hospitals Trust. Subscription increases in 1965 were not applied to them, 'as the service we are able to give . . . is limited.' Conflict over recognition flared in 1967, reaching the verge of strike and Dáil questions. Even without recognition the women gained advances. Some male cleaners joined, gaining increases. Recognition was 'pursued through the machinery available at the International Labour Office.' The employer's refusal to recognise a union was rare enough, and the Labour Court intervened on the WUI side, as in a newly organised provender mill in Co. Roscommon, where wage increases of £3 were won in addition to full recognition. The problem in the Hospitals Trust was that when the crunch came, women cleaners did not want to strike.

In 1969 the WUI sought legislation to 'impose a statutory obligation on employers' to recognise a worker's choice of union and to negotiate with it.' The recognition battle with Hospitals Trust was 'an annual event' at the union Conference. Cassidy (Staff) saw it as 'asking for a State sledgehammer to crack a very small nut.' After twenty years of trying, only 150 out of 800 employees had joined. Many had 'some form of physical disability' and worked under conditions where 'fear with a capital F' fouled the atmosphere. The management adamantly refused recognition, even though they dealt with unions in their other employments, Irish Glass Bottle and Waterford Glass. P. J. McGrath appeared to suffer from 'tritsophrenia', putting the phone down rudely whenever WUI callers managed to get through. The WUI considered blacking the sale of Hospitals Sweepstakes tickets around the world but desisted.

In the spring of 1968 a sharp dispute occurred in RTÉ. The issues were artificially distorted by media speculation. The WUI, with considerable membership in the station, sought to maintain and improve terms and conditions but did not 'seek to impose political, cultural or news demands' on the Authority. Equally, it could not 'allow itself to be used by political interests at the possible expense of its members' welfare and security.' The union issued a clear statement, seeking the reinstatement of dismissed members and gaining widespread acclaim for its forthrightness and clarity. A satisfactory outcome was achieved.[24]

TULLAMORE AND GALWAY

Vincent Wynter succeeded Michael Moore as Tullamore District Secretary in 1962. The Branch had 'fallen back' when Moore was unwell, but 'outstanding progress' was recorded in 1963, with membership at 'its highest figure ever.' Beyond the original area, Tullamore to Carlow and Athy, Portumna to Longford, expansion occurred in Galway among local Government, hospital, clothing, manufacturing and university technicians. In 1965–6 membership extended south and west to Ballingarry coalmines, Tipperary and Bord na Móna and considerably extended after check-off was agreed. In 1966 the South-East Branch was established in Athy, with Seán Breslin as Secretary. The wui still felt that provincial organisation was problematic. By January 1968 membership in Galway had risen to between 600 and 700. It became increasingly hard to service from Tullamore, and the Western Area Branch was established on a trial basis.[25]

CLERICAL WORKERS

Congress set up a Clerical and Professional Workers' Advisory Council to strengthen white-collar organisation. The Chairman was Denis Larkin, wui Industrial Secretary. In 1960 J. Cashen did not accept that Labour Court recommendations for white-collar workers resulted from honest considerations but rather reflected perceived industrial strength. In 1957 it had recommended that Batchelors' management trainees 'look elsewhere for employment at the end of their three years' training, enabling the company to cheaply replace them.'

In Dublin District Milk Board it considered those on £431 a year to be 'well-paid'. In the National Blood Transfusion Service it felt 'three-year contracts sufficient.' Larkin asked what members expected from the Labour Court. Its only obligation was to settle disputes; it was not governed by social tenets.

In 1961 Frank Corrigan (No. 15) wanted a Congress Charter for clerical workers. In 1964 200 members of the clerical staff of the *Irish Independent* joined. They had no fixed scales and very low salaries. The Printing Trades Federation wanted no new rates in the industry. After conciliation, strike notice was served and it was activated after Christmas. Pickets were not placed, but the newspaper quickly closed. A new offer, retrospective to 7 September, was accepted. The wui praised its new members for the 'intelligent way' they prevented the management's designs to divide them. It could 'well be studied' by those of 'longer standing' as an example of 'union strategy and strike tactics.'

Perhaps because newspaper staffs were joining, the three Dublin dailies, after consulting each other, refused to publish an advertisement appealing for clerical workers to join No. 15 Branch if not already members. The grounds for refusal, strangely, were that the advertisement was 'in contravention of the terms of the national Agreement on the 12% increase.' The ictu disputed this, but the newspaper managers were prepared to publish the offending advertisement only if the wui made 'certain amendments'. It declined to do so.

A strike by the Irish Graphical Society in the *Irish Independent* in the summer

of 1965 cost the WUI more than £800 a week, as members of the clerical staff honoured pickets. In 1967 No. 15 Branch had 3,000 members. The Quinn Tribunal,
which investigated comparable salary scales in state and state-sponsored companies,
sought to deny increases to those earning above £1,200 per year. Except in state or
local authority employments, union opposition defeated this; the WUI breached it
by gaining increases for the Aer Lingus clerical staff.[26]

THE MAINTENANCE DISPUTE

More than 6,000 WUI members were directly affected by the 'Maintenance Dispute',
begun in January 1969, either through their refusal to pass pickets or through the
running down of plant. The handling of the dispute and the failure of ICTU notification and consultation procedures caused anger and resentment. There were calls
for reform. The WUI saw craft unions as 'adopting some of the worst features of
capitalistic competition and so-called private enterprise initiative, in prosecuting
Sectional claims with a complete disregard to the damage which the activities may
inflict on the broad mass.' Correspondence from the ICTU Industrial Officer, Barry
Desmond, on 20 January was considered a breach of procedures for notifying
unions of impending disputes, as agreed at the 1968 Congress. This was denied by
Desmond, supported by Con Murphy's conclusion in his subsequent inquiry. The
National Group of Maintenance Craft Unions had 'no written constitution and no
formal relationship' with Congress. Desmond informed all general unions of the
notice, and on 23 January the ICTU Executive asked that pickets be held for a week.
Major unions ignored Congress's request.[27]

At the Labour Court fifteen or sixteen unions agreed to defer action pending
further talks, but the Amalgamated Engineering Union and National Engineering
and Electrical Trade Union broke ranks, placing pickets the following morning.
It resulted in 'utter chaos.' WUI members followed the union line of respecting
pickets but were prevented from claiming social welfare while awaiting decisions on
admissibility. Matters quickly became serious, and Jack Harte suggested a levy
under Rule 81 (C), as funds were 'seriously depleted.' An overdraft with Provincial
Bank for £30,000 was agreed and a levy imposed from 7 March, although Denis
Larkin, reflecting the confusion and angst within the GEC, thought that 'to impose
a levy now would be bad from a psychological point of view.' Conversely, to impose
a levy after the return to work might be worse.

An objective look at the union's finances was urgent. By 5 March a further
£15,000 overdraft was sought. The WUI showed a deficit of £33,965 in 1969, the
dispute costing 'in excess of £67,000.' Denis Larkin knew that 'money itself does
not win disputes,' but—some general unions might have argued—having access to
others' money might blind workers against defeat. The strike could best be seen as
a 'very useful or rather expensive exercise,' provided the right lessons were learnt
and just solutions applied. The WUI had 'no quarrel' with craft unions, nor did it
question the legitimacy of their claim, but their methods were open to much constructive criticism. The 'law of the jungle' should not apply to union activity.

Annoyance spread beyond discontent with Congress. The WUI's re-affiliation to Dublin Trades Council was debated, with 'more control' over union Delegates sought. The union reaffirmed its 'emphatic condemnation of the misuse of the pickets and its adamant refusal to recognise unofficial pickets.'

The Maintenance Dispute coloured all views, and there was fear of repressive legislation. Unofficial pickets were described as a 'menace', but Joe McGrane (Staff) argued that each case needed to be judged on its merits. Willie Doyle (No. 9) bemoaned the lack of moral courage that prevented members walking past unofficial pickets.[28]

PRODUCTIVITY AND PROFIT-SHARING

In 1960 there were calls for staff members to be trained in work study, job evaluation and productivity skills. Jack Harte (Guinness) referred to ILO materials and to the fact that expertise was available to ITGWU members. Larkin pointed out that 'you don't always get more money by having an expert to argue your case.' J. Dorgan (No. 13) wanted a 'system of profit sharing' in industry, various speakers citing Pope Leo XIII as the first man to call for it. It became union policy. J. Ruddock (No. 12) wanted worker-members on all state and state-sponsored boards.[29] There were consistent calls for greater worker democracy, even if thinking was woolly.

THE COMMON MARKET AND EMPLOYMENT

The prospect of Ireland's membership of the Common Market exercised the WUI in 1961. It was a threat to Irish manufacturing. For G. Fitzsimons (No. 3) the challenge was to 'organise intelligently' and seek worker participation to improve efficiency. Lower wages would be a thing of the past. Joe McGrane cited Pope Pius XII's concerns that 'complete internationalism' would 'submerge entirely national identities and sovereignty.' No conclusion was reached, but clear fault lines in members' thinking were identified.

Jack Harte (Guinness) condemned the Government policy of 'selling Ireland' as a low-wage economy. Larkin said he had 'not yet seen anywhere a statement inviting foreign industrialists to come here because there is an adequate supply of cheap labour.' The IDA talked of 'intelligent, readily adaptable and educated labour.'

In 1962 the WUI wondered whether the economy could, at last, 'take off.' The Committee on Industrial Organisation needed to carefully research the impact of membership of the Common Market. While not utterly hostile, the WUI urged caution. Larkin thought it was a 'poor debate', with positions predetermined by people's politics. With the rejection of the British application in 1962 attention turned to what the future held for Ireland. Members, in common with the public, found the arguments difficult to follow, especially as at first 'circumstances beyond our control' imposed a decision on us. The union paid tribute to the 'ideals' upon which the Common Market was based. Ireland should not merely coat-tail Britain but should be prepared to join irrespective of Britain. Neutrality was compromised in this rush to be 'European', another complication in a complex debate.

The WUI nailed its ideological colours to the mast in 1963. Many 'so-called' economists asserted that capitalism automatically solved all problems, 'so long as soft-hearted or soft-headed people did not interfere' by being 'unduly troubled by the inevitable human suffering which was a necessity for human progress.' Planning could ameliorate capitalism's problems. Time and two world wars had proved 'the planners correct and free enterprise devotees wrong'. Economic progress did not just happen. The union insisted on a planned approach to speed the 'old accustomed plodding pace.' Membership of the Common Market would occasion structural unemployment and redundancy. The problem was economic underdevelopment, whether Ireland was in the EEC or not. If the Second Programme for Economic Expansion was to attain its target of 78,000 jobs by 1970, the state needed to plan with 'unrelenting drive and determination.' If that did not happen the 'Second Programme would remain a programme on paper.' It was 'strictly not a plan.'

In 1967 the WUI welcomed economic upturn. Its source was not 'money, or machinery or land' but people, who alone could 'activate the inert economic factors of money, land and machinery.' People needed to be confident that their efforts would produce results. When recovery was under way, workers needed to be clear about the direction they wanted society to take. Redefined targets in the *Report on Full Employment* were welcomed. The final paragraph was considered worthy of repetition in the union's Annual Report.

> In the last resort, then, the questions raised in this report concern the will and conscience of the whole community. To harden the will and arouse the conscience of the community will require dynamic leadership and sustained backing from political and religious leaders, from trade unions, from employers' Associations, and from all other organisations and institutions which influence and form public opinion and public attitudes. Without such leadership, particularly in the political field, the policies which will raise living standards and expand employment will not be chosen and implemented.

Larkin could have drafted it himself.[30]

LEGISLATION
In 1965 P. Dunne (No. 2 Branch) called for a redundancy compensation scheme, reflecting concerns about technology and consequent loss of jobs. Paddy Cardiff (Staff) called for prior consultation before redundancy, the provision of alternative employment, compensation at the rate of one week for each year of service and manpower policy providing job placement and retraining.

In 1967 the WUI felt that even a Senior Counsel would struggle to explain exactly what a union could or could not do in pursuit of a trade dispute. Ministerial threats to transform the Labour Court drew sharp, angry responses. Denis Larkin cautioned that the intention was to turn the Labour Court into an arbitration Court, to outlaw unofficial pickets and to issue group rather than individual licences for trade unions, which would make it illegal for unions to act unilaterally. Both Congress and the Labour Party had to strongly oppose this.[31]

SAFETY AND HEALTH

In 1960 C. O'Reilly (No. 6) wanted diesel exhausts to be 'overhead and not underneath,' as workers inhaled fumes, and T. O'Neill (Guinness) wanted crews of two in all commercial vehicles. In 1963 the WUI affiliated to the National Industrial Safety Organisation. In 1967 J. Gaffney of the NISO urged the Annual Conference to activate Safety Committees. He was 'loudly applauded', but the echo of his speech in the creation of Safety Committees was not discernible.

In 1969 the WUI sought the extension of the Factories Acts to state employees and for a Factory Inspector, when visiting factories, to consult the elected safety Delegate, 'who will accompany him on his rounds.' Factory Inspectors' reports should be issued to the Safety Committee.[32] Safety consciousness was slowly rising but was yet to embrace comprehensive policy demands.

LARKIN MEMORIAL FUND

Although the Larkin Memorial Fund was closed in 1960, the Dublin Trades Council fund was still open. However, it was 'so small that it is a problem to know what could be done with it.' The removal of the Crampton Memorial from College Green and its replacement with a Larkin memorial was considered by Dublin Corporation. It was proposed that the Larkin Memorial Fund 'be finalised as soon as possible' in 1961. If either Ashe Hall or Parnell Square were to be renovated, a library named after Larkin could be provided. Peter Purcell (No. 4) looked ahead to 1963 and called for an appropriate celebration of the Lock-Out. The Larkin Memorial Fund's £4,300 was eventually used to provide a Rehabilitation Unit attached to St Laurence's Hospital, Dublin, a worthy cause but one far short of original expectations.[33]

The fiftieth anniversary of 1913 drew a significant response from the WUI, both 'on its own initiative' and with Dublin Trades Council and the Congress Commemoration Committee. A 'magnificent parade' to Glasnevin on Sunday 3 February, followed by Mass in the Pro-Cathedral, was 'an outstanding achievement.' Smithers talked of the expression 'He was a '13 man'—a badge of honour younger members needed to comprehend. He concluded a lengthy tirade against indiscipline with the 'great union slogan "EACH FOR ALL and ALL FOR EACH." For too many members it was only "ALL FOR EACH" that applied.' It was an odd way to celebrate 1913, but Smithers clearly felt it necessary.

T. Coffey (No. 8) asked whether the ITGWU had been approached to put up a plaque to Larkin in the new Liberty Hall. J. C. Walsh (No. 2) pointed out that the Labour Party Conference made no reference to Larkin or to 1913. The WUI published Donal Nevin's 1913: *Jim Larkin and the Dublin Lock-Out*, 'a labour of love' for its author, ably assisted by Hilda Larkin. Although well received, it lost money.

An Rás Tailteann asked the wui to sponsor a prize, as the 1963 Rás was dedicated to the Lock-Out's fiftieth anniversary. No mention of Larkin meant that a vexed gec made no grant. More successful was an Industrial Exhibition in the rds, sponsored by Dublin Trades Council. Even this lost £1,354.[34] The wui issued a commemorative badge.

Reflecting on 1916, Smithers complained that all the nation's children had not been cherished equally. It was not 'carping, sterile criticism but in order to spur our people to rid ourselves of the social injustices and wrongs.' Annual Larkin Commemoration parades, held in January each year, were discontinued in 1968 for lack of numbers. No replacement event was organised.

In October 1969 5,000 copies of Emmet Larkin's *James Larkin: Irish Labour Leader,* first published in 1965, were offered by the publishers or they would be pulped. The wui took some.[35]

EDUCATION

During the first ictu Congress the Jim Larkin Dramatic Group presented James Plunkett's *The Risen People* in the Gas Company Theatre. In December, under Jim Fitzgerald's direction, the group took over the Gate Theatre for a week. Organised through the European Productivity Agency, ictu seminars examined textiles and leather, factory safety, economic development, and productivity. A new three-month Gaeltacht scholarship was provided, a longer stay giving children a better understanding of Irish.

In 1960 a special course was organised for staff and honorary Officials to improve negotiating skills. The gec established an Educational Committee. In 1961 Smithers said the wui had 'played a leading role in workers' education,' giving 'at all times the utmost assistance' to the Adult Education Association. The new Committee would further this work. Progress was made on establishing Records and Research Departments in Head Office, providing Officials with a 'handy reference, loose-leaf book containing essential wage rates, working hours, overtime rates, etc.', constantly updated. Peter Purcell (No. 4) wanted an Education Officer appointed. Séamus Bleakley (Athlone) sought more ictu courses in provincial towns and scholarships for union schools to enable unpaid local Officials to attend.

In 1968 Cardiff pointed out that less than £1,500 was spent on education, 'a very, very small sum,' with only two basic courses and one advanced course run catering for about 105 students. Expressing frustration with worker education, Larkin said the People's College, sponsored by the ictu, had 'failed to achieve its purpose.' The union supported Scéim na gCeardchumann, which strove 'to create in the minds of Irish workers an appreciation of our Irish culture, history and language.'[36]

PUBLICATIONS

Sales of *Bulletin* showed a marked improvement in 1960, particularly in Nos. 1, 2, 15 and Guinness Branches, thanks to 'an active Committee working with the editors.' Its 'contents and appearance . . . improved,' with 'a steady stream of topical reports,' but there were also calls for it to be closed because of losses. J. Berkley (No. 5)—although 'he did not purchase it himself'—said, 'There is nothing in it.' Cardiff (Guinness) sought improvements rather than suppression. Tommy Kavanagh (Chairman of the Finance Committee) revealed losses of £257 in 1957, £553 in 1958 and £647 in 1959. After a sub-Committee was set up, sales rose by 100%. Expenditure was reduced to £486 in 1960, as against £649 in 1959, with income of £125 giving a net loss of £360. 'Even the strongest critics' and the 'most economy-minded' could 'hardly regard' such a sum as 'unjustified' for what was 'widely regarded, both inside and outside the union, as one of the better, if not the best, trade union journal in this country, judged from the viewpoint of real trade unionism.' In 1963 Kavanagh stated that the loss was £2,592 4s 2d between 1957 and 1962. The announcement occasioned no debate. *Bulletin* was produced by Hilda Larkin and Joseph O'Connor, although this 'was not part of their normal union duties.' They were 'under no obligation' and 'frequently' worked 'in their own time.' However, income in 1964 amounted to only £5 9s 8d, and Kavanagh acknowledged that if the costs rose above £500 'in any year we would consider whether or not to continue its publication.'

In April 1965 *Bulletin* ceased publication. Although at many Conferences 'Delegates strongly insisted' that publication be maintained, only a 'small number' enquired about its closure. 'Apparently, those who insisted on it being brought out each month did not notice its disappearance.'[37] In its absence, the 1966 Conference called on Congress 'to produce a magazine' for general sale and to 'resume publication of *Trade Union Information.*'

Table 101: *Bulletin*, income, expenses and balance (£)

	Expenses	Income	Balance
1957	381	84	(297)
1958	617	64	(553)
1959	676	26	(650)
1960	517	125	(392)
1961	296	35	(261)
1962	499	58	(441)
1963	n.a.	n.a.	(—)
1964	477	5	(472)
1965	—	—	—
Total	3,463	397	(3,066)

Source: WUI, Reports of General Executive Committee and Annual Delegate Conference, 1957–65.

STAFF AND PREMISES

Patrick Forde's death in October 1959 denied the union a foundation member who had battled alongside Larkin in 1913. Barney Conway, Tony Brack, Seán Nugent and Bob Foley all retired. The WUI had 'never had a more loyal and devoted Official' than Nugent. He joined in 1913 and became an Official in 1929. 'No sacrifice of money, time or personal convenience' was beyond him.

In 1961 a contributory superannuation scheme was introduced for staff members under fifty-five, the GEC thus treating them 'not less fairly than persons in other pensionable employments' and meeting a long-standing obligation. The WUI owned three premises in 1960: 29 Parnell Square and 5A College Street in Dublin and 4 Church Street in Tullamore. An adequate large meeting hall was lacking, and architectural reports and costings were obtained for building a hall in Dublin. Thomas Ashe Hall was an 'attractive property to purchase,' as Larkin first lay in jail in Dublin in a cell there when it was the Central Police Station. The Conference demanded a 'better Union Hall or an extension to existing premises.' The cost was estimated at £100,000 to £120,000, money that represented roughly two years' membership contributions. Ashe Hall, after much agonising, was rejected as unsuitable for conversion to modern offices and was sold in 1966 for £55,000.[38]

In 1962 the deaths at comparatively young ages of Thomas Doyle, Secretary of No. 15 Branch, and Michael Moore, District Secretary, Tullamore, were shocking. Doyle was 'devoted to the national and social well-being' of workers, 'unselfish, hard-working, self-sacrificing' and possessed 'moral and physical courage.' Moore worked in the Grand Canal Company before becoming a full-time Official in 1951, building up an impressive membership from scratch. In December 1962 Christy Troy, a long-standing GEC member, died. He was Chairman of the Operative Butchers and an 'active, loyal and self-sacrificing member,' having learnt at 'the feet of the "Big Man"'. He toiled tirelessly despite physical handicap. In November 1962 George Nathan passed away, a founder and long-standing GEC member.

A number of staff members left, some regrettably under a cloud, causing considerable reorganisation. P. Kinch (No. 6) wanted all staff recruited 'from the ranks.' The GEC opposed. Thomas Kavanagh (Finance Committee) reported that wages and pensions represented 40% of total income, when an ideal figure would be 33%. A Central Cash Office to lighten work loads was created. The WUI Staff Association felt that the position of Senior Clerk, advertised in the press, should be filled internally and that Smithers was 'foolish to try and establish something which has not got the good will of the staff.' The GEC were shocked by this stance. Austin Stack was appointed from outside but with Paddy Duffy as Assistant.

Many Branches had transferred from Ashe Hall to Parnell Square by 1964. The union acknowledged that 'while it is unlikely that levels of remuneration and conditions of employment' for the staff would ever equal those secured for members in 'top class private employment,' they were 'generally satisfactory.' Regular attempts by the staff to achieve parity with ITGWU employees were rejected. Like was not being compared with like: in all senses the ITGWU was a much bigger organisation.[39]

Barney Conway's death on 2 January 1965 marked the 'end of an era.' He had 'fought and suffered' since 1909 and was an 'outstanding member of Larkin's Old Guard,' a 'pioneer trade unionist, Irish Citizen Army man, 1913 veteran,' who did 'honourable service in prison for his class and country.' He was a 'confidant and friend of Jim Larkin' and 'comrade and friend of us all.'[40]

On 20 March 1966 Billy Eustace, General Treasurer, died 'after a fairly long illness.' A bakery van driver and a founding member, he was a close friend of Larkin, 'unswerving in his loyalty' and 'ever ready to help and advise.' Although General Treasurer, Eustace was unpaid as such, his wage coming from his position as Central Cash Office clerk. 'Actual control and direction' of finances was 'carried out by the General President.' The position of General Treasurer died with him.

On 10 March 1966 Seán Nugent passed away.

In 1967 the WUI employed a staff of forty: three General Officers, twenty Branch Secretaries and Assistants, a clerical staff of fourteen and three caretakers and cleaners. The ratio of Officials to members was 1:830.

Towards the end of 1969 Anthony Brack died. Originally a caretaker, he became an Official, sometimes courting controversy with his forthright manner and occasional refusal to acknowledge authority.

There was a lively debate in 1969, decrying the fact that No. 2 Branch had been used as 'a training ground for Officials.' It was alleged by Joe McGrane, one of the staff members who 'passed through' the Branch in rapid succession, that there was a problem in that staff members did not want to stay there. This was explained by the very high demands the Branch made. One Official was stretched over a number of areas, where the WUI was the minor union and others had full-time, specialised staff. The debate underlined structural and organisational tensions. Generally, staff matters were in some crisis, with the deaths of Larkin and Smithers and the ageing profile of others: Dan Byrne was sixty-eight, Sam Hannon sixty-four.[41]

RELIGION

At Annual Conferences there were occasional references to Papal encyclicals and clerical articles. In 1962 Smithers quoted extensively from *Mater et Magistra*, 'one of the great social documents of this century.' In 'broadening and elaborating' on the work of Popes Leo XIII and Pius XI, the 'fruits of this work' were demonstrated by the 'Church's firm stand on the strikes in Spain.' During the canonisation service for St Martin de Porres the WUI passed on a cheque to Cardinal Browne. A message saluted him 'not only as a great Churchman but also as an outstanding Irishman.' Browne's response was read to the Conference.

> I am most deeply grateful, Mr Smithers, for your kind words and generous gift. It is a great surprise, but I accept it with deep and genuine pleasure. There is nobody whose friendship and kindness I appreciate more than the Workers of Ireland, whose wonderful devotion to their Faith is a noble example to the entire world.

Martin de Porres 'was a worker,' and Browne knew he had 'only to ask your help and you will be always willing to help me.' He could not resist reminding Delegates not to stray from the path. 'You should at all times recall that you are acting on behalf of thousands of working men and women; that your decisions will be their legislation.'

Smithers quoted from encyclicals again in 1963, demonstrating Papal support for collective bargaining and workers' involvement. By 1969 the climate had changed, and Vincent Keane (No. 4) successfully moved, without debate, that church services for deceased members should 'include other religious denominations.'[42]

SOLIDARITY

On 24 March 1960 the GEC endorsed Dublin Trades Council's protests against racial discrimination in South Africa and recorded 'their opposition to discrimination in any part of the world against other human beings on the grounds of their race, creed or colour.' M. McGregor (Guinness) was disappointed at the 'couldn't care less' attitude to the 'merciless and tyrannical' South African Government. Resolutions were not enough: 'trade unionism on an international scale' could bring an end to 'the horrible evil of Apartheid' by a 'boycott on the handling of South African goods.'[43] No-one followed McGregor to the rostrum, but he had laid a foundation stone for a long campaign by Irish workers against apartheid.

Reflecting much-changed times, in November 1966 the GEC approved arrangements for a visit to the Soviet Union. Larkin led a Delegation in July 1967. A return visit from a Soviet Delegation was put into question by the Soviet invasion of Czechoslovakia.

The WUI affiliated to the International Union of Food and Allied Workers' Associations, based in Geneva, initially through No. 7 (Tobacco Workers) Branch but from 1963 its entire membership in food, brewing, distilling and aerated waters. Larkin and Smithers represented the union at its 14th Congress in Stockholm on 27–28 May 1964. This was the first WUI international affiliation since membership of the Red International in the 1920s.

In 1967, the WUI disaffiliated, ironically as the international union held its Congress in Dublin. The problem arose from demands from other sectors to be affiliated to other internationals. The cost, at between £2,000 and £3,000 a year, was considered too high.[44]

POLITICS

Denis Larkin and Frank Cluskey were elected to Dublin Corporation, and 'full use' was made of their services 'in respect of housing, child welfare, health services, etc.' and for members employed by the Corporation. Still, the WUI had no actual 'political objectives or affiliations,' even if its outlook could be identified as clearly Labour. In 1961 W. Lynch (No. 8) requested that Larkin run in his old constituency, 'as the workers feel they have lost a very good representative.' J. McGuinness (No. 2) opposed, as our General Secretary cannot serve two masters. He cannot be in the Dáil and the Union at the same time. One must fall a victim. We have a very able Deputy in the Dáil—Denis Larkin. When we lost Christy Ferguson we lost a great little soldier and a great Organiser.

Larkin said he had no intention of being a candidate, but either the union confined itself to industrial activity or took a firm decision on its political stance. He stated:

I am a Labour man. I have been all my life and will continue to be one. But I cannot be in the Dáil and do my work in the Union at the same time.

Kay Fallon asked the GEC to 'devise ways and means' of affiliating to the Labour Party, to give effect to political motions that came up 'year in and year out.' She called on all 'trade unionists to resolve their ideological and political differences and unite' within the Labour Party. The Party's fiftieth anniversary was celebrated in Clonmel, an ideal time to affiliate. J. Craig (No. 13) opposed, as it was 'interfering with my liberty of action,' while M. Cassidy (No. 7) opposed on his Branch's behalf, as the Labour Party had no support in Dublin. The motion was referred back.[45]

Denis Larkin contested Dublin North-East on 30 May 1963 to fight against 'anti-working class measures.' J. Ruddock (No. 12) moved that Amnesty be invited to address the Conference, and that the WUI should affiliate. Seán MacBride spoke. The WUI addressed the issue of 'The Political Responsibility of the Trade Unions', observing that they were 'playing an ever-more important role in the affairs' of the state. Workers were not only trade unionists but also citizens and voters. The Labour Party's poor political representation was regretted and needed to be urgently strengthened. A strong Dáil opposition was required.

Alderman Seán Moore addressed the 1964 Conference as Lord Mayor of Dublin. John Breen in 1953 and Denis Larkin in 1958 were previous members who were Lord Mayor.[46]

In 1964 S. Lennon (No. 12, Civil Aviation) moved affiliation to the Labour Party. It was carried, with only eleven dissenters, after lengthy debate. Formal application was made on 1 December for 25,000 members, effective from January 1965. In the 1965 election three members ran for the Labour Party, receiving financial assistance: Frank Cluskey (Dublin South-Central), P. J. Coughlan (Dublin South-West) and Denis Larkin (Dublin North-East). Cluskey and Larkin were among twenty-two Labour TDs returned. As to selecting WUI Delegates for Labour Party Conferences, P. Coughlan (No. 3) wanted them to be of five years' standing, active in a Labour Party Branch and to be paid only 'actual out-of-pocket expenses.'

The first Party Conference at which the WUI was represented was in Liberty Hall on 15–17 October 1965—an ironic venue, given that the ITGWU was not yet re-affiliated. At the 1966 WUI Conference Brendan Corish, Leader of the Labour Party, was guest speaker. He brought fraternal greetings and signposted political actions. By 1969 the Labour Party's growth and its decision to field 100 candidates in a national election strategy was seen as a function of the WUI's, and subsequently the ITGWU's, affiliation.

Níall Greene (No. 12 Branch and Finance Secretary of the Labour Party) called for long-term commitment, as, for the first time, the prospect of a Labour Government could be talked about, if not immediately then within the foreseeable future. In the General Election eleven members were selected as Labour candidates, with Justin Keating (North County Dublin) and Frank Cluskey (Dublin Central) successful. Cluskey was retained by the WUI on a 'consultative and advisory basis' after his election. Michael D. Higgins was a notable candidate in Galway West. £5,459 was expended from the Political Fund. Jack Harte was an unsuccessful Seanad candidate. There was anger at the loss of Seán Dunne's seat in Dublin South-West, where 'quarrelling' and the 'emergence of a Coalition plank' proved costly.

The WUI thought leading Party members were 'either changing or had already changed their attitude to Coalition.' Dunne's death was another blow so soon after those of Larkin Junior and Smithers.[47]

As serious trouble broke out in Northern Ireland in August 1969 the GEC had a lengthy discussion on whether to provide financial aid for families in Belfast and Derry. Tom Geraghty suggested that the General Officers visit the North and hand a cheque for £1,000 'to whatever organisation they considered appropriate.' Denis Larkin 'saw no point.' They had no members there. £500 was given through the ICTU Northern Ireland Committee and Dublin Trades Council Relief Fund.[48]

Chapter 28 ~

CONCLUSIONS

LOST POSSIBILITIES

The ITGWU grew steadily from 136,179 to 162,181 members. The WUI's growth was less impressive, from 28,904 to 33,352. Geographical and numerical growth brought new problems. The emphasis was on 'service'.

Extra full-time staff and more benefits, coupled with steady inflation, meant that expenditure rose dramatically. The ITGWU's costs rose from £183,031 in 1960 to £542,962 in 1969, the WUI's from £127,465 to £633,389. Paddy Clancy insisted on a rigorous analysis of all industrial, financial and administrative systems, resulting in new ITGWU management practices and the creation of the Development Services Division.

In 1964 John Carroll oversaw the appointment of six National Industrial Group Secretaries, each responsible for 25,000 to 30,000 members, to lead negotiations and organisation. This added another link to an already lengthy chain, but the net effect was to equip the ITGWU with a national industrial leadership supported by sophisticated 'back-up' services. Only by 1969 had check-off and pre-emptive closed-shop Agreements begun to significantly distance members.

Watching these developments, James Larkin became convinced that the WUI's stagnation necessitated serious consideration of amalgamation. An ageing staff profile, apparent dearth of up-and-coming talent and insignificant property and investment portfolios created the view that, should it delay amalgamation, a relatively strong position, derived from Larkin's own high prestige, would diminish. Not all agreed that the obvious amalgamation—with the ITGWU—was welcome or necessary. Some believed, and not just because of old animosities, that developing a second large general union to compete with the ITGWU might serve the movement far more effectively, and strengthen Congress.

Relations progressed from agreement on transfers and exchange of ideas to formal merger discussions after 1966. The deaths of Conroy and Larkin in 1969 halted matters. The ITGWU became bullish about its own expansion, its National Groups and Development Services Division and possibly felt that it was acquiring a critical mass that would inevitably absorb the WUI. The WUI in turn began to seek to resist that possibility through absorbing other Associations, not just to deny 'One Big Union' but because it made sense if it was to meet members' increasingly complex demands. Nevertheless, the failure to merge was undoubtedly an oppor-tunity lost. That Larkin considered that a merged union might be called the Irish Transport and General Workers' Union says much for the man and his motivation. Whether the WUI Conference and ballot would have agreed can only be speculated upon.

The ITGWU's Northern Ireland members suffered from the decline of waterfront and clothing industries, but the Northern Ireland Civil Rights Association and reac-tive sectarian violence placed Belfast, Derry and Newry members on centre stage. The ITGWU, and particularly Michael Mullen, pressured the Irish and British Governments, the Labour Party and Congress to concede the civil rights agenda, increase investment and remove the Unionist veto. Suggestions that a 32-County Socialist republic was the solution dominated the Conference.

Women's equality emerged as a central issue. If unions were to challenge soci-ety's patriarchy, first they had to reform themselves.

Table 102: ITGWU and WUI membership, 1960–69

	ITGWU	WUI		ITGWU	WUI
1960	136,179	28,904	1965	150,414	30,048
1961	140,334	29,230	1966	148,804	31,309
1962	146,339	29,329	1967	153,415	30,716
1963	143,498	29,833	1968	156,277	31,373
1964	149,915	29,361	1969	162,181	33,352

Source: National Archives, Registrar of Friendly Societies, files 275T and 369T.

Despite new national structures, the emphasis in the ITGWU was on revitalising Branch and work-place activity. Grievance-handling and negotiating procedures were part of widely introduced comprehensive work-place Agreements. Shop stewards and industrial staff needed training in representational skills to success-fully operate them. There was resistance by employers, particularly from newly arriving transnational Corporations. In this context the ITGWU's victory in EI at Shannon was highly significant. The Government and employers' bodies were still favourably disposed to union recognition. Effective work-place representation was seen as part of the country's industrial learning curve, facilitating good employer-worker relations, productivity-related wage bargaining and co-operation with change to improve efficiency and product quality.

Table 103: ITGWU and WUI, income, surplus and credit balance (£), 1960–69

	ITGWU			WUI		
	Income	Surplus (deficit)	Credit balance	Income	Surplus (deficit)	Credit balance*
1960	183,031	81,414	1,238,934	58,589	8,390	78,413
1961	190,318	32,841	1,304,828	61,067	954	76,862
1962	223,392	97,616	1,443,409	67,761	13,768	96,799
1963	260,596	52,067	1,532,351	74,697	3,748	125,506
1964	292,852	94,414	1,660,815	85,589	2,592	123,550
1965	330,934	40,015	1,743,146	101,080	13,130	137,973
1966	433,160	88,628	1,841,193	120,696	(7,351)	131,772
1967	517,334	106,924	1,894,749	119,977	29,354	165,562
1968	501,527	110,895	1,878,942	126,923	620	178,618
1969	542,962	(29,170)	1,780,937	136,864	(33,965)	164,119

*This is the value of WUI investments; no figure for credit balance is given.

Source: ITGWU, Annual Reports, 1960–69, and WUI, Reports of General Executive Council, 1960–69.

DISPUTES

The 1960s were the 'decade of upheaval.'[1] Most major disputes—in banks, construction, the ESB and among maintenance craftsmen—did not directly involve the ITGWU or WUI. As the country modernised, inter-union and demarcation disputes seemed anachronistic and obstructive. For the ITGWU the formation of the Dublin Busmen's Union was a bitter pill, a triumph for Sectionalism. Considerable time, attention and money had been devoted to bus workers. It raised serious warnings for Liberty Hall. Had members ceased to identify with an enlarging and apparently more distant organisation?

A comparison of ITGWU and WUI Dispute Pay shows similar patterns, allowing for differences in scale. The ITGWU spent £802,187, an average of £80,218 a year or 21% of income; the WUI, £224,259, equal to £22,245 a year and also 21% of income. The ITGWU pursued the goal of a threshold income of £500 a year, achieved by a combination of money wages, social welfare and taxation. National Wage Agreements decreasingly achieved meaningful redistribution of the nation's growing wealth. Larkin, in particular, suggested exchanging wage militancy for increases in the social wage, commitments to employment, economic planning, the full development of natural resources and worker democracy.

By 1969 some saw the ICTU as disappointing. The ITGWU continuously carped over the allocations of funds, lack of value for its affiliation fees and, worst of all, Congress's apparent failure to provide leadership or to control affiliates. The

Maintenance Dispute brought matters to a crisis. The ITGWU moved for disaffiliation. The WUI's greater reliance on and support for Congress was strained, but
Liberty Hall's attitude contributed to re-emerging distance between the two unions.

Table 104: ITGWU and WUI Dispute Pay, 1960–69

	ITGWU			WUI		
	Income (£)	Dispute Pay (£)	Dispute Pay as proportion income (%)	Income (£)	Dispute Pay (£)	Dispute Pay as proportion income (%)
1960	183,031	7,904	4.3	58,589	3,933	6.7
1961	190,318	47,137	24.8	61,067	14,924	24.4
1962	223,392	9,692	4.4	67,761	3,383	5.0
1963	260,596	67,938	26.1	74,697	13,795	18.5
1964	291,852	33,814	11.6	85,589	12,113	14.1
1965	330,934	100,338	30.3	101,080	18,361	18.1
1966	433,160	112,686	26.0	120,696	42,907	35.5
1967	517,334	81,806	15.8	119,977	6,074	5.1
1968	501,527	85,592	17.0	126,923	39,972	31.5
1969	542,962	255,280	47.0	136,864	68,797	50.2

Source: ITGWU, Annual Reports, 1960–69; WUI, Reports of General Executive Committee,
1960–69.

POLITICS

The WUI affiliated to the Labour Party in 1965; the ITGWU re-affiliated in 1968. 'The
seventies would be Socialist'; a Labour Government was possible. At last there
would be a chance that union policies on planned economic development, fiscal
and welfare reform, education, health and housing could be realised. Despite trau-
matic divisions and anger caused by the Maintenance Dispute, the ITGWU and WUI
entered the 1970s in optimistic mood. There was a global atmosphere of protest
and change, of youth and energy. At last, trade unionism would gain access to the
tables of power and radically reform society.

Chapter 29 ~

DEVELOPING AN UNDER-STANDING: THE ITGWU IN THE 1970s

MEMBERSHIP, ORGANISATION AND FINANCE

In 1970 the General Secretary, Michael Mullen, reported that Branch remittances had increased, although 35% of members still paid only 1s 6d per week or less. (See table 105.) Rates of benefit were 'unequalled', but members needed to contribute at higher levels to reap those rewards. In 1970 only 10% were Class 1 members, 16% Class 2, 26% Class 3, 19% Class 4, 20% Class 5, 8% Class 6, 0.6% Class 7 and 1.5% Class 8. It was a pattern that was slow to change.

Income, while it rose by 7%, was overshadowed by the 26% increase in expenditure. Mullen felt that a 10% annual membership growth was attainable. There were calls for a Craft Section, and for organisation to be extended to England, Scotland and Wales. A superannuation benefit and house purchase loan scheme were suggested, reflecting a more prosperous membership, whatever about their practicality. More down to earth was the annual plea by Vincent Moran (Limerick No. 2) for the Deduction at Source or 'check-off' of contributions. It was finally heeded.

Contributions were raised by approximately 6d. The increases were well received. A comprehensive legal aid scheme and personal accident benefit, granting up to £2,000 in cases of fatal or disabling accidents, were introduced. Financial membership rose by 7% to 122,170, a solid achievement. Consultants examined all administrative and management practices.[1]

In 1971 John Reilly (Ballina No. 1) complained about a lack of attention from National Group Secretaries. Service in the west was better in 1918–24, when P. J. O'Brien visited, in the 1930s, when Cathal O'Shannon and James Gilhooly were on the beat, or even when Paddy Armstrong provided 24-hour service to part-time Branches in Cos. Mayo and Roscommon. The platform strongly challenged this assertion.

Total assets exceeded £2 million for the first time, although financial membership declined slightly. By December, 44,000 members or 30% were on check-off.

Consultants' recommendations were designed to improve the collecting of contributions and the payment of benefits, to develop internal reporting systems,
including trend data, to enable more effective decision-making by the NEC, to adopt
a better investments policy, to determine the appropriate level of administrative
staff and to introduce computerisation.

Two hundred members of the Irish Civil Service Institute were 'anxious to transfer' but were not thought appropriate. In 1972 the membership increased by 7%,
mostly in new companies. Despite check-off, arrears still ran at 13%. New or
improved premises were opened in Kilkenny, Midleton, Tullamore and Youghal.
Premises, however, were 'quite useless without the vital element of human horse-
power.' Additional Officials were appointed. In 1973 Mick McDermott (Dublin No.
16) thought that contributions should be raised to 'an hour's pay per member per
week . . . let's cut out the messing around.' Liam Beecher (Cork No. 6) reflected that
in 1918 workers paid 4d to 6d per week from wages—a small fraction of present
levels. More and more Branches sought subsidies from Head Office, no longer able
to make ends meet from their 25% local retention. In addition, £104,512 was provided to Dublin Branches as Liberty Hall rent subsidies.[2]

Table 105: Subsidies to ITGWU Branches (£), 1972

Derry	5,578	Dublin No. 15	1,578
Dublin No. 1	4,708	Newry	1,561
Dublin No. 14	4,679	Limerick No. 2	1,550
Dublin No. 3	3,970	Laois-Offaly	1,511
Dublin No. 13	3,584	Dublin No. 4	1,470
Mallow	3,500	Lucan	1,280
Dublin No. 7	3,053	Sligo	1,239
Shannon	2,919	Cork No. 2	986
Cork No. 5	2,845	Kilkenny	928
Dublin No. 2	2,744	Athy	890
Limerick No. 1	2,638	Tralee	856
Dublin No. 17	2,537	Ballinasloe Mental Hospital	760
Cork No. 4	2,530	Bray	701
Athlone	2,352	Cork No. 3	602
Dublin No. 5	2,259	Waterford No. 2	600
Waterford No. 1	2,229	Dublin No. 6	521
Drogheda	2,218	Dublin No. 9	496
Dundalk	2,088	Limerick county	333
Galway	2,000	Cóbh	250
Cork No. 1	1,950	Wexford	250

Dublin No. 11	1,922	Dublin No. 8	198
Dublin No. 16	1,873	Clonmel	73
Carlow	1,819	Kingscourt	45
Dublin No. 12	1,805	Tullamore	10
Cork No. 6	1,694		

Source: ITGWU, Report of Proceedings of Annual Delegate Conference, Ballybunnion, 5–8 June 1973, p. 212.

In 1973 membership increased by 7,727, with 88% paid up and 56,000, or 38%, on check-off. Dispute Pay fell sharply, but total expenditure still outstripped income. A novel development was the first Gaeltacht Branch, that of Doirí Beaga, Co. Donegal, its Secretary the colourful Seán Ó Cearnaigh. There was an immediate increase in the use of Irish in the journal and at Annual Conference. In 1974 contributions were raised by 5p, to 30p per week at the top level. There was little opposition except from members whose wage increases took them into a higher category. Gone were the days when the first week's wage increase went ungrudgingly to the union.

Membership rose by 5% to 140,213 after a 'concerted effort at organisation,' with expansion among professional and supervisory groups significant. More than 65,000 were on check-off. An audit control system was introduced to supervise Branch finances.

In October a wage campaign was directed at professional, managerial and academic grades through Dublin No. 2 Branch, which increased from 2,300 members in 1972 to 6,000. A 'Union of Interest' was created with the United Commercial Travellers' Association and the ESB Meter Readers' Association, neither resulting in merger. Talks with the Irish Union of Distributive Workers and Clerks were also unproductive. The Irish Airlines and Executives Staffs' Association was 'anxious to become associated or possibly members,' and, notwithstanding its 'association with the WUI,' approval was given. A proposed Craft Federation with six building unions—which got as far as agreeing a written constitution—'appeared to be dead' by March. Reasons varied, but the organising by the ITGWU of a Limerick joinery triggered collapse.

Equivocation regarding the recruitment of senior administrative employees ceased when Pat Rabbitte was asked to 'indulge in organising professional and managerial staffs' in November through a 'Professional Managerial Unit' within Dublin No. 2 Branch. Stephen Treacy became craftsmen's Official in January in 1975, although his old union, the National Union of Sheet Metal Workers, did not, as expected, follow. Some complained that this pandered to Sectionalism within a low-paid general workers' union.[3]

The Irish Branches of the National Union of Gold, Silver and Allied Trades transferred as a Section in Dublin No. 13 Branch in April 1976, their Secretary, Mick Browne, joining the staff. In August 1977 the Irish Shoe and Leather Workers' Union merged, its General Secretary, Michael Bell, becoming National Group Secretary. This amalgamation was the first funded under the Trade Union Act (1975).

Contributions were raised, those on £60 now paying 60p per week, entitling them to £20 per week in Dispute Benefit. Financial membership fell to 141,079, however, mainly through redundancies. A National Fishermen's Branch explored new waters, and members of the administrative staff in the University Colleges of Cork and Galway transferred their associations. In Galway the University authorities tried to 'destroy the credibility of the Union,' which expected that more 'enlightened management attitudes could surely have been anticipated within a university.' A strike was completely successful. Given autonomous status, the Professional Managerial Unit brought in university employees, the Shannon Free Airport Development Company Staffs Association, the City and County Managers' Association, regional tourism managers, the Local Authority Inspectorate and part-time employees of Bord na gCon, achieving improvements in pay and conditions. There were fears about the effect that 'such people' would have within the ITGWU.

In August 1976 Dan Shaw, Group Secretary, died after a long illness. A native of Castlecomer, he became an Official in July 1956 and trained in Cork and Dublin before becoming Secretary of the Sligo Branch in 1959. In October 1965 he became Wicklow District Secretary and in 1973 National Industrial Group Secretary for construction, mining and some public services. His loss was deeply regretted.[4]

Financial membership increased by 11,654 to 152,733 in 1977. The Association of Scientific, Technical and Managerial Staffs was rumoured to be either 'seeking to merge or set up independently' in Ireland. Were this true the ITGWU would be either partner or opponent.

Some bank employees, members of the non-Congress Irish Bank Officials' Association, sought transfer. The NEC gave the go-ahead. Talks with the Electrical, Electronic, Plumbing and Telecommunications Union began in March but were not successful. In 1978, 5,739 new members brought the total to 158,160. The new Branches were Belfast No. 2 (Clerical), Galway Psychiatric Hospital, North of Ireland Boiler Operators and Shannon Airport and Industrial Estate.

Members of the Irish Union of Distributive Workers and Clerks recruited in various Branches of Dunne's Stores were ordered to be handed back. Arguments that these workers would be non-union rather than rejoin the IUDWC cut no ice: Head Office policy was not to accept IUDWC transfers. In talks with the Ancient Guild of Incorporated Brick and Stone Layers the ITGWU offered assistance as the bricklayers' Cuffe Street premises were demolished. Talk of merger was far from the mark, and matters were complicated by the smaller union's insistence that financial commitments were made, which was denied. Discussions took place with the National Land League on 'matters of mutual interest.' Mullen saw commonality with small working farmers as the Centenary of Davitt's Land League loomed.[5]

In 1979 the ITGWU Brass and Reed Band played in provincial centres to celebrate the seventieth anniversary. Dublin District Council wanted to increase its Band Levy from 5p to 10p per annum in November, financial problems constraining the Band.

Merger invitations were extended to the Irish National Union of Vintners', Grocers' and Allied Trades' Assistants, the Irish Bakers, Confectioners and Allied Workers Amalgamated Union, the Irish Union of Distributive Workers and Clerks and the IWWU, while the Irish Federation of Musicians requested a 'similar document to that being balloted on by Irish Actors' Equity.'

Concerns were expressed about the union's poor public image, and RTÉ was asked to provide a 'weekly programme on trade union affairs,' a request made almost continuously ever since.

The ITGWU reviewed membership over the 1970s, encouraged by growth from 114,174 in 1969 to 167,239 in 1979. The increase, 53,065 or 46%, came mostly through check-off. New entrants came from workers awakening to unionisation—clerical, administrative, technical and managerial—and were welcomed. The ITGWU actively sought to use the provisions of the Trade Union Act (1975), condemning 'splintering' and non-Congress unions. Once outside Congress, normal procedures for transfers went out the window and cannibalism was possible.

Table 106: ITGWU membership, income, expenditure, surplus and General Fund credit balance (£), 1970–79

	Membership	Income	Expenditure	Surplus (deficit)	Credit balance
1970	122,171	618,633	504,770	113,863	1,903,406
1971	116,739	814,741	693,094	121,647	2,017,949
1972	125,185	892,219	716,392	175,827	2,230,434
1973	132,912	1,015,675	759,328	256,347	2,479,838
1974	140,213	1,255,661	1,079,800	175,827	2,701,476
1975	144,083	1,578,955	1,414,905	164,582	2,860,166
1976	141,079	1,776,235	1,636,284	139,951	3,004,360
1977	152,733	3,243,489	2,798,866	444,624	3,441,115
1978	158,160	3,435,358	3,473,138	133,442	3,569,431
1979	167,239	4,180,319	3,841,809	338,510	3,814,077

Source: ITGWU, Annual Reports, 1970–79.

The emphasis was on 'service' rather than 'organisation.' The union's staff increased substantially—'almost in direct proportion' to membership increases. Full-time Branches were created in previously part-time areas, such as Mayo, Longford, Killarney and Donegal, usually after the arrival of transnational factories. The Development Services Division was the jewel in the servicing crown.

The 1979 Annual Report ended on an optimistic note. Growth in membership and services was 'gratifying, particularly having regard to the background against which it was achieved.' It left the ITGWU 'in a sound position to look forward to the undoubted challenges of modern technology and world-wide recession' that lay ahead.[6] Such optimism, while laudable, ignored fundamental flaws inherent in the method of recruitment that would plague all unions.

Income grew by a staggering £4½ million, but concomitant rises in expenditure meant that surpluses, although achieved in every year, were small, except in 1977 and 1979, at £444,624 and £338,510, respectively. The General Fund credit surplus grew from £1.9 million to £4.1 million, suggesting health and vigour. However, rising costs were a cause of concern as recession deepened. Most alarmingly, staff costs ballooned, from £152,536 in 1970 (representing 25% of expenditure) to £2,235,543 in 1979 (53%). Committed, talented staff members were an undoubted asset, but when service, pension and long-term non-pay costs were considered, problems waited in the longer grass of the 1980s.

WOMEN

In 1970 Paddy Armstrong (Dublin No. 13) called for the ratification of ILO Convention No. 100 'relating to the principle of equal pay for work of equal value.' Only nine women Delegates out of 252 heard him. Ethel Phillips thought that 'in all future claims' women should 'be equal with men.' Despite moves towards equal pay in National Wage Agreements, differential rates were still being negotiated.

In 1972 Tralee wanted equal rights and opportunities for women, and 'where necessary industrial action taken' to achieve them. In negotiations for the Thirteenth Wage Round the ITGWU rejected the first proposals, partly because commitments to equal pay were insufficient. In the final deal, the Employer-Labour Conference accepted in principle the Interim Report on Equal Pay of the Commission on the Status of Women and took steps 'for the phased implementation' of some of its recommendations. Male workers could not introduce claims exclusively for themselves or to 'restore their relative earning power.' Rates should be struck for job rather than for men or women. Equal-pay claims could be made throughout the course of the Agreement where women performed the same jobs, similar jobs where the differences were small or infrequent, or equal in value with those of men, or where pay was differentiated according to marital status. This language became very familiar once equal pay legislation was introduced.

The Labour Court appointed an Equal Pay Commissioner. Where job evaluation was necessary, both sides agreed to co-operate. Where differentials were based on shift or night work—from which women were legally banned—problems arose but were not insurmountable. Where differences were 95% the gap could be completely closed, otherwise it could be narrowed by 17½% of the difference. 'Inability to pay' cases could be referred under clause 17, 'Special Economic Circumstances'. While not dramatic or totally satisfactory, this was a breakthrough on equal pay.[7]

Marie Jones (Dublin No. 8) complained of the complexity of procedures. Carroll acknowledged her frustration but pointed out that in pursuit of an equal pay claim conceded by the Labour Court the strike weapon was always available. Sixty-eight women attended six workshops on the Commission on the Status of Women. Mary

Maher's 'Woman Worker' column in *Liberty* demonstrated hopes that membership of the EEC would quicken the pace of equality.

In 1971 the difference in hourly rates for female industrial workers against male rates was 77% in France, 76% in Italy, 70% in West Germany, 68% in Belgium, 61% in the Netherlands and 56% in Luxembourg, while it was 56½% in Ireland. Maher concluded: 'We've broken a few old traditions this month by linking up with the Common Market. Maybe it's time we broke a few more, by demanding re-training facilities in the male-dominated industries, and an end to discrimination against women in job placement.'

Attitudes to female union staff (usually referred to as 'girls', irrespective of age) changed too. In April 1973 the NEC noted that sixteen married women were on six months' extension, two applying for further extensions. Previously, women automatically left the union's employment on marriage. The all-male NEC decided that 'in future we should allow married women to continue in permanent employment until such time as pregnancy makes it impossible for them to do so.'

Women's average earnings in 1974 were £23.03 per week, compared with men's at £45.71, figures balanced a little as women worked 36.4 hours for this income, men 43.4. Kennedy declared that equal pay for women was something they were 'dedicated to.' The ITGWU won equal pay claims through the Equal Pay Commissioner and the Labour Court. Despite this, 'only a tiny proportion' received their 17½% instalment under the 1972 National Wage Agreement and 33⅓% instalment under the 1974 Agreement. Even this was confined mainly to public servants. Employers' delaying tactics pushed the implementation date for equal pay beyond 1975.[8]

The ITGWU welcomed the Anti-Discrimination (Pay) Act (1974), even though it was 'not sufficiently comprehensive and not sufficiently positive' to guarantee full equality. It urged the adoption of a Charter for Women's Rights to provide for the 'right of women to have full access to all types of employment regardless of marital status,' equal opportunity in 'education, training and re-training, inclusive of day-release facilities,' the 'removal of all legal and bureaucratic impediments to equality in regard to tenancies, mortgages, pension schemes, taxation, jury service, hire-purchase Agreements, social welfare benefits, and rights in respect of children'; day nurseries with adequately trained staff; and 'recognition of motherhood and parenthood as a social function' demanding 'social entitlements such as maternity leave, protection of women's interests during pregnancy' and 're-entry to employment.' Ria Farren (Dublin No. 7) moved her own charter: equal pay for work of equal value; statutory National Minimum Wage; equal job and promotional opportunities for men and women, regardless of marital status; the abolition of the Marriage Bar; equal training, day-release and re-training opportunities; the provision of creches and day nurseries by local authorities and employers; improved canteen and take-away meal facilities; eighteen weeks' maternity leave on full pay; no dismissal during pregnancy or maternity leave and no loss of security, pension or promotional prospects; and a campaign to encourage women to join trade unions.

Anne Speed (Dublin No. 2) connected inequality and low pay. Why were there so few, if any, equal pay claims being served? She concluded a thought-provoking and challenging contribution by tackling the 'thorny problem' of 'family planning or that nasty word contraception.' 'Without the right to control our means of reproduction or fertility, we have no way in which we can plan our future or our career.' She was the first to introduce the Conference to such concepts as 'women's right to choose' and serious consideration of contraception, not all values that met an open embrace by the still—on social issues at least—largely conservative membership.

1975 was International Women's Year. The European Trade Union Confederation pushed the EEC to increase legislative action for equality. The ITGWU broadened the agenda to include Travellers' rights. A seminar on 8–9 March provided a union forum for women's views. The final session, chaired by May O'Brien (Dublin No. 6/8), was 'Towards a Union Policy.' International Women's Year was viewed with mixed feelings. 'Little may appear to have been achieved,' but it was considered worth while. The lack of progress was still, however, partly blamed on women themselves. That it had ended did not mean 'that we promptly forget about women.' It 'should have been the start of a definite commitment' by unions 'to make sure that something positive is done for women.' Women 'provided a source of cheap labour' for too long. This could not continue 'if we are serious in our trade unionism.' But it had to be repeated:

> women must involve themselves. If they fail to do this they will have lost any inroads IWY [International Women's Year] may have made. So we ask women trade unionists as a New Year resolution for 1976 to get involved. There is no other way.'[9]

Congress adopted the ITGWU Working Women's Charter in 1976. (See p. 644.) Anne Speed demanded, 'Let us mobilise our strength as a union to win equality for women now,' regretting that the Anti-Discrimination (Employment) Bill made 'no mention of pregnancy at all' and did not provide maternity leave. In addition, FUE and state obfuscation stymied the act's impact.

On 15 January 1976 more than 1,000 assembled in the Mansion House to rally against proposed amendments to equal pay legislation. Carroll joined Ruairí Quinn and Barry Desmond of the Labour Party in demanding full, unamended implementation. A petition of protest with more than 35,000 signatures was handed to the Government, whose 'squalid attempt' to 'evade its moral and political obligation to women' and obtain derogation failed.

The battle was not over but shifted to the collective bargaining arena. The ITGWU demanded that the movement 'not be found wanting.' To promote awareness and improve case presentation the union ran job evaluation and equal pay courses. Successful, often bitterly fought cases, particularly in Midleton and Killarney, proved their worth. The first report of the Commission on the Status of Women, in December 1972, was check-listed by the Women's Representative Committee in May 1977. Progress was acknowledged in social welfare, equal pay legislation, family law reform and jury service, but significant areas of discrimination against women remained untouched: the penal taxation of married women; the absence of maternity legislation; no child care; a lack of information and advice on family planning; and inadequate Unemployment Assistance for single women. The ITGWU broadcast the findings of the Women's Representative Committee and increased its lobby for change.

In August 1977 the Labour Court 'drove a coach and horses' through the Anti-Discrimination (Pay) Act when reversing an Equal Pay Officer's decision in Arklow Pottery. The male comparator received a higher rate on grounds other than sex, on compassionate grounds receiving the full labourer's rate even though physically unable to carry out the duties. The ITGWU concluded that 'in the current atmosphere of extreme FUE hostility to equal pay' the Court's invitation 'is bound to be received with glee by employers.' It was 'increasingly obvious' that the Act alone 'cannot gain complete equal pay.' Industrial action in support of equality was ordered.

The Employment Equality Act (1977) necessitated the removal of Marriage Benefit from the ITGWU Rules for women joining from 1 July.[10]

In February 1978 a *Liberty* 'Equal Pay and Pensions' supplement encouraged women members to push for equal pay and improved pensions and to use the Employment Equality Act. Data demonstrated the depth and breadth of work-place discrimination, and members were advised how to bring equal pay or equal treatment cases. Progress was made on maternity leave, although Ireland lagged well behind other EEC countries. Best Agreements were twenty-six weeks' leave on full pay in Sunday newspapers and P. J. Wall's, while twenty weeks was won in Willis Books, Hodges Figgis and Boland's Flour Mills, mostly for clerical staff. In 1979 the ITGWU sought technical amendments to the acts as employers fought, inch by inch, by 'despicable tactics' of every possible delay and appeal.[11]

Table 107: Women in the ITGWU, 1970–79

	Total membership	Women members	Women as proportion of total (%)
1970	162,478	54,159	33.3
1971	155,614	51,872	33.3
1972	155,879	51,959	33.3
1973	157,918	52,638	33.3
1974	156,418	52,139	33.3
1975	157,392	52,463	33.3
1976	154,388	51,464	33.3
1977	166,034	56,344	33.3
1978	176,429	58,809	33.3
1979	185,566	61,855	33.3

Source: National Archives, Registrar of Friendly Societies, file 275T.

Throughout the 1970s women's membership remained a static third, a convenient piece of arithmetic for the Registrar of Friendly Societies, to whom returns were made. These figures, the only ones available, show that an additional 7,696 women joined.

NORTHERN IRELAND

Joe McBrinn (NEC, Belfast) thanked the 1970 Conference for its 'financial help, supply of clothing, food and housing accommodation.' One member's son, Liam Lynch, was murdered in the Ardoyne area of Belfast while protecting his family. There was no 'crisis' in the North, however: 'it was always the same.' The problem, hidden so long under British and Irish Government carpets, surfaced with a vengeance. Joe Meehan recalled, after forty-eight hours with no sleep, sitting in Belfast Branch Office 'when the door opened and in walked the General Secretary' and NEC. Their gesture made a deep impression.

Conor Cruise O'Brien TD introduced a more reflective mood, not pleasing all Delegates. 'The problem of the Border not only should not be solved by force, it cannot be solved by force.' Attempts 'to solve it that way' would 'not result in unity.' Violence would 'only result in dead bodies,' mainly of working people, a 'legacy of increased hatred and fear ... probably in new forms of Government,' and 'Ireland divided into green and orange.' Settlement should not be forced on 'two thirds of the people' or licence given for restrictive legislation in the South. Unification depended on strengthening the labour movement, with civil rights a necessary precondition.

Stephen McGonagle (Derry) sought areas of Agreement and reform of repressive, sectarian legislation. Citing the constructive work of the Northern Ireland Committee of the ICTU, he asked whether Delegates were with him. There is no formal record of their response, but it was affirmative, albeit laced with anger and frustration.

Northern Branches had industrial successes. McGonagle acted as Vice-Chairman of the Derry Commission, administering local Government services and implementing the Development Plan for Derry, adding profile and prestige to the ITGWU. John McAleavey (Newry) traced the sense of isolation and despair that led to serious rioting. It was 'years of low wages, no jobs, the sailing back and forth to England for employment.' An ICTU motion moved by Mullen and Cruise O'Brien condemned 'without reservations' all those responsible for the dreadful toll of misery and human suffering.' The creation of the Ulster Defence Regiment was condemned as a return to institutionalised bigotry; but had the Republic got its own anti-sectarian house in order? Problems over community schools evidenced a continued Catholic domination. The real sufferers were the slum dwellers of Shankill, Falls and Bogside. The trade union movement must liberate them. There was an air of serious contemplation and foreboding. Worse was to come.

Ambivalence on violence might be detected in calls for the abolition of the Offences Against the State Act and the 'immediate release of all Irish political prisoners' in England and Northern Ireland. Cruise O'Brien questioned what a political prisoner was. Did such motions aid trade union unity? A lengthy queue formed to explain matters to him.

Meehan expressed tiredness of 'this clap-trap about trade union unity,' citing 10,000 shipyard workers marching to demand the introduction of internment. Brendan Corish confirmed that Cruise O'Brien stated Labour Party views, not a confirmation that assuaged an angry hall.[12]

In 1971 Carroll and McGonagle travelled in Europe to win union support against internment. Matt Guinan of the Transport Workers' Union of America sent financial aid through the Irish Red Cross for Northern refugees. The ICTU issued the first of many constructive, reasoned policies, *Peace, Employment and Re-construction in Northern Ireland*, which the ITGWU endorsed. Attitudes hardened, especially after the killing of fourteen civilians in Derry on Bloody Sunday, 30 January 1972. The ITGWU saw events as British 'get-tough' policy whose seeds went back 'to the coming to power of the British Conservative Party in 1970.' The 'more backward looking elements,' pushed into the background in the previous twenty years, 'came forward.' This explained 'the sell-out to the racialists in South Africa and Southern Rhodesia,' the aggressive attitude to unions and 'abrasive "stand on your own feet" approach to social welfare.' Citing the 'Insight Team' of the *Sunday Times,* the ITGWU accepted that internment was introduced to smother all Stormont opposition. It insisted that 'eventual reunification' was 'the only long-term solution.' They must resist sectarianism; the Northern minority were not to be manipulated in the interests of Southern interest groups; and territorial unity was secondary to the unity of people. Civil rights and civil liberties were central. Britain's role was divisive and disruptive. Incongruously, the ITGWU published the Northern Ireland section of its report in Irish, 'Na Sé Chontae.' McGonagle suggested that 'listening' was a missing ingredient on both sides.[13]

After Bloody Sunday the ITGWU felt 'we are personally involved.' It stepped up support for the NICRA and a settlement based on views taken from the union's founders, 'a line going back through the Land League, the Young Irelanders and Fintan Lawlor [*sic*]' and the United Irishmen, 'a history of genuine Catholic and Protestant co-operation.' It 'looked for much more than mere political independence.' For Tone, Davis, Lalor, Davitt and Connolly, 'separation from England' was the 'necessary prerequisite for creating a genuinely just, egalitarian society.'

This placed the ITGWU firmly in one camp. Its Belfast members were seen as intensely republican, although not all were. One NEC member, Joe McBrinn, served eighteen months in prison in England for alleged arms conspiracy. His release and 'vindication' underlined Unionist suspicion. McBrinn was marked absent from NEC meetings, 'detained at Her Majesty's Pleasure.' Once he was released, the threat of internment should he return to Belfast left him unemployed in Dublin.

Spontaneous and angry demonstrations of protest took place throughout the country after Derry. ITGWU members were often the organising force. An 'unscheduled mass protest' outside the British Embassy in Merrion Square, Dublin, reflected massive anger.

In March the union launched a campaign against internment, sending a petition to the Prime Minister, Edward Heath. It was not 'directed against fellow workers and citizens regardless of creed or nationality.' It demanded 'an end to internment without trial completely and without qualification.' Internment was 'not only in breach of the United Nations Declaration of Human Rights' and 'European Convention of Human Rights, but is contrary to all civilised standards of human justice.' It was 'sectarian and divisive' and caused 'great suffering in many families.' The union demanded the 'removal of the uncivilised Special Powers Act' and stated its intention 'to do everything within our power, personally and collectively, at home and abroad,' to remove the 'major impediment to an early political solution.' The ITGWU Derry Bloody Sunday Appeal raised £16,164.

At the Annual Conference Kennedy declared that 'we have never made any secret of the fact that we aspire and actively strive for the reunification of our country.' A lengthy, emotional discussion ensued. Paddy Devlin (Belfast) made his first Conference appearance, 'not sure whether I am an MP or not.' He warned of imminent civil war and unequal arms balance between the factions. Although acknowledging its defensive role, he urged the Provisional IRA to cease its bombings to let talks begin. Youghal wanted British troops withdrawn and the abolition of Stormont. The ITGWU abhorred the 'new dispensation of indifference, of affluence,' that disregarded Northern Ireland, or wished it would disappear. There were spill-over effects: the loss of lives in Dublin and Monaghan, loss of hotel and tourism jobs, and mounting security costs. Victims, Catholic or Protestant, were mostly of the working class.[14]

A total cessation of violence was necessary if 'ordinary politics' was to have an opportunity. Direct Rule from London and Diplock (non-jury) Courts did not improve matters. 'Military solutions' were unworkable. Opening premises in Newry, Kennedy appealed for tolerance and calm. Few listened.

On more mundane matters, a 'ginger group' on Belfast Docks, led by 'outside influences', produced *Dockers' Voice*, a militant paper critical of ITGWU Officials. Copperfastening a growing relationship with the SDLP, Gerry Fitt and Austin Currie joined the Belfast Branch, John Hume and Ivan Cooper in Derry, and Paddy O'Hanlon in Newry.[15] The Sunningdale Agreement between the parties and British and Irish Governments was agreed on 6–9 December 1973. It provided for a 'power-sharing' Executive, which was allowed to collapse after the loyalist workers' stoppage in May 1974. The ITGWU felt that the British Government had surrendered to the 'forces of reaction and triumphalism.' Kennedy said that 'any form of society that has to be maintained by the use of guns is a sick society.' The Belfast Branch demanded repatriation of the Price Sisters and all political prisoners. Carroll condemned both republican and loyalist violence. He saw Unionist violence as part of a long tradition and certainly not just a reaction to the IRA.

Today's picture of Ian Paisley leading masked men in Ballymena is yesterday's image of the upper-class British Officer in the Curragh suborning the Home

Rule Bill. No, the Loyalists, having been trained in the tradition of Lord Craigavon, needed no tuition from the IRA.

The Ulster Workers' Council had nothing to do with trade unions. It simply deepened divisions.

Meehan expressed the depth of anger, resentment, bitterness and despair within the minority, pointing out that in the rush to praise Sunningdale some on the Nationalist side saw it as a sell-out. Little hope of solution was offered. Bombings in Birmingham induced the British Government to rush through the Prevention of Terrorism Act. The NEC extended immediate sympathy to the Lord Mayor of Birmingham. The union supported demands by the ICTU for a Bill of Rights and the introduction of All-Ireland institutions. Kennedy insisted on the right 'to live free from threats of violence, intimidation and discrimination ... to associate freely and to advocate political change by peaceful means' and the right to 'well-paid work,' decent housing, full and free education and adequate social services. Much of this applied equally to the Republic.[16]

In September 1974 the ITGWU strongly opposed moves for an 'Ulster TUC.' It was sectarian and designed to weaken united ICTU action.

In 1975 the Labour Party was accused of reneging on agreed policy. Unless it moved for the repeal of internment, ITGWU members would be consulted 'on whether continued affiliation to the Party is desirable.' Charlie Taggart (Belfast) was among a joint Delegation of the Northern Ireland Committee of the ICTU and European Trade Union Confederation seeking support for the 'Better Life for All' campaign. It sought the right to live free from violence, sectarianism, intimidation and discrimination, security of employment and well-paid work, good housing, equality of educational opportunity and adequate social services. The ITGWU 'was one of the largest contributors' to the campaign fund.

The NEC reviewed its Northern Ireland presence. 'Foran, Kennedy, Larkin and Connolly' had 'played a crucial role in organising Catholic and Protestant' when 'no union existed to serve their interests.' The ITGWU, 'without forsaking any of its beliefs and assumptions,' could 'again establish a significant role.' Competing unions were, however, only too happy to play the green card, confining ITGWU membership to declining industries.

Huge demonstrations in 1976 were led by the 'Peace People'. Though recognising the strong yearning for peace, the ITGWU found their aims too narrow, apolitical and ultimately of little consequence. It 'was made more of outside the North than within it,' as evidenced by their Nobel Peace Prizes.

The report of the European Commission on Human Rights condemned Britain for the inhuman and degrading treatment of prisoners. It acknowledged that not all violence emanated from paramilitary sources. 'State or institutionalised violence' was perpetrated. The collapse of the Constitutional Convention brought political matters back to square one. The ITGWU cheered Roy Mason's departure as Secretary of State. He was 'abrupt in manner and oriented towards the military,' generating no confidence.

Fair Employment legislation and two Industrial Relations Orders established the Labour Relations Agency and much-needed employment rights. It was progress, as was Paddy Devlin's appointment as Organiser. Membership increased, even if it occasioned inter-union disputes in Belfast Corporation and Antrim Crystal. On 8 October 1977 a new part-time Branch was established in Ballycastle. The ITGWU was the first union to successfully conduct ballots for recognition through the Labour Relations Agency. Brian McCann (Belfast) said that 'at first, we didn't want Paddy Devlin.' It was 'like Ian Paisley joining the ATGWU!' Devlin's energy, commitment and success in expanding sterile Branches won everyone over.[17]

In 1976 Seán Ó Cearnaigh (Doirí Beaga) set the cat among the pigeons by calling for the repeal of articles 2 and 3 of the Constitution of Ireland 'as a means of bringing to an end the National Conflict.' Conor Cruise O'Brien, a hate figure for many, was the 'most articulate liberal in the Southern Government.' Northern membership was collapsing because of its identification with republican nationalism. McBrinn dismissed his motion as 'bunk' but displayed contradictory feelings when stating that British withdrawal would spell economic disaster. The NEC felt that the revocation of the articles 'could be taken as a confession of failure.' The motion was lost.

Devlin attacked Ó Cearnaigh and challenged him to move changes to the Rules. His motion struck at the heart of what the ITGWU stood for, a 'Sovereign Irish Socialist Republic.' He outlined advances made, a new understanding with the ATGWU, and economic demands.

In May 1977 the stoppage organised by the 'United Unionist Action Council', a 'motley group of para-military groups and disaffected Unionists' supported by Paisley, failed. It was not because of 16,000 troops but because workers decided not to give in to the 'intimidation and violence' that had destroyed the Executive in 1974. The Better Life for All campaign won adherents and changed minds. British policy remained militarist while tying the North closer to itself. Devlin thought the majority had the right to determine things but did not have a monopoly. An Emergency Motion called for an independent inquiry into the 'death by hanging of Brian Maguire, AUEW-TASS Branch Secretary, in Castlereagh Interrogation Centre.'

The ITGWU made a 'most comprehensive' submission to the Hotel and Restaurant Wages Council in 1979, was prominent in three major campaigns against cuts, and demanded the reorganisation of Belfast Harbour Commissioners. Such industrial normality was difficult as killings continued unabated. On 27 August Lord Mountbatten and companions were killed at Mullaghmore and eighteen soldiers blown to pieces at Warrenpoint. Demands for a right of 'hot pursuit' for British soldiers directly threatened Irish sovereignty, and 'more draconian emergency legislation' was enacted. Britain continued to treat symptoms, not cause. The ITGWU condemned the killings, also joining people in their disgust at the 'hysterical and crude outburst of virulent anti-Irish racialism in the British media,' which ignored the 'journalistic principles of objective reporting and responsibility not to incite.'

Séamus Mallon suggested that the Taoiseach, Jack Lynch, was 'making it easy' for Britain to drop the 'Irish dimension', which added to the pressure that saw him replaced by Charles Haughey. The ITGWU regretted that the national question was transformed 'into a plaything of conservative politicians' and 'used to deceive and divide the Left.' The union's views remained unaltered: national independence was integral to social emancipation. An indication of Britain's 'intention to disengage from Ireland and encourage unity' was a 'first necessary step' in uniting the Irish working class and realising its Socialist vision.[18]

CONGRESS

Having threatened to disaffiliate from Congress in 1969, the ITGWU fully debated its criticisms in 1970. It was agreed that ICTU Delegate Conferences should be recognised as the 'supreme authority' for determining policy, which would be effectively applied. Rationalisation was considered essential. In 'straightforward terms' this was 'acceptance of the underlying principle' of the ITGWU resolution.

Dónal Lehane (Cork No. 4) insisted that Congress did not provide services commensurate with affiliation costs, and could not or would not exercise adequate control over affiliates' industrial action. In September 1971 Carroll walked out of a meeting of the ICTU Executive because a discussion of Northern Ireland was not allowed. The ITGWU argued that the Northern Ireland Committee should allow All-Ireland representation, as the Annual Conference allowed Delegates from North and South. Congress dragged its heels. The ITGWU was seen as pushing a republican agenda too hard. Privately, it fully examined its relationship with Congress, especially in the light of the Development Services Division. Mick Finn (Tralee) wondered 'if, by expanding services,' they were 'interfering with the objective of rationalising' the movement. This was asked beyond the ITGWU. Jim Blake (Cork) came from the opposite angle: they were 'not getting value for money'; why 'should we pay for services from ICTU that we were getting from the DSD?' He resented proposed increases in Congress fees. Joe McBrinn (Belfast) and Andy Burke (Dublin No. 4) also questioned the logic of the Development Services Division: it let Congress 'give services free to other unions.' Jimmy Cullen (Dublin No. 9) suggested that the staff of the Division be hired to Congress to recoup costs. Debate was wrapped in the cloak of a sentiment that Congress rarely, if ever, did the ITGWU any favours. It was slow to forward state funding for union-run education. In February 1974 the NEC suggested withholding Congress affiliation fees until money owed was paid over. Paddy Clancy claimed that Congress 'had not only a financial dependence on our Union but a physical one as well.' The 'same went for the Labour Party.' Had this been openly heard by Congress or party it would have been resented as Liberty Hall arrogance.[19]

In September 1974 Congress received £100,000 in state grants. The ITGWU was due £18,000. Ruaidhrí Roberts, General Secretary of the ICTU, well aware of the tensions this allocation raised, suggested that joint premises be considered for ICTU education and research with the Development Services Division. There is no record of any ITGWU response. Some NEC members would have entertained the notion, but Paddy Clancy, Head of the Development Services Division and widely seen as the 'fourth General Officer', was vehemently opposed. In January 1977 the ITGWU offered to pay its Congress fees less sums owed it as niggling rancour persisted. In May the NEC complained that the ITGWU's support for Congress gave the 'kiss of life' to some unions. Conscious of alienating allies, Clancy cautioned that 'something positive' must be done to avoid a situation 'where we appeared to be always complaining at meetings of Congress.'

After the Ferenka dispute and internecine conflict with the Marine, Port and General Workers' Union, Kennedy, 'as an Officer of Congress, as well as General President' of the ITGWU, extended a 'sincere invitation' to all unions outside Congress 'to join or rejoin.' The Psychiatric Nurses' Association of Ireland, a breakaway from the ITGWU in 1969, affiliated to the Local Government and Public Services Union, so gaining access to Congress. Complaints were made that some members were heavily in arrears with the ITGWU. Meetings were sought with Congress, and if they did not take place the ITGWU 'would have to reconsider' its 'whole position vis-à-vis Congress.' Relations were in a downward spiral.[20]

Tensions were inevitable, given the ITGWU's numerical dominance in the Republic. Its greater resources were the subject of envy.

RELATIONS WITH OTHER UNIONS

Kennedy assured the 1970 Conference that talks with the WUI were 'proceeding in a spirit of good will and understanding.' Denis Larkin, General Secretary of the WUI, was a welcome fraternal guest. He was joined by two observers from six building craft unions, with which the ITGWU hoped to work in 'closer harmony and co-operation.' Mullen saw the ITGWU's responsibility as 'to be generous and to draw to ourselves in a friendly and brotherly fashion' all unions that had the 'common bond of nationalism and who look to us in times of crisis to honour our heritage.' Discussions opened with the Building Workers' Trade Union (Ancient Guild of Incorporated Brick and Stone Layers' Trade Union), the Stonecutters' Union of Ireland, the Irish National Painters' and Decorators' Trade Union, the Irish National Union of Woodworkers, the Irish Society of Woodcutting Machinists and the Operative Plasterers' and Allied Trades Society of Ireland, 'with a view to a new craft Federation dedicated to the principle of maximum co-operation in all spheres of action.' A 'formal constitution' was anticipated. The Federation of Irish Industrial and Building Operatives (Comhaltas Ceardchumann Tionscail agus Oibrithe Tógála na hÉireann) was established, with John Mulhall (INPDTU) as President, Patrick Duffy (Bricklayers) Vice-President and Seán Ó Murchú (ITGWU) Secretary. Craft unions represented 10,000 members, the ITGWU 25,000 craft members.[21]

Denis Larkin was the first Larkin to address an ITGWU Conference since 1923. A month earlier Kennedy addressed the WUI. Larkin reflected on Conroy and his brother James's roles in the unification of Congress. Regrettably, they had attended only one meeting between the ITGWU and WUI. When both Executives first met it was agreed that few fundamental differences existed. Kennedy was coy over a possible merger. The ITGWU Annual Report made no reference to talks.

In 1971 Kennedy thought that ITGWU and WUI members were disappointed that 'talks may not yet appear to have borne fruit.' Both were preoccupied with urgent business. The ITGWU Rules were amended in 1972 to allow for negotiation with groups or unions. Proposals for merger or transfer were subject to a ballot vote. There was no further mention of either the WUI or the Craft Group.

Larkin attended the 1974 Conference but did not speak. He featured in front-page photographs in *Liberty* addressing the annual dinner of Dublin District Council. In July 1974 Larkin's ICTU presidential speech openly asked British unions whether the time had come 'to cut the apron strings' and allow Irish trade unionists to determine their own destiny. In May 1975 Kennedy decided, with the NEC's approval, not to accept an invitation to the WUI Conference. Merger prospects were dead.[22]

In October 1971 Cantrell and Cochrane Staff Association joined the Association of Scientific, Technical and Managerial Staffs, instead of the ITGWU, as expected. The management allowed a plant meeting where the ITGWU was 'vilified and black-guarded'. Six members of the staff objected, and an apology was sought. A stoppage resulted, but to no avail. The ITGWU complained that 'an English-based union could come into an establishment where we had members already organised' and, with the management's 'connivance', force employees into their union.

Throughout 1971 and 1972 the ITGWU opposed the affiliation to Congress of the Association of Cinema and Television Technicians, a British union. These workers were already catered for. In 1972 'ginger group activities' were reported in Limerick, and although the Branch Secretary, Vincent Moran, assured the NEC that all was well, Dan Shaw was despatched to keep an eye on matters. Norman Kennedy, ATGWU, said that 'considerable numbers in Limerick wished to transfer' and requested Matt Merrigan 'to forward names.' A simultaneous ATGWU picket on Dunlop in Cork did little for mutual cordiality.

When needs must, however, general unions rallied together. After the Amalgamated Union of Engineering Workers objected to the ITGWU organising craftsmen, talks were held with the WUI and ATGWU to defend general union rights in the area. The ITGWU applied for membership of the National Federation of Craft Unions and 'let unions we have cordial relationships know' to gain support. In 1974 the ITGWU complained about 'infiltration' by the MPGWU in Foynes and Limerick.[23] The ITGWU organised Wellworthy, Dungarvan, but the ATGWU claimed 'squatters' rights': it represented Wellworthy employees in Britain. Pressure mounted when British ATGWU dockers threatened to black products and supplies for Waterford. Kennedy met the General Secretary of the TGWU, Jack Jones, to bring reason to bear.

As this was happening, Matt Merrigan, for the ATGWU—who regularly declared his principled opposition to pre-emptive closed-shop Agreements—and Larkin, for the WUI, wrote jointly to the FUE and the IDA complaining that 'neither Union was obtaining its fair share of new industry.' Pots were calling kettles black.

Competition between unions was often more surreptitious. In May 1975 the NEC was shocked to discover that the National Association of Transport Employees was the major railway union. Disbelievingly, it asked, 'How did this happen?' The knee-jerk reaction was to detail Chris Kirwan, Group Secretary, to see if NATE would amalgamate rather than to examine factors that led to disaffection. NATE was 'to merge elsewhere.'

In April 1976 discussions opened with the Irish Women Workers' Union, despite an open understanding that it was destined for the WUI; and 'off-the-record' talks were held with the ASTMS, the rumour being that its Irish Officer, Noel Harris, would become a Group Secretary, 'if he could bring his members with him.' An inter-union Agreement was signed with the Electrical Trades Union (Ireland).[24]

In January 1976 *Liberty* celebrated Larkin's Centenary. In 1979 Kennedy recalled the union's seventy years, concluding that no reference to its foundation 'could possibly be complete without paying tribute to its early inspiration, Big Jim Larkin.' He referred to the Larkin Monument to be unveiled in O'Connell Street as a 'fitting tribute by the workers of modern Ireland.' Such sentiments reflected the ITGWU's maturity.[25]

WAGES AND DISPUTES

In 1970 Carroll used the EEC Social Charter as a rod with which to beat the Government and employers. It began as a 1954 Council of Europe commitment and was re-framed in 1961 after consultation with the International Labour Organisation. Irish membership of the EEC was imminent. What would Ireland put in its report? That 100,000 were unemployed? That thousands worked for less than £13 a week, which the ITGWU reckoned a minimum standard? That many children left school early to become cheap factory fodder? That there was a housing crisis, low social welfare standards and inadequate general and mental health services? That safety, health and welfare at work was neglected and poor industrial relations were but one aspect of workers' disaffection and alienation?

Pearse O'Sullivan (Tralee) sought a 'status quo' clause in all Agreements to 'eradicate this great evil' of unofficial or 'lightning strikes,' reflecting the jittery feeling among Delegates after the Maintenance Dispute. Many unofficial disputes were caused by 'ham-fisted' handling of minor problems by managements. His idea would create valuable 'breathing space'. The ITGWU spent £81,048 on strikes, the most significant being a seven-week stoppage at Roadmaster Caravans, Kilkenny, and the 22-week national cement strike, accounting for £49,006.

The Twelfth Wage Round gathered momentum in the spring. The Employer-Labour Conference failed to reach Agreement, and the Government issued its own guidelines on 16 October, providing for a limit of 6% with, for adult males, a floor of 24s (£2) a week and ceiling of 36s (£1 16s). Price controls were to be placed on housing and on general retail prices, insurance, banking, professional fees and rents.

The NEC expressed its opposition to proposals for wage freezes in the Thirteenth Round. It removed the fundamental and inalienable right to strike. Having taken such powers, the Government might be reluctant to surrender them. In applying controls to Twelfth-Round Agreements that provided for more than 6% the Government was 'endeavouring to legalise dishonesty,' giving a 'green light to employers to repudiate Agreements.' Workers' living standards would be depressed, while measures to control other incomes were negligible. Concern for lower income groups was false, as proposals gave 50% higher increases to those above £30 a week, compared with those on less than £20. They discriminated against women by denying equal pay.

The ITGWU sought the moral high ground. After the Maintenance Dispute it 'indicated publicly' that it 'would honour all Agreements in full.' This was welcomed by employers and the Government, who 'realised that industrial relations would be reduced to a shambles if the parties to these Agreements were permitted, for any reason, to dishonour their obligations.'

With no sense of dishonour, the Government proposed to sabotage the Agreement. Congress met the Taoiseach on 29 October, and the Government withdrew the limitation on wages from the Prices and Incomes (Temporary Provisions) Bill. Thirteenth-Round terms were then agreed and described as a national wages Agreement. Carroll mused that it 'may well prove to be a major factor in the restoration of our country's economic health.'[26]

In 1971, £154,211 was dispensed on strikes, £60,754 going to Unidare, Dublin, where 1,088 workers were out for ten weeks. From 1 July 1972 the Fourteenth Round (National Wage Agreement) began. Kennedy said that the 'ITGWU has never been enchanted with the principle of a National Agreement as a permanent method of fixing wages.' In some circumstances a 'free-for-all' was better.

Table 108: ITGWU Dispute Pay (£), 1970–79

1970	81,048	1976	76,229
1971	154,211	1977	263,306
1972	135,529	1978	402,239
1973	40,881	1979	145,179
1974	191,420	Total	2,101,094
1975	167,101		

Source: ITGWU, Annual Report, 1970–79.

In any future National Wage Agreements Dublin District Council sought an escalator clause, with increases added to tax-free allowances. Special provisions for workers operating productivity and incentive schemes would 'combat employers sheltering behind national Agreements in order to avoid having to pay additional money for the productivity element of local Agreements.' National Wage Agreements should protect 'incomes rather than employment,' with wage increases balanced by price control and more progressive fiscal policies. Debate demonstrated that some members thought only in personal or Sectional terms.

In February it was decided that Congress should enter new talks. Terms were rejected by a Special Delegate Conference on 23 June 1972 and by Congress on 24 June. Revised terms were quickly negotiated and accepted, 81,579 to 27,508. Kennedy drew conclusions from the Conference and ballot. Members were 'in favour of the principle of a National Wage Agreement,' and in a 'free-for-all' many lower-paid workers 'would not benefit to anything like the same extent' and it would be disadvantageous to the 'working-class movement as a whole.'[27] His view had changed.

In 1972 Dispute Pay was £135,529. There was 'ready acknowledgement that despite their deficiencies the Thirteenth and Fourteenth Round . . . contributed much to stability' and industrial peace and moderated inflation. Workers' share of the national cake had not increased, however.

After membership of the EEC the farming community saw a dramatic rise in incomes. Workers demanded the same. Carroll felt the Employer-Labour Conference was used to control wages and salaries but the National Prices Commission failed to achieve what was required. He asked Congress to open negotiations with state, employers and other representative interests to establish 'a national development and planning authority', in which unions would be an 'implementing partner.' A National Economic Council was agreed in July 1971. Two years and membership of the EEC had elapsed since. The worry was that the 'lowest level of social, political and economic activity' would apply 'because of the primacy of materialism for its own sake.' The ITGWU firmly believed that 'we must seek to regain control of our own social and economic destiny as a matter of grave urgency.' Tralee and Castleblayney wanted a statutory minimum wage of £25, and Dublin District Council wanted the Fourteenth Round ended early. Laois-Offaly wanted future Agreements limited to twelve months' duration, a classic reaction to rampant inflation. More than sixty Delegates addressed the wages debate, reflecting tensions between urban and rural Branches, between low paid and better paid and between men and women.[28]

In late 1973 the Fourteenth Round concluded for most. The ITGWU was 'not committed to opposing' another National Wage Agreement, but Fifteenth-Round proposals were rejected, by 47,286 to 39,164, with Congress Delegates following suit on 29 January 1974, 295 to 103. Amended terms were ratified on 7 March. Employers were quick to use the 'inability to pay' clause. Press criticism of wage increases was loud.

Kennedy's response was unequivocal.

I want to make it perfectly clear, that while we are always prepared to discuss the economy with the Government, or any other interested parties, and to explore all proposals which would help to resolve or ease the unemployment and inflation problems, we must say here and now—HANDS OFF THE NATIONAL PAY PACT!

'Rigid resistance' would be offered to employers negating the Agreement, especially as pre-tax profits showed a rise of 32% and money earnings increased by 19%, while inflation ran at 20%, resulting in falling living standards. Carroll observed that pressure had mounted 'to make the workers become the conscience of the nation in regard to the worsening state of our economy.' While not to blame, workers nevertheless carried an undue burden through inflation and unemployment. Oil prices were the major external factor feeding inflation.

Within the ITGWU, rising dispute and general costs created talk of 'tightening internal financial procedures' and taking better 'control of the management of Strike Pay.' A bus strike cost the union more than £100,000, and it was observed that some members were 'going sick before strike notice expired as pay-related benefit gave them more than Strike Pay.' Should this influence the level of Strike Pay?

In October, with Sixteenth-Round talks in the air, a survey of members produced an Outline Approach to Wages Policy. Any new Agreement should retain living standards by quarterly increases linked to the Consumer Price Index, give higher flat-rate increases to lower-paid workers, last for only nine months, provide increases in social welfare, continuously review income tax, ensure equal pay 'without delay,' and progress policies on education, housing, women's rights, children and poverty.[29]

In 1975 thirty-five members in Credit Finance struck over the dismissal of their Shop Steward. Their recognition battle against obdurate employers was significant with regard to the organising of white-collar workers. It ended after a ten-week sit-in with complete victory. In Thom's Directories an equally bitter strike concluded with the company closing, serving 'to remind us forcefully that the spirit of Martin Murphyism lives on.' Dispute Pay totalled £167,101.

In April a four-page *Liberty* supplement enabled members to make an informed judgement regarding proposals for a Sixteenth-Round National Wage Agreement. Most turned to the 'ready reckoner' to calculate what increases they might gain. This presentation became normal but on this first occasion set new standards of informing union democracy. It contrasted with other unions that did not even ballot members, let alone issue comprehensive explanatory materials. ITGWU members accepted the terms, by 67 to 32%, and on 15 April, Congress endorsed them, 281 to 117. Early complaints were that employers could plead 'inability to pay' and that information provided to Labour Court assessors could not be seen by Workers' Representatives. Such secrecy inevitably created suspicion. The NEC felt that National Wage Agreements were a 'sick joke', with an 'orderly queue forming in the Labour Court over inability to pay.'

In the Budget of 26 June the Government announced an embargo on 'special increases' in the public service. Congress immediately declared this to be in breach of the National Wage Agreement. It was referred to the Adjudication Committee, with somewhat ambiguous findings.[30]

In February 1976 Congress received a mandate to enter talks on a National Wage Agreement, 254 to 101, although any pay pause—the employers' basic demand—

was ruled out. Meanwhile 'one of the most vicious strikes ever experienced in this union' terminated after sixteen weeks for Securicor's cash-in-transit drivers. Thirty-five men rejected the management's unilateral alteration of conditions. The company closed the business.

On 3 July terms for a National Wage Agreement were narrowly rejected by a Special Congress, 202 to 211. Carroll reminded all that the ITGWU was 'not committed to the principle,' considering each proposal on its merits. Members rejected the terms by two to one. A sticking-point was that up to 100,000 workers had not received their entitlements under the previous Agreement. Enthusiasm for debate was such that the Conference went well past its scheduled finishing time. New interim terms, together with the promise of tripartite talks on economic and social matters, emerged and were put to a ballot. *Liberty* published its now usual guide, full text and 'ready reckoner'. There was no NEC recommendation, however, merely an invitation to vote. Neither General Officers nor NEC decided to 'accept or reject an offer like this.' That 'would not be right.' Important decisions were 'made by you—the member.' The NEC did finally recommend acceptance. On 11 September 1976 Congress accepted the amended Agreement, 309 to 90, a union ballot having already accepted. Carroll talked of the 'emergency' of unemployment. This time around it was in the 'yes' camp. It might not be so in future.[31]

In February 1977 members balloted on Eighteenth-Round proposals, recommended by the NEC. The ITGWU had reservations but thought it the best available in all circumstances, mainly through the good offices of the Minister for Labour, Michael O'Leary. Congress accepted on 22 February, 249 to 155. Carroll, sniping at some who 'were opposed to National Wage Agreements no matter what they contained,' said the ITGWU had no such 'hang-ups'. It voted in favour, 91,341 to 56,483. Increasingly, members sought preconditions: a National Minimum Wage, the automatic indexing of increases, retention of relativities and flat-rate increases.

Éamonn Lawless (NEC) put his name to a press article, albeit in a personal capacity, attacking National Wage Agreements, creating quite a stir. At the next NEC meeting he fell on his sword. He 'had spent twenty-one unhappy days' agonising over matters and thought 'there was nothing substantial coming from the ICTU.' He was unhappy with the income-tax concessions, green pound and job creation, which was 'dealt with in a very skimpy fashion.' He 'just had to get his feelings out' and 'could not see where he was breaking Rule.' He was 'most anxious not to hurt anyone' on the NEC and, 'more important, did not wish this Union, which he loved as much as anyone else, [to] suffer by any action of his.' He moved that NEC decisions, once taken, should bind all, a concept of 'cabinet responsibility' applied to this day.

A recognition dispute with the bookmakers Kilmartin ran until October. Pickets were first placed on 12 March, when 187 members of Dublin No. 2 Branch struck over deplorable working conditions, the management's refusal to negotiate improvements, and inadequate compensation to a former Shop Steward. The owner died shortly after the dispute began, complicating matters. In early summer, all were made redundant. The employer pleaded inability to pay the terms of the National Wage Agreement recommended by the Labour Court. Forty-six refused redundancy and maintained the strike. A sit-in followed the company's offer to pay the Agreement terms only to those accepting redundancy. The company opened some Branches on a lease basis, using non-union labour. Thirty-three members carried the strike into its ninth month. After thirty-seven weeks—believed to be the longest strike by women workers—only twenty-eight of the original 187 members remained. In addition to statutory redundancy, the company paid them all three weeks for every year of service. If Kilmartin's were ever to reopen, the ITGWU had negotiating rights and former employees had first call on employment. Six bookies' shops that opened during the strike employed the final twenty-eight members. The strike cost the union £61,000.[32]

Des Geraghty led a debate in *Liberty* on the merits of National Wage Agreements versus 'free-for-alls' (free collective bargaining). Central bargaining was required but should not be a further pay Agreement except as part of a broader package. A planned approach to industry and company-level bargaining were required to end reactive, *laissez-faire* trade unionism that expended massive energy to get nowhere.

In March 1978 the NEC recommended rejection of the Nineteenth Round after 'careful and detailed examination.' Clause 8 'dictated' conditions under which 'industrial action must be conducted.' It was 'both repugnant and unnecessary,' constituting an 'unprecedented interference' with unions' freedom. The wage terms were considered reasonable but did not do enough for low pay. Despite clear rejection by members—73,422 to 32,423, a majority against of 40,999—ICTU Delegates voted to accept, 240 to 215. Some unions, supposedly in principle against National Wage Agreements, scuttled into the 'yes' lobby they had long derided. The ITGWU quoted, with considerable irony, the popular song, 'When will they ever learn?' Many unions with a membership far smaller than the ITGWU's majority against the Agreement voted for, without balloting their members. The *Irish Press* shouted: 'SMALLER UNIONS WIN. BIG UNIONS BEATEN ON PAY.' Twelve weeks' back money persuaded many, and it was suggested that unions with few resources did not fancy a potentially expensive 'free-for-all'.

Liberty Hall adopted a sanguine attitude. 'What will the ITGWU do now?' Living in a democratic society, they would abide by the Congress decision.

Within the confines of the Agreement and the obnoxious clause 8, the ITGWU pursued 'Higher Earnings for the Lower Paid' (HELP), intended to raise all wages above the £50 barrier. The National Wage Agreement could be used. Branches were instructed to seek the additional 2% flat-rate increase under clause 7 (1), to refer matters to the Labour Court if need be under clause 7 (3), to claim further amounts if productivity could be demonstrated under clause 7 (4) and to vigorously pursue equal pay, imaginatively using the 'work of equal value' provision of the Anti-Discrimination (Pay) Act (1974). In addition it sought reductions in income tax on low pay and improved social welfare benefits. Human-interest stories of HELP successes featured in *Liberty,* stimulating greater activity.

A one-day seminar on 6 November, an 'Outline Approach to Wages Policy', was held. Wages could not be determined in isolation. Members had to 'accept the need for a co-ordinated policy approach over the whole field of socio-economic issues affecting them.' Central to this was 'a three to five year plan.' Short-term and long-term objectives could be pursued with the 'necessary machinery to monitor and measure progress.' Meanwhile HELP 'proceeded . . . as quickly as possible.' The seminar endeavoured to maximise returns from the National Wage Agreement.[33]

In 1978 Dublin District Council wanted recommendations for or against National Wage Agreements to come only from Special Conferences 'convened specifically for that purpose.' The NEC previously made recommendations. Campaigns were then mounted to ensure that members followed. It would be more democratic if the Delegate Conference considered and debated proposals. The NEC could lead discussion and offer opinions. The NEC moved rejection, the hall surprisingly concurring. It demonstrated the tensions created by ever-tightening National Wage Agreements.

In September the ITGWU led 20,000 marchers in Waterford in defence of jobs in National Board and Paper Mills, part of demands for the protection of employment. On 14 November the ICTU, on a show of hands, decided against entering talks with a belligerent FUE. Carroll said that entering talks before the content of the Budget and the implications of the European Monetary System were known 'would be crazy.' He demanded minimum guarantees of the indexation of income tax allowances, greater tax equity, with farmers and the self-employed brought into the tax net, effective measures against tax evasion, a wealth tax, twice-yearly adjustments in social welfare payments, a free, comprehensive health service, a national income-related pension scheme and the implementation of HELP. Rewards for productivity, maintenance of employment, equal pay, reduced working hours and improved paid holidays lengthened a long list.

There was a 22-week strike in Kildare Chilling, a 28-week battle in Arigna coalmines, a 26-week unofficial stoppage at Tynagh Mines and a five-week unofficial strike in the mill at Tara Mines. Poor ore prices caused losses in Tara Mines, and new wage schemes were negotiated. Seventy mill workers pursued a Sectional claim. The workers signed personal declarations that they would abide by procedures, against the ITGWU's advice. The near exhaustion of Tynagh Mines meant that men wanted matters settled. Unofficial action lasted from June to Christmas, with settlement terms for closure agreed after a Section 24 Labour Court investigation. At Arigna 230 members struck for a wage increase after it was given to fitters, gaining 63% increases for underground shovellers.[34]

In January 1979 attention focused on HELP. Having rejected the Nineteenth Round but seeing it narrowly accepted by Congress, the ITGWU was determined to succeed. As Budget time approached, provincial Branches lobbied TDs to 'call halt' to the annual hit at the vulnerable. In March, Mullen said that flat-rate increases, not percentage increases, would have to feature, with flexibility to allow bargaining at the local level. Tax reform was imperative. The Government ignored the opportunity presented by the Budget to introduce a wealth tax. Lower-paid workers lost out in relative and absolute terms.

The ITGWU had had enough. Narrow, increasingly rigid national wage agreements had had their day. Agreements that simply gave more 'paper money' to workers, who then gave it back to the Government and the rich through extra taxes and rising prices, were pointless. Mullen declared that 'future advances' would be 'firmly based upon economic and social reality and must not be influenced by a cynical version of the "Numbers Game".' Wages would 'not be improved simply by proclaiming higher figures than the last mentioned by another group' or by competing claims to re-establish questionable differentials . . . Our future strategy must be a serious continuation of our war against privilege and injustice.'

By May proposals for a 'National Understanding for Economic and Social Development' emerged, a radically different approach involving the Government as Government. The ITGWU urged members, 'Vote No!' It would not be 'rushed into making a hasty and unalterable decision.' It did not accept that the proposals represented what the Taoiseach said was 'the very limit of what the country could reasonably afford.' Objection was made to percentage increases. The rich would get richer.

Andy Burke (NEC) thought the restrictive paragraph 9 'dynamite for our Union.' It was 'out of line with HELP.' The ITGWU demanded renegotiation and interim settlement. The NEC nevertheless welcomed the 'principle underlining' the National Understanding. The union's involvement had to 'broaden and deepen.'

Rejected by Congress, the National Understanding appeared dead. The ITGWU Conference rallied members behind comprehensive campaigns at the work-place and the national level. The ballot vote showed a majority of 59,070 against out of 108,433 votes cast. It was felt that 'both Connolly and Larkin recognised that it was not sufficient' just 'to combine, only to defend its members in a fundamentally unjust society.' They 'must also be organised to attack the root causes of those injustices.' It could 'well be that 1979 will represent a new turning point in the history of our organisation and that of the whole trade union movement.' The NEC wanted unity of purpose and action. 'We have the organisation and the ability.' It now had to 'develop the will to use it intelligently.'

Amended terms were accepted, albeit with complaints about inadequate tax reform and a need to clarify what was meant by National Enterprise Agency and National Hire Agency. The oil crisis contributed to the NEC's change of heart, economic uncertainties abounding. It hedged its bets, suggesting acceptance only as a 'basis upon which we can build.' It might represent 'the beginning of a new era' or, if the Government failed to make a significant response, might 'equally be a period of massive disillusionment.' Either way, the ITGWU saw the National Understanding as beginning a process, not an end in itself.

Benefits came quickly. The Minister for Social Welfare, Charles Haughey, accepted that pay-related contributions should not be deducted from redundancy payments, and the Minister for Labour, Gene Fitzgerald, drafted safety regulations on brucellosis. These small beginnings were evidence of what the new arrangement could achieve. Failure of the Government to save BIM Boatyards, the bungling of Van Hool bus-building and the general tolerance of private-sector incompetence quickly created disillusion. The ITGWU forcefully reminded the Government of its obligations.

So novel was the National Understanding that Congress produced a special report in November to acquaint unions with what might be wrung from it.[35]

ALL-OUT PICKETS

On 18 March 1969 the Minister for Finance requested Congress not to seek increases based on the settlement of the Maintenance Dispute. Congress asked to meet the Minister for Labour and Minister for Finance jointly. A Working Party was established, which reported after meetings on 27 and 28 May that there would be movement on low pay and equal pay. The ICTU Public Services Committee accepted proposals that, ultimately, provided increases of 25s for manual grades.

The main result of the Maintenance Dispute was the Congress 'All-Out Picket' system, adopted in 1970. If any union wished to be supported when on strike, application was made to the ICTU Disputes Committee for an All-Out Picket. It would be denied if other unions could show reason, but if granted—either with no opposition or because the Disputes Committee overruled objections—the All-Out Pickets were considered to be binding on all other unions, in effect an official picket for all. The proposals, while breaking traditional attitudes that all pickets were sacred, were designed to reintroduce internal discipline and to demonstrate that, by the unions putting their own house in order, legislation was unnecessary. All-Out Pickets became effective from 1 October.

The ITGWU was often falsely accused of being the champion of All-Out Pickets. It strenuously opposed an All-Out Picket in a dispute by RTÉ with its craft group in May 1976. The ITGWU 'naturally' honoured the pickets, but 'the whole question of the procedure to govern the granting and continuance of All Out Picket approval' was questioned.

The Ferenka dispute in 1977 brought picketing back into the limelight. *Liberty* commented that for many unconnected with the movement 'the very mention of the word "union" conjured up images of pickets and strikes.' The reality was far from that, but the ITGWU was concerned that 'industrial anarchy' could ensue if every unofficial picket was obeyed willy-nilly. To some, such comments reeked of betrayal, but these same critics, when their own interests were threatened, made the same appeals for matters to be processed through procedures. That was all the ITGWU asked for.[36]

THE CEMENT STRIKE

A strike in Cement Ltd in Drogheda and Limerick dragged from 1 February to 29 June 1970. Jim Moonan (Drogheda) thanked Branches for their financial and moral support. Police escorts were given to lorries carrying smuggled cement over the border. Press reports that unions were not backing members were 'untrue, unjust and unfair.' Joe Meehan (Belfast) and D. O'Mahony (Cork No. 5) testified to port workers' solidarity in keeping cement out. Éamonn Wall (Cork No. 6) spoke of parading through Cork streets on behalf of cement workers, 'but I am not going to be associated with parades organised by pseudo-groups, organised by Maoists, by the Cork Workers' Defence Committee, God bless the mark,' and 'people that we had to expel.' The Cork Workers' Defence Committee called a General Strike. When it did not occur it picketed Connolly Hall. Wall fingered the ATGWU, as only in their ports did cement enter the country. In mid-April a sub-Committee of the Construction JIC explored a settlement, resulting in a Labour Court recommendation on 7 May that provided for £2 10s, back-dated to 1 January, with a further £1 from 1 June. Women's pay would increase by £2 5s from January and 17s 6d from June. Annual leave, rest periods, compassionate leave, service pay, production bonus, shift work and pensions were addressed. It was rejected on 29 May.

After intervention by the Minister an officer of the Labour Court, D. Lyons, met the parties on 8 and 15 June and drew up further settlement proposals, which were accepted by a ballot of ITGWU and ATGWU members on 26 June.[37]

MOGUL

The Mogul dispute arose over the alleged larceny of a packet of cigarettes. The Labour Court recommended reinstatement, but members wanted compensation for their lost time. They balloted for a strike, which began on Monday 31 May 1971. The ITGWU felt it was pointless dealing with the local management. It met representatives of the Canadian owners on 7 July and produced acceptable terms: the member to be reinstated as a bit-sharpener, without prejudice. Mogul made *ex gratia* payments of £300 to each worker; the union and employer agreed to approach the Mines and Quarries Inspectorate regarding safety compliance, complaints over overtime shift schedules were investigated, annual leave entitlements reviewed, and there was no victimisation.[38] On the morning of Saturday 3 July, however, 'an explosion took place' at the transformer, killing a local man who was in the vicinity. The damage obliged workers to take their three weeks' annual leave while repairs were carried out. The ITGWU felt the expensive lesson learnt was that the sacking or dismissal of an employee should be the employer's last resort.

NURSES

On Sunday 7 November 1971 psychiatric nurses withdrew from every District hospital over the elimination of temporary service and appointments due, agreement on claims of dual-qualified nurses and senior administrative nursing grades, unresolved Twelfth-Round claims and compensation for working on Saturdays, Sundays and public holidays. The Employer-Labour Conference met on 5 November to attempt a resolution. The ITGWU observed that 'psychiatric nurses are not by tradition ultra-militant or "strike-happy"'. The limit of their endurance was far exceeded. The management disregarded JIC procedures, refusing to negotiate. The Minister for Health had, for twelve years, talked of initiatives on temporary service. No progress was evident. A formula agreed in Cavan-Monaghan was acceptable to nurses throughout the country, but the Minister declined to act.

After a five-day stoppage a settlement was reached, resulting in 10% salary increases, with a minimum increase of £90 a year; the payment of a third equal-pay instalment to women from 1 April 1973; a forty-hour week from 1 April 1973; a marriage allowance of £125 a year for widowed psychiatric nurses; leave with pay and travelling expenses for trainee nurses attending examinations; new salary and career structures for nurses holding occupational therapy diplomas; and special allowances for attendance on Saturdays, Sundays and public holidays. Written submissions were made to the Working Party established by the Minister in late 1970 on organisation within the Psychiatric Service, and ITGWU members were appointed to regional health boards. Committees were set up in hospitals to deal with continuing change. The strikers guaranteed emergency cover, and the procedure operated 'without a hitch', except in hospitals where multiple unions operated. Here 'real difficulties' were experienced, underlining the 'threat from disunity'. Claims for 'non-nursing staff' followed and resulted in a forty-hour week, Sunday and night allowances, shift premiums at time and one-sixth, and Twelfth-Round increases from 1 January 1972 with a minimum of £2, giving minimum rates for men of £18.65 to £21.62 per week and for women £15.66 to £18.40.[39]

CIÉ

In 1971 the McKinsey Report, *Defining the Role of Public Transport in a Changing Environment*, recommended rationalisation or even complete closure of the railway system. The ITGWU opposed, drawing attention to the aspects of the report that talked of social advantage and railway expansion. Labour Court recommendation 2452, addressing one-person operation on buses, was rejected by the ITGWU and the National Busmen's Union.

In January 1973 the ITGWU wanted a sworn public inquiry into the management of CIÉ. Fares rose faster than prices in the previous seven years, and yet the insistence on one-person operation without satisfying workers' fears of job losses and insufficient earnings was persistent. A 'breakthrough for busmen' was achieved in September 1973 when the Labour Court conceded the ITGWU's claims for time and one-sixth for workers on rotating duties and similar payments for weekend working. It brought £800,000 and £181,000 a year, respectively, for members. The claim operated from 1 April 1974. The union commented that it was 'not often that this union crows about its achievements,' as Officials had a 'natural reticence about going about swaggering' about what they won for members—as, 'after all, that is what they are put there to do.' On this occasion, outdoing the NBU was too important to hide.

In December 1976 further problems on Dublin buses were firmly blamed on the management's obduracy. The ITGWU called for the dismissal of the Chairman of CIÉ and 'several other people in positions of authority' who were 'responsible for the present debacle.' Government ineptitude had permitted the running down of Dublin services. A new problem faced bus workers in 1978 when violence to drivers and conductors became commonplace. The ITGWU sought greater protection for workers.[40]

RTÉ

A craftsmen's dispute put RTÉ off the air in 1976. The ITGWU complained that the ICTU awarded an All-Out Picket but 'appeared to give little weight to the opposition' registered by seven hundred members. Worse, RTÉ 'ignored the public sector embargo' and Government 'guidelines for the public sector in relation to special claims.' It 'appeared to be prepared to make cannon-fodder out of RTÉ employees in the fight to upset Government policy on special increases within the public sector.'[41] The ITGWU asked Congress to reconsider its All-Out Picket strategy.

A second dispute, this time for ITGWU technicians, was resolved through the Employer-Labour Conference, but the union insisted on meeting the RTÉ Authority to discuss means of rationalising industrial relations procedures. There were fifteen unions in RTÉ, the ITGWU representing more than 50% of the work force.

FERENKA

The Ferenka plant at Annacotty, outside Limerick, was placed on a three-day week in February 1975. Orders were falling, and 1,400 workers had uncertain employment. Jobs were scarce in Limerick, and it was regarded locally as a disaster. The ITGWU was surprised at the 'great deal of hostility' offered by the management when attempting to extend organisation to the staff. Ferenka had 'always professed itself to hold progressive attitudes about unionisation,' making its 'anti-union attitude' to white-collar staff 'all the more difficult to appreciate.' In May 1973 six unofficial strikes in six months occurred, and there were complaints that the Branch Secretary, Vincent Moran, spent 'a lot of his time in this particular job.' The ITGWU met the senior management in an attempt to improve matters. There was a 'marked absence of knowledge on the part of the supervisors as to their functions.' Consultants advised the management on personnel, and the ITGWU tried 'to get a room on the premises' and 'time off for our Reps.' There was 'no desire apparent on the part of the members for a separate or part-time Branch of their own.' In 1975 Ferenka cut its work force from 990 to 740, although the number rose again to 1,000 in 1976. Matters had not improved by February 1977, when Moran wanted Ferenka members taken out of his Branch. The Marine, Port and General Workers' Union began to recruit the disaffected.[42]

On 28 October 1977 protective notice was given to all employees. The ITGWU placed national press advertisements to correct what it saw as erroneous and malevolent reporting. The sacking of six workers led to unofficial action. The union used all established procedures, but Labour Court conciliation could not proceed, because unofficial action persisted. The MPGWU—not affiliated to Congress—stepped up its organisation. The attitude of the ITGWU was unequivocal: 'The behaviour of the MPGWU in this matter is without precedent.' It had 'involved itself in a dispute which is the concern of a sister union' and 'declared an unofficial strike to be official—all with the aim of recruiting new members and in complete dis-regard of a democratically approved Agreement between the management and workers of Ferenka.' Did the MPGWU intend to ride rough-shod over Agreements throughout the country? If it did, Ferenka was of importance to the whole move-ment. The MPGWU left Congress because it was 'unwilling to abide by the principle of independent arbitration,' something it now advocated in Ferenka. Its interference added tremendous pressure and did 'not permit calm and informed discussion.' 'Outrageous statements' were made about poor representation by the ITGWU, but 'these simply could not be squared with the facts.'

A circular to workers described gains in wages, conditions and disciplinary claims made by the union, which had 'yet to be refuted because empty assertion and rhetoric have crumbled in the face of it.' Philip Byrnes, the Leader of the unofficial action, had previously been reinstated through the intervention of the ITGWU. Basic wages had risen from £24.50 to £34.92 per week, and, although the company per-suaded the Labour Court of its 'inability to pay' Sixteenth-Round increases, they were paid on a phased basis from July 1975 to February 1976. By the first phase of the Eighteenth Round wages were at £46.02 and would rise to £49.71. There were gains too on shift premiums, overtime, holidays, mortality, pension and sickness pay schemes, and the benevolent fund. In three dismissal cases referred to the Labour Court, reinstatement resulted each time.

Problems had mounted by October 1977. 'Grave disappointment' at the Branch Secretary's performance was expressed. The Ferenka Shop Steward, Tom O'Dwyer, was appointed *pro tem.* Carroll gave an 'excellent' performance on television, despite the clouding presence of the MPGWU. Disappointingly, Limerick Trades Council gave 'credence to a non-Congress union,' and yet 'some of our own Officials did not consider it worth their while to attend' the Trades Council.

Eddie Lawless (NEC) urged the ITGWU to 'identify with workers and challenge management when they are wrong.' Perhaps 'our Officials were not attending to their jobs in a proper manner.' Intervention by the Minister led to a document, 'Proposals to Enable a Resumption of Normal Working at Ferenka and Avoid a Closure of the Plant', which suggested an independently chaired Tribunal to 'exam-ine causes of the present discontent' and report by 31 March 1978. Pending this, full working would resume, the six suspended men would report back for work and the Labour Court would investigate the 'indefinite suspension of Mr Phil Byrnes.' All concerned would be bound by the Court's recommendation, Byrnes paid his normal rate pending the final outcome, the Court would appoint an officer 'to hold elections for production Reps,' who were 'not to be regarded as trade union repre-sentatives but representatives of the workers,' and an officer of the Court would act as Chairman. Most controversially, and a hard pill for any union to swallow, was that no worker was compelled to be a member of any union, and no dues were to be deducted or union meetings held during working hours or on company premises. The company would apply the terms of the National Wage Agreement. Finally, there would be 'no stoppages' from 21 October 1977 to 31 March 1978. The

ITGWU felt it had no choice but to accept, not least given the company's alleged financial problems.[43]

The Minister for Labour, Gene Fitzgerald, intervened on 31 October with 'close down imminent.' The fears were realised, with 1,400 jobs lost. ENKA, the parent company, was in deep financial difficulty. For the ITGWU it was 'the greatest industrial catastrophe of the year.' It despatched a forlorn Delegation to the Netherlands to try to salvage something.

Ill-informed comment blamed the ITGWU. The FUE quickly condemned unions generally and lectured Congress on changes needed in its constitution. It had 'not been so quick to call news Conferences to deplore the numerous close-downs of businesses due to bad management practices.' The ITGWU had never declared a strike, continued to represent members by abiding by the ICTU constitution that the FUE wanted changed, and did not make recognition a precondition of a settlement.

When the whole affair was over the ITGWU placed on record 'our appreciation of those members who, despite intimidation and threats, remained loyal.' Much 'noise' was made about low rates of pay, but the union had successfully brought the case to the Labour Court. All improvements were accepted by ballot vote. The union made no apology for its policy 'in consultation with our Representatives and members.' It was the 'correct one and subsequent events' showed 'this to be true.'

An interesting postscript came in August 1978. A few workers were retained to maintain the abandoned plant. The liquidator refused to pay increases under the Nineteenth Round, on the grounds of inability to pay, Ferenka being insolvent. The ITGWU pointed out that the liquidator was now the employer, not Ferenka. It won the case, creating a precedent.

The union could not resist making an obvious point. 'It would be only too easy to imagine what would have happened if the men had not had the backing of a union in this situation.' It was proud of this important success, as 'liquidation very seldom gives us anything to rejoice about.'

The whole affair proved difficult for the ITGWU to shake off. Bitter feelings persisted, particularly in Limerick, and many opportunist opponents made constant use of 'Ferenka' to damage the union's image. Little credit was given anywhere to the valuable work done in picking up the pieces, such as winning £740,000 in redundancy pay rather than the £390,000 offered. When this work was being done, the most strident critics had packed their tents and left the scene.

In March 1981, as prospective investors examined the old Ferenka site, the ITGWU met personnel of the Industrial Development Authority 'to keep the MPGWU out'— a comment on all parties concerned.[44]

CONSTRUCTION

Progress made for construction workers throughout the 1970s was handicapped by recession and public-sector cuts. The industry's anarchic organisation persuaded the ITGWU to call for reforms in its direction, control and financing, with significant improvements in safety and health. In January 1978 a *Liberty* 'Construction' supplement made the case for direct-labour units and the introduction of a national pension scheme. Some demands were well ahead of their time: Safety Representatives should have powers to regularly inspect sites and always after a fatality, notifiable accident or dangerous occurrence and should be able to inspect employers' safety records.

On 24 July 1978 Dublin City Council voted, 23 to 13, to retain a Direct Labour Unit. Dublin Trades Council had campaigned against Fianna Fáil's attempts to abolish it. The ITGWU saw direct labour as developing public enterprise as well as contributing to Dublin's stock of socially affordable housing.[45]

McDONALD'S

On 15 March 1979 the ITGWU attempted to gain recognition in McDonald's hamburger outlets in Grafton Street and O'Connell Street, Dublin. The company refused to talk about improving its basic rate of 85p an hour and successfully sought an injunction against pickets. Two Officials, Noel Dowling and Tony Mulready, were arrested and were charged under the Conspiracy and Protection of Property Act (1875), a wonderful display of judicial imagination in inhibiting workers from pursing a trade dispute. McDonald's history and 'ethics' were exposed. Few realised that, rather than this being an aberration, the future was being glimpsed.

The Union of Students in Ireland cautioned members against accepting jobs in McDonald's. Dublin Trades Council joined the ITGWU in support rallies. The union was cheered by the 'massive demonstration in Dublin' against the 'internationally notorious anti-Union' company and noted that 'the fight was not in vain and we are happy to report that the dispute was brought to a successful conclusion.' A Labour Court recommendation on 5 August made no reference to wages or conditions and made the point that only a minority of the workers were unionised. It acknowledged, however, that it was 'an important principle of natural justice' that a worker had 'the right to be represented by a person of his or her choice' and to 'be represented by a Trade Union Official if they so wish.' It recommended that McDonald's agree to recognise' the ITGWU 'for negotiating purposes both individually and collectively.'[46] It was an important victory but, given the high turnover of employees, not one that could be maintained.

THE LABOUR COURT AND LABOUR LAW

In November 1977 the ITGWU thought the Labour Court was 'almost totally lacking in independence.' It was housed in the offices of the Department of Labour and therefore subject to close Ministerial influence. The civil servants who staffed the Court at the Minister's discretion could be easily moved. The transfer of the Conciliation Officer, Diarmaid Mac Diarmada, in 1975 angered unions. Government wage policy and minimum statutory provisions weighed heavier in the Court's considerations than concepts of social justice. Information was not disclosed to unions, despite there being some legal provisions for this, and endless 'inability to pay' claims weakened the Court's credibility.

The ITGWU pressed for changes. In 1977 it wanted Joint Labour Committees abandoned in favour of a statutory National Minimum Wage. The organising potential of JLCs, not necessarily contained in minimum-wage legislation, meant that debate was far from clear-cut. In 1978 the ITGWU criticised the Court's delays in arranging Conferences and hearings and issuing recommendations. It suffered from a general conservatism and caution. The practice of issuing truncated recommendations to catch up with backlogs was unwelcome. In areas requiring imagination the Court rarely made ground-breaking recommendations unless there was 'established industrial practice.' As increasingly tight National Wage Agreements either restricted new claims or brought them into the Labour Court, a vicious circle was created, whereby the Court would not go beyond 'established industrial practice' but practice was static because matters could proceed only through the Court.

The ITGWU's analysis of recommendations, backed by an information bank on wages, conditions, fringe benefits and non-wage items, meant that union negotiators made sophisticated submissions, often overwhelmingly winning their case on any objective merit, only to finish as another log in a jammed stream. Frustration was palpable.[47]

In 1970 Michael Mullen moved that the Minister for Labour 'introduce without delay' legislation to 'restore to the Irish Trade Union movement the legal standing it enjoyed prior to the Educational Company judgement.' 'Day after day' workers were 'threatened and goaded into not joining' a union, but this never resulted in prosecution. The law turned a blind eye to workers' constitutional rights yet awarded injunctions like confetti to employers on any spurious grounds. John Carroll regretted that promised legislation on unfair dismissals and terms of employment was not forthcoming. In a worldwide outcry for civil and human rights, Irish workers were entitled to 'first-class citizenship'. In 1971 Dublin District Council called for the abolition of the Offences Against the State Act. Séamus Pattison TD added his opposition to the Forcible Entry and Occupation Bill, which could seriously impinge on Freedom of Association.

In 1973 the NEC called for reform of the Companies Act (1963) to guarantee workers' minimum rights in the event of merger, liquidation or takeover. They were well down the list after directors, creditors and shareholders, despite being physical and intellectual investors in any company. It would be long before EU Transfer of Undertakings Regulations and employers' insolvency legislation addressed this issue.

No-strike elements of National Wage Agreements annoyed Delegates. Seán Ó Cearnaigh (Doirí Beaga) demanded that the right to strike 'never be subject to negotiation in any proposed NWA.' The present 'ambiguity' led to confusion and demoralisation. In August 1976 Kennedy expressed concerns over the Conditions of Employment (Temporary Provisions) Bill, which would restrict the Irish Bank Officials' Association (a non-Congress union) from obtaining increases above the National Wage Agreement (to which it was not party), on pain of severe legal sanction. The IBOA was urged to affiliate to Congress; but the restriction of bank workers' rights was seen as the thin end of a potentially broad wedge.

The Unfair Dismissals Act (1977) was welcomed as a major advance. Calls for May Day and Good Friday to be made public holidays and for annual leave entitlements to be statutorily increased were expressed annually. Good Friday as a public holiday would eliminate the confusion of many employments being closed while others worked normally. The Minister for Labour, Michael O'Leary, granted an extra public holiday but at Halloween—the 'witches' sabbath'—instead of May Day.[48]

A merger with the Irish Shoe and Leather Workers' Union in September 1977 was the first processed under the Trade Union Act (1975), which provided financial incentives to encourage rationalisation. As soon as the Act came into operation the ITGWU approached Cork Operative Butchers' Society, the Irish Union of Distributive Workers and Clerks, Irish Actors' Equity Association, the Irish Federation of Musicians, the National Union of Gold, Silver and Allied Trades and the Transport Salaried Staffs' Association. Half resulted in mergers, demonstrating the act's effectiveness.

Calls for extending the protection of the Trade Disputes Act (1906) to public-sector workers grew in 1977. More than forty *ex parte* injunctions were served in 1976. The ITGWU suggested, as new pay talks took place: 'Let us lay down a precondition that if the law is not changed, we shall not co-operate on other issues.' The Commission on Industrial Relations in 1978 'was not greeted with any particular enthusiasm.' Employers pushed for an interim report, as they saw it strengthening their hand, but the ITGWU cautioned, correctly, that 'speed is not the essence': 'erratic action against unofficial strikes, proscribing strikes in essential industries, while leaving workers at the prey of employers, would be a recipe for disaster and would be fought tooth and nail by the Trade Union Movement.'[49]

INDUSTRIAL DEMOCRACY

The 1970s opened with real expectations that industrial democracy was inevitable. Excitement at membership of the EEC led to an examination of Scandinavian and German models that provided for works councils and granted workers a meaningful role in a company's decision-making. Carroll cautioned that employers might concede some measure of their control but would 'do this in a way calculated to quieten the workers' voice but not to accord real power.'

In 1972 the Research Department produced the first significant contribution to policy, *Industrial Democracy Paper No. 1*. With the Labour Party in Government with Fine Gael, pressure for industrial democracy grew, with unions demanding reform in state and state-sponsored bodies. In 1975 Congress was asked to 'launch a vigorous campaign' for legislation to provide for workers' control in all industries 'which fail to meet the right of its workers to a full week's work with full and just remuneration.' Statutory rights for workers 'to seek comprehensive information' on 'earnings, profits, unit costs, financial status, future production and investment plans,' together with substantial penalties for non-disclosure, were sought.

In October 1972 more than 600 members in Semperit Tyres, Ballyfermot, Dublin, were offered the same 'advanced industrial democracy' as in the Austrian parent company. Negotiating through the International Chemical and General

Workers' Federation, the ITGWU achieved the establishment of a worker-management Committee with equal representation, heralded by Carroll as a 'major breakthrough in Irish industrial relations.' Union interest or understanding was poor, however. The NEC complained in 1974 that the feedback from Branches to a circular on industrial democracy was 'deplorable', with 'not a single original thought.' They harboured the view that industrial democracy could 'not be a success in the Capitalist system.' Sadly, amid claims of malpractice, members suspended the position of full-time Semperit Shop Steward in 1978, a blow for the wider recognition of shop-floor representation.

In 1976 the ITGWU asked Congress to draft a policy on workers' participation. Mullen, citing EEC directives, guarded against mere 'cosmetic changes' and demanded 'a real transfer of power.' Reservations were expressed, and union thinking was reactive and cautious.

In February 1979 the ITGWU outlined the EEC Fourth Directive on Company Law, relating to the disclosure of company information. Members were advised 'not to rely on law' to make progress, but in truth few Officials or members sought advances, lacking confidence, information, expertise and, most crucially, direction from union leaders.

Rosheen Callender, Research Officer, demanded, 'Open the books,' and gave details of comprehensive union demands for the reform of company law, full implementation of the Fourth Directive and negotiating agendas for Officials and Shop Stewards.[50]

ECONOMIC POLICY

In 1971 Frank Lewis (Nenagh) wanted all mines brought under state control so that their profits could 'be used to the advantage of the people.' He exploded the myth that Ireland had no natural resources. For every £27 wages earned by miners, the employers made £194 in net profit, tax-free. The Tralee Branch demanded the rejection of the Buchanan Report on economic development and spatial growth. In 1972 the ITGWU demanded a 'national programme' under a National Planning Authority to cure the ills of unemployment and emigration.

Dublin District Council wanted to 'oppose all applications from aliens seeking entry into this country for employment.' The NEC opposed: it was 'unfair', inequitable and, given membership of the EEC, probably illegal.

Michael Killeen, Managing Director of the IDA, outlined the practical problems of job creation in the 'most difficult year since the 1950s': Northern Ireland troubles and depression, uncertainties around EEC membership, the burning of the British Embassy, continued high unit wage costs and inflation, and the depressed state of the European and American economies. He wanted higher productivity and new industry.

Paddy Armstrong (Dublin No. 13) wanted the 'struggle for the right to work' placed at the forefront. He cited the defence by the Upper Clyde Shipbuilders of their jobs as inspiration.[51]

In 1973 Letterkenny demanded public control of the 'thousand million pounds deposited' in Irish banks 'belonging to the dead generations who left no next of kin,' while Dublin No. 7 wanted all banks and insurance companies nationalised. After 10,000 redundancies in 1972, John O'Brien (Waterford No. 2) called for a reduced working week without loss of pay to create jobs.

Contradictory motions were sometimes adopted, raising questions about the Conference's ultimate purpose. The union's economic demands were summed up in the *Liberty* headline 'Wanted—an Economic and Social Plan.' Controls were exercised only on wages and salaries, while other incomes, prices, investment and fiscal policy were ignored.

In 1974 the ITGWU sought to commit Congress to a Special Conference to 'initiate a five year social and economic plan,' with papers circulated two months in advance. Carroll said that 'the broad mass' were 'becoming deeply concerned at the lack of any real effort' by the ICTU 'to frame, enunciate and pursue a national trade union social and economic programme.' The evidence was of 'ad hockery.' He harked back to the 1967 ITGWU Workers' Charter and wondered why its contents had not more deeply permeated bargaining on the National Wage Agreement. Pressure mounted from Delegates for Socialist solutions. Reflecting the concerns of small-farmer members, Tomás Ó Baoill (Ballinasloe) wanted protection to prevent more being driven from the land. Here were the two ends of the ITGWU membership, urban and rural, Socialist and conservative.

The Minister for Industry and Commerce, Justin Keating, told the 1974 Labour Party Conference that a smelter would be built to process Tara Mines' ore—music to ITGWU ears. The union had demanded this, with state-run enterprise for gas and oil finds thought to be imminent. In November the ITGWU launched a 'Save Irish Jobs' campaign—'A new approach this Christmas.' Unemployment stood at 76,000, with pessimistic forecasts that it would rise to between 85,000 and 90,000 before spring. If £50 million were spent on Irish produce, 2,000 jobs would be saved. Members were asked, as purchasers and workers, to demand correct labelling, to complain to shops about the non-availability of Irish goods, and to warn against the effects of a 'foreign spending spree'. The union were 'realists'. Ireland had 'to buy and sell abroad to survive. We are not self-sufficient.' Many raw materials had to be imported. 'We need the stimulus of fair competition to build up the efficiency of our own manufacturing firms.' Since the war, however, more was bought than sold, and a recent 'foreign spending spree' was 'paid for in the loss of thousands of Irish jobs.' From 1 July 1974 British goods had complete duty-free access under the Anglo-Irish Free Trade Area Agreement. In 1977 EEC countries would have almost full access. 'Never before was it so vital to support our own products. Most Irish firms will not be able to export if their home-based market is cut from under them. Make sure you are not contributing to this state of affairs.'[52]

In 1975 the NEC condemned the failure of the Budget to address unemployment and wanted emergency assistance for construction, a reduction in VAT and a National Planning Authority. Congress was asked to lead a Right to Work campaign. The

ITGWU considered setting up 'unemployed Committees at Branch, District and national levels' to retain the involvement of unemployed members. Another 'Guaranteed Irish' campaign was mounted in December.

In 1976 the National Economic and Social Council noted that emigration had virtually ceased, the flight from the land was continuing and the population increasing, necessitating the creation of 340,000 new jobs—34,000 net new jobs per year—if unemployment was to be reduced from 7% to 4% by 1986, all far beyond any targets previously reached. The ITGWU thought a 'back-to-work' movement was needed and a new commitment to Ireland that, if the private sector was unwilling or unable, should be led by public investment. The Government's 'lamentable failures' were decried. Full use of natural resources, greater commitment to 'backward and forward linkage', 'technical transfer' by transnationals and the development of enterprise with a low import content were union solutions.

Restrictive motions on making double job-holding illegal, giving preference to Irish workers and buying Irish-supported by import controls, reflected a growing negativity induced by increased unemployment and a lack of belief in future growth.

The 1977 Conference adopted similar motions. On Saturday 12 March 2,000 people took part in a Dublin Trades Council protest march. The slogans were classic 1970s ones: 'Economic planning to end unemployment! Expand state industry! State development of all national resources! No cuts in public services!'[53] Employers' mantras were challenged: high wages did not cause unemployment; if low wages were the answer, India would be a workers' paradise; state industry did work; and the unemployed were neither lazy nor spongers. ITGWU members and banners were prominent, but 2,000 marchers hardly shook the Government.

The Fianna Fáil Government's Green Paper, *Development for Full Employment* (1978), provided 'nothing to discuss.' There were vague, unsecured promises of job creation. Wages 'strategy' consisted of 'workers accepting what they are given, knowing their place and being thankful they have a job.' Social 'strategy' was simply 'screw the workless' and the poor. Further taxes, even on Children's Allowances, were promised, while the removal of food subsidies would drive down real incomes. 'Sacrifices' were the order of the day, although workers, as ever, were to be the sacrificed, not the sacrificing. It would not provide jobs. There would have to be 'income sharing'—'a polite term for cut-backs in earnings'—in an already low-wage economy. Matters 'were not helped by unions calling for hours reductions and no overtime,' as this simply shared out existing jobs.

Following a seminar, a Wages and Economic Policy paper was prepared for the Annual Conference, a seminal contribution to the debate. Where, given current Government policy, would 30,000 new jobs per year come from, merely to absorb those coming off the land and a rising population? Carroll thought we had an 'unemployment cancer beyond all curing.' There was no 'acceptable level' of unemployment.

In 1979 Michael Bell, National Group Secretary, demanded an embargo on imported hides as Irish Leathers planned 370 redundancies in Dungarvan, Gorey and Portlaw. More than 1,000 people marched through Gorey on 6 and 12 January, led by Bell and Des Corish, Wexford Organiser. Strike notice was served, and hopes remained that some jobs could be salvaged.

The Conference adopted umpteen motions on generating employment, including a National Development Agency, State Construction Company, national tanning industry, revitalisation of railways and all manner of exploitation of natural resources. An ITGWU Co-operative Society would help workers establish co-operative enterprises, an idea not pursued but taken up by the FWUI through Workers' Unity Trust. The Government abandoned all job creation targets, the oil crisis firing inflation and world recession. The Department of Economic Planning and Development was a sick joke as far as the ITGWU was concerned. It produced no plans and forever reined back on wildly optimistic claims for development and jobs. Its passing confirmed its pointlessness.

The National Understanding required the setting up of 'Sectoral Committees' to assess 'technological, marketing and related developments for future employment' and for 'efficiency and growth' before the end of the year. In November 'one or two such Industry Committees' were to be 'set up shortly on a pilot basis.' Government ineptitude and unwillingness to genuinely embrace economic planning was nothing if not consistent.[54]

TRANSNATIONALS

In 1970 Tony Dunne (NEC) wanted all 'private companies who receive state grants to publish profit and loss accounts.' This became a hardy annual. Carroll called for union representation on industrial development boards and for transnational corporations to 'accept local trade union practice.' The widespread belief was that they came, took all the benefits, and left, without a 'by your leave.' Despite bitter experiences with EI, SPS, Potez and Mogul, the ITGWU welcomed foreign industrial investment. There was a need to understand transnational Corporations and develop international strategies and alliances.

Charles 'Chip' Levinson, Secretary-General of the International Federation of Chemical and General Workers in Geneva—one of a number of International Trade Union Secretariats to which the ITGWU was affiliated—'hit Dublin like a ton of bricks' in mid-December 1971. He addressed a large audience in Liberty Hall. Global investment was now 'the name of the game,' and billions of dollars 'moved about the world, crossing national borders, uncontrolled by national Governments, and largely uncontrollable.' It fuelled international inflation and wiped out jobs, as the target for investment was 'high technology, automated, capital-intensive industries producing new growth products where there are fewer jobs.' Wage demands squeezed profit margins, and the confluence of improving communications, air and sea transport meant that investment was highly flexible and switched at very short notice to where profit returns were highest. Levinson argued for 'co-determinism' to allow workers, nationally and internationally, to apply brakes to capital's unfettered progress.

All this shocked an audience raised in battle with small local employers or national bargaining units in domestic industries such as creameries. Levinson argued for international union solidarity to an Irish movement fragmented into more than 100 different unions. Even the 'regional concept of the European Economic Community,' a highly controversial and divisive issue for Ireland, was 'yesterday' as regards the emerging global economy.

On reading Levinson's speech in *Liberty,* the sharp intake of breath is audible. It was new information, conceptually fresh, and demanded imaginative responses. Carroll remarked: 'In the years ahead we will be joining more and more in the multinational ball game.' Levinson did 'not have all the answers,' but he raised 'some extraordinary provocative questions and it would be wrong for us to retire mesmerised and chicken out of the debate. You won't survive on yesterday's economics, says Chip Levinson, my ideas are tomorrow. Maybe we should listen.' Levinson addressed the Conference again in 1979, urging workers to recognise that international solidarity was no longer merely a pious aspiration but an absolute necessity. It was a call that, while well understood, still awaits a meaningful response.[55]

EUROPE

In 1971 the ITGWU felt there was insufficient information to enable it to determine its attitude towards membership of the EEC. The Development Services Division produced a booklet outlining the pros and cons. Fundamental concerns were to protect and expand industrial development, to reduce unemployment, to retain full control over economic and social policy, to adopt comprehensive social pro-grammes for health, pensions, and social welfare, to fully protect offshore fisheries and natural resources and to resist restrictive trade union laws. The ITGWU was apparently prepared to go in, 'given certain assurances.'

Brendan Corish, Leader of the Labour Party, spoke at length in support, worrying that we were like Halifax Town trying to get into a Division in 'which we were not capable of playing.' We were not prepared for EEC membership. With most unions, the ITGWU voted at a special ICTU Conference against the terms of membership negotiated by the Government. No ITGWU speaker championed the proposal. The evidence suggested that rich Regions got richer and poor Regions, like Ireland, poorer. After a two-day debate on 27–28 January, Congress rejected support for membership by 119–155. It would lead a 'trade union campaign of opposition.'

There were substantial differences within the movement. The WUI favoured membership, as did some public-service unions. 'Besides expressing the genuine and heartfelt fears of thousands of Irish men and women,' the ITGWU saw itself as making 'an important contribution to the quality of democracy in this country.' The referendum would be the 'most important event since the founding of the State.' An ITGWU press advertisement succinctly summarised its position:

Vote No! Many jobs would be lost in the EEC: The small farmer, the backbone of the rural community would be wiped out: We would lose control over our own affairs: Our alternative is a trading association with the EEC, retaining our independence: The Irish economy could not withstand the blast of uncontrolled competition with dumping, job dislocation, high prices and resulting emigration.[56]

May's *Liberty* was 'devoted to the case for opposing Ireland's entry.' It urged:

Hold on to your jobs. EEC NO. Let's decide our own future.
Kennedy said:
We foresee, if Ireland joins, an economic catastrophe in which large numbers of Irish workers will lose their jobs and the capacity of the country's economy, on which we depend for our standard of living will be seriously undermined.
Why does the ITGWU back the Irish Congress of Trade Unions in opposing Ireland's entry to the EEC?

1. Competition
   Our developing economy is far too weak to compete in free trade conditions with the industrial giants of Europe.
2. Jobs
   There will be widespread unemployment as a result of completely free entry of mass produced foreign goods into our home market.
3. Prices
   The cost of living will rise so high as to cause grave hardship to large sections of our community.
4. Independence
   We will lose full control over our future in economic, social, cultural and political affairs.
5. Farms
   The small farm community will go to the wall.
6. Emigration
   Unemployed Irish emigrants will be forced into slum labour ghettoes of Common Market cities.
7. Culture
   The oppressive open competition of European industrial society does not suit the Irish people.

It concluded that 'the emigrant ship will once more become a national symbol in the EEC.' In 1971 the ITGWU produced a 24-page booklet, *The Question Posed: How Would You Fare in the Common Market?* distributed in tens of thousands.

All was to no avail. The people decided on membership from 1 January 1973, by 83%.

Chickens came home to roost before this, as 1,200 spinning and weaving jobs were lost in October 1972. A Conference of textile members was held in Liberty

Hall, and a 'task force'—then a new concept—was demanded by Michael Gannon, National Group Secretary. Sicco Mansholt's parting comments as President of the EEC, delivered three days into Ireland's membership, were seized upon by the ITGWU. He said the Community 'had not come up to the public's expectations,' that integration led to many social stresses between rich and poor Regions, and that the institutions were undemocratic. The ITGWU wondered what the effect of such comments might have been if delivered before the referendum.

In 1973 Carroll bemoaned the negative impact of membership: additional job losses, rising inflation, little indication of any economic planning from the Government or efforts to avail of EEC social policy or regional planning.

With the Labour Party in Government, expectations rose. Carroll was an ICTU nominee to the EEC Economic and Social Committee, beginning a personal, thirty-year involvement in European policy formation. He spearheaded ITGWU policy, maintaining qualified opposition but, once in and accepting the democratic wish, using EEC structures to better things for Irish workers. An encouragement was the apparent strength of European unions and Social Democratic parties. In 1971 union density was 61% in Belgium, 52% in Ireland, 50% in Denmark, 48% in Britain, 41% in Luxembourg, 37% in West Germany, 32% in the Netherlands, 23% in Italy and 20% in France. The ITGWU welcomed the establishment of the European Trade Union Confederation and determined to play whatever role it could. It still harboured misgivings, hosting an Irish Sovereignty Movement seminar on 'Ireland and the Changing EEC' on 15 July 1974, addressed by Daltún Ó Ceallaigh, ITGWU European Officer, Anthony Coughlan and Ian Mikardo, Chairman of the British Labour Party.[57]

By 1975 the ITGWU's predictions appeared grimly correct: 'our textile industry is damn near bunched; our footwear industry is as bad and our clothing industry is not much better.' The Government should place import restrictions, despite the threat of retaliation by larger countries. It all raised a question: 'So what sort of a European Union is this? Does it all mean that when you are one of the big boys you thumb your nose at Brussels when it suits you? But when you're a poor relation like Ireland, you have to play the game in typical UK, chin-up style and sink with our floundering economic ship.' Dumping on the Irish market was disastrous for jobs. A 'people's Court' would serve to deal with 'those parasites' whose 'only concern is the rake-off they get from importing foreign goods.' A Special Conference was demanded to consider withdrawal from the EEC. A survey of members revealed that 53% wanted renegotiation; 85% felt they were too poorly informed, despite 90% having 'a lot of' or 'some' interest in Europe; and 80% thought job losses resulted from membership, although 60% thought these would level off. If Britain were to pull out, 25% thought Ireland should follow. Of those responding, 30% said they had voted for membership, 37% against, while 21% had not voted.

The EEC Commission Information Service helped to finance the survey, the first occasion on which the ITGWU employed European funding. Ó Ceallaigh supplied a constant stream of articles on Europe, most reflecting a 'critical and challenging stance.'

In 1977 Fergal Costello (Dublin District Council) moved for 'withdrawal from the Common Market.' The slogan 'Into Europe—Into Jobs' had gone horribly wrong. The NEC wanted a reassertion of neutrality and cautioned against links between the EEC and NATO. As for withdrawal, it 'still opposed' the EEC but was wary of mounting a lone campaign. The motion was defeated.

In November 1979 a European Trade Union Confederation solidarity meeting was held in Liberty Hall to coincide with Ireland's Presidency of the EEC. An open letter was addressed to the Taoiseach (see p. 645) containing detailed policy suggestions for the creation of regional employment, decrying the rush to militarism, with advanced thinking on conservation and the need to seek alternatives to oil and nuclear energy.

Having adjusted to EEC membership, the ITGWU determined to forge alliances to gain success for European policy. The National Understanding laid down some markers but was merely a beginning. Mullen concluded a paper on jobs by firing a shot across the Government's bows. 'The time has come to cry a halt to this decline in the fortunes of our country and our class and to let the EEC know at the highest levels that we are no longer prepared to endure the hardship its is inflicting on us.'[58]

SOCIAL POLICY

In 1970 Christy Bonass (Dublin No. 6/8) wanted pensions to be 'transferable' between employments—a novel concept; Vincent Moran (Limerick No. 2) wanted workers indirectly affected by a trade dispute to receive social welfare benefits; and Tom O'Brien (Dublin No. 5) demanded the stamping of cards to be the priority in any bankruptcy. O'Brien wanted a crash building programme, realistic rent controls and assistance for low-income families in obtaining accommodation. The Tánaiste, Brendan Corish, heard demands for a social welfare service of European standard that would grant immediate substantial increases in benefits, provide free optical and dental treatment, introduce family income supplement, automatically increase social welfare payments in line with the cost of living, abolish the £1,600 ceiling, and take higher contributions from employer and state. People's Advice Bureaus would disseminate information.

The replacement of Home Assistance by a Supplementary Welfare Allowance run by the Health Boards in 1977 met long-standing union demands. Persons on strike could claim supplementary allowances for dependants, although Strike Pay beyond a certain limit was deducted. The ITGWU sought direct meetings with the Minister for Health and Social Welfare, Charles Haughey, to complain about delays and confusion in the application of the new scheme. In August 1979 the ITGWU launched demands for a 'comprehensive public health service, available for all citizens, irrespective of income or means,' based on the belief that 'health care and specialist services should be freely available for those who need them most.' Those preventing such a health-care system being established were 'upholding private profit from public misfortune,' the small minority who 'make exorbitant profit from our present two-tier health service.' The Social Welfare (Amendment) Act and the Health Contributions Act (1978) came into force in April 1979, introducing a fully Pay-Related Social Insurance system, free hospital maintenance for all in public wards, irrespective of income, and the abolition of old distinctions between 'manual' and 'non-manual' employees. The income limit was set at £5,500 per year, a crucial point beyond which people would be liable for full consultants' fees and on which their benefits would be calculated.

Unions gave a limited welcome, but the income limit was a matter for serious negotiation. Commitment to a £7,000 ceiling was part of the National Understanding. This turned out to be most confusing, and an 'interim scheme', announced late in the year, was seen as flagrantly reneging on promises and 'flouting the spirit' of the National Understanding. The crunch for the ITGWU was that 'the demand for a free health service—that is, a comprehensive service which is free at the point of use—had still not been met by the end of the 1970s. Its achievement is still a task for the 1980s!'[59]

TAX

In 1973 eight Branches called for comprehensive reform of PAYE, the start of a mounting campaign as wage increases lifted workers into higher tax bands. In February they sought a 'major overhaul of the current taxation system' and 'more equitable distribution of the tax burden,' which would 'require income taxation of farmers,' capital gains tax and the complete removal of lower-income earners from the tax net. It became a mantra. In January 1978 *Liberty's* headline was 'Cut tax evasion.' Farmers, business people and professionals were either not in the tax net at all or were contributing at far lower rates than PAYE workers. The Irish Farmers' Association 'successfully conned' many into believing that unions were 'anti-farmer'. There was ill-informed talk of urban-rural divides. The ITGWU strongly rejected this, pointing to such policies as banning live cattle exports. Satisfying wealthy ranchers and dealers was ultimately anti-agriculture, and union demands for the development of food-processing were more in line with rural development and sustaining communities.

The 1977 Conference attacked the IFA, championed the National Land League and called for an alliance between small farmers, food workers and rural communities. Paddy Greene (Castleblayney) wanted one-day protest strikes 'in each town' to bring pressure for PAYE reform. There were countless similar motions.[60]

In March 1979 the NEC announced a series of national protest marches, the first on Sunday 11 March from Liberty Hall to the Department of the Taoiseach. PAYE workers paid 87% of income tax, while the 'big farmers' lobby does as it pleases in relation to tax.' Tens of thousands attended rallies led by the ITGWU. Mullen accused the RTÉ Authority of effectually 'censoring the voice of industrial Ireland,' but the whole country was aware of the campaign. It was not 'fomenting town-country conflict,' despite what IFA leaders and politicians suggested: it merely 'called for tax reform.' Many workers no doubt marched for tax cuts, but the ITGWU made it clear that 'we are NOT calling for cuts in overall taxation and revenue and WILL OPPOSE any reductions in public expenditure and services.'

In close co-operation with Congress and local Trades Councils, especially that of Dublin, the demands were straightforward: a tax code applied fairly to all workers, farmers, professionals, businessmen and other self-employed; the index-ing of personal tax allowances and tax bands; equality of treatment for married people; the payment of all income tax on a current-year basis or equivalent; an anti-evasion campaign by the state and the elimination of loopholes that facilitated tax avoidance; the reintroduction of a wealth or resource tax; higher rates of capital gains and capital acquisition taxes; a surcharge on unearned income; and increases in and extension of Corporation tax. Mullen saw it as a 'war against privilege [and] injustice.'

Not satisfied with the tax elements, the NEC rejected the first proposals for a National Understanding in April. The proposals did not provide a 'total overhaul', full indexing of income tax allowances and tax bands or reintroduce wealth tax. The NEC welcomed the joint ICTU-Government Working Party on tax but saw a £39 payment to PAYE workers 'only as an interim acknowledgement of the justice of the PAYE campaign.'

May Day saw further widespread marches demanding a 'total review' of tax and warning the Government and employers that proposals for a National Understanding, then being considered, were 'doomed to failure' if they did not include significant reform.

In September the ICTU Co-ordination Committee decided to expand the campaign by conducting a national petition, lobbying local Councillors and TDs, promoting local meetings, writing to provincial newspapers, establishing local action Committees linked with community organisations and seeking a 'number of prominent people' as campaign sponsors. The National Understanding provided a one-off tax refund amounting to between £43.75 and £105, depending on income and tax bands, resulting from a £175 increase in tax-free allowances due in week 34, 23 November 1979. A sweetener, it made no permanent impact.

Addressing the Annual Conference, Mullen argued that 'no amount of verbal nonsense such as the EEC terminology referring to "social partners" can hide the actual inequalities in our society.' It was a spongers' society. Spongers could evade their legal obligations to pay tax. He attacked Professor Martin O'Donoghue, Minister for Economic Planning, who dismissed the PAYE protests. 'It would be totally unrealistic in a healthy democracy to let any group imagine that it could unilaterally select certain proposals which suit them. It must be conveyed to the people that some of their decisions demonstrated a lack of patriotism and social concern and lack of economic reality.' Mullen derided those who moved wealth abroad to evade tax, the consistent failure or refusal of private enterprise to gener-ate jobs, the high cost of basic foodstuffs, and suggestions of legislation to restrict the right to strike. He roused his audience and warned the Government: 'The rights to organise and represent Irish workers were won by men and women who faced batons and guns with courage . . . In the face of new assaults . . . we shall not flinch but respond in a united fashion.'

Dick Kenny (Kilkenny) criticised the 'indiscriminate' and 'political' use of strikes during tax campaigns, suggesting that such actions were unconstitutional and illegal and breached union Rules. Mullen largely agreed with him but stressed that the ITGWU had called no strikes. It invited members to join stoppages and protests voluntarily, suggesting that lessons had been learnt from Paddy Lane and the IFA. Actions had been taken through Dublin Trades Council and the ICTU Co-Ordination Committee. Any protest against the Government was useless, however, if the majority of demonstrators then voted for the policies they protested against.[61]

PENSIONS

The ITGWU led the unglamorous pursuit of adequate pensions. Nursing and professional Branches sought modifications of statutory schemes. In 1973 the ITGWU demanded a complete pensions review, ensuring that all workers would be covered and that there would be an escalator clause linked to wages and transferability between employments. Rosheen Callender, ITGWU researcher, examined the Green Paper on pensions, demanded equality of treatment for women, and urged simultaneous improvements in the provision of state pensions and the pursuit of non-contributory pensions as part of work-place agendas. In addition, an analysis of pension schemes was provided to negotiators and Worker Representatives. Demands were made for an adequate construction industry pension scheme in 1978 and publicity given to a survey by Irish Pensions Trust that demonstrated widespread discrimination against women.[62] A *Liberty* 'Equal Pay and Pensions' supplement illustrated areas for reform and gave up-to-date case law to encourage claims.

SAFETY, HEALTH AND WELFARE

In 1970 Carroll moved a motion 'recognising that the health of workers is of prime importance.' He sought 'a mandatory form of socio-industrial medicine' as an adjunct to the health service 'on a national basis' to ensure a 'prognostic and treatment service.' More importantly, he wanted amendments in the Factories Acts 'so as to ensure that Safety Committees are a legal requirement in all employments with ten or more workers.' He drew attention to the need to control industrial pollution in European Conservation Year. People, having 'had so little for so long,' were blind to health and safety issues that accompanied new industrialisation.

Paddy Dooley (Dublin No. 9) complained that, although the law provided the opportunity to set up Safety Committees, and 'although I harass my Committee,' workers did not seem to care. A queue of speakers reflected a rising safety consciousness, but a mere twenty additional Safety Committees were set up in 1971, seventeen in Dublin. In 1973 Carroll characterised their absence as part of the country's 'industrial immaturity'. The Factories Act (1955) applied to 15,880 premises, but there were only 145 Safety Committees. Was it part of a wider malaise? At ordinary union meetings attendances were 'generally poor'. Those 'who complain 'most' about things 'which are not to their liking are usually the ones who don't bother attending.'

In June 1974 the ITGWU Industrial Engineering Department attended the World Safety Congress in Dublin. Two staff members were nominated to permanent EEC sub-Committees on health, safety and the environment and qualified for membership of the British Institute of Safety Officers. *Liberty* drove safety consciousness, reflecting the union's specialist knowledge. Eileen King's study of 'Noise in Industry and its Effects' and 'Industrial Accidents Don't Happen—They are Caused' were typical. The remedies included vigilance, care and improved housekeeping; but a Safety Committee was the essential in accident prevention schemes.

The Industrial Inspectorate pointed out that 1 million worker-days were lost through strikes in 1970, the worst year ever, and yet the same number were lost every year through accidents and ill health. The ITGWU wondered, 'Man-days lost as a result of strikes get plenty of publicity through the media—we hear and read about them from every source, but little (or nothing) is written or heard of death and injury caused by the industrial accident—one wonders why?'[63]

In May 1975 an Industrial Environment Service was launched, with Mullen declaring 'war on noise.' A Safety Programme would 'make effective safety arrangements' wherever there were ITGWU members, seek the overhaul of safety legislation, demand increased powers for factory industrial safety councils, reinforce factory inspection, and increase training for Safety Committees and Safety Officers. Training schemes would deal with what safety is, manual handling, hazard-spotting and good housekeeping, personal protective equipment, Safety Committees, first aid, and legal matters. The service was a first in Ireland.

Eight broad objectives of EEC guidelines on 'safety, hygiene, health and protection at work' were announced in July as the union increasingly looked to Europe for direction. The Occupational Injuries Benefit Scheme was explained, together with ITGWU legal benefit, but the emphasis was now on 'being safety-conscious' and on prevention, not compensation. The death of Seán McGuinness (Dublin No. 5) while working at the RDS led to the signing of one of the first safety Agreements and the appointment of an on-site Safety Officer. Negotiated by Eric Fleming, it covered exhibition Organisers, contractors and site unions.

A high-level Committee to examine the health effects of asbestos was demanded as concern grew for work-place exposure to carcinogens and toxins. The ITGWU campaigned for brucellosis to be declared a notifiable industrial disease. The Government published guidelines for meat plant workers in 1979. The ITGWU thought them inadequate.[64]

NUCLEAR ENERGY AND THE ENVIRONMENT

Carroll 'had some outspoken things to say' at a plenary meeting of the EEC Economic and Social Committee in Brussels in September 1976. He drew attention to work-place health and safety and to broader environmental concerns. In comments advanced for their time he announced that nuclear technology was, apart from the atomic bomb and nuclear fission for military purposes, the plaything of big finance. Nature had provided the sun, winds, rains and rivers which we could use for our energy purposes if we cared to apply the technology.

He railed against the effects of thalidomide, PVC and asbestos, and the callous condemning to death or disability of thousands of workers in the name of profit when the producers knew of side-effects and concealed them. Unions needed comprehensive environmental policies.

In August 1978 Carroll addressed a rally at Carnsore Point, Co. Wexford, protesting against the proposed nuclear power plant. In September members of the ITGWU Band were prominent among 15,000 marchers who protested against the vandalising of the Viking site at Wood Quay, Dublin, to make way for civic offices, Carroll addressing the throng. With the Leader of the German Green Party, Petra Kelly, Carroll wrote *A Nuclear Ireland?* It significantly influenced the debate on energy options. Sydney Krober, an American authority on nuclear energy, purchased 500 copies. Mixed thinking was seen in 1979 when, as well as rejecting nuclear energy, a policy based on conservation, coal, turf, oil and gas was recommended.[65]

DEVELOPMENT SERVICES

In 1970 Kennedy announced that 'in furtherance of the democratic process' and 'in order to provide the best possible services, benefits and facilities' and 'to keep them abreast of modern developments and happenings,' the NEC had created the Development Services Division. It would 'lift the Union into the forefront' not alone of trade unions 'but in the economy generally.' It had Education and Training, Statistics and Research, Public Relations and Publishing, Work Study and Production Advice Departments, all staffed by professionally qualified persons. It arose from 'pressure by members for the adoption of modern scientific practices and methods.' They required a 'brain bank composed of a group of dedicated experts' on whom front-line industrial staff could 'rely to feed them with information and intelligent comment.'

Paddy Clancy, Head of the Promotion and Field Advisory Division of the Irish National Productivity Committee and previously Chairman of the Liberty Study Group, became Head of the Division. Department Heads were: Communications, Brendan Clarke (journalist and PRO for An Foras Talúntais and the IDA); Education and Training, Thomas McCarthy ('well known and respected in Irish education circles' as Senior Psychologist, City of Dublin Vocational Education Committee); Industrial Engineering Officer, Dónal O'Sullivan (ICTU Work Study Adviser, Head of Management Services at the School of Management Studies, Rathmines, and Treasurer of the Labour Party), and Research Officer, Manus O'Riordan (economics and politics graduate). Gaining the serialisation rights of Andrew Boyd's *The Rise of the Irish Trade Unions* was a 'considerable scoop' for *Liberty*.[66]

Table 109: ITGWU education and training courses, 1972–9

	Courses	Participants		Courses	Participants
1972	17	323	1977	68	1,305
1973	34	926	1978	63	1,062
1974	52	992	1979	71	1,450
1975	67	1,327	Total	421	8,364
1976	49	979			

Source: ITGWU, Annual Reports, 1971–9.

Education and training got under way in earnest in 1972 with Shop Stewards' courses in Athlone, Belfast, Donegal, Dublin, Dunleer, Killarney, Limerick and Sligo, while a thirty-day advanced course dealt with industrial relations, labour law, communications, economics, company law and accountancy. The Development Services Division was to be housed at 15–17 Eden Quay, adjacent to Liberty Hall, but this proved unsuitable, and 10 Palmerston Park, Rathmines, was acquired. The Eden Quay premises had cost £45,000 and were sold for £67,000.

A tabloid-style *Liberty* appeared from October 1972, featuring a lively correspondence page, a 'Woman Worker' column (in contrast to a 'Woman' Page'), Political Diary, and many new features giving a more immediate, 'newsy' feel. The Research Department produced a *Handbook of Economic Statistics* for Officials and *Industrial Democracy Paper No.* 1. The Industrial Engineering Department undertook seventy work assignments, examining bonus schemes and productivity, time and manning standards, job evaluation, safety, health and ergonomic problems. In 1973 a Shop Stewards' course was run in An Bun Beag, Co. Donegal.

Concerns at the cost of the prestigious Development Services Division were assuaged when Mullen stated that they amounted to 0.76p per member. The ITGWU sought additional funding, stating that the 'real blame' for inadequate funding lay 'not with the Department of Labour but with ICTU which has displayed no initiative whatsoever in either supporting the submission or negotiating its settlement,' a mockery of the Congress decision to seek all possible funding for specialist services.[67]

The tutors Des Geraghty, Dónal Lehane and Des Mahon began training in March, dealing with educational psychology, sociology and principles of teaching. They were joined in September 1973 by Mattie O'Neill and Jim Buckley, when DC Friends of Ireland donated $50,000 for education work. Evening and day-release courses in 1974 dealt with communications, productivity concepts and women. The appointment of three additional tutors from outside the union was an adventurous step, bringing fresh thinking. In April 1975 Mullen wanted 'day-release with pay' in all Agreements, a necessary advance if the union was to reach the broadest audience. Whether the FUE and employers were keen to concede this would be tested.

Table 110: ITGWU industrial Engineering Department assignments, 1971–9

1971	40	1976	257
1972	70	1977	240
1973	98	1978	328
1974	200	1979	358
1975	207	Total	1,798

Source: ITGWU, Annual Reports, 1971–9.

In 1974 the Department of Labour gave £90,000 in grants for union education, '£65,000 to Congress and £15,000 to be divided among six applicant unions.' Paddy Clancy complained that the attitude of the President of Congress to the Minister was 'most abusive and unnecessary.' The ITGWU claimed £20,000 from Congress and expected another £20,000 from AnCO (An Chomhairle Oiliúna, the Training Council). In April 1976 the first advanced courses outside Dublin were run in Arklow, Clonmel, Kilkenny and Tralee. Courses were designed to close gaps in emerging skills, both for individual self-improvement and class reasons. The ITGWU could 'not sit back and let the new technology, thinking and particularly jargon swamp us.' Despite this, attendance at evening classes disappointed. A fellowship was created in University College, Dublin, in association with the EEC Trade Union Information Section to prepare case studies. In 1977 the ITGWU provided confidential adult literacy and numeracy training for members and their dependants. In November Rosheen Callender's book *Account for Yourself,* a workers' guide to reading and understanding company accounts, received critical acclaim. *ITGWU Industrial News* reported gains in wages and conditions, together with a *Publicity Guide for Trade Unionists,* equipping Officials and activists with advice on how to deal with the media. In May 1979 the EEC Transport Regulations were explained to road haulage drivers, such concepts as tachographs and restricted hours being novel.[68]

In May 1977 St Vincent's School, Glasnevin, Dublin, was purchased with a view to moving the Development Services Division from Rathmines to provide improved facilities, including residential training. These plans foundered, however, and Glasnevin was sold in May 1980. In 1978 an 'Optimum Agreement' impressed the NEC, which felt it should be distributed to all Officials as part of an Officials' handbook. A document produced by the National Council for Educational Awards was welcomed, describing 'bridges' for low-achieving school-leavers and adult learners and giving recognition for work experience and general involvement in society.

The Industrial Engineering Department's assignments grew rapidly. Increasing time was spent serving the ICTU Protective Legislation Committee. Pamphlets on Ferenka, involvement in International Trade Union Federations, a bibliography on equal pay, recent labour law, social welfare benefits and income tax allowances and youth employment were published, and *Liberty* increased its circulation by more than 1,000.

The Research Department produced numerous valuable guidance notes for negotiators. A Working Party to advise the Minister on the implementation of ILO Convention 140, Paid Educational Leave, was set up. The ITGWU hoped its negotiation of release for course participants 'with no loss of earnings' would extend by way of the Employer-Labour Conference to a national Agreement. Staff training broadened to include administrative and clerical personnel and 'potential female industrial staff.'

A members' art competition, run in association with the National College of Art and Design, was won by Jer O'Leary, later renowned as banner artist and actor. Members' complaints about poor media coverage had foundation but reflected bias rather than a lack of effort by the union.

Twenty-one issues of *Industrial News* were published, with more than 200 press statements and special publicity drives on the National Understanding, PAYE, European Trade Union Confederation Action Week, Údarás na Gaeltachta elections, McDonald's, and amalgamation with Actors' Equity. The ITGWU Information Officer, Daltún Ó Ceallaigh, was director of the ICTU Tax Reform Campaign.[69]

YOUTH

A seminar organised by the European Trade Union Confederation on youth unemployment, held in Dún Laoghaire in April 1976, triggered interest from the ITGWU. Dublin No. 2 Branch elected the first Youth Committee. A National Youth Policy was demanded in 1976 and 1978. A Minister for Youth was sought to address young people's legal status and for granting full rights at eighteen, to immediately implement the recommendations of the Committee on Reformatories and Industrial Schools (the Kennedy Report) and to implement changes in youth education, health and social services.

In 1979 Michael Wall was appointed Youth Officer. Working in the Education and Training Department, he studied the patterns of youth employment and union membership, developed induction training, investigated youth issues, and organised socio-educational activities to encourage the involvement of youth.[70]

PREMISES

A bomb shattered Liberty Hall on Friday 1 December 1972, part of a wider attack in which two busmen—George Bradshaw and Tom Duffy—were killed in Sackville Place and dozens injured. The ITGWU established a fund for the men's dependants. The bomb was directed 'at the union and all that it stands for.' Opposing the Offences Against the State Act (Amendment) Bill (1972) the following morning in the Seanad, Fintan Kennedy reminded Senators that Michael Mullen had called for opposition the previous Tuesday, likening these events to South Africa, Rhodesia or Portugal. The blasts assisted the passing of the iniquitous legislation, although the Labour Party stood firmly against.

No glass was left in the Hall, and repairs cost £60,000. A sanguine NEC 'agreed to explore the possibility of putting Scotch tape on all windows.'[71]

On 25 September 1976 the five-storey Connolly Hall opened at Lapp's Quay, Cork. In addition to office accommodation and meeting-rooms, space was provided for 'recreation, sports and education.' It was built at a time of economic recession, underlining the ITGWU's ambitions and belief in the economy. Economising was considered, but Connolly Hall was seen as a necessary investment in and reward for Cork members.

Architecturally, Connolly Hall had its inevitable critics. The ITGWU was unapologetic. 'It is a feature of modern architecture that it should be controversial, particularly when one is building on a site which is surrounded by architecture of a past age.' Its construction featured 'a low import content' and was 'labour-intensive.' Mullen noted that 'if one stood the building on end, it would be about thirty feet higher than Liberty Hall which probably meant that Cork would beat Dublin lying down.' The auditorium was named Thomas Kennedy Hall.

New premises were built at Ardee, Blanchardstown, Clonmel, Eden Quay, Newry, Portarlington and Shannon.[72]

Having taken over the Parliament Street Club, Dublin District Council ran a Sports and Social Club, offering tennis, basketball, football, a putting green, pitch and putt, judo, swimming and PT at grounds at Rutland Avenue, Crumlin, purchased in 1970. A club house was built and there were great hopes for significant social activity. The results of the fund-raising Annual Football Coupon became a feature of *Liberty*, along with news of competitions and activities. The driving forces were Eddie Storey and Eddie Lawless. All did not run smoothly, however. In November 1973 the NEC decided that it would not guarantee debts of more than £25,000 on the club.[73]

INTERNATIONAL SOLIDARITY

In 1971 solidarity was expressed with Spanish trade unionists who struck in protest at the imprisonment of Basque Nationalists. In February 1973 a telegram of sympathy was sent on the murder of Amilcar Cabral, Leader of the African Party for the Independence of Guinea and Cape Verde. Fighting Portuguese imperialism, Cabral was on the verge of declaring his country free. The work of Gorta was promoted to draw attention to Third World hunger and exploitation.

In 1973 Fintan Kennedy and Kader Asmal, Chairman of the Irish Anti-Apartheid Movement, attended ILO and UN Social Committees on Apartheid in Geneva, where motions condemned South Africa. In December, lengthy articles in *Liberty* dealt with the Pass Laws, the brutal repression of black trade unionists and apartheid's general wantonness, developing consciousness and solidarity. The ITGWU demanded 'NO TOUR' to South Africa by the British Lions to isolate the regime.

In September 1976 200 trade unionists attended a seminar on apartheid to support the South African Congress of Trade Unions. The speakers included Michael O'Leary (Minister for Labour), John Gaetsewe (exiled General Secretary of SACTU), Brendan Harkin (President of the ICTU) and Pat Rabbitte (ITGWU). Beginning on

21 March 1978 was International Anti-Apartheid Year. The ITGWU gave increased support to the Anti-Apartheid Movement. Asmal addressed the Annual Conference.

> If it does not seem presumptuous, this is a historic motion. In making history let us commit ourselves in the way that only workers can, to express our support—not our sympathy, *support*—and solidarity to the oppressed people of South Africa who themselves are making history. This is the demand of history. We must not fail them.

The ITGWU opposed the world tug-of-war championship planned for Dundalk in September 1978 because of the presence of a racially selected team from South Africa. The Government was asked to withdraw all collaboration with South Africa, and the Conference committed the union to supporting all 'effective trade union action' against the 'slave system of Apartheid.' In September 1979 Kennedy wrote to the Government asking that it ban the Springboks' Irish tour and promised to join the Irish Anti-Apartheid Movement's mass demonstrations.[74]

In October 1972 the union played host to the Ireland-USSR Friendship Society, an indication of the thawing of hostile attitudes within the ITGWU hierarchy to Socialist countries. Delegations to and from the Soviet Union became commonplace. To mark the sixtieth anniversary of the Russian Revolution *Liberty* published a two-part article on Irish Labour's response written by John Swift, former Leader of the Bakers' Union and President of the Irish Labour History Society. In 1978 Dublin Trades Council mooted abandoning the annual Connolly Commemoration on 12 May or nearest Sunday in favour of May Day. Michael O'Riordan, General Secretary of the Communist Party of Ireland, explained that while the Communist Party had revived the practice of celebrating May Day 'after a lapse of many years in the not-so-conducive atmosphere of the Cold War,' it nevertheless favoured the continuation of both celebrations, as 'internationalism and Connolly are inseparable.' Abandoning Connolly Day, with its national connotations, would bow to the same sorts of pressure that once caused the abandonment of May Day for its internationalism. Dublin members agreed. Five thousand people attended the May Day rally, Mullen stating that it was evident that 'the men whom Larkin said were crucifying Christ on the streets of Dublin' had still not loosened their grip.

In 1979 the ITGWU demanded that neutrality be reaffirmed and that involvement through the EEC in NATO or any other military pact be avoided.[75]

AN tOIBRÍ AND *NEW LIBERTY*

In 1976 Cumann Dhoirí Beaga (Doirí Beaga Branch of the ITGWU) proposed an Irish-language paper, *An tOibrí*. The NEC approved. In 1977 its driving force, Seán Ó Cearnaigh, became involved in a 'rank-and-file' paper, *New Liberty*. *An tOibrí* was in trouble. Its costs of £3,500 were covered by the NEC, but the union's name was taken off the title-piece in September 1978, 'as we were not the editors.' Its production was 'exclusively in the hands of Ó Cearnaigh.' The thirteenth issue contained a 'gross attack' on the NEC, presented as 'having been undemocratically elected,' and support for *New Liberty*. An undertaking to provide a literal translation in advance for issue 14 was not complied with; and Clady Knit, with which the ITGWU was locked in dispute, claimed that the 'union would close the firm' and that there was 'obscene behaviour of Gardaí to women strikers.' The ITGWU was accused of giving ambulance drivers poor service. Legal advice was sought on Clady, and Ó Cearnaigh was asked to amend material. He refused and 'sent an abusive letter to Paddy Clancy,' fuelling the fire.

In 1979 Ó Cearnaigh and Paddy Murphy (Dublin No. 13) were charged with trying to start unofficial action in Telectron, Gaoth Dobhair, in support of similar action in Dublin. It was the first time in ten years that NEC charges were brought against individuals. Ó Cearnaigh did not deny them but claimed that his tactics worked, as increases were secured and relations were again cordial. 'I make no apologies for my behaviour which has always been in the interests of my members and the Union.' The 'charges' could 'only provide comfort' to the union's enemies. 'It is not too late to withdraw them.' The NEC suspended both men from holding office under Rule 14.[76]

POLITICS

Michael O'Leary and Barry Desmond, Labour TDs, addressed the 1970 Conference, but Mullen was at pains to persuade Delegates that 'politics' did not necessarily mean 'party politics . . . Our involvement in political activity is not in any sense a party political or sectarian commitment.' If workers were to gain employment 'here and not in Birmingham or Düsseldorf,' political activity was essential.

Michael McEvoy (Dublin No. 7) wanted those 'paying the Political Levy' to be able to vote for Delegates to Labour Party Conferences, while the Youghal Branch wanted affiliation rescinded if the Labour Party entered Coalition. Brendan Corish, Leader of the Labour Party, outlined the *realpolitik,* the effective choices.

In 1972 there were further calls to disaffiliate. The Shannon Branch was motivated by the Labour Party's absence from the anti-EEC campaign in rural areas and its lukewarm attitude on the Offences Against the State Act. Herbert Devoy (Thomastown) asked those who ferociously attacked any Labour TD who addressed them what they had ever done to advance Socialist politics. He had been in the IRA, attempting to win a 32-county Socialist republic, but never bombed factories to throw men out of work, robbed banks or shot policemen. Conversely, Joe Meehan (Belfast) asked if the Labour Party was sacrosanct and above criticism. Up to 1969 nobody in Dáil Éireann 'even mentioned us.' Mullen appealed for Shannon to withdraw the motion, which they did, content that their point was made.

At the Labour Party Conference Joe McBrinn, a member of the NEC of the ITGWU, insisted on speaking. He felt there was a 'deliberate attempt' to 'make sure that no-one rocked the boat.' He criticised Cruise O'Brien's and Desmond's 'proBritish stand.' His maverick action quietly pleased some ITGWU leaders.[77]

During the 1973 election a huge 'VOTE LABOUR' sign hung from Liberty Hall and a car and driver were provided for Corish. The ITGWU, despite strong reservations, finally supported the Coalition Government of Fine Gael and the Labour Party. Its fourteen-point Programme of Intent 'contained many of the policies which successive Conferences' had 'been pressing for.' The election was a 'huge triumph for the people,' but the ITGWU was not 'giving a blank cheque to the Government, nor even to its Labour Party components.'

Hopes were high 'for a strong national movement towards a socially conscious society.' If Fine Gael 'leading lights who become Ministers can shed their doctrinaire Toryism and put people before money and property' it could 'prove the most enlightened Government' in the country's history. Corish was congratulated but warned not to forget his roots and 'the whole purpose' for which the Labour Party existed. Fine Gael spots would not change overnight.

Corish outlined his priorities: the quarter of the population who lived on or below the poverty line; the imbalance whereby only half was spent on social welfare here of what was spent in Northern Ireland; to employ as many of the 75,000 unemployed as possible; to reduce the housing list of 15,000 families; and to improve support for 50,000 disabled people.

Liam Beecher (Cork No. 6) wanted 'continued affiliation to any political party' to be subject to ballot. Having gently shaken the hornet's nest, he withdrew, but it underlined how fragile Labour affiliation was. Members were urged to 'Vote Labour': 'The Party that puts people before money and property. The Party with a comprehensive programme for social progress. The Party of the under-privileged and the unemployed. The Party of the worker.'[78]

At the 1974 Conference Brendan Corish, now Tánaiste, and John Hume covered the political spectrum. The ITGWU felt that 'it would have been better' had the Labour Party rejected its economic document *Protecting the Future.* Criticism of the union's demands was rejected by Mullen. It had 'shown a disciplined adherence to a national Agreement' when 'shell companies, speculators, bankers and the golden boys of the multinationals' had 'really stirred it up.' As to the seventies being Socialist, Mullen concluded, 'our allegiance must not be to a narrow self-satisfied, capitalist one-third of the globe but to the greater mass of mankind at home and overseas. They deserve far better from an old Socialist party.' Corish's inexplicable failure to mention internment angered the hall.

In 1976 Killarney called for disaffiliation, a shock, given that it was Michael Moynihan's Branch. Patsy Cronin explained that the Budget had resulted in 300 resignations from the union. Dublin District Council, 'mindful of the poor performance' of ITGWU-sponsored TDs, wanted greater accountability before grants were given. Killarney were defeated.

In 1977 the ITGWU opposed the Fianna Fáil 'giveaway' manifesto, especially those elements that attempted to link exaggerated promises with union commitments to low pay increases. The electorate were more easily bought. The Labour Party was cast from office.

There was growing discontent. The Socialist Labour Party emerged, and the Labour Party could 'not afford to lose their talent.' The ITGWU asked if it was 'too late for Frank Cluskey to hold out the hand of friendship.' Seán Ó Cearnaigh (Doirí Beaga) was not supported as the Labour Party candidate in Co. Donegal. In October Michael O'Leary was engaged as political consultant.[79]

In 1978 Fergal Costello (NEC) moved that affiliation to the Labour Party be suspended during any future Coalition. The voting was close, 91 to 98, despite anger that the Labour Party had 'propped up Fine Gael.' The Labour Party's Dublin vote fell from 29% in 1969 to 22% in 1972 and to 17½% in 1977. Costello characterised the Labour Party as the 'servile adjunct of Fine Gael.' While he acknowledged certain reforms initiated by the Labour Party, he severely criticised Cruise O'Brien's love of repressive legislation and O'Leary's attempt to defer the implementation of equal pay. Both owed their election in part to ITGWU support.

Éamon Thornton (Dublin No. 7) spoke for many: the political 'voice of organised workers should be a strong, clear, responsible, progressive and, most of all, independent voice.' Belfast and Derry Branches sought to expel Cruise O'Brien in October 1979. They had widespread support.

In elections for the European Parliament the Labour Party secured four seats and the SDLP one in Northern Ireland, all ITGWU members: John O'Connell and Michael O'Leary (Dublin), Liam Kavanagh (Leinster), Eileen Desmond (Munster) and John Hume (Northern Ireland). The ITGWU was little impressed and felt that 'Ireland's veto in the Council of Ministers is a better protection of the State's interests than the motley groups in the Assembly.' Neil Blaney, Síle de Valera, T. J. Maher, Ian Paisley, Richie Ryan and John Taylor were among the 'motleys'.[80]

ICTU CHARTER OF RIGHTS FOR WOMEN

The Irish Congress of Trade Unions recognises and demands the right of everyone, irrespective of race, ethnic origin, creed, political opinion, age, sex or marital status to have the means to pursue their economic independence and to full participation in the social, cultural and political life of the community, in conditions of freedom, dignity and equal opportunity.

The ICTU will, therefore, campaign for the following Charter of Rights for women and appeals to all trade unionists to do their utmost to further the principles set out in this Charter:—

Education
Complete equality of opportunity and access to all levels right through the educational system.

Job Opportunity
Complete equality of access to employment. All efforts should be made to eliminate any discrimination based on sex or marital status regarding access to employment.

Equal Pay
Equality of basic pay, bonuses and fringe benefits. There should be a national minimum income to alleviate the real problem of low pay.

Vocational Training
Access to all apprenticeships and all vocational training and guidance and a programme of positive encouragement for the involvement of women in training should be introduced.

Retraining
Special measures to give refresher and retraining courses for all women who wish to re-enter the labour force.

Promotion
Equal promotional opportunities for both men and women in all fields and under the same conditions.

Health and Safety
Working conditions to be without deterioration of previous conditions, the same for all workers. Special protective legislation for pregnant women where necessary.

Sick Pay and Pensions
Equality of treatment with regard to sick pay and the same pension conditions for every worker irrespective of sex.

Maternity
Twenty-six (26) weeks paid maternity leave on full pay. No dismissal during pregnancy or maternity leave. The working woman should be allowed to prolong her maternity leave for up to one year and the rights linked to her employment should not be forfeited, particularly as far as employment security, promotional prospects, pensions and other rights are concerned.

Child Care
Provision for Sate controlled crèches, day nurseries and nursery schools with adequately trained personnel. Provision of after-school and holiday care facilities and school meals.

Social
Comprehensive family planning services should be freely available and easily accessible to all. All necessary measures should be adopted to ensure that all persons have access to the necessary information, education, and means to exercise their basic right to decide freely and responsibly on the number and spacing of their children.

Social Security
The elimination of all discrimination against women in the field of social security.

Legal
All appropriate measures should be taken to ensure to women equal rights with men in the field of Civil and Criminal Law.

WE DEMAND ACTION
Open letter to the Taoiseach, 29 November 1979.

Dear Taoiseach,
We are writing to you as the current President of the EEC Council of Ministers and European Council and as part of a Community-wide action being co-ordinated this week by the European Trade Union Confederation to protest at the social and economic crisis which confronts us.

The Irish Transport and General Workers' Union wishes to make it known to the Heads of Government Summit in Dublin this week its grave concern at the worsening economic and social situation in the EEC, which has hit Ireland particularly hard.

Just prior to our entry into the EEC, the Paris Summit of 1972 promised a new perspective in which regional imbalances and social disparities would be greatly reduced, while economic growth in the Community continued. Instead, we have witnessed regional differences becoming more acute rather than less, and this situation is liable to get even worse with the accession of new member States such as Greece, Portugal and Spain. As for social policy, this has attempted to put the best face on deprivation, but has made no substantial progress towards eliminating it. And these failures have occurred against a backdrop of sharply increased unemployment, steep price rises, and general economic decline.

Despite this crisis, all the signs are that the Summit meeting intends to concern itself primarily with Britain's financial relationship with the EEC and to exclude any significant consideration of the grave social problems facing the Community. This confirms yet again how out of touch EEC leaders are with the everyday life of the great mass of people.

It is obvious that the doctrinaire, free enterprise ideas of the Rome Treaty are totally inadequate in the face of the difficulties which 40 million trade unionists in the EEC now confront, and especially the 6 million unemployed, 85,000 of whom are to be found in Ireland alone.

There is an urgent need for a new approach which will stress:
—public expenditure on job creation in the shape of house building and other forms of social construction;

—more public outlay on social services such as health, welfare, education, cultural development and environmental protection;

—use of deficit Budgeting and full exploitation of the taxable base of society in an equitable way as the PAYE campaign is advocating;

—the need to raise the real incomes and spending power of the low-paid such as the ITGWU has sought to do with its HELP (Higher Earnings for the Lower Paid) campaign;

—a genuine and planned regional policy, taking special account of countries like Ireland which cannot make large internal transfers;

—an industrial policy which ensures the transition from declining to growth industries without social dislocation and structural unemployment;

—an energy policy which stresses job creating measures such as conservation and development of alternative sources to oil and nuclear power, especially in high unemployment areas such as ours;

—more public surveillance and control of multinational companies as regards investment and pricing policy;

—increased participation by workers and their representatives in industrial and State decision-making.

The ITGWU is especially concerned at the build-up of a military-industrial complex in Western Europe where there is an increasing integration at the practical level between NATO and the EEC, especially in the arms industry. This is a danger both to our neutrality and to international peace and should be firmly opposed. Moreover, foreign policy integration within the EEC on matters not relating to the Rome Treaty is a threat to the independence of member States and should cease forthwith.

We call upon the Irish Government as the current holder of the EEC Presidency to convey to the Summit meeting that these are matters which should be to the forefront and the policies which are necessary to uplift the conditions of workers in the EEC countries, and moreover, that the Irish Government intends to take the necessary steps in this direction.

Yours sincerely,

Senator Fintan Kennedy, General President; John F. Carroll, Vice President; Michael Mullen, General Secretary on behalf of the National Executive Council.

Source: *Liberty*, December 1979.

Chapter 30

NATIONAL UNION THROUGH FEDERATION AND UNDERSTANDING: THE WUI IN THE 1970s

MEMBERSHIP, FINANCE AND ORGANISATION

The Committee examining internal organisation reported in 1970. Branch investigations were conducted, scrutinising finance, organisation and administration. New premises were bought in Quinnsborough Road, Bray. General expansion occurred, especially in the South-East Area, Droichead Nua and Cashel. On the negative side, rationalisation, mergers and redundancies ate into traditional bases. The reports of the Apathy Group were to produce 'constructive results, rather than useless recriminations.' Paddy Cardiff, Secretary of the Education Committee, managed matters.

There were calls to cut Conference Delegations from one for every 100 members to one for every 200, to improve efficiency and to make it possible to take the Conference outside Dublin. With regard to the problem of apathy, cutting Delegations seemed contradictory, and it was defeated.

New contribution scales were adopted, ranging from 8p to 25p a week, Dispute Benefits increasing to between £3.50 and £8.50. Money on disputes was never begrudged, but there was an increased incidence of payments to members arising from disputes in which they were not directly involved or were not a party. Efforts to curtail expenditure continued despite increased contributions. Steady improvement was maintained in 1971 in Bray-Dún Laoghaire, Nos. 1, 6, 8, 12 and 18, the Meat Federation, Central Area, South-East and Western Branches. The WUI benefited from involvement in trade union Groups in Aer Lingus, RTÉ, the ESB, Bord na Móna and the public service.[1]

For the first time, each Branch's total income was published, ranked as follows: No. 4, £28,484; No. 1, £14,263; No. 9, £13,675; Meat Federation, £12,778; No. 12, £12,564; No. 15, £11,123; Tullamore, £9,331; No. 2, £9,182; No. 18, £9,161; No. 13, £6,711; No. 5, £5,687; No. 3, £5,361; Athy, £4,801; No. 7, £3,241; Galway, £3,097; Bray, £3,004;

Dún Laoghaire, £2,204; No. 8, £1,842; Trim, £1,085; Athlone, £1,721; No. 17, £204; and Enniscorthy £34.

Tom Geraghty (No. 2) criticised affiliated Associations: 'These people are operating a trade union membership on the cheap.' Though a member of the GEC, he knew nothing of their financial arrangements, what services they availed of and at what cost, or what exactly the benefit was to the WUI. J. Thomas (No. 2) thought they represented 'snobs and snobbery.' James Bannon (Foras Talúntais Technical Staff Association) thought his group would eventually fully merge, but in the meantime they paid for any services. In 1972 there were thirteen affiliates, the terms of their Agreement varying, itself a source of confusion and complaint.

Addressing the 1972 Conference in Wexford, the General President, John Foster, said it 'would be rather difficult to say precisely why' the Conference had previously been confined to Dublin. Wexford was appropriate, given the 1911 Lock-Out. He mentioned four men who 'figured most prominently, over the six months of the ultimately triumphant struggle: Big Jim Larkin, James Connolly, Richard Corish and Francis Cruise O'Brien.' P. T. Daly's heroics got no mention. Tom Geraghty (No. 2) quickly focused attention, as 'Conference democracy was impeded' by the slow production of relevant documents, denying the opportunity for analysis. Thomas Kavanagh (Trustee) said the WUI had 'close on 3,000 members in associated and affiliated groups,' receiving £6,765 a year from them.[2]

In 1972–3 members of the UCD academic staff joined. General Electric workers in Dublin transferred from the ITGWU after a favourable ruling by the ICTU Disputes Committee. Expansion in the country, while possible, still induced caution by the GEC. Nevertheless the 1973 Conference was held in Athlone, showing that the WUI was 'now firmly established in the Midlands.' Leo Gibson (No. 12) voiced a general complaint before the Conference began: documents were inadequate. He suggested that no future Conference should begin without advance circulation of the GEC report and necessary materials. Tom Geraghty echoed these sentiments, as he had done in the previous two years, and thought 'it needs to be brought home at this stage to our General Secretary, that he will realise that he projects the image of the Union.' Trickle became torrent as speakers rose to echo complaints, yet referral back was rejected, 46 to 84, perhaps to accommodate business rather than condone tardiness.

The General Secretary, Denis Larkin, accepted that 'criticism has been expressed; I won't comment on it.' He was up for re-election the following year; 'members could decide.' An Emergency Motion condemned him 'for his failure to publish and issue the GEC Reports to Delegates' and called for all documents to be supplied ten days in advance in future. Failure to do so would result in the Conference being delayed.

In 1974 the Voluntary Hospitals Clerical and Administrative Association and the Radiographers' Association opted for full membership. Foster reminded Delegates to the Golden Jubilee (fiftieth anniversary) Conference that 'it was in a tenement room in Dublin's Townsend Street on the 4th of January 1909' that Larkin 'first launched the ITGWU,' and 'it was in the tenement homes of Dublin's unskilled labourers that Larkin's gospel of working-class solidarity found the most ready and militant response.' He traced the development of the ITGWU and the creation of the WUI. They had 'endeavoured over the years, to promote good will and co-operation' between unions.

An excess of income over expenditure of £114,039 was recorded, the first six-figure surplus. Larkin cautioned that this was slightly false, as only £343 was spent on disputes. Motions calling for increased payments to Shop Stewards and Collectors were lost. Liam Maguire (No. 12) insisted on access by wheelchair to union premises and demanded the Government's endorsement of ILO Convention 135 through legislation, article 1 of which declares:

> Workers' Representatives in their undertakings shall enjoy effective protection against any act prejudicial to them including dismissal based on their status or activities as the Workers' Representative or on union membership or participation in union activities, insofar as they act in conformity with existing laws or collective Agreements.[3]

In 1975, contributions were raised to 40p for those on £35 per week or over, with correspondingly lower rates down to 15p for those on less than £15. Dispute Pay rose accordingly, from £14 down to £7 per week. Larry Sweetman (No. 2), although not opposing the increases, wanted to know what to tell members. The explanation was found in ever-rising costs. Income rose by 10½%, expenditure by 27%. Total net assets increased to £656,215, but underlying financial trends were not encouraging. Economic recession occasioned a decline in membership in 1976 and a shift in balance from the private to the public sector. The call was for greater recruitment. Yet excess of income over expenditure was healthy. In 1971 it was 33.5%, in 1972 34.3%, in 1973 40%, in 1974 28.7% and in 1975 30.8%.

Problems arose with the Aer Lingus and Aer Rianta Executive Staffs' Association, full membership being held up by the fact that some WUI members held similar positions in the company to members of the Staff Association. A slight increase in membership occurred in 1977. Anxious for expansion, the Conference demanded an investigation of all options. Liam Maguire wanted a 'full-time Recruitment Officer' and to 'immediately open offices' in Cork and Shannon. It was the old dilemma: should they break from their Dublin-centric structure?

In 1968–9 the WUI was 'virtually broke' but neglected potential growth. There was talk of workers 'crying out' for unionisation, although in reality what was being identified was largely disaffected ITGWU and other unions' members. Cardiff dampened things by pointing out that expansion required firm bases. The cost of one Official in a Region was £10,000 a year—a thirteenth of total income. He complained that the WUI was not getting its share of pre-emptive closed-shop Agreements in transnational factories: they were hoovered up by the ITGWU. Michael O'Halloran (No. 15) cautioned that 'big is not necessarily beautiful' and that 'talk about aggressive expansion of membership' was 'dangerous . . . without knowing why we want to expand.' Foster pointed out that with Denis Larkin's retirement a 'new chapter' was beginning. Cardiff, the succeeding General Secretary, warned that members would be recruited only 'if they could be properly serviced.' Maguire favoured 'selective amalgamation' but stuck to his guns regarding the motion. It was referred back. The WUI remained cautious about making a geographical leap.[4]

In 1978 the WUI cut links with the Irish Airlines Executive Staffs' Association. The two had 'not been very close' for five years and there were 'certain disagreements.' Matters came to a head when the association entered into an Agreement that it would undertake certain work in disputes between the WUI and the company, in exchange for certain payments. Cardiff met them and 'asked them to conform with' the 'practice of good trade unionism . . . unfortunately quite a few of their members did not conform.' The association protested to Congress about 'being disaffiliated.' The WUI felt the workers it represented would be better 'organised directly.' Membership of the WUI was not available at any price.

Financially, the 1970s proved rewarding, a surplus of £538,262 accumulating between 1973 and 1977. The value of investments rose from £242,239 in 1973 to £566,415 in 1977. Figures, however, could be misleading. Increases in membership income, virtually the sole source of income, rose by a mere £22,900, or 4½% in 1977, the lowest increase since 1961. The previous five years showed a very different pattern: 1972, increase of £234,573 (12½%); 1973, £285,532 (22%); 1974, £315,448 (10½%); 1975, £404,039 (28%; 1976, £536,014 (33%). The division of members between the different contribution rates in 1977 (table 111) showed that nearly three-quarters were on the maximum rate, leaving 'little room for manoeuvre.' Increases in expenditure were much higher than in income: 1972, £15,808 or 11½% higher than the previous year; 1973, £16,987 (11%); 1974, £47,030 (27%); 1975, £61,234 (28%); 1976, £52,295 (19%); 1977, £75,231 (22%). This caused concern. Worse, overhead expenses, excluding Dispute Pay, were 73% of income, a continuation of an upward trend since 1972 (66%), 1973 (60%), 1974 (69%), 1975 (69%) and 1976 (62%). The response was to raise contributions, generally by 10p per week, with attendant increases in benefits. Membership was 35,162.[5]

Table 111: WUI income, expenditure and surplus (£), 1970–79

	Income	Members' subscription	Socials and draws	Expenditure	Salaries and benefit	Legal fees	Surplus (loss)
1970	152,786	151,320	—	127,465	61,053	41	25,321
1971	208,678	207,342	—	151,656	73,024	216	57,022
1972	234,971	233,781	—	160,573	78,535	52	74,398
1973	285,532	283,314	—	171,493	88,883	28	114,039
1974	315,448	312,666	—	284,345	109,402	78	31,103
1975	404,039	403,120	—	288,002	154,799	8	116,037
1976	536,014	535,215	—	378,137	187,867	33	157,877

1977	558,914	557,360	—	439,708	210,121	—	119,206
1978	593,819	590,365	—	692,577	257,214	69	(98,758)
1979	827,238	824,088	—	633,389	344,310	7	193,849

Source: WUI and FWUI, Reports of Annual Delegate Conference, 1970–79.

A lengthy dispute in Aer Lingus left the GEC with little alternative but to seek increased contribution rates. Delegates, rather than expressing resistance, accepted them, with Dermot Boucher (No. 15) thinking them too low and Mick Dowling (No. 4) suggesting some form of indexation to guarantee income as wages rose. There was only one voice against.

Confirmation of the merger with the Federation of Rural Workers brought the 1979 membership to just below 50,000. On 25 May 1978 the Irish Airline Pilots' Association announced that it wanted to terminate its affiliation. It had acquired its own Negotiating Licence six years previously and felt the time 'was appropriate' to assert its independence. It expressed 'tremendous gratitude' to the WUI, which acceded to its request. Whether this decision was in any way related to the WUI clerical and technical workers' strike in Aer Lingus in 1978 was not suggested.

After the merger of the Federation of Rural Workers to form the Federated Workers' Union of Ireland, Foster addressed the largest Conference ever, with more than 400 Delegates from all corners of the Republic. Income had increased by 6% but expenditure by 14%, with administration and expenses, excluding Dispute Pay, accounting for 78% of income. Total net assets, including cars, buildings, equipment, investments and cash, amounted to £849,708. Dispute Pay, however, was £230,307, by far the largest sum dispensed and a reminder that the union was always vulnerable to significant strikes.

In May 1979 the Guinness Staff Association approached the union for support in its application for affiliation to the ICTU. At an ICTU meeting to examine the organisation of new companies the WUI expressed 'no objection to pre-production Agreements.'[6] Membership broke the 50,000 landmark.

Table 112: WUI membership by contribution category, September 1977

Contribution	Number of members	Proportion of total membership (%)
15p	714	2.03
20p	1,106	3.15
25p	1,759	5.00
30p	2,829	8.05
35p	2,620	7.45
40p	26,134	74.32

Source: WUI, Report of Annual Delegate Conference, 1978, p. 286.

Table 113: WUI and FWUI membership, 1970–79

	ICTU affiliation	RFS figure		ICTU affiliation	RFS figure
1970	35,000	34,536	1975	35,000	34,252
1971	35,000	34,706	1976	35,000	34,477
1972	35,000	34,790	1977	35,000	35,859
1973	35,000	35,048	1978	35,000	35,941
1974	35,000	35,358	1979	35,000	44,588

Sources: ICTU, Annual Reports, 1970–80; National Archives, Registrar of Friendly Societies, file 369T.

DENIS LARKIN

Denis Larkin retired as General Secretary on 30 April 1977. He openly acknowledged that 'I got my well-deserved portion of blame, at times I deserved it, and from time to time my portion of credit.' He held no ambition for office but had answered the call. He left the WUI more secure. His successor, Paddy Cardiff, paid tribute. Denis had lost not only his brother, James, but the General President, John Smithers, robbing him of experienced mentors. He also lost his wife, Annie, his life and political partner. He overcame all these losses. His leadership of Congress Delegations at talks on National Wage Agreements was legendary for his capacity to produce solutions from the air.

Denis began his farewell address by observing that when he met members in the future it would be merely as a 'fellow-member', an odd experience, given a working life as an Official. He had often been in struggle on their behalf but also in struggles with them—it had been that sort of open relationship and one that had, ultimately, endeared him to all. Larkin had his limitations, famously as regards administration, but he was respected by industrial staff for his support and commitment and his unquestionable commitment to his class.

Cardiff carried the burden of being the first General Secretary from outside the Larkin family. William A. (Bill) Attley was elected Deputy General Secretary at the 1977 Conference.[7]

FEDERATION

Discussions with the Federation of Rural Workers, begun in 1975, concluded with a 'transfer of engagements' examined by the GEC on 7 January 1978 and adopted on 19 July. The merger resulted in a new name, the Federated Workers' Union of Ireland. It was facilitated by the 'close and friendly ties' that 'always existed' between the two unions, ties that Cardiff claimed brought them close during failed talks with the ITGWU and others in the 1960s. The Trade Union Act (1975) provided new possibilities, and he and Paddy Murphy of the FRW investigated them. They were 'getting together for practical reasons,' finance not an immediate concern for either.

The FRW remained as a discernible, semi-autonomous unit as FWUI Rural Workers' Group. Murphy was Acting General Secretary, but Jimmy Tully, General Secretary, on leave of absence in Dáil Éireann and the Government, waived his right to return.

There were reservations about the change of name, but Denis Larkin, speaking as an observer, made the point that Young Jim, when the merger talks with the ITGWU were at their most intense in 1967, was not too concerned with name changes but with more 'fundamental principles, the system of organisation . . . basis of election' to the GEC, 'basis of representation at' the Conference and 'continuing to hold the power of the union among the rank-and-file.' He for one would be proud to be a 'Federated Workers' Union of Ireland' man.

FRW members voted by 94% in favour of transfer, and the new union was registered on 29 March 1979.[8]

RELATIONS WITH THE ITGWU

In April 1970 Fintan Kennedy renewed contacts with Denis Larkin and suggested that the NEC of the ITGWU meet the GEC of the WUI. The General Secretary of the ITGWU, Michael Mullen, sent a 'copy of the proposed document on contributions, benefits, etc.' and invited a WUI speaker to the ITGWU Delegate Conference in Kilkee. The GEC concluded: 'We'd better invite one of them.' Matters seemed to be moving again.

Simultaneously, discussions with the Irish Shoe and Leather Workers' Union were advanced after approaches from Michael Bell and Paul Alexander. Financial details were exchanged, and Alexander, due to retire, was keen to progress matters. Seán Tracey TD (Labour Party) would probably succeed him as President. By September, however, the trail went cold.

Talks were also held with the Irish Women Workers' Union. At the Conference Tom Geraghty, discussing attempts by the ICTU to promote rationalisation, thought that 'until such times as these big unions,' the WUI and the ITGWU, 'show that by being in that union they are going to get better service than they are getting in the smaller unions,' those in 'smaller unions are not going to agree to come in with us. So the problem lies with ourselves.'

Larkin reported that talks with the ITGWU were continuing, but there were 'no specific proposals.' P. J. Madden (National Hospitals Branch) warned against the 'highly established bureaucratic' ITGWU, while W. Lynch (No. 8 Branch) went back to Larkin's repudiation of 1923. Delegates were chary about possible merger. Larkin informed them that they had discussed matters of mutual interest, such as relative contribution rates and benefit scales. His experience in Jameson's of members opting to pay 1s to 1s 3d, as opposed to ATGWU rates of merely 6d, was that members did not want a 'cut-price union'. The ICTU could do more to equalise contribution rates, especially those of British unions. Fintan Kennedy told Delegates that it was the 'earnest desire of both Unions to arrive at a mutually satisfactory understanding' and 'work together in the closest possible unity, harmony and co-operation.' The ITGWU was simultaneously meeting the Executives of six craft unions. He extended fraternal greetings but significantly did not mention merger or amalgamation. Responding, Larkin traced the background of joint talks and the need for further rationalisation. Kennedy thought 'we are making history today.' He was a fraternal guest at the wui throughout the 1970s.[9]

Little more emerged in 1971. Continuing friendly relations minimised 'incidents of strain and disagreement,' though some might have felt that 'at times ... sufficient efforts are not being made by both sides to reduce it.' Although 'no further positive progress' was recorded, there was no apparent 'desire to terminate discussions.' J. O'Dwyer (Trim) sought 'the same facilities and the same privileges' as those given by the itgwu, a further indication of the degree to which the two unions kept an eye on each other.

In 1971, Eddie Phelan (gec) insisted that only a ballot of the full membership could determine anything. Larkin confirmed that this was so, but no such need was imminent. Officers of the wui and islwu met again in April. Larkin 'thought the discussions were going well.' He read newspaper reports that 'amalgamation with the itgwu was only a matter of time,' but 'Senator Kennedy had contacted him saying that this information did not come from his Union.' Larkin circulated Branch Secretaries, appealing for confidentiality. In fact little real progress was being made.

Kennedy again addressed the wui Conference, being 'struck by the extreme similarities between our two organisations.' There appeared to be 'no vital point of variance in our objectives.' Potential membership of the eec made union unity all the more vital, and the itgwu was affiliated to seven international Union Groups. Talks had 'lapsed somewhat in recent times,' primarily because of other preoccupations, but it was his 'fervent hope' that they would resume.

Replying, Larkin retraced the history of Congress and appealed for the lessons of unity to be learnt. Delegates were again given an impression of impending merger.

An indication of frostier relations came when the itgwu Premises Manager wrote suggesting that they were going to call a room in Liberty Hall after Larkin and requesting a 'picture of the first General Secretary to hang in the room.' Rather sniffily, the gec recorded that the 'matter will receive consideration as soon as the gs hears from the appropriate go [General Officer].' Merger with the islwu was more likely, and Alexander addressed the Conference, where Larkin presented him with a photograph of himself with Larkin Junior. He talked openly of impending merger.[10]

In 1973 Denis Larkin suggested that, with membership of the eec, 'one would have expected that unions with headquarters in Britain' would 'have, without being asked, recognised the necessity to encourage the development of unions which are wholly Irish-based and controlled.' The opposite happened. Some 'Amalgamated' unions began organising in the Republic for the first time. This was a surprising contribution. It might have been expected at an itgwu rather than a wui assembly. Tom Redmond (Bray) reminded Delegates of the thorny issue of Partition in relation to British unions.

At the Golden Jubilee Conference in 1974 Larkin read fraternal greetings from Kennedy. There was, however, no more talk about merger or joint activity. A second message came from the Congress of the Central Council of Trade Unions of the USSR.

In 1976 the WUI enthusiastically supported the ICTU's Shregle Report on rationalisation. Merger with the ITGWU had long receded. The Irish Shoe and Leather Workers' Union also fell from the radar, its talks with the ITGWU perhaps spiking other wheels. In 1977, Peter Keating (Staff) raised serious criticisms of the ITGWU's actions in disputes in Hughes Brothers Dairies, psychiatric hospitals and Poolbeg power station, where, despite ignoring ICTU procedures, Strike Pay was paid, placing the WUI in a disadvantageous position. Keating claimed the ITGWU kept Two-Tier Picketing policy on the 'statute book of Congress' yet ignored it when it suited. It was guilty of double standards. In Hughes Brothers he further alleged violent behaviour against WUI members. Michael Collins suggested that the ITGWU 'were controlling Congress.'

Denis Larkin made it clear that complaints were made to Congress but warned that if 'a guerrilla war with the ITGWU' were to break out 'indefinitely then I think we will find ourselves in quite a serious situation with no eventual good to either side.' Tom Geraghty (GEC) referred to Dublin Corporation disputes and the differing attitudes of the WUI, ITGWU and IMETU. He decried the ITGWU's 'double faced attitude' regarding Two-Tier Picketing. P. Sherry (No. 6) wanted ICTU All-Out Pickets cancelled and a referendum of members to decide whether the FWUI should remain in affiliation, as the 'present picketing system is against all principles of trade unionism.' Geraghty, while approving the sentiment, thought withdrawal from Congress would be a sledgehammer to crack a nut. Cardiff pointed out that they were defeated on the issue at Congress. The FWUI's opposition was, in any case, less to the policy and more to 'other unions who will not operate the picketing policy honestly.' Members rebuffed the guidance of the GEC and adopted the motion.

In November 1979 scheduled meetings between Cardiff and Michael Mullen were twice cancelled at short notice, with nothing new put in the diary. The exact purpose of the meetings was unclear. More than 200 ITGWU members in St Colman's Hospital, Letterkenny, and St Camillus' Hospital, Limerick, were ordered to be handed back by the Congress Disputes Committee, so it may well be that Cardiff and Mullen were merely to redefine territorial boundaries. The Association of Scientific, Technical and Managerial Staffs had to be strongly reminded in late 1979 that the Medical Laboratory Technologists' Association was an affiliated FWUI member after meetings were addressed in Cork, Galway and Waterford. The Secretary of the Association, Cyril Keogh, nipped potential poaching in the bud.[11]

In 1970 Christy Worth (Trustee) called for the WUI's re-affiliation to the International Union of Food Workers for 11,000 members in the food industry. Both the ITGWU and Irish Bakers were affiliated, emphasising the WUI's isolation. Thomas Duffy (Trustee) opposed, on the grounds of value for money. The ICTU provided sufficient international contact.

Impending membership of the Common Market concerned the Conference, however, and, after a lively debate Christy Worth was criticised, as a GEC member, for moving a motion against union policy and incurring the £400 affiliation expense.[12]

WOMEN

In March 1970 the WUI sent three members to the ICTU Women's Advisory Committee. Josephine Walsh (No. 12) demanded that the WUI state 'its determination to press onward with its aims of securing equal pay for equal work for all female workers.' She cited ILO and British TUC policies. A White Paper on membership of the Common Market had warned of the high costs of awarding women equal pay. Theresa Egan (GEC) decried the 'lip service' of such motions, pointing out that Congress had sought a report on equal pay in 1967. They still awaited it. Cardiff denied it was 'lip service'. Equal pay was won for psychiatric workers, and RTÉ and Aer Lingus had committed themselves to it. Women's general rates had moved from 70% of male increases in the Tenth Round to 90% in the Twelfth Round.

Walsh criticised Cardiff, feeling he regarded 'the achievement of parity for women' as something only to 'be considered when it does not interfere with any claims from male members.' He had indeed suggested that male and married rates be fixed first, to provide a yardstick against which women's wages could be expressed proportionately.

The WUI made an extensive submission to the Commission on the Status of Women. In 1972 L. Kelly (No. 15) moved that 'immediate practical steps' be taken on equal pay and equal rights in response to the Commission's interim report. In the Fourteenth Round they were urged 'not to capitulate to Management pleas of economic expediency as an excuse for not implementing parity pay.' Larkin was criticised for suggesting that there were 'still economic barriers' to equal pay as part of general stalling tactics. Kelly insisted: 'We demand equal pay, equal promotional opportunities and an end to all discrimination against women workers in employment.' Equal pay had 'wider implications than the same pay for the same work.' The most 'blatant injustices' existed in traditionally defined 'female-oriented work', and 'a radical appraisal of job evaluation must be initiated immediately.' Married women were victims of 'cowardly policy' on a 'grace and favour basis.' Sacking women on marriage should be illegal. The GEC was asked 'to stop being patronising.'

Larkin, clearly irked, pleaded, 'For God's sake will you try and sometimes give credit to the work being done by your Union.' He reiterated their commitment, but they were 'limited by economic factors which we cannot just push aside.' Walsh demanded pressure on the Government to introduce legislation, liaison with the ICTU on implementing equal pay through job evaluation, and a more decisive role for the Labour Court. No-one demurred.

In 1973 two out of twenty-six members of the industrial staff were women: Joan Carmichael, Secretary of No. 15 Branch, and Pádraigín Ní Mhurchú, Branch Assistant in No. 12. The staff Marriage Bar was abolished. Women were appointed not because they were women but because they were the most suitable.

In 1975 J. Dowling (No. 15) sought equality in training and placement schemes Breda Donohoe (No. 15) wanted the Anti-Discrimination (Pay) Act (1974) amended to provide that the 'minimum male rate shall be the minimum rate for all workers' in the job. Tom Redmond (Bray) reaffirmed male support for equal pay, urging uninterrupted progress to end 'discriminatory practices against women.'

In 1976 the ICTU Charter of Rights for Women was adopted—'another important stage in [an] organised effort to eradicate the many forms of discrimination' in society. Congress vigorously insisted that Ireland not seek derogation from its obligations under EEC Directive 117 on equal pay. There were complaints that the Anti-Discrimination (Pay) Act (1974) was a blunter instrument than expected.

By 1977 widespread advances on equal pay were reported, either complete or phased introduction. Carmichael's decision to leave the union was widely regretted, Paul Boushell (No. 12) stating that the 'movement cannot do without Joan Carmichael and her like; they are rare enough.' The Employment Equality Act (1977) required the abolition of the WUI's Marriage Benefit. Bernadette Barry (No. 16) demanded a 'State financed fully comprehensive Family Planning Service.' Contradictions between the legal position and society's behaviour, and weakness among political parties in providing effective leadership, were severely criticised.[13]

Table 114: Women in the WUI, 1970–79

	Membership	Women	Women as proportion of total (%)
1970	34,536	10,521	30.4
1971	34,706	11,868	34.1
1972	34,790	11,897	34.1
1973	35,048	11,928	34.0
1974	35,358	12,919	36.5
1975	34,252	n.a.	n.a.
1976	34,477	11,521	33.4
1977	35,859	13,205	36.8
1978	35,941	13,070	36.3
1979	44,588	13,236	29.6

Source: National Archives, Registrar of Friendly Societies, file 369T.

Women's membership increased by 3,836 in the 1970s but was not reflected in the proportion of the total. After merger with the predominantly male Federation of Rural Workers, the proportion of women declined. In numerical terms, however, women were an ever more visible and vocal element of the union.

WAGE ROUNDS

In 1969 the WUI expressed fears that wage increases negatively affected competitiveness. With the Anglo-Irish Free Trade Area Agreement and impending membership of the EEC before the Twelfth Round was complete, there had to be detailed
thinking 'on this thorny problem of incomes and prices.' In 1970 Foster acknowledged that, in regard to purchasing power, unions were 'conspicuously less
successful.' Real wages rose by only half of money wage increases. An 'inflationary
spiral' had implications for job creation and was 'above all the enemy of the lower
paid and weaker sections of the community.' While ruling out any statutory
response, he suggested that a voluntary response might be acceptable.

The WUI supported demands by the ICTU for a prices and incomes policy. The
Bray Branch asked the GEC to 'initiate a campaign of industrial action' to prevent
the Fianna Fáil Government's 'attempt to depress' living standards 'through their
latest wage freeze proposals.' It was 'noted.'

After the Maintenance Dispute the Employer-Labour Conference was created,
in which, for the first time, representatives of the state as employer and representatives of state-sponsored and public companies were included. Under the auspices
of the Employer-Labour Conference discussions led to a National Wage Agreement.
The proposals accompanied concerns over 10% inflation and unemployment of
70,000 in April 1971. Anglo-Irish free trade rendered employment in textiles, clothing, footwear and food parlous. Worse would follow from membership of the EEC.
The 'task of finding answers to the many vital questions' had 'once again been left'
to the unions. Responses required unity of thought and action.

Under Professor Basil Chubb the Employer-Labour Conference discussed a
National Wage Agreement as the Minister for Finance announced a Prices and
Incomes Bill, with a wage freeze from 16 October 1970. The WUI decided on 11
December to support proposals for a National Wage Agreement, provided the Prices
and Incomes Bill was withdrawn. Features of the proposed Agreement included
the necessity to 'moderate substantially' the rate of increase in costs and prices, to
improve efficiency, and industrial peace. Unions attempted to protect and improve
workers' living standards, an increasingly difficult task in a developing, international economy. Industrial relations, judged by strikes and lost days, were bad, but
problems stemmed from employers' denial of the 'concept of equality.'[14]

In 1971 Tom Geraghty insisted that the GEC should have no 'authority to
sanction or accept a general wage increase' without the approval of a Special
Delegate Conference. For Geraghty the essence of democracy was accountable leadership. John L'Estrange (No. 2) pointed out that in accepting the Twelfth Round
on behalf of 35,000 members the GEC had accepted repressions. A lengthy and at
times vivid debate ensued. Larkin pointed out that the GEC had accepted
Agreements on members' behalf since 1964, without complaint. The GEC had to
consider the legislative threat and the drain on funds should major strikes ensue
from rejection of the National Wage Agreement. He concluded: 'We do not vote.
The people who vote are the members that you elected at Annual Delegate

Conference and if you cannot trust them at times of national emergency to speak collectively in your name, well, I think you should not put them there.' F. O'Farrell (No. 2) rebuffed Larkin's justification: it was not whether National Wage Agreements were good or bad, it was the principle of consultation and participation. The motion was lost, but the principle it contained was not lost sight of.

S. Currin (GEC) praised Larkin's role in the crisis talks of December 1970 that resulted in the National Wage Agreement, despite the fact that his wife had died on 5 December. Final discussions took place on 9–11 December. Larkin stoically remained on the bridge, attempting to secure the WUI's position.[15]

In 1972 the WUI complained that, despite frequent calls for the 'need for an organised, disciplined, militant' movement, 'we appear to be still inward-looking and selfish to an increasing degree.' The movement 'continually gave lip service' to the cause of old-age pensioners, 'our blind fellow-citizens, our widows and our orphans' but avoided 'being involved in any organised and conscious effort on their behalf.' They remained 'mesmerised' by 'our own individual or Sectional interests with little regard for the good of our community.' More than ninety unions facilitated Sectionalism and division. National Wage Agreements showed some capacity to moderate inflation, but there was precious little response from the Government on tax and employment.

In 1973 Jo Walsh (No. 12) suggested that the WUI should not enter future Wage Agreements unless the Government stabilised prices. After lengthy, acrimonious debate this was carried. The failure of the National Prices Commission spurred the motion, but negotiators argued that hands should not be tied before talks. Mick Dowling (No. 4) wanted the Fourteenth Round brought forward six months 'to hasten the termination date and in order to offset the spiralling prices.'

Members rejected proposals for a National Wage Agreement in January 1973, a decision reinforced by the ICTU Special Conference on 30 January, where the vote was 103 to 295. The WUI immediately ordered Branches to pursue local claims, while the Minister called employers and unions together through the Employer-Labour Conference. New proposals emerged, which were accepted (9,090 to 5,226) and were endorsed by Congress. Larry Bateson (South-East Area) wanted each Branch to count and declare its own votes in future ballots. This stirred deep emotions, with many speakers, including the GEC, opposing, on the grounds that it was divisive. The floor resisted pressure from the GEC and adopted it, 98 to 76. P. Costello (Dún Laoghaire) wanted increases under the National Wage Agreement to 'be common to all' and not a percentage. Surprisingly, given many low-paid workers in the hall, it was soundly defeated.[16]

Aer Lingus complained to the Employer-Labour Conference that the WUI was in breach of the 1974 Agreement. Much publicity was given to the Steering Committee's decision against the WUI. No publicity was given to the increases conceded on the threat of unofficial action, however. Similar complaints were made against the WUI and ITGWU in Irish Distillers.

As the Agreement wound down, employers increasingly pleaded 'inability to pay.' A Delegate Conference in December 1974 nevertheless supported talks. A much tighter, more restrictive National Wage Agreement emerged, accepted by 281 to 117 votes at Congress on 15 April 1975, the wui having voted by 72 against 20%. A breakdown by Branch was given.

In 1976 Tom Redmond (Bray) called for an examination of the 'economic effects' of National Wage Agreements. Had lower-paid workers benefited? Had living standards improved? And what impact had they had on prices and employment? Events after the endorsement of the 1974 Agreement were taken 'too lightly.' Originally rejected, the Agreement was accepted after improvements in its monetary terms, but in other respects the deal was worse. In 1975, despite supporting indexation, the Government, not least as employer, sought to renege on its commitments. The 1976 National Wage Agreement was rejected, largely because many public sector workers had not yet secured entitlements under the previous Agreement. On 11 September 1976, however, by 309 to 90, an improved interim Agreement was accepted. Unofficial actions revealed its unsatisfactory nature, irrespective of attitudes towards unofficial action.

Before another National Wage Agreement in 1977 members wanted commitments from the Government on increased income tax allowances, stricter price and profit controls and import restrictions in industries badly hit by unemployment. A rancorous debate followed. Cardiff observed that in the gap between the last two Agreements no union rushed into the breach to serve claims. He tried to balance demands that were purely industrial—wages—with those that were political—taxation—and all against a basic desire to maintain jobs. The wui moved to broaden the bargaining scope in Congress but were defeated. It was surely time to return to that debate and exchange industrial power for political gains through a significantly widened Agreement.

Jim Larraghy (No. 15) opposed, because credence was given to the idea that National Wage Agreements strengthened the position of the low-paid, whereas they 'did not serve any of our interests.' National Wage Agreements were 'destroying' the movement's 'independence, fighting spirit and democracy' and diminishing the strike weapon. Cardiff said he had no great regard for single-level plant bargaining. It rarely benefited the lower-paid.

Proposals for a 'National Understanding for Economic and Social Development' were accepted by the fwui in a national ballot but rejected by a 'substantial majority' at a special ictu Congress on 23 May 1979. The fwui was disappointed. It had long believed it had to progress beyond wages to achieve advances in workers' real and social wage. The National Understanding concept was 'sound'. The wui felt that paye tax protests, particularly as pushed by Dublin Trades Council, meant the proposals were neither fully understood nor properly debated. The itgwu and craft unions campaigned against, with the former calling for renegotiation.

On 12 June the Government unilaterally declared a 7% pay settlement for six months after the expiry of the 1978 Agreement before further talks on 22 June with the fue produced modified pay terms. Congress said it would recommend these if the Government would reinstate the National Understanding, which was agreed on 18 June. The GEC felt that no new ballot was required and voted in favour at a special ICTU Congress on 25 July, when the National Understanding was accepted by 297 to 135. The GEC kept a close and critical eye on progress on all National Understanding fronts, receiving monthly reports and examining every detail.

John McAdam (No. 12) declared 'complete opposition to the unilateral pay guidelines which Fianna Fáil is seeking to impose' and called for Congress to 'withdraw from centralised bargaining.' Fianna Fáil's public sector pay diktat would have negative repercussions in the private sector. Its tactics were, in any case, a 'scapegoat for its own economic failures.' Tom Geraghty thought it 'a sad day' that such a commentary was needed. The Government was following a slippery slope to disaster, using police in the post office workers' strike and 'the unnecessary and political gimmick' of soldiers in the Dublin Corporation craftsmen's strike. Cardiff assured Delegates that the FWUI had 'always resisted and opposed any unilateral imposition or interference in the area of pay by the Government.' The motions were carried, reflecting the union's anger and resentment.[17]

DISPUTES

In 1970 there were problems achieving the terms of a 1968 firefighters' settlement in Dún Laoghaire, mainly through the 'attitude of the Chief Officer,' before satisfaction was gained. Serious matters arose in Gentex, Athlone, where Shannon Yarns closed. Through the Minister for Industry and Commerce the WUI unsuccessfully strove to retain a spinning plant. It could only increase redundancy payments for three hundred workers losing their jobs. The Athlone Branch was halved. In 1971 Cardiff moved an amendment to the Rules to provide for the election of Strike Committees in any dispute for organising and preparing pickets, co-ordinating activity, paying out Strike Pay and directing and monitoring the dispute with the Branch Secretary. All activity was necessarily subject to the GEC's control. This refined an existing Rule but was a further legacy of the Maintenance Dispute. It arose from reports of the Apathy Group that sought greater clarity

Although there were few strikes in 1974, two disputes cost the union more than £66,000. A strike in Irish Distillers, begun in December 1974, was protracted and required intervention by the Employer-Labour Conference. Dispute Pay in 1975 was the highest since 1969 and the second-highest in the WUI's history. A thirteen-month 'protest strike' in Newbridge Industries, Droichead Nua, saw union and members individually dragged through the Courts on 'various injunctions and counter-injunctions.' Eventually, in May 1977, thirty workers won back their jobs. Remarkably, the strike was fought without Strike Pay. The WUI established that dismissed members were not technically on strike, enabling them to receive social welfare payments. Pickets were allowed to publicise the facts of the case but not to interfere with trade or business.

In 1978 £230,307 was spent on Dispute Pay, mostly on the Aer Lingus strike, the biggest amount ever spent.

Table 115: WUI Dispute Pay, 1970–79

	Income (£)	Dispute Pay (£)	As proportion of income (%)
1970	127,465	9,245	7.2
1971	151,656	13,301	8.7
1972	160,573	6,410	3.9
1973	171,493	343	0.2
1974	284,345	66,165	23.2
1975	288,002	8,588	2.9
1976	378,137	46,428	12.2
1977	439,708	32,768	7.4
1978	692,577	230,307	33.2
1979	633,389	3,139	0.4

Source: WUI, reports of General Executive Council, 1970–79.

Dispute Pay up to 1977 totalled £187,248 but was still £43,059 below that dispensed in 1978. The Aer Lingus action was highly significant and, the union having emerged successfully from it, an immense boost to the WUI's self-confidence. The postal dispute in early 1979 created problems. Membership in Irish Hospitals Trust was let go, as no business could be done, with further sackings in the optical trade. Tom Geraghty suggested that discreet enquiries be made to ascertain whether the Post Office Workers' Union required financial assistance.[18]

THE LABOUR COURT

Generally a stout supporter of the Labour Court, the WUI voiced growing concerns in 1977. Recommendations suggested that the Court was either being denied or surrendering its independence. An absence of summaries of both sides' arguments in recommendations—allegedly because of a shortage of clerical resources—drew adverse comment.

A 'major incident' that 'shakes the confidence' of unions was the appointment of John Horgan, a personal adviser to the Minister, Michael O'Leary, as Deputy Chairman. Larkin wrote to Congress to complain on 28 January, although he emphasised that the union had 'nothing personal against this gentleman.' They found it 'hard to understand' the appointment 'against the background of qualification' and 'inadequate practical experience in Industrial Relations.' Congress sent a protest to the Minister on 11 February. O'Leary replied that he had intended to more fully consult Congress and the FUE and accepted that 'perhaps the fault lay with me.' He promised that when the Fourth Division was created, consultation would occur. The WUI felt the Minister's reply was 'unsatisfactory and barely comprehensible' and called for the Labour Court to be physically removed from Department of Labour premises.[19]

In 1978 Eddie Glackin (No. 2) noted the abuse of the Labour Court by employers that was tolerated. It was calculated 'to delay legitimate claims being conceded.' There were 'inordinate delays', the 'unaccountability' of ICTU nominees, 'rubber-stamping' of Government wage edicts and an 'imbalance of decisions.' He wanted a critical examination of Labour Court practice.

DUBLIN FIRE BRIGADE

In 1972 Tom Geraghty (No. 2) condemned fire legislation as 'criminal'. The Fire Brigade Act (1940) was outdated, was inadequate and provided no fire prevention measures. A fire in Noyek's timber yard and offices in Parnell Street resulting in seven deaths brought matters to public attention. Geraghty had attended the disaster as a firefighter. Deaths would have been preventable had effective legislation existed and been enforced. The WUI issued a press statement in March, bemoaning the lack of proper equipment and training in Dublin Fire Brigade. Through the Fire Brigades Union the WUI sent a Delegation to inspect British fire services and invited the Corporation (City Council) to take part. It declined. Geraghty felt strongly about the problem; 'what we saw over there and the information we brought back has convinced me that the people sitting in the Dáil are criminals.' They could push through legislation on a Prisons Bill in one or two days; in contrast, on fire safety there was 'no legislation since 1940 to bring in proper protection for our fellow-workers.' The WUI demanded a national board to investigate the fire service and to draft effective, modern legislation. A queue of speakers supported him.

In 1973 W. McQuaid (No. 2) condemned the union for 'lack of service,' the result of 'frustration, mainly by members of the Fire Brigade,' over two unresolved claims that rumbled on for four and seven years, respectively. It was aimed at members whose non-attendance weakened the union and Officials who did not carry out their duties. He complained that the report of the WUI-ITGWU firefighters' trip to Britain had not been published by the union, despite the GEC's instruction to do so. The General Secretary had, however, written to the Minister. The Fire Service Section resigned in protest in January, resulting in the GEC admonishing the General Secretary. It was not just about firefighters. Seven deaths in Parnell Street were a direct result of inadequate legislation. Ambrose O'Rourke and Pádraig Canny (Staff) opposed the 'outrageous attack' on the staff and Shop Stewards. Matters remained heated, and the motion was lost.

In 1975 Geraghty reported on his experiences on the Fire Brigade Review Board. Its report was still not published, although presented in January. The Chief Fire Officers' Association had spread scare stories about the collapse of the fire service, but this was nonsense.[20] The forty-hour week was finally implemented for firefighters in September 1976, having been part of a Labour Court recommendation in 1974. Throughout the 1970s the WUI strengthened links with the Fire Brigades Union and was prominent on all fire-related issues.

IRISH HOSPITALS TRUST, MEAT FEDERATION AND CLONDALKIN PAPER MILLS

The recognition dispute in Irish Hospitals Trust rumbled on for thirty years until finally 'settled satisfactorily' in 1975. The unswerving loyalty of members was praised. Settlement came only after the serving of strike notice and intervention by the ICTU Industrial Officer, Tom McGrath. There was a further strike in 1977, when members attempted to secure increases due under the 1975 and Interim National Wage Agreements. Recognition proved to be 'shadow', not 'substance'. Given that the company's activities were subject to the Public Hospitals Acts and state supervision, this was a disgrace. The management showed little interest in settling matters and ignored Labour Court and other procedures. The 1977 Conference adopted an Emergency Motion pledging full support for an official strike in pursuit of Recommendation 42411 and asking all unions to rally to the cause, while strongly protesting to the Government. Jim Quinn (No. 2) described the mean battle 'with the richest family in this country', whose 'personal wealth increases by £8,000 per day'. The Hospitals Trust had become a litmus test for the WUI's capacity to prevail.

In 1976 Ken Quinn (No. 14) called for a national investigation into the 'state of the Meat Industry' to safeguard and expand employment. Eoghan Harris (No. 15) saw the solution as nationalisation, something the Meat Federation had not called for. Harris cited Comhlucht Siúicre Éireann: 'They now have to grow their own beet to guarantee a certain minimum level of supply.' In the long run 'if that avaricious class is to be dealt with, the means of production, as Michael Davitt said, the land, has got to be taken from them and put into the hands of state companies so that a guaranteed supply of cheap food and downstream processing of meat, dairy products etc., can be arranged.' Quinn lifted the lid of a scandal that resulted in Tribunals of investigation into many rotten practices.

In 1977 a nine-week strike in Clondalkin Paper Mills was triggered by the management's 'dishonouring a manning Agreement' and insisting on unilateral action. Two members were sacked, and the management ignored grievance procedures. The WUI won its demands, and an independent Committee was set up to examine the causes of the dispute and the industrial relations structures in the company.[21]

AER LINGUS

In late 1971 Aer Lingus employees moved to form an Association, indicating tensions with the WUI. The Civil Aviation Branch was an important Branch, and every effort was made to assuage doubts and to provide first-class service. The problems were primarily with clerical workers, but the Irish Airline Pilots' Association, an affiliate, lodged money with the High Court and secured its own Negotiating Licence. The GEC was vexed: it should have been told first. New legislation would debar those with fewer than five hundred members and £1,000, so the IALPA acted quickly. The WUI paid the £1,000.

The 'most serious dispute in the history of the Branch' began in April 1976 when 1,200 Superintendent, clerical, stenographic and allied grades lodged claims for 'unilaterally extracted productivity, cost of living and movements in the public sector.' The management proved obdurate, resisting interventions by Cardiff and the Labour Court. The strike began on 14 March 1978. It was not at first intended to place pickets, but it became clear that the Irish Airlines Executive Staff Association—also affiliated—intended to carry out the work of those on strike. The position was reviewed. An ambiguous interim Labour Court recommendation was rejected, as was a final one. Professor Charles McCarthy was invited to mediate, and after a 'considerable number of marathon sessions' over three weeks, terms emerged that 'proved highly satisfactory' to the union. A lump sum of £450 was paid on account of past productivity; 5% added to the scales, with a commitment to discuss future productivity (all productivity, past and future, to be measured by the Irish Productivity Centre); improved conditions of employment were agreed; and £125 was 'paid to members who supported the strike.' After seven weeks it was a significant victory, especially given that 'the Government itself was directly involved' and the efforts of the management 'to break the membership.' After the strike the WUI disaffiliated the Irish Airlines Executive Staff Association. Paul Boushell thought the thirty-year-old Branch had 'come of age' and was more cohesive, as cabin crew and ground staff all willingly supported their clerical colleagues. The Labour Court had 'quite clearly been interfered with.' W. Jones denied the notion that they had fought the battle on their own: the way the whole union rallied was 'an eye-opener'. Cardiff congratulated members who withstood the company's 'psychological warfare', which included 'bombarding and blocking the switchboard of the union.' The *Irish Press* printed a headline 'Hostesses to go back to work', a story with absolutely no foundation but a clear intention. In February 1979 the Irish Airlines Executive Staff Association approached the WUI about re-affiliation.[22]

NURSES AND BRÚ CHAOIMHÍN

In 1979 Marie Cassidy (No. 18) wanted nurses' pay and conditions to be equivalent to other 'professional categories', such as 'radiographers, social workers, occupational therapists and physiotherapists.' She thought this 'non-contentious' and cited WHO and ILO recommendations on nurses' pay and conditions to show how out of alignment standards were. Marie Dennis (Western Area) talked of increasing nurse-patient ratios, particularly on night duty. Attley, Deputy General Secretary, appealed for a referral back to allow a full investigation by the GEC and the development of an effective strategy in tandem with other unions. The WUI's significant membership in the general health service were silent, not only on support for the nurses' position but also on concern for their own future and that of the health service. A Nurses' Committee was created in No. 18 Branch, organising a national seminar and publishing a *Nursing Bulletin*.

In 1979 the GEC reported 'regret' over the 'activities of a small minority' in Brú Chaoimhín, a nursing home in Cork Street, Dublin, arising from an unofficial dispute. So seriously was it viewed that Cardiff issued a statement to 'place the factual position on record.' The member at the heart of matters had been dismissed three years previously, having already had five union interventions on his behalf. After 'strenuous' efforts he was reinstated. Four further written warnings regarding time-keeping and general behaviour followed, culminating in seven days' dismissal notice. With no support for action from members forthcoming at a general meeting, matters proceeded to a Rights Commissioner. Two days after the dismissal, however, fourteen members placed unofficial pickets, which were ignored by the majority.

After a number of weeks the picketers approached the WUI to seek their reinstatement, for the original dismissal to go to a Rights Commissioner, and for industrial relations in Brú Chaoimhín to be subject to union investigation. Hardship payments for Christmas were sought. Despite strong resistance from the Eastern Health Board, the WUI secured agreement on all points, only for the group to reject the terms, refuse to return to work and organise a 'sit-in' in the Personnel Department. A further 'sit-in' at WUI Head Office followed, with statements to the press intended to embarrass the union. Pickets were placed on the home of the Minister for Health. The GEC, on receiving a request from the National Hospitals Branch, suspended the members concerned.

On 24 January 1979 the group occupied Head Office, frightening members of the staff. There was no alternative but to call in the Gardaí. Arrests were eventually made, at the request of the workers themselves, although the WUI was adamant that it had no desire to press charges. A petition was published in the national press condemning the union for using the Forcible Entry and Occupation Act against members, an act that unions lambasted whenever it had been used by employers in industrial disputes. Larry Doyle, General Secretary of the Automobile, General Engineering and Mechanical Operatives' Union, was among the signatories. After appeals to the union, the reinstatement of the group was negotiated, and work resumed on 12 February. The GEC did not prefer charges against members of the group.

Jack Kelly talked of a 'crisis', complaining about interference from other unions, with Attley confirming that for some the issue was not the reinstatement of an individual but the 'introduction of another union.' Cardiff bluntly named AGEMOU as having given cards and financial assistance to those concerned, facts that he deplored in the extreme.[23]

LABOUR LAW AND THE COMMISSION ON INDUSTRIAL RELATIONS

The WUI opposed the ICTU All-Out Picket system, 'mainly on the grounds that in circumstances where unofficial pickets were continuing and increasingly were being recognised by trade unionists' the policy 'appeared to be unrealistic.' Tom Geraghty thought the 1971 Conference was asleep, as it offered no comment. The ICTU had no policy on redundancy or on the EEC, but it had one on picketing! 'To me they accept the position within a capitalist system' and 'agree to work within these narrow boundaries.' Congress, he said, felt that 'part and parcel, if not their main policy is to act as policeman for the Department of Labour.' The All-Out Picket policy was 'an attempt to kill, for once and for all, the great tradition on which this movement was built, the tradition of Larkinism—the tradition of "an injury to one is the concern of all."' It originated 'in the mind of a Civil Servant.' Vincent O'Hara (No. 15) disagreed: Congress, he said, adopted the policy in the interests of workers, not employers or state. The WUI repeated its opposition, but Larkin pointed out that half the first six applications for All-Out Pickets came from No. 15 Branch!

In 1974 M. Ryan (No. 4) wanted it removed as 'divisive, confusing and unworkable.' The same motion was lost at Congress but carried by the WUI. In 1977 it was demanded that 'no member of the WUI should be requested to pass a WUI Official picket.' Cardiff opposed such a 'dangerous motion', as strike tactics had to be free of any predetermination.[24]

Throughout the 1970s the WUI continuously sought to improve workers' statutory entitlements, particularly by increasing redundancy payments and paid annual leave. Larry Bateson (South-East Area) wanted Congress to lead a campaign to declare May Day a national holiday. The WUI argued that all submissions to the Commission on Industrial Relations should be channelled through Congress. This showed its commitment to Congress but might have been seen in the ITGWU and elsewhere as a means of clipping their capacity to offer an independent voice. All Branches were asked for their views in June 1978.

The WUI ultimately made an independent submission. It pointed out that much 'wage-push' pressure arose from factors within Government control: more progressive taxation, greater access to free health care, higher social welfare entitlements, equality of educational access and opportunity, and an adequate, national income-related pension scheme. The Trade Disputes Act (1906) was defended—although considered beyond the terms of the Commission's reference—but changes to counter the effect of the Educational Company judgement and restrictions on the abuse of injunctions were urged. Management incompetence, the low priority attached to personnel management, poor communications, lack of training, alienation and failure to 'utilise the resources of good will, intelligence and knowledge' of workers were among the WUI's criticisms of employers. It readily acknowledged problems on the union side, however, particularly the inadequate training of Officials and Shop Stewards, urging greater state support for training and work-place facilities. It restated its belief in rationalisation, although it offered no proposals for how this could be achieved, no doubt seeing it as a matter for the movement itself. It felt that the Labour Court should be physically removed from the Department of Labour, that Industrial Relations Officers should be recruited from each side of industry and be better trained, and that greater resources should be provided to the Labour Court. Increasing numbers of 'no-strike clauses' in National Wage Agreements created a situation where employers folded their arms and let all matters proceed to the Labour Court, where their expectation of a conservative outcome was well rewarded. The WUI concluded with a swingeing criticism of the role of the media in industrial relations.[25]

EMPLOYMENT AND EUROPE

In 1970 the wui demanded a considered response to the introduction of free trade, fearing widespread unemployment in weak industries. Ireland's application for membership of the eec raised serious union concerns. Would national sovereignty be reduced? What would happen to employment in agriculture, industry and services? Could a different path from that of Britain be contemplated if necessary? This anxiety arose because of Ireland's isolated geographical position, continued mass emigration and high unemployment, low growth rate (the lowest in Europe) and poor standards of housing, education and social welfare.

In 1971 the wui sought legislative control of monopolies to combat the inevitable loss of jobs resulting from mergers and takeovers and as a contribution to price control. M. Harris (No. 7) wanted the Conference to declare that 'this Union is against the country becoming a member of the eec.' Free trade, in his eyes, would give the 'freedom of the Labour Exchange.' Tom Garry (No. 9) argued that a Special Delegate Conference should determine such a matter. After lengthy and emotive discussion, this was agreed for Dún Laoghaire on Saturday 15 January 1972.

M. Harris (No. 7) moved his anti-eec motion. What followed was a high-level debate, peppered with data, constructive and cogent argument, and much emotion—not always totally controlled. Michael Collins (No. 1) supported, as many did, mainly for fear of mass unemployment from free trade and industrial restructuring. Michael Mullen (No. 2) feared that 'the country's affairs' were being handed over to a 'centralised bureaucratised structure which is not susceptible to public control.' He demanded a nationwide campaign against membership. Some, like P. Corbett (No. 9), thought the debate too early, as everything would ultimately be determined by Britain's position: if they went in, Ireland would, and if they did not, Ireland would not. S. Cluskey (No. 2) opposed membership of the eec on moral grounds. He had travelled to Antwerp, Hamburg, Rotterdam and Amsterdam and witnessed dreadful immorality of both heterosexual and homosexual kinds. Others, such as R. Estridge (No. 1) and T. Ryan (No. 15), wanted to join the eec to avail of new economic, social and cultural opportunities. Jim Quinn (No. 2) wanted Ireland 'to stand on our own feet,' the Swedish experience being regularly cited as an alternative. Michael Horgan (Irish Airline Pilots' Association) recounted his first-hand experience of the advantages of European involvement. Justin Keating td (No. 15), foreshadowing the McKenna Judgement, objected to Government money being used to influence public opinion purely in favour of membership. He favoured 'something short of full membership,' to protect certain vital economic interests.

Cardiff, 'speaking as a member' rather than General Secretary, outlined the eec's post-war rationale, a context previously ignored. The alternatives, he thought, were alignment with either America or the ussr; he 'would not have either of them.' It was 'clear that geographically, ideologically and culturally we are Europeans.' It seemed to him 'inevitable', and 'clear to each and every one of us, that we must take the decision to join.' There was 'almost a conspiracy of silence on the advantageous aspects to the Common Market,' much of it based on the 'ordinary fear and lack of confidence in the Irish nation.' He did 'not subscribe to this lack of confidence.' He concluded an effective speech by reference to the Social Charter and the continuing evolution of Europe.

Tom Geraghty (No. 2) and Tom Redmond (Bray) followed with stinging speeches against, based on fears of the loss of sovereignty and independence. Tom Garry (No. 9) thought the motion 'ill-considered, ill-conceived, shallow and suicidal' and dismissed all those who reduced a complex debate to alternative slogans. Brendan Halligan (General Secretary of the Labour Party) worried that Ireland would become a labour pool for the Continent.

Denis Larkin, again speaking as a member, opposed. Keating had rightly styled Ireland the smallest, poorest and furthest-removed element of the European economy. He would 'cut us off from any attempt for co-operation.' M. Harris summed up his arguments. He would always stand against 'divorce, contraception and pornography,' all apparently inevitable consequences of membership of the EEC.

After a historic debate, the result was declared: 62 for, 74 against, two spoiled votes and one abstention. The WUI had decided its support for membership of the EEC, distinguishing itself from most of the labour movement, an outcome favouring the leadership and a defeat for the left.

At an ICTU Special Delegate Conference on 27–28 January 1972 support for membership was rejected, 158 to 113, with commitment to a 'trade union campaign of opposition,' to be chaired by Fintan Kennedy, General President of the ITGWU. An appeal for funds was sent to affiliates in February. Given the WUI's decision, it could not offer financial support to the Congress campaign nor play an active role, whatever individual members might do.[26]

In 1972 W. Jones (No. 12) moved that lower-paid workers be removed from liability for income tax. Tom Geraghty showed that 1% of the population owned 30% of the wealth and that 1,400 people controlled 7.6% of wealth. This data was a powerful argument for a progressive tax regime. V. Murtagh (No. 13) wanted income tax bands broadened to take account of rising incomes and costs, the beginnings of a clamour for tax reform. Tom Garry (No. 9) cautioned Delegates against Socialist terms and solutions, because 'the political balance' was 'very definitely' in favour of 'free enterprise society', a 'fact of life.' He cited economic realities they faced in Guinness in order to maintain a brewery in 1980.

In 1973 Jim Quinn (Trustee) pointed out that workers were forever being asked to exercise wage restraint, yet there was no control of profits, capital gains, directors' or professional fees. J. Normile (GEC) raised hackles by suggesting that the motion was meaningless, because nothing would be done. 'Don't cod yourselves either, because the Executive of this Union, the whole Union, is an affiliate' of Congress, which 'backs the Labour Party, which is part of a Coalition, two of whose Taoiseach's nominees to the Senate are . . . two of the biggest speculators and two of the biggest wealth holders in this country—that is Lord Iveagh and McGrath . . . They have wormed their way into this nest too!' Despite the rancour, the motion was carried.

Garry introduced balance by citing Donal Nevin's seven objectives announced at Congress: the achievement and maintenance of full employment; a steady rise in living standards; equality of opportunity; a fair distribution of income and wealth; the elimination of poverty; comprehensive and adequate welfare services; and improvements in the quality of life and the environment. Attaining these targets meant more than simple tax cuts and demanded an integrated, sophisticated fiscal policy, including 'stricter measures governing bank charges and mortgage interest rates.' Such demands were those of a membership experiencing rising incomes and expectations.

In 1974 Jim Quinn (No. 2) attempted to re-ignite the EEC debate. He called for Ireland to 're-negotiate our position.' Government claims had not been substantiated. British renegotiation was cited, and the motion quietly passed. Tom Redmond (Bray) wanted the nationalisation of oil, gas and mineral resources and a smelter. This demand became standard policy.

In 1975 the WUI's commitment to fully promoting Irish-manufactured goods and to introducing import quotas and tariffs was no surprise. Garry said that planning should have the twin aims of eliminating poverty and comprehensive social development. Not all agreed. C. Harris (No. 7) dismissed Garry's contribution as 'pie in the sky Socialism. It is all theory. You pass the examination that way.' He reminded Garry that in supporting membership of the EEC he had promised full employment. Jim Quinn failed 'to see where Tom Garry gets his ideas from.' There was a strong need for planning and to consider breaking the link with sterling. Eoghan Harris (No. 15) warned that 'planning' in itself contained no Socialist principle. Removed from any class purpose, it had 'no meaning whatsoever.' Garry's amendment could have been written by the FUE. Larkin wondered how so many members, who were in fundamental agreement, could spend so much time debating apparent differences that essentially did not exist. Garry reluctantly withdrew.

Lively, intelligent debate demonstrated differences of emphasis within the union between centre and left. On this occasion the left had their day. The demand for the revocation of the Government Agreement with Tara Mines and for state control of the 'exploration and exploitation' of natural resources, together with the construction of a smelter, underlined this Socialist agenda.

In 1975 S. Edge (No. 13) wanted 'EEC standards of wages and conditions,' now that he 'was a European citizen.' He saw what farmers had achieved. Irish workers had no Minister travelling to Brussels on their behalf. Michael O'Leary and other Coalition Ministers, instead of lecturing workers, 'should do what they were elected to do, look after the poor people of Ireland [and] control the profits.' J. O'Connor (No. 15) wanted a fifty-mile fishing exclusion zone and full development of the industry.

Sniping at the EEC gave way to a fusillade from Tom Redmond (Bray). He was 'bitterly disappointed' in the failure of the 'promises of prosperity' made during the EEC referendum campaign. The Government should be urged to adopt 'selective industrial protection', oppose further integration, resist the Farm Modernisation

Scheme, reject controls that prevented Irish action to safeguard and foster employment and, should Britain withdraw, should follow suit. Tom Garry (No. 9) said a 'sovereign decision by a sovereign people' had been taken. The motion called for a 'process to subvert the decision of the Irish people.' Larkin appealed for referral back and unity in the hall. Heat within the WUI on the EEC was still palpable, and Redmond, having more than made his point, tactfully accepted Larkin's pouring of oil.

In 1976 unemployment was the concern. The target of 30,000 new jobs per annum seemed impossible. The WUI saw things as 'bleak' but felt that matters could at least be improved to end the 'wanton waste of our National resources of manpower and skills.' Paul Mulhern (No. 1) demanded that the Government 'produce and implement' a national plan to eliminate unemployment in five years. If necessary, Congress should 'arrange a national strike' in support. Garry opposed the call for a strike. It would be more effective to make it the Labour Party's price for Coalition in the 1977 General Election.

Paul McIntyre (No. 4) wanted the full development of Kinsale gas under ESB control. Attacks on public enterprise led John Maguire (No. 12) to demand an ICTU co-ordinating Committee to seek the expansion of the sector and counter an ever-hostile press. Members considered this important, particularly those working in the state sector under the burdens of under-capitalisation, imposed debt and poor management.

Tom Redmond (Bray) took matters to their logical conclusion by demanding 'public ownership of banks and financial institutions' and investment in labour-intensive industries, such as construction. He wanted a National Economic Plan, substantial expansion of the public sector and services, controls over the import and export of capital, and—through legislation if necessary—the forcing of industrial investment by banks.

Eddie Glackin (No. 2) led an informed and lively debate, his final comments epitomising the frustration felt by Delegates. 'The capitalist class is going to be convinced by the force and power of the working-class movement and by nothing else, and we want to get that into our minds.' It would 'require a struggle, and a long, hard struggle, to get across our policy, not just passing resolutions. We want to get out and fight for them.' The motion was carried, but whether Delegates wanted to stand behind Glackin's call was not as clear-cut.

Progressive maritime policy demanded a Marine Minister and a long-term plan for Irish Shipping. BIM boatyards were privatised in 1979, but little interest was shown in attempts by the FWUI and ITGWU to hold the line. 'Worst of all' was the 'failure to interest' the FWUI Conference when an Emergency Motion was ruled out. Meetings with the management, lobbies and Delegations to Brian Lenihan, Minister for Fisheries, 'achieved very little.'

John McAdam (No. 12) called for a National Development Corporation in 1978 and Oliver Donoghue (No. 15) for a 'state economic strategy based on expansion of the public sector' and the creation of new state-owned companies to fully develop natural resources, agriculture and fisheries. 'As long as private enterprise is happy, Fianna Fáil is happy . . . all the better if they can provide their business friends with labour at the expense of the unemployed and the taxpayer.' J. Gannon (No. 13) wanted the WUI to take a 'more critical attitude to working practices' such as over-time that 'limit employment opportunities.'

Cardiff rose to assure pessimistic younger speakers who felt that nothing became of pious resolutions. Something did, albeit through a slow, at times almost invisi-ble process of influencing policy. The IDA, significant social welfare improvements and investigations of welfare and pensions were all attributed to union pressure. Until there was a majority for Socialist policies inside the Dáil, the drip-drip-drip of moving resolutions was vital.

Membership of the EEC was raked over in 1978 when motions calling for with-drawal were defeated. The Marine Officers' Association (No. 16 Branch) wanted maritime development as part of greater state involvement. Attacks on public-service pay and performance were strongly resisted, with calls for a specialist Division of the Labour Court to handle pay and united action to combat Government, employer and media propaganda.[27]

SOCIAL POLICY AND CIVIL LIBERTIES

D. King of the Irish Wheelchair Association addressed the 1971 Conference to estab-lish firm, voluntary financial support from members. Opposition to the Criminal Justice Bill and the Forcible Entry and Occupation Bill was vehemently expressed. As both were potential weapons against workers, Congress was called upon to mount the widest possible demonstrations. In 1972 Liam Maguire (No. 12) moved the establishment of a Trade Union Housing Co-operative, pointing out that the ITGWU had adopted a similar strategy. Larkin, while not disagreeing, said that more than 'mere lip service' was required. Paul Boushell (No. 12), 'recognising that the moral code of the majority forbids certain codes of social behaviour,' argued that 'contraception, acceptable in conscience and religious conviction to a minority,' should be available as a 'civil right.' There was much debate of civil rights in the Northern Ireland context. Potential reunification demanded extension of such rights in the Republic. There were increasing concerns for the extension and reform of social welfare.

The 1974 Conference called for the abolition of ground rents and support for any who resisted them. Oliver Donoghue (No. 15) wanted the nationalisation of banks, building societies, insurance companies and all other financial institutions as part of a debate on house ownership and provision. While he acknowledged advances made in social welfare payments, they applied to existing, inadequate levels. Proposed cut-backs were stiffly opposed. Frank Cluskey's position as Minister of State for Social Welfare enabled the WUI to claim that 'nowhere in the whole area of Government activity' were developments 'more in line with the thinking and policy of our Union.' The discussion paper on a national income-related pension scheme was welcomed. The Social Welfare (Supplementary Allowance) Act (1975) was heralded as a measure that effectually repealed the Public Assistance Act (1939) and 'removed from our Social Welfare Legislation the last traces of the Poor Law,' an attitude to poverty that had always been 'utterly rejected' by unions. Much of the pressure for reform came from members 'employed in the administration of the existing Home Assistance Service.' The National Committee on Pilot Schemes to Combat Poverty, established in May 1974, was welcomed and much expected from it.

Jack Kelly (No. 18) opposed health cuts in 1976 and demanded full consultation with health workers' unions. He described how deeply the cuts affected services and the quality of care. Concerns about health care were not sufficiently understood by Delegates to be of prime urgency. In 1977 Jo Walsh (No. 12) moved a lengthy motion on civil liberties, which described 'obvious injustices in our society,' namely the 'continued existence of the death penalty,' the 'outdated system' of admission and release from mental institutions, the neglect of child welfare in legal matters, discrimination against the 'illiterate, the poor and the undefended' within the administration of justice, increasing complaints of ill treatment in police custody, the need for an independent investigation of prisoners' complaints, restrictions on artistic expression through censorship and customs laws, the lack of a proper legal aid scheme, limitations on media rights of comment and disclosure, and 'continuing civil, legal and administrative discrimination against women in every area of life.' Support was expressed for the Irish Council for Civil Liberties and demands made that Congress should insist that the European Convention on Human Rights be fully applied. Obvious parallels with demands for a Bill of Rights for Northern Ireland were drawn.

In 1978 Charles Callan (No. 15) deplored the 'continuing erosion of civil rights' and welcomed the efforts of the Irish Council for Civil Liberties 'to counter this tendency,' although an amendment that proposed affiliating the union was defeated.

In 1979 Michael Collins led a debate on the £5,000 ceiling for eligibility for health services and demanded a 'free, comprehensive' system. In 1979, coincidental with the Pope's visit to Ireland, the WUI gave £1,000 to a number of charities to mark UN Year of the Child.[28]

TAX

In 1976 W. Jones (No. 12) sought legal advice about contesting the 'constitutional validity' of income tax legislation. His concern was the contradiction between compulsory disclosure for some, notional incomes for others, and no disclosure obligations on others. Farmers were particularly criticised, but there was general discontent about the disproportionately rising tax burden on workers and specific anomalies and discrepancies that discriminated against working married couples.

In a pre-Budget submission on 17 January 1977 the WUI clearly set out its taxation policy, demanding annual adjustments of personal income allowances, a more equitable distribution of tax liability, including increases in personal allowances and tax thresholds and reduction of rates, tax on farm profits, a surcharge on investment income, and the integration of taxation with social welfare payments. J. O'Connor (No. 15) condemned the 'arrogance of the IFA-CIF-CC [Irish Farmers' Association, Construction Industry Federation, Chambers of Commerce] triumvirate' and rejected their attacks on workers before calling for the 'taxation of all farmers, professional and self-employed' at rates no less than PAYE rates. Eoghan Harris (No. 15) recited Barry Desmond's Dáil questions regarding net transfers of European, central Government and local authority funds to the farming community in the previous year. The answer was £241.6 million, while PAYE workers contributed £365 million. Comparative tax rates were 15% on urban workers and 2% on farmers, figures that enraged the audience. The ITGWU had suggested that small farmers might join the union, but WUI Delegates had no doubt at all as to the class perspectives of farmers, big or small.

In 1978 Mick Dowling (No. 4) called for a 'revolutionary revamping of the whole taxation system' to provide for transparent tax equity and demanded that Congress press for a wealth tax. Many paying the least tax led the increasing cries for cutbacks in public expenditure.

More than 200,000 workers marched in the Dublin Trades Council tax protest on 20 March 1979. The GEC expressed private reservations about the trades council's role, clearly wanting stronger ICTU leadership. Jim Quinn argued that 'the whole matter of a protest had started in Parson's of Howth,' gathering its own momentum. The WUI's support was qualified by not providing Strike Pay, maintaining essential services, and not making compensation payments for time off. Congress subsequently reissued its Declaration on Taxation and established the National Campaign on Taxation Reform. James Larkin, an Assistant Branch Secretary, was seconded as assistant campaign director. Dublin Trades Council's decision to hold a further protest on Tuesday 1 May was rejected by the GEC, and Congress had its reservations. Thousands of FWUI members nevertheless participated. The FWUI felt the decision of Congress to oppose a strike in support of tax reform was correct, in view of the impending negotiations with the Government, but concluded that no trade unionist 'would argue that there is no case for taxation reform of the PAYE system.' The GEC cautioned: 'However, care must be taken to ensure that pressure is not applied to the extent that existing services are curtailed or that indirect taxation replaces direct taxation.' Within the GEC Tom Geraghty led criticism of Congress's 'conservatism'. Members were 'anxious to show their strength,' to put pressure on the Government, and efforts were 'being made to hive it off.' Cardiff did not want to see the authority of Congress 'brushed to one side.'

The GEC reluctantly agreed to support the Trades Council's demands for a May Day stoppage. It felt that a proper debate about proposals for a National Understanding was being clouded by Trades Council agitation. The General Officers were allowed a 'few minutes' private conversation on the matter' before proposing that, as 'Congress had recommended against the one-day stoppage,' but 'recognising that members might, of their own volition, chose to support the DCTU demonstration at 3 p.m. on 1 May,' the GEC felt it 'imperative to point out that essential services be maintained.'

Motions calling for tax reform came thick and fast in 1979. P. Doyle (No. 9) suggested that income tax be abolished and replaced by a 'pay as you spend' tax. Support for the National Income Tax Reform Organisation was called for, because the 'momentum' of the trade union campaign had 'flagged.' Mary Kavanagh (No. 18) wanted all old-age pension and social welfare payments to be completely free of tax.[29] The GEC asked members to give the fullest support to the mass demonstrations of 15–16 December 1979 organised through the ICTU Tax Campaign Committee.

SAFETY, HEALTH, AND WORKERS' PARTICIPATION

Work-place safety and health did not feature strongly in WUI agendas of the 1970s. In 1977 Austin Byrne (No. 1) moved an interesting motion calling for research into the effects on workers of having to continuously wear protective clothing. Members attended ICTU training courses, but health and safety were not significant items of the agenda.[30]

In 1975 C. Creevy (No. 6) called for industrial democracy in all state and state-sponsored companies. Calls for workers' participation were part of the WUI suite. Paul Boushell (No. 12) wanted time to be spent defining the union's position; then they could demand what they wanted from the Minister. T. Kenna (No. 9) wanted a restructuring of the boards of state-sponsored bodies, with a third to be elected by employees, a third appointed by the Government and a third nominated by Congress. This was in line with union policy, which sought 'full economic freedom for the Irish worker,' and Labour Party policy from 1969 on industrial democracy. In 1977 there were calls for a Special Conference on industrial democracy, the Scandinavian model of state planning and enterprise seemingly appealing.[31]

EDUCATION AND TRAINING

In 1969–70 the Central Education Committee ran basic and advanced Shop Stewards', public speaking and procedural courses, completed by fifty-nine members. 'Suitably inscribed Certificates' were presented at the 1970 Conference to those completing courses, granting the participants recognition, encouraging others and demonstrating the value placed on members' education. Two seminars were conducted on the report of the Apathy Working Party. Larkin remained a member of the Board of the College of Industrial Relations, encouraging members to participate in its courses. Where 'such a dearth of facilities' for union education existed, 'we cannot afford to ignore the help offered by educational bodies' outside the movement. They did 'not forget' that it was their responsibility 'to train and inform our own members and Officials.' A serious problem was gaining members' release from their employments. Union education courses were 'not brainwashing of members by Officials,' nor 'giving people an opportunity to bedazzle their open-mouthed colleagues at work with multi-syllable words or high-sounding jargon': they were intended to improve members' and Officials' capacity to serve the union.

In addition to WUI schemes, members attended ICTU Shop Stewards' courses, special Aer Lingus courses and EEC briefings. The WUI ran a two-day seminar, 'The

EEC: Is There an Alternative?' and produced three booklets, *Work Study, Procedure,* and *Shop Stewards' Guide.* Everything was overseen by the Central Education Committee. In 1971 affiliation to Ruskin College, Oxford, was proposed; it did not happen.

B. Canavan was appointed Education Officer in 1972. WUI numbers passing through the three-year industrial relations course in the College of Industrial Relations increased. In 1974 the GEC set up a Committee to inquire fully into the union's education and training needs, resulting in a joint submission to the Minister for Labour with the FRW. Lack of funds prevented progress, but four new projects were identified: new and proposed legislation, motivation and leadership, workers' participation, and communications. Three seminars were held: 'New and Proposed Legislation', 'Worker participation' and 'Communications', all addressed by invited experts. It was agreed to second both a work study adviser and a training adviser from Congress to work jointly with the WUI and FRW.

In 1976 John Graham, a long-standing activist in Guinness, was appointed full-time Training Officer. WUI classes began to be organised on a day-release rather than evening basis, and numbers rose dramatically. New subjects included leadership training for Officials, parliamentary procedure, disputes and picketing procedure, job evaluation, work study and equality.

In 1977 the WUI called for 'interdenominational, co-educational comprehensive schools' to be opened, part of long-term concern among members for greater educational opportunity and access. Eddie Glackin (No. 2) wanted week-long courses for full-time staff members dealing with the EEC, natural resources, the economy and trade union law.[32]

PUBLICATIONS

In 1972 it was felt that a newspaper would eliminate confusion and misinformation among members. The least they should have was a Press Relations Officer. Jim Quinn blamed apathy and thought a paper essential if they were 'to stay alive. Everything is against us.' M. Byrne (Carlow) recalled the fate of *Bulletin*: 'We couldn't give it away.' Larkin dampened enthusiasm by asking for rejection, 'not because we are opposed' but because what was called for was in effect a daily newspaper, which was beyond their means. It was rejected.

Willie Doyle (Guinness) immediately moved the reintroduction of *Bulletin*. It had died a 'natural death', but it was time to try again. Larkin asked that it be referred back, as '85% of the content' was 'written by the [previous] General Secretary. Nobody was interested.' An Information and Records Service was inaugurated in June 1975. Work was co-ordinated between Paddy Cardiff and Paddy Murphy, General Secretary of the FRW, and Michael Fitzgerald, appointed Information Officer in 1975, who developed the 'Red Book'—a handbook complied from a survey of records of working conditions in all industries and services, a very useful, annually updated tool for negotiators. As merger with the Federation of Rural Workers loomed, the WUI wondered whether it could maintain the FRW's journal, *Starry Plough*.[33]

YOUTH

In 1974 Mick Dowling (No. 4) thought that 'young people are the lost, neglected section' and wanted the appointment of Junior Shop Stewards and a Youth Officer, an annual ICTU Youth Conference, 'increased social, cultural and recreational facilities' for young people and the expansion of education courses. Jim Quinn (No. 2) opposed 'sectionalism'. Cardiff also opposed: it was proving difficult enough to maintain existing structures without creating new ones.

Youth again featured strongly in 1977, with demands for greater employment opportunities, improved access to training and education, better social facilities and guidance, and an acknowledgement that young workers were tomorrow's movement.[34]

LARKIN MONUMENT

Outline planning permission was secured in Golden Jubilee Year, 1974, to erect a monument to James Larkin 'directly opposite what was once the Imperial Hotel' (Clery's Department store) in O'Connell Street, Dublin. The noted sculptor Oisín Kelly submitted designs, and many organisations notified their desire to be involved. A grant was received from Dublin Corporation on 29 November 1977, but delays were caused by problems in securing a suitable single granite block. The first attempts resulted in the block splitting under the material's sheer weight. The Golden Jubilee Committee arranged a production of Eoghan Harris's *Ballad of Jim Larkin* at the Gaiety Theatre, Dublin, on 22 September. Silver medallions were presented to those whose membership predated 1929 and bronze medallions to 25-year members. In 1976, in conjunction with the Irish Labour History Society, a lecture series commemorated Larkin's Centenary, published as *Saothar* no. 4 (1978). Foster reminded Delegates of 'our unique and historic relationship with Jim Larkin,' which was 'never more evident' than 'in our social thinking.' A commemorative postage stamp was issued in March through the offices of Conor Cruise O'Brien, Minister for Posts and Telegraphs. A fund to finance the Larkin Monument was advertised in the press.

The Jim Larkin Memorial Statue was unveiled by President Patrick Hillery on 15 June 1979, the eve of the first Conference of the Federated Workers' Union of Ireland. Denis Larkin thanked the union for allowing 'Jim Larkin to return to O'Connell Street.' He reiterated his brother's appeal for unity, 'co-operation, tolerance and understanding and above all [the belief] that human life is sacred.'[35]

PREMISES AND STAFF

The union's staff in 1970 consisted of twenty-four Branch officers, fifteen clerical employees and three caretaker-cleaners. Salaries exceeded £50,000 for the first time, total income being £152,786. The Staff Superannuation Scheme was improved and, as a result, future recruitment was confined to those under fifty. Complaints that wages were unsatisfactory were accepted by the GEC, which agreed that they were 'by no means too generous.' The WUI felt it provided a high level of service.

Tom Geraghty (No. 2 Branch) thought there were too many Officials allocated in a haphazard way. His idea of service was 'the type of self-help service from active rank-and-file members . . . That is the type of service I was talking about, and that is the type of service members in the Union want.' It 'killed apathy' and was 'the type of service that this Union was built on.' There was 'too much dependence on full-time Officials, people crying out for full-time Officials because they won't do the work themselves.' It led to apathy, 'where people are allowing full-time Officials to do the functions of the Shop Stewards.' Larkin concurred.

For many years the wUI was 'not viable' financially and survived on overdrafts and voluntary sacrifice. In 1971 a staff pension scheme brought existing super-annuation provisions 'more into line with current practice.'

The defection of Joe McGrane to become Personnel Manager of the *Irish Independent* was regretted; he was regarded as 'having potential.' No fewer than four Officials switched to personnel or the public service, causing discontinuity and low-ering morale. Disgruntled members were told that 'it has always been the policy of this Union to recruit the best possible applicants.' It had 'proved successful over the years if it is to be judged by the high level of performance of the Officials' but car-ried with it the 'dangers that good quality Officials are in demand.' Unions offered 'security of employment which is not matched in other areas' and 'opportunities for the development of character and judgement,' together with great 'job satisfac-tion'. The 'best of good luck' was offered to those who 'decided to leave the fold.'

In 1972 K. Ennis (No. 3) thought members should be given preference over 'out-siders'. Not all agreed. P. Mulhearn (No. 1) thought it 'narrow-minded' for 'one of the most democratic' unions. The 'best Officials' should always be chosen, irrespective of origin. Many members were concerned that outside recruitment meant less com-mitment, but the majority of those leaving were internal appointments. It was felt that rigorous job demands placed pressures on the staff, especially on those with families; but there were still questions about motivation and political commitment.

In 1975 Denis Larkin told the Conference that negotiations were advanced for purchasing 29 Parnell Square and the adjoining 15–16 Granby Row for £70,000. In January 1979 a consultant valued the property at £1.3 million.[36]

'Prolonged and difficult' negotiations took place with the Staff Association in 1975–6, resulting in new salary scales, a 35-hour week for the clerical and adminis-trative staff and general improvements. The staff agreed not to seek parity with the ITGWU. In 1977 R. McGrogan (Bray) moved that any Official who was nominated to the Seanad or as director of a state company should 'pay into the union funds, any fees or salaries' received. H. McKay (GEC) opposed, pointing out that some fees were as low as £800, which, after tax, meant that 'you are not left very much.' The idea—which was policy in the ITGWU—was lost.

OPPOSITION TO APARTHEID

In January 1970 members in RTÉ 'refused to comply with GEC requests for a boycott' of the Springboks' tour. As it was 'not dictation but request,' no action was taken.

A large union Delegation supported the protest march. Michael Mullen (No. 2) moved that there should be no Government sponsorship of any business or sporting organisation that co-operated or dealt with 'countries whose Governments openly encourage discrimination on grounds of colour, religion or politics.' Christianity allowed for no discrimination between mankind, and members should demonstrate with their feet as part of 'a vigorous and promising campaign against Apartheid' that would 'help the more liberal-minded people in South Africa who love their Government to replace their leaders by men and women of courage and humanity.' Such actions would be in 'the great tradition of Ireland.' Racists in South Africa and Rhodesia should be 'as outcasts.' Eoghan Harris (No. 15) linked the motion to Northern sectarianism, saying that the 'resolution cannot be read at a distance.' Its implications stretched 'from the Falls Road to Derry to here.' Cardiff asked that it be referred back, as discrimination on political grounds made implementation a problem. Delegates thought there was little 'impractical' about it and adopted it.

P. Smith (Tullamore), while agreeing that 'there should be no colour bar in sport,' objected to Officials standing outside the Lansdowne Road stadium requesting members not to attend Springbok games. Vincent O'Hara wondered why the same boycott did not apply to teams sent by 'Socialist, atheistic Communists . . . we should remember this, the South Africans crush freedom only in South Africa but the bastards from the Kremlin crush all freedom outside of Russia—Hungary, Poland, Czechoslovakia.' Despite (or perhaps because of) O'Hara's contribution, the motion was defeated.

The WUI enthusiastically supported UN International Anti-Apartheid Year and the Declaration on Apartheid and South Africa issued in March 1978 in order to 'isolate and weaken the present racist and repressive regime' and 'assist our oppressed African fellow-workers in their struggle for liberation.' The WUI affiliated to the Irish Anti-Apartheid Movement.[37]

Politics

In 1970 Michael Collins (No. 1) wanted WUI Labour Party candidates to be subject to scrutiny. Some sponsored candidates defected to Fine Gael. How could anyone accepting the Labour Party's social policy turn around and 'run along with Mr Cosgrave's hobby horse on a social justice policy?' Of greater concern was the changing attitude to Coalition. The WUI gave £5,459 to candidates in 1969 in the hope of a Labour Government. M. Mulhall (No. 9 Branch) thought that one potential benefit from a merger with the ITGWU was the possibility of the New Union creating its own political party.

The WUI participated in the Labour Party Special Conference in December 1970 that departed 'almost completely from the attitude of independence' that had developed the Party so well in Dublin. The loss of rural seats in 1969—the election in which 'the seventies will be Socialist'—panicked country members. The WUI opposed Coalition. That said, the union regretted 'groups whose loyalty and allegiance lies elsewhere' as negative factors at a time when Fianna Fáil's disarray was seen to offer real opportunity for the left. After the 1972 General Election Justin Keating (No. 15 Branch) became Minister for Industry and Commerce and Frank Cluskey Parliamentary Secretary to the Minister for Social Welfare. Joe Bermingham (South-East) was elected TD for Kildare.

Tom Geraghty suggested that adopted motions be sent to sponsored public representatives, their actions reported to the GEC, and future sponsorship considered in the light of their actions. Delegates were divided, with those involved in the Labour Party conspicuous in demands for referral back. With a guarantee of full GEC discussion on political affiliation, Geraghty retreated with his prize.

In 1976 criticism of affiliation to the Labour Party emerged. Paul Boushell (No. 12) asked that the Party's performance, albeit as minor Coalition partner, be examined against union policy on employment, natural resources, state enterprise, social welfare, tax, and equal pay. The outcome should be brought before a Special Conference to which all WUI Labour TDs should be invited. The GEC supported the idea.

Eddie Glackin, while opposing disaffiliation, wanted any sponsorship to be withdrawn from candidates who supported repressive legislation, such as the Criminal Law (Jurisdiction) Act (1976) and Offences Against the State Act. Both had been used against workers in disputes. An intense debate followed, largely examining the Labour Party in Coalition, rather than whether the WUI should financially support candidates or under what conditions sponsorship would be given.

On 23 April 1977 an Adjourned Annual Delegate Conference considered two motions dealing with affiliation to the Labour Party. Jim Quinn and Eddie Glackin (No. 2) raised questions under the heading of the Political Fund about Labour Party TDs voting for the Criminal Law Amendment Act. Tom Redmond (GEC) said that matters were processed through Congress seeking repeal of the 'infamous legislation.' Delegates were given comprehensive details of WUI and Labour Party policies; a discussion paper on Economic and Social Development; all legislation enacted since 1972 'relating to WUI policies'; motions adopted at union and ICTU Conferences, 1970–76; and developments in social welfare policy and services. Paul Boushell criticised the Parliamentary Labour Party, warning that 'we give notice that our views must be heeded to a greater extent than is currently being done.'

T. Dunleavy expressed a not uncommon view of Coalition when he said the Labour Party had 'joined up with a shower of gangsters that are completely opposed to the working class.' Cluskey was absolved from the general condemnation.

Larkin pointed out that few WUI members were Labour Party members. Few voted Labour. Michael Collins (GEC) catalogued the Labour Party's achievements, balancing the debate. While welcoming criticism, he expressed wariness at those whose criticism stemmed from the fact that 'you belong to another political party.' Brendan Halligan TD felt the Labour Party had made and would make a 'unique and significant contribution' to economic and social policy. Dermot Boucher (No. 15) suggested that the whole debate, while worthy, was unreal, as it would have little if any influence on the Labour Party. Cluskey disagreed. 'Wishing something' to happen did not make it happen, and there was no substitute for political engagement and activity. The support of ordinary people was required before any policy could be implemented. That support had to be canvassed and won. Joe Bermingham TD (South-East Area) reminded everyone that he came to the Labour Party through the WUI. They were two sides of the same coin. Senator Jack Harte spoke in similar vein, saying that his first loyalty was to the union. Cardiff spoke of his opposition to Coalition. He proudly pointed to the WUI's influence on Congress in widening the central bargaining agenda. A similar impact was evident inside the Labour Party. While not a convert to Coalition, he acknowledged the progress made in important areas and the more open attitude of Ministers towards union delegations. The motion was carried, with bi-annual consultation being favoured.

The second motion dealt with Coalition. Arguments were repeated, but the Labour Party's Conference had recently rejected opposition to Coalition. Not surprisingly, the WUI motion was defeated.[38]

NORTHERN IRELAND

An Emergency Motion in 1970 condemned the 'gun-running recently uncovered in Government circles.' The WUI had 'no desire to see Irish workers fighting each other' and wanted 'solidarity between workers north and south.' Past Fianna Fáil involvement with Charlie Kearns and George Plant, Seán South, Fergal O'Hanlon and Tommy Doyle, 'who was a Secretary of this Union,' was recounted. A caution against civil war was sounded. For much of the previous twenty years Fianna Fáil had control of social welfare, unemployment and hospital benefits and had allowed them to become some of the lowest in Europe. These 'were the barriers against unification, not religion.' Charles Haughey would be better making a stand against land speculation than running guns. The debate became hot, with claim and counter-claim. Eoghan Harris (No. 15) cited Lenin and Connolly; others asked, who was to defend Catholics from Paisleyite mobs? The motion was adopted unanimously.

In 1971 an Emergency Motion called for the Government to press for intervention by the United Nations 'to protect the oppressed population of occupied Ireland.' An emotive debate followed. There was a desire to react as trade unionists and reach out to fellow trade-Unionists. Larkin referred to the ICTU Northern Ireland Committee's good work in keeping violence from work-places. After Bloody Sunday in Derry, 30 January 1972, the GEC placed a notice in the press:

> In expressing shock and horror on behalf of all members of this Union at what can only be termed the brutal murder of thirteen human beings in Derry on Sunday, the GEC desires to tender sincere sympathy to their relatives and the relatives of all killed or injured since August 1969, in Northern Ireland.
>
> The GEC further considers that the day of the funeral of the latest victims should be a day of special mourning in Ireland, North and South, and that in the case of the members of this Trade Union it recommends that they should cease work for a period not exceeding two hours on the morning of the day of the funeral.

The GEC further recommends that its Union representatives should make arrangements for Masses and/or other religious services to be held near to the workers' places of employment to coincide with the cessation of work.

The GEC finally has decided to request the ICTU to make an urgent approach to the British TUC seeking support for immediate action towards providing new political initiatives designed to bring about peace in the country.

The WUI condemned the Prisons Acts and Offences Against the State Act (1972), seeing the latter as a move towards internment without trial. Ray Cass (Staff) alleged double standards by those who condemned bigotry and sectarianism in the North on the one hand yet condoned terrorist actions, or at least intentions, on the other. Those who supported 'our people' were giving credence to groups who 'seek to undermine the democracy that exists down here.' Cluskey saw the IRA, Official or Provisional, as a 'true menace to the working class,' and condemned violence from whatever quarter. He opposed the Offences Against the State Act, as he did not think a serious threat to democracy existed to justify it. The motion was rejected, 64 to 92.

Tom Redmond (Bray), 'knowing that the working class has a vital role to play' in Northern Ireland, congratulated the Northern Ireland Committee of the ICTU on its 'Peace and Construction' programme. He called on the Government 'to condemn in all forums, including the United Nations, the British Government's policy of repression' and urged the British Government to accept the 'demands of the Civil Rights Movement.' He talked of the 'working class' rather than 'our people' or Catholic and Protestant and praised Belfast Trades Council and Congress for developing non-sectarian human rights policies. He quoted the policy of the NIC: 'We recognise that a democratic state requires powers to protect its security and the liberty of its citizens. Legislation appropriate to this purpose which protects the principles of innocence until guilt is proved should take the place of civil authority's Special Powers Act.' Mick Dowling (No. 4) demanded a 'Bill of Human and Democratic Rights as demanded by the Northern Ireland Civil Rights Association', the ending of internment without trial, the withdrawal of British troops to barracks, the abolition of Stormont and a statement of a date for withdrawal by Britain.

In 1974 Redmond urged the implementation of a Bill of Rights—British TUC policy in Northern Ireland. The NIC's 'Better Life for All' campaign was praised as a major contribution to peace. Emily Barr (No. 12) called for support for the Women's Peace Movement; Eddie Glackin (No. 2) rejected 'peace at any price': the only true peace movement was that of the trade union movement. Ross Connolly (Bray) supported the Northern Ireland Committee's six-point programme for peace, jobs and democracy, wanting a greater appreciation of the charter throughout the union. His concluding remarks were poignant and no doubt pricked many consciences. 'We cannot extend the hand of brotherhood to the workers of Chile if we don't extend it to the workers of the North, and we cannot weep for the dead of Soweto if we do not also weep for our murdered comrades in the North.'

In 1977 Foster cited extensively from Young Jim Larkin's celebrated ITUC Presidential Address in 1949, *A Common Loyalty: The Bridge to Unity*. It seemed an appropriate antidote to the high emotions and tendency towards tribalism. Time judged the remarks thoughtful and appropriate, challenging but offering a real prospect for mutually agreed solutions. He urged a mutual exchange of views and, 'where possible, joint endeavours' in economic development, trade, transport and cultural extensions, so that 'our people' could 'learn in a practical manner the possibilities and advantages of co-operation.' He concluded: 'Above all, let us not feel that any effort to find a bridge, however slender, across the gulf dividing the ordinary people, North and South, is a betrayal of principle or a compromise of positions.' Foster mused: 'How different things might have been' if 'only Young Jim had the power and authority in 1949 to translate his words into meaningful national politics,' or if either side of the divide 'had only listened more attentively.' Foster's quiet constraint, cloaked in Larkin's words, was not to be underestimated in bringing a more considered approach not just to the national question but to a range of divisive issues that sowed disunity within the WUI.

In 1979 John Tierney (No. 15) dismissed Fianna Fáil and Fine Gael policies as 'undemocratic'. They involved 'implicit and explicit attempts to force the majority' into 'unity or federation with a confessional denominational Southern state.' He wanted respect for that majority, a Bill of Rights for the minority and an end to 'interference by Southern politicians.' Michael Mullen (No. 2) saw Northern Ireland as 'artificially contrived' and devoid of 'democratic rights'. For Redmond, Tierney's motion was 'poison' and 'must be so overwhelmingly defeated that it never appears again.' Matters were defused when referral back was agreed, 119 to 66, the same for calls for the 'restoration of special-category status' for the H blocks and for prisoners in Armagh Women's Prison. Support for the 'Better Life for All' campaign was carried in a heated and divisive atmosphere. Hearts had ruled minds, but few were left under any impression other than that the majority felt a clear commitment to unity and independence.

Having attended a meeting of the ICTU Resident Committee in Northern Ireland, Paddy Cardiff suggested that they arrange exchange trips between Shop Stewards on both sides of the border to increase mutual understanding. Unlike the ITGWU, the WUI had no members in Northern Ireland. The spirit and intensity of the debates reflected general concerns within the movement for an end to violence and for a peaceful settlement.[39]

Chapter 31 ∿

CONCLUSIONS

MEMBERSHIP

Despite the decline in traditional industries, manufacturing employment grew in the 1970s as transnationals invested heavily, their eyes on European markets. The WUI supported Irish membership of the 'Common Market', while the broad movement, particularly the ITGWU, urged opposition. The promised jobs and economic boom failed to materialise, and criticism of the EEC mounted, exacerbated by significant unemployment and inflation.

Membership of the ITGWU and WUI grew by 23,088 and 10,052, respectively. The expansion of the ITGWU came through closed-shop Agreements in transnational Branch plants (with other unions complaining that they were 'not getting their share') and among professional and white-collar workers. Recruitment to the WUI was pronounced in the public sector. The merger with the Federation of Rural Workers transformed the WUI (now FWUI) into a 'national' body.

Incomes rose dramatically, the ITGWU's by £3,561,686, the WUI's by £674,452. Check-off brought most members into full, continued compliance. Growth had its price, however, financially and organisationally.

Table 116: ITGWU and WUI membership and income, 1970–79

| | ITGWU | | WUI | |
	Members	Income (£)	Members	Income (£)
1970	162,478	618,633	34,536	152,786
1971	155,614	814,741	34,706	208,678
1972	155,879	892,219	34,790	234,678
1973	157,918	1,015,675	35,048	285,532
1974	156,418	1,255,661	35,358	315,448
1975	157,392	1,578,955	34,252	404,039
1976	154,388	1,772,235	34,477	536,014
1977	166,034	3,243,489	35,941	558,914
1978	176,429	3,435,358	35,941	593,819
1979	185,566	4,180,319	44,588	827,238

Source: National Archives, Registrar of Friendly Societies, files 275T and 369T.

The emphasis was on 'service'. In the ITGWU full-time offices opened around the country. Expenditure rose by £3,337,039, and in 1979 staff costs accounted for £2,235,543. The equivalent WUI figures were £283,257 and £344,310. The ITGWU's surpluses totalled £2,064,620, the WUI's £790,094. However, the underlying cost patterns suggested a living beyond means. Members were constantly asked for higher subscriptions, admittedly from rising money wages. In turn they demanded expensive services, such as education and training. The real price, however, was the invisible distancing of the membership. Multiple factors explained this: check-off denied members the conscious act of 'paying their card' and weekly contact with Shop Steward or Collector; pre-emptive Agreements resulted in personnel officers recruiting members to the union, through a signature on a deduction-at-source form, rather than Shop Stewards; National Wage Agreements led many to believe that increases came from the Government rather than through union intervention; and the 'Tribunalising' of industrial relations saw grievances increasingly referred to Rights Commissioners, the Labour Court or Employment Appeals Tribunal and to full-time Official, rather than being settled within the work-place.

Table 117: ITGWU and WUI expenditure and staff salaries, 1970–79

	ITGWU			WUI		
	Expenditure (£)	Staff salaries (£)	As proportion of expenditure (%)	Expenditure (£)	Staff salaries (£)	As proportion of expenditure (%)
1970	504,770	152,536	30.2	127,465	61,053	47.8
1971	639,094	145,201	22.7	151,656	73,024	48.1
1972	716,392	192,191	26.8	160,573	78,535	48.9
1973	759,328	220,315	29.0	171,493	88,883	51.8
1974	1,079,800	311,774	28.8	284,345	109,402	38.4
1975	1,414,905	500,652	30.5	288,002	154,799	53.7
1976	1,636,284	631,907	22.5	378,137	187,867	49.6
1977	2,798,866	1,419,942	50.7	439,708	210,121	47.7
1978	3,473,138	1,776,614	51.1	692,577	257,214	37.1]
1979	3,841,809	2,235,543	58.1	633,389	344,310	54.3

Source: ITGWU, Annual Reports, 1970–79; WUI, reports of General Executive Council, 1970–79.

The 'new working class' was qualitatively different from the class-conscious slum-dwellers who created the union. Many were rural and new to unionisation, and their entry to regular, paid employment often represented upward social mobility. Unprecedented increases in living standards and in expectations, mortgages and consumerist values fed individualism. Transnationals purposely recruited employees from considerable distances rather than their immediate locality, inhibiting organisation, communication, and instinctive solidarity. The 'service model' unconsciously placed members outside their union as consumers of its services, rather than embracing them within it as integral, participating components of its organisation.[1]

Little of this was apparent to leaderships presiding over ever-larger memberships and hugely expanding Budgets. The wui did identify 'apathy' and the itgwu drove members' education, but both pursued 'better service' rather than 'better organisation'. The £2 million rise in the itgwu's credit balance and £250,000 rise in the wui's investment values were blinding lights. Magnificent structures became Hollywood sets: impressive to behold but, seen from behind, flimsy structures of little substance. A saving grace was that employers, still tolerant of unions, gazed at set fronts too.

Women were exceptions to the rule of diminishing involvement. An analysis of discrimination against women led to an investigation of all social inequality. Union women's under-participation was integral to their repression. Increasingly, they led debates on structures and participation, challenged tired decision-making processes and brought fresh voices and ideas to Branches and Conference. The itgwu drafted the Women's Charter for International Women's Year, and equality legislation made possible claims for equal pay and equal treatment, notwithstanding dogged resistance by employers.

Table 118: ITGWU and WUI credit balance (£), 1970–79

	ITGWU	WUI*		ITGWU	WUI*
1970	1,903,406	166,270	1975	2,860,166	273,711
1971	2,017,949	219,947	1976	3,004,360	302,983
1972	2,230,434	243,996	1977	3,441,115	566,415
1973	2,479,838	242,239	1978	3,569,431	460,314
1974	2,701,476	234,516	1979	3,814,077	414,054

*This figure is for value of investments.

Source: ITGWU, Annual Reports, 1970–79; WUI, reports of General Executive Council, 1970–79.

UNDERSTANDING

Missed opportunities for fusion between the itgwu and wui were forgotten. Differences emerged over attitudes to Congress, particularly allegations by the wui about the itgwu's abuse of All-Out Pickets. Expansion undoubtedly led Executive eyes away from merger. Paddy Cardiff certainly believed that a few large unions were healthier than 'One Big Union.' Yet the National Understanding gave evidence of common thinking. The need for rationalisation and a more efficient use of resources posed obvious questions. Equally obvious answers were ignored.

Patterns of Dispute Pay were similar. The itgwu spent £2,101,094 (an average of 10½% of income), the wui £416,694 (9.1%). Disputes arose from frustrations with narrow National Wage Agreements, closures, demarcation as technology advanced, and unresolved grievances. The 1978 Aer Lingus dispute galvanised the WUI, creating huge well-being and purpose, while Ferenka generated alienation and ill-will within, and to, the ITGWU. Liberty Hall acquired a reputation for being 'soft' and non-militant—at least among unfriendly opponents. An analysis of dispute data and comparative union wage rates completely negates this view. The HELP campaign demonstrated imagination and originality. The ITGWU gave no *carte blanche* to employers or Government on National Wage Agreements. Members decided their response through Special Conference and national ballots, leading policy away from the pointlessness of Connolly's 'pure and simple' trade unionism. When the ITGWU voted against National Wage Agreements, some opposed 'in principle' to central Agreements scuttled through lobbies they previously apparently despised.

Cardiff took pride in the National Understanding, not because it was the perfect answer but because it created a template for change, widening bargaining to address all income, economic and social policy. Regular rejection by the ITGWU of National Wage Agreements wrung extra concessions from the Government and employers, deepening the first National Understanding. After 1976 members engaged in sophisticated debate on national bargaining against 'free-for-alls', informing the 'understanding' model.

Table 119: ITGWU and WUI Dispute Pay, 1970–79

	ITGWU		WUI	
	Dispute pay (£)	*As proportion of income (%)*	*Dispute pay (£)*	*As proportion of income (%)*
1970	81,048	13.1	9,245	6.0
1971	154,211	18.9	13,301	6.3
1972	135,529	15.1	6,410	2.7
1973	40,881	4.0	343	0.1
1974	191,420	15.2	66,165	20.9
1975	167,101	10.5	8,588	2.1
1976	76,229	4.3	46,428	8.6
1977	263,306	8.1	32,768	5.8
1978	402,239	11.7	230,307	38.7
1979	145,179	4.2	3,139	0.3

Source: ITGWU, Annual Reports, 1970–79; WUI, reports of General Executive Council, 1970–79.

POLITICS

The Labour Party participated in Government from 1973 to 1977, disappointing the ITGWU and WUI. Handicapped by poor national finances, the Party was criticised for attempting to renege on equal pay, supporting repressive emergency legislation and succumbing too passively to Fine Gael's parsimony and right-wing ideology. Violence in Northern Ireland exacerbated matters, with the Party expected to constrain British intransigence and militarism. Coalition was rejected. The seventies were far from Socialist.

By 1979 the FWUI owned its Parnell Square premises, operated throughout the country and seemed financially secure. The ITGWU appeared impregnable. But appearances were deceptive. At an apparent moment of great strength, unrecognised fault lines lay hidden below the surface.

SIPTU GENERAL OFFICERS, 1990–2009

John Carroll, General President, 1990

William Attley, General President, 1990–1994, General Secretary, 1994–1998

Edmund Browne, General President, 1990–1997

Thomas Murphy, Vice-President, 1990–1994

Thomas Garry, General Secretary, 1990–1994

Christopher Kirwan, General Secretary, 1990–1991

Jimmy Somers, Vice-President, 1994–1997, General President, 1997–1999

Des Geraghty, Vice-President, 1997–1999, General President, 1999–2003

John McDonnell, General Secretary, 1998–2002

Jack O'Connor, Vice-President, 2000–2003, General President, 2003–present

Joe O'Flynn, General Secretary, 2002–present

Brendan Hayes, Vice-President, 2004–present

WUI General Executive Committee, 1949: back, *l–r*, Patrick Murray, John Quinn, George Nathan, Christy Troy, J. Bennett, J. Duffy and Dan Byrne; front, *l–r*, John Lennox, T. A. Browne, Breda Kearns, John Smithers (General President), James Larkin (General Secretary), and Patrick Forde. (WUI Silver Jubilee Souvenir, 1949)

" Don't tell me they'd ever realise their strength and think of putting up a candidate in every constituency in the next election, and voting solidly Labour ! "

Dev hopes workers continue to fail to realise the obvious. (*Liberty Magazine*, April 1959, SIPTU Archive)

ITGWU celebrates creation of Irish Congress of Trade Unions. (*Liberty Magazine*, March 1959, SIPTU Archive)

ITGWU NEC 1958–1959: front, *l-r*, Edward Linehan (Cork 1), Sheila Williams (Dublin 4), Paddy O'Brien (Dublin 1), Edward Browne (Vice-President), John Conroy (General President), Fintan Kennedy (Assistant to the General Secretary), George Gillis (Dublin 2), George Judge (Limerick), Mattie O'Neill (Dublin 9); back, *l-r*, Michael Moynihan (Killarney), Michael O'Halloran (Cork 2), Laurence White (Waterford), Joe Meehan (Belfast), James Kelly (Dublin 3), Nixie Boran (Moneenroe). (SIPTU Archive)

ITGWU NEC 1981: front, *l-r*, Paddy Mooney (Dublin 2), John Gannon (Lucan), Michael Sheehan (Mallow), John Carroll (Vice-President), Fintan Kennedy (General President), Michael Mullen (General Secretary), Fergal Costello (Dublin 7), Andy Burke (Dublin 4); back, *l-r*, Seán Roche (Waterford 2), Martin Kennedy (Nenagh), Thomas Colgan (Laois/Offaly), Seán Murphy (Cork 4), James Lawlor (Dublin 15), Mick Finn (Tralee), Peter Glass (Dublin 12), Jim Doherty (Cork 5), Tony Kelly (Convoy). Absent from photograph Gerry Donaghy (Dundalk). (SIPTU Archive)

Liberty Magazine front cover urges members to vote No to the EEC, May 1972. (SIPTU Archive)

WUI Head Office, Parnell Square, Dublin, 1972. (SIPTU Archive)

SEANAD ELECTION 1965

Three prominent representatives of the Irish Transport & General Workers' Union have been nominated to contest the Seanad Election in Trade Union and Labour interests.

MR. JOHN CONROY,
General President, has been unanimously selected by the National Executive Council of the Union and nominated on the **Labour Panel** by the Irish Congress of Trade Unions.

MR. MICHAEL MOYNIHAN,
member of the National Executive Council for many years and Secretary of Killarney Branch for a long period, has been nominated on the **Agricultural Panel** by the Labour Party.

SENATOR CON. DESMOND,
retired Official of Cork No. 1 Branch has been nominated on the **Administrative Panel** by the Labour Party.

All three have given long and valuable service to the Trade Union and Labour Movement and have outstanding qualifications to continue to serve the best interests of Irish Workers and the Irish nation as members of the Seanad. Accordingly, the National Executive Council of the Union requests that all members and all those interested in the welfare of the Irish workers will extend the fullest possible support and co-operation and assistance in helping to have all three elected.

ITGWU members march against EEC membership: 'Some industries will certainly be badly dislocated. Shareholders will switch their investments, but workers have a more discouraging prospect ahead of them'. (*Liberty Magazine*, May 1972, SIPTU Archive)

Chapter 32 ～

UNITED IN UNION: THE ITGWU IN THE 1980s

MEMBERSHIP, ORGANISATION AND FINANCE

In December 1979 *Liberty* reflected on the 1970s. Decisions affecting workers were taken further and further from the shop floor. PAYE protests and other discontent increased social tensions.

There were still regrettable inter-worker disputes, when the 1980s required unity of purpose and action. In February 1980 the Limerick Branch of AUEW (TASS)—850 local authority engineers and cognate grades—transferred *en bloc* to form the Local Authority Professional Officers' Branch. It did 'not relate to any dissatisfaction' with TASS but to its 'inability to secure effective negotiating rights on their behalf.' The ITGWU was already represented within the Conciliation and Arbitration Scheme.

In July the 210-member Professional Footballers' Association of Ireland joined, linking with Actors' Equity under Dermot Doolan. The Galway City Branch wanted structures to reflect IDA and health board Regions. On 7 December Michael Mullen opened the Dan Shaw Centre in Navan, an ambitious project providing offices, meeting-rooms, hall and social facilities.

The ITGWU suffered a shocking loss on Friday 22 February when Séamus B. Kelly, a National Group Secretary, was killed in a car accident at Fermoy (ironically colliding with a union member for whom he had just negotiated an increase). Kelly had joined in 1948 and was appointed a Branch Official in 1954, gaining rapid promotion to Head Office Movements Department and in 1957 to Branch Secretary of Dublin No. 7 Branch. A National Group Secretary from 1964, he contested the General Secretaryship against Mullen in 1969. He was widely regarded as a 'General Officer in waiting', and his reputation as a negotiator was substantial. His death cast a long shadow.[1]

In the wake of Ferenka and criticisms from *New Liberty*, the NEC wondered, 'Were we losing grip?' Fergal Costello (Dublin No. 7) thought poor structure meant that 'warning signs were seen too late.' The solution to every problem was 'not to put in an Official.' Mick Finn (Tralee) thought 'some Officials had contempt for' the General Officers and NEC as morale deteriorated.

Paddy McKenna, Head of Finance, warned in January 1981 that economies were needed: they would 'not survive if we are going to run the Union at a loss or on a break-even basis.' The absorption of the Irish Racecourse Bookmakers' Assistants' Association was effected on 5 June, although its 274 new members hardly solved the union's problems. The Irish Federation of Musicians and Associated Professions was accepted, its 1,400 members coming on the same instrument of transfer as the Racecourse Bookmakers' Assistants. Their main asset, their club, 'was vested in the Trustees.' Financial membership increased by 5,113 to 172,353.

Three new Cork Branches were created, with full-time offices put into Longford and Kildare. While check-off brought great financial benefits, the NEC was 'concerned at the possible adverse effects' for communication with members. Decasualisation of the docks eliminated the union's traditional base, blunting its one-time industrial spearhead. The Delegate Conference suggested organisation among Irish workers in Britain.

With more than 25,000 white-collar workers, the ITGWU was seldom recognised as the largest such union. Dublin No. 2 Branch was divided, a new Dublin No. 19 Branch catering for the public sector. In June an NEC sub-Committee to hear members' appeals regarding lack of service and grievances over decision-making announced 'an important step towards . . . greater democratisation.' A low point was the members' ballot in Travenol, Castlebar, about which Official should service them. Two full-time Branches in Co. Mayo serviced similar memberships, geographically and industrially. The affair reflected poorly on union management.[2]

Table 120: ITGWU financial membership, income, expenditure and surplus (£), 1980–89

	Financial membership	Income (£)	Expenditure (£)	Surplus (deficit) (£)
1980	172,352	5,186,959	5,088,224	98,735
1981	169,798	6,294,113	5,764,005	530,108
1982	169,354	7,304,444	7,399,776	(95,332)
1983	158,344	7,822,410	7,831,471	(9,331)
1984	155,090	8,262,110	8,697,034	(434,924)
1985	139,690	9,042,323	8,733,653	308,653
1986	136,394	10,033,378	9,665,167	368,211
1987	133,777	10,175,457	10,256,923	(81,466)
1988	148,255*	11,014,645	10,256,923	589,310
1989	157,622*	10,743,842	10,417,985	325,857

*These are the figures of the Registrar of Friendly Societies and probably relate to book rather than financial members.

Source: ITGWU, Annual Reports, 1980–89.

In February 1982 more than 1,500 employees of the PMPA, Irish Life, Irish National and New Ireland insurance companies transferred from the Irish Union of Distributive Workers and Clerks, together with the Secretary of the Insurance and Finance Branch, Pat Meade. A month-long strike in PMPA ended in complete victory. Des Geraghty, National Group Secretary, led five hundred protesters to the office of the Minister for Industry and Energy, Albert Reynolds, seeking a reversal of the closure of Avoca Mines. There was a grim picture of factory closures, cut-backs and redundancies. Inevitably, financial membership fell, by 444 to 169,354. This did not fully reflect the recessionary effect, a time lag existing before members ceased to be counted. The figure of £159,752 for remission of contributions told a chilling tale. In 1983 membership losses were more apparent, a decrease of 11,010 reducing the total membership to 158,344.

The ITGWU resisted the temptation to poach members from other unions and restored good relations with the IUDWC. There were calls for greater involvement by unemployed members through separate Branches or Sections or reduced contributions. This drew attention to a difficulty: unions organised the employed and found it difficult to cater for the unemployed.[3]

Decline continued in 1984, with membership dropping to 155,090. The prospects were not encouraging. When two Group Secretaries, Paddy Donegan and Mick Gannon, retired they were not replaced. On 22 January 1985 a circular catalogued 10,000 redundancies. Branches were urged to rein in expenditure, particularly on Conferences. On 21 June a second circular cautioned that 'nothing on the horizon' suggested 'any dramatic improvement.' Recruitment leaflets were printed and Officials asked to identify white-collar, part-time, women and young workers, with specific materials aimed at nursing, clothing, textiles and engineering. A special *Liberty* acted as recruitment leaflet in a nationwide drive. On 30 July a third letter complained that the 'response had been abysmal, to say the least of it.'

Little thought was given to the fact that circulars did not recruit members. Many Officials had little or no organising experience. No skills training was offered. 'Recruiting' was not understood as not being 'organising'. On 13–14 September meetings of Branch Secretaries were held—no consideration being given to Branch Assistants or administrative and support staff. Financial membership fell to 119,871, meaning a final figure of about 137,000, a drop of 20,000 since 1983. Staff numbers fell by forty-eight from September 1982, effecting savings of £980,000. Members of the staff were assured that

> it is **imperative** to stress that **not one** of the 48 staff reductions referred to was caused by **redundancy**. They resulted from retirements, three secondments and four [members of the] staff terminated their employment. **Nobody was dismissed from the Union's employment nor was anyone made redundant.**

The 289 remaining employees were urged to 'please get cracking on the organisational campaign' and 'Recruitment Blitz.' On 13 December the NEC expressed 'major concern' despite 'the support received in tightening up substantially on expenditure.' There was little optimism.[4]

In 1986, if Class 8 (retired) members were included, the picture was alarming. At 173,000 members in 1982, the figure had dropped to 162,000 in 1983, 160,000 in 1984, 146,000 in 1985 and 143,000 in 1986. It was better if those receiving remission of contributions were counted: 190,000 in 1982, 178,000 in 1983, 170,000 in 1984, 160,000 in 1985 and 157,000 in 1986. Whichever way the sums were done, however, the figures spoke alarmingly for themselves. Recruitment drives had mitigated the problem, and new enrolments were encouraging: 11,289 in 1982, 10,813 in 1983, 13,955 in 1984, 18,436 in 1985 and 18,801 in 1986. Between 1982 and 1986 financial membership fell from 169,798 to 136,394, a collapse of 33,404. At 1983 contribution levels this represented a fall of £1.8 million a year, £2.4 million at 1986 rates.

General circulars of 18 November and 11 December 1986 asked Branches the following questions:

1. What steps have been taken by your Branch regarding membership recruitment in the past year?
2. What were the results?
3. What enquiries have been received by your Branch regarding membership and/or appropriate rates and conditions as a result of (*a*) the Branch's own local campaign, and (*b*) the Union's national campaign (including newspaper advertisements)?
4. What can you report to us on the particular question of recruiting part-time workers?
5. What are other unions locally doing on these issues and what sort of competition are they presenting?
6. Do you have any useful suggestions to make about recruitment and organisation?

Natural wastage and reorganisation effected wage savings of £1.3 million. The balance in the Industrial Contingency Fund stood at £1,025,392 in 1986, an impressive figure until it is set against Dispute Pay of £557,000 that year, and small enough should serious, national action occur. The future looked bleak.

The imperative remained to 'maximise our efficiency in operational costs and infrastructures' so as to provide 'the best possible service.' There was no talk of becoming an 'organising union'. The emphasis remained on servicing, reflected in two new benefits: educational scholarships for members and their children, and medical insurance.

In 1987 the membership was 133,777. The NEC surveyed the insidious New Right influence that demanded cuts in public expenditure, privatisation, competitiveness and 'labour market flexibility'. These were anti-union policies. The labour market was changing towards service jobs, part-time, agency and contract workers and temporary and work experience schemes. Employers moved from national-level to company-level bargaining, as 'central Agreements had given ICTU an unreasonably strong power position not only in the labour market but in society as a whole.'

'Human resource' management techniques, team briefing, profit-sharing, direct employee involvement and hostility to unions were the new suite. The FUE shifted from providing 'countervailing power' to unions to promoting derecognition and de-unionisation. The Confederation of Irish Industry inculcated public opinion with New Right values. Understanding this did not stop the decline in membership but could inform new strategies. Wages as low as £1 an hour were found among unorganised workers in Cork, one of many shocking discoveries as union lights shone into the labour market's darker corners.[5]

Contributions were raised by 20p per week in 1985 and 1986, with a further increase of 20p deferred until October 1987 after a Special Conference in November 1986. Some members complained, but a General Fund deficit of more than £300,000 warranted the increases. In January 1985 net current or liquid assets 'amounted to less than £100,000.' The General Secretary, Chris Kirwan, said: 'True, we did have fixed assets valued at £2.7 million and investments valued at £1.1 million,' but the overdraft was £157,000, and an accommodation of £800,000 was needed 'to take account of our cash flow situation.' Matters improved and net liquid assets amounted to £2.7 million in 1987, made up of cash and short-term investments, £1.3 million in the Industrial Contingency Fund and an £800,000 General Fund, despite Dispute Pay of £1.4 million in the previous three years. Without increased contributions, the situation would have been disastrous. Additional benefits were considered important: education scholarships, household insurance and life assurance, hospital benefit, and five information clinics.

Joe Ronan (Kilkenny) wanted greater recognition and protection for shop stewards, expressing a general view, at least among the more committed, that centralised bargaining had effectually eliminated their role. They were crucial to the ITGWU's existence. The Annual Conference was dominated by full-time staff, and he asked what impact this had on the morale and self-confidence of rank-and-file representatives. Carroll accepted some criticism, but the NEC fought shy of radical structural reform.

Addressing the last ITGWU Conference in 1989, Kirwan cautioned against anyone feeling 'that everything is okay' regarding 'finance and membership.' Coy about providing actual figures, he acknowledged that numbers were still declining. The Industrial Contingency Fund, consisting of 5p out of any additional increase in contributions, was a comforting cushion, with £2,900,724. Not to 'be utilised for day-to-day administration costs,' it was 'earmarked solely' for disputes and campaigns.

Young, part-time and contract workers had not featured on the organisational radar in better times, but needs dictated that they now be pursued. In the recruitment of such workers the ever-sinking floor was finally being pulled up again. Minimum statutory rights were sought for the most vulnerable groups, ultimately to the benefit of all.[6]

SIPTU

An indication of closer relations between the ITGWU and FWUI was Denis Larkin's obituary by the General Secretary of the FWUI, William Attley, published in *Liberty News* in 1988. Even James Larkin reappeared outside Liberty Hall again on May Day, although played by an ITGWU activist, Jer O'Leary, as part of commemorations of the Lock-Out. Reflecting on 1913, Carroll recognised that the enemies, while still the old familiar ones, had changed. The lesson of the Lock-Out was that it 'tried to out-law a culture counter to capitalism.' It failed, 'partly because it was so crude and ham-fisted.' The contemporary attack was 'more subtle and all the more dangerous because of it.' Old Divisions made less and less sense.

A joint ITGWU-FWUI national essay and project competition for schools, a gala concert and the production of Tomás Mac Cana's *Scrawled in Rage* in Liberty Hall acted as 'confidence-building' measures between the two unions. Identical issues of *Liberty News* and *Unity* put the terms of the Programme for National Recovery to members in the autumn of 1987, the first public manifestation of mutual activ-ity, though perhaps not apparent to the journals' separate readerships.

The ITGWU carried out a root-and-Branch survey of structures and services. 'Part of this exercise' was a series of discussions with the FWUI. The two unions 'identified the same problem areas.' The talks were 'well advanced,' and Carroll was 'satisfied they will be successful.' Young Jim Larkin's and John Conroy's dream was thwarted by 'their untimely deaths,' which 'impeded that natural evolution . . . it is on the way again.' They had to move closer while respecting 'each other's traditions.' Carroll added, 'on a personal note,' that 'it is my hope, indeed, even my dream, to see the reality of that come about even in my own time.' He hoped 'to include my colleagues in the FWUI to accept January 1990 as the cardinal date for this new OBU.' In this spirit, agreement in principle was reached in the autumn of 1988 'to amalgamate and face the future as the Services, Industrial, Professional and Technical Union,' reuniting the 'one trade union family which had been sired by Larkin, Connolly and their contemporaries.'

Addressing the final ITGWU Delegate Conference, Carroll detected a 'certain poignancy', the 'metaphorical tummy quiver' as the unknown lay ahead. The 'bonding' of the ITGWU and FWUI was 'as natural as night follows day.' It was 'really a re-marriage of two very well suited partners.' A *Liberty News* editorial was headed 'One Big Union—A beginning' and recorded other 1980s mergers, which, while welcome, all 'involved relatively few workers.' Talks between public-service unions and the emergence of the Manufacturing, Science and Finance (MSF) Union created a changed atmosphere in which the FWUI-ITGWU talks seemed natural.[7]

Kirwan saw the speed of the merger as 'a magnificent achievement on the part of all concerned'; it must 'not be viewed as a hurriedly rushed-through exercise,' as critics implied. The extent of the vote against was testimony to those who, in his view, opposed 'for opposition's sake.' The merger process 'was, in its own right, a tremendous and worthwhile exercise.'

A *Liberty News* supplement in March 1989 introduced the 'Union of the Future.'

'Alive to the potential of creating a bureaucratic monster,' the individual member was placed at its heart. Each member was entitled to vote for General Officers, the National Executive Council and eight new Regional Executive Committees, with reserved places for women if necessary. A range of consumer benefits and a Social Solidarity Service were provided. A postal ballot gave members a 'unique opportunity to usher in a dynamic new period' in labour history, 'ending the long-standing division' and maximising the use of resources, an obligation that would intensify with the Single European Market in 1992. The NEC urged members: 'To meet all of these challenges, we need a strong organisation—but we also need a responsive organisation capable of representing the membership accurately and effectively.' SIPTU would 'be all of that and more—drawing upon the resources, the democratic traditions and the determined spirit of two great unions.' There was really only one choice: vote 'Yes.'

ITGWU members voted by 88% in favour, FWUI members by 84%. The only regret on Liberty Hall's side was the loss of the name Irish Transport and General Workers' Union. There were reservations about 'SIPTU', with jokes about it sounding 'insipid', or 'septic'. The decisive outcome greatly boosted both Executives. For Carroll, forty-six years serving the ITGWU, there were mixed emotions. If any tears were shed they were 'tears of joy and celebration because we are moving forward—not to the demise of our great Union but to its rebirth and renewal' under SIPTU.

The ICTU discussed 'Trade Unions and Change' in 1989, identifying a need to organise the traditionally neglected: low-paid, part-time, temporary, contract, agency and home workers. Negotiating work-place change and seeking to share the benefits of extensive technology, new work systems and forms of work organisation were crucial, as was 'getting our message across' to workers who took trade union-ism for granted or who too readily imbibed the New Right philosophy that 'trade unions had no future' or were 'no longer necessary.' There was a strong sense of a 'new era'. Restructuring a fragmented, wastefully competitive movement was central to workers' capacity to respond adequately.[8]

FINTAN KENNEDY AND MICHAEL MULLEN

For years there was a sense of permanence and strength about the ITGWU leadership. This was broken on 14 January 1981 when Fintan Kennedy retired as General President, aged sixty-five. Following his father, Thomas, as an ITGWU General Officer, he served as General Secretary from 1959 to 1969 and as General President from 1969. Trade union unity was his central tenet on countless Committees. An iron fist could be revealed within a velvet glove when the need arose to defend the ITGWU or workers' rights or to resist employers' or Government excess. His daughter Jean maintains a family involvement, working in SIPTU College. He died unexpectedly on 24 March 1984. John Carroll succeeded him as General President, while six candidates contested the vacant Vice-Presidency. Tom O'Brien won, but his tenure was cut tragically short by his death on 10 November 1981. Christy Kirwan succeeded him in February 1982.

Michael Mullen's death in Frankfurt on Monday 3 November 1982 caused deep shock. The ITGWU felt that 'his unique combination of personal qualities' was irreplaceable. 'Mickey' Mullen defended global human rights and civil liberties, opposed racism, and championed Irish unity and independence. Elected General Secretary in 1969, he was proud of the Development Services Division, established in 1972, and the Cultural Division, established in 1980. He was elected Labour Party TD for Dublin North-West in 1961, the only Dublin Labour Deputy, but on his election as General Secretary of the union resigned all political office. Appointed a Senator by the Taoiseach, Liam Cosgrave, in 1973, he resigned from the Parliamentary Labour Party over the Criminal Law (Jurisdiction) Act (1976). At his graveside John Carroll described him as 'an instinctive Socialist ... proud of his working-class origins' and a tireless campaigner, particularly for inner-city Dublin. Mullen had been 'broker' in the 'Gregory Deal' in 1982. Kirwan was elected as Mullen's successor, defeating Des Geraghty by 206 votes to 140.[9] Edmund (Eddie) Browne defeated Des Geraghty to become Vice-President in June 1983.

SEVENTY-FIFTH ANNIVERSARY

Addressing the Seventy-Fifth Anniversary Conference, Carroll recalled that 'small band of dockers and carters' led by 'James Larkin as its dynamic Leader.' As for the WUI, 'we were both born of the one body of working men and women reaching out for economic and social freedom.' There was 'very little difference between us'; their names had 'much in common, as indeed do our constitutions and objectives.' The FWUI was congratulated on its sixtieth anniversary. He suggested that talks between them be resumed. Among many guests were the Irish-American Labour Coalition. In classic Larkinite tones, Carroll concluded: 'We, too, today, need to stir the hearts and the heads of working people and to rekindle the passion for social justice and equity. When that passion reaches its peak then we are fulfilling our destiny.' An essay competition for senior primary school classes and all secondary schools, run with the FWUI, was organised to 'pay tribute to the sacrifice ... in that titanic battle' and to 'pass on to a new generation a sense of that period.' The FWUI and ITGWU jointly placed gravestones over the Lock-Out martyrs Alice Brady, John Byrne and John Nolan in Glasnevin, and special editions of *Liberty* and *Unity* were published.[10]

WOMEN

In January 1980 the Trade Union Women's Forum issued a pre-Budget submission seeking equality of treatment in the tax and social welfare systems and particularly an end to discrimination against working married women. The ITGWU endorsed these demands. The ICTU Women's Advisory Committee sought community-based and work-place nurseries in a submission to the Government on child care. The demand came from the Working Women's Charter in response to increasing need as more mothers entered the labour force.

The ITGWU reported progress on maternity leave, with sixty-nine private-sector firms granting between thirteen and twenty-six weeks' paid leave, many achieved after the breakthrough of Labour Court recommendation 5123 in April 1979. Rosheen Callender pointed out that, despite the Anti-Discrimination (Pay) Act (1974) and the pursuit of cases, women's industrial earnings were still only 56% of those of men, hourly earnings 65%. Both gaps narrowed only by 4% in four years. Long delays, legal loopholes and employers' systematic delaying tactics minimised the impact of the legislation.

The Conference discussion paper 'Equality for Women' described comprehensive demands and actions. Equal pay, for most women, was not yet a reality. The ITGWU accepted the criticism of the Commission on the Status of Women that it did not do enough to encourage women's participation. Reserving NEC places for women was proposed as 'an initial step—and no more.' Change would not occur 'simply by evolution, or because people are well-intentioned,' and certainly not by passing resolutions. An action programme 'to systematically tackle all outstanding areas in which sex discrimination—direct or indirect' was vital. The ITGWU's structures needed to be opened to women to 'help us to tackle sex discrimination in society generally with greater effectiveness and credibility.' Women's low pay dragged down all workers. Previous well-motivated and laudable efforts were 'unplanned and un-coordinated,' leading to women's 'frustration, despondency and isolation.' Efforts would now be 'more planned and systematic.'

'Equality for Women' was 'an important document' for the entire movement, the 'first detailed study of its kind' by an Irish union. Sixty thousand ITGWU women were poorly reflected within its decision-making structures. Nóirín Greene (Dublin No. 2) demanded a Women's Committee, an annual seminar and reserved NEC places.[11]

Sylvia Meehan of the Employment Equality Agency welcomed discussion as an honest acceptance that much remained to be done *within* the movement. Equality was in everyone's interest. Attention had to be given to work grading and wage rates, the evaluation of qualifications and work-related requirements, fringe benefits and work-related rights linked to seniority and service, and criteria for training and promotion. Equality for women had 'come at the right time, with the HELP Campaign, to root out and eradicate core impediments to equality of access and opportunity. Women should ask, 'Has my union the capacity and will to pursue such agendas?' ITGWU women could 'give a positive "Yes".'

Senator Mary Robinson wanted an 'action plan and action strategy,' employing legislation in an assertive collective-bargaining campaign. Jean Roche (Dublin No. 6) addressed male Delegates who felt alienated: 'Women are your comrades. Our combined strength can bring about changes that will benefit men as well as women as a class and not as individuals ... An offence to one is an offence to all.' Men had 'a moral obligation to protect' any member 'whose position is weak.' If this was 'not done, the Union as a whole will be weakened.' 'Equality for Women' laid the keel for women's equality within the ITGWU.[12]

Technical aspects of successful equal-pay claims featured in *Liberty*, with such concepts as entitlement, what must be proved, what was 'like work', 'reasons other than sex' and procedural issues proving of value to negotiators and claimants. A feeling arose that 'you had to be an expert or a lawyer' to take equality cases, which inhibited Officials and members in initiating claims, a victory for employers' tactics of 'appeal everything.'

In December a Special Delegate Conference on 'Positive Action on Equality for Women' was held. The 'vast majority' in attendance were women. What was 'an unusual occurrence in any union, not just ours,' was still newsworthy. Workshops increased participation as compared with 'normal' Delegate Conferences. Branches demanded equality education and training, the identification and removal of obvious impediments to women's attendance at meetings—timing, child care, transport, an equality aspect to collective bargaining agendas, Women's Conferences, a National Equality Committee, and a Women's Officer. Within society, changes were sought in the provision of and access to education, the removal of the ban on night work in manufacturing, paid maternity leave, child care and improvements in social welfare and with the demand that 'all trade unionists should ensure that responsibility for work in the home is shared equally between the sexes.'

In March 1981 the NEC agreed to appoint a Women's Affairs Official, the first such full-time appointment in Ireland. A Women's Advisory Committee followed in September.[13] Tony Nolan (Limerick No. 1) called for the ban on women doing night work to be lifted. Not all agreed: Frank Graham (Dublin No. 15) saw it as a 'backward step for women.' The Maternity (Protection of Employees) Act (1981) granted fourteen weeks' paid maternity leave, albeit through social welfare benefits. There was predictable rearguard resistance from employers. The ITGWU wanted further progress, urging that the Working Party on Child Care promised under the National Understanding should actually meet. A negative consequence was that unions took their eyes off the ball and ceased to negotiate maternity leave with no loss of earnings directly from employers. The Shannon Branch called for financial support for the Society for the Protection of the Unborn Child. Carroll asked that the proposal be withdrawn: the NEC was not aware of SPUC's full programme. It did not want headlines saying the ITGWU 'is for abortion or against abortion.' The debate was acrimonious. The motion was lost and was immediately followed by a Clare County request that family planning services be overhauled, carried without debate.[14]

History was made twice in June 1982. Nóirín Greene, president of Dublin No. 2 Branch, became the first woman elected to the NEC since Sheila Conroy in 1955, and May O'Brien, Branch Assistant, Dublin No. 6/8 (Tailoring and Clothing), was appointed Women's Affairs Official, assisted by a Women's Affairs Committee elected in September: Mary Adams (Derry), Mary Burke (Clonmel), Bernie Delargey (Dublin No. 13), Cathy Kealy (Dublin No. 4), Doris Kelly (Dublin No. 2), Carmel Harrington (Bantry), Maureen McNicholas (Castlebar No. 1), Marie Rock (Carlow) and Margaret O'Sullivan (Cork No. 1). Poor attendance at a workshop on 'Achievements Towards Equality' was blamed on Branch Secretaries not giving it priority, an indication of the long road still ahead.

In October 1983 the first Consultative Conference on Women's Affairs asked that quotas be considered throughout the ITGWU's structures. May O'Brien, addressing her first Delegate Conference, was not afraid to criticise the slow pace of internal change. On reserved NEC seats for women the viewpoints of the Women's Affairs Committee and the NEC did 'not coincide.' The ITGWU contested reserved seats on the Executive Council of Congress but would not concede them to its own women. A magazine, *Equality Review,* provided case law and other developments and was widely sought beyond the ITGWU.

May O'Brien brought a new focus to previously neglected questions, such as family planning, women's health, discrimination in social welfare, child care, divorce and family law issues, rape, part-time work and low pay, and maternity leave. Although accepting the vote on the constitutional ban on abortion, the ITGWU expressed regret at the lack of 'tolerance and compassion' shown to women who bore children out of wedlock. It commented on cases in Athlone, Dún Laoghaire, Granard, New Ross and Tralee. Eileen Flynn's case showed that women were 'prone to be judged equally badly, not on their qualities or qualifications but on a moral judgement on their private lives.'[15]

Table 121: Women in the ITGWU, 1980–89

	Membership	*Women*	*As proportion of total (%)*
1980	188,722	62,907	33.3
1981	189,146	62,900	33.2
1982	188,702	62,900	33.3
1983	177,148	59,000	33.3
1984	173,894	57,900	33.2
1985	158,494	52,832	34.0
1986	155,198	51,732	33.3
1987	151,230	50,410	33.3
1988	148,255	49,918	33.6
1989	157,622	54,717	34.7

Source: National Archives, Registrar of Friendly Societies, file 275T.

In 1985 equality for married women was achieved in the social welfare code 'at the cost to married men on social welfare benefits—surely the ultimate in cynical manoeuvring.' The ICTU Women's Charter, which originated in the ITGWU, built upon the original 1975 Charter. (See p. 745) It tackled the highly divisive social issues of contraception and divorce, domestic violence, sexism in the media and sexual harassment. May O'Brien produced 'Equal Pay: How Does the Law Work?' The ITGWU pursued equal pay, employing the technical expertise of Eugene Kearney

(Industrial Engineering Department). The NEC held its ground on not conceding reserved places: it would be better if women broke through on their own terms.

In 1986 the Women's Affairs Committee felt that 'at last they were seeing measurable progress,' in the 'teeth of the worst possible economic and political situation.' The ITGWU women's presence at Congress was now rank-and-file women, not staff members, as other unions sent. Nóirín Greene won a reserved seat on the ICTU Executive Council.

Assertiveness training, first used at a five-day residential school at An Grianán in Termonfeckin in April, spurred women. A weekend at Magee College, Derry, on 'Low Pay and Health' was held in association with the National Union of Public Employees. All this experience was reflected in high levels of contribution at the fourth Consultative Women's Affairs Conference, held in Liberty Hall in November. Some success was gained on the social welfare front, the ITGWU having rejected equalisation on the basis of penalising men. Youghal Carpets, Lissadell Towels, Toyota, Krups and Metropole Hotel proved notable equal-pay victories, setting important precedents. Joint projects were carried out with Well Woman Clinics, Cherish, the Rape Crisis Centre, the Divorce Action Group, the Irish Cancer Society and Third World organisations, reflecting the ITGWU's holistic approach.

The defeat of the constitutional referendum on divorce disappointed. The union had urged a 'Yes' vote. The result had serious social, personal and legal implications for thousands of adults and children, victims of broken relationships. The legal ban on women doing night work in manufacturing was removed in 1987.[16]

In 1988 only twenty-four women attended the annual Delegate Conference. The union's success rate in equal-pay cases had risen to 80%. Cases were handled 'without fear because we know our business,' meaning that negotiated settlements were more likely. The ITGWU called for screening for cervical and breast cancer and an increased awareness and treatment response for AIDS and hepatitis B. Hugh Cox (Laois-Offaly) warned against treating women's affairs as a side-show. They were central, and women could become a 'pivotal dynamic' within the labour market and the union. Des Derwin (Dublin No. 13) objected to the fact that the only woman to appear on the platform was a 'conservative politician' on the first morning and wondered why the ITGWU still had no reserved NEC seats. The NEC's arguments were assuaged when Doris Kelly (Dublin No. 2) and Mary Oakes (Mullingar) were directly elected at the last ITGWU Conference in 1989.[17] The number of women members had fallen from 62,907 in 1980 to 54,717 by 1989, although remaining a constant third. Total membership of the FWUI was 39,004, underlining women's significance within the ITGWU.

NORTHERN IRELAND
Right-wing Tory Government in Britain spelt problems for Northern Ireland. New laws weakened gains made through the Industrial Relations Order (1976), constrained picketing and opened union funds to actions for damages by employers. Restrictions were placed on recruitment and recognition. The ITGWU Northern

Secretary, Paddy Devlin, maintained momentum, increased membership and participation and publicised low pay by actively pursuing Wages Councils to lift standards. Devlin's energy and imagination won equal pay for 150 women in Greenmount Appliances, Newry, the first case heard under Northern Ireland equality legislation. Devlin advanced the parallel agendas of equal pay and low pay and was appointed to the Low Pay Unit, the only non-MP. Decasualisation of the docks eroded numbers.

The hunger strike of Martin Meehan, a union member, led the ITGWU to invite Amnesty International to investigate. In 1980 Michael Mullen talked of Northern Ireland as 'an artificial entity,' riven by sectarianism and supported by the Unionist veto. Thatcher's talks with the Taoiseach were regarded with extreme caution. She was 'no friend of the Irish working class,' or any working class for that matter.

A Congress Action Day on employment and opposition to public spending cuts was a resounding success on 2 April. Fifteen thousand people marched in Derry, and ITGWU marchers were prominent in Strabane. In April the case of Bobby Sands MP raised 'concern'. The NEC restated that 'reform of the prison system must come about on humanitarian grounds with the rights and dignity of all prisoners respected at all times.' H blocks campaigners visited Liberty Hall in May to discuss their five-point claim. They wanted the ITGWU to pressure the Taoiseach and support a work stoppage. As with other unions, the ITGWU fell short of that but sent telegrams of protest to Thatcher, the ICTU, the European Trade Union Confederation and the British TUC.

Unlike the unequivocal attitudes of the late 1960s, early 1970s attitudes to the republican movement were now qualified. Sands's death was regretted, as were the 'deaths of all unfortunate victims.' His mother's call to 'avoid any action which would be likely to escalate the violence' was commended. Mullen argued that British 'intransigence' heightened tension and increased sectarianism, 'precisely the conditions under which paramilitaries on all sides flourish.'

The Tories' 'savage attacks' on social and economic life continued. They abolished the Supplementary Benefits Commission, scrapped the Central Advisory Council for the Disabled (despite 1981 being International Year of the Disabled) and planned to do away with thirteen other bodies. The Government could not estimate the savings involved, but the ITGWU recognised that 'one thing is sure, it won't bother to estimate the social and economic harm' that its cut-backs caused. Devlin pointed out that unemployment was higher than after the Wall Street Crash in 1931.[18]

Significant gains were made for hospital maintenance workers in a landmark case. On 10 December boilermen 'cut steam' at Musgrave Park Hospital, Belfast, and were replaced by blacklegs; 140 men in other hospitals walked out. After intervention by the Labour Relations Agency, all demands were won. Thatcher's anti-union Employment Bill was bitterly opposed by the ITGWU within the Northern Ireland Committee. Devlin saw it as 'the first step towards a non-unionised economy in Britain.'

A dispute in Norbrook Laboratories, Newry, lasted six months after union recognition was denied. The Branch Secretary, Martin King, appeared in Court 'for behaviour that is normal in the context of industrial relations.' Damages of £7,500 were awarded to the company and a permanent injunction imposed on King. In the context of the British Employment Bill, the judgement was a 'major infringement of the traditional immunity' provided by the Trade Disputes Act (1906) for Officials 'in the performance of their duties in a legally held dispute.' The ITGWU was thus the 'first and indeed the only' union 'subjected to such an attack through the Courts.' After intervention by the Labour Relations Agency, Norbrook finally granted recognition, reinstated twenty-five dismissed activists, paid agreed redundancy payments to selected members of the staff and accepted an investigation of general company relations by the Labour Relations Agency. In the Court of Appeal the original judgement was overturned and the slate wiped clean.[19]

The Anglo-Irish Agreement of 1985 laid the foundations for peace, but continued recession sent membership of the ITGWU 'tumbling'. Belfast had 1,215 financial members in 1984, 1,195 in 1985 and 989 in 1986. Derry had 1,195 in 1984, 1,503 in 1985 and 1,583 in 1986; Newry had 816 in 1984, 784 in 1985 and 907 in 1986. Matters remained static in 1987, while the ICTU adopted 'Equality of Opportunity for Northern Ireland'. A 'Charter for Equal Opportunities' urged unions to establish Equality Committees, hold courses, eliminate sectarianism and sexism, keep work-places free of emblems, flags, pin-ups or graffiti that could give offence, discipline members proved guilty of sectarian or discriminatory behaviour, draw up check-lists for negotiators and monitor progress.

In 1986 an anti-sectarian and anti-intimidation campaign, 'Peace, Work and Progress', was launched. The ITGWU identified closely with it. In 1988 rallies were held in support of Harland and Wolff and Short Brothers as Thatcher's breaker ball coldly dismantled industry. A Fair Employment Bill promised legal recognition of the MacBride Principles.

Within the 'cauldron of unease, disquiet and continued disruption occasioned by acts of horror and violence,' beleaguered Branches continued to be 'well serviced' by Officials and activists, who demonstrated immense personal courage. The 'uneven scales of British justice' were condemned and support given to campaigns for the release of the Birmingham Six and the Guildford Four. In 1989 Jack Nash spearheaded a significant equality victory for 700 women in Daintyfit plants in Irvinestown, Limavady and Plumbridge, working closely with the National Union of Tailors and Garment Workers.[20]

CONGRESS

In 1980 difficulties arose with the Amalgamated Transport and General Workers' Union, whose 'intransigent attitude' led the ITGWU to process all further transfer applications through Congress, 'even if we lose.' The Inter-Relation Agreement signed in 1945 was dead. Simultaneously, the ITGWU sought the expulsion of the Local Government and Public Services Union because it took in the Psychiatric Nurses' Association of Ireland. More rows with the ATGWU occurred in

Telecommunications, in Kilroy Brothers and in Cork and Letterkenny Regional Hospitals. Some apparently found it easier to poach others' members than to organise the unorganised. A meeting was sought with the ATGWU's Irish Officer, John Freeman. The extent of either his desire or his capacity to influence events among his members in the Republic was unclear, although in any other Region of that union the senior officer's command would be absolute. British unions frequently allowed their Irish membership an autonomy sometimes even at odds with their 'national' policy. To circumvent this, Kennedy and Mullen travelled to London for talks with the General Secretary of the TGWU (the ATGWU's parent organisation), Moss Evans. They got no favours through formal channels, with Congress appearing to be 'placating' the ATGWU. The ITGWU complained that the constitution of Congress was not being 'adhered to by all affiliates.' Lengthy discussion at the GEC of the FWUI showed how widely this dispute affected the movement generally.[21]

In spite of regular disputes with Congress, Fintan Kennedy, at his last NEC meeting in December 1980, said 'he believed in' Congress and the 'unity of the Irish workers and the entire working class.'

Problems with the Local Government and Public Services Union grew in 1981 as 850 local authority engineers transferred over. Tom McGrath, Industrial Officer of the ICTU, attempted to broker peace. In July 'two very amicable meetings' were held with the FWUI and ATGWU 'in respect of new employments.' It was agreed that '[standard] Agreements covering wages and hours of work be drawn up and submitted for approval.' The bounty of new manufacturing plants was to be more evenly shared. The ITGWU sought to amend clause 47 of the constitution of Congress to enable those dissatisfied with their union to secure a two-thirds majority in order to switch allegiance. The ITGWU clearly felt it would benefit from looser arrangements. The Conference did not agree.

The ITGWU extended its international affiliations, the most comprehensive of any Irish organisation, indicating a keenness to keep abreast of European developments and to integrate with the international movement.[22]

Squabbling with the Irish Union of Distributive Workers and Clerks ceased in March 1984 after a 'pact' was signed defining 'spheres of influence'. Matters came to a head after Clery's staff transferred to Dublin No. 2 Branch in 1983. In 1985 calls for discussions with British unions regarding peace and unity were dismissed by Denis Carr (Dublin No. 6/8) as a waste of time. There was no evidence that British Labour gave a 'tinker's damn' about Ireland. He wondered why they still operated here and invited them to 'leave us to look after ourselves.' The ITGWU observed that 'we rightly condemn management for inefficiency and weakness' yet tolerate it within the movement: 'Let is put our own union house in first-class order so that we can maximise our effectiveness.'

In 1987 fifteen unions accounted for 80% of the Republic's 475,000 union members, with thirty unions having fewer than 1,500 members. Carroll said that Liberty Hall was 'ready and willing' to reduce this confusing structure to ten efficient and effective units. He invited the FWUI and ATGWU 'to seriously consider doing likewise.'[23] Older minds were cast back to the ITUC Commissions and the Trade Union Act (1941).

WAGES, DISPUTES AND THE PROGRAMME FOR NATIONAL RECOVERY

A Conference on 7 March 1980 honed the ITGWU's wages and employment policy: a National Minimum Wage, to be reviewed annually; local bargaining clauses in national Agreements to allow workers to share in gains arising from productivity, new technology or work reorganisation; the protection of employment; the early completion of equal pay; reductions in the working week; and additional paid holidays. The position paper 'Economic and Social Policy' was adopted. It demonstrated how HELP (Higher Earnings for the Lower Paid) had influenced the content of the National Understanding, but inflation wiped out advances. Pay for those on £50 per week rose by 23.6% if all increases were paid and for those on £60, 20.8%, but inflation had risen by 23% in the previous fifteen months. Those on £50 experienced a wage freeze, those on £60 a real wage cut. Clause 4 supposedly provided an opportunity for local bargaining but fell victim to the Labour Court's 'very rigid interpretation.' The 'balance of Branch opinion' favoured the 'principles underling centralised bargaining,' but there was 'strong disapproval of percentage increases coupled with restrictive causes.'

In May, Congress entered talks with the Government and employers. The ITGWU observed that 'during every recession, workers are told that their main contribution to "national recovery" and "everybody's economic interest" is to exercise wage restraint and moderation.' This was always the 'main message during every run-up to a new national wages deal. When both occur simultaneously, the cry was deafening and drowned out everything else.' Wage restraint was not the only or the most effective policy response. Even if it were, why not call for 'incomes restraint?'

In September the ITGWU saw the money terms of the Second National Understanding as 'no real improvement.' The 'lower paid were not adequately catered for . . . job creation promises [were] unreal,' and Sectoral Industrial Committees, promised in the first National Understanding, had not got off the ground. The 'inability to pay' clause was 'a let out for many' and an additional one day's annual leave 'not enough.' Despite this, the NEC recommended acceptance, by 12 votes to 2.[24]

Kennedy was pleased that, through the National Understanding, unions had 'assumed a degree of responsibility for Government policies,' rectifying growing dissatisfaction with narrow National Wage Agreements. It challenged unions to 'put their house in order,' and the Tripartite Committee was an indication of their ability to do so.

The Second National Understanding for Economic and Social Development was agreed by Congress in October 1980. It lacked an 'inability to pay' element, but clause 6 allowed individual firms to seek to arrive at different terms with their workers through agreed procedures. Members were asked to 'make it work,' not 'simply as another pay deal but as a broad framework' for social and economic progress, 'despite recession.' Pay limitations could be balanced by concerted efforts on workers' participation, health and safety, welfare, disclosure of information, maternity leave, and education and training.

A nice touch was the sight of Matt Merrigan's ATGWU Delegation voting in favour on the front cover of *Liberty*. He explained (quoting Owen Sheehy Skeffington) that 'people in a democracy have a right to do wrong.' Wry smiles stretched well beyond Liberty Hall. 'Mattie on this occasion had the unenviable task of telling the Conference that the ballot vote of his members had revealed a majority for acceptance of the proposals, against his advice. Aren't we all too familiar with that experience?'

The FUE met the Government in November and extracted concessions that enabled it to 'comply' at 'minimal cost to themselves.' The ITGWU protested that this assailed the spirit of the National Understanding and cautioned against attempts to weaken it or to introduce anti-union legislation. Calls for a National Minimum Wage provoked consideration whether this could be 'safety net or snare.' European experience was mixed.[25]

The ITGWU supported calls by Congress for an additional 2.7% increase on the second phase in May 1981 as real wages rapidly declined. Although it welcomed the National Understanding concept, 'unfortunately the word failed to become flesh.' After Charles Haughey came to power it 'became particularly debased.' His regime was a mixture of 'cynicism and demagogy.' It allowed Garret FitzGerald to dismiss the National Understanding with 'what amounted to contempt.' Efforts to gain advances from the new Coalition 'met with studied indifference.' It encouraged employers to 'mount an even more vicious campaign' against living standards. An 'orgy of spurious theoretical justification for this offensive' was spouted by the 'economics profession'; the National Economic and Social Council wanted an eighteen-month pay freeze. FitzGerald's 'Three Wise Men' showed that living standards fell by 13% during the National Understanding.

The ITGWU concluded:

In this so-called 'free-for-all' situation members themselves will decide by the ballot-box how best to embark upon this struggle on a co-ordinated industrial basis. Once the democratic process has been observed they can be assured of full backing. Both Government and employers stand warned.[26]

The ITGWU rightly believed that 'one worker's sacrifice is another's gain' and that there was '*no mechanism*, in our society, for translating pay freezes, or reductions in overtime, or early retirement,' into 'new jobs' or improving low pay. Opposition to, or least serious scepticism about, future Agreements was evident. The platform won the referral back of critical motions, preserving its bargaining position but impressed by the strength of members' feelings.

In 1982 the Government was accused of reneging on its commitments under the National Understanding. Carroll reminded Delegates that the ITGWU's position papers informed its movement towards National Understandings from narrow

National Wage Agreements. He appealed for the freedom to enter talks, reassuring Delegates that each set of proposals would be considered purely on its merits and in the context of prevailing circumstances.

As talks broke down, the focal point of bargaining shifted back to the local level, 'for the first time in over ten years.' The ITGWU considered that 'our organisational structure' was 'better equipped' than any other union, both in full-time staff and the 'availability of specialised back-up services,' to 'maintain employment and living standards.'[27] It was a claim that would be severely tested.

In January 1982 the ITGWU regarded proposals on public-service pay as 'moderate' but recommended them as the best on offer. By autumn the Government reneged on the deal as part of savage cuts. The ITGWU led 8,000 people in demonstrations in Cork and 5,000 in Longford. It warned that the FUE would encourage private-sector employers in similar demands for pay freezes and cuts. A study of 1,154 settlements covering 126,000 members showed Agreements lasting an average of 14.6 months for basic pay increases of 16.3%, with 43% of cases gaining an extra day's annual leave.

In creameries the union's National Committee agreed 'not to co-operate in the unprincipled movement of milk from one co-op to another.' Rationalisation led to the poaching of milk between co-ops. It was an 'understandable trade union position' that members on the ground vigorously supported. In the Kantoher-Golden Vale case co-operation between Shop Stewards 'proved to be impossible because of historical bitterness' between the co-ops and 'worker indoctrination by management.' As the losses on Golden Vale milk exceeded a million gallons and jobs were threatened, workers blockaded supplies to Kantoher. A 'tortuous formula' settled matters: milk went to Shannon Dairies, then to Kantoher Co-op, which promised 'to give the milk back to Golden Vale. Indeed, an Irish answer to an Irish problem.' The withdrawal of Kerry Co-op from national negotiating structures shortly before the Twenty-Second Round did not impede a 'good Agreement' but was the thin end of a wedge that destroyed national bargaining structures. The emphasis was placed on work-place bargaining in pursuit of 'lean production'.[28]

A Public Service Pay Agreement was concluded in 1983 for fifteen months, inclusive of a six-month pay pause. Members and Officials had limited, if any, experience in directly dealing with employers. ITGWU figures showed that 906 Agreements, covering 135,000 members, provided an average of 11.9% over 13½ months. Pay pauses, redundancies, cuts and worsened conditions featured widely.

In January a 'sharp drop in take-home pay' was reported since 1980, 13% of real wages for single workers and 15½% for married workers with two children. Additional slices of take-home pay were forfeited in tax and PRSI contributions. 'Free-for-all' wage bargaining proved expensive rather than 'free'. Dispute Pay nevertheless totalled £771,698 in 1982–3.

Table 122: ITGWU income and Dispute Pay, 1980–89

	Income (£)	Dispute pay (£)	Dispute grant (£)	Total dispute pay (£)	As proportion of income (%)
1980	5,186,959	400,201	43,750	443,951	8.5
1981	6,294,113	216,281	13,573	229,854	3.6
1982	7,304,444	427,029	13,830	440,859	6.0
1983	7,822,410	342,669	17,657	360,356	4.6
1984	8,262,110	514,120	20,350	534,470	6.7
1985	9,042,323	317,242	5,437	322,679	3.5
1986	10,033,378	557,717	2,013	559,730	5.6
1987	10,175,457	462,913	29,458	492,371	4.9
1988	11,014,645	195,648	5,485	201,133	1.8
1989	10,743,842	138,931	5,851	144,782	1.3

Source: ITGWU, Annual Reports, 1980–89.

Clondalkin Paper Mills closed on 22 January 1982 but were purchased by the state. Nothing much then happened and workers sat in until February 1983, when announcements were made about possible reopening. John Carroll and Paddy Cardiff of the FWUI demanded an inquiry into the Minister's handling of matters after John Bruton declared that unless viability could be shown there would be no reopening. On 3 November two workers began a hunger strike, and the mills were reoccupied in a last-ditch endeavour to save them. The hunger strike concluded on Wednesday 16 November with an announcement that a Canadian company, Freedham McCormack, was to restart production, with thirty to forty employed. The ITGWU wondered whether Bruton's 'unilateral abrogation' of commitments made to Congress were an example of 'calculating duplicity or crass stupidity'? The affair raised broader questions about whether any invitation to discuss economic and industrial relations with the Government was of value.[29]

In 1983 recognition was sought from Condron's Concrete, Tullamore. The owner adamantly refused to deal with the ITGWU or the Labour Court or to acknowledge political interventions from his own party representatives. Many firms refused to do business with Condron's, but materials were moved at dead of night in unmarked vehicles and in open defiance of pickets. The Branch Secretary, Seán Sheehan, and his Committee fought nobly, but the longer the dispute lasted the more bloody-minded the employer and the scab work force became. The Labour Court found 'no good reason' why the ITGWU should not be recognised. In August a Condron's lorry rammed a union car which was stoned by people hidden by the roadside, one of a number of violent incidents. A National Strike Fund was set up in October as hopes of a settlement faded. After fourteen months, in April 1984 an anonymous mediator finally effected a settlement. It involved temporary closure and compensation for the dismissed men.

Better news came after a twelve-week strike in Christy's Hotel, Blarney, Co. Cork, and Blarney Woollen Mills after seven workers were sacked for joining the ITGWU. Thirty-two members, thirty of them women, picketed seven days a week, twenty-four hours a day, to bring the employer to the negotiating table. The Branch Secretary, Joe O'Callaghan, won reinstatement, a comprehensive Agreement and substantial increases.

In two Pizzaland restaurants in Dublin two managers, member of the union's Professional and Managerial Branch, were suspended. Overtures by the Labour Court were ignored, scabs were imported from Britain and pickets were continuously harassed. Victory was secured with reinstatement and an honouring of Agreements. All three strikes were symptomatic of a growing anti-unionism.

After Dunlop in Cork closed there was a sit-in for 'decent severance payments'— a plaintive gesture by those who had given a lifetime to the company. Poor management delayed the switch from cross-ply to radial tyres, compounded by the choice of textile rather than steel bases, causing closure. Dunlop could 'well afford to improve' inadequate severance terms 'with hardly a ripple in their accounts.' A further 800 jobs went when Ford closed.[30]

In 1984 Government pay guidelines were rejected 'out of hand' as 'unreal' and 'quite irresponsible.' The ITGWU supported the withdrawal of Congress from the National Prices Commission. The Government was accused of interfering with the principle of voluntary free collective bargaining, the 'cornerstone' of industrial relations. Claims under the Twenty-Fourth Round were lodged as Government fiscal policy fuelled inflation. Jobs could not be created without markets, and depressing consumer demand worsened matters.

In 1985 Carroll reflected on the loss of centralised bargaining. The 'social partners' had acknowledged the worth and merit of a social contract. The National Understandings coincided with 'musical chairs' Government. Political instability had not helped central Agreements get 'fully into gear'. They 'set the framework' upon which effectively planned economic and social development could have been built 'and still point the way to this possibility.' Despite some union opposition it was the Government and employers who killed off the concept. If the Coalition did not want them, Carroll reasonably commented, 'there is surely good cause for our side to reflect on the reasons.'

Congress published *Confronting the Jobs Crisis: The Framework for a National Plan*; but with no prospect of a Labour Government, how would it be implemented? Carroll pitched strongly for another National Understanding; neither employers nor Government heeded his call. Low-pay strategies were rejected as not contributing to job creation and not socially acceptable. Hourly rates were among the EEC's lowest and working hours the longest. Productivity was high and rising.

The Twenty-Fourth Round produced wage increases of about 9%, slightly ahead of inflation at 6–7%, and witnessed a tough battle to defend the public sector. Éamonn Gilmore (Professional and Managerial Branch) rejected claims that all economic ills stemmed from 'high pay'. There was a sense of drift and a desire to synchronise efforts in order to maximise impact and returns.[31]

The ITGWU spent £534,470 on Dispute Pay in 1984, 6.7% of income, and a further £322,679 in 1985. An Industrial Contingency Fund set aside £353,863. An unemployment and tax campaign ran from September, financed from this source for £14,077. The Convoy Branch wanted the 'Fighting Fund' to be used for the low-paid, to win improvements and attract new members.

The number of strikes rose again in 1986, and Dispute Pay was £579,730. Most strikes were against job losses. Employers continued dismantling national bargaining structures, such as JICS, reverting to plant bargaining in creameries, meat-processing and flour-milling. Battles were fought, sometimes literally, in Dublin Corporation, CIÉ and Veha in Wicklow.

The Veha dispute arose from the wrongful selection for redundancy of three clerical members, one of whom, Dónal Dunne, was Shop Steward. It continued until 8 May, when, rather than concede, the owner placed the company in receivership, with the 'tragic loss of all the jobs.' Workers voted to defend union principles despite the owner's bloody-minded threat of closure and rejected 'the Labour Court's golden handshake.' 150 members were out for forty weeks, at a cost to the union of £178,593 in Dispute Pay.

A Lock-Out of two hundred workers in the Shelbourne Hotel was imposed in 1983 after the dismissal of a barman and culminated in a rationalisation programme and ninety-four voluntary redundancies. A strike for improvements in basic pay and 'Sunday equivalent' for those with liability for a seven-day week began on 4 October 1986 after the rejection of a Labour Court recommendation. The owners, Trust House Forte, proved obdurate employers. Dublin No. 4 Branch Strike Committee were 'commended for their creativity and resourcefulness in winning great public sympathy for their case' and sustaining picketers' morale. Materials included *Shelbourne Strike News,* a mock menu showing existing rates and industry norms, and a bilingual 'rugby ticket' urging French and Irish supporters not to patronise the hotel. When pickets were placed on the 'most distinguished address in Ireland' they naturally became the 'most distinguished pickets.' After intervention by Bishop James Kavanagh a settlement was reached, with wages raised from £68 to £111 per week and from £83 to £133.80 for various grades, plus service charge. The Hibernian Hotel closed in 1984 with the loss of 160 jobs, so the Shelbourne victory was a welcome boost.[32]

A change of Government in 1987 brought no change in policy except in one crucial area: 'the willingness expressed' by the new Taoiseach, Charles Haughey, to enter talks with Congress on economic growth, jobs, tax reform, public finance, pay, social services, health and education. Carroll saw these as 'imperative to get the country's economy back on track.' The 1987 General Election left the labour movement 'more powerless than ever before,' with a block of 146 Dáil seats supporting New Right policies. The ITGWU felt 'it remained for the trade union movement to use its bargaining power in the effort to undermine the right-wing economic consensus.' The result was the 'Programme for National Recovery', adopted in November, a new form of centralised Agreement, expanding the scope of National Understandings. It protected living standards, working hours were reduced as a contribution to job creation, and specific job targets were agreed. There would be no compulsory redundancy in the public service, an end to forced lay-offs in local authorities, and the establishment of a national bargaining forum. 'Recognition of the right of the ICTU to participate in national economic and social planning' was paramount.

The NEC saw the Programme for National Recovery not as 'an ideal solution' but an acceptable compromise, given widespread talk of pay freezes, savage cuts in public expenditure, wholesale privatisation and social welfare cut-backs. 'Few doubt that, left to their own devices, this Government would have stuck rigidly to that path.' The Agreement did 'not bind the trade unions to silence and inactivity on any Government policies we oppose,' nor was it a rubber stamp for Fianna Fáil. Members were asked, What is the alternative? The NEC argued that 'as long as 90% of the electorate continue to vote for essentially right-wing political parties,' ideal solutions were beyond the horizon.

The biggest selling point of the Programme for National Recovery was that 'spokespersons for Fine Gael and the Progressive Democrats have complained that the Government has already conceded too much.' The Agreement allegedly threatened democracy and usurped the Dáil's authority. Members accepted the 'strongly recommended' package, albeit by a narrow majority of 2,127 out of 74,482 votes cast. It was carried in Congress by 181 to 114.[33]

Average settlements under the Twenty-Sixth Round were 5.9%, covering 100,000 workers, with minor improvements for the low-paid. The Programme for National Recovery ran for four years, from August 1987 to December 1991. There was provision for reducing working hours to thirty-nine. Carroll was 'mindful of the reservations' members had, and the ITGWU was 'especially vigilant' to ensure that the provisions of the Central Review Committee were honoured. The union was 'to the fore' in condemning the FUE's opposition to the £4 floor, 'which seemed to be carrying weight with the Labour Court,' to deny many covered by JLCs. 'We defeated that attempt resoundingly and exploited the value' of the Central Review Committee in the process.

Dispute Pay in 1987 was £492,371 as battles continued against redundancy, closure and rationalisation. In the B&I Line two disputes disrupted a troubled company, and one of many 'survival plans' was negotiated. In 1982 2,000 were employed in the company, from 900 in 1988.The deregulation of air fares severely affected cross-channel ferry traffic. The survival plan was drastic and not acceptable to the employees, who fought tenaciously to retain the Liverpool route. It was finally endorsed on 11 December, with the Government approving an additional £11 million in equity.[34]

In 1988, 409 settlements under the Twenty-Seventh Round catered for 40,000 members averaging 4¾%, 501 under the Programme for National Recovery, 77,000 workers averaging 4.45% despite the Agreement's provision that it should have been 2.89%. Dispute Pay, at £201,133, was the lowest of the decade.

Women in Premier Disposables, Naas, fought to improve wages of £1.60 an hour and to gain overtime pay, better hours and equality with male colleagues. Pickets placed from mid-September were passed, and the employer dug in. Courageous commitment from the young women and the support of the Kildare Branch won out. A five-week strike over suspensions and a lock-out in Memorex, Clondalkin, ended successfully in December.

Dispute Pay fell to £144,782 in 1989. The Programme for National Recovery induced industrial peace, even if Congress led criticisms of the general delivery of initial promises. A 25-point action plan was submitted for creating larger Irish companies capable of withstanding global competition; the conversion of building and machinery grants into employment grants; corporate taxes that rewarded the creation of employment; an end to the embargo on recruitment in the public sector; improved training and the creation of more apprenticeships; an assault on the black economy; the introduction of price controls, tax equity, a minimum wage and profit-sharing; and significant improvements in social welfare. Chris Kirwan led the Congress Delegation to the Government.[35]

NURSES

In the spring of 1980 a nurses' dispute drew predictable press claims that they no longer cared about patients. The National Nursing Council observed that recognition of the essential nature of nurses' work occurred only when strikes threatened. It was certainly not recognised in their pay.

In January 1981 a National Nursing Conference, 'Health and the Nurse in Modern Society,' was part of an endeavour to lead health policy. A National Nursing Officer, Pat Brady, was appointed in 1981. The Association of Administrative Psychiatric Nurses affiliated, creating the Association of Nursing Officers, representing senior nurses. As the decade progressed, there was concern for conditions, staff levels and recruitment embargoes. Health cuts were constantly opposed. In 1987 the staff of St Finan's Hospital, Port Laoise, voted to strike 'to secure improved standards of health care' for patients. Those who had not resigned or emigrated could no longer be party to inadequate treatment. They hoped that a withdrawal might provoke a meaningful response.[36] They hoped in vain.

AUGHINISH ALUMINA

A strike at the Alcan construction site at Aughinish, Co. Limerick, the country's largest civil engineering project, made headlines in May 1980. Since operations began, in September 1979, the ICTU Construction Group had a full-time Official on site, Dan Millar (Electrical Trades Union), and from March, Tony Walsh (ITGWU, former Ferenka member) joined him. As on all sites, the men wanted their problems solved before the completion of the job. Many, especially in specialist areas, were migratory workers, some flown in weekly. The Union Group welcomed an independent inquiry into management practice, but by June the entire operation closed. Stalemate persisted. Steel-fixers employed by Wimpey Hegarty placed un-official pickets on 29 April. Matters remained unresolved until 9 July. Eleven weeks were spent on complex negotiations by two specialist sub-Committees, one on structures, the other on bonuses. More than 2,000 were employed, 800 of them ITGWU members.

After the return to work the union reflected on the value of the project, not least at a time of mass unemployment and redundancy, and thought it 'time for practical and progressive trade union leadership.' It would 'be a major test of our ability to industrialise' and use industrial strength intelligently.[37]

OIL TANKER DRIVERS

In October 1980, ITGWU oil tanker drivers struck. It began as a 'common industrial relations problem' in Texaco in June but grew into a 'major national issue with serious political, industrial and economic implications.' After the first National Understanding the ITGWU sought substantial wage increases and an increase in shift premiums, reduced hours, restoration of a week's holidays for those with more than twenty years' service, double time for all rest-day working, conversion of the pension scheme from contributory to non-contributory, free petrol, and danger money when transporting hazardous products. The management insisted that matters could be processed only under the National Understanding. The company would not be taken for the industry's 'soft under-belly'. Nothing was heard until men in all oil companies imposed an overtime ban and work to rule on 1 September, although direct discussions were held only with Texaco. The ITGWU advised the men that, as the members had democratically decided to accept the National Understanding, such action was inadvisable. The drivers reverted to 1967 conditions, refusing to leave depots without a helper or do shift work.

The Labour Court vainly attempted to restore the status quo pending fuller investigations, the companies criticising its intervention in an unofficial dispute. On 15 September the Chairman of the Labour Court, Maurice Cosgrave, confirmed that it was the first investigation while unofficial action was in progress in the Court's 34-year history. The men demanded a recommendation within one week and compensation for lost time, conditions the Court was unwilling and unable to comply with. The men met on Saturday 20 September, with Officials asked not to attend. 343 voted to continue the unofficial action, 48 against.

Such was the impact on fuel supplies that the Minister called the FUE and ICTU to meet on Tuesday 23 September. It was recommended that normal working resume on 26 September, with both sides attending a full hearing on the same day, any financial benefits to apply retrospectively. A payment 'on account' of £250 was offered against any sums accruing if overtime and rest-time working resumed. Dublin Shop Stewards met on 25 September and countered with demands for immediate direct negotiations with a view to the resumption of work, the employment of helpers, a non-productivity basic rate of £90 per week, standard time and methods of operation to be discussed, and all shift work to be optional. The management refused to talk while unofficial action persisted.

On Sunday 28 September, Con Murphy, Rights Commissioner, acting personally, brought the sides together. Acknowledging the 'serious emergency' in oil supplies, he proposed that all return with crews of two for one week, normal standards applying and payments at 31 August rates. After a week, pre-August conditions, particularly driver-only vehicles, would apply until the Labour Court made a recommendation after beginning an investigation on 6 October (assuming normal working). Neither the ITGWU nor the Committee were to cite these arrangements as a precedent. The companies accepted. The men rejected, suggesting instead 'alternate one week with two men, one week with one' until a final settlement. Murphy withdrew.

On Monday 29 September pickets were placed on oil termini in Cork, Galway and Limerick. Men who had hitherto steadfastly refused to join unofficial action ceased work. It was clear that this decision was taken on Friday 26 September in the event that Murphy's intervention failed.

The Government used emergency powers and introduced the army, thus exacerbating matters. 'Hysterical outbursts in the mass media' raised feelings higher. As the dispute remained unofficial, ITGWU leaders were unable to get to the heart of matters or to deal directly with the employers. The NEC constantly advised a return to enable normal procedures to operate.

Finally the ITGWU asked the Minister, under Section 24 of the Industrial Relations Act (1946), to direct an intervention by the Labour Court. After two days, on 2–3 October, the Labour Court recommended an 'immediate resumption of normal working,' the employers to offer £350 to each man, offset against final terms, and the involvement of the Irish Productivity Committee in a comprehensive investigation of all claims, which would take six weeks. The men's Representatives at the Court agreed to recommend this to nationwide meetings, by 19 to 9, the three Dublin men voting in favour.

On Saturday 4 October, Dublin agreed to put the recommendation, although Shop Stewards opposed it. The Labour Court's proposals were excepted in all centres except Dublin but rejected on aggregate, 338 to 393. On Monday 6 October the NEC, 'regretting' the rejection, requested 'all workers to desist from any action' that made matters 'more difficult for us to resolve.' Only a return to work would allow normal procedures to apply, a resolution to be sought, the 'rights of the trade union movement' protected and army intervention ended. Dublin No. 2 Branch, which organised clerical staffs, actively supported the drivers, criticising the union's tactics. The NEC noted that the Branch Secretary, John Kane, 'invariably found himself at odds with the Union'—an interesting observation in the light of Kane's subsequent challenges for General Officership.

Murphy was again directed to mediate. After 'long and tedious discussions' on Sunday 12 October he recommended that normal working resume at once; a one-off payment of £150 for co-operation in restoring normality, in addition to the £350 recommended by the Court; an assessment by the FUE and ICTU, to be completed by 14 November; and basic rates to be compiled for investigation and comparison. The national negotiating Committee of the strikers recommended this to General Meetings on Tuesday 14 October. It was accepted, 568 to 194.

Normal working resumed, except in Texaco, where material handled by the army complicated matters until 18 October. The FUE-ICTU assessment was carried out by Des Branigan. The Labour Court recommended increasing 'consolidated basic pay' by £4.15 per week.

Afterwards the NEC sought submissions to an internal inquiry, 'because this matter is so important.' *Liberty,* in an article headed 'Media Horror . . . No Shock!!' analysed press coverage. Typical and frequent terms in headlines were 'irresponsible', 'unjustified' and 'prolonged the agony.' None contributed anything positive to the national atmosphere or facilitated a settlement. The 'vicious campaign' against the drivers was 'quite merciless'. Whenever this blew itself out attention was turned on union Officials, naturally ignoring the umpteen proposals suggested by them. In 'its handling of this dispute, the national press went beyond the bounds of fairness and reason.'

A Conference motion condemned the use of the army and called for non-cooperation should it recur. The debate was emotional and confused. Carroll made it clear that, without 'reservation, qualification or anything else,' they opposed the use of the military. But defiant unofficial action created problems. The motion was defeated.

The Head of the Development Services Division, Paddy Clancy, was Commissioned to draw up a report. It apportioned blame but was not made public; the 'great pity was that it was totally and absolutely unnecessary.' 'Gross neglect' by the management was criticised, but the handling of the dispute by the ITGWU came 'a close second in the lack of leadership qualities.' Senior Officials should be 'called to account,' not least for their failure to appreciate a 1975 Labour Court recommendation that in effect provided the same terms as the ultimate settlement. Since the conclusion of the dispute the National Group Secretary, Chris Kirwan, had been elected Vice-President of the union.

The power of the tanker drivers was broken when the employers sub-contracted their fleets, the drivers becoming owners. The FWUI debated the dispute in great detail, although it had not been directly involved. It acknowledged official ITGWU efforts to settle matters. The General Secretary, Paddy Cardiff, felt that unofficial action was 'extremely dangerous' for 'democratic procedures'. At a meeting of Congress with the Taoiseach and the Minister for Labour he asked that the use of the army be delayed and that the Labour Court investigate. He thought the ITGWU was 'confused' and unable to resolve the issue. The GEC strongly opposed intervention by the army as a 'problem that concerns all unions.' The FWUI refrained from public comment but raised matters continuously in private with Congress.[38]

CIÉ

With CIÉ's 'popularity rating' at 'an all-time low,' the McKinsey Report was published in January 1981. It was all too disappointing and did not address the bias against public enterprise, the under-capitalisation and debt burden of the company, or the lack of imaginative planning. Bill McCamley, a driver, drew attention to bus workers' ill health, resulting from stress and poor conditions. The *Financial Times* claimed that 'stress costs more than strikes.' Bus workers were taken for granted, by company and public alike.

The ITGWU replied to McKinsey, opposing proposed railway closures, not least because they would cost as much as keeping them open for another twenty-five years. It called for further investment in new services, the control of private road haulage and bus operators, and a recognition of public transport as a potential dynamic for economic growth and an essential element in regional development and energy conservation. When, in August, it became known that railway passenger services to Belfast, Cork, Dublin and Limerick would be curtailed, with no freight haulage, there was an 'instant furore'. 'Positive and determined objections' were made to the dismantling of CIÉ. Union multiplicity in the company did not help.

The Minister for Communications, Jim Mitchell, turned the financial screws on CIÉ in June 1983, slashing Budgets and ordering job cuts. Figures showed that the company 'lost' more than £500 million between 1968 and 1982; the projected loss in 1983 was £115 million. The unions disputed these figures by adding in considerations of under-capitalisation, transferred debts and cost-benefit analysis.

Whatever way the sums were done, fierce pressure was put on wages and conditions. Labour Court recommendation 9628 on 23 March 1985 addressed one-person operation on Dublin buses. Labour Court recommendation 9901 in August provided for voluntary implementation with a 33 % bonus, conversion payments, a five-day week within two years, safety measures, income continuance provisions, feeder buses, and a Tribunal to deal with disputes. After initial rejection, CIÉ began to suspend men as they refused to comply. More than 200 members were suspended, resulting in the ITGWU persuading the Court to again intervene, which finally agreed one-person operation, in Dublin at least, with acceptable compensation and a consideration of workers' concerns.

In 1985 CIÉ recorded a profit of £6.7 million. Even industrial relations improved, with a mere nine stoppages, compared with fifteen in 1984 and 31 in 1983. Poor management-worker relations were characterised by 2,343 meetings with unions, Rights Commissioners and the Labour Court in the year. The Transport (Re-Organisation of CIÉ) Act (1986) divided the company into Iarnród Éireann, Bus Átha Cliath and Bus Éireann, with effect from 2 February 1987.[39]

DUBLIN CORPORATION, TARA MINES AND HANLON'S

A Refuse Collectors' strike in Dublin Corporation began on 26 May 1986. An All-Out Picket was quickly awarded but was left in abeyance while an intervention by the Employer-Labour Conference attempted a settlement. It recommended improved basic pay by £5 from 1 May and a further £6 from 16 February 1987, lump sums of £250 to be paid on 26 June for assisting with the rapid clearance of rubbish; and workers to be given flexibility. The terms were recommended by the ITGWU, FWUI and IMETU and accepted by both sides. The army had been called in very rapidly to dispose of refuse, leading to confrontation between pickets and the gardaí and army, most famously in the 'Battle of Moore Street'. The ITGWU reflected that it 'proved to be a very emotive issue and one which we hope not to see repeated in a normal industrial dispute.'[40]

A craftsmen's strike in Tara Mines began on 25 June 1981 and involved 550 members for the rest of the year. The craftsmen sought parity with miners, a problem arising from a plant bonus Agreement of 1976 that left the craftsmen £11 per week worse off. The Minister for Labour, Liam Kavanagh, brought about a settlement in February 1982 that provided additional tool money and tonnage bonuses. Animosity arose as craftsmen got jobs elsewhere or even took short-time contracts abroad while general workers dutifully observed pickets.

In Hanlon's of Longford, ambulance manufacturers, the management rejected a Labour Court recommendation that short-time working, operating since November 1986, continue and remaining work be shared. It argued that quality dropped and customers lost confidence, and wanted a redundancy package. Strike notice expired on 8 May. The owner, Noel Hanlon, immediately sought High Court injunctions to restrict pickets. Attempts at conciliation through Con Murphy, Rights Commissioner, and the local bishop failed. Congress granted an All-Out Picket in an attempt to force a settlement. Pickets were stretched to prevent imported chassis being finished by supervisors and non-Unionists, while the company ran to the Courts in the Republic and Northern Ireland. A final Labour Court recommendation in October provided for recognition of the union and no victimisation on either side, with workers recalled as work built up. It was a nasty dispute, characterised by the employers' intransigence.

Hanlon failed to honour the Agreements entered into. Intervention by the Labour Court produced proposals for thirty-six compulsory redundancies and a payment of £60,000. This was rejected, 131 to 7. Matters deteriorated. Hanlon dug in, introducing a no-strike clause and binding arbitration. On 1 June 1988 the workers made the following appeal:

> Noel, the workers in your Company say emphatically you do not have to move to Liverpool. The enterprise has been built up by the combined efforts of workers and management over the years. Longford needs Hanlons and Hanlons needs Longford. Today the workers call on you to rescind your decision to move to Liverpool and meet with our representatives to negotiate an honourable and fair settlement.

Bishop Colm O'Reilly, Bishop of Ardagh and Clonmacnoise, sought assistance from Albert Reynolds TD, and after intensive negotiations a lengthy proposal emerged that dealt with Hanlon's right to manage, redundancy and recognition. On 7 June it was rejected, 125 to 7.

On 20 June, Hanlon's went into liquidation, with assets of £1.55 million and liabilities of £1.95 million. All outstanding statutory entitlements were referred to the Employment Appeals Tribunal.

There were no victors. It had been a 'withdrawal of capital' and 'managerial suicide' after a confrontation since the autumn of 1986. More than 170 workers finally gained redundancy and minimum notice payments in 1989.[41]

TAX

PAYE protests were vigorously renewed in 1980. The ITGWU pressed General Kitchener into service on a poster suggesting that on 22 January 'YOU SHOULD BE THERE!' Mullen said that increases in oil prices and poor agricultural performance could not justify inequitable taxation. Thousands of tiddlers among the low paid and social welfare recipients were dragged into a tax net that let bigger fish swim blithely through. Foot dragging by Congress would not be tolerated. The ITGWU maintained maximum pressure to move the campaign forward, demonstrating 'political courage'. This remark reflected the fact that tens of thousands marched in protest against Fianna Fáil or Fine Gael actions but then voted for them in successive elections.

No-one predicted the enormity of the demonstrations. More than 700,000 people marched in the largest protest in the country's history. Surely such a torrent of popular protest could not be ignored! The National Understanding had succinctly stated workers' expectations, and Budget Day, 27 February, was seen as Deadline Day. 'Taxation is not only a major instrument of economic management and development. It is a means of redistribution of wealth and income and of financing the state's obligations.' For the ITGWU the 'essential requirement' was the 'achievement of equity as between taxpayers', the reduction of inequalities and the promotion of greater economic efficiency and growth. The time 'had passed for political gimmicks, Commissions of Enquiry or a national debate.' The campaign was not about tax cuts. They had received a massive mandate through street protests.

At a Special Conference on 7 March the ITGWU wanted a speedy conclusion of the work of the Commission on Taxation. It was a classic Government manoeuvre to obfuscate. The union demanded a minimum guarantee of indexation of allowances and bands, bringing farmers, the self-employed and the rich into the tax net, improved and effective anti-evasion measures and a wealth tax.[42]

Predictably, the Budget did not meet workers' demands. It did concede the principle of 'income splitting' between couples for tax purposes, which was welcomed. In January the Murphy case in the Supreme Court determined that the aggregation of married couples' earned income for tax purposes was unconstitutional. In April the Court also decided that, although the Murphys could receive a tax rebate backdated to 1978/9, no-one else could, the fact that they had paid their tax being taken as acceptance that it should have been paid. This penalisation was seen by the ITGWU as 'another slap in the face.' Worse, tax revenue from PAYE workers had risen by 40% over the previous year and accounted for 86% of all income tax paid. The ICTU Co-ordinating Committee was asked to maintain the campaign, 'with whatever action is necessary until the just demands' were met.

In April 1981 the NEC did not approve of members walking off the job to join May Day demonstrations. This 'would be tantamount to unofficial action and would just result in unnecessary loss of earnings.' In addition, given that the right parties—employers and workers—and right subject matter—wages, conditions or employment—were not present, all trade union Executives had problems sanctioning action that was not a trade dispute within the meaning of the Trade Disputes Act (1906). With no immunity, it left union funds open to actions for damages by ill-minded employers.

May Day numbers were 'counted in hundreds rather than thousands.' Carroll complained that the 'reaction on the part of the people in charge of the demonstration' (Dublin Trades Council) had 'left a lot to be desired. Indeed, we were told to get to the end of the parade.' Kennedy thought the marches forced the Government's hand and secured substantial benefits for PAYE workers in the Budget.[43]

In January 1982 Ireland paid the highest taxes within the EEC. The ITGWU felt that the tax marches had 'failed', as 'little has been done to root out . . . parasites' evading their responsibilities. In July the NEC expressed 'grave reservations' about the report of the Commission on Taxation. Its 'dominant philosophy' was the 'abolition of progressive rates of income tax,' strong measures in favour of the accumulation of private capital, and a reduction in employers' PRSI contribution and business taxes. It demanded that the Government 'ensure that all sectors of the community are treated equally.'

Speaker after speaker at the Delegate Conference rose in support of reform. Proposals for a single low rate of tax on all incomes were radical, but expenditure taxes were 'unworkable', and many inequities remained. Capitalists did well in the suggested reforms: there was no wealth tax and reduced company taxes. The ITGWU was disappointed if not surprised: the Commission's political purpose had been well served.

Extensive cuts in public-sector spending, announced on 30 July, underlined the failure, as the Government attempted to renege on commitments on pubic-sector pay. At the Delegate Conference there was exasperation with marches. Members demanded 'action not more colourful parades.'

From March 1983 the ITGWU fought a 'major campaign' against the 'Fine Gael-Labour Government's Finance Bill', on three fronts: 'in Leinster House, among the general public and in industry.' Amendments were moved in Dáil and Seanad by Michael Bell TD and Senator Chris Kirwan; tens of thousands of leaflets supported a nationwide lobby of TDs and Councillors; and there were 'work stoppages and overtime bans.' A half-day stoppage on 13 April was a 'powerful expression' of workers' 'anger and dissatisfaction.' The ITGWU parted from the softer ICTU line and gave leadership to members, and many more besides, in stepping up pressure on the Government. At the Annual Conference John Dwan (Waterford) reminded all of the ten-point demand for the protection of living standards. He wanted leaflets and notes, local Conferences, national debates led by General Officers, a 'definite hit list' instead of the vague 'more jobs', and a discussion of all policy options for resisting redundancies, closures and general job loss. The most popular slogan was 'Tax the Greedy, Not the Needy', its obvious appeal creating confusion. Many undoubtedly marched for tax cuts rather than tax reform.[44]

In 1986 the NEC reviewed the union's 'most outspoken' advocacy, especially since 1982, and condemned another Budget for its failure to provide tax reform. It called on the Coalition Government 'to submit itself to the electorate' for 'an assessment and evaluation of its office.' Kirwan put it simply: 'Let the people decide!' Many wanted stoppages weekly, to be stepped up 'in frequency and duration until equity is achieved.'

The 1985 campaign left much to be desired, with many leaflets and special editions of *Liberty News* 'never seeing the light of day.' Carroll asked, 'So how do we articulate national policy?' He suggested that the whole debate be written up and circulated to Branches to bring everything back to a Special Conference in November. They could decide on a 'national ballot vote for either Sectional strikes, area strikes, national strikes, industrial strikes, geographical strikes, daily strikes, weekly strikes, ongoing strikes, or a total national strike.' The Conference agreed. 57,683 members voted in the ensuing ballot, 28,484 (49.2%) voting for 'Option A: continue to press for tax equity and job creation by representations to the Government and the lobbying of political parties; and urge similar actions by the ICTU.' As the vote was spread evenly over the four alternative proposals, this was perhaps not quite the outright rejection of direct action that it seemed.

Meanwhile the ITGWU produced figures showing that the 'level of PAYE/PRSI burden as% of married workers on average male industrial wages with two children' had risen from 18½% in March 1979 to 27% in March 1987. A tax amnesty in 1988 brought a windfall of £500 million for the Revenue Commissioners but angered workers, who felt that prosecutions, fines and interest for tax-dodgers would be more appropriate. Carroll attempted to assuage members by pointing out that Congress consistently put their case to the Government, both through the Programme for National Recovery and pre-Budget submissions. Albert Reynolds's 1989 Budget signalled '(Big) Business as Usual.' An 'alternative Budget', drafted by Dick Spring and Barry Desmond, observed that after two years in office Fianna Fáil had sacked 4,000 health workers and closed 4,000 hospital public beds, almost bankrupted the VHI, abolished farm tax, froze child benefit, abolished local services, got rid of 2,500 teachers and attacked free education, cut social welfare and abused the National Lottery. After a decade of protests about tax equity, this was a sorry record.[45]

THE COMMISSION ON INDUSTRIAL RELATIONS

In 1979 the ITGWU gave a 'broad welcome' to the Commission on Industrial Relations. Its primary task should be 'defining the proper collective bargaining framework' and 'drawing up proposed guidelines for good industrial relations,' rather than indulging right-wing cries for the curtailment of union rights. Mullen warned against 'any attempt to improve our system of industrial relations by restrictive legal intervention.' Industrial relations problems did not stem from inadequacies in law but from workers' 'frustration and sense of injustice.' The 'get-rich-quick' mentality was the root cause, compounded by media misrepresentation of unions.

Mullen asked, 'What happened to all our proposals for improving collective bargaining practice? Why have we still not achieved our demand for access to RTÉ for trade union programmes to provide insight and information . . . related to the world of work?' Why did children leave school with 'absolutely no concept' of 'how to participate in democratic decision making?' Why was paid time off for adults to improve their education so slow in being granted? Why was industrial democracy and access to company information blocked at every turn? Why had the Labour Court not been reformed, or the Conciliation Service improved? Such questions merely generated 'reactionary' responses.

When the Government refused to amend the Trade Disputes Act (1906) to extend the right to strike to the public service the ICTU withdrew from the Commission on Industrial Relations, thus contributing to its lack of impact. Unions greeted the Report of the Commission in near-silence. The 'main thrust' was 'an attempt to hamstring' the movement 'still further', with suggestions that 'legal immunity' be withdrawn in unfair dismissal, redundancy, employment equality and equal pay claims. There was no mention of the abuse of injunctions nor a reproach for Lock-Outs by employers. The NEC condemned employers' increasing resort to law and underlined the value of the voluntary character of industrial relations that had, generally, served all sides well. It would be a foolish Minister who would attempt to act on 'such a one-sided and unbalanced document.' So it proved.[46]

The Payment of Wages Act (1980) permitted payment by cheque or other non-cash methods. The Truck Acts (1831 to 1896) obliged employers to pay workers in 'coin of the realm' and forbade certain deductions to prevent unscrupulous employers exploiting workers. Security concerns, the extension of personal banking and the development of non-cash money transfers led to demands by employers for repeal of the Truck Acts' restrictions. Unions approved but insisted on voluntary measures to enable workers to opt for non-cash payment. One problem, particularly in rural communities, was that cashing cheques allowed shopkeepers, publicans or others to know what people earned—or, worse, opened up the possibility of spouses finding out!

In May 1980 the ITGWU published *Labour Law in Ireland* by Naomi Wayne, an ITGWU tutor, which made an outstanding contribution as negotiating aid and training manual. (Officials regularly saw the book consulted on the other side of the table.) In 1982 there was extensive criticism of the Unfair Dismissals Act (1977).

Increasingly it had become a licence for employers to dismiss workers cheaply and avoid industrial action. In December the ITGWU publicised an EEC directive providing rights for part-time workers. Virtually all labour law applied only to those working more that 18 to 21 hours per week, thus excluding thousands of part-timers, especially women.

In 1985 the proposals of the Minister for Labour, Ruairí Quinn, for reforms in industrial relations and trade union law were an invitation 'to move into the unknown.' 'Strike rights instead of immunities' were on offer. The ITGWU feared that changes could 'provide many feast days for the Irish legal fraternity' and establish the 'most restrictive and objectionable industrial disputes case law.' They did not doubt Quinn's sincerity, but 'nobody gives us nothing for nothing.'

As recession bit deeper there were countless requests for improvements in redundancy legislation and a reform of insolvency law to allow workers receive money owed, statutory entitlements and contributions to pension schemes. In 1987 Carroll quoted from the International Confederation of Free Trade Unions Annual Survey of Violations of Trade Union Rights, cataloguing global 'abuses, harassments, denial of negotiation rights, spancelling of trade union freedoms and so on.' It was not confined to 'Third World' or 'dictator-led' countries but was an increasing feature of western Europe. Thatcher was gleefully mowing down long-established union rights. He warned that 'we must remain very vigilant' while being prepared to adapt to 'today's scene and tomorrow's reality.' He indicated what was in store: growing aggression by employers; the decentralisation of wage bargaining; 'flexibility' to cover a multitude of changes in manning levels, work loads, job descriptions, flexible time, sabbaticals, etc.; changes in the organisation of work so that 'teamwork' replaced hierarchical control by supervisors and foremen, exploiting company loyalty against unions; the growth of temporary, part-time and contract work; and the influence of Japanese industrial relations, with house associations or non-union equivalent.[47] 'No-strike Agreements' were increasingly sought. Carroll preferred 'peace Agreements' but suggested that they demanded 'trust and belief and openness' and 'full disclosure of information and participation in decision-making.'

The decline in conciliation settlements—49% in 1979—increasingly turned the Labour Court into a process of first resort rather than last resort. The Court hit back at criticisms that it was very restrictive in its interpretation of National Wage Agreements. They were accepted voluntarily by employers and unions: was it not reasonable to apply them to the letter? Clause 4 of the National Understanding, however, was a step too far. The Court described it as 'totally, unnecessarily and harmfully restrictive.' It was 'small wonder' that this report of the Labour Court received little publicity. The Government and employers were angered by the remarks.

In 1988 it was proposed that the Labour Relations Commission would separate conciliation from the Labour Court. Some feared this would undermine the Court's authority. Dublin No. 2 Branch called on Congress to establish a Working Party to examine the Labour Court's shortcomings of inordinate delays, lack of staffing, general conservatism of decisions and poor record on legal entitlements, particularly equal pay. Little had changed; but the imminent creation of the Labour Relations Commission overrode matters.

An interesting dichotomy revealed at Annual Conferences was that members who wanted little or nothing to do with trade union or industrial relations law were increasingly content to turn to law on matters of employment rights.[48]

EMPLOYMENT

In 1980 the ITGWU adopted 'Economic and Social Policy', the product of question-naires and consultation throughout the union. It demanded access to economic decision-making at the work-place, industrial and national level. Promised National Understanding sectoral Committees had not been created. Employment-creation targets of 25,000 jobs per year seemed unattainable. Thousands of clothing and textile workers marched in Dublin in July to protest against cheap imports, job losses and the absence of Government policy. The ITGWU called for the expansion of state enterprise and the fullest possible development of natural resources, on land, underground and offshore.

In September the Republic faced its 'most difficult economic situation ever.' The ITGWU mounted its annual 'GUARANTEED IRISH UNION LABOUR' campaign, while accepting that membership of the EEC prohibited isolationist policies or tariff barriers. Workers were encouraged to push for greater 'added value', quality production and higher efficiency—new and challenging demands. The logic was 'if we work for improvements within the collective bargaining system' we 'can proceed to advocate with more credibility our defence of the public sector, our opposition to legal intervention in the collective bargaining system and our genuine commitment to policies of full employment.'

On Christmas Eve the Government abandoned plans for a smelter to process Irish ore. The NEC attacked 'creeping Thatcherism' in February 1981 as uncertainty sur-rounded CIÉ, Comhlucht Siúicre Éireann and Ceimicí Teoranta. It demanded vibrant investment through the promised National Enterprise Agency. The Telesis Report on industrial policy 'nailed' Government failures, especially in Dublin. The culprit was not the IDA—'the most dynamic, active and effective marketing agency in the world market'—but the absence of strategy. The ITGWU sought redrafting of the Multi-Fibre Agreement, an end to foreign dumping, and strategic plans for Regions, such as Derry-Donegal and Dublin, where further job losses were predictable.

Industrial Group Secretaries reported endless rationalisation, redundancies and short-time working as manufacturing was swamped by global recession. Unemployment reached 125,000, or 11%, in February, the highest in the EEC. By April it was 'evident' that 'all traditional approaches to job creation' had failed. Radical new thinking was needed. The ITGWU mounted an 'intense campaign' to keep Tuam sugar factory open. The Government announced a stay of execution in September, but this fell far short of a constructive plan for Tuam or the company, adding further evidence to the Telesis fuel. The Government was asked to declare a national emergency.

The FUE demanded that manufacturing be kept in private hands, despite the constant failure of private enterprise. Worse, the state had 'been forced to prop up' industry 'with a variety of grants, allowances and subsidies' while denying the public sector 'the opportunity to engage in profitable and productive industrial enterprise.' Successive Conferences demanded tax penalties on speculation, the abolition of tax loopholes and 'full public control of the banks and financial institutions.' Tax reform was central to the rarely debated alternatives to demands from the Confederation of Irish Industry, the FUE and the media. The CII insisted that state companies should be made to meet 'straightforward commercial criteria,' demonstrating a capacity for black humour: 'while they rant and rave about Government subsidies to State companies' they ignored the £500 million given to the private sector in 1981 alone. For the CII there was 'one rule for the public sector and another for the private sector.' The ITGWU demanded that the Department of Economic Planning and Development be re-established, to draw up a plan that the Tripartite Committee on Employment—provided for under the National Understanding—could respond to.

In 1982 Fianna Fáil and Fine Gael both produced 'plans', 'The Way Forward' and 'Jobs in the Eighties', which were 'waved up and down' during what appeared to be a continuous election. Union voices were in the wilderness. The 'well-deserved victory' for Avoca miners, heralded in January 1983, was three weeks' pay for every year of service rather than statutory redundancy, and this rather than their jobs. Such was the climate of despondency. The crisis was so deep that emergency responses were needed. The ITGWU wanted investment in agriculture, beef production, boatbuilding, clothing, offshore oil and gas, tourism and construction and an effective application of the 1% PRSI and youth levies or their abolition. Congress imposed a ½p a week levy to finance Centres for the Unemployed, the first one opening in Finglas, Dublin, in February.

On 15 June construction unions called a Day of Action to demand increased capital spending and 30,000 local authority houses. Wicklow Branches mounted 'ACTION'—Arklow Campaign to Industrialise our Neighbourhood—to combat the 'catastrophic job losses', producing a promotional booklet for prospective industrialists. The closure of Avoca Mines, Nítrigin Éireann, Noritake, Shanks and Nuplast brought 2,000 redundancies to a town of 8,500 people.

In 1984 John McDonnell (Mallow) called for an Agricultural Development Authority to maximise export income and the job potential of food production. Kings Wear Workers' Co-operative was founded in Naas by workers made redundant on 24 January 1983. British trade union pressure to ban imports had ironically triggered the original closure. Norman Croke, Secretary of the Kildare Branch, urged a New Year's resolution: 'When you think of work wear, think Kings Wear—and show our British comrades that we too can Buy National by Buying Irish.'

The Planning Board, 'always viewed with healthy scepticism' by unions, simply 'repeated the same tired old clichés on wages and competitiveness' in April, ignoring the Economic and Social Research Institute's 'very positive attitude to the job-creation potential of the public sector.' If low wages really were the key, how did 'Professor Ryan and his colleagues' explain the success of high-wage economies, such as Germany? The board produced a 'rag-bag of half-promises.'

The *White Paper on Industrial Policy,* published in July, and *Building on Reality,* 1985–1987, were both dismissed as useless, simply reaffirming Government props for the failed private sector. The organisation Socialist Economists, in *Jobs and Wages: The True Story of Competition,* showed that design, quality, marketing and punctual supply were far more significant in international competition than wage costs. They argued for moving from 'low-wage economy' thinking—where Ireland could never compete with Third World rates—to high value-added production. Wage militancy was rejected in favour of improved levels of workers' participation and the encouragement of innovation, new technology, diversification and investment in research and development—all relatively new concepts for trade unionists.

Congress produced *Confronting the Jobs Crisis: The Framework for a National Plan.* It proposed a rolling four or five-year plan, with active worker-management Sectoral Committees, overseen by a Department of Economics and Social Planning—not Finance. Linkages between foreign and home enterprise would be encouraged, with a state construction company, extensive afforestation, support for co-operatives, and inter-relationship between pay, tax, social services, education and health. The NEC demanded 'urgent and emergency corrective measures' in 1985, part of a lengthy, if understandably repetitive, debate, and published its own views, 'Unemployment: The Trade Union Alternative'. Employment in manufacturing fell from 230,500 in December 1979 to 186,300 in September 1985, a loss of 44,200 jobs.

From September 1985 to the Budget in January 1986 the ITGWU campaigned through protest meetings, leaflets, circulars and a special edition of *Liberty News* as well as by writing to every TD and Councillor. Thousands participated, but the union acknowledged that 'we would be deluding ourselves' if we though it a 'resounding success.'

In Cork in December Carroll told an audience of 5,000 that 'if the Government does not change its policies, we will work to change the Government.' The Government, however, was safe in the knowledge that sufficient turkeys could be guaranteed to again vote for Christmas.

After rejecting the Budget, the ITGWU and ICTU sent a joint public letter to the Taoiseach. 'On behalf of the trade unionists, the unemployed and the PAYE tax payers of Ireland, we call on your Government to take immediate action' to 'end the scourge of mass unemployment . . . reform the taxation system' to ensure equity of contribution and collection and 'ensure that social welfare benefits . . . at least keep pace with the rate of inflation . . . We demand jobs—not excuses! We demand tax reform—not promises!'

RTÉ stymied the campaign by refusing to carry ITGWU advertisements on radio or television: it could broadcast nothing 'directed towards any political end.' As sadly predicted, unemployment exceeded 250,000 by December 1986. Even that figure was moderated by rising emigration. The Government was content to 'explain away the jobs crisis rather than tackling it.' Union anger rose. Some explanation was found in international factors, but from December 1979 to December 1986 unemployment rose from 88,600 to 250,200. Comparison with other European countries showed how poor Irish responses were.

Nothing illustrated the problem better than the drop in manufacturing employment, from 230,500 in December 1979 to 185,700 in September 1986, a fall described by the National Economic and Social Council as being 'the result of the type of industrial . . . policies pursued rather than the product of any set of immutable historical forces.' The ITGWU rejected the 'metaphysical' or 'meteorological' schools of economics that talked of a 'climate for investment' or 'spirit of enterprise.' NESC agreed that the state had to play a more active role, 'which is what the Union has been advocating for years.' Ray MacSharry's Budget was dismissed by *Liberty News*: 'No Ray of Hope!' Carroll saw it as 'anti-employment.'

Table 123: Comparative unemployment rates in Europe (percentage of civilian working population), 1979–86

	Dec. 1979	*Dec. 1986*
Luxembourg	0.8	1.7
Federal Republic of Germany	3.3	8.1
Denmark	5.5	8.2
France	6.5	11.5
United Kingdom	5.2	11.9
Netherlands	4.2	12.3
Belgium	9.1	13.0
Italy	7.8	13.9
Ireland (Republic)	7.8	19.5

Source: ITGWU, Annual Report for 1986, p. 39.

In 1987 the NEC gave £1,000 to each of the eleven ICTU Centres for the Unemployed. In 1988 the Delegate Conference called for the maximum return from the Programme for National Recovery in reducing working hours, developing equality, stamping out the black economy, defending the public sector and reversing cuts. Much understandable scepticism was evinced, but Browne expressed pride in the Agreement, which had secured much of the ITGWU's recent mandate. It was something that had 'not been repeated' elsewhere. The British movement had not 'even come close to realising' it.

Éamonn Gilmore (Professional and Managerial Branch) wanted to 'disturb the national silence on emigration' as between 30,000 and 35,000 people left the country every year—the equivalent of the city of Galway disappearing—many illegally to the United States. The Economic and Social Research Institute estimated that between 1983 and 1992 some 250,000 left, with all the consequent family heartache and loss of able people to economy and society. In 1988 green shoots of recovery were visible and unemployment fell slightly, by 6,000. MacSharry's Budget was another immense disappointment, the Programme for National Recovery having raised expectations. At least Congress now had direct avenues through which to seek change.

Dissatisfaction with job creation under the Programme for National Recovery led Carroll to suggest that Congress's role might be reviewed. Pay moderation had not yet translated into new employment, despite the windfall from a £500 million tax amnesty. In 1989 the Athlone, Galway, Letterkenny and Mayo Branches all called for withdrawal from talks to replace the Programme for National Recovery unless job targets were realised. Such strength of feeling was understandable.[49]

DEFENDING THE PUBLIC SECTOR

Attacks on the public sector reached fever pitch in the mid-1980s. Browne attacked the New Right's importing of monetarism and Thatcherism, noting that twenty-one state-sponsored bodies employed '80,000 people with capital employed of £6.6 billion and a turnover of £3.9 billion.' The ICTU's document 'What Must Be Done: A Charter for Progress' demanded proper funding for public enterprises with their social obligations truly costed, additional funding from equity rather than foreign borrowing, all state incentives for private enterprise to be equally available to public enterprise, no doctrinaire restrictions on the right of public enterprise to compete nor obligations to purchase at uneconomic prices from the private sector, no more 'political hacks' on boards, the creation of joint Management-Union Committees to develop planning, the dismissal of managements or directors known to be hostile to public enterprise, an end to civil service and political interference, the expansion of public enterprise into natural resources and new technology, chemicals and pharmaceuticals, forestry and food production, and the development of international services. The Congress study 'Public Enterprise—Everybody's Business' was a fount of data and ideas and countered the poison pumped out by the media that was deep-rooted and difficult to eradicate. The Government 'decision to delete the trade union labour clause from public contracts' was 'a direct incentive to tax dodging, lumping and social welfare abuse.' Many were 'driven into the Black Economy' while the Government ignored the 'long-standing recommendations of the sectoral development report' on construction. EEC competition rules made implementation difficult, but the absence of political will was the key.

1987 was 'the year that monetarism came to Ireland with a vengeance,' severely affecting the ITGWU, half of whose members were in the public service or state-sponsored enterprises. A voluntary redundancy package, 'Government Proposals for Redeployment', effectually terminated public service workers' 'security of tenure.' The elimination of An Foras Forbartha and the Health Education Bureau and the attempted elimination of the National Social Services Board revealed the

Government's ruthlessness. Fianna Fáil campaigned on the slogan 'Health cuts hurt the old, the sick and the handicapped' and then callously proved the point. There were meetings, pickets and street protests led by nurses in uniform. Many protesters, however, had voted for Fianna Fáil and blindly would again. The quest was for 10,000 redundancies, although where this number was plucked from was never explained.

In November 1986 the Secretary of the Department of Finance, addressing a Conference of the Institute of Public Administration on 'Managing Public Money', said: 'I have no great faith in rationalistic approaches to expenditure control . . . devoting much time and effort to management techniques . . . is only a distraction.' Such breathtaking comment suggested that the inmates were running the asylum. It explained why well-considered, detailed and costed union policies made such little impression on those whose concept of policy creation consisted of blindfolded Officials attempting to pin tails on donkeys. The human costs were extreme, particularly in health. Fianna Fáil's 'U-turn on its health manifesto' became 'a by-word for political dishonesty.' It led to unprecedented unity in the Alliance of Health Service Unions from May 1987. Only the Irish Medical Organisation remained aloof, though many doctors participated individually.

In January 1986 the closure of eight hospitals was announced, with proposals to cut nurses' pay. More than 1,000 temporary nurses lost their jobs. The 1987 Budget left all health boards compelled to make cuts. On 1 April the most severe cuts yet were announced: between March and December fourteen hospitals and 1,470 beds were closed. The Dublin Nursing Branch recruited 200 new members. The Alliance of Health Service Unions held large demonstrations on 21 May with demands for workers' involvement in a 'Plan for Health'. The Minister talked of 2,000 jobs to go. A national day of protest followed on 24 June with rallies in Cork, Dublin, Galway, Letterkenny, Limerick, Sligo, Tralee and Tullamore, most led by the ITGWU. Support came through Trades Councils, the ESB and the Construction and Local Authority Groups of Unions as well the public. Three AHSU demands were put to the Department, the management claiming inability to do anything: no further dis-employment until there is progress in discussions, changes to time-scales that would maximise the protection of services, and no unilateral suspension of exist-ing Agreements. Simultaneously, talks on what became the Programme for National Recovery began.

On 16 July a package was announced for Dublin and the Western Health Board, but the management was unable to deliver it: the Department of Finance dictated to the Department of Health. Cut-backs continued, and the seeds of a health crisis that would continue into the next century were sown.

The lesson of the Alliance of Health Service Unions was that unity was vital. Inter-union rivalry was pointless and counter-productive. The ITGWU felt that the AHSU failed to realise 'one of its primary objectives which was to forge links with community organisations concerned with the delivery of a quality health service.' Two thousand beds were lost. Unions dealt with individual claims for reallocation and early retirement. The payments were not unattractive to many temporary and casual workers; and local managements—often members of AHSU unions—in panic applied considerable pressure to entice such workers—also AHSU members— to take the bait. The ITGWU ruefully acknowledged that, 'as calculated by Government,' the AHSU 'could not sustain the public protests.' It was a cleft stick for the unions: leading a campaign against cuts on the one hand, servicing genuine fears and demands from members facing job loss, reallocation, transfer and general uncertainty on the other. Privately, ITGWU Officials commented on the built-in sectionalism (based on grade, profession, institution or geographical location) and the hierarchical thinking within health unions. The AHSU had been a loose alliance, not the makings of an industrial union, wherein lay the dilemma for realising long-term ITGWU demands for a health service free at the point of use.

A further difficulty was the Irish Nurses' Organisation, which negotiated rates of pay for student nurses £1,000 below agreed rates. This was 'bad enough,' but 'it was done without the courtesy of even advising' the ITGWU. Relations deteriorated and, 'even by the standards of recent years, became very bad.'

In 1988 Browne protested about the continuing attacks on the public sector, resolving to oppose privatisation and contracting out. Dublin No. 7 Branch led the opposition to local charges, although the union wanted more funding for local Government. In 1989 the development of 'autonomous work groups' in Bord na Móna was viewed with alarm.[50]

EUROPE

The European Trade Union Confederation met in parallel with the EEC Council of Ministers in Dublin on 29–30 November 1979. It expressed disappointment at the Council's failure to grasp the nettle regarding employment. The ITGWU backed the demands of the ETUC for the maintenance of workers' spending power, increases for the low-paid, the protection of acquired rights, investment programmes to generate employment and the development of communal services and facilities, especially through increased Regional Funds.

In 1983 John Meehan (Castlebar No. 1) moved that Ireland negotiate withdrawal from the EEC. Views were mixed, although experience since membership confirmed the ITGWU's position that it was a 'rich men's club.' Éamonn Gilmore won the day, accepting that an acceptance by referendum by 80% against 20% would be hard to overturn, and efforts might be better spent seeking to give direction to more pro-gressive policies. While the ITGWU's misgivings continued, increasingly attention turned to Europe for labour law and enlightened social policy. In 1987, however, the ITGWU worried that right-wing propaganda was heralding the Single European Act as the answer to all problems. The Irish member of the European Commission, Peter Sutherland, and 'other apologists' were 'skilfully playing down' possible adverse effects of the harmonisation of indirect taxes on living standards, not least through the application of value-added tax to food. Through the European Trade Union Confederation the ITGWU fought for the promised 'social Europe.' As to the

Single European Act, members were urged, 'For jobs' sake—vote No!' The union hoped for renegotiation on terms more favourable to Ireland. The old Citizen Army slogan of 1914, 'We Serve Neither King Nor Kaiser—But Ireland,' was resurrected to remind members that union policy was to support neutrality 'as an instrument for promoting world peace and ending the arms race,' opposing military alliances such as NATO. A detailed set of answers to questions posed was published in a 'Vote No!' edition of *Liberty News*.

In Tralee 1989 Carroll asked about Europe after 1992: what were the implications for jobs and industrial policy? Could structural reforms, reforms in the Common Agricultural Policy and industrial policy solve the jobs crisis? What would happen to state aids to industry, and would the harmonisation of indirect taxes push up food prices? Did international trade unionism need to be developed?[51] Answers were not provided, and great uncertainty awaited SIPTU.

NEW TECHNOLOGY

Concerns over 'new technology' surfaced in 1980. Dublin District Council, 'although not opposed,' wanted to minimise its impact on jobs by reducing working hours, increasing holidays and providing greater release for further education. The Professional and Managerial Branch thought that without union involvement new technology would be 'disruptive and divisive.' Protections against downgrading and de-skilling, the maintenance of working conditions, in-service training and the maximum distribution of benefits and savings accruing were sought.

In 1981 Pat Rabbitte chaired a New Technology Committee. Technology was necessary to uplift the industrial skills base, but adequate information in advance, full consultation and Agreement and a guarantee of job security were preconditions for change. Paid educational leave, the adequacy and duration of weekly payments rather than lump sums for redundancy, health and safety issues, productivity increases to create shorter working hours and the regular monitoring of impact and consequences were called for. The NEC proposed a Council on New Technology, comprising representatives of the Government and the social partners, to properly manage the application of information technology.[52]

SOCIAL POLICY

The ITGWU honed its social policy at a Conference on 7 March 1980. It called for twice-yearly adjustments in social welfare payments, taking account of the Consumer Price Index; a national income-related pension scheme; differentials between long-term and short-term benefits to be eliminated; and a comprehensive health scheme without income limitation. The ITGWU supported Willie Bermingham's charity 'Alone', lobbying Dublin City Council and the Eastern Health Board. The Social Welfare (Pay-Related Benefit) Regulations (1979) entitled striking workers to have their insurance contributions credited for the duration of any strike. If claims were not made, payments would be reduced, because 'average weekly earnings'—used for calculating entitlement in the period of any subsequent claim—would be reduced. These new regulations were broadcast to members. There was no evidence that 'credit' provisions contributed in any way to levels of strike activity.

'Without further delay' the ITGWU wanted the National Pension Scheme outlined in the Green Paper. Éamon Thornton (Dublin No. 7) called for the provision of child care and nursery schooling, to accommodate the ever-growing number of working mothers and to address inequities in access to education. An increased income limit for hospital services to £7,000 provided in the National Understanding was seen as an advance, although there was widespread evidence of misinformation by hospitals to those on incomes between £5,500 and £7,000 to secure the unnecessary payment of consultants' fees. The social welfare system was seen as one that 'degrades'. It needed complete overhaul.

'Poverty and Social Policy', an Irish contribution to an EEC survey, was launched in January 1982. It revealed that one household in four—approximately 600,000 people—existed below the poverty line. The ESRI's publication *Economic and Social Circumstances of the Elderly in Ireland* demonstrated how chronic poverty was among older people. It was the 'Year of the Aged', but the absence of Government policy or concern was such that most people could 'scarcely have been aware of the fact.'

There were constant stories of 'social welfare abuse'. Garret FitzGerald claimed that 'up to £70 million per annum was being fiddled through false claims,' headline-making stuff. Refutations scarcely got coverage. There was clever distortion of figures produced in Gerry Hughes's ESRI report, *Social Insurance and Absence from Work*, and, although the ITGWU was 'to the forefront of efforts to counter such anti-welfare propaganda,' public opinion bought the pup. This 'undoubtedly facilitated general acceptance of savage social welfare cut-backs which were to become a feature of 1983.'

One advance was made. Under Section 35 of the Social Welfare Act (1981) the payment of benefit to those on strike was automatically disallowed. During a prolonged strike in Clover Meats, Waterford, this was challenged. Workers were unemployed because 'they found themselves unable to agree to management rationalisation proposals that they saw as totally unacceptable.' At the end of the dispute Paddy Gallagher TD (Workers' Party) secured the payment of disallowed benefits and a commitment from the Government that the law would be amended.

The Minister for Health and Social Welfare, Michael Woods, delayed, but a similar case in Comer Yarns, Kilkenny, put him back under pressure. A Bill was introduced that was fought, line by line, by Fine Gael, clearly influenced by the FUE. The Social Welfare (No. 2) Act (1982) provided for a Social Welfare Tribunal. On 31 December 1982 the Tribunal's first recommendation was in favour of Comer Yarns workers, a 'success story' in which 'members and Officials played an important part.' Although it was an official strike, the company was deemed to have acted unfairly by imposing different conditions and refusing to reopen until a new package was accepted. The workers had been unreasonably deprived of their employment from mid-March to June 1982 and were entitled to full Unemployment Benefit or Assistance. After ten months, perseverance paid off. Despite this, the ITGWU still regarded Social Welfare Appeals as 'very rough justice.'[53]

In February 1984 the ITGWU made a detailed submission to the Commission on Social Welfare, arguing for the integration of tax and social welfare to provide everyone with a guaranteed minimum income. Such 'individualisation' would remove 'adult dependence.' At a time when society 'most needed an expansion of social services' they were being restricted or dismantled. The ITGWU attempted to play a positive role, locally and nationally, 'in resisting such negative developments,' but the 'cuts mentality' proved pervasive.

The Commission on Social Welfare reported in 1986. It was set aside as political parties prepared for an election. The ITGWU submission addressed the whole system, identifying its failure to tackle the causes of poverty and to protect people from its effects, 'its almost incredible complexity,' its inequities, the persistence of widespread sex discrimination, the 'lack of respect for claimants' dignity' and the scope and method of funding, 'which was not always seen as fair.' It wanted greater equity, simplification, greater efficiency and humanisation; additional payments for the special needs of handicap and disability; improved child support; better pay-related benefits, including a national income-related pension scheme; the extension of PRSI to all employers and the self-employed; the removal of all forms of discrimination; improvements in supplementary welfare; and an urgent reform of appeals structures. The union responded to the report's sixty-five recommendations, supporting the improvement of basic payments, the inadequacy of family supports, broadening the social insurance base and improving provision. Disappointment was expressed at the rejection of 'our long-term approach.' By the end of the year there was little official response.

Another milestone was the establishment of the 'long-awaited' National Pensions Board. Congress made a significant contribution to its work, much of it drawn from the work of Rosheen Callender, ITGWU Research Officer. EEC obligations to provide equal treatment in social welfare were more or less resolved by November, under constant pressure from unions and community groups.

A 'comprehensive health service free at the point of delivery' was again demanded in 1987. The Delegate Conference deplored the savage health cuts and opposed the growing 'two-tier' system. The 'largest union in the health service' was urged to campaign through 'industrial action and where appropriate the democratic process' to gain maximum public support. The NEC condemned the Government and demanded the 'extension of the Second Programme to combat poverty and illiteracy,' equal opportunities for women and equality in education, implementation of the EEC action programme on education and training for new technology, social integration of the handicapped, the provision of 'positive and progressive action on health and safety,' an improved awareness and treatment for cancer, a 'social welfare and health code just and humane in all its aspects' and a 'comprehensive education programme on AIDS.' Kirwan said that the ITGWU would frame a 'Charter for Social Progress', around which unions could lobby; in the short term it needed to be a 'Charter for Social Defence'. There had been 'a return to the Victorian values of the workhouse—so beloved of Margaret Thatcher.'

Disagreement between Fine Gael and the Labour Party over cuts led to an election and the return of a minority Fianna Fáil Government. Its promised 'better way' was even more savage cuts. The Programme for National Recovery provided for 'greater social equity in terms of access to social benefits and to health and education services.' The value of social welfare payments would be maintained, with increases for the lowest income groups; PRSI for the self-employed would be introduced by 1988; and there would be changes in the appeals systems, upward adjustments in family income supplements and closer liaison with voluntary organisations. Given that 1.3 million people depended wholly or partly on social welfare, the constraining hand on cuts placed by the Programme for National Recovery cannot be underestimated.

Another 30,000 people abandoned ship through emigration; but at least now there was some receptacle for union policies other than wastepaper bins. In Irish Country Bacon Ltd in Roosky, Co. Roscommon, 210 workers won an important victory at the Social Welfare Tribunal when, after a stoppage from January to March, the Tribunal recognised that 'employers have a responsibility to avoid unnecessary work stoppages' by conforming to 'good industrial relations principles.' All Unemployment Benefit or Assistance for the period was paid. Participation in Government by the Progressive Democrats heralded the 'unequivocal advocacy of the politics of the New Right.'

In 1988 the Combat Poverty Agency 'revealed a range and depth of poverty that was alarming, undeniable' and 'had to be taken seriously': more than a third of the population existed below 'objective' poverty limits. Its conclusions were not earth-shattering: the unemployed were among the poorest; social welfare payments were inadequate, especially for long-term recipients, the aged and handicapped; low pay affected family health, access to education and living standards; poverty traps existed throughout the system; whatever about fraud, the non-take-up of benefits was extremely widespread because of lack of information, social stigma and difficulties in gaining access to benefit; women, especially single mothers, were at the bottom of most scales; and delivery left much to be desired.

In 1989 Carroll listed the ITGWU's economic and social aspirations, which should govern social relations in any decent society: the right of the unemployed to jobs; the right of school-leavers to the opportunity to develop their potential by training and career opportunities; the right of those on social welfare to an adequate level of subsistence; the right of the physically and mentally handicapped to equality of treatment with all other citizens; the right of the underprivileged to the full dignity of first-class citizenship; the right of women to have their role in all aspects of society fully respected, acknowledged and applied; the right of children to freedom from discrimination arising from matters of birth and social status; and the right of all citizens to combine in the creation of a just society. These were goals they 'would bring into SIPTU.' They were goals that few disagreed with but that many never voted for.[54]

WORKER PARTICIPATION

A Department of Labour discussion paper on workers' participation was issued in March 1980. It stressed the need for consensus. Suggestions for one-tier and two-tier systems, works councils, relations between any participation structures and existing industrial relations models and financial information and exchange were welcomed. The ITGWU felt that 'the risk of institutions being imposed in conformity with EEC Directives' would have to be realised 'before any serious advance will be made.' Lack of understanding and concerns about how it would affect traditional union practices were as great an impediment to progress as employers' fears: the Minister 'may be a long time waiting for "consensus" to break out.' As powerful vested interests bleated for 'wage restraint' in the Twentieth Round, the ITGWU pointed out that the EEC Fourth Directive on company law reform and disclosure should have been implemented in Irish law by 25 July 1980. Not even a Bill was published by August, as unions were lectured 'about reason, restraint and responsibility.' Companies operated behind a veil of secrecy, with no obligations to workers or the public, while simultaneously accepting massive state aid, direct and indirect, and constantly demanding more. The only thing missing from the ITGWU case was any degree of surprise.

Tony Tobin, locomotive driver, and Tony Flynn, Dublin bus conductor, were among the first four Worker-Directors elected to the Board of CIÉ under the Worker Participation (State Enterprises) Act (1977). In 1981 the ITGWU insisted on 'explicit recognition, in law, of the duty of company directors to take account of the interest of employees at all times,' the 'immediate recognition of the right of employees and their representatives' to have regular and continuing access to 'all company information,' adequate safeguards against such information being deliberately false or misleading, no 'escape clauses' on the 'spurious grounds of "confidentiality", commercial secrecy or potential loss of competitiveness,' and better protection for workers when companies closed, with money owed being 'paid in full, as the first priority of any winding up.'

Employers fiercely challenged proposed EEC legal changes obliging firms to tell workers of the economic and financial situation, the development of business and sales, employment trends, production and investment programmes, rationalisation plans, manufacturing and work methods, and anything that would have a substantial effect on employees. Industrial democracy faded as an issue.

In 1988 Frank Wallace (Cóbh) wanted it back on centre stage, included in union courses, and a national promotional agency. When a Worker Participation (State Enterprises) Bill was produced in 1989 there was no massive enthusiasm.[55]

SAFETY AND HEALTH

In 1980 Eileen King continued to stimulate safety consciousness in *Liberty*, describing specific hazards and precautionary measures. The Safety in Industry Act (1980) updated the Factories Act (1955) and introduced two new concepts: an obligation on all employers to produce a Safety Statement, setting out arrangements for safeguarding safety and health, the co-operation required from workers, training facilities, and Rules regarding accidents and dangerous occurrences; and a requirement that all factories have a Safety Committee and Safety Representative or Delegate. The Safety Statement introduced hazard identification and risk assessment. The ITGWU felt that mandatory Safety Committees with a built-in worker majority were a breakthrough, providing a real opportunity to become involved in work-place decision-making. Given the tiny number of Safety Committees set up since 1955, a significant change of outlook was required.

The ITGWU began a massive training programme. £50,000 was allocated to provide one-day briefing workshops and follow-up three-day training. Supported by Congress, representation was made to the Government for funding; 'Governments cannot be allowed to pass social legislation, which imposes a financial burden on the movement, without recognising the importance of the Union's contribution to the effective realisation of the objective of the legislation.' 2,277 members attended 131 courses throughout the country, receiving the acclaimed booklet *Safety in Industry*.

In 1981 the extension of the Safety in Industry Act to all work-places was demanded, together with obligations on all employers to explain work-place hazards. Dónal O'Sullivan (Industrial Engineering Department) was one of three Congress appointments to the Commission of Inquiry on Safety, Health and Welfare at Work (Barrington Commission). In 1984 the ITGWU wanted the speedy implementation of the Barrington Report, which had been 'gathering dust.'[56]

In 1986 Harry Murphy (Dublin No. 3) opposed a ban on smoking in public places. A tobacco worker, he was defending jobs in manufacturing, packaging, advertising, sales and distribution. Those opposing the 'right to smoke' were a minority. The Industrial Engineering Department published a national survey of the Safety in Industry Act, *How Safe is Irish Industry?* It drew attention to dust, fumes and noise as prime concerns. Standards and compliance were much higher in employments where Safety Committees operated.

The Safety, Health and Welfare at Work Act (1989) was warmly welcomed. It triggered another significant training drive. For the first time all workers, all employers and self-employed and all work-places were covered by legislation. The loss of mandatory Safety Committees with built-in worker majorities was regretted. Expectations were that the new Act, 'enabling' rather than 'prescriptive' in nature, would facilitate significant involvement by workers in the identification and assessment of hazards, their elimination or control through engineering, safe systems or, as a last resort, personal protective equipment, and the raising of safety-consciousness. A computer-based 'dial-o-fax' service was provided by the Industrial Engineering Department, providing up-to-date information on the toxic effects of 250,000 chemical compounds.[57]

DEVELOPMENT SERVICES DIVISION

The 1980 Conference asked that 'radio and television should also be used more extensively to provide insight and information, in a lively and entertaining manner,' on work-place matters. The circulation of *Liberty* rose to 17,000, and Dublin daily papers competed to get 'first copy on publication date' in order to publish reaction or to reproduce features. In 1981 the Tralee Branch sought legislation to provide paid leave for workers engaged in 'collective bargaining, trade union education, civic duties and adult education.' In May 1982 *The Formative Years: A History of the Irish Transport and General Workers' Union, 1909–1923*, by C. Desmond Greaves was published. In 1983 submissions for a diploma course in industrial relations to be accredited by the National Council for Educational Awards were prepared and two books on teaching industrial relations published. Releases for courses dried in 1984 as employers withheld support.

In 1985 *Liberty News*, a quarterly magazine, replaced *Liberty* as part of cost controls. A bumper Conference edition contained a supplement, 'Unemployment: The Trade Union Alternative', and 60,000 posters supporting the Tax and Jobs Campaign. Day-release problems hampered education and training in 1986, with the situation worse in the public sector. Agreement between the ICTU and FUE improved matters in the private sector. FÁS technical assistant grants, which refunded 50% of direct training costs to the union, were cut to 30% early in 1986. Appeals and renegotiation raised this figure back up to 40% but underlined the 'difficulty experienced' in 'having more adequate funding made available.'

To get the union's message across on standards, tax and employment, a series of advertisements, 'Don't Let the Boss', dealt with low pay in catering, contract cleaning, security and retailing. Another campaign dealt with shorter working time, and 'Ten Questions for Charlie, Garret, Dick, Dessie and Tomás' were posted on advertising hoarding around the country, supported by 20,000 ordinary posters and 400,000 leaflets. The ITGWU announced 'a major scholarship scheme through one competition for children of members.' For ten years, with assistance from District of Columbia Friends of Ireland, the ITGWU provided scholarships to the College of Industrial Relations. The new scheme, costing £100,000 a year, granted four scholarships for higher education for members' children at £4,000 each, fifty scholarships of £200 for post-primary education for members' children and two higher-education scholarships for members at £4,000 each. Calls were made for trade unionism and the world of work to be included in the schools' transition year curriculum and for Branches to 'take whatever education steps are necessary' to transform members 'from being merely fee paying members into trade unionists.'[58]

CULTURAL DIVISION

Irish Actors' Equity Association amalgamated on 19 December 1979. Dermot Doolan said it would 'bring a new dignity to the writer, the performer and the artist.' Maurice O'Doherty, RTÉ newsreader and President of Equity, thought it gave actors greater industrial strength and 'their proper place' within the movement. Equity retained an independent status within a Cultural Division. An Arts Council report, *Living and Working Conditions of Artists in Ireland*, publicised the poverty, terrible conditions and general insecurity of many people engaged in the arts.

Equity included actors and performers in theatre, film and television, ballet dancers and freelance members in advertising and general performance. In 1980 Doolan invited all 'those artists who are unorganised', the painters, sculptors and 'those in what we call the plastic arts' to recognise that 'there is a place for you in the new Cultural Division.' In a 'spirit of good will and harmony' the ITGWU offered British Actors' Equity in Northern Ireland its full backing, including an office, secretarial service and the 'good offices of Paddy Devlin'. It was not accepted.

On 30 March actors, meeting in the Peacock Theatre, threatened a strike in RTÉ against cuts. Support came from the International Federation of Actors.

Better news was the Irish Theatre Company's continued success. The state-owned touring company with worker participation celebrated its fifth anniversary with Ibsen's *Enemy of the People* and Thornton Wilder's *Our Town*. The support of the FWUI was enlisted in opposing the affiliation of British Actors' Equity to Congress in 1981, despite fears that opposition would assist those calling for a separate Ulster TUC. The matter was resolved when British Equity gave an undertaking not to operate in the Republic.

The ITGWU demanded that local radio be under public control to safeguard broadcasting standards and the conditions of those employed. A full public debate was called for if the public ownership and control of any element of broadcasting, unchallenged since 1926, was to be handed to 'bankers, financiers and businessmen.'

In 1982 Equity was involved in back-foot resistance to prevent the closure of the Irish Theatre Company and Ardmore Studios. Of deeper concern was RTÉ's crisis when the Government refused to increase the television licence fee, despite a 40% increase in prices in two years, threatening the very existence of the service. Loss of income to illegal radio stations that the Government refused to regulate or control exacerbated matters. The ITGWU's protests were detailed, ably led within the NEC by Fergal Costello, an RTÉ cameraman. The Delegate Conference devoted much time to demanding improved funding for the performance arts. The Cultural Division developed 'A Policy for the Arts in Ireland', drawing on UNESCO's documents 'The Status of the Artist' and 'Opinion on Community Action in the Cultural Sector'.

On 9 October the inaugural meeting of the All-Ireland Federation of Performers' Unions, as agreed by the 1980 ICTU Congress, was held in the Cultúrlann, Head Office of Comhaltas Ceoltóirí Éireann, in Monkstown, Co. Dublin. Irish Actors' Equity was joined by the Irish Federation of Musicians and Associated Professions, the Northern Ireland Musicians' Association and British Actors' Equity.[59]

DISABILITY

John Grant (Waterford No. 1) sought employment schemes for handicapped people and full protection once in work. There were 100,000 adult handicapped. In

1974 the EEC adopted policies for involving the mentally and physically handicapped fully within communities. In 1975 the United Nations issued a Declaration of the Right of Disabled Persons. Unions agreed quotas within employments, but there was resistance by managements. Congress adopted policies, but all workers needed to do more for their less fortunate fellows, in employment, in the community and nationally. Dublin No. 2 Branch produced a discussion paper on work-place disability in February 1981, supporting calls for a quota scheme in all state employments of 3% and demanding a Minister with responsibility for the handicapped. It was a neglected area, and this was one of the first trade union initiatives.[60]

STAFF

From 1970 staff numbers rose consistently as full-time Branches were opened. The 'cold wind of economic depression' began to be felt after 1980 as membership and income fell. The NEC considered structural changes to defend levels of service and benefits, especially Strike Pay. There were tough clashes between the Staff Association and the NEC, which decried 'misrepresentation and smear propaganda' by some 'hacks' supplied with 'misinformation and gossip' from inside the union. The Staff Association was accused of not appreciating the scale of the problem.

In turn, the staff accused the NEC of exaggerating the crisis in order to resist valid demands for equal pay, regrading and increases. Newspaper headlines about staff redundancies contributed to tetchy relations. Few on either side reflected on the increasing 'dependence culture' being bred within the ITGWU, as 'service' became the mantra. Members naturally expected this service to be immediately available at the end of a phone; their perception of their own, voluntary role in servicing fellow-members diminished. Deduction at source significantly reduced local contact, and work-place Collectors virtually disappeared. The number of Shop Stewards declined as centralised bargaining and 'Tribunalisation' propelled grievances and claims centrifugally from work-place to third-party institutions and the care of full-time Officials. There was talk of 'slot machine' trade unionism: you pay your money and expect a product, but saw no participative role for yourself.

Beyond the immediate issue of costs and administrative structures, Carroll referred to the claim that 'on a non-trade union platform' some 'appointed staff' had called for the 'sweeping aside' of the union leadership. He angrily pointed out that all members of the staff were elected or were appointed by those democratically elected. He famously concluded: 'Of course, if any such appointed Official found it impossible to give the required loyalty to and support for the Union's agreed policies and elected leadership, well, that person can easily resolve such a personal dilemma as he or she has the absolute personal freedom, as the old saying goes, to either shape up or ship out.' It was a phrase that would haunt him. It addressed internal divisions according to political differences and drew applause and condemnation from different camps.

Further evidence of tensions came with motions in 1986 from Dublin District Council and Dublin No. 2 Branch asking the NEC to withdraw the 'Code of

Conduct' for 'employee candidates' for General Officer. It should be replaced with an Agreement that all Branches be notified of all candidacies, all invitations to address Branches to be accepted, and all candidates to have one piece of election literature delivered to each Branch. Both motions were rejected by the Delegate Conference, but they revealed a sense of grievance among some members of the staff.[61]

YOUTH

Michael Wall was appointed Youth Project Leader on 1 February 1980, the movement's first whole-time Youth Official. A campaign, 'Don't Be Ripped Off—Know Your Rights', was launched in July 1981 to advise young people and school-leavers of their work-place rights and give details of the Protection of Young Persons (Employment) Act (1977). The ITGWU slammed the Government charade that anything new or meaningful was being done to tackle youth unemployment. Union concerns also covered drug abuse and symptoms of youth alienation. In 1970, 113 had been charged with drug offences, a figure that rose to 991 in 1980. New legislation to stop supply and provide care for victims was demanded. In 1984 there was strong condemnation of the misuse of the Youth Employment Levy and neglect of the plight of long-term young unemployed.

Tony Walsh (Limerick No. 3) was Congress nominee to the Youth Employment Agency, and he offered a detailed explanation of its role and function, citing criticisms along the way. The levy was a 'cynical con trick', the funds being used to finance existing projects or being siphoned off by employers to subsidise labour rather than new jobs or training. There were calls for youth involvement in 'social and restorative work' schemes and concerns that youth placements were being used, particularly by local authorities, as cheap labour, undermining wages and conditions.

In 1985 Congress adopted a Youth Charter (see p. 746), fully supported by the ITGWU, which attempted to root out the sources of discrimination against young people. In 1987 Kirwan reported that the NEC was considering a Youth Committee but noting disappointing attendances in Dublin and Limerick, where the matter was discussed. Which came first, 'structures or commitment?' In 1988 developments were turgid, many Branches not sending anyone to a Youth Conference.[62]

INTERNATIONAL SOLIDARITY

On Friday 26 January 1980 the Irish Anti-Apartheid Movement held a rally in Liberty Hall, addressed by Oliver Tambo, President of the African National Congress of South Africa, as part of International Anti-Apartheid Year. The ITGWU supported opposition to the Springboks' tour by 'acquainting the public about the reality of the situation,' circulating leaflets and gathering a petition throughout the movement. Resolutions were forwarded to the Irish Rugby Football Union and the Taoiseach. *Liberty* promoted the message, and signs on Liberty Hall declared 'STOP THE TOUR.' Opposition was 100%, and a torchlight parade to St Stephen's Green on Friday 6 February and at many local rugby clubs by local Branches made this patently clear. Despite opposition from all corners of society—churches, politicians (with the 'dubious exceptions' of Ian Paisley and John Taylor), sporting and community organisations—the IRFU persisted. The Anti-Apartheid Movement held a huge demonstration on Saturday 7 March to coincide with the Lansdowne Road match, with full ITGWU backing.

The Delegate Conference demanded 'an effective trade embargo' against South Africa. Another seminar held in Liberty Hall in January promoted the 1975 Helsinki Agreement. Michael Mullen (a founder-member of the Irish Anti-Apartheid Movement) outlined support for Irish neutrality and asked that Ireland use its 'unique' international standing to promote peace, security and co-operation between peoples. He cited Connolly's opposition to the First World War to demonstrate the union's long tradition of supporting peace and interaction between nations.

In September members were encouraged to lobby for greater state aid for Third World development, training schemes for aid workers, exchange visits between workers or their unions, and direct union contributions to aid projects. In November 1982 the Irish Anti-Apartheid Movement set up the Michael Mullen Trust as a tribute to an 'unremitting opponent of race prejudice, apartheid and colonialism.' Backed by the South African Congress of Trade Unions, the Trust assisted South African trade unionists in financing education and training and encouraged Irish campaigns against apartheid.

In the autumn of 1985 Solomon Grundy's and Captain America's restaurants signed an Agreement with the ITGWU not to handle South African goods. In the light of the Dunne's Stores strike over the same issue, Congress met the Taoiseach to discuss imposing sanctions on South Africa. The ITGWU was one of many 'Maritime Unions Against Apartheid' that met in London on 30–31 October to impede South African oil deliveries.

In the early 1980s the ITGWU was active in the Congress Third World Committee and instituted bilateral relations with Philippine unions, exchanging Delegations and providing funding and resources for assisting them. Pirooz Daneshmandi and John Flannery (Dublin No. 14) put solidarity into practice as Irish Brigade volunteers gathering the Nicaraguan coffee harvest in 1988.

Éamon Thornton and Fergal Costello (Dublin No. 7), concerned at the creeping return to Cold War and to nuclear arms proliferation, wanted Ireland to 'give real meaning' to its neutrality by adopting 'a more positive role' on peace and disarmament. Resistance should be given to NATO, closer involvement made with non-aligned countries, and constant international pressure mounted for peace.

Irish neutrality was seriously undermined by the Government's weakly going along with the US-inspired boycott of the Moscow Olympic Games in 1980, despite the wishes of the people. The ITGWU called for 'financial and moral support' for the Olympic Council of Ireland to allow Irish participation. Tony Tobin (Dublin No. 11) pointed out that, despite Government opposition, should any medals be won by Irish participants there would be a stampede of Ministers at the airport to welcome the heroes home.

In 1982 Anne Wilkinson (Letterkenny) moved support for Solidarność in Poland. Reservations were expressed about western manipulation; it was surely suspicious that Governments that rushed to support Solidarność simultaneously denied basic rights to their own working class.

In 1986 Carroll was shocked to discover, as the Conference hall cleared, that seventeen copies of the *Sun* were found, despite the battle raging in Britain with Rupert Murdoch. He advised 'those of you who have papers which are the product of the company which is engaged in warfare with unions' in Britain: 'would you either burn them, or whatever you do, don't leave them on the tables here and don't bring then into this hall!' The ITGWU offered practical and financial solidarity to the striking British workers.[63] *Liberty News* regularly published news of international labour and trade union repression.

Members of the Iron and Steel Trades Confederation were deeply impressed by Irish solidarity during their strike for a 'living wage' and against 'savage cuts'. In May 1980 *Liberty* reported the attendance of members of the Irish Labour History Society at a Conference of the Welsh Society for the Study of Labour History and a trip to the coal face of Penrhiwceiber Colliery in the Cynon valley. In 1984 Nóirín Greene (NEC) moved an Emergency Motion pledging support to British mineworkers, reminding Delegates of the £1,000 a week for fourteen weeks given to locked-out Dublin workers by the South Wales Miners' Federation in 1913—a huge sum. Irish support efforts in 1926 had repaid some of that debt, but hunger again stalked the coalfields, and fresh support was needed. From 26 to 28 April 1986 a miners' choir, Côr Meibion Onllwyn, was sponsored to tour Ireland as a gesture of thanks for Irish, and especially ITGWU, support. Much of it originated when Tadhg Philpott persuaded Cork Council of Trade Unions to accept speakers from the Welsh Area of the National Union of Miners in May 1984.[64]

POLITICS

In January 1980 the Taoiseach, Charles Haughey, made an electrifying television broadcast in which he announced his intention to reduce the public-sector borrowing requirement. The ITGWU expected the worst; but Haughey lost his nerve.

Ireland's official asset position had deteriorated by £800 million, but Haughey and the Minister for Finance, Gene Fitzgerald, simply concealed matters. The 1981 estimates were massaged to conceal a projected deficit of £947 million. The crisis dominated the General Election of June, and another Coalition of Fine Gael and Labour was returned. The Carlow Branch wanted the union's disaffiliation from 'any political party'. Similar motions, aimed at the Labour Party, were inspired by members who supported Fianna Fáil or Fine Gael. Jim Kinneally (Cork No. 2), an Independent Councillor, at least cited reasons for losing faith in the Labour Party: it had voted with right-wing parties in Cork Corporation to deny firefighters a wage increase that was due. 'How can the Labour Party expect the support of working people if they don't practise what they preach?' Martin Kennedy (Nenagh) suggested that the union revive its Liaison Committee with Labour, wanting greater interaction.

Coalition Government brought 'creeping Thatcherism'. The Minister for Labour, Liam Kavanagh, and Minister for Health and Social Welfare, Eileen Desmond (members of the ITGWU and FWUI), created the Youth Employment Agency and in the January 1982 Budget insisted on a 25% increase in social welfare payments to meet inflation. The Department of Finance's insistence on VAT on children's clothes and footwear brought down the Government.

As an election loomed in February, the ITGWU announced its preference for an independent Labour line, opposed VAT on textiles and footwear, demanded the restoration of subsidies on milk and butter and condemned the taxing of short-term social welfare benefits. Mullen wanted a 'much more politically conscious membership.'

The Letterkenny Branch opposed Labour Coalition with any 'capitalist party'; it should speak with 'an independent Socialist voice.' The General Election, on 11 June, nearly produced an overall majority for Fianna Fáil. In Dublin the Labour Party lost three seats, including that of the Leader, Frank Cluskey. Michael O'Leary (a former ITGWU Official) succeeded him. The 'Gaiety Agreement', despite the ITGWU's opposition, accepted a Coalition strategy with Fine Gael, whose manifesto had 'echoed Reagan and Thatcher in its monetarist emphasis.' The Labour Party's influence was negligible, in ITGWU eyes, both wealth tax and the proposed National Development Corporation sinking quickly from sight. Pro-Coalitionists' arguments that the Labour Party had to accept some unpleasant measures in return for the implementation of some 'Socialist' policies 'was rendered painfully invalid in the first six months' of Government.

Endless debate on Coalition became 'more intense'. Its one consistent achievement was to benefit Fine Gael. Bemoaning 'Labour's loss of political independence,' the union felt that 'politics is now dominated by two catch-all parties, tied socially and financially to large private business interests and offering virtually identical policies.' Only degrees of ability to deliver on patronage and lingering Civil War attitudes determined the allocation of votes. Politically, things looked bleak. Nine of the Labour Party's fifteen TDs were ITGWU members.[65]

Table 124: First-preference votes (%) and number of seats, 1948–89

	Labour Party		Fianna Fáil		Fine Gael		Others	
1948	11.3	(15)	41.9	(68)	19.8	(31)	21.7	(22)
1951	11.4	(16)	46.3	(69)	25.7	(40)	13.7	(16)
1954	12.1	(19)	43.4	(65)	32.0	(50)	9.5	(8)
1957	9.1	(12)	48.3	(78)	26.6	(40)	13.6	(14)
1961	11.6	(16)	43.8	(70)	32.0	(47)	11.1	(9)
1965	15.4	(22)	47.7	(72)	34.1	(47)	2.8	(3)
1969	17.0	(18)	45.7	(75)	35.1	(50)	3.2	(1)

1973	13.7	(19)	46.2	(69)	30.5	(54)	3.0	(2)
1977	11.6	(17)	50.6	(84)	35.1	(43)	7.3	(4)
1981	9.9	(15)	45.3	(78)	36.5	(65)	8.3	(8)
1982 (Feb.)	9.1	(15)	48.4	(81)	38.0	(63)	4.2	(7)
1982 (Nov.)	9.6	(16)	45.2	(75)	42.2	(70)	3.0	(5)
1987	7.2	(12)	48.8	(81)	33.1	(55)	13.2	(22)*
1989	9.0	(15)	46.4	(77)	29.3	(55)	11.4	(19)

*Includes the Progressive Democrats.
Source: ITGWU, Annual Report for 1981, p. 17; www.oireachtas.ie.

In 1982 the ITGWU criticised the Labour Party's 'embarrassingly poor performance' in Government. The lowest ebb was when Labour TDs lined up to support the Budget, which hit society's poorest the hardest. Carroll received 'much personal abuse' for speaking out against 'Tweedledum and Tweedledee'.

The year witnessed two General Elections and three Governments, none tackling mass unemployment. After the Coalition Government 'foundered on the rocks of a harsh and insensitive Budget' the Labour Party officially fought on independent Socialist policies, as endorsed by the Administrative Council, but the Leader, Michael O'Leary, 'placed the emphasis on vainly defending the terms of the disastrous Bruton Budget.' The Labour Party hit a new low point, with only 9% of first-preference votes, while Fianna Fáil and Fine Gael increased their share, 'demonstrating yet again that Coalition' revitalised 'Fine Gael at Labour's expense.'

MacSharry's sleight of hand in promising 'boom and bloom' in place of 'gloom and doom' did not fool people for long. On 30 July he announced huge public-sector cuts and a pay freeze. 'The Way Forward', Fianna Fáil's indication of four more years of austerity, cost it the confidence of the Workers' Party and Tony Gregory, precipitating another election. The Labour Party Conference decided that the Party should offer a Socialist alternative, pleasing the ITGWU. Coalition would be decided after the election, 'in the interests of Party unity.' Within days of the Conference O'Leary not alone resigned the leadership but joined Fine Gael—an extraordinary action.

The Labour Party increased its representation to sixteen seats, with two serving ITGWU Officials, Michael Bell and Frank Prendergast, returned in Louth and Limerick East, respectively. At the Party Conference in December to decide on the terms of Coalition to be negotiated between the new Party Leader, Dick Spring, and Garret FitzGerald, the ITGWU voted against, as there was a 'marked absence of substantial Labour policies.' The 'likelihood of further electoral disadvantage resulting from another period as little more than lobby fodder for a fundamentally conservative dominant partner in Government' was high. 'Unfortunately our view was not shared by a majority.'

Dublin No. 7 Branch wanted 'all financial contributions' withdrawn from the

Labour Party 'until such time' as it 'implements ITGWU policy.' After a lively debate in which the majority, while agreeing with the criticism, urged Delegates to stay loyal to the Labour Party but to increase pressure within the Party, it was defeated, 208 to 44.[66]

In 1983 the ITGWU noted the 'remarkable capacity' of politicians to 'devote vast amounts of time and energy to issues of a secondary or trivial nature—while virtually ignoring the most fundamental problems facing the country.' A Day of Action was urged against the absence of effective policies, generating the largest demonstrations since the 1980 tax marches. Michael Bell moved six union amendments to the Finance Bill, and before its final reading direct meetings were sought with the Tánaiste, Dick Spring, Tomás Mac Giolla (Workers' Party) and Charles Haughey (Fianna Fáil). It was all to no avail. When the Labour Party again entered Coalition with Fine Gael, 'against the advice of our union and many others,' the ITGWU hoped the Party's participation 'would provide a necessary curb on the worst excesses of Fine Gael'; the Budget demonstrated that that influence was 'negligible'. The 'scale of the onslaught on PAYE workers' was such that 'even with an immediate 10% increase in pay, their standard of living' would still fall by between 7 and 11%. The Labour Party's betrayal was decried.

The ITGWU mounted a campaign against the Government from March, lobbying TDs, moving amendments to the Finance Bill in Dáil and Seanad, putting thousands on the street, distributing tens of thousands of leaflets, and organising work stoppages. The choices were clear for the ITGWU, if not for the Labour rump in the Government:

> The challenge is there for all our politicians. We can tackle unemployment in a positive way to stimulate economic activity or we can adopt the negative book-keeping approach of the Government which seems intent on applying the same kiss of death to our economy as the Iron Lady has done in Britain and in the North.

After delays in reopening Clondalkin Paper Mills, Frank Cluskey, Minister for Trade, Commerce and Tourism, resigned over the rescue package for Dublin Gas. The ITGWU approved his action. 'Detailed consideration' would be given to the union's 'future relationship' with the Labour Party.

Kirwan reiterated differences with the Labour Party but pointed out that they were 'as nothing when compared to the fundamental and irreconcilable differences on economic and social policy' with Fianna Fáil and Fine Gael. Praise was reserved for Michael Bell, who had consistently pursued ITGWU policy in the Dáil.

The Galway City Branch wanted the Labour Party to commit itself to a non-Coalitionist policy. Kevin Monaghan (Convoy) appealed for members to join the Party and fight for Socialism from within. Eric Fleming (Dublin District Council) wanted greater liaison with sponsored TDs and noted the 'current spate of requests for exemptions from the Political Levy.' Dermot Hayes (Clare) praised O'Leary 'for having the courage to go over to a right wing party' and invited other 'present Ministers' to do likewise. There was disgust with the Labour Party in Government, but left-wing speakers persuaded the floor to seek to admonish and influence, not to disaffiliate. The NEC's verdict on the Government's first year was 'deplorable.'[67]

In 1985 Carroll pointed out that the Labour Party's sixteen affiliated unions contributed only about £19,000 directly, £10,000 of it from the ITGWU. The Labour Party did not benefit in 'any massive or extraordinary or particular sense from money' from these affiliations. The majority of union members obviously did not vote Labour. He repeated criticisms of Coalition but accepted that decisions were taken democratically at Party Conferences. Éamonn Gilmore wanted a 'Coalition of the Left.' Generally, criticism of the Labour Party was from the left. The failure of Coalition Government was 'complete.'

In 1986 calls were made for the Labour Party to break with Fine Gael, 'precipitate a General Election' and 'prove to workers that they no longer support the monetarist policies that have brought so much misery.' The election did not come until 1987. In February the Tánaiste, Dick Spring, along with Barry Desmond, Liam Kavanagh and Ruairí Quinn (all union members), resigned because they refused to accept Budget cuts in health, social welfare and education advanced by the Taoiseach, Garret FitzGerald. Change of Government brought no respite, just 'retrenchment, cuts and more cuts,' not least because the right-wing Progressive Democrats entered the Dáil with fourteen seats, two more than the Labour Party. The Fianna Fáil Minister for Finance, Ray MacSharry, made the most extensive cuts in current and capital expenditure in the 1980s.

The union was happier with the Labour Party's independent opposition to (as Spring described it) a 'minority Government with the largest majority in Western Europe.' A column in Liberty presented readers with a political alternative. Norman Croke (Kildare) argued for a 'political awareness programme' in 1988, 'recognising the dichotomy' between 'our members' actions and expectations as trade unionists' and their 'voting pattern in support of right-wing political parties.' An objective of the union contained in its Rules was the 'furtherance of political objectives of any kind.' Although members were urged to vote Labour and lobbied for Socialist policies, there was no continuing political activity within Branches. Croke insisted that change was far more effective when produced from the bottom up than enforced from the top down.

The Labour Party Trade Union Group responded by appointing a full-time Co-Ordinator, Flor O'Mahony. As ITGWU members were voting to create SIPTU in March 1989, Spring was setting the Labour Party's programme for the 1990s before them: opposition to Thatcherite New Right policies, the promotion of public enterprise and restructuring of industry through a National Development Corporation and Employee Shareholders' Funds, tax equity, a universal child benefit of £40 and a strong lobby for regional and structural funding to balance the expected negative impact of the Single European Act. All were policies adopted at ITGWU Conferences.[68]

ICTU CHARTER OF RIGHTS FOR WOMEN, 1985

The ICTU recognises and demands the right of everyone, irrespective of race, ethnic origin, creed, political opinion, age, sex, marital status or sexual orientation to have the means to pursue their economic independence and to full participation in the social, cultural and political life of the community in conditions of freedom, dignity and equal opportunity. Congress further recognises that the elimination of past and present sex discrimination requires positive action and therefore resolves to pursue a programme of positive action to achieve full equality for women in society.

The ICTU will therefore campaign for the following Charter of Rights for Women and calls on all trade unionists to do their utmost to further the principles set out in this Charter.

- The *Right of Women to Work* regardless of marital status, including the right to return to work after a period of absence.
- *Equal pay for work of equal value* and the introduction of a *national statutory minimum wage* to alleviate the real problem of low pay.
- *Equality in conditions of employment* and the elimination of all forms of direct and indirect discrimination with regard to *sick pay* and *pension schemes.*
- *Equal access to job opportunities,* promotion and work experience.
- *Full statutory protection* and pro-rata pay and benefits for part-time workers.
- Elimination of *discriminatory age-limits* in the public and private sectors.
- *Equal access to all levels of education,* the elimination of all forms of sexism and a positive programme aimed at promoting equality and ensuring equal opportunities for both sexes.
- *Special training programmes* to encourage more women into higher skilled jobs and non-traditional occupations.
- The *working environment* to be adapted to ensure the health, safety and welfare of women workers.
- *The reorganisation of working time* through the introduction of more flexible working arrangements and an overall reduction in working hours.
- 26 *weeks maternity leave on full pay,* the latter 12 weeks to be taken by either parent. A minimum period of 15–20 days leave for family reasons.
- Eradication of *sexual harassment* in all its forms.
- *Protection of women's health* by dealing with the major issues affecting it, including stress, domestic violence, pre-menstrual tension and menopause. The provision of a comprehensive service for women's health to be made available on a local basis, this service to incorporate contraception, ante-natal and post-natal care, comprehensive screening facilities for cancer and other diseases, and a health education service.
- Recognition of *divorce* as a basic civil right. An end to the constitutional ban on divorce and the introduction of divorce legislation.

- An end to the *portrayal of women by the media* in a sexist and stereotyped manner.
- The provision of *comprehensive childcare* facilities to be provided free and controlled by the State including after-school and holiday care facilities and school meals.
- The elimination of all forms of direct and indirect discrimination against women in the *social welfare code*. A fundamental review of the concept of dependency which would recognise the independent status of each individual.
- Provision of *comprehensive contraception* freely available and accessible to all. All necessary measures should be adopted to ensure women have access to the necessary information and means to exercise their basic right to control their fertility.
- That all appropriate measures should be taken to ensure that *civil and criminal law* protects and supports the rights of women.

ICTU YOUTH CHARTER, 1985

The ICTU recognises and affirms the right of Youth to participate fully in the social, economic, political and cultural life of the community in conditions of peace, prosperity, freedom and dignity, regardless of sex, race, creed, or political opinion.

Congress identifies the right to work as the most pressing social need of our time, so that young persons can have a basis for financial independence, social status and participation in society.

Congress affirms the urgent need for special measures to alleviate the particular difficulties faced by young women, young travellers, the homeless young, disabled youth, and disadvantaged youth.

The ICTU therefore pledges itself to campaign for the following Charter of Youth and calls on all trade unionists to do their utmost to further the demands set out in this Charter.

Employment
- The right to work which can only be achieved by Government implementing the trade union policies for radical changes in the economy and society.
- A national statutory minimum wage to protect young workers from exploitation.
- Reorganisation and reduction in working hours, thereby improving employment opportunities for young persons.

Education
- Equality of access to a comprehensive, publicly-funded and accountable democratically-controlled education system at all levels. In particular finance must be provided and measures take to increase the participation of working-class youth in third-level education.

- A scheme of education allowances to enable working-class youth to remain on at second-level education.
- Reform of education curricula, so as to eliminate sexism, promote an understanding of social, economic and political issues including trade unionism, encourage the development of a critical and evaluative mind, and lay the foundation for education as a life-long process.
- Action to ensure that the education does not reinforce existing class structures.
- The reduction in pupil/teacher ratios through the employment of unemployed teachers.

Youth Schemes
- A single agency such as the Youth Employment Agency should have responsibility for the co-ordination and supervision of Youth Schemes.
- The introduction of a single framework Youth Scheme incorporating integrated modules for training, work experience and relevant education related to the target group, with guaranteed places for ALL unemployed youth.
- Trade unions must have an input at the design stage and a monitoring role for the scheme, which should meet minimum criteria as to content and standards. The Scheme should be financed by the Youth Employment Levy.
- Special provision should be made for second-chance education for early school-leavers and disadvantaged youth.
- Adequate allowances must be provided for trainees who should have the right to join trade unions.

Training
- Expansion of quality training programmes for youth which should include training in new technology and provide for the acquisition of transferable skills and an end to sex stereotyping.
- Extension of the designated apprenticeship system to additional skill areas.
- Guarantee for all apprentices and trainees of the opportunity to complete their training.

Participation
Youth involvement in:
- Society
  Facilities for Youth to participate fully in the social, cultural, political and economic aspects of society.
- Trade Unions
  Recognising the potential role of Youth in the Trade Union Movement, individual trade unions must take steps to encourage the involvement of young persons at all levels of the movement.
- Schools/Colleges
  Consultation of Youth in the schools and colleges on issues that affect them and participation where appropriate.

- Workplace
  The opportunity for young workers to influence their workplace environment
  and to participate in decisions affecting their jobs and their future.

Youth and the Law
- Removal of the status of illegitimacy.
- Freedom from discrimination arising from sexual orientation.
- Provision of special treatment centres for drug abusers in custody.
- Increased emphasis on non-custodial sanctions and community rehabilitation for young offenders.
- The age of criminal responsibility to be raised to 15 years of age.

Health and Social Welfare
- Young persons to be eligible to the full range of welfare and health benefits.
- Provision of a comprehensive programme of sex education and family planning services.
- A programme of health education for young persons with particular emphasis on prevention of substance abuse (e.g. alcohol, drugs, etc.)
- Provision of adequate treatment facilities for drug abusers.

Protective Legislation
- Strict enforcement of the Protection of Young Persons (Employment) Act to prevent exploitation of young workers.
- Stringent application of health and safety regulations for the protection of young workers including trainees.

Youth Services
- The introduction of a comprehensive National Youth Service to meet the recreational, educational and development needs of young persons.
- Existing facilities for recreation and social education, particularly in the education sector, should be made available to youth, and in particular the young unemployed.
- Comprehensive programme for community-based facilities for youth.

Peace
- Removal of the threat of nuclear annihilation and an end to the arms race so as to provide a secure future for youth.
- A reaffirmation of neutrality.
- An end to terrorism and violence.

Social Justice
- Action to remove special inequality.
- Special measures to improve the position of disadvantaged youth.
- Creation of an awareness of the special problems of the Third World and the need for an adequate response by society.

Chapter 33 ∿

FROM FEDERATION TO AMALGAMATION: THE FWUI IN THE 1980s

MEMBERSHIP, ORGANISATION AND FINANCE

The holding of the Annual Conference in Cork in 1980 trumpeted the FWUI's geographical and numerical expansion. It was now a 'national' organisation. Tom Geraghty moved a further increase in contributions, for although the finances seemed reasonably secure, underlying trends gave no grounds for complacency. A loss in 1978 of nearly £100,000 shook the system. Brian Carney (Finance Committee) pointed out that 'net asset value per member was down to £1.52.' New premises were built in Tullamore and extensive repairs and renovations made to Parnell Square.

The Rules relating to Marriage and Retirement Benefit were deleted, reflecting their declining take-up, while legal advice suggested that they were discriminatory. Marriage Benefit payments fell from £1,208 in 1970 to £920 in 1975 and £720 in 1979. Retirement payments fell from £370 in 1970 to £550 in 1975 and £310 in 1979. The loss of 238 jobs in Westport Textiles was the exception to rising membership, despite recession.

The first Biennial Delegate Conference of the Rural Workers' Group took place in Monaghan on 22–23 November. By 1982 five new Branches had arisen from the integration of the Federation of Rural Workers: No. 19 (AnCO), No. 20 (Department of the Public Service, local authorities and forestry), No. 21 (Northern), No. 22 (Southern), No. 23 (Mid-West) and No. 24 (East). Income exceeded £1 million for the first time. At 17%, however, the excess of income over expenditure was the lowest since 1975. Expenses, less Dispute Pay, reached 82% of income, the highest for many years: 1975, 70%; 1976, 62%; 1977, 73%; 1978, 78%; and 1979, 76%. It took the gloss off the million. Increased salaries, wages and social insurance were the cause. Paddy Cardiff, General Secretary, pointed out that costs ran at about 82%; a healthy recommended figure for unions was 65%. This could not be maintained, and calls for Equality and Youth Officers were tempered. The appointment of an Administrative Assistant to the General Secretary was approved and the vacancy filled in June by Charles Callan.

The Aer Lingus strike had cost the union more than £250,000. Similar action from the FWUI's other 'big battalions' and the financial situation could quickly become critical. Increased contributions were agreed, the highest, for those on £100 a week or more, being £1. There was little opposition.[1]

Table 125: FWUI surplus and General Fund balance, 1980–89

	Surplus (deficit) (£)	As proportion of total income (%)	General fund balance (£)
1980	174,891	17.34	1,238,899
1981	124,936	8.70	1,435,510
1982	21,575	1.47	1,463,578
1983	110,141	6.99	1,573,719
1984	225,816	14.78	1,730,168
1985	(94,585)	(5.68)	1,763,371
1986	121,906	6.57	1,855,301
1987	225,816	10.93	2,064,529
1988	60,113	2.89	2,074,289
1989	618,625	23.33	2,651,612

Source: FWUI, reports of annual Delegate Conferences, 1981–9.

A letter from Dermot Boucher (No. 15 Branch) published in *Hibernia* criticised Cardiff for his handling of the Conference, suggesting that he acted against GEC policy. Cardiff was inclined 'to do nothing about it,' but the GEC felt the FWUI was damaged, and it was referred to a solicitor.

The Irish Airlines Executive Staffs' Association, whose affiliation was cancelled in 1978, frantically endeavoured to accumulate 500 members so as to secure a Negotiating Licence. Frank O'Malley, Secretary of the Aer Lingus Branch, complained that the Association's policy 'of strike-breaking has worsened': it referred to strikes as 'industrial vandalism'. Congress was encouraged to oppose its application before the High Court. No licence was awarded, and the FWUI opposed its affiliation to the ITGWU or any other body. The Association was offered re-affiliation in November 1981, after the ESB Officers' Association indicated that it would accept it. Congress agreed not to sanction any transfer. The Association rejected the FWUI and attempted to obtain 'accepted body' status under the Trade Union Acts. The pill of observing future FWUI pickets was still too hard to swallow.

Despite continued recession, membership held in 1982. It did not surprise the GEC, and there was a growing self-assuredness. The union 's 'image' was 'determined, militant but yet disciplined and responsible.' This did 'not emerge by accident' but from training and education, good communications, leadership and 'utilisation of the talents and abilities available.' But there was 'never room for complacency.'

Tom Dunne became Administrative Secretary to the General Secretary in January 1982, after Callan took up a post in AnCO. The Irish Agricultural Advisers' Organisation, affiliated since 1970, became full members in 1983. Its General Secretary, John Howley, became Secretary of the IAAO Branch. A letter from the Irish Union of Distributive Workers and Clerks suggested closer co-ordination on 'organisation, industrial, social and economic policy.' This was 'not related to amalgamation' but to considerable pressures on the IUDWC.[2]

In 1983, while income reached its highest level ever, £1,379,973, expenditure accounted for 93% of it, causing alarm and necessitating calls for an increase of 20p in contributions. Opposition was voiced but the increase was agreed. The transfer of the IWWU became effective from 1 September 1984, its outgoing General Secretary, Pádraigín Ní Mhurchú, becoming a Workers' Representative on the Labour Court. Further increases in contributions were made in 1984, bringing the top rate, for those earning £100 or more, to £1.20 a week. There was 'a backlash in some Branches.'

The General Secretary, Bill Attley, referred to two internal reports, one on finance, the other on structures, designed to forecast where the FWUI might be five years hence and to maximise efficiency and effectiveness. An underlying problem was that the 'membership had declined,' which meant that the union's 'ability to provide the ever-expanding services to our members, while at the same time implementing a militant industrial policy,' was 'impaired'. The FWUI was coy about declaring its membership, details being omitted from GEC reports; but given that it had absorbed the Irish Agricultural Advisers' Organisation and the IWWU, the drop was clearly considerable.

The GEC felt a need to 're-state and indeed clarify' what unions were established for. The first edition of the union's new paper, *Unity,* urged greater solidarity, involvement and questioning by each member. It was a traditional appeal to members to use the democratic structures to ensure that the organisation first and foremost truly reflected their wishes.[3]

Table 126: Travelling, hotel and motor expenses (£), 1980–89

1980	66,191	1985	165,018
1981	101,271	1986	167,372
1982	116,134	1987	187,684
1983	131,131	1988	188,938
1984	148,854	1989	187,427

Source: FWUI, reports of General Executive Council, 1980–89.

In 1984 income exceeded £2 million, a 25% increase, while expenditure, at £1,461,206, had risen by 14½%. Increased contributions were nevertheless sought, bringing the top rate to £1.40 for those on over £100 per week, applied from June

1986. Comparable rates were: ASTMS, 95p; NATE, £1; IDATU, £1.15; ITGWU, £1.25; IMETU, £1.25; LGPSU, £1.75. With only minor reservations expressed, the proposal was carried. The fall in membership was 'serious' in 1985. Manufacturing losses ran into four figures. Balancing this, a merger with the National Association of Transport Employees was concluded. Founded in 1952 when the National Union of Railwaymen withdrew from Ireland, NATE organised railway and transport employees. Its membership in Northern Ireland Railways allowed the FWUI for the first time to become an All-Ireland organisation.

There were regular complaints about the format of the Annual Conference, with suggestions about the size of delegations, venue, duration, length of speeches and number of motions, all constructively offered by delegates, who appreciated and enjoyed their annual gathering. In 1986 Larry Hogan (No. 4) regretted a 'high level of apathy' and 'serious lack of communication' between levels within the union. He wanted 'adequate time' for 'discussion on matters of jobs, work quality and living standards.' He waited two days for a debate on his motion regarding jobs in the food industry in 1984, but it was never reached, while an Emergency Motion on the visit of Ronald Reagan and 'about six pages of contraception was spoken.' Others suggested that too much time was taken up by 'divorce, abortion, contraception, political involvement, etc.' Tempers frayed, but delegates clearly wanted broad social debate.[4]

The Revenue Commissioners fined the FWUI £500 for a 'minor breach' of regulations relating to failure to submit P35 forms (employer's payroll return). After an internal inquiry one member of the staff was suspended and the 1985 statement of accounts revised to ensure accuracy. The accounts could not be presented to the Conference in May and it was necessary to reconvene on 1 November. It was revealed that between January 1978 and May 1986 'an unspecified sum of money could have been misappropriated.' The Gardaí were informed and they began a fraud investigation. An audit by Stokes Kennedy Crowley, presented to the GEC on 3 October 1986, showed an overstatement of assets to the extent of £379,270, accounted for by an understatement of liabilities, unexplained cash deficiencies, penalty interest charged because of late PAYE and PRSI payments, and additional charges. All liabilities were paid off but resulted in a deficit in 1985 of £94,585, as opposed to an actual surplus of £284,685. Stokes Kennedy Crowley made recommendations regarding internal audit procedures, and the union's auditors were changed. No further increase in contributions was sought, but a proposed increase of 10p from July 1987 was approved. Tom Garry acknowledged that a 'serious misstatement' of union accounts had 'occurred and might go back as far as 1977.' One staff member was dismissed after inquiries were complete.[5]

In 1987 the United Stationary Engine Drivers', Cranemen's, Firemen's, Motormen's and Machinemen's Trade Union, founded in 1827, merged. It recognised the 'benefits of being part of an organisation with the necessary resources' to deal with change. An Aer Lingus Clerical Branch was created in 1986, while No. 13 lost 400 members through redundancy as New Dublin Gas was placed in receivership. In 1986 the FWUI returned to surplus and running the union from current income, 'in spite of our serious difficulties over the last year.' Jim Quinn nevertheless cautioned that economies were necessary, as administrative expenditure, less Dispute Pay, accounted for 92% of income, a figure consistent with the previous four years. Membership income, up by 9%, reflected the increase of 20p in contributions and the loss of 600 members. An overdraft of £150,000 on the current account required remedial action.

Garry, attempting to assuage members' understandable fears after the discovery of serious maladministration, said the union had been advised to appoint a Financial Controller. It decided to select one itself, despite having 'no background in picking financial people.' It asked the Irish Productivity Centre, because it was a 'non-profit body', jointly sponsored by the ICTU and FUE. Éamonn Tully was appointed. Quinn welcomed the lengthy debate, as usually the accounts 'went through on the nod.' They merited the scrutiny and concern they had received that year. A further contribution increase brought the top rate to £1.60 for those on £100 a week. The Rule Book was amended to rid it of sexist terminology.[6]

Membership losses were bad enough, but by 1988 concerns grew at the insidious impact of individualism, 'the strict conservatism of old, rooted in the belief that it is up to the individual to better themselves,' and that the market cured all ills. The FWUI accepted that market economics was a 'strong discipline against inefficiencies' but it 'always created massive inequalities.' Insecurity and isolation, alienation and crumbling organisation, combined to allow assertive managements to 'divide and intimidate' and demand deregulation of the labour market. Organisation, in the GEC's view, did 'not get the attention it deserves.'

All Bord na Móna members were allocated to the Peat Industries Branch in Tullamore, serviced by Kevin MacMahon. Jim Quinn announced that total assets were valued, for the first time, at more than £2 million. Administrative costs remained high, rising at 11% above inflation.

A further increase of 10p in contributions was sought from 1 January 1989. It was seen 'as absolutely critical.' Some objected, while others thought it not enough, calling for an additional category of higher payment for those earning more than £200 per week.

Membership fell from 50,000 in 1980 to 43,000 in 1988, but the staff remained the same. In response to demands for wider services, a range of car, home, travel and health insurance services was provided in association with Savings and Investments Ltd. Reorganisation of the Western Area created Divisions for Agriculture and Mariculture, Education, Food, Health, Manufacturing and Services.[7]

In 1989 the membership rose to 41,932, the largest declared figure since 1981, reversing a downward trend that saw membership fall, at its worst, by 6,935 or 15%. The FWUI would transfer a healthy, growing base to SIPTU.

SIPTU

In 1980 an ICTU Committee examined organisation in new firms. The FWUI wanted 'equal representation' for all unions when companies set up operations in Ireland, a position shared by the ATGWU. The ITGWU was thought to gain undue advantage, but its national spread gave it exclusivity in many areas. Allegations that it adopted low rates in order to secure organisation were not supported by facts. In December the GEC reported on the 'row' between the ITGWU and ATGWU, which 'had to be kept confidential.' It centred around new firms, the 'inflexibility of Clause 47D' of the constitution of Congress regarding transfers, and non-implementation of recommendations of the ICTU Disputes Committee in Tedcastle's, Kilroy's, Cork Regional Hospital and Data Products.

The FWUI, ATGWU and ITGWU met in January 1981 to discuss matters. In an apparently unrelated gesture, the FWUI hosted a reception for the General President of the ITGWU, Senator Fintan Kennedy, on the occasion of his sixty-fifth birthday, inviting senior staff members of the FWUI, ICTU, ITGWU and Post Office Workers' Union.

In July 1981 further discussions were held with the ATGWU and the ITGWU on recruitment under the headings of pre-production Agreements, agreed minimum rates and standard Agreements. The 'openness' of the ATGWU and the ITGWU was valued, but it would 'prove difficult to achieve agreement.'[8]

By 1988 clashes with the ITGWU were more common. The FWUI had become a 'national' union, offering greater competition. Self-confidence grew, and the impression, at least to outsiders, was that it was weathering the economic storm far better. Membership losses were fewer and more balanced by gains; and financially, if not yet on the same scale as Liberty Hall, Parnell Square was less troubled and had seen its property and investment portfolios grow. Yet consistent FWUI policy, from Young Jim Larkin's time, was rationalisation. 'Explanatory' consideration was therefore given to 'co-operating with the ITGWU on a wide range of issues of concern to both': education and training, services to the unemployed, financial packages, equality and campaigns among part-time and temporary workers. All this notwithstanding, the FWUI recognised that in the short term both had to 'ensure that they remain strong independent Unions.'

The first public manifestation of the new collaboration was the simultaneous production of identical issues of *Unity* and *Liberty News* in 1987, placing the terms of the Programme for National Recovery before the members.

ITGWU General Presidents were fixtures as fraternal Delegate to FWUI Annual Conferences. In 1988 the Vice-President, Eddie Browne, General Secretary, Chris Kirwan, and NEC members Andy Burke, Martin Kennedy and Seán Roche also attended. Their appearance was not very conspicuous, as they were among more than twenty guests representing the ATGWU, MPGWU, Bakers' Union, National Union of Tailors and Garment Workers, Fire Brigades Union and Northern Ireland Public Service Alliance.

To commemorate the seventy-fifth anniversary of the 1913 Lock-Out the FWUI and ITGWU held a Gala Concert in Liberty Hall, 2–3 August 1988; promoted a schools essay competition; and erected headstones on the derelict, unmarked graves of the 1913 martyrs Alice Brady, James Byrne and James Nolan. A thaw was setting in fast between two ancient protagonists.

Garry acknowledged the talks with the ITGWU but was, understandably, cagey about detail. The FWUI had accepted an invitation from the NEC of the ITGWU to talks 'without preconditions, with a view to healing the historical rift between both Unions,' and because 'such a request could not be ignored, not only for the sake of history but also for more pragmatic reasons.'⁹

A second simultaneous edition of *Unity* and *Liberty News* presented the SIPTU proposal to members in March 1989. Attley argued that 21st-century problems could not be tackled with nineteenth-century structures. The 'extraordinary speed' of negotiations was surprising. No corners were cut, however, such was the level of agreement. While urging support for SIPTU, Attley asked that a 'proud history' not be forgotten and that the WUI's 'wisdom and fighting spirit' be carried forward. A union 'has to have a soul and it also has to be effective.'

Proposed regional structures were a big selling-point within the FWUI presentations of SIPTU, the members being assured of local autonomy, strike sanction granted by regional Executives, and no unit being bigger than 40,000 members. This, together with the application of new technology, would 'create paradoxically the reality of the "great little Union" with the advantage of scale on one hand and "small size at local level" on the other.'

Concerns at the impact of the Single European Market in 1992 underlay the GEC's thinking. As the talks progressed there was no sense of the coming economic boom that might have reversed everyone's rush to circle wagons. Equally, it was 'only eleven years from the new Millennium,' and there was a strong sense of the need for change. SIPTU was new, conceptually and structurally.

A Special Delegate Conference on 15 April approved the proposals. A significant number of Delegates spoke not against the principle of amalgamation but against specific Rules, insufficient time to reflect, and frustration that it was 'either take it or leave it' on the whole package. The vote, from 8 to 19 May, was 249 to 36. The GEC concluded its pitch by recognising that, 'while many old friends will have difficulties,' they would accept that unions were 'not works of art but living vibrant organisations.' All were being asked to 'participate in a historic decision to establish a new trade union with new radical structures, which enhances the democratic concept of their own union and which will ensure the continuation of the tradition of Connolly and Larkin in a modern trade union of the future.'

Parallel to talks with the ITGWU the FWUI concluded an Agreement with the Marine, Port and General Workers' Union to merge, effactually adding to SIPTU's creation. An 'overwhelming majority' of FWUI members 'clearly embraced' the idea of developing a new dynamism' in SIPTU. Over the previous five years it was a 'constant battle to maintain the morale and courage' of members against unemployment, redundancy, emigration and social deprivation. The parting FWUI view was that 'SIPTU must not fail!' The task set was demanding, but the 'reward will be a movement relevant and powerful in the cause of workers and their families.'¹⁰

PADDY CARDIFF, JOHN FOSTER AND PADDY MURPHY

John Foster retired at the 1982 Conference, proud that the FWUI had grown considerably under his presidency and particularly that 42% of the members were now outside Dublin. A 'safe pair of hands', Foster was inconspicuous but diligent and a source of calm strength. In the contest to succeed him, Tom Garry defeated Tom Geraghty and Frank O'Malley.

Health problems forced Paddy Cardiff's retirement on 9 July 1983. He was succeeded by William Attley. Cardiff announced his decision at the GEC meeting of 15 January and listened as members extolled his virtues and expressed their surprise and sadness. He had 'emulated the Larkin tradition.' Cardiff said that his mother had observed that he 'was a child that could never be made cry. Today he had come the closest ever to that situation.' He brought his military experience to bear, his focus on discipline and organisation, education and training. The WUI grew significantly through strategic mergers and considered expansion, marking Cardiff out as a very significant figure. His desire to expand the content of National Wage Agreements assisted the emergence of National Understandings. It was a matter of deep regret that, while he was President of the ICTU, National Understandings ceased. Temperamental and tough, Cardiff was a good man to have in your corner and a dreaded opponent. A row with him, however, was forgotten when over. He respected loyalty and commitment to the cause.

On 31 May 1988 the Assistant General Secretary, Paddy Murphy, retired. It was the end of an era. He had dedicated his life to rural workers in the FRW and then the FWUI. He was a tenacious negotiator, armed with a celebrated attention to statistical detail and comprehensive supporting facts. He 'did not easily concede the entitlements sought,' displayed courage, and once 'initiated "soup kitchens" for bog workers' to save them from the ignominy of being starved into submission. He was a Labour Party activist and spent many years on the European Social Committee, beavering away on the fine print of matters that benefited rural communities from the Atlantic to the Carpathians.

Other significant staff members who retired before SIPTU's coming were Jack McCarthy, Meat Federation; Vincent Wynter, Central Area; and the redoubtable Peter Keating, most famous for his stoic support of Clondalkin Paper Mills. He served on the Barrington Commission on Safety, Health and Welfare at Work, the Interim Board for Safety, Health and Welfare at Work and the founding Board of the Health and Safety Authority.[11]

WOMEN

In November 1980 Cardiff progressed discussions with the IWWU as far as the 'brass tacks' of merger. Its General Secretary, Maura Breslin, did not enjoy great health, and she suggested a secondment from the FWUI to assist her. Pádraigín Ní Mhurchú was the 'only Official' that Cardiff could think of, as 'they have never had a male Official in the IWWU.' Ní Mhurchú would 'do a first-class job,' and to 'let the IWWU disintegrate would be a crime.' The move gave the FWUI a unique insight into the emerging amalgamation. Maura Breslin retired in June 1982 and Ní Mhurchú succeeded her, altering her FWUI employment relationship.

In 1981 Mary Dowling (No. 17), recognising that women were a third of the membership, wanted a full-scale report to provide women with greater participation and responsibility. Úna Claffey (No. 15) wanted reserved GEC seats. The FRW had been accommodated with 'special structures'—why not women? Cardiff produced some 'balancing figures': out of 13,500 women there were 262 women Shop Stewards, 290 on Section Committees and 44 on Branch Committees. In No. 4 Branch, where women were 60 to 70% of the membership and had 'the opportunity to dominate,' they did not—a comment some women would take as an indication that he was missing the point. He opposed reserved seats.

In 1981 Claffey wanted 'a campaign of positive action' to increase women's participation, the ICTU Working Women's Charter to be central to all future negotiations, the inclusion of equality clauses in all Agreements, improved equality training, and creche facilities at Annual Conferences. The FWUI declined to support the Trade Union Women's Forum, seeking 'information about it' from Congress. Assurances from Donal Nevin, General Secretary of Congress, cut little ice, as Pádraigín Ní Mhurchú reported that the TUWF had 'not done anything for two or three years.' The FWUI was reluctant to sponsor a non-elected body.

Table 127: FWUI women membership, 1980–89

	Membership	Women	As proportion of total (%)
1980	44,959	13,236	29.4
1981	45,939	14,357	31.2
1982	45,666	14,462	31.6
1983	43,620	13,628	31.2
1984	42,842	14,612	34.1
1985	41,674	14,435	34.6
1986	40,630	13,231	32.5
1987	41,662	13,447	32.7
1988	39,004	n.a.	n.a.
1989	41,932	n.a.	n.a.

Source: National Archives, Registrar of Friendly Societies, file 369T.

Ita Gannon thought the GEC Report 'Women's Participation within the FWUI' was 'patronising and unsympathetic to the liberation of women.' It had to be 'heavily criticised.' The listing of 'apathy' as the first reason for women's under-involvement was insulting. Who would dare say that black Americans were not more active in unions because they were apathetic? There was no equality element in training courses. A specific Official was needed.

Cardiff defended the report. Responses to the Branch circular had been very negative. For all the fine speeches, no significant decisions emerged. Jo Walsh (Union Trustee) was the only woman on the Committee, which concluded that women's lack of involvement was due to apathy, social conditioning, family responsibilities, and lack of confidence and experience. It decided against a Women's Equality Officer, as the union's record 'in practical gains and establishing important precedents for female members' was 'ample proof of the competence' of all Officials 'to deal effectively with the progress of women's rights.'

While the wui had elected women to its GEC as far back as 1951, no women had been elected since 1971, with the exception of M. Hayes, Trustee since 1974. A survey in 1982 revealed that women constituted 15% of all voluntary Officials. Four Branches, previously FRW Sections, either had no women or less than 1%, while 54% of women members were concentrated in No. 4, 12, 15, 17 and 18 Branches. Women's participation in seminars and courses had improved significantly since 1977, but attendance at Annual Conferences remained frustratingly stagnant: 8½% of Delegates in 1979, 13% in 1980, 9½% in 1981 and 11% in 1982. Travel, the time of meetings and domestic commitments inhibited women's attendance.

On wages, 88% of women reported having equal pay, 7% had not, while the remaining 5% worked in employments with no comparable male jobs. Of the 7% without equal pay, one-seventh were the subject of claims under the Anti-Discrimination (Pay) Act (1974) that, for one reason or another, had failed. The great majority were beneficiaries of union-negotiated equalisation Agreements.

Table 128: Proportion of women on equal pay, not on equal pay or not comparable (%), by Branch, 1982

	Equal	Not equal/Not comparable
No. 1 & 8	91	9
No. 2	10	90
No. 3 & 7	99	1
No. 4	100	—
No. 6	54	36
Meat Federation	21	79
No. 9	—	—
No. 12	100	—
No. 13	98	2
No. 15	100	—
No. 16	100	—
No. 17	47	53
No. 18	100	—
No. 19	86	14

No. 20	—	100
No. 21	96	4
No. 22	100	—
No. 23	—	—
No. 24	—	—
Bray-Dún Laoghaire	100	—
Western Area	68	32
Central Area	55	45
South-East Area	52	48
Trim	—	100

A breakdown of equal pay was provided by Branch. Most women enjoyed equal pension rights, and virtually all employments had a written equality Agreement, based on an FWUI model equality clause. On maternity leave, 5% had full pay while on negotiated leave of twelve to fourteen weeks, 57% had full pay less social welfare entitlements, while the remaining 38% were covered by the Maternity (Protection of Employees) Act (1981).

Despite apparent progress on equal pay, women's weekly earnings in manufacturing rose only from 56% of that of men in 1970 to 71% by 1980, reflecting age structure, the concentration of women in lower grades, persistent concepts of 'men's and women's work,' and less service by women, who tended to break service after the birth of their first or subsequent children.[12]

The FWUI concluded that women's union participation was 'roughly the same as women's participation in the labour force.' It was 'reasonably good' and had improved in all areas. More positive action at the Branch level was still required, however. The union's record on maternity leave and equal pay was a 'proud achievement but Officials were encouraged to immediately pursue claims for the minority who still did not have equal pay.'

The first Women's Consultative Conference took place on 30 October 1982 and a Women's Advisory Committee was elected: Éilís Boland (No. 15), Vera Byrne (No. 3), Maria Cassidy (No. 7), Ann Fennell (No. 18), Angela Hannon (Western Area), Dympna Harper (No. 19), Kate Kirwan (No. 17), Eileen Molloy (No. 7), Moira Neylon (No. 13) and Josephine Walsh (No. 12), chairwoman.

In 1984 the FWUI published the findings of its survey again, together with its work within the ICTU Women's Committee, and submissions on job-sharing, sexism in education and motions adopted at the Women's Consultative Conference. With 16,485 women members, only the ITGWU, ATGWU and Confederation of Health Service Employees had more. Motions requested specialist education and training for women, reserved GEC places (the ICTU had adopted this practice), the ending of all discrimination within social welfare on grounds of sex, and action on health and safety, family planning and the ICTU Women's Charter. All this was included in the FWUI's submission to the Dáil Committee on Women's Affairs, which started from the belief in the 'right of women to work outside the home, whether married of single,' achievable only by the equal availability of jobs to women, irrespective of their marital status; recognition of the 'true financial, commercial and social value of what is usually described as women's work'; full implementation of equal remuneration; an end to the exploitation of part-time workers (the FWUI was leading the organisation of contract cleaners) and improved safety, health and welfare at work for women. For women in the home the FWUI wanted equal treatment within social welfare, recognition of the home care of elderly or sick relatives and substantial increases for deserted wives and widows. In society, the demands were for sex education in schools, comprehensive family planning education, the availability of contraception, an end to the 'pandering to religious constraints' and to 'profiteering' by the medical profession, adequate provision of child care, an end to discrimination against women in law, the introduction of divorce legislation and an end to sexism in advertising and the media.[13]

The transfer of the IWWU's engagements significantly increased women's profile. Janet Hughes became Secretary of the Women Workers' Branch. The FWUI complained of decisions by Equality Officers and the Labour Court that a defence against equal pay was for the employer to prove that the claimant's work was higher in value that that of her male comparator. This interpretation was a 'flagrant breach of the spirit' of the Anti-Discrimination (Pay) Act.

The third Women's Consultative Conference on 20 October 1984 bemoaned the lack of cases taken under the Employment Equality Act (1977), demanded legislative protection for part-time and contract workers and the provision of child care. It insisted that the three-year experiment within the union on women's rights be maintained for a further five years, with national and Branch Women's Committees. A seminar on job-sharing was sparsely attended, and with more men than women. It undermined the women's case. Mary Sherlock (No. 16) submitted a comprehensive paper on 'Childcare is a Trade Union Issue', referring to the Department of Health's findings on child abuse, identifying the inadequacy of child-care facilities and the lack of state supervision, the case for pre-school playgroups and the findings of the Report on Childcare Facilities, 1983. The FWUI endorsed the demands of the ICTU Working Women's Charter for implementation of the EEC directive on equal treatment in the provision of social security and approved Ruairí Quinn's statement of 29 November, 'Government policy statement on equality of opportunity between men and women in employment'. There was no lack of a union focus on equality.

In 1985 'alarming trends' that demonstrated continued discrimination against women were challenged, a debate on the Health (Family Planning) (Amendment) Act presented examples of 'bigoted intolerance', and a record number of women came to the rostrum. Women's participation in Delegate Conferences rose sharply. In numbers, ironically, it declined: in 1982, 54; in 1983, 51; in 1984, 43. There were continued demands for child care and support for ICTU campaigns to outlaw sexual harassment launched in January 1986. Caroline McCamley (No. 15) sought measures for women's well-being: free contraception and family planning advice, support organisations that dealt with rape and incest victims, domestic violence, the Well Woman Centres and Open Line.[14]

On 11 March 1986 Mai Clifford's death was the loss of a much-loved stalwart. Born in 1918, she began work in Terenure Laundry, joined the IWWU, later working in the Shelbourne Hotel and St Luke's Hospital, and fought in the 'laundry girls' strike' of 1945. As President of the IWWU in January 1980, while waiting for the vast throng of PAYE protesters to assemble at the GPO, she transformed the song 'One Day at a Time' into a Labour anthem.

On 17 October 1987 the Biennial Women's Seminar was on the theme 'The Future for Women'. The long, hard slog involved in winning equal pay claims, tortuous industrial relations and legal procedures being fully exploited by stalling employers was exemplified by the ultimate triumph in 1988 of twenty-nine women who had lodged their claim against the Department of Posts and Telegraphs on 4 December 1981. Twenty-two had either retired or been reallocated. The matter was referred to an Equality Officer in 1982, then to the Labour Court and the High Court, where Mr Justice Keane acknowledged that the women had a claim for equal pay with a comparator male labourer on £29 a week more. The FWUI financed taking the case to the European Court of Justice, which gave legal rulings and returned the case to the High Court, which awarded costs against the women's employer, now An Bord Telecom. The whole 'silly matter' cost the taxpayer more than £40,000 in legal costs and the employer £293,000 in equal pay. Ironically, their regrading meant the remaining women were obliged to transfer to the Postal and Telecommunications Workers' Union.[15]

An important victory for the Women Workers' Branch in 1988 was 'organising into a cohesive force the contract cleaners' of Dublin city and county. In endeavouring to make a 'quantum leap' in wages and conditions, these mainly women members voted for industrial action in support of a Labour Court recommendation. No action was ultimately needed, because of the 'tremendous and overwhelming response' from members 'engaged in secure employments.' Their victory included 'extremely good pay and conditions, redundancy, pension and sick pay schemes, cervical cancer screening' and 'a wide range' of benefits. The employers, forced to agree to a Joint Labour Committee in 1985, refused to nominate anyone to the agreed Working Party on Conditions of Employment in 1986, as the FWUI pursued a registered Agreement. They continued to filibuster, holding up Labour Court proceedings first to demand the right of legal representation—a dubious entitlement but conceded by the Court—and then, in unprecedented fashion, objecting to the presence of Pádraigín Ní Mhurchú as Worker Representative. Two conciliation Conferences before strike notice expired on 11 January 1989 broke the impasse, although the 'considerable shock' among employers when they found themselves 'totally isolated' contributed hugely to the victory. It was a breakthrough in the unionisation of atypical workers.

In 1989 Janet Hughes was given responsibility for the Women's Committee, among complaints that its 'role has become fudged' and activity had 'tapered off' amid a 'perceived lack of support' from the senior staff. Activities were planned in education and training, equality claims and joint ventures with the ITGWU and National Union of Public Employees.[16]

ANNIVERSARIES

To celebrate the seventieth anniversary of the Lock-Out the Oscar Theatre in Sandymount, Dublin, produced James Plunkett's *The Risen People* for a week, and the assembly room in Parnell Square was named Larkin Hall. The FWUI proudly celebrated its sixtieth anniversary in 1984. Garry welcomed the General President of the ITGWU, John Carroll, to the union Conference and congratulated Liberty Hall on its seventy-fifth anniversary. Reflecting changed and changing times, Garry 'put on record that whatever differences . . . may have existed in the past' were 'now a matter of history and no longer relevant to our relationship.' The FWUI was 'no ordinary' union, being built on 'great principles': that workers could 'only advance their rights and interests through unity and solidarity with each other.' The best expression of unity was the trade union movement. Workers' struggle to be free and independent was 'a worldwide movement,' one worker's loss of freedom being a 'threat to the freedom of all.' The most effective means of organising unity was 'through the philosophy of democracy and non-violence'; and the 'construction of strong and effective' trade unions with sufficient power and influence was the 'only available means open for workers to attain full economic and social freedom and, when attained, maintain it.'

In 1982 David Pettigrew of the Northern Ireland Arts Council was Commissioned to create a bronze bust of James Larkin Junior.[17]

CONGRESS

The FWUI affiliated to Congress for 50,000 members from 1980. On 6 November 1981 an Inter-Union Relation Agreement was signed between the FWUI, ITGWU and ATGWU. Disagreements would be referred through the Inter-Relations Committee, with no transfers without prior agreement or if members were in arrears. For any transfer an 80% majority was also required.

In October the ICTU Industrial Relations Committee granted the FWUI negotiating rights within the ESB, with no opposition from the ITGWU, National Engineering and Electrical Trade Union or United Stationary Engine Drivers' Trade Union. The ATGWU, which did not attend the hearing, did object, together with the ESB management, and made life difficult by either not attending or walking out of meetings attended by the FWUI.

FWUI reports always cited ICTU policy statements at great length. The FWUI regarded itself as a significant contributor to Congress and strongly felt that policy initiatives should be made through it. This contrasted with the ITGWU, which felt it was its right to establish independent policy lines, even if those lines were parallel to, though not identical with, Congress. Policy differences raised interesting questions about what the relationship between SIPTU and Congress should be. The ITGWU, with greater resources than the FWUI, was in a better position to contribute its own policy responses. The FWUI did make policy initiatives when it felt the need. Similarly, it was a more conspicuous presence in Dublin Council of Trade Unions than the ITGWU. In 1988, Paddy Trehy was unopposed as President of the Trades Council.[18]

WAGES

Cardiff reported on negotiations for a Second National Understanding in September 1979, noting employers' disunity and divisions between 'those whose jobs were not in a strong position, labour intensive, low technology' as against those holding a stronger hand. After a second breakdown the Taoiseach, Charles Haughey, pressured the employers to go back to the table. Cardiff thought it 'of paramount importance' that National Understandings be maintained.

After a lengthy debate the GEC voted in favour, 6 to 4—hardly a ringing endorsement. Jim Quinn expressed unease with a process that was, to some extent, 'usurping the functions of the political parties'—a common criticism, usually coming from the opposite wing of the park. A ballot on 22 October accepted the Second National Understanding, 18,241 to 4,495. Members wanted a detailed analysis of what exactly emanated from National Understandings. Although supporting the principle, many still suspected a confidence trick. Cardiff wondered 'where we are going.' The FWUI 'tried to get away' from narrow National Wage Agreements 'right from the start.' There were forty-nine items in the National Understanding, and a study would be time-consuming. The FWUI's support was a critical one. A White Paper on pensions and the removal of anomalies within pay structures in the public service were demanded.[19]

On 26 September 1981 a Special Conference reviewed the National Under-standing, supporting exploratory talks in the ICTU, a decision upheld by a Special Congress on 28 September, 316 to 116. The employers insisted on a pay pause, linking increases closely with productivity and banning all comparability or relativity claims. No satisfactory progress was made, but after an intervention through Professor Basil Chubb the Government made a unilateral announcement that Congress would not accept unless in direct discussion with employers. On 27 November 1981 Congress rejected the employers' offers, not least in the context of an expected inflation rate of 20 to 25%, with both proposed increases and restrictions attached unacceptable. At direct talks with the Government on 15 October, Congress sought assurances on planning and the maintenance of public-sector employment, acceptance of tax equity, the implementation of outstanding commitments under the National Understanding and the establishment of Joint Monitoring Committees. Some progress was reported, but, in the absence of agreement, workers were pushed back to watch the action from the wings rather than centre stage.

The FWUI thought it 'extremely regrettable' that attempts to negotiate a Third National Understanding failed. The concept was viciously attacked by employers and 'looked upon less favourably by some politicians who wished to confine' the movement to 'a centralised narrow wages policy.' 'Even more regrettable' were attacks from unions whose 'basic motivations arose from purely narrow sectional interests divorced from consideration of the movement as a whole.' The FWUI felt that 'National Understandings were a brave, original and creative attempt to broaden the scope' of collective bargaining: 'Historically and in retrospect they will be so viewed.' Cardiff, incumbent President of the ICTU, was downcast. No. 15 Branch jumped the gun by circulating a motion calling for public-sector negotiations, invoking a strong reprimand from the GEC. The ICTU Public Services Committee did, however, negotiate a public-sector pay Agreement covering non-commercial state-sponsored bodies, which in turn 'set the effective minimum level' for private-sector pay. When Fianna Fáil resumed office in 1982, however, it reneged on the Agreement, suspending the third phase and seeking renegotiation. Compromise and payment were eventually concluded in January 1983.[20]

In August 1982 protest marches were held against the public service pay embargo, initiated by the ITGWU in Cork but eventually held under the auspices of the ICTU Public Services Committee. The Government wanted deferment of an agreed 5% until at least January 1983 and no increases at all in 1982 or 1983. Meetings were sought with the Taoiseach. All agreed that the national finances were in a critical state, but Cardiff thought more intelligent handling of matters by the Government might have brought a different response.

It was estimated that the embargo would affect 23,000 members. Cardiff reminded the GEC that the FWUI's financial position was not great: there was £120,000 in the deposit account, £96,416 due from a pension premium and a cash balance of £23,680. The sale of premises in Gardiner Place might raise £57,000, but should widespread action occur the sale of investment stock and an overdraft might be necessary. Settlement terms emerged in October.

In the private sector the next five years were a constant battle against 'downsizing', 'lean production', the removal of non-wage benefits, continuous demands for greater productivity and the emergence of direct employee involvement that saw Personnel Managers replaced by 'human resource' managers. Officials were stretched to hold the line, employers wiping the bargaining wall smooth of once-familiar footholds of relativity, bonus schemes, consolidated rates—all manner of outcrops that could be gripped, not least to break a fall.

In 1987, just as the right-wing agenda seemed about to triumph, with recession at its lowest ebb, the ICTU brought about the Programme for National Recovery 'against all the odds' and 'temporarily side-tracked' those elements in society hostile to unions. The FWUI's guard remained high, however. Employers continued 'to pursue the central core of their policy of marginalising and weakening organised labour.' Once weakened, 'the voice of the ordinary individual is no longer heard,' and 'hard-won rights' to have 'some say in how their life might be shaped is removed.' The Programme for National Recovery met long-standing union objectives: real increases in living standards, employment creation, help for the lower-paid, shorter working hours, tax relief for PAYE workers, the extension of PRSI to farmers and the self-employed, no more compulsory public-sector redundancies, social welfare increases and hope for the long-term unemployed. This last 'break-through' was justification enough for accepting the deal. The FWUI claimed that Congress was 'successful in convincing the elected Government of the day to sit down and treat them as equals in designing a policy' for recovery. Larkin Junior's legacy and Cardiff's hopes were realised.

Those who never gave credence to union arguments saw threats to parliamentary democracy. Unions remained free to attack the Government, but the country's crisis was of such proportions that an imaginative, consensus approach demonstrated the Government's courage. The FUE preferred the bargaining focus to remain within the work-place; centralised bargaining gave unions, at the national and the industrial level, 'an unreasonably strong position.' The Agreement was presented to members in simultaneous issues of *Unity* and *Liberty News*. Both the GEC and the NEC of the ITGWU argued that it was the 'best deal available'.

In 1989 the FWUI reflected that 'many of us believed that the problems facing the Irish economy were of such magnitude that it was impossible to imagine' a halt in the 'continual slide in the living standards' of members at work and 'for the vast army of the unemployed.' Recovery was dramatic and a total vindication of the FWUI-ITGWU-ICTU line. Congress criticised the Government for its ill-conceived voluntary severance scheme in the pubic service, seeing its abandonment as the acid test of the sincerity of the Government's commitment to the Programme for National Recovery.[21]

DISPUTES

Dispute Pay in 1980 was meagre, £6,894, reflecting industrial peace brought by National Understandings. The closure of International Meat Packers in Ringsend, Dublin, cost 300 jobs. In 1981 Dispute Pay rose to £41,105. A strike in Cantrell and Cochrane, Cork and Dublin, occurred in January. An ICTU All-Out Picket was applied to the company's Belfast plant, the first All-Out Picket board to cross the border. The Belfast stoppage quickly ended the dispute.

In HB Ice Cream another All-Out Picket was poorly supported, except in Dundalk, where the FWUI had members. They 'found it nearly impossible to get ITGWU Officials to honour' the pickets. The management tried to import ice cream from England, but a trip to meet Shop Stewards in Wall's British factory quickly stopped that; and after intervention by the Employer-Labour Conference full victory was secured.

Strike sanction was given in Aer Lingus in May 1982 in a relativity claim for operative members, having its origins in 1966. A two-week strike took place in Trinity College, Dublin, in the spring of 1983, the first in the college's 400-year history. The authorities refused to honour an Agreement to pay Dublin Corporation scales, which had been increased, agreed as part of the Public Service Agreement. The college tried to fight the public sector pay embargo in isolation. Success came by subtly detaching the college from the Agreement.

The expulsion of two Aer Lingus cabin crew members, leaders of the '1980 Group' who were pursuing an equality claim on their Committee's recommendation, led to High Court injunctions being served on the union. The case was settled out of Court but created animus. A three-week strike in An Bord Iascaigh Mhara could not prevent the company's offices being moved from Ballsbridge to Dún Laoghaire but gained acceptable compensation.[22]

Table 129: FWUI Dispute Pay, 1980–89

	Total expenditure	Dispute Pay (£)	As a proportion of expenditure (%)
1980	833,384	6,894	0.8
1981	1,064,487	41,105	3.8
1982	1,358,389	77,212	5.6
1983	1,529,103	58,897	3.8
1984	1,892,297	220,391	11.6
1985	2,483,681	52,343	2.1
1986	2,422,380	144,467	5.9
1987	2,587,747	113,382	4.3
1988	2,901,919	137,291	4.7
1989	2,616,191	n.a.	n.a.

Source: FWUI, reports of annual Delegate Conferences, 1980–89.

Most battles were about 'trying to defend existing conditions.' Employers used the 'Russian roulette' system of industrial relations, threatening to close unless a 'no strike' clause and 'rationalisation' were accepted—the latter a 'code word for reducing the conditions that exist' for those remaining and redundancy for many more. The Government and media, blithely ignoring the facts, insisted that the root of all evil was trade unions, and that all protective legislation should be removed. They gazed with relish on Thatcherite success in smashing British labour. The FWUI looked to Congress for leadership to counter black propaganda.

In 1985 a ten-week strike reduced the number of sackings and improved terms in Bord na Móna at Littleton (Co. Tipperary) and Lullymore (Co. Kildare). In 1988 Tom Geraghty, tired and battered from the Dublin firefighters' dispute, condemned the 'regular use of the armed forces for strike breaking' and the 'role played by leading Officials in Government Departments in organising' it. Tactics in Ireland were less blatant than Thatcher's frontal attacks, but they had seen a secret Department of Justice document issued on 21 January, 'where senior civil servants from four Departments sat down and drew up contingency plans which involved the use of the army.' These people were 'members of trade unions.' The worry was that the use of soldiers would 'be considered the norm.'[23]

The FWUI dispensed £851,892 on Dispute Pay in the 1980s. It was a considerably higher outlay than in the 1950s (£13,927), 1960s (£241,244) or 1970s (£410,5694).

CLONDALKIN PAPER MILLS

In 1982 unions in Clondalkin Paper Mills—the FWUI (No. 1 and No. 17 Branches), ITGWU, AUEW-TASS, Bookbinders and craft unions—prepared to negotiate on redundancies, a seven-month pay freeze, an 18% wage increase over thirty months and new conditions. 'Bit by bit' reluctance to accept new conditions was eroded 'until there was nothing left to concede.' Henry Lund, who took over the mill, accepted a 45% investment from Fóir Teoranta, the Government's capital fund, the rest coming from the company (45%) and the work force (10%), but the company wanted 100% control. In a meeting with Government agencies and the Minister Lund asked for time to consider a new offer to secure the company, but the following morning a liquidator took control, something Lund already knew.

Two days before the closure Tom McGrath of the ICTU arranged a deal with Fóir Teoranta, but the terms were altered at the last hour by the company to an unacceptable extent. A 35-member Workers' Action Committee was formed for a 'political fight to get the mill opened,' but 'from the outset the media turned on the workers.' Demonstrations were held outside the Dáil as the Government fell, wives and children drilling home the significance of the closure for their community. Dockers blacked the import of paper, workers pledged support, but the mill remained closed.

With Haughey's Government in 1982 the workers thought they were 'home and dry', as Fianna Fáil 'had given all the assurances written and verbal that we could hope to get.' Within three months, on 9 June, the Minister for Industry and Energy, Albert Reynolds, would reopen the mill, without fail. He did not. Reynolds gave an undertaking to Congress and the Workers' Committee, guaranteeing payment to the liquidator of 10% of the purchase price 'within seven days of receiving the signatures of all ex-CPM employees,' thus enabling the Government 'to receive an unencumbered mill.' Two 'snags' were found, relating to water rights and the ownership of a small parcel of land. Dick Spring assured workers that arrangements with the previous Government would be honoured.

Requests for strike sanction, ultimately granted, caused much anxiety in the GEC. It worried that sanction might allow the Minister or the new owners to renege on Agreements to reopen. Blanket embargoes on paper imports were a problem, because the Talbot Decision imposed legal restrictions on such action. In any case, most paper came through Larne. Worse, in the final analysis 'it would be difficult' to make the mill a 'viable proposition.' Any dispute would terminate when the Government took control.

In January 1983 the Fine Gael Minister for Industry and Energy, John Bruton, denied any knowledge of a commitment to reopen. He needed time to investigate. Workers were in 24-hour occupation, and on 8 March, International Women's Day, wives and partners joined them in a gesture of solidarity.

Removing the workers was necessary to enable the liquidator to sell assets, and injunctions were taken out against six occupants. The injunctions were not contested. The men would not acknowledge their contempt and were committed to Mountjoy Prison. The night before their incarceration the Executive Council of Congress met Government representatives and demanded that the paper mill be purchased. Under this pressure and the threat of 'massive strikes in support of those jailed,' the Government yielded and paid the liquidator 10% of the £1¾ million, the balance due on 22 March. The GEC urged the vacation of the premises in February.

On 22 June, Bruton told the workers that 'the only way the Mill will open is to have private enterprise participate with' the Government. Purchasing did 'not commit us to open it.' Congress expressed grave concern at the Government's delay and called for 'early re-opening.' It secured a personal undertaking from the Taoiseach, Garret FitzGerald, that a decision 'one way or the other' would be given in August. Like other political promises, it was broken.

Pickets were placed on the Stationery Office in Beggar's Bush (now the home of the Irish Labour History Society Archives); but, although workers refused to handle paper, it was 'not enough to force the Government's hand.' An embargo on handling paper in all public enterprises 'fell flat on its face.' In November two members of the Workers' Committee, Myles Speight and Brian Nolan, decided, of their own accord, to go on hunger strike. The FWUI dissociated itself from this tactic but maintained general support. The hunger strike lasted two weeks and ended when the Government announced that a Canadian purchaser was found.

The GEC agreed that unless the Labour Party voted with Fianna Fáil for reopening it would consider suspending its affiliation. The Labour Party, in Government with Fine Gael, had declined to do so.

The FWUI Branch Secretary, Peter Keating, became synonymous with Clondalkin. He appealed to Delegates to support the struggle, as it raised issues regarding employment, company law and exploitation ranging well beyond the mill. The prospect of 230 jobs in the mill in late 1985 was one of the 'very few bright spots' for employment. Keating's tenacity kept Clondalkin open.

Leinster Paper Mills—the original name and now the new name for Clondalkin Paper Mills—would reopen in May 1986. After four years of delay the Government finally agreed to provide nearly £4 million for renovation. Nearly 200 workers were employed by the spring of 1986. Whereas previously both the FWUI and ITGWU catered for general workers, a 'near unanimous decision' by ballot determined that the FWUI would be the 'sole union'.

The paper mill was in trouble in late 1986, and lay-offs were enforced. For the union, 'the only problem' for the mill was 'under-capitalisation.' A further battle loomed. The mill ceased operations in December. Its 'financial base' was 'unsound' from the start, and bank interest bled the company dry. In March 1987 a receiver was appointed but was opposed by the workers, who secured his removal, an act that 'created a precedent.' Rory O'Farrell of Touche Ross came in, and Leinster Paper Mills was sold to Dynasty of Canada for £4.2 million. By December the deal collapsed. Another Canadian Corporation, Roman, expressed interest, and the FWUI sought the Minister for Industry and Commerce, Albert Reynolds, to act as intermediary. His speed of action would not have blurred a photograph. All that kept the mill shut was the absence of political will.

Keating pursued an increasingly lost cause. It seemed that no Irish company was prepared to enter an annual market worth £300 million in paper imports. The receiver sold the machinery for export to Morocco, ending the whole sorry saga. 'Every scrap of paper' used in Ireland now had to be imported. Even in retirement in April 1989 the old warrior Keating still hoped that 'some good must come from all the efforts to maintain a Paper Mill in Clondalkin.'[24]

THE BATTLE OF MOORE STREET

In September 1981 a strike was sanctioned in Dublin Corporation against the decision to run down its Design and Construction Section. Despite apparent ambivalence by the Irish Municipal Employees' Trade Union and the ITGWU, the FWUI took the lead and the issue was resolved. The GEC concluded that, among the lessons learnt, was that the 'actions of the IMETU and ITGWU do not always match up to their stated policies.' The FWUI's General Officers, the ICTU, the Employer-Labour Conference and the Department of the Public Service were all involved with Branch Officers and Shop Stewards, a large drain on time and resources.

On 17 January 1985 the three unions discussed strategy. The IMETU suggested that those with pay relativities with the Corporation—the VEC, Dún Laoghaire Corporation and Eastern Health Board—be involved from the start. The FWUI and ITGWU instead proposed that an ICTU All-Out Picket be sought. The Fire Brigade Section was unhappy about a lack of consultation but would comply. The application of the All-Out Picket was delayed, however, to 25 February. Only one union objected, the Sheet Metal Workers' Union, which had twelve members employed. Congress said it would grant an All-Out Picket after the aggregate result of General Meetings on 10 February.

FWUI members voted, by 354 to 107, to reject the Corporation's offer and to strike, but the IMETU voted in favour, 581 to 513, and the ITGWU likewise, 379 to 150. The aggregate result was thus for acceptance, 1,067 to 1,017. The IMETU announced that it was now 'going alone', disregarding the previous tripartite approach. This put the FWUI in 'an impossible position.' On 12 February a meeting narrowly reversed its decision and accepted the offer, 262 to 247, 'because we had no option.' The FWUI rather bitterly concluded that 'major issues' had to be learnt by the three unions.

Recruitment in some areas of Dublin Corporation was non-existent after 1982. Casualisation by stealth occurred, with part-time workers replacing full-time workers in play centres, a policy disappointingly upheld by the Labour Court. The FWUI rejected a 'ridiculous' Twenty-Fifth Wage Round offer from the management. The Branch Secretary, Eddie Glackin, attacked the Minister, Ruairí Quinn, suggesting that his theme was that 'Corporation workers in full-time, well-paid jobs were keeping the unemployed out of work.' Glackin wanted to move the vote of thanks after Quinn's address to the 1986 Conference dinner, but Attley 'was not too keen on the idea.' Although wearing his FWUI tie, Quinn had warned that Glackin 'should not feel he had him by the neck,' to which Glackin—reflecting members' frustration—assured the Minister that the 'pressure point that needs to be squeezed to get the maximum response is a bit lower than the neck': a politician's neck was the 'hardest portion of their anatomy.'

From finishing time at midnight on Conference Sunday, members withdrew from work. Glackin concluded with a rallying cry: 'If the Minister or anybody else is concerned about local authority employment, let them start by paying proper wages to the workers that they have there and forget about these slave-labour half-jobs: they are not going to come into Dublin Corporation.'

Having exhausted all procedures, including the Labour Court, the strike began on 26 May. It lasted three weeks, until intervention by the Employer-Labour Conference produced a revised offer of £5 a week from 1 May and £6 from 16 February 1987, plus a lump sum of £250. All three unions accepted this on 15 June, although subsequently the Corporation reneged on the £250 payment. Matters had to be pursued on a time-consuming individual basis. The ferocity of feeling during the dispute caught the public imagination, providing tabloids with a field day. The GEC concluded: 'Members will have vivid memories of the dispute, including the "Battle of Moore Street".' It was to the 'eternal credit of the Strike Committee for the way they organised and conducted the dispute.' There was a palpable sense of pride throughout the FWUI, not least in the hole punched through the Government's public-sector pay guidelines. The union had publicised low pay and gained substantial public support for poorly paid council workers.

In 1987 cut-backs and 'structured overtime' became central, contentious issues for Dublin Corporation staff. A breach of the Housing Attendants Agreement in May led to a lengthy dispute, with members put off the payroll.[25]

DUBLIN GAS COMPANY

An official strike in Dublin Gas Company from 15 October to 13 November 1984 arose over the renewal of the contractors' Agreement in the Distribution Department. Complex technical detail clouded the essential kernel of the dispute: when employers attacked the 'most fundamental tenet on which industrial relations are based—the observance of Agreements'—unions had 'no alternative but to confront such situations with all the power at their disposal.' From 1 September the management continued to use contractors, although the Agreement had run out; allocated work to contractors without agreement; supplied those contractors; failed to give twenty days' notice of lay-offs; and continued to use contractors even though the Agreement said that all contracting would stop from the first day of any official action. The intervention of the Employer-Labour Conference was eventually required to settle matters. A receiver was sought on 11 April 1986 and a 'survival plan' produced in July. Four hundred redundancies were announced, wages frozen, and travel time, mileage allowances, sickness payments, overtime and shift allowances eliminated or reduced, together with other worsened conditions. A 'viability Agreement' emerged after strike notice in September and was reluctantly accepted. Frank Cluskey's 'constant' and 'exemplary' support and his threat to withdraw support from the Government induced the Taoiseach, Garret FitzGerald, to increase the amounts for redundancy, publish details of where public money had gone, and generally facilitate agreement, including public ownership of the company.[26]

IRISH SHIPPING AND B&I

In 1984 the FWUI received an assurance that the troubled Irish Shipping Ltd—the state-owned shipping fleet—'had a long future ahead of it' and submitted claims under the Twenty-Fourth Round. A submission to the Joint Oireachtas Committee on Commercial State-Sponsored Bodies appealed for application of the Worker Participation (State Enterprises) Act, greater care in the appointment of Board members and the need for independent examination of the 'company's decision making and management structure.'

In November the liquidation of Irish Shipping was announced. The FWUI claimed six weeks' pay per year of service for severance and other statutory entitlements, opposed the appointment by the High Court of an official liquidator and established the Minister's responsibility for members stranded in Mombasa and Taiwan. Politically, demonstrations and Dáil pickets were mounted, and direct meetings were sought with the Minister for Communications, Jim Mitchell, and Minister for Labour, Ruairí Quinn. A letter from the Taoiseach, Garret FitzGerald, thanked the seamen, 'who have served the country well,' and recognised that they and their families were 'innocent victims'. Washing his hands, he blamed the company's charter policies, entered into 'without the knowledge or approval' of the Government or the Minister, which bankrupted it. The FWUI traced a shameful episode of bungling ineptitude, political indifference and a capacity to be economical with the truth that was breathtaking in scale. A national scandal was avoided only because of public indifference and a failure to comprehend the significance of the country's maritime situation. Garry contrasted the treatment of Irish Shipping with that of the Insurance Corporation of Ireland. Ships' crews were left stranded around the globe without warning, and pensions were 'savagely and miserably reduced.' The restoration of full pension rights was demanded. In both Irish Shipping and the Insurance Corporation the senior management, who had made dreadful errors, seemed unaccountable and personally immune to the consequences of their actions. The FWUI opposed the liquidation and fought for the retention of an Irish merchant fleet. Mitchell's washing of hands was a 'cop-out.'

In 1985 Con Rigney and Brendan Smith (No. 15) demanded a formal inquiry, contrasting the 'disgraceful' treatment of pensioners with the 'payoff of £66,000 and a pension of £27,000 per annum awarded to one of the major culprits in this scandal, Mr Willie O'Neill.' A queue of speakers formed in support. A submission to the Mitchell Committee on Maritime Requirements was 'ignored', a fate that befell most union suggestions. Public, media and Dáil turned deaf ears and blind eyes. In 1986 at a meeting with the Tánaiste, Dick Spring, it was pointed out that O'Neill, former Chairman of Irish Shipping, had received the equivalent of six weeks' salary for every year of service. Why not the workers? Another demonstration, in November 1987, was to no avail.

An interesting development was the support of Workers' Unity Trust for a co-operative, Irish Marine Services, established by former members. In 1989 the FWUI still campaigned and brought individual cases to the Employment Appeals Tribunal, a time-consuming business. It was a sad comment on the Government and public servants that such actions were necessary.

In 1987 the FWUI complained that the management of the B&I Line ignored procedures, issued ultimatums and threatened closure. Yet on 'each and every occasion' on which members took industrial action to resist such bullying it 'brought the wrath of the popular newspapers down on the heads of these workers.' The success of such tactics could 'not be underestimated.' Nowhere had this been more apparent than in the B&I when the FWUI fought to defend jobs. Worse, they were also 'subjected to a picket from other workers within B&I protesting against the Union's actions to stand up for its members.' A strike in March 1987 to secure safe and adequate manning levels was successful.

Further financial problems brought conflict and a drastic survival plan, to run until 1989, involving a 5% wage cut and changes of conditions. It was FWUI ships' officers who led resistance to job cuts, with, in an 'unprecedented move', members of other unions marching to Parnell Square 'to put pressure on' union officers 'to abandon their support of the Ship's Officers.' Unmoved, the FWUI won the day; but such splits in the trade union timbers of B&I would have serious long-term implications for the seaworthiness of the vessel *Solidarity*.[27]

IRISH HOSPITALS TRUST

The closure of Irish Hospitals Trust was among the sadder membership losses. Competition from the National Lottery meant that the end of the 'Irish Hospitals Sweepstake' came on 1 March 1986. A sting in the tail was the inadequacy of redundancy payments after income from the sale of the property, sold back to the Government, was taxed, leaving much less than anticipated in the kitty. Despite assurances from successive Ministers, sufficient money was not forthcoming. Maura Doolin, a stalwart activist, called for decent treatment for redundant members in 1987. Even after the creation of SIPTU Officials were 'working continuously' on behalf of union members to secure an 'undistributed Prize Fund' which 'effectively belongs to no one.' A Bill was submitted to the Government, suggesting its allocation among former employees, and the union was hopeful. The old troops were 'not forgotten' in the pursuit of justice.[28]

FIREFIGHTERS

In 1987 Dublin Corporation's decision to reduce operating levels in Dublin Fire Brigade was strongly resisted. It placed 'the lives of those who work in the Brigade' and the 'citizens of Dublin City in jeopardy.' It was not a dispute about pay but support for a 'proper fire service' and 'adequate health and safety protection' for firefighters. The GEC congratulated the strikers for their 'courageous stand'. A most 'heartening aspect' was the international solidarity from fire brigade unions in Britain, Europe and the United States, especially members of the Fire Brigades Union in Northern Ireland. The action demonstrated the union's commitment to supporting the members' democratic decision 'in defiance of Government policy.'

Until this dispute the Fire Service was relatively free of the 'jackboot of cut-backs'. Two issues collided: reneging by the management on a negotiated manning Agreement and a disagreement over overtime. On 24 November the management announced that thirty-nine men were approved for redundancy under the public service package, although no consultation had taken place. The FWUI Committee immediately began a campaign of lobbying politicians and flooding the media. At a Special Meeting on 10 December members decided to withhold co-operation with restructuring. Between 2 and 6 January 1988 forty non-cooperating members were removed from the payroll. On 11 January members voted to strike, 579 to 47, a margin attributed to the 'particularly belligerent and inflammatory public relations approach of the Corporation.'

The strike began on 22 January and 'was absolute bar one individual.' Retained (part-time) members in North County Dublin came out. Dún Laoghaire members were locked out from 29 January for confining themselves to the borough. The Corporation was assisted by the army, Gardaí and Government Departments. A 'major military style operation complete with propaganda and suppression of news' was mounted against the union.

Members 'remained solid and resilient.' Weekly cheques came from firefighters in Cork, Drogheda, Dundalk, Galway, Limerick, Sligo and Waterford, from Northern Ireland and from overseas, greatly boosting morale. Labour Court proposals on 19 February were rejected, 515 to 49, leading to direct intervention by the Minister for Labour, Bertie Ahern. A package emerged on 29 March and was accepted, 570 to 51. It provided for the recruitment of twelve additional firefighters on 8 July; a minimum manning level of six hundred, with an annual review each November; a guaranteed number of third officers and District officers, with eight new posts at station officer level; the maintenance of agreed pay structures; and reinstatement without loss of those suspended. It was a thundering victory, not just for the FWUI but for the movement and particularly for the strength of the new Programme for National Recovery. The FWUI hoped it would 'encourage others to resist unilateral action' by employers.

At the 1988 Conference Tom Geraghty thanked all for their support. More than £40,000 was collected, with some remaining in the hands of the Strike Committee. He handed a cheque for £5,000 to the General Secretary of the Fire Brigades Union,

Ken Cameron, 'to be handed on to the National Union of Seamen to support their battle to stay in existence.'

Less pleasant was some members' strike-breaking. Ambulance crews employed by health boards agreed to additional rosters before the strike to cover work normally handled by Dublin Fire Brigade, and controllers in the Eastern Health Board took over the 999 service usually manned by fire brigade personnel. Geraghty was forthright: 'What a dreadful indictment of this movement that members of the union would set out deliberately to strike-break,' to 'consistently undermine' the dispute 'in spite of the requests from Officials from this Branch, in spite of directions from the General Secretary to cease their action.' They did 'not have any major effect' on the dispute but had 'a terrible effect' on morale.

The men received praise for achieving their objective, the 'maintenance of a properly manned Fire and Ambulance service.' The Corporation tried to roll back training and manning Agreements hard won by the union in the wake of the Stardust disaster. 'Old rivalries' between the FWUI and IMETU were forgotten as 'firefighters stood united behind the DFB Pipe Band, displaying discipline, commitment and sacrifice.' The Corporation quietly got on with the task of attempting to renege on the settlement.

RADIO TELEFÍS ÉIREANN

RTÉ experienced acute financial problems in the 1980s, its very survival at risk. The demotion of a producer, Pat Feeley, occasioned a lengthy dispute, complicated by a parallel wage claim for presentation assistants. Tensions within the GEC led to suggestions that the RTÉ tail wagged the FWUI dog.

In November 1981 the management refused to pay the Sales Manager, Brian Higgins, an increment because of his 'unacceptable level of trade union activity.' Strike sanction was granted, although the ballot was not overwhelming. Agreement was reached without a strike, but matters became acrimonious, with Higgins (GEC) challenging the union's decisions. In 1987 hard questions were asked of staff and management relating to cost-cutting and living within means. Section 31 of the Broadcasting Act was a matter of extreme contention. The FWUI sought legal advice about whether it infringed the rights of broadcasters under Section 10 of the European Convention of Human Rights. A picket was placed on the Minister's office on the renewal of the ban on Sinn Féin members being allowed on air.

Gerry Gregg (GEC) wrote to the *Sunday Tribune* in support of Section 31, prompting the General Secretary to write to all industrial staff to clarify that the union's policy was opposition. John Caden (No. 15) complained of a 'smear campaign' against himself, Gregg and Eoghan Harris because of their 'total opposition to the murderous Provo campaign.' The Branch Secretary, Bernard Browne, thought it strange that 'exactly the same' report that was presented to the Branch AGM should now be the vehicle for a Delegate attacking the Branch. He denied that any individuals were smeared because of their politics. It was a smokescreen to cover the challenge some were making to democratic decisions taken by the Branch and endorsed by the GEC, including the sanctioning of industrial action.

Caden was obliged to leave the union on promotion to senior management, and Browne thought it sad that, having been a solid member for many years, he should leave 'on the basis of allegations which are wholly unsubstantiated and simply not factual.' Gregg said the FWUI's opposition to Section 31 was clarified in Salthill in 1986, calling for its replacement to include anti-sectarian and anti-racist provisions. Betty Purcell (No. 15) said there was a McCarthyite atmosphere in RTÉ. Anyone who did not 'row in behind the supporters of the Workers' Party' was likely to be smeared as a Provo supporter. It was unusual for such dirty linen to be washed in the public laundry of a Delegate Conference.

Further problems arose among producers over the allocation of Budgets and costs. Harris, never slow to express his opinion, attacked the RTÉ Section Committee at a joint FWUI-Equity meeting in November 1987, and resigned from the union. He later withdrew his resignation, which the union had accepted. Attley, writing to Bernard Browne, said this in 'no way excused his public attack on democratically elected representatives.' The Section Committee had the GEC's full support; 'these unwarranted attacks' damaged the 'interests of the membership.' A personal campaign by some members in RTÉ had caused difficulties for the FWUI as a whole, as their views, in many public minds, had not been distinguished from the union's formal position.

In 1982 the blame for 'an unnecessary strike' was laid squarely at the door of the management. The FWUI wanted the introduction of extensive new technology to be done in a planned manner through agreement, a joint assessment scheme to determine job grading, the settlement of a claim for productivity among library staff begun in 1979 and a 13% pay rise for clerical staff, whose pay had fallen out of line with agreed comparators. Despite negotiations beginning in 1981 the management's intransigence prevented progress at conciliation or the Labour Court, not least because the company refused to attend the hearing. An offer finally emerged fifteen minutes before a strike began. Although problems were deferred, a 3½-day stoppage was needed before there was a satisfactory settlement.

The discipline of RTÉ members was again necessary in 1988, together with others in FÁS and the Eastern Health Board. Such 'lack of solidarity' was regarded as serious, weakening the union's actions 'to the very core.' Those who had 'participated with management in strike breaking' were swiftly dealt with. It was gravely disappointing and a 'measure of the deterioration in trade union standards' that those disciplined were offered membership of other ICTU-affiliated unions.[29]

ATYPICAL WORKERS

Concerns about 'atypical' workers grew in the mid-1980s. 'Flexible' work arrangements and the decline of 'permanent, pensionable' jobs created organisational difficulties. Part-time, contract and zero-hours workers were 'potentially the soft underbelly' of the labour market, being more likely to break a strike and tolerate poor pay and conditions. Janet Hughes (Women Workers' Branch) spoke of distributing 21,000 leaflets around Dublin in March 1986 in an attempt to create awareness and extend organisation. They got little return but discovered the frighteningly low standards many workers had to accept. The black economy was integral to exploitation by employers. Fear of unemployment was rife, as was a lack of belief in trade unionism. Previous poor experiences of unions were reported regularly. They had to recognise the extent to which 'we are seen as part of the problem.'

Attley complained about the 'hum in the hall' during the debate. Did it indicate a lack of concern? Perhaps atypical workers were unorganised because no-one cared.

The FWUI received written complaints from other unions claiming exclusive rights to organise in certain areas, and yet the workers remained unorganised.[30]

INDUSTRIAL RELATIONS REFORM

In 1980 'widespread disillusionment' and mistrust of the Labour Court were expressed. Pádraigín Ní Mhurchú complained that Officials faced a 'major credibility problem' when suggesting to members that matters be referred to the Court. There were constant delays, obfuscation, conservative findings and under-resourcing. The 1983 Conference wanted legislation to enable workers who were victims of their company's bankruptcy or insolvency to be 'given status of first creditor' and be able to receive all statutory entitlements, tax, PRSI and pension contributions, with stiff penalties for defaulters.

In 1987 Garry spoke at length about his hopes for industrial democracy, the need to include a 'participation clause' in every negotiated Agreement, and the benefits of access to financial information. Employers were in the ascendant, however.

In 1988 Patricia King, Assistant Branch Secretary of No. 15 Branch, succeeded in getting an amendment order to the Protection of Employees (Employers' Insolvency) Act (1984) passed, entitling any claimant over sixty-six to full entitlements to minimum notice, redundancy and pay from the Employment Appeals Tribunal, a small but significant improvement.[31]

EMPLOYMENT AND EUROPE

The FWUI strongly supported the economic policy of Congress but codified its thoughts in 'Economic and Social Planning'. It condemned Governments for neither defining nor adequately quantifying their attempts at 'planning' and relying exclusively on 'private enterprise as a mean of generating wealth and employment.' This had 'failed.' Public enterprise was created only when the private sector either 'could not, or would not,' fulfil particular requirements but was spancelled by under-capitalisation or restrictions on their operation. The solution to mass unemployment and emigration did not lie in 'unqualified criticism or praise' of either public or private sectors: it lay in 'an aggressive extension of both, although the essential elements must be 'planned private enterprise expansion, extension of the Public Sector and a planned harmony' between them. This echoed Young Jim Larkin.

While some value in the three Programmes for Economic and Social Development and various White Papers was recognised, indicative planning was insufficient. The FWUI wanted fixed, achievable targets at the national, regional and sectoral levels, the establishment of a National Planning Council with sufficient resources and powers and essential social objectives factored into a proper economic plan. The National Planning Council must be independent, have sufficient powers and be fully representative of the public and private sectors, including co-operatives, agriculture, and Congress. A National Enterprise Agency would be a natural creation of the National Planning Council. This 'preamble' of ideas captured the essence of FWUI policy, honed over many Conferences, moved and supported by the ICTU.[32]

The FWUI was, to a considerable extent, a 'public service union', and Cardiff suggested an annual seminar to co-ordinate policy and negotiating responses. Garry related how Seán Lemass, in response to Young Jim Larkin's calls in the 1950s for planning, said that 'every time he heard the term economic planning he reached for his gun.' If the FWUI felt they were 'pioneers' of the concept, many in powerful positions were still ready to draw their weapons.

Eugene Fitzsimons (No. 17) initiated a lengthy debate on redundancy policy. Peter Keating argued that it was quite clear: for those who wished to fight, the sanction for industrial action would be given. Fitzsimons suggested a 'national week of activity culminating in an all-Ireland link-up in a Peoples' March for Jobs.' Nearly 300,000 people were unemployed in Ireland as a whole. Delegates responded with enthusiasm. Paul Smyth (No. 18) wanted opposition to all redundancies, a 35-hour week with no loss of pay, a crash programme of public works and the nationalisation of all banks and insurance. The Labour Party should be promoting this in the Dáil. Cardiff called for referral back, sympathising with the motion but questioning its practicalities. The Delegates, angered and frustrated by continuing depression, would have none of it and adopted the motion.

In 1984 the FWUI opposed the Government's document 'Building on Reality, 1984–1987'. Given 'our historically poor economic performance,' any 'National Plan' should surely have contained 'some re-structuring of economic policies, combined with a radical plan for re-distribution of incomes, wealth and opportunities?' Unions had co-operated in the national interest to grow the economy. 'Building on Reality', 'a scandalous abdication of responsibility,' exemplified the monetarist policies of the Fine Gael-Labour Coalition. ICTU policy, contained in 'Confronting the Jobs Crisis', was a far more serious and worthwhile proposal. Attley thought the Government should call its plan 'Building on Unreality'. In essence it proposed further unemployment and emigration. Neither the Government nor employers were 'prepared to accept us as essential partners' in solving the nation's ills, which made translating union policy into practice very difficult.[33]

Little changed, and unemployment and emigration increased. In 1986 Tom Redmond (No. 17) demanded that all 'our industrial and political strength' be used to 'counter the New Right,' that the public sector be defended, part-time and contract workers recruited, new communications opened with youth and women, and workers' co-operatives expanded. There was little to disagree with. The motion was long-sighted, its concerns being those that would be central to unions in the next century.

In 1986 the FWUI fully supported Congress's document 'Public Enterprise—Everybody's Business'. The Food Branch mounted a Buy Irish campaign to attack the 'national scandal of Irish people continuing to fund imports at the expense of home produced goods.' The emergence of the inappropriately named Progressive Democrats gave further political voice to 'economic Social Darwinism', a 'doctrine to defend the position of the rich and the powerful.' Getting union alternatives across was even more problematic.

In 1987 a plethora of motions condemned privatisation, which increased job losses, lowered standards, diminished revenue and accountability and led inevitably to non-union labour. In 1987 calls to renegotiate the Single European Act were carried 'overwhelmingly', qualifying the union's earlier endorsement of the EEC. Attley thought that had been a 'correct decision' and that few on the left any longer saw a role for Ireland outside Europe, even if such issues as neutrality and foreign policy were controversial.

In 1988 speakers cited their own family tragedies resulting from emigration. It was a short, poignant debate. Unemployed Centres were supported, although Hilda Breslin saw them as treating symptom rather than cause.[34]

TAX CAMPAIGN

The GEC wholeheartedly supported the pre-Budget tax demonstration of Tuesday 22 January 1980, while requesting that 'all essential services be maintained,' placing details of such arrangements in the press. More than 750,000 marched in the largest co-ordinated public demonstration in the country's history.

The GEC saw Congress as 'extraordinarily weak' after it called for non-cooperation with the Commission on Taxation. This was a hard conclusion, as the FWUI placed great faith in Congress and preferred to do its campaigning business through it. Cardiff warned of the dangers of public expenditure cuts and a switch from direct to indirect taxes. It was essential that matters be dealt with nationally or they would 'have trouble with the Trades Councils'.

At the Conference Eoghan Harris (No. 15) rejected the 'red herring of a Commission on Taxation' and demanded the 'immediate' taxing of farmers and self-employed and the 'professional classes and workers on an equitable basis.' Cardiff favoured the Commission, believing the ICTU members, Donal Nevin and Dan Murphy, would vigorously present the movement's case. Harris said the 'biggest Commission ever held' was on the streets and turned taxation 'into a class issue.' P. Bolger (Mid-West) wanted street demonstrations to continue and congratulated Dublin Council of Trade Unions. Cardiff would have none of it, defending the central role of Congress, vital in translating street anger into positive policy. He worried that dwindling numbers on marches damaged their cause. Greater co-ordination between the Trades Council and Congress was needed. Finally, the election posed questions about how many of the 750,000 who marched for tax reform then voted against it.[35] An atmosphere of impotence was palpable within the hall.

In June 1981 further stoppages at the discretion of the Executive Committee of the Trades Council were called for. The FWUI was alarmed, pointing out that the Trades Council had no authority to sanction industrial action. They were mindful of the Supreme Court's Talbot decision, seeing 'dangerous implications' in the proposals. They should be withdrawn. The FWUI had a record of support for actions on taxation, but the 'reaction from ordinary members' was increasingly against more stoppages. Poorly attended demonstrations damaged union credibility. The FWUI won the argument and the motion was withdrawn. In 1982 steam was rapidly escaping from the tax-reform engine. Expectations dropped. The Commission on Taxation served its political purpose of emasculating protests and providing an opportunity for the FUE to call for reductions in PRSI and for reforms to benefit the minority. Cardiff expressed concerns in April that the campaign to reduce PRSI would betray differences between workers in the private and public sectors. While the FWUI would 'fully support' May Day protests, it would avoid stoppages and await the report of the Commission.

Pressure continued for half-day stoppages and protest marches. The FWUI strengthened its Trades Council Delegation, electing Kevin Lynch as Leader and Matt Merrigan as Secretary. Another 100,000 marched in Dublin before the 1983 Budget in April; more than 70,000 marched in other parts of the country. Congress and the FWUI opposed the demonstration when first proposed by Dublin Trades Council on 27 February. Attley reminded members that the campaign was for tax equity, not cuts, and cautioned about the dangers of a PRSI campaign that would reduce the amount of money available before it affected Government policy. The Finance Bill would control avoidance, if implemented. The campaign's direction now had to be about broadening the tax base.

A plan for another demonstration on 1 July—on this occasion including unemployment and public-sector cuts—was opposed by the FWUI, which thought that the Finance Act (which became law on 4 June) had enacted enough of the ICTU-led amendments.

In 1984 Brian Hanney (Western Area) moved that, 'in view of the fact that the last protest march was a disorganised shambles,' a proper national campaign be mounted. He cited the German metalworkers' successful campaign to reduce working hours. Issue was taken with his term 'disorganised shambles', but he insisted on the value of self-criticism. Attley reminded everyone that when PAYE was first introduced, workers saw it as an equitable tax system. It had been corrupted by successive Governments. The GEC had reservations about elements of the Commission on Taxation's proposals, particularly the possible abolition of employers' PRSI contributions. This would leave a shortfall of £400 million, which would no doubt mostly be made good by further impositions on PAYE workers. Low capital tax and a single VAT rate of 15% on all items were also regressive.[36]

By 1986 ICTU marches and demonstrations had 'only limited success' and fell 'into disrepute.' Attley contrasted this with the successes of farmers and the self-employed. The big difference was that, while both unions and farmers could mass numbers on the streets, unions were 'unable to deliver our membership politically.' The Government appreciated that, if it stood firm and waited, protests would 'fizzle out to an undignified death.' Members had to be politicised or campaigns had limited value. The Government's failure or refusal to effect tax reform tired union opposition, presumably the intention.

Energy was still summoned to defend Deposit Interest Retention Tax (DIRT) from the headlights of New Right demands for regressive tax policies. The 'so-called Job Search Scheme' was regarded as a 'crude device designed to reduce the numbers' on the live register and to 'save' £11¼ million.' It reflected no credit on those who conceived it (Fine Gael) or on those who 'now so vigorously' sought to implement it (Fianna Fáil). In 1986 PAYE workers contributed £1,900 million, or more than 83% of the total tax intake of £2,380 million. The FWUI worried about the proliferation of 'Axe the Tax' stickers.

In 1987 some motions were not even debated, others adopted passively, almost ritualistically. Expectations of change had been reduced. Capital slept more easily.[37]

SOCIAL POLICY

In 1980 Michael Doyle (No. 16) called for an Anti-Poverty Programme and the defence of those threatened by cuts. He praised Combat Poverty, first introduced in 1972 when Frank Cluskey was Parliamentary Secretary to the Minister for Social Welfare. An FWUI Social Policy Conference publicised poverty and demanded that the national exchequer replace any EEC money that might be withdrawn. The housing crisis required the provision of more units at affordable costs or rents. The FWUI's priorities were: full employment, incorporating adequate rewards, with a dynamic facility for skills training and retraining; comprehensive health care available to all on the basis of need, with special emphasis on health education and preventive medicine; a guaranteed family income below which no family would fall; comprehensive educational facilities available to all at every level, academic and technical, with special emphasis on post-school cultural pursuits; adequate housing with an emphasis on construction training and environmental concerns; and a community 'in which equality of means in respect of the basic necessities of life, and of opportunity, are combined with free democratic institutions and planned economic activity. The union's values were noble, its aspirations achievable; missing was the political will and support to implement them. This did not invalidate the exercise nor lessen its value in contributing to society's debate on exclusion.

In 1983 Delegates queued up to condemn social welfare and health cuts, albeit in an atmosphere of part despair, as few thought callous politicians would heed them. This was repeated in 1984, with demands to retain hospitals or services threatened with closure in Monaghan, Bantry and Galway. There was a sense of going through the motions. A hospital charge of £10 was resisted in 1986. The health service, built by PAYE taxpayers, was 'being dismantled.' By the Government's own reckoning, the minimum income for a single person in 1985 was £50 to £60 a week, which put the level of Unemployment Assistance, £35.10 in July 1987, into a shameful context. Laudable recommendations of the Commission on Social Welfare rested on the same shelf as many previous progressive reports. The provision of Social Welfare offices was resisted, while the 1978 Green Paper *Social Insurance for the Self-Employed*, a possible income generator, was ignored. No-one challenged the concept of a minimum, adequate income, but nothing was done to implement it. The FWUI despaired of progress. Speakers wanted the abolition of the three-day waiting period, equal treatment, improved minimum payments and the restoration of cuts. An Emergency Motion condemned 'indiscriminate cuts', the decimation of services and a two-tier health service and demanded a campaign led by Congress to defend the health service.[38]

DISABILITY AND LIAM MAGUIRE

Liam Maguire (No. 12) addressed the 1980 Conference, challenging Delegates' attitudes to disability. He raised questions about access, services, incomes and employment for the physically handicapped. He demanded the FWUI's involvement in United Nations Year of Disabled Persons, 1981, asking whatever happened to commitments to a 3% quota for the employment of handicapped people in the public sector made in 1977. Maguire's long, flowing locks and inimitable, colourful oratorical style roused the hall.

The FWUI contributed significantly to raising the disability agenda, encouraging Congress to adopt radical supportive policies. In 1981 Mairéad Hayes (No. 12) demanded that the FWUI 'do everything in its power' to secure implementation of the UN Declaration of Human Rights for Disabled Persons, signed by Ireland on 9 December 1975. This included entitlement to measures to allow the physically disabled to become as self-reliant as possible, to receive social rehabilitation, education and training to develop their maximum potential and facilitate their social integration, the removal of all stigma attaching to mental handicap and the provision of all needs for them, their parents and families.

Maguire wrote to the GEC in November 1982, complaining about lack of access to union premises. In 1983, coming from a hospital bed, he graphically demonstrated the impact of health cuts by relating his experiences of delays, incompetence, neglect and apparent unconcern from consultants. It was a harrowing account and should have shamed those who stroked their pens to effect cuts.

John Liam Maguire died on 16 September 1983. A true champion of the disabled was silenced. He had served on the Aer Lingus Branch Committee for fifteen years and on the GEC from 1974 to 1978 and was the founder of the Trade Union Study Group on Industrial Democracy at the airport. He was 'a strong man with tremendous drive and ability,' who 'felt compassion for his fellows' and who gave 'unstintingly of himself to others.' Marie Cassidy (No. 18) wanted the ICTU Charter of Rights for the Disabled pursued in Maguire's memory. John McAdam said that 'Liam educated the disabled to the trade union movement' and 'trade unions to the rights of the disabled.'

In 1985 the Parnell Square Head Office was made fully accessible, with an office set aside for disabled members named in Liam Maguire's memory. The President of Ireland, Dr Patrick Hillery, opened the facilities on 9 January 1987 in a ceremony jointly hosted by the FWUI and the Irish Wheelchair Association.[39]

SAFETY AND HEALTH

The FWUI was underwhelmed by the Safety in Industry Act (1980). Its submission on safety and health to Congress called for a 'unified system with one major Act, covering all workplaces.' Citing the British Health and Safety at Work Act (1974) as a model, it wanted an Act to hold all employers and self-employed responsible for ensuring that regulations were upheld within work-places, an occupational health service and the replacement of the voluntary National Industrial Safety Organisation with a statutory National Safety, Health and Work Commission. The submission addressed noise, the safety of firefighters, dangerous substances, forestry, agricultural and local authority workers and research into accidents and social welfare compensation. It was well-considered and ahead of its time, prefiguring much that was incorporated in the Safety, Health and Welfare at Work Act (1989). Disappointingly, it was not more assertive on rights for Safety Committees and statutory powers for Safety Representatives and Delegates.

In 1983 the Training Officer, John Graham, acknowledged that health and safety received little attention within courses. Impatience with delays in implementing the report of the Barrington Commission surfaced after 1984. Tobacco workers complained about health warnings being printed on cigarette packets, the Minister placing 'Tobacco Manufacturers in the same league as drug pushers.' The Government was 'hell bent to stop cigarette smoking,' had 'broken commitments to the industry' and would 'not listen to workers' whose jobs were at risk. Frank Mills (No. 16) called for a national campaign to promote awareness of AIDS, protection of the confidentiality of HIV sufferers, no compulsory testing within work-place medicals, and no discrimination 'on the grounds of HIV status, haemophilia or sexual orientation.' It was International AIDS Day as he addressed the 1988 Conference. No. 18 Branch was the first to run AIDS awareness events, and Jack Kelly (GEC) posed some difficult ethical questions regarding confidentiality and the concomitant rights of colleagues exposed to unknown risk.[40]

EDUCATION, TRAINING, RESEARCH AND MEDIA

The inglorious Brú Chaoimhín row led to calls for a Press Liaison Officer in 1980. The FWUI was sensitive to the flagrant misrepresentation over Brú Chaoimhín. The press were invited to the Annual Conference from 1979, and a greater effort was made to improve the FWUI's public image, but they baulked at a Press Officer.

In 1988 expanded research and information services provided for unemployed members. The Information Section represented members at social welfare and health board appeals. It was not clear how these heavy demands would be met, once agreed upon. The FWUI trained 200 members in 1981, the ICTU 700 and the ITGWU 3,000.

A 'high point' in FWUI education and training was reached in 1982–3 with a 50% increase in attendance, 'phenomenal by any standards.' A fall from such heights was examined under the headings of the extent and effectiveness of training and the economic and industrial relations climate.

In 1984 there were calls to fill a 'major gap' with a union journal, filled by the appearance of *Unity* in December. Jane Foreman (No. 19) called for a 'programme of political education for all members.' Some members did not even like trade unions.' *Unity* was inspired by the impressive 'Union News', published by the IDA Section of No. 15 Branch. Office facilities were provided for the the Irish Labour History Society and AnCO Survey of Trade Union Records in 1986, culminating in the publication of *Select Guide to Trade Union Records in Dublin*.[41]

YOUTH AND AGED

Bernadette Berry (No. 16) called for a Youth Officer in 1981. The GEC opposed, as it was an incursion on its authority to make all staff decisions. Cardiff claimed that the FWUI 'possibly' had the 'highest ratio of staff to union membership' of any union, 1:1,200. He expected 'every Official to be a Youth Officer, Equality Officer and even to look after middle-aged fellows like myself.' Berry vainly looked around the hall in search of youth and appealed for positive action to engage young workers. Her appeal fell on deaf ears.

In 1982 motions called for the Youth Employment Levy to be used to create jobs for young people. In 1985 Garry pointed out the irony that in the year designated International Youth Year by the United Nations, thousands of young Irish people were forced to emigrate. The FWUI had no Youth Committee, and the question was left in abeyance. Seán Whelan (No. 12) urged the GEC to 'initiate a campaign among young people, whether employed, unemployed or students,' to inform them of the 'achievements, role and objectives' of unions and to mount a drive to recruit young people, calling on Congress for assistance. The youthful Whelan was one of the few 'deemed to be in that age bracket' at the 1986 Conference, thus making his point. Attley accepted the tenor of the motion but repeated a typical GEC response that implementation depended not on more Committees but by a union-wide commitment. An 'Introduction to Trade Unionism' course for young members was one positive response.

In October 1988 the ICTU adopted a Charter of Rights for the Elderly in conjunction with the National Federation of Pensioners' Associations. (See p. 791) The FWUI prided itself on having fought long and hard for improved state pensions, widows' pensions and social welfare advances for the elderly and their carers.[42]

PREMISES

The FWUI Head Office premises at 31 Parnell Square, formerly owned by the Ancient Order of Hibernians, were privately offered for sale to the union by the Dominican Order in July 1981. Considerable repair was needed. The GEC initiated a Building Fund in April 1983, and in October, Larkin Hall was officially opened with three performances of James Plunkett's *The Risen People*. 30 and 32 Parnell Square were secured, the first by lease and the second by purchase. New premises opened in Monaghan, signalling the FWUI's Ulster presence, and on 14 December 1985 in Kilkenny. By 1987 the FWUI owned 48 Fleet Street (former IWWU Head Office), 15–16 Granby Row and 29, 31 and 32 Parnell Square, Dublin, Church Street, Tullamore, 8 Dean Street, Kilkenny, and 25 Lower Salthill, Galway, and rented offices at 30 Parnell Square, 6 Prince of Wales Terrace, Bray, Leinster Street, Athy, and the Diamond, Monaghan. Merger with the National Association of Transport Employees brought 33 Parnell Square into the union's ownership, and new premises were acquired at 7 Marine Terrace, Bray.[43]

WORKERS' UNITY TRUST

The FWUI levied members 10p per week from 1 January 1986 for three years to raise funds for the establishment of or participation in co-operative production and distribution and the publication of newspapers, books and pamphlets. Ross Connolly linked the proposal to the newly created ICTU Centres for the Unemployed. Despite some confusion, slight reservations about a further weekly demand and acceptance that this 'would not solve the unemployment problem' but was a 'practical response,' it was unanimously agreed, and Workers' Unity Trust was established, operating out of 48 Fleet Street, Dublin.

Mike Fitzgerald, Information Officer, was seconded to act as Director, with Ross Connolly as Treasurer. An Advisory Service was provided in association with the National Social Service Board. Discussions were held with every employment, manpower and social agency, with funding promised from the European Social Fund. Among the first to receive support were Winstanley Footwear, a co-operative established by redundant workers; Aonad Computer Co-operative, Dublin; and an Arts and Community Development in Monaghan. The FWUI was immensely proud of Workers' Unity Trust: 'Alone of the Irish Trade Unions, we have recognised, in addition to the valuable work which it has to do, a responsibility to deal with the changed circumstances brought about by this recession, in that we have an obligation to do what we can for members of the Union who become unemployed.' It was evidence that the 'Larkinite spirit still exists and flourishes.'

In December 1986 Workers' Unity Trust was awarded charitable status, and Eddie Glackin was seconded as Executive Director. A booklet, *How to Set Up a Workers' Co-operative,* was published, along with numerous materials informing unemployed members of their welfare and legal entitlements. Enthusiasm for Workers' Unity Trust and its initiatives was plain. More worker co-ops opened in 1988, Athy Co-op Foundry and Ballymun Organic Market Garden the most significant. Material support was provided to ICTU Unemployed Centres in Ballymun, North Strand, Tallaght, Galway, Kilkenny, Limerick, Sligo and Waterford. Nine co-operatives were assisted with loans and with business and technical advice, and an interest-free loan was given to the Northern Ireland Co-op Development Agency, with an eye to cross-border projects and EEC and Ireland Fund subventions. By 1988 eight worker co-ops were operational, supported by loans of £100,000. A Resource Centre opened in Fleet Street, and training courses on enterprise development, social welfare and unemployment were held. As SIPTU loomed it was hoped that the New Union would add significant resources to what would become the Irish Trade Union Trust. Workers' Unity Trust was one of the merger's selling-points to ITGWU members.[44]

INTERNATIONAL SOLIDARITY

The decision of the Irish Rugby Football Union to tour Apartheid South Africa was vigorously opposed by the Irish Anti-Apartheid Movement, to which the FWUI was affiliated, and by virtually every element of society, from politicians to churches. With no regard for this united public opinion, the IRFU's action was 'misguided and insensitive.' The GEC decided to oppose the tour and to grant £50 to the Irish Anti-Apartheid Movement, but it was left to each employment to decide their stance. Similar practical problems arose in Dublin port when Kader Asmal, Chairman of the Anti-Apartheid Movement, requested the blacking of South African vessels.

Garry visited the Philippines on an ICTU Delegation in 1983, being struck by the 'determination and courage against a most oppressive, cruel regime,' propped up by the US Government and transnational companies—the same companies that were protected from revealing information to their Irish employees by Fianna Fáil and Fine Gael MEPs voting against the Vredeling Directive.

When the Dunne's Stores strike against handling South African produce took place, the FWUI offered material and financial support to the strikers and to the Irish Distributive and Administrative Trade Union, whose General Secretary, John Mitchell, said that 'the degree of fraternity shown . . . if it were universal, would place the Trade Union Movement as a whole in a much stronger position.' £500 was given to the Michael Mullen Memorial Fund to encourage trade union activity in South Africa. Marek Garzeckie, Chief Shop Steward of Solidarność at Polish Radio, Warsaw, addressed the 1983 Conference. Exiled since 1981, he outlined the work of Solidarność and the support that Irish workers could give. In 1984 the FWUI protested against the award of a doctorate of law to President Ronald Reagan because of 'his attacks on the living standards and rights of American workers.'

A Miners' Distress Fund to support the British miners in 1984–5 was set up. The FWUI collected money, conveyed food to Wales and facilitated holidays for miners' children in Monaghan and Dublin. In 1980 the FWUI gave £2,000 and material support to the Sheffield Steel Strike Committee.[45]

POLITICS

In 1980 Stephen Edge (No. 13) wanted support from the Labour Party to protect employment in the town gas industry by maintaining Government subsidies, getting the go-ahead for An Bord Gáis to begin construction of a national grid, and giving priority to Dublin Gas in receiving supply. It was typical of members seeking party political support for sectional, albeit highly valid, interests. For the Branch Secretary, Tom Crean, all jobs 'were on a knife edge.' Unfavourable international comparison of gas prices per therm were damaging: a national gas grid was as important as electricity or water supply and would greatly enhance the country's infrastructure.

The Conference demanded a 'register of interests' of Deputies and Senators. The loss of Frank Cluskey's seat in Dublin South-Central in 1981 was a major disappointment. Cluskey was 'their TD.' The union granted him £5,000 towards national election expenses and £2,000 personal expenses, as it did in 1977. The FWUI believed the Labour Party Trade Union Affiliated Group was paying dividends but wanted greater activity. Sixteen candidates were supported, at a cost of £6,500, on a strongly anti-Coalition line. A circular letter from the new Leader, Michael O'Leary, was considered a 'disgrace to say the least.' The GEC felt that no money should 'be sent centrally' to the Labour Party, to 'adequately express our disapproval of the Coalition position.' Individual grants totalling £4,200 were agreed, favouring those 'who had served this Union.'

Jim Quinn asked if it would mean they supported people who 'had put VAT on clothing and removed subsidies on butter and milk?' Jack Kelly suggested that opposition to the Labour Party came from GEC members who belonged to 'other parties.'

Cardiff wrote to O'Leary explaining why no money was given centrally. He made a 'fairly firm attack' on taxing children's footwear and on tax equity and supplied copies to each candidate. He 'indicated that if the dictates of their consciences was such that they were unable to accept the grant on this occasion, it would be fully understood by the GEC.' Not surprisingly, 'apparently the problem of conscience had not arisen with any members of the Union seeking election to Dáil Éireann.'[46]

Cluskey was back in the Dáil in 1982. Tom Redmond argued that the Labour Party in Coalition harmed workers. How best could they influence the Labour Party and spend the political fund? The 'politicisation of members' was more important than sponsoring candidates. Cardiff said that class interests were 'not served by division,' and 'irrespective of the current direction the Party was taking' it should be remembered that it was 'our' Party and that 'unity and solidarity on the political front' were vital. The collapse of the Labour Party's vote during the 1970s indicated that change had to be made.

Some championed the Socialist Labour Party, Democratic Socialist Party and Workers' Party; but Redmond's intention was not to break the link: he wanted to redefine and reinforce it. Michael D. Higgins and Ruairí Quinn spoke as FWUI TDS, the former welcoming dialogue, the latter talking about the 'lonely years' spent in 'principled Socialist opposition.' Cardiff saw current problems as stemming from the change of leadership, O'Leary replacing Cluskey. Paul Smyth (No. 18) moved that the Labour Party should fight 'all future elections on its own Socialist programme' and not enter Coalition with Fianna Fáil or Fine Gael. They needed to 'reclaim' the Party 'from the likes of Michael O'Leary and Barry Desmond who have just taken it over and use it as their own electioneering machine.'

Cardiff reminded the hall that the FWUI was not a political party, merely a union. It had always voted against Coalition. There were no tears when Dick Spring replaced O'Leary as Leader. Jack Harte was sponsored as Seanad candidate throughout the 1980s. Redmond reminded all of the WUI's Marxist past and called for a Socialist analysis of union political activity, not just electoral politics. Attley thought that the 'only good Michael O'Leary did for the Labour Party was to leave it.' There was need for a political wing, but Clondalkin Paper Mills was an example to show that they did not necessarily fare better when dealing with so-called friends in the Government than with apparent enemies.

The GEC adopted a position that if the Labour Party did not support a Fianna Fáil proposal to re-open Clondalkin Paper Mills the FWUI would suspend its affiliation.[47]

The FWUI was one of fourteen affiliated unions and a 'leading member' of the Labour Party Trade Union Affiliation Group. This 'small number' of affiliated unions reflected a 'lack of understanding' within unions 'for the need for a political arm.' Publications, lectures, seminars and events were needed to boost awareness. The group assisted in assembling pre-Budget submissions and other policy documents, reflecting ICTU policy. 'Endless destructive criticism' was not the solution but a detailed analysis of obstacles that inhibited the Labour Party from becoming a political force. Few unions gave more that the £14,088 spent by the FWUI in 1982. Affiliation fees were £1,888. A rather bland report concluded that it was 'quite clear that organisation' was a problem; the union could do much to assist but did not flesh out what.

TDS sponsored by the FWUI were Ruairí Quinn (Minister for Labour), Joe Bermingham (Minister of State at the Department of the Taoiseach), Frank Cluskey, Eileen Desmond, Frank McLoughlin and Mervyn Taylor, while Jack Harte and Michael D. Higgins were Senators and Brendan Halligan and Justin Keating members of the European Parliament. The GEC 'noted with considerable pride that a distinguished member,' Frank Cluskey, resigned as Minister for Trade, Commerce and Tourism 'on a matter of principle, namely are our resources to be used to benefit all our people or a small privileged few?' The natural gas 'deal' was unacceptable to him because of its implications for other natural resources, such as oil. He had done the 'country a distinct service.' The GEC saw Cluskey's resignation as serving a purpose. Dick Spring became Minister for Energy, and the 'proper utilisation of Ireland's natural resources' was 'very much highlighted in the public mind.' The hand of the Labour Party Government members was strengthened on issues such as the dismantling of Bord na Móna.[48]

In January 1984 it was felt that the Labour Party's Coalition with Fine Gael 'cannot serve the interests of the working class.' On every issue 'Fine Gael monetarism' won the day. To 'defend working people from further cut-backs, social inequality and mass unemployment' the Labour Party needed 'independent policies and the building of mass support for them.' The FWUI called on the Parliamentary Labour Party 'to withdraw from Coalition to enable this development to start.' Cluskey gave the lead when withdrawing from the Government. They had to campaign outside the Dáil on employment, tax, the defence of social welfare, health, the removal of VAT from clothing—in other words 'real Socialist policies.'

The FWUI opposed the expulsion of supporters of the Militant group from the Labour Party. It defended the right of party members 'opposed to Coalition' to 'express their own ideas without harassment.' It was felt that the Labour Party 'was in crisis.' Party observers could be under no false impression. The FWUI mood was anger and disillusion. Again, however, no suggestions emerged about how the Party could be strengthened. The FWUI readily acknowledged the assistance some Labour TDs gave. It placed the following motion before the 1985 Party Conference, confirming the 'national objective of full employment':

That the Labour Party rejects the pessimism and lack of confidence it implies of other political Parties and those in the media and elsewhere who argue that the goal of full employment is now beyond the capacity of the Irish people to achieve.

The Labour Party must re-assert its political philosophy that full employment can be achieved through the introduction of appropriate economic and social policies, through the application of real, comprehensive economic and social planning, and through the full mobilisation of the nation and its natural and technical resources.

FWUI members felt that the Labour Party 'had nothing in common' with unions. Congress was asked to 'discuss the need for an effective political arm' or 'build an alliance' with other unions, tenants and community associations and women's groups. The general tenor again reinforced strong, leftward criticism of the Labour Party.[49]

In 1986 the GEC concluded that the 'Labour and Trade Union Movement' must 'rebuild the Party.' The Labour Party Trade Union Affiliation Group made this point strongly to the Party's Commission on Electoral Strategy. Continued Coalition with Fine Gael was condemned, and it urged a 'ten year moratorium' on participation in Coalition. It was trade unionists—Connolly and Larkin—who created the Party. The FWUI concluded by quoting Larkin Junior's recognition in 1947 that most of labour's problems had political solutions: 'there was no way' unions could be 'non-political'. 'If we are going to achieve ourselves that freedom from poverty, from unemployment, that freedom from low wages, the denial of opportunity to our children, then we have not only got to have strong unions, we have got to have strong political parties of the working class.'

Attacks on the Labour Party's role in Government and its 'appalling failure' to create jobs were heartfelt in 1987. It had gone into office with unemployment at 50,000 and left with 250,000 idle, not counting those who emigrated.

Eoghan Harris said that, as a member of the Workers' Party, it was 'like being a Protestant on a train to Cork listening to Catholics talking about moving statues all the time.' Hearing Labour supporters 'confess their sins' was 'tedious and boring.' The Workers' Party might be more deserving of support than the Labour Party.

The reorganisation of the Labour Party Trade Union Affiliation Group, within which the FWUI was 'to the forefront', saw a 'most radical step taken': the appointment of a full-time Political Officer, Flor O'Mahony. The GEC increased the Political Levy from ½p to 1p.[50]

NORTHERN IRELAND

In 1980 Michael Mullen (No. 2) rose to demand that the FWUI restate Larkin's 'traditional policy': 'being in favour of a United Ireland opposed to Partition.' He wanted the Labour Party to pressure British Labour to force the British Government to move matters peacefully to a conclusion. Tom Redmond—breaking GEC Rules—opposed referral back; and, despite Cardiff's intervention and admonishment, the Conference adopted the motion.

A letter from the National H Blocks Committee 'posed some problems' for the FWUI, which usually left Northern affairs to the ICTU Northern Ireland Committee. Decisions were postponed until a special GEC meeting reviewed all WUI and FWUI policy resolutions. A statement was agreed, by 9 to 4, in November. (See p. 790) It was left to individual members whether they took part in H blocks demonstrations. It was a historic GEC meeting, the first called exclusively to discuss the national question.[51]

Conferences condemned strip-searching, supported political status for prisoners, and consistently endorsed ICTU Northern Ireland campaigns, such as 'A Better Life for All'. The death of Aidan McAnespie, a union member, brought events closer to home. On 21 February 1988 he was shot in the back, 'whether it was a ricochet or deliberately aimed' by a British soldier, walking from GAA grounds near Aughnacloy, Co. Tyrone, on the Monaghan border. He had twice complained to the FWUI about British army harassment, but, 'apart from ensuring [that] the situation would not affect his employment,' the union was 'not in a position to help him directly.' This was the sort of helplessness familiar to many oppressed Northern citizens. The FWUI called for a permanent body, in consultation with unions, to 'monitor what happens at the various Border crossover points.' Garry re-emphasised:

This trade union condemns the use of violence by any source . . . We condemn the killing of any Irish man or Irish woman for whatever reason. No-one has a right to kill a sister or brother Irish citizen, not the British Army, the IRA or the UDA, or any other self-styled grouping.

He called for support for the Northern Ireland Committee's campaign 'Peace, Work and Progress' and insisted that 'what happened at Enniskillen must never be forgotten.'

Jim Monaghan condemned the use of emergency legislation and the infringe-ment of civil liberties by army and police searches of private dwellings, activities stemming from republican activity in the South. The FWUI wanted the Birmingham Six, Maguire Family, Judith Ward and Guildford Four cases to be taken to the European Court of Justice.[52]

FWUI STATEMENT ON THE H BLOCKS, NOVEMBER 1980

The policy of the Federated Workers' Union of Ireland as expressed in motions adopted at successive Annual Conferences and in conformity with the policy of the Irish Congress of Trade Unions as the representative body for the whole Trade Union Movement in Ireland, is to oppose absolutely and firmly any recourse to force or violence as a means of resolving the problems of Northern Ireland, irrespective of the purpose or motivation of such violence. Our move-ment stands for reconciliation between the communities there and rejects any form of coercion. In particular it is concerned to protect working class interests as expressed through the Trade Union Movement and repudiates those who by word or act would in any way jeopardise the unity of workers that has been painfully maintained in our movement. Trade Union solidarity and working class unity is the only way forward for peace, reconciliation and human rights in Northern Ireland. The policy enshrined in the Northern Ireland Committee ICTU Better Life for All Campaign must be the basis for any Trade Union pronounce-ment at this difficult time.

The FWUI, in the tradition of our first two General Secretaries, Big Jim Larkin and James Larkin Junior, has always been concerned about prison conditions. Indeed, James Larkin Junior was the main author of a pamphlet, *Prisons and Prisoners in Ireland,* which was issued in 1946 and which pioneered the fight for the human rights for prisoners and better conditions in prisons. The FWUI deplores the degrading and inhuman conditions in the Maze and Armagh Prisons and begs all concerned to find a solution to the dire problems that have been created there. We support all reasonable demands for reforms in the prison system including the right of the prisoners to wear civilian clothing of their choice. We also call for changes in the judicial system to bring it into conform-ity with the accepted norms and procedures operating in democratic countries.

In the context of these policies repeatedly urged and consistently pursued by the Trade Union Movement in Ireland, the FWUI pleads with the prisoners and those who, on humanitarian and other grounds, claim sympathy with them in their plight, to bring about an end to the Hunger Strike. The FWUI also calls upon the Government of Ireland to influence the British Government to take the necessary action to implement the essential reforms in the Prison System and changes in the judicial system to bring it into conformity with the accepted norms and procedures operating in Democratic countries.

Source: FWUI, minutes of General Executive Council, 26 November 1980.

ICTU CHARTER OF RIGHTS FOR THE ELDERLY, OCTOBER 1988

- The Right to live independent, active and full lives without discrimination on grounds of age.
- The Right to an adequate income, substantial enough to provide a decent standard of living.
- The Right to equity in taxation. Provision in the income tax code relating to the elderly should be regularly reviewed.
- The Right to adequate, secure and suitable living accommodation in the community. A range of housing options to be available to the elderly including sheltered housing, purpose built flats, voluntary housing Associations and controlled private rented accommodation. Subsidies and grants should be provided to encourage families to keep elderly relatives in the family environment.
- The Right to proper Nursing Homes Service for the very frail and physically incapacitated. All Nursing Homes should be subject to statutory regulations to guarantee proper treatment of patients, including professional nursing care.
- The Right to hospitalisation and medical services. These services to be provided through a comprehensive public health programme based on a positive commitment to the health of the elderly. Home nursing and public health nursing services should be expanded. Hospital and medical services impose a heavy financial burden on many elderly persons not entitled to medical cards. This situation should be remedied.
- The Right to a properly funded Home Help service providing for the care of the elderly and organised in co-ordination with local community care services.
- The Right to participate in formal and informal adult education.
- The Right to proper pre-retirement facilities including paid time-off for retirement planning courses, flexible working hours, job-sharing and early retirement.
- The Right to participate and be represented in appropriate bodies dealing with matters concerning the elderly.
- The Right to protection against violence. Local Community Alert Programmes which can be of assistance to the elderly, particularly those living alone, should be developed.
- The Right to travel and recreational facilities providing opportunities for self-expression, personal development and fulfilment.

Chapter 34 ⌒

| CONCLUSIONS

MEMBERSHIP AND FINANCE

Continuous redundancies and the pursuit by employers of 'lean production' made life difficult for unions. The membership of the ITGWU declined by 14,730, the FWUI by 3,027. Conversely, union incomes rose dramatically, the ITGWU's by £5,556,883, the FWUI's by £2,226,541. Regular increases in contributions were sought as expenditure climbed. The ITGWU's costs rose by £5,655,118, the FWUI's by £1,782,807. With the exception of 1985, when it declared a loss of £94,585, FWUI heads stayed well above water. The ITGWU declared a surplus in six years, totalling £2,220,874, against four deficits totalling £621,053. Both unions' credit balance (general surplus) rose, the ITGWU's by £1,833,420, the FWUI's by £1,412,713.

Table 130: ITGWU and FWUI membership and income, 1980–89

| | ITGWU | | FWUI | |
	Membership	Financial income (£)	Membership	Financial income (£)
1980	172,352	5,186,959	44,959	1,008,275
1981	169,798	6,294,113	45,939	1,189,423
1982	169,354	7,304,444	45,666	1,379,973
1983	158,344	7,822,410	43,620	1,630,244
1984	155,090	8,262,110	42,842	2,118,743
1985	139,690	9,042,323	41,674	2,389,096
1986	136,394	10,033,378	40,630	2,544,286
1987	133,777	10,175,457	41,662	2,813,219
1988	148,255*	11,014,645	39,004	2,962,932
1989	157,622*	10,743,842	41,932	3,234,816

*These are the figures of the Registrar of Friendly Societies and probably relate to book rather than financial members.

Source: ITGWU, Annual Reports, 1980–89.

Table 131: ITGWU and FWUI expenditure, surplus and credit (General Fund balance) (£), 1980–89

	ITGWU			FWUI		
	Expenditure	Surplus (deficit)	Credit	Expenditure	Surplus (deficit)	Credit
1980	5,088,224	98,735	4,102,350	833,384	174,891	1,238,899
1981	6,294,113	530,108	4,455,563	1,064,487	124,936	1,435,510
1982	7,304,444	(95,332)	4,453,045	1,358,398	21,575	1,463,578
1983	7,822,410	(9,331)	4,443,614	1,529,103	110,141	1,573,719
1984	8,262,110	(434,924)	4,008,790	1,892,927	225,816	1,739,168
1985	9,042,323	308,653	4,317,460	2,483,681	(94,585)	1,763,371
1986	10,033,378	368,211	4,757,607	2,422,380	121,906	1,855,301
1987	10,175,457	(81,466)	4,676,142	2,587,747	225,816	2,064,529
1988	11,014,645	589,310	5,609,911	2,901,919	60,113	2,074,289
1989	10,743,842	325,857	5,935,770	2,616,191	618,625	2,651,612

Source: ITGWU, Annual Reports, 1980–89; FWUI, reports of National Executive Council, 1980–89.

There were increasing concerns about membership trends and finance, but the motive for merger in 1989 did not appear to be rooted—as, arguably, most union mergers ultimately are—in either chronically declining memberships or financial crisis. That said, before the adoption of the Programme for National Recovery in 1987 things looked bleak. The employers' offensive was in full swing, and increasing public expenditure cuts threatened jobs. Membership rallied with the greater stability of the Programme for National Recovery and the beginnings of recovery.

Inside the ITGWU tensions existed between staff and NEC as financial concerns dictated cuts and wage restraint. Politically motivated factors induced John Carroll's famous 'shape up or ship out' comments, an indication of stress and disunity.

Women were a considerable dynamic. Although the number of women in the ITGWU declined from 62,907 to 54,717, they remained a third of the total, a larger number than most ICTU affiliates' total membership. Nóirín Greene was elected to the NEC in 1982 and to a reserved position on the ICTU Executive in 1985, as May O'Brien was appointed the first full-time Women's Affairs Official, supported by an elected Women's Affairs Committee. The NEC declined to concede reserved positions, but the election of Doris Kelly (Dublin No. 2) and Mary Oakes (Mullingar) in their own right in 1989 possibly justified this position. In the FWUI women were a constant 13,500 or one-third of the membership. Women's Conferences failed to persuade the GEC to appoint a full-time Women's Officer or to create reserved places. Both unions vigorously fought for equal pay and equal treatment.

DISPUTES

The dismantling of National Understandings was a particular blow to the incumbent President of the ICTU, Paddy Cardiff. Both unions had, in differing ways, fought for the concept and regretted the return to work-place bargaining. The employers' attack after 1981 was unrelenting and, with unemployment reaching a peak at 226,000, cast unions into a defensive posture. There was palpable relief when the Programme for National Recovery was agreed.

Table 132: ITGWU income and Dispute Pay, 1980–89

	ITGWU		FWUI	
	Dispute Pay (£)	As proportion of income (%)	Dispute Pay (£)	As proportion of income (%)
1980	443,951	8.5	6,894	0.6
1981	229,854	3.6	41,105	3.4
1982	440,859	6.0	77,212	5.5
1983	360,356	4.6	58,897	3.6
1984	534,470	6.7	220,391	10.4
1985	322,679	3.5	52,343	2.1
1986	259,730	5.6	144,467	5.6
1987	492,371	4.9	113,382	4.0
1988	201,133	1.8	137,291	4.6
1989	144,782	1.3	n.a.	n.a.

Source: ITGWU, Annual Reports, 1980–89; FWUI, reports of National Executive Council, 1980–89.

The supposedly non-militant ITGWU spent a staggering £3,430,185 on Dispute Pay, the FWUI £851,982. Most disputes were over survival plans, rationalisation and redundancy. Despite the enormously difficult bargaining environment, wage levels were reasonably well maintained. There was considerable local activity, particularly in the private sector, exposing the under-development or inexperience of Shop Stewards and work-place structures. Union responses were to talk of 'recruitment' but not yet organisation. The decade concluded with a sense of the movement breathing more easily, but it had yet to grasp the essential problems posed by new forms of work organisation, direct employee involvement and declining density. Survival was very much the prize. Perhaps it was imagined that, when economic crisis passed, things might return to 'normal'.

POLITICS

Politics moved to the right. Under Frank Cluskey's leadership the Labour Party obtained fifteen seats in 1981, a very disappointing outcome given the massive PAYE protests. Once again, tens of thousands who marched voted against themselves in the next election. Michael Mullen acted as broker for the 'Gregory Deal', securing Fianna Fáil's continuance in power. The Labour Party was static in the two General Elections of 1982, in February and November, although Michael O'Leary's brief leadership dragged the Party to new depths in union eyes. Under Dick Spring the Party entered Coalition with Fine Gael. Increasingly difficult economic conditions and mounting violence in the North combined to give the Government a rough ride.

By 1987, union antipathy to Coalition was absolute. The Labour Party fell to twelve seats before a slight recovery to fifteen in 1989. Access to decision-making through the Programme for National Recovery was not anticipated from Haughey's Fianna Fáil. It broke a number of moulds. Unions found it easier to deal with Fianna Fáil than with a Fine Gael-led Coalition, receiving a more sympathetic ear. Not yet referred to as 'social partnership', Garret FitzGerald was among leading voices dismissing the Programme for National Recovery as a threat to parliamentary democracy. In the absence of a powerful Dáil Labour presence, broadly based central Agreements allowed unions to implement far more of their policy and simultaneously constrain managements and the New Right while forlornly awaiting the Labour Party's electoral success.

PART 5

Organising the millennium, 1990–2009

CONTEXTS

Economic and social contexts

The Republic's economy was characterised as the 'Celtic Tiger'. Fuelled by more than €10 billion in European Union infrastructural funds, low Corporation tax, sound economic management and 'social partnership', the economy was transformed until, in 2000, Ireland was among the world's wealthiest countries Unemployment fell to 65,400, 3.6% of a work force of 1,791,900. Income tax was nearly half the 1980s level, and rising consumption, particularly in housing, led an annual growth of 5–6%. Although income per capita surpassed many western European countries, the concern was to balance inflation, personal tax and Government spending.

Unions complained that wealth was not shared equally, 'social inclusion' becoming a policy keynote as fiscal restraints accompanied the adoption of the euro in January 1999. Growth eased after 2001 but surged again to reach 5% in 2005. The population of the Republic grew from 3.526 million in 1991 to 3.626 million in 1996, 3.917 million in 2002 and 4.24 million in 2006. Natural increase was boosted by significant immigration, particularly from new EU member-states in eastern Europe after 2002. In 2006, 419,733 non-Irish citizens were among 4,172,103 inhabitants. Unions embraced diversity and, in SIPTU's case, appointed Polish and Lithuanian staff to directly contact exploited immigrant workers. In 2007 global recession slowed the economy. The Celtic Tiger was increasingly considered to have roared its last.[1]

Table 133: Immigration and emigration (26 Counties), 1990–2007 (selected years)

	Immigration	Emigration	Net
1990	33,400	56,300	−22,900
1995	31,200	33,100	−1,900
2000	52,600	26,600	26,000
2001	59,000	26,200	32,800
2002	66,900	25,600	41,300

2003	60,000	29,300	30,700
2004	58,500	26,500	32,000
2005	84,600	29,400	55,100
2006	107,800	36,000	71,800
2007	109,500	42,000	67,300

Source: Central Statistics Office.

Unemployment remained a major concern, running at 12.9% in 1990 and reaching a peak at 220,100, or 14.6%, in 1993. 'Social partnership' contributed to a rapid economic turn-around. Unemployment fell to 65,400, or 3.6%, by 2001. The wage terms of Agreements, while crucial and determining elements, were but a fraction of ever more comprehensive deals. A 'fourth pillar' representing community and voluntary groups joined the process, and finely detailed social welfare, housing and educational reform were significant achievements, much informed by SIPTU researchers. Health remained a running sore, tolerated by the electorate as an 'Irish institution'—an open disgrace in a wealthy society.

In Northern Ireland the Belfast Agreement of 1998 brought peace. The 'peace dividend' saw unemployment fall from more than 17% in 1990 to 3.8% inSeptember 2007. The public sector accounted for 63% of economic activity, however, as traditional manufacturing disappeared.

Table 134: Unemployment, 1990–2008

	Unemployment	Labour force		Unemployment	Labour force
1990	172,400	1,332,100	1999	96,900	1,688,100
1991	198,500	1,354,400	2000	74,900	1,745,600
1992	206,600	1,371,800	2001	65,400	1,781,900
1993	220,100	1,403,200	2002	77,000	1,840,000
1994	211,000	1,431,600	2003	82,100	1,875,500
1995	177,400	1,459,200	2004	84,200	1,920,300
1996	179,000	1,507,500	2005	85,600	2,014,800
1997	159,000	1,539,000	2006	91,400	2,108,300
1998	126,600	1,621,100	2007	98,800	2,194,100

Source: Central Statistics Office.

Union contexts

The Irish trade union movement was envied by other western movements pinned on the back foot by New Right policies. Even Scandinavia, once the benchmark, sent missions to study social partnership. Not everything in the garden was rosy, however. SIPTU in particular began to criticise inadequate wage rises and social exclusion. During alleged 'partnership', however, one partner, the employers, displayed increasing antipathy to another, the unions. Where once co-existence and charges of corporatism were the norm, there was derecognition, de-unionisation and a marked reluctance to concede SIPTU's demands for legislative support for the illusory constitutional right to join a union.

The membership of SIPTU and of the movement rose consistently. There were 153,116 more trade unionists in 2007 than in 1990. SIPTU grew by 32,713 financial members and 40,944 book members. A starker picture emerges, however, if union density—the proportion of workers in unions who could be in unions—is examined.

Table 135: Wage Rounds, 1946–2008

28th (1990)—Programme for Economic and Social Progress: 4% on basic pay in first year, with minimum increase of £5; 3% in second year, minimum £4.25; 3¾% in third year, minimum £5.75; 'exceptional cases' local bargaining clause for 3% of basic pay.
29th (1994)—Programme for Competitiveness and Work: Private sector, increase of 9% in basic pay over 3 years; construction, 5-month pay pause, then 8% increase over 33 months, deal lasting 39 months; public service: 5-month pay pause, then 8% rise in basic pay over 3 years to June 1997, and maximum 3% rise in pay for productivity in public service carried over from PESP.
30th (1997)—Partnership 2000 for Inclusion, Employment and Competitiveness: First phase, 2½% for 12 months; second, 2¼% for 12 months, with local bargaining elements, 2% in second six months; third, 1½% for 9 months; fourth, 1% for 6 months.
31st (2000)—Programme for Prosperity and Fairness: 5½% of basic pay for first 12 months, with minimum of £12; 5½% for second 12 months, minimum £11, and 4% in last 9 months, minimum £9. National Minimum Wage of £4.70 per hour from 1 July 2001, £5 from 1 October 2002.
32nd (2003)—Sustaining Progress: Private sector: 3% of basic pay for 9 months, 2% for six months and 3% for 3 months; benchmarking in the public sector. A mid-term review in June 2004 resulted in (phase 1) 1½% for six months, 2% for those on €9 per hour or less, (phase 2) 1½% for 6 months, and (phase 3) 2½% for 6 months. In the public service, 1½% from December 2005, 2½% from 1 June 2006.
33rd (2006)—Towards 2010: 3% of basic pay from 1 December 2006; 2% from 1 June 2007; 2½% from 1 March 2008; and 2½% from 1 September 2008.

Sources: Kieran Jack McGinley, 'Neo-Corporatism, New Realism and Social Partnership in Ireland, 1970–1999,' PhD thesis, Trinity College, Dublin, 1999; Patrick Gunnigle, Gerard McMahon and Gerard Fitzgerald, *Industrial Relations in Ireland: Theory and Practice* (Dublin: Gill & Macmillan, 1999), chap. 6.

Table 136: Trade union membership, 1990–2007

	ICTU	*SIPTU*	*SIPTU as proportion of ICTU (%)*	*SIPTU (RFS)*	*SIPTU (RFS) as proportion of ICTU (%)*
1990	679,000	163,940	24.1	207,227	30.5
1991	682,000	167,170	24.5	208,417	30.5
1992	679,000	174,128	25.6	209,703	30.8
1993	679,000	170,282	25.0	213,159	31.3
1994	677,650	176,631	26.0	213,476	31.5
1995	682,211	176,235	25.8	218,936	32.0
1996	690,140	179,019	25.9	226,170	32.7
1997	699,191	178,931	25.5	230,006	32.8
1998	725,946	187,484	25.8	237,462	32.7
1999	710,067	191,484	26.9	243,064	34.2
2000	738,126	197,353	26.7	248,938	33.7
2001	759,360	195,419	25.7	247,960	32.6
2002	745,127	193,617	25.9	246,911	33.1
2003	766,647	196,537	25.6	250,351	32.6
2004	754,899	191,336	25.3	249,454	33.0
2005	800,057	195,116	24.3	246,634	30.8
2006	799,593	196,653	24.5	248,171	31.0
2007	832,116	199,781	24.0	253,271	30.4

RFS: Registrar of Friendly Societies.

Source: ICTU and SIPTU, Annual Reports, 1990–2007; Natalie Fox, ICTU.

Employment and work-force densities showed an accelerated decline from 1990. Union density fell 18% in the twelve years to 2006, having reached a peak in the late 1970s and early 1980s, at more than 60%, but reduced to approximately 36%. In the private sector it was even more stark, reaching 29%.[2]

This decline was not confined to Ireland but was similar throughout Europe, Australia and the United States. SIPTU's response was to transform itself from 'service' to 'organising' union.

Table 137: Union density, 1945–2007

	Membership	Employment density (%)	Work-force density (%)
1945	172,340	27.7	25.3
1955	305,620	45.7	41.6
1965	358,050	52.4	48.8
1975	449,520	60.0	53.2
1980	527,960	61.9	55.3
1985	485,050	61.3	55.3
1990	474,590	57.1	45.0
1995	504,459	53.1	41.1
1999	561,800	44.5	38.5
2000	586,800	45.0	n.a.
2001	595,086	43.0	n.a.
2002	625,744	44.2	38.0
2003	624,150	43.0	36.1
2004	603,104	42.5	34.6
2005	649,255	41.3	35.2
2006	625,000	38.0	32.5
2007	628,000	36.0	31.5

Source: DUES data series on trade unions in Ireland, 1925–99, University College, Dublin; Central Statistics Office; Manus O'Riordan, 'Some Issues in Tracking Union Density' (SIPTU, 2007).

Political contexts

The election of Mary Robinson as President of Ireland in December 1990 and Dick Spring's leadership in the Labour Party's best result ever of thirty-three seats in 1992 appeared to presage a long-awaited breakthrough for Socialist politics. The Labour Party's Coalition with Fianna Fáil angered many; their fears were realised in 1994 when revelations of corruption in the beef industry and other industries led to the collapse of the Government.

The Labour Party entered a 'Rainbow' Coalition with Fine Gael and Democratic Left; it was punished in 1997, losing sixteen seats.

The Party has been treading water since, holding twenty seats under Ruairí Quinn in 2002 (having gained four after the merger with Democratic Left) and Pat Rabbitte in 2007, the Mullingar Accord again revitalising Fine Gael. Without political influence, workers' interests remain marginalised. Without social partnership, workers' ability to influence the broad economic and social agenda would be severely diminished.

Chapter 35 ~

PARTNERSHIP, PROGRESS AND PEACE: SIPTU IN THE 1990s

MEMBERSHIP, ORGANISATION AND FINANCE

On 1 January 1990 fireworks flashed from the Dublin Civic Offices at Wood Quay to mark the birth of the Services, Industrial, Professional and Technical Union. The media called it a 'super-union' of 200,000 'book' members. It was promoted through newspapers, extensive hoarding advertising and commercials broadcast on RTÉ, UTV and Channel 4. SIPTU's National Executive Council met in the National Concert Hall on 4 January (the date in 1909 when the ITGWU was registered) and formally ratified all office-holders: Joint General Presidents, William Attley and John Carroll; Vice-Presidents: Edmund Browne and Tom Murphy; General Secretaries: Tom Garry and Chris Kirwan. In addition, three Assistant General Officers were appointed: Paul Clarke (Public Sector), Jimmy Somers (Private Sector) and Tommy Walsh (Development and Organisation).

In Dublin, where the greatest overlap occurred, Branches were merged under titles rather than numbers. A Special Conference determined SIPTU's attitudes to a successor to the Programme for National Recovery and adopted a Political Fund.

The initial financial membership of 161,631 rose to 163,940 by December. The emphasis was on recruitment through promoting services and benefits. Union density in the Republic was 56%—77% in the public sector, 45% in the private sector. Assertive anti-union strategies and new forms of work organisation threatened these figures.

If merger was designed to overcome financial problems it was not, at first sight, successful. A deficit of £378,179 was recorded, the first of nine in the decade. If transfers to the Industrial Contingency Fund are factored in, however, the picture is very different and a surplus of £1,181,045 is shown. The Industrial Contingency Fund was a sensible strategy, as events proved. Deficits, however artificial, demonstrated fragility even for a union of SIPTU's size. Dividing book assets of £19,884,121 (comprising a credit balance of £12,842,905 and investments valued at £7,041,216) by the number of financial members produced only £121.29 per member.

In 1991 membership rose to 167,170. The Irish National Painters' and Decorators' Trade Union voted by 7 to 1 to amalgamate from 1 October, becoming the INPD Trade Group, with Gerry Fleming as National Official. A deficit of £439,796 was recorded.

The death of Paddy Murphy on 22 April was the loss of a 'mentor and adviser of wisdom, courage and dedication.' Active since 1946, he had been the last General Secretary of the Federation of Rural Workers. At the Delegate Conference Paddy McKenna, Head of Administration, retired, being replaced by John Fay.

SIPTU reflected on 1992 as 'undoubtedly one of the most controversial years' in recent history. The Taoiseach, Charles Haughey, resigned in March and Fianna Fáil lost nine seats, if not power, in the subsequent election; controversy arose over the Treaty of Maastricht; and the Supreme Court ruling in the X case led to three referendums in November. SIPTU campaigned continuously to preserve the Programme for Economic and Social Progress in the public sector, to defend Aer Lingus and to achieve the 3% local bargaining element in the private sector. Remarkably, membership rose by 7,012, to 174,182.

Michael Brady, aged 104, passed away, having been for almost sixty-five years Secretary of the Balbriggan Branch. He was 'believed to have been one of the longest continuously serving elected trade union Officials in the world.' A historic joint seminar was held with the Fire Brigades Union, 'Firefighters: The European Dimension', in Derry.[1]

A Special Biennial Delegate Conference in May 1993 discussed economic problems, centralised bargaining, industrial policy, jobs, and workers' participation; social insurance, pensions, tax and social welfare, equality and housing; local bargaining and human resource management; and privatisation. Transitional Regional Conferences were held from September to November 1994 to establish permanent structures and Executives.[2] Membership fell to 170,282 in 1993 but recovered somewhat to 172,631 in 1994. This gave the lie to the view that 'trade union membership and influence is in terminal decline.' The profile was changing, however, from 'job-for-life' members to those in less secure employments.

Table 138: Organisations to which SIPTU was affiliated, 1994

National

Amnesty International—Irish Section
Economic and Social Research Institute
Irish Anti-Apartheid Movement
Irish Association of Brass and Military Bands
Irish Labour History Society
Labour Party
National Association of Mentally Handicapped
National College of Industrial Relations
National Industrial Safety Organisation

People's College
Retired Council of Ireland

Europe
Committee of Transport Workers' Unions
European Committee of Food and Allied Workers' Unions
European Federation of Agricultural Workers' Unions
European Federation of Building and Woodworkers' Unions
European Federation of Chemical and General Workers' Unions
European Metalworkers' Federation

International
International Federation of Actors
International Federation of Audio-Visual Workers
International Federation of Building and Wood Workers
International Federation of Chemical, Energy and General Workers
International Metalworkers' Federation
International Textile, Garment and Leather Workers' Federation
International Transport Workers' Federation
International Union of Food and Allied Workers' Associations

Source: SIPTU, Report of National Executive Council, 1993–4, p. 13–14.

Unemployment rose from 293,700 in December 1992 to 297,100 in 1993. Financial problems accompanied membership losses. New accounts systems were introduced, and net deficits in the General Fund were offset by surpluses in Provident and Contingency Funds and sales of premises. The loss of the Nolan Transport case in the High Court (see p. 823) exposed the union's finances. Staff Pension Trustees invested £30,000 in a venture capital project for job creation in line with recommendations of the Murray-Walsh Report on Irish Pensions.

In 1994 Jimmy Somers was elected Vice-President in succession to Tom Murphy, defeating John Kane, Tom Walsh and Norman Croke.[3]

Table 139: SIPTU membership, 1990–99

1990	163,940*	1995	176,235
1991	167,170	1996	179,019
1992	174,128	1997	178,931
1993	170,282	1998	187,484
1994	172,631	1999	191,484

*Initial membership was 161,631.

Source: SIPTU, Annual Reports, 1990–99.

Membership rose to 176,235 in 1995, recruitment adding 14,746, underlining a considerable turnover. Organising drives identified retail distribution, electronics and specified sites, assisted by Branches for Docks, Marine and Transport; Film, Entertainment and Leisure; Drink, Tobacco and Wholesale Distribution (absorbing the Guinness Branch); and county-based Health Services. SIPTU had more than 6,000 Shop Stewards and a staff of 311—168 industrial, 143 administrative and support. 'Special benefits' included Tax Check, a service securing tax refunds, competitive insurance, and consumer savings.[4]

Membership rose to 179,019 by 1996, but warning bells sounded. Union growth rates fell well below employment growth. The Strategic Development Initiative added recruitment to its tasks, as only 8,403 new members came in. In December the NEC adopted the SDI's consolidated report, *SIPTU, 2000: A World-Class Union*. A rise in contribution rates, approved in 1995, improved finances, but a slight membership decline followed in 1997. The transfer of the Automobile, General Engineering and Mechanical Operatives' Union added 2,100 members, while a draft Agreement was signed with the Marine, Port and General Workers' Union. A demand for 'better housekeeping' added 2,000 members, while more than 900 workers in the Community Employment Scheme joined. The State and Related Agencies Branch was created from Sections of non-commercial state-sponsored and education Branches.

Edmund Browne retired as General President and was succeeded by Jimmy Somers, who defeated a rank-and-file candidate, Carolann Duggan (Waterford), 51,651 to 37,940, in SIPTU's first direct election for a General Officer. Duggan's campaign, although ruffling feathers, showed the union's democracy and opportunity. The election for Vice-President was more fraught; Des Geraghty finally achieved office after defeating four rivals, two of them women. Three National Industrial Secretaries were appointed: John Kane, Matt Merrigan and Joe O'Flynn.[5]

Table 140: SIPTU income, expenditure and surplus, 1990–99

	Income	*Expenditure*	*Surplus (deficit)*	*Surplus (deficit)*
				+ Industrial Contingency Fund
1990	14,014,194	14,390,373	(378,179]	1,181,045
1991	14,819,883	15,259,679	(439,796)	1,279,420
1992	15,182,257	15,894,955	(712,698)	1,040,863
1993	15,914,580	18,629,509	(2,714,929)	(661,170)
1994	16,612,536	18,323,032	(1,710,496)	211,960
1995	17,254,623	17,853,264	(598,641)	463,239
1996	17,698,820	18,112,528	(413,708)	578,896
1997	18,732,170	18,677,136	55,034	362,542
1998	20,127,852	20,147,389	(19,537)	345,392
1999	21,105,742	21,403,411	(297,699)	32,137

Source: SIPTU, Annual Reports, 1990–2007.

In 1998 a 'housekeeping incentive scheme' rewarded Shop Stewards who recruited ten or more members by presenting them with a watch. The Security Services Branch tackled a neglected industry, and Dublin Transport and NATE Division amalgamated as Rail Services. In 1999 4,000 extra members came largely through amalgamations with the Irish Print Union and MPGWU. Nearly 400 ATGWU and MSF members in the Agricultural Credit Corporation transferred to the Insurance and Finance Branch. John McDonnell was elected General Secretary in succession to Bill Attley. 'SIPTU People', the first nationally co-ordinated and locally run recruitment campaign, was launched in September, led by Clare Bulman, Eddie Higgins and Gerry McIntyre. Planning, teamwork and specialist training courses underlined the drive from a new Organising Unit. The adaptation of the red-hand badge created a new image, and thirty leaflets, some in foreign languages, were aimed at employment groups. Jimmy Somers retired as General President in November and was succeeded by Des Geraghty.[6]

STRATEGIC DEVELOPMENT INITIATIVE

In 1994 SIPTU launched the Strategic Development Initiative to develop the union's full potential and achieve the highest possible standards of pay and conditions through maximising flexibility, organisational strength and enhancing the qualifications and experience of the staff. SIPTU became a 'learning organisation', guided by well-informed, planned activities. SDI project groups examined communications, equality, information technology, recruitment, Shop Stewards, staff development and training, staff relations and union structures. Liberty Forum, a lunchtime lecture series, was held from April to June 1995, and training modules established under the EU NOW (Women in a Trade Union: Making Policy Practice) and ADAPT programmes in association with the Adult Education Department of University College, Galway. Team-building, understanding change, strategy and personal development featured under ADAPT. A thirty-minute video, *The Changing World of Work,* dealt with SIPTU's responses to change. The bulletin *Renewal* kept members informed. Des Geraghty directed the SDI processes.

SIPTU Report was published from September 1996, providing information on industrial relations, macro-economics, the European Union, pay and conditions, and safety and health, and the quarterly *Connection* described NEC deliberations.[7]

In 1996 the Minister for Enterprise and Employment, Richard Bruton, launched 'SIPTU 2000: A World-Class Union', an ADAPT project run in association with Dublin City University and University College, Cork, piloted in Derry, Donegal, Dublin Engineering, Mallow, Mayo and Wexford Branches, with Danish and Swedish partners. The SDI Shop Stewards Project Group sought improved induction training for members, a review of Shop Stewards' Commission and greater definition of core union values. An iconic SIPTU poster depicted Earth as seen from space and the message:

In an ever-changing world, some things are constant . . .
SOLIDARITY—recognising our mutual interdependence;
EQUITY—ensuring a fair distribution of rewards;
EQUALITY—removing discrimination and prejudice;
DEMOCRACY—promoting full participation in decision-making.
The SEED from which our Union grew is the guiding principle for the renewal of SIPTU.

A *Newsline* supplement, 'Your Union at Work', provided information on SIPTU within the work-place, Shop Stewards, Regions, NEC and policy-making processes, support services, SIPTU Bonus and Scholarships, and other endeavours. SIPTU Bonus promoted members' consumer benefits.

From 1997 Branch education and Training Representatives and eighteen equality advisers and eight mentors were trained through NOW and UCG's Open Learning Centre. Eddie Higgins succeeded Geraghty as SDI Co-Ordinator, producing a representative's pack; Employee Assistance Programme and Partnership Forum for staff; the development of representative and Equality Representative; tasks relating to the change-over to the euro; and the SIPTU-NUIG Alliance.[8]

REGIONS

SIPTU was divided into eight Regions over a four-year transition period. In September 1994, 149 candidates contested elections for the Regional Executive Committees to replace the Transitional RECs. All candidates were profiled in *Newsline* in a huge exercise in democracy and a demanding task for the staff members who maximised participation.[9]

Table 141: SIPTU Regions and regional Secretaries, January 1990

Region 1 (Dublin Public Sector): 17.39%; Brendan Hayes.
Region 2 (Dublin Private Sector): 19.54%; Martin King.
Region 3 (South-East: Cos. Carlow, Kilkenny, Waterford Wexford, Wicklow): 8.98%; John Dwan.
Region 4 (South-West: Cos. Cork, Kerry, Limerick, Tipperary): 23.68%; John McDonnell.
Region 5 (Midlands: Cos. Kildare, Laois, Longford, Meath, Offaly, Westmeath): 9.23%; Jack O'Connor.
Region 6 (West: Cos. Clare, Galway, Mayo, Roscommon, Sligo): 10.46%; Janet Hughes.
Region 7 (Northern Counties: Cos. Cavan, Donegal, Leitrim, Louth, Monaghan): 8.91%; Bob Brady.
Region 8 (Northern Ireland): 1.81%; Jack Nash.

Region 1 (Dublin Public Sector)
Under its first President, Kay Garvey, Region 1 lobbied against aspects of the Broadcasting Act and tackled profound change in Team Aer Lingus, B&I and Dublin Gas. A major loss was Paul Boushell, an activist in Civil Aviation Branch, who died after a long illness in October 1991. In 1992 SIPTU's National Forestry Committee negotiated terms for the introduction of autonomous work groups in Coillte. A Lock-Out of more than 1,000 RTÉ members occurred when resistance to attempts by the management to 'impose unilateral changes' was made. As with the orchestras' strike in 1991, solidarity was total, with mass pickets, benefit gigs and events creating a 'tremendous sense of camaraderie'—not part of the management's intention. The break-up of Dublin County Council into three new administrative counties occasioned lengthy negotiations regarding transfers and the preservation of conditions and practices. In 1998 the Region broadcast information about additional voluntary contributions within the state industrial sector, hoping to maximise the take-up of a scheme long sought by SIPTU.[10]

Region 2 (Dublin Private Sector)
Under its first President, Andy Burke, the Region's main challenges were job losses and significant work-place change. Increased aggression by employers was evident. Securicor brought SIPTU to the 'steps of the High Court,' where a financial settlement was made, emphasising the need for care and the observance of procedures demanded by the Industrial Relations Act. The law's uneven-handedness and employers' disregard for industrial relations procedure was demonstrated. The Hotels Branch celebrated its seventy-fifth anniversary in 1993, recording a turbulent history in a special publication. The sudden closure of the troubled Packard Electric plant in April 1996 provoked anger. SIPTU and the ATGWU worked hard on a business plan for re-engaging more than 400 workers laid off since June 1995, when the rug was pulled. A task force attempted to secure alternative employment, while negotiations squeezed another £2½ million in severance terms. The loss of Semperit in Ballyfermot, Dublin, was another blow, not least as profits had increased. Production was switched to a low-wage plant in Central Asia, an ominous sign of things to come. In 1998 the Hotels Branch initiated a National Organising campaign. Workers were increasingly non-national and unaware of their rights and entitlements.[11]

Table 142: SIPTU financial membership by Region, 1990–99

	1990	1991	1992	1993	1994	1995	1996	1997	1998	1999
1	28,509	30,164	31,468	30,412	29,662	29,736	30,230	29,933	31,591	31,951
2	32,033	32,719	34,210	31,882	32,782	32,779	34,260	32,865	34,074	33,017
3	14,719	14,481	14,991	14,252	14,744	15,016	14,759	15,101	16,120	16,663
4	38,820	38,917	40,121	40,086	40,469	42,149	42,565	42,860	45,146	45,191

5	15,131	15,615	15,636	15,727	16,020	16,314	16,674	16,836	18,199	17,129
6	17,148	18,000	18,691	18,502	19,400	20,791	21,579	22,275	22,643	23,602
7	14,607	14,700	14,864	15,569	15,254	15,991	15,996	15,542	15,932	14,827
8	2,967	2,574	274	1,135	1,008	983	971	917	2,502	2,261
Total	163,940	167,170	174,128	170,282	172,631	176,235	179,019	178,931	187,484	191,484

Source: SIPTU, Annual Reports, 1990–98.

Region 3 (South-East)

Operating from Kilkenny under its first President, Tommy Byrne (Carlow), the Region fought a lengthy recognition battle in Lett's, Wexford, a fish-processing plant, concluded in January with the union's objectives met; but by the end of the year only half the members remained, as the company experienced difficulties. A membership decline reflected constant closures and redundancies. In 1992 the Waterford Branch put a ban on Social Employment Schemes, seeing them as cheap compulsory labour and expressing concern over their terms and conditions. This resulted in a code of practice for the approval and supervision of future schemes. The decision of Wexford County Council in 1995 to cut £100,000 from the Budget of its fire service was strongly resisted. Retained and full-time firefighters throughout the country rallied to support their colleagues. The strike lasted fifteen weeks before a settlement. After John Dwan's retirement Jack O'Connor became Regional Secretary, and in 1998 the first calls for a 'properly resourced Organising Department' were made as part of a 'detailed Organising strategy.'[12]

Region 4 (South-West)

Edward McGrath chaired the largest Region, operating from Connolly Hall, Cork. It identified the need for a specialist white-collar Branch and Recruiting Official; successfully defended members in Sunbeam and Kerry Fashions, Cork and Tralee, when threatened with redundancy; resisted contracting out in Golden Vale and Dairygold; and won a twelve-week strike in Liebert, Cork, for the reinstatement of a member. Equal pay claims were won in Irish Crown, Clonmel Chemicals and CMP. The closure of Western Digital in Cork in July 1991 cost more than 400 jobs, but 2,000 members were recruited. The Region's membership of 38,828 was divided between food and chemicals (11,000), textiles and construction (10,000), local authorities and health (9,000), transport, computers and electronics (5,500) and catering and leisure (3,000). The Region was active in monitoring both the EC Common Agricultural Policy and the General Agreement on Tariffs and Trade (GATT), identifying their effect on agribusiness, where employment fell from 57,000 in 1979 to 38,000 in 1992. Seminars were held on unemployment, championing co-operative production. A five-month strike in Three Lakes Hotel, Killarney, in 1997 ended in redundancy settlements—an unsatisfactory conclusion but one that did not deter attempts to unionise the next season. Dick Spring thought it 'an

incomprehensible, appalling situation' and supported the strikers. In 1999 continued job cuts in Apple, Cork, caused anger.[13]

Region 5 (Midlands)

Tom Crowe, President, operating from Tullamore, led the rationalisation of struc-
tures in his own county, Kildare, and the new Offaly and Peat Industries Branches.
Recruitment preoccupied the Region, together with resisting job cuts and con-
tracting in Bord na Móna. In 1992 a 'noteworthy success' came in Peerless Rugs,
Athy, with seventy-five women gaining equal pay of £35 a week, backdated to 1
August 1981. In 1999 the closure of Avon Arlington and the uncertain future of Tara
Mines dominated.[14]

Region 6 (West)

Michael Cullen, President, led the Region, centred on Galway, in a fruitless defence
of Arigna Mines, which closed with the loss of two hundred jobs, and the transfer
of Aran Ferry Services to private ownership. The highly motivated SIGNAL
Committee defended Shannon Airport, 'unquestionably' the biggest issue in 1991.
The Chairperson of SIGNAL, Christy Normoyle, sadly died as activity he inspired
began to capture national headlines. Congress adopted SIPTU's motion demanding
the retention of the Shannon stop-over. The Region was closely involved in plans
to open a Breast Cancer Research Institute, a campaign launched by President Mary
Robinson, with Tom Garry in attendance. In 1992 alliances were made with the Irish
Farmers' Association and Irish Creamery Milk Suppliers' Association in defence of
jobs in Halal-Ump in Cos. Mayo and Sligo. The purchase of the plants by Avonmore
brought a satisfactory outcome. SIGNAL's campaign won a victory with the retention
of the compulsory stop-over. SIPTU had provided financial and material assistance,
organised a Dublin demonstration by Shannon staff, put 5,000 people on the streets
of Shannon Industrial Estate and another 530,000 in Limerick and petitioned the
Minister, demonstrating a successful role for regional structures. 'Action West:
Community Action for Jobs' saw SIPTU leading demonstrations in Ballina, Ennis,
Galway, Roscommon and Sligo. In 1995 a 'Gender and Development' workshop led
to exchanges with SPALI in Manila. In 1996, 320 members in University College
Hospital, Galway, resisted the sub-contracting of catering contracts. In 1997 the
Regional Secretary, Janet Hughes, became a Rights Commissioner. A strong cham-
pion of equality and human rights, she was the most senior female staff member,
and her departure was regretted. She was succeeded by George Hunter. In 1998
Mayo No. 1 and No. 2 Branches produced a basic information guide for new
members, *Welcome to SIPTU*.[15]

Region 7 (Northern Counties)

Charlie Faulkner had the unenviable task of leading a Region operating
from Monaghan and embracing all the Border counties, attaining cohesion and
purpose while the normal business of disputes and equality claims was pursued.

The expansion of Fruit of the Loom in Inishowen brought boom times, thousands of new members and full-time offices in Buncrana. McCarren's Bacon, Cavan, announced substantial rationalisation in March 1996 without consultation, and a row rumbled through the Labour Relations Commission and Labour Court. A strike began on 16 August 1996, with the Social Welfare Tribunal granting Unemployment Benefit on the grounds that the management 'acted unreasonably.' Matters were not resolved in 1997. In April 1998 the Regional Secretary, Bob Brady, retired and was replaced by George Hunter. A 22-month picket on McCarren's Bacon, Cavan, was finally removed in June after agreement on severance. The once-booming Fruit of the Loom became 'Fruit of the Gloom' as more than 700 members waited anxiously to hear their fate while the company debated transferring operations to low-wage countries. Their worst fears were realised at Christmas.[16]

Region 8 (Northern Ireland)

In 1990 book membership was 3,581 former ITGWU members and 206 from the NATE Division of the FWUI: Belfast, 861; Derry 1,474; and Newry 1,516. For the first time SIPTU had a distinct Northern Ireland identity, allowing direct nomination to cross-border bodies and more positive recruitment drives. Death threats made workplace activity difficult. Séamus Sullivan, aged twenty-four, was shot dead at Belfast City Council's refuse collection depot in Springfield Avenue. A three-day stoppage registered disgust and abhorrence. 'Compulsory competitive tendering' threatened jobs in Belfast and Newry, worsened by a decision to wind down Wages Councils. SIPTU predominantly represented low-paid workers, and these developments affected livelihoods and family incomes. New premises at 3 Antrim Road, Belfast, were purchased. The Regional Secretary, Jack Nash, moved to Dublin in January 1993, and Robert Brady succeeded him. 1992 ended with a sectarian attack on the Dockers' Club in Pilot Street, Belfast, where a cross-community event was raising money for the Northern Ireland Hospice. Only courageous action by those manning the doors prevented gunmen gaining access to the building and potentially killing scores. Mark Rodgers and James Cameron were shot dead in November 1993 as they arrived for work at Kennedy Way Cleansing Depot, victims of tit-for-tat sectarian violence. The Gresteel massacre and Shankill Road bombing brought matters to a sickening low point, shocking a public thought to be inured to such crimes. Congress organised a Community Day for Peace on 18 November 1993, which brought 80,000 people onto the streets. At the same time thousands in work-places in the Republic and school-children throughout the country stood for a period of silence. The Congress slogan was *Peace—The perfect present at Christmas.* Jack Nash played a leading role in this activity. After the ceasefires of autumn 1994 Congress drafted 'Investing in Peace', a comprehensive programme for maximising the 'peace dividend'. It was not so peaceful on the industrial front, where Wages Councils were abolished and the Trade Union Reform and Employment Act (1993) changed procedures for Deduction at Source. In addition, compulsory competitive tendering was enacted. The Regional Conference centred on 'Building the Peace', with John Hume a guest speaker.[17]

Peace was maintained in 1995. Counteract, the ICTU's anti-sectarian unit, set up in 1990, commented that, with ceasefires, 'work is only beginning.' SIPTU received its Certificate of Independence under trade union legislation. A presentation was made in Belfast to 'acknowledge the loyalty' and courage of members and staff 'throughout the troubles times.' The bombs in Canary Wharf, London, in February 1996 were responded to by peace rallies held simultaneously throughout Ireland on 25 February, co-ordinated by 'Solidarity to Organise Peace' (STOP): 60,000 marched in Dublin, 30,000 in Cork and 15,000 in Belfast. The Job Seekers Act was bitterly opposed as another unnecessary blow for the most vulnerable. In Raelbrook Shirts, Derry, members occupied their canteen in October to protest against redundancies announced with no consultation. In 1997 Bill Attley called for an end to violence, a Bill of Rights and economic investment, supporting the Northern Ireland Committee's Programme for Investing in Peace.[18] In 1998 a membership decline caused an anxious NEC to call 'for greater efforts' from all to combat not just the effects of the 'difficult social and political environment' but the legislative requirement that 'members re-affirm their authorisation' for check-off annually. This imposed 'considerable strains', as 'the demands of book-keeping compete periodically with the demands for servicing.'

SIPTU welcomed the Belfast Agreement. The Regional Secretary, George Hunter, praised SIPTU's contribution to peace and called for greater dialogue, right down to the work-place level. The Omagh bombing was strongly condemned by the NEC, which tendered its condolences to the victims' families. SIPTU strongly urged a 'Yes' vote in the referendums resulting from the Belfast Agreement, 'for peace, prosperity and partnership' and 'for unity by peaceful persuasion.' John Hume, a union member, was warmly congratulated on his Nobel Peace Prize, given jointly with the First Minister Designate, David Trimble. In 1999 SIPTU welcomed the establishment of the Human Rights Commission and North-South Co-operation Unit. Irish Trade Union Trust became involved in the Museum of Tolerance and Dublin and Belfast Trades Councils' City Bridges project, dealing with sectarianism, discrimination and multiculturalism.[19]

WOMEN AND EQUALITY

SIPTU began with 70,000 women members. All elected structures provided reserved places. An Interim Women's Committee, chaired by Mary Burke (Clonmel) identified issues and training needs. The first Women's Conference, on the theme 'Are Unions Relevant to the Twenty-First Century?' was held in November 1990. The prime target was the removal of the eighteen-hour threshold for part-time workers, reduced to eight by the Worker Protection (Regular Part-Time Employees) Act (1991). National improvements in cervical cancer screening were sought. Equal pay cases were won at Lissadell Towels, Carrickmacross, and Irish Crown, Cork, after lengthy industrial and legal processes, with Mary Robinson acting for SIPTU. In 1991 'Making Equality a Reality' examined poverty and its effects on family and community, the impact of the Single European Market on women, equality legislation, health and safety, and positive action. May O'Brien retired as Women's Affairs Official in 1992. Nóirín Greene succeeded her as Equality Officer. SIPTU's success rate in equality and sexual harassment cases was 90%. Awareness programmes equipped members with skills for identifying and managing claims within work-places and provided Officials with quality intelligence. The 1992 Delegate Conference in Waterford was on the theme 'SIPTU Making Equality a Reality'. May O'Brien was a slightly unexpected appointment as Women's Affairs Official in 1982, but her understated manner proved highly effective in moving equality forward. She was a superb technician—assisted by Eugene Kearney (Industrial Engineering) —in handling equal pay and equality claims, allying an encyclopaedic legal knowledge with imaginative argument and dogged persistence. She sat on the Employment Equality Agency. Her memoir of her first days in Liberty Hall is a joy.[20]

An equal pay claim on behalf of eighty women in Verbatim, Limerick, was thwarted by the management 'refusing legitimate Union requests for entry into the premises in order to obtain information in pursuit of the claim.' Where union membership, a constitutional right, was effectually thwarted workers were simultaneously denied any capacity to pursue a statutory equality entitlement, raising serious questions about the effectiveness of the Anti-Discrimination (Pay) Act. In the 1992 referendum on the 'rights to travel and information' on abortion SIPTU campaigned against the first amendment, for the second and third. The 'NOW' (New Opportunities for Women) Project, funded by the European Community, was used by the Women Workers' Branch to develop skills among contract cleaners. A guidance leaflet on work-place sexual harassment, 'Working with Dignity', was launched at the Women's Forum in Limerick in 1993. Assertiveness training was provided in Dublin, Donegal, Ennis, Sligo and Wexford. In 1995 SIPTU published 'Model Agreement Policy Statement for all Employees (Equality of Opportunity) and (Freedom from Sexual Harassment)', 'Bullying, Intimidation and Harassment in the Workplace', 'Sexual Harassment Is No Joke', and 'Guidelines to the Maternity Protection Act (1994), Adoptive Leave Act (1995) and Maternity Protection Act (1994) (Implementation of the EU Pregnancy Directive)', which were adopted in numerous employments. A weekend seminar, 'Equality and Partnership: Europe's Greatest Challenge', was held in Magee College, Derry, in addition to the Women's Forum in Cork.

In 1996 the Women's Forum sought 'mainstreaming equality'. The National Women's Committee organised Irish holidays for Belarussian children, part of a long-lasting involvement with Chernobyl Children's Irish Aid Programme. Significant equal pay cases were won in C&D Petfoods, Edgeworthstown, and St Patrick's College, Drumcondra, and for Trinity College cleaning workers, who secured more than £500,000 in back pay. Following allegations that women Delegates were subjected to sexual harassment at the Delegate Conference, the NEC investigated; it found no case reported but made it clear through its public statements and *Newsline* that SIPTU 'was opposed to sexual harassment anywhere; was concerned to eliminate it in the work-place and within the Union,' and would take appropriate action if complaints were proved. In 1998 a Gender Equity

Committee developed a plan for achieving full equity within the union by 2010. The first Equality Representatives graduated from the 'NOW' SIPTU-NUIG project, and a journeywoman painter, Bronwyn Clohissey, became Equality Official in the Irish National Painters' and Decorators' Group.[21]

In August 1998, after Nóirín Greene left SIPTU, Rosheen Callender became National Equality Secretary, identifying progress on a minimum wage and tax and welfare reforms and securing all Partnership 2000 commitments on poverty, inequality and social inclusion. The Equality Unit published Donncha O'Connell's *Equality Now!: The SIPTU Guide to the Employment Equality Act* (1998) and Barbara Kelly's *Social Partnership: What Have Women Achieved?*

Racism became a concern as tensions were identified within an increasingly multinational work force. SIPTU strongly challenged popular myths about asylum-seekers and immigrants, promoted multiculturalism and defended non-nationals from exploitation. It demanded that asylum-seekers be given the right to work and that work permits be the property of workers, not their employers. Within all work-places SIPTU championed all workers' right to dignity at work.[22]

CONGRESS
Congress celebrated its Centenary in 1994. SIPTU supported the events, particularly the May Public Holiday Weekend festival, its highlight the Centenary Cavalcade in Dublin. Five SIPTU Officials were elected to the ICTU Executive in 1999: Des Geraghty (Vice-President) and John McDonnell (General Secretary) as Executive Council members, Jimmy Somers (General President) as Treasurer, Rosheen Callender (Equality Secretary), who topped the poll for reserved seats for women, and Eric Fleming (Construction Branch) as Trades Council representative.[23] Relations between the new 'super-union' and Congress were strong.

SOCIAL PARTNERSHIP
Consultation took place in August and September 1990 as the Programme for National Recovery concluded. The NEC's document 'Shaping Our Future: An Agenda for Progress' identified alternatives. On pay, a basic floor at least matching inflation and 'specifically weighted in favour of the lower paid' while allowing workers in more profitable companies to pursue additional claims was sought. Action on jobs was demanded, with the involvement of workers in decision-making and with an emphasis on 'the potential of local community enterprises and co-operatives to create jobs.' A simplified tax code with two bands—a standard rate of 25% and a top rate of 48%, with those on low incomes removed altogether—was advocated. Noting that 90% of the report of the Commission on Social Welfare still awaited implementation, SIPTU wanted action, although acknowledging that the Programme for National Recovery had maintained the real value of welfare payments. Comprehensive reform of the health service, a reduction in class sizes and the appointment of guidance teachers were central. An hour's reduction in the working week and two additional days' annual leave were demanded.

SIPTU led calls for a review of the Programme for National Recovery. A special ICTU review agreed, by only 180 to 141, to let the programme run its full term. Criticism centred on high inflation, which eroded wage terms. On 27 September, Congress Delegates voted overwhelmingly to enter talks. Provisions for negotiating a 39-hour week proved problematic, as many employers had shopping-lists to set against the concession. The amendment of holiday legislation would have avoided this. Significant pay increases for construction workers resulted from a joint review by Congress and the Construction Industry Federation.[24]

The 'Programme for Economic and Social Progress' was ratified early in 1991. SIPTU regarded it as 'much more than a Programme for National Recovery Mark 2.' By 'extending the boundaries of accepted trade union interest and influence' the union hoped that matters would progress beyond mere aspirations. SIPTU aimed to 'make the Programme work.' A local bargaining mechanism under clause 3 provided for an additional 2% at the work-place level. This, and flat-rate rather than percentage increases, addressed important criticisms of the Programme for National Recovery. Its acceptance by 57,103 to 33,244 showed that a high level of scepticism remained. Congress ratified the Agreement by 224 to 109. The Minister for Finance, Albert Reynolds, announced in the summer that the Government's finances were so imperilled that increases in public-sector pay due in January 1992 could not be met. The new Minister, Bertie Ahern, intended to cap wages in 1992 and 1993 and introduce savage welfare cuts. SIPTU, with the ICTU Public Services Committee, sponsored a national poster campaign, 'Why pick on public servants for the squeeze? Honour the PESP—it's only fair.' This created a great resonance with the public. With a Congress Day of Action on 28 January looming, Ahern retreated, offering to maintain the cash limit to 1 December, then pay full retrospection. SIPTU's 45,000 public-servant members endorsed this overwhelmingly.

Opposition to Charlie McCreevy's 'Dirty Dozen' welfare cuts and demands for action on jobs strained the Programme for Economic and Social Progress to the hilt. As with the 39-hour week, the 3% local bargaining clause allowed employers to screw concessions. SIPTU members stood firm in 54% of cases, but in others much was conceded, sometimes negating the 3%. The Labour Court fully endorsed the employers' 'trade-off' argument. Low pay was dealt with by a 'minute note after the printed report was published, 'perhaps a bad omen; 'only four cases were referred to the Labour Court.'[25]

On 22 September 1993 a Special Delegate Conference voted overwhelmingly to open talks on a national Agreement, 'subject to a prior Government commitment to withdraw the 1% income levy (imposed in the 1993 Budget) and "Dirty Dozen" social welfare cuts.' The resulting 'Programme for Competitiveness and Work' made broad commitments on employment, agribusiness and rural development, macroeconomic policy and tax reform, development partnership, and social equity. By December 1994 SIPTU had concluded 480 Agreements, covering 150,000 workers. Attitudes to national Agreements were informed by evidence from the Research Department that under the 'free-for-all', 1981–7, total employment fell by 76,000, or

7%, while manufacturing employment fell by 35,000, or 14%. Unemployment rose from 100,000 to 250,000. Real earnings rose by about 5% for industrial workers; but for all workers the real value of take-home pay fell by 7%, mainly as a result of increased PAYE and PRSI, which rose for a married man with two children from 16% to 25%. Under the Programme for National Recovery, 1987–90, total employment rose by 46,000, or 4%, and manufacturing employment by 15,000, or 7%, while the live register of unemployment fell by 20,000, or 8%. Average manufacturing earnings increased by 13%; but, after allowing for inflation, real increases were 3%. As the PAYE and PRSI burden was eased slightly, the real value of take-home pay rose by 5%.

Under the Programme for Economic and Social Progress things worsened, as employment creation stagnated, the live register increasing by 90,000. Average manufacturing earnings rose by 14%—after inflation a mere 4%—resulting in the real value of take-home pay rising by about 4%. Serious questions were asked about successor Agreements.[26]

An encouraging aspect of settlements under the Programme for Competitiveness and Work in 1995 was the improvement in pension and sickness pay schemes in both the private and the public sector. Rosheen Callender, Research Officer, provided expertise, and the Irish Trade Union Trust developed advisory skills. Lack of progress on local-level partnership, a poor share for workers of record profits and 'no guaranteed legal right to trade union representation' led Bill Attley to suggest in December that a 'decade of national deals may be over.' Positive aspects were improvements in living standards and reduced inflation, lower interest rates and a reduction in the national debt; economic growth the envy of Europe, based on increased competitiveness; membership of European monetary union; and increasing union partnership. Against were an inadequate workers' share of the boom, the non-implementation of Government PAYE, PRSI and social welfare commitments, unacceptable unemployment, the lack of progress on union recognition, and increasing casualisation. A Special Delegate Conference on 12 September 1996 approved the opening of talks, by 289 to 58. A submission for a National Minimum Wage, 'Five Pounds Per Hour and Staying Behind No More!', was made as the talks progressed. SIPTU's acceptance of 'Partnership 2000' was narrower than before, 57 to 43%. It was an impressive tribute to industrial and administrative staff and Branch activists, who got out 114,622 votes, 65,515 against 49,107, the closeness reflecting concerns about the 'credibility of other social partners.' By December settlements had been made for 90,285 members.

New forms of work organisation preoccupied Officials. SIPTU took a lead, providing training for management and members. Negotiating work-place compliance with the Organisation of Working Time Act (1997) and avoiding losses to members was niggling and time-consuming.[27]

In 1998, 1,017 settlements under Partnership 2000 covered 124,098 members. Many won significant improvements in fringe benefits. The NEC cautioned against the view that centralised bargaining meant that SIPTU was effectually 'on auto-pilot.'

It was not as simple as 'the local Union Branch asks for the increase and the employer grants it.' Partnership 2000 'established a broad framework,' but there were 'many local, regional or sectoral variables.' In Kvaerner Cementation, Thurles, the employer's practice of deducting employers' PRSI contribution and £50 a week towards workers' holiday pay was stopped only after workers joined up. More than thirty-five employments concluded Agreements on gain-sharing, and more than a hundred won new or improved pension or sickness pay schemes.

Progress was maintained in 1999 with the application of the Craft Analogue.

An intensive consultation process took place regarding Partnership 2000's successor. A progress report was published and a questionnaire circulated, asking members to allocate priorities to twelve areas: increased take-home pay; tax; job security; housing costs; real increases in living standards; equality; pension schemes; better health care; union recognition; low pay; child care; and safety and health. In response, 32% wanted national bargaining, 11% local bargaining and 57% a combination of both. The Delegate Conference endorsed SIPTU's twelve-point programme, 'Pay Increases for Fairness at Work and Justice in Society'.

Talks had barely begun when the December Budget resulted in Congress suspending its involvement. Des Geraghty said the Budget was 'an indefensible attack on low-income families' and 'ran counter to the Tax strategy agreed the previous month by all Social Partners, including the Government.' The Taoiseach turned turtle, and talks resumed, with low pay a central consideration. SIPTU contributed much to the pressure, reinvigorating its alliance of social and community groups and issuing its 'Decent Dozen' demands.[28]

Table 143: SIPTU's twelve-point programme 'Pay Increases for Fairness at Work and Justice in Society'

(1) **Pay**

It is quite clear that the economy can sustain substantial pay increases for all workers, based on past and future rates of economic growth and labour productivity. A particular priority for SIPTU will be to significantly improve the absolute and relative position of those on less than average industrial earnings through substantial flat rate pay increases and the attainment of a statutory Minimum Wage of £5 an hour.

(2) **Tax Reform**

SIPTU's tax policy for workers gives priority to further improving the living standards of lower to middle income earners by a real tax reform which removes all workers on £5 an hour from the tax net altogether and ensures that 80% of PAYE tax payers contribute at no more than the standard rate. Real tax reform must, however, also bring about a system that is fully transparent, provides an equitable treatment for both labour and capital, eliminates illegality and applies a range of penalties including imprisonment and interest arrears and fines on the privileged minority who have been systematically defrauding the National Exchequer.

(3) Participation

The refusal by employers to agree to meaningful participation at the level of the individual employment must be overcome. Rights of information and consultation must be vigorously pursued as well as the right to a significant share in the profits and productivity gains which workers themselves have brought about.

(4) Union Representation

In order to guarantee the rights of workers to be professionally represented by a union, there must be full, immediate and effective implementation of the Report of the High Level Group, with provision for a review of such effectiveness. There must also be provision of proper facilities for Shop Stewards and employee representatives in the workplace.

(5) Equality

The elimination of inequality based on gender, race, disability or other personal characteristics must be brought to completion. The promotion of social equity must also be pursued through a programme of measures—both nationally and within the workplace—to ensure equality of opportunity for all in an inclusive multi-cultural society.

(6) Quality of Life

The quality of life must be enhanced by ensuring that the health, safety and welfare of all workers is both guaranteed and enforced. The demands of work and the needs of families must also be reconciled through family friendly employment practices, including state provision and workplace Agreements on childcare, paid parental leave, greater flexibility in the organisation of working-time and increased annual leave.

(7) Atypical Workers

The ICTU commitment to co-ordinate the development of an integrated plan of campaign for the rights of atypical workers must be implemented. The quality of working life and job security of part-time, temporary, contract and other atypical workers must be enforced through standard codes; the poverty traps in the social welfare system experienced by such workers must be eliminated; and minimum wage legislation must be effectively enforced with particular regard to such vulnerable groups.

(8) Pensions

There must be adequate social welfare pension coverage for all supplemented by an extension of occupational pension coverage for all workers to an approved standard. The integration of many occupational pension schemes with social welfare pension provision must not be allowed to offset or negate overall pension improvement. There must be further progressive improvement of pension benefits in profitable employments and well-funded schemes.

(9) Affordable Housing

The housing crisis must be addressed through substantially increased expenditure on social housing, price control, rent control and increasing the supply of building land in line with SIPTU policy on the provision of affordable housing.

(10) Lifelong Learning

Lifelong learning must be promoted through achieving full and free access to all levels of the educational system for PAYE workers and their families; the provision of paid educational leave; the negotiation of workplace Agreements on education and training; and the provision of focused training support for workers in traditional and threatened industries.

(11) Health

The health service must be thoroughly reformed and expenditure significantly increased to reduce waiting lists and eliminate undue delay through the development of a system which provides proper access and cover for all, irrespective of income.

(12) Social Welfare

There must be a substantial increase in the levels of social welfare benefits in line with revised anti-poverty targets; and the further improvement of the social welfare system itself through developing new schemes in priority areas such as carer's allowances and paid parental leave.

WAGES AND DISPUTES

Disputes in 1990 cost the union £158,893, a mere 1.1% of income, reflecting the industrial peace of the Programme for National Recovery. Union protests over the Broadcasting Bill and the threat to jobs in RTÉ were brought home by hour-long stoppages in July. Actors' Equity played a football match outside the Dáil between a 'Ray Burke Eleven' and a 'Fair Play Squad'.

In 1992 the sale of United Meat Packers threw 500 members in Ballyhaunis, Ballaghaderreen, Charleville and Camolin out of work. SIPTU protested strongly. Many jobs were saved when Avonmore took over. In construction, new relativities were established between craftsmen and general operatives, part of SIPTU's continuing advance for building workers. Issues in more than 5,000 employments were settled without the need for industrial action.

Exceptions were Pat the Baker, Ward International (Athlone) and Nolan Transport. After the rejection of a Labour Court recommendation that Pat the Baker recognise the union in Cherry Orchard, Co. Dublin, a strike began in March 1993. In June the company closed and withdrew its services to Granard, Co. Longford, with pickets following. In a sign of things to come the 'company spent huge amounts of money on advertising campaigns, security and surveillance, top legal assistance and use of two public relations companies to distort the issues.' Had this been spent either on the Cherry Orchard bakery or on meaningful attempts at resolution the matter would have been amicably resolved. A severance settlement was agreed in December. Members were asked to 'use your loaf' and 'next time you go shopping remember your SIPTU colleagues on the breadline.' *Breadline News* maintained spirits against 'Pat the Strike-Breaker'.

From 4 October 1993 to 1 June 1994 members resisted the efforts of Ward International to make 'major deleterious changes in conditions.' Intervention by the Labour Court finally settled the matter, although the Shop Steward was 'made redundant.'

Table 144: SIPTU Dispute Benefit, 1990–99

	Dispute Benefit (£)	Dispute Grants (£)	Benefit + grants (£)	As proportion of income (%)
1990	158,923	—	158,923	1.1
1991	129,748	6,983	136,731	0.9
1992	295,248	10,776	306,024	2.0
1993	162,001	6,397	168,398	1.0
1994	112,066	3,319	115,385	0.6
1995	93,377	7,939	101,316	0.5
1996	267,161	10,639	277,800	1.5
1997	138,590	23,812	162,402	0.8
1998	115,596	12,785	128,381	0.6
1999	910,581	25,347	935,928	4.4

Source: SIPTU, Annual Reports, 1990–99.

In 1995 Dispute Pay was £93,336, with £50,222 going to Dunne's Stores members nationally in a row over Sunday trading and 'zero-hours' contracts. Sadly, even in the wake of the strike the management's 'grudging attitude' suggested that 'Dunne's had not fully learned the lessons.' A national campaign sought guidelines on sub-contracting in construction and improved enforcement by the Construction Industry Monitoring Agency. Short stoppages publicised violence against bus drivers. There was another, thirteen-day national strike in Dunne's in August and September 1996, the victory securing 'for the first time in Dunne's fifty-year history' an agreed grievance procedure with reference to the Labour Relations Commission and Labour Court. The loss of 800 jobs at Packard Electric in Tallaght was bitterly resisted. The Electronics Branch led the fight, together with the ATGWU, but to little avail. General Motors refused to reconsider. A lengthy strike began on 31 August in the Royal Dublin Hotel, where many of the workers were Spanish, aimed at raising appallingly low basic wages.

The Government's plan to break up CIÉ into Bus Éireann, Bus Átha Cliath and Iarnród Éireann was challenged. SIPTU and the NBRU took part in a protest march in September, amid concerns over job losses and anger at the lack of consultation. In 1997 a strike by more than 4,000 local authority, health board and voluntary hospital craftsmen over their analogue pay claim drew support from 30,000 general operatives. A seven-week strike in Greencore achieved improved basic rates for members in Carlow, Mallow and Thurles.[29]

Table 145: SIPTU Industrial Contingency Fund (£), 1990–99

	Income	Expenditure	Balance
1990	1,559,224	381,692	3,831,570
1991	1,719,216	232,963	5,317,823
1992	1,753,561	458,841	6,612,543
1993†	2,053,759	364,095	8,302,207
1994	1,922,456	1,646,494	8,578,169
1995	1,061,880	330,483	9,309,566
1996	992,604	302,170	10,000,000
1997	307,508	307,508	10,000,000
1998	364,929	364,929	10,000,000
1999	329,836	788,170*	9,211,830

*£788,170 transferred to General Fund for nurses' strike.
†Transfer of €1,000,000 from General Fund.
Source: SIPTU, Annual Reports, 1990–2007.

WORK-PLACE CHANGE

Rapid change in the work-place was driven by the converging trends of single-market competition, globalisation and new technology, the 'flexible firm' and 'lean production', and advancing 'human resource' management that swung towards direct involvement with employees and away from traditional collective bargaining. Congress produced 'Managing Change: Negotiators' Guide', while Martin Naughton, a SIPTU Tutor, developed customised training and negotiating packages, providing in-plant courses for members and management. SIPTU acknowledged the desirability of change, attempting to maximise the return to members. This closely fused the industrial and education functions, feeding experiences of best practice straight into negotiating briefs.

Concepts of 'partnership' were not always popular with members. Scepticism was rife. Naughton insightfully concluded that what was happening was a 'a production process dressed up inside a social or industrial relations process.' He sought to ensure that the sheep saw everything, no matter how much employers attempted to pull down the wool.

At the 1995 Biennial Conference Browne greeted social partnership as successful—at the national level; at the local level it was a 'mirage'. He called for deeper engagement to manage work-place change. The Transnational Information and Consultation of Workers Act (1996) transposed the EU European Works Councils Directive into Irish law. SIPTU rapidly engaged companies to which it applied, providing training and information. A Special Conference in Galway in 1997 set an agenda for a network of European Works Councils representatives. Training and policy development with SIPTU worker directors continued in parallel. In 1998 significant numbers of Agreements on new forms of work organisation were made, including a reform of corporate structures developed under an ADAPT project. More than 100 companies agreed 'enterprise partnerships', dealing with financial involvement, adaptability, flexibility and innovation, competitiveness, health and safety, and conflict-solving and avoidance.[30]

NURSES

A 'long-awaited' nurses' pay review began in 1994, with a 1% 'good faith' award from 1 April, to be 'offset against the outcome of negotiation.' Beyond wages, concerns about the health service led SIPTU to observe that 'while the Minister was busily launching his Strategy for Effective Healthcare in the 1990s' those 'charged with its delivery were encountering severe difficulties' in securing its implementation. Traditionally strong among psychiatric nurses, SIPTU appealed to greater numbers of disgruntled general nurses as pressures built. SIPTU Nursing Council secured an additional £1 million for improvements in health and safety, raising awareness of violence against nurses. Under the heading 'Enough is Enough', nurses conducted one-day stoppages to publicise overcrowding and the chronic shortage of beds in accident and emergency departments. *Newsline* published posters suggesting that 'even angels can't get by on a wing and a prayer', calling for 'fair play, fair pay and no delay.' In February 1997, 7,600 SIPTU nurses joined 20,000 colleagues in the Nursing Alliance to campaign for significant improvements in pay and conditions. SIPTU voted for industrial action. The Nursing Officer, Noel Dowling, mooted a Commission to investigate the complexities of nurses' pay. A final settlement included £50 million for increases.

In 1998 the Alliance of Nursing Unions demanded the implementation of the report of the Commission on Nursing. Following a rejection of the terms of the Labour Relations Commission by nine to one, SIPTU's 9,000 nurses balloted for strike. After nine days on picket lines the Alliance of Nursing Unions suspended action to allow for a ballot on a Labour Court recommendation. SIPTU members accepted, by 62 to 38%, a ratio similar to other unions. Apart from pay increases the dispute secured improved career structures and opportunities. SIPTU had 'expended considerable energy and resources in pursuing justice' for nurses, a total of more than £1 million. Extensive public solidarity was generated. Firefighters, gardaí, prison officers and public all provided refreshments to pickets.[31]

THE INDUSTRIAL RELATIONS ACT (1990) AND NOLAN TRANSPORT

In 1993 SIPTU expressed concerns that 'findings of the judiciary were inconsistent with the assurances given' by the then Minister for Labour, Bertie Ahern, when the

Industrial Relations Act (1990) passed through the Oireachtas. *Nolan Transport (Oaklands) Limited v. Halligan and Others* came before Mr Justice Barron in the High Court in 1994. In December the judge granted a perpetual injunction and substantial damages against SIPTU. Fifty applications were received from Nolan's drivers, and a General Meeting was held on Sunday 17 January. Two members, Jim Halligan and Henry Nolan, were sacked on 19 January as SIPTU's claims were received by the company in New Ross. While members were balloted for a strike, the company approached workers individually to set up a Non-Union Works Committee. This 'had the effect of arresting the flow of applications,' although thirty joined.

On 31 January twenty members voted to strike, with three against. Seven days' notice was served on 4 February. The company refused to respond either to SIPTU or to the Labour Relations Commission. A review on 7 February produced no change of heart by the men. After the meeting, however, 'five members came back into the meeting room.' They 'were frightened and had decided to resign' from the union. Within a few hours of pickets being placed on 11 February a High Court writ was served at Liberty Hall and on Halligan, Nolan and Tony Ayton, the Branch Assistant, in their personal capacities. SIPTU members were also rostered away on long trips and isolated from one another; fearing a lost cause, most, on returning, passed the picket lines.

Chris Halligan (brother of Jim) and one other joined the picket, which was assaulted on Tuesday 16 February by non-striking drivers. On 17 February sixteen of the company's lorries blocked New Ross bridge, a 'direct attempt to force the Union to abandon the dispute.' The tactic backfired by generating widespread support for the strikers. The entire NEC joined the picket in a public show of solidarity, while behind the scenes work with the Labour Relations Commission and private mediators attempted a settlement. Halligan's unfair dismissal case was successful, Nolan's was not.

In March 1994 the High Court refused to award the company an interlocutory injunction, but in June a full High Court action opened, with judgement delivered in December. Mr Justice Barron held that SIPTU 'was not engaged in a *bona fide* trade dispute' and therefore 'not entitled to the protection of the immunities contained in the 1990 Act.' The 'pre-strike ballot had been falsified' and a 'campaign of "malicious falsehood"' waged against the company. SIPTU thought the judgement was 'inconsistent with the intention' of the Act, as stated by Ahern. He had assured Congress, privately and in the Dáil, that 'only an aggrieved member' of a union 'could mount a challenge to the outcome of a secret ballot,' immunities were 'not dependent on the holding of a secret ballot,' and a 'legal action could not be taken against' a union 'arising from its activities in contemplation or furtherance of a trade dispute.' The judgement was appealed to the Supreme Court.

In two other cases the Courts awarded interlocutory injunctions to constrain picketing, despite the supposed limitations in the Act on granting them, 'one of the few concessions made to trade unions in the Act.' SIPTU concluded: 'If this was merely an exercise of purely academic interest, these developments would be problematic. Unfortunately, their impact extends far beyond the confines of the Court right out into workplaces around the country.' The Act 'as practised in the Courts rather than as promised in the Dáil' was 'shown to be seriously defective.' It curtailed union activity but left employers unrestricted. Justification for the restriction on the union was the alleged abuse by a 'small group of "mavericks"', but the law now 'encouraged "maverick" employers' to resist workers' legitimate claims 'to exercise their Constitutional rights to join a trade union.' SIPTU wanted union representation guaranteed by law, 'by a Constitutional amendment, if necessary.' It was 'not acceptable' that workers could be 'deprived of their livelihood' or should 'suffer serious physical abuse simply by virtue of their trade union membership.' Barron's judgement rendered the dispute invalid, picketing had to cease, and considerable damages were awarded against SIPTU. Action against the perpetrators of violence against picketers was not forthcoming.

SIPTU established a Working Party to explore the constitutional and legislative options for recognition. The paper 'Our Legal Rights under Attack: Trade Unions and the Law: A SIPTU View' was adopted by the Conference. The 'quality, range and detail' of the debate was 'impressive', as was the 'anger and frustration—expressed in a controlled and constructive way.' Opinion shifted from amending article 40 of the Constitution of Ireland to legislative enactment, codes of practice or enforceable Agreements. SIPTU concluded, with ironic but pointed reference to the Northern peace process:

> It is surely inconsistent that the current concept of social partnership—a partnership based on joint and equal participation—is to undermine and diminish one partner by a calculated and forceful programme of denial. SIPTU, having observed the refusal by the Government and employers' organisations to accede to trade union requests to acknowledge the problem of recognition in the Programme for Competitiveness and Work, calls on the social partners to decommission their weapons of attack on the trade union movement before any talks for a successor to the Programme for Competitiveness and Work commence.

In 1996 frustration led SIPTU to conclude that where the 1990 Act 'was supposed to assist the orderly conduct of industrial relations including those involving trade union recognition,' the opposite was the case. It insisted that Partnership 2000 include a high-level group to review matters. Jimmy Somers said he would not put his name to any resultant recommendation unless there was 'substantial and significant' progress on recognition and no 'fudging, dodging or parking the issue somewhere for another ten years.'

There was little advance on recognition in 1997. Tommy Broughan (Labour Party) unsuccessfully moved a Trade Union Recognition Bill in the Dáil. The High-Level Group met throughout 1998, its proceedings strongly influenced by concomitant developments in Ryanair and the Nolan Transport judgements.

The Supreme Court reversed the High Court ruling in the Nolan case, determining that SIPTU was engaged in a *bona fide* trade dispute and therefore entitled to immunity. Mr Justice O'Flaherty said that an unfortunate aspect was that the company 'appeared to have approached it on the basis that either all the workers joined the union or none of them joined and that the decision was to be made by the majority of the workers.' It was 'well established in Irish law,' however, that the constitutional right to join or not to join a union was invested in each individual. 'No worker can be forced to join a union against his will, and likewise no worker can be denied his right to join a union which is prepared to accept him. These are matters of Constitutional right and are not capable of being resolved by a majority vote unless all workers have freely agreed to have the said matter so resolved.'

SIPTU was subject to criticism regarding how it conducted the ballot. Ballot papers 'should set forth the issue clearly with ideally an independent person supervising the whole operation.' All injunctions were discharged. No damages were awarded, and each side bore its own—considerable—costs. New procedures emerged from the High-Level Group, allowing for binding Labour Court recommendations on pay and conditions for workers where an employer refused recognition or refused to engage in voluntary collective bargaining. The NEC supported its proposal and called for amendment of the Industrial Relations Act. Somers pointed out that the High-Level Group had not exchanged these changes against any curtailment of a worker's right to strike.[32]

RYANAIR

A majority of Ryanair's ground handling staff sought membership in November 1997. SIPTU wrote to the management seeking talks on pay increases, proper grading structures, overtime rates, health and safety issues and representative procedures. The management refused to engage in dialogue, leading to a series of one-day stoppages from January. A survey by the *Sunday Independent* showed that 91% of the public thought Ryanair should negotiate. Cross-Party Dáil support was expressed, with the Taoiseach and Tánaiste urging Ryanair to enter dialogue. Éamon Gilmore TD (Democratic Left) called for a boycott, while the Secretary of the Aviation Branch, Paul O'Sullivan, contrasted the company's big profits with its policy of low pay. A rally at Dublin Airport closed all services as thousands attended or refused to pass pickets. The comedian Brendan O'Carroll staged a mock boxing match on his film set between flyweight baggage-handlers and heavyweight management.

In March the management withdrew security clearance from ground handling agents, and pickets had to be placed at the airport entrances. This led to a complete shutting down of the airport. Intervention by the Government secured agreement on a return to work after a special inquiry team was appointed. Reporting in July, it found that Ryanair was untruthful in some of its statements and that the matter could have been resolved had it been referred to the Labour Court with the management's participation. Ryanair continued to refuse any third-party engagement.

The report rejected the company's claims that Ryanair's development would be threatened by granting recognition.

In December patient SIPTU members decided to await the report of the High-Level Group on Trade Union Recognition before further action. Four workers who had been sacked made 'an amicable settlement' before the question reached the Employment Appeals Tribunal, media reports suggesting that there would be 'financial compensation.'[33]

GREAT SOUTHERN HOTELS AND AER LINGUS

In 1990 a battle was waged against the privatisation of Great Southern Hotels, hitherto owned by CIÉ. A decision was made to sell them off in 1987 after the Labour Party withdrew from Coalition with Fine Gael. On 3 August 1990 a decision was made to sell them to Aer Rianta. An expansion programme was to follow—all good news for members. The 1991 SIPTU *Better Hotels Guide* was part of a recruitment drive, publicising hotels that provided good terms and conditions.

The Cahill Plan, launched in June 1993, presented Aer Lingus workers 'with a daunting list of demands for considerable sacrifices.' A projected loss of £188 million by the group in 1992/3 concentrated minds. A single injection of Government equity of £175 million was conditional on acceptance of the survival plan, including 1,280 redundancies, pay cuts, reductions in overtime and shift rates, and the sub-contracting of non-core catering, transport and baggage-handling. In July members demanded no compulsory redundancies, no privatisation or sub-contracting, no basic wage cuts, consultation before change, an equity stake in return for payroll savings, and costs to be made equally across the board, including the management. The media dismissed these demands as unrealistic.

The final Agreement, accepted by 1,710 to 576, provided for 780 voluntary redundancies, no contracting out or basic pay cuts, no change in overtime pay and improved early retirement packages, £15 million in non-payroll savings, and 10% of the company's value to be given to the workers—5% immediately in shares and 5% in cash on return to profitability. While not happy with the job losses, SIPTU was to 'be congratulated for their decisive leadership in difficult circumstances.' In addition to defending members to the best of their ability, Officials had 'improved the prospects for the future' of Aer Lingus—not only as a commercial operation but as 'a valuable strategic resource for the entire Irish economy.' A similar battle was fought in TEAM, the aircraft maintenance subsidiary.[34]

GOODMAN INTERNATIONAL

The first company to take advantage of the Companies Amendment Act (1990) was the Goodman Group, an examiner being appointed rather than a liquidator. Congress, through the Programme for National Recovery, raised concerns about the beef industry with the Government. SIPTU demanded diversification, greater added value and controls over the blatant exploitation of workers, particularly the increasing numbers on contract. A rescue package was approved by the High Court on 28 January 1991, with similar arrangements north of the border for Anglo-Irish Beef Processors. After securing jobs, SIPTU pressed for full commitments under the Programme for Economic and Social Progress for all workers. On 24 May 1991 the Tribunal of Inquiry into the Beef Processing Industry was announced.

In October SIPTU held a national seminar on reform of the Common Agricultural Policy, demands being made for improved production and, more importantly, the development of added-value products to aid Irish industry.[35]

THE ECONOMY AND EUROPE

Unemployment rose in 1991. Manufacturing employment was 195,200 in December, a fall of 29,100 since 1980. Attley attacked the Government for 'sleep-walking their way through the jobs crisis.' Suitably stung, the Taoiseach, Charles Haughey, invited Congress to discuss matters, resulting in a Special Employment Task Force, with union involvement; a Working Party to review industrial policy, chaired by Jim Culliton; an extra 2,500 on Social Employment Schemes and 1,000 more apprentices; a marketing drive for tourism; and a Committee of State-Sponsored Bodies to consider the maximisation of employment.

In 1991 a tripartite Sectoral Committee, of which Bill Attley and Manus O'Riordan (SIPTU Head of Research) were members, produced 'Ireland's Increasing Share of European Economic and Sectoral Development', identifying growth targets; as was to become usual, it was largely ignored by the Government and industrialists.

SIPTU welcomed the Culliton Report, reminding everyone that ten years earlier it had enthused about the Telesis Report while the Government and industry sat on their hands. The creation of Forbairt, to promote indigenous industry, was praised, as were Culliton's comments on the low costs of capital. SIPTU wanted an integrated European Community industrial policy to bring Ireland in from the cold.

In 1992 members were urged to vote for the Treaty of Maastricht, 'despite many reservations.' A national poster campaign drew attention to unemployment, urged the purchase of Irish goods and promoted SIPTU in the public consciousness. On 6 October SIPTU led a number of nationwide demonstrations on unemployment, and in 1994 it campaigned to retain jobs in Irish Steel, one of many attempts to preserve the company. ICTU Centres for the Unemployed came on stream, all actively supported by local SIPTU Branches.

By 1995 Ireland experienced economic boom. Export-led growth of more than 7% was non-inflationary, enabling the Government to comfortably meet the Maastricht criteria for membership of European monetary union. Both money and real wages rose, albeit by small amounts, adding to domestic consumption. Job creation rather than unemployment began to make headlines. The number of manufacturing jobs rose by 10,000 in 1994 and by 9,000 in 1995. Total employment rose by more than 100,000 over the duration of the Programme for Competitiveness and Work, which had a target of 60,000. Members were involved in local area initiatives and county enterprise boards.

Economic growth accelerated again in 1997, a tide lifting all boats. The abolition of duty-free sales within the European Union was opposed to defend jobs in airport and seaboard retail outlets. Significant growth in 1998 was reflected in employment rising by more than 72,000. The long-term unemployment rate tumbled to 3.1%. The Irish Trade Union Trust offered a Solidarity Service, providing information on redundancy and social welfare, job creation and preservation, and partnership. SIPTU publicised the 'Dark Side of the Jungle', where the 'Celtic Tiger is an endangered species.'

In 1998 Congress urged a 'Yes' vote on the Treaty of Amsterdam, based largely on commitments on employment and social rights that outweighed concerns about neutrality. Employment increased by 75,000 in 1999, although there were still significant redundancies in Apple Computers, Cork, in Krups, Limerick, in Avon Arlington, Portarlington, in IEC Electronics, Longford, and in Donegal Shirt Company and Fruit of the Loom.[36]

TAX, SOCIAL WELFARE AND HEALTH

The 1991 Budget did not address SIPTU's demands for a reversal of social welfare cuts. Encouraging commitments were given under the Programme for Economic and Social Progress, but little progress was made. The income ceiling on health contributions was removed, so everyone paid 1¼% on gross earnings. This did little to alleviate the shortage of beds and inadequate services.

A week before Christmas the Minister for Social Welfare, Brendan Daly, acting as Scrooge, announced the taxing of disability and occupational injuries benefits, the denial of Unemployment Benefit to those taking voluntary redundancy or early retirement, and various acts of callous cheeseparing. SIPTU strongly opposed the tax amnesties, Edmund Browne pointing to the blatant contradiction between an amnesty for wealthy cheats and a 1% income levy on PAYE taxpayers. 'Broken promises' from the Government meant that in 1996 the tax burden still bore heavily and unfairly on PAYE workers. Greater benefits of boom resulting from the Programme for Competitiveness and Work should have accrued but were stymied by the Government reneging on tax reform commitments.

If 1991 was a 'disappointment', 1992 was a 'disaster' for social progress. McCreevy's 'Dirty Dozen' cuts introduced degrading means tests and tightened qualifying conditions. Back payments to women denied equality since 1984 began to be grudgingly paid out. The Labour Party's much-improved performance in the November General Election held out hopes for change. Participation in talks to follow the Programme for Economic and Social Progress were dependent on the removal of the Dirty Dozen. Some advances were made under the Programme for Competitiveness and Work, but changes to PRSI in the 1994 Budget removed many benefits workers had already paid for. The removal of Ahern's 1% income levy was the focus of strong pressure, with SIPTU demanding relief for the lower paid. It went in the Budget.

Wage restraint sharpened the economy's competitive edge, but inflation eroded living standards—hardly an appropriate reward for workers' selflessness. Eight years after the Commission on Social Welfare the implementation of priority rates was welcome, but a greater share for workers was demanded. A 1995 Conference workshop demanded a 'thorough-going reform' of tax and social welfare, with the recovery of all lost ground.

Manus O'Riordan saw the 1996 Budget as being 'far from a fair share' and a penalisation of workers and the unemployed in order to satisfy European criteria for a single currency. Greater commitments to tax and social welfare were made in the 1997 Budget, with tax relief for the lower-paid, increased personal allowances and a delay in the impact of top rates, together with the elimination of some poverty traps. SIPTU saw Partnership 2000 as having been crucial in winning such gains. Jimmy Somers called for an end to 'Golden Circles', warning that the 'very fabric of our democracy' would be 'undermined irreparably' if some were seen to be above the law. The Ben Dunne and Michael Lowry cases drew attention to unsavoury connections between big business and politics. *Newsline* characterised Haughey and Lowry as 'D'unbelievables'.

McCreevy's Budget cast him as 'Santa Claus for the rich' and significantly increased social inequality. SIPTU's disgust was summed up in the expression 'That's rich,' with a table in *Newsline* showing differences between the union's proposals and Budget changes, ranging from £276 a year for those on £12,000 (SIPTU £356, McCreevy £80) to actual gains for those on £45,000 and above. The 'rich get richer' also applied to social welfare.

In 1998, following a 'highly unsatisfactory Budget', SIPTU created a 'broad campaigning alliance' with the ICTU Centres for the Unemployed, the Irish National Organisation of the Unemployed, the National Youth Council, the Conference of Religious of Ireland (CORI) and the Inner City Organisations Network. A 'Checklist for Charlie' summarised their demands; and, although he was unable to resist some sniping at the 'poverty industry', McCreevy's next Budget significantly increased personal tax allowances and began converting them into tax credits—both SIPTU demands—and improved some welfare payments.

SIPTU tabled six proposals for 'investing in children' in September 1999: increased income support for children by substantially raising child benefit; promoting child care as an anti-poverty measure for low-income families; tackling educational disadvantage; increasing personal tax allowances to benefit the low-paid; investing in heath and housing to benefit low-income families; and making the prevention and reduction of child poverty a priority for the National Anti-Poverty Strategy, National Children's Strategy and National Development Plan.

In April 1994 the Minister for Health, Brendan Howlin, produced *Shaping a Healthier Future*. It contained many 'worthy' ambitions but left the 'implementation . . . open-ended.' A change of Government buried the strategy. The 'health crisis' became a sordid national spectacle. SIPTU campaigned strongly against abuses of the C45 tax scheme in construction. Rampant inflation and profiteering shot housing prices through the roof and made it increasingly difficult for first-time buyers, especially lower earners. With the Civil and Public Services Union, SIPTU held a seminar on affordable housing, publishing the results to generate debate. While the Celtic Tiger roared loudly, SIPTU complained that waiting lists grew longer. More than 35,000 people awaited treatment. Health was a constant sore, beyond political commitment or resolution.[37]

EMPLOYMENT LAW
In 1993 the Minister for Labour, Ruairí Quinn, finally made May Day a public holiday—well, the first Monday in May anyway. SIPTU strongly criticised Mary Harney's failure to consult it on the terms of reference and composition of the Commission on Minimum Pay in 1997. The Conference concentrated on eliminating low pay and demanded a minimum wage of £5 an hour. Congress backed SIPTU's demand. In general, progress on employment rights was considered satisfactory.[38]

SAFETY AND HEALTH
SIPTU explained the Safety, Health and Welfare at Work Act (1989) through ten-day courses developed in association with the Health and Safety Authority. The Local Authority Professional Officers' Branch organised a seminar, 'The Environment: What Can We Do?' at Trinity College, Dublin, in 1991, reflecting concerns for environmental issues. On 7 July 1990 four fishery protection officers and members of SIPTU—Dominic Meehan, Benno Haussmann, Barry O'Driscoll and Barra Ó Loingsigh—lost their lives off Ballycotton, Co. Cork. SIPTU demanded improvements in safety standards and mourned their loss. As part of European Year of Safety, Hygiene and Health Protection at Work the SIPTU Industrial Engineering Department received funding to survey Dublin Safety Committees. This first empirical research on work-place participation under the 1989 Act made disappointing reading. It showed that managements' compliance and unions' promotion of health and safety to be two sides of the same problem of neglect. Francis Devine, a SIPTU Tutor, organised three concerts for the HSA, featuring Dick Gaughan, the Fallen Angels and Eric Fleming's Work and Play Band (the latter Secretary of the Construction Branch) on 'Singing for Safety' in Belfast, Cork and Dublin. 'Safety First . . . and Last! Understanding the Law', a SIPTU guide to the Safety, Health and Welfare at Work Act, was published as a *Newsline* supplement.[39]

In 1994 the Health and Safety Authority previewed its *Guidelines on Violence in the Workplace,* amending material in the light of SIPTU members' experiences in transport, services and health care. Dónal O'Sullivan, a significant figure in safety, retired as Head of the Industrial Engineering Department. In October SIPTU reacted swiftly to Ruairí Quinn's suggestion that compensation awards to injured workers be capped, pointing out that amounts of compensation were not the problem but the absence of adequate prevention. Three AIDS/HIV awareness booklets were produced by Dublin Region (Private Sector) in association with the Health Promotion Unit and Dublin AIDS Alliance. After a fire at Hickson's chemical plant in Cork, SIPTU met the Minister and the HSA to seek improved environmental policies. SIPTU was prominent in securing funds for pilot schemes to improve safety in construction and in the Construction

Employees' Health Trust, exposing 'Sites for Sore Eyes' in *Newsline*. Tom Kelly, at Tara Mines, became Ireland's first full-time Safety Representative. Throughout 1995 SIPTU publicised the 300 work-place deaths since 1990 and demanded additional Inspectors, 'blitz' inspections of high-risk industries, stiffer enforcement and penalties and maximum publicity for convictions. *Newsline's* front-page image of coffins stated: '3,000 deaths in 25 years: Northern Ireland? No. Irish workplaces.' This put the issue firmly in perspective and underlined the Government's indifference.

The Health and Safety Authority held its September 1996 Board meeting in Liberty Hall to recognise the union's contribution to promoting safety-consciousness and to honour SIPTU's two HSA Board members, Sylvester Cronin and Eric Fleming. More than 2,000 building workers benefited from a course in Construction Skills Certification, negotiated by SIPTU. Co-ordinated action took place on Zoe Developments' Dublin sites following the death of James Masterson, the third worker killed in its employment. Mr Justice Kelly told Liam Carroll, Zoe's Controlling Director, that he was 'not entitled to make profits on the blood and lives of your workers.'[40]

In 1997 the Industrial Engineering Department provided environmental services and facilitated work-place anti-bullying Agreements. Bullying 'took off as a trade union issue,' and the NEC set up a Working Party to develop policies, assisted by Trinity College Anti-Bullying Centre and the HSA. A specialist Health and Safety Unit was established in SIPTU College, supported by a National Committee led by Sylvester Cronin. In 1999 a major demonstration by construction workers led to a Construction Safety Partnership, with representation from the ICTU, the Construction Industry Federation, FÁS and the HSA. A national rally was led by Eric Fleming after the death of Michael McGinty in Dublin. Within hours, Gavin Brady, aged nineteen, was killed in Cavan.[41] A 'Prime Time' programme on RTÉ, 'Dying for a Living', publicised asbestos problems at Tegral plants in Athy and Drogheda.

Following highly emotive contributions at the 1993 Conference SIPTU engaged in a campaign against drug abuse. It urged the Government to set up a special Commission and, in Dublin, worked with the Inner City Organisations Network to promote drug awareness, recovery and treatment programmes, co-ordinated by Paul Clarke and Paddy Behan. SIPTU was a central element in the Dublin City-Wide Drugs Crisis Campaign and held a one-day Conference in Liberty Hall on 'Fighting Back Together.' In 1995 the NEC demanded a long-term strategy to deal with heroin addiction, and in May 1996 staff and members attended addiction Counselling courses provided in association with the Council for Addiction Information and Mediation. In 1999 City Wide published *Responding Together: The Crisis Continues*, and SIPTU lobbied for resourced action on drugs.[42]

SIPTU COLLEGE

In 1990 the Education and Training Department moved to the former FWUI premises in Parnell Square as Palmerston Park became SIPTU Head Office. More than 700 Shop Stewards attended training courses. 1,600 attended in 1991, including all

Regional Executive Committees. 'World-Class Manufacturing' and 'Total Quality Management' featured in 1992 as SIPTU raised awareness of human resource management and new forms of work organisation, developing bargaining agendas and organisational responses. Tom McCarthy retired as Head of Education and Training in 1990 and was succeeded by Des Mahon. Kay Marron (Women Workers' Branch) pioneered adult literacy courses within her Branch and Liberty Hall. An annual James Larkin Memorial Lecture was initiated in association with Dublin City University, with world-class speakers delivering addresses.[43]

More than 100 education courses were held in 1993, involving 2,000 participants, numbers exceeded in 1994 when there was a 'concentration on innovation' and 'trainee-centred methodology'. Subjects included the Occupational Pension Scheme Regulations (1993) and pensions and sickness pay schemes, the Programme for Competitiveness and Work, World-Class Manufacturing and Total Quality Management, media studies, women's equality and staff development. The SIPTU Guide for Union Representatives was published in October 1994, attracting exceptional public interest. A national seminar on privatisation, sub-contracting and competitive tendering in the public sector, held in Liberty Hall in November, showed the engagement of the Education and Training Department in policy development. Seven different scholarship schemes operated for members and their children. SIPTU made national and Branch responses to the Green Paper on Education and were represented at the National Education Convention by Francis Devine, presenting the view that the Government should 'educate people for a full life in their community; base Irish education on a comprehensive statutory footing; enable and foster equality of opportunity and eliminate any inequity on a gender or social class basis; bring parents, community and industry into management structures; broaden second-chance education; cater for social disadvantage; and prepare and publish a financial plan.' A national workshop on education, held in Marino Institute of Education, Dublin, was published in 1996 as *Education: Meeting the Needs of All: A Trade Union Response to the Government's White Paper on Education.*[44]

In 1995 the SIPTU-NCEA certificate in trade union studies was launched. The third-level award contained elements on trade unionism, collective bargaining, trade unions and change, employment law, health and safety, and social and economic issues and was pioneered in Cork, Dublin, Letterkenny and Navan. Forty-one graduated in 1997. A specialist facility for education and training, research and industrial engineering was opened at Canal House in Kilmainham, Dublin. There were smirks when it was grandly styled SIPTU College, but events proved how far-sighted the decision was. It was the busiest year ever for training. In 1998 SIPTU College established networks of representatives for education and training, partnership, equality, pensions, work study and time study, and health and safety. Education and Training Representatives initiated local activities. The college was formally opened by the General Secretary, Bill Attley, on 20 February.

In 1999 fifty-three members were awarded NCEA diplomas in trade union studies (business studies). A third school was held in association with the Fire

Brigades Union in Newcastle, Co. Down, on 'Attacks on the Fire Service.' Branch Development Funds were employed to promote local educational initiatives, including briefing days for Shop Stewards. Nine partnership enterprise teams were established through ADAPT, and SIPTU College published *Participation and Partnership in Changing Work Organisation*.[45]

PUBLICATIONS

A *Sunday Business Post* supplement celebrated SIPTU's first anniversary on 4 January 1991. Internally, *Newsline* appeared on May Day 1990, and a lavish 1991 calendar portrayed members at work. In 1992, 3,363 printed news items covered SIPTU, a small proportion positively so! Officials' training in media handling was developed, while the national poster Buy Irish campaign was eye-catching and promoted public awareness of SIPTU values. *Newsline* was remodelled from magazine to tabloid newspaper, aiming at a circulation of 50,000. The 'Right to Entertain' support for RTÉ strikers was praised as imaginative, humorous and pointed. 'The Plane Truth' supported the Aer Lingus Equity Campaign. Computerisation was advanced, and by 1994 'desktop publishing' made possible the in-house production of *Newsline*. By 1997 on-line industrial data-bases provided details of annual leave, bonus schemes, compensatory payments, disturbance allowances, European Works Councils, paid time off, pay (rates for clerical and general), pensions, redundancy settlements, service pay, shift premiums, sickness pay, working time and world-class management.[46] In 1998 SIPTU's web site, www.siptu.ie, was expanded to provide information on history, structures, policy, international contacts, specialist services, and press statements.

CULTURE

In 1991 Eric Fleming co-ordinated Congress and Dublin Trades Council's May Work and Play Festival, filling Liberty Hall with music, song and joyous children. For 'Dublin, European City of Culture' James Plunkett's *Wits, Rogues and Dreamers* was produced; a plaque was unveiled in Aungier Street on the house where Robert Tressell (Robert Noonan), author of *The Ragged-Trousered Philanthropists*, was born; and a plaque in commemoration of Irish International Brigaders killed in the Spanish Civil War was unveiled at Liberty Hall by the Lord Mayor, Michael Donnelly. Concert programmes, posters and tickets were produced to support the locked-out members of the National Symphony Orchestra and RTÉ Concert Orchestra. Under the heading 'Strike a Chord', the orchestras held two concerts during their Lock-Out, which ended on 15 February after a Labour Court recommendation.

A Cultural Division Executive was elected in 1992, with Brian Keenan (Association of Artists in Ireland) as Chairperson. In 1993 the Irish Writers' Union affiliated. Celebrations of the 1913 Lock-Out were held, and the Donegal Branch marked Peadar O'Donnell's Centenary with a Conference and a specially commissioned Robert Ballagh print, and *Newsline* published the winning entry in a schools essay competition by Tanya Nic Gairbheith, 'Peadar Ó Domhnaill: Sóisialaí, Óglach,

Scríbhneoir, Eagarthóir.' The 1994 Congress Centenary celebrations included James Plunkett's *The Risen People,* produced by Peter and Jim Sheridan at the Gaiety Theatre, Dublin, with Jer O'Leary memorably portraying Larkin.[47]

The cultural event of 1996 was the unveiling of Éamonn O'Doherty's James Connolly statue in Beresford Place by President Mary Robinson. Facing Liberty Hall, Connolly surveys the scene of many meetings, proud and purposeful, a constant reminder to everyone entering or leaving Liberty Hall not to neglect their historic duty. SIPTU generously supported the statue, which was commissioned by Congress.

The Minister for the Arts, Culture and the Gaeltacht, Michael D. Higgins, delivered the Larkin memorial Lecture on 'Bread and Roses: Culture and Democracy'. In 1997, largely through the energy of Donal Nevin, the fiftieth anniversary of Larkin's death was marked in Belfast, Dublin and Ennis with 'Salute to Big Jim', a celebration in poetry, prose, music and song devised by Nevin. John Gray and Emmet Larkin delivered commemorative lectures in Belfast and Dublin; a plaque was unveiled on 41 Wellington Road, Ballsbridge (where Larkin lived for a time), by the Lord Mayor; and an exhibition, 'James Larkin: Orator, Agitator, Revolutionary' was held in the National Library. In addition RTÉ Radio broadcast a Thomas Davis lecture series, Robert Ballagh made a limited-edition print for the Labour Party Trade Union Group, and 750 Larkin statuettes were cast by Royal Tara, Galway.

In 1998 SIPTU sponsored Donal Nevin's *James Larkin: Lion of the Fold* and a Liberty Hall production of Seán O'Casey's *Red Roses for Me.* Tommy Grimes (NEC) secured SIPTU's support for a monument at Crossakeel, Co. Meath, to Jim Connell, author of 'The Red Flag', and Helena Sheehan (Education Branch) produced the CD *Songs of Irish Labour.* Together with the Irish Labour History Society, SIPTU honoured the former Secretary of Irish Actors' Equity, Dermot Doolan, through the publication of the union's history.[48]

IRISH TRADE UNION TRUST

The Irish Trade Union Trust fulfilled the union's objective (laid down in the Rules) of the 'development of a Social Solidarity Service for unemployed, disabled or retired members.' Following a review in 1992 it concentrated on job creation and preservation and redundancy-linked services. Area-based partnerships were the central element, with ITUT providing advice and training. Ross Connolly retired from the service of ITUT. A Trade Union Network for Employment was created through Euroform, operated with Welsh and Danish partners. More than fifteen new co-operatives were established in 1993–4, with Printwell Co-operative Society Ltd winning 'Co-op of the Year.' A Disability Advisory Service began in 1993 with assistance from a former Official, Michael Gogarty, a member of the ICTU Disability Advisory Committee, Commission on the Status of People with Disabilities and Forum for People with Disabilities. The *Report of the Commission on the Status of People with Disabilities* in 1996 won union support.

In 1998 SIPTU held a national seminar, 'The Politics of Disability', at the Marino Institute. SIPTU's TRUST (Trade Union Support and Training) Project produced

Disability Equality: Guidelines for Union Negotiators, and SIPTU College ran courses in association with the Irish Council of People with Disabilities.[49]

In 1995 ITUT took charge of the Retired Members' Section, chaired by Jim Quinn, participating in the Senior Citizens' Parliament, formally opened by President Mary Robinson in November 1996. Paddy Donegan, a former ITGWU Group Secretary, was elected first President of the Parliament. More than 5,000 people made use of ITUT's services on job-seeking, interview skills, and preparing a CV, while 'The Rights Stuff' in *Newsline* provided continuing advice.

SIPTU celebrated International Year of the Older Person in 1999 by providing a lobby on behalf of the aged, fully participating in the Senior Citizens' National Parliament and drawing up a national register of retired members. A huge ITUT success was the £3.3 million contract won by the workers' co-op Whitefern and its partners JIT Logistics in 1997 to deliver Irish Biscuits products. ITUT, and Naomi Brennan in particular, were 'midwife' at the birth of the company. A redundancy service was provided in 1999.[50]

STAFF AND PREMISES

In November 1990 the first new SIPTU premises were opened in Limerick and named after Fintan Kennedy. The union's premises in Clara, Co. Offaly, were presented to the local Branch of Comhaltas Ceoltóirí Éireann, and the IWWU premises at 48 Fleet Street, Dublin, were sold to Amnesty International in 1994. Sites in Cóbh, Gorey, Kilkenny (Dean Street), Mitchelstown, Tullamore (Kilbride Street) and Youghal were also offloaded. New premises at Forster Place, Galway, and in Longford were acquired, while the Galway premises at Mainguard Street, Prospect Hill and Lower Salthill were sold.

In 1995 Branches transferred from Parnell Square to Liberty Hall, and new premises were opened in Monaghan. An Information Technology Unit advanced the computerisation of records and internal communication. In 1999 new premises were opened in Dundalk, while old premises in Dundalk (Seatown) and Enniscorthy were sold.[51]

Table 146: SIPTU **staff salaries and industrial Conferences, 1990–99**

	Staff salaries (£)	*As proportion of expenditure (%)*	*Meetings and Conferences (£)*
1990	8,256,224	57.3	1,313,493
1991	8,457,841	55.4	1,497,954
1992	8,955,501	56.3	1,473,399
1993	11,130,255	59.7	1,002,209
1994	10,979,411	59.9	643,823
1995	11,134,279	62.3	764,754

1996	11,292,010	62.3	786,801
1997	11,692,585	62.2	974,466
1998	12,621,665	62.6	853,858
1999	12,677,084	59.2	979,623

Source: SIPTU, Annual Reports, 1990–2007.

At the 1995 Conference staff salary scales were included for the first time in annual financial reports; they have been published ever since. In 1999 a Staff Relations Secretary, Patricia King, was appointed to carry out a personnel function. Customised training programmes were established for newly recruited members of the staff, together with improved media training. SIPTU Staff Partnership Forum was created. Staff costs accounted for about 60% of expenditure.[52]

SOLIDARITY

SIPTU offered solidarity to Philippine workers, child victims of Chernobyl, and Third World development. In 1996 Martin Naughton (tutor) worked with the National Confederation of Eritrean Workers at the request of the International Union of Food Workers, providing training on new forms of work organisation. *Workers' Rights in the Global Economy: The Need for a Social Clause,* jointly produced by SIPTU and Trócaire, was launched by the Tánaiste and Minister for Foreign Affairs, Dick Spring, in Liberty Hall on May Day 1997. In 1998 SIPTU members in Bus Éireann in Tralee drove an ambulance and supplies to Belarus. One of the outstanding long-term fund-raising efforts for Chernobyl was led by Sheila Rogers from Carndonagh, Co. Donegal, supported by the National Women's Committee. To mark the fiftieth anniversary of the Universal Declaration of Human Rights the General Officers, Somers, Geraghty and McDonnell, signed an Amnesty International appeal for one million signatures to present to the General Secretary of the United Nations, Kofi Annan. SIPTU encouraged as many members as possible to sign. Kevin Kinsella, Food Branch, led eleven forty-foot container lorries on a mercy mission to Kosovo in 1999 after a collection jointly organised by Tesco and Trócaire.[53]

POLITICS

In December 1990 SIPTU voted by 13,112 to 5,780 to adopt a Political Fund, with 50p per member per year being transferred unless the individual member opted out. The low poll—less than 19,000 out of 163,940 financial members—testified to a general apathy or a failure to understand that the Political Fund and the Labour Party were not synonymous.

SIPTU welcomed the 'palace coup' that saw Charles Haughey ousted, followed in November 1992 by Albert Reynolds's leadership of the worst Fianna Fáil election performance in more than fifty years. *Newsline* published the front-cover exhortation 'Vote Labour No. 1' and 'continue your preferences to other candidates of the Left'—a rare acknowledgement of other Socialist candidates. Dick Spring urged a 'fresh start for Ireland' while there were '300,000 reasons to vote Labour' in dole queues every week.

Endless and extremely emotional debate on abortion caught much attention— to the detriment, some argued, of the jobs crisis. Fine Gael boycotted a Dáil jobs forum. The Labour Party entered talks with Democratic Left to create the basis of a centre-left Coalition, but with 'only Fianna Fáil responding positively' it concluded a deal with a party that many of the electorate thought they had voted against. The election of Mary Robinson, also a SIPTU member, as President of Ireland in 1990 was greeted enthusiastically. In 1992 Des Geraghty was given leave of absence to substitute for Proinsias de Rossa as Workers' Party MEP.[54]

SIPTU participated in the Labour Party Trade Union Group, of which John O'Brien (Wicklow Branch) was Secretary. In addition to affiliation and Conference fees SIPTU gave significant material assistance. In 1994, when the Labour-Fianna Fáil Coalition collapsed, SIPTU met Spring to impress upon him the 'crucial importance of tax adjustments for low-paid PAYE workers' and the 'removal of taxation on Unemployment and Disability Benefits.' Great pressure was put on the Labour Party before Ruairí Quinn's 1995 Budget, which was greeted as one of 'mixed blessings'. Criticism centred on the incapacity to generate employment even as the economy boomed.

Spring delivered the prestigious Larkin Memorial Lecture on 22 February, speaking on 'A New Framework for Agreement in Northern Ireland', an aspect of Labour policy with which SIPTU was in complete accord. On economic and fiscal issues SIPTU brought its criticisms to the Labour Party Conference in Limerick, led by Jimmy Somers. SIPTU was unequivocally in favour of a 'Yes' vote in the divorce referendum in 1995. Comprehensive information was provided to members.

Quinn's 'flawed Budget' of 1996 was slated as having failed to honour commitments under the Programme for Competitiveness and Work. Somers expressed members' 'disappointment and anger.' Quinn's 1997 Budget drew more approval. More than £144,000 was provided in grants for SIPTU candidates in the 1997 Dáil and Seanad elections. In 1999 £41,050 was dispensed in Dáil and EU election grants. In 1998 the Party Leader, Ruairí Quinn, began 'Partyline' in *Newsline*, a regular channel of communication between Party and member. SIPTU welcomed the merger of Democratic Left with the Labour Party.[55]

Chapter 36 ∾

ORGANISING THE NEW MILLENNIUM: SIPTU IN 2000

MEMBERSHIP, ORGANISATION AND FINANCE

In 2000, financial membership was 197,353. A mutual support Agreement was signed with the Union of Students in Ireland. Students could obtain access to advice on employment rights, and SIPTU publications and membership cards were available to 250,000 USI members. A National Retained Firefighters' Committee and National Firefighters' Council were established.

After a deficit in 1999 the new year began with a surplus of £111,206. Jack O'Connor was elected Vice-President in May, with the 'largest personal tally in the Union's electoral history.' After a public meeting in the National Stadium in January, Jerry Brennan's personal initiative, following the announcement by the Minister of State at the Department of Transport, Robert Molloy, that he would issue new licences 'plate for plate', SIPTU created a Dublin Taxis Branch, with 800 members, initially within the Marine Port Group.

In 2001, membership fell. Recruitment targets in construction, health and services were reached but were offset by job losses. Finances remained stagnant, causing concern to the NEC. *SIPTU Financial News* provided information about discounted savings and insurance schemes.

In 2002, membership fell again. Many new jobs were 'atypical' in nature, or employers virulently anti-union, making organisation difficult. Within informed union heads, alarm bells rang. Strategic Development Initiative mainstreamed its recommended actions. The change to the euro was explained through the 'Eurowise' and 'EU PRINCE' projects, while more Equality Representatives were trained through the SIPTU-NUIG Alliance.[1]

Table 147: SIPTU **financial membership and women members, 2000–2007**

	SIPTU figure	*RFS figure*	*Women*
2000	197,353	248,938	102,065
2001	195,419	247,960	101,744

2002	193,617	246,911	93,826
2003	196,537	250,351	95,150
2004	191,336	249,454	99,782
2005	195,116	246,634	93,734
2006	196,653	248,171	94,305
2007	199,781	253,271	97,510

Sources: SIPTU, Annual Reports, 2000–2008; National Archives, Registrar of Friendly Societies, file 598T.

In 2002 increased contributions merely offset reduced income. The disposal of fixed assets raised a surplus, but this was clearly of short-term benefit. Joe O'Flynn was elected General Secretary in succession to John McDonnell, defeating Noel Dowling (National Industrial Officer) and the rank-and-filer Des Derwin. It was a close contest and a testimony to members' interest and democratic involvement. McDonnell's diligence, absolute commitment to union ideals and mannerly disposition marked him out as a popular, trusted and highly regarded figure. In September 2003, Des Geraghty retired as General President, being succeeded by Jack O'Connor. Geraghty's tenure was characterised by energy, original thinking and innovation.

A significant development in 2003 was the Trade Union Federation, an alliance between SIPTU and the Technical, Engineering and Electrical Union, the country's largest craft union, to promote mutual interests, improve and share services, and optimise co-operation and synergy. The TUF Membership Services Scheme was launched on 1 November 2004.

The upward trend in membership resumed in 2003. The Musicians' Union of Ireland developed opportunities to build on existing memberships in the National Symphony Orchestra and RTÉ Concert Orchestra. Finances reflected growth.[2]

SIPTU concentrated on organisation as 'paramount' in ensuring that 'any attempts to diminish standards of employment are resisted.' The decline of traditional manufacturing saw membership fall to 191,336, the lowest since 1999. The National Organising Unit, led by Noel Dowling, was created as SIPTU committed itself to transforming from a servicing to an organising union. The first campaigns were among home helps and construction workers. Although showing a surplus, finances troubled planners, as significant additional resources would be required to fuel organisational efforts.

Brendan Hayes (Dublin Regional Secretary) was elected Vice-President in a straight contest with Des Derwin, 61,058 to 17,791. Membership climbed to 195,116 in 2005, better 'housekeeping' and organising bearing fruit. Lithuanian, Polish and Russian-speaking Organisers were appointed, the first foreign nationals appointed to industrial positions in Ireland. The West of Ireland Construction Branch opened. A co-operation Agreement with Impact was signed in February to maximise common strategies, co-operate at the local level and develop policies. John Fay, SIPTU Head of Administration and Finance, retired after forty-one years' service.[3]

Table 148: SIPTU income, expenditure and surplus (€), 2000–2007

	Income	Expenditure	Surplus
2000	21,066,535	20,311,850	754,685
2001	27,085,091	26,412,213	672,878
2002	28,662,996	28,260,908	402,088
2003	31,122,183	29,706,995	1,415,188
2004	34,982,495	33,019,918	1,962,577
2005	35,515,384	33,169,089	2,346,295
2006	39,261,070	35,329,947	3,931,947
2007	40,107,102	35,379,673	4,732,429

Note: From 2001, accounts change from Irish pounds to euros.

Source: SIPTU, Annual Reports, 1990–2007.

AN ORGANISING UNION

In 2003 the National Organiser, Noel Dowling, led the 'All together stronger campaign', urging members, 'It's your union—keep it strong.' The message of the 2005 Conference was 'Organise! Organise! Organise!' The General Officers exhorted members to commit themselves to 'Organising for Progress.' Members agreed to increase Dispute Benefit for those forced to take action and strengthened the Industrial Contingency Fund. Above all, members accepted the organising imperative and sanctioned necessary expenditure on education and training, research and economic analysis, legal advice and representation. SIPTU was 'always reluctant to seek a higher contribution' and continuously sought to restrain costs; but 'if we are to defend workers' rights and conditions' in an increasingly difficult environment 'we must resource the Union adequately.' Members were advised to claim income tax credit on their union dues. Joe O'Flynn announced extensive internal restructuring to meet the challenges of the changing work-place and facilitate organising, insisting that a 'modern trade union is not simply a glorified insurance company.'[4]

Chastened by the Gama (see p. 864) and Irish Ferries (see p. 861) experiences, and increasingly concerned about declining union density, particularly in the private sector, SIPTU announced in 2006 that the 'key to ending the scourge of exploitation of vulnerable workers' was organisation: 'by combining together in a disciplined and co-ordinated fashion, workers can develop the necessary leverage' to ensure that they were 'not overlooked by Government or employers.' O'Connor warned that 'Irish Ferries is a taste of things to come—unless we organise.' SIPTU adopted a 'more strategic approach—based on employment trends emerging on sectoral and geographic bases.'

The Cavan Branch won €342,000 at the Employment Appeals Tribunal for mushroom-pickers after proving breaches of employment rights. Meetings were conducted in Latvian, Lithuanian and Polish. The 'Invisible no more' and 'Be fair to those who care' drive, supported by 'protest postcards', voiced the cause of home helps and domestic workers. Until 2000, home helps were the lowest-paid public employees, at £3 an hour. SIPTU raised this to €7.87, with a lump sum of €1,270. By 2004 their rate was €9.40. The Musicians' Union of Ireland organised buskers and arranged with the Gardaí that performers holding a union card would not be prosecuted or treated as vagrants. Christy Moore supported the initiative, reminding everyone: 'Don't forget your Union . . . if you want to go to work.' The courage shown in these areas by workers, Irish and foreign, was inspiring, as many were new to trade unionism.

Membership climbed to 196,653 in 2006, the highest since 2000. Among them were 9,000 Shop Stewards, Safety Representatives, Equality Representatives, lay tutors, pension Trustees, Works Councillors, Worker Directors and Committee activists at the Section, Branch, regional and national levels.

Membership figures by themselves are not fully representative of the dynamic that is any union but particularly of SIPTU. The union's Organising Unit produced a range of leaflets, all addressing the

> simple principle that unity is strength—and the greater that strength then the more the influence our members will have in their workplace and in society. So we all have a responsibility to ensure that our Union continues to grow.

'Getting Organised' was now 'everybody's business.'

By December €350,000 had been won in compensation for mushroom workers. A co-operation Agreement was agreed with the ATGWU. At Congress the General President, Jack O'Connor, and Dublin Regional Secretary, Patricia King, were elected Vice-Presidents.[5]

SIPTU COMMISSION

On 29 May 2008 Joe O'Flynn was re-elected General Secretary, defeating Kieran Allen (Education Branch), 45,216 to 12,455. O'Flynn took it as an 'endorsement of my work . . . over the past six years' and 'a strong mandate for the next six.' This would involve implementing the recommendations of the Commission of Review. The Commission examined SIPTU's structures under its Chairperson, Mike Crosby, an international expert on organisation, former Federal Secretary of Australian Actors' Equity and Director of the Organising Centre of the Australian Council of Trade Unions, now working for the Service Employees International Union in the United States.[6] The Commission's terms of reference were to 'review all aspects of organisation, structures, practice and activity in the context of the dynamics of economy and society' and the 'lessons of international experience in organising.' It outlined measures it 'deems appropriate to maximise the union's capacity to maintain and build trade union density' and to 'make such recommendations as appropriate to implement and resource these measures within a reasonable timescale.'

On Wednesday 25 June the NEC unanimously adopted the Commission's recommendations. Regions were to be abolished and replaced with industrial Divisions for Health, Public Administration, Manufacturing, Services and Community Sector; Divisional Secretaries and Committees would develop national strategies; Member Service Centres would handle grievances with activists, leaving Organisers free to concentrate on building work-place density and visibility; from 2012 one General Officer will be a woman (necessitating the resignation of the Vice-President, Brendan Hayes); 25% of union contributions will be placed in an Organising Fund; political and community Organisers will facilitate campaigns; and inter-national alliances will be made with like-minded unions.

A Special Conference of 30 July adopted 170 recommendations to fundamentally transform SIPTU. This was arguably the most historic Conference in the union's 100-year history.

REGIONS

Heralded as a unique SIPTU feature, regional structures became subject to increasing reservations. They undoubtedly assisted in 'bedding down' SIPTU, and Regional Conferences extended participation to a far greater extent than traditional structures. Organising needs, however, suggested that industrial structures were more effective. This was reflected in the appointment of National Industrial Organisers and campaigns on work-place issues. Some argued that Regional Committees added a layer of expenditure, with real decision-making still in the hands of the General Officers, NEC and Biennial Conference.

Region 1 (Dublin)

Almost 900 Delegates, representing 76,245 members, attended the first combined Dublin Regional Conference in 2001, Ireland's largest union gathering. In 2002 attempts to save Irish Glass Bottle sadly concentrated on amounts of redundancy. The Branch Secretary, Gerry Lynch, saw 375 lost jobs as a 'betrayal' of workers who had accepted far-reaching changes in work practices. SIPTU argued strongly that the Government should intervene, given the capacity of the Ringsend plant for recycling and waste management, all to no avail; the Government insisted it was a 'private matter'. With the election of Brendan Hayes as Vice-President, Patricia King became Regional Secretary. Opposition to Government plans for decentralisation concerned public-sector members as well as the general public, who worried about the scattering of state agencies from the capital.[7]

Region 2 (Midlands and South-East)

In 2000 Mike Jennings succeeded Jack O'Connor as Regional Secretary. Considered to have a hard act to follow, Jennings proved himself innovative and energetic. In

2001 SIPTU campaigned for a South-East University, based on Waterford Institute of Technology but embracing Cos. Wexford and Kilkenny. A George Newsome Memorial Essay Competition was run in secondary schools. The Region called for an Immigrant Workers' Rights Unit within the Labour Relations Commission, with the detention of nineteen Moldovans working in Kildare Chilling illustrating the problem. In 2002 a vigorous defence of south-east railway services fought to maintain the Rosslare Harbour–Waterford and Waterford–Limerick Junction links and 543 jobs. Strong support for the Cancer Services Campaign was given, contrasting provision in Dublin and Waterford. The closure of IFI and Richardson's plants in Arklow, Belfast and Cóbh cost 620 jobs, and, despite the 51% state involvement, notice to workers was inadequate and the battle for compensation unnecessarily complicated. On 1 January 2002 Region 3 (South-East) and Region 5 (Midlands) merged as Region 2 (Midlands and South-East). Two new Construction Branches were created, Midlands and South-East, and a seminar held to commemorate Joe Hill's ninetieth anniversary in November 2005. The closure of the Carlow sugar factory, regarded in the town as a betrayal, ended an important era of indigenous industry. Jennings left in April 2007, becoming General Secretary of the Irish Federation of University Teachers, and was succeeded by Christy McQuillan, long-serving Secretary of the Meath Branch, who transferred from Sectoral Organiser, Transport and Logistics.[8]

Table 149: SIPTU financial membership by Region and Branch, 2000

Region 1 (Dublin Public Sector)

Broadcasting	1,136
Bus Átha Cliath	1,160
CIÉ Clerical and Supervisory	72
City and County	3
Aer Lingus	3,795
Civil Aviation	2,438
Community and Education	97
County Councils	1,583
Dublin Health Services	5,553
Education	1,972
Energy	850
FÁS	1,392
Health Service Professionals	2,769
Irish Actors' Equity	1,039
Local Authorities	2,457
Local Authority Professional Officers	1,328
Portrane Psychiatric Hospital	161

Railway Services	2,358
Richard Byrne Dundrum Psychiatric Hospital*	115
St Brendan's Psychiatric Hospital	128
State Agencies	1,861
State-Related Agencies	931
Total	33,198

Region 2 (Dublin Private Sector)

Administrative, Supervisory and Sales	3,090
Apparel and Allied	672
Chemicals	1,644
Construction and Allied Trades	5,283
Docks, Marine, Transport	1,525
Drink, Tobacco, Distribution	2,223
Services	1,580
Electronics and Engineering	2,461
Film, Entertainment and Leisure	1,390
Food	2,854
Hotels, Restaurant and Catering	3,312
Insurance and Finance	2,148
Printing and Allied Trades	1,884
Professional and Managerial	636
Security Services	1,889
Women Workers	2,339
Total	34,950

Region 3 (South-East)

Arklow	797
Bray	733
Carlow	2,009
County Wexford Health	369
Eniscorthy	354
Gorey	316
Kilkenny Industrial and Manufacturing	1,925
Kilkenny Public Sector	1,662
Muine Bheag	203
South-East Construction—Waterford	6,285
Wexford	2,100

Wicklow	533
Total	17,286

Region 4 (South-West)	
Administrative, Professional and Technical	1,759
Askeaton	341
Bandon	247
Bantry	404
Clonakilty	245
Clonmel	1,778
Cóbh	703
Cork No. 1	3,011
Cork No. 2	2,103
Cork No. 3	1,250
Cork No. 6	2,984
Cork No. 7	2,801
Cork No. 8	2,650
Cork General Nurses	443
Cork Psychiatric Hospital	223
Dunmanway	398
Foynes	81
Kerry Nurses and Allied Grades	947
Killarney	1,689
Kinsale	100
Limerick No. 1	3,830
Limerick No. 2	3,674
Limerick Nurses	514
Macroom	729
Mallow No. 1	2,263
Mallow No. 2	95
Midleton	827
Mitchelstown	897
Nenagh	1,859
Rathmore	134
St Stephen's Psychiatric Hospital	258
Skibbereen	278
South Tipperary	52
Templemore	41

Thurles	731
Tipperary	1,124
Tralee	4,102
Youghal	745
Total	47,265

Region 5 (Midlands)

Administrative, Clerical, Technical and Services	1,113
Athlone	1,779
Athy	590
Kildare-Leixlip	2,895
Laois	1,431
Longford	1,323
Meath	1,860
Mullingar	1,572
Mullingar Psychiatric Hospital	482
Offaly	2,116
Peat Industries	864
South-East Area	1,107
Total	17,132

Region 6 (West)

Ballinasloe	1,028
Clare County	1,811
Conamara	787
Galway No. 1	2,471
Galway No. 2	2,915
Galway No. 3	862
Galway Health Services	321
Mayo No. 1	2,667
Mayo No. 2	3,398
Mayo Health Services	682
Roscommon	788
Roscommon Health Services	348
Shannon Aviation	1,034
Shannon Free Airport Development Company	155
Shannon Industrial	1,491
Sligo	2,681

Sligo Health Services	343
Total	23,782

Region 7 (Northern Counties)	
Bailieborough	210
Ballyshannon	76
Buncrana	901
Cavan	2,895
Doirí Beaga	913
Donegal	2,819
Donegal Nursing	406
Drogheda	1,700
Dundalk	1,370
Dungloe	105
Kilcar	36
Leitrim	577
Louth Nursing	360
Monaghan No. 21/22	1,926
Monaghan Nursing	352
Total	4,646

Region 8 (Northern Ireland)	
Belfast	459
Derry	940
Newry	765
Total	2,164

Source: SIPTU, Annual Report for 2000, p. 60–62.

*Richard Byrne was a long-serving officer in Dundrum Psychiatric Hospital Branch, which was named in his honour in 1997.

Region 3 (West)

In 2000 Mayo No. 2 Branch produced a members' magazine, *SIP2view,* carrying Branch development news. The campaign to retain Shannon Airport's dual gateway was maintained in 2003, as 40,000 jobs were at risk. It involved political parties, employers, development and community organisations and the regional media. 'EQUAL Ireland' training initiatives took place in partnership with Institutes of technology and NUIG. Branch Development Funds promoted seminars, workshops and organising activities. In 2003, 500 jobs were lost when A. T. Cross and Square D closed in Ballinasloe, a terrible blow to the local economy. Campaigns in 2005 dealt with organising hotels, opposition to the breaking up of Aer Rianta, and drug and alcohol abuse. The West of Ireland Construction Branch, launched under Noel Kilfeather, had enrolled 1,000 members by 2006.[9]

Table 150: SIPTU financial membership by Region, 2000–2007

	2000	2001	2002	2003	2004	2005	2006	2007
1	33,198	33,328	67,343	69,345	67,212	67,887	69,121	76,663
2	34,950	34,999	—	—	—	—	—	—
3	17,286	16,960	33,992	33,831	33,626	33,762	34,038	35,588
4	47,265	46,877	46,855	47,309	46,386	47,086	46,788	47,010
5	17,132	16,835	—	—	—	—	—	—
6	23,782	23,754	23,434	23,444	22,590	23,822	25,063	26,150
7	14,646	13,587	15,043	14,608	14,045	14,376	14,288	14,370
8	2,967	1,992	—	—	—	—	—	—
Total	163,940	197,353	193,617	196,537	191,336	195,116	196,653	199,781*

*Total membership includes other units: AGEMOU; Irish National Painters and Decorators; Irish Print; Marine, Port and General Workers; and Dublin Taxis, amounting to approximately 8,000.

Note: From January 2002 Regions 1 and 2 became a single Dublin Region; Regions 3 and 5 became Midlands and South-East Region; Regions 7 and 8 became Northern Region.

Source: SIPTU, Annual Reports, 2000–2008.

Region 4 (South-West)

In 2000, workers in Irish Express Cargo, Limerick, joined, triggering a long recognition dispute that went through the Labour Relations Commission and the Labour Court, finally resulting in agreed procedures and pay increases for nearly five hundred members in Limerick, Cork and Dublin in 2003. The dispute created a number of precedents and was testimony to the loyalty and commitment of the original forty members, who stayed with the process, continuously adding to their number. In November 2000 Joe O'Flynn succeeded the retiring Kevin O'Connor as Regional Secretary. A campaign on the health service, 'We're Sick of Waiting', was run throughout 2002. Construction workers and home helps were also recruited in significant numbers. In 2002 Tony Galvin, long-serving Shop Steward in Krups, Limerick, which closed in 1999 with the loss of 1,300 jobs, returned to the site as a trainer with FÁS Southill Jobs Club, set up by the Limerick Enterprise Development Partnership. Gene Mealy succeeded Joe O'Flynn when the latter became General Secretary. In 2003 the first substantial history of an ITGWU/SIPTU Branch was published with Ger Lewis's impressive *Loosening the Chains: The Story of the Nenagh Branch*.[10]

A shattered Liberty Hall after bombing. (*Liberty Magazine*, December 1972)

Liam Maguire, WUI GEC member and activist for rights for the disabled, 1979. (Photograph Derek Speirs, SIPTU Archive)

Nóirín Green (Dublin No. 2 Branch) congratulated at Conference in 1982 on becoming second woman to be elected to ITGWU NEC by Sheila Conroy, first woman elected to NEC in 1955. (SIPTU Archive)

FWUI General Executive Committee, 1984–1985: back, *l–r*, Ross Connolly, Kay Geraghty, Tom Geraghty, Larry Hardy, Pat Daly, Paddy Murphy (Assistant General Secretary), Tom Murphy (Deputy General Secretary), Tom Browne, Eddy Phelan, Jim Bannon, John Shorthall, Tom Redmond, Michael Cullen; seated, *l–r*, Larry Bateson, Jo Walsh, Kathleen Monaghan, May Clifford, Tom Garry (General President), William Attley (General Secretary), Frank Keelehan, Dympna Harper, Jim Quinn and Jack Kelly. (*Unity*, Winter 1984, SIPTU Archive)

Contract cleaners picket the entrance to college grounds in pursuit of equality. (*Liberty News*, Winter 1985, SIPTU Archive)

Union activist, actor and banner artist Jer O'Leary reincarnates Big Jim Larkin. Jer's son Diarmuid stands on the left. (*Liberty News*, March–April 1988, SIPTU Archive)

ITGWU Women's Committee attend ICTU Women's Conference, 24 February 1989: back, *l–r*, Maria Farrell (Dublin No. 2), Attracta Behan (Galway County), May O'Brien (Women's Affairs Official), Mary Burke (Clonmel); seated, *l–r*, Margaret Sullivan (Cork No. 1), Mary Ormiston (Kingscourt), Marie Cunningham (Clare County), Liz Worrall (Bray), and Ellen Shiels (Carlow). (SIPTU Archive)

SIPTU Assistant National Executive Officer Jimmy Somers with successful presidential candidate and union member Mary Robinson, high in Liberty Hall, 1990. (SIPTU Archive)

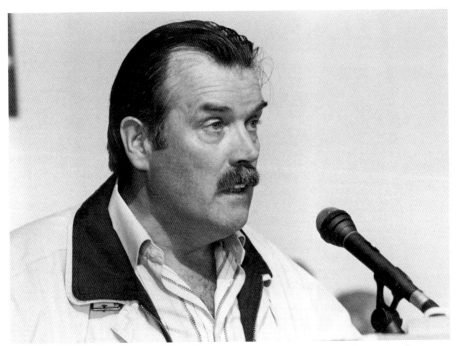

WUI, FWUI and SIPTU Executive member and firefighter Tom Geraghty addresses Conference, 1992. (SIPTU Archive)

Nolan's Transport picket, New Ross. (*SIPTU Report, 1993–1994*, SIPTU Archive)

Presentation of print of Peadar O'Donnell by Robert Ballagh to Tom Garry, General Secretary, SIPTU; Seán Reilly, Branch Assistant, and George Hunter, Branch Secretary, Donegal County Branch; Bob Brady, Northern Regional Secretary; and Jim Kemmy TD, 1994. (SIPTU Archive)

SIPTU Construction Branch Secretary Eric Fleming leads chanting in support of Irish Ferries workers, Dublin, December 2005. (SIPTU, *Annual Report 2005*, SIPTU Archive)

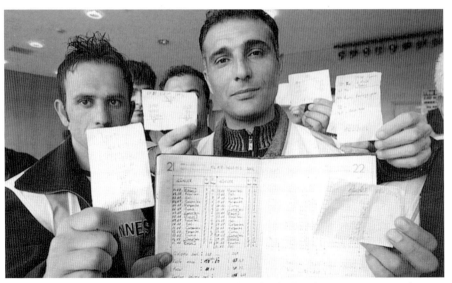

Turkish GAMA Construction workers display their 'pay slips'—hand written on pieces of paper—at press conference in Liberty Hall. (Photograph Leon Farrell, SIPTU, *Annual Report 2005*, SIPTU Archive)

Crew members and relatives march in defence of decency in Irish Ferries dispute, 2004. (Photograph Tommy Clancy, SIPTU Archive)

Region 5 (Northern)

The City Bridges project gathered pace in 2000. Funded by the International Fund for Ireland, it developed anti-sectarian programmes, raised awareness, established cross-border community contacts, enhanced the trade union role in such communities and built support structures. Job losses in the Hawkesbay clothing factory in Ardee heralded accelerating de-industrialisation. In 2001 SIPTU participated in actions by the Northern Ireland Committee of the ICTU for a minimum wage and developments in north-south co-operation. John Hume's retirement as Leader of the SDLP in September drew appreciative statements for a member who had made an outstanding contribution to peace. On 25 January 2002, 25,000 people took to the streets to protest against the shooting of Danny McColgan , a postal worker, by the UDA, organised by the Northern Ireland Committee. The General President, Des Geraghty, attended the Belfast rally. The plight of Richardson's workers in Belfast after the closure of the plant caused anxiety and anger with the Irish Government's failure to meet its moral obligation as a major shareholder. Matters worsened when it was revealed that the pension scheme was in arrears by more than £15 million. In 2004 SIPTU identified with the Congress policy 'A Shared Future' and participated in campaigns against the privatisation of water and sewerage. The Regional Secretary, Jack Nash, was nominated as a Worker Representative on the Labour Court and left the union. In September, John Hume became the first recipient of SIPTU's Spirit of Solidarity Award.

In 2005 the Belfast, Derry and Newry Branches were consolidated into a single Northern Ireland Branch, with Kevin McKinney concentrating on Belfast and Derry and John King covering Newry. SIPTU's commitment to Northern Ireland was evidenced in the opening of renovated Belfast premises. Activities were organised under 'EQUAL Ireland', 'Learning at a Time, Place and Pace that Suits the Modern Adult Worker Learner', using 'blended learning' techniques with members made redundant in NEC Ballivor, C&D Petfoods and Polyglass. Much community work was carried out through ITUT and City Bridges, and a 'Good Relations in the Workplace Guide' and training pack were launched by the General Secretary, Joe O'Flynn, in Belfast. The death of John Cassells in August 2006 robbed SIPTU of an outstanding stalwart. A tugboat man and Shop Steward in Cory Towage for thirty-five years, he was Chairperson of the Northern Ireland Branch, a member of the NEC and a beacon against sectarianism and violence.[11]

WOMEN AND EQUALITY

The Equality Unit published *The PPF [Programme for Prosperity and Fairness]: What's in It for Women and Low Paid Workers?*, identifying follow-up actions. An Equality Network was launched on 8 March, International Women's Day. The SIPTU-NUIG Alliance commissioned the sculptor John Behan to fashion *Equality Emerging,* a statue depicting a figure struggling through barriers to reach equality. The Equal Status Act (2000) extended legal protection against discrimination on nine grounds to those obtaining goods or services. In 2001 'Gender Equality in

SIPTU', compiled by Annette Atkinson, examined women throughout union structures, confirming their significant under-representation at senior levels. The Programme for Prosperity and Fairness provided a 'most sophisticated framework for progress and real change' at the company level on equality. Two National Framework Committees on Equal Opportunities and Family Friendly Workplace Arrangements translated ideas into work-place actions. The National Women's Forum informed SIPTU's 'Genderagenda', and a Workers' Charter of Rights for the Twenty First Century was launched on 8 March 2001.

In 2002 the Equality Committee engaged political parties on equality aspects of their manifestos. All attended a meeting except the Progressive Democrats (which declined without giving a reason). An Official, Mags O'Brien, was seconded to the ICTU's Gender and Pay Project in 2003 to develop a 'Toolkit' for 'Negotiating for Equality', a product of the National Framework Committees under the Programme for Prosperity and Fairness. A Working Party on Domestic Violence, created after the 2001 Conference, published guidelines on its consequences for work-places in 2004. In 2005 the rugby international Reggie Corrigan launched SIPTU's *Stopping Violence and Abuse*. Improvements in maternity benefit were won but little or no advance made on temporary agency workers, family-inclusive social insurance or child care. Much work was done with Congress to ensure the most positive improvements in the Equality Act (2004), which implemented three EU Equality Directives. A quarter of the seats on the ICTU Executive Council were reserved for women from 2005, raising questions about similar representation in SIPTU.[12]

In 2005 SIPTU published *Childcare in Ireland: A Trade Union View* to underline its long-term demands for improvements in the provision of child care and equal treatment for working mothers. An analysis of barriers and obstacles to career opportunities for women of non-officer grade in Dublin hospitals was published as *Equality for You: Filling the Knowledge Gap*. A National Women's Forum in Tralee in April dealt with 'Organising for Equality by Embracing Diversity', published as *Organising Diversity*. In 2006 a CD for negotiators, *Equality How?* was produced by SIPTU College and the Equality Unit to address the technical complexities of presenting effective equality claims. In 2007, as part of European Year of Equal Opportunities for All, the National Women's Forum dealt with 'age and gender'. Continuing commitments to improvements in child care were secured under Towards 2016.

In April 2008 the National Equality Secretary, Rosheen Callender, retired. She made an immense contribution since joining the ITGWU as Senior Researcher in 1973, fundamentally influencing pension, social welfare, equality and diversity issues, not just within SIPTU but in society as a whole.[13] From 2010 the Women's Committee would become an Equality Committee and a standing NEC Committee.

DIVERSITY

A SIPTU poster was produced for Anti-Racism Workplace Week, 'At Work in Ireland, At Home in SIPTU'. A code of practice against racism was drawn up by Congress and the Irish Business and Employers' Confederation under the Programme for Prosperity and Fairness. SIPTU strenuously promoted tolerance and multiculturalism in all its public statements and work-place practice. Union materials were published in Czech, Filipino, French, Italian, Latvian, Lithuanian, Polish, Portuguese, Romanian, Russian and Spanish to assist foreign workers in gaining access to their rights. An informal Anti-Racism Working Group, set up in 2000 by the National Equality Secretary, Rosheen Callender, became SIPTU Anti-Racism Group in November 2001. During National Anti-Racist Week it produced the well-known poster 'You're Welcome in Our Workplace.' The group fed into working groups on racism, refugees and asylum-seekers under the Programme for Prosperity and Fairness and the Steering Group for Development of the National Action Plan against Racism. On International Day Against Racism in March 2002 events were held in the Liberty Hall Centre, and Anton McCabe, Navan, became the first recipient of SIPTU's Anti-Racism Award, a unique depiction of the red hand emblem by Rowan Gillespie.[14]

In 2002 the Equality Unit secured funding from the Equal Opportunities Framework Committee under the Programme for Prosperity and Fairness and carried out research work through the SIPTU Equality Project Team. It gathered data on members' nationality, first language and all equality-related information, identifying the changing membership profile. SIPTU published *Representing Immigrant Workers* and held a 'Drop In, You're Welcome to Liberty Hall' open day for migrant workers in 2003.

Serious criticisms of the Immigration Bill that was rushed through the Dáil in 2004 were raised, not least given the absence of a promised Work Permits Bill. Mike Jennings led efforts to expose employers who exploited immigrant labour. SIPTU Anti-Racism Group issued 'No to racism—In the workplace and in the social welfare system' during Anti-Racism Week in November, demanding equal treatment, an end to bonded labour and the 'habitual residence condition', both seriously discriminating against migrant workers. Rosheen Callender was a member of the National Action Plan Against Racism's Special Initiative on Migration and Interculturalism. *Organising Diversity,* a report by the National Women's Forum, brought together a compendium of information, best practice and negotiating viewpoints in 2005. In 2006 SIPTU Anti-Racism Group was subsumed into a broader Migrant Workers' Policy Steering Group, created to engage more of SIPTU's 20,000 non-national members. With ITUT, SIPTU published 'Diversity in the Workplace: A Guide for Shop Stewards' and supported Congress's Guidelines for Combating Racism and Planning for Diversity. Training initiatives were taken by SIPTU College and within employments.[15]

SIPTU's first foreign staff members were appointed to the Organising Unit— Kazik Anhalt, Barnaba Dorda and Joanna Ozdarska (Polish) and Evelina Šaduikyte (Lithuanian)—to facilitate contact with and the organising of migrant workers.

SOCIAL PARTNERSHIP

Negotiations for a successor to Partnership 2000 concluded on 7 February 2000 with the 'Programme for Prosperity and Fairness' against a backdrop of unprecedented economic growth. Five operational frameworks covered living standards and workplace environment; prosperity and economic inclusion; social inclusion and equality, 'successful adaptation to continuing change'; and renewing partnership. Pay elements included a Benchmarking Body to examine the totality of public-sector pay. A National Minimum Wage was set at £4.40 an hour, increasing to £4.70 on 1 July 2001 and £5 from 1 October 2002. On income tax, a commitment was made that 'overall increases in net take-home pay of up to 25% or more over the lifetime of the PPF [Programme for Prosperity and Fairness]' would result from combined pay and tax provisions; all earnings below the National Minimum Wage would be withdrawn from the tax net; and 80% of taxpayers would not pay at the highest rate. Social inclusion would see a minimum social welfare payment of £100, with improved child benefit, social housing and health services. Equality measures included positive action, guidelines on domestic violence, improved family policies and child-care facilities, and action on racism. The Programme for Prosperity and Fairness was accepted by SIPTU, 80,989 to 36,428, and ratified by Congress, 251 to 112. It was the biggest SIPTU vote, 69%, for any partnership Agreement, and from the highest poll. SIPTU triggered a review clause when inflation exceeded 3% as early as July, resulting in a further 2% payable from 1 April and extra tax concessions. By December more than 113,369 members benefited from settlements.[16]

In 2001 many members won increases above the terms of the Programme for Prosperity and Fairness, something Jack O'Connor saw ultimately as a comment on the original Agreement's inadequacy. In addition to increases in basic wages, Agreements on profit-sharing, gain-sharing and employee share ownership were widely concluded. In 2002 169,464 members were part of settlements under the programme, with 160,384 getting the 'extra 2%' and 53,984 gaining increases above the Agreement. This was a tribute to the efforts of Officials and Shop Stewards. SIPTU estimated that average take-home pay rose by 35% under the Agreement, 'the biggest rise in real pay ever negotiated.' Even in real terms, increases were an impressive 19.3%. Despite €5 billion worth of tax cuts, those on the minimum wage remained in the tax net.

Negotiations for a successor to the Programme for Prosperity and Fairness continued until January 2003, when the NEC recommended acceptance of 'Sustaining Progress', although another regressive McCreevy Budget came close to sinking things. Paraphrasing Harry Potter film posters, SIPTU advertised 'Charlie Rotter' and outlined his 'latest dirty dozen' cuts in supports and assistance to finance transfers to the wealthy. The union Conference on 25 February expressed misgivings, but with economic uncertainty rising and many benefits accruing in what the NEC insisted would be a short-term Agreement, members voted by 77,020 to 28,128 to accept and Congress by 195 to 148. Some commentators suggested a sharp division between the public and the private sector. An analysis by SIPTU showed that 67.1% of Dublin private-sector members were in favour, compared with 70.2% of public-sector members. The talks were 'the most difficult round of negotiations in living memory.'[17]

By December, 380 settlements were made for 49,413 members, with 1,634 gaining more than the Agreement. Tax adjustments as part of partnership Agreements ended with Sustaining Progress. The real value of take-home pay rose by 11½% under Partnership 2000 and by 10% under the Programme for Prosperity and Fairness—actually more like 16% with the pay drift that occurred. Under Sustaining Progress increases would be 6 to 7%, comparing favourably with 5% under the Programme for National Recovery and 5½% under the Programme for Economic and Social Progress. European Industrial Relations Observatory tracked pay in 2003 and 2004. Ireland headed the tables for average annual increases in basic pay and in real value.

Sustaining Progress was divided into two eighteen-month Agreements, expiring in June 2004 for private-sector workers and in December 2004 for the public sector. Jack O'Connor would not attend talks in April because of the 'absence of any reference to the rights and interests of workers in public transport and aviation' in Mary Harney's address to the Conference of the Progressive Democrats. He insisted on a balance between the 'objective of a dynamic competitive economy with that of fairness and promotion of workers' rights and interests in the workplace.'

SIPTU and the TEEU re-entered talks on 21 May because the Government expressed a willingness to honour transport and aviation workers' rights and to discuss employment rights generally. The negotiations concluded on 18 June with further increases of 5½ to 6% won and an extra 0.5% for those on less than €9 an hour. SIPTU accepted these terms, by 62,279 to 25,619, and the ICTU by 267 to 110. By December, 108,000 members had gained increases. Attention focused on Performance Verification Groups throughout the public sector, designed to assess whether industrial peace was achieved in exchange for payments under benchmarking. In its 2004 Budget submission SIPTU outlined 'ten priorities' for McCreevy (with little expectation, given his record). The demands were to develop a fairer tax system by widening the tax base; to take a serious initiative on child care; to develop strategies for eliminating child poverty and educational disadvantage; to invest in lifelong learning; to tackle the excessive costs of building land and end speculation and profiteering; for a comprehensive insurance-based health service; for innovative solutions for the care of the elderly and disabled within the community; for adequate pensions for all; to improve living standards for those at work and on social welfare; and to honour Ireland's commitment to UN targets for overseas development assistance. 'Sustaining Progress, Part 2' was recommended to members in July and expected to provide real pay increases ranging from 4.7 to 5.6%—better than any Agreement since 1987. The members accepted, 62,279 to 25,619.

Resting on no laurels, SIPTU submitted a ten-point pre-Budget demand in November. It wanted single workers' tax credits increased by €550 and the standard tax band increased by €2,500; the income level for exemption from the health contribution raised from €356 to €479 and exemption from the 4% rate of PRSI increased to €386 a week; a minimum tax credit of €20 a week towards the cost of child care; maternity benefit raised from 70 to 80% of reckonable earnings; more flexible arrangements for the payment of carers' benefit; the introduction of parental leave benefit; the raising of all social welfare benefits by €21 a week and old-age pensions to at least €188; the abolition of the 'habitual residence' condition; and new pensions accounts established for all children born after 1 January 2005 by adding €15 to child benefits.[18] Negotiations on a successor to Sustaining Progress began in the autumn of 2005.

On 25 October, Congress decided that the 'timing was not right for talks and more work needed to be done.' On 4 December the National Implementation Body, monitoring developments in Irish Ferries, said it was 'particularly mindful of the concerns which have been expressed about the maintenance and protection of employment standards in the Irish labour market.' It conveyed its concern 'that the situation which has now evolved has the potential to damage significantly the climate of trust and stability which has developed over the years in the context of Social Partnership.' The National Implementation Body was established to ensure the implementation of 'the industrial relations stability and peace provisions of the PPF [Programme for Prosperity and Fairness]' and was representative of the Government, IBEC and the CIF and the ICTU, chaired by the Department of the Taoiseach. Reflecting widespread concerns about the 'adequacy of employment pro-tection measures' and their enforcement, notwithstanding commitments in Sustaining Progress to a flexible labour market, the NIB recommended that talks recommence but that they should 'comprehend in particular the incentives and disincentives within public policy which might influence decisions to substitute lower paid workers for those currently employed.' It recognised the need to 'ensure that inspection and enforcement systems in respect of mandatory employment standards are effective' and that the 'position of vulnerable workers who have re-located to Ireland from abroad should be the subject of particular focus in these enforcement issues.' It wanted 'a balance between employment protection and labour market flexibility' and urged all parties to engage with the Labour Relations Commission to complete new arrangements. This process was not concluded by 31 December. SIPTU was encouraged by the NIB's statements, but O'Connor led tough negotiations in order to translate concerns into adequate policy.[19]

In January 2006 SIPTU voted overwhelmingly to enter fresh talks, and in April 'Towards 2016' was endorsed, by 72 to 28%. *Liberty* published a detailed supple-ment, 'So Now it's Over to You.' O'Connor explained that lengthy negotiations arose from SIPTU's insistence that 'the issues of exploitation, displacement and the proper enforcement of labour standards' be addressed.

On 5 September, Congress voted by 242 to 84 to accept the Agreement, which pro-vided an agenda for the modernisation of the public service, employment rights and compliance measures; commitments on pensions, work-place learning and partner-ship initiatives; and health and child-care measures. There were immediate concerns about how inflation might erode the Agreement's monetary elements. The 2006 Budget was criticised as being 'unnecessarily cautious' and contributing further inflation. For

O'Connor, the 2007 Budget made no improvement, as it 'lived down to expectations.'

SIPTU Research published *Inequity in the Tax System: Who Benefits?* emphasising the fact that the tax code worsened social inequality. O'Connor felt that 'without justice', social partnership had 'no future', as increasing elements in the process continuously turned a blind eye to exploitation and exclusion.[20]

In 2008 lengthy negotiations for a successor to Towards 2016 stalled as the Government threatened pay pauses, employers questioned trade unions' credibility as bargainers, and SIPTU insisted on legal rights for collective bargaining. In August 2008 talks on a successor Agreement collapsed. O'Connor reflected that the Government's support for SIPTU's anti-inflationary pay strategy was not forthcoming. IBEC's aggressive attitude threatened industrial unrest unnecessarily, and its insistence that 'those least able to carry the burden of the economic downturn would shoulder it' would 'simply not wash.'

By 31 August, with no apparent prospect of talks being reconvened, SIPTU had already secured settlements of 3% for motor trade employees in direct bargaining. If this really was the end of social partnership it had come suddenly and without any great gnashing of teeth on the state's part. Matters were retrieved when proposals for a new deal emerged in September.

WAGES AND DISPUTES

Very few strikes occurred in 2000. Industrial peace accompanied a booming economy. A protracted strike by 140 members in the National Car Testing Service secured a Dublin allowance of £37 and improved conditions throughout the country. Pickets on East Link and West Link toll bridges won terrific public support, not least given the £30 million profit declared by National Toll Roads PLC. Victory brought an extra 3% over the terms of the Programme for Prosperity and Fairness and a reduction in hours from 41 to 37½. Substantial wage increases were won for building workers through a revised grading structure, victory for a lengthy campaign to raise wages and allow workers to share in huge industry profits.

Table 151: SIPTU **industrial contingency fund (€), 2000–2007**

	Income	Expenditure	Balance
2000	204,000	204,000	9,211,830
2001	297,119	297,119	11,696,611
2002	297,119	297,119	11,696,611
2003	297,118	297,118	11,696,611
2004	562,118	312,118	11,946,611
2005	1,329,859*	329,859	12,946,611
2006	1,483,267*	483,267	13,946,611
2007	1,422,160*	422,160	14,946,611

*Transfer of €1,000,000 from General Fund.

Source: SIPTU, Annual Reports, 1990–2007.

For the public, a confusing dispute arose from action by the Irish Locomotive Drivers' Association and the train drivers' productivity deal negotiated by SIPTU-NBRU, necessitating rank-and-file members of those unions putting the record straight in print.[21]

Led by John Kane, National Industrial Secretary, SIPTU met Officials of the Department of Agriculture in January 2001 to discuss short-time working in beef plants arising from the BSE crisis. A Working Party was set up to provide for displaced workers. In 2002 a four-month dispute in Irish Glass Bottle Company followed the management's decision to close the plant, 'the first act of betrayal by the company since it followed exhaustive negotiations on a major restructuring.' The second came when the management rejected a Labour Court recommendation on severance pay, which led to a strike. A National Day of Action ratcheted up pressure on Ardagh PLC, the holding company. A revised offer moved in the direction of the Labour Relations Commission but was rejected by the workers. After intervention by politicians and IBEC, significant further improvements were wrung from the company and were accepted. The plant, however, remained closed, a blow to Ringsend and the end of an era.

Tommy Glennon's lonely four-month vigil outside Sheridan Precast in Tyrrellspass, Co. Westmeath, was rewarded with an €8,000 redundancy settlement in December. Tommy, the sole union member, had to wear hearing protectors, as the management placed noisy machinery beside him in an effort to deter him. A three-month strike in Spring Valley Nursing Home, Enniscorthy, concluded in November when the management finally attended the Labour Relations Commission.[22]

2003 was quiet industrially. In Shannonside Northern Sound Radio, however, nine members struck from 2 May after the management issued redundancy notices to two employees. The intention was to dismiss the leading union activists, the management having first withheld recognition in 2001. On 17 July the matter was concluded when three members accepted voluntary redundancy.

An important dispute began in Oxigen Environmental on 14 October. Three years' correspondence from SIPTU was unanswered, and workers decided they wanted professional representation, the implementation of their statutory entitlement to a 39-hour week, a review of overtime rates, proper sickness pay and pension schemes, fair and just grievance procedures, and improved pay. Members in Dublin City Council voted to take half-day solidarity action on 6 November, but the Oxigen management remained obdurate. The dispute ended in February 2004 with agreement on a special 'protocol' on handling 'common issues' agreed through two facilitators.

In July 2004 eighty members in Brinks Allied refused to operate a new 'drive away' policy, whereby, in the event of an armed robbery, drivers were to abandon their grounded colleagues. The matter was not resolved until September, when new procedures were agreed and workers received €375 for loss of earnings. The company's rejection of Labour Court recommendations was a significant and disturbing development, not least as it was an IBEC affiliate.

Independent Newspapers ignored all partnership processes to push through redundancies, 'respectfully' declining to meet the National Implementation Body, something SIPTU saw as a 'critical moment' for industrial relations. Throughout the year SIPTU resisted Dairygold's decision to cut 500 jobs. The company's Christmas message to employees was to demand lower wages and longer hours.[23]

Table 152: SIPTU Dispute Benefit, 2000–2007

	Dispute Benefit (€)	Dispute Grants (€)		As proportion of income (%)
2000	285,456	—	285,456	1.3
2001	346,865	1,270	348,135	1.2
2002	720,266	14,000	734,266	2.5
2003	317,430	—	317,430	1.0
2004	202,838	—	202,838	0.5
2005	61,310	—	61,310	0.1
2006	242,375	—	242,375	0.6
2007	98,998	—	98,998	0.2

Source: SIPTU, Annual Reports, 1990–2007.

There were few disputes in 2005, but Gama and Irish Ferries dominated. In Doyle Concrete-Steelite in Kildare, industrial action began in October when the management refused to attend the Labour Court to discuss redundancy. After intensive negotiations, and before a proposed rally on 20 November, the management withdrew redundancy notices to permit a return to work, reinstate negotiated rates and apply them to non-nationals. This appeared to settle the matter, but 'subsequent developments proved otherwise.' In 2006 major battles were against job losses in Greencore, the continued struggle in Doyle Concrete-Steelite, Maria Goretti Nursing Home, Limerick (where the Gardaí had to called on thirteen occasions 'because of intimidation by management' of the picket line), and Clubman Omega.[24]

CAMPAIGNS

Members in the health service campaigned in 2000 to improve Accident and Emergency provision in Beaumont Hospital, Dublin, to up-skill ancillary employees through NVQ training schemes, and in Wexford to improve facilities in Wexford General Hospital. SIPTU's National Strategy Group, set up in 1999, maintained pressure to safeguard the future of Aer Rianta and qualified opposition to the Aviation Regulation Bill (2000). Other campaigns dealt with retaining public ownership of Great Southern Hotels, regulating the private security industry, and improving conditions for home helps. Reform of the health service was the main 2001 campaign. A novel demonstration was held by Eastern Vocational Enterprises, a subsidiary of the Eastern Regional Health Authority. The actor Jack Lynch, posing as a cash-in-transit security guard, arrived at the Department of Health and Children in Hawkins Street, Dublin, to collect £1½ million in wage arrears. By the end of the afternoon the money was transferred to a specific bank account, to be paid the week following May Day. Dublin Taxi Branch campaigned for a Tribunal to investigate the impact of taxi deregulation.[25]

In February 2002 Des Geraghty launched a health service reform campaign, demanding a single waiting list—no discrimination between private and public; more hospital and medical staff appointments; a more integrated approach to primary care between GPs and health specialists; the restoration of adequate funding; and improved future resources. An action pack was widely distributed. The National Nursing Convention in 2004 debated 'Heath Service Reforms—Are We Prepared for the Challenge?'

In February 2002 the Minister of State at the Department of Transport, Robert Molloy, agreed to set up 'an independent panel to examine the financial losses which taxi drivers had experienced since deregulation,' after consistent lobbying by SIPTU. The Taxi Hardship Panel was criticised by Jerry Brennan, Taxi Branch Official, as not going far enough. In 2003 SIPTU was the central campaigner against the privatisation of CIÉ. In January transport unions held a four-hour protest stoppage against the Minister's proposals, but further actions were necessary on 16 September, 14 October, 18 November and 8–9 December. A 'no-fares day' was held on 18 July. Dialogue hung by a thread as the year closed, with little resolved. In December the Minister for Transport, Séamus Brennan, insisted, in the *Irish Independent,* that competition would take place on 25% of Bus Átha Cliath routes, the start of what would ultimately be a complete process. The Dublin Bus Branch held a two-hour meeting on 22 January 2004. A four-hour stoppage took place on 16 February as the talks stalled. The Government displayed little interest in expediting matters.

Just as talks at the Labour Relations Commission agreed some sort of path forward, Brennan told the Fianna Fáil ard-fheis that fifty bus routes, involving 200 vehicles and 600 workers, would be privatised by December. Assurances from the Taoiseach in March were matched by suggestions from the Progressive Democrats that their continuation in Government would be threatened if the 'liberalisation' of Bus Átha Cliath did not occur. This led to Jack O'Connor refusing to lead SIPTU in pay talks under Sustaining Progress. A complete review of all bus services in the greater Dublin area was announced on 12 May. SIPTU responded with its own position paper. Brennan continued to issue licences to private operators, and negotiations through the Labour Relations Commission were constantly undermined by his actions. Once he was replaced in a Government reshuffle in September, things improved, and talks continued in a less confron-tational atmosphere.

The 'Cry for Health' Campaign was relaunched in the autumn of 2004, SIPTU members within and beyond the health service being asked to mount pressure on politicians to solve the chronic problems.

SIPTU's long-standing opposition to 'double-taxation' domestic service charges was reaffirmed at the 2003 Conference. Linking them to privatisation, they were all the more abhorrent. Support was offered to the Dublin West TD Joe Higgins (Socialist Party) and Councillor Clare Daly when they were imprisoned for not paying their charges as a 'totally disproportionate and unjustifiable response' by Fingal County Council. SIPTU supported the TEEU's proposal at Dublin Council of Trade Unions for a campaign against bin charges and a demonstration on 11 October against the jailings.

In 2005 SIPTU publicised the Competition Authority's decision to curb union representation for actors, artists, musicians and freelance writers. The authority outlawed an Agreement between the Actors' Equity Branch of SIPTU and the Institute of Advertising Practitioners, which set down minimum rates and conditions. With the National Union of Journalists, SIPTU called for legislative amendment to overthrow the ruling.

In 2006 SIPTU demanded the removal of all non-commercial state-sponsored agencies from plans for decentralisation. By October only 56 out of almost 1,400 state agency employees had opted for transfer. SIPTU called for a halt before more resources were wasted.

Industrial action was endorsed for members in FÁS, Enterprise Ireland, the Arts Council and Fáilte Ireland, indicating the strength of feeling. SIPTU also campaigned for improved standards in the security industry; the promotion of the community sector (300 people attended a seminar in December in Liberty Hall); to prevent the sale of Great Southern Hotels; and, as ever, reform of the health service.

In September 2006 Anne Speed became National Campaigns Organiser, underlining the union's commitment to putting issues before the public in a co-ordinated and assertive manner. The Dublin Health Services Branch augmented this initiative by creating a 'fighting fund' through a 50p weekly levy. Paul Bell, Sectoral Organiser, explained that the union intended to 'tell the public why a SIPTU health worker was a better health worker.'

A campaign to defend the rights of agency workers was launched at a public meeting in Liberty Hall in November 2007. Fianna Fáil, Fine Gael, the Green Party and Progressive Democrats all declined to attend, eloquent testimony to their collective lack of interest in the most exploited in society.[26]

AIRPORTS

Intervention by the Labour Court just before the third of a series of one-day stoppages on 12 April 2000 granted SIPTU more than 80% of the assurances it sought as Aer Lingus was again convulsed by management plans for rationalisation and cost-cutting. SIPTU strongly denied that the claims were 'catch-up' to cabin crew rates. Jack O'Connor, Vice-President, said the motive was 'equity of treatment between all grades.' There were tensions within SIPTU's membership. Clerical employees pointed out that awards to others that did not stem from local productivity removed any constraints they felt by normal procedures in pursuit of their own claims. After a five-day stoppage Servisair ground handling crews at Cork and Dublin won improved pay. SIPTU continued to publicise Ryanair's employment practices but made no headway in recruiting members. In July 2002 Cityjet handling members engaged in a dispute after the management refused to discuss improvements in pay and conditions. More than 60% of the workers were temporary, part-time or agency workers, with wages 35% lower than in comparable companies. At the end of the year the issue was not resolved, with strike-breakers and a 'Staff Forum' introduced, as well as higher wages and a pension scheme— both items it was originally claimed would break the company. After balloting in September, members in Aer Lingus, Aer Rianta, Servisair and FLS in Cork, Dublin, Galway, Knock and Shannon took solidarity action with Cityjet.

In 2003 SIPTU led a campaign to resist the construction of a privately owned terminal at Dublin Airport and to prevent the dismantling of Aer Rianta, announced on 10 July. In 2004 SIPTU published 'A Reckless Act of Institutional Vandalism', a critique of Séamus Brennan's proposals for Aer Lingus. In March the company announced a 30% operating profit of €83 million and the National Implementation Body was asked to examine industrial relations problems.

The Progressive Democrats announced that their continued participation in Government was threatened unless bus routes were liberalised and Aer Rianta broken up. O'Connor's response was to refuse to participate in talks on Sustaining Progress unless written assurances were given. In June the Chief Executive of Aer Lingus, Willie Walsh, said he would not sign the employee share option plan unless outstanding issues were resolved. The Government set up a Committee, and SIPTU led resistance. In July, without warning, Aer Lingus announced a further 1,325 job cuts. Matters rumbled on until, on 16 November, Walsh and two senior Executives announced their resignation. O'Connor reiterated calls for the management's and Government's plans to be re-examined. More than 1,600 workers expressed an interest in voluntary severance.

Aer Rianta occupied centre stage throughout 2004. Work stoppages were announced for 18 March and 2, 20 and 26 April to slow Brennan's charge and allow for rational negotiation. Ryanair took an action in the High Court against SIPTU on 16 March to further muddy the waters. Two days earlier the Taoiseach, Bertie Ahern, assured SIPTU that there would be no 'race to the bottom' in state-sponsored jobs: 'existing undertakings would be honoured.' Stoppages were halted. After marathon talks, on 18 June it was agreed that three separate companies would be created, solely to produce business plans. Disagreements almost immediately arose about whether these new boards had operational control.

On 22 June the State Airports Bill (2004) was published, providing for the breaking up of Aer Rianta and seen as 'advancing the PDS' agenda . . . ideologically driven and ill-conceived.' Paul Sweeney, former SIPTU Research Officer employed by the ICTU, defended Aer Lingus, pointing out that the privatisation of Eircom had been a strategic mistake in 1999; the sale of the airline would be similarly unsound. In July 2005 SIPTU published 'A New Flight Path for Aer Lingus: The Alternative to Selling

Our National Airline', to forcefully and intelligently make the case for retaining public ownership. SIPTU called for the airline and twelve other commercial state enterprises, instead of being sold off, to be transferred to a State Holding Company, through which equity could be raised in financial markets without surrendering strategic control. The Aer Lingus pension scheme had an aggregate deficiency of £350 million, adding to workers' concerns and uncertainty.

SIPTU strongly supported the right of the Dublin Airport Authority to build the second Dublin Airport terminal. While welcoming the commitment of the Minister for Transport, Martin Cullen, that the DAA would own a new terminal, it cautioned about the potential problems arising from the requirement that any new facilities would be open to competitive tendering.

The sheer grind of continuous negotiating, lobbying and campaigning on airport issues absorbed huge SIPTU resources. This was not fully appreciated by members and not at all by the public, in whose ultimate interests SIPTU acted.

Campaigns to resist the part-privatisation of Aer Lingus and the restructuring of airports continued in 2006. A hostile bid from Ryanair led the Aer Lingus management to announce yet another plan, involving reductions in staff and remuneration.[27]

IRISH FERRIES

Throughout 2004 SIPTU engaged in discussions with Irish Ferries about rationalisation. *Liberty* published a prophetic headline in March: 'Rough waters ahead.' The company sought savings of €3.4 million, incorporating fifty-two job cuts and amendments to sickness leave and other conditions. In February the Labour Court suggested that both sides return to the Labour Relations Commission and that Congress would construct a unified negotiating position. The Seamen's Union of Ireland, representing 480 seamen, refused to negotiate alongside SIPTU, representing 177 officers and 120 seamen. The great fear was that separate negotiations would allow the company to play one group off against another.

On 24 February the management suspended its Dublin–Holyhead sailings by the *Jonathan Swift* and its Rosslare–Pembroke and Rosslare–Cherbourg sailings by the *Isle of Inishmore,* blaming lack of progress in the talks and inter-union difficulties. More than 450 sea-going workers (mostly seamen) out of 777 were temporarily laid off without pay. Intervention by Congress secured joint negotiations, and crews were reinstated on 4 March. Negotiations were completed in July, with a saving of €3.4 million attained by voluntary redundancy, reduced crew ratios and the loss of fringe benefits.

Towards the end of the year the management demanded a further 150 job cuts and the sub-contracting of the Rosslare–Normandy services to a third-party employment agency. The sales staff was to be streamlined, with bookings concentrated on the internet. SIPTU and the Seamen's Union of Ireland expressed anger and urged the Minister to intervene, not least to provide a level playing field with heavily subsidised French ferries. SIPTU served strike notice on the Rosslare–

Cherbourg sailings, to expire on 2 December. The management responded by taking the *Normandy* out of service on 25 November, stranding a hundred passengers. SIPTU officers conducted a 24-hour strike on 2 December, and learnt that the *Normandy* was being refurbished in Belfast, crewed by agency workers.

An indefinite strike began on Monday 6 December. On Sunday 5 December the management instructed crews at Holyhead and Pembroke not to board passengers or freight but to put to sea for unspecified destinations. They refused, pointing out that they were obliged only to sail agreed routes. The vessels remained tied alongside. Both sides argued that this was in breach of the 1994 registered employment Agreement. SIPTU called in the National Implementation Body, which recommended on 15 December that the strike be called off, lay-offs cease and the parties return to the Labour Relations Commission. SIPTU agreed and called off the action.

At the talks, cuts of €2.4 million were offered, which, while less than the company's demands, would return the French routes to viability. Negotiations continued into 2005, with SIPTU 'determined to make a stand' to prevent Irish Ferries transferring Irish jobs to low-cost foreign operators. Waters had been stormy in 2004, but a tempest awaited SIPTU seafarers in 2005.

A Philippine beautician, Salvacion Orge, working on board the *Isle of Inishmore* was discovered to be earning €1 an hour. The company's response was to terminate her services rather than rectify its 'error'. A confidential settlement was eventually agreed. Crew members donated more than €1,000 to her. In contrast, the Managing Director of Irish Ferries, Éamonn Rothwell, was enjoying a salary of €350 an hour, having received an increase of €35,000 a year, to bring his annual salary to €687,000. The holding company, Irish Continental Group, declared a profit of €14.6 million in 2004—this after spending €12 million restructuring its French routes. Such facts attracted huge adverse publicity to the company. The company, however, appeared impervious to criticism.

In February the Labour Court recommended that the company continue to directly employ deck and engine officers and that the position be reviewed at the end of the season. SIPTU accepted this, but the management did not. SIPTU balloted the ships' officers. Even before the result was declared the management put all employees on protective notice. Had the unions behaved in a similar fashion, press headlines would have bellowed about 'wildcat' action. The company's action was unemotive, well thought out and long in the planning, as evidenced by the re-registering of the *Normandy* in the Bahamas and the sub-contracting of crewing in May. A demonstration in Cherbourg was joined by French and British unions through the International Transport Workers' Federation.

In June the management and SIPTU agreed to appoint independent assessors, Greg Sparks of Farrell Grant Sparks and Martin King of Ampersand Consulting, to comprehensively review Irish Sea and Continental operations. For six weeks neither side would take any further action.

In September Sparks and King recommended a 5% pay cut across the board, new work rosters, and sub-contracting to be confined to catering and cleaning, saying that 'there was no evidence of competitive pressures,' as Irish Ferries' share of an admittedly declining market was static, at 38%. The management rejected this and on 19 September announced a redundancy package for 543 seamen on Irish Sea routes, offering up to eight weeks per year of service, inclusive of two weeks' statutory payment. It would replace Irish crews with cheap eastern Europeans at €3 an hour. Conditions attached to the redundancy offer included no threat of industrial action and that it be accepted by 2 October, a mere two weeks away. If not accepted, the management 'would have no option but to completely exit' the Irish Sea. It insisted on 'the right to replace any/all ranks, grades, categories of staff as they leave with a third party arrangement for EU sourced staff.' SIPTU served two weeks' strike notice.

Following the intervention of the Taoiseach, the management reluctantly agreed to talks at the Labour Relations Commission. The Government said there was ultimately nothing it could do if Irish Ferries proceeded, but SIPTU pointed to health and safety concerns that could have been pursued, such as working time, mandatory shore leave, language competence, medical tests for those working long hours, and safety drills. Here was a role for the Health and Safety Authority, had the Government wished.

The talks at the Labour Relations Commission made no progress. At SIPTU's biennial Delegate Conference in Cork in October, Irish Ferries was linked to job displacement, exploitation, and the 'race to the bottom' for employment standards. On 3 November 10,000 people responded to a rally in Dublin. A Labour Court recommendation backed SIPTU and instructed Irish Ferries to honour its 2004 Agreements and resume negotiations. In short, it called for a collectively negotiated settlement, pointing out that the 1994 registered employment agreement between SIPTU ships' officers and the company was 'clear' and 'binding on both sides.' Irish Ferries said the recommendation was 'incapable of acceptance' and stepped up the dispute by bringing agency crews on board ship, backed by a covert security presence. Again these were decisions not made on a whim. Officers responded by barricading themselves in the engine rooms of the *Isle of Inishmore* and *Ulysses.* These were not young, headstrong militants but mature, highly qualified and professional ships' masters. Their reaction resulted from deep anger and frustration with an employer that was stripping them of all dignity as well as threatening hundreds of livelihoods.

On 4 December the National Implementation Body issued a lengthy and unequivocal statement. The Chief Executive of the Labour Relations Commission, Kieran Mulvey, invited both sides to talk. Jack O'Connor proposed that Congress lead a national day of protest, and 168,000 people joined 'Threshold of Decency' marches: 100,000 in Dublin, 20,000 in Cork and Waterford, 15,000 in Limerick, 3,000 in Athlone and Sligo, 2,500 in Galway and Tralee, and 2,000 in Rosslare. Irish Ferries' response was to remove the two-week 'good will' element of the severance offer, amounting to a quarter of the total, if work did not resume by 13 December. The *Jonathan Swift* service would be reduced to summer only, with immediate lay-offs.

On 14 December an Agreement was reached that broadly met SIPTU's objectives. It was accepted at a General Meeting, and lawyers were called in to draft a framework Agreement to protect employees contracted to work through Dobson Recruitment Agency. While crewing ratios and wages were higher than the management wished, the reality dawned that most workers were now non-union, foreign, and poorly paid; those who remained faithful to SIPTU were isolated, disillusioned, and vulnerable. The less said about the role of the Seamen's Union of Ireland the better.

That state funding was available for the Irish Ferries 'redundancies' occasioned further widespread disgust in 2007. Everything confirmed the SIPTU poster: 'Irish Ferries waives the Rules.'

Irish Ferries was an iconic battle. It was 'not just another industrial dispute': it raised public consciousness to the unacceptable levels of exploitation and the dangers of the EU Services Directive, and raised union morale. Few will forget the spontaneous and prolonged applause from the public as marchers tramped down O'Connell Street. Paul Smyth, Tony Ayton, Noel Dowling, Brendan Hayes, Patricia King, Jack O'Connor and many others provided leadership to gallant members in holding a line at sea before land defences for every other worker were swamped. To that extent, all Irish workers are in the debt of SIPTU ships' officers and seamen for their courageous stand. International support, co-ordinated by Norrie McVicar of the International Transport Workers' Federation, was crucial and substantial.

An interesting tailpiece was the transfer of SIPTU's Contingency Fund of more than €8 million from Bank of Ireland after the bank declined to state whether or not it supported job displacement in the light of comments made by its chief economist, Dan McLoughlin, during the dispute. The NEC transferred funds after calling on the bank to 'heed the request from the Labour Court to maintain the status quo in relation to a dispute over the bank's defined-benefit pension scheme for its employees.' The National Employment Rights Authority and action against 'Compulsory Replacement' were enacted under Towards 2016, beneficial legacies from SIPTU's Irish Ferries and Gama battles.[28]

GAMA CONSTRUCTION

Press and politicians dismissed SIPTU's claims of widespread exploitation of immigrant workers as exaggerated, 'anecdotal' and isolated. Gama Construction 'challenged the wishful thinking.' Exploitation was 'systematic, sophisticated and practised by a major employer.' Gama was a members of the Construction Industry Federation and Dublin Chamber of Commerce and employed 1,300 workers in Ireland, 10,000 throughout Europe. Even the 'most blinkered apologists for an unregulated labour market' were shocked by the combination of Gama and Irish Ferries. The public were appalled. The discovery owed much to chance, further underlining the problem.

In November 2004 three members of the Building and Allied Trade Union at Balgaddy, Co. Dublin, occupied a crane to protest about the non-payment of three weeks' wages. Both the Labour Court and the High Court upheld the contention of Gama Construction that it was not the employer. Councillor Mick Murphy (Socialist Party) circulated leaflets in Turkish, seeking further information. Deputy Joe Higgins told the Dáil in February 2005 that

> this company imports workers who do not speak English from their home base, controls their passports and work permits, accommodates them often in company barracks, demands 'grotesque' working hours, and, incredibly, pays them between €2 and €3 an hour, €5 below National Minimum Wage and far below Registered Employment Agreement rates of €12.96.

Higgins opened the door to public debate. More Gama workers came forward. An investigation of earlier complaints by Inspectors of the Department of Enterprise, Trade and Employment found that Gama met all their legal obligations. This demonstrated 'a lack of rigour' by the Minister, Mary Harney, who had led a trade mission to Turkey to invite Gama to tender for public contracts. She also blocked the appointment of additional Labour Inspectors at the negotiations on Sustaining Progress.

New inspections showed that some money was paid into Finansbank in Amsterdam. More than €30 million was lodged, amounting to more than €45,000 per worker. This money was transferred to Turkey but still only accounted for the discrepancy in basic wages; so unions submitted claims for unpaid overtime. Gama mounted a successful legal challenge to prevent publication of the Inspectorate's report, continuing to draw a grubby veil over the facts, although Mícheál Martin said he would forward the file to both the Revenue Commissioners and the Garda Fraud Squad.

It was revealed that Gama had been granted 889 work permits between January 2004 and March 2005, even though it was agreed that such permits would not be issued for construction workers, as sufficient labour from within the European Economic Area was available. In addition to using the Courts, Gama increased pressure on workers by threatening repatriation and evictions. SIPTU made emergency arrangements and sought urgent state support through the Department of Social and Family Affairs. Images of 1913 soup kitchens came to mind.

As SIPTU and others attended talks at the Labour Relations Commission, the *Irish Times* revealed that Gama was given 70% of the exemptions granted under a scheme to exempt employers from paying social insurance for foreign employees. Price Waterhouse Cooper resigned as Gama's auditors, as the company had not forwarded information relating to alleged breaches of employment law.

After three weeks, proposals by the Labour Relations Commission were rejected by the workers, and the dispute proceeded to the Labour Court, which recommended a lump sum of €8,000 per year of service in respect of unpaid overtime (most workers had three years' service, and all workers would receive a minimum of €2,000), with all workers getting an *ex gratia* payment of one month's pay on completion of the contract. A distrustful General Meeting withheld acceptance until the workers knew how the management would implement the recommendation.

Noel Dowling, National Organiser, paid tribute to the men and to Joe Higgins and his Socialist Party comrades. Regrettably, every politician mentioned in this account was returned to the Dáil in the next election—except for Higgins.[29] The whole affair stank of corrupt practice at the highest levels and added great weight to SIPTU's case for the improved enforcement of employment rights.

UNION RECOGNITION

Social partnership was increasingly welcomed as the dynamic of the Celtic Tiger economy. Yet, ironically, union recognition rose to the top the agenda. The Industrial Relations (Amendment) Bill (2000), criticised by SIPTU as inadequate, at least attempted to introduce some resolution of the problem. The Industrial Relations Act (1990) Code of Practice on Voluntary Dispute Resolution Order (2000) and the Code of Practice on Grievance and Disciplinary Procedures Order (2000) were enacted to provide an alternative to 'bitter recognition' disputes. They did not meet union aspirations, proving cumbersome and slow and facilitating employers' obfuscation and avoidance. A landmark case was won for licensed eel fishers on the Shannon, but they were found not to be 'workers' as defined by the legislation.

Improvements in procedures were a central demand in discussions for a successor to the Programme for Prosperity and Fairness. Jack O'Connor insisted that there would be 'no accommodation—without representation' in pay talks, the Cityjet dispute illustrating the union's frustrations.[30]

The Industrial Relations (Amendment) Bill, published in 2003, a commitment under Sustaining Progress, greatly shortened procedures. O'Connor commissioned an internal survey of the industrial staff to inform the case for reform, emphasising experiences of frustrating delays, disingenuous management resistance and, ultimately, the denial of *bona fide* claims.

The Industrial Relations (Miscellaneous Provisions) Act (2004) came into force in May, its revised time-scale cutting the time a case could take through all procedures to six months. SIPTU was quick to make use of the Enhanced Code of Practice on Voluntary Dispute Resolution Order (2004) to gain improvements in pay and conditions for newly organised members, even if there was still no provision for union recognition as such. SIPTU publicised procedures in simple language in leaflets and posters as part of the 'All Together Stronger' campaign. Notices in *Liberty* outlined the five steps as 'Representation rights for all!' Seventeen recognition Agreements were won in 2006 under the legislation, with a further sixteen cases enjoined.[31] A challenge by Ryanair to the legislation was heard in the Supreme Court in 2008, severely holing the Orders below the waterline.

NEW FORMS OF WORK ORGANISATION

Under 'Framework 5' of the Programme for Prosperity and Fairness thirty-eight companies concluded partnership Agreements with SIPTU in 2000. Issues included forms of financial involvement, co-operation with new work practices, equality, conflict solving and avoidance, safety and health, representational arrangements, adaptability, flexibility and innovation, and employee involvement. A Partnership Network co-ordinated activities throughout SIPTU by disseminating information on best practice, European developments, and ideas for change. A four-part documentary, 'Mind Your Own Business', commissioned by SIPTU and involving the ICTU and IBEC, was broadcast by RTÉI in May, examining company partnership projects. All this demonstrated SIPTU's leadership in the field. The publication of *Mind Your Own Business: Economics at Work* proved a useful tool for increasing the number of members engaged in partnership.

The Craft Analogue Agreement, settled in 2003, provided a one-off payment of €2,000 to about 26,000 ancillary health service workers in exchange for extensive change and modernisation, with basic increases back-dated to December 2001. A new 'broad-banding' system was used to provide for four grades, supplemented by job rotation and absentee arrangements.[32] SIPTU's attempts to join the Government in building partnership in state and state-sponsored bodies in order to provide world-class quality at competitive prices were frustrated by Séamus Brennan's 'strange idea of partnership.' His actions and speeches seemed at odds with the Taoiseach's views, not least as expressed within Sustaining Progress. A deliberate attempt to provoke confrontation was the most generous assessment of Brennan's actions, apart from questioning his capacity to actually grasp matters. The Employees (Provision of Information and Consultation) Act (2006) passed slowly through the Dáil. SIPTU College organised a national briefing workshop.

Responses to training were mixed, perhaps betraying the weakness of workplace information and consultation structures, management resistance and the lack of effective union demand.[33]

SOLIDARITY

SIPTU, and the ITGWU before it, were long-standing affiliates of the International Transport Workers' Federation. Many port-based Officials regularly assisted stranded foreign seamen. SIPTU College hosted a workshop of maritime unions in September 2000 to discuss appointing an ITF Inspector. In April 2001 Tony Ayton was seconded to become Ireland's first Inspector. He and his successor, Ken Fleming, won more than $1.1 million in unpaid wages for crews berthing in Irish ports. The scrapping of an EU directive aimed at deregulating port services throughout Europe was rejected by the European Parliament and welcomed as a victory for union opposition, particularly SIPTU's ITF liaison. On 18 June 2008 in Stockholm an ITF Flags of Convenience Conference, representing 654 affiliates and 4½ million workers in 148 countries, congratulated SIPTU on its success in combating the abuse of seamen and maintaining a campaign on flags of convenience and ports of convenience.[34]

SIPTU maintained numerous international connections, formal and informal. In 2002 firefighters raised €275,000 for dependants of their New York colleagues who lost their lives in the attack on the World Trade Center on 11 September 2001. The money was presented by Brian Murray and John Moody, members of the National Full-Time Fire Fighters Committee, to Kevin Gallagher, President of the Uniformed Association of Fire Fighters, and Jack Ginty of the Uniformed Officers' Association before an Ireland-United States football international at Lansdowne Road, Dublin.

Solidarity was offered to Palestinian firefighters, and SIPTU participated in a Palestine Awareness Week with ITUT, producing 'Boycott Israeli Goods' badges. In 2003 SIPTU joined mass protests against the Iraq War, condemning the American invasion as a breach of international law. SIPTU affiliated to the Irish Anti-War Movement, and Des Geraghty addressed the huge rally of 15 February.

SIPTU was an official partner for the 2003 Special Olympics. Many Branches engaged in support activities, providing volunteers. A cheque for €10,345 was presented to Rita Lawlor of the Hotels, Restaurants and Catering Branch, a former Special Olympian, Global Messenger for the Games and joint presenter of RTÉ's nightly coverage. Solidarity was ever ready for victims of such disasters as Chernobyl, the 2004 tsunami and the Pakistani earthquake. SIPTU donated €250,000 to the ICTU tsunami Appeal.

In June 2005 Liberty Hall displayed huge banners declaring *Make poverty history,* insisting that the Government meet its target of 0.7% of GNP on overseas development aid. In 2006 SIPTU expressed concerns for the Rossport Five, with the licensing terms for the Corrib pipeline being questioned by Pádraig Campbell, SIPTU National Offshore Committee. In December a co-operation Agreement was signed with the Polish union Solidarność.[35]

THE ECONOMY AND EUROPE

Despite the booming economy, 2000 saw 1,343 jobs lost in Fruit of the Loom, Co. Donegal, and in Dundalk Guinness's Macardle Moore packaging plant, Hawkesbay Sportswear and MKIR Panasonic, where 260 jobs were lost. Manufacturing jobs were migrating to North Africa, eastern Europe and Asia, where labour costs were lower. Growth in GNP was a 'heady 10.4%' but slowed to 5% in 2001, most notably after the New York bombings. In 2002 SIPTU thought the Celtic Tiger was finally running out of steam, a slowdown inducing warning shivers. Briefing sessions were held to advise members about the changeover to the euro.

SIPTU urged members to vote 'Yes' in the referendum on the Treaty of Nice. Despite some reservations, it wanted to express solidarity with workers applying for membership of an enlarged European Union, more extensive social measures and legal force to a Charter of Fundamental Rights. An Irish 'No' vote halted the process of enlargement. *Liberty* published 'for' and 'against' articles and attempted to encourage understanding and debate.

In 2005 SIPTU published *The Frankenstein Directive,* a guide to the dangers of the EU Services Directive (Bolkestein Directive). Seminars were held in January 2006, and Jack O'Connor led a Delegation to attend demonstrations organised by the European Trade Union Confederation outside the European Parliament in

Strasbourg. In November the modified Services Directive showed much improvement, and the Bolkestein proposals were buried. SIPTU would pay careful attention to the transposition of the directive into Irish law.

On 30 May 2008 the NEC recommended support for the Treaty of Lisbon 'if the Government here commits [itself] to legislation for an entitlement to the benefits of proper Collective Bargaining,' so that 'workers in Ireland would have the benefit of one of the key "balancing" elements which will apply to virtually every other citizen in Europe if the Treaty is ratified.' The NEC would not 'support a "watered down" version' of the treaty that would expose workers to the 'free-market aspects' while being denied the 'balancing protection of real collective bargaining.' After the rejection of the treaty by the Irish people, SIPTU maintained its campaign for implementation of the 'Social Progress' Protocol.[36]

SOCIAL WELFARE, HEALTH AND PENSIONS

Alterations in adult dependants' allowances were announced in December 1999, resulting from SIPTU pressure, especially from the Women Workers' Branch. Actors' Equity failed to persuade the Minister that the unique employment circumstances of actors justified special treatment. The Government's failure to index the income thresholds at which 4% PRSI and 2% health levies became payable was an increasing concern. This 'devalued' SIPTU's achievement of December 1999 (which had in effect forced the Government to rewrite the 2000 Budget and give lower-paid workers an extra £5 per week, on average, as a precondition for entering negotiations on the Programme for Prosperity and Fairness), but it also wiped out the value of the special 2% payable under the Agreement in April 2001 for thousands just below those thresholds, which remained at £226 for PRSI and £280 for the health levy. In 2000 SIPTU put 'its money where its mouth is' by providing land in Townsend Street, Dublin, to the National Association of Building Co-operatives for sixteen apartments. Geraghty called for a Housing Forum under the Programme for Prosperity and Fairness.

The Pensions (Amendment) Act (2001) established the National Pensions Reserve Fund and the appointment of seven Commissioners. SIPTU contributed to the 1998 report of the Pensions Board and criticised Charlie McCreevy's choice of Commissioners, six men and one woman 'made up mostly of Irish and international bankers and businessmen and no serving trade unionist.' It was another slight to social partnership. The fact that, 'between them, two Commissioners, through their companies, owned about one-third of the Irish stock market,' and the Chairperson's company was in 'considerable difficulty' by the end of the year, 'did nothing to diminish' the union's concerns. SIPTU cautioned members against the trend whereby employers altered pension schemes from defined-benefit schemes, where payments were guaranteed, to defined-contribution schemes, where the level of payment was at the mercy of financial markets. A Pensions Advisory Service, co-ordinated through ITUT, was provided to members. Pension Trustees were urged to oppose the new accounts standard FRS 17, with accountancy bodies and the pensions industry, as it threatened the independent status of pension scheme accounts, created an inappropriate link with the financial affairs of individual companies and drove employees towards defined-contribution schemes and away from defined-benefit ones. O'Connor saw the report of the Public Service Pensions Commission as a 'mixed bag', welcoming the retention of defined-benefit pension schemes, better AVC flexibility, the extension of coverage to atypical workers, and statutory guarantee of post-retirement pension increases. He strongly endorsed the minority report drawn up by the Commission's trade union members. A special SIPTU Personal Retirement Savings Account was launched to assist members for whom occupational pension schemes were not feasible. When PRSA schemes came on stream in 2003 SIPTU members were ahead of things. Major improvements in the construction industry pension scheme were won in November, although union pressure was maintained against construction pension fraud.

In 2004 SIPTU launched a national pensions initiative. O'Connor called for a system of mandatory contributions to occupational pension schemes by employers if the Government's voluntary approach did not achieve the target of 70% pension coverage by 2006. He also asked the state to open pension accounts for all children born after 1 January 2005. Liberty Hall displayed a huge banner, *A good pension is essential . . . Don't leave work without one!* The long-standing campaign to improve pensions for low-paid public-service workers bore fruit in April with improvements in access, payments and scope. Lengthy negotiations were led by Brendan Hayes (Regional Secretary), Matt Merrigan (National Industrial Secretary) and Rosheen Callender (Equality Secretary). The Pensions Board began a review of non-compliance within the construction industry pension scheme after continuous representation by SIPTU.

In September the Government announced the main recommendations of the Commission on Public Service Pensions: cost-neutral early retirement; integration formula and integration *pro rata*; access by teachers to a revised spouses' and children's scheme; notional added years; the reckoning of allowances for pension purposes; and compound interest rates. SIPTU welcomed the moves, not least for their contribution to the 'pensions climate'. The Public Services Superannuation Act (2004) and the Social Welfare Act (2004) extended the non-gender equality grounds into those areas, but 'no real legislative progress' of the kind sought by SIPTU in the pensions area was achieved. The Social Welfare and Pensions Act (2005) amended previous acts and implemented the EU IORPS (Institutions for Occupational Retirement Pensions) Directive in the activities and supervision of such pensions. The recommendations of the Pension Board on National Pensions Strategy were effectually ignored in the Budget. Further progress on pensions was provided within Towards 2016.[37]

LABOUR STANDARDS

In 2001 SIPTU welcomed the Carers' Leave Act, the Pensions (Amendment) Act and the Protection of Employees (Part-Time Work) Act. All had been sought by SIPTU.

In September a campaign for improving statutory redundancy payments was launched, specific amendments being drafted by the SIPTU Labour Law Monitoring Group. A national day of protest was held on 4 October 2002, with demonstrations in Dublin, Cork, Limerick, Waterford, Galway, Cavan, Roscommon and other towns, attracting thousands and placing the issue high on the agenda following the Programme for Prosperity and Fairness. Changes came on 25 May 2003, providing for the payment of a lump sum based on two years for every year of service, irrespective of age, plus one week. The Trade Union Federation's *Guide to Labour Law for Union Representatives* followed, an acclaimed 253-page compilation of statutory entitlements. In 2004 SIPTU won two significant cases in Dunne's Stores, Cavan and Letterkenny, and for contract cleaners through the JLC under the Protection of Employees (Part-Time Work) Act (2001). The union called for resistance to the 'race to the bottom', making the protection and extension of employment rights central to talks for a new pay Agreement in May.[38]

O'Connor demanded a new 'Department of Labour' in March 2005. The absence of a focused Department enabled greater levels of exploitation and corruption. A strengthened Labour Inspectorate was urgently required. When, without consultation, the Government decided to open the economy to the citizens of EU accession states there were concerns about the absence of adequate inspection and enforcement safeguards to prevent their exploitation. The Gama and Salvacion Ogre cases underlined these fears. Research by the union showed how ineffective labour inspection was and how inadequate the deterrents were. SIPTU demanded a substantial increase in the number of Inspectors to seventy-five, proper legal and professional support for the Inspectorate, statutory links with the trade union movement through a liaison body and significantly increased penalties. Almost immediately eleven Inspectors were added, to bring the total to thirty-two. The bludgeoning of workers' rights by Irish Ferries rallied public opinion that a 'threshold of decency' should not be crossed; SIPTU insisted that it be addressed before proceeding with an Agreement to succeed Sustaining Progress.

Under 'Towards 2016', approved in September 2006, a new statutory Office of the Director of Employment Rights Compliance was established, with an increase in the Labour Inspectorate from thirty-one to ninety.[39] Michael Halpenny and Tom O'Driscoll were appointed to a new SIPTU Legal Rights Unit in 2008.

SAFETY AND HEALTH

The Construction Safety Partnership Plan was launched in 2000, involving Congress, the Construction Industry Federation, the Health and Safety Authority, FÁS, the Department of Finance, the Department of the Environment and Local Government and the Department of Enterprise, Trade and Employment. The plan established the 'Safepass' scheme, and it was hoped that all building workers would acquire a Safepass identity card. Sylvester Cronin, Eric Fleming and Andrew McGuinness of SIPTU were members of the Construction Safety Partnership Plan.

SIPTU strongly criticised the second report of the Special Working Group on Personal Injury Compensation, not least for its detachment of compensation from cause. A primary objective was to reduce the compensation costs. Sylvester Cronin, SIPTU Health and Safety Adviser, argued that this would disproportionately benefit negligent employers who did little to improve their accident prevention. Work-place accidents cost the economy more than £2 billion a year, but the cost of insurance was only 3% of this. Focusing on these costs addressed only the tip of the iceberg. A holistic approach, with accident prevention at its core, was needed. The Personal Injuries Assessment Board was criticised for favouring employers, not least by the apparent exclusion of direct union involvement. 'Such an arrangement would be patently unfair and indeed would load the dice against the injured worker.'

The Task Force on the Prevention of Workplace Bullying reported in 2001. Eschewing a legislative approach, an Advisory Committee of the Health and Safety Authority drew up codes of practice and a Dignity at Work Charter, all launched in March 2002. SIPTU's Anti-Bullying and Harassment Unit published three documents in 2004, the product of extensive surveys of industrial Officials' experience: 'Operational Instructions', 'SIPTU Guidelines', and 'Guidelines for Conducting an Investigation of Bullying in the Workplace'. In addition, a diploma in mediation skills was offered to members of the staff through SIPTU College. Approximately 1.4 million working days were lost in 2003 through accidents and ill health; the comparative figure for strikes was 37,482. If the media and employers gave the same attention to work-place safety and health as they did to the disappearing phenomenon of strikes, more progress would be made in eliminating hazards. An average of fifty-eight people were killed at work each year; to this figure could be added more than 300 deaths stemming from exposure to carcinogens in the work-place and those of victims of heart disease, stress and work-related road accidents. SIPTU demanded an appropriate Government response.

Thousands of building workers were obliged to make a 'dignified protest' in Dublin against inaction by employers and the HSA, which contributed to twenty-two work-place deaths. SIPTU's slogan was 'Safe sites—not death traps.'

Matters worsened in 2003. A cautious welcome was given to the Safety, Health and Welfare at Work Bill (2004). Eric Fleming pointed out that the HSA would have extra work but no extra resources. Fatalities and accident rates in 2005 demonstrated the growing vulnerability of foreign workers. SIPTU's Safety Representatives Network examined the Safety, Health and Welfare at Work Act (2005), making submissions to the Minister and, through SIPTU College, providing briefings. Regional seminars were held in 2006, supporting the Safety Network. Tying in with 'SIPTU, the Organising Union', workers were reminded that 'Organised workplaces are safer workplaces!' A poster campaign marked a 'safety check-up' for safety representatives under the slogan 'Safe working: it's no more than we bargain for—no less than we deserve.'

The tragic deaths in Bray of two SIPTU firefighters, Brian Murray and Mark O'Shaughnessy, led to demands for an independent inquiry in an Emergency Motion at the biennial Delegate Conference.[40]

SIPTU COLLEGE

SIPTU's Basic English Scheme, run in association with the National Adult Literacy Association, resulted in NCVA certificates in communications for participants in 2000. SIPTU College published guides on 'Negotiating European Works Councils' and 'Introducing Annualised Hours'. Employment-based training expanded further in 2001, together with a Conference on 'Public Ownership versus Privatisation' in November. 'English as a Second Language' was addressed, with the assistance of ITUT, in Beaumont Hospital, and the Basic English Scheme was availed of by numerous immigrants. SIPTU College's web site was launched in October 2004, a novel feature being access for primary and second-level teachers to resources for teaching pupils about the world of work. The web designer was Pat Coughlan, a tutor.

In 2005, in line with the Working Group on Shop Steward Development, SIPTU College introduced a programme of 'sequential training': step 1, introduction, to be given at the work-place or Branch level by lay tutors; step 2, basic five-day courses for Shop Stewards and activists on organisation and recruitment and health and safety; step 3, intermediary and advanced five-day courses; and step 4, advanced Shop Stewards' training, leading to a HETAC certificate in the law and practice of Irish industrial relations. Full FETAC accreditation was provided for a certificate in union skills.

Norman Croke succeeded Martin Naughton as Head of SIPTU College. Imparting organising skills became central to the college's activities in 2006. Thirty-nine lay tutors were trained to assist in providing best organising practice. The 'SKILL' project provided educational grants for health service support staffs, at the second and third levels, and resulted from initiatives by SIPTU. 'IDEAS' (Institute for the Development of Employees' Advancement Services), established in February 2001, engaged in providing Safepass and customised employment-based training, catering for 2,500 students in 2005. Matt Merrigan, National Industrial Secretary, initiated 'WIELD' (Workplace Initiative for Employee Learning and Development), which would train 1,700 workers, 500 of them SIPTU members, by 2006.[41] In 2009 the first Officials received the HETAC Certificate in Labour Law.

COMMUNICATIONS

Newsline's last issue was in February 2001. From April a 'News on Line' service featured on the web site. *SIPTU Report* continued in printed form. In January 2002 *Liberty*, now a two-monthly newspaper, met members' insistence on a printed journal. In 2006 SIPTU adopted Solidatas, a membership recording and information system developed by Miller Technology, linked most offices to broadband, equipped members of the staff with laptop computers, and updated www.siptu.ie.[42] In May 2008 Barbara Kelly, stalwart Public Relations Official, retired, and Séamus Shiels, trojan Publications and Public Relations Officer, left the union. Their service was marked by diligence, innovative application and outstanding dedication.

HERITAGE

The erection of a monument to John Doherty in Buncrana realised the ambition of the local historian Séamus 'Shirts' Doherty, Bridie Burns (Trustee), Maisie Grant and Francis Devine. Weekend events honoured Doherty, factory reformer, radical trade unionist and people's advocate. Manus O'Riordan's *Liberty Hall as a Cultural Centre: The Early Years* traced its artistic contribution as the Taoiseach, Bertie Ahern, opened Liberty Hall Centre for the Performing Arts.

In 2002 an international Conference on 'The State of the Performing Artists and Their Role in the Life of the Nation' took place in Liberty Hall to celebrate the fiftieth anniversary of Irish Actors' Equity. *Larkin,* 'a dramatic new musical,' was presented by the musical workshop DAYMS in a successful representation of Big Jim. The weekly Clé Club, a folk session, opened in October with Al O'Donnell.

In 2003 Irish Actors' Equity, the Film and Broadcasting Branch and the Musicians' Union of Ireland led opposition to the ending of Section 481 tax relief for the film industry. More than 4,000 jobs in film production and 3,000 in transport, catering and tourism were in jeopardy. The scheme was not a tax avoidance scheme for the wealthy but an attraction for vital foreign investment. The 2004 Budget continued the relief until 2008.

In 2003 the Irish National Painters' and Decorators' Group hosted the Robert Tressell Festival, and there were events commemorating the 1913 Lock-Out. Jer O'Leary was Larkin at a Bloody Sunday re-enactment in Beresford Place. Conference Delegates in Galway were raised to their feet by a presentation of their 1913 heritage and an address by James Larkin 'Jack' Jones, veteran International Brigader and General Secretary of the Transport and General Workers' Union. In association with Dún Laoghaire Heritage Project a headstone was erected over the grave of James Byrne, Branch Secretary and a neglected 1913 martyr, in Dean's Grange. A striking portrait of Seán O'Casey by Michael Kane was unveiled in Liberty Hall.

In 2005 Donal Nevin's masterly *James Connolly: A Full Life* was published by Gill & Macmillan in association with SIPTU. In 2007 the union made a significant financial contribution to *Connolly—The Movie* and funded Nevin's *Between Comrades,* Connolly's correspondence. A series of SIPTU events in Belfast and Dublin commemorated the 1907 Belfast dockers' and carters' strike, most permanently by republishing John Gray's classic, *City in Revolt.*[43]

IRISH TRADE UNION TRUST

ITUT's Outreach Service was availed of by 1,325 members in 1997, by 1,401 in 1998, by 1,982 in 1999 and by 1,319 in 2000, indications of economic disasters amid unprecedented boom. ITUT's Redundancy Information Guide and Retirement Guide was updated annually. The Declaration of Older Persons' Rights for the New Millennium was drafted by the National Association of Widows and the People's College, both led by the SIPTU stalwart Sheila Conroy, and endorsed by the union. In 2002 the Equality Unit and the Dublin Health Services Branch examined equality issues in ten hospitals.

In 2003 the Jim Larkin Credit Union, set up in 1963 by the WUI, was accommodated in Liberty Hall. The Retired Members' Section campaigned for travel concessions on Luas trams in Dublin and issued a quarterly newsletter, *Watchword*. Through ITUT, SIPTU pressured the Government to honour its commitment to the 3% quota for the employment of disabled workers in the public service. The proceedings of the National Disability Conference, held in October 1999, were published as *Getting It Right* in March 2000. Terry Bryan (Waterford) produced *Disability: A Trade Union Challenge,* showing that disabled people still found employment hard to obtain, despite the boom. The EU Council of Ministers adopted a Directive on Non-Discrimination in Employment and Occupation; and, assisted by the Inter-national Labour Organisation, SIPTU completed a Code of Practice on Managing Disability in the Workplace. The Disability Act (2005) was welcomed, but SIPTU saw more potential in the statutory codes of practice. In July SIPTU supported the demand of Congress for an extra €3.4 billion to be spent on a care strategy for children, the disabled and the elderly. In 2006 SIPTU launched a strategy document on caring for older people at the Health Forum of the Retired Members' Section.[44]

STAFF AND PREMISES

In 2000 the Dan Shaw Centre in Navan was disposed of, with a commitment to rebuilding within the site. In 2001 staff development training took place on equality enforcement, media skills and Labour Court, Labour Relations Commission and Employment Appeals Tribunal practice. The renovation of Liberty Hall's auditorium began. The theatre had 400 seats and the most up-to-date lighting and sound facilities, while the Connolly Hall had eighty seats seats and the Larkin Hall 180. A new bar facility, Cois Life, opened. In 2004 the old Painters' and Decorators' Union premises in Aungier Street, Dublin, were sold and the new Dan Shaw Centre in Navan opened. Rooms dedicated to Francis Ledwidge had beautiful satinised glass panels, designed by Susan Campbell, depicting him as labour agitator, poet and soldier. The auditorium and leisure centre in Connolly Hall were leased to the Cork School of Music for twenty-five years until a new college is built.

Table 153: SIPTU staff salaries and industrial Conferences, 2000–2007

	Staff salaries (€)	As proportion of expenditure (%)	Meetings and Conferences (€)
2000	12,985,969	63.9	733,474
2001	17,339,282	65.6	1,031,695
2002	18,015,719	63.7	1,059,572
2003	18,750,638	63.1	1,365,915
2004	19,708,109	59.6	1,222,425
2005	20,370,509	61.4	1,403,044
2006	22,517,709	63.7	1,060,809
2007	23,034,410	65.1	1,278,723

Source: SIPTU, Annual Reports, 1990–2007.

SIPTU had a full-time staff of 325 in 2006: 3 National Executive Officers, 17 Regional and National Industrial Secretaries or Department Heads, 20 Sectoral Organisers, 76 Branch Organisers, tutors, researchers and industrial engineers, 90 Assistant Branch Organisers and Personal Secretaries, 6 location-based Organisers, 166 administrative and clerical workers, and 17 porters and cleaners. SIPTU was a significant employer in its own right, contributing to national and local economies. Reflecting change, the priority of all members of the industrial staff was reflected in their title of Organiser.[45]

LIBERTY HALL

In 2005 the NEC began a consultative process regarding Liberty Hall. The options were to carry out a minimum or a major refit of the building, to move to the Docklands or Dublin West, or to demolish and rebuild on the 'oul spot by the river.' In November 2006 the NEC approved demolition and replacement at Beresford Place. For O'Flynn, the new building would be a 'milestone rather than a millstone,' a 'tremendous resource for the Union, rather than a liability.' Structural, safety and environmental issues had arisen with Liberty Hall as building regulations, design and demand moved on from 1964, when the new Liberty Hall rose so challengingly from the Liffey banks. It became a symbol of working-class confidence and permanence. SIPTU is determined to demonstrate that same confidence in an equally iconic structure.

The Dublin Region published a pamphlet to commemorate the role of Liberty Hall in the 1916 Rising as part of the ninetieth anniversary. O'Connor unveiled a plaque commemorating that role, and City Pavements Pageants Collective re-enacted the march from Liberty Hall to the GPO. In November 2007 Gilroy McMahon, famous for their design of the Croke Park stadium, won the competition to be architects for the Liberty Hall project.[46]

POLITICS

The 2002 General Election was used by SIPTU to publicise the health crisis. Members were urged: 'The Government has squandered the fruits of the boom: Ireland needs LEADERSHIP FOR A CHANGE: VOTE LABOUR.' The National Women's Committee invited all parties to a public meeting in Wynn's Hotel, Dublin, to answer questions of concern to women and trade unionists. The responses were published in *Liberty*, with each Labour Party candidate profiled. The Progressive Democrats did not bother to attend.

After the election SIPTU published details about how the Fianna Fáil-PD Coalition had measured up on its commitments regarding the health service. It made for disappointing, if predictable, reading.[47]

A Political Fund Commission was established in 2002, chaired by the former General Secretary John McDonnell, to 'consider the use of the Union's Political Fund' and to develop an overall political agenda. Under the Rules, members contributed 63 cents a year to the Political Fund. While a portion went on affiliation to the Labour Party, an increasing proportion financed campaigns such as those on the health service and improving redundancy payments.

After nationwide consultations, the 2003 Conference supported the Commission's recommendations that affiliation to the Labour Party should continue. Future union candidates would have to sign a 'charter of values' or risk losing financial support. A Political Liaison Committee, chaired by the General Secretary, was approved, rather than a full-time Political Liaison Officer. Grants to candidates other than those of the Labour Party who were prepared to sign the charter of values were not dismissed as a possibility.

A former ITGWU Official, Pat Rabbitte, succeeded Ruairí Quinn as Leader of the Labour Party after the disappointing General Election performance. SIPTU fully supported his aim of 're-energising Labour.'[48]

In 2004 more than sixty members stood for the Labour Party in local elections, all profiled in *Liberty* with the Labour Party's four European Parliament candidates. Liberty Project was launched by SIPTU and the Labour Party in 2005 to celebrate labour in Irish history, particularly around Easter Week. Activities in April included the launch of a Larkin Family Photographic Archive CD. In 2007 SIPTU members were urged to 'make your vote count.'

SIPTU was happy that the Iraq War was an election issue and published the following pledge:

> We, the undersigned, give a firm commitment that, if elected, we will not partic-
> ipate in any Government that allows Shannon Airport or other Irish facilities to
> be used by the United States to conduct war in Iraq or any other imperialist war.

A special General Election issue of *Liberty* in May urged members: 'Don't trust to luck: use your vote . . . for fairness at work and justice in society.' Party views were analysed on workers' rights, health, education and work-place learning, tax equity, child care, occupational pensions and older people, waste and water, global warming and energy, and transport. Once again, many workers voted for the enemy.

Another former ITGWU Official, Éamonn Gilmore, succeeded Rabbitte as Leader of the Labour Party on 6 September 2007.[49]

A NEW WORKING WOMEN'S CHARTER OF RIGHTS FOR THE TWENTY FIRST CENTURY

To celebrate and mark International Women's Day, 2001, SIPTU's Equality Unit has updated the Working Women's Charter which was produced by women in the ITGWU in 1975 and adopted by the ICTU in 1976. This new Charter of Rights looks 'beyond equality' to a better quality of life, both inside and outside every workplace, for every worker, irrespective of age, sex, race, religion, disability or other personal characteristics. A summary of the points below is shown overleaf.

NOT ONLY EQUALITY, BUT QUALITY TOO

- Equal enjoyment of fundamental social, economic and human rights by everyone—irrespective of age, disability, ethnic origin, race or religion; sex, marital status, family status, sexual orientation, or political opinion; membership of the traveller community or of a trade union.
- These fundamental rights to include equal access to basic necessities such as housing, healthcare and education at all levels; equal access to all forms of employment; positive action to facilitate equal labour market participation by under-represented groups; paid educational leave for workers, more in-service training and a national system of life-long learning accessible to all.
- Equal (gross) pay and a higher National Minimum Wage; no discrimination in relation to fringe benefits and other conditions of employment.
- Equal treatment in relation to take-home pay; and an adequate guaranteed individual income for all citizens, whether at work, at home or in retirement, through a fairer and more integrated system of taxes and transfers, geared to improving the position of lower-paid workers and others on low incomes.
- The right to work—in conditions that are conducive to achieving an appropriate work-life balance at all stages of the life-cycle, including flexible working hours and a standard 30-hour week for all.
- The right to work—in a safe and healthy working environment free from all forms of physical and psychological hazard including stress, bullying, intimidation and harassment; with the provision of childcare and other 'family-friendly' facilities; the lengthening of paid maternity leave; and the introduction of paid paternity and parental leave.
- The right to stop work—temporarily—to have children and/or care for dependants, or for other reasons—without loss of an independent income or social insurance and pension rights; and full legislative protection for all non-full-time workers with regard to holidays, leave, PRSI, pensions etc.
- The right to stop work—permanently—and to retire on an individual income capable of ensuring dignity, self-sufficiency and independence in old age; and the facility to finance this, with Exchequer and/or employer support, from an early age to ensure adequacy.
- A modernised system of social protection that supports all citizens, whether on a short-term or long-term basis, in a manner which both guarantees income adequacy during absence from the workforce and facilitates and encourages take-up of appropriate employment.
- Equal decision-making rights in the workplace, the boardroom, the pension Trustee Board and other bodies; as well as in the legislature, judiciary and Executive of the state.
- Enjoyment of multi-culturalism and diversity in the workplace and society generally; and international solidarity with, and active support for, disadvantaged workers world-wide, including the many millions of men, women and

children suffering the indignity and even torture of human trafficking, bonded labour and other modern-day versions of slavery.

NOT ONLY EQUALITY, BUT QUALITY TOO

In this year of 2001, SIPTU pledges itself to work for the social and economic liberation of all workers irrespective of sex, age, race, religion, disability, marital status, family status, sexual orientation, political opinion, membership of the traveller community—or of a trade union . . .

Our ten key objectives can be summarised as below, with further elaboration of each point overleaf:

1. Fundamental social, economic and human rights for all—to include equal access to education, employment and the necessities of life in the 21st century;
2. Equal pay and conditions and a higher minimum wage;
3. Equal treatment as regards take-home pay; and an adequate guaranteed individual income for all;
4. The right to work flexible and family-friendly hours; and a standard 30-hour week for all workers;
5. The right to work in a safe, healthy environment, free from all forms of physical and psychological hazard; with the provision of such essential facilities as high-quality, affordable childcare;
6. The right to stop work, temporarily, for caring or other reasons, and not be punished through loss of promotion, pension, PRSI or other rights;
7. The right to stop work permanently, on an individual retirement income capable of ensuring dignity, self-sufficiency and independence in old age;
8. A modernised social protection system that is genuinely worker-friendly and family-friendly;
9. Equal representation and decision-making rights on all work-related bodies such as company and pension Trustee boards; and in the legislature, judiciary and Executive of the state;
10. Promotion of multi-culturalism and diversity in all parts of Irish society; solidarity with, and support for, disadvantaged workers world-wide.

Chapter 37 ~

| FORWARD

THE UNION IN IRISH HISTORY

From the moment of its creation, the union understood that its purpose was historic. It transformed a supine labour movement, embracing Socialism and national self-determination. Almost immediately it became central to the national consciousness, winning international recognition and respect. It is associated in the public imagination with Larkin and Connolly, 1913, the Irish Citizen Army, and the printing of the 1916 Proclamation. Liberty Hall became the symbol of workers' struggle and achievement. The union's deeds and personalities inspired writers from O'Casey to Plunkett and artists from Orpen to Ballagh. Few unions can have had such a tempestuous first fifteen years.

Geographical and membership growth after 1916 was staggering, reaching a peak at 130,000 in 1922. Members were attracted by the ability of the ITGWU to raise wages and improve conditions and its identification with the national and land movements. Organisation and Organisers pursued the Workers' Republic, providing leadership to the spontaneous influx.

From 1924, however, the ITGWU suffered a decline. Wages were savagely cut by employers and the Government. Larkin's return from America resulted in a split and the formation of the WUI. Left criticism suggests failed opportunities after 1917 to foment Socialist revolution, but forces beyond the ITGWU were part of the complex reasons why those who fought most keenly for an independent Irish state were disinherited by it after it was partially achieved. Internal dissension diminished the union and labour movement, already reeling under the burdens of mass unemployment and depression. Survival rather than syndicalist ambition became the imperative.

In 1932 the ITGWU's membership was 14,125, the WUI's 16,780. By 1939 the WUI was standing still, but the ITGWU was back to its 1923 strength, without the abandoned farm labourers. O'Brien and Foran had steered the ITGWU back to calmer waters. Ambitions receded. The union's priority was defending members' living standards and lobbying for employment rights, rather than the Workers' Republic.

The ITGWU's £50,000 interest-free loan to the Government in 1940 is seen either as a magnanimous gesture motivated by concern for the national economic well-being or, as many suggested, a *quid pro quo* for Fianna Fáil's complicity in assisting

O'Brien's attempt to achieve 'One Big Union' by statute. Larkin enjoyed an Indian summer as a street agitator, leading opposition to the Wages Standstill Orders and raising workers' political awareness. O'Brien's reaction to Larkin's admission to the Labour Party and the participation of the ITUC in the World Congress split the movement industrially and politically, the ITGWU creating the Congress of Irish Unions and the National Labour Party. On O'Brien's retirement in 1946 and Larkin's death in 1947 their final legacy was manifest in complete organisational division. The ITGWU had nonetheless raised wages beyond the Tribunal system limits, and grew during the war. The WUI declined to 8,000 members.

After the war, service increasingly supplanted organisation in union strategy, dominated by Catholic social teaching. Voluntary wage constraint was offered to unresponsive state and employers as Ireland missed the boat of European economic reconstruction and growth. Young Jim Larkin and John Conroy were central to moves towards unity, finally achieved with the creation of the ICTU in 1959. The union split might have healed after 1966 but for their deaths. The ITGWU had grown to 150,000 while the WUI hovered around 30,000.

Insistent union demands for economic planning, the development of natural resources and state enterprise, and improvements in education, health, housing and social welfare slowly penetrated political agendas, despite the reluctance of workers to vote for policies they readily adopted as trade unionists. 'Industrialisation' through transnational branch plants brought significant increases in membership. 'Check-off' generated security of union income but distanced members, further alienated by centralised bargaining and the tribunal-isation of grievances. Social factors diminished class consciousness and voluntarist commitment. Exchanging wage restraint for advances on wider economic and social agendas began with the National Understanding of 1979 and, after the employers' offensive of 1981–7, the birth of what became social partnership with the Programme for National Recovery in 1987. The union was a central dynamic for these policies. The 'Celtic Tiger' brought unprecedented growth in employment and incomes but raised questions of social exclusion. Union membership, although numerically higher than ever, declined in density after 1990, diminishing bargaining power in the eyes of the Government and employers. SIPTU's response was to transform itself from 'service' to 'organising union', a return to Larkin and Connolly's instinctive organising model.

HIDDEN FROM HISTORY

Contemporary society appreciates SIPTU's contribution to social partnership, to defending the 'threshold of decency.' Yet the overwhelming amount of union activity remains hidden, unrecorded in annual or Conference reports, Executive minutes or journals. Hundreds of thousands of work-place claims, conducted by Shop Stewards, Section Committees and Officials, advance wages and conditions, improve health and safety, resist bullying and discrimination, defend procedures or secure individual grievances, almost all without resort to industrial action or referral to third parties. This daily grind is the essence of representation, the cutting edge of recognition. It is almost completely unacknowledged, even by those directly benefiting from activity on their behalf. Within this mundane grind, extraordinary self-development takes place. Activists acquire social skills, representational and bargaining techniques, public speaking and report-writing expertise, and enhanced self-esteem. For 'ordinary' men and women who began the union—'unskilled' labourers with little formal education—self-development was crucial. Nowadays, many members have graduate and postgraduate qualifications but still acquire social training from their union involvement. Their contribution to community and society through and beyond their union activity—voluntary and unpaid—has been immeasurable.

UNION BENEFITS

What did the union achieve? No person alive on 4 January 1909 or born after that date has not benefited in some way from the union's existence—certainly within the Free State and Republic if not the entire country. The transfer of money wages from wealthier sections to poorer, improvements in social wage, demands for planned economic development, all ultimately benefited all of society. Sadly, most beneficiaries had and have no awareness that their improved living standard and quality of life resulted from union endeavours. A simple equation is to ask what the difference would be between a society with the union and one without. Under any heading, the left-hand column of that equation is in surplus. A challenge for 21st-century society is to realise how impoverished—probably literally so for thousands—society would be if the New Right have their way and trade unionism diminishes.

From Democratic Programme to social partnership, the union was central to progressive economic and social policy, not least in the absence of Socialist Government. Thousands who took to the streets in support of union policy—as in the PAYE protests of the late 1970s and early 80s—then voted for parties opposing their demands. It was to the unions that many then turned for defence. The 'Threshold of Decency' march during the Irish Ferries dispute was a case in point. Thousands lined the pavements applauding the protesters—a significant demonstration of true union recognition; yet right-wing Government persists.

Women, in demanding equal pay and equal treatment, forced the union to examine the roots of all discrimination. The Working Women's Charter, first drafted by the ITGWU in 1975, informed demands for the reform of patriarchal oppression well beyond the work-place. The union was a major dynamic for women's equality. More recently it has embraced diversity and championed the rights of other minorities: the aged, disabled, immigrants, lesbians and gays, Travellers, and youth.

UNION MYTHS

Trade unions—the ITGWU and SIPTU in particular—are subject to much criticism from within the movement, often being characterised as non-militant, undemocratic and bureaucratic. The data does not support such allegations. By 2007 the union had spent millions on Dispute Pay, an unparalleled outlay within Ireland. Union militancy and financial strength meant that the vast majority of claims were settled without recourse to strike. Indeed most members never experience industrial action. No national dispute levy was ever imposed, all claims being met from funds. The union's rates were the best in every industry in which it operated, often much higher than those of supposedly more militant unions. National Agreements were frequently rejected by members, at least as first proposed, after extensive briefing through Conference, Branch consultations, publication and explanation of offers, and national ballots. Once agreed by Congress, even without union consent, the maximum return was sought, and frequently terms better than those agreed were widely secured. The WUI and ITGWU both sought to expand bargaining beyond 'pure and simple' wages. National Understandings and social partnership were conceived and detailed on union drawing-boards.

Congress was the vehicle for national bargaining, though relations with Congress were occasionally strained. The WUI displayed greater commitment, perhaps as a counter to the ITGWU's size and influence. The ITGWU's success and drive produced hostile, not to say envious, attitudes. On occasion Liberty Hall had greater industrial and support services than a Congress limited by the movement's fragmentation. Its calls for rationalisation were distrusted as attempts to enforce OBU or to eject British organisation. SIPTU is the essence of the rationalisation vital if the organising model is to be embraced. Rather than snipe or begrudge, others would be better served by emulating the union's achievements for the benefit of all workers and the wider society.

Table 154: Dispute Pay, ITGWU, WUI (FWUI), and SIPTU, 1920–2007

	ITGWU	WUI/FWUI	SIPTU
1909–1917 (£)	200,000		
1918–1929 (£)	296,131	17,362	—
1930s (£)	61,466	21,279	—
1940s (£)	98,949	15,644	—
1950s (£)	235,375	83,726	—
1960s (£)	802,187	221,264	—
1970s (£)	2,101,094	416,694	—
1980s (£)	3,730,185	851,982	—
1990s (£)	—	—	2,491,288
2000–2007 (€)	—	—	2,290,808

Source: ITGWU, WUI, FWUI and SIPTU, Annual Reports, 1918–2007.

In addition to Dispute Pay, the union provided other direct cash benefits to members. Mortality Benefit allowed a dignified burial and provided relief at times of acute family distress. The range of benefits expanded throughout the union's history, including unquantifiable elements of education and training, industrial engineering, health and safety advice, scholarships and legal aid. For members, the union was always 'good value for money.'

Table 155: ITGWU benefit payments (£), 1918–89

	Mortality	Sickness and marriage	Retirement	Unemployment
1918–1930	36,981	—	—	—
1931–1940	13,058	—	—	—
1941–1950	20,549	—	—	—
1951–1960	41,704	890	1,829	—
1961–1970	93,342	20,838	31,363	48,770
1971–1980	237,592	233,228	88,483	313,001
1981–1989	289,226	1,137,551	47,560	326,999
Total	732,452	1,382,497	169,235	688,770
Average per year	10,316	43,203	5,641	31,308
Total expended in benefits, 1918–1989 £2,972,954				

Source: ITGWU, Annual Reports, 1918–1989.

The union was well managed. Unlike many national institutions, it has published fully audited accounts from its inception. This transparency is part of unique union democracy. All decisions on industrial action, changes of Rule, adoption of policy and election of officers are by ballot. Right down to the work-place level, members are consulted on issues affecting them and freely elect their own representatives. It is a democratic model rarely complimented by commentators or historians. It is the essence of good union management. Trade unionism is based on a collective view of society. When individualism, sectionalism or greed prevail, the union is asked to defend the exploited, seek legal reform or overturn Government cut-backs. Diminished density casts this ability in doubt. For anyone who recognises the value of the union's lobby within society their first duty, if not already unionised, is to join a trade union, even in an individual capacity.

RESERVATIONS
It has not all been a 'glorious march'. Liberty Hall is accused of allowing the 'revolutionary moment' from 1916 to 1923 to pass, consciously abandoning syndicalism and opting instead for the calmer waters of reformist economism. It was not that simple. The union's preoccupation, by rule and practice, was defending

members at the point of production. This, arguably, it did well, within the limits of trade union bargaining. However, the ITGWU's identification with 'Ireland' induced a sense of 'responsibility' towards the 'national interest'. Workers' interests were sacrificed to those of the state. Other interest groups—employers, farmers, capital generally—had and have no concern for the 'national interest'. What was the union, and the broader movement, to do? The Workers' Republic was achievable only with commitment from the masses. Was that ever truly present?

O'Brien in particular is accused of a compact with the Government, especially Fianna Fáil, to achieve 'One Big Union', the union's institutional interests apparently dominating organisational and class concerns, all masked by O'Brien's loathing of Larkin. The union's commitment to Ireland was reflected in its purchase of state and local authority securities, the employment of hundreds of Officials, and an investment in buildings. When Liberty Hall was rebuilt it was the largest civil engineering project in the country and a considerable statement of belief in an Irish economy apparently doomed by underinvestment and underdevelopment.

Workers' education was needed. The union, through its newspapers, from the *Irish Worker* to *Liberty* and *Unity*, promoted a consistent, Socialist message, but these publications were not always widely read. Workers' education schemes were infrequent—experiments such as the James Connolly Labour College and the Workers' Educational Institute notwithstanding. When the Liberty Study Group, the ITGWU Development Services Division and FWUI Central Education Committee revived matters from the 1960s the emphasis was on service, not organisation. The politicisation of members—although inherent in all union activity—was never given sufficient priority or adequately resourced.

Politically the union, as affiliate and supporter, was part of the Labour Party's failure to achieve power. Most members clearly never voted Labour. Few joined the Party. Some insisted that the union have no political affiliation, concentrating resources on traditional industrial activity and maintaining an independent bargaining position with the Government. With no apparent sense of contradiction, many arguing this were the first to demand action by the union against regressive policies imposed by right-wing parties that the same members had voted for. Political ambivalence was rife, in both the ITGWU and WUI, from the war until the late 1960s.

Union Rule Books, while allowing for political activity, impose restrictions. Unions are not political parties, but they could have done more to advance members' politicisation. Equally, few if any Labour Party leaders addressed the same weakness, seriously engaged with or made demands of the union. The union advised members on membership of the EEC—the WUI and ITGWU adopting opposite views—defending proportional representation, or on social issues such as contraception, divorce and abortion. There was clear unease at these moments, however. The union's political role itself became an issue, with some members too readily offended.

The union, from its origin, was 'Irish'. It always had an 'All-Ireland' membership. In reality, however, organisation in Northern Ireland was a rump, neglected and seldom considered. The republican Larkin never took the WUI there. Although occasionally focused by Stephen McGonagle or Paddy Devlin, strategic thinking was limited and spasmodic. 'Partitionist' consequences of the 1940s Congress and Labour Party splits emphasise the point. The union argued that British organisations should face the contradiction of adopting policies supportive of Irish self-determination at their 'national' Conferences while maintaining, even extending, their presence in Ireland.

'Partitionism' was not the sole preserve of the ITGWU. The Northern conflict saw the union make demands of the Irish and British Governments, but the agenda was political, not organisational, reactive rather than active. In the contexts of the Belfast Agreement and the SIPTU Commission a determined strategy for Northern Ireland is essential for developing Irish labour's maximum potential.

The union—the ITGWU and SIPTU particularly—always maintained an international viewpoint, through affiliation to such bodies as the International Transport Workers' Federation and countless acts of solidarity. In 1984–5 the sense of 'repaying the debt' of 1913 was a significant factor in generating huge financial and material aid for British miners. Efforts by the Women's Committee for Chernobyl victims have been outstanding. SIPTU is rightly considering how to further develop international action by forging alliances with sister unions. Globalisation necessitates greater international solidarity between workers.

UNSUNG HEROES

Leaders, naturally, make headlines and are recorded in any history. Conversely, thousands of 'unsung heroes' escape any record. If readers want to identify real union heroes and heroines they should examine images of strikers, mass demonstrations, women and children attending soup kitchens. Anonymous workers in Dublin and Cork factories and hotels, Munster farmsteads, Connacht meat plants, Ulster hospitals and docks and Leinster mines, bogs and mills joined, defended and advanced the union. They did so at the risk of being dismissed or locked out, evicted or starved, or having to emigrate. They did so because they fundamentally believed in collective action, in the right to dignity in the work-place, and that society should be marked by justice, equity, equality and fairness. Their collective, largely unrecorded commitment was the union's bricks and mortar.

Names can be randomly snatched from the stream. For the ITGWU: Charles J. Supple, courageous 1920s Secretary of the Athy Branch; Charles Ridgway, imprisoned hotel workers' leader; James Gilhooley, Arigna miner robbed of high office by an early death; John Kane, Dublin No. 2 Branch Secretary, widely regarded as 'the best officer we never had'; Fergal Costello, outstanding NEC member; straight-as-a-die Pat McKiernan, Cavan; May O'Brien, first Women's Officer; Carmel King, 'the union in Drogheda'; Tom O'Dwyer, renowned winner of hopeless cases; and rank-and-file stalwarts such as Pa Dunne (Dublin), Mary Burke (Clonmel), Maisie Grant (Buncrana), Albert Jackson (Belfast), Jack Doolan (Mullingar), Mel Sexton, (Longford), and Johnny Treacy (Waterford). For the WUI: Breda Kearns, stalwart

Secretary to the two Jim Larkins; Margaret McLoughlin, typist and Dublin Trades Council Delegate; the Dublin activists Billy Burke, Barney Conway, Paddy Duff, Stephen Edge, Kay Fallon Geraghty, Jack Harte, Thomas Kavanagh, Peter Purcell and Jim Quinn and such country stalwarts as Lal Daly and Vincent Wynter. For SIPTU: Philip Funchion, tireless Kilkenny Branch Secretary; Tony Ayton, ITF Inspector; Paul Smyth, Irish Ferries ships' officers and Oxigen Refuse Collectors; Ryanair baggage handlers; and members who fought for jobs in Peerless Rugs, Irish Glass Bottle, the health service and aviation. Not all were victorious but all were selfless, honourable, and courageous. All were unsung.

History may call on any of us to be the next to be unsung!

THE FUTURE

From its inception the union recognised its 'historic' purpose. That purpose had different yet ultimately identical expressions: Larkin's 'divine gospel of discontent'; Connolly's Workers' Republic; Young Jim's vision of union-run banks and building societies, co-operative enterprises, hospitals and rest homes, educational institutions and holiday camps; Jack O'Connor's determination to organise the future. However historic any union might be—and the ITGWU, WUI and SIPTU certainly were—it is essentially an organisation of present and future. Karl Marx observed that 'the philosophers have only *interpreted* the world, in various ways; the point, however, is to *change* it.' Just as the union's founders understood that their historic purpose was 'to change it', so today's and tomorrow's members must acquire that same appreciation. Reading union history should not just provide facts and figures but inform and inspire.

Union membership carries entitlements and obligations. In centenary year, members should commit themselves to becoming history-makers, to write the next chapters. If they do not successfully do so they will have betrayed their inheritance. It is a legacy of which each and every member can be proud. It is fragile and constantly under attack from the same forces that batoned people from the streets in 1913 and sought to starve them into submission. The only defence against that fragility is committed organisation and the belief that an injury to one is the concern of all.

The union's history must continue to be written by informed, intelligent opposition to self-interest, sectionalism and exploitation of the many by the few, within Ireland and internationally. Ennobled by others' past deeds, let today's and tomorrow's members maintain the same dignity and integrity in struggle.

Organise your own history.

APPENDIXES

Appendix 1 ~

RULES OF THE IRISH TRANSPORT AND GENERAL WORKERS' UNION, 1912

No copy of the original ITGWU Rules appears to have survived. C. Desmond Greaves published those registered on 10 October 1912, suggesting that 'from extracts of the first Rules kindly supplied to me by Professor Emmet Larkin it is quite clear that there is virtually no difference.' It seems appropriate to reproduce them here in their entirety, 'exactly as they appear in the original.'[1] The Rules, certainly during Larkin's time, were hardly applied.

Preface

Trade Unionism in Ireland has arrived at a certain stage of growth when this question confronts us—What is to be our next step in fostering its future development? Are we going to continue the policy of grafting ourselves on the English Trades Union movement, losing our own identity as a nation in the great world of organised labour? We say emphatically, No. Ireland has politically reached her manhood; industrially she is in swaddling clothes. And it is our purpose, come weal or woe, to cherish the infant with the milk of economic truth; clothe her in the school of experience; educate her in the solidarity of the workers of Ireland with their fellows the world over; in the hope that in the near future she may become sensible of her dignity and powerful enough to voice her own demands. The workers in Ireland must realise that society is changing rapidly, the capitalist class in Ireland is being reinforced by the influx of foreign capitalists, with their soulless, sordid, money-grubbing propensities. It behoves the Irish workers to realise the power of the employing class, who are not only well organised industrially but practically monopolise the political power in this country as they do in all other countries at present. The old system of sectional unionism amongst unskilled workers is practically useless for modern conditions (this also applies to the skilled workers). When you consider that there are at least 800,000 so called unskilled workers unorganised, surely it must be recognised that the necessity for such an organisation as this we invite you to enrol in is self-evident. The Irish Transport and General Workers' Union offer to you a medium whereby you may combine with your fellows to adjust wages and regulate hours and conditions of labour, wherever and whenever possible and desirable by negotiation, arbitration, or, if the conditions demand it, by withholding our labour until amelioration is granted. Further, we demand political recognition for the enforcement of our demands. Our immediate programme being a legal eight hours' day; provision of work for all unemployed, and pensions for all workers at 60 years of age; adult suffrage; nationalisation of canals, railways and means of transport; the land of Ireland for the people of Ireland. Our ultimate ideal: the realisation of an Industrial Commonwealth.

By the advocacy of such principles and the carrying out of such a policy, we believe we shall be ultimately enabled to obliterate poverty, and help to realise the glorious time spoken of and sung by the Thinkers, the Prophets, and the Poets, when all children, all women, and all men shall work and rejoice in the deeds of their hand, and thereby become entitled to the fullness of the earth and the abundance thereof.

RULES

Rule I—Name of Union and Registered Office
Irish Transport and General Workers' Union.

Rule II—Objects of the Union
The organisation is for the purpose of raising the standard of social life of the workers, and the raising of funds to provide for:—
(a) Dispute Pay in the case of Strike or Lock-out, or as the result of obeying the lawful demands of the Union at the rate of 10s. per week;
(b) Legal assistance for the purpose of enforcing the application of industrial laws and the recovery of wages;
(c) A Funeral Allowance for members;
   And generally to regulate the relations between employers and employed, to encourage co-operation and enterprise amongst its members.

Rule III—Who May Join
The Union shall consist of any number of persons, of not less than 16 years of age, who accept the principles and methods of the Union, and who are not eligible to join a skilled Trade Union; or skilled workmen who desire to help the Union may become members providing they show that they are members of their own Trade Union; or whenever any body of members believe that the interest of their occupation require special technical organisation such body may be affiliated upon accepting the principles of the Union and conforming to its Rules.

Rule IV—Entrance Fee
The Entrance Fee from any District or locality shall be fixed by the General Secretary and Executive in consultation with the local Branch, who may raise or lower the fee as they deem necessary for the betterment of the Union. Penny each shall be charged for contribution card and Rule Book, and 3d. for badge.

Rule V—Union Contributions
Clause A.—General Fund and Legal Assistance.—Section 1
Those who wish to provide for Dispute Pay, funeral, labour representation, and legal assistance, shall pay the sum of 4s. 8d. per quarter. Such payments to be made in the following manner:— 4d. per week and a quarterly levy of 4d.

Section 2.—3s. 7d. per quarter, such payments to be made as follows:— 3d. per week and 4d. quarterly levy.

Section 3.—2s. 6d. per quarter payments to be made as follows:— 2d. per week and 4d. quarterly levy.

The benefits for such payments to be in proportion to contributions paid (See Rules IX and XI).

No person shall be allowed to qualify under lower rate of contributions and benefits, who in the opinion of the Executive is receiving a weekly wage sufficient to pay higher rate of contributions.

Clause B.—Honorary Members (approved by the General E.C.) who shall pay a minimum of one guinea per annum.

Such Honorary Members will have no vote or any power to interfere with policy of Union.

Rule VI—When Entitled to Benefit
Members shall be entitled to legal assistance after paying six consecutive weeks' contributions, and Dispute Pay after paying 52 weeks' consecutive contributions. Members shall be entitled to half Funeral Benefits after paying twenty-six consecutive weeks' contributions, and full benefit after paying fifty-two consecutive weeks' contributions.

Rule VII—Arrears of Contributions
(a) Members more than eight weeks in arrears shall be fined 6d.—such fine to be considered arrears—and be out of benefit until such arrears be paid, and forfeit all claim to benefits of Union.
(b) All arrears owing by any member when claiming benefit from the funds shall be deducted from any payment made to such member.

Rule VIII—Clearance Card for Members Transferring to another Branch
Members removing from the neighbourhood in which their Branch is situated must obtain from the Secretary of their Branch a Clearance Card, stating date of entry, class to which member belongs, amount of benefits during current fifty-two weeks, and the arrears at the time of transfer. Such Clearance Card must be deposited with the Secretary of the Branch nearest the member's new place of residence within fourteen days of the date of clearance.

Rule IX—Disputes
Members paying under Section 2, Rule V., 3d. per week will receive in case of dispute, Lock-Out, or victimisation, subject to E.C.'s ruling, 8s. for ten weeks, 4s. for ten weeks, 2s for ten weeks.

Members paying under Section 3, Rule V., 2d. per week will receive in Cases of dispute, Lock-Out, or victimisation, subject to ruling of E.C., 5s. for twelve weeks, 2s. 6d. for twelve weeks.

Every member of the Union paying full subscriptions, in benefit, who may be locked-out by an employer, or withdrawn from employment by the Union in consequence of any trade dispute, on satisfying the Branch and the General E.C., as to the bona fide nature of the dispute, shall receive the sum of 10s. per week for ten weeks, 6s. for ten weeks, 3s. for ten weeks. Any member claiming strike or Lock-Out pay must sign the Vacant Book each day. Members failing to sign shall forfeit benefit for such days.

Should any member obtain employment for three days in any one week he shall not be entitled to any Dispute Pay for that week.

For each day under three days that the member obtains employment the day or days so worked shall be deducted from the Dispute Pay.

No Dispute Pay shall be paid until six days after ceasing work and the members have signed the book for that period.

After the first week odd days may be paid.

Dispute Benefit to cease on the day employment is resumed.

Any member on the dispute or Lock-Out fund having employment offered and refusing the same shall not be entitled to any further benefit during such dispute or Lock-Out.

No notices to cease work shall be recognised by the General Executive unless their consent has been obtained prior to such action, provided time for consideration has been given by the firm employing our members.

In sudden and unavoidable disputes the General Executive shall have discretionary power to grant or withhold Dispute Pay.

The General Secretary shall have power to negotiate when our members are in dispute, and the General Executive may close any dispute when they consider it advisable in the interests of the Union.

When a dispute occurs a Strike Committee must be elected by the members in such dispute. Such Strike Committee shall be subject to the control of the General Executive.

With every request to the General Executive to serve notices to cease work the Branch Secretary must forward to Chief Office:—

The number of members who voted for and the number who voted against the dispute;

The number of workmen directly affected by the dispute;

The number of members entitled to benefit, with their Chief Office number;

The number of members not entitled to benefit; and

The number of non-members, if any, and the position of similar workmen in the District.

The Branch, subject to the General Executive, shall have power to fine or expel any member acting in these or any other matters against the interests or well-being of the Union.

Any member working four weeks consecutively shall be ineligible to resume of dispute for that dispute.

Any member working during a dispute after having received instructions not to do so shall be fined a sum not exceeding £1, or is liable to be expelled.

A Strike is a stoppage of work caused by members refusing to work for any particular employer, but such stoppage must have received the sanction of the General Executive before any benefit can be paid.

A Lock-out is where members are laid idle by an employer attempting to impose or introduce conditions on his workmen which the General Executive has authority to resist.

In cases where members are prevented from following their usual employment in consequence of a labour dispute over which the Union has no control, such case may be brought to the notice of the General Executive, and they may decide whether such be supported, and, if so, to what extent.

Rule X—Legal Assistance and Accidents

Every member of the Union, in benefit, who desires to take legal action for compensation in case of accident, of recovery of wages, or for enforcing the application of any industrial law which may have for its object the protection of the members, must report the case, through the Branch, to the Central Office, and, if approved by the General Executive, the case shall receive the legal assistance of the Union.

A member who sustains an accident while following his usual employment shall at once send details of the accident, together with the name and address of his employer and foreman, along with a doctor's note, to the Branch Secretary. Should a member be killed, or too seriously injured to send in a report to the Branch Secretary, notice may be given by any other member or any other person to the Branch Secretary. In each case such information shall be immediately sent on, along with the doctor's note, by the Branch Secretary to the Chief Office on the form provided for the purpose.

Rule XI—Funeral Benefit or Benefits

At the death of a member in benefit the wife, nominee, or next-of-kin, shall receive in accordance with the following scale:—

Members of twelve months' standing, and who shall have paid twelve months' contributions, shall be entitled to Funeral Benefit as follows:—

At 4d. per week—Member, £6; wife, £3. 3d. per week—Member, £4; wife £2. 2d per week—Member only (male or female), £2 after twelve months' membership.

Members of six months' standing, and who shall have paid six months' contribution, shall be entitled to half benefits.

Death Certificate—Every application for death allowance must be accompanied by a certificate, signed by a registrar of deaths. The above-mentioned certificate shall be given to the Branch Secretary, who shall forward them to the Chief Office within 24 hours of its receipt by the Branch Secretary.

Rule XII—Financial Assistance to Labour Members

The General E.C. is empowered to grant sums of money in aid of the support of any Labour member on any public elective body, provided the said Labour member is not connected with any political party.

Rule XIII—Branch Meetings, Trades Councils, and Branch Funds

A Branch shall consist of not less than twenty members and as many as may be approved by the District Committee, where one exists, or by the General Executive in cases where there is no District Committee.
Each Branch may hold weekly meeting.

Branches are empowered to levy their members not more than one halfpenny per week to allow of affiliation with the local Trades Councils and other Labour bodies, and for benevolent purposes towards members.

Rule XIV—Issuing Circulars or Attempting to Injure the Union

No address or circular shall be issued by any Branch excepting where such address or circular has been approved by the General Executive. Any member or members of a Branch violating this Rule shall be fined 2s. 6d. each, and shall also be immediately suspended from all benefits of this Union for one month after fine has been paid. But if the General Executive of the Union so decide, such member or members may be excluded from membership of the Union.

Should a member be found guilty of attempting to injure the Union, the Branch shall have power to suspend him and report his conduct to the District Committee, where one exists; or, in case the Branch is not included in any District, to the General E.C., who shall investigate the nature of his or her offence, and the D.C. or General E.C. shall then have power to fine the member an amount not exceeding 10s. for a first offence and £1 for a second offence; or, if the nature of the offence is such as to constitute a grave injury to the Union, the member may be expelled without the option of a fine. The member, in case of being fined or expelled by the District Committee, shall have the right of appeal to the General Executive Committee. When any member is expelled by the District Committee or General Executive he shall forfeit all claims to the benefits of the Union.

Rule XV—Branch Officers

The Branch Officers shall be Chairman and Secretary (who shall also act as Treasurer), and shall be nominated at a General Meeting of the members of the Branch elected by ballot, and hold office during the pleasure of the Branch. No person to be elected to any Branch office until he has been a member of the Union for twelve months. This is not to apply to new Branches. No member to be eligible to hold office, or continue to hold office, who is more than eight weeks in arrears.

Rule XVI—Branch Committees

A Branch Committee of not less than four members shall be formed, who, along with the Branch President and Secretary, shall transact all business referred to them by the Branch, and see to the due observance of the Rules of the Union. All officers and members of Committee shall be elected by ballot.

XVII—Duties of Branch Chairman

Every Branch Chairman shall preside at all meetings of his Branch. He shall see that the business is conducted in accordance with the Rules, he shall decide points of order; he shall take and (after confirmation by the Branch) sign all minutes. The Chairman shall preside at all meetings; during a dispute see to proper payment of benefits, and also the due observance of all Rules, and shall aid in the efforts to secure a settlement.

XVIII—Duties of the Branch Secretary and Salary

Every Branch Secretary shall attend all meetings of his Branch at the time on which the Branch may decide. He shall keep an account of the contributions of the members in a book provided for that purpose, and sign members' contribution cards for each contribution. He shall keep the accounts of the Branch in a clear and intelligible manner, and keep all documents, accounts, receipts, books, and papers in such manner as the

Branch may appoint. He shall pay all benefits in accordance with the Rules, taking an official receipt for each payment made on behalf of the Branch. He shall make application to the Chief Office for such monies as are needed to meet all legal claims. He shall conduct such correspondence as belongs to his office, and forward a weekly return of all income and expenditure and forward all monies in hand with the exception of £5 in case of Branches under 500 and £10 in case of Branches of 500 members and over. He shall also furnish the Central Office with such detailed information on matters pertaining to the Union as may be required by the General E.C. from time to time. All fines and levies incurred by members of the Union must be accounted for by the Secretary. In cases of dispute or Lock-Out the Secretary must see to the member affected signing the book daily. He shall check such record, keep a correct amount of all monies received and paid out. No money to be paid without a duly signed receipt on the Dispute Pay Sheet. He shall report to the General Secretary, and communicate any information tending to be helpful in settling the dispute.

Branch Secretary's wages shall be such as fixed by Branch, subject to endorsement of Executive Committee.

XIX— The Duties of Branch Collectors and Salary
Collectors shall be appointed by Branches for the purpose of collecting the weekly contributions of members where a number are employed together. The Collectors shall sign all members' cards, and enter all monies received thereon. No amount paid by a member and not so entered can be accredited by the Union. Collectors shall pay over to Branch Secretary all monies received by them at the meeting of the Branch following after the date on which such monies are collected. Collectors shall receive as remuneration for their services 5% of the amount they collect.

XX—District Committees
Where a number of Branches consider it advisable for the better organisation or improvement of the Union, a District Committee may be formed and they shall have local autonomy within the Rules, and, where the Rules are silent, under the instruction of the General Executive. They may meet when circumstances and conditions require, and shall receive the cost of travelling to and from the place of meeting.

XXI—Officer of District Committees' Duties
The Officers of the District Committee shall be:—
(a) Chairman, who shall preside at all meetings of the District Committee, and sign all minutes after confirmation.
(b) Secretary, who shall keep the District Accounts and minutes, conduct all correspondence appertaining to his office, and generally carry out the instructions of his Committee.

The Chairman and Secretary shall be elected at and from a meeting of the District Committee, and shall receive such remuneration as may be recommended by the D.C. and endorsed by the General E.C.

Rule XXII—General Executive Committee
The General Executive shall be composed of one Delegate from Munster, one from Connaught, two from Ulster, four from Leinster (and General President and General

Secretary), and shall be elected each year in November, and take office on January 1st following. They shall meet at least four times in each year quarterly and such other times as occasion may require. Each member of the General E.C. shall receive 12s. 6d per day while attending the E.C. meetings with third-class fares to and from the place of meeting.

Each Branch of Union can nominate one, and not more than one, candidate for Executive; but all members are entitled to be nominated for the office of General President and General Secretary.

Any paid Official having to travel to the E.C. meeting shall receive the sum of 6s. per day and third-class fare to and from place of meeting.

Rule XXIII—Duties of the General Executive Committee

The General Executive shall have the management and control of the Union in accordance with the Rules. It shall have the power to order a levy for any Trade Union purpose or for Labour representation after giving seven days' notice to Branches and a majority vote of the members being in favour of the same; the votes to be taken at the next Branch meeting following the one on which the notice is received. It shall have power to federate the Union nationally or internationally subject to a majority vote of the members. The General Executive shall have power to decide on questions where the Rules are silent and to interpret any doubtful Rule, and its decision shall be binding, unless an appeal is made by the Referendum to the whole body of members. The General Executive shall have the power to veto any strike, and order members to return to work after any trade dispute. It shall the sole control of all funds.

Rule XXIV—General Executive Committee and Organisation

The General Executive shall supervise all arrangements at the Central Office and control the Executive Officers. It shall supervise the work of organisation, and if required, appoint special Organisers for special work.

Rule XXV—Election and Duties of General President

There shall be a General President elected every two years, in December, by a ballot vote of the members, and take office on January 1st following. The General President shall, in conjunction with the General Secretary, be responsible for the organisation and extension of the Union. He shall be allowed such assistance by the General Executive as may be necessary, and receive such remuneration as may be decided upon from time to time by the members on the recommendation of the General E.C.

Rule XXVI—Election and Duties of General Secretary

There shall be a General Secretary elected every two years, in December, by a ballot vote of the members, and take office on January 1st following. He shall, in conjunction with the General President, conduct the business of the Union in accordance with the Rules, and act under the instructions of the General Executive. He shall be allowed such assistance at the Central Office as may be necessary in order that the business of the Union may be conducted in a proper manner, and receive such remuneration as may be decided from time to time by the members on the recommendation of the General E.C. He shall send a report of each General E.C. meeting to the Branch Secretaries within one month of such meeting. An Assistant Secretary shall be appointed by the Executive.

Rule XXVII—Election of Union Trustees

There shall be three Trustees, who shall be elected every two years, in December, by a ballot vote of the members, and take office on January 1st following. The President and General Secretary shall be ex-officio Trustees.

Rule XXVIII—General Treasurer

The Treasurer of the General Fund shall be elected every two years, in December, by a ballot vote of the members, and take office on January 1st following, and receive such salary as fixed by the Executive (not exceeding the sum of £20 per year). He shall see that all monies of the Union (excepting £20 to be left in the hands of the General Secretary) received shall be banked according to Rule, and shall, when required by the Executive, deliver to whoever may be appointed all monies or properties belonging to the Union that he may have in his custody or possession.

Rule XXIX—Duties of Union Trustees

The Trustees shall have the general control of the finances of the Union, and shall have the power to refuse to sign any cheques for payment which are not in accordance with the Rules; but shall not refuse to make payments or sign cheques for payments which are in accordance with the Rules.

Rule XXX—Banking of Union Funds

The funds of the Union shall be banked in a Joint Stock Bank in the names of the three Trustees. Each cheque for the withdrawal of money from the bank shall be signed by the General President and one Trustee, or by three Trustees, and each cheque shall be countersigned by the General Secretary. When the funds at the bank have reached such a sum as is considered sufficient by the General E.C. of the Union all amounts above such sum shall be invested by the Trustees in Co-operative Securities or Municipal Corporation Stock.

Rule XXXI—Inspection of Books

Every member having an interest in the funds of the Union shall, at any reasonable time and on giving due notice, have the right to inspect the books of the Union and the list of members at the Registered Officer.

Rule XXXII—Nomination for Funeral Benefit

A member may by writing under his hand, delivered at or sent to the Registered Office or Branch Secretary's address, or made in a book kept for the purpose, nominate a person to whom any sum of money payable by the Union on the death of such member at his decease shall be paid: provided the person so nominated, and not being husband, wife, brother, sister, nephew or niece of the nominator, is not an officer of the Branch where the nominator is a member.

For each such nomination one shilling shall be paid, and sixpence for each revocation or variation, which money shall go to the General Fund of the Union.

A payment made to a person who at the time appears to the majority of the Committee to be entitled thereto on the death of a member, shall be valid and effectual against any demand made upon the Union. Recovery of the money to rest with the next-of-kin or lawful representative from the person receiving the same.

When the Union has paid money to a nominee in ignorance of a marriage subsequent to the nomination, the receipt of the nominee shall be a valid discharge to the Union.

Rule XXXIII—Alteration of Rules
The Rules shall only be altered by the General E.C. after amendments have been asked for and sent in by the Branches, such amended Rules to be finally voted on by the members.

Rule XXXIV—Dissolution of Union
The Union may be dissolved, and its funds divided, with the sanction of five-sixths of the votes of the financial members.

Rule XXXV—National Convention
A National Convention of the Union shall be summoned every year. Summonses for the Convention shall be sent out to Branches three months before the date of meeting. Notices of motion for the Convention must reach the General Secretary two months before the date, and an agenda paper of Convention business must be sent to Branches one month before the date of its assembling. Secretaries of Branches are required to summon a General Meeting of their members for the purpose of electing Delegates and considering the agenda as soon as possible after the necessary papers reach them. Except where a General Meeting is ordered the decision of the Convention so summoned shall constitute and be construed as the ruling of the Union. Such Convention to be held in the same town as, and on the day following the Irish Trades Congress, if possible.

Rule XXXVI—Annual Audit and Election of Auditors
The accounts of the Union shall be audited in January of each year by two members elected by ballot in the preceding December, such Auditors to receive remuneration at the same rate as members of the General E.C., or by a registered accountant.

The Registered Office is in Ireland, at No. 18 Beresford Place, Dublin, in the City of the County of Dublin. In the event of any change in the situation of the Registered Office notice of change shall be sent within fourteen days to the Registrar in the form prescribed by the Treasury Regulations in that behalf.

Peter Ennis
Stephen Clarke
John Bohan
Joseph Kelly
John O'Neill
Thomas Hewson
Thomas Foran
James Larkin

Appendix 2 ∽

AMALGAMATIONS, MERGERS
AND BREAKAWAYS

1: THE IRISH TRANSPORT AND GENERAL WORKERS' UNION

Amalgamations and mergers

Tracing organisations that merged or amalgamated with the ITGWU is difficult, especially from 1917 to 1923. Many folded into the Transport Union by local decision, with
no formal transfer of engagements. This was especially true when Branches of British
unions decided that henceforth they were ITGWU members. The ITGWU created other,
ostensibly independent unions, such as the Irish Textile Workers' Union (Belfast, 1910),
Irish Foundry Workers' Union (Wexford, 1911) and Irish Women Workers' Union. In
later periods, mergers or amalgamations become easier to identify, as formal transfer
procedures were followed.

1909
National Union of Dock Labourers
The National Union of Dock Labourers of Great Britain and Ireland was founded in
Glasgow in 1890, registered in 1898 (no. 195T), and was affiliated to the ITUC, 1894–1921.
It became the National Union of Dock and Riverside Workers and a constituent
founder-member of the (Amalgamated) Transport and General Workers' Union in 1922.
In December 1908 the ITGWU was born out of NUDL Branches in Belfast, Cork, Dublin,
Dundalk, Waterford and Wexford. The ITGWU took over NUDL registers, memberships,
even office accommodation—without, it must be acknowledged, any real complaint.
The ITGWU was registered on 4 January 1909 (no. 275T).

1911
Irish Textile Workers' Union
The Irish Textile Workers' Union was formed by Connolly, as an ITGWU subsidiary, to
organise women textile workers in Belfast. It became a Branch of the Irish Women
Workers' Union, but after the Rising membership of the union among Ulster textile
workers ceased.

Irish Women Workers' Union
The Irish Women Workers' Union was founded, with Delia Larkin as Secretary, on 5
September. Larkin interpreted the word 'person' in the Rules of the ITGWU to mean
'man', and therefore women could not be members and so required a separate organisation. The IWWU established n independent status after 1917, was registered in 1918 (no.
332T) and continued in existence until its merger with the FWUI in 1984. It was a constant ITUC affiliate, 1912–59, and of the ICTU, 1959–84.

1912

Cork Carmen and Storemen

In April 1911 the ITGWU No. 13 Branch was called the Storemen and Carmen's Union, with an office in George's Street, Cork. The Cork Carmen and Storemen was founded in 1903 and in 1908 transferred to the National Union of Gas Workers and General Labourers. It transferred its Branch, but the ITGWU collapsed in Cork until its revival after the 1913 ITUC Congress in the city. Cork Carmen and Storemen were represented at the 1913 ITUC Congress by Daniel Lynch. It transferred a second time after this as No. 20 Branch.

Irish Foundrymen's Union

The Irish Foundrymen's Union was formed after the Lock-Out in the Wexford foundries, 1911–12, as Connolly's vehicle to allow the employers recognise a union other than the ITGWU. It was affiliated to the ITUC, 1912–13, as Wexford Iron Workers, integrating with the ITGWU in 1913. Richard Corish was Secretary.

1914

Dublin Coal Factors' Association

Founded and registered in 1912 (no. 301T), its objects were 'to procure better and cheaper coal for its members; establish and maintain a minimum price for coal; procure cheap rates for the repair and purchase of drays, harness, sacks and feed; and create a coal co-operative confined to members.' Based in Liberty Hall, it was dissolved in 1914. In 1913 it had 163 members, an increase from 55 in 1912. It regularly advertised in the *Irish Worker*. The Association had moved from Liberty Hall by 1920 and became an independent union.

Dublin Operative Poulterers' Trades Union

Founded on 8 January 1903 and registered (no. 224T), in April 1913 it became the Poulterers' and Fishmongers' Trade Union but 'broke up' on 11 August 1914, and its registration was cancelled on 16 June 1921. In 1914 the ITGWU Fish and Poultry Section reported its absorption. Its membership in 1913 was 40 and in 1914 was 39.

Kilmacow Trade and Labour Benefit and Protection Society

Formed in 1905, it was registered in 1907 (no. 256T). It dissolved in 1914, most probably into the ITGWU.

1915

Dublin Paviours' Protective Society

Founded in 1904, it was registered in 1909 (no. 271T) and affiliated to the ITUC, 1908–10; its registration was cancelled in 1915. It was most probably absorbed into the ITGWU, as its leading representative was P. T. Daly.

Kilkenny Brewery Labourers' Trade Union

Registered in 1904 (no. 231T), its registration was cancelled in 1915 when it went into the ITGWU. Its Registrar of Friendly Societies file in the National Archives is empty.

Workers' Union
The Tralee Branch of the Workers' Union, with 160 members, transferred to the newly formed Tralee Branch of the ITGWU in October 1915. The Workers' Union's few Irish members appear to have followed.

1916
Castlebellingham Operative and Labourers' Friendly Society
Registered as a Friendly Society in 1894 (no. 891FS), it dissolved in 1916, most probably into the ITGWU.

Rathmines and District Workers' Union
Registered in 1905 (no. 240T), it dissolved in 1918; it may have been absorbed by the Irish Municipal Employees' Trade Union but most probably by the ITGWU. It gave £1 to the Silk Weavers in 1913. Its membership was 120 in 1910, 74 in 1911, 56 in 1912, 104 in 1913, 115 in 1914, 103 in 1915 and 113 in 1916.

United Labourers' Society, Tralee
Affiliated to the ITUC in 1896–1916, it went into the ITGWU in 1916.

1917
Blanchardstown Land and Labour League
George O'Driscoll, later a member of the NEC of the ITGWU, formed Blanchardstown Land and Labour League, but it had 'been unsuccessful.' On 11 March he invited Foran to address a meeting, and the Blanchardstown Branch of the ITGWU was founded, one of the first instances of a Land and Labour League or Association transferring in.

Bruff Trade and Labour League
Bruff Trade and Labour League, Co. Limerick, transferred in November.

Churchtown Labour League
Churchtown Labour League, Co. Cork, appears to have joined in the spring.

Clonmel Trade and Labour League
Founded in 1892 (no. 852FS), it changed its name to Clonmel Trades and Labour Society in 1906. Its registration was cancelled in 1917 when it was subsumed into the ITGWU.

Dublin Tile, Mosaic and Faience Fixers' Association
Registered in 1912 (no. 294T), its registration was cancelled in 1917 when it was absorbed into the ITGWU.

Foremen's Union
The National Foremen's Association, a British union, was formed in 1917, changing its name in 1942 to the Association of Supervisory Staff and Engineering Workers and then to the Association of Supervisory Staff, Executives and Technicians before eventually becoming part of the Association of Scientific and Managerial Staffs in 1968. The Irish membership was negligible at this time. This Foremen's Union appears to have been a

wholly controlled ITGWU subsidiary. In 1923 George Spain was Secretary, with an address in Liberty Hall. It disappeared after 1924 in the general ITGWU collapse.

Killorglin Labourers' Society
It is not clear what the exact title of a 'local society at Killorglin', Co. Kerry, was. It joined in January.

Limerick Dockers' Society
The Limerick Dockers' Society joined the ITGWU on the creation of the Limerick Branch of the ITGWU, led by Patrick Horrigan, who became an ITGWU official.

National Association of Theatrical and Kinematograph Employees
The Dublin Branch organised itself as the ITGWU Theatre and Cinema Branch in December.

Regular Hotel Workers' International Trade Union (Dublin)
Formed and registered on 23 June 1912 (no. 295T), its registration was cancelled in 1917. It divided its assets among the members, but by then the ITGWU was organising hotel workers. Its membership was 50. It affiliated to Dublin Trades Council.

1918
Ballinasloe Land and Labour Union
Ballinasloe Land and Labour Union merged with the ITGWU to become a Branch in September.

Bennett's Bridge Labour Union
The Bennettsbridge Branch of Kilkenny Labour Union became an ITGWU Branch in July. In 1977 a plaque was unveiled to its founders, James Lawlor and Michael Kelly.

Carlow Land and Labour Association
A meeting of Carlow and Laois Land and Labour Associations was held in Maryborough (Port Laoise) on 4 February 1917. Carlow Land and Labour Association quickly folded into the ITGWU after a Carlow Branch was established on 2 June.

Castledermott Land and Labour Association
Castledermott Land and Labour Association was amalgamated in June as an ITGWU Branch.

Drombana Creamery Workers' Society
Drombana Creamery Workers' Society organised a strike in February over the dismissal of a butter-maker. The creamery was kept open by scabbing farmers' sons but ran up a large loss until a settlement was agreed in March. Drombana Creamery workers, and those in an auxiliary creamery at Killonan, Co. Limerick, transferred to become the Drombana Branch.

Dublin Municipal Engine Drivers', Firemen, Cranemen and Motormen's Trade Union
This union was registered in 1914 (no. 311T) but dissolved in 1918 when it merged with
the ITGWU.

Hotel and Club Workers' Union
The Hotel and Club Assistants' Association of Ireland, founded in 1888, was registered
in 1893 (no. 143T) and dissolved in 1909; perhaps the remnant 'rallied to form a Branch
of the ITGWU' in May. Note also the Hotel and Club Assistants of Ireland Mutual Benefit
Society in the Registrar of Friendly Societies in 1882 (639 members), the Hotel and Club
Employees' Friendly Benefit Society, Registrar of Friendly Societies, 1902 (1,038 members) and the Hotel, Restaurant and Club Employees' Society of Ireland, Registrar of
Friendly Societies, 1909 (1,180 members), any of which could have been part of the
organisation that became the Hotel and Restaurant Branch in 1918.

Irish Glass Bottle Makers' Trade and Protection Society
This union was founded in 1867 as the Irish Glass Bottle Makers' Society, represented
at the ITUC Congress in 1894–1918. It merged into the ITGWU.

Job Carriage Drivers' and Coffin Makers' Protective Association
This Association was founded on 11 December 1916 and registered (no. 322T); on 5 May
1918 the 'Society no longer exists as an independent organisation' and joined the ITGWU.

Kildare Labour Union
Amalgamated with the ITGWU in July.

Kilkenny City and County Labour Union
Merged in July and brought 1,200 members. Also known as Kilkenny Trade and Labour
Union, it had a previous existence, registered in 1895 (no. 167T), cancelled in 1905.

King's County Land and Labour Association
King's County [Offaly] Land and Labour Association transferred in January.

Migratory Labourers' Union
After failed attempts by the WU to organise tattie-hokers (potato-pickers) in Achill and
Erris, Co. Mayo, Michael Masterson, a resident of Belmullet, set up the Migratory
Labourers' Union. After the arrival in the area of W. J. Reilly, Sligo ITGWU, it transferred
in. Masterson became their Delegate, based in Glasgow.

Newtown Drogheda Land and Labour Association
Merged in September.

North Tipperary Trades and Labour Association
Nenagh and District Labourers' and Artisans' Association was registered in 1895 and
followed an earlier Nenagh Labourers' Association. In 1898 it may well have been one
of the founding elements of the North Tipperary Trade and Labour Association, which
affiliated to the ITUC in 1901. In March the Association became the Nenagh Branch of
the ITGWU.

Operative Stonecutters of Ireland Trade Union
Founded as the Operative Stonecutters of Ireland in 1891, it was registered in 1894 (no. 151T), based in Cork, and was affiliated to the ITUC, 1894–1910. The City of Dublin Stonecutters was founded and registered in 1900 (no. 219T) and in 1907 amalgamated with the Operative Stonecutters. It merged with the ITGWU with roughly 300 members. The registration was cancelled in 1926, and William O'Brien wrote to the Registrar of Friendly Societies on 23 March 1927 to state that 'the organisation . . . ceased to exist many years ago.' It is not clear when it re-established an independent identity, but it affiliated to the ITUC in the 1930s. It was a Branch of the Building Workers' Trade Union c. 1945–52. The Stonecutters' Union of Ireland was registered in 1963 (no. 529T), amalgamating with the Ancient Guild of Incorporated Brick and Stone Layers' Trade Union in 1966. Another City of Dublin Stonecutters' Trade Union was registered in 1910 (no. 282T), the registration cancelled in 1915. The membership of the Operative Stonecutters of Ireland Trade Union was 469 in 1911, 486 in 1912, 472 in 1913, 415 in 1914, 402 in 1915, 318 in 1916 and 302 in 1917. Before amalgamating with the Incorporated Brick and Stone Layers the Stonecutters' Society applied to join the WUI in 1965.

Rathmines and District Workingmen's Union
Registered in 1905 (no. 240T); dissolved into the ITGWU.

South Kildare Labour Union
'A vigorous organisation' based in Athy, merged in August.

1919
Amalgamated Union of Saddlers and Harness-Makers
Founded in 1890, it was affiliated to the ITUC, 1895–7. The members joined after June, when increases were gained.

Birr Land and Labour Association
Amalgamated in January. It is not known whether this was the Birr or Offaly Land and Labour Association.

Carpet Planners of the City of Dublin
Founded in 1898 and registered on 20 February 1898 (no. 200T), it was represented in the ITUC, 1911–14, and affiliated to Dublin Trades Council. It dissolved in 1919, having been absorbed in July. The membership was 24 in 1911, 25 in 1912, 33 in 1913, 35 in 1914, 33 in 1915, 47 in 1916, 39 in 1917 and 65 in 918.

City of Dublin Marble Polishers
Founded in 1881, it was absorbed into the ITGWU.

Clare Land and Labour Association
Reportedly transferred in July.

Clonmahon Land and Labour Association
Merged in April.

County of Limerick Trade and Labour Association
Attended the ITUC Congress in 1918 but merged in 1919–20.

Dublin Mineral Water Operatives' Society
Transferred in July. There were two earlier bodies, both called the Mineral Water Operatives' Trade Union, one registered in 1886 (no. 73T) and dissolved in 1890, the other formed in 1896, registered in 1897 (no. 182T) and dissolved in 1897. The Dublin Mineral Water Operatives' Society was registered in 1906 (no. 248T) and dissolved in 1919. The highest membership was 212, in 1917. It gave Dublin Trades Council's 1913 Lock-Out Fund £16 10s and the Silk Weavers £5. Membership was 86 in 1911, 117 in 1912, 91 in 1913, 90 in 1914, 118 in 1915, 114 in 1916 and 212 in 1917.

Dublin Operative Poulterers' Trade Union
Founded in 1903 and registered (no. 224T), it changed its name to Poulterers' and Fishmongers' Trade Union in 1913. In the ITGWU from 1918, its registration was cancelled in 1928.

Dublin Regular Farriers' Society
Founded in 1670, later the City of Dublin Operative Farriers. It was affiliated to the ITUC, 1910–19, and to the ITGWU in June 1919.

Dublin Saddlers' and Harness Makers' Trade Society
Founded in 1791, but modern existence was from 1 January 1903, registered on 14 October 1903 (no. 228T), It was represented at the ITUC Congress, 1894–1918, and dissolved in July 1919 after merger with the ITGWU. It was part of the Saddlers', Harness Makers', Collar Makers', Bridle Cutters', Mill Band Workers' and Leather Workers in Saddlery Trades Union, 1901–1903. It donated ten guineas (£10 10s) to the ITGWU in 1913. Membership was 75 in 1910, 73 in 1911, 74 in 1912, 76 in 1913, 80 in 1914, 75 in 1915, 68 in 1916, 62 in 1917, 82 in 1918, and 98 in 1919.

Ferns Trade and Labour Association
Ferns [Co. Wexford] Trade and Labour Association merged in March to become a Branch.

Irish Land and Labour Association
Various county Land and Labour Associations merged in 1919, having been affiliated to the ITUC, 1895–1919.

Irish Stationary Engine Drivers', Cranemen, Firemen and Motormen's Trade Union
Registered in April 1909 (no. 277T), it had Branches in Arklow, Limerick and Waterford and was affiliated to the ITUC, 1909–20. It had a close association with the ITGWU for a long period, news of its meetings and activities appearing in the *Irish Worker,* before it was fully absorbed. Membership was 206 in 1911, 253 in 1912, 338 in 1913, 248 in 1914, 240 in 1915, 270 in 1916, 362 in 1917, 455 in 1918 and 693 in 1919. It had absorbed the Independent Stationary Engine Drivers' Union in December 1912, 'when a number of the members joined our Union on 6 January 1913.' The Independent Stationary Steam

and Gas Engine Drivers', Steam and Electrical Crane and Motor Drivers', Greasers', Firemen and Trimmers' Trade Union was launched on 17 October 1909, registered on 27 October 1909 (no. 280T) and was dissolved in 1912, dividing its assets of £59 among the members. It had 64 members in 1910 and 57 in 1911. It re-emerged as an independent body before merging with the Irish Engineering Industrial Union in 1921.

Leix Land and Labour Association
Leix [Laois] Land and Labour Association, based in Maryborough (Port Laoise), merged in February, bringing 2,500 members.. Thomas Farren was accredited with doing 'missionary work' among the Association, opening ITGWU Branches in Ballybrittas, Borris-in-Ossory, Castletown, Mountmellick and Mountrath.

Limerick Harbour Workers' Society
Amalgamated in March.

Mullingar Trade and Labour Union
Represented at the ITUC Congress in 1918 but merged after that.

Queenstown and District Government Labourers' Union
Queenstown [Cóbh] and District Government Labourers' Union was registered in 1912 (no. 239T) and dissolved in 1920. Membership was 380 in 1912, 270 in 1913, 278 in 1914, 287 in 1915, 376 in 1916, 441 in 1918 and 391 in 1919.

Wexford Labour Union
As result of the 'Bunclody Agreement' in July 1919 the ITGWU acquired Branches in Boleyvogue, Camross, Clologue, the Harrow, Kilteely, Monamolin and Taghmon from the WLU.

1920
Brewery Workers' Association (Cork)
Known also as the Breweries Workingmen's Society and Cork Brewery Workmen, it was represented in the ITUC, 1895–1919, and came into the ITGWU after a strike in March 1920. The dispute was resolved in May, and the 'sum of £125 as a condition of amalgamation with benefit was accepted' by the NEC. Cork Brewery Workingmen's Association was formed 1889 and merged with the National Union of Gasworkers and General Labourers in 1908.

Derry Tailoresses
There is some indication that this body merged in July. The ITGWU paid £73 10s to Derry Tailoresses on 27 July 1920. It is not clear whether they were a local society or a Branch of the Amalgamated Society of Tailors and Tailoresses.

Dublin Portmanteau Makers' and Leather Workers' Trade Union
Not apparently registered; merged in May or June. Thomas Kennedy was a member.

Irish Agricultural and General Workers' Union
Known as the Irish National Trade and Labour Union (Enniscorthy), it was founded on
1 January 1918, registered on 29 June 1918 (no. 334T) and became the Irish National
Agricultural and General Workers' Union on 29 June 1919, 'owing to the amalgamation
of other bodies with this union.' It was affiliated to the ITUC, 1918–19, and registration
was cancelled in 1928. O'Brien wrote to the Registrar of Friendly Societies that 'no union
in existence from March, 1920, all members joined Transport Workers' Union, between
August, 1919 and this date.' It had 6,000 members in 1917 and 5,500 in 1918. Richard F.
King was Secretary and John R. (Seán) Etchingham, Trustee. It included the County
Wicklow General Labourers' Association, founded in 1917 by James Everett and James
de Courcey, which amalgamated with the Wexford Branch of the Irish National
Agricultural and General Workers' Union in 1919. In fact the merger took place after a
meeting in Enniscorthy on Sunday 13 June 1920, when the Irish Agricultural and General
Workers' Union agreed 'to join on terms of half benefit to paid up members on payment
of one shilling entrance fee per member.' Where both unions had Branches in the same
place they met after the merger to appoint the Branch Secretary, and if matters could
not be decided the members would be balloted. James Everett and Doran met the
ITGWU Organisers O'Donoghue, Heron and Metcalfe on 22 June 1920 'to agree upon
transfer of membership etc.' At Aughrim in June 1920, 160 INAGW men 'came over' at
a meeting addressed by Archie Heron.

Louth Land and Labour Association
Transferred in November.

Moate Trade and Labour Society
The transfer of the Moate (Co. Westmeath) body was agreed by the NEC on 10 June
1920. It also had an Approved Insurance Society, taken into the ITGWU National Health
Insurance Society. Moate Trade and Labour Society registered as a Friendly Society in
1912 (no. 1244), although it clearly carried out trade union functions.

National Amalgamated Union of Shop Assistants, Newry Branch
Transferred to the ITGWU in November.

National Union of Dock, Wharf and Riverside Labourers, Passage West
The Passage West (Co. Cork) Branch of the NUDWRL transferred in August.

National Union of Gas Labourers and General Workers, Cork Branch
The Branch came over in August, bringing dockers from Cork, Passage West and
Midleton.

Operative Butchers' and Assistants' Trade Union
The Operative Butchers were founded in 1828; from 1870 the society had premises in
Great Britain Street (Parnell Street), Dublin, later in Capel Street. It was registered on
19 December 1890 (no. 102T), became the Operative Butchers' and Assistants' Trade
Union in 1901 and Dublin Operative Butchers' Benefit Union, 1920, and attended the
ITUC Congress in 1901 and 1917; registration was cancelled in 1920. The Secretary in

1910, John Long, was elected by avoiding the 'black ball'. P. J. Hickey, Secretary in 1913, a clerk in McDonagh's, Chatham Street, abolished the yearly share-out and developed a reserve fund. The butchers 'decided to transfer their membership' to the ITGWU in July 1920, but 'preparatory to this course a meting of the operatives has been arranged for the purpose of the correct interpretation of the Constitution of this Union [ITGWU].' The Butchers' Union 'had more money per head' than the ITGWU, and Liberty Hall 'could not understand why we wished to merge into their Union.' It was the inspiration of Larkin and 1913. The Butchers' Secretary was subsequently Frank Cluskey, and after the creation of the WUI in 1924 they became a founding Branch. Membership was 108 in 1912, 127 in 1913, 118 in 1914, 92 in 1915, 149 in 1916, 188 in 1917, 302 in 1918, 379 in 1919, and 384 in 1920. It set up an Approved Society under the National Health Insurance Act in 1914.

St Stephen's Insurance Society
Engagements were transferred to the ITGWU National Health Insurance Approved Society at the NEC meeting of 10 June.

Tipperary Workingmen's Protective and Benefit Society
Founded by Michael Callaghan in 1911 and based around the town of Tipperary. It transferred in June and broke away in 1932 before re-merging in 1943.

United Builders' Labourers and General Workers of Dublin Trade Union
Formed as the Dublin United Builders' Labourers in August 1896, it was registered in August 1897 (no. 85T) and was represented at ITUC Congresses, 1894–1918. It was also known as the United Builders' Labourers of Ireland Trade Union (1891), the United Labourers of Dublin (1901) and the United Building Labourers and General Workers of Dublin Trade Union (1912) and colloquially as 'the Hoxies' (perhaps from an archaic word meaning 'muddy'). There were allegations of blacklegging by members in 1913. It was absorbed in November or December, when registration was cancelled. Membership was 710 in 1910, 715 in 1911, 1,108 in 1912, 1,610 in 1913, 1,408 in 1914, 1,130 in 1915, 1,150 in 1916, 1,406 in 1917, 1,576 in 1918, 1,516 in 1919 and 997 in 1920. The ITGWU paid £1,000 to the union on 12 October 1920, presumably as settlement of debts. Members voted by 714 to 12 in favour of amalgamation, with 22 spoiled votes. At a meeting on 31 October 1920 in the Trades Hall, Thomas Kennedy (ITGWU) and Patrick Moran (Secretary, UBLTU) mooted the proposed transfer; the Executive Committee recorded that 'it was decided to accept the transfer of the Union, including the National Health Insurance Section, if the members agreed to this course on a ballot vote, and that thereupon all members on strike and receiving full benefit from the UBLTU be paid Strike Pay at the rate of 15/- per week commencing 5 December, those receiving reduced benefit to receive 10/- per week.' Both Moran and William Harris were kept on the payroll, the latter also receiving payments from the UBLTU National Health Insurance Approved Society. At a ballot in the Banba Hall on 4 December 1920 the builders' labourers' strike was ended by a vote of 685 to 13, the numbers suggesting that before the absorption of the UBLTU the ITGWU had few labourers in membership. The Builders' Labourers' Section operated out of 17 High Street. Early in 1921 the Builders' Labourers and existing members in builders' providers and the Marble-Polishers and Stonecutters were brought together as the ITGWU Dublin No. 5 (Building) Branch.

Vintners' Assistants' Association
The Cork Branch came over in August.

Workers' Union, Cork Dockers' Branch
Transferred in August.

1921
Amalgamated Society of Farriers
Transferred in October. The society, founded in 1903 (registered no. 227T), had its Head Office in Manchester. It affiliated to the ITUC in 1911.

Amalgamated Society of Pork Butchers (Limerick and Waterford)
Founded in 1890, it was represented in the ITUC in 1895–7 and 1919–21.

British Seafarers' Union
A Conference in Liberty Hall on 21 September agreed that the ITGWU should immediately organise all seamen resident in Ireland and 'act as agents in all Irish ports for the B.S.U.' An Agreement was made for the joint recognition of union cards, and a Conference was held in Liverpool with the BSU, ITGWU, All Seamen's Vigilance Committee, Coastwise Officers' and Mates' Association and Cooks' and Stewards' Union. While it was not a merger, the relationship with the BSU—at a time of mass defection from the National Sailors' and Firemen's Union in Ireland—allowed the ITGWU to develop a strong Marine Section. It was a short-lived liaison, as a subsequent meeting under the auspices of the National Transport Workers' Federation came to naught.

Dundalk Operative Labourers' Friendly Society
Registered as a Friendly Society in 1872 (no. 141F), it long regarded itself as the 'superior' body in the town, engaging in bitter disputes and disagreements over membership, organisational rights and mutual card recognition (or, more commonly, non-recognition). It transferred to the ITGWU on 12 November.

Iron and Steel Erectors
It is not clear whether this was a local society or a Branch of a British union. It was taken in as a Section of Dublin No. 1 Branch on 15 September.

Longford Land and Labour Association
It is not certain when transfer took place, but the Longford Land and Labour Association Approved Society was taken into the ITGWU National Health Insurance Approved Society in May 1921.

Mosaic and Tile Fixers' Association
Registered in 1918 (no. 327T), with registration finally cancelled in 1928. It became a Section of Dublin No. 1 Branch on 8 September.

National Sailors' and Firemen's Union of Great Britain and Ireland
Many members of the NSFU in Belfast and Dublin left and formed the Marine Section of the ITGWU in October. The Dundalk Branch of the NSFU transferred in late October.

National Union of Dock Labourers, Newry
The Newry Carters transferred in November.

National Union of Dock, Wharf and Riverside Labourers, Cork and Waterford
All members in Cork and Midleton defected in June or July, and transfer was complete by November, with the Cork Secretary, James Hickey, given a position in the ITGWU. Waterford NUDRWL members followed.

National Union of Railwaymen, Dublin
Dublin dockers on the Holyhead ships of the London and North-Western Railway formally transferred from the NUR in November, giving the ITGWU complete control of Dublin port. Thirty railway shop men transferred from the NUR in Bray on 3 December.

National Union of Vehicle Builders, Dublin
Dublin Branch members transferred in June or July.

Typographical Association, Dublin
Machinemen in the *Irish Independent* transferred on 5 August.

Workers' Union, Kilsaran
Chemical workers in Kilsaran Branch of the WU transferred on 26 November. Indeed WU chemical workers generally appear to have transferred.

1922
Amalgamated Society of Woodcutting Machinists
The Dublin Branch held a ballot on merger, having been accepted in April. It is not clear what happened. The Branch eventually seceded to form the Irish Society of Woodcutting Machinists in 1933, registered in 1934 (no. 408T). The most likely event is that the ASWM Branch joined but, as a consequence of an internecine row with Larkin after 1923, simply reverted to the ASWM before its independent action in 1933.

Dublin Silk and Poplin Trade Union
The Dublin Silk Trade Society was founded in 1680 and re-formed in 1728. It became Dublin Silk and Poplin Trade Union and registered in 1918 (no. 328T). It is recorded as having merged in February but appears to have re-established an independent identity and in 1925 joined the Irish Union of Distributive Workers and Clerks, although maintaining a separate registry until 1937. Michael Mallin, ITGWU Official in Inchicore and executed as a Citizen Army member after Easter 1916, was the Silk Weavers' Secretary.

Gardeners' Society
'Defunct' members transferred in January in Parteen, Co. Clare.

Irish Asylum Workers' Trade Union, Grangegorman, Cork and Wexford
A ballot of members in Grangegorman Mental Hospital, Dublin, in October resulted in 156 voting for transfer, 27 against; 57 did not vote. It joined Dublin No. 3 Branch. The Cork and Enniscorthy Branches transferred *en bloc* in March.

Irish Automobile Drivers' and Mechanics' Union
Founded and registered as the Irish Automobile Drivers' Society in 1911 (no. 286T) and Irish Automobile Drivers' and Mechanics' Union, represented at the ITUC, 1916–22. Membership was 149 in 1911, 162 in 1912, 138 in 1913, 98 in 1914, 117 in 1915, 132 in 1916, 248 in 1917, 830 in 1918, and 1,571 in 1919. It made no returns after 1919. In September 1922 it was agreed that 100 members 'on full benefit with clear cards' would be transferred as full members of the ITGWU, a further '50 on half-benefit,' and the 'remainder can come as new members on entrance fee of 2/7 providing [it is] within two weeks of decision.' Those not transferring within two weeks would be charged a '10/1 entrance fee.' The Secretary of the IADMU, Ciarán J. King, was taken onto the Head Office staff as a clerk, and the Organiser, Liam Slattery, employed until 31 December 'to enable him to get other employment.' Even this Agreement was conditional on the approval of the Motor Section of Dublin No. 1 Branch. The IADMU was later revived to become the Automobile, General Engineering and Mechanical Operatives' Union.

Irish Ordnance Workers' Trade Union
Founded in 1918 and registered in 1919 (no. 339T) but dissolved by 1922, when it was either absorbed into or unable to compete with the ITGWU.

Meath Labour Union
Represented at the ITUC, 1919–22, it came in after an interview with the Secretary of the 'Meath Herds' Union' in August and a decision to 'accept members of that body as a section on payment of 2/6 entrance fee and a half year's contributions for each member, and on payment of same they be admitted to full benefit.' With other rural organisations, it had reacted against the ITGWU's Socialism. In 1918 it briefly initiated the Association of Rural Workers and Workmen's Labour Unions.

1923
Limerick Pork Butchers' Society
Founded in 1890, the society agreed to transfer on 12 September as half-benefit members, having 316 on strike. It retained a separate Executive and premises, although a Section of the Limerick Branch.

Marine Workers' Union
Agreed in May with the ITGWU to 'recognise each other's cards.' The Irish members were served by the ITGWU.

National Sailors' and Firemen's Union
Founded in 1894, its name was changed to the National Union of Sailors, Firemen, Fishermen, Cooks and Stewards in 1899 and National Union of Seamen in 1926. In April the Cork members transferred, followed by wholesale transfers to the Maritime Section in Belfast, Dublin, Dundalk, Newry, Waterford and Wexford.

Waterford Pork Butchers' Society
120 members transferred in September, 'all the men being at present on strike.'

1924
Clonmel Operative Coopers' Trade Union
Registered in 1921 (no. 352T); registration was cancelled in 1924 and the union transferred over.

National Union of Boot and Shoe Operatives
Founded in England in the 1870s, its first Irish Branch was established in 1874, registered in 1902. It was affiliated to the ITUC (later CIU), 1894–1953, and in 1971 merged with the Amalgamated Society of Leather Workers, the National Union of Leather Workers and Allied Trades and the National Union of Glovers and Leather Workers to form the National Union of Footwear, Leather and Allied Trades. The Dublin Branch of the National Union of Boot and Shoe Operatives was admitted to Dublin No. 3 Branch 'as half benefit members' in March 1924.

United Stationary Engine Drivers
Became a Section of Dublin No. 1 Branch in January.

1925–1926
Irish Asylum Workers' Trade Union
Founded in 1917 and registered in 1920 (no. 345T), it was represented at the ITUC, 1918–25. It became the Irish Mental Hospital Workers' Union in 1922. It formally merged with the Amalgamated Transport and General Workers' Union on 31 January 1926, but the Registry files suggest a possible merger with the ITGWU, and many members certainly transferred to the ITGWU. Membership was 1,917 in 1919, 2,122 in 1920, 2,050 in 1921, 1,575 in 1922, 1,568 in 1923, 1,418 in 1924 and 1,235 in 1925. The Secretary of the ATGWU Mental Health Workers' Section was M. J. O'Connor, last General Secretary of the IMHWU. The report of the Executive Council of the ITUC&LP, 1925–1926, said that the IMHWU membership was 'absorbed by the ITGWU and ATGWU.'

1926
Amalgamated Transport and General Workers' Union, Newry and Galway Docks Branches
'All members on full benefit' were transferred, with a separate Branch Secretary, 'except seamen.'

1927
Limerick Dockers' Society
Founded in 1905 after the collapse of an earlier Limerick Dock Labourers' Union, 1863–1900. At a meeting on Sunday 10 July it decided to join the ITGWU by Sunday 7 August. It continued as a semi-autonomous body until 1931.

1931
Limerick Dock Labourers' Society
Transferred to the ITGWU in March, functioning as the Dockers' Section of the Limerick Branch, with 'the local Society going out of existence.' This confirms the previous entry.

1934
Kilrush Dockers' and General Workers' Union
Founded and registered in 1931 (no. 338T), cancelled in 1934, when it came over.

1935
Cork Builders' Labourers' Local Society
Established on 11 November 1932 and registered (no. 411T). It opposed the ITGWU and had 150 members in 1934 (90 men and 60 women). It complained that they were not recognised on the job at Fair Hill in 1935; 'all members have left to join I.T.G.W.U.,' with a few to the ATGWU. It complained that the Master Builders' Association and Cork Workers' Council conspired against them. There was no formal merger, but all members, bar perhaps moving lights, returned to the ITGWU.

1937
National Union of Dyers and Bleachers
Originally the Amalgamated Society of Dyers, Bleachers, Finishers and Kindred Trades, it affiliated to the ITUC in 1928. The Dublin Branch transferred as a Section of Dublin No. 6 Branch in September.

1938
Dublin Coal Factors' Association
Founded in 1936 and registered in 1938 (no. 430T), it rejoined Dublin No. 1 Branch.

Dublin United Tramway and Omnibus Inspectors' Association
Registered in 1934 (no. 414T), it dissolved in 1938 and its members came over. Membership was 87 in 1934, 100 in 1935, 100 in 1936 and 90 in 1937. At a Special General Meeting on 31 January 1938 'this Association was dissolved and the funds [£455] divided to the members.'

Tipperary Amalgamated Society of Masons, Painters and Plumbers
Founded in 1934 and registered in 1938 (no. 420T); its registration was cancelled in 1938 on transfer over.

1941
Limerick Corporation Employees' Union
Founded as Limerick Corporation Servants' Society in 1905, it was represented at the ITUC, 1896–7 and 1929–40. Some members may have transferred individually to the Irish Municipal Employees' Trade Union.

1942
Ardagh Trades and Labour Union
Registered in 1934 (no. 404T); registration was cancelled after its transfer.

Cork Coopers' Society
Founded in 1700 as a constituent of the Mutual Association of Journeymen Coopers. It was represented at the ITUC from 1895. Unable to raise the money for a Negotiating

Licence under the Trade Union Act (1941), it transferred all 43 members to the ITGWU in May.

1943

Limerick Operative Plasterers', Slaters' and Tilers' Society
Transferred in February 1943 after being unable to finance a Negotiating Licence.

Tipperary Workingmen's Protective and Benefit Society
Registered in 1932 (no. 391T). There were numerous local Workingmen's Protective and Benefit Societies throughout Co. Tipperary, which appear to have grown out of, and faded back into, the ITGWU in the 1930s. The registration of this society was cancelled in 1938 but it came over only in 1943.

Waterford Operative Coopers' Society
Registered on 10 January 1884 (no. 60T) and dissolved in 1942. It was represented at the 1897 ITUC Congress and transferred to the ITGWU in March 1943 after being unable to finance a Negotiating Licence. Membership was 23 in 1912, 12 in 1917, 20 in 1920, 16 in 1925, 10 in 1930, 13 in 1935, 12 in 1940.

1944

Ennis United Labourers' and Protective Benefit Society
Formed on 10 November 1910 and registered on 2 May 1934 (no 407T), it was dissolved in 1944 and accepted in November, when it was referred to as Ennis United Labourers' Association. 'Paid up members of the Association' were granted 'immediate benefit on the basis of one year's membership' in the ITGWU. The union's own account to the Registrar of Friendly Societies was that in October 1943 it became a 'Branch of the I.T.G.W.U.,' as the 'members decided that when they were not in a position to take out a Negotiating Licence they had no alternative [but] to dissolve the Association.' Membership was 411 in 1934, 381 in 1935, 351 in 1936, 401 in 1937, 350 in 1938 (258 men, 92 women), 307 in 1939 (220, 87), 408 in 1940 (330, 78), 414 in 1941 (273, 141) and 404 in 1942 (206, 198). The Secretary was D. Bourke.

1948

CIÉ Clerical Staffs' Association
The CIÉ Clerical Association sought amalgamation in 1947 and 1948. Liberty Hall finally agreed to accept the transfer of all members in Dublin CIÉ garages but not those employed in the company's Head Office. These members made a further application but were refused. Presumably they finally transferred to the Railway Clerks' Association.

1949

Cumann Teicneoirí Innealtóireachta
Founded in 1949 and affiliated on 9 August 'to enable them to overcome the problem of Negotiating Licence.' Mostly ESB draughtsmen and originally members of the Association of Engineering and Shipbuilding Draughtsmen, part of a movement of workers from British unions in reaction to the British Parliament's Ireland Act (1949). It gave 7d out of its weekly contributions of 3s (19½%) to the ITGWU, readjusting its arrangement and entitlements in July 1953. Its Leader was John Thomson.

Irish Municipal Employees' Trade Union, Limerick
Most IMETU members in Limerick Corporation transferred in October.

1950
Amalgamated Transport and General Workers' Union, Waterford Pork Butchers
All ATGWU members in Clover Meats, Waterford, transferred to the Limerick Pork Butchers' Society, an integral part of the ITGWU, in February.

1951
Stockbrokers' Clerks' Association
It is not clear if this was a formal organisation, but they became members in August.

1953
Clothing Workers' Union (Derry)
A breakaway from the National Union of Tailors and Garment Workers in 1951, merged with the ITGWU in October 1953. It had 4,300 members; 3,316 voted for amalgamation, 212 against. Its leader was Stephen McGonagle.

1958
Irish Railwaymen's Union
Formed on 1 January 1943 and registered (no. 472T). It ceased to function in September 1958, when the 'bulk of the members sought membership of N.A.T.E.,' some going to the ITGWU and 'a few to the W.U.I.' The General Secretary explained that 'early in the year it became evident that the Union, whose income had not met expenditure for some time, could no longer carry on. From that time, March 1958, members began to defect and it was eventually agreed to 'discontinue the Union.' It sought to be absorbed. Membership was 1,585 in 1943, 1,359 in 1944, 1,887 in 1945, 2,442 in 1946, 2,390 in 1947, 2,028 in 1948, 2,084 in 1949, 1,866 in 1950, 1,046 in 1951, 1,036 in 1952, 938 in 1953, 693 in 1954, 660 in 1955, 670 in 1956, 403 in 1957, nil in 1958. The ITGWU had guaranteed money for it to gain a Negotiating Licence in October 1942. It first transferred in numbers in 1948.

1971
Federation of Irish Industrial and Building Operatives' Trade Union / Comhaltas Ceardchumann Tionscail agus Oibrithe Tógála na hÉireann
This was a federation between the ITGWU, the Ancient Guild of Incorporated Brick and Stone Layers' Trade Union and Stonecutters' Union of Ireland (itself combined in the Building Workers' Trade Union), the Irish National Painters' and Decorators' Trade Union, the Irish National Union of Woodworkers, the Irish Society of Woodcutting Machinists and the Operative Plasterers' and Allied Trades Society of Ireland. The craft unions brought 10,000 members to the federation and the ITGWU 25,000. Each union continued to work independently, but all could avail of specialist ITGWU services in education, communications, industrial engineering and research. Three members of each union made up a monthly Executive, with John Mulhall (General Secretary, INPDTU), President, Patrick Duffy (General Secretary, AGIBSLTUI), Vice-President and Seán Ó Murchú (Group Secretary, ITGWU), Secretary. It collapsed within a couple of years.

1972
Association of Asylum Attendants
An Association of workers in the Central Mental Hospital, Dundrum, Dublin, it was finally allowed to join a trade union in 1972 and immediately transferred to the ITGWU and significantly improved its members' terms and conditions. In 1997 the Dundrum Mental Hospital Branch of the ITGWU was renamed the Richard Byrne Branch in memory of a long-serving Branch Officer.

1973
Irish Cinema Managers' Association
Taken in as a Section of Dublin No. 2 (Clerical and Professional) Branch in February.

1974
City and County Managers' and Assistant Managers' Society
The society transferred its engagements and was organised as an autonomous Branch within the Professional and Managerial Unit in March.

1975
ESB Meter Readers' Association
The Association entered a 'union of interest', receiving the services of a full-time Official. Problems arose, however, and 'considerable difficulty was experienced in endeavouring to clarify their position in relation to insurability,' while the ESB was 'very unresponsive to representations and requests for meetings.'

Irish Commercial Travellers' Federation, Irish Press Sales Staff
Irish Press Sales Staff Section of the ICTF transferred over.

United Commercial Travellers' Association
A British Friendly Society, it entered a 'union of interest' Agreement, receiving the services of a full-time Official. It was clear, however, 'that they were not interested or were not free within their constitution to form a union,' and the matter fizzled out.

1976
Comhaltas Lucht Riaracháin agus Leabharlanna (Administrative and Library Staff Association), University College, Galway
The Association organised administrative and clerical employees and transferred its 130 members in February, retaining an autonomous identity within the Professional and Managerial Division, Dublin No. 2 Branch.

Administrative Staff Association, University College, Cork
130 members transferred in July 1976 and were organised in the Professional and Managerial Division, Dublin No. 2 Branch.

Irish Share Fishermen's Association
The Association transferred in September 1976, creating the National Fishermen's Branch. The Branch had some initial success, with representatives at its first AGM in

Liberty Hall on 23 September 1980 from Balbriggan, Castletown Bearhaven, Cóbh, Dingle, Dún Laoghaire, Galway, Howth, Killybegs and Skerries and its own full-time Official, Kevin Page, but by 1980 it had collapsed.

National Union of Gold, Silver and Allied Trades

Founded in Sheffield in 1910 as the Amalgamated Society of Gold, Silver and Kindred Trades, there was a Dublin Branch from the beginning. In 1969 it absorbed the Society of Goldsmiths, Jewellers and Kindred Trades. The Irish membership transferred to the ITGWU when the parent union amalgamated with AUEW-TASS. Membership was 207 in 1920, 84 in 1930, 111 in 1940, 177 in 1950, 186 in 1960 and 250 in 1970. On merger with the ITGWU in July 1976 it had 350 members. They became a Section in Dublin No. 13 Branch, and Mick Browne, the NUGSAT Irish Secretary, became a Branch Assistant.

Shannon Free Airport Development Company Executive Staffs Association

Joined in spring through the Professional and Managerial Unit.

1977

Irish Shoe and Leather Workers' Union

Founded in Dundalk and registered in 1953 (no. 509T), it was represented in the ITUC and ICTU, 1953–77. It was amicably created from the National Union of Boot and Shoe Operatives in 1952, with the Irish Shoe and Leather Workers' Union formed on 1 January 1953. Northern Ireland members remained in the NUBSO but were serviced from Dundalk by the ISLWU. Membership was 330 in 1921, 263 in 1930, 3,596 in 1940, 3,500 in 1950, 4,451 in 1960 and 4,185 in 1970. In February 1978 the ITGWU discovered that the ISLWU's financial membership was 2,855. The first Irish Branches of the NUBSO were in Dublin and Cork in 1890 and Drogheda in 1894. The merger was the first conducted under the terms of the Trade Union Act (1975).

Local Authority Inspectorate

It is not clear what formal organisation the Local Authority Inspectorate had, but it transferred in as part of the Professional and Management Unit.

Regional Tourism Managers

Transferred in as part of the Professional and Management Unit.

1978

Irish Airlines Executive Staffs' Association

The Association was 'anxious to become associated or possibly members' in January 1974, when it was 'in association with the WUI.' The NEC nonetheless decided 'approval given to proceed,' and the arrangement with the WUI was suspended in 1978.

1979

Irish Actors' Equity Association

Founded in 1941 as the Writers', Actors', Artists' and Musicians' Association and registered in 1945 (no. 486T), renamed Irish Actors' Equity Association in January 1949. Membership was 371 in 1945, 250 in 1955, 469 in 1965 and 469 in 1975. It was affiliated to the ITUC, then CIU and ICTU, 1948–79, and merged with the ITGWU on 19 December 1979, having voted by seven to one to do so. It formally moved into Liberty Hall on 1 January 1980 and Actors' Equity's registration was cancelled on 5 March. As WAAMA it affiliated to the ITUC in September 1948 and on becoming Actors' Equity in 1949 transferred to the CIU.

1980
Amalgamated Union of Engineering Workers (Technical and Supervisory Section), Limerick
The Limerick Branch of AUEW-TASS, consisting of 850 local authority engineers and cognate grades, transferred *en bloc* in February to form the Local Authority Professional Officers' Branch. The transfer did 'not relate to any dissatisfaction with their union but rather to the inability of AUEW (TASS) over a long period, to secure effective negotiating rights on their behalf.' The ITGWU had representation within the Conciliation and Arbitration Scheme.

Professional Footballers' Association of Ireland
The 210-member Association joined in July, linking with Equity under Dermot Doolan. Two years of unproductive talks on a new Agreement with the Football Association of Ireland had led to the decision to affiliate. The Chairperson was Jim Jackson, and the Honorary Secretary was the legendary Mick Leech. At some point the PFAI withdrew and re-established an independent status.

Society of Irish Playwrights and Screen Writers' Guild
Part of the Cultural Division on 1 January. The formal Agreement for the Association of Irish Playwrights was completed in October 1987.

1981
Association of Administrative Psychiatric Nurses
The Association, many of whose members were already members of the ITGWU, formally affiliated in 1981 after rejecting an alternative offer from the Irish Nurses' Organisation. The ITGWU appointed a full-time National Nursing Officer and created the Nursing Council. At the AAPN Annual Conference in Killarney the union acknowledged the separate and special needs of senior nurses and established the Association of Nursing Officers as an autonomous body.

Association of Artists in Ireland
A 'new organisation,' the AAI became part of the Cultural Division in September. It had seventy members, with Robert Ballagh as Chairperson and Ken Dolan Secretary. In October 1987 the AAI made a new Agreement providing greater access to ITGWU services.

Association of Nursing Officers
After the merger of the Association of Administrative Psychiatric Nurses in 1981 the ITGWU recognised the separate requirements of senior nurses, in both psychiatric and general hospitals, and established the ANO as an autonomous body, serviced by a full-time Nursing Officer.

Dublin Junior Teachers' Association
The Association, representing teaching staff in convent junior schools, was formed in
1965 and had an associate relationship with the WUI. It joined the Professional and
Managerial Unit.

Irish Racecourse Bookmakers' Assistants' Association
Founded on 22 March 1938 and registered on 1 May 1943 (no. 447T), the Association
was represented in the CIU and later ICTU, 1945–80. Membership was 160 in 1943, 120 in
1950, 172 in 1955 and 133 in 1960. At the time of the merger, 5 June, it claimed its largest
membership of 274.

1982
Irish Federation of Musicians and Associated Professions
Founded as the Irish Federation of Dance Musicians in 1936, it was not registered until
1944 (no. 483T), then became the Irish Federation of Musicians in 1946 and the Irish
Federation of Musicians and Associated Professions in 1968. It was accepted in July 1982,
but the merger collapsed. The Association had 1,400 members at the time of merger, its
highest claimed total being 3,000, although the file of the Registrar of Friendly Societies
gives 1,724 in 1961 as the highest figure. The members 'voted overwhelmingly' to merge
with the ITGWU in March and April 1982.

Irish Union of Distributive Workers and Clerks, Insurance Staffs
More than 1,500 insurance workers in PMPA, Irish Life, Irish National and New Ireland
transferred from the IUDWC. After argument, the transfers were fully sanctioned by the
ICTU and resulted in the creation of Dublin No. 19 (Insurance and Finance) Branch.
The IUDWC Branch Secretary, Pat Meade, became Branch Secretary.

1987
Association of Irish Composers
The Association became part of the Cultural Division agreed by the NEC on 23–24
October.

Unions applying unsuccessfully to join the ITGWU

1920
Flax Dressers' Trade and Benevolent Trade Union
Formed in 1872 and registered in 1873 (no. 10T), it became the Flax Dressers' and Linen
Workers' Trade Union in 1912. It was affiliated to the ITUC, 1894–1914. Registration was
cancelled on the Northern Ireland Registry in 1922, the union having apparently merged
with the WU in 1920. It made an unexpected enquiry regarding amalgamation in May.
The ITGWU wondered if it was 'a sign of a coming revolt,' as such an enquiry must have
'upset the Counsels of a Tory Executive Committee.' Nothing came of it.

Irish Clerical Workers' Union
Formed in 1917 as a breakaway from the National Union of Clerks, it became the Irish
Clerical and Allied Workers' Union in 1920. It was invited to merge in April 1920, when

such figures as J. M. MacDonnell ('Malcolm MacColl', editor of the *Watchword of Labour*) and Thomas Johnson were prominent. It asserted its independence when registering in 1922 (no. 355T) and was affiliated to the ITUC, 1918–24. It petered out, and the registration was cancelled in 1928. Most members joined the Irish Union of Distributive Workers and Clerks. The ICWU received financial support from the ITGWU, written off as a bad debt in 1925.

1921
Dublin Silk and Poplin Trades Union
Applied to join in December 1921, when it was accepted, together with its National Health Insurance Approved Society. Why amalgamation was not completed is unclear, but it probably withdrew after the Larkin split in 1923 and before the merger with the Irish Union of Distributive Workers and Clerks.

1922
Irish Engineering Industrial Union
The union was founded in 1920 and registered in 1922 (no. 358T). Also known as the Irish Engineering, Shipbuilding and Foundryworkers' Trade Union, it quickly absorbed three other unions: (1) the Irish Stationary Engine Drivers (part of which had been in the ITGWU); (2) the Operative Society of Mechanical Engineers, Whitesmiths, Iron Workers, Pipe Fitters, and Brassfounders, Locksmiths and Bellhangers, etc., founded as the Dublin Whitesmiths, Locksmiths, Bellhangers, Domestic Engineers, Art Metal Workers and General Iron and Pipe Fitters in 1893, registered in 1903 (no. 267T), and affiliated to the ITUC, 1916–17, and later known as the Operative Society of Mechanical, Heating and Domestic Engineers, Whitesmiths, Ironworkers and Pipe Fitters; and (3) the Dublin United Brassfounders', Finishers' and Gasfitters' Society, dating from 1817 and affiliated to the ITUC, 1894–1918. The IEIU quickly fractured, with the Irish General Railway and Engineering Union breaking away in 1922 and the Electrical Trades Union (Ireland) in 1923. The IEIU became the IEIETU in 1947/8. The Executive of the IEIU sought an alliance with the ITGWU in December 1921, which led to suggestions of a joint Executive (rather along the lines of the Trade Union Federation between SIPTU and the NEETU in 2001). Foran and O'Brien insisted that the IEIU come in as a Craft Section, and the discussions broke down.

1942
Federation of Irish Rail and Road Workers
Established in 1934 and registered (no. 406T). On 4 November 1942 it let three members of its staff go, as the 'failure to take out a Negotiating Licence was final disaster.' The membership was 3,104 in 1934, 3,499 in 1935, 273 in 1936, 1,471 in 1937, 2,847 in 1938, 3,244 in 1939 and 2,900 in 1940. During 1935 'a strike occurred which was lost. The result was a complete collapse due to refusal of Companies to recognise' the union. It proposed to the ITGWU that it 'should take over their membership.' This was discussed by the NEC on 27–28 August 1942, which merely agreed to interview the General Secretary. It appears that some members were taken in, but the ITGWU supported the formation of the Irish Railwaymen's Union. The registration of the FIRRWU was cancelled in 1944, by which time the IRU had been registered, in 1942 (no. 472T), and it quickly affiliated to the CIU. The ITGWU provided the IRU with the money for a Negotiating Licence.

1947
Ulster Transport and Allied Operatives' Union
The UTAOU sought to amalgamate in February. As it was engaged in a 'bitter feud with the Amalgamated Transport and General Workers' Union,' the Vice-President of the ITGWU, William McMullen, advised the NEC that he was 'personally of the opinion that amalgamation with us would not be in the best interests of the Ulster Union.' The ITGWU was engaged in a series of membership disputes with the ATGWU, and amalgamation with the UTAOU was clearly considered unwise. It was informed in March. A Delegation visited Liberty Hall in August 1952 to suggest large-scale transfers, but the members of the Delegation were subject to disciplinary action, as a result of which many members left, mostly to join the General Union of Municipal Workers.

1949
Association of Shipbuilding and Engineering Draughtsmen
120 members sought to transfer, but the NEC decided that they were 'not encouraging the application as they were more appropriate to an Engineering Union.'

Guild of Irish Journalists
A breakaway from the National Union of Journalists, accepted as a CIU affiliate, after which the ITGWU stopped organising journalists and transferred its journalist members to the Guild.

1951
Garda Síochána Representative Body
In July 1951 *Liberty* reported 'our regrets to those members of the Gardaí who asked us to organise them, but, as pointed out, they are precluded from trade union Association.' It is not clear whether the request came from individual gardaí or from a formal Association. Either way, the Trade Union Act (1941) and policing legislation would have made it impossible for the ITGWU to accept them. A Representative Body for Guards existed before the creation of the Garda Representative Association and the Association of Garda Sergeants and Inspectors in 1978.

1953
Association of Irish Clerks
The Association approached the ITGWU to join, with the suggestion that a special white-collar Branch be created to cater for them. The union's policy, however, was stated to be one of 'confining recruitment to employments where we had industrial power to enforce just claims,' and that it would be 'unwise . . . to be committed to the indiscriminate organisation of clerical staffs.'

1954
Killarney Hackney Drivers' Association
Half the Association's seventy members applied to transfer in February, but the NEC declined their request, on the grounds that it would be 'difficult to represent them.'

1958

Irish Taxi and Hackney Owners' Association
The Association sought affiliation in August, but the NEC was to 'reply in the negative and to tender what advice deemed necessary and desirable.'

National Union of Furniture Trade Operatives
The Dublin Upholstery and Bedding Branch, with 350 members, voted by 69 to 5 to transfer in October. Two other Branches, representing a further 350 workers, did not proceed. The ITGWU insisted that it needed a memorial signed by a majority of all members before a transfer could be effected.

1965

Dublin Regular Coopers' Society
The society made an approach in January with a view to transferring. After it had requested information about structures and benefits, the matter withered on the vine.

United Stationary Engine Drivers
The United Stationary Engine Drivers approached about a possible transfer of engagement in December, and a deal was worked out and effected on 1 April 1965, with the USED's full-time Official becoming a member of the ITGWU staff. Problems arose at the last minute, however, delaying the merger, and by May the NEC reported that it had 'not been possible to clear up the difficulties and problems that had arisen regarding the transfer, as a single entity, of the members of this Union.' By June everything was off, and the USED, which had moved into the newly opened Liberty Hall, moved out again, although relations were 'still quite cordial.' There the matter ended.

Professional Officers' Association
This body, representing such professionals as accountants, architects and solicitors, made an approach in January about transfer. The matter was handed to Dublin No. 2 (Clerical, Supervisory and Professional) Branch. It was referred to the ICTU Working Party and appears to have faded away.

1971

Irish Civil Service Institute
Two hundred members were 'anxious to join' in November, but the NEC decided that they were not appropriate to the union and could be better serviced elsewhere.

National Union of Sheet Metal Workers of Ireland
Founded in 1836 as the City of Dublin Tinsmiths and Sheet Metal Workers' Society, later the Dublin Tinsmiths and Sheet Metal Workers and Dublin Tin and Sheet Metal Plate Workers and registered in 1942 (no. 466T) as the National Union of Sheet Metal Workers and Gas Meter Makers of Ireland, it became the National Union of Sheet Metal Workers of Ireland in 1967. It was affiliated to the ITUC, later to the CIU and ICTU, continuously from 1900. It entered amalgamation talks, ultimately unsuccessful, in October.

1974
Building Craft Federation
Between 1969 and 1971 a number of building craft unions came close to merging with
the ITGWU, with matters progressing as far as a written constitution. The unions were
the Building Workers' Trade Union (Ancient Guild of Incorporated Brick and Stone
Layers' Trade Union), the Irish National Painters' and Decorators' Trade Union, the
Operative Plasterers and Allied Trades Society of Ireland, the Irish National Union of
Woodworkers and the Irish Society of Woodcutting Machinists. Matters stalled and
were ended when the ITGWU took in wood factory workers in Limerick, although there
were more complex underlying factors.

Irish Dental Association
The Irish Dental Association sought merger in May, but matters never progressed
beyond initial talks.

1975
ESB Meter Readers' Association
A 'union of interest' was set up with the Association, but it fizzled out.

1977
Electrical, Electronic, Plumbing and Telecommunications Union
Unproductive talks were held regarding members of the EEPTU in the Republic, all of
them plumbers.

1978
Irish Commercial Travellers' Federation
Founded in Cork in 1919 and registered in 1922 (no. 359T). It operated as a Branch of
the Irish Union of Distributive Workers and Clerks, 1936–44, but never formally merged.
It was affiliated to the ITUC and ICTU from 1947. In 1981 it became the Sales, Marketing
and Administrative Union of Ireland. (In ITGWU reports it is erroneously referred to as
the United Commercial Travellers' Association.) Membership was 116 in 1922, 37 in 1930,
174 in 1940, 885 in 1950, 1,121 in 1960 and 1,683 in 1970.
    A 'union of interest' was created with the Federation, and the Professional and
Managerial Unit brought negotiations for merger 'to the final stages.' However, members of the ICTF in a secret ballot opted to continue as a separate union.

Unions breaking away from, or set up in opposition to, the ITGWU

1910
Irish Railway Workers' Trade Union
Established in the Trades and Labour Hall on 10 December 1910 by John Saturnus Kelly.
It stood for the state ownership of 'our railways, tramways and canals,' for safeguarding
members 'against the evil effects of strikes, Socialism and syndicalism,' and for all disputes to be settled by arbitration. It claimed 500 members in 1911, 133 in 1912, 152 in 1913,
142 in 1914, 87 in 1915, 93 in 1916, 94 in 1917, 94 in 1918, 95 in 1919, 96 in 1920, 96 in 1921,
124 in 1922, 129 in 1923, 131 in 1924, 131 in 1925, 132 in 1926, 132 in 1927, 133 in 1928, 133 in

1929 and 30 in 1930. Kelly complained to the Registrar of Friendly Societies about the 'unprecedented reign of terror of "Larkinism" in the city for the last two years' and in 1914 thought that 'now that it is crushed out forever by the force of true Irish Trade Unionism we hope that the members will return to this—the only Irish Trade Union that can render them any service.' In 1915 he tilted against the same windmills, his lance now the 'true doctrine of Christian Trade Unionism for Constitutional Trade Unionism.' Workers never quite accepted his message, although he was returned in elections in Inchicore.

1911
Belfast Transport and General Workers' Union
A short-lived Orange union fostered by employers and directed by Councillor Finnigan.

Galway Workers' and General Labourers' Union
Set up after Larkin agitated among supine local workers after the 1911 Congress of the ITUC in Galway. An independent local society was set up, mainly among dockers, and it decided to appoint a full-time Secretary. Against all trends, it opted not to throw in its lot with Liberty Hall but, in December 1912, after encouragement from James O'Connor Kessack, Larkin's successor as NUDL Organiser, it became No. 20 Branch of the NUDL. Only small NUDL Branches in Belfast, Derry and Drogheda survived. This schism with Liberty Hall—and it would appear that ITGWU militancy scared the locals—was to become a continuing saga as, in the 1920s and 30s, Galway members played hokey-cokey, coming and going between the ITGWU and ATGWU.

1913
Irish Dockers' and Workers' Union
Formed on 3 January 1914 and registered on 17 February 1914 (no. 309T), it dissolved in 1916, a short-lived attempt to set up a rival, yellow union arising out of the City of Dublin Steam Packet Company dispute in the spring of 1913, before the Lock-Out. It involved Richardson, Quigley and, most disappointingly, Thomas Greene, first Secretary of Dublin No. 1 Branch of the ITGWU in 1909. Greene and James Fenton had resigned by May, and the union collapsed as the Lock-Out terminated. It claimed to have had 130 members at the start, rising to 150. It was discontinued from December 1916.

Irish National Workers' Union
Registered in 1913 (no. 302T), cancelled in 1915. It was a short-lived yellow union.

Workers' Union, Kingstown
Father Flavin, a priest in Kingstown (Dún Laoghaire), was 'crucial to the destruction of the union [ITGWU]' in the Borough. He did not publicly attack it but organised a working men's Sodality of the Sacred Heart, which attracted between 600 and 700 members. Flavin condemned the ITGWU's use of the sympathetic strike, as it led to 'victimising the innocent.' These innocents he recruited into a Workers' Union of his own, which, by the end of the Lock-Out, had more than 300 members, divided into sections representing coal porters, municipal labourers and building labourers. He later boasted to Archbishop William Walsh that he had recruited seven-eighths of the coal porters from

the ITGWU. He persuaded the sixty-eight municipal labourers to withdraw from the
ITGWU as early as 1910. Many of Flavin's 'members' were recruited from the United
Builders' Labourers' Union. He insisted that he had been invited to undertake these
recruiting measures by disillusioned workers, and he had 'joyfully consented.' His
Workers' Union Rule Book provided for holding secret strike ballots. Flavin's 'concern'
at the death after a hunger strike of the Secretary of the Kingstown Branch of the ITGWU,
James Byrne, and his family should probably be taken with a considerable pinch of salt.

1914
New Labour Union
Founded in Swords, Co. Dublin, by Joseph Early in the spring of 1914. Greaves suggests
that it was closely connected with the United Irish League, which had done much to halt
the wages movement in Co. Dublin, an overlooked part of 1913 lost in the shadow of the
Lock-Out. The New Labour Union, set up to directly oppose Liberty Hall, appears to
have had a short existence.

1917
Irish Women Workers' Union
Founded in 1911 as an ITGWU Section, it was reorganised in 1917 and registered as an
independent union in 1918 (no. 332T). It was affiliated to the ITUC and ICTU, 1912–84, and
in 1984 amalgamated with the FWUI. Membership was 5,300 in 1918, 2,933 in 1930, 5,614
in 1940, 6,966 in 1950, 5,250 in 1960 and 3,550 in 1970. The Irish Nurses' Union and
Domestic Workers' Union were subsidiary organisations, the former becoming the Irish
Nurses' Organisation.

1918
National Tramway and Vehicle Workers' Association
Workers in Dublin United Tramways Company, members of the ITGWU since 1913, sur-
prisingly joined the NTVWA in February 1918. It was a founding component of the
ATGWU in 1922. There were extensive clashes between the ITGWU and ATGWU in Dublin
tramways in the 1920s, 30s and 40s, with most men joining the ITGWU or WUI.

1919
Ulster Workers' Trade Union
Registered in 1919 (no. 341T), registration dissolved in 1928. It was a Unionist organisation, directed not only against the ITGWU but at any 'Bolshevik or Fenian' influences. It
was specifically directed against the ITGWU at Caledon, Co. Tyrone, ultimately driving
it out.

1920
Dublin Coal Factors' Association
Registered in 1918 (no. 330T), moved out of Liberty Hall on 25 February 1920 to assert
its independence. It became the Dublin Coal Factors' Union in 1919, but its registration
was cancelled in 1928. Its membership was 18 in 1918, 93 in 1919 and 60 in 1920. Another
Dublin Coal Factors' Association was founded in 1936, registered in 1938 (no. 430T),
again dissolving in 1938, and finally Dublin Coal Distributors' Union, registered in 1941
(no. 451T), which survived until 1948.

1921

Irish Stationary Engine Drivers', Cranemen, Firemen and Motormen's Trade Union
Registered in April 1909 (no. 277T), it had Branches in Arklow, Limerick and Waterford
and was affiliated to the ITUC, 1909–20. It was closely associated with the ITGWU for a
long period, news of its meetings and activities appearing in the *Irish Worker*. It appears
to have been absorbed in 1919. Having re-emerged as an independent body, it merged
with the Irish Engineering Industrial Union in 1921.

1923

United Builders' Labourers' Trade Union
Registered in 1923 (no. 360T), registration cancelled in 1943. According to the *Voice of
Labour*, 6 September 1924, its re-formation took place after the Marino strike, and, hav-
ing opted out of the ITGWU, the alternative to the WUI was to re-establish its old body.
It did not survive the Trade Union Act (1941), and members most probably joined the
WUI. It was refused affiliation to the ITUC in 1939.

1924

Association of Ex-Officers and Men of the National Army Trade Union
This organisation remains a mystery. Registered in 1924 (no. 371T) and most active during the dispute at the Shannon Scheme in 1925, it was in effect used by the authorities as
a strike-breaking, anti-ITGWU organisation. Its registration was cancelled in 1930.
Frustratingly, its file in the National Archives is empty. The *Voice of Labour* published a
notice of the organisation supplying scabs to break a strike in Sutton Sandpit in April
1926.

Independent Co-operative Trades Union
Based in Moate, Co. Westmeath, and led by the renegade Labour TD Seán Lyons. It
sought affiliation to the ITUC in 1924. It was registered the same year (no. 368T), giving
a Dublin address, but registration was cancelled by 1928. The 'co-operation' Lyons
preached was with employers and against the ITGWU—in which he had once been a
Branch Secretary—and the WUI.

Irish National Union of Free State Workers
Formed 'among ex-soldiers' in Cóbh and rejected as an affiliate by the ITUC&LP. It
undercut ITGWU wages and conditions. It was probably the same organisation as the
National Association below.

National Association of Free State Workers
Registered in 1924 (no. 365T) but dissolved in 1926. Most probably an organisation similar to the Association of Ex-Officers and Men of the National Army Trade Union, and
probably the same as the Irish National Union above.

Workers' Union of Ireland
Founded and registered in 1924 (no. 369T) by James Larkin after his expulsion
from the ITGWU; it became the Federated Workers' Union of Ireland in 1979 after its
amalgamation with the Federation of Rural Workers. It amalgamated with the ITGWU
on 1 January 1990 to form SIPTU.

1925
Cork Unemployed Workers' Union
Founded in 1925 and registered (no. 375T). There is little information about it other than that it was encouraged by Cork Workers' Council and charged only 6d per month. Its target was primarily the ITGWU, which complained about it in May 1926. It had a fleeting existence. Whether or not it was a forerunner of the Cork Builders' Labourers' Local Union (below) is not clear. It dissolved in 1928.

National Association of Motor and Steam Lorry Drivers and Mechanics
An 'appeal in picturesque but ungrammatical language' was addressed to motor drivers to join this new organisation in November 1925. The ITGWU observed that the 'tendency to revert to craft and sectional organisation is the inevitable outcome of the indefensible tactics of the disruptionists'—in other words, some trade Unionists were opting out of both ITGWU and WUI on a 'plague on both your houses' platform. Whether this organisation either survived or was revived as the Irish Automobile Drivers and Automobile Mechanics' Union (see under 1939 below) is not clear. James Mitchell, previously President of the IADAMU and in 1925 an Official of the WUI, was probably involved.

Kilkenny Local Labour Union
A reference to James Reade forming a local Labour Union in Kilkenny in October 1925 was published in the *Voice of Labour*, but there is no other information. In March 1926 Reade was seeking to form an ATGWU Branch, his original plan presumably abandoned. It opposed the ITGWU.

1926
Hotel Employees' Association
Planned over six months by Dublin hoteliers to break the influence of the ITGWU, the backdrop being the festering strike in the Metropole Restaurant and Cinema. Hoteliers promised £250 to the new body and selected six workers as representatives. Two— Graham and O'Shea—repudiated it, and C. O'Callaghan took no part in its activities, leaving Halpin, Brophy and Moore as stooges. Kidney (an employer) was Treasurer, Fred A. Moran (Moran's Hotel) was Organiser, and M. Freyne, Secretary. Its office was in Duke Street. The ITGWU saw the Association as 'organised and controlled by employers for the maintenance of a Free Labour Bureau.' All employees were then recruited through the ITGWU. The Association was defeated in the famous Five Houses dispute in Dublin, June–July 1926. Freyne was sacked in May.

United Union of British and Irish Ex-Servicemen
Registered in 1926 (no. 381T) but dissolved by 1930. It was formed to secure preference in employment for ex-servicemen, particularly in state employments, in opposition to the ITGWU.

1931
Irish Mines, Quarries and Allied Workers' Union
Formed in December 1931 among coalminers around Castlecomer, Co. Kilkenny, and led by Nicholas 'Nixie' Boran as a breakaway from the ITGWU. It affiliated to the Red

International of Labour Unions but not to the ITUC. It led 400 men in a strike for an increase of 3d per ton in October 1932 and succeeded in gaining 2d. It was a pyrrhic victory, however, as funds were exhausted and clerical opposition fierce. It dissolved back into the ITGWU, and Boran became a member of the NEC.

Kilrush Dockers' and General Workers' Union
Founded among ITGWU members on 28 October 1931 and registered (no. 338T), it dissolved on 31 January 1934 back into the ITGWU.

United General Workers' Union
William Gleeson, Secretary of the Nenagh Branch of the ITGWU, took the Larkinite side in the split of 1923–4 and was for a period Nenagh Branch Secretary of the WUI. After the demise of the local ITGWU and WUI by 1930, Gleeson led the New Union. It is not clear how long it operated, but when the ITGWU was revived in 1940 all workers were back in the Liberty Hall fold. The UGWU appears to have had previous members of both the ITGWU and WUI in its ranks.

1932
Cork Builders' Labourers' Local Union
Established on 11 November 1932 in opposition to the ITGWU and registered in 1934 (no. 411T). It complained that the Master Builders' Association and Cork Workers' Council conspired against it. It was dissolved on 22 August 1935, when most members left to join the ITGWU.

Limerick City Workers' Union
Formed on 7 May and 1932 and registered (no. 392T). To be a member it was necessary to have been 'born in the city or suburbs of Limerick,' a qualification no doubt motivated by severe unemployment. Membership was 271 in 1932, 129 in 1933, 100 in 1934, 161 in 1935, 118 in 1936 and 107 in 1937. It was gone by December 1938, having been refused affiliation to the ITUC.

Tipperary Workingmen's Protective and Benefit Society
The society had amalgamated in 1920 but reasserted its independence and was registered in 1932 (no. 391 T). Registration was cancelled in 1943, and it went back into the ITGWU.

United Stationary Engine Drivers', Cranemen, Firemen, Motormen and Machinemen's Trade Union
In 1932 the long-standing Engine Drivers' Section of the ITGWU formed an independent union, and it was registered (no. 394T). Between 1938 and 1943 it was known as the Irish Power Operatives' and Allied Workers' Trade Union, before reverting back to its original title. It affiliated to the CIU in 1958 and thence the ICTU. In 1942 it absorbed the Limerick Engine Drivers' and Firemen's Union, an ancient union dating from 1882 and represented at the ITUC Congress in 1896. In the mid-1960s it agreed to re-merge with the ITGWU and actually had offices in the new Liberty Hall when it opened in 1965. Problems arose, however, and the merger was cancelled, with the USED moving out. It expanded membership in paper mills and other mills, canneries and construction

works. It had 83 members in 1932, 249 in 1940, 734 in 1950, 706 in 1960 and 501 in 1970. It was refused affiliation to the ITUC in 1938, as, having consulted a number of unions, most notably the ITGWU, the Executive thought its 'small membership could be catered for adequately by a Union already affiliated.' In 1987 it merged with the FWUI.

1933
Athlone Local Workers' Union
Registered in 1933 (no. 402T) and dissolved in 1937, this was a short-lived rival to the ITGWU.

Dockers' and Carters' Union
Little is known about this short-lived organisation other than that it shared offices with the Irish Seamen's Union in Commons Street, Dublin, before merging with it in July 1933 to form the Irish Seamen's and Port Workers' Union. The DCU was a 'by-product' of the 1933 seamen's strike, which led to the creation of the Irish Seamen's Union and was 'made up of hundreds of dock workers,' who hitherto were casual and unorganised and, most probably, alienated by the fratricidal strife between the ITGWU and WUI.

Irish Seamen's and Port Workers' Union
Founded at a meeting on 23 May 1933 among Irish seamen, mostly members of the National Union of Seamen (a British union), in opposition to the new Agreement between the NUS and the Shipping Federation. It was first called the Seamen and Firemen's Union of Ireland and had offices at 1A Commons Street, Dublin. A strike began on 28 June, and membership spread to Cork and other ports, with the NUS assisting the Shipping Federation in opposing it. The total closure of the ports brought matters to a head, and a settlement reached on 15 July secured the union's future. It quickly spread beyond seamen, however, taking in the Dockers' and Carters' Union (above) on 23 July 1933 and changing its name to the Irish Seamen's and Port Workers' Union. It was registered in 1934 (no. 409T) and in 1955 became the Marine, Port and General Workers' Union.

1934
Stonecutter's Union of Ireland
The Stonecutter's Union of Ireland re-affiliated to the ITUC in 1934. It was still an integral part of the ITGWU in 1925 but clearly struck out independently after that date. It was part of the Building Workers' Trade Union, 1945–62, before registering as a separate body in 1963 (no. 529T). It merged with the Ancient Guild of Incorporated Brick and Stone Layers' Trade Union in 1966, having first approached the WUI in 1965.

1935
Irish Mental Hospital Employees' Union
Established on 1 July 1935 and registered (no. 417T), with 141 members, including 38 women. It was dissolved on 2 June 1937, having failed to attract members from the ITGWU.

1936
Thurles Sugar Company Union
When the campaign opened in Mallow a strike was 'fought with great vigour.' When the Thurles sugar factory next opened, workers, 'seduced by local pressure,' were 'persuaded to establish a blackleg and strike-breaking organisation.' The Industrial Court failed to settle the matter. What became of this yellow union is not known, but the workers soon rejoined the ITGWU.

Tipperary Amalgamated Society of Masons, Painters, Plasterers and Plumbers
Formed in 1934 and registered in 1936 (no. 407T). The registration was cancelled in 1938 and merged back into the ITGWU.

1938
Irish Motor Mechanics' Trade Union
Formed in 1938 and registered in 1939 (no. 437T), it was dissolved in 1943. The members probably went individually into AGEMOU (below).

1939
Automobile, General Engineering and Mechanical Operatives' Union
Formed and registered in 1939 (no. 441T) as the Irish Automobile Drivers' and Automobile Mechanics' Union. It was refused affiliation to the ITUC in 1938 and was directed to 'seek association with' unions already catering for drivers and mechanics. IADAMU replied: 'We have no intention of merging with any other Union,' least of all the ITGWU. It was affiliated to the CIU and ICTU, 1945–97. It became AGEMOU in 1962 and went into SIPTU in 1997.

1948
National Union of Boot and Shoe Operatives
Virtually all the ITGWU Boot and Shoe Section of the Killarney Branch, including the Secretary, left to join the NUBSO in April 1948.

1963
National Bus and Rail Workers' Union
Founded in 1963 as the Dublin City Busmen's Union and registered in 1963 (no. 530T), it became the National Busmen's Union in 1964, National Busworkers' Union in 1980, and National Bus and Rail Workers' Union in 1979 when taking in railway workers from the ITGWU and NATE.

1969
Psychiatric Nurses' Association of Ireland
Registered in 1969 (no. 545T) and affiliated to the Local Government and Public Services Union in the 1980s. When the PNA sought a Negotiating Licence in the spring of 1970 the ITGWU 'sought to get WUI to join with us and IWWU in a common approach to the Minister,' as the 'granting of this licence would be inimical to the interests of Psychiatric Nurses and harmful to the rationalisation of the trade union movement.' Denis Larkin of the WUI did not agree with this direct approach and insisted on matters going through Congress, which reported back that 'little or nothing could be done.' In June

1970 a Negotiating Licence was granted, and the NEC of the ITGWU 'learned from the Department [of Labour] that there were approximately 27 members involved in this licence application.' The ITGWU said the PNA began as a professional Association, 'concerning itself only with nursing standards, etc.,' but in the 1969 salary negotiations it had 'acted as a ginger group.' It dismissed the new body: 'some prominent members of the PNA were more concerned with divorcing themselves from our Union because of our affiliation to the Labour Party more than for any other reason.'

1982
Irish Federation of Musicians and Associated Professions
Merged with the ITGWU but reversed its decision, ceased to function in 1990 and re-registered as an independent union on 1 January 1994. It ceased to exist in November 2002 and divided the proceeds from the sale of its premises in Lower Gardiner Street, Dublin—rumoured to be £1 million—among the remaining member in proportion to the length of their membership. SIPTU established the Musicians' Union of Ireland on 30 January 2003.

FEDERATED WORKERS' UNION OF IRELAND

Amalgamations and mergers

1929
Dublin Regular Chimney Cleaners' Trades Union
Little is known of this union. It marched in the Dublin trades procession of 1864 and had sixty members. It claimed to have originated from a guild and carried an ancient emblem on its badge with the words *God loves justice*. Its members were mostly employed by Dublin Corporation, hospitals and other institutions. It affiliated to the WUI, and its wonderful badge has *WUI* stamped above its emblem with *RCCTU* around the rim. The City of Dublin Regular Chimney Cleaners' Friendly Society was registered as a Friendly Society in 1882 (no. 632) and a second body with the same name in 1911 (no. 1243), its registration cancelled in 1916.

1942
Dublin Fire Brigade Men's Union
Founded in 1892 in Tara Street Fire Station and registered in 1905 (no. 244T) and was affiliated to the ITUC, 1913–23, at times represented by P. T. Daly. Membership was 40 in 1911, 32 in 1921, 32 in 1931 and 25 in 1941. It was dissolved on 26 April 1942 and is thought to have gone into the Irish Municipal Employees' Trade Union, but it had a close relationship with the WUI, and some members transferred.

1944
Boilermen's Section, Irish Engineering and Foundry Union
The Section transferred, led by Christy Ferguson and Peter Coates (an Irish Citizen Army veteran).

1947
Brewery Employees' Association (Guinness)
Transferred in May, after approaching the ITGWU.

Muintir na Mara
East coast fishermen's organisation begun in Howth 1947. It approached the WUI for support from the Fish and Poultry Section in not handling imported herrings while its members tied up their boats in protest at exploitation by auctioneers. It sought to affiliate 500 members and was accepted by the GEC in July. Unfortunately, while WUI members were laid off through lack of herrings in markets and processing plants, Howth boats landed their catches in the Isle of Man at good prices. The WUI rebuffed any attempts at a merger.

1948
Irish Woodcutting Machinists' Union
Formally applied to affiliate in July 1948, with two hundred members in Cork, Limerick and Waterford. It is not clear what obstructed the merger, but it never occurred.

Shipconstructors' and Shipwrights' Association
The Dublin Branch transferred, completing the transfer in 1949. As late as 1957 the Association would not enter a card recognition Agreement with the WUI, as the latter had 'taken a seceding Branch' into membership, even though all twenty-six members of the SSA had 'transferred as a body' and 'had clear cards.'

1950
Irish Airline Pilots' Association
Founded in 1946 and registered in 1948 (no. 499T). It affiliated in April 1950 (referred to in WUI documents as the International Airline Pilots' Association). It became an affiliated Section in 1957 for a fee of £200 per annum, altering its status from full members of the union. Had 80 to 90 members in April 1957, paying 2s a week. It wanted to pay only £150 a quarter, but the WUI suggested £200 in return for secretarial assistance, office accommodation and stenography. No benefits would apply after 1 January 1957. In 1971 it had 282 members, paying £650 a year for advisory and negotiation services. Registration was cancelled in 1951. The Association again took out its own Negotiating Licence in 1971 and on 25 May 1978 terminated its affiliation, expressing 'its tremendous debt of gratitude' to the WUI 'for all the help it had given to the Association in its formative years.'

Irish Pharmaceutical Employees' Association
Registered in 1950 (no. 505T) but cancelled in 1951. Originally the Chemists' Branch of the Irish Union of Distributive Workers and Clerks, it established its own organisation. After a mass meeting and a ballot in February 1950 it transferred. In 1971 it had 134 members and paid £400 a year for secretarial and negotiating services. It changed its name to the Association of Pubic and Hospital Pharmacists at that time.

1953

Assistance Officers' and Superintendent Assistance Officers' Association
Transferred after a postal ballot from the Irish Local Government Officials' Union and became an affiliated Section; final affiliation was made in June 1956. In 1957 it paid 4s per month per member. In 1971 it had 209 members and paid 10p per member per week to the WUI. It fully merged in 1972.

Civilian Aeronautical Instructors' Association
Previously members of a professional Association and, from November 1950, the Irish Conference of Professional and Service Associations, it joined in spring.

1955

National Society of Brushmakers
The United Society of Brushmakers existed from 1894 to 1959; the Dublin Branch was established c. 1955. It merged into No. 3 Branch in 1958 after declining membership.

1956

Irish Superintendent Assistance Officers' and Assistance Officers' Association
The Association was accepted as an affiliated group in January.

Irish Liver Assurance Employees' Union
WUI members in the Dublin office of the Royal Liver Assurance had for years sought unsuccessfully to gain recognition. In 1956 they transferred into the Irish Liver Assurance Employees' Union in Cork, which in turn became an affiliated Section of the WUI. In 1971 the union had 498 members and paid 10p per member per week for negotiation and secretarial services, and all benefits except marriage and Funeral Benefit. They finally became full members on 1 June 1976, being absorbed into No. 16 Branch. They got a skilled negotiator, clerical assistance and Dispute Pay. The GEC's formal invitation was that the 'ILAEU be invited to join with our 190 members of the Royal Liver Society as full members of the union, constituting, if desired, a separate Section.'

1958

Physiotherapists' Association
Little is known about this body, other than that it applied for and was granted affiliate status.

1960

John Player and Sons Staff Association
The Dublin Branch affiliated as an autonomous Section in August 1960, with 120 members. Men paid 5s monthly, women 3s, and four-fifths was to be returned to WUI Head Office, the remainder creating a Local Fund. It became a single Association only in 1966. In 1968 another John Player's Staff Association was formed but was strongly discouraged by the WUI.

Radio Éireann Staff Association
With the establishment of the RTÉ Authority, radio employees were no longer civil

servants and formed the Radio Éireann Staff Association, which in turn affiliated. The first Secretary was James Plunkett Kelly, a Radio Éireann staff member but formerly Branch Secretary, Gas Workers' Branch.

1961
Medical Laboratory Technologists' Association
In 1971 the Association had 420 members and paid £500 plus costs per year for negotiation and secretarial services. The title was changed to Irish Medical Scientists' Association, and it sought its own Negotiating Licence in August 2005, affiliating directly to the ICTU.

St James's Gate Technical Assistants' Association
Guinness Technical Assistants' Association represented laboratory workers in the brewery and voted to affiliate in February. It had 62 members and paid 2s per week.

1962
Irish Free State Pilots' Association
Formed in 1935 and registered in 1936 (no. 422T), it became the Irish Pilots' and Marine Officers' Association in 1949. It affiliated and dissolved its independent status.

Vocational Education Clerks' Association
In 1971 the Association had 48 members and paid £100 a year for secretarial and negotiation services.

1964
Association of Chief Administrative Officers of Hospitals
In 1971 the Association had 20 members and paid £10.40 a quarter for secretarial and negotiation services.

Association of Hospital and Public Pharmacists
It appears to have first made contact in 1958. It confirmed its affiliate status in 1964.

Institute for Industrial Research and Standards Staff Association
An application was received in January 1964. After the Association negotiated with the employer and accepted an increase after a visit to the Labour Court, all without informing the WUI, its affiliate status was cancelled in June 1968.

Irish Independent Clerical Association
Affiliated in April with 130 members.

Irish Pharmaceutical and Medical Representatives' Association
Accepted as an affiliate in June, and terminated its Association in September 1968.

Voluntary Hospitals Clerical and Administrative Staffs' Association
First accepted as an affiliated group in February, it opted for full membership in 1974.

1965

An Foras Talúntais (Agricultural Institute) Technical Officers' Staff Association
Affiliation was reaffirmed by ballot in 1971, when it had 321 members, paying 7½p per member per week for negotiation and secretarial services. They opted to become full members in 1975.

Association of Irish Radiographers
Applied to become an affiliate in January. In 1971 it had 147 members and paid 10p per member per week for secretarial and negotiation services. They opted for full membership in 1974.

Association of Professional Officers in Local Authorities
Applied to become an affiliate in January.

Dublin Institute of Advanced Studies Staff Association
Applied to become an affiliate in February.

Irish Marine Officers' Association
Little is known of this body. In 1980 its 668 members were trying to seek independent Branch status from the GEC.

Junior Teachers' Association
Formed in 1965 with 100 members and applied to become an affiliate in June 1965. A Dublin Junior Teachers' Association joined the ITGWU in 1981.

Stonecutters' Union of Ireland
Approached to become full members in January and accepted. The merger was clearly never concluded, as the union merged with the Ancient Guild of Incorporated Brick and Stone Layers' Trade Union in 1966.

1966

Irish Airlines Executive Staffs' Association
Accepted as an affiliate in January on terms of £3 per member per annum. In 1971 the IAESA, or Aer Lingus Executive Staffs' Association, had 232 members and paid £3.50 per member per year for negotiation and secretarial services. Relations were described in 1975 as unsatisfactory, and discussions to resolve differences were held. 'Having heard a report on the activities of some members' of the IAESA during a dispute, the WUI terminated the Agreement in 1978, although it appeared that nothing was ever put in writing between the two. An application by the Association for a Negotiating Licence was opposed in the High Court by the ICTU on behalf of the FWUI and was refused in May 1981.

Mercantile Marine Officers' Section
A Section created after an Agreement with the Merchant Navy and Airline Officers' Association, London, and transfer of members and responsibilities.

Town Clerks' Association of Ireland
Applied to affiliate in September 1966.

1969
National Rehabilitation Placement Officers
In 1971 it had 16 members and paid 12p per member per week for secretarial and nego-
tiation services.

1970
Racing Staffs' Association
Approached in November 1962 and accepted as an affiliate on 3 June 1970 at a charge of
£50 per quarter, the Association being 'responsible for collecting their own money.' In
1971 it had 80 members and paid £50 a quarter for negotiation and secretarial services.
In January 1963 the title was Racecourse Employees' Association, and it was agreed to
take it in as a group for negotiating purposes at a fixed annual sum.

1974
Aer Rianta Sales and Catering Managerial Association, Shannon
Affiliated in 1974 and opted to become full members in 1975.

1976
Irish Liver Assurance Employees' Union
Finally became full members on 1 June, having been affiliated from 1956.

1978
Racing Board Tote Staff Association
Affiliated, but little is known about the organisation.

1979
Federation of Rural Workers
Founded in 1946 and registered (no. 493T), it was represented in the ITUC and ICTU,
1948–79. After the transfer of engagements in 1979 the WUI became the FWUI.

Irish Association of Dental Prosthesis
Approached in November with a view to affiliate its 250 members, some of whom were
self-employed.

1984
Irish Women Workers' Union
The Irish Women Workers' Union was founded in 1911 as an integral part of the ITGWU
and registered in 1918 (no. 332T) and was represented in the ITUC and ICTU, 1912–84.
Subsidiary organisations were the Irish Nurses' Union and the Domestic Workers'
Union. The merger with the FWUI took place on 1 September, creating the Women
Workers' Branch. The IWWU had 1,600 members.

1986
Irish Agricultural Advisors' Organisation
The IAAO WAS founded in 1922 as the Agricultural and Technical Instruction Officials' Association and was briefly within the Irish National Teachers' Organisation in 1923 and the Irish Local Government Officials' Union, 1925–9. In 1932 it became the Irish Agricultural Officers' Organisation and in 1970 the Irish Agricultural Advisors' Organisation, when it affiliated. It finally merged in 1986. John Howley, General Secretary of the IAAO, became Branch Secretary of the Irish Agricultural Advisers' Branch. In 1982 it had 720 members.

1987
National Association of Transport Employees
Founded and registered in 1953 (no. 508T) after withdrawal from the National Union of Railwaymen. It was represented in the CIU and ICTU, 1953–87. The merger was completed on 3 April 1987.

United Stationary Engine Drivers, Cranemen, Motormen and Firemen's Trade Union
A number of unions catered for stationary engine drivers. The United Stationary Engine Drivers, Cranemen, Motormen and Firemen's Trade Union was registered in 1932 (no. 384T) and was represented in the CIU and ICTU, 1958–87. From 1938 to 1943 it was the Irish Power Operatives and Allied Workers' Trade Union. It took in the Limerick Engine Drivers' and Firemen's Union in 1942. It merged from 16 March.

1989
Marine, Port and General Workers' Union
Founded in 1935 as the Irish Seamen's and Port Workers' Union, registered in 1934 (no. 409T), it was affiliated to the ITUC, later CIU and ICTU, 1936–98. It changed its name to Marine, Port and General Workers' Union in 1955. Membership was 5,150 in 1934, 7,344 in 1940, 3,220 in 1950, 3,803 in 1960 and 4,808 in 1970. The Irish Seamen's Union broke away in 1957 and registered (no. 518T); it dissolved in 1959. The Seamen's Union of Ireland was then formed and registered in 1959 (no. 520T); it was affiliated to the ICTU, 1959–2007. Agreement for a merger was obtained as the talks concluded to found SIPTU; the MPGWU thus effectually voted to merge with SIPTU, although its members were balloted merely on the proposal to merge with the FWUI.

Unions attempting to join, break away or disaffiliate from the FWUI

1948
Irish Woodcutting Machinists' Union
Formed in 1933 as the Irish Society of Woodcutting Machinists when the Dublin Branch of the Amalgamated Society of Woodcutting Machinists seceded. It was registered in 1934 (no. 408T). It was affiliated to the ITUC and later the CIU and ICTU, 1938–79, and in 1979 merged with the Irish Union of Woodworkers to form the National Union of Woodworkers and Woodcutting Machinists. It was a founding component of the Building and Allied Trades Union in 1989. In July 1947 the 'Irish Woodcutting Machinists' Union' applied to affiliate. It had 200 members in Cork, Limerick and Waterford. It is not clear why this merger never materialised.

1956
County Cork Vocational Schools Caretakers' Association
The Association sought to join in September, but the GEC told the twenty-member organisation that its 'best interests would not be served by joining our union.'

1978
Irish Airlines Executive Staffs' Association
The WUI terminated its Agreement with the IAESA after its unacceptable behaviour during a dispute with Aer Lingus. It reapplied to affiliate in February 1979 but also sought advice from the ICTU regarding a Negotiating Licence. It was accused of poaching WUI members in 1980 as it frantically attempted to acquire the five hundred members needed for a Licence. The High Court rejected its application in May 1981. The ESB Officers' Association offered membership, provoking the FWUI to again offer it affiliate status in November 1981. This was rejected, and the Association moved to achieve 'accepted body' status under the Trade Union Acts (1941–1976). It went into the ITGWU.

Irish Airline Pilots' Association
The Association took out its own Negotiating Licence in the early 1970s and on 25 May 1978 terminated its affiliation.

SERVICES, INDUSTRIAL, PROFESSIONAL AND TECHNICAL UNION

Amalgamations and mergers

1991
National Union of Tailors and Garment Workers
The Tailors and Garment Workers' Union was formed in 1920 by the amalgamation of the Scottish Operative Tailors' and Tailoresses' Association and the United Garment Workers' Union. In 1932 it merged with the Amalgamated Society of Tailors and Tailoresses to form the National Union of Tailors and Garment Workers. In 1939 it absorbed the United Ladies' Tailors' Trade Union and in 1972 the Waterproof Garment Workers' Trade Union. In 1991, when the NUTGWU merged with the General, Municipal, Boilermakers' and Allied Trades Union, members in the Republic opted to transfer to SIPTU. William O'Brien, General Secretary of the ITGWU, 1924–46, was active in the Amalgamated Society of Tailors and Tailoresses until joining the ITGWU in 1917.

1992
Irish National Painters' and Decorators' Trade Union
Registered as Metropolitan House Painters in 1890 (no. 99T) and represented at the ITUC, 1894–1907. It wound up and was re-established on the same day as the Dublin Metropolitan House Painters' Trade Union and re-registered in 1911 (no. 290T). In 1918 it became the Irish National Painters', Decorators' and Allied Trades Union and in 1926 the Irish National Painters' and Decorators' Trade Union. It claimed to be the successor of the Guild of St Luke the Evangelist, formed in 1670, and St Luke's Regular Operative House Painters of the City of Dublin Society, 1860. It was affiliated to the

ITUC and then to the CIU and ICTU, 1913–91. Membership was 534 in 1892, 500 in 1900, 487 in 1910, 494 in 1920, 293 in 1930, 214 in 1940, 733 in 1950, 927 in 1960 and 1,628 in 1970. It amalgamated with SIPTU in 1992. (Negotiations and agreement in principle had been made with the ITGWU in September 1989 on the understanding that the merger would be with SIPTU.) Other unions involved in the painting trade were the Dublin Whiteners' Trade Union, founded in 1829, registered in 1892 (no. 129T), amalgamated with the INPDTU 1919–23, registration cancelled in 1937; the Limerick Operative House Painters' Trade Union, which became a constituent of the Building Workers' Trade Union, 1942–59, amalgamated with the INPDTU in the late 1960s; the Cork House Painters, formed 1924 and registered (no. 370T), in 1966 amalgamated with the INPDTU; and the United House and Ship Painters' and Decorators' Trade Union, Ireland, formed and registered in 1927 (no. 392T) affiliated to the ITUC, then CIU and ICTU, 1930s to 1972, which dissolved in 1972, most of its members joining the INPDTU.

1993
Irish Writers' Union
The Irish Writers' Union (Comhar na Scríbhneoirí) was founded on 1 January 1987. Membership grew to about 300 in the mid-1990s, dipped from 2000 but has revived since 2005. It includes most prominent Irish writers.

1997
Automobile, General Engineering and Mechanical Operatives' Union
Founded as the Irish Automobile Drivers' and Automobile Mechanics' Union in 1939 (no. 441T); represented in the CIU and ICTU, 1945–96, became AGEMOU in 1962. It brought 2,000 members into SIPTU.

1998
Irish Print Union
Founded as Dublin Typographical Provident Society in 1809, registered in 1935 (no. 416T). It became the Irish Graphical Society in 1965 and in 1984 the Irish Print Union by amalgamation with (1) the Electrotypers and Stereotypers, Dublin and District, founded in 1891, registered in 1923 (no. 362T), originally a constituent of the Electrotypers and Stereotypers, Great Britain and Ireland, affiliated to ITUC, CIU and ICTU, 1930–84, and (2) the Irish Bookbinders' and Allied Trades Union, formed in 1920, registered in 1924; in 1936 the Dublin Branch of the National Union of Printing, Binding and Paper Workers (formerly the Bookbinders' and Machine Rulers' Consolidated Union) amalgamated and the union became the Irish Bookbinders' and Allied Trades Union, affiliated to the ITUC, 1930s to 1945, CIU, 1945– 59 and ICTU, 1959–84.

Marine, Port and General Workers' Union
Founded in 1935 as the Irish Seamen's and Port Workers' Union, registered in 1934 (no. 409T); affiliated to the ITUC, then CIU and ICTU, 1936–98. It changed its name to Marine, Port and General Workers' Union in 1955. Membership was 5,150 in 1934, 7,344 in 1940, 3,220 in 1950, 3,803 in 1960 and 4,808 in 1970. The Irish Seamen's Union broke away in 1957 and registered (no. 518T), dissolved in 1959. The Seamen's Union of Ireland was then formed and registered in 1959 (no. 520T) and was affiliated to the ICTU from 1959.

Professional Footballers' Association of Ireland
Registered in 1960 (no. 527T) and was represented in the ICTU, 1960–64. It had an affiliate status with the MPGWU, and transferred with the same status to SIPTU.

2000
Union of Students in Ireland
A 'mutual support Agreement' between SIPTU and the USI was approved at the Ennis Conference of the USI in April. A Joint Standing Committee examined lobbying, youth policy, employment and education, training, health and safety, and employment rights for student and first-time workers. Regrettably, matters fizzled out.

2003
Musicians' Union of Ireland
Formed as an autonomous union within SIPTU.

Unions breaking away from or set up in opposition to SIPTU

1998
Irish Locomotive Drivers' Association
Launched on 28 September 1998 with members of the former National Locomotive Drivers' Group of ITGWU and the NBRU. Registered with the Registrar of Friendly Societies but, having 120 members or less, unable to obtain a Negotiating Licence. It was accepted by the ATGWU as No. 3/57 Branch.

Appendix 3 ⌖

OUTLINE HISTORIES OF SIPTU AFFILIATES

On the ITGWU's forty-fifth anniversary in January 1954 the WUI noted that itself, the IWWU, the ISPWU and the ITGWU all 'grew from that one seed—the seed of militant trade unionism sowed by Jim Larkin among the unskilled workers.' Short sketches are provided here for some main or current SIPTU components. Some are drawn from *Select Guide to Trade Union Records in Dublin* by Sarah Ward-Perkins (1996); other published sources are listed and, where appropriate, contemporary details given. Further information is available at *www.siptu.ie.*

Association of Artists in Ireland
After the amalgamation of Irish Actors' Equity Association with the ITGWU in 1979 to create a Cultural Division in 1980, the Association of Artists in Ireland joined with the Society of Irish Playwrights in expanding the Division's breadth in 1981. The AAI, with seventy members, aimed to improve the working conditions and the status of individual artists. It held seminars on the artist and the law, met the Department of Social

Welfare to fully establish artists' entitlements and to develop policies for improving matters, and received briefings from Officials of the Revenue Commissioners on the Finance Act (1969), which provided income tax exemptions and relief for artistic work. It examined problems for working artists arising from VAT on the sales of work. The Chairperson of the Association, Robert Ballagh, said it 'aimed to professionalise the profession' and to progress beyond the 'gentlemen's agreement' basis of most arrangements with art dealers and agents.

The AAI was recognised by the Arts Council as the artists' representative body and received funding. It affiliated to the International Association of Art, sponsored by UNESCO, on which Ballagh served as Treasurer. On its merger Ballagh was Chairperson, Ken Dolan, Secretary, Eithne Jordan, Treasurer, and Betty Ballagh, part-time administrator. James Allen, Catherine Carman, Patrick Hall, Leo Higgins, Michael O'Sullivan and Vivienne Roche served on the Committee, which produced *Artletter*, a periodic newsletter. Research by the Arts Council showed that 'plastic artists' had a 'very precarious existence.'

The AAI assisted an art competition through *Liberty*, thrice won by Jer O'Leary, and hoped to tour exhibitions around Branches. The Vital Campaign for the Arts, launched in 1985 together with Equity, the Association of Irish Composers and the Society of Irish Playwrights supported Crisis in the Arts. In October 1987 the Agreement with the ITGWU was reaffirmed, with the AAI receiving greater access to research, communi-cations and computer facilities. The General President of the ITGWU, John Carroll, addressing the 1988 AGM of the AAI, talked of the need for 'special support systems' for artists, explaining that 'support systems mean the provision of resources, financial and physical, to enable artists to concentrate on their creativity without having economic needs impede their progress.' The ITGWU called for greater funding for the arts, condemned the cutting of Dublin Corporation's grants to the Hugh Lane Municipal Gallery of Modern Art (Dublin City Gallery) and continuing problems with VAT. It viewed with 'alarm' the removal of any reference to artists' tax exemption from self-assessment tax forms.

As part of the Cultural Division, the AAI was disappointed that a Cultural Fund—something akin to the Provident Fund or Political Fund—was not developed in order to fund artistic events and performances in union premises. Under some 'political' pressure the AAI moved offices from Liberty Hall to Temple Bar, which, together with Dermot Doolan's retirement, led to a rupture with SIPTU and a withering of the Cultural Division. Eventually, after some acrimony, Arts Council funding was withdrawn and the AAI went out of existence. In 2007 its functions were carried out by two bodies, Visual Arts Ireland and the Irish Visual Arts Relief Organisation, Ballagh chairing the latter.

- Brian Trench, 'Artists sign up with Union', *Artletter*, no. 1, n.d.
- 'Support systems', *Art Bulletin*, no. 26, July–September 1988.

My thanks to Robert Ballagh.

Association of Irish Composers

The Association of Irish Composers was a founding component of the ITGWU Cultural Division in 1980. The union's assistance 'in securing a degree of economic security for artists of all kinds' was 'of great value.' In return the AIC hoped to 'foster an appreciation and understanding of our music through recitals and discussions.' It hoped that 'cross-fertilisation between the various arts bodies' would 'prove of great value to us all.' In 1982 the AIC achieved full consultant status in the Performing Rights Society, and plans were made to form two limited companies, AIC itself and Irish Composers' Centre.

AIC, Copyright House, Pembroke Row, Dublin 2; (01) 4961484.

Automobile, General Engineering and Mechanical Operatives' Union
The Irish Automobile Drivers' Society was founded in 1910 and registered in 1911 (no. 286T). In 1917 it became the Irish Automobile Drivers' and Automobile Mechanics' Union, its membership climbing from under 200 to 1,571 by 1919. The Motor Permits Strike of 1919–20 proved disastrous, bringing the IADAMU into conflict with the ITUC, with which it was affiliated, and the ITGWU, with which it competed. Effectually bankrupt, it sought a merger with various unions before, reluctantly, merging with the ITGWU in 1922. Ciarán J. King, its last General Secretary, joined the ITGWU Head Office staff. He then became the first General Treasurer of the WUI.

The Irish Automobile Drivers' and Mechanical Operatives' Union was registered in 1939 (no. 441T). It was affiliated to the CIU, 1945–59, and thence the ICTU. In 1962 it became AGEMOU. Its membership was 654 in 1939, 1,879 in 1950, 2,169 in 1960 and 3,904 in 1970. AGEMOU brought 2,000 members into SIPTU on its merger in 1997. It had a chequered history with Congress, a capacity to run foul of other unions leading to occasional suspensions. The destruction of Dublin's car assembly industry cost it many members. The creation of the Union of Motor Trade, Technical and Industrial Employees in 1984 took more than 1,500.

AGEMOU Trade Group, North Frederick Street, Dublin 1; (01) 8744233; fax (01) 8747076; agemou@siptu.ie; www.siptu.ie.
My thanks to Christy Cullen, Barney Maguire and Charlie Mooney.

Butchers' societies
Butchers, as with other Dublin craft unions, claimed origins dating from the mediaeval guilds. A Butchers' Society was founded in 1828 and in 1870 had premises in Great Britain Street (Parnell Street), subsequently in Capel Street. It was registered in 1890 (no. 102T) and titled the Operative Butchers' and Assistants' Trade Union in 1901. It affiliated to the ITUC in 1901 and 1917 but cancelled its registration in 1920. Membership was 108 in 1912, 127 in 1913, 118 in 1914, 92 in 1915, 149 in 1916, 188 in 1917, 302 in 1918, 379 in 1919 and 384 in 1920. The Secretary in 1910 was John Long, elected by avoiding the 'black ball'. (Frank Cluskey Senior mused that 'the colouring matter on the black balls must have come off from constant use due to the reluctance on the part of the Committee to admit anyone into their charmed circle.') P. J. Hickey, Secretary in 1913, a clerk in McDonagh's of Chatham Street, had a 'brilliant, analytical mind and his judgement was responsible in effecting a complete change' in union policy. These qualities and 'an innate sense of courtesy earned him the respect of all.' He abolished yearly share-outs of 'money in the chest' and developed a Reserve Fund. The chest was 'an enormous oak affair bound on each corner with heavy brass plates and had three different locks. Three Trustees each held a key so all three had to be present at the opening ceremony.' Cluskey reflected that 'banks might go bust, nations might experience the throes of financial convulsions, but the chest was immune from all such upheavals and

stood there as a symbol of security and stability and inspired a degree of confidence in the money system that a Rothschild might envy.'

The Butchers 'decided to transfer their membership' to the ITGWU in July 1919, but 'preparatory to this course' an operatives' meeting was arranged for the 'purpose of the correct interpretation of the Constitution of this Union [ITGWU].' The Butchers' Union 'had more money per head' than the ITGWU, and Liberty Hall 'could not understand why we wished to merge into their Union.' It was the inspiration of Larkin and 1913.

Cluskey would hang around Liberty Hall 'in the hope of getting a glimpse of Jim.' He was lodging with an aunt, Mrs Carney, a deeply religious woman, and she removed a picture of Larkin from over Cluskey's head, saying 'there could be neither luck nor grace where such a picture was.' He had to secrete his *Irish Worker* 'to save it from the fire.' Cluskey and John McCann met Thomas Foran, President of the ITGWU, to discuss a merger. Foran showed them around Liberty Hall, and in one room was a map of Ireland covered in little flags, each representing a union Branch. Cluskey gasped: 'Larkin is a wonderful man!' to which Foran replied, 'What is wonderful about him? 1913 ended in a bottle of smoke! Today we settle everything by negotiations'—a statement 'akin to blasphemy' to Cluskey. He considered advising members against transfer but was consoled by thoughts of Larkin's return from America. He clearly never forgot the conversation, however, as the Butchers became founding members of the WUI in 1924.

In 1945 'men and women of the trade fought for more than twelve long weeks in the first battle' to secure a fortnight's holidays with pay. The solidarity of women shop assistants was remarkable, as they had nothing to gain, already having secured the holidays. They 'gave life' to the slogan 'Each for all and all for each.' In 1947 the WUI discussed proposals from the North of Ireland Operative Butchers' and Allied Workers' Association to form a national butchers' union. The Association was affiliated to the ITUC, 1947–65, but eventually merged with the ATGWU in 1965. Overtures were made to butchers in Limerick and Waterford, who were ITGWU members, and to Cork Operative Butchers' Society. A series of meetings and exchanges of information came to nothing.

The Butchers had at least two social clubs, for in 1948 the GEC requested that they be closed from one o'clock during Connolly Commemorations in May, presumably to encourage members to attend parades. In April 1954 the Pork Branch left Mallin Hall to move to WUI Head Office in Parnell Square.

- Frank Cluskey, 'Trade unionism and the Dublin butchers: A record of growth and militancy,' *Report*, no. 13, August 1953, p. 6–7; 'Trade unionism and the Dublin Butchers: Further recollections,' *Report*, no. 14, September, 1953; 'Trade unionism and the Dublin Butchers: Further recollections,' *Report*, no. 15, October 1953.
- Charlie Phipps, 'Memories of Mallin Hall,' *Report*, no. 22, May 1954.

Federation of Rural Workers

After its catastrophic defeat on the land in 1923 the ITGWU resisted further attempts to organise farm workers, including rejecting invitations by the ITUC to do so in the late 1930s. ITGWU consciences were absolved by its campaign to create the Agricultural Wages Board and demands for rural housing and improved social welfare benefits. Farm labourers were supposedly 'unorganisable' or next to impossible to 'retain in organisation.'

The ITUC turned to the ATGWU to take up the task, but they found it beyond them. Congress did not abandon its concerns; its initiative led to the creation of the FRW in

1946 (no. 493T). James Larkin Junior was first President and Seán Dunne Organiser, then General Secretary. The wui transferred all its rural members into the frw, feeling it could develop specialist services required to do the job that the rapidly expanding but essentially urban wui struggled to provide. It was a noble gesture and no doubt accounted for continued close relations between the two unions. The first General Secretary, George Pollock, was an influential figure in the inevitable confrontation with farmers in Cos. Dublin, Kildare, Meath and Wicklow and elsewhere. Organisation quickly spread to local authority, turf and forestry workers, members being allocated to county Branches. Other General Secretaries were Jimmy Tully, 1953–72, Patrick Murphy, 1972–88, and finally Paul Clarke, serving as Rural Group Secretary of the fwui and siptu. Both Dunne and Tully became Labour tds, Tully serving in Government, reflecting a strong frw Association with the Labour Party.

After Ireland joined the eec the frw campaigned for rural rights and regional development and generally championed the cause of agriculture, often taking a line at variance with the Irish Farmers' Association. Murphy became an acknowledged expert on all European matters relating to workers' interests. Membership was 1,431 in 1946, 2,127 in 1950, 2,165 in 1955, 2,919 in 1960, 5,650 in 1965, 6,301 in 1970 and 10,000 in 1979. The union merged with the wui in 1979, creating the fwui. Murphy became Assistant General Secretary. Membership expanded geographically, and long-standing Branches in Athy, Bray, Galway and Tullamore were augmented with new Branches and premises in Kilkenny and Monaghan. The fwui acquired a genuinely 'national presence'.

- Daniel G. Bradley, *Farm Labourers' Irish Struggle, 1900–1976*, Belfast: Athol Books, 1988.
- Daniel G. Bradley, '"Speeding the plough": The formation of the Federation of Rural Workers,' *Saothar*, 11 (1986), p. 39–53.
- Ross M. Connolly, 'Memories of a union Organiser in County Wicklow,' *Labour History News*, 2, autumn 1986, p. 7–9.
- Patrick Murphy, *The Federation of Rural Workers, 1946–1979: The Twilight Years, 1943–1946*, Dublin: fwui, 1988.

Horse Racing Ireland Tote Employees' Association

The Racing Board Tote Staff Association became the Irish Horse Racing Association, Tote Employees' Association and Horse Racing Ireland Tote Employees' Association and has 350 members.

Racing Board Tote Staff Association, Toby Cullen, Loughtagalla, Thurles, Co. Tipperary.

Irish Agricultural Advisors' Organisation

The Irish Agricultural and Technical Advisers' Association grew out of the Agricultural and Technical Instruction Act (1899). It briefly affiliated to the Irish National Teachers' Organisation in the 1920s and after 1926 amalgamated with the Local Government Officials (Ireland) Trade Union. The Vocational Education Act (1932) restructured agricultural education, and on 6 May 1932, at the rds Spring Show, the iaao was born, with Úna Byrne as vigorous chairwoman. It had four Sections: Agricultural Instructors' Association, Horticultural Instructors' Association, Instructors in Poultry Keeping Association, and County Agricultural Executive Officers' Association. Its journal,

Adviser, flourished from 1959 to 1963. Todd Comerford became the first full-time General Secretary, 1966–80, succeeded by John Howley from the Irish Veterinary Union.

In 1970 it became the Irish Agricultural Advisors' Association, and in 1985 Eugene Mealy, recruited from the Irish Distributive and Administrative Trade Union, replaced Howley. The IAAO merged with the FWUI 1986. The Chairman was the highly regarded P. J. Woulfe, whose outstanding contribution was acknowledged when he tragically died in 1997.

- Gene Mealy, 'P. J. Woulfe: An appreciation', *Newsline,* May 1997.
  My thanks to Gene Mealy.

Irish Actors' Equity Association

The Writers', Actors', Artists' and Musicians' Association (WAAMA) was formed in 1941 at a meeting in Jury's Hotel, Dame Street, Dublin. Seán Ó Faoláin was the first President. It registered in 1945 (no. 486T) and affiliated to the ITUC in 1948. In 1949 WAAMA was transformed into a purely actors' organisation, the Irish Actors' Equity Association (Cumann Ionannta Aisteoirí na hÉireann). It switched allegiance to the CIU through its close association with the ITGWU, which organised back and front of house theatre employees. Membership was never huge: 372 in 1945, 20 in 1955, 469 in 1965, 530 in 1970 and 706 in 1975. Actors' Equity did, however, win significant disputes with Radio Éireann, the National Theatre Company (Abbey Theatre) and Radio Telefís Éireann, establishing standard contracts and significantly raising wages and conditions for actors. Strikes were necessary on occasion, with Equity picket lines manned by well-known radio, television and stage actors. It secured worker representation on the board of the state-funded Irish Theatre Company.

On 19 December 1979 Actors' Equity decided, by 7 to 1, to amalgamate with the ITGWU. The General Secretary, Dermot Doolan, who held office from 1947 to 1985, speaking at the formal transfer of engagements, said the merger would 'bring a new dignity to the writer, the performer and the artist.' Maurice O'Doherty, RTÉ newsreader and President of Actors' Equity, thought it gave actors greater industrial strength and 'their proper place' within the movement. Equity retained an independent status as part of the ITGWU Cultural Division in 1980.

In recent years rulings by the Competition Authority have adversely affected Equity's role in setting minimum wages and standards for members and functioning as an employment agency for unemployed actors. Actors' Equity is active in the International Federation of Actors.

Irish Actors' Equity, Liberty Hall, Dublin 1; (01) 8586403; fax (01) 8743691; equity@siptu.ie; www.equity.ie.
- Francis Devine, *Acting for the Actors: Dermot Doolan and the Organisation of Irish Actors and Performing Artists, 1947–1985* (Studies in Irish Labour History, 3), Dublin: Irish Labour History Society, 1997.
- Mattie O'Neill, 'The Cultural Division,' *Liberty* 75 (Diamond Jubilee Issue), June 1984, p. 56–8.
- 'A new horizon for writers, performers and artists,' *Liberty,* January 1980.
My thanks to Jane Boushell, Des Courtney and Dermot Doolan.

Irish Liver Assurance Employees' Trade Union

Royal Liver Friendly Society was founded in Liverpool by nine men in July 1850. It quickly grew to a huge organisation, with members all over Britain and Ireland. With expansion came a large staff, both in Head Office and Branch offices and 'out in the field.' In 1890 the National Union of Insurance Workers attempted to represent some employees, but the Manchester Association of Liver Workers transformed into the Royal Liver Agents' and Collectors' Union. By 1897 it had members in Dublin. By 1922 the Royal Liver Employees' Union was in difficulty. Irish members wanted their own organisation.

An Irish Royal Liver Employees' Union was unsuccessfully attempted, although the Irish Union of Distributive Workers and Clerks and the National Amalgamated Union of Life Assurance Workers also recruited Irish agents. The National Federation of Insurance Workers grew out of 'house unions' in insurance companies and merged within the NAULW in 1964 to form the National Union of Insurance Workers. The Insurance Act (1936) amalgamated Irish insurance companies. Irish members of the Prudential Staff Union refused to join the IUDWC, as it was a 'general union', and formed the Assurance Representatives' Organisation in Cork, quickly taking in Irish Liver agents.

The RLEU did not seek a Negotiating Licence under the Trade Union Act (1941), and Irish members sought an Irish union, many joining the ARO. In 1948, however, in the AOH Hall, Cork, the ILAEU was created. Branches were set up in Bandon, Fermoy, Killarney, Tralee and Waterford. There were still divisions among Irish Liver employees, however, and in 1955, in addition to those in the ARO and ILAEU, more joined the WUI, serviced by Thomas Doyle. A Joint Council was set up between the ILAEU and WUI, serviced by the National Organiser, Christy Ferguson.

In 1956 the ILAEU formally affiliated to the WUI and on 1 June 1976 was absorbed into No. 16 Branch. The GEC's formal invitation was that the 'ILAEU be invited to join with our 190 members of the Riyal Liver Society as full members of the union, constituting, if desired, a separate Section.'

- Francis Devine, '"A quaint curiosity": The history of the Irish Liver Assurance Employees' Trade Union, 1948–1975,' *Saothar*, 24 (1999), p. 100–110.
- William O'Brien, *The Foundation and Development of the Irish Liver Assurance Employees' Union*, Dublin: Irish Liver Assurance Employees' Trade Union, 1975, p. 92.

Irish National Painters' and Decorators' Trade Union

The INPDTU claimed an origin in the Guild of St Luke the Evangelist, incorporated in 1670. It catered for painters, cutlers and paper-stainers. From 1814 to 1869 the Friendly Brothers of St Luke of the City of Dublin met in South King Street, operating pension and mortality funds. A breakaway, St Raphael's Society of House Painters, operated from Clarendon Street, 1827–38. In 1860 the Regular Operative House Painters' Society built its own hall at 27 Aungier Street, the premises being occupied until 1953. In 1877 the title 'Trade Union' was adopted.

In 1890 the union was wound up but immediately restarted as the Dublin Metropolitan House Painters' Trade Union. It became the Irish National Painters', Decorators' and Allied Trades Union, 1919–26, then amalgamated with the Glaziers and

Whiteners. The United House and Ship Painters' and Decorators' Trade Union of Ireland broke away, existing from 1926 to 1972.

The INPDTU took in local painters' unions in Cork and Limerick and, when the UHSPDTU collapsed, absorbed its members. Gerry Fleming was General Secretary when it merged with SIPTU in 1991, with Paddy Coughlan, Thomas Lundy and Martin Leahy as the industrial staff. It brought in 6,000 members. Illustrious members included Peadar Macken, 1878–1916, founding member of the Socialist Party of Ireland, Labour alderman and member of the Executive of Sinn Féin; John Mulhall, General Secretary, 1941–81; Peadar Kearney, 1882–1941, who wrote 'The Soldier's Song' with Patrick Heeney; and Stephen, Brendan and Dominic Behan.

Irish National Painters' and Decorators' Trade Group, Liberty Hall, Dublin 1; (01) 8586409; fax (01) 8586487; construction.div@siptu.ie; www.siptu.ie.
• Charles Callan, *Painters in Union: The Irish National Painters' and Decorators' Trade Union and Its Forerunners,* Dublin: Watchword, 2008.
• Charles Callan, 'The Regular Operative House Painters' Trade Union: Labour relations and working conditions in the Dublin house-painting trade, 1860–1890,' *Saothar,* 7 (1981), p. 28–39.
• Charles Callan, '"They stooped to conquer": Inter-union rivalry in the painting trade, 1892–1910,' *Saothar,* 25 (2000), p. 45–55.
• Charles Callan, 'Painters and the Dublin building trades lockout of January–April, 1931,' *Saothar,* 28 (2003), p. 63–76.
• Charles Callan, '"We got it for everybody": The Irish National Painters' and Decorators' Trade Union and the forty hour week strike of 1964,' *Saothar,* 30 (2005), p. 47–58.
• Charles Callan, 'Peadar Macken, 1878–1916,' *Saothar,* 31 (2006), p. 121–3.
• 'Painters and Decorators say "Yes" to SIPTU,' *Newsline,* autumn 1991.
My thanks to Charles Callan and Paddy Coughlan.

Irish Print Union

A printers' Association may have existed in Dublin from 1760. The Amicable Benefit Society, 1793, collected contributions, paid benefits and agreed wage scales. Members often met in the Brazen Head or Carteret's Head pubs, and, as a consequence, funds collected were known as 'head money'. The Amicable Society went underground during the Emmet Rising in 1803. In 1809 former members established the Dublin Typographical Provident Society in Castle Street. In 1836 the Irish Typographical Union was set up, giving way in 1844 to the National Typographical Association. In 1847, amid trade depression, Dublin voted itself out of the NTA and continued as the DTPS.

In 1861 the Provincial Typographical Association, inaugurated in Sheffield, enveloped the DTPS, against the Committee's wishes. It was a loose confederation, and the DTPS withdrew in 1868. Dublin Typographical Benevolent Fund and Printers' Pension Society was created in 1869. An internal conflict over the use of boy labour resulted in Laurence E. Knox setting up a rival union in 1859, which was eventually settled by compromise.

The DTPS was a member of the United Trades Association in 1863. A disastrous strike weakened it in 1878, but it resisted absorption by the Typographical Association, a British union. By the early twentieth century the DTPS was very weak, with many unemployed members. Under W. J. Whelan, Secretary, and Seán P. Campbell, Treasurer, it gradually recovered. It finally registered in 1935 (no. 416T). It was affiliated to the ITUC from the late 1890s and to the CIU from 1945 to 1959, with W. J. Whelan serving as President, 1947–8. Membership was 800 in 1892, 1,038 in 1900, 1,050 in 1910, 1,000 in 1920, 1,050 in 1930, 1,139 in 1940, 1,242 in 1950, 1,476 in 1960 and 1,743 in 1970. In 1965 the name was changed to the Irish Graphical Society.

As the trade underwent rapid technological change, amalgamation with the Electrotypers and Stereotypers, Dublin and District and the Irish Bookbinders' and Allied Trades Union resulted in the creation of the Irish Print Union in 1984 (no. 581T). The ESDD was formed in 1891 as part of the Federated Society of Electrotypers and Stereotypers of Great Britain and Ireland. In 1923 it became an independent organisation and registered (no. 362T). It was affiliated to the ITUC in 1938 and the CIU, 1945–59, subsequently the ICTU. The highest membership was 112.

The Irish Bookbinders' and Allied Trades Union was formed in 1920 as the Irish Bookbinders' and Paper Rulers' Trade Union, registering in 1924 (no. 367T). In 1936 the Dublin Branch of the National Union of Printing, Binding and Paper Workers, formerly the Bookbinders' and Rulers' Consolidated Union, amalgamated to form the IBATU. From the early 1930s it was affiliated to the ITUC and, from 1945 to 1959, the CIU. Membership reached a peak in 1950 at 1,050. In 1970 the membership was 874. After attempts to merge with the National Union of Journalists failed, the IPU became the Print Trade Group of SIPTU in 1998 following a vote for merger of 1,221 to 647.

Irish Print Group, 35 Lower Gardiner Street, Dublin 1; (01) 8743662; ipg@siptu.ie.
- Curran, Owen, *Two Hundred Years of Trade Unionism, 1809–2009*, Irish Print Group, SIPTU, Dublin, 2009.
- Brian Donnelly, 'Records of the Irish Graphical Society,' *Saothar*, 9 (1983), p. 111–15. *My thanks to Owen Curran.*

Irish Racecourse Bookmakers' Assistants' Association
Founded in 1938, the IRBAA was registered in 1943 (no. 471T). It was affiliated to the CIU from 1948 (occasionally neglecting to pay its affiliation fee) and the ICTU, 1959–81. It amalgamated with the ITGWU in 1981, with its highest membership of 274, previously reporting 200 in 1945, 200 in 1950, 200 in 1955, 167 in 1960 and 125 in 1965. The last four Secretaries were Walter Mullineaux, 1943; James Coffey, 1944–9; James McLaughlin, 1949–93; and Tommy Byrne, 1993–4, having previously been Chairman, 1958–64.
- 'Racing Branch mourns Jimmy McLoughlin,' *Newsline,* June 1993.
- 'Tommy Byrne: An appreciation,' *Newsline,* November 1994.

Irish Shoe and Leather Workers' Union
The Irish Shoe and Leather Workers' Union was formed on 1 January 1953 after an amicable arrangement with the National Union of Boot and Shoe Operatives, a British union, whereby its 5,000 members in the Republic would form an Irish union. Three thousand members in Northern Ireland remained with the NUBSO but, uniquely, were serviced by the ISLWU, which registered in 1953 (no. 503T), with its Head Office at St Crispin's Hall, Seatown, Dundalk. In 1977, taking advantage of the Trade Union Act (1975), the ISLWU transferred 3,500 members and twenty Branches into the ITGWU.

The NUBSO had been formed in 1874 as the National Union of Operative Rivetters and Finishers, seceding from the Amalgamated Cordwainers' Association as tensions rose between traditional hand-stitching and new mechanical methods. Branches of the NUBSO were set up in Dublin and Cork in 1885 and in Drogheda in 1894. There were several unsuccessful attempts to set up Irish unions: the City of Dublin Union of Hand Sewn Boot and Shoe Makers, registered in November 1920 (no. 347T) to June 1928, the Irish National Union of Boot, Shoe and Leather Workers, October 1924 to June 1928 (no. 372T), and the Irish Shoemakers' and Repairers' Trade Union, November 1936 to October 1941 (no. 421T). The Drogheda Branch of the NUBSO was revived in the late 1930s and soon had more than 600 members. In 1949 the Dundalk members tried to move *en bloc* to the ITGWU; but eventually the ISLWU emerged.

Three ISLWU officers made a significant contribution to the general movement: two General Secretaries, Hugh Crilly, 1953–67, from the Black Bull, Drogheda, and Michael Bell, 1967–75, Drogheda, and Labour TD for Louth; and the General President, Paul Alexander, a native of Belfast, 1953–72. The founding Vice-President was the well-known Waterford hurler Charlie Ware. The ISLWU was affiliated to the ITUC, 1953–9, and thence to the ICTU. It claimed 4,820 members in 1953, 4,451 in 1960 and 4,185 in 1970.

• Michael Bell, 'The Irish Shoe and Leather Workers,' *Liberty* 75 (Diamond Jubilee Issue), June 1984, p. 55.

Irish Women Workers' Union

The IWWU was founded in April 1911, with Jim Larkin as President and his sister, Delia Larkin, Secretary. It was an autonomous ITGWU Section. Larkin decided that 'person' in the Rule Book meant 'man' and therefore a separate women's organisation was needed. It was financed and housed by the ITGWU, then in 1912 moved to offices in Great Brunswick Street (Pearse Street). Delia Larkin contributed a women workers' column to the *Irish Worker* and ran theatre, dancing and choral groups, touring in Britain to raise funds. The union ran a clothing co-operative in Liberty Hall, manufacturing, among other things, the famous 'Red Hand Shirt'. Branches were established in Cork and Dundalk and by Connolly among mill workers in Belfast under the title Irish Textile Workers' Union.

Delia Larkin left the union in 1915, and Connolly invited Helena Molony to maintain it. After the Rising, Molony sought assistance from Louie Bennett, who in turn enlisted her friend Helen Chenevix, and these two effectually managed the IWWU until 1955, when 85-year-old Bennett finally retired. In 1917 a wholly independent IWWU claimed 2,300 members in printing, box-making, laundries and textiles. Constance Markievicz was Honorary President. The union used the suffrage paper *Irish Citizen* and later its own journal, *An Bhean Oibre,* to champion working women.

By 1930 membership had risen to 2,900, to 4,630 in 1935 and to 5,614 in 1940. Bennett (1931 and 1947–8), Chenevix (1950–51) and Molony (1936–7) all served as President of the ITUC, a tremendous recognition for women at a time when few women even attended the Congress. The IWWU moved to 48 Fleet Street, Dublin, in 1948. In 1950 it sought the creation of an ITUC Women's Advisory Committee as campaigns for equal pay and employment equality gathered pace. Chenevix briefly succeeded Bennett as General Secretary, 1955–7, followed by Kay McDowell, 1957–70, and Maura Breslin, 1970–82. Membership reached a peak in 1950 at 6,966, however, and had declined to 3,550 in 1970 as traditional industries were ravaged by new technology.

The union never really organised outside Dublin and became marginalised as women asserted themselves in other unions and employment equality legislation was enacted. Arrangements were made to merge with the FWUI, and Pádraigín Ní Mhurchú was seconded to oversee matters as the last IWWU General Secretary. After the merger on 1 September 1984 Ní Mhurchú became an officer of the Labour Court.

The IWWU played a leading role in the campaign for a fortnight's paid holiday, epitomised by the laundry workers' strike of 1945. Mai Clifford, an IWWU stalwart, when President of Dublin Council of Trade Unions famously entertained more than half a million PAYE demonstrators at the GPO on 22 January 1980 by singing 'One Day at a Time'—this after she had carried out the Executive's request to 'make twenty-four red armbands' for the demonstration.

The merger with the FWUI ended a unique 'union for women organised by women'. By contemporary standards the IWWU did not always espouse radically feminist views, but it maintained a lone voice from a women's viewpoint within the movement. It had a good record on calling for the reform of safety and health legislation and defending women's employment rights, threatened by the Conditions of Employment Act (1936), although it could be ambivalent on the rights of married women working and in arguing for improved Children's Allowances and women's health and education. The IWWU was one of only a handful of exclusively women's trade unions known to have existed in the world.

- Rosemary Cullen Owens, *Louie Bennett,* Cork: Cork University Press, 2001.
- Ellen Hazelkorn, 'The social and political views of Louie Bennett, 1870–1956,' *Saothar,* 13 (1988), p. 32–44.
- Ellen Hazelkorn, 'Louie Bennett, 1870–1956,' *Saothar,* 25 (2000), p. 98–100.
- Mary Jones, *These Obstreperous Lassies: A History of the Irish Women Workers' Union,* Dublin: Gill & Macmillan, 1988.

Irish Writers' Union

The Irish Writers' Union (Comhar na Scríbhneoirí) was founded on 1 January 1987 and the Irish Writers' Centre in 1991. The founding Chairperson was Jack Harte. Also involved were James Plunkett Kelly (James Plunkett), once a WUI Official in Dublin Gas Company, and Sam McAughtry, Belfast. The membership grew to about 300 in mid-1990, dipped around 2000, but has revived since 2005 and includes most prominent Irish writers. On 22 March 2002 Jack Harte was awarded life membership. In his ground-breaking collection of short stories, *Murphy in the Underworld* (1986), he created a character out of his own experiences as a union member. In the 1970s he was Chairperson of the County Dublin Branch of the Teachers' Union of Ireland. With John F. Deane, Conleth O'Connor and others he set up Profile Press to publish new fiction and poetry. From this, in 1979, developed Poetry Ireland, 'a kind of poets' union,' to establish poetry on a respectable, paid footing. Efforts were also made to revive the ailing Irish PEN club. For the first time in many years an Irish writer, Deane, attended a PEN meeting abroad, in Lyon, where he met Uffe Harder of the Danish Writers' Union, and the idea of the Irish Writers' Union and Irish Writers' Centre was born. The IWU campaigned for tax exemption for artists and public lending right for writers (to receive royalties when a book is borrowed from a public library). This was achieved in November 2007 under the Copyright and Related Rights (Amendment) Act.

The Chairperson of the IWU, Conor Kostick, reflects the general view among members that they are 'very aware of our affiliation to SIPTU.' The IWU aims to organise writers in Ireland, to advance writing as a profession and form of work, to improve remuneration and conditions, to provide advice, assistance and support, to contribute to education policy and the art of writing and the use of literature within the education system and to provide a means for the expression of writers' collective opinion. It acts as watchdog on contracts and royalty payments for members, or for their estate, and negotiates with Arts Councils, Bord na Leabhar Gaeilge and CLÉ (the publishers' Association), amongst others, on behalf of writers, achieving a disputes procedure for writers who feel they have been treated unprofessionally by publishers. Membership 'runs from one April Fools' Day to the next.' A newsletter, *Final Draft*, informs members of activities, campaigns and events. Liz McManus TD is a member.

Irish Writers' Union, 18 Parnell Square, Dublin 1; (01) 8721302; iwu@ireland-writers.com.
• John F. Deane, 'Jack Harte tribute,' *IWU Newsletter*, no. 58, April 2007.
• Tony Hickey, 'James Plunkett: A tribute,' at www.ireland-writers.com/news.htm.
My thanks to Conor Kostick.

Marine, Port and General Workers' Union

Founded in 1933 as the Irish Seamen's and Port Workers' Union and registered in 1934 (no. 409T), it became the Marine, Port and General Workers' Union in 1955. Seamen left to form the Seamen's Union of Ireland in 1959. The membership was 5,150 in 1934, 3,220 in 1950, 6,204 in 1955, 3,803 in 1960, 4,808 in 1970 and 4,000 in 1980. Larkin played a supporting role in the foundation of the ISPWU, but it was accepted by the ITGWU and during the Second World War was bailed out financially by Liberty Hall. This may explain why the union affiliated to the CIU until the formation of the ICTU in 1959. Well-known leaders included Seán O'Moore, Des Branigan, Jimmy Dunne, Frank Ellis and Séamus Redmond. Under Redmond the MPGWU often trod a lone path outside the Congress fold, but it re-affiliated 1982. Bitter clashes took place with the ITGWU during the Ferenka dispute in Limerick in the 1970s. Having decided to merge with the FWUI before 1990, it took a further eight years before eventual merger with SIPTU in 1998. Michael Hayes was the last General Secretary.

MPGW Group, 35 Lower Gardiner Street, Dublin 1; (01) 8740327; mpgw@siptu.ie.
• Joe Deasy, 'Séamus Redmond,' *Saothar*, 21 (1996), p. 18–19.
• Séamus Redmond, 'We Ain't Got a Barrel of Money': History of the Marine, Port and General Workers' Union' (unpublished paper).
My thanks to Michael Corcoran, Michael Hayes and Gerard Whyte.

Medical Laboratory Scientists' Association

Laboratory technicians were first organised in 1958 as a Section of the WUI No. 15 Branch. Previously, technicians joined the majority union in each hospital. In the late 1950s technicians demanded improvements and a harmonisation in pay and conditions in rapidly expanding hospital laboratories. The WUI Technicians' Section was only a partial success, with fewer than fifty members, as most technicians were reluctant to join. The General Secretary of the WUI, James Larkin, suggested that the affiliation model be used; this allowed vocational groups to enjoy the benefits of a larger union yet to retain their own Association. The Medical Laboratory Technicians' Association was founded in 1961 as a professional Association and WUI affiliate. Membership rose from 70 in 1961 to 150 in 1963.

In 1968 a pay claim was submitted to employers and was rejected. Members voted for industrial action, and a limited but well-organised and successful strike took place in 1969. It was the only time in the Association's history that it resorted to a national strike to achieve its goals. The MLTA made use of the WUI's Negotiating Licence, so there was no need to register in its own right.

Changes brought about by the Industrial Relations Act (1990) and the amalgamation of the FWUI and ITGWU to form SIPTU changed the landscape for affiliates. This lack of registration and licence was brought into sharp contrast following a disastrous showing in the first benchmarking process. Medical scientists had just achieved the 'holy grail' of pay parity with biochemists in the report of an expert group when, because of a 'technical oversight', the Benchmarking Body awarded medical scientists a 2.4% pay increase and biochemists 12%. Long-awaited parity disappeared overnight, and members pressured the Executive to strike to recover it. As an affiliate, the MLSA assumed that SIPTU's Negotiating Licence covered it, as with the WUI, only to discover that the Industrial Relations Act (1990) did not recognise its affiliated status. It was therefore barred from taking industrial action.

An independent review was commissioned, and, following extensive consultation with members and a number of unions, it finally recommended continued affiliation to SIPTU but the establishment of the MLSA as an independent union. It registered in 2004 (no. 610T) and obtained a Negotiating Licence in July 2005, and it affiliated to the ICTU in 2005.

Cyril Keogh was the first National Secretary, 1961–92, followed by Helen Franklin, 1993–2003, and Terence Casey, 2003–. Tom Moloney was Deputy Secretary, 1965–95. The membership was 70 in 1961, 150 in 1963, 900 in 1980, 950 in 1991, 980 in 1992, 1,000 in 1993, 1,185 in 1996, 1,376 in 1997, 1,428 in 1998, 1,521 in 1999, 1,547 in 2000 and 1,935 in 2007. The union moved from Parnell Square to Liberty Hall in 1995 and became the Medical Laboratory Scientists' Association in 1997 to better reflect members' role. The report of an expert group in 2001 changed laboratory technicians' job title to medical scientist.

MLSA, Liberty Hall, Dublin 1; (01) 8586472; mlsa@siptu.ie; www.mlsa.ie.
My thanks to John Kane.

Musicians' Union of Ireland

The Musicians' Union of Ireland was launched in January 2003 as a SIPTU Branch, representing classical, contemporary, traditional, country and western, folk, jazz, pop and rock musicians, both full-time and part-time. It offers protection from exploitation and bullying and seeks to negotiate improved financial services for musicians. The core membership includes the RTÉ National Symphony Orchestra and RTÉ Concert Orchestra, previously organised in the ITGWU (later SIPTU) for more than twenty years. They were joined in 2001 by members of the RTÉ Vanbrugh Quartet. However, the drive to create a specific organisation for musicians was based on an ambition to unite all musicians in a single organisation, evidenced by a successful campaign to organise and protect street musicians in Dublin. Among those pledged to support the MUI are the influential traditional musicians Dónal Lunny and Andy Irvine (President, 2009), the popular musician Seán Hession, the folk singer Johnny McEvoy, the pianist and conductor Noel Kelehan and the composer, performer and teacher Mícheál Ó Súilleabháin.

The MUI explores all opportunities for co-operative action with Actors' Equity, the other representative body for performing artists. It produces an annual directory of musical artists, teachers and directors and a quarterly newsletter, *Sound Post* (available electronically). It resisted the use of cheap labour at Wexford Opera Festival, but—as with unions representing journalists, actors and other freelance workers—it struggles against rulings by the Competition Authority that prevent the negotiation of rates of pay for such workers. (Legislation amending this ruling is pending.)

Musicians' Union of Ireland, Liberty Hall, Dublin 1; (01) 8586404; musicians@siptu.ie; www.siptu.ie/musicians/SoundPost.
- Francis Devine, '"Fullers' Silk Stocking Blackleg Band": James Larkin and the Musicians' Union, 1930–1932,' *Sound Post*, spring 2008.
- Francis Devine, 'Striking the right note, Part 1: The ITGWU and the RESO in the 1950s,' *Sound Post*, summer 2008; 'Part 2: The ITGWU and the Dublin Theatre Royal Dispute, 1952/1953,' *Sound Post*, autumn 2008.

My thanks to Des Courtney and John P. Swift.

National Association of Transport Employees

In 1871 the Amalgamated Society of Railway Servants was founded in Leeds, its title redolent of the servile nature of railwaymen engendered by the industry's semi-military command structure. Branches were opened in Belfast (1885), Dublin (1887), Cork (1889) and Limerick (1890). It held its Annual Conference in Belfast in 1891 and in Dublin in 1912, in recognition of its large Irish membership. In Dublin the ASRS changed its title to National Union of Railwaymen after amalgamating with the General Railway Workers' Union and United Pointsmen and Signalmen's Society. During the 1911 railway strikes, and on other occasions, Larkin and the ITGWU offered solidarity and assistance, although Liberty Hall also organised general-grade railway operatives.

The ASRS was affiliated to the ITUC from 1894. Separate Irish badges, Rule Books and structures were created by the ASRS and NUR and an Irish Branch journal, *New Way*, was published. At its peak, in 1920, the NUR had 20,000 Irish members. Its All-Ireland membership did not prevent it identifying closely with struggles for Irish self-determination, and the union was central in the Munitions of War Strike in 1920. The ASRS was involved in the Taff Vale Case and Osborne Judgements, legal decisions overturned only by the enactment of the Trade Disputes Act (1906) and Trade Union Act (1913), which allowed unions immunity in trade disputes and the right to establish political funds and affiliate to political parties. The ASRS and NUR were staunch Labour Party supporters. William Vennard, an NUR Official from Portadown, became an Organiser with the ITGWU in 1920s, recruiting many railway workers.

A number of breakaway Irish railway unions emerged after 1922, some short-lived, others longer-lasting, but none hugely damaged the NUR's Irish presence. In 1947 the union challenged Section 3 of the Trade Union Act (1941) and won a Supreme Court judgement that the Section was unconstitutional. Its fear was that the proposals would deny it a Negotiating Licence, in favour of the ITGWU.

After the British Government's Ireland Act (1949) in particular, increasing numbers of NUR members defected to the ITGWU, which created a special Railway Branch, Dublin No. 11. In 1951, at its AGM in Hastings, after a five-hour debate and bowing to pressure from Irish railwaymen to control their own affairs, the NUR took a noble decision to withdraw, offering support to the new organisation created by its members and presenting it with its property and capitation. (The three Irish Delegates voted to stay, however, as did twenty-three Branches.) The Irish Division of the NUR became the National Association of Transport Employees in 1953 and was registered (no. 508T). NATE incorporated the NUR Branch structures and representation methods. In comradeship, the NUR presented NATE with £80,000 and Head Office premises at 33 Parnell Square and residences in Kimmage and Botanic Avenue, Dublin. 'In a rare gesture,' the NUR also sent NATE 'a copy of every circular, document, publication, etc., it sent nationally to its own Branches.' The two unions retained strong fraternal relations and also exchanged Conference Delegates.

In contrast, bitterness arising from the 1950 railway strike lingered with the ITGWU for long afterwards, until the creation of the ICTU's CIÉ Trade Union Group. NATE membership climbed from 8,027 in 1953 to more than 9,000 in 1955, although official returns showed 7,033 in 1955, 5,657 in 1960, 4,039 in 1965 and 3,972 in 1970.

In 1968 a second British railway union, the Associated Society of Locomotive Engineers and Firemen, withdrew. About 65% of ASLEF members joined NATE, while 35% went the ITGWU. In Northern Ireland members transferred to the Amalgamated Engineering Union. Declining membership after 1970 reflected falling railway employment, although hackney cab drivers, canal and other transport workers balanced this. Northern Ireland members were lost to the ATGWU and those in the Republic to the ITGWU and later the National Busworkers' Union, which changed its name to National Bus and Rail Workers' Union. In 1987 NATE merged with the FWUI, its Head Office in Parnell Square, Dublin—the old NUR Irish office—being convenient to the FWUI premises. William T. Chapman of the Cork Bus Branch was the first General Secretary of NATE, 1953–70 (having suggested the union's title), followed by Frank Smyth (Belleek, Co. Fermanagh, 1971–8), Michael Cox (Roscommon, 1978–89) and Bernard Byrne (Dublin), Divisional Secretary, 1989–93.

In 1993 the combined pre-merger NATE, ITGWU and FWUI railway members were brought together, 'although not all members were happy.' Bernard Byrne was succeeded by Tony Tobin, with Terry Cowap servicing Northern Ireland Railways. Cowap tragically died on 2 April 2002, and Northern members transferred to the Belfast Branch of SIPTU.

- Anthony J. O'Brien and Bernard Byrne, *National Association of Transport Employees, Golden Jubilee, 1953–2003*, Dublin: SIPTU, 2003, p. 56.

My thanks to Bernard Byrne and Michael Casserly.

National Union of Gold, Silver and Allied Trades

Founded by William Kean in Sheffield in 1910, the Amalgamated Society of Gold, Silver and Kindred Trades drew together a number of small trade bodies in London, Birmingham and Dublin. Kean was General Secretary, 1910–53, President of the TUC, 1935, and a member of the General Council, 1921–45. In 1969 the National Union of Gold, Silver and Allied Trades absorbed the Society of Goldsmiths, Jewellers and Kindred Trades. In 1976 Dublin and Cork members transferred to the ITGWU, while the moribund Belfast Branch disbanded. NUGSAT merged with the AUEW-TASS in 1982, and in 1988 TASS merged with the Association of Scientific, Technical and Managerial Staffs to form the MSF Union. The first Dublin Secretary of the ASGSKT was J. Costello, succeeded by R. Adaire.

From the 1920s to the 1960s the main figure was Patrick Ryan, apprenticed 'to the silver polishing' at Makeley and Wheeler in Fade Street, Dublin, in 1910. He joined the union in 1913, strongly influenced by Larkin. He represented watchmakers on the City of Dublin Vocational Education Committee and started a superannuation fund for members in 1938. In 1952 he organised the presentation of a silver gilt medallion to the Dublin Trades Union Council, 'to be worn by the President on all occasions,' and in 1960 a gold chalice to Pope John XXIII. NUGSAT held its Annual Conference in Dublin in 1959 as a tribute to Ryan.

Cork joined the ASGSKT in 1916, with T. Creavan as Secretary. He was succeeded by Willis until his death in 1949. Belfast joined in 1919, with 160 members, under G. Reaney. NUGSAT affiliated to the ICTU in 1965, with William O'Neill as Secretary and more than 200 members. Jimmy Kelly succeeded O'Neill until his appointment as a WUI Official. Mick Browne was the Secretary of NUGSAT on its merger with the ITGWU in 1976 and joined the Liberty Hall staff. The membership was 207 in 1921, 84 in 1930, 111 in 1940, 177 in 1950, 186 in 1960 and 250 in 1970. 1975 was a disastrous year in the Republic, as two large jewellery firms halved their work force and the largest silverware manufacturer closed in obnoxious circumstances, owing workers more than £20,000. Hopkins and Hopkins had once made ITGWU badges. NUGSAT became a Section of Dublin No. 13 Branch.

• Éamonn O'Brien, 'A touch of gold', *Liberty*, May 1976.
My thanks to Jimmy Kelly.

Professional Footballers' Association of Ireland

Registered in September 1960 (no. 527T), the Professional Footballers' Association of Ireland was affiliated to the ICTU, 1960–64. With its 210 members it joined the ITGWU in July 1980, linking with Irish Actors' Equity in the Cultural Division. Two years of unproductive talks on a new Agreement with the Football Association of Ireland led to the PFAI's disaffiliation. In 1998, after an Extraordinary General Meeting, it became a Branch of the Marine, Port and General Workers' Union and in 1998 part of SIPTU. In 2002 it received a grant from the Fédération Internationale des Associations de Footballers Professionnels (FIPRO). Fran Gavin became full-time General Secretary in January 2002 until December 2006, when he took up a position with the FAI. He was succeeded by Stephen McGuinness in 2007. Previous General Secretaries included Mick Lawlor and Mick Leech.

PFAI, National Sports Campus, Abbotstown, Dublin 15; (01) 8999350; info@pfai.ie; www.pfai.ie.
My thanks to Frank Devlin, Fran Gavin, John Givens, Stephen McGuinness and Sharon Smith.

Society of Irish Playwrights and Screen Writers' Guild

The Society of Irish Playwrights was a founding member of the ITGWU Cultural Division in 1980. Its members are engaged in writing and producing plays, documentaries and other theatrical entertainments, and its objects are to 'bring a living theatre' to members, to stage productions in union-owned buildings, to involve members in productions, to 'improve the living standards of writers, actors and all connected with the Theatre' by providing regular outlets for their talent and to 'encourage and foster writing and theatrical talent' among members generally. It produced a newsletter, negotiated improved rates for radio plays with RTÉ and received a grant from the Arts Council towards the costs of administration.

Society of Irish Playwrights and Screen Writers' Guild, 18 Parnell Square, Dublin 1; (01) 8721302.

United Stationary Engine Drivers

There have been many Irish stationary engine drivers' unions, one claiming existence from 1840. The United Stationary Engine Drivers' Trade Union was registered in 1891 (no. 119T), changing its name to United Stationary Engine Drivers', Cranemen's and Firemen's Trade Union in 1900. Its registration was cancelled in 1906, however, while a New Union under the same name was registered in 1907 (no. 254T). This was dissolved in 1909 but was followed later the same year by the Irish Stationary Drivers', Cranemen, Firemen and Motormen's Trade Union, which was registered (no. 277T) and was represented at ITUC Congresses in 1909 and 1920. It merged with the Irish Engineering Industrial Union in 1921.

The Independent Stationary Steam and Gas Engine Drivers', Steam and Hydraulic Crane and Motor Drivers', Greasers', Firemen's and Trimmers' Trade Union was registered in 1902 (no. 221T), changing its name in 1906 to the Independent Stationary Steam and Gas Engine Drivers, Steam and Electrical Crane and Motor Drivers', Greasers', Firemen's and Trimmers' Trade Union. It was affiliated to the ITUC, 1906–8, but was dissolved in 1909. The Independent Stationary Steam and Gas Engine Drivers', Steam and Electrical Crane and Motor Drivers', Greasers', Firemen's and Trimmers' Trade Union was registered in 1909 (no. 208T) but was dissolved in 1913; most members are thought to have gone to the Irish Stationary Engine Drivers. Many, however, probably formed the Dublin Municipal Engine Drivers', Firemen, Cranemen and Motormen's Trade Union, registered in 1914 (no. 311T). It operated out of Liberty hall, had its meetings and notices published in the *Irish Worker,* and probably became the ITGWU Engine Drivers' Section after the union was dissolved in 1918.

In 1932 the long-standing Engine Drivers' Section of the ITGWU decided to form an independent body, the United Stationary Engine Drivers', Cranemen, Firemen, Motormen and Machinemen's Trade Union, which was registered (no. 394T). Between 1938 and 1943 it was known as the Irish Power Operatives' and Allied Workers' Trade Union before reverting back to the original title. It affiliated to the CIU in 1958 and thence to the ICTU. In 1942 it absorbed the Limerick Engine Drivers' and Firemen's Union (dating from 1882 and represented at the ITUC Congress in 1896). In the mid-1960s it agreed to re-merge with the ITGWU and had offices in the new Liberty Hall in 1965. Problems arose, however, and the merger was cancelled, with USED moving out. It expanded its membership in paper mills and other mills, canneries and construction works. It had 83 members in 1932, 249 in 1940, 734 in 1950, 706 in 1960 and 501 in 1970. The General Secretaries were James Keyes (1932), John Byrne (1933), Fergus O'Flanagan

(1934), Robert Murphy (1937–9), Joseph Flanagan (1940–63) and Robert Redmond (1964–87). In 1987 it merged with the FWUI.

Appendix 4 ∿

PEN PICTURES OF UNION PERSONALITIES

Individuals are listed alphabetically and by the union in which they ended their time: James Larkin is therefore in the WUI Section rather than the ITGWU. I have been assisted by Charles Callan (Irish Labour History Society), the ILHS web site (www.ilhsonline. org) and 'Biographical Notes' in Donal Nevin, *Between Comrades: James Connolly: Letters and Correspondence,* 1889–1916 (2007). All those living were consulted regarding their entries.

ITGWU

Edward Browne. Born in Limerick, 1904; joined the ITGWU in 1929 when working in flour mills, a sympathetic strike on 6 April providing a fiery baptism. He was President of the Limerick Branch when John Conroy was Branch Secretary, an Association that continued until their deaths in 1969; Branch Assistant, Limerick, 1938–42; Branch Secretary, 1942–53, organising Rineanna (now Shannon) Airport; Vice-President, 1953–69. A hurling and rugby enthusiast, he played for Shannon. He died in April 1983, aged seventy-nine. Fintan Kennedy said it was 'mainly due to his efforts that the Union decided to re-affiliate to the Labour Party in 1967,' a decision made at Annual Conference in Limerick. He travelled the country securing support.
• 'Edward Browne', *Liberty,* Golden Jubilee, May 1959.

Winifred (Winnie) Carney. Born in Bangor, Co. Down, 1887, the only child of a marriage that broke down when she was young. She qualified as a secretary-typist and joined Conradh na Gaeilge in her twenties. A friend of Marie Johnson, wife of the Labour Party Leader Thomas Johnson, she was introduced to Connolly and became full-time Secretary to the Belfast Branch of the ITGWU, 1911. As Connolly's Personal Secretary she accompanied him during the 1916 Rising in the GPO, the 'Secretary with the Webley'. She joined Cumann na mBan in April 1914 and was Adjutant of the Citizen Army. She was president of the Belfast Branch of the IWWU and with Ellen Gordon signed the manifesto 'To the Linen Slaves of Belfast', 1913, as Secretary of the Irish Textile Workers' Union. She contested the Victoria Division of Belfast for Sinn Féin in the General Election of December 1918; worked for the ITGWU, occasionally in Head Office but mostly in Belfast, until she married George McBride in September 1928. She was active in Belfast Labour College and the National Council of Labour Colleges. She died in 1943, a 'loyal comrade, strongly dedicated to the cause; a quiet, serious person, unassuming and reserved, almost timid in appearance and puritan in attitude, a careful and conscientious worker.' She was an ITGWU women's pioneer, displaying courage and determination.

- Helga Woggon, *Silent Radical: Winifred Carney: A Reconstruction of Her Biography* (Studies in Irish Labour History, 6), Dublin: Irish Labour History Society, 2000.
- Helga Woggon, *Ellen Grimley (Nellie Gordon): Reminiscences of Her Work with James Connolly in Belfast* (Studies in Irish Labour History, 7), Dublin: Irish Labour History Society, 2000.

Patrick J. (Paddy) Clancy. Born in Waterford on 23 August 1927, son of an ITGWU activist Denis Curran and Nora Curran, Kilrossanty. His grandfather Thomas Clancy, from Spanish Point, Co. Clare, was an active Land Leaguer. Educated at Mount Sion, he joined Bord na Móna as Shipping Officer, organising the staff into Dublin No. 2 Branch. In the Head Office in Droichead Nua he was a colleague of Ruaidhrí Roberts, ATGWU, later General Secretary of the ICTU. In 1964 he joined the Irish National Productivity Centre, becoming Director of Development and Human Resources. He was Chairperson of Dublin No. 2 Branch, a member of the NEC, 1963–78, member of the ICTU Executive, 1977–82, and Treasurer, 1982–4. In 1956 he created the Liberty Study Group within No. 2 Branch to provide education and training. This expanded until 1960, when the NEC gave Liberty Study Group a national role running seminars, training workshops and classes and publishing training guides. In the 1960s he presented an analysis to the NEC making a case for the Development Services Division in 1970, the country's first specialised, professionally run education, training, research, communications and industrial engineering facility. Clancy became head of the Division until his controversial departure in 1985. A visionary, he was regarded as the 'fourth General Officer.' He was close to Michael Mullen, and together they influenced the adoption of progressive policies and staff appointments. Clancy envisaged a broad role for trade unions, supporting National Understandings. A natural shyness and a desire to avoid the limelight meant that, while extraordinarily influential, he remained a 'back-room boy.' His mistake was that he never sought the office that his talents, perceptions of the union and forward thinking merited. His departure left the ITGWU organisationally and intellectually weaker. He died on 14 September 2003.
- 'Death of Paddy Clancy', *Liberty,* September 2003.

James Connolly. Born of Co. Monaghan parents in Cowgate, Edinburgh, on 5 June 1868. He was a printer's devil, a bakery worker and a general labourer. Influenced by John Leslie and the Edinburgh Social Democratic Federation, he sought political solutions to inequality and poverty. He stood for election as a Socialist candidate and was associated with James Keir Hardie's Scottish Labour Party; in 1896, on Leslie's suggestion and with a loan of £50 from Hardie, he founded the Irish Socialist Republican Party. It published the *Workers' Republic,* linking social and national emancipation for Irish workers. In 1902 and 1903 Connolly unsuccessfully stood as as Socialist candidate for the Wood Quay Ward of Dublin Corporation (City Council), endorsed by Dublin Trades Council, to which he was the Delegate of the United Labourers' Society.

In 1903 Connolly and his family emigrated to the United States. He organised for the Socialist Labor Party and the IWW and founded the Irish Socialist Federation, editing *The Harp.* He stayed in close touch with William O'Brien and Irish Socialists, learning of the founding of the ITGWU and Cumannacht na hÉireann (the Socialist Party of Ireland) in 1910. O'Brien persuaded him to return as Organiser for the SPI in 1910, and

Larkin appointed him ITGWU Ulster Organiser in July 1911. In Belfast he created the Irish Textile Workers' Union among women mill workers but became increasingly active on the national ITGWU stage, successfully negotiating a settlement of the Wexford Lock-Out.

At the 1912 Congress of the ITUC he moved the creation of the Labour Party. He fought the Dock Ward for Belfast Corporation in 1913, unequivocally calling for Socialism and national self-determination. During the 1913 Lock-Out in Dublin he was Acting General Secretary of the ITGWU while Larkin was detained or campaigning in Britain, proving an effective and canny industrial strategist. In 1914 he was disgusted with international Socialism's collapse into support for the Great War. He saw an opportunity for Ireland to strike a blow for freedom. Having succeeded Larkin as Acting General Secretary in the autumn of 1914 he increasingly concentrated on preparations for an insurrection as Commandant of the Irish Citizen Army. In 1915 a printing press was installed in Liberty Hall, from where the *Workers' Republic*—replacing the suppressed *Irish Worker*—published articles about revolutionary and guerrilla warfare while Liberty Hall became an arsenal. He did not neglect his union activities, establishing an Executive and insisting on financial discipline and accountability and providing industrial leadership right until the Rising.

One of seven signatories of the Proclamation of the Irish Republic, he led the detachment that took over the GPO. As Commandant-General he directed operations of the Dublin Division. He was court-martialled and, despite severe wounds, was shot by firing squad on 12 May 1916, strapped in a chair in Kilmainham Jail.

- Kieran Allen, *The Politics of James Connolly*, London: Pluto Press, 1991.
- W. N. Anderson, *James Connolly and the Irish Left*, Dublin: Irish Academic Press, 1994.
- C. Desmond Greaves, *The Life and Times of James Connolly*, London: Lawrence and Wishart, 1961.
- Austen Morgan, *James Connolly: A Political Biography*, Manchester: Manchester University Press, 1989.

John Conroy. Born in Co. Wicklow c. 1904. A factory and coal worker, he joined the ITGWU in 1920 and in 1922 moved to Dublin as a building worker before becoming Secretary of the Wicklow Branch, 1923–4. Appointed to Head Office, 1925–6, he was Branch Secretary in Limerick, 1926–42, and Head of the Movements Department, 1942–6, Vice-President, 1946–53, and General President, 1953–69. He was President of the CIU, 1951/2 and 1958/9, and first President of the ICTU, 1959/60. He served on numerous JICS and JLCS, on Bord Fáilte Éireann and the Atomic Energy Committee. Fintan Kennedy said he 'was a solid man, a man of strong views, of forceful dedication and absolute belief in the concept of social justice. He brooked no opposition to this belief and fought courageously and vehemently to awaken the public conscience to the ills of our society in which injustice and inequalities were so prevalent . . . He was of the good old stock and he was rough-hewn, down to earth, gruff at times, merely to hide an interior of sensitive feeling for those he was honoured to represent.' When he was first elected to national office 'the general public hardly knew his name,' but he was certainly well known inside the ITGWU. He was not flamboyant, delivered speeches slowly and deliberately, and was renowned for his discipline, intolerance of waste, and reluctance to suffer fools gladly. He married Sheila Williams, the first woman elected to the

NEC, in July 1959. His death on 13 February 1969, together with that of James Larkin Junior on 18 February, effectually ended the possibilities of the ITGWU-WUI merger at that time.

- 'John Conroy,' *Liberty*, Golden Jubilee, May 1959.

Sheila Williams Conroy. Born in Bantry, Co. Cork, on 22 April 1918, she began her working life in the Victoria Hotel, Cork, in 1942, organising the workers into the union. She moved to Dublin in 1944 and worked in the Capitol Restaurant; in 1951 was a member of Dublin No. 4 Branch Committee, having shown leadership during the year-long 'Four Houses' strike, although the Capitol was not directly involved. She was the only woman at the Annual Conference in Killarney in 1952, moving a proposal on equal pay. Encouraged by the Branch Secretary, Michael Mullen, she contested a place on the NEC in 1955, succeeding (by one vote) in becoming the first woman elected. The *Evening Herald* announced: 'Thirty-seven men and a girl!' She topped the poll in 1958, but, having married John Conroy, General President, in July 1959, she was a victim of the Marriage Bar and was forced to resign.

After Conroy's death in February 1969, to give her life some purpose she worked for Our Lady's Hospital for Sick Children, Crumlin, Dublin, and joined the Irish Widows' Association, 'becoming its greatest asset,' turning it into a national body. Ruaidhrí Roberts, General Secretary of the ICTU, invited her to become part-time Secretary and Organiser of the People's College, of which she is now President. She was a member of the first Commission on the Status of Women, 1972, and of the RTÉ Authority, 1973–82, of which she was Chairperson, 1976, promoting educational broadcasting and adult education and an 'open door' policy, when members of the staff could come and see her if they had ideas or problems, opening up communications between separate layers of the organisation.

- Marianne Heron, *Sheila Conroy: Fighting Spirit*, Dublin: Attic Press, 1993.
- Ruaidhrí Roberts and R. Dardis Clarke, *The Story of the People's College*, Dublin: People's College, 1986.
- 'Tribute to Sheila Conroy' at www.siptu.ie/equality/NationalWomensForum2007.

Patrick Joseph (Paddy) Devlin. Born in Lady Street in the Pound Loney District off the Falls Road, Belfast, on 8 March 1925, the eldest of seven. Slum conditions made for tough times. His mother, Anne, was a fervent Nationalist, his father, Patrick, a Labour man and trade Unionist in Andrews' Mill. The young Patrick Joined Fianna Éireann, progressing to the Belfast Brigade of the IRA. Interned in Belfast in September 1942, he read and questioned, admiring Billy McMullen, Jack Macgougan and Danny McDevitt, who were attempting Socialist alternatives to sectarianism. After failing as a milk roundsman from his inability to collect money from impoverished customers, he joined Andrews' Mills and the ITGWU and, in 1950, the Irish Labour Party. He won the Falls Ward seat on Belfast City Council in 1956 in a straight fight with Gerry Fitt; defeated in 1958, he joined the Northern Ireland Labour Party, of which he became Chairman in 1967. Active in the Northern Ireland Civil Rights Association, he was an important community worker in west Belfast, seeking to mediate, moderate and construct, generating enemies among former republican comrades, especially Provisionals. Devlin wanted people on the streets, not bombs and bullets.

He was elected MP for Falls for the NILP in 1969, but the Party's refusal to abandon its Unionist line disappointed him. He was a founder-member of the Social Democratic and Labour Party in 1970 with Ivan Cooper, Austin Currie, Gerry Fitt, John Hume and Paddy O'Hanlon. In the 'power-sharing' Executive he was Minister for Health and Social Services. Regarded as unorthodox but highly effective, he was approachable and hard-working, telling his civil servants, 'Just call me Paddy!'

In deep frustration he resigned his office shortly before the Ulster Workers' Council stoppage collapsed everything. He resigned from the SDLP in 1977 in anticipation of his expulsion, subsequently engaging in the United Labour Party (1979), Labour Party of Northern Ireland (1984) and Labour '87. He felt that the SDLP had abandoned the 'social' aspect and had become 'too green.' Appointed ITGWU Northern Organiser in 1975, he quadrupled the membership before his retirement in 1985. At first it was an unpopular appointment, particularly among disaffected Nationalist members, but he came to be highly regarded for energising the union and, against all predictions, recruited more Protestants than Catholics. He was proud of this, 'not to be making a sectarian or big-oted point' but to demonstrate the 'professional trade union service' offered.

He was awarded a master of science degree at Cranfield College of Technology in 1981 for a study of the 1930s unemployed struggles, published as *Yes, We Have No Bananas*. His autobiography, *Straight Left*, won literary and history awards. He received honorary doctorates from the University of Ulster and Queen's University, Belfast, in 1999. He revived Sam Thompson's play *Over the Bridge* at the Arts Theatre, Belfast, in 1985 and presented his own play, *Strike*, based on the Belfast Docks, in 1989. He loved football and boxing. He was made a Commander of the Order of the British Empire in 1999 for promoting unity, although his name was withheld from published lists. He died on 15 August 1999.

Although he was a controversial, at times argumentative figure, Devlin's sincerely held commitment to class politics cannot be doubted. He was personally and politi-cally courageous. Much of what he attempted has come to pass, marking him out as someone ahead of his time. His wife, Theresa, and family were significant supporters, and participants, in his endless activities, their home often accommodating politicians, journalists and those afraid to go home or made homeless by the conflict. His revital-isation of the ITGWU in Northern Ireland was a significant contribution.

- Paddy Devlin, *Straight Left: An Autobiography*, Belfast: Blackstaff Press, 1993.
- Paddy Devlin, *The Fall of the N.I. Executive*, Belfast: P. Devlin, 1973.
- Paddy Devlin, *Tuzo, Whitelaw and the Terror in Northern Ireland*, Belfast: SDLP, 1975.
- Francis Devine, 'Paddy Devlin: Socialist tribune,' *Newsline*, 23 July 1996.
- Francis Devine, 'Just call me Paddy,' *Newsline*, November 1999.
- Francis Devine, 'Paddy Devlin,' *Saothar*, 25 (2000), p. 9–11.

Thomas Farren. Born at 20 St Stephen's Street, Dublin, in 1879 or 1880. He was Secretary of the Stonecutters' Union of Ireland, 1908–17, and, following the formation of the Dublin Labour Party in 1912, one of six members returned to Dublin Corporation, elected for the Usher's Quay Ward. In the 1913 Lock-Out he was Treasurer of Dublin Trades Council and Labour League Strike Fund, in 1915 President of Dublin Trades Council and Labour League and one of seven Labour members on the O'Donovan Rossa Funeral Committee. He was the first Irish Labour Party parliamentary candidate, contesting the by-election in the College Green Division, Dublin, after the death of J. P. Nannetti (Irish Party). He was Treasurer of the Irish Neutrality League, an attempt, initiated by Peadar Macken, to form a joint anti-recruiting campaign between the Trades Council, Irish Volunteers and Citizen Army. He took no part in the Rising but was arrested and held at Richmond Barracks, Inchicore, Dublin, until 20 May.

In 1917 he was one of three Labour representatives on the official Irish Food Control Committee. In February 1918, with Thomas Johnson, Thomas Foran and William O'Brien, he joined the All-Ireland Food Committee established by Sinn Féin. The 300-member Operative Stonecutters of Ireland Trade Union merged with the ITGWU in 1918, and Farren became Organiser, at £2 10s per week. In December, Cathal O'Shannon and Farren were in the minority that strongly favoured running Labour candidates and not leaving Sinn Féin an open field. Farren was President of the ITUC&LP, 1919–20, overseeing the motor permits strike and the General Strike against militarism. In November 1920 Farren, Johnson and ITGWU Officials were arrested in raids on Liberty Hall. He was Secretary of Dublin Workers' Council, 1921–5, and was re-elected to Dublin Corporation, 1920–24. In mid-1922, with other ITUC&LP leaders, he unsuccessfully attempted to avert civil war, intervening between Government and anti-Treaty forces, then in Mountjoy Prison. In December he was one of five Labour Senators elected, with Michael Duffy also an ITGWU member, holding the seat until the Seanad was abolished by the Fianna Fáil Government in 1936.

From 1921 he was Secretary of No. 5 (Building) Branch until retirement on grounds of ill-health in 1950. He died in Our Lady's Hospice, Harold's Cross, on 26 March 1955. The NEC minutes sadly reported that the Farrens were in poor straits, and financial assistance was provided for their last days.

James Fearon. Born in Castle Street, Newry, Co. Down, in 1874. After a spell in the British army he settled in Glasgow and met Larkin while working in iron-ore works. He joined the NUDL and, with Larkin, organised dockers and seamen in Ardrossan, Belfast, Bowness, Cork, Drogheda, Dublin, Dundalk, Glasgow, Leith, Newry, Warrenpoint and Waterford. Bill McCamley argues that 'while Larkin must get the credit for being the dynamic behind the unprecedented drive to unionise the unskilled,' it 'must not be forgotten that Fearon played a major supporting role.' Fearon did the 'bull work,' his nickname, 'Round the Ring', saying much.

He was Secretary of the Glasgow Branch of the NUDL until 27 September 1907, when he set up the Newry Branch. Inseparable from Larkin, he may have represented Cork at the founding ITGWU meeting there in December 1908 and is listed as Vice-President in the 1911 Rules. He engaged in rough-house strikes in Cork and was sentenced to six months' imprisonment with hard labour. He suffered a breakdown and spent time in Downpatrick Asylum before returning to Scotland.

It has been claimed that the Citizen Army originated from his Workers' Militia in Cork, though Greaves dismisses that event as a faction fight between stevedores. In Scotland he was active in the National Unemployed Workers' Committee, housing campaigns and, very probably, the Communist Party of Great Britain. He returned to Newry in 1922 and, with his brother John, to the ITGWU and the Communist Party of Ireland. It is not clear what role he played in the union split or indeed when he returned to Scotland, but he died in Glasgow on 24 October 1924.

Young Jim Larkin, speaking in New York in 1947, said: 'While we pay tribute to men like Connolly and Larkin, whose names are international and have become part of our history, let us also remember the men of the rank-and-file, who not only fought in the cities of Dublin and Cork, but died in the struggle in the city of Glasgow—died of a broken heart, worn out in the battles of his class.'

- Bill McCamley, *The Third James: James Fearon, 1874–1924: An Unsung Hero of Our Struggle* (Studies in Irish Labour History, 4), Dublin: Irish Labour History Society, 2000.

Thomas Foran. Born in Golden Lane, Dublin, in 1883. A warehouseman, he joined the NUDL in 1907, becoming a founding ITGWU member in January 1909 and President. In 1913 he became full-time, drawing wages from the ITGWU National Insurance Approved Society until 1915. A central figure in the Lock-Out, he paid out strike pay from TUC funds with John O'Neill, Secretary of Dublin No. 1 Branch, using unpaid surpluses to secure Liberty Hall in 1914. He was Vice-Chairman of the Irish Citizen Army from March 1914 but took no part in the Rising. Imprisoned in England, after his release he led the reorganisation of the union as Acting General Secretary. Not associated with great speech-making or theoretical writing, Foran is credited with writing *The Lines of Progress* (1919), more probably written by J. J. Hughes. Foran supported the policy of 'One Big Union.' He was a member of the National Executive of the ITUC&LP and subsequently ITUC, 1915–39, President of the ITUC&LP, 1921, President of Dublin Trades Council, 1918, unpaid Acting Secretary of the National Health Insurance Society, 1919–20, a Senator, 1923–36 and 1938–48, and at his death a member of the Council of State. As General President of the ITGWU, 1909–39, he had a 'sixth sense in sizing up a meeting, whether of men or employers, and a capacity for hard work which was an example to all who worked with him.' He had 'an ability to impart knowledge to Organisers.' Greaves saw him as unsung hero, bringing 'common sense and immense energy,' as a 'central figure, the man who was there all the time, quiet, persistent and un-flamboyant.' He frequently worked to near-exhaustion. He was an able and tough negotiator, directly handling members' claims throughout his presidency. Foran was the constant from 1909 to 1939, anchoring the movement during the 1913 Lock-Out, the 1916 Rising, the huge expansion of 1917–23 and the spilt with Larkin in 1923–25 as well as during his near-collapse, 1925–32, and recovery until 1939. He died on 18 March 1951.

The CIU stated that 'workers have lost one of their greatest champions, a man whose unselfish devotion to duty and whose high ideals will be an inspiration to all who serve the Cause of Labour and the Cause of Ireland.'

- 'Thomas Foran,' *Liberty,* Golden Jubilee, May 1959.
- D. R. O'Connor Lysaght, 'Labour Lives, 7: Thomas Foran, 1883–1951,' *Saothar,* 30 (2005), p. 99–100.

Archibald (Archie) Heron. Born in Portadown, Co. Armagh, in 1894, son of a doctor, a Protestant Liberal. Educated locally, at eighteen he was active in Dublin as a full-time Organiser for the Irish Republican Brotherhood. With Seán Mac Diarmada he met James Connolly in the DBC Café in Dame Street and tried to interest him in the IRB. Active in the IRA, 1919–21, and then the Free State army, 1922–3, he was an ITGWU Organiser, 1918–24, editor of the *Voice of Labour,* 1921, and Financial Secretary, 1924–8.

He stood unsuccessfully in March 1924 in the County Dublin by-election, doubling the Labour vote. In August 1925 he attended the Summer School of the International Federation of Trade Unions in Prague. He was active in the James Connolly Labour College, 1919–21, and Workers' Educational Institute, 1925–7. In 1925 the Irish Labour Party and TUC set up local Labour Clubs, and he was appointed Organiser, setting up 140 Branches in 1926 (among them Galway, chaired by Pádraic Ó Conaire). He was Labour candidate in Mayo North (1923), Leitrim-Sligo (June and September 1927) and Dublin County (1933) before his success in Dublin North-West (1937) but failed to hold the seat in 1938. He was General Secretary of the Civil Service Clerks' Association, 1928–40, and of the Irish Local Government Officials' Union, 1940–44, before his dismissal (not for any impropriety but a casualty of internal strife). He was Organiser for the Labour Party in the late 1940s and Brendan Corish's Director of Elections in Wexford in 1947. He contested Dublin North-East in 1948 for National Labour. In 1950 he was appointed Labour Relations Officer of the Department of Local Government, later of the Department of Industry and Commerce, attached to the Factory Inspectorate to promote Safety Committees under the Factories Act (1955). He was married to Ina Connolly, one of James Connolly's daughters. He died in Dublin on 10 May 1971.

James Hickey. Born in Mallow, Co. Cork, in 1888. A docker in Cork, he led the Cork Branch of the National Dock, Wharf and Riverside Labourers' Union into the ITGWU in 1923. An influential Branch Secretary, he contributed intelligently to Annual Conference; was Secretary of Cork No. 1 Branch, 1923–51; Lord Mayor of Cork, 1937–9 and 1943, and longest-serving member of the Corporation, 1934–51. Labour TD for Cork Borough, 1938–43, he was defeated as National Labour Party candidate, 1943 and 1945, and re-elected for the Labour Party, 1948 and 1951. The Taoiseach, John A. Costello, nominated him to the Seanad, 1954–7. A gifted man, he had a grasp of economics, introducing planning concepts to the union. As Mayor he made international headlines in February 1943 when he refused a civic reception for the captain and crew of a German warship, the *Schlesien*. He was a director of the *Catholic Standard*, remitting his fee to the union. He died on 7 June 1956.
- Michael O'Riordan, Address to the National Conference, Irish Labour Party, Cork, 30 September 2001, at www.Communistpartyofireland.ie/spainn-en.html.

Fintan Kennedy. Born on 14 January 1916 in Dublin, son of Thomas Kennedy (below); educated at Catholic University School, gained the diploma in economic science from Harvard University and the ILO. He joined Head Office under Cathal O'Shannon, 1938, was Head of Movements Department, 1948–58, and Assistant to General Secretary, 1958, before being elected General Secretary, 1958–69. He was General President, 1969–81, President of the ICTU, 1965/6, and Treasurer of the ICTU, 1966–82. He served on numerous JICS and JLCS, the Factories Advisory Committee and the Employment Appeals Tribunal and was a member of Seanad Éireann, 1969–82. He was regarded as a 'gentleman', his mannerly bearing disguised a tough, uncompromising negotiator and shrewd strategist. A staff tribute recognised that, 'in spite of all the strains and responsibilities of office, to us you have always been a gentleman, distinguished by your unfailing courtesy and respect for those you have worked with.' He retired on 14 January 1981 and died suddenly on 24 March, 1984. His daughter, Jean Kennedy, maintains the family involvement, working in SIPTU College.

• 'Fintan Kennedy,' *Liberty*, Golden Jubilee, May 1959.

Thomas Kennedy. Born in Dublin in 1887. When he was seventeen he joined a union but at the age of nineteen emigrated to Scotland, meeting Larkin in the NUDL. He was associated with John Wheatley's Catholic Socialist Society, becoming 'one of the most forceful and energetic propagandists.' He returned in 1907 and was involved with William O'Brien in the Committee of the Socialist Party of Ireland in bringing Connolly back to Ireland. In the 1911 census he is described as a trunk maker. He joined the ITGWU shortly after its foundation, was active during the Lock-Out and briefly served on the Executive of the Citizen Army in 1914. He was closely involved in the reorganisation of the union, 1917–18, and was an Official of No. 3 Branch (Thomas Street) and a member of the Executive Council. He acted as General Treasurer, 1922–3, when O'Brien served in the Dáil and was Vice-Chairman of the Labour Party, 1923; elected Vice-President of the union, 1924, and General President, 1939. On O'Brien's retirement in 1946 Kennedy became General Secretary. He was a member of the Executive of the ITUC and President in 1944, a position from which he resigned when the ITGWU seceded to form the CIU in 1945; was President of the CIU, 1945/6, a Labour member of Dublin Corporation, 1920–24 and a member of Seanad Éireann, 1934–8 and 1943–7.

During the Black-and-Tan War and after the establishment of Dáil Éireann he was a judge of the Dáil High Court, South Dublin District. He attended the International Labour Conference in Geneva, 1931, and events in England, Scotland, France, and Denmark. He served on the Economic Commission, 1928, the Summer Time Commission, 1939, the Advisory Councils for Flour Milling, Bread Prices and Building and the flour-milling, woollen and worsted, bacon-curing and boot and shoe JICS. He sat on Trade Boards and was closely involved in the drafting of the Conditions of Employment Act (1936) and Holidays (Employees) Act (1939). In 1946 he led the CIU Committee on the Industrial Relations Act.

'All his life' Kennedy was 'an upholder of the cause of the Common People, in whose memories and of all who knew him he will live, as he will live in the history of the Irish labour movement, a history from which his name will be as inseparable as that of the Union itself and in which both names will shine with equal brilliance.' He was 'both kind and modest, with considerable skill as a negotiator and great tenacity of purpose, yet he also had the ability to reconcile groups with apparently opposite views.' He died on 18 September 1947.

• 'Thomas Kennedy,' *Liberty*, Golden Jubilee, May 1959.

Edward (Éamonn) Lynch. Born in Cuskinny, Queenstown (Cóbh), Co. Cork, 1890. Educated locally, he was an apprentice painter in the dockyards in 1904, President of the Queenstown Branch of the National Amalgamated Society of Operative House and Ship Painters and Decorators, 1911–12, and a member of the Socialist Party of Ireland, 1909–12. When the SPI merged with other groups in 1912 to form the Independent Labour Party of Ireland he became Secretary of the Queenstown Branch. He met Connolly during the 1913 ITUC Congress, and his local knowledge assisted in the organising of laundry workers. A good singer (something Connolly valued), he 'sang his way into all assemblies, councils and Congresses.' He contributed to the *Workers' Republic,* using the pen-name 'Argus'.

He was Organiser for Cork, 1917–21, until his transfer to Head Office as 'Organiser of the Organisers'. The plan was thwarted when he was arrested in Cork in February 1921. Released and re-arrested a week later, he was interned until the end of November. He attended the Summer School of the International Federation of Trade Unions in Prague, August 1925, and was elected a member of Cóbh Town Council and Cork County Council for the Labour Party, serving until 1931. He stood unsuccessfully in Cork East in September 1927 and in 1932. From 1 November 1930 he was Secretary of the ITUC, and when its paper, *Irishman,* changed to *Watchword* he replaced Cathal O'Shannon as editor.

In 1930 Lynch began studies for entrance to King's Inns and in 1934 qualified as a barrister. In 1936 the ITUC established a twelve-member Commission on Reorganisation, Lynch acting as Secretary. It reported in 1939 but the report was not adopted; its unintended outcome came in 1945 with the formation of the CIU. Lynch drafted and presented the ITUC submissions to the Banking Commission in 1934, which led to the establishment of the Central Bank of Ireland in 1943. He was a Labour Party Senator, 1938–43. In 1940/41, during William O'Brien's presidency, Lynch resigned as Secretary of the ITUC.

From the early 1940s to 1961 he was on the staff of the *Irish Times,* working in editorial, filing and journalism. He lived in Greystones, Co. Wicklow, was a keen golfer, sailor and shooter, a noted local historian and speaker and a member of the Grand Master's Lodge of the Masonic Order. He never married. He died suddenly on 29 March 1962.

Michael McKeown. Born in Drominteer, Co. Armagh. He emigrated to England, working as a foundryman and docker at Birkenhead. With Richard McGhee and Edward McHugh he was one of the 'Three Macs', founders of the National Union of Dock Labourers in 1889. McGhee was General President, McHugh was General Secretary and McKeown was Vice-President. In 1889 he was a Leader of the Liverpool dock strike, becoming National Organiser of the NUDL. He spoke at Dublin's first May Day rally in the Phoenix Park, 1890, and in 1891 established the Belfast Branch of the NUDL. He led a three-month strike of Cork dockers and organised Limerick railway and creamery workers. Belfast cross-channel dockers left the NUDL after McKeown spoke on a platform in Glasgow with Michael Davitt. He got work as a tallyman and in 1901 was promoted to Superintendent.

In 1907 he was elected to Belfast City Council, Smithfield Ward, for the United Irish League (Irish Party) and as a Poor Law Guardian, gaining a reputation as a fine orator and persuasive advocate. A native Irish-speaker, McKeown was involved in cultural activities. He was also deeply religious and remained aloof from the movement's Socialist elements. When Larkin arrived as NUDL Organiser in 1907 he asked McKeown to become Secretary of the Belfast Branch. Both were central figures in the dockers' and carters' strike and were deeply suspicious of the General Secretary, James Sexton. Through McKeown's influence, Alex Boyd and Lindsay Crawford (Independent Orange Order) and Joe Devlin MP and Tom Sloan MP became involved.

McKeown represented Belfast at the foundation meeting of the ITGWU on 28 December 1908. He was Secretary of the Belfast Branch, organising Newry, Sligo and

Dundalk, also forming an IWWU Branch there in 1912. With Connolly's appointment as Ulster Organiser in 1911, McKeown was used more widely and was a prominent figure in the Wexford foundry strikes. Standing for Labour in 1913, he lost the council seat won in 1911.

During the 1913 Lock-Out and on the eve of his imprisonment in Mountjoy Prison in November, Larkin nominated McKeown and P. T. Daly to manage the ITGWU. In July 1914, at about the time that Larkin first offered his resignation from the ITGWU, he sacked McKeown 'on the spot' for his outspoken criticism of Daly. McKeown went back to work as a stevedore 'but could not compete with the other bosses employing sweated labour,' and he found other work. Re-elected a Nationalist Councillor, opposing Labour, he remained in public life until his death in Warrenpoint on 14 May 1932, aged seventy-eight.

Paddy Devlin acknowledged McKeown as the ITGWU 'founding father': 'he came so close to being a Leader that we in the labour movement can now view him with a deep sense of loss.'

- Paddy Devlin, 'Michael McKeown: A founding father,' *Liberty* 75 (Diamond Jubilee Issue), June 1984, p. 14–15.
- William McMullen, 'Early days in Belfast,' *Liberty* 75 (Diamond Jubilee Issue), June 1984, p. 10–13, and www.siptu.ie/AboutSIPTU/History/EarlyDaysinBelfast.
- Eric Taplin, *The Dockers' Union: A Study of the National Union of Dock Labourers, 1889–1922*, Leicester: Leicester University Press, 1986.

William (Billy) McMullen. Born in Lilliput Street, Belfast, in 1888, his father, Joseph, from Co. Monaghan farming stock, his mother from Co. Cavan. She died when William was five, and his father opened a shop, first in Lilliput Street, then in the Shore Road. After elementary schooling, McMullen worked in the shipyards and before he was twenty became active in the Independent Labour Party. He was influenced by Larkin and the Belfast Dock Strike, 1907. When Connolly arrived in Belfast as Ulster Organiser of the ITGWU in 1911 McMullen became a loyal, energetic Assistant. In 1912 he moved to Dublin and helped form a Branch of the Independent Labour Party of Ireland. He spoke at a meeting protesting against the exclusion of Ulster from Home Rule in 1914, joining Connolly on a public platform for the first time and developing what became a famous and much-admired speaking style. Unemployment forced his emigration to England and Scotland during the Great War; on his return to Belfast in 1920 he became Secretary of the Belfast Branch of the ITGWU. He was elected Poor Law Guardian for the NILP in Smithfield Ward, 1924, a City Councillor in January 1925 and in June 1925 Stormont MP for West Belfast; despite coming at the bottom of the poll, with 2,869 first-preference votes, transfers from Joe Devlin, the only Nationalist Party candidate, carried him home.

In Parliament he challenged the Ulster Unionist Party over unemployment and in 1928 he joined the rest of NILP in walking out, earning a suspension. He opposed the boundary settlement and argued for national unity, a position he held all his life. He stood in the Falls in 1929 but was defeated by Richard Byrne, Nationalist, 6,941 to 5,509. The NILP published *Northern Worker*, in which it claimed that Byrne, a publican, was a slum landlord. Byrne secured an injunction to stop distribution two days before the election.

McMullen did not stand in the 1933 General Election but contested the by-election in June 1934 for Belfast Central after Devlin's death and finished second. He attended

the Republican Congress in Dublin in 1934, earning admonishment from a disapprov-
ing NEC. He was National Organiser, 1937, elected Vice-President in 1939 and General
President from 1946 until his retirement in 1953. He was President of the ITUC, 1927–8,
and of the CIU, 1953/4, and a member of Seanad Éireann, 1951–3. He retired, under age,
after the 1953 Conference. He was a director of the Joint Great Northern Railway Board
and of CIÉ. He died in December 1982, aged ninety-five.
- William McMullen, *With James Connolly in Belfast,* Dublin: ITGWU, n.d.; reprinted
  Belfast: Donaldson Archives, 2001.
- 'William McMullen,' *Liberty,* Golden Jubilee, May 1959.

Constance Markievicz, née Gore-Booth. Born in London in 1868 but reared on the
family estate, Lissadell, Drumcliff, Co. Sligo. She studied art at the Slade School in
London, 1893, and Paris, 1898–1900, where she met Casimir Dunin-Markiewicz, a Polish
count, whom she married in London in 1900. After periods in Ukraine and London
she settled in Dublin in 1908, joining Sinn Féin and Inghinidhe na hÉireann. She
founded Fianna Éireann in 1909 and during the Lock-Out helped run soup kitchens in
Liberty Hall. She was made an honorary member of the ITGWU and President of the
IWWU. She fought in the College of Surgeons in 1916 as a captain in the Citizen Army,
second in command to Commandant Michael Mallin. Her subsequent death sentence
was commuted to life imprisonment; she was released from prison in June 1917. In 1918
she became the first woman elected to the House of Commons, for St Patrick's Division,
Dublin, but, as a Sinn Féin member, refused to take her seat. She was Minister for
Labour in the first and second Dáil, was imprisoned during the Civil War and returned
to the Dáil, 1923 and 1927, for Dublin Borough South. Regarded as a great friend of the
ITGWU, she joined Fianna Fáil on its formation in 1926.
- Anne Haverty, *Constance Markievicz: An Independent Life,* London: Pandora, 1988.
- Anne Marreco, *The Rebel Countess: The Life and Times of Constance Markievicz,*
  London: Weidenfeld and Nicholson, 2000.
- Mary Moriarty and Catherine Sweeney, *Markievicz: The Rebel Countess,* Dublin:
  O'Brien Press, 1991.
- Diane, Norman, *Terrible Beauty: A Life of Constance Markievicz,* Dublin: Poolbeg
  Press, 1991.
- Jacqueline van Voris, *Countess de Markievicz: In the Cause of Ireland,* Amherst
  (Mass.): University of Massachusetts Press, 1967.

Michael (Mickey) Mullen. Born in Dublin in February 1919 into a working-class and
strongly Labour family. His father, a glass-blower, died from pneumonia when Michael
was fourteen, propelling the boy into paid employment as a butcher's messenger. When
he was seventeen he started in Ever-Ready Batteries at Portobello Harbour, Dublin,
where he joined the ITGWU, becoming Shop Steward within the year and a member of
Dublin No. 1 Branch Committee. A member of Fianna Éireann, he graduated to the
IRA in the 1940s but left in 1945 to join the Labour Party; he later reflected: 'I learned the
facts of life and realised that Socialism was the only way out of the morass my people
found themselves in.'
   He was Branch Assistant, Dublin No. 1 Branch, 1945–50, and Secretary of Dublin
No. 4 (Hotel and Catering) Branch, 1950–64. A bitter, hard-fought strike broke out from

October 1950 to June 1951, imposing great hardship on catering workers, who sought a 10% service charge to end their reliance on tips. Many lost not only their income but their accommodation, as they were 'living in'. Mullen provided leadership and a strong hand to maintain discipline and morale. He was Secretary of Dublin District Council, 1956–64, a significant figure among the industrial staff.

Elected to Dublin Corporation, 1960–69, alderman, 1967, and Labour Deputy for Dublin North-West, 1961–9. From 1961 to 1965 he was Dublin's only Labour Deputy; spokesman on Posts and Telegraphs and on Transport and Power, 1965–9; Senator, 1973–7, appointed by the Taoiseach, Liam Cosgrave. He was National Industrial Group Secretary, 1964–6, Senior Adviser to the NEC, 1966; elected General Secretary in 1969, when he ceased political activity.

His stewardship coincided with a rapid growth in membership, the introduction of Deduction at Source, expansion into 'white-collar' areas and extension among manufacturing throughout the country. The Development Services Division, from 1972, and Cultural Division, from 1980, were radical initiatives. He supported the appointment of openly Socialist candidates to industrial and support staff; served on the ICTU Executive, 1969–82, on the Board of CERT, and as a director of Aer Rianta and Bord Fáilte Éireann. In 1982 he was the 'guarantor' of the 'Gregory Deal' between the Taoiseach, Charles Haughey, and the Dublin Central independent TD Tony Gregory.

He was an 'outspoken, sometimes controversial personality,' and none could doubt his support for the underprivileged. Putting his money where his mouth was, in 1977 he arranged that his Dáil pension be divided between the Irish Council for Civil Liberties and organisations assisting handicapped children. He strongly supported the Irish Anti-Apartheid Movement and, as a Labour Senator, opposed the Criminal Law Jurisdiction Act (1976), losing the Labour Party whip, although later readmitted. His desire for Irish unity and independence was patent, and he supported the Northern Ireland Civil Rights Association. He was prominent in the H blocks hunger strike crisis in 1981, seeking to promote agreement and to pressure the British and Irish Governments. Attending a Conference in Frankfurt when taken ill, he died on 3 November 1982.

Tributes came from all quarters, many no doubt grudgingly paying formal respect to an adversary; others, such as Tomás Mac Giolla (Workers' Party), Michael O'Riordan (Communist Party of Ireland) and Dan McCarthy (National Land League) recognised a kindred spirit who built bridges with organisations that pursued similar agendas for the poor and dispossessed, urban or rural, domestic or international. At his graveside John Carroll described him as 'an instinctive Socialist . . . proud of his working-class origins' and a tireless campaigner, particularly for inner-city Dublin. There were claims that Kennedy, Carroll and Mullen, General Officers from 1969 to 1981, did not get on well. There were certainly occasional difficulties, but the general effect was one of creative tension and much innovation, to the extent that their collective term is now looked back on as something of a 'golden age'.

- John Armstrong, 'Leaders pay tribute to Mullen's life [and] work,' *Irish Times*, 2 November 1982.
- 'Michael Mullen, 1919–1982,' *Liberty*, November 1982.
- 'Mullen—fighter for the underprivileged,' *Irish Times*, 2 November, 1982.

Mary (May) O'Brien. Born in Donnybrook, Dublin, on 30 May 1932, the second of five children of Richard, a chauffeur, and Margaret (née Small). She joined the staff of the ITGWU in 1947 as clerk-typist, No. 6/8 (Clothing and Textiles) Branch. The General President, John Conroy, put many hurdles in her path as she attempted to become an industrial Official. She finally succeeded in 1972, becoming a Branch Assistant, one of only two women Branch Officials. She was the first Women's Affairs Official in 1982, her appointment seen as 'safe' and unthreatening to an establishment still not completely convinced of the equality agenda. Their judgement was misplaced. In a quiet, undemonstrative manner, supported by the Women's Affairs Committee, she raised the profile of women, delighted in encouraging their advancing participation; pioneered assertiveness training and turned the Women's Conference into a training ground for the Annual Conference; produced *Equality News,* reporting industrial, legal and case precedents; moved proposals challenging discrimination within society; and, with assistance from Eugene Kearney (Industrial Engineering), won equal pay and equal treatment cases through diligent application of her knowledge of equality legislation and the committed perseverance of claimant women, inspired by her encouraging leadership. Lissadell Towels, Carrickmacross, was the scene of an eight-year battle against bitter opposition by IBEC and every appeal possible; committed members, female and male, never swerved.

She was a member of the Employment Equality Agency, the Employment Appeals Tribunal and the ICTU Women's Affairs Committee and a regular contributor to many women's platforms. She was a mould-breaker, encouraging others within work-place and home. The election of Doris Kelly and Mary Oakes to the NEC was a victory for her strategy of encouraging women to do it for themselves.

On her retirement in 1992 her legacy was a stronger women's presence, broken glass ceilings, and industrial successes for equality—a worthy Women's Officer. Her sister, Frances O'Brien, worked in the ITGWU and later SIPTU, 1964–2001, as Administrative Assistant in the Cash Office, No. 2 (Clerical), No. 7 (Cinema and Theatre, later Film and Broadcasting) and FÁS Branches and in Region 2 (Dublin Private Sector).

• May O'Brien, *Clouds on My Windows: A Dublin Memoir,* Dingle: Brandon, 2004.

Thomas (Tom) O'Brien. Born in Dublin on 6 December 1933; educated at Boys' National School, Rathfarnham, College of Commerce, Rathmines, and College of Industrial Relations. His father, Thomas O'Brien, was active in Dublin No. 9 Branch; O'Brien followed him into CIÉ in 1950, joining the ITGWU rather than the NUR and, although only a boy, standing with them in that year's bitter railway strike. He was elected to Dublin No. 11 Branch Committee and appointed Branch Assistant in Dublin No. 1 Branch in 1960, being responsible for road haulage, docks, motor assembly, bottled gas, Aer Lingus and Unidare. He was Secretary of Dublin No. 5 (Construction) Branch in 1965 after Tom McCarthy's death; Secretary of Dublin District Council, 1974–7, and National Group Secretary, Construction, 1977. He was a trade union Trustee in the Construction Industry Pension Scheme and a member of the AnCO Community Youth Training Committee and numerous national and international bodies. Elected Vice-President on 26 May 1981, sadly he died on 10 November, aged forty-seven, having served only five months. A big man in all senses, he was a strong negotiator, a purposeful Leader and highly popular among members.

William Xavier (Bill) O'Brien. Born on 23 January 1880 in Ballygurteen, Clonakilty, Co. Cork. He moved to Dublin in 1897, qualified as a tailor, and until 1918 was a member of the Amalgamated Society of Tailors and Tailoresses. Associated with James Connolly from 1896, with his brothers Dan and Tom he joined the Irish Socialist Republic Party. He served on the Executive of Dublin Trades Council, 1909–19, was President in 1914 and Secretary of the Lock-Out Committee, 1913–14. He was a member of the Executive of the ITUC&LP and ITUC, 1911–45, and President in 1913, 1918, 1925 and 1941; Secretary of the ITUC, 1918–20; Secretary of Dublin Labour Party, 1911–15; Chairman of the Labour Party, 1933–9; and TD for Dublin South, June 1922 to August 1923, and for Tipperary, 1927, 1937 and 1938.

He was elected to the ITGWU Executive in January 1918, was General Treasurer, 1919–24, and General Secretary, 1924–46. A member of the Irish Neutrality League and Anti-Conscription League, he fought the Stockport by-election in 1920 while interned in London.

NEC minutes and union publications reveal little about him, as he scarcely features. It is not doubted, however, that his hand firmly gripped the ITGWU tiller. His obsessive contempt for Larkin never wavered and resulted in O'Brien leading the ITGWU out of the Labour Party in 1945, ostensibly on the grounds of 'Communist infiltration' but more certainly out of animus to Larkin after he was admitted to the Party. Similarly, he was central to the moves that created the CIU in 1944 as he sought the withdrawal of British unions.

On his retirement in 1946 the movement was bisected, industrially and politically—hardly a high point. Where Larkin was impassioned, perhaps irrational, O'Brien was calculating and deliberate. Nevertheless, with Foran, O'Brien held the ITGWU together during its dramatic collapse after 1923 and, through sound management, saved it from extinction and turned it into an organisation of more than 60,000 members. De Valera appointed him one of the first directors of the Central Bank of Ireland in 1943, and he was reappointed until he was aged eighty-six in 1966. He died on 30 October 1968, aged eighty-eight.

- Arthur Mitchell, 'William O'Brien, 1881–1968, and the Irish labour movement,' *Studies*, 20 (1971).
- D. R. O'Connor Lysaght, 'The rake's progress of a syndicalist: The political career of William O'Brien, Irish labour Leader,' *Saothar*, 9 (1983), p. 48–62

Cathal O'Shannon. Born Charles O'Shannon in Randalstown, Co. Antrim, reared at Draperstown, Co. Derry. His father and brother were active in the Amalgamated Society of Railway Servants on the Londonderry–Lough Swilly Railway. He attended St Columb's College, Derry, where he began writing newspaper articles. His first job was as a clerk in a Belfast shipping company; he joined Conradh na Gaeilge and the Dungannon Club, meeting Seán Mac Diarmada, Bulmer Hobson and Denis McCullough, and was sworn into the IRB, aged 18. He was Secretary of the Belfast Branch of Sinn Féin, a founder-member of Belfast Fianna Éireann and a worker under James Connolly in the Belfast Branch of the ITGWU from 1912. He mobilised Republicans in Coalisland, 1916, and was interned in Wales and England with Terence MacSwiney, Tomás Mac Curtáin, Seán T. O'Kelly and Ernest Blythe. He was a member of the Executive of the ITUC&LP, 1918–23, and President, 1921/2, Cork District Secretary of the

ITGWU, 1917, Organiser in 1918 and Assistant Secretary from March 1919. He wrote for the *Irish Worker, Workers' Republic, Peasant, Claidheamh Soluis* and *Sinn Féin* and edited the *Voice of Labour* and *Irishman*. His pseudonym was 'Craobh Dearg'. He went on hunger strike in Mountjoy Prison, Dublin, in 1920 but strove, with William O'Brien, Tom Johnson and Tom Farren, to prevent civil war.

He represented the ITUC at the International Socialist Congress in Bern in 1919 and was Labour TD for Louth-Meath, 1922–3. He was Secretary of the ITUC, 1941–5, Secretary of the CIU, 1945–6, and a Worker Representative on the Labour Court, 1946–69. He continued to write prolifically for the *Irish Press* and *Liberty* and edited *Fifty Years of Liberty Hall* (1959). He died on 4 October 1969.

- 'Cathal O'Shannon,' *Liberty,* Golden Jubilee, May 1959.
- Emmet O'Connor, 'Labour lives: Cathal O'Shannon,' *Saothar,* 24 (1999), p. 89–90.

William Patrick (W. P.) Partridge. Born in Sligo on 8 March 1874, son of an Englishman who came to Ireland as an engine-driver on the Midland and Great Western Railway; his mother was from Athlone. The family moved to Ballaghaderreen, Co. Roscommon, in 1874. He completed his fitter's apprenticeship at the MGWR Works, Broadstone, Dublin, in 1897. He was active in the Amalgamated Society of Engineers, working at the Ross and Walpole foundry and Dairy Engineering Company and the Great Southern and Western Railway Company works at Inchicore, Dublin, 1898, and moved to Kilmainham. He was Treasurer of Inchicore Branch of Conradh na Gaeilge; active in the Labour Electoral Association and Director of Elections for the successful Labour candidate, William Reigh (Coach Makers' Society), Kilmainham, 1902. He was elected Labour Councillor for Kilmainham in 1904, campaigning on anti-corruption and health issues, for better housing, direct labour and changing the council's meeting hours to accommodate workers. He resigned in 1906, was dismissed from the GSWR in August 1912 and worked briefly in Carrick-on-Suir.

When the ITGWU leased Emmet Hall in Kilmainham in the autumn of 1912 Larkin appointed Partridge as caretaker-manager. The hall became a labour centre and allowed Partridge to work on ASE business. He was re-elected to the City Council in 1913. Twice arrested during the 1913 Lock-Out, he travelled with Thomas MacPartlin and Councillor Thomas Lawlor to address the special TUC Congress convened in Manchester to discuss Dublin. He was ITGWU Southern Organiser in 1915. Active in the Irish Citizen Army from its inception; as a captain, although unwell, he fought in St Stephen's Green and the College of Surgeons with Constance Markievicz and Michael Mallin. Detained in Richmond Barracks and Kilmainham Jail, he was sentenced to fifteen years' penal servitude. Released on medical grounds on 20 April 1917, suffering from Bright's disease, he died at Ballaghaderreen on 26 July and is buried in Kilcolman Cemetery, where a monument was finally erected over his grave in August 2006.

- Hugh Geraghty, *William Patrick Partridge and His Times (1874–1917)*, Dublin: Curlew Publications, 2003.
- Hugh Geraghty, 'William P. Partridge: Labour Councillor and Citizen Army captain,' *Labour History News,* 1991, p. 9–11, 22.
- Hugh Geraghty and Peter Rigney, 'The engineers' strike in Inchicore Railway Works, 1902,' *Saothar,* 9 (1983), p. 20–30.

Francis (Frank) Purcell. Born in Kilcock, Co. Kildare. He worked in St Patrick's College, Maynooth, organising the staff into the union, 1917. He was Secretary of Kilcock Branch, 1920–22, before joining Head Office Movements Department. Active in the IRA in the War of Independence, he was interned in the Rath Camp, Co. Kildare. Neutral in the Civil War, he suffered short imprisonments and detentions by both sides in the course of his organising. He developed into a 'dependable, thoughtful, careful and conscientious Official,' always ready to 'take good example' from others; outwardly 'steady, good-tempered, unperturbed,' concealing an 'anxiety of mind and sometimes natural vexation of spirit and conscience.' He possessed moral and physical courage in abundance. He was Secretary of Dublin No. 4 (Hotels and Restaurants) Branch, 1931; transferred to Movements Department, 1943; elected General Secretary, 1948. He was Secretary of the National Labour Party from 1944 and was 'responsible for the general direction' of *Liberty*. Died shortly after his retirement in 1959. Fintan Kennedy's appointment as Assistant to the General Secretary in 1958 indicated Purcell's failing health.

• 'Frank Purcell', *Liberty*, Golden Jubilee, May 1959.

WUI AND FWUI

John Bohan. First Secretary of ITGWU No. 3 Branch (High Street, Dublin); represented the union at the ITUC Congress, 1910–11. Elected to Dublin Corporation in 1912, he lost the seat in 1915. He was a member of the Executive from 1915 but was a constant thorn in Liberty Hall's side, seemingly wanting an autonomous existence and slow to make financial returns.

After the Rising the divisions became more pronounced. Bohan actively supported Delia Larkin, P. T. Daly and Michael Mullen (Mícheál Ó Maoláin) in their opposition to the Executive. He was elected to the Executive of the ITUC in 1919 and to Dublin Corporation in 1920. In 1924 he became Secretary of No. 1 Branch of the WUI. Larkin quickly discovered that Bohan could be just as independent-minded and as difficult as his previous employers had found him. In 1930 the WUI took a Court action to retrieve money, books and premises. After his dismissal by the WUI, Bohan reapplied for membership of the ITGWU; he was admitted 'as a new member' in March 1931 but never again held office.

Bohan was a talented individual (with the emphasis on 'individual'). He appears to have held property in High Street and Inchicore in his own name that the ITGWU and WUI contested. It is not clear what his trade was, or when he died.

Patrick (Paddy) Cardiff. Born in Basin Street, off James's Street, Dublin, on 8 November 1925. Both parents were Larkinites, his father a member of the WUI and his mother of the IWWU. The father served with the British army in the Great War. He inculcated a love of reading in Cardiff, who left the Christian Brothers' School in James's Street before he was fourteen to work in a heel-tip factory in Basin Lane. In the late 1930s and early 40s he worked, when he could get it, as a general labourer and around the fruit and vegetable markets. In 1943 he went to England and joined the King's Liverpool Regiment (in a battalion known as the 'Liverpool Irish') and he remained in the army after the war, serving in India, until 1948. His military experience was obvious in his insistence on thoughtful preparation, planning and discipline in everything he engaged in.

On returning home he laboured with McLaughlin and Harvey, mainly in the Guinness Brewery, joining the No. 8 (Building) Branch of the WUI and attending evening classes at the Catholic Worker's College, 1955–1962. He became active in No. 9 (Guinness Brewery) Branch. James Larkin Junior was a huge influence. Cardiff was a member of the GEC until he was appointed Secretary of No. 4 (Food, Sugar and Confectionery) Branch in 1964; and in 1968, following John Smithers's death, he narrowly failed to be elected General President. When James Larkin Junior died, in 1969, Cardiff was elected Deputy General Secretary. From May 1977 to 1983 he was General Secretary. Poor health compelled his retirement.

Under his stewardship, education, training and information were developed; Workers' Unity Trust was created; and the union expanded to become a National Organisation through mergers with the Federation of Rural Workers, Irish Agricultural Advisors' Association, IWWU and NATE. A strong supporter of the ICTU and of tripartite centralised national Agreements, Cardiff fought to expand Wage Agreements into more wide-ranging accords encompassing job creation, infrastructural development, education, health, social welfare, housing, tax reform, worker participation, training and equality, leading to the National Understandings of 1979–81. It was a great disappointment that, when he was President of the ICTU, 1982/3, the national udnerstandings collapsed. He served on the boards of An Post, Bord na Móna and the National Economic and Social Council. He was a member of the Merchants' Quay Branch of the Labour Party and took a keen interest in the Labour Party Trade Union Affiliated Group. He retained a strong Catholic faith but was intolerant of sectarianism and utterly opposed violence for any purpose. He was regarded as supportive and considerate but at times impatient and truculent and was not someone to 'mess with.' He died in Dublin on 3 June 2005.

- Paddy Cardiff, 'Reform: What needs to be done?' in Pollock, *Reform of Industrial Relations,* p. 110–23.
- Francis Devine, *Understanding Social Justice: Paddy Cardiff and the Discipline of Trade Unionism,* Dublin: Irish Labour History Society, 2002.

John (Jack) Carney. Born in Ireland in 1889, according to a 1920 Court hearing, or in Duluth (Minnesota) or Liverpool, according to Emmet Larkin. (Carney told him that his mother, while emigrating to America, delivered him on Merseyside.) After being orphaned he was reared by grandparents in Liverpool, where he first heard Larkin speak. He was active with Larkin in Belfast in 1907 and appears to have been employed by the ITGWU from 1911, helping Larkin with the *Irish Worker* and Connolly in the Belfast Municipal Election campaign in 1913, when he was briefly imprisoned.

He travelled to New York in June 1916, teaming up with Larkin and his paper, the *Irish Worker,* and campaigning for Eugene V. Debs's Socialist Party presidential campaign. Larkin and Carney were active in the IWW. He settled with his wife, Mina, in Duluth, editing *Truth.* In 1919 he supported the 'Left-Wing Manifesto' of the Socialist Party, leading to the creation of the Communist Labor Party in Chicago in August 1919, and he was a member of it Executive. He was charged with sedition in 1919 and under Illinois Sedition Law in 1920. Mina edited *Truth* during his absences until October 1920, when he moved to Butte (Montana) to edit the *Daily Bulletin* and then to Chicago, editing the *Voice of Labor.* He was imprisoned in November 1922 but was pardoned after ten days and, with Mina, became active in the Larkin Defense Committee, run by John Fitzpatrick of the Chicago Federation of Labor.

Carney sailed back to Ireland with Larkin on 2 April 1923, signing on board as a 'French chef' but ending in the stokehold. He returned to America and edited *Labor Unity* in San Francisco until he was sent to Moscow in 1925 as Larkin's Comintern representative, remaining as the Irish Worker League's permanent representative. In September 1927 he assisted with IWL election campaigns for Larkin, Young Jim Larkin and John Lawlor. He edited the *Irish Worker* from 1931 and the *Irish Workers' Voice* (published by the Communist Party of Ireland) from 1936.

From the late 1920s he was a WUI Official, but when the Executive decided that members of the staff could not speak on platforms supporting the Spanish Republic, he resigned. During the Second World War he worked in London for Australian Associated Press and was a member of the House of Commons press corps. Mina Carney presented her bust of Larkin to the Hugh Lane Municipal Gallery of Modern Art (Dublin City Gallery) in 1930. Jack Carney died on 21 March 1956.

That Emmet Larkin dedicated his classic biography of Larking to Carney in 1965 says much for the relationship between the two, the dedication being because 'more than anyone else' he gave the author 'an understanding of what Jim Larkin was all about.'

- Jack Carney, 'Jim Larkin in America,' in Nevin, *James Larkin: Lion of the Fold.*
- Richard Hudelson, 'Jack Carney and the *Truth* in Duluth,' *Saothar*, 19 (1994), p. 129–39.
- Virginia Hyvarinen, 'Research notes: Jack Carney,' unpublished manuscript, c. 1990 in ILHS Archives.
- Emmet O'Connor, *Reds and the Green: Ireland, Russia and the Communist International, 1919–1943,* Cork: Cork University Press, 2004.

Francis (Frank) Cluskey. Born on 8 April 1930 in St Ignatius' Road, Drumcondra, Dublin, son of Frank Cluskey Senior (journeyman butcher and WUI Branch Secretary). Young Cluskey attended Francis Xavier National School, Dorset Street, and St Vincent's Christian Brothers' School, Glasnevin, and began his butchery apprenticeship in 1946. Always active, he became Branch Secretary of the Operative Butchers, 1954–65, when it merged with the ITGWU to become the Meat Federation. He was a quintessential 'Larkinite', his vision never confined to mere 'bread-and-butter' issues, believing that the arts and education were essential in defeating poverty. Active in the WUI Dramatic Society, 1950s to 1960s, he contributed to *Bulletin* and was Chairman of the Central Education Committee. His sister May Cluskey became a respected theatre and television actor.

He was elected to Dublin Corporation (City Council) in 1960 and in 1958 unsuccessfully contested the Dublin South-Central by-election caused by the resignation of Jack Murphy, the Unemployed Workers' TD, and was unsuccessful again in 1961. In the 1965 General Election he was elected for the Labour Party in Dublin South-Central, Larkin Junior's old seat. When Lord Mayor of Dublin in 1968 one of his first actions was to confer the Honorary Freedom of the City on Mícheál Mac Liammóir and Hilton Edwards. Cluskey's Mayoral term was cut short when the Corporation was abolished and a Commissioner appointed.

In 1969, following Larkin Junior's death, he contested the Deputy General Secretaryship, his political involvement perhaps putting off traditionalists who wanted a total commitment to the union. He was chief whip of the Labour Party, 1965–73, and spokesman under several briefs. In 1973 in the Fine Gael-Labour Coalition Government he was Parliamentary Secretary with responsibility for Social Welfare under the Tánaiste and Minister for Health and Social Welfare, Brendan Corish. He introduced many important reforms and new provisions: the qualifying age for old-age pensions was reduced from seventy (it has stood still at sixty-six since Cluskey's time); workers laid off or unable to work because of a strike or Lock-Out in which they are not directly involved became eligible for Unemployment Benefit or assistance; Children's Allowance was made payable directly to the mothers; and new provisions included allowances for unmarried mothers (as single mothers were then called), deserted wives and prisoners' dependants, as well as pensions for women aged fifty-eight who were the principal carers of parents or relatives. The Combat Poverty Agency was also established. Cluskey always credited Corish with making these innovations possible.

After the 1977 General Election he succeeded Corish as Party Leader. He was an effective Leader (though hampered by lack of funds and perennial dissension) and an accomplished parliamentarian. He lost both seat and leadership in June 1981; was member of the European Parliament for Dublin, 1 July 1981 to late 1982; and regained his Dáil seat in February 1982, holding it until November 1982.

In the subsequent Fine Gael-Labour Government he served as Minister for Trade, Commerce and Tourism, his only Government appointment. On 8 December 1983 he resigned over the provision of natural gas and public funding to the privately owned Alliance and Dublin Consumers' Gas Company (which was later taken into public ownership), showing great loyalty to the work force—primarily FWU members. He fell ill during the 1987 General Election and spent the next two years in hospital. He died in the Eye and Ear Hospital, Dublin, on 7 May 1989.

Bernard (Barney) Conway. Born in Dublin on 18 April 1882. A labourer and docker, he joined the NUDL in 1907 and was a founder-member of the ITGWU in 1909, serving on No. 1 Branch Committee and as a Delegate to Dublin Trades Council. He was twice arrested during the Lock-Out for attacking blacklegs. A member of the Citizen Army in 1916, he fought in the War of Independence and the Civil War, being interned at Gormanston, Co. Meath. In 1924 he led the 'Forty-Five' who occupied Liberty Hall and was a founder-member of the WUI.

He was elected to Dublin Corporation in 1940 and was an Alderman and Deputy Lord Mayor (under Martin O'Sullivan). He was a Delegate of No. 1 Branch from 1924 until 1958, when he retired. He did 'honourable service in prison for his class and country,' was a 'confidant and friend of Jim Larkin' and 'comrade and friend of us all.' His death on 2 January 1965, aged eighty-three, marked the 'end of an era' for an 'outstanding member of Larkin's Old Guard': 'To the older members he was a friend and comrade; to the younger members an inspiration, a guide and fatherly adviser. In the tactics and strategy of the trade union movement he was a source of helpful knowledge and experience. He was a militant, fighting trade Unionist; yet in his personal life he was a quiet big man, the friend of all and respected by all.'

Patrick (P. T.) Daly. Born in Dublin in 1870, son of a printer. He served his time as a compositor and became active in Dublin Typographical Provident Society; DTPS

Delegate to Dublin Trades Council, 1902, and President, 1904. He helped print the *Workers' Republic*. He was Secretary of the 1798 Centenary Committee and a member of the IRB, rising to be one of the three-member Supreme Council. At the 1900 ITUC Congress he proposed the formation of a Labour Party but was a founding member of Sinn Féin in 1905 and a member of its National Council, 1906–10. He was the manager of Cló-Chumann, 1904; because the DTPS did not allow managers he 'got some of his friends' to form the 24-member Paviours' Society and represented it on Dublin Trades Council. He was editor and manager of the Trades Council's *Irish Labour Journal*, 1909 (beating Connolly to the post); the paper collapsed after four months, with an overdraft of £50. He was Secretary of the ITUC, 1909–18, being defeated by William O'Brien. Appointed Acting General Secretary of the ITGWU in June 1910 while Larkin was imprisoned, he spent much of his time in Belfast. Larkin appointed him Organiser, 1911–14, his finest hour being the Wexford Lock-Out, 1911–12, when he suffered several serious assaults and incarceration in Waterford Prison.

Before Larkin departed for the United States he recommended that Daly become Acting General Secretary, but after pressure from O'Brien and Connolly he made him instead Secretary of the National Health Insurance Approved Society. He was not re-elected in 1919 and was replaced by Foran, General President. He allied himself with Delia Larkin and Michael Mullen (Mícheál Ó Maoláin) to agitate against this decision, challenged the new union Rules and expressed opposition to those seen as usurping the absent Larkin's authority. The Sligo Branch, which Daly claimed to have joined in 1912, nominated him as Acting General Secretary in 1917, further exacerbating tensions with O'Brien. He received a testimonial from Richmond and Portrane Asylums against Dublin Trades Council policy. Delegates overturned an Executive ruling, and many unions formed the Dublin Workers' Council in protest. Daly remained Secretary of Dublin Trades Council. After the healing of the split in 1929 with the creation of Dublin Trades Union Council, he remained the full-time Secretary.

He assisted in the creation of the WUI and appeared on IWL platforms but does not appear to have been a WUI Official. In later life he was a member of the ATGWU. He represented the Dublin Fire Brigade Men's Union and Meath Labour Union at Congress. He was a member of Dublin Corporation for Rotunda Ward, 1904–8, for North Dock, 1910–19, and North City and North Dock, 1920–25 and 1932–3, also representing the Corporation on Dublin Port and Docks Board, Grangegorman Mental Hospital and Jervis Street Hospital boards. He died on 20 November 1943, fittingly, perhaps, on the steps of the DTUC hall in Lower Gardiner Street.

Daly has been much maligned. The embezzlement of IRB funds is undeniable, and drink may at one time have been an issue. Connolly did not trust him, and Daly became the focus for Larkinite opposition, certainly in O'Brien's mind. He was, however, a diligent administrator, capable orator and intelligent presenter of a case. He stayed true to the cause and by the time of his death had earned the grudging respect of all, including, privately at least, former enemies.

· Séamus Cody, 'The remarkable Patrick Daly,' *Obair*, 2 January 1985, p. 10–11.

William (Billy) Eustace. Born in Dublin. He was a van driver in the bakery trade and a founding member of the WUI. A 'close friend' of Larkin, he was 'unswerving in his loyalty' and 'ever ready to help and advise' fellow-workers. General Treasurer 1928–66, he was unpaid, his wage coming from his position as clerk in the Central Cash Office. The 'actual control and direction' of finances was 'carried out by the General President,' and the position of General Treasurer died with Eustace. He was the general factotum in Mallin Hall. He died on 20 March 1966 'after a fairly long illness.'

Christopher (Christy) Ferguson. Born in Dublin in 1903. His father, Simon, was a boilermaker's helper and his mother, Julia, a charwoman. Neither parent was literate. They lived in Church Street; during the Lock-Out, when Ferguson was nine, numbers 66 and 67 collapsed, killing three adults and four children. Ferguson was active in Fianna Éireann, 1919–21. He took the anti-Treaty side in the Civil War; interned in Newbridge Camp, he escaped through a tunnel. He was an apprentice boilermaker with the Great Southern and Western Railway at Inchicore workshops, 1918–25; in 1924 he was arrested for supporting the WUI strike in the works. He was involved in the 1920s Dublin unemployed activity and the Workers' Party of Ireland, 1926–7. A member of the Revolutionary Workers' Groups, he attended the International Lenin School, Moscow (using the pseudonym Christopher Bristol), in 1930 but returned after a month, pleading 'nervous exhaustion'; he was categorised as a 'declassé astute opportunist' and expelled from the RWG. He worked in the British Midlands and London before returning to Dublin in the late 1930s; was active in the Irish Engineering and Foundry Union and Chairman of the Boilermakers' Section when it transferred to the WUI in 1944. On 7 January 1947, as Delegate of the Engineering Branch to Dublin Trades Council, he proposed action against high prices and low wages, and he was Vice-Chairman of the Lower Prices Council, which campaigned vigorously in the 1950s.

When Larkin Junior became General Secretary, Ferguson was appointed National Organiser on 19 February 1947. Membership rose rapidly, from 13,225 to 28,745 in 1957, a product of his energetic drive and capacity to recruit directly and to persuade groups to join, such as Guinness, Irish Airline Pilots' Association, civil aviation workers, paper mills, transport workers and clerical, administrative and professional employees in private, voluntary and public employments. He was an able negotiator and an expert at compiling and presenting Labour Court cases. From 1952 to 1954 he edited *Report,* and he jointly wrote (with Sheila Greene) the *Irish Times* Saturday column 'Pin Pointing Politics' under the pseudonym 'Aknefton'. He had a keen interest in workers' education and was Deputy Chairman of the People's College Adult Education Association. His death occurred on 4 February 1957, a shock to family and union comrades.
- Barry McLoughlin, 'Proletarian academics or party functionaries?: Irish Communists at the International Lenin School, Moscow, 1927–1937,' *Saothar,* 22 (1997), p. 63–79.

John Foster. Born in Dublin on 20 October 1916. A psychiatric nurse in Grangegorman Mental Hospital, Dublin, he joined the WUI on 1 March 1937, involving himself in a claim negotiated by Big Jim Larkin. In 1950 John Smithers, General President, drew together members in St Brendan's (Grangegorman), St Ita's (Portrane), St Dympna's (Carlow), St Patrick's (Dublin) and Stewart's (Dublin) hospitals to form the National Hospitals Committee. He was Chairman, then Secretary, of the National Hospitals Branch, 1955. In October 1962 he was prevailed upon to become full-time Branch Secretary after the transfer of some clerical members from No. 15 Branch. Difficulties with his release from nursing arose, and he remained part-time.

By 1968 the Branch was among the largest and most representative, organising nurses and auxiliary staff in St James's and St Mary's (Dublin), Western Regional Hospital (Galway), Wexford, Kilkenny and Carlow (general and psychiatric) and Cork and South Tipperary (general). After his election as General President at a Special Delegate Conference on 16 November 1968 he continued to be involved with the National Hospitals Branch and affiliated physiotherapists, pharmacists and radiographers, No. 16 Branch being designed for them. He prided himself on having presided over a steady expansion and particularly the fact that 42% of members were outside Dublin when he retired. He was re-elected, unopposed, in 1973 and 1978. He served on the Local Authorities and Health Services Conciliation and Arbitration Scheme, was Chairman of the ICTU Appeals Board, Chairman of the Trade Union Board of Sponsors, College of Industrial Relations, and was a member of An Bord Altranais, the National Blood Transfusion Service Board, Alcoholic Rehabilitation Centre, National Prices Commission, National Health Council, and National Social Service Council. He was a member of the Executive of Dublin Trades Council in the 1950s.

Foster was diligent, quietly effective and an able and shrewd negotiator, and was noted for the support he gave industrial colleagues once action was agreed upon, and was considered a gentleman in his dealings with people. He could, however, be tough and uncompromising, his fundamental commitment to trade unionism and the poor without question. He retired as General President of the FWUI at the 1982 annual Delegate Conference on 23 May 1982 and died in July 1997.

James Plunkett Kelly. Born in Bath Street, Sandymount, Dublin, on 21 May 1920, son of a Larkinite father, Patrick, a car mechanic, chauffeur and ITGWU activist, and Cecilia Cannon. He was educated at Synge Street Christian Brothers' School, in 1937 joined Dublin Gas Company as a clerk and the WUI, a courageous action then for a 'white-collar worker'; with his friend Paddy Phelan he met Larkin in Unity Hall, and he admitted them. He was appointed Secretary of the Gas Workers' Branch on 1 April 1946, his office adjoining Big Jim's; he felt that the great man treated the youngest Official 'with an old man's indulgence'. In the tradition of 'bread and roses' he admired Larkin's wanting 'for the underprivileged not just material sufficiency, but access to culture and the graces of living as well.'

Christy Ferguson described Kelly as a 'lanky, blonde young man who marks your cards and attends to your woes,' his double life clearly a source of pride to the union. 'Did you ever hear of James Plunkett of the *Bell, Penguin New Writing, Irish Bookman, Irish Writing* and another dozen or so periodicals? That is our own J. P. Kelly. Did you know that he plays the violin and the viola—on a standard to find him a berth in Radio Éireann? He is a critic too—of music, literature and the theatre.' He left the WUI to follow a literary path. His radio play *Big Jim* formed the basis of *The Risen People*, a dramatisation of the Lock-Out, produced in the Abbey Theatre in 1958. The character of Mulhall was based on Barney Conway. Jim Sheridan's Gaiety production was part of the 1994 Congress Centenary celebrations. The play was transformed into the best-selling novel *Strumpet City* (1969), and a powerful drama by RTÉ television in 1980, with Peter O'Toole as Larkin.

With other artists, writers and journalists he travelled to the Soviet Union in 1955 and was denounced by the *Catholic Standard* for daring to visit a 'godless' society. Some wui members called for his dismissal as an Official but he won a vote of confidence. Asked later what he could have learned about Soviet society in four weeks, he replied: 'Not much—but I learned a lot about Ireland.'

In 1955 he became Assistant Head of Drama and Variety in Radio Éireann and in 1960 one of Telefís Éireann's first two producer-directors. He resigned in 1985. In retirement he read and wrote incessantly, though he never found writing a comfortable process. In 1986 he felt that trade unionism had 'lost its soul.' He was presented with the Butler Literary Award by the Irish-American Cultural Institute in 1993 and on his eightieth birthday in 2000 was made a life member of the Irish Writers' Union.

In *Report,* January 1953, in profiles of 'Union Staff', Ferguson wrote: 'Many people have become educated by their participation in the trade union movement, many people never became educated at all—as far as trade unionism is concerned; but in James Plunkett Kelly we have a queer and original fish—the man who became part of the trade union movement because he read books!'

- James Plunkett, *Strumpet City,* Dublin: Gill & Macmillan, 2006.
- Francis Devine, 'A queer and original fish!' *Liberty,* June 2003.

John Kenny. He succeeded John Lawlor as President of the wui in 1929. A docker and a boxing champion, he was Staff Major of the wui Brass and Reed Band. He was succeeded as President by John Smithers in 1946.

Ciarán J. King. General Secretary of the Irish Automobile Drivers' and Mechanics' Union from 1920 to 1922, when it merged with the itgwu, he was a clerk in Head Office, 1922–3. King and John O'Shea worked with Larkin when he took over Liberty Hall. When it was repossessed the staff refused to work with King, and he was sacked. He remained in Jim Larkin's room until 2 November 1923, when he was finally ejected. He was a founder member of the wui and General Treasurer 1924–6.

Denis Larkin. Born in Rostrevor, Co. Down, in 1908, second son of Big Jim. He attended Pearse's school, St Enda's, and first worked in a large trading concern in London. On his return he became a clerk in Unity Coal Company, 1928; from 1938 he was Acting Secretary of the Gas Workers' Section, in 1947 District Secretary, in 1957 Assistant General Secretary and in 1968 Acting General Secretary. He was co-opted to Dublin Corporation for the Labour Party in April 1949 and elected in his own right in 1950; was a member of the Housing Committee until he no longer sought office, 1967. He was General Secretary from February 1969 to April 1977, a member of the ituc Executive, 1948–9, of the ictu Executive Council, 1969–7, President of the ictu, 1973/4, Lord Mayor of Dublin, 1955, and Labour td for Dublin North-East, 1954–61 and 1965–9. He served on the ictu Resident Executive Committee, Demarcation Tribunal, Industrial Relations Committee, Trade Union Organisation Committee and International and etuc Committee, the Committees on Social Policy in the eec and Housing Policy and the Working Committee of the Employee-Labour Conference. He was Congress nominee to the National Economic and Social Council, the European Social Fund Committee, AnCO, the Executive of the etuc, the Mental Health Association of Ireland, the Statistical and Social Inquiry Society of Ireland and An Foras Forbartha. He died on 2 July 1987.

Larkin's administrative ability was the subject of public criticism, but his industrial skill was unquestioned, his fundamental Socialist belief undoubted. He was popular, inspiring loyalty through his dedication to the cause. He 'epitomised the best traditions of the labour movement in his integrity, his loyalty and his passionate commitment for the less favoured in society.'

• William A. Attley, 'Denis Larkin,' *Liberty News*, summer 1987 (reproduced from the *Irish Times*).

James Larkin. Born in Liverpool on 21 January 1874. He joined the National Union of Dock Labourers in 1901. After taking a leading part in a strike in Harrison's in 1905, despite being a foreman, he was appointed General Organiser of the union in 1906. He ran the local and General Election campaigns for the General Secretary, James Sexton, and rapidly increased the membership in England, Scotland and Ireland, arriving in Belfast in January 1907. By May the union had gained such strength that Thomas Gallaher, the 'Tobacco King', launched a counter-offensive. Port workers remained solid behind Socialist beliefs and above sectarianism, sustained by Larkin's presence and fired by his uncompromising oratory.

'Larkinism' was contagious. Friction with Sexton resulted in his expulsion from the NUDL on 8 December 1908. He was founding General Secretary of the ITGWU in 1909, editing the *Irish Worker*, raising class-consciousness and setting the union apart. His supreme achievement was his leadership of the 1913 Lock-Out in Dublin, which 'raised the workers of Dublin from their knees.' He left for a fund-raising tour of America in 1914, supported the IWW and spoke at Joe Hill's funeral in Chicago in 1915. Convicted of criminal anarchy, he became convict no. 50945 in Sing Sing Prison, New York, in 1920.

On his release in 1923 and his return to Ireland he challenged the ITGWU leadership and Rules. The matter went to the Courts, and a defeated Larkin was expelled. He was General Secretary of the WUI, which his brother Peter founded in June 1924. The bitterness engendered caused internal labour conflict, and William O'Brien ensured the WUI's isolation from Congress. The WUI was admitted to Dublin Trades Council in 1936 and the ITUC in 1945 but only after the ITGWU broke away to form the Congress of Irish Unions.

Larkin led the wartime opposition to the Trade Union Act (1941) and the Wages Standstill Order. In September 1923 he formed the Irish Worker League, which became the Irish Section of the Communist International. In 1924 he was elected to the Executive Committee of the Comintern, and the WUI affiliated to the Red International of Labour Unions. He backed away from the attempted formation of a Communist Party in 1925; won a Dáil seat in September 1927 in Dublin North but was disqualified as a bankrupt; ran as a Communist in 1932 and as Independent Labour in 1933; was elected to Dublin Corporation in 1936; and won and lost his Dáil seat, 1938–9, before being returned as Labour TD, 1943–4. O'Brien, angered by the Labour Party's acceptance of Larkin, led the ITGWU Deputies out to form the National Labour Party, alleging Communist influence. Larkin died on 31 January 1947.

Emmet Larkin has written that when Larkin died, 'most people outside Ireland were surprised, for they had assumed he had been dead for a long time.' He remains the most controversial character in Irish labour history. His inspiration of the downtrodden and dispossessed, the victories he led in Belfast and Dublin and his partnership with Connolly in establishing a revolutionary labour movement remain fine legacies.

- Emmet O'Connor, *James Larkin*, Cork: Cork University Press, 2001.
- James Plunkett, 'Jim Larkin,' in J. W. Boyle (ed.), *Leaders and Workers*, Cork: Mercier Press, 1966.
- James Plunkett, 'Jim Larkin and the risen people,' in Nevin, *Trade Union Century*.

James Larkin (Junior). Born in Liverpool in 1904, son of Big Jim. He attended Patrick Pearse's St Enda's School in Rathfarnham, Co. Dublin, before working on the *Voice of Labour*, edited by Cathal O'Shannon. After 1924 he worked in WUI Head Office. He attended the International Lenin School in Moscow, 1927–30, returning to the WUI and *Irish Worker*, which was suppressed under the Public Safety Act. Following his father's death in January 1947 he succeeded him as General Secretary and played a leading role within the ITUC, being central to its reunification in the ICTU in 1959, and was President, 1960–61. In 1927 he unsuccessfully contested County Dublin as Independent Labour (Irish Worker League) candidate; was a City Councillor, 1930–33, and Labour TD for Dublin South, 1943–8, and Dublin South Central, 1948–57, when he left politics to concentrate on the union. He was Leader of the Parliamentary Labour Party in 1948. His Presidential Address to the 1949 ITUC Congress was published as *A Common Loyalty: The Bridge to Unity*. He died on 18 February 1969. With him went hopes of a merger between the WUI and the ITGWU.

Larkin was a 'skilled negotiator, polished advocate, an intellectual with a brain as keen as a butcher's knife.' He is credited with 'modernising' the movement and bringing 'thinking' and 'intelligence' to wage-bargaining and the pursuit of an enhanced social wage. His legacy was more significant, if less dramatic, than his father's.

- Barry McLoughlin, 'Proletarian academics or party functionaries?: Irish Communists at the International Lenin School, Moscow, 1927–1937,' *Saothar*, 22 (1997), p. 63–80.

Peter Larkin. Born in Liverpool in 1880, youngest brother of Big Jim. In the 1890s, during religious riots, he helped organise the Catholic Democracy League and was drum major in a Fife Band. He assisted James during the 1907 Belfast dockers' and carters' strike and was active in the Liverpool Dock Strike, 1911. He emigrated to the United States and organised timber and cannery workers for the IWW before returning in 1913 and engagement in the Dublin Lock-Out. He went again to the United States in 1914 and then to Australia. In Sydney in September 1915, with eleven other IWW activists, he was found guilty of conspiracy and sedition and sentenced to ten years' imprisonment with hard labour. Released after four years, he became Organiser for the Australian Communist Party. In 1923 he returned to America, joining the agitation for Larkin's release, and then to Ireland, where he took part in the opposition to Liberty Hall. On 15 June 1924—apparently against the express wishes of James, who was in Moscow—he announced in Beresford Place the formation of the WUI. On his return, James became General Secretary on 25 August.

After a brief spell in London, Peter was National Organiser of the WUI, 1927–31. Restless and erratic, he was a constant thorn in the side of those in authority, within and without the movement. A dedicated syndicalist, he believed in rank-and-file control and saw unions as revolutionary tools if in the right hands and preserved from the dangers of bureaucracy. He died on 15 May 1931.

- Donal Nevin, 'Peter Larkin,' in *James Larkin: Lion of the Fold*, p. 439–44.

John Lawlor. Born in America in 1860 or 1861, of Irish parents. Little is known of his youth, education or occupations or when he came to Ireland. By the early 1880s he was a leading handball player and Irish champion in the summer of 1886. He played the American Casey for the 'Championship of the World' and £200 at Dan Horgan's Court, Duncan Street, Cork, on 4 August 1887. Described as 5 feet 9 inches and weighing 9 stone 12 pounds, he was then twenty-seven or twenty-eight. Casey was leading when the match was brought to a close by the intervention of the crowd. Lawlor lost to Casey in New York before challenging him, 'or anyone else,' for the title the following year. After getting no response Lawlor claimed the world championship; he won a gold medal inscribed *Championship of World,* 1891, and returned home in 1897 with a horse he was presented with. He set up a cab business, operating mainly from Broadstone Station, Dublin.

He was the Delegate of the Cab and Car Owners' Society on Dublin Trades Council and Labour League. On 29 May 1911, on behalf of the Labour Representative Committee, he was elected to South Dublin Poor Law Guardians for Wood Quay Ward. After a venomous attack by James Nugent, UIL candidate and head of the Ancient Order of Hibernians, on the Labour candidate Thomas Farren in the College Green by-election (for J. P. Nannetti's seat), Lawlor resigned from the AOH. He was a member of the Executive of Dublin Trades Council and Labour League from 1910 and President, 1916–17. In January 1920 he was one six Labour and DTCLL nominees elected to Dublin Corporation (with Thomas Lawlor, P. T. Daly, Daniel McGee, John Farren and Dermot Logue). In the General Election of August 1923 Lawlor and Daly were Dublin Trades Council candidates in Dublin North; Lawlor polled 573 and Daly 2,075 votes (compared with the 1,653 of Éamonn O'Carroll of Official Labour). He was first President of the WUI, 1924–9, and unsuccessfully stood for the IWL (of which he was an Executive member) in the 1927 General Election, polling 2,857. His intervention undoubtedly lost a Labour seat held since June 1927 by Thomas Lawlor (Irish Municipal Employees' Trade Union). He died on 26 June 1931.
• Tom McElligott, *The Story of Handball: The Game, the Players, the History,* Dublin: Wolfhound Press, 1984, p. 23–35.

John Lynch. Born into a fishing family in Magherow, Co. Sligo, in 1876, he was a deck hand on harbour tugs and lighters between Rosses Point and Sligo. He joined the IRB in Glasgow and was closely associated with Seán Mac Diarmada and Connolly. He was founding Secretary of the Sligo Branch of the ITGWU, 17 September 1911, and a Delegate of the National Sailors' and Firemen's Union. He led a bloody General Strike in Sligo in 1913 and was elected to the ITGWU Executive for Connacht, 1913–16. He was nearly killed in July 1917 by Laurence Graney and his sons as revenge for 1913 events.

In 1918 he organised Achill tattie-hokers (potato-pickers), travelling to Glasgow to contact the Scottish Farm Servants' Union. He was imprisoned after the Arigna Soviet in 1919; on his release from Belfast Jail in April more than 2,000 people paraded him from Sligo station. He was long a thorn in the side of Liberty Hall, not forwarding remittances and siding with P. T. Daly and Delia Larkin in 1919. In 1923–4 he invited Larkin to Sligo; he was expelled from the ITGWU in February 1925 after attempting (unsuccessfully) to form a WUI Branch. An unrepentant 'Connollyite, Dalyite and Larkinite,' he served on the GEC. He was elected to Sligo Corporation in January 1913 and was an alderman and Mayor, 1931–2, 1932–3. He died in 1939.

On May Day 2003 a plaque was unveiled by Alderman Declan Bree on the Sligo quays. It reads: *To the memory of Alderman John Lynch, 1876–1939, Socialist and trade Unionist.*

Patrick (Paddy) Murphy. A native of north County Dublin, he joined the FRW on its formation in 1946 and from 1948 was a full-time Official, working alongside Young Jim Larkin, Seán Dunne, William Norton, John Swift and James Tully. He was successively Vice-President, President and General Secretary. With Paddy Cardiff he negotiated the merger with the WUI to create the FWUI in 1979. He was a member of the Executive Council of the ITUC, central to the reunification talks that created the ICTU in 1959 and a member of the Executive of the ICTU, 1959–88.

His encyclopaedic knowledge of procedures and legalities meant that he was called upon to play a vital behind-the-scenes role in amalgamation talks between the FWUI and ITGWU: 'with no small justification, Paddy Murphy could have claimed—if modesty had not forbade him—to have been one of the senior "midwives" at the birth' of SIPTU. Modest, unassuming, hard-working and personally undemonstrative, even shy, he was a tough, uncompromising negotiator, always armed with fact and reasoned argument. A great student of industrial relations, he observed trends in decisions of the Labour Court and Tribunals, patterns of wage settlements and changes in management techniques and arguments. His view was always fresh, and open to change. He adored statistics and legal data and could reproduce them from the top of the head with clarity and accuracy.

A Labour member of Dublin County Council for more than twenty years, he 'presided over the biggest expansion of low-cost housing' for working people in the country's history. He was responsible for countless amendments to legislation, advising Congress and any other union that sought his Counsel. He attended the European Economic and Social Affairs Committee until his death on 22 April 1991.

- William Attley, 'Patrick Murphy,' *Newsline*, spring 1991.
- Frank Keelaghan, 'Paddy Murphy: An appreciation,' *Newsline*, June 1991.

John Smithers. He served in the British army before fighting with the IRA in the War of Independence. He was a founding member of the WUI in 1924 and a Shop Steward. When John Kenny retired, in 1943, Smithers became General President, full-time from 1947, when some felt the union would 'not last another twelve months.' He died during the ICTU Congress on 27 May 1968.

Larkin Junior thought Smithers was 'an ordinary kind of guy. He is no spellbinding orator; he is no flamboyant labour Leader; he is no great political figure. He is one of yourselves, an ordinary Dublin worker . . . a union man all his life.' This summed up a loyal, dedicated and self-effacing stalwart. Donal Nevin contrasted him with Christy Ferguson: 'one a traditionalist, the other an iconoclast; Smithers cool, Ferguson fiery. Ferguson told the story of two internees held in Newbridge Camp during the Civil War. 'One was a "decent guy", the other a "smart guy".' The decent guy dug a tunnel, the smart guy escaped. Ferguson happened to be the smart guy who escaped through the tunnel; the decent guy, Smithers, who dug the tunnel, did not.

SIPTU

William A. (Bill) Attley. Born on 5 April 1938, reared at Rathcoole, Co. Dublin, attending the local National School and Lucan Technical School. He worked in Killeen Paper Mills and joined the Lucan and Dublin No. 16 (Printing) Branches of the ITGWU. In 1968 he was appointed Secretary of the newly merged Bray and Dún Laoghaire Branch of the WUI. In 1977 he was elected Deputy General Secretary and in 1982 succeeded Paddy Cardiff as General Secretary. On the formation of SIPTU he was, for a week, Joint General President with John Carroll, then with Edmund Browne, until appointed General Secretary in 1994. He retired in April 1998. He was a member of the Executive Council of the ICTU, 1982–90, and Treasurer, 1990–98.

He takes pride in his initiating role in the adoption of the Programme for National Recovery in 1987, the foundation-stone of social partnership. He was directly involved in framing and developing the next two Agreements, turning the country 'away from its adversarial Anglo-Saxon industrial relations model' towards a more European one. Free collective bargaining, in his view, did not deliver, and he wanted a greater voice for workers in dividing the national cake. The 'success of this partnership model' is taken for granted. There were few industrial relations disputes, but in 1987, per capita, 'Ireland had the worst strike record in Europe.'

With John Carroll, Attley spent three years preparing for SIPTU. In his time AGEMOU, IAAO, INPDTU, IPU, IWWU, MPGWU, NATE and USED merged, underlining his desire for rationalisation.

A well-known League of Ireland referee, Attley remains involved with the Football Association of Ireland and the European Union of Football Associations (UEFA), leading progressive changes in the training, assessment and development of referees. He was a member of the European Trade Union Confederation, Employer-Labour Conference, FÁS, Córas Tráchtála, Council of the European Social Fund and European Economic and Social Committee. Regarded as a strategic thinker, he is accessible and personable, open to how ordinary members felt. He is not afraid to lock horns, privately or publicly, in defence of his position, ultimately winning respect from friend and foe.

• 'SIPTU's midfield general,' *Newsline*, April 1998.

Edmund Browne. Born in Dublin on 11 April 1937; educated at the College of Commerce, Rathmines, the National College of Industrial Relations and Michigan State University. He worked with Dublin No. 7 (Film and Theatres) Branch of the ITGWU from 1952; Head Office and was Secretary of Dublin No. 7 Branch, 1963, and National Industrial Group Secretary with responsibility for hospitals, catering, entertainment, banking, security, distribution and fire services, 1964. He was elected Vice-President in 1983 and Joint Vice-President of SIPTU in 1990. When John Carroll retired, on 8 January 1990, Browne became Joint General President (with Bill Attley) and General President, 1994–7. He was a member of the Executive Council of the ICTU, 1984–9, Treasurer, 1989–95, and President, 1996/7. He served on Bord Fáilte, the Central Review Committee of Partnership 2000, the Employment Appeals Tribunal, the European Coal and Steel Consultative Committee, the Irish Horse Racing Authority and Dublin Port Authority. He was an ardent member of the ITGWU Brass and Reed Band as a noted clarinettist and, complete with Bavarian costume, of the the the Egerlander Band.

He was central to SIPTU's Strategic Development Initiative. He was widely regarded as a leading negotiator, with the ability to grasp the most complicated case, often apparently from the barest details, and notoriously wanted ideas 'on a single page'.

- Edmund Browne, 'Trade unions and the management of change,' in Patrick Gunnigle and William K. Roche (eds.), *New Challenges to Irish Industrial Relations* (LCR Seminar Series), Dublin: Labour Relations Commission and Oak Tree Press, 1995, p. 47–58.
- 'Thanks, Eddie!' *Newsline*, May 1997.

John F. Carroll. Born in an old coachhouse at Summer Hill, Dublin, on 8 January 1925. When he was ten the family moved to Parnell Street, still in terrible conditions. He was educated at St Canice's and O'Connell Christian Brothers' Schools. His father, John, was 'clearly identified with the Communist Party' and the ITGWU. He joined the Medical Corps of the Free State army after the Civil War, then worked in Dublin Corporation, where he suffered an injury that left him incapacitated and unable for full-time employment. His mother worked to supplement the family income, a sacrifice that made an indelible impression on her son and accounted for his lifelong commitment to women's equality. When he was fourteen his father brought him to join the ITGWU Brass and Reed Band, beginning his lifelong association with the union.

He was offered a job as an Official with Dublin No. 4 (Hotels and Catering Branch) in 1944, then worked in Dublin No. 6/8 (Clothing), in Head Office and, briefly, as Secretary of Carlow Branch, before he was appointed Head of Industrial Movements in 1958, drafting proposals for the National Industrial Group Secretary system as Chief Industrial Officer, 1964.

He was elected Vice-President in 1969 and General President, 1981–90, served as Joint General President of SIPTU, 1–8 January 1990, and as a member of the Executive Council of the ICTU, 1971–90, and President, 1986/7. He sat on JLCS, the National Prices Commission, Censorship of Films Appeals Board, RTÉ Authority, EEC Economic and Social Committee (chairing its Social Section), IDA Grants Committee and Central Committee of the International Metal Workers' Federation. He gained a Diploma in Industrial Engineering from Columbia University, New York.

Always portrayed as 'aloof' or 'distant', his essential reserve hid a thoughtful, sincere man with an absolute commitment to social justice and the working class. Although serving SIPTU for only one week, its creation is his historical legacy to a movement he unstintingly served for forty-six years and one that, with Bill Attley, he had striven hard for three years to bring about.

- Evanne Kilmurray, 'Behind the public face of John Carroll,' *Newsline*, May 1990, p. 8–9.

Paul Clarke. Born in Drimnagh, Dublin, on 22 June 1945, attending St Michael's and Synge Street Christian Brothers' Schools. His grandfather, Philip Clarke, was an ITGWU activist in Boland's Mill and a member of the Citizen Army, killed in the Royal College of Surgeons in 1916. Clarke was an apprentice printer, 1964, active in Dublin Typographical Provident Society; a journeyman, 1967, then worked as production editor at Pergamon Press, Oxford, joining the National Union of Journalists. In Dublin he worked in Creation Print, 1969–74; was Father of the Chapel in the Irish Graphical

Society and a members of the Executive. After redundancy he was a child-care worker in St John of God's residential home for children with intellectual disabilities, where he revitalised the WUI Section of No. 18 (Hospitals) Branch. Victory in a toughly resisted equal-pay claim broke new ground under the Anti-Discrimination (Pay) Act (1974). He was appointed Branch Assistant in No. 18 Branch, February 1978, Branch Secretary, 1980, and Branch Secretary, No. 22 and 23 Branch, establishing premises in Monaghan.

After Paddy Murphy retired as General Secretary of the FRW, Clarke became Assistant General Secretary of the FWUI. He joined the Labour Party after membership of the Communist Party of Ireland, 1972–5, and Socialist Labour Party. In January 1990 he was Assistant National Executive Officer of SIPTU, having been part of the amalgamation team. He was founding Chairperson of Dublin Citywide Drugs Crisis Campaign, linking SIPTU with the Inner City Organisations Network and community groups, and a member of the Employment Appeals Tribunal. He retired in 1998 and moved to Co. Leitrim.

• 'Clarke's farewell,' *Newsline*, May 1998.

Thomas (Tom) Garry. Born in Oldcastle, Co. Meath, in 1934, reared in Dún Laoghaire and Glasthule, Co. Dublin, having been adopted by Dawn McDonald from Dún Laoghaire Orphanage when he was twenty-five days old. She died when he was six, but her best friend, Nora Byrne, took responsibility for his care. Both women would be proud of the fine grounding they provided.

After primary education in St Joseph's National School, Glasthule, he started as a boy messenger in Guinness in 1949 but was refused membership of the WUI until 1952, when he was eighteen. He progressed from number-taker to labourer in the Transport Department. He was Departmental Chief Shop Steward in 1964 and Branch Chairman, a full-time position, from 1970, and Branch Secretary from March 1976, succeeding Jack Harte. He was elected General President of the FWUI in 1982, succeeding John Foster. He was inspired by Young Jim Larkin, whom he saw as 'essentially a teacher'. He was Secretary of the Central Education Committee, 1976–82.

On the creation of SIPTU he was Joint General Secretary (with Chris Kirwan) and General Secretary from September 1991 to June 1994. He was a member of the ICTU Executive and the Board of the Irish Productivity Centre. On his retirement he moved to Co. Wexford.

A fine negotiator and administrator, Garry was passionate about education and membership development and deeply committed to the union project. He had a 'simple view' of trade unionism, 'believing that it alone could make a difference to the lives of countless working people.' With Jack Harte, he developed close ties with Frank Cluskey and Dublin South-Central. He was a member of the founding Board of the Combat Poverty Agency, a member of the Irish Commission for Justice and Peace and of the National Social Science Board. Dick Spring noted his 'sincere philosophy of care and compassion for the weakest members of our society,' while Bill Attley appreciated that Garry's 'self-betterment' was used, before all else, 'to better the people he represented.'

• 'The boy from the black stuff,' *Newsline*, June 1994.

Desmond (Des) Geraghty. Born in Cornmarket in the Liberties of Dublin on 27 October 1943. His father, Tom, was a Larkinite Republican and his mother, Lily O'Neill, a Communist Party activist. Both eventually joined the Labour Party. Geraghty worked in Ireland and Britain in the 1960s, holding membership of the Electrical Trades Union and Electrical Trades Union (Ireland) and the Irish Post Office Engineering Union while working for Dictagraph and Irish Telephones. In 1967 he was a cameraman in RTÉ, joining the No. 7 Branch of the ITGWU. He was Assistant Secretary of No. 1 (Docks and Transport) Branch, 1970, a Tutor in the Education and Training Department, 1973, Publications and Communications Officer, 1977, and in 1981 National Industrial Group Secretary with responsibility for construction, the OPW, local authorities, health boards, forestry, energy, offshore drilling and related manufacturing, with more than 44,400 members. He was SIPTU National Industrial Secretary with responsibility for European affairs, participation and national industrial issues and central to the Strategic Development Initiative, drawing down European funding for staff and membership training under ADAPT and NOW. He was Vice-President, 1997, and General President from November 1999 to September 2003.

   He was active in Dublin Housing Action Committee in the late 1960s, a member of Official Sinn Féin, of Sinn Féin the Workers' Party and of Democratic Left before its merger with the Labour Party in 2000. From 1991 to 1994 he was seconded as Workers' Party, subsequently Democratic Left, member of the European Parliament, serving on its Economic, Industrial and Monetary Committees and acting as industrial spokesperson for the EU United Left Group. He contested a Seanad seat in 2002. He was a member of the Executive of the ICTU, 1997–2005, and the Boards of RTÉ, 1995–2002, FÁS, 1999–2003, National Competitive Council, 1997–2002, National Economic and Social Council, 2000–2003, Enterprise Strategy Board, 2003, and Poetry Ireland. He was elected a shareholder of the Abbey Theatre and was a member of the Affordable Homes Partnership for Greater Dublin.

   An original and creative thinker, Geraghty's union legacy has sometimes been debated. It may be speculated how much more effective it might have been had he been elected to senior office earlier. Establishment forces were not displeased by his unsuccessful attempts. His tangible achievements were in the fine detail of the Programme for Prosperity and Fairness and Sustaining Progress, in the Liberty Hall Centre for Performing Arts and in the instigation of SDI and the IDEAS Institute. In the ITGWU, promoted concepts of industrial democracy and transnational bargaining produced Optimum Agreement, a negotiating model based on current best practice and standards. He initiated HELP (Higher Earnings for the Lower Paid) and constantly argued for 'political bargaining', the genesis of moving union debate away from sectional, narrow wage bargaining towards exchanging industrial strength for advances on the broadest social and political agendas, much of what became 'partnership'. An internationalist, he sought to create solidarity of actions and ideas with unions around the world, understood the potential and need for European action, and opposed imperialism at every opportunity. He was teeming with ideas, and a lengthier national leadership would have provided greater scope for building an even deeper legacy, an undoubted loss to union and movement.

   A talented flute player, piper and singer, Geraghty founded the Clé Club, a folk club run in Liberty Hall since 2003. He made countless broadcasts on radio and television and is published widely.

   His brothers were activists: Seán (Fleet Street electrician); Tom (firefighter and stalwart member of the GEC of the WUI and FWUI); Séamus (Secretary of the Waterford Branch of the ATGWU); and Hugh (AEEU and TEEU activist and CIÉ Group Secretary of the ICTU).

- 'I'm only retiring from the job—not from the struggle,' *Liberty,* September 2003.
- Des Geraghty, *New Century Socialism: Fighting for Justice in the Jungle,* Dublin: Democratic Left, 1998.
- Des Geraghty, *Forty Shades of Green: A Wry Look at What It Means to be Irish,* Dublin: Real Ireland Design, 2007.
- Des Geraghty and Norbert Gallagher, *Guide to the EU Directive on Works Councils,* Dublin: Irish Productivity Centre, 1997.

Éamonn Gilmore. Born in Caltra, Co. Galway, 24 April 1955; educated at Garbally College, Ballinasloe, and University College, Galway. He was active in the Union of Students in Ireland as National President, 1976–8. He joined the ITGWU in 1978 and, after brief spells in Dublin No. 4 and Dublin No. 14 Branches, became Acting Secretary of the Galway Branch, 1978–9, Secretary of Tralee Branch, 1979–81, and Professional and Managerial Staffs Branch, 1981–9. He was heavily involved in organising tax protests in Galway, resisting redundancies and closures in Co. Kerry, and arguing to defend affiliation to the Labour Party. The ITGWU years were 'among the most satisfying,' providing 'great grounding in understanding working class needs, issues and politics.'

He was active in Sinn Féin the Workers' Party, elected to Dublin County Council, 1985, and Dáil Éireann, 1989, being returned ever since. On becoming a TD, his ITGWU employment ceased.

In 1992 he joined with Proinsias de Rossa and five other Workers' Party TDs to create New Agenda, subsequently Democratic Left. Between 1994 and 1997 he was Minister of State at the Department of the Marine in the 'rainbow' Coalition. With Brendan Howlin he was a central figure in the negotiations that led to the merger of Democratic Left into the Labour Party in 1999. Following the resignation of Rabbitte he was unopposed as Leader of the Labour Party on 6 September 2007, where he said he 'will focus on Labour policies and Labour's future rather than electoral pacts with any other party or preoccupation with the Labour "brand".' An intelligent, articulate advocate, he has shown personal courage and integrity on many issues and is not afraid to champion unpopular causes.

Brendan Hayes. Born in Dublin in 1953. His father was an ITGWU activist in No. 16 (Printing) Branch. He attended O'Connell School and University College, Dublin, qualifying as a teacher before his appointment as WUI Assistant Branch Secretary on 27 August 1975. He was Secretary of No. 3 (General Workers), No. 7 (Tobacco), National Hospitals and FÁS Branches and was SIPTU Regional Secretary, Dublin Public Service, 1990, and of combined Dublin Region, 2001. He was elected Vice-President in February 2004. He managed the Branch network computerisation and maintains a keen interest in technology. He is a trade union nominee to the Government Task Force on the Long Term Unemployed and on the Public Service Pensions Commission, Public Service Benchmarking and Analogue Agreements. He played a leading role in the eight-year campaign to secure improved pension entitlements for low-paid public servants and was active in similar campaigns for the private sector.

A member of the Labour Party since his student days, he was one of the minority who campaigned (as did the WUI) for membership of the EEC in 1972. A believer in 'social activism', he is deeply respected as an innovative, meticulous negotiator with a capacity for strategic thinking. Unassuming and not noted for rousing public speaking, he appears to be content out of the limelight. He served as Secretary of the Gender Equity Committee—established by the NEC to increase women's participation—and, underlining his commitment to change, will move aside in 2010 to enable the first woman to become a SIPTU national officer, a noble gesture typical of his commitment to the union rather than to self.

Christopher (Christy) Kirwan. Born in a single tenement room in Meath Street, Dublin, on 14 September 1926; educated at Meath Street National School and Crumlin Secondary School. He gained a Higher Diploma in economics from UCD, a Diploma from the National College of Industrial Relations, the Diploma in Industrial Relations and Management from Rutgers University, New Jersey, and a Certificate in American Studies, Meridan House, Washington.

He did a 'few menial jobs' before joining the British army, 1944–9. On his return he was relief clerk in the Great Northern Railway, working in Clones and Castleblayney. He joined the Irish Rail Union, but just before the 1950 railway strike he organised six hundred GNR men into the ITGWU Dublin No. 1 Branch, acting as part-time Secretary. He was appointed Secretary of Dublin No. 11 Branch, 1953, Movements Division, Head Office, 1959, and National Industrial Group Secretary with responsibility for transport and energy, 1969. He was Vice-President in succession to Tom O'Brien, March 1981, the last General Secretary of the ITGWU, February 1983, and Joint General Secretary of SIPTU, 1990–91. He was a member of the ICTU Executive, 1983–91, Treasurer, 1984–9, and President, 1990/91. He was a member of the Human Sciences Committee of the Irish Productivity Centre, the General Council of the International Transport Workers' Federation, of Dublin Port and Docks Board and Nítrigin Éireann, and a member of Seanad Éireann, nominated by Dick Spring and appointed by Garret FitzGerald, 1982–7. Opposition to the Finance Bill cost him the Labour Party whip.

He was Chairman of FÁS and a member of the boards of NCIR, Aer Rianta and the International Transport Workers' Federation and Vice-President of the EC Coal and Steel Consultative Committee.

His interests are military history and boxing, and he is a Trustee of the Irish Amateur Boxing Association. He gave few interviews and seldom sought the limelight. He maintained the railway organisation, despite competition from the NUR and NATE and from ASLEF, and saw himself as 'National Rail Officer'. He opposed the activities of the Workers' Party inside the ITGWU. His forthrightness and straight-to-the-point manner led to the title of 'the Sheriff' in Liberty Hall. He defended what he saw as the union's interests as defined by the Delegate Conference and brooked no opposition.

- Evanne Kilmurray, 'Mr President', *Newsline*, July 1990.
- 'Chris retires "undefeated"', *Newsline*, autumn 1991.

John McDonnell. Born in Mallow, Co. Cork, on 11 October 1942, attending St Patrick's National School and Patrician Brothers' Academy before starting work in the sugar factory in 1960. In 1972 he completed the Diploma in Social and Economic Science in University College, Cork, and a degree in Economics and Social Policy in 1990. As a general operative in Erin Foods he was a Shop Steward and Branch Committee member from the mid-1960s until he was appointed Assistant Secretary of Mallow No. 1 Branch in February 1974. Within three weeks he was Branch Secretary after two Officials left for jobs with the management. The Branch grew from 1,800 to 3,000 members and gave him access to national-level bargaining for sugar and creameries. 'Milk wars', the rationalisation and privatisation of co-ops, national strikes and the dismantling by employers of national bargaining units made times difficult, with occasional internal conflict with members in other Districts. He insisted that agriculture and agri-business feature in union policy. He was Secretary of ITGWU Region 4 (South-West), 1990–8, where he co-ordinated 45,000 diverse and geographically scattered members and created the first Education and Training Centre outside Dublin in Connolly Hall, Cork, 1997.

He was elected General Secretary in April 1998, serving until September 2002. He oversaw major changes in the Rules, revitalised neglected youth structures and sought improvements in statutory redundancy pay and the minimum wage. He was a member of the ICTU Executive, 1999–2002, and Treasurer, 2001–3. He chaired the SIPTU Commission to consider affiliation to the Labour Party, reporting in 2003.

He joined the Labour Party in recent years, previously seeing membership within the local community as presenting obstacles to union work. A belief in class politics was understood. Self-effacing, eschewing politicking and from a small-town base, he was not typical national officer material. His appeal was a patent commitment to the cause, prodigious hard work, and the capacity, as a team player, to engage those around him. A 'safe pair of hands', he was a solid, trusted performer, bringing a different viewpoint to Dublin tables: that of low-paid rural workers and neglected, under-resourced provincial townspeople. His contribution over three decades was a model of consistent incorrigibility and often overlooked achievement.

• 'Your good health, John,' *Liberty*, December 2002.

Thomas (Tom) Murphy. Born in Dublin on 18 May 1934 and reared in Inchicore. His father, William, worked in Donnelly's bacon factory in Cork Street; his mother, Margaret Tynan, whose father worked in Guinness, was a shop assistant. When he was young the family moved to Co. Wexford. His father died of TB in 1943, leaving Margaret with six children, aged eleven to eighteen months. Murphy attended Glenbrien National School, Enniscorthy; at fourteen he worked as a shop assistant before joining Bord na Móna at sixteen. Working around the country, he joined the Federation of Rural Workers. In 1952 he emigrated to England, worked with British Railways in Leicester and was active in the National Union of Railwaymen. In 1954 he became a maintenance worker with London Underground, serving on the Branch Committee of London No. 7 Branch of the NUR and on London District Council. He was Assistant Secretary of London District Executive Committee and a Delegate to London Trades Council.

He studied at Ruskin College, Oxford, 1958–60, gaining the Diploma in Economics and Politics. Returning home in 1962 he worked for the engineering company of J. and C. McGloughlin in Pearse Street and Inchicore and for CIÉ at the North Wall. He was Branch Chairman with NATE, 1967, and full-time Organiser, 1971. In 1978 he was appointed Branch Assistant of No. 2 (Local Authorities) Branch, WUI, and Branch Secretary later that year. He was elected Deputy General Secretary in 1984 and appointed Vice-President of SIPTU in 1990, with special responsibility for industrial policy. He was a member of the Executive Council of the ICTU, 1990–93, and of the Employment Appeals Tribunal, 1984–2001. An acknowledged expert on rules and procedures, he played a central role in the negotiations leading to SIPTU.

He likes horse racing and follows Wexford hurling. Regarded as a 'gentleman', he has a placid manner that belies a shrewd, tough negotiator. Unafraid to be truthful, he did not always endear himself to members or fellow-negotiators. Pragmatic, he sought solutions rather than courting popularity. Employers learnt not to under-estimate his abilities, tenacity or fundamental belief in core trade union values. He retired on 17 May 1994.

· 'Tom bows out', *Newsline,* May 1994.

John (Jack) O'Connor. Born in Lusk, Co. Dublin, on 24 January 1957; left school at fifteen to work in agriculture, construction and the local authority sector. He was politically active at sixteen in the Trotskyist movement; left-wing politics introduced him to trade unionism. He was active in the Federation of Rural Workers at seventeen; meagre resources rendered it heavily dependent on voluntary Organisers. He joined the Labour Party, serving as constituency officer, Dublin North, and was a founder-member of Labour Left. He was a Shop Steward and Branch Committee representative before his appointment as Secretary of No. 25 Branch of the FWUI, 1980, and of No. 2 (Local Authorities) Branch, 1986, representing firefighters, port workers, public-sector and council employees. He became SIPTU Regional Secretary for the Midlands, 1990, and South-East, 1997. In 1996 he was Chairperson of the SDI Shop Stewards' Project Group that recommended Branch Development Funds. In contrast to his earlier union experience, the workers he represented were now predominantly in the private sector.

He was elected Vice-President of SIPTU in 2000 and General President in 2003, returned unopposed in 2006. He has been a member of the Executive Council of the ICTU since 2000, Vice-President since 2007 and President 2009.

With the other General Officers of SIPTU, Brendan Hayes and Joe O'Flynn, he is committed to the 'organising model' of trade unionism. Strongly believing in consensus-building within the movement, he emphasises collective leadership and the involvement of the membership. His declared priorities are combating the exploitation of workers, promoting people's right to participate in collective bargaining, advancing the training and skills agenda, and asserting the economic as well as the moral superiority of 'fairness at work and justice in society'.

Joseph (Joe) O'Flynn. Born in Cork on 26 February 1958. His father, Terence, was active in Cork No. 3 (Construction) Branch of the ITGWU and Cork No. 6 when he was a welder before his death in 1983. His mother, Christine Harland, organised contract cleaners through Cork No. 7 Branch and was active on regional, National Women's and Retired Members' Committees. After attending Sawmill Street Technical School and Cork Institute of Technology, O'Flynn qualified as a mechanic, joining the ITGWU when he was sixteen, becoming a Shop Steward and Branch Committee member before his appointment as Branch Assistant, Cork No. 8 Branch, at the age of twenty-two; Secretary of Cork Administrative, Professional and Technical Staffs Branch, 1991–7, adding Cork No. 2 in 1995 and six part-time nursing Branches; National Industrial Secretary, 1997; and Regional Secretary in Region 4 (South-West), 2000–02.

Long active in the Labour Party, he was elected first Labour City Councillor in Cork South-East, 1991–2003, serving as Lord Mayor, June 1998 to July 1999. He contested the Cork South-Central by-election in 1994. Elected General Secretary in October 2002 and re-elected in 2007, and ICTU Treasurer from 2003. He is a director of three SIPTU-affiliated bodies: IDEAS Institute, Irish Trade Union Trust and Liberty Hall Centre for the Performing Arts. A 'hands-on' officer, his persuasive, personable style hides a shrewd and, if needs be, tough administrator. Managing the change to 'organising union' and the demolition and reconstruction of Liberty Hall will be a tough stint but a challenge that he welcomes, and measures up to.

Patrick (Pat) Rabbitte. Born on 18 May 1949 in Ballindine, Claremorris, Co. Mayo; he crossed the fields to attend the now-derelict Cullane National School. After St Colman's College, Claremorris, he gained degrees in English, politics and law at University College, Galway. He was National President of the Union of Students in Ireland, 1972–4. (For the press and opponents he and Éamonn Gilmore were 'the Student Princes'.) Appointed to the ITGWU County Galway Branch, 1974, he transferred to Dublin No. 2 Branch, 1975, and Professional and Managerial Unit, 1976, and was then Secretary of Dublin No. 13 (Electronics) Branch, 1979. He was National Industrial Group Secretary, 1980, with responsibility for 45,000 public-service, nursing and white-collar workers. In the mid-1980s he argued for continued affiliation to the Labour Party, though he left in 1976, opposing Coalition. He was elected to Dublin County Council, 1985, and Dáil Éireann, Dublin South-West, 1989, for Sinn Féin the Workers' Party, being returned since. On entering the Dáil his ITGWU employment ceased.

After Tomás Mac Giolla retired in 1988 Rabbitte wanted to move the Workers' Party from alignment with the Soviet Union and international Communist movement. In 1992 he was one of six TDs who broke away to form New Agenda, later Democratic Left. In the 'Rainbow Coalition' of Fine Gael, Labour and Democratic Left, 1994–7, he held the so-called 'super' Junior Ministry, giving him the right to attend meetings of the Government but not to vote. As Minister for Commerce, Science and Technology he established the National Drugs Strategy, published the first White Paper on *Science, Technology and Innovation*, brought in legislation to allow credit unions to grow, and expanded consumer protection. In January 1999 Democratic Left merged with the Labour Party.

In October 2002 he defeated two other SIPTU members, Éamonn Gilmore and Brendan Howlin, to become Party Leader. He made the 'Mullingar Accord' with Enda Kenny of Fine Gael, entering the 2007 General Election in a firm pact; despite encouraging signs early in the campaign, the strategy failed to produce an alternative Government. He resigned as Leader on 23 August 2007 and is Party spokesman on justice.

A highly regarded Official, he demonstrated diligence and imagination. A distinguished, often highly amusing but always acutely perceptive critic of the Government, he turned a searchlight on corrupt practices, double standards and weak performance.

James (Jimmy) Somers. Born on 2 November 1939 in Dublin and reared in Cabra. His father, 'Jimmy the Busman', was well known locally and was active in the ITGWU No. 9 (Bus) Branch and the Labour Party, raising funds to build party premises in Cabra, 1948–9. After working on railways in Ireland and Britain, Somers was appointed Branch

Assistant in Dublin No. 2 (Clerical) Branch, 1960, then served No. 9 Branch, No. 3 (food, drink and tobacco), Head Office, Galway and Dublin No. 1 (oil, docks, road freight, aviation) and was first Secretary of No. 17 (civil aviation) Branch, 1972–1983. Membership in Dublin Airport, where the WUI was dominant, grew from 200 to 1,500.

From 1977 he was was Secretary of Dublin District Council, engaging in protests on tax, employment and the health service. He enjoyed the cut-and-thrust of debate in Dublin District Council, a great Shop Stewards' forum (and lost under SIPTU). He became National Industrial Group Secretary for food, drink, tobacco, hotels, catering, chemicals, pharmaceuticals, fertilisers and distribution in 1983, establishing nationwide connections and heading 'free-for-all' negotiations. His great support outside Dublin stemmed from this. He was Assistant National Executive Officer of SIPTU until elected Vice-President in 1994, the union's first directly elected General Officer; was General President, 1997–9. A member of the ICTU Executive, 1993–9, he was Treasurer, 1999–2001. He was a member of the High-Level Group on union recognition, 1997–9, which led to the Industrial Relations (Amendment) Act (2001), and a member of the Labour Relations Commission from 1995 to 2000, when he became a Worker Representative on the Labour Court, 2000–2005. He was a member of Bord Fáilte, the Conventions Bureau of Ireland, JLCS, JICS, Forbairt and various international union Executives.

Long active in the Labour Party, he missed a seat on Dublin City Council by eleven votes in 1974; contested Dáil elections in Cabra, Dublin, in 1973, 1981 and 1983; and was co-opted to the City Council, 1983–6. Active in Dublin Central, he was a member of the Labour Party Executive.

Modest and unassuming, he was in ways an unlikely national Leader. His election was a tribute to his diligence, clear passion, commitment and straight talking. Personable and warm, he endeared himself to all who knew him but could be tough as a Conference Chairperson or negotiator. His wife, Alice, Administrator of the People's College and a founding member of the Labour Women's Council, was a constant support and political companion—part of a dedicated team. No doubt under-rated for a consistent contribution and sound delivery of every brief given, he welcomed social partnership, having strongly argued his case as a General Officer when SIPTU's doubts about social partnership were most acute.

- 'Thank you, Jimmy: Union General President retires,' *Newsline*, November 1999.

Appendix 5 ∾

UNION OFFICERS AND SIPTU NATIONAL COMMITTEES

ITGWU

General President
Thomas Foran, 1909–39; Thomas Kennedy, 1939–46; William McMullen, 1946–53; John Conroy, 1953–69; Fintan Kennedy, 1969–81; John F. Carroll, 1981–9.

Vice-President
Thomas Kennedy, 1924–39; William McMullen, 1940–46; John Conroy, 1946–53; Edward Browne, 1953–69; John F. Carroll, 1969–81; Thomas O'Brien, 1981; Edmund Browne, 1981–9.

General Secretary
James Larkin, 1909–23; William O'Brien, 1923–46; Thomas Kennedy, 1946–7; Frank Purcell, 1947–59; Fintan Kennedy, 1959–69; Michael Mullen, 1969–82; Christopher Kirwan, 1982–9.

Acting General Secretary
P. T. Daly, 17 June to 1 October 1910; James Connolly, November 1914 to 12 May 1916; Thomas Foran, May 1916 to 1917.

Assistant Secretaries
James J. Hughes, 1917–19; Cathal O'Shannon, 1917–19.

General Treasurer
Patrick Smyth, 1912–18; William O'Brien, 1918–24.

Financial Secretary
Archibald Heron, 1925–9.

Political Secretary
Cathal O'Shannon, 1924–5.

WUI AND FWUI

General President
John Lawlor, 1924–9; John Kenny, 1929–43; John Smithers, 1943–68; John Foster, 1968–82; Thomas Garry, 1982–9.

General Secretary
James Larkin, 1924–47; James Larkin Junior, 1947–69; Denis Larkin, 1969–77; Patrick Cardiff, 1977–83; William A. Attley, 1983–9.

Deputy General Secretary
Denis Larkin, 1967–9; Patrick Cardiff, 1969–77; William A. Attley, 1977–84; Thomas Murphy, 1984–9.

General Treasurer
Ciarán J. King, 1924–6; John Lawlor, 1926–7; John Kenny 1927–8; William Eustace, 1928–66.

SIPTU

General President
John F. Carroll, 1990; William A. Attley, 1990–94; Edmund Browne, 1990–97; Jimmy Somers, 1997–9; Des Geraghty, 1999–2003; Jack O'Connor, 2003–.

Vice-President
Thomas Murphy, 1990–94; Jimmy Somers, 1994–7; Des Geraghty, 1997–9; Brendan Hayes, 2004–.

General Secretary
Thomas Garry, 1990–94; Christopher Kirwan, 1990–91; William A. Attley, 1994–8; John McDonnell, 1998–2002; Joe O'Flynn, 2002–.

SIPTU NATIONAL COMMITTEES, SEPTEMBER 2008

National Executive Council
Jack O'Connor (General President), Brendan Hayes (Vice-President), Joe O'Flynn (General Secretary); *Dublin:* Paddy Cahill (Drinks, Tobacco and Wholesale Distribution), Tom Gill (State and Related Agencies), Paul Hansard (Construction and Allied Trades), David Johnston (Hotels, Restaurants and Catering), Jack Kelly (Health Services), Jack McGinley (Dublin Education), Margie McQuaid (Services), Barry Nevin (Civil Aviation), Peter O'Connor (Administrative, Supervisory and Sales Assistants); *Midlands and South-East:* Margaret Egan (Athlone), Mark Flynn (Waterford), Martin Meally (Kilkenny Industrial and Manufacturing), Martin Rowe (Wexford), Tom Russell (Kildare-Leixlip); *West:* Battie Doohan (Roscommon), Pádraig Heverin (Mayo Health Services), Helen Murphy (Galway No. 2); *South-West:* Danny Crowley (Cóbh), Pat Harrington (Cork No. 3), Mary O'Rourke (Cork No. 8), Mary Reddin (Limerick No. 2), Stephen Tobin (Tralee); *North:* Fiona Doherty (Derry), Séamus Kelly (Monaghan No. 20/21), Rosabel Kerrigan (Donegal County), Brendan O'Donnell (Letterkenny); *National Trustees:* Brian Bird (Cork No. 7), Jimmy Brennan (Carlow), Séamus Briscoe (North-East), Noel Clune (Shannon Aviation), Noel Pocock (Health Service Professionals).

National Women's Committee
Chairperson: Liz O'Donohoe (Athy); Vice-Chairperson: Lily McConnon (North-East); Eithne Brady (Longford), Mary Brady (Dublin Health Services), Jacqueline Brennan (Wexford), Margaret Cooney (Nenagh), Caroline Curraoin (State Agencies), Maura D'Arcy (Ballinasloe-Galway No. 3), May Dowling (Hotels, Restaurants and Catering), Susanna Griffen (Tralee), Ramone Jurkonyte (Food), Mary Kavanagh (Local Authorities), Suzanne Kelly (Waterford), Margaret McDermott (Monaghan No. 20/21), Edel Moran (FÁS), Mary O'Connell (Clare Heath Services), Phyllis O'Kane (Shannon Industrial), Siobhán Quirke (Cork General Nursing), Ann Reid (Administrative, Supervisory and Sales), Rosa Seda (Actors' Equity), Mary Somers (Cork No. 7), Ber Stone (Cork No. 8), Mary Ward (Donegal Nursing).

Regional Executives
Region 1 (Dublin)
President: Kieran Jack McGinley (Education); Vice-President: Deirdre Smyth (Chemicals, Health Care and Distribution): Secretary: Patricia King; Des Derwin and Liam Griffin (Electronics and Engineering), Christy Dunne and Joe Marsden (Health Services), Michael Fowler (Printing Trades), Christy Gleeson, John Judge and Mary Kavanagh (Local Authorities), Matt Henry (County Councils), Christy Hughes (AGE-MOU Division), Liam Hughes (Film and Entertainment), Willie Hynes (Aer Lingus), Robert Jolley (Rail), Dee Kelly (Hotels, Restaurant and Catering), Gerry Kelly and Rose O'Reilly (Food), Paul Kelly (Marine Port), Pauline King (Contract Services), Bill McCamley (Dublin Bus Branch), Ray McHugh (Broadcasting), Tony Merriman (Energy), Michele Monahan (Health Professionals), Dave Murphy (Construction), Garret O'Brien (Insurance and Finance), Rynagh O'Grady (Actors' Equity), Lynda Scully (Community Sector), Dermot Tobin (Administrative and Supervisory), Tom Walsh (State-Related Agencies), Christy Waters (Security).

Region 2 (Midlands and South-East)
President: Pat Cody (Wexford Health Services); Vice-President: Theresa Walsh (Wexford); Secretary: Christy McQuillan; Peadar Bermingham, Éamon Kinsella and Josephine O'Brien (Carlow), Gerry Brauders (Arklow), John Brosnan (Kildare-Leixlip), Bernard Cox, Jim McCauley and Edel O'Neill (Longford-Westmeath), Tony Cunningham, Suzanne Kelly, Philip Myler and Stephen O'Donohoe (Waterford), Frankie Doolan (Athlone), Cathy Duff (Midland Nursing), Frank Kavanagh and John Kavanagh (Kilkenny), Pat Lalor (Laois), Joe Lambe and P. J. McCabe (Offaly), Anton McCabe, Donie McEnroe and Tina O'Brien (Meath), Dick Maher and Elizabeth O'Donohoe (Kildare-Athy), Paschal Maher (Peat Industries), Gordon O'Toole (Kildare-Athy), Dolores Sheeran (Offaly).

Region 3 (West)
President: Tom Costello (Galway No. 1); Vice-President: David Breen (Mayo No. 2); Secretary: Joe Cunningham; Philip Bishop (Roscommon), Annette Carpenter and Pat Scully (Galway No. 2), Joe Casey and Mary Dolan McLoughlin (Sligo), Michael Clair (Shannon Aviation), Michael Connellan (Clare), Brendan Duffy (Galway No. 1), Vincent Grant and Michael Ruane (Mayo No. 1), Marlyn Kirby (Mayo Health Services), Maureen McNicholas (Mayo No. 2), Ray Mitchell (Shannon Industrial), John O'Connell (Ballinasloe), John Wade (Galway No. 3).

Region 4 (South-West)
President: Tim Daly (Cork No. 5); Vice-President: Marguerite Neville (Cork No. 1); Secretary: Gene Mealy, Patsy Barry (Cork No. 8), Dónal Cahill (Cork No. 7), John Connolly (Bantry), Tony Doody (Limerick Nursing), Brian Duff (Cork No. 6), Frank Fehilly (Cork No. 2), Tim Fitzgerald (Mallow), Raymond Humphries (Clonmel), Bernard McCaul (Midleton), Brenda Mendiola (Cork No. 7), Denis Mulcahy (Nenagh), William O'Brien (Tipperary), Tim O'Connor (Tralee), Maurice O'Donoghue (Administrative, Professional and Technical), Carmel O'Leary (Cork No. 6), Christy O'Sullivan (Cork No. 3), Thomas Quinlivan (Limerick), Stephen Tobin (Tralee).

Region 5 (Northern)
President: Patrick Hannon (Donegal Nursing); Vice-President: Josephine Bailey (Belfast); Secretary: Joe Cunningham; Séamus Califf and Jim Lyng (Cavan), Peter Crosby and Cathal Faulkner (Monaghan No. 20/21), Fiona Doherty (Derry), Michael Ferry, Veronica McNutt and Séamus Murphy (Donegal County), Phelim Jennings (Newry), Bernadette Macken (Louth Nursing), Lily McConnon and Hugh Rafferty (North-East), Séamus Murray (Leitrim), John Smith (Monaghan Nursing).

Retired Members' Committee
President: Jim Quinn; Vice-President: Tadhg Philpott; Secretary: Ross M. Connolly; Project Manager: Paddy Moran.

Appendix 6 ❧

UNION PARLIAMENTARY MEMBERS, 1922–2008

President of Ireland
Mary Robinson (ITGWU and SIPTU member), 1990–97.

Dáil Éireann and Seanad Éireann
The following table lists all union members elected to Dáil Éireann, Seanad Éireann, Northern Ireland Parliament (Stormont) and the European Parliament for the Labour Party, National Labour Party, Independent Labour Party or SDLP. Union members have also been returned for conservative parties but did so without union support; those listed here were either serving union Officials or formally sponsored by the union.

The ITGWU was affiliated to the Labour Party until 1944, when it led a breakaway to form the National Labour Party, and from 1967; the WUI was affiliated from 1966, and SIPTU from 1990. The National Labour Party re-merged with the Labour Party in June 1950. Leaders of the Labour Party have been Thomas Johnson, 1922–7; T. J. O'Connell, 1927–32; William Norton, 1932–60; Brendan Corish, 1960–77; Frank Cluskey, 1977–81; Michael O'Leary, 1981–82; Dick Spring, 1982–97; Ruairí Quinn, 1997–2002; Pat Rabbitte, 2002–7; and Éamon Gilmore, 2007–. Corish, O'Leary and Spring were all supported by the ITGWU, Cluskey and Quinn by the FWUI and SIPTU, and Rabbitte and Gilmore (after Democratic Left merged with the Labour Party) by SIPTU, both having been ITGWU Officials. Cluskey and O'Leary were also full-time Officials. Richard Corish was the first ITGWU member elected as a Sinn Féin Deputy, in Wexford, 1921.

Since 1919 there have been thirty sessions of Dáil Éireann:
1st: 21 January 1919 to 10 May 1921
2nd: 16 August 1921 to 16 June 1922
3rd: 9 September 1922 to 9 August 1923
4th: 19 September 1923 to 23 May 1927
5th: 23 June 1927 to 25 August 1927

6th: 11 October 1927 to 29 January 1932
7th: 9 March 1932 to 2 January 1933
8th: 8 February 1933 to 14 June 1937
9th: 21 July 1937 to 27 May 1938
10th: 30 June 1938 to 31 May 1943
11th: 1 July 1943 to 10 May 1944
12th: 9 June 1944 to 12 January 1948
13th: 18 February 1948 to 7 May 1951
14th: 13 June 1951 to 24 April 1954
15th: 2 June 1954 to 12 February 1957
16th: 20 March 1957 to 15 September 1961
17th: 11 October 1961 to 18 March 1965
18th: 21 April 1965 to 22 May 1969
19th: 2 July to 5 February 1973
20th: 14 March 1973 to 25 May 1977
21st: 5 July 1977 to 21 May 1981
22nd: 30 June 1981 to 27 February 1982
23rd: 9 March 1982 to 4 November 1982
24th: 14 December 1982 to 21 January 1987
25th: 10 March 1987 to 25 May 1989
26th: 29 June 1989 to 5 November 1992
27th: 14 December 1992 to 15 May 1997
28th: 26 June 1997 to 25 April 2002
29th: 6 June 2002 to 20 April 2007
30th: 14 June 2007–

ITGWU members who have held Government posts
Brendan Corish: Social Welfare, 1954–7; Tánaiste and Health, 1973–7; *Barry Desmond:* Health and Social Welfare, 1982–7; *James Everett:* Posts and Telegraphs, 1944–8; Justice, 1954–7; *Liam Kavanagh:* Labour and the Public Service, 1981–2; Labour, 1982–3; Environment, 1982–6; Tourism, Fisheries and Forestry, 1986–7; *T. J. Murphy:* Local Government, 1944–8; *Conor Cruise O'Brien:* Posts and Telegraphs, 1973–7; *Michael O'Leary:* Labour, 1973–7; Tánaiste and Industry and Energy, 1981–2; *Dick Spring:* Tánaiste and Environment and Energy, 1982–7.

WUI, FRW and FWUI members who have held Government posts
Frank Cluskey: Trade, Commerce and Tourism, 1982–3; *Eileen Desmond:* Health and Social Welfare, 1981–2; *Justin Keating:* Industry and Commerce, 1973–7; *Ruairí Quinn:* Labour and the Public Service, 1983–7; *James Tully* (FRW): Local Government, 1973–7; Defence, 1981–2.

SIPTU members who have held Government posts
Niamh Bhreatnach: Education, 1993–4, 1994–7; *Proinsias de Rossa*[1]: Social Welfare, 1994–7; *Michael D. Higgins:* Arts, Culture and the Gaeltacht, 1993–4, 1994–7; *Brendan Howlin:* Environment, 1994–7; *Ruairí Quinn:* Industry and Commerce, 1993; Enterprise and Employment, 1993–4; Finance, 1994–7; *Dick Spring:* Tánaiste and Foreign Affairs, 1993–4; Tánaiste and Foreign Affairs, 1994–7; *Mervyn Taylor:* Equality and Law Reform, 1993–4; Equality and Law Reform, 1994–7.

Union members who were Ministers of State or Parliamentary Secretaries

Joe Bermingham: Minister of State at Department of Finance, 1981–2, 1982–7; *Joan Burton:* Minister of State at Department of Social Welfare, 1993–4; Foreign Affairs, Overseas Development Aid, 1994–7; *Frank Cluskey:* Parliamentary Secretary to Minister for Social Welfare, 1973–7; *Brendan Corish:* Parliamentary Secretary to Minister for Defence, 1948–51; Social Welfare, 1954–7; *Eithne Fitzgerald:* Minister of State at Department of Finance, 1993–4; Office of the Tánaiste and Department of Enterprise and Employment, 1994–7; *Éamonn Gilmore:* Minister of State at Department of the Marine, 1994–7; *Liz McManus:* Minister of State at Department of the Environment and Department of the Taoiseach, 1994–7; *Michael Moynihan:* Minister of State at Department of Trade, Commerce and Tourism, 1982–7; *M. P. Murphy:* Parliamentary Secretary to Minister for Agriculture and Fisheries; *Gerry O'Sullivan:* Minister of State at Department of the Marine, 1992–3; *Séamus Pattison:* Minister of State at Department of Social Welfare, 1982–7; *Ruairí Quinn:* Minister of State at Department of the Environment, Urban Affairs and Housing, 1982–3; *Pat Rabbitte:* Minister of State at Department of Enterprise and Employment with responsibility for Commerce, Technology, Consumer Affairs and Government, 1994–7; *Dan Spring:* Parliamentary Secretary to Minister for Local Government, 1956–7; *Dick Spring:* Minister of State at Department of Justice, 1982–7; *Emmet Stagg:* Minister of State at Department of the Environment, 1993–4; Transport, Energy and Communications, 1994–7.

Union members who were Ceann Comhairle or Leas-Cheann Comhairle

Patrick Hogan: Leas-Cheann Comhairle, 1928, 1932–4; Ceann Comhairle, 1951–68; *Dan Morrissey*[2]: Leas-Cheann Comhairle, 1928–32; *Seán Treacy:* Ceann Comhairle, 1973–7, 1987–97 (became an independent, 1987); *Séamus Pattison:* Ceann Comhairle, 1997–2002.

ITGWU Dáil Deputies[3]

— Michael Bell, Louth: November 1982 to 1987; 1987–9; 1989–92; 1992–7; 1997–2002.
— Michael Bradley, Cork County: 1922–3.
— Henry Broderick, Longford-Westmeath: 1927; 1927–32.
— John Butler,[4] Waterford: 1922–3; 1923–7.
— Henry Byrne, Laois-Offaly: 1965–9.
— Patrick Clancy, Limerick: 1923–7; 1927; 1927–32.
— Hugh Colohan, Kildare-Wicklow: 1920–23; Kildare: 1923–7, 1927; 1927–32.
— Brendan Corish, Wexford: 1945–8; 1948–51; 1951–4; 1954–7; 1957–61; 1961–5; 1965–9; 1969–73; 1973–7; 1977–81; 1981–2.
— Richard Corish, Wexford: 1922–3; 1923–7; 1927; 1927–32; 1932–3; 1933–7; 1937–8; 1938–43; 1943–4; 1944–5.
— Stephen Coughlan, Limerick East: 1961–5; 1965–9; 1969–73; 1973–.
— Conor Cruise O'Brien, Dublin North-East: 1969–73; 1973–7.
— Robert Day, Cork Borough: 1922–3.
— Barry Desmond, Dún Laoghaire-Rathdown: 1969–73; 1973–7; 1977–81; 1981–2; February–November 1982; November 1982 to 1987; 1987–9.
— Edward Doyle, Carlow: 1923–7; 1927; 1927–32.
— James Everett, Kildare-Wicklow: 1922–3; Wicklow: 1923–7; 1927; 1927–32; 1932–3; 1933–7; 1937–8; 1938–43; 1943–4; 1944–8; 1948–51; 1951–4; 1954–7; 1957–61; 1961–5; 1965–8.

— Michael Ferris, Tipperary South: 1989–92; 1992–7; 1997–2002.
— John F. Gill, Laois-Offaly: 1927.
— David Hall, Meath: 1923–7; 1927.
— Archibald Heron, Dublin North-West: 1937–8.
— James Hickey, Cork Borough: 1938–43; 1948–51; 1951–54.
— Patrick Hogan, Clare: 1923–7; 1927; 1927–32; 1932–3; 1933–7; 1937–8; 1943–4; 1944–8; 1948–51; 1951–4; 1954–7; 1957–61; 1961–5; 1965–9.
— Brendan Howlin, Wexford: 1987–9; 1989–92; 1992–7; 1997–2002; 2002–7; 2007–.
— Liam Kavanagh, Wicklow: 1969–73; 1973–7; 1977–81; 1981–2; February–November 1982; November 1982 to 1987; 1987–9; 1989–92; 1992–7.
— Seán Keane, Cork East: 1948–51; 1951–3.
— Patrick Kerrigan, Cork City: 1977–9.
— Michael Lipper,[5] Limerick East: 1977–.
— T. D. Looney, Cork South-East: 1943–4.
— Gilbert Lynch, Galway: 1927.
— John Lyons, Longford-Westmeath: 1922–3.[6]
— Patrick MacAuliffe, Cork North: 1944–8; 1948–51; 1951–4; 1954–7; 1957–61; 1961–5; 1965–9.
— Pádraig Mac Gamhna (Patrick Gaffney), Carlow-Kilkenny: 1922–3.
— Gerrard McGowan, Dublin County: 1937–8.
— Daniel Morrissey,[7] Tipperary: 1922–3; 1923–7; 1927; 1927–32.
— Michael Moynihan, Kerry South: 1981–2; February–November 1982; November 1982 to 1987; 1989–92.
— Michael Mullen, Dublin North-West: 1961–5; 1965–9.
— John Mulvihill, Cork East: 1992–7.
— M. P. Murphy, Cork West: 1951–4; 1954–7; 1957–61; 1961–5; Cork South-West: 1965–9; 1969–73; 1973–7; 1977–81.
— T. J. Murphy, Cork West: 1923–7; 1927; 1927–32; 1932–3; 1933–7; 1937–8; 1938–3; 1943–4; 1944–8; 1948–9.
— Thomas Nagle, Cork North: 1922–3; 1923–7.
— William O'Brien, Dublin South: 1922–3; Tipperary: 1927, 1937–8.
— John O'Connell, Dublin South-West: 1965–9; 1969–73; 1973–7; Dublin Ballyfermot: 1977–81.[8]
— John O'Donovan, Dublin South-Central: 1969–73.
— John O'Leary, Wexford: 1944–8; 1948–51; 1951–4; 1954–7.
— Michael O'Leary,[9] Dublin North-Central: 1965–9; 1969–73; 1973–7; 1977–81; 1981–2; Dublin Central: February 1982–.
— Cathal O'Shannon, Louth-Meath: 1922–3.
— Gerry O'Sullivan, Cork North-Central: 1989–92; 1992–4.
— J. P. Pattison, Carlow-Kilkenny: 1933–7; 1937–8; 1938–43; 1943–4; 1944–8; 1948–51; 1951–4; 1954–7.
— Séamus Pattison, Carlow-Kilkenny: 1961–5; 1965–9; 1969–73; 1973–7; 1977–81; 1981–2; February–November 1982; November 1982 to 1987; 1987–9; 1989–92; 1992–7; 1997–2002; 2002–7.
— Nicholas Phelan, Waterford: 1922–3.
— Frank Prendergast, Limerick East: November 1982 to 1987.

— Timothy Quill, Cork North: 1927.
— Joseph Sherlock,[10] Cork East: 1981–2; February 1982 to 1987; 1987–9; 1989–92; 2002–7.
— Daniel Spring, Kerry North: 1943–4; 1944–8; 1948–51; 1951–4; 1954–7; 1957–61; 1961–5; 1965–9; 1969–73; 1973–7; 1977–81.
— Richard (Dick) Spring, Kerry North: 1981–2; February–November 1982; November 1982 to 1987; 1987–9; 1989–92; 1992–7; 1997–2002.
— Richard Stapleton, Tipperary: 1943–4.
— David Thornley, Dublin North-West: 1969–73; 1973–7.
— Patrick Tierney, Tipperary North: 1957–61; 1961–5; 1965.
— Seán Treacy,[11] Tipperary South: 1961–5; 1965–9; 1969–73; 1973–7; 1977–81; 1981–2; 1982; 1982–7; 1987–9; 1989–92.

WUI Dáil Deputies[12]

— Joseph Bermingham, Kildare: 1973–7; 1977–81; 1981–2; February–November 1982; November 1982–1987.
— Frank Cluskey, Dublin South-Central: 1965–9; 1969–73; 1973–7; 1977–81; February–November 1982; November 1982 to 1987; 1987–.
— R. J. Connolly, Louth: 1943–4; 1948–51.
— Brendan Halligan, Dublin South-West: 1976–7.
— Michael D. Higgins, Galway West: 1981–2; February–November 1982; 1987–9; 1989–92; 1992–7; 1997–2002; 2002–7; 2007–
— John Horgan, Dublin County South: 1977–81.
— Justin Keating, Dublin County North: 1969–73; 1973–7.
— Denis Larkin, Dublin North-East: 1954–7; 1957–61; 1965–9.
— James Larkin (Senior), Dublin North: 1927–8; Dublin North-East: 1937–8; 1943–4.
— James Larkin (Junior), Dublin South: 1943–4; 1944–8; Dublin South-Central: 1948–51; 1951–4; 1954–7.
— Frank McLoughlin, Meath: November 1982 to 1987.
— Ruairí Quinn, Dublin South-East: 1977–81; February–November 1982; November 1982 to 1987; 1987–9; 1989–92; 1992–7; 1997–2002; 2002–7; 2007–.
— Emmet Stagg, Kildare North: 1987–9; 1989–92; 1992–7; 1997–2002; 2002–7; 2007–.
— Mervyn Taylor, Dublin South-West: 1981–2; February 1982 to 1987; 1987–9; 1989–92; 1992–7.

FRW Dáil Deputies

— Daniel Desmond, Cork South: 1948–51; 1951–4; 1954–7; Cork Mid: 1961–5 (FRW Official).
— Eileen Desmond,[13] Cork Mid: 1965; 1965–9; 1973–7; 1977–81; Cork South-Central: 1981–2; February–November 1982; November 1982 to 1987.
— Seán Dunne,[14] Dublin County: 1948–51; 1951–4; 1954–7, 1961–5; 1965–9; Dublin South-West: 1969–70.
— James Tully, Meath: 1954–7; 1961–5; 1965–9; 1969–73; 1973–7; 1977–81; 1981–82.

SIPTU Dáil Deputies[15]

Listed above under ITGWU but also sponsored by SIPTU were Michael Ferris, Brendan Howlin, Liam Kavanagh, Brian O'Shea, Gerry O'Sullivan, Séamus Pattison, John Ryan,

Joe Sherlock and Dick Spring. Similarly, WUI members sponsored by SIPTU were Ruairí Quinn, Emmet Stagg and Mervyn Taylor.

— Niamh Bhreatnach, Dún Laoghaire: 1992–7.
— Declan Bree, Sligo-Leitrim: 1992–7.
— Joan Burton, Dublin West: 1992–7; 2002–7; 2007–.
— Brian Fitzgerald, Meath: 1992–7.
— Eithne Fitzgerald, Dublin South: 1992–7.
— Patrick Gallagher, Laois-Offaly: 1992–1992.
— Éamonn Gilmore,[16] Dún Laoghaire-Rathdown: 1989–92; 1992–7; 1997–2002; 2002–7; 2007–.
— Kathleen Lynch,[17] Cork North-Central: 1992–7; 2002–7; 2007–.
— Liz McManus,[18] Wicklow: 1992–7; 1997–2002; 2002–7; 2007–.
— Breda Moynihan Cronin, Kerry South: 1992–7; 1997–2002; 2002–7.
— Willie Penrose, Westmeath: 1992–7; 1997–2002; 2002–7; 2007–.
— Pat Rabbitte,[19] Dublin South-West: 1989–92; 1992–7; 1997–2002; 2002–7; 2007–.
— Seán Sherlock, Cork East: 2007–.
— Jack Wall, Kildare South: 1997–2002; 2002–7; 2007–.

Union members of Seanad Éireann[20]
Sessions of the Seanad have been: (Free State) 1922–5, 1925–8, 1928–31, 1931–4, 1934–6; (Constitution of Ireland) Second, 1938; Third, 1938–43; Fourth, 1943–4; Fifth, 1944–8; Sixth, 1948–51; Seventh, 1951–4; Eighth, 1954–7; Ninth, 1957–61; Tenth, 1961–5; Eleventh, 1965–9; Twelfth, 1969–73; Thirteenth, 1973–7; Fourteenth, 1977–81; Fifteenth, 1981–2; Sixteenth, 1982; Seventeenth, 1983–7; Eighteenth, 1987–9; Nineteenth, 1989–92; Twentieth, 1992–7; Twenty-First, 1997–2002; Twenty-Second, 2002–7; Twenty-Third, 2007–.

After 1928 Michael Duffy, Thomas Foran and Thomas Farren sat as independents. Foran (1938–48) and Thomas Kennedy (1943–7) also did. I think the same applied to the leading ITGWU Officials from the late 1940s to 1967.

— Edward Browne, 1960–61.
— Robert Malachy Burke, 1948–51.[21]
— John F. Carroll, 1981–2; 1982; 1983–7.
— Bill Cashin, 1993–7.
— R. J. Connolly, 1973–7.
— Mary Davidson, 1950–51, 1954–7; 1957–61; 1961–5; 1965–9.
— Con Desmond, 1961–5.
— Eileen Desmond, 1969–73.
— Michael Duffy, 1922–; 1925–8; 1928–1; 1931–4; 1934–6.
— Patrick Dunne, 1981–2.
— Thomas Farren, 1922–5; 1925–8; 1928–31; 1931–4; 1934–6.
— Michael Ferris, 1973–7; 1981–2; 1982; 1983–7.
— Jack Fitzgerald, 1961, 1961–5, 1965–9, 1969–73, 1973–7.
— Thomas Foran,[22] 1922–5; 1925–8; 1928–31; 1931–4; 1934–6; 1938–43; 1943–4; 1944–8.
— Patrick Gallagher, 1997–9.

— Brendan Halligan, 1973–6.
— Jack Harte, 1973–7; 1977–81; 1981–2; 1982; 1983–7; 1987–9.
— James Hickey, 1954–7.
— Michael D. Higgins, 1973–7; 1983–7.
— Patrick Hogan, 1938–43.
— Brendan Howlin, 1983–7.
— Justin Keating, 1977–81.
— Alan Kelly, 2007–.
— Fintan Kennedy, 1969–73; 1973–7; 1977–81.
— Thomas Kennedy, 1934–6; 1943–4; 1944–8.
— Patrick Kerrigan. 1973–7.
— Christopher Kirwan,[23] 1983–7.
— Éamon Lynch, 1938–43.
— Tim McAuliffe, 1961–5; 1965–9; 1973–7; 1971–7; 1981–2.
— Michael McCarthy, 2002–7; 2007–.
— William McMullen, 1951–2, 1953.
— Patrick Magner, 1981–2; 1983–7; 1993–7.
— Seán Maloney, 1997–2002.
— Michael Moynihan, 1973–7; 1977–81.
— Michael Mullen, 1973–7.
— John O'Leary, 1957–9.
— Flor O'Mahony, 1981–2; 1982; 1983–7.
— Phil Prendergast, 2007–.
— Frank Purcell, 1954–7; 1957–60.
— Mary Robinson (Mary Bourke until 1970), 1969–89.
— Ruairí Quinn, 1973–7; 1981–2.
— Joseph Sherlock, 1993–7.
— Jack Wall, 1993–7.
— Alex White, 2007–.

Northern Ireland

Union members elected to the Parliament of Northern Ireland, 1921–73, Northern Ireland Assembly, 1973–5, Northern Ireland Constitutional Convention, 1975–6, and Northern Ireland Assembly, 1982–6.

— Ivan Cooper, Mid-Ulster (SDLP): 1973–5.
— Austin Currie, Fermanagh and South Tyrone (SDLP): 1973–5.
— Paddy Devlin, Belfast Falls (NILP): 1969–73; Belfast West (SDLP): 1973–5.
— Hugh Downey, Belfast Dock (NILP): 1945–9.
— Gerry Fitt, Belfast Dock (Irish Labour Party): 1962–5; (Republican Labour): 1965–9; 1969–73; Belfast North (SDLP): 1973–5.
— John Hume, Londonderry (SDLP): 1973–5, 1982–6.
— William McMullen, Belfast West (NILP): 1925–9.
— Murtagh Morgan, Belfast Dock (Irish Labour Party): 1953–8.
— Paddy O'Hanlon, South Armagh (Nationalist): 1969–73 (SDLP from 1970), 1973–5.

British House of Commons
— Gerry Fitt,[24] Belfast West (Republican Labour): 1966–70, 1970–74; (SDLP): 1974; 1974–9; 1979–84.
— John Hume, Foyle (SDLP): 1983–7, 1987–92; 1992–.

European Parliament
— Frank Cluskey, Dublin: 1981–3.
— Conor Cruise O'Brien, Dublin: 1973.
— Proinsias de Rossa, Dublin: 1989–92; 1999–.
— Barry Desmond,[25] Dublin: 1989–94.
— Eileen Desmond, Munster: 1979–81.
— Des Geraghty,[26] Dublin: 1992–4.
— Brendan Halligan, Dublin: 1983–4.
— John Hume, Northern Ireland: 1979–84; 1984–9; 1989–94; 1994–9; 1999–2004.
— Liam Kavanagh, Leinster: 1973–81.
— Justin Keating, Ireland: 1973; Leinster: 1984.
— Bernie Malone, Dublin: 1994–9.
— John O'Connell, Dublin: 1979–81.
— Michael O'Leary, Dublin; 1979–81.
— Flor O'Mahony, Dublin: 1983–84.
— Séamus Pattison, Leinster: 1981–3.
— David Thornley, Dublin; 1973–7.
— Seán Treacy, Munster: 1981–4.

I am grateful to Barry Desmond and Charles Callan for assistance with this appendix.

Appendix 7 ∿

STATISTICAL TABLES

Irish Transport and General Workers' Union

Table 156: Membership, 1909–89

	ITGWU	*RFS*	*Congress**	*Women*
1909	1,200	2,500	*n.a.*	*n.a.*
1910	5,000	5,000	*n.a.*	*n.a.*
1911	18,089	18,000	*n.a.*	*n.a.*
1912	22,000	24,135	*n.a.*	*n.a.*
1913	30,000	22,935	*n.a.*	*n.a.*
1914	15,000	15,000	*n.a.*	*n.a.*
1915	10,000	10,000	*n.a.*	*n.a.*
1916	5,000	5,000	*n.a.*	*n.a.*
1917	15,000	14,920	*n.a.*	*n.a.*

1918	67,827	67,827	*n.a.*	*n.a.*
1919	102,823	101,917	*n.a.*	*n.a.*
1920	120,000	101,970	*n.a.*	*n.a.*
1921	100,000	100,000	*n.a.*	5,000
1922	82,243	100,000	100,000	*n.a.*
1923	89,000	89,000	100,000	*n.a.*
1924	67,000	67,000	70,000	*n.a.*
1925	50,984	42,000	50,000	*n.a.*
1926	40,000	42,000	40,000	*n.a.*
1927	22,000	37,500	20,000	*n.a.*
1928	18,857	35,000	20,000	*n.a.*
1929	15,453	35,000	20,000	*n.a.*
1930	14,608	33,400	20,000	1,100
1931	14,500	32,580	20,000	1,000
1932	14,123	32,400	20,000	1,000
1933	14,660	35,000	25,000	2,500
1934	16,670	30,000	25,000	2,500
1935	20,951	36,000	30,000	4,000
1936	24,810	36,000	32,000	4,000
1937	28,514	36,000	36,000	6,000
1938	33,095	36,000	36,000	6,000
1939	36,444	36,000	36,000	6,000
1940	36,825	36,000	36,000	6,000
1941	35,271	36,000	36,000	6,000
1942	31,228	36,000	36,000	6,000
1943	30,615	36,000	36,000	6,000
1944	34,853	51,874	36,000	10,374
1945	37,970	53,185	51,874	10,634
1946	39,717	61,260	80,000	12,000
1947	46,477	78,380	80,000	15,676
1948	120,000	89,054	95,000	17,811
1949	130,000	101,609	108,000	20,322
1950	100,000	116,257	130,000	23,251
1951	124,000	128,191	130,000	25,638
1952	79,000	127,480	148,442	25,496
1953	79,957	119,377	148,442	23,875
1954	82,314	122,903	150,000	24,581
1955	83,500	126,180	150,000	25,346
1956	84,252	126,707	150,000	25,342
1957	84,860	124,183	150,000	24,837

1958	82,336	125,571	150,000	25,314
1959	83,256	127,571	150,000	25,830
1960	150,000	136,179	150,000	27,236
1961	150,000	140,334	150,000	28,067
1962	150,000	146,339	150,000	29,268
1963	150,000	143,498	150,000	28,697
1964	150,000	149,915	150,000	29,983
1965	150,000	150,414	150,000	30,083
1966	150,000	148,804	150,000	29,760
1967	105,408	153,415	150,000	n.a.
1968	108,270	156,277	150,000	n.a.
1969	114,174	162,181	150,000	54,060
1970	122,170	162,478	150,000	54,159
1971	116,730	155,614	150,000	51,872
1972	125,185	155,879	150,000	51,959
1973	132,912	156,918	150,000	52,638
1974	140,213	156,418	150,000	52,139
1975	144,083	157,392	150,000	52,463
1976	141,079	154,388	150,000	51,464
1977	152,733	166,034	150,000	56,344
1978	158,160	176,429	150,000	58,809
1979	167,239	185,566	150,000	61,855
1980	172,353	188,722	150,000	62,907
1981	169,798	189,146	150,000	62,900
1982	158,344	188,702	150,000	62,900
1983	155,090	177,894	150,000	59,000
1984	139,690	173,894	150,000	57,900
1985	136,394	158,494	150,000	52,832
1986	133,777	155,198	150,000	51,732
1987	155,000	151,230	150,000	50,410
1988	148,255	148,255	150,000	49,918
1989	157,622	157,622	150,000	54,717

Notes: ITGWU figures: May 1910, 3,000; January 1911, 5,000; January 1912, 18,009; Easter 1916, 5,000 (some accounts show higher numbers, between 7,000 and 8,000); January 1917, 14,500; February 1918, 25,000; June 1918, 43,788; May 1919 and August 1919, 66,000; January 1920, 102,823; May 1920, 120,000; April 1923, 82,243; April 1924, 72,000.

*The ITGWU was affiliated to the ITUC, 1909–44, to the CIU, 1944–59, and to the ICTU, 1959–89.

Sources: ITGWU, Annual Reports, 1918–1989; ITUC, Annual Reports, 1909–1959; CIU, Annual Reports, 1945–59; ICTU, Annual Reports, 1959–89; National Archives, Registrar of Friendly Societies, file 275T.

Table 157: Income, expenditure and annual balance (£), 1918–89

	Income	Expenditure	Surplus (deficit)
1918	27,699	18,986	8,713
1919	74,726	63,379	11,346
1920	100,011	62,848	37,163
1921	81,584	45,596	35,997
1922	96,007	64,506	31,501
1923	84,122	160,427	(76,305)
1924	50,137	40,417	9,270
1925	32,880	36,883	(4,003)
1926	27,182	24,617	2,565
1927	21,292	19,231	2,062
1928	17,866	14,783	3,083
1929	17,368	14,506	2,862
1930	16,901	12,505	4,396
1931	16,994	14,653	2,341
1932	17,380	10,158	7,222
1933	19,340	11,891	7,449
1934	24,389	19,377	5,012
1935	27,482	26,590	892
1936	30,471	19,962	10,509
1937	35,081	34,224	857
1938	37,340	19,956	17,384
1939	37,494	16,974	20,520
1940	37,969	21,304	16,665
1941	33,533	17,342	16,191
1942	33,649	18,787	14,682
1943	37,137	17,427	19,710
1944	39,960	16,245	23,715
1945	41,072	21,806	19,266
1946	49,720	21,868	27,852
1947	61,298	74,861	(13,563)
1948	74,074	35,427	39,277
1949	85,404	46,910	38,494
1950	97,686	55,532	42,154
1951	106,799	108,742	(1,943)
1952	109,533	103,897	5,656
1953	153,979	55,876	98,103

1954	159,907	64,970	94,937
1955	166,129	96,179	69,950
1956	166,469	84,203	82,266
1957	166,564	104,656	61,908
1958	166,177	93,194	72,983
1959	170,407	121,355	49,052
1960	183,031	101,617	81,414
1961	190,318	157,477	32,841
1962	223,392	125,776	97,616
1963	260,596	208,529	52,067
1964	292,852	197,438	94,414
1965	330,934	290,919	40,015
1966	433,160	344,532	88,628
1967	517,334	410,419	106,924
1968	501,527	390,632	110,895
1969	542,962	572,132	(29,170)
1970	618,633	504,770	113,863
1971	814,741	693,094	121,647
1972	892,219	716,392	175,827
1973	1,015,675	759,328	256,347
1974	1,255,661	1,079,800	175,861
1975	1,578,955	1,414,905	164,582
1976	1,776,235	1,636,284	139,951
1977	3,243,489	2,798,866	444,623
1978	3,435,358	3,473,138	133,442
1979	4,180,319	3,841,809	338,510
1980	5,186,959	5,088,224	98,735
1981	6,294,113	5,764,005	530,108
1982	7,304,444	7,399,776	(95,332)
1983	7,822,410	7,831,471	(9,331)
1984	8,262,110	8,697,034	(434,924)
1985	9,042,323	8,733,653	308,653
1986	10,033,378	9,665,167	368,211
1987	10,175,457	10,256,923	(81,466)
1988	11,014,645	10,256,923	589,310
1989	10,743,842	10,417,985	325,857

Source: ITGWU, Annual Reports, 1918–89.

Table 158: Credit balance (£), 1918–89

1918	17,929	1954	614,286
1919	29,038	1955	760,598
1920	66,202	1956	858,700
1921	102,199	1957	639,741
1922	133,700	1958	1,048,128
1923	58,462	1959	1,123,284
1924	68,183	1960	1,238,934
1925	64,180	1961	1,304,828
1926	66,745	1962	1,443,409
1927	66,052	1963	1,532,351
1928	69,135	1964	1,660,815
1929	71,997	1965	1,743,146
1930	76,393	1966	1,841,193
1931	78,734	1967	1,894,749
1932	87,956	1968	1,878,942
1933	95,405	1969	1,780,937
1934	100,405	1970	1,903,406
1935	101,297	1971	2,017,949
1936	111,807	1972	2,230,434
1937	113,845	1973	2,479,838
1938	131,229	1974	2,701,476
1939	151,874	1975	2,860,166
1940	169,039	1976	3,004,360
1941	199,691	1977	3,441,115
1942	216,874	1978	3,569,431
1943	237,058	1979	3,814,077
1944	261,294	1980	4,102,350
1945	285,592	1981	4,455,563
1946	320,559	1982	4,453,045
1947	313,420	1983	4,443,614
1948	355,965	198	44,008,790
1949	403,623	1985	4,317,460
1950	454,207	1986	4,757,607
1951	459,905	1987	4,676,142
1952	476,905	1988	5,609,911
1953	584,495	1989	5,935,770

Source: ITGWU, Annual Reports, 1918–89.

Table 159: Income and Dispute Benefit, 1918–89

	Income (£)	Dispute benefit (£)	Dispute grant (£)	Benefit and grant as proportion of income (%)
1918	27,699	8,407	—	—	30.4
1919	74,726	40,571	—	—	54.3
1920	100,011	36,847	—	—	37.1
1921	81,593	20,409	—	—	44.1
1922	96,007	33,139	—	—	32.8
1923	84,122	128,724	—	—	153.0
1924	50,137	10,906	—	—	21.8
1925	32,880	7,117	—	—	21.7
1926	27,182	3,042	—	—	12.3
1927	21,292	2,445	—	—	11.5
1928	17,866	989	—	—	5.5
1929	17,386	1,276	—	—	7.3
1930	16,901	983	—	—	5.8
1931	16,994	4,450	—	—	26.2
1932	17,380	425	—	—	2.5
1933	19,340	1,394	—	—	7.2
1934	24,389	7,000	—	—	28.7
1935	27,482	13,509	—	—	49.2
1936	30,471	6,871	—	—	22.6
1937	35,081	18,948	—	—	54.0
1938	37,340	5,234	—	—	14.2
1939	37,494	2,652	—	—	7.1
1940	37,969	5,054	—	—	13.3
1941	33,533	745	—	—	2.2
1942	33,649	288	—	—	0.9
1943	37,137	430	—	—	1.2
1944	39,960	252	—	—	0.6
1945	41,072	4,581	—	—	11.2
1946	49,720	3,447	—	—	6.9
1947	61,289	54,992	—	—	89.7
1948	74,704	9,813	—	—	13.1
1949	85,404	19,347	—	—	22.7
1950	97,686	20,870	—	—	21.4
1951	106,799	70,322	—	—	65.8
1952	109,553	57,298	—	—	52.3

1953	153,979	6,682	—	—	4.3
1954	159,907	6,100	—	—	3.8
1955	166,129	22,789	—	—	13.7
1956	166,469	1,971	—	—	1.2
1957	166,564	22,719	—	—	13.6
1958	166,177	9,631	—	—	5.8
1959	170,407	16,993	—	—	9.9
1960	183,031	7,904	—	—	4.3
1961	190,318	47,137	—	—	24.8
1962	223,392	9,692	—	—	4.4
1963	260,596	67,938	—	—	26.1
1964	291,852	33,814	—	—	11.6
1965	330,934	86,858	13,480	100,338	30.3
1966	433,160	85,553	27,133	112,686	26.0
1967	517,334	73,410	8,396	81,806	15.8
1968	501,527	63,617	21,975	85,592	17.0
1969	542,962	231,730	23,550	255,280	47.0
1970	618,633	74,908	6,140	81,048	13.1
1971	749,339	145,201	8,525	153,726	20.5
1972	892,219	128,643	6,500	135,143	15.1
1973	1,015,675	37,931	2,950	40,881	4.0
1974	1,255,661	181,361	10,059	191,420	15.2
1975	1,578,955	158,306	8,795	167,101	10.5
1976	1,776,235	74,956	1,273	76,229	4.2
1977	3,243,489	244,473	18,833	263,306	8.1
1978	3,435,358	391,347	10,992	402,339	11.7
1979	4,180,319	111,704	33,475	145,179	3.4
1980	5,186,959	400,201	43,750	443,951	8.5
1981	6,294,113	216,281	13,573	229,854	3.6
1982	7,304,444	427,029	13,830	440,859	6.0
1983	7,822,410	342,669	17,657	360,356	4.6
1984	8,262,110	514,120	20,350	534,470	6.7
1985	9,042,323	317,242	5,437	322,679	3.5
1986	10,033,378	557,717	2,013	559,730	5.6
1987	10,175,457	462,913	29,458	492,371	4.9
1988	11,014,645	195,648	5,485	201,133	1.8
1989	10,743,842	138,931	5,851	144,782	1.3

Source: ITGWU, Annual Reports, 1918–1990.

Table 160: Aggregate Dispute Pay (£), 1909–89

1909	200,000*	1961	875,331
1918	294,855	1971	2,019,275
1931	65,53	71981	3,286,204
1941	114,785	Total	7,078,376
1951	222,409	Average per year	88,480

*ITGWU estimate.
Source: ITGWU, Annual Reports, 1918–89.

Table 161: Salaries and wages, organisation and travel expenses, 1918–89

	Salaries and wages (£)	As proportion of expenditure (%)	Organisation and travel (£)	As proportion of expenditure (%)
1918	2,378	12.5	1,225	6.4
1919	7,795	12.2	3,761	5.9
1920	10,712	17.0	3,613	5.7
1921	10,731	23.5	2,407	5.2
1922	11,048	17.1	2,763	4.2
1923	11,918	7.4	5,814	3.6
1924	12,331	30.5	4,747	11.7
1925	7,692	20.8	3,404	9.2
1926	6,950	28.2	2,344	9.5
1927	5,220	27.1	1,469	7.6
1928	3,305	22.3	1,239	8.3
1929	2,991	20.6	1,247	8.5
1930	2,771	22.1	1,020	8.1
1931	2,020	13.7	811	5.5
1932	2,006	19.7	988	9.7
1933	2,300	19.3	1,155	9.7
1934	3,381	17.4	1,021	5.2
1935	3,303	12.4	1,123	4.2
1936	3,480	17.4	1,664	8.3
1937	3,656	10.6	1,526	4.4
1938	3,573	17.9	1,480	7.4
1939	3,845	22.6	1,183	6.9
1940	3,836	18.0	1,518	7.1
1941	3,660	21.1	935	5.3
1942	3,891	20.7	913	4.8

1943	4,517	25.9	1,398	8.0
1944	5,281	32.1	1,548	9.4
1945	5,286	24.2	1,687	7.7
1946	5,701	26.0	2,028	9.2
1947	6,604	8.8	2,625	3.5
1948	7,478	21.1	2,783	7.8
1949	9,277	19.7	2,668	5.6
1950	10,060	18.1	4,123	7.4
1951	11,795	10.8	5,476	5.0
1952	13,272	12.7	5,069	4.8
1953	14,459	25.8	6,190	11.0
1954	14,589	22.4	5,909	9.0
1955	15,275	15.8	7,255	7.5
1956	16,523	19.6	7,594	9.0
1957	18,404	17.5	8,475	8.0
1958	19,753	21.1	6,667	7.1
1959	19,976	16.4	8,740	7.2
1960	20,194	19.8	10,193	10.0
1961	23,388	12.2	13,267	6.9
1962	27,355	12.3	11,612	5.2
1963	31,594	12.1	16,693	6.4
1964	38,910	13.3	17,100	5.8
1965	52,902	15.9	20,434	6.2
1966	70,093	16.2	24,080	5.5
1967	73,955	14.3	26,158	5.0
1968	84,422	16.8	34,815	6.9
1969	90,327	16.6	28,692	5.3
1970	152,536	24.6	38,402	6.2
1971	145,201	17.8	46,153	5.7
1972	192,191	21.5	42,245	4.7
1973	220,315	21.7	43,391	4.3
1974	311,774	24.8	64,524	5.1
1975	500,652	31.7	102,565	6.5
1976	631,907	35.5	98,895	5.6
1977	1,419,942	43.7	223,245	6.9
1978	1,776,614	51.7	263,979	7.7
1979	2,235,543	53.4	335,497	8.0
1980	2,762,497	53.2	427,602	8.2
1981	3,286,612	52.2	480,217	7.6

1982	4,022,580	55.1	655,661	8.9
1983	4,752,462	60.7	774,262	9.9
1984	5,300,175	64.1	732,994	8.8
1985	5,454,096	60.3	749,986	8.3
1986	5,576,144	55.6	789,447	7.8
1987	6,016,091	59.1	879,160	8.6
1988	6,089,755	55.2	878,236	7.9
1989	6,005,870	55.9	718,220	6.6

Source: ITGWU, Annual Reports, 1918–89.

Workers' Union of Ireland and Federated Workers' Union of Ireland

Table 162: Membership, 1924–89

	RFS	ITUC/ICTU		RFS	ITUC/ICTU
1924	15,754	—	1957	28,745	25,000
1925	16,741	—	1958	29,090	25,000
1926	17,231	—	1959	29,631	30,000
1927	14,531	—	1960	28,904	30,000
1928	15,095	—	1961	29,230	30,000
1929	16,159	—	1962	29,329	30,000
1930	16,909	—	1963	29,833	30,000
1931	17,117	—	1964	29,361	35,000
1932	16,781	—	1965	30,048	35,000
1933	17,363	—	1966	31,309	35,000
1934	16,693	—	1967	30,716	35,000
1935	15,763	—	1968	31,373	35,000
1936	14,776	—	1969	33,352	35,000
1937	16,997	—	1970	34,536	35,000
1938	16,720	—	1971	34,706	35,000
1939	16,408	—	1972	34,790	35,000
1940	15,681	—	1973	35,048	35,000
1941	12,542	—	1974	35,358	35,000
1942	10,780	—	1975	34,252	35,000
1943	9,451	—	1976	34,477	35,000
1944	8,803	8,000	1977	35,859	35,000
1945	9,129	8,000	1978	35,941	35,000
1946	10,080	8,000	1979	44,588	35,000
1947	13,225	9,500	1980	44,959	50,000

Year			Year		
1948	17,251	15,000	1981	45,939	50,000
1949	21,427	15,000	1983	43,620	50,000
1950	24,217	20,000	1984	42,842	50,000
1951	26,376	25,000	1985	41,674	51,000
1952	28,035	25,000	1986	40,630	51,000
1953	27,469	25,000	1987	41,662	51,000
1954	28,090	25,000	1988	39,904	54,000
1955	28,320	25,000	1989	41,932	55,000
1956	28,939	25,000			

Note: In 1979 the Workers' Union of Ireland amalgamated with the Federation of Rural Workers to form the Federated Workers' Union of Ireland. The WUI was affiliated to the ITUC, 1945–59; the WUI and FWUI were affiliated to the ICTU, 1959–89.

Sources: WUI and FWUI, Annual Reports, 1947–89; ITUC, Annual Reports, 1909–59; ICTU, Annual Reports, 1959–89; Registrar of Friendly Societies, file 369T.

Table 163: Women members, 1924–89

	Number	Proportion of total (%)		Number	Proportion of total (%)
1924	—	—	1957	7,539	26.2
1925	—	—	1958	7,585	26.0
1926	—	—	1959	7,715	26.0
1927	1,071	7.3	1960	7,501	25.9
1928	945	6.2	1961	7,713	26.3
1929	1,480	9.1	1962	7,742	26.3
1930	1,115	6.5	1963	7,925	26.5
1931	1,245	7.2	1964	7,618	25.9
1932	1,005	5.9	1965	7,963	26.6
1933	925	5.3	1966	8,284	26.6
1934	—	—	1967	8,090	26.3
1935	—	—	1968	11,981	38.1
1936	1,898	12.8	1969	10,907	32.7
1937	2,028	11.9	1970	10,521	30.4
1938	1,993	11.9	1971	11,868	34.1
1939	2,140	13.0	1972	11,897	34.1
1940	2,257	14.3	1973	11,928	34.0
1941	1,870	14.9	1974	12,919	36.5
1942	1,988	18.4	1975	—	—

1943	1,774	18.7	1976	11,521	33.4
1944	1,502	17.0	1977	13,205	36.8
1945	1,464	16.0	1978	13,070	36.3
1946	—	—	1979	13,236	29.6
1947	2,686	20.3	1980	14,357	31.9
1948	3,836	21.8	1981	14,462	31.4
1949	5,044	23.5	1982	14,435	31.6
1950	6,291	25.9	1983	13,628	31.2
1951	7,053	26.7	1984	14,612	34.1
1952	7,195	25.6	1985	14,435	34.6
1953	7,118	25.9	1986	13,231	32.5
1954	7,604	27.0	1987	13,447	32.2
1955	7,600	26.8	1988	—	—
1956	7,699	26.6	1989	—	—

Source: National Archives, Registrar of Friendly Societies, file 369T.

Table 164: Income and expenditure (selected items) (£), 1924–89

	Income	Expenditure	Balance
1924	9,479	9,006	(9,007)
1925	11,942	11,204	(4,790)
1926	6,051	5,288	(4,491)
1927	12,540	7,063	(4,027)
1928	4,337	6,807	(1,019)
1929	6,335	7,164	(1,019)
1930	7,811	6,167	(829)
1931	7,957	7,538	1,236
1932	6,303	4,714	2,825
1933	7,482	6,598	3,709
1934	7,892	7,947	3,634
1935	8,678	8,701	3,630
1936	8,098	6,916	4,811
1937	15,541	15,088	5,268
1938	12,710	12,499	5,476
1939	10,996	10,894	5,578
1940	10,542	10,558	6,064
1941	9,145	9,255	5,413
1942	10,794	9,606	6,027

1943	11,127	10,686	6,468
1944	13,496	13,340	6,615
1945	15,029	18,480	3,164
1946	18,080	14,599	6,644
1947	25,358	18,540	13,462
1948	32,017	21,899	23,952
1949	31,637	25,751	29,837
1950	34,482	24,174	40,145
1951	37,597	27,248	49,371
1952	38,825	28,413	59,783
1953	35,859	29,413	66,261
1954	35,892	32,038	71,115
1955	39,791	31,903	78,003
1956	50,571	36,987	91,587
1957	49,900	40,230	101,252
1958	53,932	43,572	109,252
1959	58,345	55,738	111,895
1960	63,380	55,206	120,069
1961	64,851	67,231	117,690
1962	67,761	53,417	96,790*
1963	74,697	70,431	125,506
1964	85,589	82,390	123,506
1965	101,080	87,949	137,973
1966	120,696	119,066	131,772
1967	119,977	90,623	165,562
1968	126,923	126,544	178,618
1969	136,684	168,894	164,119
1970	152,786	127,465	166,270
1971	208,678	151,656	219,947
1972	234,971	160,375	243,996
1973	285,532	171,493	242,239
1974	315,448	284,345	234,516
1975	404,039	288,002	273,711
1976	536,014	378,137	302,983
1977	558,914	439,708	566,415
1978	593,819	692,577	469,314
1979	827,238	633,389	414,054
1980	1,008,275	833,384	471,515
1981	1,189,423	1,064,487	386,287

1982	1,379,973	1,358,398	366,243
1983	1,630,244	1,520,103	370,751
1984	2,118,743	1,892,927	477,486
1985	2,389,096	2,483,681	652,764
1986	2,544,286	2,422,380	723,390
1987	2,813,219	2,587,747	801,193
1988	2,962,032	2,901,919	890,678
1989	3,234,816	2,616,191	1,023,072

*From this point the figure is for value of investments.
Source: National Archives, Registrar of Friendly Societies, file 369T, Workers' Union of Ireland.

Table 165: Members' receipts, Dispute Pay and staff salaries as proportion of total income, 1924–89

	Members' receipts (%)	Dispute Pay (%)	Staff salaries (%)
1924	97.7	55.0	18.5
1925	78.1	78.2	21.0
1926	98.2	0.7	46.2
1927	57.3	1.0	33.2
1928	100.0	26.7	59.5
1929	82.8	23.0	31.6
1930	73.7	10.0	41.7
1931	100.0	18.7	28.3
1932	99.9	15.5	27.6
1933	100.0	21.3	40.8
1934	100.0	31.2	33.4
1935	100.0	29.8	31.4
1936	100.0	8.6	37.9
1937	100.0	39.1	19.6
1938	100.0	21.5	31.2
1939	100.0	16.8	38.2
1940	100.0	13.9	38.6
1941	100.0	1.2	44.5
1942	100.0	0.1	38.0
1943	100.0	0.0	45.6
1944	88.4	2.8	39.2
1945	89.1	47.8	33.2
1946	87.6	3.6	27.9
1947	89.7	4.9	29.8

1948	91.3	1.5	31.8
1949	89.8	12.8	34.4
1950	97.5	2.9	31.2
1951	96.8	5.3	33.0
1952	96.2	1.2	32.8
1953	95.5	2.7	36.9
1954	94.7	4.2	38.2
1955	93.6	2.2	36.8
1956	94.5	0.6	33.2
1957	94.2	0.4	35.3
1958	93.6	3.2	35.9
1959	93.9	13.2	34.2
1960	92.4	6.2	33.9
1961	88.9	23.0	34.5
1962	98.6	6.7	36.8
1963	98.8	18.5	36.6
1964	98.8	14.1	38.4
1965	98.6	18.1	32.0
1966	93.0	35.5	29.3
1967	99.2	5.1	32.5
1968	99.2	31.5	33.3
1969	99.1	50.2	36.9
1970	99.0	6.0	39.9
1971	99.3	6.3	34.9
1972	99.6	2.7	33.4
1973	99.2	0.1	31.1
1974	99.1	20.9	34.6
1975	99.7	2.1	38.3
1976	99.8	8.6	35.0
1977	99.7	5.8	37.5
1978	99.4	38.7	43.3
1979	99.6	0.3	41.6
1980	99.6	0.6	46.1
1981	99.6	3.4	47.1
1982	99.7	5.5	51.3
1983	98.6	3.6	51.6
1984	96.1	10.4	44.4
1985	93.0	2.1	45.5
1986	95.1	5.6	46.2

1987	95.4	4.0	46.1
1988	94.3	4.6	43.4
1989	94.9	*n.a.*	43.1

Source: National Archives, Registrar of Friendly Societies, file 369T, WUI and FWUI.

Services, Industrial, Professional and Technical Union

Table 166: Membership, 1990–2007

	SIPTU	ICTU *affiliation*	RFS	*Women*
1990	200,000	205,000	207,227	74,601
1991	208,417	206,001	208,417	79,198
1992	209,703	197,502	209,703	76,687
1993	213,159	197,502	213,159	81,004
1994	213,476	197,502	213,476	81,120
1995	218,936	197,502	218,936	86,917
1996	226,170	197,502	226,170	88,206
1997	230,006	197,502	230,006	92,024
1998	237,462	197,502	237,462	97,501
1999	243,064	197,502	243,064	102,086
2000	248,938	206,871	248,938	102,065
2001	247,960	206,871	247,960	101,744
2002	246,911	206,871	246,911	93,826
2003	250,351	206,871	250,351	95,150
2004	249,454	206,871	249,454	99,782
2005	246,634	206,871	246,634	93,734
2006	248,171	206,871	248,171	94,305
2007	253,271	206,871	253,271	97,510

Sources: SIPTU, Annual Reports, 1990–2009; ICTU, Annual Reports, 1990–2009; Registrar of Friendly Societies, file 598T.

Table 167: Dispute Benefit, 1990–2007

	Dispute Benefit (£)	*Dispute Grants (£)*	*Benefit and grants as proportion of income (%)*	
1990	158,923	—	158,923	1.1
1991	129,748	6,983	136,731	0.9
1992	295,248	10,776	306,024	2.0
1993	162,001	6,397	168,398	1.0

1994	112,066	3,319	115,385	0.6
1995	93,377	7,939	101,316	0.5
1996	267,161	10,639	277,800	1.5
1997	138,590	23,812	162,402	0.8
1998	115,596	12,785	128,381	0.6
1999	910,581	25,347	935,928	4.4
2000	285,456	—	285,456	1.3
2001	346,865	1,270	348,135	1.2
2002	720,266	14,000	734,266	2.5
2003	317,430	—	317,430	1.0
2004	202,838	—	202,838	0.5
2005	61,310	—	61,310	0.1
2006	242,375	—	242,375	0.6
2007	98,998	—	98,998	0.2

Note: From 2001 accounts change from Irish pounds to euros.
Source: SIPTU, Annual Reports, 1990–2007.

Comparative figures for ITGWU, WUI and FWUI, SIPTU, and other unions

Table 168: Memberships, 1909–2007

	ITUC	CIU	ICTU	ITGWU	WUI/FWUI	ITGWU/SIPTU as proportion of Congress (%)
1909	89,000	—	—	1,200	—	1.3
1910	n.a.	—	—	5,000	—	n.a.
1911	50,000	—	—	18,000	—	36.0
1912	70,000	—	—	22,000	—	31.4
1913	100,000	—	—	30,000	—	30.0
1914	110,000	—	—	15,000	—	13.6
1915	n.a .	—	—	10,000	—	n.a.
1916	120,000	—	—	5,000	—	4.1
1917	150,000	—	—	15,000	—	10.0
1918	250,000	—	—	67,000	—	26.8
1919	270,000	—	—	66,000	—	24.4
1920	229,000	—	—	100,000	—	43.6
1921	196,000	—	—	100,000	—	51.0
1922	189,000	—	—	100,000	—	52.9
1923	183,000	—	—	100,000	—	54.6
1924	175,000	—	—	89,000	15,800	50.8

1925	149,000	—	—	61,000	16,750	40.9
1926	123,000	—	—	40,000	17,200	32.5
1927	113,000	—	—	35,000	14,500	30.9
1928	103,000	—	—	30,000	15,100	29.1
1929	92,000	—	—	20,000	16,200	21.7
1930	102,000	—	—	20,000	16,900	19.6
1931	102,000	—	—	20,000	17,200	19.6
1932	95,000	—	—	20,000	16,700	21.0
1933	95,000	—	—	20,000	17,300	21.0
1934	115,000	—	—	25,000	16,700	22.7
1935	125,000	—	—	30,000	15,700	24.0
1936	134,000	—	—	30,000	14,800	22.3
1937	146,000	—	—	32,000	17,000	21.9
1938	161,000	—	—	36,000	16,700	22.3
1939	162,000	—	—	36,000	16,400	22.2
1940	163,000	—	—	36,000	15,600	22.1
1941	173,000	—	—	36,000	12,500	20.8
1942	164,000	—	—	36,000	10,000	21.9
1943	183,000	—	—	36,000	9,000	19.6
1944	187,000	—	—	36,000	8,000	19.2
1945	146,000	—	—	—	8,000	n.a.
1946	147,000	—	—	—	8,000	n.a.
1947	151,000	—	—	—	8,000	n.a.
1948	181,000	131,400	312,400	95,000	15,000	30.4
1949	196,000	143,600	339,600	108,000	15,000	31.8
1950	197,000	169,622	366,622	130,000	15,000	35.4
1951	210,000	170,601	380,601	130,000	25,000	34.1
1952	214,000	179,223	393,223	148,442	25,000	37.7
1953	209,000	183,385	392,385	148,442	25,000	37.8
1954	211,000	189,575	400,575	150,000	25,000	37.4
1955	218,000	193,479	411,479	150,000	25,000	36.4
1956	221,000	192,905	413,905	150,000	25,000	36.2
1957	222,000	199,991	421,991	150,000	25,000	35.5
1958	226,000	187,968	413,968	150,000	25,000	36.2
1959	224,000	187,340	411,840	150,000	25,000	36.4
1960	—	—	432,000	150,000	30,000	34.7
1961	—	—	439,000	150,000	30,000	34.1
1962	—	—	440,000	150,000	30,000	34.0
1963	—	—	441,000	150,000	30,000	34.0
1964	—	—	453,000	150,000	30,000	33.1

1965	—	—	465,000	150,000	30,000	32.2
1966	—	—	472,000	150,000	30,000	31.7
1967	—	—	483,000	150,000	30,000	31.0
1968	—	—	491,000	150,000	30,000	30.5
1969	—	—	499,000	150,000	30,000	30.0
1970	—	—	510,000	150,000	30,000	29.4
1971	—	—	523,000	150,000	30,000	28.6
1972	—	—	539,000	150,000	30,000	27.8
1973	—	—	547,000	150,000	30,000	27.4
1974	—	—	570,000	150,000	50,000	26.3
1975	—	—	576,000	150,000	50,000	26.0
1976	—	—	550,000	150,000	50,000	27.2
1977	—	—	564,000	150,000	50,000	26.5
1978	—	—	604,000	150,000	50,000	24.8
1979	—	—	621,000	150,000	50,000	24.1
1980	—	—	661,000	150,000	50,000	22.6
1981	—	—	663,000	150,000	50,000	22.6
1982	—	—	641,000	150,000	50,000	23.4
1983	—	—	640,000	150,000	50,000	23.4
1984	—	—	643,000	150,000	50,000	23.3
1985	—	—	652,000	150,000	51,000	23.0
1986	—	—	666,000	150,000	51,000	22.5
1987	—	—	670,000	150,000	51,000	22.3
1988	—	—	670,000	150,000	54,000	22.3
1989	—	—	663,000	150,000	55,000	22.6
1990	—	—	679,000	205,500*	—	30.2
1991	—	—	682,000	206,000	—	30.2
1992	—	—	679,000	197,502	—	29.0
1993	—	—	679,000	197,502	—	29.0
1994†	—	—	677,650	197,502	—	29.1
1996	—	—	690,140	197,502	—	28.6
1999	—	—	710,067	197,502	—	27.8
2002	—	—	767,297	206,871	—	26.9
2007	—	—	833,486	206,871	—	24.8

*SIPTU affiliation figure.

†ICTU figures available biannually.

Sources: ITGWU, Annual Reports, 1918–89; WUI and FWUI, Annual Reports, 1947–89; ITUC, CIU and ICTU, Annual Reports, 1909–2008; National Archives, Registrar of Friendly Societies, files 275T and 329T.

Table 169: Comparative membership of general unions (Congress figures), 1909–89 (selected years)

	ITGWU	ATGWU*	IWWU	ISPWU†	WUI‡
1909	5,000	—	—	—	—
1913	30,000	—	—	—	—
1920	100,000	—	—	—	—
1925	61,000	8,000	3,000	—	16,000
1930	20,000	15,000	2,500	—	17,000
1935	30,000	25,000	4,000	3,000	16,000
1940	36,000	35,000	6,000	4,000	16,000
1945	40,000	35,000	5,000	1,000	8,000
1950	130,000	40,000	6,000	2,950	20,000
1955	150,000	40,000	6,000	5,087	25,000
1960	150,000	45,000	6,000	6,000	30,000
1965	150,000	50,000	6,000	6,000	30,000
1970	150,000	60,000	3,000	5,000	30,000
1975	150,000	60,000	3,000	5,000	35,000
1980	150,000	60,000	3,000	4,000	50,000
1985	150,000	55,000	—	4,000	50,000
1989	150,000	55,000	—	4,000	55,000

*The ATGWU was founded in 1922.
†The ISPWU became the MPGWU.
‡Not affiliated to ITUC until 1945.
Source: ITUC, CIU and ICTU, Annual Reports, 1909–1990.

Appendix 8 ∽

DELEGATE CONFERENCES

Irish Transport and General Workers' Union

1924	Cork, 8–9 August	1957	Bundoran, 12–14 June
1925	Newry, 5–7 August	1958	Ballybunnion, 11–13 June
1926	Galway, 5–6 August	1959	Dublin, 19–22 May
1927	Dublin, 4–5 August	1960	Buncrana, 7–10 June
1928	Belfast, 9–10 August	1961	Salthill, 13–16 June
1929	Limerick, 29–30 July	1962	Killarney, 5–8 June
1930	Dublin, 27–28 July	1963	Waterford, 4–7 June

1931	Waterford, 27–28 July	1964	Cork, 9–12 June
1932	Cork, 25–26 July	1965	Kilkee, 8–11 June
1933	Killarney, 2–4 August	1966	Liberty Hall, 7–10 June
1934	'Marine', Wicklow, 26–28 May	1967	Limerick, 2–5 May
1935	'Marine', Wicklow, 25–27 May	1968	Arklow, 14–17 May
1936	Dublin, 23–25 May	1969	Wexford, 14–17 April
1937	Cork, 5–7 June	1970	Kilkee, 9–12 June
1938	Waterford, 25–27 June	1971	Galway, 8–11 June
1939	Bray, 17–19 June	1972	Waterford, 6–9 June
1940	Galway, 8–10 June	1973	Ballybunnion, 5–8 June
1941	Drogheda, 16–18 July	1974	Bundoran, 4–7 June
1942	Dundalk, 7–8 June	1975	Wexford, 3–6 June
1943	Cork, 18–19 July	1976	Killarney, 8–11 June
1944	Bray, 4–5 July	1977	Cork, 31 May to 3 June
1945	Galway, 5–6 June	1978	Sligo, 30 May–2 June
1946	Galway, 3–5 July	1979	Salthill, 29 May to 1 June
1947	Youghal, 18–20 June	1980	Wexford, 27–30 May
1948	Killarney, 2–4 June	1981	Killarney, 26–29 May
1949	Mosney, 22–24 June	1982	Castlebar, 1–4 June
1950	Galway, 21–23 June	1983	Tralee, 31 May to 3 June
1951	Sligo, 20–22 June	1984	Liberty Hall, 29 May to 1 June
1952	Killarney, 18–20 June	1985	Cork, 28–31 May
1953	Youghal, 8–10 June	1986	Cork, 27–30 May
1954	Kilkee, 9–11 June	1987	Killarney, 27–29 May
1955	Mosney, 15–17 June	1988	Salthill, 31 May–3 June
1956	Salthill, 20–22 June	1989	Tralee, 30 May–2 June

Workers' Union of Ireland and Federated Workers' Union of Ireland

1947	Dublin, 8 June
1949	Dublin, 19 June
1950	Dublin, 21 May
1951	Dublin, 3 June
1952	Dublin, 24–25 May
1953	Dublin, 30–31 May
1954	Dublin, 29–30 May
1955	Dublin, 21–22 May
1956	Dublin, 26–27 May
1957	Dublin, 18–19 May
1958	Dublin, 17–18 May

1959	Dublin, 23–24 May
1960	Dublin, 29–30 May
1961	Dublin, 27–28 May
1962	Dublin, 26–27 May
1963	Dublin, 25–26 May
1964	Dublin, 23–24 May
1965	Dublin, 29–30 May
1966	Dublin, 14–15 May
1967	Dublin, 13–14 May
1968	Dublin, 4–5 May; Special Conference 16 November
1969	Dublin, 7–8 June
1970	Dublin, 9–10 May
1971	Dún Laoghaire, 23–24 October
1972	Wexford, 27–28 May
1973	Athlone, 26–27 May
1974	Dublin, 20–22 September
1975	Galway, 24–25 May
1976	Dún Laoghaire, 30–31 October
1977	Dublin, 11–12 June; 1977 Adjourned ADC, Dublin, 23 April
1978	Dún Laoghaire, 7–8 October
1979	Dublin, 16–17 June
1980	Cork, 13–15 June
1981	Dublin, 20–21 June
1982	Dublin, 22–23 May
1983	Dublin, 21–22 May
1984	Malahide, 19–20 May
1985	Malahide, 18–19 May
1986	Salthill, 23–25 May 1986; Reconvened ADC, Malahide, 1 November
1987	Malahide, 23–24 May
1988	Malahide, 28–29 May
1989	Special DC, Malahide, 15 April

Services, Industrial, Professional and Technical Union

1991	Killarney, 28–31 May	2001	Tralee, 2–5 October
1993	Tralee, 25–28 May	2003	Galway, 26–29 August
1995	Killarney, 3–6 October	2005	Cork, 4–7 October
1997	Ennis, 7–10 October	2007	Tralee, 2–5 October
1999	Killarney, 5–8 October		

NOTES

Abbreviations
ILHSA   Irish Labour History Society Archive
NA   National Archives
NLI   National Library of Ireland

Preface (p. ix)
1. Devine, *Understanding Social Justice* and *An Eccentric Chemistry*.
2. Devine and O'Riordan, *James Connolly, Liberty Hall and the 1916 Rising*, and Croke and Devine, *James Connolly Labour College*.
3. 'SIPTU Guide for Union Representatives' (2008) and preparations for HETAC accreditation of higher certificate in employment law and industrial relations in Ireland, delivered to staff from January 2008.

Acknowledgements (p. xi–xii)
1. They are held in the National Library of Ireland, Irish Labour History Society Archive and Pearse Street Library, Dublin. See Francis Devine, 'Labour press holdings, Pearse Street Library, Dublin,' *Saothar*, 32 (2007), p. 69–71.
2. Peter Rigney, 'Some records of the ITGWU in the National Library of Ireland,' *Saothar*, 3 (1977), p. 14–15, and Bob Purdie, 'The Kennedy/O'Brien Papers recently acquired by the NLI,' *Saothar*, 12 (1987), p. 88–90.
3. Mary Carolan, 'Expanding trade unionism: The ITGWU Library,' *Saothar*, 11 (1986), p. 101–3. The ITGWU Library is now SIPTU College Library.

Chapter 1 (P. 1–4)
1. Its full title, reflecting the amalgamating process behind it, was Amalgamated Society of Engineers, Machinists, Smiths, Millwrights and Patternmakers. It still exists, after many mergers and changes of name, as a component of Unite, now Britain's largest union, formed in 2007.
2. Lynch, *Radical Politics in Modern Ireland*.

Chapter 2 (P. 5–9)
1. Greaves, *The Irish Transport and General Workers' Union*, p. 4–6; Redmond, *The Irish Municipal Employees' Trade Union*.
2. Michael McKeown, a docker from Birkenhead, was Vice-President of the National Union of Dock Labourers, 1890, and subsequently National Organiser. Taplin, *The Dockers' Union*, p. 36, 45, 52, 168. McKeown became an ITGWU Organiser. See also Newby, *The Life and Times of Edward McHugh*, and Taplin's entries for McGhee (1851–1930) and McHugh (1853–1915) in Joyce Bellamy and John Saville, *Dictionary of Labour Biography*, vol. 5 (Basingstoke: Palgrave, 1979), and *Oxford Dictionary of*

National Biography (Oxford: Oxford University Press, 2004); also 'Irish leaders and the Liverpool dockers: Richard McGhee and Edward McHugh,' *North West Labour History Society Bulletin*, 9, 1983–4, p. 36–44. The membership of NUDL Branches in 1891 was: Belfast, 541; Carrick-on-Suir, 10; Cork, 74; Drogheda, 449; Dublin 290; Dundalk, no return; Dungarvan, 3; Enniscorthy, 3; Limerick, 5; Newry, 209; Sligo, 136; Warrenpoint, 22; Waterford, 61; and Wexford, 206.

3. Donal Nevin, 'Early years in Liverpool,' in *James Larkin*, p. 133–8. Few now insist that Larkin was born in Tamnaharry, Burren, Co. Down, in 1876, a claim that Larkin himself gave credence to during his own life but that only his grandson would insist on: James Larkin, *In the Footsteps of Big Jim*; Taplin, *The Dockers' Union*, p. 68. See also Eric Taplin, 'James Larkin, Liverpool, and the National Union of Dock Labourers: The apprenticeship of a revolutionary,' *Saothar*, 4 (1978), p. 1–8; and Eric Taplin, 'Liverpool: The apprenticeship of a revolutionary,' in Nevin, *James Larkin*, p. 17–22.

4. Taplin, *The Dockers' Union*, p. 69–; National Union of Dock Labourers, Executive Report for the Year Ending 31 December 1906, cited by Taplin, p. 71; James Sexton, *Sir James Sexton*, p. 203–4.

5. Greaves, *The Irish Transport and General Workers' Union*, p. 12–13. The Delegates were Thomas Cupples, John Quinn and John Davidson—names that would feature in subsequent ITGWU ledgers. John Gray, 'City in revolt: Belfast, 1907,' in Nevin, *James Larkin*, p. 23; National Union of Dock Labourers, Executive Report for the Year Ending 31 December 1907, cited by Taplin in *The Dockers' Union*, p. 72–3.

6. Taplin in Nevin, *James Larkin*, p. 22.

7. John Gray, 'City in revolt: Belfast, 1907,' in Nevin, *James Larkin*, p. 205–6.

8. Gray, *City in Revolt*.

9. Irish Trades Union Congress, Report of 15th Annual Congress, Belfast, 8–10 June 1908, p. 25, 36, 42–3. On housing reform, Larkin supported the motion but called for the 'socialisation of land and dwellings,' saying that 'no man had any legal, moral or divine right to own anything in the way of property or land'; on the brushes issue, p. 39; seconding E. L. Richardson's motion on insurance, p. 53; seconding the motion on factory reform, p. 57.

10. NLI, William O'Brien Papers, ms. 1,679 (16), note attached to the *Peasant*, 16 May 1908, and ms. 16,273; NA, CSORP 26, 870 (1908), cited by Cody et al., *The Parliament of Labour*, p. 63; and Francis Devine in Donal Nevin, *James Larkin*, p. 30–37.

Part 1 (p. 11–15)

1. O'Connor, *A Labour History of Ireland*, p. 104.

2. Fleming and O'Day, *Longman Handbook of Modern Irish History since 1800*, p. 489–515.

3. Fleming and O'Day, *Longman Handbook of Modern Irish History since 1800*, p. 489–515.

4. Fleming and O'Day, *Longman Handbook of Modern Irish History since 1800*, p. 570–71.

5. Francis Devine and Emmet O'Connor, 'The course of labour history,' *Saothar*, 12 (1987), p. 2–4.

6. ITGWU, Annual Report for 1918, p. 5–7.

Chapter 3 (p. 16–26)

1. Greaves, *The Irish Transport and General Workers' Union*, p. 25 and NA, Registrar of Friendly Societies, file 275T; *Freeman's Journal*, 14, 18 Jan. 1909; *Irish Nation and the Peasant*, 2 Jan. 1909. Like today, unless they were in dispute trade unions were rarely considered newsworthy. NLI, William O'Brien Papers, ms. 15,705 (2); an examination of these diaries, however, suggests that not all entries were necessarily made contemporaneously, and so this entry may have been added at a later date. Greaves, *The Irish Transport and General Workers' Union*, p. 26–7. See evidence of O'Brien in Saorstát Éireann, High Court of Justice, Chancery Division, Master of the Rolls, 1923, No. 446, in NLI, ITGWU, C. Desmond Greaves Papers, arc. 6157, box 3. See also ITGWU, Rules, 1912, Rule 1. Badges are in Francis Devine collection, Dublin; see also John B. Smethurst and Francis Devine, 'Trade union badges: Mere emblems or means of membership control?' *Saothar*, 7 (1981), p. 83–96.

2. Clarkson, *Labour and Nationalism in Ireland*, p. 221, n. 4; O'Casey, *Drums Under the Windows*, p. 223.

3. O'Brien, *Forth the Banners Go*, p. 54–. Joseph Harris was a Dubliner but had been active for the Upholsterers' Union on Belfast Trades Council. He then organised for the Workers' Union but, having taken in textile operatives, ran foul of Mary Galway. The affiliation of the Workers' Union to Belfast Trades Council was rejected, and he turned his attention to Dublin. Having failed to persuade Larkin to allow seceded Irish Branches of the Workers' Union into the nascent ITGWU, Harris became an opponent. The Workers' Union was disaffiliated from the Irish Trades Union Congress, and Harris disappeared. See Hyman, *The Workers' Union*. Larkin said 'he intended first to organise the Transport Workers in every port in Ireland before asking any man to sacrifice his position. When he had accomplished that he would then ask assistance of others to make a general workers' union.' NLI, O'Brien Papers, ms. 16,274, diary entry.

4. *Freeman's Journal*, 18 Jan. 1909; Greaves, *The Irish Transport and General Workers' Union*, p. 28. See also Sexton, *Sir James Sexton*; NLI, William O'Brien Papers, ms. 15,679 (16).

5. Emmet Larkin, *James Larkin*, p. 49–50; Francis Devine, 'Larkin and the ITGWU, 1909–1912,' in Donal Nevin, *James Larkin*, p. 32.

6. NLI, O'Brien Papers, ms. 16,273; O'Shannon, *Fifty Years of Liberty Hall*, p. 15.

7. Bohan was Secretary of Dublin No. 3 Branch and O'Neill of Dublin No. 1 Branch; Kelly was General Treasurer; Clarke and Hewson were members of Dublin No. 1 Branch Committee; and Ennis was caretaker of Liberty Hall.

8. Irish Transport and General Workers' Union, *The Attempt to Smash the Irish Transport and General Workers' Union*, p. xii.

9. *The Harp*, Mar. 1909; NLI, O'Brien Papers, ms. 13,908, Connolly to O'Brien, 5 July 1909; *Irish Nation and the Peasant*, 2 Jan. 1909.

10. *Evening Telegraph* (Dublin), 10 Jan. 1909; *News Letter* (Belfast), 15 Jan. 1909; *Freeman's Journal*, 13 Jan. 1909, cited by William McMullen, 'Early days in Belfast,' *Liberty*, June 1977; ITGWU, Annual Report for 1918, p. 5; Patterson, *Class Conflict and Sectarianism in Belfast*, p. 77.

11. *Freeman's Journal*, 14, 15 and 18 Jan. 1909, 15 Feb. 1909; NA, CO 904/77, microfilm MFA 54/39, Inspector-General's Report, Feb. 1909.

12. *Freeman's Journal*, 17 and 19 Feb. 1909, 2 Mar. 1909.

13. NLI, ms. 12,781, minutes of Dublin Trades Council, Mar. 1909; Irish Trades Union Congress, Report of 15th Annual Meeting, Limerick, 30 May to 2 June 1909; report also published in *Irish Labour Journal,* 19 June 1909, p. 13–: 'In their last report your Committee made reference to Belfast Dock Labourers' Lock-Out, in which Mr. Larkin was engaged as an Official of the National Union of Dock Labourers. Subsequently further trouble of a similar nature arose both in Dublin and Cork, which led to friction between the Officials of the National Union and Mr. Larkin, culminating at a later date in the starting in the three centres mentioned of another union under the name of the "Irish Transport Workers' Union" with Mr. Larkin as Organiser, and which, your Committee are informed was largely made up of former members of the National Union. Your Committee were neither appraised nor consulted regarding these transactions. At their meeting of 13th February they received a letter signed Michael MacKeown, Secretary, "Irish Transport Workers' Union," from 11 Victoria Street, Belfast, requesting them "to appoint a Sub-Committee to inquire into the merits of the dispute between the Irish Transport Workers' Union and the National Union of Dock Labourers in Belfast—the members of the last-named union are at present blacklegging on the members of the former union." After considerable discussion, the matter was remitted to the Belfast Trades Council, and it was further decided, Mr. Larkin dissenting, that, pending a settlement of the dispute, no invitation to attend the Congress be sent to the Transport Workers' Union.' The Committee was Mitchell (Belfast), Patrick Murphy (Cork Trades Council), MacCallion (Derry) and Daly (elected from the floor), with E. W. Stewart, Michael O'Lehane (Drapers' Assistants) and E. L. Richardson representing the Parliamentary Committee.

14. Greaves, *The Irish Transport and General Workers' Union,* p. 39; NA, CO 904/77–79, microfilm MFA 54/39–41, Inspector-General's Report, May–Sep. 1909. Lumps of coal were used as missiles. *Cork Examiner,* 14–17 June 1909; *Dublin Trades and Labour Journal,* 26 June 1909; *Cork Examiner,* 19 June 1909, *Irish Labour Journal,* 14 Aug. 1909; Keogh, *The Rise of the Irish Working Class,* p. 142, and McCamley, *The Third James,* p. 18–19.

15. Paul Starrett, 'The ITGWU in its Industrial and Political Context, 1909–1923,' DPhil thesis, University of Ulster, 1986, p. 35. See also *Saothar,* 12 (1987), p. 92–3.

Chapter 4 (P. 27–51)

1. NA, Registrar of Friendly Societies, file 275T. Greaves, *The Irish Transport and General Workers' Union,* p. 55, extrapolating from the 1915 rolls, finds that 160 joined in 1909 and 120 in 1910 and that an estimate of the strength of the Branch was 2,700 at the end of the year. *Irish Worker,* 29 July and 19 Aug. 1911.

2. *Irish Worker,* 24 and 31 May, 3 and 10 June, 19 and 26 Aug. and 7 Oct. 1911; Greaves, *The Irish Transport and General Workers' Union,* p. 66–7. Keena's labourers, 2s; David Allen (billposting), 2s; sandwich-men, 3d a day; Taylor's Mineral Water, 2s; Bewley's and Draper's, wine stores and ink manufacturers, 2s; Halligan's, millers, 2s; draymen, 5s; Paul and Vincent, granted 2s, having 'anticipated the men's demands'; Barrington's Soap Works, 2s; Dixon's Soap and Candles, 2s; Gallagher's, master carriers, 6s; Brooks Thomas, builders' providers, 2s; Watkins, Jameson, Pim, brewers, 2s; D'Arcy's Brewery, 2s; Burns and Laird Line, dockers' increase. Greene topped

the poll, with 703; O'Toole was third elected; Lawlor topped the poll; and O'Carroll was second elected out of four. Greene's letter of resignation said it was because of the 'amount of responsibility' arising from his union duties and those of a Poor Law Guardian. He wished the union well and said he had 'always considered it a pleasure to be connected' with Larkin.

3. *Irish Worker*, 13 Jan. 1912, 17 Feb. 1912, 16 Mar. 1912, 6 Apr. 1912, 22 June 1912, 24 and 31 Aug. 1912, 5 Oct. 1912; Greaves, *The Irish Transport and General Workers' Union*, p. 81–2. The premises were at 35 Lower George's Street. The Engineering Machinists, whose Secretary was M. Devlin, had members in Dublin Port and Docks Board, Tonge and Taggart, Spencer, and Ross and Walpole, while the Printing Section, whose Secretary was D. Phillips, had members in Thom's, Hely's, Eason's, Sackville Press, Shuley's, Faulkner's, and Humphrey and Armour's.

4. The signatories of the Rules were James Larkin, Tom Foran, John Bohan, John O'Neill, Peter Ennis (caretaker, Liberty Hall), Joseph Kelly, Stephen Clarke and Thomas Hewson. For descriptions of these meetings see Greaves, *The Irish Transport and General Workers' Union*, p. 344, n. 4, and Helga Woggon, *Ellen Grimley (Nellie Gordon): Reminiscences of Her Work with James Connolly in Belfast*, (Dublin?, 2000). A meeting was held in the Supper Room of the Mansion House under the auspices of the Lord Mayor, Lorcan Sherlock, and attended by Officials of the ITGWU and Dublin Trades Council. *Irish Worker*, 31 May 1913, 26 July 1913 and 2 and 27 Aug. 1913. Nevin, *Trade Union Century*, p. 433.

5. Greaves, *The Irish Transport and General Workers' Union*, p. 52–5, insists that it was Larkin who selected Daly in his place, which is most probable, as Larkin was all-powerful in the union. *Irish Worker*, 7 Oct. 1913; NLI, ITGWU Special List A8, dossier on Daly; O'Brien Papers, ms. 15,672 (3), part 1; Séamus Cody, 'The remarkable Patrick Daly,' *Obair*, 2, Jan. 1985, p. 10–11.

6. O'Brien, *Forth the Banners Go*, p. 65–; Greaves, *The Irish Transport and General Workers' Union*, p. 52–3.

7. Irish Trades Union Congress, Report of 17th Congress, 17–18 May, Dundalk, 1910; Report of 18th Congress, Galway, 5–6 June 1911; Report of 19th Congress, Clonmel, 27–28 May 1912, p. 12–13, 45, 61; Report of 20th Congress, Cork, 12–13 May 1913, p. 3–4, 77–8; *Irish Worker*, 8 June 1912; Greaves, *The Irish Transport and General Workers' Union*, p, 44–50, 58. The Delegates were James Larkin, Joe Metcalfe, Mick McCarthy, Barney Conway, Michael Brohoon and William Fairtlough, Dublin No. 1 Branch; John Bohan and Thomas Burke, Dublin No. 3 Branch; Edward Gibson, Dublin No. 16 Branch (Aungier Street); James Connolly, Belfast; James Stanford and P. T. Daly, Sligo; and James Byrne, Kingstown [Dún Laoghaire].

8. *Irish Worker*, 12 and 19 Aug. 1911, 9 Sep. 1911, 23 Dec. 1911, 6 Apr. 1912. See also Jones, *These Obstreperous Lassies*, p. 2–5. Delia preferred 'affiliated' to the ITGWU. Jones, p. 4, cites a letter by O'Brien in the *Irish Times*, 1 May 1955. After 1918 O'Brien insisted that 'person' in Rule 5 meant either male or female. See also Theresa Moriarty, 'Larkin and the women's movement,' in Nevin, *James Larkin*, p. 95, citing William O'Brien, 'The ITGWU and the IWWU: A bit of history,' NLI, O'Brien Papers, ms. 13,970.

9. *Irish Worker*, 15 and 22 July 1911. His speech ranged over the gunboat attack on dockers in Hull twenty years previously and Mark Daly's brutal suppression of miners in Butte, Montana. The 'scab' firms were Heiton and Company, J. J. Carroll,

Flower M'Donald, S. N. Robinson, Coal and Steamship Company, and Arley Coal Company. Union firms included Dublin Steamship Company, W. W. Robinson and Son, Nuzum Brothers, John M'Carthy, Dublin Coal Company, Diamond Coal Company, Dickson, and P. Murphy. Shipping firms approved by the union were Bristol Steamers, Messrs Dickson, Henry McDermott, Patrick O'Carroll (Inchicore), Michael Murphy, Cardiff Steamers, Gale Line of Steamers, and Manchester Line of Steamers.

10. *Irish Worker,* 29 July 1911, 19 Aug. 1911, 23 and 30 Sep. 1911, and 7 Oct. 1911. Francis Devine, 'Larkin and the ITGWU, 1910–1912,' in Nevin, *James Larkin,* p. 36–7; Preface, ITGWU Rules, 1912.

11. *Irish Worker,* 15 July 1911, 2, 9 and 16 Sep. 1911, 28 Oct. 1911, 4 and 11 Nov. 1911. The Managing Committee of the infirmary passed a motion of sincere regret that Daly 'was greatly inconvenienced by the action of our gate-porters.' The motion was seconded by McNamee of Co. Meath. It was suggested that a hurling match be arranged between Dublin and Meath and held at Jones's Road for the Lock-Out, but it is not clear whether this occurred. Further collections were taken at other games, such as the Wexford county final, played at Ballyhogue, and Davidstown United v. Wexford Volunteers, played at Enniscorthy on 26 November. *Irish Worker,* 25 Nov. 1911.

12. *Irish Worker,* 11, 18 and 25 Nov. 1911, 2 Dec. 1911, 10 and 17 Feb. 1912, 9 Mar. 1912, 6 Apr. 1912. Presumably the men were wearing the only button available, the ITGWU one. Connolly said: 'We are not sticklers for the button as such but we will not allow the employers to dictate to the men as to what they will or will not wear. We will have another button.' The influence of Jim Connell's song 'The Red Flag' is fairly obvious in this chorus.

13. *Irish Worker,* 24 Feb. 1912, 2 Mar. 1912, 6 and 13 Apr. 1912; Greaves, *The Irish Transport and General Workers' Union,* p. 274; and Bill McCamley, 'Fearon and the Citizen Army,' *Liberty,* Sep. 1982. The address stated: 'We, the members of the IFWU, fellow-workers and sympathisers in Wexford, desire you to accept this address and presentation as a token of appreciation of your services in their behalf and in the cause of labour generally, and also as a mark of the recognition of the sacrifices you made for them and the unjust prosecution to which you have been subjected for vindicating their right to organise. When you came to Wexford you found an utter lack of organisation among those who toiled and helped to build up the trade and industries of the town, and when the fight began with the workers for joining the only union that was at the time open to them, you threw yourself heart and soul into the struggle on the side of labour. Your advice and Counsel gave solidarity and unity. Your unsparing efforts won the sympathy and material help of organised labour throughout Ireland and across the water—largely providing the funds that enabled them to hold out for six months and your personality inspired them and nerved them in their darkest hours. Your determination to suffer imprisonment when you were so unjustly sentenced for your espousal of the workers' cause strengthened them when strength was most needed, and now, thanks to you, they have won the right to have a recognised labour organisation. With gratitude we recall your services, sacrifices and leadership in our prolonged fight and we look on ourselves as bound to you by the brotherhood of comradeship in agitating for

workers' rights of Association in suffering, and of participation in our struggle and in our victory. Joseph Kingsberry, T. C., (Chairman); John Kehoe (Treasurer); Richard Corish (Secretary),' *Irish Worker*, 27 Jan. 1912, 17 Feb. 1912, 6 and 13 Apr. 1912.

14. *Irish Worker*, 26 Aug. 1911, 16 Sep. 1911. The movers were Campbell and James Flanagan, ITGWU.

15. *Irish Worker*, 14, 21 and 28 Oct. 1911, 18 and 25 Nov. 1911, 23 Dec. 1911, 6 July 1912, and 23 Nov. 1912.

16. *Irish Worker*, 25 May 1913, 15 June 1913. See Jones, *These Obstreperous Lassies*, p. 7–8; Francis Devine, 'Early slaves of the linen trade,' *Liberty*, Feb. 1976, p. 3; Morgan, *Labour and Partition*, p. 152–6, 165–7, 175; and, for Marie Johnson, see Gaughan, *Thomas Johnson*, p. 18–26; Greaves, *The Irish Transport and General Workers' Union*, p. 88–9.

17. *Irish Worker*, 30 Mar. 1912, 13 Apr. 1912, 29 Mar. 1913, 26 Apr. 1913, 31 May 1913; Greaves, *The Irish Transport and General Workers' Union*, p. 78–9. They were Laurence Garvey, Bernard Kelly, James Roycroft, John Roycroft, Michael Roycroft, Francis Scanlon, John Scanlon, Edward Verdon Senior, Edward Verdon Junior and Henry Verdon. See also Cunningham, *Labour in the West of Ireland*, p. 160–64.

18. Cunningham, *Labour in the West of Ireland*, p. 151–6, 168, 187; John Cunningham, 'A glimpse of the Galway Workers' and General Labourers' Union, 1913,' *Saothar*, 15 (1990), p. 109–12. Taplin, *The Dockers' Union*, p. 104, states that the Galway Dockers' Society became No. 20 Branch.

19. *Irish Worker*, 10 and 17 June 1911, 1, 8, 15 and 29 July 1911, 10 June 1912; Greaves, *The Irish Transport and General Workers' Union*, p. 59. See also L. H. Powell, *The Shipping Federation, 1890–1950: The First Sixty Years* (London: Shipping Federation, 1950).

20. *Irish Worker*, 1, 8 and 15 July 1911, 19 and 26 Aug. 1911; Greaves, *The Irish Transport and General Workers' Union*, p. 60–66. For full details of the railway strike see Conor McCabe, 'The context and course of the Irish railway disputes of 1911,' *Saothar*, 30 (2005), p. 21–31.

21. The Provisional Committee of the Dublin Employers' Federation was Edward H. Andrews, R. W. Booth JP, S. P. Boyd JP, John Brown, William Crowe, H. M. Dockrell, F. J. Fisher, D. Frame, R. K. Gamble (Chairman), Sir W. J. Goulding, T. R. McCullagh, John McIntyre, J. D. MacNamara, James Mahoney, Lawrence Malone, Frank V. Martin, William Martin Murphy JP, Thomas A. O'Farrell, J. A. Pearson, William Perrin, J. E. Robinson, J. Sibthorpe, William Wallace JP, and J. Young. *Irish Worker*, 29 July 1911.

22. *Irish Worker*, 8 Feb.1913, 1 and 15 Mar. 1913, 5 Apr. 1913; NLI, O'Brien Papers, ms. 13,908 (iii), O'Brien to Connolly, 22 Mar. and 5 June; Greaves, *The Irish Transport and General Workers' Union*, p. 85–; Emmet Larkin, *James Larkin*, p. 115–. Those who attended were Alderman J. C. McWalter, W. P. Partridge, Thomas Lawlor, T. M. O'Beirne, Miss Harrison, and L. O'Neill (all town Commissioners), Larkin, MacPartlin, Walter Halls, William O'Brien, Delia Larkin, James Connolly and Tom Foran.

23. *Irish Worker*, 15 Mar. 1913, 14 and 26 Apr. 1913. The Organiser of the Tramwaymen's Union was Quigley. Constant men, in addition, were to get 1s an hour for Sunday work to 6 a.m. and on Monday a meal hour after five hours but paid if worked.

Casuals were to get 5s for a ten-hour day, on Saturdays 5s till 2 p.m., 9d an hour thereafter, on Sundays 1s an hour and one meal hour. Checkers were to get a minimum wage the same as dockers. Sailors and firemen were to get 33s 6d per week and ordinary seamen and boys an increase of 2s 6d per week.

24. *Irish Worker*, 31 May 1913, 7, 14, 21 and 28 June 1913, 12 and 26 July 1913, 23 Aug. 1913, 11 and 25 Oct. 1913, 1 Nov. 1913, 31 Jan. 1914; Greaves, *The Irish Transport and General Workers' Union*, p. 90–91. For a broader account see Eugene Coyle, 'Larkinism and the 1913 County Dublin farm labourers' dispute,' *Dublin Historical Record*, 58, 2, autumn 2005, p. 176–90. The venues were Balbriggan, Baldoyle, Howth, Kilbarrack. Kilmainham, Kingstown (Dún Laoghaire), Sutton, Kilbarrack, Portmarnock and Swords.

25. *Irish Worker*, 27 May 1911, 28 Oct. 1911, 30 Dec. 1911; NLI, O'Brien Papers, ms. 15,651; Greaves, *The Irish Transport and General Workers' Union*, p. 64; Keogh, *The Rise of the Irish Working Class*, p. 163; O'Connor, *A Labour History of Ireland*, p. 163; and John Newsinger, 'A lamp to light your feet: Jim Larkin, the Irish Worker and the Dublin working class,' *European History Quarterly*, 20, 1990, p. 63–9. Those attending included Thomas Murphy (Carpet Planners and President of Dublin Trades Council), Bernard Hoskins, Michael McKeown, Miss Devoy, James O'Farrell, William O'Brien, P. T. Daly and James Larkin. Connolly to O'Brien, cited in Irish Transport and General Workers' Union, *The Attempt to Smash the Irish Transport and General Workers' Union*, p. 163.

26. *Irish Worker*, 24 Feb. 1912, 8 Feb. 1913, 26 July 1913, 2 Aug. 1913. Greaves, *The Irish Transport and General Workers' Union*, p. 343, n. 10, says he was unable to establish who gave Liberty Hall its name but points out that the 'expression occurs in Goldsmith's *She Stoops to Conquer* in an English context' and was used by the writer 'Captain [Frederick] Marryat in *Midshipman Easy* in order to satirise radicalism. It is a tale of the sea, and probably Larkin read it like most other Victorian schoolboys.'

27. *Irish Worker*, 20 and 27 Apr. 1912, 22 and 29 June 1912.

28. *Irish Worker*, 27 May 1911, 13 Jan. 1912, and 4, 11, 18 and 25 Jan. 1913. Lynch was returned in Sligo and James Goodison, Dick Corish, Myles Bergin, John Walsh and Mick Martin in Wexford.

29. *Irish Worker*, 4 Jan. 1913.

Chapter 5 (P. 52–65)

1. Fergus D'Arcy, 'Larkin and the Dublin Lock-Out,' in Donal Nevin, *James Larkin*, p. 38–47; Greaves, *The Irish Transport and General Workers' Union*, p. 92–121; Keogh, *The Rise of the Irish Working Class*; Nevin, 1913; Newsinger, *Rebel City*; and Yeates, *Lockout*.

2. *Report of the Constitution Review Group* (Dublin: Stationery Office, 1997).

3. NLI, O'Brien Papers, ms. 27,034; Keogh, *The Rise of the Irish Working Class*, p. 401.

4. Yeates, *Lockout*, p. xvii–xxx.

5. See McCamley, *Dublin's Tram Workers*.

6. Registered as 100T in 1890, the Dublin and District Tramwaymen's Trade Union actually affiliated to the Irish Trades Union Congress, 1894–1896, but had collapsed by 1905. See Ward-Perkins, *Select Guide to Trade Union Records in Dublin*, p. 248; NLI, LO p83, 'Meeting of motormen, etc.'; *Irish Worker*, 26 July 1913, 6 Dec. 1913.

7. See Andy Bielenberg, 'Entrepreneurship, power and public opinion in Ireland: The career of William Martin Murphy,' at www.ucc.ie/chronicon/bielen.htm; Dermot Keogh, 'William M. Murphy and the Origins of the 1913 Lock-out,' *Saothar*, 4 (1978), p. 15–34; Donal Nevin, 'The clash of titans: James Larkin and William Martin Murphy,' in *James Larkin*, p. 47–55; Dónal McCartney, 'William Martin Murphy: An Irish press baron and the rise of the popular press,' in Brian Farrell (ed.), *Communications and Community in Ireland* (Cork: Mercier Press, 1984); and Morrissey, *William Martin Murphy*.

8. Cited by Breandán Mac Giolla Choille in 'Dublin labour troubles,' *Intelligence Notes*, 1913–16, *Preserved in the State Paper Office* (Dublin: Stationery Office, 1966).

9. Members of the Irish Women Workers' Union set off in brakes for a picnic at the Scalp.

10. John Newsinger, "'The Devil it was who sent Larkin to Ireland': *The Liberator*, Larkinism and the Dublin Lockout of 1913,' *Saothar*, 18 (1993), p. 101–6, and "'The curse of Larkinism': Patrick McIntyre, the *Toiler* and the Dublin Lock-out,' *Éire-Ireland*, 30 (3), 1995, p. 90–102.

11. NLI, William O'Brien Papers, ms. 13,921, Larkin to C. W. Bowerman, TUC, 13 Oct. 1913; ITGWU Special List A8, ms. 13,913 (1). The Bottle Makers had 45 members affected and were paying 15s a week; Brick and Stone Layers, 475 out and weekly levy on the rest; General Union of Carpenters, 65 out, paying 14s; Farriers, 9 out and 'financial position good'; Iron Founders, 40 out, 5s; Marble Polishers, 14 out, small levy; Iron Moulders, 56 out, 6s levy; Packing-Case Makers, 32 out, 8s, 'able to pay'; United Smiths, 20 out, 'able to pay'; Amalgamated Painters, 4 out, not entitled, as 'came out without sanction'; Electricians, 10 out, able to pay; Paviours, seven out, 'no funds'; Mineral Water Operatives, 2 out, 10s, 'able until Christmas'; Plasterers, 74 out, 120 still working; Plumbers, 12 out, able to pay; Saddlers, 3 out, 'continue for some time'; Sawyers, 128 out, can pay; Slaters, 40 out, 12s, 'pay for some time'; Stationary Engine Drivers, 98 out, 15s, 'pay for some time'; Amalgamated Society of Railway Servants, 300 out, 15s and 10s, able to pay. The figures for the UBLTU were 568 at 5s and 572 at 4s, a total of 1,140 on 22 December 1913, 1,146 on 29 December, 1,180 on 6 January, 1,164 on 12 January, and 1,154 on 20 January; Jimmy Sweeney, 'The Dublin lock out, 1913: The response of British labour,' *Saothar*, 6 (1980), p. 104–8; Jonathan K. Saunders, *Across Frontiers: International Support for the Miners' Strike* (London: Canary, 1989), p. 82–93, 207–10. Pádraig Yeates draws attention to the sterling efforts of J. A. Seddon and Harry Gosling of the TUC in the food effort and in attempting settlements.

12. NLI, ms. 7,298, ITGWU, No. 1 Branch Minute Book, Oct. 1913 to June 1914; NLI, ITGWU Special List A8, ms. 13,913 (1) and ms. 15,676 (1); NLI, William O'Brien Papers, ms. 15,681 (1). The UBLTU received £283 on 1 November, £144 on 8 November, £177 on 15 November, £249 on 22 November, £254 on 29 November, £250 on 6 December, £230 on 13 December, £252 on 20 December, £257 on 3 January and £266 on 10 January. The Bricklayers, for the same dates, received, £103, £103, £103, £103, £114, £118, £130, £132, £132 and £135. The Plasterers received £7 on 1 November and then £17 to 20 December and £22 and £30 in January. The Paviours received £1 15s on 2–29 November, then 15s to the end. The ASCJ got £50 for 15 November to 20 December, then £60. The SED received £13 on 22 November, £30 on 29 November, £20 on 6 December, £21 for 13–20 December and thereafter £27 10s. The

Stonecutters got sporadic payments: £7 10s on 22 November, £1 10s on 13 December and £11 10s for 3–10 January. The Amalgamated Painters got £5 for 22–29 November and the ASE £1 15s for 3–10 January. The NSFU got £80 on 10 January. The United Builders' Labourers' Union received £3,371 1s 9d, the Brick and Stone Layers' Trade Union £1,606 9s, the Amalgamated Carpenters' Society £510, the Stationary Engine Drivers' Society £246 16s 10d, the Operative Plasterers' and Allied Trades Society of Ireland £245, the National Sailors' and Firemen's Union £195, the Stonecutters' Union of Ireland £69 5s, the Paviours' Society £13, the Amalgamated Painters' Society £10, the Amalgamated Society of Engineers £6 15s and the Marble Polishers' Society £1 2s 6d. Administrative deductions were low, at £212 8s 4d, and a cash balance of £33 4s 5d remained. See O'Riordan, *Next to the Revolution*.

13. *Irish Worker*, 11 and 25 Oct. 1913.
14. *Irish Worker*, 22 and 29 Nov. 1913, 13 and 20 Dec. 1913.
15. Greaves, *The Irish Transport and General Workers' Union*, p. 120.
16. *Irish Worker*, 22 Nov. 1913, 13 and 27 Dec. 1913; *Freeman's Journal*, 14 Nov. 1913; *Irish Times*, 14 Nov. 1913. The reference to Ulster was to Carson's open drilling of the Ulster Volunteer Force. It has been suggested that the Citizen Army had its origins in the dockside battles in Cork in 1909, or in the resistance to police repression in Wexford, 1911–12, but it finally came after the events in Dublin of Bloody Sunday, 31 August 1913, with various vague suggestions being made in September and October. John Hanratty recalled that in mid-October five hundred strikers went to the ITGWU social premises at Croydon Park, Clontarf, to register, but nothing happened until after Connolly's November speech. See D. R. O'Connor Lysaght, 'The Irish Citizen Army, 1913–1916: White, Connolly and Larkin,' *History Ireland*, Mar.–Apr. 2006, p. 16–21; J. R. White, *Misfit*. White was born in Broughshane, Co. Antrim, in 1879, son of Field-Marshal Sir George Stuart White, 'Hero of Ladysmith.' Jack followed the family's military tradition, joined the British army, saw action in the Anglo-Boer War and was decorated for bravery in 1901. He resigned his Commission in 1909, opposed Carson's 'bigotry and stagnation' and, with Roger Casement, attempted to rally Protestant opinion to Home Rule. Drawn to Dublin, he met Connolly and converted to socialism. He joined the Irish Volunteers but after the Easter Rising went to Wales and after involvement in a miners' dispute received a prison sentence of three months. He was associated with the Socialist Party of Ireland, 1919, the Irish Worker League, 1923, Workers' Party of Ireland, 1926, and Revolutionary Workers' Groups, 1933. In London he was active with Sylvia Pankhurst's Workers' Socialist Federation, and he was a founder-member of the Irish Secular Society, 1933. In 1936 he joined the Republican Congress and organised a Dublin Branch consisting of former British servicemen (the other five Branches in the city corresponded to IRA battalions). He claimed to have participated in the Spanish Civil War, but there is no supporting evidence. In London he joined the anarchist group that produced *Freedom* and was 'one of the Organisers of the regular meetings at the National Trade Union Club' against Italian fascists and for Spanish anarchists. He was associated with Emma Goldman and various anarcho-syndicalist groups until his death in 1946.
17. NLI, ms. 7,298, ITGWU, minutes of Dublin No. 1 Branch, Jan.–July 1914. Robbins, *Under the Starry Plough*, p. 27–.

18. *Irish Worker,* 28 Nov. 1914.
19. Francis Devine, 'The 1913 Lock-Out: A brief history,' at www.siptu.ie/AboutsIPTU/ History/The1913Lock-Out.
20. Irish Trades Union Congress, Report of 21st Congress, Dublin, 1–3 June 1914, p. 37; *Irish Worker,* 17 Jan. 1914.
21. *Irish Worker,* 24 Jan. 1914.

Chapter 6 (P. 66–81)

1. NLI, ms. 7,298, ITGWU, minutes of Dublin No. 1 Branch, 22 and 27 Feb. 1914, 3 and 17 Mar. 1914, 14 and 28 Apr. 1914. Members of the sub-Committee were John Cunningham, William Fairtlough, Joseph Byrne, Patrick Doyle and James Foran. Barney Conway proposed the action. Three men—W. Moore, D. Ward and P. Doyle—appeared before the Committee to explain that they had been 'deceived' and 'would not follow the O'Connell Band until permitted by the Union.'
2. NLI, ITGWU Special List A8, ms. 13,910. He also enquired after the welfare of Lynch's family. NLI, ms. 13,931, correspondence, 26 Oct. 1914 to 7 Dec. 1915; *Irish Worker,* 21 Mar. 1914; Irish Transport and General Workers' Union, *The Attempt to Smash the Irish Transport and General Workers' Union,* p. xviii–xix. The Bill included Jem Young (Irish middleweight champion) v. Jem Smith, Canning Town; Frank Dwyer, Dublin, v. Young Thorogood, Canning Town; Kid Doyle, Dublin, v. Young Burke, Birkenhead; and Young Bell, Liverpool, v. Tom Graham, Birmingham.
3. *The Worker,* 2 Jan. 1915. The representatives were James Byrne, John Dillon, John Farrell, Thomas Fitzsimons and Patrick Maguire (coal-porters), Cooling (City of Dublin Steam Packet Company), Matthew Byrne, Andrew Molloy and John Milloy (cross-channel), Michael McCarthy, Thomas O'Brien and Charles Smith (general carriers), Jack Dunne (Morgan Mooney), Michael Fitzpatrick (Ballybough Manure), Jack Killeen (Midland Railway); unascribed men were Barney Conway, Patrick Collins, Jack Cunningham, Michael Cunningham, Patrick Doyle, William Fairtlough, Patrick Forde, Simon Kelch, Joseph Kelly, James Smith, John Toole and Patrick White.
4. NLI, ms. 7,303, ITGWU, minutes of Dublin No. 1 Branch, 20 and 28 July 1915, 11 and 25 Aug. 1915; *Workers' Republic,* 14 and 28 Aug. 1915, 4 Sep. 1915. An exception was the assistance, 'if possible,' that was agreed for Francis Sheehy Skeffington 'to send him on a tour of America to recruit his health.' James Nolan's widow died in October 1915, leaving three children aged between two and eight. *Workers' Republic,* 23 Oct. 1915.
5. NLI, ms. 7,303, ITGWU, minutes of Dublin No. 1 Branch, 8 Dec. 1915, 2 and 5 Jan. 1916; *Workers' Republic,* 15 Jan. 1916. Sections and representatives were: coal fillers and banksmen (P. Maguire, John Dillon, John Farrell, Thomas Fitzsimons and P. Mathews), cross-channel dockers (M. Byrne, Thomas Duff, Andrew Early and J. Cooling), general carters (Thomas O'Brien and Mick McCarthy), grain carters (Simon Kelsh and William Fairtlough), casual grain (Barney Conway and James Gannon), bushellers (Thomas Mills), chemical workers (William O'Toole and John Gannon), deepwater casuals (P. Murtagh), gas workers (James Cunningham and William Darby), fish markets (Joseph O'Neill) and Dublin Corporation (James Nolan). Other Sections were engineers and railwaymen. The Trustees were to be

Joseph Kelly, Michael Cunningham, Joseph Metcalfe and William Fairtlough.

6. NLI, ms. 7,303, ITGWU, minutes of Dublin No. 1 Branch, 24 Nov. 1915; Cathal O'Shannon, 'Historic site,' *Irish Times,* 1 May 1965; NLI, ITGWU Special List A8, ms. 15,67; Irish Transport and General Workers' Union, *The Attempt to Smash the Irish Transport and General Workers' Union,* p. xv–xvii, 132.

7. 'Shellback', in 'Jim Larkin and the future of the Red Hand,' *Irish Worker,* 27 June 1914 and 11 July 1914, argued that the lesson of Larkin's resignation was that 'we *must* keep him and we must make him secure in his position by putting him financially and socially on a level, if not superior, to a military or a Salvation Army leader'.

8. *Irish Worker,* 11 July 1914, 10, 17 and 24 Oct. 1914; *Workers' Republic,* 11 Sep. 1915, 30 Oct. 1915, 11 and 25 Dec. 1915. In attendance were William O'Brien (President, Dublin Trades Council), Thomas Farren (Treasurer), John Simmons (Secretary), John Farren, Thomas Murphy and Richard O'Carroll. Irish Transport and General Workers' Union, *The Attempt to Smash the Irish Transport and General Workers' Union,* p. xv. See also Ken Coates and Tony Topham, *The History of the Transport and General Workers' Union, Volume 1: The Making of the TGWU: The Emergence of the Labour Movement, 1870–1922, Part II: 1912–1922: From Federation to Amalgamation* (Oxford: Basil Blackwell, 1991), p. 536–40.

9. NLI, ms. 7,303, ITGWU, minutes of Dublin No. 1 Branch, 14 and 21 July 1915; *Irish Worker,* 21 May 1914, 13 June 1914; *Workers' Republic,* 29 May 1915, 12 and 19 June 1915, 3 July 1915.

10. NLI, ms. 7,303, ITGWU, minutes of Dublin No. 1 Branch, 20 Oct. 1915, 17 Nov. 1915, 29 Dec. 1915; *Workers' Republic,* 2 and 16 Oct. 1915, 6, 13 and 20 Nov. 1915, 25 Dec. 1915.

11. *Workers' Republic,* 1 Jan. 1916, 5 Feb. 1916, 1 Apr. 1916. Stokers got 2s 4d, engine men 3s, water gas makers 2s 4d, machine men 2s 3d, coal workers 4s, yard men 2s, and boys 1s. Constant boats got 3s a week, making 37s per week, with overtime at 8d an hour; casual boats got 6s a week, 7s a day and overtime at 1s an hour, and H. M. Leask, forage merchants, also granted 3s 6d to all (among those in this list were Foran and other members of the Executive Council), National Union of Life Assurance Agents £1, Dublin Fire Brigade Men's Union £2, and the printing staff of the *Workers' Republic* 16s 6d. John Farren, Treasurer of Dublin Trades Council, acknowledged £54 14s 6d, with £5 10s coming from the North Wall Branch of the National Union of Railwaymen and £10 from the Society of Coachmakers in Britain.

12. NLI, ms. 7,303, ITGWU, minutes of Dublin No. 1 Branch, 2 and 16 Feb. 1916, 29 Mar. 1916; *Workers' Republic,* 8 and 15 Jan. 1916, 12 Feb. 1916, 1 and 15 Apr. 1916.

13. NLI, ms. 7,303, ITGWU, minutes of Dublin No. 1 Branch, 28 July 1915, 4 Aug. 1915, 27 Oct. 1915, 17 Nov. 1915; *Workers' Republic,* 17 and 31 July 1915, 7 Aug. 1915, 30 Oct. 1915, 13 Nov. 1915. It was agreed that Foran and Connolly could 'organise the Women Workers in whatever way they think fit.' On 4 August, Connolly complained about the 'conduct of some of the women' in the IWWU and Women Workers' Co-operative Society, and it was agreed that 'these people [are] not to be allowed into the Hall any more.' The Committee were Mrs Reilly, Mrs Norgrove, Mrs Nolan, Miss M. Geraghty, Miss M. Ryan, Miss J. Shannon and Miss Kinch.

14. *Workers' Republic,* 12 June 1915, 5 Sep. to 30 Oct. 1915, 13 Nov. 1915, 1 Jan. 1916, 26 Feb. 1916. See also Francis Devine, 'Liberating the Kingdom: The Transport Union in

Kerry, 1915–1990,' in *An Eccentric Chemistry*, p. 5–16.

15. NLI, ms. 7,303, ITGWU, minutes of Dublin No. 1 Branch, 8 Sep. 1915; *Workers' Republic*, 17 July 1915. John Farrell and Mick McCarthy moved, and on 15 Sep. Foran's wages were set at 33s a week, on a motion of Joseph Kelly and Mick McCarthy.

16. ITGWU, Annual Report for 1918, p. 5–6; *Irish Worker*, 15 Aug. 1914; *The Worker*, 26 Dec. 1914; *Workers' Republic*, 23 Oct. 1915, 1 Jan. 1916.

17. NLI, ITGWU Special List A8, ms. 13,931, circular from James Connolly, Acting General Secretary; *Workers' Republic*, 4 Dec. 1915; 1 Jan. 1916.

Chapter 7 (p. 82–90)

1. 'Remembering the labour movement in 1916,' *Liberty*, n.s., vol. 5, 2 July 2006, p. 24–5; '1966,' *Liberty*, vol. 29, no. 3, Jan. 1966, p. 1–2; NA, Bureau of Military History, Witness Statement 546, Rosie Hackett.

2. For varied accounts of Easter Week see John W. Boyle, 'Irish labor and the Rising,' *Éire-Ireland*, vol. 11, 3, autumn 1976, p. 122–31; Max Caulfield, *The Easter Rebellion* (London: Frederick Muller, 1963); Tim Pat Coogan, 1916: *The Easter Rising* (London: Cassell, 2006); Seán Cronin, *Our Own Red Blood: The Story of the 1916 Rising* (Dublin: Irish Freedom Press, 2006); Owen Dudley Edwards and Fergus Pyle (eds.), 1916: *The Easter Rising*, London: MacGibbon and Kee, 1968); Michael Foy and Brian Barton, *The Easter Rising* (Stroud, Glos.: Sutton, 2004); Jonathan Githens-Mazer, *Myths and Memories of the Easter Rising: Cultural and Political Nationalism in Ireland* (Dublin: Irish Academic Press, 2006); Diarmuid Lynch, *The IRB and the Insurrection* (Cork: Mercier Press, 1957); F. X. Martin (ed.), *Leaders and Men of the Easter Rising: Dublin, 1916* (London: Methuen, 1967); Kevin B. Nowlan (ed.), *The Making of 1916: Studies in the History of the Rising* (Dublin: Gill & Macmillan, 1969); Leon Ó Broin, *Dublin Castle and the 1916 Rising*, (London: Sidgwick and Jackson, 1966); L. G. Redmond-Howard, *Six Days of the Irish Republic: An Eyewitness Account of 1916* (London and Dublin: Maunsel, 1916, reprinted Millstreet: Aubane Historical Society, 2006); Annie Ryan, *Witnesses: Inside the Easter Rising*, (Dublin: Liberties Press, 2005); Desmond Ryan, *The Rising: The Complete Story of Easter Week*, (Dublin: Golden Eagle Books, 1957); Charles Townsend, *Easter 1916: The Irish Rebellion* (London: Penguin, 2005).

3. Ó Cathasaigh, *The Story of the Irish Citizen Army*, p. 9, 14–15, 44–5. D. R. O'Connor Lysaght, in 'The Irish Citizen Army, 1913–1916: White, Connolly and Larkin,' *History Ireland*, Mar.–Apr. 2006, p. 16–21, points out that Richard O'Carroll, bricklayers' Leader and the Leader of the Labour Party in Dublin Corporation, died in 1916 as a member of the Irish Volunteers, not of the Citizen Army. The Vice-Chairmen were James Larkin, P. T. Daly, W. P. Partridge, Thomas Foran and Francis Sheehy Skeffington; Treasurers: Richard Brannigan [Braithwaite] and Constance Markievicz; Committee: T. Blair, John Bohan, T. Burke, P. Coady, P. Fogarty, P. J. Fox, Thomas Healy, Thomas Kennedy, J. McGowan, P. Morgan, Frank Moss, Michael Mullen [Mícheál Ó Maoláin], P. O'Brien, Christy Poole and John Shelly. The five 'out' were Markievicz, McGowan, Moss, Partridge and Poole. White became an Organiser for the Irish Volunteers. Lysaght argues that Larkin, recognising that the ITGWU could not take state power and being sceptical about political parties,

believed that 'to build an organisation of armed workers seemed much more promising.' Greaves, *The Irish Transport and General Workers' Union,* p. 126; Robbins, *Under the Starry Plough; Irish Worker,* 8 Aug. 1914.

4. *Workers' Republic,* 26 Feb. 1916, 4 Mar. 1916, 1 Apr. 1916.

5. Greaves, *The Irish Transport and General Workers' Union,* p. 152; Billy Mullins, *Memoirs of Billy Mullins, Veteran of the War of Independence* (Tralee: Kerryman, 1983), p. 48; Geraghty, *William Patrick Partridge and his Times,* p. 257–8; Sinéad Joy, *The IRA in Kerry,* 1916–1921 (Cork: Collins Press, 2005); Helga Woggon, '"Not merely a labour organisation": The ITGWU and the Dublin dock strike, 1915–1916,' *Saothar,* 27 (2002), p. 43–54.

6. NLI, ms. 7,303, ITGWU, minutes of Dublin No. 1 Branch, 8 and 9 Apr. 1916; *Workers' Republic,* 22 Apr. 1916; Greaves, *The Irish Transport and General Workers' Union,* p. 164–5.

7. Those killed were John Adams, St Stephen's Green, 25 April.; Louis Byrne, City Hall, 24 April; Philip Clarke, St Stephen's Green, 25 April; Seán Connolly, City Hall, 24 April; Edward Cosgrave, GPO, 25 April; Charles Darcy, Parliament Street, 24 April; J. J. Fox, St Stephen's Green, 25 April; George Geoghegan, City Hall, 26 April; Daniel Murray, Camden Street, died from wounds on 13 May; Thomas O'Reilly, between City Hall and Liberty Hall, 27 April; and Frederick Ryan, Harcourt Street, 27 April Connolly and Mallin were executed. The fifteenth victim was the elusive A. Weeks, who appears to have come to Dublin to avoid Conscription and turned up at Liberty Hall on the afternoon of Monday 24 April, asking to join the insurgents. Donal Nevin, in *James Connolly: A Full Life,* p. 646, says: 'A stranger applied for permission to join the insurgents. He wore an IWW (Wobblies) button on his coat. He said he had come over from England, that he had a conscientious objection to fighting for capitalistic and imperialistic Governments but that he also had a conscientious objection to being left out of a fight for liberty. This man whose identity is unknown—his name might have been Allen—fought bravely during the week. He was wounded in the evacuation of the GPO on Friday and died the following day.' John Ihle identifies the man as Abraham Weeks, who arrived 'a day late and from the direction of Greenville Hall,' and probably fought in St Stephen's Green. Ihle suggests that it was 'easy to see how a Jewish socialist in 1916 could see his future' in the Ireland being fought for and that he prefigured other Jews who fought in the War of Independence, 'when the dreamers of Zionism and Irish autonomy stood together in mutual support.' John Ihle, 'One Jew's role in Irish history,' at jta.org/news/ article/1999/11/30/13986/yearslaterlife. Speaking in Dáil Éireann on 23 February 1944, in a debate on military service pensions and allowances, Oliver Flanagan commented that 'we had not got the rancher, the capitalist, the financier or the Jew in the Old IRA. We had the plain, poor, honest people.' James Larkin rejoined: 'Yes, you had. The first man to die in Dublin was a Jew. The first man shot in Dublin was a Jew.' This was not correct (in that the first victim on the insurgent side was Seán Connolly), but he was undoubtedly referring to Weeks. *Parliamentary Debates: Dáil Éireann: Official Report,* vol. 92, col. 1521–63. Flanagan persisted in his anti-Semitism by remarking that, 'from my experience of some Jews, they have been opposed to everything national.' Earlier in the debate Larkin decried the lack of acknowledgement of the Citizen Army. 'Nobody ever speaks of the ICA. I am

afraid there would not have been any IRA if the ICA had not gone into action. No reference is made to them and there is no suggestion that they were ever in existence.' He then detailed the neglect of some old Citizen Army men. This list included P. Dougherty, referred to as Michael Dougherty, who 'died [in] 1920 from the effect of wounds received in 1916.' *Irish Worker,* 3 May 1924. The *Watchword of Labour* published an obituary for Michael O'Doherty, 'one of the fighting Old Guard of the Transport Union,' the Carters' Section, who had been wounded in twelve places in the GPO but who 'survived and died last week' (10 January 1920).

8. The *Helga* was anchored at Sir John Rogerson's Quay. After an ineffectual start, its eighteen-pounders quickly reduced Liberty Hall to a shell. Given that the leadership and all arms and ammunition had gone, the deed was symbolic. The caretaker, Peter Ennis, was stirred by the noise, opened the doors and was fired upon. He finally made a celebrated dash along Eden Quay, dodging bullets, to the cheers of onlookers. The *Irish Times* report suggests that he completed the distance in a time that would have troubled Olympic time-keepers. *Irish Times,* 27 Apr. 1916, and Robbins, *Under the Starry Plough,* p. 239–44, which includes the *Helga's* log of events.

9. Greaves, *The Irish Transport and General Workers' Union,* p. 169.

10. Greaves, *The Irish Transport and General Workers' Union,* p. 171–8.

11. ITGWU, Annual Report for 1918, p. 5–7.

12. *Irish Worker,* 14 Mar. 1914. See Nevin, *James Connolly,* p. 485–501, for a discussion of Connolly and his attitudes to Home Rule and Partition.

13. Irish Labour Party and TUC, Report of 24th Annual Meeting, 1918, p. 9.

14. 'The heritage of Easter Week,' *Irish Worker,* no. 41, 19 Apr. 1924.

15. NLI, O'Brien Papers, ms. 15,673 (1) and (5), 5th Annual General Meeting of Dublin Employers' Federation.

Chapter 8 (p. 91–129)

1. ITGWU, Annual Report for 1918, p. 6; NLI, ms. 7,299, ITGWU, minutes of Dublin No. 1 Branch, 4, 10 and 18 June 1916, and ITGWU Special List A8, ms. 15,671. Those present were Michael McCarthy (Chairman), Joseph Kelly, Joseph O'Neill, William Darby, James Byrne, Patrick Stafford, John Nolan, John Gannon, Thomas O'Brien, William Fairtlough, James Smith, Michael Cunningham, Councillor Michael Brohoon, Andrew Early, Thomas Duff, T. Fitzsimons, and Joseph Metcalfe, who acted as secretary *pro tem.* The inspection team was Joseph Kelly, Fairtlough and Brohoon. NLI, ms. 7,299, ITGWU, minutes of Dublin No. 1 Branch, 18 June 1916. A row with the Liberty Hall barber resulted in the caretaker, Peter Ennis, being instructed to take possession of his premises, 'by force if necessary.' The shop was reopened after the meeting of 18 June. O'Shannon, *Fifty Years of Liberty Hall.*

2. John Dillon Nugent (1869–1940), for the Irish Party, defeated Thomas Farren (ITGWU and Labour), 2,445 to 1,816, to become MP for the College Green Division, Dublin, on 11 June 1915 in a by-election after the death of J. P. Nannetti. The election was fought on 1913 issues, Nugent having taken a leading part in preventing children going to England and in supplying strike-breakers. He contested the St Michan's Division, Dublin, in 1918 and lost to Michael Staines (Sinn Féin) but was Nationalist MP for Armagh at Stormont, 1921–5, losing in 1925. He was National

Secretary of the Ancient Order of Hibernians and head of Hibernian Insurance. Connolly observed that Nugent's selection 'was a studied insult to the Dublin working class.' Its arm would be 'nerved by remembrance of the poisonous lies and slanders poured upon it' during the Lock-Out. It would 'remember the thousands of homes into which Nugent brought hunger and misery by the active assistance and encouragement given to the employers. It will think of all the poor victimised girls and women whose places were taken by the scabs procured by Nugent's agents. It will reflect that when it was sought to reduce the working class of Dublin to the vilest slavery, to break up their unity and disorganise their forces, it was John Dillon Nugent that stood forth as their bitterest foe and the most valued supporter of those who sought to enslave them.' Nugent's 'malign influence' sowed 'the seeds of discord and hatred amongst Irishmen' and prevented 'national unity for truly national purposes.' He 'set Irishman against Irishman, brothers against brothers,' had 'broken up family ties and the ties of community, and been the ready agent of every evil thing that sought to darken the national soul and sully the character of the race. He is the incarnation and flowering of the results upon Irish character of seven centuries of slavery.' *Workers' Republic,* 12 June 1915.

3. NLI, ms. 7,299, ITGWU, minutes of Dublin No. 1 Branch, 21, 26 and 28 June, 9, 12, 26 and 30 July, 2 Aug. 1916. The Committee would be Foran, Fairtlough, Brohoon and McCarthy. The Delegates were Foran, Brohoon and Metcalfe. NA, CSORP/1916/25248; *Irish Opinion,* 12 and 19 Jan. 1918; Liam Beecher, 'Cork's role in ITGWU growth over the years,' *Liberty,* Oct. 1975. O'Reilly was given £2 so that she could avoid giving her son 'a pauper's grave as he was a very good member before he fell.' NLI, ITGWU Special List A8, ms. 27,037; Foran to O'Connell, 24 Oct. 1916, 13 Nov. 1916, 5 Dec. 1916; Foran to Lynch, 31 Oct. 1916; *Irish Opinion,* 12 Jan. 1918.

4. Joseph McGrath (1887–1966) was born in Dublin and joined the IRB. He fought in Marrowbone Lane in 1916 and was imprisoned in Wormwood Scrubs and Brixton Prisons, London. He organised bank robberies during the War of Independence, and allegedly kept some of the proceeds. He was a member of the first Dáil Éireann as Sinn Féin TD for St James's Division, Dublin. In October 1921 he travelled to London as one of Michael Collins's personal staff. In the Civil War he took the pro-Treaty side and was Director of Intelligence, later head of the Criminal Investigation Department. He was Minister for Labour in the second Dáil and Provisional Government, 1922, and Minister for Industry and Commerce in the first and second Executive Councils, 1922–4. He resigned from Government and Dáil in April 1924. Having begun in the building trade, in 1925 he was Labour Adviser to Siemens-Schuckert on the Shannon Hydro-electric Scheme, opposing the ITGWU and assisting with the creation of a yellow union, the Association of Ex-Officers and Men of the National Army. In 1930 he founded the Irish Hospitals Trust, whose success made him an extremely wealthy man. He died in Dublin in 1966.

5. ITGWU, Annual Report for 1918, p. 7; NLI, ms. 7,299, ITGWU, minutes of Dublin No. 1 Branch, 15 July 1916, 10 and 24 Sep. 1916, 26 Nov. 1916, 29 Apr. 1917, 27 May 1917, 3, 10 and 24 June 1917, 22 and 29 July 1917, 26 Aug. 1917, 9 Sep. 1917, 12 and 21 Oct. 1917, 5 May 1918; ITGWU Special List A8, ms. 27,037, Foran to Lynch, 22 Sep. 1916; Special List A8, circular, 10 May 1917, printed letter heading, 6 Nov. 1917; *Irish Opinion,* 5 Jan.

1918; Irish Labour Party and Trades Union Congress, Report of 23rd Congress, Derry, 6–8 Aug. 1917, p. 39, 51.

6. ITGWU, Annual Report for 1918, p. 8–9; NLI, ms. 7,299; ITGWU, minutes of Dublin No. 1 Branch, 6 Jan. 1918, 17 Feb. 1918, 2 Mar. 1918; *Voice of Labour,* 19 Jan. 1918, 9 Feb. 1918, 9 Mar. 1918, 20 Apr. 1918, 11 and 25 May 1918, 27 July 1918. The TUC had 4,532,085 affiliated members. Had the ITGWU been affiliated it would have been the eighth-largest affiliate—a remarkable fact given the events of 1913 and 1916. (The others were the Miners' Federation of Great Britain, 650,000; National Union of Railwaymen, 402,000; Workers' Union, 331,000; National Union of General Workers, 302,390; Amalgamated Society of Engineers, 260,000; National Amalgamated Weavers' Association, 174,000; and National Amalgamated Union of Labour, 140,000.) NLI, ITGWU Papers of C. Desmond Greaves, Arc. 6157, Box 3, Foran v. Larkin, 15 Jan. 1924; *Voice of Labour,* 20 July 1918, 3 and 24 Aug. 1918, 14 Sep. 1918. See 50th Annual TUC, Derby, 2–7 Sep. 1918, p. 3–25.

7. ITGWU, Annual Report for 1918, p. 9; *Voice of Labour,* 4, 11 and 25 Jan. 1919, 1 Feb. 1919, 15 and 22 Mar. 1919, 1 May 1919, 21 June 1919; *Watchword of Labour,* 27 Sep. 1919. Foremen cutters got 70s a week; number 2 man, 60s; layers, 55s, with overtime at time and a quarter, 6–9 p.m., and time and a half, 9–12 p.m. The Sections listed were account Collectors, artificial limb makers, bank porters, bottle makers, brewers, builders' providers, carters, chemical trades, coal workers, confectioners, Corporation and public boards, distillers, dockers, drug workers, engineering and shipbuilding, fish market men, foundries, French polishers, gardeners, gas workers, grain trades, grocery and wine trade, laundry workers, mail drivers, marble polishers, millers, mineral water operatives, music trade employees, oil trades, potato factors, poulterers, printers' assistants, railwaymen, rope workers, soap makers, stone cutters, tobacco pipe makers, and window cleaners. NLI, ITGWU, Special List A8, ms. 27,039; Paddy O'Brien, 'Early days of the ITGWU in Kerry,' *Liberty,* June 1981.

8. ITGWU, minutes of Resident Executive Committee, 28 Nov. 1920, 8, 9 and 16 Mar. 1921, 27 Apr. 1921, 1 July 1921.

9. ITGWU, Annual Report for 1919, p. 5–6, 24; *Voice of Labour,* 1 and 8 Mar. 1919, 24 Apr. 1919, 17 and 31 May 1919, 7 and 21 June 1919, 5 and 12 July 1919, 13 and 20 Sep. 1919. Hayes was 'deported.' The Organisers were Daniel Branniff, Kilkenny; Tadhg Barry, Cork; John Dowling, Limerick; Thomas Farren, Dublin; Éamon Hayes, Thurles; Michael Healy, Boyle; Archibald Heron, Maryborough [Port Laoise]; Denis Houston, Belfast; Helen Hoyne, Dublin; Éamon Lynch, Cork; Joseph Metcalfe, Bray; Michael Murphy, Mullingar; Máire Mullen, Cork; Francis McCabe, Dublin; Thomas Nagle, Waterford; Maurice Neligan, Tralee; Séamus O'Brien, Limerick; Peter [Peadar] O'Donnell, Monaghan; Michael O'Donoghue, Enniscorthy; W. J. Reilly, Sligo; and Éamonn Rooney, Drogheda. Under the Defence of the Realm Act, ITGWU, minutes of Resident Executive Committee, 22 Jan. 1920.

10. ITGWU, Annual Report for 1919, p. 6–9; ITGWU, Annual Report for 1920, p. 5–9, 11, 28. John Dowling, Limerick; Thomas Farren, Head Office; James A. Henderson, Galway; Denis Houston, Dundalk; John McGrath, Mallow; Joseph Metcalfe, Head Office; Thomas Nagle, Cork; Séamus F. O'Brien, Waterford; Michael O'Donoghue, Enniscorthy; and Charles F. Ridgway, Belfast. ITGWU, minutes of Resident Executive Committee, 3 June 1920; Annual Report for 1921, p. 5–7; minutes of Resident

Executive Committee, 6 Oct. 1920, 9 and 16 Jan. 1921, 25 May 1921, 10 June 1921. The UBLU had borrowed £1,000 from Liberty Hall. NLI, ITGWU Special List A8, ms. 27,042 (1), 18 Oct. 1920; *Voice of Labour*, 2 Aug. 1919; *Watchword of Labour*, 21 Feb. 1920, 3, 10, 17 and 24 Apr. 1920, 22 and 29 May 1920, 31 July 1920, 21 Aug. 1920, 5 Sep. 1920, 9 Oct. 1920, 20 Nov. 1920. Clonmel Trades Council expelled the NUDL, Irish Labour Party and Trades Union Congress. Report of National Executive, 1920–21, p. 13–14. It was agreed that those who were prisoners 'other than for crimes' should have their cards kept clear, maintaining full benefits and having positions kept open for them. Thus Hill from the Executive Council and Séamus O'Brien, Organiser, could return, once released, to their old positions. A Register of Interned Members was kept. Paddy Devlin, 'Long shadows cast before,' *Liberty*, June 1982.

11. ITGWU, Annual Report for 1921, p. 9–12; Annual Report for 1922, p. 5–11, 26; *Voice of Labour*, 21 and 28 Jan. 1922. Other Organisers were James Baird, Waterford; Denis Houston, Wexford; Éamon Lynch, Cork; Joe Metcalfe, Bray; Séamus F. O'Brien, Limerick; Thomas O'Reilly, Head Office; Thomas Redmond, Mullingar; and C. F. Ridgway, Head Office. Minutes of Resident Executive Committee, 31 Dec. 1921, 9 Jan. 1922, 5 Feb. 1922, 4 and 20 Sep. 1922, 18 Dec. 1922. James Baird and Thomas Farren, Head Office; John Dowling, Waterford; Denis Houston, Wexford; Joseph Metcalfe, Bray; Thomas Nagle, Cork; Séamus F. O'Brien, Limerick; Thomas J. Redmond, Mullingar; and C. F. Ridgway, Dundalk. Liam Slattery, Organiser, was taken on until Christmas to enable him to obtain other work. All this depended on the approval of the Motor Section, Dublin No. 1 Branch! I am grateful to Pádraig Yeates for these references from the minutes of the Irish Engineering and Industrial Union, 31 Dec. 1921 and 4 Feb. 1922. NLI, O'Brien Papers, ms. 15,687, Mícheál Ó Coileáin to O'Brien, 6 July 1921; Irish Labour Party and Trades Union Congress, Report of 27th Congress, Dublin, 1–4 Aug. 1921, p. 95–106.

12. Irish Labour Party and Trades Union Congress, Report of 28th Congress, Dublin, 7–10 Aug. 1922, p. 125–7; Report of 29th Congress, Dublin, 6–9 Aug. 1923, p. 81–2.

13. ITGWU, minutes of Resident Executive Committee, 25 Sep. 1920, 12 Dec. 1920, 9 Jan. 1921, 6 Dec. 1921. Hoyne had overstayed her annual leave, and her subsequent work 'should be carefully noted.' She sought and was given a reference. NLI, ms. 7,99, ITGWU, minutes of Dublin No. 1 Branch, 2, 5 and 9 July 1916, 29 Aug. 1916, 3 Sep. 1916. The ITGWU gave them a loan of £2 for their ITUC Delegation, 2 August 1916.

14. ITGWU, Annual Report for 1921, p. 9–10; minutes of Resident Executive Committee, 17 Oct. 1920, 5 Nov. 1920, 15 June 1921.

15. ITGWU, minutes of Resident Executive Committee, 25 Mar. 1921.

16. ITGWU, Annual Report for 1918, p. 8; *Voice of Labour*, 3 and 24 Aug. 1918; D. R. O'Connor Lysaght, 'Thomas Foran, 1883–1951,' *Saothar*, 30 (2005), p. 99–100.

17. Foran moved that, although Redmond 'had no intention' of pocketing the money, he never again 'do any work outside his duty as Delegate,' and the Casual Coal Section was called to discuss matters. NLI, ms. 7,299, ITGWU, minutes of Dublin No. 1 Branch, 9 July 1916, 18 and 22 Oct. 1916, 1, 4, 12 and 19 Nov. 1916.

18. NLI, ms. 7,299, ITGWU, minutes of Dublin No. 1 Branch, 22 Apr. 1917; *Voice of Labour*, 28 Sep. 1918, 7 Dec. 1918; Irish Labour Party and Trades Union Congress, Report of Special Congress, Dublin, 1 Nov. 1918, p. 95–9; Paddy Devlin, 'Long shadows cast before,' *Liberty*, June 1982.

19. ITGWU, Annual Report for 1919, p. 7.

20. *Watchword of Labour,* vol. 1, no. 9, 22 Nov. 1919.

21. *Watchword of Labour,* vol. 1, no. 10, 29 Nov. 1919.

22. *Watchword of Labour,* vol. 1, no. 17, 17 Jan. 1920.

23. *Watchword of Labour,* vol. 1, no. 22, 21 Feb. 1920.

24. ITGWU, Annual Report for 1921, p. 5–8; Irish Labour Party and Trades Union Congress, Report of National Executive, 1920–1921, p. 35–7.

25. ITGWU, Annual Report for 1922, p. 6, 10.

26. NLI, Special List A8, ms. 27,044. The original appeared in the *Irish Independent,* 9 Feb. 1922.

27. NLI, ms. 7,299, ITGWU, minutes of Dublin No. 1 Branch, 2 Sep. 1917; ITGWU, Annual Report for 1918, p. 7–8; *Irish Opinion,* 1 Dec. 1917; *Voice of Labour,* 8 and 15 June 1918, 13 July 1918; Irish Labour Party and Trades Union Congress, Report of 24th Congress, Waterford, 5–7 Aug. 1918, p. 13–14.

28. ITGWU, Annual Report for 1921, p. 8–11; Irish Labour Party and Trades Union Congress, Report of National Executive, 1920–1921, and 27th Congress, Dublin, 1–4 Aug. 1921, p. 45, 136–8, 179–81.

29. ITGWU, Annual Report for 1922, p. 8–10; minutes of Resident Executive Committee, 3 Aug. 1922, 12 Sep. 1922. *Voice of Labour,* 7 Jan. 1922, 25 Feb. 1922, 4 and 25 Mar. 1922. The Delegates were J. O'Reilly (Lansdowne), M. Lennon, R. Ryan and J. Callanan (Clonmel), J. Spillane (Kanturk), D. Clifford (UDC), M. P. Linehan (Mallow), Thomas O'Dwyer (Knocklong), P. Ferris, T. Ferris and J. Kinnane (Bansha), T. O'Brien J. Sheehan (Grange), P. Kearns, T. O'Brien and N. Heffernan (Cutteen), M. Hanrahan and M. Coleman (Bruree), D. Kinane (Bruff), W. Guerin (Elton), J. Savage, J. Moloney and M. Sheedy (Kilmallock), J. Quinn, T. McCarthy and M. Shelley (Tipperary), D. Hayes and S. Ryan (Bansha) and T. O'Connell (Ballycarron). Irish Labour Party and Trades Union Congress, Report of 28th Congress, Dublin, 7–10 Aug. 1922, p. 125–7.

30. *Voice of Labour,* 11 and 18 May 1918, 1 June 1918, 13 July 1918, 13 Aug. 1918, 7 and 14 Sep. 1918, 2 and 16 Nov. 1918. Cathal O'Shannon claimed that the Branch was a result of the Anti-Conscription Strike in April. Henry Hanna KC, who had been prosecution Counsel at O'Shannon's court-martial in Belfast in 1917, was arbitrator; J. R. Lardner KC MP was the employers' spokesman, and O'Shannon 'had the honour of representing the workers.' 'Coming, sir—with victory,' *Liberty,* Sep. 1959.

31. NLI, ms. 7,299, ITGWU, minutes of Dublin No. 1 Branch, 14 Apr. 1918. The 'trusted person' was Father Albert. *Irish Opinion and Voice of Labour,* 6 Apr. 1918; *Voice of Labour,* 27 Apr. 1918, 19 and 26 Oct. 1918; Irish Labour Party and Trades Union Congress, Report of 24th Congress, Waterford, 5–7 Aug. 1918, p. 10, 37–45.

32. ITGWU, Annual Report for 1921, p. 8; Liam Beecher, 'Cork harbour strike of 1921, parts I–III,' *Liberty,* Sep.–Nov. 1976. The ITGWU's address was 80 Oliver Plunkett Street.

33. ITGWU, Annual Report for 1921, p. 11; Annual Report for 1922, p. 8; minutes of Resident Executive Committee, 29 June 1921, 17 Sep. 1921, 2 Sep. 1921, 7 May 1922; *Voice of Labour,* 7 and 14 Jan. 1922. Those invited to the Conference were the British Seafarers' Union, All Seamen's Vigilance Committees (Liverpool Committee to supply addresses), Coastwise Officers' and Mates' Association (Head Office, Garston, Liverpool) and Cooks' and Stewards' Union (J. Cotter, Secretary).

34. Irish Labour Party and Trades Union Congress, Report of National Executive, 1920–1921, p. 26–30.

35. Irish Labour Party and Trades Union Congress, Report of National Executive, 1920–1921, p. 30–32.

36. Irish Labour Party and Trades Union Congress, Report of 27th Congress, Dublin, 1–4 Aug. 1921, p. 78.

37. Irish Labour Party and Trades Union Congress, Report of 27th Congress, Dublin, 1–4 Aug. 1921, p. 140–46.

38. Irish Trades Union Congress and Labour Party, Report of 23rd Meeting, Derry, 6–8 Aug. 1917, p. 14–28, 70; Report of 24th Congress, Waterford, 5–7 Aug. 1918, p. 23–7.

39. Irish Labour Party and Trades Union Congress, Report of 23rd Meeting, Derry, 6–8 Aug. 1917, p. 5–13, 49–50, 55–8, 99. The Delegates were Joe Metcalfe and Mick Brohoon (Dublin No. 1 Branch), John Bohan and Tom Kennedy (Dublin No. 3 Branch), James Flanagan (Belfast), Denis Houston and D. Carey (Cork) and Alderman John Lynch and Michael Lynch (Sligo). John Lynch was also listed as representing the National Sailors' and Firemen's Union. Another Delegate list, p. 22–3, lists the ITGWU personnel as Foran, Brohoon, Houston, Richard Corish (Wexford) and Michael Lynch. Report of 24th Congress, Waterford, 5–7 Aug. 1918, p. 19–22, 53.

40. Irish Labour Party and Trades Union Congress, Report of 24th Congress, Waterford, 5–7 Aug. 1918, p. 7–.

41. Irish Labour Party and Trades Union Congress, Report of 24th Congress, Waterford, 5–7 Aug. 1918, p. 47–8, 67.

42. Irish Labour Party and Trades Union Congress, Report of 27th Congress, Dublin, 1–4 Aug. 1921, p. 74–5.

43. Irish Labour Party and Trades Union Congress, Report of National Executive, 1920–1921, p. 21.

44. Irish Labour Party and Trades Union Congress, Report of 27th Congress, Dublin, 1–4 Aug. 1921, p. 129–32.

45. Irish Labour Party and Trades Union Congress, Report of 28th Congress, Dublin, 7–10 Aug. 1922, p. 214–22; Report of National Executive Council, 1922–1923, p. 8–10; ITGWU, minutes of Resident Executive Committee, 23 Dec. 1922.

46. Irish Labour Party and Trades Union Congress, Report of National Executive, 1920–1921, p. 39–47.

47. Voice of Labour, 11 Mar. 1922.

48. ITGWU, Annual Report for 1921, p. 12; Irish Labour Party and Trades Union Congress, Report of 27th Congress, Dublin, 1–4 Aug. 1921, p. 194–6.

49. NLI, ITGWU Special List A8, ms. 27,042, 14 Feb. 1921.

50. ITGWU, Annual Report for 1918, p. 6, 9; Irish Trades Union Congress and Labour Party, Report of 23rd Meeting, Derry, 6–8 Aug. 1917, p. 28–30, 40, 54; Éamonn Wall, 'Memories of Connolly Hall,' Liberty, Oct. 1972, and Liam Beecher, 'Cork's role in ITGWU growth over the years,' Liberty, Oct. 1975.

51. Irish Labour Party and Trades Union Congress, Report of 27th Congress, Dublin, 1–4 Aug. 1921, p. 175–6.

52. Irish Labour Party and Trades Union Congress, Report of National Executive, 1921–1922, p. 10–12.

53. Irish Trades Union Congress and Labour Party, Report of 23rd Meeting, Derry, 6–8 Aug. 1917, p. 5–13, 31–2, 44–8, 51–3; Report of 24th Congress, Waterford, 5–7 Aug. 1918, p. 27–36. Thomas Lawlor observed of the twenty-four: 'And some are of military age too.' Hall (Belfast) suggested that the sailors' union should refuse to take them in their ships, and O'Brien hoped they would refuse to take scabs too.

54. ITGWU, Annual Report for 1922, p. 6–8; Irish Labour Party and Trades Union Congress, Report of 28th Congress, Dublin, 7–10 Aug. 1922, p. 182–6; Pádraig Yeates, 'Labour and the first Free State Dáil,' *Liberty*, Sep. 1982.

Chapter 9 (p. 130–42)

1. ITGWU, Annual Report for 1923, p. 5; Irish Labour Party and Trades Union Congress, Report of National Executive, 1922–1923, p. 12–15.

2. ITGWU, Annual Report for 1923, p. 5, 10–15; Annual Report for 1924 and Proceedings of Annual Conference, Newry, 6–7 Aug. 1925, p. 20; NLI, ms. 7,307, ITGWU, minutes of Dublin No. 1 Branch, 6 Sep. 1923; Irish Labour Party and Trades Union Congress, Report of 29th Congress, Dublin, 6–9 Aug. 1923, p. 99–100. J. P. Hughes (Kilrush) and William O'Brien were other ITGWU speakers.

3. ITGWU, Annual Report for 1923, p. 7–9; Irish Transport and General Workers' Union, *The Attempt to Smash the Irish Transport and General Workers' Union*. Legal expenses in 1923 were £1,208, compared with £1,339 in 1922 and £867 in 1924; 'Memories of Connolly Hall,' *Liberty*, Oct. 1972; Liam Beecher, 'Cork's role in growth over the years,' *Liberty*, Oct. 1975.

4. ITGWU, Annual Report for 1923, p. 6.

5. ITGWU, Annual Report for 1923, p. 6–7; NLI, ms. 7,306, ITGWU, minutes of Dublin No. 1 Branch, 6 Feb. 1923, 21 and 25 Mar. 1923, 10 and 31 May 1923, 7 and 26 June 1923, 19, 26 and 30 Aug. 1923. The names and the proposers were: M. Carroll (F. McCabe, J. Brennan), P. Toale (F. Cullen, J. O'Brien), J. White (P. Toole, P. Byrne), P. Spain (P. Walsh, M. O'Brien), P. Doran (L. Johnston, D. Brophy), J. Dempsey (P. Dixon, W. Brien), P. Murray (R. Carrick, M. Harvey), J. Horan (J. Kelly, J. Hanlon), J. Nolan (M. Ellis, P. Murray), J. Mitchell (P. Farrell, P. Whelan), W. Stone (F. Robbins, D. O'Leary), S. Kelsh (A. Early, M. Brien), J. O'Brien (J. Dillon, J. Burke), T. Connor (C. McCann, J. Mangan). Roddy Connolly was present but, as a member of less than one year's standing, was ineligible for election. Butler resigned on 6 September 1923, although the Committee asked him to reconsider.

6. *Irish Worker*, 22 Sep. 1923, 6, 20 and 27 Oct. 1923, 3, 17 and 24 Nov. 1923, 1 Dec. 1923, 22 Mar. 1924.

7. ITGWU, Annual Report for 1923, p. 10–11; NLI, ms. 7,307, ITGWU, minutes of Dublin No. 1 Branch, 12 July 1923, 12 Aug. 1923, 15 Nov. 1923, 6 Dec. 1923. Those in attendance in August were T. Butler (Chairman), John O'Neill (Branch Secretary), J. Boylan, P. Brady, W. Brown, F. Cullen, M. Donnelly, P. Doody, P. Doran, E. Dowling, A. Doyle, J. Geoghegan, P. Gray, H. Hynes, H. Kane, J. Kane, J. Manweiler, P. Martin, W. Mitchell, J. Murphy, T. Nagle, J. O'Brien, Joseph O'Neill, J. Osbourne, P. Osbourne, W. Purcell, P. Rock, P. Spain, J. Sullivan and J. Tobin.

8. ITGWU, Annual Report for 1923, p. 12–13; Irish Labour Party and Trades Union Congress, Report of National Executive and 29th Congress, Dublin, 6–9 Aug. 1923, p. 22, 97.

9. Éamonn Wall, 'Memories of Connolly Hall,' *Liberty,* Oct. 1972.
10. Irish Labour Party and Trades Union Congress, Report of 29th Congress, Dublin, 6–9 Aug. 1923, p. 59–60, 68.
11. ITGWU, Annual Report for 1923, p. 5, 15. They were John Butler (Waterford), Patrick Clancy (Limerick), Hugh Colohan (Kildare), Richard Corish (Wexford), Edward Doyle (Carlow), James Everett (Wicklow), David Hall (Meath), Patrick Hogan (Clare), Daniel Morrissey (Tipperary), T. J. Murphy (Cork West) and Thomas Nagle (North Cork).

Part 2 (p. 143–7)

1. Kieran Allen, 'Forging the links: Fianna Fáil, trade unions and the Emergency,' *Saothar,* 16 (1991), p. 48, and Lee, *Ireland,* p. 314.
2. Lee, *Ireland,* p. 571, 583–7. James B. Wolf, in '"Withholding their due": The dispute between Ireland and Great Britain over unemployed insurance payments to conditionally landed Irish wartime volunteers,' *Saothar,* 21 (1996), p. 39–46, provides additional data.
3. Fleming and O'Day, *Longman Handbook of Modern Irish History since* 1800, p. 571, 583–7.

Chapter 10 (p. 148–75)

1. *Irish Worker,* 26 Apr. 1923, 30 June 1923, 7 and 21 July 1923, 11 Aug. 1923, 13 Oct. 1923, 17, 24 and 31 Nov. 1923, 15 Dec. 1923. The figures were from the return to the Registrar of Friendly Societies, and Larkin states that the figures were attested by William Fairtlough, Joseph Kelly and Patrick Murray (Trustees), Joseph Casey and J. Smyth (auditors) and Patrick Smyth (Treasurer). £65 8s 11d was received in the week of 7 July. Another message of support came from Hare Park District Camp, Curragh, 5 August 1923, when a 'meeting of the ITGWU ... unanimously pledge ourselves to support the General Secretary' in his fight against the Executive. The breakdown was: Senator Michael Duffy, £51 10s 1d; Daniel Clancy, £39 17s; Michael McCarthy, £30 10s 7d; Thomas Kennedy, £54; Thomas Ryan, £79 4s 6d; and W. Hill, £50 3s 10d.
2. *Irish Worker,* 23 and 30 June 1923, citing action between Foran, O'Brien and the ITGWU Executive and Larkin. The other signatories were Thomas Foran, Thomas Butler, P. Hanratty, Thomas Kennedy, Patrick Nolan and John O'Neill. The motion was proposed by Patrick Ducie and William O'Brien. A further charge was that Kennedy had refused legitimate claims for Mortality Benefit. The Committee was Peter Nolan (docker), Michael Lyons (carter), Peter Mooney (farrier), J. Boyle (Paper Section), W. Kelly (coal), Michael Brohoon, Michael Ward (Chemical) and Patrick Murray (Cross-Channel). The meeting also withdrew its Delegates from the Workers' Council, discharged the existing Branch Committee and declared that '100 members appointed by the General Secretary would run matters until new elections could be arranged.' The representatives were Smith, Keating and Sheeran.
3. *Irish Worker,* 28 July 1923, 4 Aug. 1923, 15 Sep. 1923, 6, 13 and 20 Oct. 1923, 15 Dec. 1923, 5 Jan. 1924, 29 Mar. 1924, 5 and 19 Apr. 1924. Larkin referred to the 'bogus Congress' and the eighty-three Delegates 'calling themselves' the ITGWU, 11 Aug. The signatories were M. Usher (Chairman), Thomas H. Redmond, George Nathan, James

Flanagan and Patrick Brophy (Secretary). Birr, Borrisokane, Borris-in-Ossory, Cloghjordan, Kinnitty, Moneygall, Nenagh, Rathdowney, Shinrone, Templemore, Thurles and Toomyvara were represented at the Co. Tipperary meeting.

4. *Irish Worker*, 16 and 23 Feb. 1924, 1, 8 and 22 Mar. 1924, 10 May 1924, 19 July 1924. ITGWU, Annual Reports for 1922–1927. In 1926 the figure was £405 and in 1927 £187. The message came from the Grocers' Porters' Section, Dublin No. 3 Branch.

5. *Irish Worker*, 31 May 1924, 14, 21 and 28 June 1924, 5 July 1924; ITGWU, Annual Report for 1924, p. 6.

6. *Irish Worker*, 10 and 24 May 1924, 7, 14, 21 and 28 June 1924, 12 and 19 July 1924; *Irish Worker*, 21 and 28 June 1924, 12 and 19 July 1924; WUI, Report of Annual Delegate Conference, Dublin, 19 June 1949, p. 6–7; ITGWU, Annual Report for 1924, p. 5; Donal Nevin, 'Larkin and the Workers' Union of Ireland,' in *James Larkin*, p. 342–52.

7. *Irish Worker*, 19 July 1924, 6 and 20 Sep. 1924, 4 and 25 Oct. 1924, 1, 8, 15 and 29 Nov., 20 Dec. 1924, 14 and 21 Mar. 1925, 4 and 18 Apr. 1925. The incidents had occurred on 7 Oct. 1924 and 13 January 1925. On appeal, the sentences were suspended. Other nicknames and remarks were Burke, 'Scab Motor Organiser'; O'Brien, carters' Delegate, 'if only he had any carters'; Gannin, ex-CID tout; 'Sodawater Keavy'; McKenna, 'the clerk who got notice to quit from O'Brien'; Harry Lauder O'Reilly; 'Baby' Ridgway; McGrath, 'the man with the detachable ribs'; Kelly, 'Thirsty from Kingstown'; and Connell, 'the Santry Sponge.' The Chairman of Dublin No. 1 Branch was J. Mallon and the Secretary was M. J. Sutton. The Branch staff was Thomas Farrelly, J. J. Lightfoot and John O'Shea, the Trustees were D. Courtenay and R. Lynch, the Delegate was John 'Jack' Dempsey, and and the Committee was Luke Doyle (oil), R. O'Donnell (builders' providers), T. Larkin (grain), M. Rawl (milling), G. Dowdall (labourers), James Doyle (gas-workers), J. Mahoney (grocers' porters), W. Morgan (mineral water), A. Ronan (coal), Thomas Spence (deep sea), H. Courtenay (coal fillers), W. Eustace (bakery), James Ralph (Corporation) and John Kenny (cross-channel docks). ITGWU, Annual Report for 1924, p. 6–7.

8. *Irish Worker*, 17, 24 and 31 May 1924; ITGWU, Annual Report for 1924, p. 5–7; 'Martin Joseph Magennis, 1891–1953: An appreciation,' *Report*, no. 7, Feb. 1953.

9. *Irish Worker*, 28 June 1924, 5 and 26 July 1924, 16, 23 and 30 Aug. 1924, 6 Sep. 1924, 18 Oct. 1924, 29 Nov. 1924, 6 Dec. 1924, 28 Feb. 1925; ITGWU, Annual Report for 1924, p. 7–8. The criticism made, Captain Moynihan of the Association of Ex-Officers and Men of the National Army Trade Union had gone to Liberty Hall for cards to work at Marino but had been refused.

10. *Irish Worker*, 5 July 1924, 9, 16, 23 and 30 Aug. 1924, 20 Sep. 1924, 6 Dec. 1924; ITGWU, Annual Report for 1924, p. 8. Crotty had been Secretary of the Breadvanmen's Society, which had joined the ITGWU, and O'Loughlin from the old Carmen and Storemen's Society. O'Brien was described as '*née* James Fitzmaurice, sometime miner in Butte, Montana.' A 'lady attached to their intelligence Department' was also part of the ITGWU conspiracy.

11. NLI, ms. 7,308, ITGWU, minutes of Dublin No. 1 Branch, 31 July 1924, 21 Aug. 1924, 11 and 25 Sep. 1924, 23 Oct. 1924, 4 and 8 Dec. 1924, 11, 15 and 22 Jan. 1925, 5 Mar. 1925. This applied to all except P. Nolan and J. Burke, who did not agree to the arrangement, and T. O'Brien, who did not attend the meeting. NLI, ITGWU Special List A8, ms. 27,048. Attacks were recorded between 7 October 1924 and 12 August 1925, with

Conway, Dempsey and O'Shea given various sentences for the assaults. Michael Connolly, 58 Lower Gloucester Street, was number 18,634; Richard Lynch, 29 North Great George's Street, 16,257; and Patrick Brady, 32 Foley Street, 5,630. Connolly had been an unsuccessful candidate for Branch Delegate, 29 January 1918, polling 139 votes against Patrick Nolan's 823 and Laurence Redmond's 763. D. Courtenay polled worse, with 77. See NLI, ITGWU Special List A8, ms. 15,676 (1).

12. Irish Transport and General Workers' Union, *The Attempt to Smash the Irish Transport and General Workers' Union*; Annual Report for 1924, and Proceedings of Annual Conference, Newry, 6–7 Aug. (Proceedings of Annual Conference), 1925, p. 5–9, 21; Report of Special Delegate Conference, Connolly Hall, Cork, 8–9 Aug. 1924; Annual Report for 1925, p. 10; Thomas McCarthy, 'The organisation of building workers,' *Liberty*, Apr. 1963; Irish Labour Party and Trades Union Congress, Report of Proceedings of Special Congress, Dublin, 14–15 Mar. 1924, p. 12–43; Report of 30th Congress, Cork, 4–7 Aug. 1924, p. 180–82; Report of National Executive, 1924–1925, p. 21.

13. ITGWU, Annual Report for 1924 and Proceedings of Annual Conference, 1925, p. 9–10, 21; Irish Labour Party and Trades Union Congress, Report of 30th Congress, Cork, 4–7 Aug. 1924, p. 131–2, 189–190, 199; Report of National Executive, 1924–1925, p. 19–20.

14. ITGWU, Annual Report for 1924, p. 7; Irish Labour Party and Trades Union Congress, Report of 30th Congress, Cork, 4–7 Aug. 1924, p. 173–9, 197–8, 206; Report of National Executive, 1924–1925, p. 32–6.

15. Irish Transport and General Workers' Union, *The Attempt to Smash the Irish Transport and General Workers' Union*, p. 43.

Chapter 11 (p. 176–203)

1. ITGWU, Annual Report for 1924 and Report of Proceedings of Annual Conference, Newry, 6–7 Aug. 1925, p. 16–; Annual Report for 1925, p. 5–6, p. 16–; minutes of National Executive Council, 23 Jan. 1925, 3–4 Apr. 1925, 19 Nov. 1925. Legal costs arose mainly as a result of actions taken against the Executive by Larkin.

2. ITGWU, Annual Report for 1925 and Proceedings of Annual Conference, 1926, p. 28–9; Annual Report for 1928 and Proceedings of Annual Conference, 1929, p. 27; *Voice of Labour*, 10 Jan. 1925, 4 Apr. 1925, 2 May 1925, 4 July 1925.

3. ITGWU, Annual Report for 1926, p. 6–7; minutes of National Executive Council, 15–16 May 1926; *Voice of Labour*, 25 Apr. 1925, 3 Apr., 1926, 1 May 1926, 5 June 1926. The ICWU appears to have collapsed in 1924, with most members going individually to the Irish Union of Distributive Workers and Clerks. For nurses see Devine, *An Eccentric Chemistry*. Nurses attended from Carlow, Cork, Ennis, Enniscorthy, Grangegorman, Limerick, Mullingar, Port Laoise and Portrane. It is not clear what happened in Letterkenny. The ITGWU actually took positive steps to induce nurses to join the union rather than the English union. Minutes of National Executive Council, 29 Jan. 1926.

4. ITGWU, Annual Report for 1926 and Proceedings of Annual Conference, 1927, p. 18. It was a 'year of distress and hardship.' Annual Report for 1927 and Proceedings of Annual Conference, 1928, p. 6, 30–32; Annual Report for 1928, p. 5; minutes of National Executive Council, 18 Mar. 1928, giving approval of rate reductions; 30

Sep. 1928. The conditions for reinstatement were further amended, 17 Jan. 1929. *Voice of Labour,* 15 Jan. 1927.

5. ITGWU, Annual Report for 1924 and Proceedings of Annual Conference, 1925, p. 19. In addition to those addressing the Conference, Éamon Lynch, Séamus O'Brien, T. J. Redmond and C. F. Ridgway were also on the staff. Patrick O'Doherty, Organiser, emigrated to the United States, and Joe Metcalfe became Secretary of Dún Laoghaire Branch. Minutes of National Executive Council, 29 Jan. 1926. Michael McCarthy, Organiser, was dismissed in January 1928 after a lengthy investigation regarding poor work and money unaccounted for, although he was still active enough to be imprisoned during the gas strike in Tralee in October. Minutes of National Executive Council, 25–6 Mar. 1926, 9–11 Oct. 1926, 21–22 Jan. 1928. Séamus O'Brien, Organiser, was offered the post of Secretary of Galway Branch, 25 June 1927, when it was decided that 'unless a considerable improvement' in membership occurred 'a considerable reduction would have to be made in the number of Organisers employed.' Denis Houston was dismissed after a row with a Labour Party candidate, A. J. Cassidy, in Donegal, 30 September 1927. In December 1926 it was decided to reduce the number of Organisers to two 'as soon as feasible,' with other employment in the union found if possible. Minutes of National Executive Council, 11 Dec. 1926; minutes of National Executive Council, 22 Nov. 1927, 17 and 21–22 Jan. 1928, 29 Apr. 1928, 30 Sep. 1928, 16 Dec. 1928, 17 Jan. 1929. He was wished 'every success.'

6. *Voice of Labour,* 3 Oct. 1925, 29 May 1926.

7. ITGWU, Annual Report for 1925 and Proceedings of Annual Conference, 1925, p. 24; *Voice of Labour,* 21 Feb. 1925, and Irish Transport and General Workers' Union, *The Attempt to Smash the Irish Transport and General Workers' Union,* p. 75. Paul Whitty's poem 'Father Albert' was published in *Voice of Labour,* 12 Dec. 1925. Among those in attendance were Archie Heron, Joe Metcalfe, Séamus Everett TD, John Dunne (Secretary, Bray United Trades and Labour Council), Laurence Redmond (Aughrim), James Murphy (NUR), Peter Holden (Avoca), John Conroy (Wicklow), Martin Kehoe (Enniscorthy), 500 members from Arklow, and representatives of the Irish National Foresters, the Ancient Order of Hibernians and the local Fishermen's Association. *Voice of Labour,* 8 and 15 Jan. 1927, the latter bearing a photograph on the front page and an obituary.

8. ITGWU, minutes of National Executive Council, 10 May 1929.

9. *Voice of Labour,* 24 Jan. 1925. 'Larkin's Right-Hand Man! P. T. Daly's Libel Action is now published in pamphlet form. A complete record of the Legal Action and Facsimiles of the Sligo Letter and Faked Books and Other Documents. An amazing revelation. Order from Literature Department 35 Parnell Square.' *Voice of Labour,* 31 Jan. 1925; ITGWU, Annual Reports, 1925–1926. In 1925 'coal, freight and insurance' cost £427 3s 5d and bank charges were £26 0s 6d; in 1926 expenses of £32 11s 6d were incurred. Against that, an income of £160 was recorded in 1925 and a further £13 17s 2d in 1926.

10. *Voice of Labour,* 7 Feb. 1925, 9 May 1925, 22 and 29 Aug. 1925. In fact a 'trade dispute' under the Trade Disputes Act (1906) could be between worker and worker. *Voice of Labour,* 5 and 12 Sep. 1925. 'We regret we are unable to insert the advertisement in the *Sunday Worker.* There appears to be a dispute between two Unions in which we

are unwilling to participate. Hoping that you will appreciate the situation which compels us to take this line.' At a meeting at Burgh Quay, Lawlor claimed the WIR had given them £300. *Voice of Labour*, 19 Sep. 1927, 7, 14 and 21 Nov. 1927, 5 Feb. 1927.

11. Irish Labour Party and Trades Union Congress, Report of 31st Congress, Newry, 3–6 Aug. 1925, p. 76–; *Irishman*, 22 Dec. 1928.

12. ITGWU, Annual Report for 1924 and Proceedings of Annual Conference, 1925, p. 35–6; Annual Report for 1925 and Proceedings of Annual Conference, 1926, p. 7, 28–30. A further attempt to introduce a rate of 4d a week for land workers, submitted by South Wexford, was defeated in 1929. See Proceedings of Annual Conference, 1929, p. 29; Annual Report for 1926, p. 5; minutes of National Executive Council, 9–11 Oct. 1926, 11 Dec. 1926; 'Mask comes off: Larkin's union organises blacklegs,' *Voice of Labour*, 13 June 1925, 17 Apr. 1926, 8 May 1926, 5 June 1926, 7 and 28 Aug. 1926 ('Obscurantism in Tralee' and 'Troglodytes who rule Tralee'), 4 and 11 Dec. 1926.

13. ITGWU, Annual Report for 1927, p. 5; Annual Report for 1928 and Proceedings of Annual Conference, 1929, p. 5, 7, 18; Annual Report for 1929, p. 5–6; minutes of National Executive Council, 30 July 1927; *Irishman*, 13 and 20 Apr. 1929.

14. ITGWU, Annual Report for 1925, p. 7; Annual Report for 1926 and Proceedings of Annual Conference, 1927, p. 18; minutes of National Executive Council, 25 Sep. 1925, 30 July 1927. *Voice of Labour*, 16 May 1925, 24 Apr. 1926, 26 June 1926 ('Shannon Scheme scandal'), 3 July 1926 ('Not fit for human beings').

15. 'Metropole for trade unionism: Workers' fight for recognition,' *Voice of Labour*, 11 and 18 July 1925. The directors were Patrick and Peter Corrigan (5 Lower Camden Street, Dublin), Aubrey V. O'Rourke (1 Rutland Terrace, Clontarf), Maurice Elliman (29 Dufferin Avenue), Patrick J. Wall (Ennistimon, Co. Clare), George J. Nesbitt ('Bessboro', Kimmage Road) and Francis B. O'Rourke (1 Hillview Terrace, Clontarf). The solicitors were W. P. Corrigan and M. A. Corrigan, although Pat Corrigan died before the strike. The first list of scabs included 'James Cranny, acting as chef; Rose Smith; two Wilsons, brothers, as kitchen men; Mrs. Antoine, Kitty Maher, Dalton, Mrs. Demange, King in the grill; Chrissie Field who scabbed in the Standard; Miss Lambe and Daly on first floor; Mrs. Martin, Mrs. Hepburn, Miss O'Mara on second floor; Rose Kenny and her cousin May Bolger; Gilsenan and Michael Kelly, cellarmen.' Wall gave evidence that Ridgway entered the kitchens and ordered the staff out, while O'Shannon was accused of 'intimidating Rose Kelly, assaulting her by catching her by the shoulder, likely to cause breach of [the] peace, fined £1, bound over [for] 6 months.' On 25 July greater detail was given: 'THE BLACK LIST: John Dixon, lift boy, age about sixteen, seems proud of being a scab; Kathleen Gregory, lives Dolphin's Barn way. Is counted as a waitress, and, as can be seen by Court case, willing to do the bidding of the boss; Kathleen Howard, another hero of McAdam's and figures in the Court. Acting as barmaid at present in Metropole; Mrs. Martin. Waitress. Husband in Army. What Army? Maggie Kenny. An import received from the shirt factory. Formerly worked in Johnston's; Miss 'Caruso' Burke, Stock-keeper; Mrs. Farrelly, 16 Mount Pleasant Square. Husband working. In case of Metropole Dispute drew the Union money up to the last and then scabbed it. Letters resigning membership of the Union have been received from the following three scabs. The letters are in similar terms, and, we assume,

had common inspirations: Nellie Hepburn, 8 Hope Street, Ringsend. Works all week in the Metropole and on Sunday works in Bray Head Hotel; Mrs. Antoine, 38 Lower Mount Street; and Miss Lambe, 5 Royal Canal Terrace, Broadstone. McLellan, waiter, from Imperial Hotel, Belfast. Scabbed it there on [British] Workers' Union, now playing the same game here; Wilson Bros., Lucan. Late permanent way workers Lucan trams; Miss K. Ivors, late Ritz and Harrison's; Gore's Cottages, Camden Row, supplies a quota: Rose Reilly, Mrs. Redmond, Letitia O'Brien. All these are presently enjoying holidays with pay, for there's no trade at all, and the directors are considering a 50% reduction in staff.'

16. ITGWU, minutes of National Executive Council, 11 Dec. 1926; *Voice of Labour*, 1 Aug. 1925, 10 Oct. 1925, 14 Nov. 1925; 2, 9, 16 Jan. ('Met—Not peace but war') 23 Jan. ('Met—The fight grows keener') and 30 Jan. 1926; 6, 13 and 20 Feb. 1926, 13 Mar. 1926, 8 May 1926. The two were Geoffrey Goodheart, conductor, and F. Stewart, instrumentalist. The officers of the HEA were P. Brophy (Chairman), M. Freyne (Secretary) and Fred A. Moran and G. W. Manning (Organisers). Freyne had been sacked by mid-May. *Voice of Labour*, 5, 12 and 19 June 1927, 7 Aug. ('Tilting the scales of justice') and 14 Aug. 1927, 29 Jan. 1927, 5 Feb. 1927; Irish Labour Party and Trades Union Congress, Report of 32nd Congress, Galway, 2–5 Aug. 1926, p. 177–8.

17. ITGWU, Annual Report for 1926, p. 6; Annual Report for 1928 and Proceedings of Annual Conference, 1929, p. 6, 29; Annual Report for 1929, p. 6; *Voice of Labour*, 3 and 10 July 1926; *Irishman*, 19 Jan. 1929.

18. ITGWU, Annual Report for 1926 and Proceedings of Annual Conference, 1927, p. 18; *Voice of Labour*, 3 Jan. 1925. The Delegates for the Limerick Junction Co-op Creamery Conciliation Board were Patrick Keogh (Garryspillane), Jim Baggot (Herbertstown), Bobbie Heuston (Oola), Mick O'Dwyer (Solloghodbeg), P. J. O'Brien and Paddy O'Doherty (ITGWU). *Voice of Labour*, 22 Aug. 1926, 20 Mar. 1926; Irish Labour Party and Trades Union Congress, Report of 31st Congress, Newry, 3–6 Aug. 1925, p. 122, 147–9.

19. ITGWU, minutes of National Executive Council, 29 Jan., 9–11 Oct. 1926, 30 Sep. 1927, 18 Mar. 1928; *Voice of Labour*, 28 Feb. 1925; Walker, *Parliamentary Election Results in Ireland*, p. 48–9. Others were Sam Kyle (ATGWU), Belfast North, and Jack Beattie (blacksmith), Belfast East. See Edward McKeown, 'Newry Branch history,' in McCamley, *The Third James*, p. 6–8.

20. ITGWU, minutes of National Executive Council, 23 Jan. 1925; *Voice of Labour*, 7 Feb. 1925, 14 Mar. 1925, 9 May 1925; *Irishman*, 26 Jan. 1929.

21. ITGWU, minutes of National Executive Council, 8–10 May 1926, 15–16 May 1926; Annual Report for 1926, p. 7; *Voice of Labour*, 25 July 1925, 8 Aug. 1925. Cork ITGWU sent similar messages, 22 Aug. 1925.

22. ITGWU, Annual Report for 1925, p. 9–10; *Voice of Labour*, 14 Feb. 1925; Irish Labour Party and Trades Union Congress, Report of National Executive, 1925–1926, and 31st Congress, Newry, 3–6 Aug. 1925, p. 41–2, 96–104, 105–6.

23. ITGWU, Annual Report for 1925, p. 9. For a fuller discussion see Croke and Devine, *James Connolly Labour College.*

24. ITGWU, Annual Report for 1926, p. 7; Annual Report for 1927, p. 7–8; minutes of National Executive Council, 23 Jan. 1925, 25 June 1927. See 'Next week's Voice,' *Voice of Labour*, 27 June 1925: there was 'nothing to equal it,' and it would 'not merely be

a journal of opinion. IT WILL BE A REAL WEEKLY NEWSPAPER FOR THE WORKERS. All the old writers will continue to contribute, and a host of new ones have promised their services'; 'The Voice's last word,' *Voice of Labour,* 7 May 1927. Ruddy, the Newry employer, won damages of £250.

25. ITGWU, Annual Report for 1927, p. 7–9; Annual Report for 1929, p. 8; Annual Report for 1930, p. 7; minutes of National Executive Council, 22 May 1925, 30 Sep. 1927, 12 Aug. 1928. Numbers 29A and 31 Eden Quay and 122 Emmet Road, Inchicore, were let, while the Tralee and Wexford premises were sold. Minutes of National Executive Council, 10 May 1929. In the former case the £600 raised was used to purchase new premises for £400, 29 July; Newbridge was put up for sale, 1 Dec. *Irishman,* 16 July 1927, 1 Oct. 1927. Article by P.C.T., 1927; 27 July 1929, 16 Nov. 1929. Prices were £2 per week, including board; children aged twelve to fifteen, 30s.

26. ITGWU, Annual Report for 1925, p. 8–9; minutes of National Executive Council, 23 Jan., 6–7 Mar. 1925, 10 July 1925, 25–26 Mar. 1926; *Voice of Labour,* 14 Feb. 1925. There were 97 rejected votes out of a total ballot of 6,863. O'Shannon owed more than 11s. Surprising individuals also got into arrears, an indication perhaps of difficult times for everyone in making ends meet. O'Shannon lapsed again in late 1926, was suspended, and reinstated after he cleared his card. Minutes of National Executive Council, 11 Dec. 1926. Cork Builders' Labourers were the first to seek exemption. *Voice of Labour,* 7 Mar. 1925. Cullen polled 8,422 in Dublin North, third behind Leonard (Cumann na nGaedheal), 17,379, and Traynor (Republican), 15,598; Lawlor polled 4,237, behind Hennessey (Cumann na nGaedheal), 24,075, and O'Mullane (Republican), 13,900. Walker, *Parliamentary Election Results in Ireland,* p. 116–17; 'Cards on the table, gentlemen, please!' *Voice of Labour,* 31 Oct. 1925.

27. ITGWU, Annual Report for 1927 and Proceedings of Annual Conference, 1928, p. 30–31; Annual Report for 1928 and Proceedings of Annual Conference, 1929, p. 6–7, 29; Annual Report for 1929 and Proceedings of Annual Conference, 1930, p. 7–8, 26; minutes of National Executive Council, 1 Apr. 1927, 25 June 1927. Cullen, Lawlor and Johnson were successful. Cork Brewery members withdrew from the Political Levy in June. Minutes of National Executive Council, 29 Aug. 1927. £150 was granted to Éamon Lynch, £100 to Hugh Colohan, Richard Corish, James Everett, J. F. Gill, Gilbert Lynch, Daniel Morrissey, T. J. Murphy, O'Brien and Tim Quill, £50 to Harry Broderick, and £100 (if selected) to Heron, Thomas O'Reilly, O'Shannon and Jim Hickey. Minutes of National Executive Council, 30 Sep. 1930, and Walker, *Parliamentary Election Results in Ireland,* p. 109–10, 119, 126, 133, 139; *Voice of Labour,* 2 Jan. 1926; *Irishman,* 3 Sep. 1927; Irish Labour Party and Trades Union Congress, Report of 32nd Congress, Galway, 2–5 Aug. 1926, p. 140–47.

28. Morrissey, *William O'Brien,* p. 252–3. Morrissey contests this view.

Chapter 12 (p. 204–20)

1. C. N. Ferguson, 'Larkin and the union, part 2,' *Report,* Aug. 1952; Donal Nevin, 'Titan at bay,' in *James Larkin,* p. 74–83.

2. NA, Registrar of Friendly Societies, file 369T; 'The new movement,' *Irish Worker,* 21 June 1924; 'Carney memoir' cited by Emmet Larkin in *James Larkin,* p. 282–3. Other members of the Provisional Committee were Denis Redmond, John Kenny, Peter Larkin and Michael Whitty, with Conway, John Dempsey, Henry Fitzsimons, Forde,

and John Ruth as Trustees. The signatories of the Rules were Vincent Atkinson, Andrew Baker, George Caliph, Bernard Costello, Michael Costello, John Doyle, Francis Rankin and Sheppard. See Hyman, *The Workers' Union*.

3. *Irish Worker*, 7 Mar. 1925, 2 and 19 May 1925; *Voice of Labour*, 7 Feb. 1925, 14 Mar. 1925, 9 May 1925, 4 July 1925 ('Larking in Limerick'). Robert 'Bob' Stewart, born in Scotland in 1877, trained as a ship's carpenter and in 1921 was a founder-member of the Communist Party of Great Britain, serving on its Executive Committee until 1936. He was sent by the Comintern to Ireland in 1924 to assist with the establishment of an Irish Communist Party. See his *Breaking the Fetters* (London: Lawrence and Wishart, 1967). Nolan showed that in the 1922 elections for Branch Delegates, presumably the last actually held, he had polled 1,454; Lawrence Redmond polled 1,155, James Byrne 670 and William Holloway 259.

4. ITGWU, minutes of National Executive Council, 11–12 July 1924; 6–7 Mar. 1931; *Voice of Labour*, 10 July 1926; *Irishman*, 8 Feb. 1929, 30 May 1929, 19 Oct. 1929.

5. *Irish Worker*, 21 June 1924, 9 Aug. 1924, 20 Sep. 1924 ('A fishy story'), 6 Dec. 1924; 'Now to deal with the Transport Union,' *Irish Worker*, 21 Mar. 1925; *Voice of Labour*, 29 Nov. 1924; '400 box like houses' would be built, their construction manna from heaven at a time of acute economic depression. *Irish Worker*, 23 May 1925; Emmet Larkin, *James Larkin*, p. 283–4; Nevin, 'Larkin and the Workers' Union of Ireland,' in *James Larkin*, p. 344; C. N. Ferguson, 'Larkin and the union, part 3,' *Report*, Sep. 1952.

6. WUI, Report of Annual Delegate Conference, Dublin, 19 June 1949, p. 7. Nevin, 'Larkin and the WUI,' in *James Larkin*, p. 344–5, suggests that Liverpool merchants wanted £12,000 or no more coal would be sent. Larkin crossed over, met them and accepted their cigars, pointing out that 'unless they continued to export coal to his co-op' the strike would collapse and they would never be paid. 'He got the coal.' C. N. Ferguson, 'Larkin and the union, part 3,' *Report*, Sep. 1952; 'Danger and opportunity,' *Irish Times*, 14 Aug. 1925. The 'economic development' in the balance was presumably the Shannon Hydro-electric Scheme; *Irish Times*, 13–28 Aug.; Emmet Larkin, *James Larkin*, p. 284–6; *Voice of Labour*, 31 Jan., 1925, 7 Feb. 1925, 5 Dec. 1925 ('The Good Shepherd'). He is erroneously cited as William. *Voice of Labour*, 15 Jan. 1927. James Everett TD, John Conroy (Branch Secretary), Hugh Byrne, R. Noctor, P. Sullivan, Joseph Doyle, Thomas Doyle and W. Vickers were all acquitted of riot.

7. NLI, O'Brien Papers, ms. 15,670, Seán McLoughlin, 'How Inchicore was lost'; O'Casey Papers, Carney to O'Casey, 27 July 1948, cited by Niamh Puirséil in 'Seán O'Casey Papers,' *Saothar*, 31 (2006), p. 129–31; *Voice of Labour*, 24 Jan. 1925.

8. See Ger Lewis, *Loosening the Chains: Nenagh Branch, ITGWU-SIPTU, 1918–1997*, (Nenagh: SIPTU, 2003), p. 47–81. Morrissey polled 5,580 and Doherty 2,955. Walker, *Parliamentary Election Results in Ireland*, p. 114–15; 117–43.

9. *Irish Worker*, 1 Nov. 1929; Charles Phipps, 'Memories of Mallin Hall,' *Report*, May 1954.

10. ILHSA, Dublin Trades Council, minutes of Executive, 11 June 1925, 12 Feb. 1926, 27 Nov. 1928; Cody et al., *The Parliament of Labour*, p. 148–50. 'Larkin's Right-Hand Man! P. T. Daly's Libel Action is now published in pamphlet form. A complete record of the Legal Action and Facsimiles of the Sligo Letter and Faked Books and Other Documents. An Amazing revelation. Order from Literature Department

35 Parnell Square,' and 'STOP PRESS: P. T. DALY LOSES AGAIN: APPEAL DIS-
MISSED WITH COSTS,' *Voice of Labour*, 31 Jan. 1925, 4 Apr. 1925, 6 Mar. 1926;
Irishman, 22 Dec. 1928; Mike Milotte, *Communism in Modern Ireland: In Pursuit of
the Workers' Republic since* 1916 (Dublin: Gill & Macmillan, 1984), p. 80.

11. *Voice of Labour*, 16 May 1925, 12 Sep. 1925 ('The tin cans go round again'). John
Lawlor claimed that locked-out men each got 5s from the WIR. Mike Milotte,
Communism in Modern Ireland: In Pursuit of the Workers' Republic since 1916
(Dublin: Gill & Macmillan, 1984), p. 78–9; Cody et al., *The Parliament of Labour*, p.
139–41.

12. *Voice of Labour*, 14 and 21 Mar. 1925, 14 Nov. 1925; Gaughan, *Thomas Johnson*, p.
271–7.

13. 'A history of the Communist movement in Ireland,' at www.Communistparty of-
ireland.ie/pairti.html. Members of the Executive of the Irish Worker League
included P. T. Daly, John Lawlor, Jack Dempsey (world heavyweight boxing champion) and Muriel MacSwiney (widow of Terence MacSwiney). Mike Milotte,
Communism in Modern Ireland: In Pursuit of the Workers' Republic since 1916
(Dublin: Gill & Macmillan, 1984), p. 70; *Voice of Labour*, 14 and 28 Feb. 1925. The
'convention' was that of the National Minority Movement, whose speaker was P.
Murray. *Workers' Republic*, 18 June 1927; Cody et al., *The Parliament of Labour*, p. 143.

14. *Irish Worker*, 8 Sep. 1923, 3 May 1924 (for Mansion House meeting on 27 April); *The
Communist International Between the Fifth and Sixth World Congresses, 1924–1928*
(London: Communist Party of Great Britain, 1928), 'Report on Ireland,' p. 133–7.
This report was written by Jack Carney, who Larkin left behind in Moscow. Walker,
Parliamentary Election Results in Ireland, p. 127–8, 131. Lawlor polled 2,857, while
the Labour candidate, Thomas Lawlor, polled 3,662, a total that without a second
candidate might have been enough; Young Jim polled 2,126, while Johnson polled
3,626. Big Jim polled 7,490, while the Secretary of the Bakers' Union, Denis Cullen,
the sitting Labour TD, got 2,044 and Thomas O'Reilly, an ITGWU Official, 665. In the
by-election, Rice polled 21,731 and Clarke 13,322. Had Larkin not stood, the
Government would probably have lost the seat. *Voice of Labour*, 24 Jan. 1925 (for the
bankruptcy hearing); *Irishman*, 24 Sep. 1927, 15 Oct. 1927, 3 Dec. 1927; C. N.
Ferguson, 'Larkin and the union, part 3,' *Report*, Sep. 1952; Emmet Larkin, *James
Larkin*, p. 286–93.

Chapter 14 (p. 225–60)

1. ITGWU, Annual Report for 1929 and Report of Proceedings of Annual Conference,
1930, p. 18; Annual Report for 1930, p. 5–7; minutes of National Executive Council,
18 Jan. 1930, 5–26 July 1930, 12–13 Dec. 1930, 16 Oct. 1931. Metcalfe, Secretary of Dún
Laoghaire Branch, was given a 'special grant of £100' for his 'long and faithful service' and O'Leary £25. Hackett was given £5 but, having been let go from Dublin No.
1 Branch, accepted employment in the ITGWU Tobacco Shop, where she remained
until its closure. In Metcalfe's case the NEC purchased an insurance book for him.
Irishman, 1 Mar. 1930, 17 and 24 May 1930. A Sligo ITGWU and Sligo Town selection
played at the Showgrounds before 'a good attendance.' It finished 2-2, with Pa
Rooney scoring for the ITGWU and Kilfeather equalising for the town. There was
also a dance and a flag day. 'A bit of union history,' *Liberty*, Jan. 1975. The members

included dockers, coal workers, carters, oil workers, flour milling, fish and poultry, laundries, drapers' porters, furniture porters, carpet planners, chemical workers, soap and candle, drug workers, ironmongery, stationary engine drivers, newspaper and printing workers, confectionery, and wine and spirit workers.

2. ITGWU, Annual Report for 1930 and Proceedings of Annual Conference, 1931, p. 18, 26; Annual Report for 1931, p. 5, 10–16; minutes of National Executive Council, 6–7 Mar., 22 May 1931. The LDLS functioned as 'the "Dockers" Section of our Limerick Branch and the local Society going out of existence.'

3. ITGWU, Annual Report for 1931 and Proceedings of Annual Conference, 1932, p. 19, 22. It was moved by J. C. Flanagan and M. Keane (Dublin No. 3 Branch). Annual Report for 1932, p. 5; Annual Report for 1933 and Proceedings of Annual Conference, 1934, p. 20; minutes of National Executive Council, 22–3 Apr. 1932.

4. ITGWU, Annual Report for 1933, p. 5, 24; minutes of National Executive Council, 12–13 May 1933, 30 June to 1 July 1933, 15 July 1933; Séamus Redmond, 'We Ain't Got a Barrel of Money': History of the Marine, Port and General Workers' Union' (unpublished paper), especially 'The birth of the union,' p. 1–42, and 'The emergence of the Irish Seamen and Port Workers' Union,' p. 43–69. I am grateful to Mick Corcoran and Michael Hayes (MPGWU) for access to this document. Although ITGWU dockers had supported the seamen, the National Executive Council decided that if they 'withdrew their labour no benefit would be sanctioned.'

5. ITGWU, Annual Report for 1933 and Proceedings of Annual Conference, 1934, p. 19–20, 23. Duffy made further reference to support by the Irish Trades Union Congress for an Agricultural Wages Board at the 1935 ITGWU Conference, p. 24; Annual Report for 1934 and Proceedings of Annual Conference, 1935, p. 19–23; Annual Report for 1935 and Proceedings of Annual Conference, 1936, p. 23, 26–7 p. 9; ITGWU, minutes of National Executive Council, 14–15 Dec. 1934, 22–23 Nov. 1935, 3–4 Jan. 1936, 13–14 Feb. 1936. A complete breakdown of Branch memberships was: Dublin No. 1: 3,265; Cork: 2,738; Dublin No. 3: 1,519; Limerick: 1,419; Dublin No. 4: 1,250; Belfast: 970; Dublin No. 6: 854; Dublin No. 8: 512; Newry: 354; Tralee: 313; Kilrush: 317; Waterford: 293; Sligo: 291; Leix-Offaly: 288; Carlow: 277; Mallow: 277; Arigna: 263; Blarney: 250; Rathfarnham: 249; Drogheda: 242; Bray: 225; Kilkenny: 198; Mullingar: 195; Enniscorthy: 139; Foynes: 128; Athlone: 125; Wexford: 118; Mullingar MH: 117; Ballysadare: 111; Dunmanway: 110; Dún Laoghaire: 109; Ballina: 105; Navan: 96; Fermoy: 77; Mitchelstown: 77; Thurles: 77; Tuam: 77; Thomastown-Bennettsbridge: 74; Cahir: 73; Westport Quay: 71; Graigue: 70; Bandon: 66; Mountmellick: 66; Fenit: 58; Carrick-on-Suir: 51; Boyle: 50; Castlebar: 48; Youghal: 48; Cavan: 46; Dungarvan: 45; Castlerea: 41; Carrick-on-Shannon: 40; Cóbh: 38; Dublin No. 2: 38; Midleton: 38; Belmullet: 37; Nenagh: 35; Blanchardstown: 32; Balbriggan: 31; Callan: 30; Ballyshannon: 29; Naas: 27; Newbridge [Droichead Nua]: 25; Rathdrum: 22; Ballinrobe: 17; Skerries: 11; Buttevant: 10; Aughrim: 9; and Clondalkin: 8. ITGWU, minutes of National Executive Council, 29–30 Mar. 1935.

6. ITGWU, Annual Report for 1936 and Proceedings of Annual Conference, 1937, p. 5–7, 24–6. Nixie Boran (Moneenroe) added grist mills, and Thomas Ryan (NEC, Waterford) and John Conroy (Limerick) also spoke. Annual Report for 1937 and Proceedings of Annual Conference, 1938, p. 20–21, 25–6, 28–9.

7. ITGWU, Annual Report for 1938 and Proceedings of Annual Conference, 1939, p. 23–4;

minutes of National Executive Council, 20–21 Oct. 1939, 18 Nov. 1939; Irish Trades Union Congress, Report of National Executive, 1937–1938, p. 38–40; Irish Trades Union Congress, Report of National Executive, 1938–1939, p. 36–8, 59–63. McMullen was on the London–Stranraer train that struck the London–Inverness express standing at the station. See www.livingarchive.org.uk/wherelinesmeet/jeff.html.

8. ITGWU, Annual Report for 1938, p. 10; minutes of National Executive Council, 24–25 June 1932, 23–24 Sep. 1932.

9. Irish Trades Union Congress, Report of 41st Congress, Derry, 31 July to 2 Aug. 1935, p. 144–51.

10. ITGWU, Annual Report for 1936 and Proceedings of Annual Conference, 1937, p. 26–7; Irish Trades Union Congress, Report of 38th Congress, Cork, 27–29 July 1932, p. 126–8.

11. ITGWU, Annual Report for 1936 and Proceedings of Annual Conference, 1937, p. 23; Annual Report for 1937, p. 9; Annual Report for 1939, p. 8; minutes of National Executive Council, 17–18 Oct. 1930, 23–24 Oct. 1936; Irish Trades Union Congress, Report of National Executive, 1930–1931, and 37th Congress, Waterford, 29 July to 1 Aug. 1930, p. 37, 86–91. William McEwan (Dublin Trades Council), W. Scott (Dublin Typographical Provident Society), McGrath and Miss O'Connor (Irish Women Workers' Union) were members of the Committee. Report of National Executive, 1935–1936, p. 44–6. Others were Seán P. Campbell (Dublin Typographical Provident Society), Denis Cullen (Irish Bakers', Confectioners' and Allied Workers' Union), Gerald Doyle (Operative Plasterers and Allied Trades Society of Ireland), Michael Drumgoole (Irish Union of Distributive Workers and Clerks), Sam Kyle (ATGWU), Helena Molony (Irish Women Workers' Union), Robert Morrow (Plumbers', Glaziers' and Domestic Engineers' Union), William Norton TD (Post Office Workers' Union), J. T. O'Farrell (Railway Clerks' Association); Michael Somerville (Amalgamated Society of Woodworkers) and C. D. Watters (National Union of Railwaymen). Report of National Executive, 1934–1935, p. 65–7; Report of National Executive, 1936–1937, p. 49; Report of National Executive, 1938–1939 and 45th Congress, Waterford, 2–4 Aug. 1939, p. 87–101, 153–5.

12. ITGWU, minutes of National Executive Council, 18 Dec. 1931, 22–23 Apr. 1932, 25–26 Nov. 1932, 26 May 1934. A decision to withdraw from the Dublin Trades Council if the WUI was admitted was taken at this meeting. ITGWU, minutes of National Executive Council, 20 July 1936. Daniel Clancy and Thomas Ryan voted with Foran, while Michael Connor, Michael Duffy, Edward Finnegan, John McLarnon, William Murphy, Michael Connor, John McLarnon and Dominick Sullivan were with O'Brien. ITGWU, minutes of National Executive Council, 2 Aug. 1936, 4–5 Sep. 1936.

13. ITGWU, Annual Report for 1931 and Proceedings of Annual Conference, 1932, p. 7, 22. A motion was adopted calling for a Committee to fully investigate the employment, conditions and wages of boys, moved by J. R. Hunter (Cahir) and T. Darcy (Dublin No. 1 Branch). ITGWU, Annual Report for 1933 and Proceedings of Annual Conference, 1934, p. 24; minutes of National Executive Council, 12–13 Dec. 1930; Report of National Executive, 1930–1931; and 37th Congress, Waterford, 29 July–1 Aug. 1931, p. 60–69; Irishman, 2 Aug. 1930. Ridgway and O'Sullivan held a Conference of dockers in January 1931, with nineteen Delegates attending from Ballina, Belfast, Cork, Dublin, Fenit, Foynes, Newry, Limerick, Sligo and Westport.

14. ITGWU, Annual Report for 1933 and Proceedings of Annual Conference, 1934, p. 7, 23–4. T. J. Murphy TD thanked the National Executive Council for its 'splendid support' of the Benduff men. Irish Trades Union Congress, Report of National Executive, 1933–1934, p. 53–6, and Report of National Executive, 1934–1935, p. 67. The other unions were the Irish Municipal Employees' Trade Union, Irish Engineering and Industrial Union and Electrical Trades Union (Ireland), as well as the Dublin Trades Union Council. Irish Trades Union Congress, Report of 38th Congress, Cork, 27–29 July 1932, p. 88–91; Report of 40th Congress, Galway, 8–11 Aug. 1934, p. 32–5.

15. Gains were made for bacon-curing; boots and shoes; building, private and public; carpets, furnishing and upholstery; cinemas; dairies and creameries; gas; electricity; horse and lorry transport; hotels and restaurants; paper manufacture; public works; timber; trams, buses and bus garages; woollen and clothing; and general workers.

16. ITGWU, Annual Report for 1934 and Proceedings of Annual Conference, 1935, p. 7–9, 20, 25; Annual Report for 1935 and Proceedings of Annual Conference, 1936, p. 8–9, 28.

17. ITGWU, Annual Report for 1936, p. 6–8; Annual Report for 1936 and Proceedings of Annual Conference, 1937, p. 23–4; Annual Report for 1937, p. 7; Annual Report for 1938, p. 8–9; Irish Trades Union Congress, Report of 42nd Congress, Tralee, 5–8 Aug. 1936, p. 31; Report of 44th Congress, Bangor, 3–5 Aug. 1938, p. 120–23; Report of 45th Congress, Waterford, 2–4 Aug. 1939, p. 140–42. See George Hunter, 'The ITGWU in Donegal,' *Liberty,* June 1974. Don Sullivan and John Anthony McElhinney, the first Branch Secretary, were the Organisers. McElhinney left to become a priest and was succeeded by William Doherty.

18. ITGWU, Annual Report for 1930, p. 6. The loan was for the Dublin Operative Plasterers' and Bricklayers' Union. Even the lowest rates restored the 1923 levels of pay. Annual Report for 1931, p. 6–7; Annual Report for 1934, p. 9–10; Annual Report for 1937, p. 7; minutes of National Executive Council, 6–7 Mar. 1931; Thomas McCarthy, 'The organisation of the building worker,' *Liberty,* Apr. 1963.

19. ITGWU, Annual Report for 1932, p. 8–9; Annual Report for 1933 and Proceedings of Annual Conference, 1934, p. 8, 24–5; Annual Report for 1934 and Proceedings of Annual Conference, 1935, p. 9–10, 22. Even the lowest rates restored the 1923 levels of pay. Annual Report for 1935, p. 10. This was achieved only after a four-week strike in July–August 1935, when six men were reinstated and given increases. Annual Report for 1936 and Proceedings of Annual Conference, 1937, p. 7, 28–9; Annual Report for 1937 and Proceedings of Annual Conference, 1938, p. 29; Irish Trades Union Congress, Report of 39th Congress, Killarney, 2–4 Aug. 1933, p. 157.

20. ITGWU, Annual Report for 1933 and Proceedings of Annual Conference, 1934, p. 6, 22–3; Annual Report for 1934 and Proceedings of Annual Conference, 1935, p. 7, 24; Annual Report for 1935, p. 7, 11; Annual Report for 1936 and Proceedings of Annual Conference, 1937, p. 31; minutes of National Executive Council, 7–8 Feb. 1935. The proposal was actually defeated, by 6 to 3. It was debated again on 22–23 November and this time rejected by 7 to 5. ITGWU, minutes of National Executive Council, 24–25 May 1935, 22–23 Nov. 1935, 3–4 Jan. 1936.

21. Irish Trades Union Congress, Report of National Executive, 1933–1934, and 40th Congress, Galway, 8–11 Aug. 1934, p. 50–53, 109–10, 122–38; Report of National

Executive, 1934–1935 and 41st Congress, Derry, 31 July to 2 Aug. 1935, p. 59–60, 121–22, 160–62. Other members were P. J. Cairns (President, Post Office Workers' Union), Helena Molony (Irish Women Workers' Union), Denis Cullen (Bakers), and Éamonn Lynch (Secretary). Irish Trades Union Congress, Report of 42nd Congress, Tralee, 5–7 Aug. 1936, p. 124–8, 156–60. All correspondence is cited in full.

22. ITGWU, Annual Report for 1933 and Proceedings of Annual Conference, 1934, p. 27; Annual Report for 1934, p. 9; Annual Report for 1935 and Proceedings of Annual Conference, 1936, p. 30, 33–4; Irish Trades Union Congress, Report of 42nd Congress, Tralee, 5–7 Aug. 1936, p. 148–9.

23. Irish Trades Union Congress, Report of National Executive, 1934–1935, and 41st Congress, Derry, 31 July to 2 Aug. 1935, p. 62–4, 162–4.

24. Irish Trades Union Congress, Report of 39th Congress, Killarney, 2–4 Aug. 1933, p. 145–8; Report of 41st Congress, Derry, 31 July to 2 Aug. 1935, p. 122–6; Report of National Executive, 1935–1936, and 42nd Congress, Tralee, 5–7 Aug. 1936, p. 47, 145.

25. Irish Trades Union Congress, Report of National Executive, 1935–1936, p. 50; Report of National Executive, 1936–1937, p. 53–60; Report of National Executive, 1937–1938, and Report of 44th Congress, Bangor, 3–5 Aug. 1938, p. 45–6, 105–7.

26. ITGWU, Annual Report for 1932, p. 8; Irish Trades Union Congress, Report of 38th Congress, Cork, 27–29 July 1932, p. 79–88; Report of 39th Congress, Killarney, 2–4 Aug. 1933, p. 85–99; Report of 40th Congress, Galway, 8–11 Aug. 1934, p. 23–32; Report of 41st Congress, Derry, 31 July to 2 Aug. 1935, p. 102–15; Report of National Executive, 1935–1936, p. 33–38 (for summary of Congress policy on unemployment, shorter hours and juvenile labour); Report of National Executive, 1936–1937, p. 28–40; 61–3; 'Reply to Mr. Lemass,' Report of National Executive, 1938–1939, and Report of 44th Congress, Waterford, 2–4 Aug. 1949, p. 66–86, 121–7.

27. ITGWU, Annual Report for 1934, p. 10; Irish Trades Union Congress, Report of 37th Congress, Waterford, 29 July to 1 Aug. 1930, p. 96–100, 108–9. Thomas Ryan (NEC, Waterford) also spoke to the motion. Report of 38th Congress, Cork, 27–29 July 1932, p. 110–11, 119–20; Report of National Executive, 1933–1934, p. 58–60; Report of National Executive, 1935–1936, p. 38–9; Report of National Executive, 1936–1937, p. 50–53; Report of 44th Congress, Bangor, 3–5 Aug. 1938, p. 99–100, 107–9; Report of 45th Congress, Waterford, 2–4 Aug. 1939, p. 135–9.

28. ITGWU, Annual Report for 1934 and Proceedings of Annual Conference, 1935, p. 20, 29–30; Annual Report for 1935 and Proceedings of Annual Conference, 1936, p. 10, 24, 30–31; Annual Report for 1936 and Proceedings of Annual Conference, 1937, p. 30; Annual Report for 1937 and Proceedings of Annual Conference, 1938, p. 25–6, 28; Annual Report for 1938 and Proceedings of Annual Conference, 1939, p. 24; Irish Trades Union Congress, Report of National Executive, 1933–1934, p. 61–4; Report of National Executive, 1934–1935, p. 70; Report of 42nd Congress, Tralee, 5–7 Aug. 1936, p. 152–5, 161–2; Report of 45th Congress, Waterford, 2–4 Aug. 1939, p. 127–30, 173.

29. ITGWU, Annual Report for 1931, p. 8; 1938, p. 10; Annual Report for 1932, p. 7; Annual Report for 1934 and Proceedings of Annual Conference, 1935, p. 10, 29. Commercially, however, there was no improvement. ITGWU, Annual Report for 1935 and Proceedings of Annual Conference, 1936, p. 31; Annual Report for 1936 and Proceedings of Annual Conference, 1937, p. 10, 34; Annual Report for 1937 and Proceedings of Annual Conference, 1938, p. 31; minutes of National Executive

Council, 9 May 1930, 12–13 Dec. 1930, 24–25 June 1932, 24–25 July 1932 (Ernest Blythe had indicated that a new claim might be favourably considered in 1930). Minutes of the NEC, 3–4 Mar. 1933, 4–5 Oct. 1935, 13–14 Feb. 1936, 3–4 Apr. 1936, 4–5 Sep. 1936.

30. ITGWU, Annual Report for 1933 and Proceedings of Annual Conference, 1934, p. 10, 26; Annual Report for 1934 and Proceedings of Annual Conference, 1935, p. 11, 21; Annual Report for 1935 and Proceedings of Annual Conference, 1936, p. 32. The motion was moved by J. McCabe (Dublin No. 1 Branch) and J. Fogarty (Dublin No. 3 Branch). Annual Report for 1936 and Proceedings of Annual Conference, 1937, p. 9, 30–31. The ITGWU subscribed £500. Annual Report for 1937 and Proceedings of Annual Conference, 1938, p. 10, 31; minutes of National Executive Council, 15 July 1933, 1–2 Dec. 1933, 27 Mar. 1934. The papers were Richard Corish, 'Housing,' Paddy Hogan, 'Unemployment,' Tom Kennedy, 'Replacement of Adult Labour by Machines,' McMullen, 'Registration of Dockers,' T. J. Murphy, 'Pensions, Widows and Orphans,' and O'Brien, 'Political Situation.' ITGWU, minutes of National Executive Council, 4–5 Oct. 1935; Irish Trades Union Congress, Report of National Executive, 1935–1936, p. 41–2. O'Brien and Lynch were among the lecturers. Report of 42nd Congress, Tralee, 5–7 Aug. 1936, p. 116–20; Report of 44th Congress, Bangor, 3–5 Aug. 1938, p. 126–7.

31. Irish Trades Union Congress, Report of National Executive, 1933–1934; Report of 40th Congress, Galway, 8–11 Aug. 1934, p. 27–9, 38–43, 65–6, 94–106; Report of 41st Congress, Derry, 31 July to 2 Aug. 1935, p. 117–21; Report of 44th Congress, Bangor, 3–5 Aug. 1938, p. 152–3; Report of 45th Congress, Waterford, 2–4 Aug. 1939, p. 150–53, 181–2. The Committee included the Earl of Listowel, Victor Gollancz, Margery Fry, Dorothy Wadman, C. C. Wang and A. D. Clegg.

32. Irish Trades Union Congress, Report of National Executive, 1934–1935, and 41st Congress, Derry, 31 July to 2 Aug. 1935, p. 85–7, 166–7; Report of National Executive, 1935–1936, p. 43–4, 89–91. The other countries were Austria, Belgium, Britain, Bulgaria, Czechoslovakia, Denmark, Finland, France, Greece, Hungary, Italy, Luxembourg, Netherlands, Poland, Romania, Saar Territory, Spain, Sweden and Switzerland. Report of 42nd Congress, Tralee, 5–7 Aug. 1936, p. 128–35.

33. ITGWU, Annual Report for 1930 and Proceedings of Annual Conference, 1931, p. 7–8, 26; Annual Report for 1931 and Proceedings of Annual Conference, 1932, p. 23; Annual Report for 1932, p. 10; minutes of National Executive Council, 9 May 1930, 17–18 Oct. 1930, 12–13 Dec. 1930, 6–7 Mar. 1931. Its authors were Tom Kennedy, Joseph O'Kelly, Charles Ridgway and Cathal O'Shannon. Paddy Hogan TD (Clare) was the first victim of this policy, being 'regarded as a new member from December 1930.' ITGWU, minutes of National Executive Council, 22 Jan. 1932, 22–23 Apr. 1932. In fact the Labour Party withdrew its endorsement of Doyle. Irish Trades Union Congress, Report of National Executive, 1931–1932; 'Foreword,' Irish Worker, 28 Feb. 1931.

34. ITGWU, Annual Report for 1932, p. 10; Annual Report for 1933 and Proceedings of Annual Conference, 1934, p. 25–6; minutes of National Executive Council, 5 Jan. 1933. £300 was given to William O'Brien (Tipperary), Thomas Ryan (Waterford) and Dominick Sullivan (Cork North); £150 was given to Harry Broderick (Longford-Westmeath), P. J. Curran (Co. Dublin), James Everett (Wicklow), Maurice O'Regan (Leitrim-Sligo), J. P. Pattison (Carlow-Kilkenny) and £100 to Richard Corish (Wexford), Paddy Hogan (Clare) and T. J. Murphy (Cork West).

The varying grants reflect the candidates' status within the union, those with problematic cards getting the least. ITGWU, minutes of National Executive Council, 15 July 1933, 26 May 1934, 29–30 Mar. 1935. The TDS were Richard Corish, James Everett, T. J. Murphy and J. P. Pattison, together with Senators Thomas Farren and Michael Duffy and the Athlone Labour man Harry Broderick.

35. They were held in Athy, Bray, Clara, Cork, Drogheda, Drumshanbo, Dublin, Dunmanway, Ennis, Galway, Kilkenny, Kilrush, Limerick, Naas, Sligo, Tipperary, Tralee, Waterford and Wexford.

36. ITGWU, Annual Report for 1934 and Proceedings of Annual Conference, 1935, p. 20, 27; Annual Report for 1935 and Proceedings of Annual Conference, 1936, p. 23–4; Annual Report for 1936 and Proceedings of Annual Conference, 1937, p. 10, 22–4; Annual Report for 1937 and Proceedings of Annual Conference, 1938, p. 9, 20–21, 30; Annual Report for 1938 and Proceedings of Annual Conference, 1939, p. 27; minutes of National Executive Council, 22–3 Nov. 1935; Irish Trades Union Congress, Report of National Executive, 1934–1935, p. 71; Report of 45th Congress, Waterford, 2–4 Aug. 1939, p. 156–7.

Chapter 15 (p. 261–83)

1. *Irish Worker*, 3 Jan. 1931, 21 Feb. 1931, 7 Mar. 1931, 11 and 18 Oct. 1931, 1 and 14 Nov. 1931, 6 Dec. 1931. For Peter Larkin see *Irish Worker*, 23 May to 27 June 1931. R. James was Secretary of the WUI Railway Section.

2. WUI, minutes of General Executive Council, 23 Feb. 1938, 9 Mar. 1938, 20 Apr. 1938; *Irish Worker*, 2 Jan. 1932; Christopher Brien, 'Fifty years of union in Bray', *Unity*, winter 1985. Three thousand badges were ordered from the Jewellery and Metal Manufacturing Company Ltd and made available to members at 6d each.

3. *Irish Worker*, 31 Jan. 1931, 22 Aug. 1931, 17 Oct. 1931.

4. *Irish Worker*, 25 Oct. 1930, 16 May 1931, 27 June 1931.

5. *Irish Worker*, 11 Oct. 1930, 'That the three several Unions (the United Builders' Labourers' Trade Union, the ITGWU, and the WUI) catering for the Building Trades agree that no member, skilled or unskilled, be permitted to work for any Building Contractor for less than 1s. 4d. per hour, etc. That rate to govern Greater Dublin and the Coastal Borough. The three several Unions further agree that no man of any of the Unions be taken into membership without the applicant producing a clear card and transfer permission from his former Union, such transfer card not to be withheld except for good and sufficient reason.' *Irish Worker*, 17, 24 and 31 Jan. 1931, 7 Feb. 1931, 4, 11 and 25 Apr. 1931, 18 July 1931. Cody et al., *The Parliament of Labour*, p. 163–6. The total vote, including that of the National Federation of Building Trade Operatives (a British union), was 2,485 to 1,533, a majority of 952.

6. WUI, minutes of General Executive Council, 23 Mar. 1938.

7. *Irish Worker*, 11 Oct. 1930, 12 Dec. 1931, 2 Jan. 1932. £3,500 of Farrell's deficit was due to a loss on the sale of the Tivoli.

8. *Irish Worker*, 6 Dec. 1930; *The Truth That Is News: Irish Press Strikers' Bulletin*, no. 1–6, n.d. [Oct.–Nov. 1932]; Seán MacBride, *That Day's Struggle: A Memoir*, 1904–1951 (Dublin: Currach Press, 2005), p. 119–20. A typical verse was: 'With regard to the doughty McGrath | Who feels he is almost a rajah | Can hire and can fire | Shove 'em down in the mire | Sure he'll get some way as the Czar!'

9. *Irish Worker,* 8 and 15 Nov. 1930, 31 Jan. 1931, 7 and 14 Feb. 1931, 11 Apr. 1931, 12 Dec. 1931, 2 Jan. 1932; Irish Trades Union Congress, Report of National Executive, 1931–1932, and 38th Congress, Cork, 27–29 July 1932.

10. Séamus Redmond, 'We Ain't Got a Barrel of Money': History of the Marine, Port and General Workers' Union' (unpublished paper), especially 'The birth of the union,' p. 1–42, and 'The emergence of the Irish Seamen's and Port Workers' Union,' p. 43–69. At the First General Meeting of the Irish Seamen's and Port Workers' Union, held in the Mansion House on Sunday 13 August 1933, James Murphy replaced Kelly, who resigned for personal reasons.

11. *Irish Worker,* 29 Nov. 1930, 6 Dec. 1930. 'Today and since 1924, this Union has committed every crime that could be laid to the charge of the most vicious organisation of strike breakers.' *Irish Worker,* 3 Jan. 1931, 21 Feb. 1931, 18 and 25 July 1931, 22 Aug. 1931, 15 Nov. 1931. 'The right to picket: Police prosecute after hearing from wui: Larkinite evidence for employers,' *Irishman,* 31 May 1930.

12. *Irish Worker,* 11 and 25 Oct. 1930; Irish Trades Union Congress, Report of National Executive, 1935–1936, and 42nd Congress, Tralee, 5–7 Aug. 1936, p. 32, 83–9; Report of National Executive, 1936–1937, and 43rd Congress, Dundalk, 4–6 Aug. 1937, p. 27, 107–15; Report of National Executive, 1937–1938, and Report of 44th Congress, Bangor, 3–5 Aug. 1938, p. 39–40, 92, 143–5; Report of 45th Congress, Waterford, 2–4 Aug. 1939, p. 120.

13. *Irish Worker,* 11 and 25 Oct. 1931, 1 and 22 Nov. 1931; 6 Feb. 1932, 12 Mar. 1932. The butchers were John Carney, 47 Moore Street; Patrick Hart, 56 Moore Street; Thomas Walsh and James Carney, Moore Street; E. Hart, 53 Parnell Street; R. Nelson, 9 Meath Street; and L. Gormley, 124 Francis Street. Advertisers included Fishing Trawlers Direct, 11 South Great George's Street; Cook's Fish and Chips, 5 Capel Street and 26 Cuffe Street; Burdock's; J. Starkey, newsagent and tobacconist, 106 Marlborough Street; J. Brady, ladies' and gents' hairdresser, 30 High Street; the 1916 Club, Irish Republican Soldiers' Federation; Talbot Boot Store; and J. McEnerney, 10 Cathedral Street.

14. Serialisation began in the *Irish Worker,* 17 Jan. 1931. Irish Trades Union Congress, Report of 44th Congress, Bangor, 3–5 Aug. 1938, p. 101–4; Report of 45th Congress, Waterford, 2–4 Aug. 1939, p. 131–4.

15. *Irish Worker,* minutes of General Executive Council, 23 Feb. 1938, 1 Oct. to Dec. 1930; and Francis Devine, '"And fighting for the team": James Larkin's unions and football' (unpublished article). The current League of Ireland side Limerick 37 commemorates Dolphin's replacement. *Irish Worker,* 24 Oct. 1931.

16. *Irish Worker,* 8 Dec. 1930, 2 May 1931, 17 Oct. 1931, 7 Nov. 1931, 12 Dec. 1931, 30 Jan. 1932, 6 Feb. 1932, 5 Mar. 1932; Irish Trades Union Congress, Report of 44th Congress, Bangor, 3–5 Aug. 1938, p. 128–32, 152–3, J. Noctor (National Union of Railwaymen) acknowledged his role in the Mount Street Club, of which he was proud, likening it to the Society of St Vincent de Paul. Report of 45th Congress, Waterford, 2–4 Aug. 1939, p. 185–7.

Chapter 17 (p. 289–317)

1. ITGWU, Annual Report for 1939 and Report of Proceedings of Annual Conference, Galway, 8–10 June 1940, p. 19–22; Irish Trades Union Congress, Report of 47th Congress, Drogheda, 16–18 July 1941, p. 129–31.

2. ITGWU, Annual Report for 1939 and Proceedings of Annual Conference, 1940, p. 5–8, 23–4. O'Brien's report was seconded by the Carlow veteran Pádraig Mac Gamhna. Annual Report for 1940 and Proceedings of Annual Conference, 1941, p. 27; Annual Report for 1941, p. 6. Industries included aerated water, asbestos, candles, carters, cement, chemicals, confectionery and sugar, construction, drugs, flour and maize, furniture, laundries, pottery, oil and petrol, printing, public service and local authorities, theatres and cinemas, timber, tramways and buses, and general workers. ITGWU, minutes of National Executive Council, 1–2 and 30 Mar. 1940. The Irish Seamen's and Port Workers' Union was given £600 and the Irish National Union of Woodworkers £160. The ISPWU was given a further £150 at the NEC meeting of 14–15 July 1940 and another £200 on 30 April 1942. The Irish National Union of Woodworkers could not pay in 1941 but was told it was all right, managing £50 before the end of the year and then clearing it on 22–24 Oct. ITGWU, minutes of National Executive Council, 11–12 Dec. 1941, 5–6 Feb. 1942.

3. ITGWU, Annual Report for 1940 and Proceedings of Annual Conference, 1941, p. 24; Annual Report for 1941 and Proceedings of Annual Conference, 1942, p. 5, 27; Annual Report for 1942 and Proceedings of Annual Conference, 1943, p. 5–6, 27–8, 34; Annual Report for 1943, p. 6–7; minutes of National Executive Council, 24–25 Mar. 1942, 27–28 Aug. 1942, 15–16 Oct. 1942, 4–5 Mar. 1943, 4–5 Nov. 1943.

4. ITGWU, Annual Report for 1944, p. 5–6; Annual Report for 1945, p. 5–6; minutes of National Executive Council, 2–3 Mar. 1944, 13–14 Apr. 1944, 20–22 Mar. 1945, 23 July 1945.

5. Irish Trades Union Congress, Report of National Executive, 1940–1941, and 57th Congress, Drogheda, 16–18 July 1941, p. 52, 127.

6. ITGWU, minutes of National Executive Council, 14 Feb. 1940; Annual Report for 1941, p. 10; Annual Report for 1945, p. 14.

7. Those benefiting included building workers, carters, carpet-planners, cinema and theatre workers, coal and other dockers, cranemen, electrical workers, fertilisers, flour millers and maltsters, foundrymen, gas workers, mental hospital staffs, municipal employees, provender millers, railway and road freight workers, ropemakers, tanners, undertakers and cemetery workers and wallpaper manufacturers.

8. ITGWU, Annual Report for 1939, p. 6–7; Annual Report for 1941 and Proceedings of Annual Conference, 1942, p. 22–5; minutes of National Executive Council, 1–2 Dec. 1939. In Co. Donegal, 2,000 hosiery workers had said that the JIC rates were too high and agreed to work at lower rates. Needless to say, such workers were not unionised.

9. ITGWU, Annual Report for 1939 and Proceedings of Annual Conference, 1940, p. 27–8; Annual Report for 1940 and Proceedings of Annual Conference, 1941, p. 22–6; Irish Trades Union Congress, Report of 45th Congress, Waterford, 2–4 Aug. 1939, p. 183; Annual Report of National Executive, 1939–1940, p. 35; Report of National Executive, 1940–1941, p. 29–31. *Parliamentary Debates: Seanad Éireann: Official Report*, vol. 25, cols. 1370–426 (27 May 1941); NA, Department of Labour files, Department of Industry and Commerce, meting with O'Brien and Kennedy, 16 Oct. 1940, cited by Kieran Allen, 'Forging the links: Fianna Fáil, trade unions and the Emergency,' *Saothar*, 16 (1990), p. 52; John P. Swift, 'The last years,' in Donal Nevin, *James Larkin*, p. 87.

10. ITGWU, Annual Report for 1939 and Proceedings of Annual Conference, 1940, p. 25–6; Annual Report for 1940 and Proceedings of Annual Conference, 1941, p. 3, 9, 22–3; Annual Report for 1941, p. 6–7; Irish Trades Union Congress, Report of National Executive, 1939–1940, and 56th Congress, Killarney, 17–19 July 1940, p. 37–44, 45–52, 89–93. The pamphlet was issued in October. ITGWU, Report of 47th Congress, Drogheda, 16–18 July 1941, p. 147–8. W. J. Keenan seconded.

11. ITGWU, Annual Report for 1941 and Proceedings of Annual Conference, 1942, p. 24, 28–41; Annual Report for 1942 and Proceedings of Annual Conference, 1943, p. 7–8, 28–30; Annual Report for 1943, p. 10–11; Annual Report for 1944 and Proceedings of Annual Conference, 1945, p. 7–8, 10, 43–50; Annual Report for 1945, p. 10; Annual Report for 1946, p. 24; Irish Trades Union Congress, Report of 57th Congress, Drogheda, 16–18 July 1941, p. 107–16; Report of National Executive, 1941–1942, and 48th Congress, Bundoran, 15–17 July 1942, p. 30–32, 50–53, 25–7, 111–21, 134–8. See Devine, *An Eccentric Chemistry*.

12. ITGWU, Annual Report for 1939 and Proceedings of Annual Conference, 1940, p. 31–2. The previous rates were 7s 6d, 12s 6d and 20s. ITGWU, Annual Report for 1940 and Proceedings of Annual Conference, 1941, p. 30. Contributions are not recorded, but thirteen speakers were heard. Annual Report for 1942, p. 5–9; Annual Report for 1945, p. 11; minutes of National Executive Council, 4–5 Mar. 1943.

13. ITGWU, Annual Report for 1945, p. 15–16; minutes of National Executive Council, 1–2 and 30 Mar. 1940, 15–16 and 26 Aug. 1941, 16 Apr. 1942, 4–5 Mar. 1943, 21–22 Nov. 1944. The Committee were: Michael Colgan (Irish Bookbinders' and Allied Trade Union), Michael Keyes TD (National Union of Railwaymen), Seán P. Campbell (Dublin Typographical Provident Society), Jeremiah Hurley TD (Irish National Teachers' Organisation), P. J. Cairns (Post Office Workers' Union); the Secretary was Cathal O'Shannon, then Secretary of the ITUC. The ATGWU was represented by Kyle, E. P. Hart and Gilbert Lynch, while Thomas Kennedy, William McMullen and William O'Brien represented the ITGWU. 'Old' Bill Murphy succeeded O'Hanlon, resigning from the National Executive Council. The six expelled were: J. Hogan, J. Kavanagh, P. Massey, W. Buckley, J. McGuirk and J. H. Lucas. C. Kavanagh was disciplined but not expelled. All later apologised and were reinstated, except for Lucas. The AGM was in the Mansion House, Dublin. Irish Trades Union Congress, Report of 47th Congress, Drogheda, 16–18 July 1941, p. 97–107; Report of National Executive, 1941–1942, p. 21–22; Report of National Executive, 1943–1944, p. 31–2.

14. ITGWU, Annual Report for 1941 and Report of Annual Conference, Dundalk, 7–8 June 1942, p. 9–10, 31; Annual Report for 1944 and Report of Annual Conference, Bray, 4–5 July 1944, p. 36; Annual Report for 1944, p. 8. The Emergency Powers (No. 260) Order (1943) (Sixth Amendment) Order (1944) covered Cos. Sligo, Roscommon and Leitrim, with an Eighth Amendment relating to Cos. Kilkenny, Laois and Tipperary.

15. ITGWU, Annual Report for 1941 and Proceedings of Annual Conference, 1942, p. 26, 35–6; Annual Report for 1943 and Proceedings of Annual Conference, 1944, p. 26; Annual Report for 1944 and Proceedings of Annual Conference, 1945, p. 34–8, 57–9; Irish Trades Union Congress, Report of 46th Congress, Killarney, 17–19 July 1940, p. 88–9, 112–14; Report of National Executive, 1940–1941, and 57th Congress, Drogheda, 16–18 July 1941, p. 31–5, 136–8, 148–9; 48th Congress, Bundoran, 15–17

July 1942, p. 93–100. Kennedy's remark was at the ITUC Executive, 31 May 1940, cited by Kieran Allen in 'Forging the links: Fianna Fáil, trade unions and the Emergency,' *Saothar*, 19 (1991), p. 50.

16. ITGWU, Annual Report for 1941, p. 7–8; minutes of National Executive Council, 13–14 June; 1941, 22–24 Oct. 1941, 24–25 Mar. 1942, 15–16 Oct. 1942; Irish Trades Union Congress, Report of 47th Congress, Drogheda, 16–18 July 1941, p. 72–9, 117–27, 150–54, 164–7; Report of National Executive, 1941–1942, p. 25–8, 48–9. The centres holding meetings were Cork (30 Nov. 1941), Athlone (7 Dec. 1941), Limerick (14 Dec. 1941), Kilkenny (4 Jan. 1942), Mullingar (25 Jan. 1942), Ennis (15 Feb. 1942), Dublin (20 Feb. 1942), Maryborough [Port Laoise] (22 Feb. 1942), Drogheda (1 Mar. 1942) and Dundalk (14 Mar 1942).

17. ITGWU, Proceedings of Annual Conference, 1942, p. 32. Pádraig Mac Gamhna (Carlow) and Thomas O'Reilly (Dublin No. 3 Branch) moved the first and J. Duggan and M. Birmingham (Cork No. 1 Branch) the second. ITGWU, minutes of National Executive Council, 4–6 June; 23 July 1945; Irish Trades Union Congress, Report of 48th Congress, Bundoran, 15–17 July 1942, p. 15–17; Irish Trades Union Congress, Report of National Executive, 1942–1943, p. 27–9 (for Memorandum of Suggestions Made by the National Executive Council, Dec. 1942, see p. 47–9); Report of 49th Congress, Cork, 21–23 July 1943, p. 101–3. Other unions involved were the Irish Bakery, Confectionery and Allied Workers' Union, Irish Union of Distributive Workers and Clerks, Irish Seamen's and Port Workers' Union, Dublin Typographical Provident Society, and Typographical Association. Report of National Executive, 1943–1944, and 50th Congress, Drogheda, 7–8 July 1944, p. 25–8, 30–31, 98–103; Report of National Executive, 1944–1945, p. 20.

18. ITGWU, Annual Report for 1944 and Report of Proceedings of Special Conference, Dublin, 20 Apr. 1945, p. 25–32, and Proceedings of Annual Conference, 1945, p. 36–7; minutes of National Executive Council, 27–28 Feb. 1945; Irish Trades Union Congress, Report of 50th Congress, Drogheda, 7–8 July 1944, p. 104–18, 139–40. Gilbert Lynch (ATGWU) and Michael Keyes TD (National Union of Railwaymen) were appointed to attend. For details see ITGWU, Report of National Executive, 1944–1945, p. 19, 22–8, 29–37, 58–73. They were the Building Workers' Trade Union; Dublin Typographical Provident Society; Electrical Trade Union (Ireland); Electrotypers' and Stereotypers' Society, Dublin and District; Irish Bookbinders' and Allied Trades Union; Irish Engineering Industrial Union; Society of Woodcutting Machinists; Irish Union of Distributive Workers and Clerks; Operative Plasterers' Trades Society of Ireland; and ITGWU.

19. Irish Trades Union Congress, Report of National Executive, 1938–1939, and Report of 45th Congress, Waterford, 2–4 Aug. 1939, p. 64–5, 157–9; Report of National Executive, 1939–1940, p. 44–5; Report of 48th Congress, Bundoran, 15–17 July 1942, p. 146–8; *Report of the Commission on Vocational Organisation* (1943), p. 184–5, 417–18.

20. Irish Trades Union Congress, Report of National Executive, 1939–1940, and Report of 46th Congress, Killarney, 17–19 July 1940, p. 47–56, 93–100, 117–20; Report of 47th Congress, Drogheda, 16–18 July 1941, p. 168–9. James Green Douglas (1887–1954) was a Dublin businessman, Quaker and Nationalist. He was active in the Irish White Cross, 1920–22, and was appointed by Michael Collins to the Committee

that prepared drafts of the Constitution of the Irish Free State in 1922. He was a member of Seanad Éireann, 1922–36, 1938–43 and 1944–54, serving on the Industrial and Commercial Panel, either through election or as a Taoiseach's nominee. See Gaughan, *Memoirs of Senator James G. Douglas.*

21. ITGWU, Annual Report for 1940 and Proceedings of Annual Conference, 1941, p. 25–6. The speakers were Philip Clarke (National Executive Council), John Conroy (Limerick), J. Flynn (Sligo), T. Horan (Mallow), T. D. Looney (Blarney), Bill Murphy (Dublin No. 9 Branch), P. J. O'Brien (Cork No. 2 Branch) and Frank Robbins (Dublin No. 7 Branch). Only Jim Hickey TD expressed reservations. ITGWU, Annual Report for 1941 and Proceedings of Annual Conference, 1942, p. 26; Annual Report for 1944 and Proceedings of Annual Conference, 1945, p. 40; minutes of National Executive Council, 14–15 July 1940, 20–21 Sep. 1940, 13–14 Dec. 1940. The movers were C. W. Browne (Limerick) and John McLarnon (Belfast). ITGWU, minutes of National Executive Council, 24–25 Mar. 1942, 13–14 June 1942, 11–12 Dec. 1942, 4–5 Oct. 1945, 13–14 Dec. 1945, 13–15 Feb. 1946, 20–22 Mar. 1946, 2–3 May 1946.

22. ITGWU, Annual Report for 1940 and Proceedings of Annual Conference, 1941, p. 30–31; Annual Report for 1941 and Proceedings of Annual Conference, 1942 p. 12, 20, 35–6; Annual Report for 1942 and Proceedings of Annual Conference, 1943, p. 33–4; Annual Report for 1944 and Proceedings of Annual Conference, 1945, p. 57–9; Irish Trades Union Congress, Report of National Executive, 1939–1940, and 46th Congress, Killarney, 17–19 July 1940, p. 55–62, 135–7; Report of 47th Congress, Drogheda, 16–18 July 1941, p. 127–9.

23. ITGWU, Annual Report for 1945, p. 12; *Parliamentary Debates: Dáil Éireann: Official Report,* vol. 98, cols. 489–90 (24 Oct. 1945).

24. ITGWU, Annual Report for 1943 and Report of Annual Conference, Bray, 4–5 July 1944, p. 28; Annual Report for 1944 and Report of Annual Conference, Galway, 5–6 June 1945, p. 57–8.

25. Irish Trades Union Congress, Report of National Executive, 1941–1942, p. 57–9; ITGWU, Annual Report for 1942 and Report of Annual Conference, Cork, 18–19 July 1943, p. 33; Annual Report for 1944 and Report of Annual Conference, Galway, 5–6 June 1945, p. 58.

26. ITGWU, Annual Report for 1939 and Proceedings of Annual Conference, 1940, p. 24, 35; Annual Report for 1940 and Proceedings of Annual Conference, 1941, p. 31. The speakers were McMullen (Vice-President), T. Lally (Galway), D. Looney (Cork No. 1 Branch), M. Regan (Cork No. 1 Branch), Robbins (Dublin No. 7 Branch) and P. J. O'Brien (Cork No. 2 Branch). Annual Report for 1941 and Report of Annual Conference, Dundalk, 7–8 June 1942, p. 9, 32–3. Paddy Dooley (Dublin No. 9 Branch) thought members should be trained at university and 'places found' for them in the union. ITGWU, Annual Report for 1942 and Proceedings of Annual Conference, 1943, p. 34; Annual Report for 1943 and Proceedings of Annual Conference, 1944, p. 36; Annual Report for 1944 and Proceedings of Annual Conference, 1945, p. 59.

27. ITGWU, Annual Report for 1939 and Proceedings of Annual Conference, 1940, p. 31; Annual Report for 1940 and Proceedings of Annual Conference, 1941, p. 26; Annual Report for 1941 and Proceedings of Annual Conference, 1942, p. 26; minutes of National Executive Council, 13–14 Dec. 1940, 5–6 Feb. 1944, 24–25 Mar. 1944, 19–20

Sep. 1944, 7–8 Nov. 1944, 13–14 Feb. 1945. The first entrants were: Head Office: T. Kennedy, W. O'Brien, W. McMullen, Joseph O'Kelly, Éamon Dalton, Francis O'Meara, Cathal O'Shannon, Dominick Sullivan, Frances Gill, James Gilhooly, Elizabeth Kelly, Kathleen Davidson, Margaret McDonnell; Belfast: Dan McAllister, Loughran; Carlow: Stephen Carroll; Cork No. 1 Branch: James Hickey, M. Flynn, Éamonn Wall, C. Desmond; Cork No. 2 Branch: P. J. O'Brien, P. Crowley, P. J. Mullane; Dublin No. 1 Branch: John McCabe, Mick McCarthy, Seán Rogan; Dublin No. 2 Branch: P. Kelly, Tom O'Brien; Dublin No. 3 Branch: Thomas O'Reilly; Dublin No. 4 Branch: Frank Purcell, Margaret O'Donnell; Dublin No. 5 Branch: Tom McCarthy; Dublin No. 6 Branch: M. O'Shaughnessy, Sarah (Sadie) Small; Dublin No. 7 Branch: Frank Robbins; Dublin No. 8 Branch: D. J. Galavan; Dublin No. 9 Branch: William Murphy, P. McDonnell; Galway: Thomas McDonagh, B. Keane; Limerick: John Conroy, Patrick Horrigan, Edward Browne; Newry: James Poucher; Sligo: James Flynn; Waterford: Thomas Dunnet; Kildare: R. G. Swanton; Leix-Offaly: John F. Gill.

28. ITGWU, Annual Report for 1939 and Proceedings of Annual Conference, 1940, p. 35; Annual Report for 1943 and Proceedings of Annual Conference, 1944, p. 35–6. Byrne also raised the matter at the National Executive Council, 15–16 Aug. 1941. See also ITGWU, minutes of National Executive Council, 7–8 Feb. 1941, 23 July 1945, 27–28 Aug. 1945, 15–16 Nov. 1945, 29–30 Aug. 1946. Furniture and effects were auctioned for a further £284 10s 6d.

29. Irish Trades Union Congress, Report of 48th Congress, Bundoran, 15–17 July 1942, p. 155–9; Report of 49th Congress, Cork, 21–23 July 1943, p. 117–22, 125–30.

30. ITGWU, Annual Report for 1939 and Proceedings of Annual Conference, 1940, p. 34–5; Annual Report for 1942 and Proceedings of Annual Conference, 1943, p. 24, 34; Annual Report for 1943 and Proceedings of Annual Conference, 1944, p. 12, 30, 34; minutes of National Executive Council, 24–25 Mar. 1942, 16 and 30 Apr. 1942, 12–14 July 1942; 4–5 Mar. 1943, 20–21 May 1943, 28–20 June 1943, 1 July 1943, 4–5 Nov. 1943, 16–17 Dec. 1943, Jan. 1944, 2–3 Mar. 1944, 13–14 Apr. 1944, 6–7 June 1944, 20–22 Mar. 1945, 21–24 Apr. 1945, 23 July 1945. Hickey's fees were paid from 1939 into the same special fund that received General Officers' Seanad fees. The NEC was still 'gravely dissatisfied' with Ryan on 17–18 Oct. 1946. Irish Trades Union Congress, Report of National Executive, 1942–1943, p. 49–50, 20–21. See Puirséil, *The Irish Labour Party*, p. 123–, and 'ITGWU and the Labour Party: The Union's Reply to the Labour Party Statement' (1944).

Chapter 18 (p. 318–30)

1. Salaries were: 1939: £5,578; 1940: £4,018; 1941: £4,072; 1942: £4,109; 1943: £5,083; 1944: £5,296; 1945: £5,004. John P. Swift, 'The last years,' in Donal Nevin, *James Larkin*, p. 88; Bradley, *Farm Labourers' Irish Struggle*, p. 74–82, and Daniel G. Bradley, 'Speeding the plough: The formation of the Federation of Rural Workers, 1944–48,' *Saothar*, 11 (1986), p. 27–38.

2. Irish Trades Union Congress, Report of National Executive, 1940–1941, and 27th Congress, Drogheda, 16–18 July 1941, p. 23–9, 107–16; C. N. Ferguson, 'Larkin and the union, part 4,' *Report*, Oct.–Nov. 1952; *Parliamentary Debates: Seanad Éireann: Official Report*, vol. 25, cols. 1371–431 (27 May 1941); John P. Swift, 'The last years,' in

Donal Nevin, *James Larkin*, p. 87–8; Cody et al., *The Parliament of Labour*, p. 171–7.

3. Irish Trades Union Congress, Report of National Executive, 1941–1942, and 48th Congress, Bundoran, 15–17 July 1942, p. 30–32, 50–53, 111–21, and Memorandum on Emergency Powers (No. 83) Order (1941), presented to the Minister for Industry and Commerce, p. 50–52; Report of National Executive, 1942–1943, and 49th Congress, Cork, 21–23 July 1943, p. 25–7, 32–4, 89–97; Report of 51st Congress, Dublin, 4–6 July 1945, p. 135–44.

4. Irish Trades Union Congress, Report of 51st Congress, Dublin, 4–6 June 1945, p. 144–7; Report of National Executive, 1945–1946, and Report of 52nd Congress, Dublin, 9–11 July 1946, p. 50–54, 60–63, 138–40, 195–6; WUI, minutes of General Executive Council, 12 July 1946. See also Cody et al.,*The Parliament of Labour*, p. 179–82, and Jones, *These Obstreperous Lassies*, p. 176–87.

5. WUI, Report of Annual Delegate Conference, Dublin, 8 June 1947, p. 7; 'As I remember Big Jim—Breda Cardiff,' in Nevin, *James Larkin*, p. 455–6; *Report*, Dec. 1952; Christopher Brien, 'Fifty years of union in Bray,' *Unity*, summer 1985; Irish Trades Union Congress, Report of 51st Congress, Dublin, 4–6 July 1945, p. 157.

6. Irish Trades Union Congress, Report of National Executive, 1939–1940, and 46th Congress, Killarney, 17–19 July 1940, p. 35, 88; Report of National Executive, 1940–1941, and 47th Congress, Drogheda, 16–18 July 1941, p. 21, 85–96; Report of National Executive, 1941–1942, and 48th Congress, Bundoran, 15–17 July 1942, p. 21–22, 81–92, 121–8. The others were Navan Trades and Labour Council, Irish Engineering and Foundry Union, Irish Automobile Drivers' and Automobile Mechanics' Union and Irish National Union of Vintners', Grocers' and Allied Trades' Assistants. Report of 51st Congress, Dublin, 4–6 July 1945, p. 164–9, 135–47. For O'Brien's view see Morrissey, *William O'Brien*, p. 328–30.

7. Irish Trades Union Congress, Report of National Executive, 1940–1941, and 47th Congress, Drogheda, 16–18 July 1941, p. 29–31, 112, 117–27, 150–51, 154; Report of 48th Congress, Bundoran, 15–17 July 1942, p. 22, 126. The motion, effectually expelling Larkin, was carried by 107 to 60. Report of National Executive, 1942–1943, p. 25–9; Sheehy Skeffington, *Skeff*, p. 107; Swift, *John Swift*, p. 113–14; Donal Nevin, '. . . Lighting a flame,' in *James Larkin*, p. 476–7.

8. Swift, *John Swift*, p. 118; Séamus Cody, 'The remarkable Patrick Daly,' *Obair*, 2, Jan. 1985, p. 10–11. Cody et al., in *The Parliament of Labour*, p. 178, acknowledge his minutes as a 'remarkably detailed record.'

9. Emmet O'Connor, in *James Larkin*, p. 102, suggests that this was a reward for his admiration for de Valera. Others were Louie Bennett (Irish Women Workers' Union), Senator Seán Campbell (Dublin Typographical Provident Society) and Senator Thomas Foran, who resigned on 17 April 1939 and was replaced by Luke J. Duffy (Irish Union of Distributive Workers and Clerks). Irish Trades Union Congress, Report of National Executive, 1938–1939, and Report of 45th Congress, Waterford, 2–4 Aug. 1939, p. 64–5, 157–9; John Swift, 'Report of Commission on Vocational Organisation (and its times, 1930s–1940s),' *Saothar*, 1 (1975), p. 54–63; Joseph Lee, 'Aspects of corporatist thought in Ireland: The Commission on Vocational Organisation, 1939–1943,' in Art Cosgrove and Dónal McCartney (eds.), *Studies in Irish History: Presented to R. Dudley Edwards* (Dublin: University College, 1979), p. 324–46. Larkin therefore missed about 292 sessions! *Report of the*

Commission on Vocational Organisation (1943), p. 185–6, and NLI, Commission on Vocational Organisation, 1939–1943, vol. 18, document 136.

10. Labour Party Administrative Council, Official Statement Relating to the Disqualification from the Labour Party of the ITGWU, cited by Emmet Larkin in *James Larkin*, p. 299–301; Mike Milotte, *Communism in Modern Ireland: The Pursuit of the Workers' Republic since 1916* (Dublin: Gill & Macmillan, 1984), p. 191–. The decision was made on 10 July 1941. It was Larkin's initiative that led to the purchase and development of St Anne's Estate, Raheny, for housing and leisure amenities.

11. NLI, William O'Brien and Thomas Kennedy Papers, ms. 33,718/I (272), cited by O'Connor, *James Larkin*, p. 109–10; Irish Trades Union Congress, Report of 51st Congress, Dublin, 4–6 July 1945, p. 116–17. Larkin polled 5,896 in Dublin North-East and Young Jim 3,049 in South Dublin. Walker, *Parliamentary Election Results in Ireland*, p. 154–61. Larkin polled 4,489, while Michael Colgan (Bookbinders), a strong anti-Communist, and Frank Robbins (ITGWU), an ancient enemy, polled 1,211 between them for National Labour—votes that would probably have seen Larkin comfortably home. Young Jim polled 3,587, his Labour running-mate Walter Beirne, with 3,571, nearly overtaking him. Joseph Hannigan, who had been Larkin's running-mate in 1943 and polled 2,345, this time ran as an independent and polled 1,824. Walker, *Parliamentary Election Results in Ireland*, p. 161–7.

Chapter 19 (p. 331–3)

1. Fleming and O'Day, *Longman Handbook of Modern Irish History since 1800*, p. 571, 583–7.

Chapter 20 (p. 340–69)

1. ITGWU, Annual Report for 1945 and Proceedings of Annual Conference, 1946, p. 34–45; Annual Report for 1946 and Proceedings of Annual Conference, 1947, p. 48–59; Annual Report for 1947 and Proceedings of Annual Conference, p. 42–54; Annual Report for 1948 and Proceedings of Annual Conference, 1949, p. 69–86.

2. ITGWU, Annual Report for 1945 and Proceedings of Annual Conference, 1946, p. 70–71; Annual Report for 1946, p. 27–30; Annual Report for 1947, p. 5–7; Report for 1948, p. 5–6; Report for 1968, p. 8–10; minutes of National Executive Council, 23–25 Sep. 1947; Congress of Irish Unions, Report of Central Committee, 1947–1948, p. 23; 'Death of William O'Brien,' *Liberty*, Nov. 1968.

3. They were: aerated water, airways, bacon-curing, bakeries, banks, boot and shoe, bottles and bulbs, brewing, building, button-making, canals, clothing, coalmining, creameries, docks, flour-milling, hosiery, laundries, linen and cotton, local authority operatives, malting, mental hospitals, oil and petrol distribution, omnibus and motor repair and maintenance, quarries, radio, road passenger and freight, shirt-making, sugar beet, sugar confectionery and food-preserving, tanning, theatres and cinemas, tobacco, and woollen and worsted.

4. ITGWU, Annual Report for 1945 and Proceedings of Annual Conference, 1946, p. 48–53; Annual Report for 1946, p. 5–7; Annual Report for 1947 and Proceedings of Annual Conference, 1948, p. 9–11, 20–21, 59, 60–63; Annual Report for 1948, p. 8–10, 33–4; Annual Report for 1949, p. 5–8, 36–7; minutes of National Executive Council, 11–12 Mar. 1947, 22–23 Apr. 1947, 29–30 June 1947, 4–5 Sep. 1947, 19 and 30–31 May 1948, 18–19 June 1948, 2–3 Sep. 1948, 3–5 Sep. 1952, 14–16 Jan. 1953; *Liberty*, Christmas

1949. Members of the CIÉ Head Office staff joined the Railway Clerks' Association, even though they too wished to transfer in late 1948. George Hunter, 'The ITGWU in Donegal,' *Liberty*, June 1974. Doherty had added Milford Flour Mills and Killybegs Boatyard to the Convoy Branch. With Nugent they set up the Kilcar Branch, after organising Gaeltarra Éireann handloom weavers and a Carndonagh Branch of shirt workers in 1948.

5. ITGWU, Annual Report for 1946, p. 20.

6. ITGWU, Annual Report for 1946, p. 19; Annual Report for 1947 and Proceedings of Annual Conference, 1948, p. 19–20, 73–5; Annual Report for 1948 and Proceedings of Annual Conference, 1949, p. 118–19, 124; Annual Report for 1949, p. 32–3.

7. ITGWU, Annual Report for 1945 and Proceedings of Annual Conference, 1946, p. 40, 65–6; Annual Report for 1946 and 1947, p. 16–18, 24, 50; Annual Report for 1947 and Proceedings of Annual Conference, 1948, p. 11–13, 15–19, 80; Annual Report for 1948, p. 26; Annual Report for 1949, p. 16–17, 30–32; minutes of National Executive Council, 21 and 27–8 May 1947, 15–16 June 1947, 15–17 Oct. 1947, 11–13 Nov. 1948, 16–17 Dec. 1948. Congress of Irish Unions, 1st Annual Meeting, Killarney, 25–27 July 1945, p. 62–7; 4th Annual Meeting, Tramore, 21–23 July 1948, p. 111–12.

8. ITGWU, Annual Report for 1947 and Proceedings of Annual Conference, 1948, p. 63–7; Annual Report for 1948 and Proceedings of Annual Conference, 1949, p. 26–8, 80–81; Annual Report for 1949 and Proceedings of Annual Conference, 1950, p. 10–12, 95–7; minutes of National Executive Council, 30 Oct. 1947, 26–7 Nov. 1947; Congress of Irish Unions, Report of Central Committee, 1946–1947, p. 23–4; Report of Central Committee, 1947–1948, and 4th Annual Meeting, Tramore, 21–23 July 1948, p. 9–14, 5–67; 5th Annual Meeting, Cork, 20–22 July 1949, p. 47–52.

9. ITGWU, Annual Report for 1946, p. 21; Annual Report for 1947 and Proceedings of Annual Conference, 1948, p. 17–18, 69–70; Annual Report for 1948, p. 32–3; Annual Report for 1948 and Proceedings of Annual Conference, 1949, p. 127–8; Annual Report for 1949, p. 17–20, 33–5; minutes of National Executive Council, 28–9 Oct. 1948, 11–13 Nov. 1948, 16–17 Dec. 1948, 31 Mar. to 1 Apr. 1949, 5–6 May 1949, 19–21 June 1949, 17–18 July 1949; Congress of Irish Unions, 4th Annual Meeting, Tramore, 21–23 July 1948, p. 90–95. Whatever about the NUR, all IRU men had to have clear cards. Christy Kirwan was closely associated with these events.

10. ITGWU, Annual Report for 1946 and Proceedings of Annual Conference, 1947, p. 22, 54–46. 76–7; Annual Report for 1947, p. 18; Annual Report for 1948, p. 32–3; Congress of Irish Unions, 2nd Annual Meeting, Galway, 3–5 July 1946, p. 171–3; 4th Annual Meeting, 21–23 July 1948, p. 99–100. Hospitals represented were Ardee, Ballinasloe, Carlow, Castlebar, Castlerea, Clonmel, Cork, Dublin, Ennis, Enniscorthy, Killarney, Kilkenny, Laois-Offaly, Letterkenny, Monaghan, Mullingar, Port Laoise, Sligo, Waterford, and Youghal, an indication of the ITGWU's national membership. See Devine, *An Eccentric Chemistry.*

11. ITGWU, Annual Report for 1945, p. 16–17; Annual Report for 1946 and Proceedings of Annual Conference, 1947, p. 26–7, 54; minutes of National Executive Council, 4–5 June 1945, 23 July 1945, 29–30 Aug. 1946.

12. Congress of Irish Unions, Report of Central Committee, 1947–1948, p. 20–21; ITGWU, Annual Report for 1949 and Proceedings of Annual Conference, 1950, p. 20–23, 104–6; minutes of National Executive Council, 26–27 Jan. 1950.

13. Congress of Irish Unions, 5th Annual Meeting, Cork, 20–22 July 1949, p. 96–8; ITGWU, minutes of National Executive Council, 17–18 Dec. 1946.

14. ITGWU, Annual Report for 1945 and Proceedings of Annual Conference, 1946, p. 41, 69–70; Annual Report for 1946 and Proceedings of Annual Conference, 1947, p. 54. 84; Annual Report for 1947 and Proceedings of Annual Conference, 1948, p. 80; Annual Report for 1948 and Proceedings of Annual Conference, 1949, p. 77–8, 126–7; Annual Report for 1949, p. 14–16; *Liberty,* Christmas 1949; Congress of Irish Unions, *A History of the Foundation of Comhar Ceard Éireann,* p. 3–25; 1st Annual Meeting, Killarney, 25–27 July 1945, p. 46–60, 79. It also adopted motions on trade union reorganisation, suggesting mergers between affiliates, although virtually no progress was made in this area. Congress of Irish Unions, Report of Central Committee, 1945–1946, p. 83–5, 88, 93–105 ('Report on objection to credentials'), and 2nd Annual Meeting, Galway, 3–5 July 1946, p. 121–39. The ITGWU speakers were Frank Robbins, Paddy Dooley and J. McElhinney. Congress of Irish Unions, Report of Central Committee, 1946–1947, and 3rd Annual Meeting, Waterford, 2–4 July 1947, p. 7–13, 45–6, 48–58; Report of Central Committee, 1947–1948, and 4th Annual Meeting, Tramore, 21–23 July 1948, p. 6–9, 17–18, 48–55, 76–80. Arthur Deakin, 1890–1955, was Acting General Secretary, 1940–1945, and General Secretary, 1945–1955; he was right-wing in politics. Congress of Irish Unions, 5th Annual Meeting, Cork, 20–22 July 1949, p. 86–95. Morrissey, a native of Co. Tipperary, was a labourer with the Great Southern Railway. In 1917 he became an Organiser with the ITGWU and a member of the Executive Council. He was elected to Dáil Éireann for Tipperary on behalf of the Labour Party in 1922, retaining his seat until he retired from politics in 1957. He was chief whip of the Labour Party, 1923, and Leas-Cheann Comhairle in 1928. In 1931 he and Richard Anthony, Cork, voted with Cumann na nGaedheal in favour of Military Tribunals, and both were expelled. He was re-elected in 1933 as Independent Labour, then joined Cumann na nGaedheal and was subsequently elected for Fine Gael. He was Minister for Industry and Commerce in the first Inter-Party Government, February 1948 to 7 March 1951, and was responsible for the establishment of the Industrial Development Authority and An Córas Tráchtála and for the nationalisation of CIÉ. He was Minister for Justice, 7 March to 13 June 1951. He did not serve in the 1954 Government, because of ill health, and retired from politics in 1957. He died on New Year's Day 1981.

15. ITGWU, minutes of National Executive Council, 13–15 Mar. 1946, 17–18 Oct. 1946, 21–23 Nov. 1946. The loan, although sanctioned, was never taken up, as the strike ended. ITGWU, minutes of National Executive Council, 26–27 Nov. 1947, 12–14 Jan. 1949, 31 Mar. to 1 Apr. 1949, 31 Mar. to 1 Apr. 1949, 5–6 May 1040, 19–21 June 1949, 17–18 July 1949.

16. ITGWU, Annual Report for 1946, p. 25–6; Annual Report for 1947 and Proceedings of Annual Conference, 1948, p. 58, 80–84; Annual Report for 1948 and Proceedings of Annual Conference, 1949, p. 130, 137; Annual Report for 1949 and Proceedings of Annual Conference, 1950, p. 12–15, 97–100; *Liberty,* Christmas 1949; Congress of Irish Unions, 2nd Annual Meeting, Galway, 3–5 July 1946, p. 159–62; 5th Annual Meeting, Cork, 20–22 July 1949, p. 61–2, 102–7.

17. ITGWU, Annual Report for 1946 and Proceedings of Annual Conference, 1947, p. 7–18, 20–21, 53–4, 70–74, 82–3. The JLCS covered aerated waters; boot and shoe

repairing; brush and broom; button-making; general waste materials reclamation; handkerchief and household piece goods; linen and cotton embroidery; packing; paper box; rope, twine and net; shirt-making; sugar confectionery and food-preserving; tailoring; tobacco; and women's clothing and millinery. ITGWU, Annual Report for 1948 and Proceedings of Annual Conference, 1949, p. 98–110, 128; Annual Report for 1949, p. 23–9; minutes of National Executive Council, 22–23 Apr. 1947; Congress of Irish Unions, 1st Annual Meeting, Killarney, 25–27 July 1945, p. 71–2; 2nd Annual Meeting, Galway, 3–5 July 1946, p. 139–55; Report of Central Committee, 1946–1947, and 3rd Annual Meeting, Waterford, 2–4 July 1947, p. 18, 62–7; 4th Annual Meeting, Tramore, 21–23 July 1948. W. Keenan and Tom O'Reilly spoke.

18. ITGWU, Annual Report for 1945 and Proceedings of Annual Conference, 1946, p. 56; Annual Report for 1946, p. 25; Annual Report for 1948 and Proceedings of Annual Conference, 1949, p. 129–30; Congress of Irish Unions, Report of Central Committee, 1945–1946, and 2nd Annual Meeting Galway, 3–5 July 1946, p. 88–9, 155–9; 5th Annual Meeting, Cork, 20–22 July 1949, p. 53–6, 107–10.

19. ITGWU, Annual Report for 1945 and Proceedings of Annual Conference, 1946, p. 68; Annual Report for 1946 and Proceedings of Annual Conference, 1947, p. 81–2; Annual Report for 1948 and Proceedings of Annual Conference, 1949, p. 104–6, 110–13, 134–5; Annual Report for 1949, p. 29–30; Congress of Irish Unions, 4th Annual Meeting, 21–23 July 1948, p. 104–6; Report of Central Committee, 1948–1949, and 5th Annual Meeting, Cork, 20–22 July 1949, p. 17–18, 62–6, 69–75.

20. ITGWU, Annual Report for 1945 and Proceedings of Annual Conference, 1946, p. 67–8; Annual Report for 1946 and Proceedings of Annual Conference, 1947, p. 80–81, 84–5; Annual Report for 1947 and Proceedings of Annual Conference, 1948, p. 81–3; Annual Report for 1948 and Proceedings of Annual Conference, 1949, p. 129; Annual Report for 1949, p. 38–40; Congress of Irish Unions, 4th Annual Meeting, Tramore, 21–23 July 1948, p. 80–82.

21. ITGWU, Annual Report for 1945 and Proceedings of Annual Conference, 1946, p. 66. James Gilhooly (Dublin No. 6 Branch) moved the first and A. Tyson (Dublin No. 8 Branch) the second, both representing the clothing trade. ITGWU, Annual Report for 1946 and Proceedings of Annual Conference, 1947, p. 78–9, 83; Annual Report for 1947 and Proceedings of Annual Conference, 1948, p. 80 83; Annual Report for 1948 and Proceedings of Annual Conference, 1949, p. 119, 127–31. Deputies Jim Hickey, James Everett and J. P. Pattison (Labour Party) had tried to assure Boran that they were strenuously lobbying to achieve his desired objective. Congress of Irish Unions, 2nd Annual Meeting, Galway, 3–5 July 1946, p. 162–3; 4th Annual Meeting, Tramore, 21–23 July 1948, p. 96–8.

22. ITGWU, Annual Report for 1945 and Proceedings of Annual Conference, 1946, p. 69; Annual Report for 1946, p. 31, 43; Annual Report for 1946 and Proceedings of Annual Conference, 1947, p. 85; Annual Report for 1947 and Proceedings of Annual Conference, 1948, p. 84–5; minutes of National Executive Council, 16–17 June 1946, 29–30 Aug. 1946, 17–18 Oct. 1946, 19–20 Dec. 1946. The union's premises were 35 Parnell Square; Liberty Hall (Beresford Place); 122 Emmet Road, Inchicore; Connolly Hall, Cork; 26 Peter Street and Palace Street, Drogheda; 91 O'Connell Street, Limerick; Lynn's Place, Sligo; Rock Street, Tralee; Newry; and Connolly Hall, Blanchardstown, Co. Dublin. A purchase figure of £18,485 was given, with gross

income of £1,669 5s 6d, outgoings (not repairs) £553 7s 1d and net income of £1,115 18s 5d. The City Manager actually denied any knowledge of what the union was referring to, 28–29 Jan. 1947. Income and expenditure on the premises, 1928–1947, came out at £137 7s net.

23. ITGWU, Annual Report for 1945 and Proceedings of Annual Conference, 1946, p. 68–9; Annual Report for 1946 and Proceedings of Annual Conference, 1947, p. 85–6; Annual Report for 1948 and Proceedings of Annual Conference, 1949, p. 47, 120–21; Annual Report for 1949, p. 37–8. The matter had been raised and dismissed, despite a 'good deal of difference of opinion,' in the General Executive Council, 30–31 Aug. 1945, 2–3 May 1946, 28–29 Jan. 1947. The members of the Committee were McMullen, P. Clarke, W. J. Keenan, P. Dooley and Frank Robbins. Two thousand copies at 1d would bring an income of £8 6s 8d, plus £10 for advertisements, minus costs of £70; so the monthly cost to the union would be £40–50. ITGWU, minutes of General Executive Council, 28–29 Apr. 1948, 16–17 Dec. 1948, 17–18 July 1949; *Liberty*, Nov. 1949, cited in ITGWU, Annual Report for 1949, p. 38. Provisional titles included *Worker, Torch,* and *Solidarity.*

24. ITGWU, Annual Report for 1946 and Proceedings of Annual Conference, 1947, p. 63; Annual Report for 1948 and Proceedings of Annual Conference, 1949, p. 92–8; Annual Report for 1949 and Proceedings of Annual Conference, 1950, p. 89; minutes of National Executive Council, 17–18 July 1949, 16–17 Sep. 1949.

25. ITGWU, Annual Report for 1946 and Proceedings of Annual Conference, 1947, p. 63; Annual Report for 1947 and Proceedings of Annual Conference, 1948, p. 24, 79, 82–3; Annual Report for 1948 and Proceedings of Annual Conference, 1949, p. 47–9, 121–3, 125; Congress of Irish Unions, 4th Annual Meeting, Tramore, 21–23 July 1948, p. 112–13 ('Cork Educational Scheme for Workers'); 5th Annual Meeting, Cork, 20–22 July 1949, p. 75–9.

26. ITGWU, Annual Report for 1948 and Proceedings of Annual Conference, 1949, p. 124. The seconder was James Gilhooley (Dublin No. 6/8 Branch). Congress of Irish Unions, 2nd Annual Meeting, Galway, 3–5 July 1946, p. 114–15; 3rd Annual Meeting, Waterford, 2–4 July 1947, p. 110–12; 5th Annual Meeting, Cork, 20–22 July 1949, p. 30–32, 107–10, 114–16.

27. ITGWU, Annual Report for 1947 and Proceedings of Annual Conference, 1948, p. 77–8; Annual Report for 1948, p. 43–4; minutes of National Executive Council, 26–27 Nov. 1947, 8–9 Jan. 1948, 11–12 Feb. 1948, 11–12 Mar. 1948, 30–31 May 1948, 28–29 Oct. 1948; Congress of Irish Unions, 3rd Annual Meeting, Waterford, 2–4 July 1947, p. 73–89; Report of Central Committee, 1947–1948, and 4th Annual Meeting, Tramore, 21–23 July 1948, p. 1416, 68–76. The successful candidates were James Everett (Wicklow), Jim Hickey (Cork), John O'Leary (Wexford), J. P. Pattison (Kilkenny) and Dan Spring (Kerry North). Unsuccessful were Stephen Carroll (Carlow), Stephen Doyle (Cork), J. Flynn (Sligo), J. McElhinney (Galway), P. J. O'Brien (Cork) and Frank Robbins (Dublin).

Chapter 21 (p. 370–93)

1. WUI, Report of Annual Delegate Conference, Dublin, 8 June 1947, p. 2–5; minutes of General Executive Council, 29 Nov. 1946 (moved by J. Burke and W. Murphy), 24 Jan. 1947, 6, 7 and 19 Feb. 1947 (moved by John Smithers, seconded by J. Burke); O'Connor,

James Larkin, p. 112. For all that they were effectually estranged after Larkin's return to Ireland in 1923, it seems clear that Larkin remained emotionally close to Elizabeth, and there was an underlying melancholy about the man. O'Casey, writing to Carney on 10 January 1947, echoed this, saying: 'I don't think he acted quite justly to Mrs. L. . . . Of course he would dream about her, for his mind is full of her now.' 'On Larkin: A miscellany: The Larkin family,' Nevin, *James Larkin*, p. 478, 487; Donal Nevin, 'Larkin and the WUI,' in Nevin, *James Larkin*, p. 347; James Plunkett, 'Big Jim: A loaf on the table, a flower in the vase,' in Nevin, *James Larkin*, p. 115.

2. Irish Trades Union Congress, Annual Report, 1946–1947, and 53rd Congress, Waterford, 29–31 July 1947, p. 21–25, 109–117, 132–40. J. Collins (Dublin Trades Union Council) and Robert Getgood MP (ATGWU, former president of Irish Trades Union Congress) paid tribute from the floor, p. 117–19. Congress of Irish Unions, 3rd Annual Report and Proceedings of 3rd Annual Meeting, Waterford, 2–5 July 1947, makes no reference to Larkin's death. ITGWU, Annual Report for 1947 and minutes of National Executive Council, 11–12 Mar. 1947.

3. WUI, Report of Annual Delegate Conference, Dublin, 8 June 1947, p. 9; Report of Annual Delegate Conference, Dublin, 19 June 1949, p. 9. The General Executive Council's nominees to Dublin Trades Council's Larkin Memorial Fund were J. Burke and J. Lennox. Minutes of General Executive Council, 14 Mar. 1947, 18 July 1947, 16 Jan. 1948, 26 Nov. 1948. The second concert brought in £220, but there were extensive costs to be met. Minutes of General Executive Council, 14 Jan. 1949. Irish Trades Union Congress, Report of 54th Congress, Cork, 7–9 July 1948, p. 186–87; Report of 55th Congress, Belfast, 26–29 July 1949, p. 180–81.

4. WUI, Report of Annual Delegate Conference, Dublin, 8 June 1947, p. 2, 19; Report of Annual Delegate Conference, Dublin, 19 June 1949, p. 9, 24; minutes of General Executive Council, 6, 14 and 28 June 1946, 12 July 1946, 23 Aug. 1946, 6, 13 and 20 Sep. 1946, 4 Oct. 1946. The National Union of Boot and Shoe Operatives was a British union. Minutes of General Executive Council, 8 Nov. 1946. The staff members interviewed were Barney Conway, J. Byrne, Tony Brack, Seán Nugent, William Eustace, M. F. O'Kelly, D. Byrne and R. Foley. Barney Conway's £4 10s was raised to £5 (also A. Brack, J. Byrne, M. F. O'Kelly, S. Nugent and R. James). Billy Eustace got £3 15s and a rent-free flat. J. Smith and R. Foley went from £2 up to £3 and Breda Kearns up to £3 5s as senior typist but now required to attend the General Executive Council. The carpenter was M. Lamb. Minutes of General Executive Council, 24 Jan. 1947, 19 and 21 Feb. 1947. The members of the Finance Committee were J. Burke, Thomas Quinn, Thomas Kavanagh, George Nathan and Billy Eustace. Minutes of General Executive Council, 28 Mar. 1947, 30 May 1947, 27 June 1947, 11 and 25 July 1947, 8, 11, 15 and 22 Aug. 1947, 19 Sep. 1947, 10, 22 and 31 Oct. 1947, 12 Dec. 1947. The successful candidates were Condron, Jim Quinn (Butchers' Porters), John Ivory (Building), Patrick Heelan (Portrane), Christy Troy (Operative Butchers) and Patrick Phillips (Hide and Skin).

5. WUI, Report of Annual Delegate Conference, Dublin, 19 June 1949, p. 4, 25; minutes of General Executive Council, 31 Oct. 1947, 7, 14 and 21 Nov. 1947, 7 and 27 Feb. 1948. The Grocers went to the INUVGATA. WUI, minutes of General Executive Council, 2 Apr. 1948, 14 and 20 May 1948, 11 June 1948, 2 and 16 July 1948, 26 Nov. 1948, 10 Dec. 1948, 1 and 29 Apr. 1949, 6 and 9 May 1949; O'Connor, *James Larkin*, p. 112.

6. WUI, Report of Annual Delegate Conference, Dublin, 8 June 1947, p. 8–9; minutes of General Executive Council, 12 and 26 July 1946, 6 Dec. 1946, 21 Mar. 1947; Irish Trades Union Congress, 53rd Annual Report, 1946–1947, p. 31–2; Report of 51st Congress, Dublin, 4–6 July 1945, p. 173–4; Report of 52nd Congress, Dublin, 9–11 July 1946, p. 48–50, 132–8; *Report of the Commission on Vocational Organisation* (1943), p. 127–8. See Bradley, *Farm Labourers' Irish Struggle,* and '"Speeding the plough": The formation of the FRW, 1944–1948,' *Saothar,* 11 (1986), p. 39–53, and Murphy, *The Federation of Rural Workers.*

7. WUI, minutes of General Executive Council, 1 Nov. 1946; Irish Trades Union Congress, Report of 51st Congress, Dublin, 4–6 July 1945, p. 144–7; 53rd Annual Report, 1946–1947, p. 74.

8. WUI, Report of Annual Delegate Conference, Dublin, 19 June 1949, p. 3; Irish Trades Union Congress, Annual Report, 1947–148, and Report of 54th Congress, Cork, 7–9 July 1948, p. 22–40, 96–115.

9. WUI, Report of Annual Delegate Conference, Dublin, 8 June 1947, p. 7; Report of Annual Delegate Conference, Dublin, 19 June 1949, p. 13–14; minutes of General Executive Council, 13 Sep. 1946, 13 Feb. 1948.

10. Irish Trades Union Congress, Report of 51st Congress, Dublin, 4–6 July 1945, p. 174–9, 190–91; 52nd Annual Report, 1945–1946, p. 29–46, 141–68, 215 57–60; 53rd Annual Report, 1946–1947, p. 53–9; 54th Annual Report, 1947–1948, p. 55–9; 55th Annual Report, 1948–9, p. 41–5. Motions of protest were adopted at the 55th Congress, Belfast, 26–29 July 1949.

11. WUI, Report of Annual Delegate Conference, Dublin, 19 June 1949, p. 2, 8, 26–8; Report of General Executive Council for 1975–1976 and Annual Delegate Conference, Dublin, 11–12 June 1977, p. 110–11; minutes of General Executive Council, 15 Sep. 1947; Irish Trades Union Congress, 53rd Annual Report, 1946–1947, and Report of 53rd Congress, Waterford, 29–31 July 1947, p. 33–9, 132–40; 55th Annual Report, 1948–1949, and Report of 55th Congress, Belfast, 26–29 July 1949, p. 46–54, 70–89, 115–28, 131–8; 56th Annual Report, 1949–1950, p. 30–33; Report of 58th Congress, Derry, 23–5 July 1952, 107–17; Congress of Irish Unions, Report of Central Council, 1949–1950, p. 7–18. See Francis Devine, 'Letting labour lead: Jack Macgougan and the pursuit of unity, 1913–1958,' *Saothar,* 14 (1989), p. 113–24, and Francis Devine and Dick Hunter, 'Jack Macgougan,' *Saothar,* 24 (1999), p. 10–13.

12. WUI, Report of Annual Delegate Conference, Dublin, 8 June 1947, p. 2, 6; Irish Trades Union Congress, 53rd Annual Report, 1946–1947, p. 26–39; Irish Trades Union Congress, Report of 52nd Congress, Dublin, 9–11 July 1946, 104–108, 112–16; 53rd Annual Report, 1946–1947, and Report of 53rd Congress, Waterford, 29–31 July 1947, p. 74–81, 183–4.

13. WUI, minutes of General Executive Council, 30 May 1947; Report of Annual Delegate Conference, Dublin, 19 June 1949, p. 22–3; minutes of General Executive Council, 6 and 27 May 1949; ITGWU, minutes of National Executive Council, 19–21 June 1949; Devine, *Understanding Social Justice.*

14. WUI, minutes of General Executive Council, 7 and 14 Nov. 1947, 14, 18 and 25 Mar. 1949, 29 Apr. 1949, 16 Oct. 1959.

15. WUI, Report of Annual Delegate Conference, Dublin, 19 June 1949, p. 23; minutes of General Executive Council, 25 Mar. 1949, 22 Apr. 1949. Irish Trades Union Congress, 51st Annual Report, 1944–1945, p. 196.

16. WUI, minutes of General Executive Council, 18 and 25 July 1947, 15 and 22 Aug. 1947. The Muintir na Mara Delegation was John 'the Man' Moore (Howth), McConnell (Balbriggan), Sharkey (Clogherhead), Cleary (Arklow) and Ferguson (Loughshinny). Séamus Rickard (Howth) was an influential figure in Muintir na Mara, not least in giving it an Irish title. Congress of Irish Unions, Report of Central Council, 1947–1948, p. 6.

17. WUI, Report of Annual Delegate Conference, Dublin, 8 June 1947, p. 15; Irish Trades Union Congress, Report of 52nd Congress, Dublin, 9–11 July 1946, p. 209–12; Report of 53rd Congress, Waterford, 29–31 July 1947, p. 141–6; 54th Congress, Cork, 7–9 July 1948, p. 115–23. Larkin no doubt made a significant contribution to the Memorandum on Workers' Co-operation in Industry, p. 57–60; Report of 55th Congress, Belfast, 27–29 July 1949, p. 90–92.

18. Irish Trades Union Congress, Report of 51st Congress, Dublin, 4–6 June 1945, p. 182–4; Report of 51st Congress, Dublin, 9–11 July 1946, p. 119–23; Report of 55th Congress, Belfast, 26–29 July 1949, 168–80. Ferguson and Tom Kavanagh also contributed to the debate. For a discussion of migrant work see James B. Wolf, '"Withholding their due": The dispute between Ireland and Great Britain over unemployed insurance payments to conditionally landed Irish wartime volunteer workers,' *Saothar,* 21 (1996), p. 23–34.

19. Irish Trades Union Congress, 52nd Annual Report, 1945–1946, p. 27; Report of 53rd Congress, Waterford, 29–31 July 1947, p. 175–6. Ferguson's figure of 146 over the previous four years is hard to comprehend. The official number of fatalities, as recorded by the Factory Inspectorate for 1943–46, was 48; for 1943, 13; for 1944, 5; for 1945, 12; and for 1946, 8. See Francis Devine, 'Social statistics for labour historians: Safety, health and welfare at work in the Irish Free State and the Republic of Ireland, 1922–1990: Measuring the problem,' *Saothar,* 25, 2000 p. 114–21.

20. WUI, Report of Annual Delegate Conference, Dublin, 8 June 1947, p. 11–12, 15; Report of Annual Delegate Conference, Dublin, 19 June 1949, p. 11; minutes of General Executive Council, 28 June 1946; Irish Trades Union Congress, Report of 52nd Congress, Dublin, 9–11 July 1946, p. 128–30; 55th Annual Report, 1948–1949, and 55th Congress, Belfast, July 1948–1949, p. 54–6, 150–51. See also Roberts and Clarke, *The Story of the People's College.*

21. WUI, minutes of General Executive Council, 1 Nov. 1946; minutes of General Executive Council, 21 Nov. 1947, 16 and 23 July 1948, 26 Nov. 1948, 1 Feb. 1949; Report of Annual Delegate Conference, Dublin, 8 June 1947, p. 12; Report of Annual Delegate Conference, Dublin, 19 June 1949, p. 24–5.

22. WUI, minutes of General Executive Council, 7 Mar. 1947, 11 June 1948. There were more complaints about Brack's behaviour in Jacob's in November. He was suspended in July 1948 when, among other things, he was eleven weeks in arrears. Minutes of General Executive Council, 10 and 17 Oct. 1947. The Staff Section was C. N. Ferguson (Chairman), James Plunkett Kelly (Secretary), Barney Conway, Miss McLoughlin and Tony Brack. Minutes of General Executive Council, 4 and 8 Aug. 1948, 28 May, 1948, 6 Dec. 1948. J. Quinn thought an Association inappropriate. Smithers's salary rose to £8 19s; Ferguson's was £8 1s and Denis Larkin's £7 18s; most Branch Secretaries £7 1s; Billy Eustace £6 6s; Breda Kearns £5 1s; and portering staff £2 13s to £3 12. Minutes of General Executive Council, 28 Nov. 1948, 21 Jan. 1949.

23. WUI, Report of Annual Delegate Conference, Dublin, 8 June 1947, p. 13; Report of Annual Delegate Conference, Dublin, 19 June 1949, p. 4–5, 11–12; Report of General Executive Council, 1975–1976, and Annual Delegate Conference, Dún Laoghaire, 30–31 Oct. 1976, p. 109; minutes of General Executive Council, 6 June 1946, 19 Mar. 1948, 16 July 1948, 3 Sep. 1948, 22 Apr. 1949, 6, 9 and 20 May 1949. Mrs Buckley (Irish Women Workers' Union) spoke on 'Connolly, man and myth.' See Puirséil, *The Irish Labour Party*, p. 133–4, citing the reminiscences of Donal Nevin.

Chapter 23 (p. 397–447)

1. ITGWU, Annual Report for 1949 and Report of Proceedings of Annual Conference, Galway, 21–23 June 1950, p. 64–81; Annual Report for 1951 and Proceedings of Annual Conference, 1952, p. 43–57; Annual Report for 1952 and Proceedings of Annual Conference, 1953, p. 38–52.

2. ITGWU, Annual Report for 1955 and Proceedings of Annual Conference, 1956, p. 39–41; Annual Report for 1957 and Proceedings of Annual Conference, 1958, p. 43–53.

3. ITGWU, Annual Report for 1952 and Proceedings of Annual Conference, 1953, p. 85–7. ITGWU, Annual Report for 1953 and Proceedings of Annual Conference, 1954, p. 59–65; Congress of Irish Unions, Report of Central Committee, 1950–1951, p. 27.

4. ITGWU, Annual Report for 1951, p. 5; Annual Report for 1958 and Proceedings of Annual Conference, 1959, p. 10–14, 95–101, 111–14; Annual Report for 1959 and Proceedings of Annual Conference, 1960, p. 7, 67–8; minutes of National Executive Council, 19–21 Nov. 1958, 9–10 Feb. 1959, 19–21 Sep. 1959, 25–26 Nov. 1959; 'Golden Jubilee,' *Liberty*, Feb. 1959; 'Jubilee celebrations at Mullingar' and 'Union honours Connolly's birthplace,' Mar. 1959; 'Jubilee celebrations at Limerick,' June 1959, July 1959; 'Big welcome for Band in Sligo,' Sep. 1959; 'Union prize Band in Enniscorthy,' Nov. 1959; 'Enjoyable evening at Buncrana,' Oct. 1959; '1959: A year to be remembered by Irish workers,' Dec. 1959. See O'Shannon, *Fifty Years of Liberty Hall*. Purcell suffered from diabetes.

5. Congress of Irish Unions, Report of Central Committee, 1950–1951, p. 27–8; ITGWU, Annual Report for 1950, p. 5–8. The event was held in the Savoy Restaurant on Thursday 9 November, with Dr O'Neill, Bishop of Limerick, James Everett TD, Minister for Posts and Telegraphs, and Kevin Bradshaw, Mayor, as guests. In 'their first great battle the pork butchers had placed themselves under the guidance of the Mother of God' and 'manifested their gratitude to Our Lady ever since.' A three-month strike in 1890 was settled after the intervention of Bishop O'Dwyer. John Conroy said it taught two lessons: unity, and that 'they refused to work any more on 15 August, the Feast of the Assumption, and that date was still observed as a holiday and holy day up to the present by the Limerick Pork Butchers.' The eight founder-members were Tom Forrestal, James Galvin, John Galvin, Pat McNamara, Edward McManus, William O'Dwyer, Mick Plunkett and Dick Ryan. *Liberty*, Dec. 1950.

6. ITGWU, Annual Report for 1951 and Proceedings of Annual Conference, 1952, p. 7–10, 44–5, 65; *Liberty*, July 1951.

7. 'The ever faithful few,' *Liberty*, Aug. 1951.

8. ITGWU, Annual Report for 1952 and Proceedings of Annual Conference, 1953, p. 6–8, 59–65, 65–7; 1953, p. 7–9; 1954, p. 5–6; minutes of National Executive Council, 12–

14 July, 3–6 Sep. 1953. P. J. Boyle was sent in.

9. ITGWU, minutes of National Executive Council, 15–17 Nov. 1954; Annual Report for 1954 and Proceedings of Annual Conference, 1955, p. 66–8, 82–3, 105–7; Paddy O'Brien, 'Early days of the ITGWU in Kerry,' *Liberty*, June 1981; Francis Devine, 'Liberating the Kingdom: The Transport Union in Kerry, 1918–1990: An outline history,' in *An Eccentric Chemistry*, p. 5–16.

10. ITGWU, Annual Report for 1955, p. 5–8; *Liberty*, Mar. 1955; 'Annual stock-taking,' *Liberty*, Apr. 1955.

11. ITGWU, Annual Report for 1956 and Proceedings of Annual Conference, 1957, p. 5–10, 91–2; 'This is your job,' *Liberty*, Sep. 1956.

12. ITGWU, Annual Report for 1957 and Report of Proceedings of Annual Conference, 1958, p. 6–8, 60–64; minutes of National Executive Council, 20–22 Nov. 1957.

13. ITGWU, Annual Report for 1958 and Proceedings of Annual Conference, 1959, p. 8–14, 106–10; 1959, p. 7–8. Government exchequer bills made up £297,325 of the total, Government bonds, £74,250; Government loans, £257,985; Dublin Corporation stock, £101,350; Dublin Corporation special loan, £87,194; Cork Corporation stock, £30,896; ESB stock, £12,500; Galway Harbour Commissioners' stock, £2,815.

14. ITGWU, Annual Report for 1959 and Proceedings of Annual Conference, 1960, p. 91–2; 'Strike threat forces careless to clear cards,' *Liberty*, July 1959.

15. Congress of Irish Unions, 7th Annual Meeting, Galway, 18–20 July 1951, p. 41; ITGWU, Annual Report for 1951 and Proceedings of Annual Conference, 1952, p. 65–70; Annual Report for 1953 and Proceedings of Annual Conference, 1954, p. 81–2, 90; Annual Report for 1954 and Proceedings of Annual Conference, 1955, p. 101; 'The NEC's first lady,' *Liberty*, Aug. 1955. The women Delegates were Mrs M. Webb, Miss V. Crudden and Miss S. Doyle (Derry), Eileen Flynn (Dublin No. 3 Branch), Sheila Williams (Dublin No. 4 Branch) and Molly O'Neill (Dublin No. 8 Branch).

16. ITGWU, Annual Report for 1955 and Proceedings of Annual Conference, 1956, p. 68–9; Congress of Irish Unions, 13th Annual Meeting, Tramore, 17–19 July 1957, p. 140–50; Annual Report for 1959 and Proceedings of Annual Conference, 1960, p. 92–3; minutes of National Executive Council, 19–21 Sep. 1959; 'NEC recommends Marriage Benefit for female members,' *Liberty*, May 1958.

17. ITGWU, Annual Report for 1952 and Proceedings of Annual Conference, 1953, p. 76; Annual Report for 1953, p. 33–4, 84–5; minutes of National Executive Council, 24–26 Sep. 1953, 5–7 Nov. 1953, 10–12 Dec. 1953; *Liberty*, Nov. 1953; Irish Trades Union Congress, 59th Annual Report, 1952–1953, p. 30–31. See also McCabe and Devine, *Navigating a Lone Channel*; *Saothar*, 22 (1997), p. 139–52; Andrew Finlay, 'Politics, sectarianism and the "failure" of trade unionism in Northern Ireland: The case of the garment workers in Derry, 1945–1968,' *Saothar*, 17 (1992), p. 78–86.

18. *Liberty*, Aug. 1955, Sep. 1958; ITGWU, Annual Report for 1956, p. 17–18; minutes of National Executive Council, 15–17 May 1957, 9–11 June 1957. The locks were never restored, and Newry's fate as a port was sealed. Among other ITGWU Officials who had been active in the IRA were Jerry Cronin and Ned McNamara (Cork), Mickey Mullen, and Christy and Mattie O'Neill (Dublin).

19. ITGWU, Annual Report for 1950, p. 5–7; Annual Report for 1951 and Proceedings of Annual Conference, 1952, p. 70; *Liberty*, Feb. 1949; Annual Report for 1952 and Proceedings of Annual Conference, 1953, p. 11–12, 40.

20. ITGWU, Annual Report for 1953 and Proceedings of Annual Conference, 1954, p. 30, 74–6; Annual Report for 1954, p. 7–37; minutes of National Executive Council, 25–26 Feb. 1953, 3–6 Sep. 1953.

21. ITGWU, Annual Report for 1955 and Proceedings of Annual Conference, 1956, p. 10, 36; *Liberty,* Apr. 1955, Aug. 1955.

22. 'The obligations of workers,' *Liberty,* Oct. 1955.

23. Congress of Irish Unions, Report of Congress of Irish Unions, 1955–1956, p. 58; ITGWU, Annual Report for 1957 and Proceedings of Annual Conference, 1958, p. 11–13, 47.

24. ITGWU, Annual Report for 1957 and Proceedings of Annual Conference, 1958, p. 64–6; Annual Report for 1958, p. 16–18; Annual Report for 1959, p. 11–12; 'PUTUO sponsors work study school at Greystones,' *Liberty,* Oct. 1958; Congress of Irish Unions, Report of Central Committee, 1958–1959, p. 12–14.

25. ITGWU, Annual Report for 1950, p. 9–12; Congress of Irish Unions, 6th Annual Meeting, Killarney, 12–14 July 1950, p. 49–57, 106–28; *Liberty,* Nov. 1950.

26. ITGWU, Annual Report for 1950 and Proceedings of Annual Conference, 1951, p. 82–3; *Liberty,* Jan. 1950; Annual Report for 1951, p. 10–12; *Liberty,* July 1951; Congress of Irish Unions, Report of Central Committee, 1950–1951, p. 7; 7th Annual Meeting, Galway, 18–20 July 1951, p. 41–52, 63–72.

27. ITGWU, Annual Report for 1952 and Proceedings of Annual Conference, 1953, p. 8–11, 44–5; Congress of Irish Unions, Report of Central Committee, 1951–1952, and 8th Annual Meeting, Waterford, 23–25 July 1952, p. 15–19, 73–97.

28. ITGWU, Annual Report for 1952 and Proceedings of Annual Conference, 1953, p. 71–2; Annual Report for 1953 and Proceedings of Annual Conference, 1954, p. 9–30, 79–83; Annual Report for 1954, p. 32–3; minutes of National Executive Council, 28 May 1952, 15–16 June 1952, 20–21 July 1952; *Liberty,* Apr. 1953; Congress of Irish Unions, 8th Annual Meeting, Waterford, 23–25 July 1952, p. 86–8; 9th Annual Meeting, Killarney, 15–17 July 1953, p. 44–58.

29. ITGWU, Annual Report for 1954 and Proceedings of Annual Conference, 1955, p. 72–3, 87–92; *Liberty,* Feb. 1955; Congress of Irish Unions, 11th Annual Meeting, 1954–1955, p. 45–50.

30. ITGWU, Annual Report for 1955 and Proceedings of Annual Conference, 1956, p. 10, 36–7, 55–7; Annual Report for 1956, p. 10–13; 'Cost of living now highest ever,' *Liberty,* Aug. 1955; 'Can Ireland afford higher wages?' *Liberty,* Sep. 1955; 'Progress on the wages front' and 'Negotiations succeed in many centres,' *Liberty,* Oct. 1955.

31. ITGWU, Annual Report for 1956, p. 13–15; Annual Report for 1957 and Proceedings of Annual Conference, 1958, p. 8–11, 46–7; 'Outstanding progress in wages campaign,' *Liberty,* Jan. 1958; Congress of Irish Unions, Report of Congress of Irish Unions, 1955–1956, p. 58–62.

32. ITGWU, Annual Report for 1958 and Proceedings of Annual Conference, 1959, p. 15–16, 114–17; Annual Report for 1959, p. 10–11.

33. ITGWU, Annual Report for 1959, p. 13–14; 'John Conroy issues a challenge,' *Liberty,* Sep. 1959, Dec. 1959.

34. ITGWU, Annual Report for 1949 and Proceedings of Annual Conference, 1950, p. 113–14; Congress of Irish Unions, Report of Central Committee, 1949–1950, and 6th Annual Meeting, Killarney, 12–14 July 1950, p. 9–18, 45–9, 66–87, 96–9, 120–25; Report of Central Committee, 1950–1951, p. 13–14.

35. Congress of Irish Unions, 7th Annual Meeting, Galway, 18–20 July 1951, p. 76–83, 122–4.

36. Congress of Irish Unions, Report of Central Committee, 1951–1952, p. 20–21; Report of Central Committee, 1952–1953, and 9th Annual Meeting, Killarney, 15–17 July 1953, p. 28–30, 54–6, 116–22; 11th Annual Meeting, Cork, 13–15 July 1955, p. 96–111; ITGWU, Annual Report for 1952 and Proceedings of Annual Conference, 1953, p. 67–9; minutes of National Executive Council, 5–6 June 1953.

37. ITGWU, Annual Report for 1953 and Proceedings of Annual Conference, 1954, p. 58–9, 94; Annual Report for 1955, p. 15–20; Annual Report for 1956, p. 18–19; Congress of Irish Unions, Report of Central Committee, 1953–1954, p. 30–43, including 'Unity Conference: Joint Memorandum on Trade Union Unity'; Annual Report for 1954–1955 and 11th Annual Meeting, Cork, 13–15 July 1955, p. 32–6, 96–111.

38. *Liberty*, Feb. 1956; Congress of Irish Unions, Report of Central Committee, 1956–1957, and 12th Annual Meeting, Kilkee, 18–20 July 1956, p. 12–13, 16–52 (including 'Report of Special Congress, 5 January 1956'), 109–21, 123–32; ITGWU, Annual Report for 1957, p. 16–20.

39. ITGWU, Annual Report for 1958, p. 29–39 ('Provisional United Trade Union Organisation'); Annual Report for 1958, p. 40–53 ('Special Delegate Conference, 5 January 1959'); Congress of Irish Unions, 14th Annual Meeting, Youghal, 17–19 July 1958, p. 163–4; 15th Annual Meeting, Salthill, 22–24 July 1959, p. 115–19.

40. Congress of Irish Unions, 7th Annual Meeting, Galway, 18–20 July 1951, p. 119–22; Report of Central Committee, 1952–1953, p. 21, 27. The unions were the Building Workers' Trade Union (which included bricklayers and painters), the Irish National Union of Woodworkers, the United House and Ship Painters' and Decorators' Trade Union, and the Operative Plasterers' Trade Society. *Liberty*, Feb. 1950, Jan.-Feb. 1953.

41. ITGWU, minutes of National Executive Council, 9–11 Nov. 1955, 14–16 Dec. 1955, 25–27 Jan. 1956, 22–24 Feb. 1956, 21–23 Mar. 1956. 'New Inter-Relations Agreement,' *Liberty*, May 1956. Others involved in the talks were John Conroy and Edward Browne (ITGWU) and John Smithers and Christy Ferguson (WUI).

42. *Liberty*, Mar. 1959; ICTU, 1st Annual Report, 1959, and Report of 1st Annual Congress, Dublin, 22–25 Sep. 1959, p. 25–7 ('To all trade Unionists').

43. ITGWU, Annual Report for 1949 and Proceedings of Annual Conference, 1950, p. 66–7; Annual Report for 1950 and Proceedings of Annual Conference, 1951, p. 82–3; Annual Report for 1951 and Proceedings of Annual Conference, 1952, p. 43–4, 72–3; Annual Report for 1959 and Proceedings of Annual Conference, 1960, p. 40–42, 67; ITGWU, minutes of National Executive Council, 29 Aug. 1951; Congress of Irish Unions, 6th Annual Meeting, Killarney, 12–14 July 1950, p. 60–66; 7th Annual Meeting, 18–20 July 1951, p. 137–40; Report of Central Committee, 1951–1952, and 8th Annual Meeting, Waterford, 23–25 July 1952, p. 10–12, 63–71.

44. ITGWU, Annual Report for 1952, p. 12–13; Annual Report for 1953, p. 30–33.

45. ITGWU, Annual Report for 1954 and Proceedings of Annual Conference, 1955, p. 72–3; Annual Report for 1955, p. 10–11; Annual Report for 1956, p. 14–17; 'The Labour Court,' *Liberty*, June 1955; Congress of Irish Unions, Report of Central Committee, 1955–1956, p. 14–16.

46. ITGWU, Annual Report for 1950, p. 12; Annual Report for 1949 and Proceedings of Annual Conference, p. 68; *Liberty*, Jan. 1958, Feb. 1950.

47. ITGWU, Annual Report for 1950 and Proceedings of Annual Conference, 1951, p. 64–5; *Liberty,* Mar. 1950; William McMullen, 'Victory at Clontarf,' *Liberty,* Apr.–May 1950; ITGWU, minutes of National Executive Council, 20–21 Apr. 1950. Dispute benefit was £3,115 18s 10d; loans, £7,339. Subscriptions from Branches totalled £640 16s 11d.

48. ITGWU, Annual Report for 1950, p. 14–23; Annual Report for 1951, p. 12–15; *Liberty,* Jan. 1951, Feb. 1951. McMullen, Conroy and Mick Dunbar (Dublin No. 1 Branch) were the Delegation. ITGWU, minutes of National Executive Council, 17–18 Apr. 1952.

49. ITGWU, Annual Report for 1956 and Proceedings of Annual Conference, 1957, p. 77–8; Annual Report for 1957, p. 22; 'Union wins CIÉ claim,' *Liberty,* Oct. 1955, Feb. 1956; 'Hardships imposed on road passenger staffs,' *Liberty,* Feb. 1958; 'Arduous year for Dublin No. 9 Branch Committee,' June 1958, Oct. 1958.

50. ITGWU, Annual Report for 1949 and Proceedings of Annual Conference, 1950, p. 116–17; 'Settlement in mental hospital dispute,' *Liberty,* May 1955; 'The mental hospital dispute,' Feb. 1956, Mar. 1956.

51. ITGWU, Annual Report for 1949 and Proceedings of Annual Conference, 1950, p. 118–19; Annual Report for 1950 and Proceedings of Annual Conference, 1951, p. 91; Annual Report for 1951, p. 16–22; minutes of National Executive Council, 20–21 July 1952. Purcell's Labour Court submission was reproduced in *Liberty,* Nov. 1951. See Norman Croke, 'Seventy five years of the Hotels, Restaurants and Catering Branch, 1918–1993: An outline history,' in ITGWU, *Hotels, Restaurants and Catering Branch, 75th Anniversary—Diamond Jubilee, 1992 Annual Report.*

52. ITGWU, Annual Report for 1951 and Proceedings of Annual Conference, 1952, p. 71–2; Annual Report for 1952 and Proceedings of Annual Conference, 1953, p. 72, 81; Annual Report for 1955 and Proceedings of Annual Conference, 1956, p. 64–5; 'Our guests,' *Liberty,* Aug. 1955; 'Outstanding progress in Dublin No. 4 Branch,' May 1958; 'The Catering Exhibition,' 'Meet the people at the exhibition' and 'Staffs and management made Catering Show a success,' Nov. 1958.

53. ITGWU, Annual Report for 1953 and Proceedings of Annual Conference, 1955, p. 86–7; Annual Report for 1958, p. 54–5. The International Confederation of Free Trade Unions, International Metalworkers' Federation, International Federation of Petroleum Workers and International Federation of Organisations and General Workers' Unions were also involved in the boycott. *Liberty,* Feb. 1950.

54. ITGWU, Annual Report for 1951 and Proceedings of Annual Conference, 1952, p. 65–7; Annual Report for 1952 and Proceedings of Annual Conference, 1953, p. 60–61, 76, 80–84.

55. ITGWU, Annual Report for 1953 and Proceedings of Annual Conference, 1954, p. 87; Annual Report for 1954 and Proceedings of Annual Conference, 1955, p. 102–3; Annual Report for 1955 and Proceedings of Annual Conference, 1956, p. 55–61, 68–9; Annual Report for 1956 and Proceedings of Annual Conference, 1957, p. 20–26, 70–71, 80, 94–96; Annual Report for 1957 and Proceedings of Annual Conference, 1958, p. 68–70. 76–8; Annual Report for 1958 and Proceedings of Annual Conference, 1959, p. 21–9, 117–19; 'Importing shamrocks,' *Liberty,* Mar. 1954; Congress of Irish Unions, 10th Annual Meeting, Galway, 13–15 July 1954, p. 67–72. ITGWU speakers included Murtagh Morgan MP and Stephen McGonagle. *Liberty,* Mar. 1955; 'Towards a co-operative commonwealth,' *Liberty,* Aug. 1955; Our economic crisis,'

Aug. 1956; *Labour Monthly*, Feb. 1957; 'Further views on unemployment,' *Labour Monthly*, Mar. 1957; 'Government has no plan for full employment,' *Labour Monthly*, Mar. 1958; 'PUTUO takes action on unemployment,' *Labour Monthly*, May 1958; 'Co-operative movement provides an outlet for true patriotism,' *Labour Monthly*, Nov. 1958, Mar. 1959; Congress of Irish Unions, Report of Central Committee, 1954–1955, and 11th Annual Meeting, Cork, 13–15 July 1955, p. 53, 122–30; 13th Annual Meeting, Tramore, 17–19 July 1957, p. 164–85, 202–6; 14th Annual Meeting, Youghal, 16–18 July 1958, p. 155–63, 166–8, 178–80; 15th Annual Meeting, Salthill, 22–24 July 1959, p. 50–63.

56. ITGWU, Annual Report for 1957 and Proceedings of Annual Conference, 1958, p. 70; Annual Report for 1958 and Proceedings of Annual Conference, 1959, p. 130; Annual Report for 1959, p. 31–9; 'Yes! We can't have bananas,' *Liberty*, Oct. 1956.

57. ITGWU, Annual Report for 1950 and Proceedings of Annual Conference, 1951, p. 87; Annual Report for 1952 and Proceedings of Annual Conference, 1953, p. 15–21, 76–9; Annual Report for 1953 and Proceedings of Annual Conference, 1954, p. 37–9, 64–5, 87–91; Annual Report for 1954 and Proceedings of Annual Conference, 1955, p. 40–41, 96–100; Annual Report for 1955 and Proceedings of Annual Conference, 1956, p. 38–9, 61; Annual Report for 1956 and Proceedings of Annual Conference, 1957, p. 26–8, 76; Annual Report for 1958 and Proceedings of Annual Conference, 1959, p. 127–8; Annual Report for 1959, p. 15–31; minutes of National Executive Council, 20–21 Apr. 1951; *Liberty*, Feb. 1957, Apr. 1959; Congress of Irish Unions, 7th Annual Meeting, Galway, 18–20 July 1951, p. 41–52, 126–27; 15th Annual Meeting, Salthill, 22–24 July 1959, p. 55–6.

58. ITGWU, Annual Report for 1952 and Proceedings of Annual Conference, 1953, p. 80; Annual Report for 1953 and Proceedings of Annual Conference, 1954, p. 77–9.

59. Congress of Irish Unions, 6th Annual Meeting, Killarney, 12–14 July 1948, p. 57–60, 104–106; 7th Annual Meeting, Galway, 18–20 July 1951, p. 128–9. Seán O'Moore (Irish Seamen's and Port Workers' Union) was made to withdraw anti-Semitic remarks when referring to bad employers.

60. ITGWU, Annual Report for 1950 and Proceedings of Annual Conference, 1951, p. 65–6; Annual Report for 1952 and Proceedings of Annual Conference, 1953, p. 76–8, 82–3. Boran moved his pneumoconiosis motion again in 1954. Annual Report for 1953 and Report of Annual Conference, Kilkee, 9–11 June 1954, p. 60–61, 85, 92; Annual Report for 1954 and Report of Annual Conference, Mosney, 15–17 June 1955, p. 74–5; Annual Report for 1955 and report of Annual Conference, Salthill, 15–17 June 1955, p. 12–13, 74–5; Annual Report for 1956, p. 32–6; Annual Report for 1957 and Report of Annual Conference, Ballybunnion, 11–13 June 1958, p. 83; Annual Report for 1958, p. 55–65; Annual Report for 1959, p. 45–6; John E. Gibson, 'Air must be kept moving,' *Liberty*, Nov. 1950, and 'Cigarettes and your health: Hard facts for the scaremongers,' Dec. 1950; *Liberty*, Mar. 1955; 'The liability of employers,' *Liberty*, Sep. 1955; Congress of Irish Unions, 8th Annual Meeting, Waterford, 23–5 July 1952, p. 133–4; 9th Annual Meeting, Killarney, 15–17 July 1953, p. 64–72; 10th Annual Meeting, Galway, 13–15 July 1954, p. 125–8; 12th Annual Meeting, Kilkee, 18–20 July 1956, p. 138–41.

61. ITGWU, Annual Report for 1949 and Proceedings of Annual Conference, 1950, p. 118; Annual Report for 1952 and Proceedings of Annual Conference, 1953, p. 63–5, 83; Annual Report for 1953 and Proceedings of Annual Conference, 1954, p. 93–4;

Annual Report for 1954 and Proceedings of Annual Conference, 1955, p. 103, 105; Congress of Irish Unions, Report of Central Committee, 1950–1951, p. 16; Report of Central Committee, 1952–1953, and 9th Annual Meeting, Killarney, 15–17 July 1953, p. 123–7, p. 30–32. Graduates were Christy Bonass, Peter Eustace, B. Farrelly, John Forde, Mick Gannon, Con Healy, James Kelly, T. J. Kennedy, Charles Larkin, Philip Lennon, James Loughrey, Colbert Moore, Jerome Morrissey, Mattie O'Neill, Joseph Power, Peter Smyth and Edward Pender.

62. ITGWU, Annual Report for 1955 and Proceedings of Annual Conference, 1956, p. 42; Annual Report for 1957 and Proceedings of Annual Conference, 1958, p. 86–7; Congress of Irish Unions, 12th Annual Meeting, Kilkee, 18–20 July 1956, p. 188–9, 196–7; Report of Central Committee, 1956–1957, and 13th Annual Meeting, Tramore, 17–19 July 1957, p. 12, 32–4, 71–2.

63. ITGWU, Annual Report for 1958 and Proceedings of Annual Conference, 1959, p. 123–4; 'Catholic Workers' College courses,' Liberty, Sep. 1955; 'Continued progress in Catholic Workers' College,' Liberty, June 1958; 'Knowledge is there for the asking,' Liberty, Sep. 1958; Congress of Irish Unions, Report of Central Committee, 1958–1959, and 15th Annual Meeting, Salthill, 22–24 July 1959, p. 17–23, 105–6. Virtually every significant Dublin trade Unionist at this time was a graduate of the Catholic Workers' College.

64. 'Full employment and the Free Trade Area,' Liberty, Feb. 1959; 'A matter of grave importance,' Liberty, Nov. 1959.

65. ITGWU, minutes of National Executive Council, 26–27 Jan. 1950, 25–27 and 30–31 Mar. 1950, 7–8 Sep. 1950; Annual Report for 1949 and Proceedings of Annual Conference, 1950, p. 90; Annual Report for 1950 and Proceedings of Annual Conference, 1951, p. 92; Annual Report for 1953 and Proceedings of Annual Conference, 1954, p. 58, 94; Annual Report for 1954 and Proceedings of Annual Conference, 1955, p. 5–6, 65, 82–3; Annual Report for 1955 and Proceedings of Annual Conference, 1956, p. 51; Annual Report for 1956 and Proceedings of Annual Conference, 1957, p. 70; Annual Report for 1957, p. 7, 24–5; Annual Report for 1959 and Proceedings of Annual Conference, 1960, p. 92. Foran tried unsuccessfully to claim £5,000 in undrawn wages, to be credited to rebuilding Liberty Hall as a Connolly Memorial Hall. ITGWU, minutes of National Executive Council, 21–23 May 1958: Athlone, Convoy, Cork, Dublin, Galway, Kilkenny, Limerick, Lucan, Mallow, Midleton, Newry, Sligo, Tralee, Waterford, Wexford and Wicklow; 'Liberty Hall closes its doors for the last time,' Liberty, Jan. 1958.

66. ITGWU, Annual Report for 1955 and Proceedings of Annual Conference, 1956, p. 43; Annual Report for 1956 and Proceedings of Annual Conference, 1957, p. 91.

67. ITGWU, Annual Report for 1949 and Proceedings of Annual Conference, 1950, p. 109–110; Liberty, St Patrick's Day 1950, Apr.–May 1950, Nov. 1950; ITGWU, minutes of National Executive Council, 20–21 Apr. 1951. Losses in 1950 were £1,869 18s 6d. Thomas Carnduff, 'Salute to the labourer,' Liberty, St Patrick's Day 1950, 'It's all in a navvy's life,' Nov. 1950, 'The worker as writer,' Feb. 1951 and 'Notes from an out of work diary,' July 1951. Thomas Carnduff (1886–1956) worked in the shipyards and served in the British army during the First World War and later in the Ulster Special Constabulary. See Songs from the Shipyard and Other Poems (Belfast: E. H. Thornton, 1924), Songs of an Out-of-Work (Belfast: Quota Press, 1932) and Poverty

Street and Other Belfast Poems (Belfast: Lapwing Publications, 1993). His plays include *Workers* (Abbey Theatre, Dublin, 1932) *Machinery* (Abbey Theatre, 1933), *Traitors* (Empire Theatre, Belfast, 1934) and *Castlereagh* (Empire Theatre, 1935). He also wrote radio plays. See John Gray (ed.), *Thomas Carnduff: Life and Writings* (Belfast: Lagan Press, 1994); ITGWU, Annual Report for 1951 and Proceedings of Annual Conference, 1952, p. 63–5; minutes of National Executive Council, 26–27 Mar. 1952. Losses were: June-December 1949, £1,318 5s 5d; 1950, £1,122 18s 6d; 1951, £1,322 5s 2d.

68. ITGWU, Annual Report for 1952 and Proceedings of Annual Conference, 1953, p. 60–63; Annual Report for 1955 and Proceedings of Annual Conference, 1956, p. 42–3, 52; Annual Report for 1957 and Proceedings of Annual Conference, 1958, p. 61–3; Annual Report for 1958 and Proceedings of Annual Conference, 1959, p. 108–11; minutes of National Executive Council, 25–26 Feb. 1954, 14–16 Jan. 1954; *Liberty*, Nov. 1953.

69. ITGWU, minutes of National Executive Council, 18–19 Mar. 1954, 26–28 Apr. 1954, 2–4 and 30 Sep. 1954, 1–2 Oct. 1954, 15–17 June 1956, 15–17 July 1956.

70. ITGWU, Annual Report for 1950 and Proceedings of Annual Conference, 1951, p. 65–6; Annual Report for 1952 and Proceedings of Annual Conference, 1953, p. 84. The mover was Frank Robbins. ITGWU, Annual Report for 1953 and Proceedings of Annual Conference, 1954, p. 56–7; Annual Report for 1955 and Proceedings of Annual Conference, 1956, p. 53–5; Annual Report for 1957 and Proceedings of Annual Conference, 1958, p. 42–3, 78–9; Annual Report for 1958 and Proceedings of Annual Conference, 1959, p. 92–3; minutes of National Executive Council, 20–21 Apr. 1950, 18–19 June 1950, 21–23 Mar. 1956, 20–22 Nov. 1956, 8–10 June 1958; Séamus Murphy, 'To Rome: Under the banner of Matt Talbot,' *Liberty,* Jan. 1949, Dec. 1950; 'Pork Butchers' presentation for College Building Fund,' *Liberty,* Dec. 1958, Sep. 1959; Congress of Irish Unions, 6th Annual Meeting, Killarney, 12–14 July 1950, p. 132–3; Report of Central Committee, 1950–1951, and 7th Annual Meeting, Galway, 18–20 July 1951, p. 7, 17–18, 22–3, 48, 96, 101–108; 9th Annual Meeting, Killarney, 15–17 July 1953, p. 69–72. See John Cooney, *John Charles McQuaid: Ruler of Catholic Ireland* (Dublin: O'Brien Press, 1999), p. 227, 251.

71. ITGWU, Annual Report for 1949 and Proceedings of Annual Conference, 1950, p. 112; Annual Report for 1951 and Proceedings of Annual Conference, 1952, p. 23–4, 73–4; Annual Report for 1953 and Proceedings of Annual Conference, 1954, p. 74–6; Annual Report for 1954, p. 43–5; Annual Report for 1955 and Proceedings of Annual Conference, 1956, p. 74, 76; minutes of National Executive Council, 18–19 June 1950, 7–8 Sep. 1950, 3–5 Sep. 1952, 10–11 Dec. 1952, 14–16 Jan. 1953, 14–15 June 1955, 1–3 Sep. 1955, 12–14 Oct. 1955, 23–25 May 1955, 15–17 June 1956; Congress of Irish Unions, 6th Annual Meeting, Killarney, 12–14 July 1950, p. 67–88; 10th Annual Meeting, Galway, 13–15 July 1954, p. 128–30. The TDS were William Norton, Michael Keyes, Martin O'Sullivan, Séamus O'Farrell, Tom Kyne and James Larkin (Labour Party) and James Everett, Brendan Corish, James Hickey, Dan Desmond, John O'Leary and Dan Spring (National Labour Party). *Liberty,* Feb. 1957; 'The turning point in the Government's life,' *Liberty,* Feb. 1958; 'I protest,' *Liberty,* Apr. 1958; *Liberty,* June 1958; 'A challenge to Labour,' *Liberty,* Oct. 1959; 'The decision to abolish PR,' *Liberty,* Oct. 1958.

Chapter 24 (p. 448–95)

1. WUI, Report of Annual Delegate Conference, Dublin, 3 June 1951, p. 18–19; Report of Annual Delegate Conference, Dublin, 30–31 May 1953, p. 2–3; Report of Annual Delegate Conference, Dublin, 29–30 May 1954, p. 45–8; Report of Annual Delegate Conference, Dublin, 26–27 May 1956, p. 1–3; Report of Annual Delegate Conference, Dublin, 23–24 May 1959, p. 6; 'It seems to me . . .' *Report*, Feb. 1953, Apr. 1954.

2. WUI, minutes of General Executive Council, 15 Feb. 1957, 21 June 1957; Report of General Executive Council, 1954–1955, p. 5, 31; Report of General Executive Council, 1956–1957, p. 4; Report of Annual Delegate Conference, Dublin, 18–19 May 1957, p. 16–17.

3 WUI, Report of Annual Delegate Conference, Dublin, 21 May 1950, p. 4–5; Report of General Executive Council, 1950–1951, p. 35, 38–40; Report of Annual Delegate Conference, Dublin, 3 June 1951, p. 26; Report of Annual Delegate Conference, Dublin, 24–25 May 1952, p. 53. They were: bakeries; beef and pork butchers and porters; biscuit-making; boot and shoe trade; brush and broom; building workers; builders' providers; canals; carters; checkers; civil aviation (pilots, stewardesses, clerical, supervisory); clerical staffs; coal workers; Corporation workers; dockers; engineering trade; ESB; fish operatives; gas; health service; hide, skin and offal; Irish Hospitals Trust; laundry workers; maltmen, brewers and distillers; marble-polishers; mental hospital staffs; paper box trade; pharmaceutical chemists; port and harbour staffs; public assistance officers; railway and road workers; shipwrights; silk workers; state employees; storemen; structural steel; sugar confectionery and food-preserving; tanneries; tobacco; wallpaper manufacture; and water workers.

4. WUI, Report of General Executive Council, 1951–1952, p. 8–9; Report of Annual Delegate Conference, Dublin, 24–25 May 1952, p. 19–22, 40–; Report of General Executive Council, 1952–1953, and Annual Delegate Conference, Dublin, 30–31 May 1953, p. 9–11, 32–8; *Report*, Mar. 1953; 'Our newest Section: Road Passenger Transport,' Apr. 1953; 'It seems to me . . .' May 1953.

5 *Report*, Jan. 1954, Feb. 1954; WUI, Report of General Executive Council, 1953–1954, p. 7–8; Report of Annual Delegate Conference, Dublin, 29–30 May 1954, p. 16–19, 33–4, 40–42; '1953: A quiet year,' *Report*, Jan. 1954.

6 'And still they come . . .' *Report*, May 1954. The question of the Brushmakers was raised at the Disputes Committee of the ITUC, as proper 'notice was not given to Brushmakers' Society' till the transfer was effected, and the WUI was chastised for not following 'good trade union practice.' WUI, minutes of General Executive Council, 8 June 1956; Report of General Executive Council, 1954–1955, p. 3–5; Report of Annual Delegate Conference, Dublin, 21–22 May 1955, p. 25–6. Gerald Doyle, Operative Plasterers' and Allied Trades' Society of Ireland (CIU), and Maher, Amalgamated Society of Woodworkers, intervened.

7. WUI, Report of Annual Delegate Conference, Dublin, 21–22 May 1955, p. 10–26, 64–7; Report of General Executive Council, 1955–1956, and Annual Delegate Conference, Dublin, 26–27 May 1956, p. 1–2, 5–6, 40–43; minutes of General Executive Council, 8 June 1956, 12 and 29 Oct. 1956; Report of General Executive Council, 1956–1957, and Annual Delegate Conference, Dublin, 18–19 May 1957, p. 2–5, 12–16. The ILAEU got a skilled negotiator, clerical assistance, and Dispute Pay. The General Executive Council's formal invitation was that the ILAEU 'be invited to join

with our 190 members of the Riyal Liver Society as full members of the union, constituting, if desired, a separate Section.'

8. WUI, Report of General Executive Council, 1957–1958, p. 2–5; Report of General Executive Council, 1958–1959, p. 6–7; Report of Annual Delegate Conference, Dublin, 23–24 May 1959, p. 10–12, 52–4, 67–8; minutes of General Executive Council, 10 Jan. 1858, 14 Mar. 1958, 2 and 15 May 1958.

9. WUI, Report of Annual Delegate Conference, Dublin, 26–27 May 1956, p. 10–12; Report of Annual Delegate Conference, Dublin, 26–27 May 1956, p. 34–6; Report of General Executive Council, 1956–1957, p. 13–16; minutes of General Executive Council, 28 Sep. 1956, when it was reported that sixty members had transferred to the ITGWU and thirty-two to the WUI. The full terms were published in Report of General Executive Council, 1955–1956, p. 3–4. 'Building trade workers: Protection through unity,' Report, July 1953; 'Tobacco workers join hands across the sea,' Report, July 1953; Report, Jan. 1954; Irish Trades Union Congress, Report of 61st Congress, Portrush, 27–29 July 1955, p. 146–60; 62nd Annual Report, 1955–1956, p. 28–31.

10. WUI, Report of Annual Delegate Conference, Dublin, 21 May 1950, p. 5; Report of General Executive Council, 1950–1951, and Annual Delegate Conference, Dublin, 3 June 1951, p. 24–5, 40; Report of General Executive Council, 1951–1952, p. 13–14; Report of Annual Delegate Conference, Dublin, 26–27 May 1956, p. 9; Report of General Executive Council, 1956–1957, p. 1–2; minutes of General Executive Council, 7 Dec. 1957, 2 Dec. 1958; 'The farm workers can thank us,' Report, July 1951.

11. Irish Trades Union Congress, Report of 57th Annual Delegate Conference, 1951–1952, p. 31; Report of 59th Annual Delegate Conference, Sligo, 22–24 July 1953, p. 151–2; Report of 60th Annual Delegate Conference, Limerick, 21–23 July 1954, p. 166–8; WUI, Report of Annual Delegate Conference, Dublin, 3 June 1951, p. 29, 42; Report of Annual Delegate Conference, Dublin, 24–25 May 1952, p. 47–8, 84. Men voted 187 to 72 for a strike; women voted 329 to 263—arguably a more noble vote, as the women had already accepted the wage offer and had nothing to gain by supporting the men. Irish Trades Union Congress, Report of Annual Delegate Conference, Dublin, 29–30 May 1954, p. 29, 55; Margaret McLoughlin, 'The Dublin Trades Union Council,' Report, June 1953; 'Congratulations and good wishes to recipients of Marriage Benefit,' Report, Aug. 1953; Report, Sep. 1953. A list of newly married women followed in 'Woman's Page,' Report, Nov. 1953; 'Woman's Page,' Report, Apr. 1954.

12. WUI, Report of Annual Delegate Conference, Dublin, 21 May 1950, p. 17–18, 23–5.

13. Irish Trades Union Congress, Report of 56th Congress, Galway, 26–28 July 1950, p. 80–83, 86–7, 113–22; 57th Annual Report, 1951–52, and 57th Congress, Killarney, 25–27 July 1951, p. 26–30, 58–63, 84–9, 97–103, 112–30. The speakers were Thomas Kavanagh, Richard Emoe and J. Byrne. WUI, Report of General Executive Council, 1950–1951, p. 42–8; Report of Annual Delegate Conference, Dublin, 3 June 1951, p. 27–33.

14. WUI, Report of General Executive Council, 1950–1951, p. 47–9; Report of Annual Delegate Conference, Dublin, 3 June 1951, p. 35–6; Report of Annual Delegate Conference, Dublin, 24–5 May 1952, p. 19–21; Report of General Executive Council, 1952–193, p. 27–8; Report, Aug. 1952.

15. Irish Trades Union Congress, Report of 58th Congress, Derry, 23–25 July 1952, p. 156–62; Report of 59th Congress, Sligo, 22–24 July 1953, p. 136–8; Report, July, Aug., Dec. 1952.

16. WUI, Report of General Executive Council, 1953–54, p. 14; 1954–1955, p. 13–15; Irish Trades Union Congress, Report of 61st Congress, Portrush, 27–29 July 1955, p. 196–203; Report of 63rd Congress, Galway, 27–29 July 1957, p. 211–21.

17. WUI, Report of General Executive Council, 1955–1956, p. 17–18; Report of Annual Delegate Conference, Dublin, 18–19 May 1957, p. 1–7; Report of General Executive Council, 1957–1958, p. 16–19; Report of Annual Delegate Conference, Dublin, 17–18 May 1958, p. 37–43; Irish Trades Union Congress, 63rd Annual Report, 1956–1957, p. 47–48, and Second Report of Provisional United Organisation of the Irish Trade Union Movement, p. 105–9; Irish Trades Union Congress, Report of 64th Congress, Killarney, 23–25 July 1958, p. 195–203.

18. WUI, Report of General Executive Council, 1958–1959, p. 3–5; Irish Trades Union Congress, 64th Annual Report, 1957–1958, and 64th Congress, Killarney, 23–25 July 1958, p. 40–44, 109, 186–8, 297–300; 65th Annual Report, 1958–1959, p. 39–40.

19. WUI, Report of General Executive Council, 1950–1951, p. 37–8; Report of Annual Delegate Conference, Dublin, 3 June 1951, p. 21–22; Report of Annual Delegate Conference, Dublin, 24–5 May 1952, p. 22–6; Report of General Executive Council, 1952–1953, p. 16–18; 'Strike in Scotts,' Report, May 1953; 'Strikers in R. and W. Scott Ltd. win through,' Report, June 1953.

20. WUI, Report of General Executive Council, 1954–1955, p. 16–22; Report of Annual Delegate Conference, Dublin, 26–27 May 1956, p. 28–9; Report of General Executive Council, 1955–1956, p. 5; Report of General Executive Council, 1957–1958, p. 22–8; minutes of General Executive Council, 27 June 1957, 16 Aug. 1957, 18 July 1958, 16 and 30 Oct. 1959, 20 Nov. 1959; Irish Trades Union Congress, 64th Annual Report, 1957–1958, Third Report of Provisional United Organisation of the Irish Trade Union Movement, p. 103–4.

21. Report, Sep. 1952, Oct.-Nov. 1952.

22. WUI, Report of Annual Delegate Conference, Dublin, 21 May 1950, p. 6; Report of General Executive Council, 1950–1951, and Report of Annual Delegate Conference, Dublin, 3 June 1951, p. 22–4, 39; Report of Annual Delegate Conference, Dublin, 24–25 May 1952, p. 27; minutes of General Executive Council, 7 June 1957; Irish Trades Union Congress, Report of 56th Congress, Galway, 26–28 July 1950, p. 98–9; 61st Annual Report, 1954–1955, and 61st Congress, Portrush, 27–29 July 1955, p. 33–7, 160–62; Congress of Irish Unions, 9th Annual Meeting, Killarney, 15–17 July 1953, p. 165–6.

23. So strongly did the WUI feel about the Labour Court's attitude that it published an 'extract from the Union's case made to the Labour Court, March 1950,' on the front cover of Report, Oct.-Nov. 1952. Arguing that increased productivity merited reward, the union concluded: 'If this Court allows it to go forth that such a position does not call for correction then it will be futile to expect workers generally to respond to appeals for increased production, knowing that any claim they make for a share of the increased values they have made will be denied and denied with the authority of the Court.' WUI, Report of Annual Delegate Conference, Dublin, 21 May 1950, p. 6, 22–3; Report of General Executive Council, 1950–1951, p. 38; Report of General Executive Council, 1951–1952, p. 14–15; WUI, Report of General Executive Council, 1954–1955, p. 21; Report of General Executive Council, 1957–1958, p. 21–22; Report, Aug. 1952; Report, Jan. 1953. Guinness employees always wanted 'autonomy'

within the union. WUI, minutes of General Executive Council, 12 Oct. 1956. In an obituary for Jack Carruthers the date for the Union Shop Agreement is given as 1957. See WUI, Report of General Executive Council, 1988–1989, p. 16–17.

24. 'Putting wings on the union,' *Report*, July 1952; WUI, Report of General Executive Council, 1951–1952, p. 15–16; WUI, Report of General Executive Council, 1954–1955, p. 20–21; Report of General Executive Council, 1958–1959, p. 20–22; minutes of General Executive Council, 20 Mar. 1959. The ballot was 335 to 121 for a strike.

25. WUI, Report of General Executive Council, 1951–1952, p. 1–2; Report of General Executive Council, 1950–1951, p. 40; Report of Annual Delegate Conference, Dublin, 21–22 May 1955, p. 67–8; 'It seems to me . . .' *Report*, Jan. 1953; 'A dangerous precedent,' *Report*, Mar. 1953, and 'The clerical workers and trade unions,' *Report*, Apr. 1953.

26. The members of the Committee were Patrick Pender (Chairman), Michael Lowbridge (secretary), Laurence Daly, Joseph Hadden, Thomas Lynam, Charles Molloy and Michael Moore. 'Tullamore: A good job well done,' *Report*, Jan. 1953; Michael Moore, 'Tullamore: A good job well done,' *Report*, Feb. 1953; *Report*, Jan. 1954; 'Spreading the good work,' *Report*, Mar. 1954; *Report*, May 1954.

27. Irish Trades Union Congress, Report of 56th Congress, Galway, 26–29 July 1950, p. 134–9, 145–53; WUI, Report of General Executive Council, 1950–1951, p. 49–50; Report of Annual Delegate Conference, Dublin, 3 June 1951, p. 2–3, and Report of General Executive Council, 1951–1952, p. 12; *Report*, Oct.-Nov. 1952.

28. Irish Trades Union Congress, 62nd Annual Report, 1955–1956, p. 32–3, and First Report of Provisional United Organisation of the Irish Trade Union Movement, p. 107–49; Report of 64th Congress, Killarney, 23–25 July 1958, p. 174–81; WUI, Report of Annual Delegate Conference, Dublin, 26–27 May 1956, p. 12–14.

29. Irish Trades Union Congress, Report of 64th Congress, Killarney, 23–25 July 1958, p. 261–3; Report of 65th Congress, 1958–1959; Report of Special Congress, 10 Feb. 1959, p. 60–81.

30. WUI, Report of General Executive Council, 1958–1959, p. 15–17; Report of Annual Delegate Conference, Dublin, 23–24 May 1959, p. 3–6, 26–8.

31. Irish Trades Union Congress, Report of 56th Congress, Galway, 26–28 July 1950, p. 70–71; Report of 57th Congress, Killarney, 25–27 July 1951, p. 105–12; Report of 59th Congress, Sligo, 22–24 July 1953, 113–16, 121–30; WUI, Report of Annual Delegate Conference, Dublin, 3 June 1951, p. 35; Report of General Executive Council, 1952–1953, p. 21–22; Report of General Executive Council 1952–1953, p. 22–3.

32. WUI, Report of Annual Delegate Conference, Dublin, 29–30 May 1954, p. 50–53; Report of Annual Delegate Conference, Dublin, 26–27 May 1956, p. 15–18; Irish Trades Union Congress, 60th Annual Report, 1953–1954, and Report of 60th Congress, Limerick, 21–23 July 1954, p. 52–6, 145–8. Thomas Kavanagh seconded.

33. WUI, Report of Annual Delegate Conference, Dublin, 18–19 May 1957, p. 22–4, 60–66; Irish Trades Union Congress, Report of 62nd Congress, Cork, 25–27 July 1956, p. 189–90, 193–208, 297–302.

34. WUI, Report of General Executive Council, 1957–1958, p. 12; Report of Annual Delegate Conference, Dublin, 23–24 May 1959, p. 69–82; minutes of General Executive Council, 11 Oct. 1958, 17 July 1959; Irish Trades Union Congress, 63rd Annual Report, 1956–1957; Second Report of Provisional United Organisation of the

Irish Trade Union Movement and Report of 63rd Congress, Galway, 27–29 July 1957, p. 110–22, 263–6; Report of 64th Congress, Killarney, 23–25 July 1958, p. 189–94, 280–82.

35. 'It seems to me . . .' *Report*, Apr. 1953; WUI, Report of Annual Delegate Conference, Dublin, 21–22 May 1955, p. 67–8; Report of Annual Delegate Conference, Dublin, 23–24 May 1959, p. 58–64.

36. WUI, Report of Annual Delegate Conference, Dublin, 26–27 May 1956, p. 50–54; Report of Annual Delegate Conference, Dublin, 16–17 May 1958, p. 64–5; Report of Annual Delegate Conference, Dublin, 23–24 May 1959, p. 56–8; 'The forgotten children,' *Report*, Feb. 1953; Irish Trades Union Congress, Report of 57th Congress, Killarney, 25–27 July 1951, p. 81–4; 58th Annual Report, 1951–1952, p. 30–33; Report of 59th Congress, Sligo, 22 July 1953, p. 95–101; Report of 61st Congress, Portrush, 27–29 July 1955, p. 186–9.

37. Irish Trades Union Congress, Report of 57th Congress, Killarney, 25–27 July 1951, p. 104–5; *Report*, Jan. 1954. The union erroneously referred to the Trade Union Act (1906). *Report*, Apr. 1954.

38. WUI, Report of Annual Delegate Conference, Dublin, 3 June 1951, p. 36–9; Report of Annual Delegate Conference, Dublin, 24–25 May 1952, p. 53–4, 55–7; Report of Annual Delegate Conference, Dublin, 29–30 May 1954, p. 35–8, 44–5; Report of Annual Delegate Conference, Dublin, 21–22 May 1955, p. 59–65; Report of Annual Delegate Conference, Dublin, 26–27 May 1956, p. 21, 24–8; Report of Annual Delegate Conference, Dublin, 18–19 May 1957, p. 42–26; Irish Trades Union Congress, Report of 57th Congress, Killarney, 25–27 July 1951, p. 89–97; Report of 60th Congress, Limerick, 21–23 July 1954, p. 171–2; Report of 61st Congress, Portrush, 27–29 July 1955, p. 178–80; Report of 63rd Congress, Galway, 27–29 July 1957, p. 210–12, 271–4; Report of 64th Congress, Killarney, 23–25 July 1958, p. 231–6.

39. Irish Trades Union Congress, Report of 58th Congress, Derry, 24–25 July 1952, p. 138–9; Report of 61st Congress, Portrush, 27–29 July 1955, p. 214–16; 62nd Annual Report, 1955–1956, p. 58–60; 64th Annual Report, 1957–1958, Third Report of Provisional United Organisation of the Irish Trade Union Movement, p. 117–18, 136–42; WUI, Report of Annual Delegate Conference, Dublin, 26–27 May 1956, p. 62.

40. WUI, Report of Annual Delegate Conference, Dublin, 21 May 1950, p. 26–7; Report of General Executive Council, 1950–1951, p. 41; Report of Annual Delegate Conference, Dublin, 24–25 May 1952, p. 71–2; Report of Annual Delegate Conference, Dublin, 30–31 May 1953, p. 3; Report of Annual Delegate Conference, Dublin, 29–30 May 1954, p. 19–23; Report of General Executive Council, 1954–1955, p. 7; Report of Annual Delegate Conference, Dublin, 26–27 May 1956, p. 36–38; Report of General Executive Council, 1956–1957, p. 8–9; Report of General Executive Council, 1957–1958, p. 7; Report of General Executive Council, 1958–1959, p. 14–15; Report of Annual Delegate Conference, Dublin, 23–24 May 1959, p. 24–6. C. N. Ferguson, 'Larkin and the Union,' *Report*, July–Oct.–Nov. 1952; *Report*, Jan. 1954; Irish Trades Union Congress, Report of 56th Congress, Galway, 26–28 July 1950, p. 111–12; Report of 57th Congress, Killarney, 25–25 July 1951, p. 155–7; Report of 59th Congress, Sligo, 22–24 July 1953, p. 148–9. See Michael Milne, 'Soccer and the Dublin working class: Doncaster Rovers in Dublin, 1952,' *Saothar*, 8 (1982), p. 97–102.

41. WUI, Report of General Executive Council, 1953–1954, p. 13–14, 35–9; Report of General Executive Council, 1954–1955, p. 11–12; Report of Annual Delegate Conference, Dublin, 21–22 May 1955, p. 46; Report of General Executive Council, 1956–1957, p. 9; Report of Annual Delegate Conference, Dublin, 18–19 May 1957, p. 20–22; Report of General Executive Council, 1957–1958, p. 13–14; Report of Annual Delegate Conference, Dublin, 17–18 May 1958, p. 18–19; *Report,* July 1952; Irish Trades Union Congress, Report of 60th Congress, Limerick, 21–23 July 1954, p. 174; Report of 61st Congress, Portrush, 27–29 July 1955, p. 183–4; Report of 64th Congress, Killarney, 23–25 July 1958, p. 294–5; Report of Special (Final) Congress, Cork, 22–24 July 1959, p. 108–11.

42. WUI, Report of Annual Delegate Conference, Dublin, 24–25 May 1952, p. 57–8; Report of General Executive Council, 1952–1953, and Annual Delegate Conference, Dublin, 30–31 May 1953, p. 3, 16–17; Report of General Executive Council, 1953–1954, and Annual Delegate Conference, Dublin, 29–30 May 1954, p. 5–6, 10, 23–6; Report of General Executive Council, 1954–1955, and Annual Delegate Conference, Dublin, 21–22 May 1955, p. 8, 34–7; Report of General Executive Council, 1956–1957, p. 8; Report of Annual Delegate Conference, Dublin, 18–19 May 1957, p. 18–19, 74; Report of General Executive Council, 1957–1958, and Annual Delegate Conference, Dublin, 17–18 May 1958, p. 8–9, 12–16, 48–9, 61–2; Report of General Executive Council, 1958–1959, p. 12–14; Report of Annual Delegate Conference, Dublin, 23–24 May 1959, p. 12–14, 51–2; Report of General Executive Council, 1959–1960, p. 10–11; minutes of General Executive Council, 11 Jan. 1957, 12 Sep. 1958; *Report,* Feb. 1953; 'Educational and training classes for Shop Stewards,' *Report,* Feb. 1954. Irish Trades Union Congress, Report of 60th Congress, Limerick, 21–23 July 1954, p. 158–9; Report of 64th Congress, Killarney, 23–25 July 1958, p. 229; 65th Annual Report, 1958–1959, p. 87–8.

43. WUI, Report of Annual Delegate Conference, Dublin, 3 June 1951, p. 35; Report of General Executive Council, 1953–1954, and Annual Delegate Conference, Dublin, 29–30 May 1954, p. 11, 27–31; Report of General Executive Council, 1954–1955, and Annual Delegate Conference, Dublin, 21–22 May 1955, p. 8, 41–3; Report of Annual Delegate Conference, Dublin, 26–27 May 1956, p. 29–34; Report of General Executive Council, 1956–1957, and Annual Delegate Conference, Dublin, 18–19 May 1957, p. 7–8, 17; Report of General Executive Council, 1957–1958, p. 6–7; Report of Annual Delegate Conference, Dublin, 17–18 May 1958, p. 21–6; Report of General Executive Council, 1958–1959, and Annual Delegate Conference, Dublin, 23–24 May 1959, p. 11–12, 13–24; minutes of General Executive Council, 20 July 1956, 30 Nov. 1956, 14 Dec. 1956, 8 and 22 Mar. 1956, 16 Aug. 1957, 15 May 1959, 2 Oct. 1959. *Report,* July 1952, Jan. 1954; Irish Trades Union Congress, Report of 56th Congress, Galway, 26–28 July 1950, p. 112–13.

44. WUI, Report of General Executive Council, 1952–1953, p. 63; Report of Annual Delegate Conference, Dublin, 29–30 May 1954, p. 5, 31–4; Report of Annual Delegate Conference, Dublin, 21–22 May 1955, p. 39–41; Report of Annual Delegate Conference, Dublin, 26–27 May 1956, p. 38–9; Report of Annual Delegate Conference, Dublin, 18–19 May 1957, p. 25–30. A motion was adopted calling for 'proper salary scales' for staff, p. 68; minutes of General Executive Council, 22 July 1957, 17 Apr. 1959; Report of General Executive Council, 1958–1959, p. 10–11; minutes

of General Executive Council, 28 Aug. 1959; 'Vaughan's Hotel to be union offices,' *Report*, Sep. 1953; 'Vaughan's Hotel taken over,' *Report*, Nov. 1953'.

45. *Report*, Nov. 1953.

46. WUI, Report of General Executive Council, 1950–1951, p. 49; Report of Annual Delegate Conference, Dublin, 3 June 1951, p. 33; Report of Annual Delegate Conference, Dublin, 21–22 May 1955, p. 6–8; Report of Annual Delegate Conference, Dublin, 21–22 May 1955, p. 49–52, 54–5; Report of Annual Delegate Conference, Dublin, 18–19 May 1957, p. 74; Report of Annual Delegate Conference, Dublin, 17–18 May 1958, p. 70, 79; Irish Trades Union Congress, Report of 62nd Congress, Cork, 25–27 July 1956, p. 288–92.

47. WUI, Report of Annual Delegate Conference, Dublin, 21 May 1950, p. 7–20. Those censured were William Clarke, Michael Denvers, Peter Wade and Richard Ward. Debarred and fined were Michael F. O'Kelly, John Lennox and William Heffernan. Report of Annual Delegate Conference, Dublin, 21 May 1950, p. 18–20. The Committee consisted of P. Brennan (Gas), C. Buckley (Dublin No. 2), J. Fitzgerald (Dublin No. 1), John Foster (Grangegorman), R. Halpin (Dublin No. 3), Miss McCormack (Dublin No. 4), C. Seery (Dublin No. 4), P. Sweeney (Dublin No. 4), P. Nolan (Rail), V. Savino (Guinness) and J. Walsh (Dublin No. 2). WUI, Report of General Executive Council, 1950–1951, p. 36–7; Report of General Executive Council, 1951–1952, p. 10.

48. Irish Trades Union Congress, 57th Annual Report, 1951–1952, p. 36–7; WUI, Report of Annual Delegate Conference, Dublin, 21 May 1950, p. 26; Report of General Executive Council, 1950–1951, p. 48–9; Report of General Executive Council, 1951–1952, and Annual Delegate Conference, Dublin, 21 May 1950, p. 9, 28–38; Report of Annual Delegate Conference, Dublin, 29–30 May 1954, p. 5; Report of General Executive Council, 1954–1955, p. 8–9; *Report*, Sep. 1952. Commiserations were extended to an unsuccessful candidate, Bháltar Breatnach, and to 'another member of the Union,' Richard Grogan, who was congratulated on his personal achievement on his election to Dáil Éireann.

49. WUI, Report of General Executive Council, Dublin, 21–22 May 1955, p. 38, 56–8; Irish Trades Union Congress, 61st Annual Report, 1954–1955, and Report of 61st Congress, Portrush, 27–29 July 1955, p. 107, 225–8.

50. WUI, Report of Annual Delegate Conference, Dublin, 26–27 May 1956, p. 55–6.

51. WUI, Report of General Executive Council, 1956–1957, p. 9–10; Report of Annual Delegate Conference, Dublin, 17–18 May 1958, p. 28; Report of General Executive Council, 1958–1959, p. 17–18; Report of Annual Delegate Conference, Dublin, 23–24 May 1959, p. 29–37; minutes of General Executive Council, 26 Sep. 1958, 17 Oct. 1958, 31 July 1959; Irish Trades Union Congress, 55th Annual Report, 1958–1959, p. 56–7. Hilda Larkin polled 2,693 votes on 22 July 1959 and in the 1961 General Election only 930. Her running-mate, Pat Coghlan, polled 754.

Chapter 26 (p. 506–50)

1. Agriculture and fishing; mining, quarrying and turf; foodstuffs, including creameries and sugar confectionery; beverages; tobacco; textiles; skins and leather; wood and cork; furniture; paper and paper products; printing and publishing; chemicals; bricks, stone, pottery and glass; metal products; electrical machinery;

transport equipment; miscellaneous manufacturing; construction; electricity, gas, water and sanitation; commerce, including retail and wholesale distribution; transport, storage and communications; public administration; professions, including hospitals, health services and education; personal services, including catering, laundries, hairdressing, undertaking and photography; entertainment and sport.

2. ITGWU, Annual Report for 1959 and Proceedings of Annual Conference, 1960, p. 51–2, 67, 90–99; Annual Report for 1960 and Proceedings of Annual Conference, 1961, p. 51–2, 80–81, 84–6; Annual Report for 1961 and Proceedings of Annual Conference, 1962, p. 104, p. 7–8, 64–5; Annual Report for 1962 and Proceedings of Annual Conference, 1963, p. 5–7, 74–5; 88–90; Report for 1963 and Proceedings of Annual Conference, 1964, p. 5–6, 123–31; 'Outstanding progress by the union,' *Liberty*, Jan. 1963, Oct. 1963.

3. ITGWU, Annual Report for 1965 and Proceedings of Annual Conference, 1966, p. 9, 138–40, 144–6; Annual Report for 1966 and Proceedings of Annual Conference, 1967, p. 9–10, 181–91; Annual Report for 1967 and Proceedings of Annual Conference, 1968, p. 13–17, 191–6; Annual Report for 1968 and Proceedings of Annual Conference, 1969, p. 193–219; Annual Report for 1969, p. 14–17; '1965 diary,' *Liberty*, Jan. 1965; 'Wishes and hopes for 1966,' *Liberty*, Feb. 1966; '1968,' *Liberty*, Jan. 1968; 'Election of General Officers,' *Liberty*, May 1969.

4. ITGWU, Annual Report for 1962 and Proceedings of Annual Conference, Waterford, 4–7 June 1963, p. 118–22. Other speeches were made by Rev. Thomas Ahearne (Waterford Cathedral), M. J. Costello (read by Brendan Daly) and Joseph O'Donnell (Harvard University). 'The year of agitation,' *Liberty*, Jan. 1969.

5. ITGWU, Annual Report for 1960, p. 4–5; Annual Report for 1968, p. 8–10; *Liberty*, Apr. 1960, 'Funeral of the late Senator Purcell,' *Liberty*, May 1960; 'Memorial to the late Senator Purcell unveiled,' *Liberty*, May 1964; 'Death of William O'Brien,' *Liberty*, Nov. 1968; 'John Conroy: A staunch champion of trade unionism,' *Liberty*, Mar. 1969.

6. ITGWU, Annual Report for 1959 and Proceedings of Annual Conference, 1960, p. 92–3; Annual Report for 1960 and Proceedings of Annual Conference, 1961, p. 104; Annual Report for 1963 and Proceedings of Annual Conference, 1964, p. 166–70; Annual Report for 1966 and Proceedings of Annual Conference, 1967, p. 225; Annual Report for 1968, p. 23–6; 'My first Annual Conference,' *Liberty*, Oct. 1964; 'Working mothers,' *Liberty*, Mar. 1965; 'Women in the background far too long,' *Liberty*, Nov. 1966; Frances Lambert, 'The Women's Advisory Committee,' *Liberty*, Nov. 1966; 'The role of women in trade unions,' *Liberty*, Aug. 1967; 'General President's call to women members,' *Liberty*, June 1968.

7. ITGWU, Annual Report for 1959 and Proceedings of Annual Conference, 1960, p. 110–12; Annual Report for 1960, p. 29–30; Annual Report for 1961 and Proceedings of Annual Conference, 1962, p. 92–8; 'An answer to the plight of Northern Ireland,' *Liberty*, Jan. 1961; 'New hope for Ireland in trade union co-operation' (Liberty Study Group seminar in Derry), *Liberty*, Nov. 1965. For McGonagle's election performance see McCabe and Devine, *Navigating a Lone Channel*.

8. ITGWU, Annual Report for 1965 and Proceedings of Annual Conference, 1966, p. 129–30; Annual Report for 1968 and Proceedings of Annual Conference, 1969, p. 296–304, 331–2; Annual Report for 1969, p. 144–8.

9. 'The Six Counties' and 'The union's concern on Northern situation,' *Liberty*, Aug. 1969; 'Belfast's ordeal by fire,' *Liberty*, Oct. 1969; *Liberty*, Christmas 1969. Two senior Officials have privately said that they had concerns about the destination of some of these payments. Humanitarian aid was not an issue, but they worried that Republican organisations may have benefited. The sums involved seem small but would be more than €100,000 today. There are many stories about Mullen's close associations with militant republicanism at this time and allegations that not all money went on 'relief.' Nothing confirming these stories appears in official records.

10. ITGWU, Annual Report for 1962 and Proceedings of Annual Conference, 1963, p. 73–4; Annual Report for 1963 and Proceedings of Annual Conference, 1964, p. 134–5, 145–51, 176, 183–4; Annual Report for 1964, p. 6–7, 22–65; *Liberty*, Oct. 1963; 'National secretaries appointed by the Union,' *Liberty*, Feb. 1964. Walter McFarlane continued as Secretary of Dublin No. 1 Branch, responsible for transport and printing; George O'Malley, Dublin No. 2 Branch, clerical and professional; Conor O'Brien, Dublin No. 3 Branch, food, drink and tobacco; Edward 'Ned' Duff, Dublin No. 12 Branch, general industrial; Patrick Armstrong, Dublin No. 13 Branch, musical and electrical; William Purcell, Dublin No. 14 Branch, engineering; and Patrick Flanagan, Dublin No. 15 Branch, general industrial and services. 'Negotiations at shop floor level,' *Liberty*, Feb. 1965. Carroll went on to talk of gathering and checking the facts of a case through interview, case assessment and presentation, and the range and limit of a Shop Steward's authority in the process. 'A Shop Steward is . . .?' *Liberty*, Mar. 1966.

11. ITGWU, Annual Report for 1960, p. 20–21; Annual Report for 1964 and Proceedings of Annual Conference, 1965, p. 129–30; Annual Report for 1968 and Proceedings of Annual Conference, 1969, p. 312–20; Annual Report for 1969, p. 17–18; 'The importance of unity,' *Liberty*, Mar. 1960; 'A dinner of the proposed Cork Council of Trade Unions,' *Liberty*, Aug. 1962; 'Trade union information,' *Liberty*, Aug. 1966; 'The future role of Congress,' *Liberty*, Feb. 1969.

12. ITGWU, Annual Report for 1964, p. 8; Annual Report for 1966 and Proceedings of Annual Conference, Limerick, 2–5 May 1967, p. 190–94; Annual Report for 1967 and Proceedings of Annual Conference, Arklow, 14–17 May 1968, p. 16–17, 188; Annual Report for 1968 and Proceedings of Annual Conference, Wexford, 14–17 Apr. 1969, p. 206–7; 'Trade union re-organisation,' *Liberty*, Mar. 1967; 'Larkin remembered,' *Liberty*, Feb. 1968.

13. ITGWU, Annual Report for 1959 and Proceedings of Annual Conference, Buncrana, 7–10 June 1960, p. 70; Annual Report for 1964 and Proceedings of Annual Conference, Kilkee, 8–11 June 1965, p. 109–10.

14. ITGWU, Annual Report for 1959 and Proceedings of Annual Conference, Buncrana, 7–10 June 1960, p. 66–83; Annual Report for 1960 and Proceedings of Annual Conference, Salthill, 13–16 June 1961, p. 10–13, 51–2; Annual Report for 1961, p. 11–12; *Liberty*, Feb. 1960, Mar. 1960, Jan. 1962.

15. ITGWU, Annual Report for 1961 and Proceedings of Annual Conference, Killarney, 5–8 June 1962, p. 8–16, 92–8; 'Unofficial strikes harmful to workers' interests,' *Liberty*, Feb. 1962; 'General Secretary on Muine Bheag dispute,' Aug. 1962; 'End of Muine Bheag dispute,' Nov. 1962.

16. ITGWU, Annual Report for 1963 and Proceedings of Annual Conference, Cork, 9–12 June 1964, p. 7–27, 36–7, 156–61; 'Government White Paper,' *Liberty*, Mar. 1963.

17. 'Recommendation on wage and salary adjustments,' *Liberty,* Feb. 1964; 'Spoliation of the National Wages Agreement,' Nov. 1964.

18. ITGWU, Annual Report for 1964 and Proceedings of Annual Conference, Kilkee, 8–11 June 1965, p. 130–39; Annual Report for 1965 and Proceedings of Annual Conference, Liberty Hall, 7–10 June 1966, p. 13–25, 122–6, 152–62.

19. ITGWU, Annual Report for 1966 and Proceedings of Annual Conference, Limerick, 2–5 May 1967, p. 12–28, 93–6, 213. Diarmaid Mac Diarmada signed the Labour Court statement.

20. ITGWU, Annual Report for 1967 and Proceedings of Annual Conference, Arklow, 14–17 May 1968, p. 20–26, 176; 'The cause of strike,' *Liberty,* Feb. 1966; 'Equality!' *Liberty,* Apr. 1967; 'Workers' Charter campaign begun,' *Liberty,* Christmas 1967.

21. ITGWU, Annual Report for 1967 and Proceedings of Annual Conference, Arklow, 14–17 May 1968, p. 178, 218–21, 224–39; Annual Report for 1968 and Proceedings of Annual Conference, Wexford, 14–17 Apr. 1969, p. 20–25, 219–88; Annual Report for 1969, p. 33–6, 232–6; 'Minister's refusal to meet deputation,' *Liberty,* May 1968; *Liberty,* June 1968; 'The plight of lower income workers,' *Liberty,* Feb. 1969; 'Wages policy reaffirmed,' *Liberty,* Mar. 1969.

22. ITGWU, Annual Report for 1961 and Proceedings of Annual Conference, Killarney, 5–8 June 1962, p. 106; Annual Report for 1963 and Proceedings of Annual Conference, Cork, 9–12 June 1964, p. 186; Annual Report for 1964 and Proceedings of Annual Conference, Kilkee, 8–11 June 1965, p. 139–40, 162–3; Annual Report for 1965 and Proceedings of Annual Conference, Liberty Hall, 7–10 June 1966, p. 146–7;. Annual Report for 1966, p. 97–107; Annual Report for 1968 and Proceedings of Annual Conference, Wexford, 14–17 Apr. 1969, p. 219–24, 332–4.

23. ITGWU, Annual Report for 1967, p. 102; 'The facts about the Shannon dispute,' *Liberty,* May 1968; 'Shannon settlement,' *Liberty,* July 1968; 'EI agree to recognise the union,' *Liberty,* June 1969; Means to an end,' *Liberty,* Aug. 1968. For IRA involvement at EI see Brian Hanley, 'The IRA and trade unionism, 1922–1972,' in Devine et al., *Essays in Labour History,* p. 171–2.

24. ITGWU, Annual Report for 1968 and Proceedings of Annual Conference, Wexford, 14–17 Apr. 1969, p. 219–24; Annual Report for 1969, p. 32–3; 'Blackmail picketing,' *Liberty,* Nov. 1968; 'The dictatorship of the minority,' *Liberty,* Feb. 1969; 'Wages policy reaffirmed,' *Liberty,* Mar. 1969; 'ICTU report on Maintenance Dispute,' *Liberty,* July 1969.

25. ITGWU, Annual Report for 1962 and Proceedings of Annual Conference, Waterford, 4–7 June 1963, p. 13–15, 87–92, 98–9; Annual Report for 1964 and Proceedings of Annual Conference, Kilkee, 8–11 June 1965, p. 50–51, 136–7; Annual Report for 1965 and Proceedings of Annual Conference, Liberty Hall, 7–10 June 1966, p. 49–51, 128–9, 149; *Liberty,* June 1960; 'Why penalise the busmen, Dr Andrews?' *Liberty,* Feb. 1961; 'The facts about the bus dispute,' *Liberty,* Mar. 1961; *Liberty,* Jan. 1963; 'Delegate Conference of bus workers,' *Liberty,* May 1961; 'The bus strike,' *Liberty,* June 1961. The 'General President's strong warning' was repeated in *Liberty,* July 1961. Ballina, Cavan, Clonmel, Cork, Drogheda, Dublin, Dundalk, Galway, Limerick, Sligo and Tralee were represented. 'Busmen and the union,' *Liberty,* Jan. 1964; 'Commission's recommendations on CIÉ pensions and sickness benefits,' *Liberty,* Apr. 1964.

26. ITGWU, Annual Report for 1964, p. 36–40; 'The organisation of the building worker,' *Liberty,* Apr. 1963; 'The building dispute,' *Liberty,* Oct. 1964.

27. ITGWU, Annual Report for 1959 and Proceedings of Annual Conference, Buncrana, 7–10 June 1960, p. 112–14; Annual Report for 1960 and Proceedings of Annual Conference, Salthill, 13–16 June 1961, p. 21–6, 116–17; Annual Report for 1961 and Proceedings of Annual Conference, Killarney, 5–8 June 1962, p. 96–8; Annual Report for 1964, p. 49; 'Improved working conditions for hotel workers,' *Liberty*, Sep. 1967.

28. ITGWU, Annual Report for 1965, p. 40–41; Annual Report for 1968 and Proceedings of Annual Conference, Wexford, 14–17 Apr. 1969, p. 69–70, 267–8.

29. *Liberty*, May 1962; 'The success story of Dublin No. 2 Branch,' Jan. 1964.

30. 'ITGWU, Annual Report for 1960 and Proceedings of Annual Conference, 1961, p. 58–62; Annual Report for 1961, p. 32–3; Annual Report for 1962 and Proceedings of Annual Conference, 1963, p. 68–9; Annual Report for 1969, p. 26–32; 'Congress criticism of Trade Union Bill,' *Liberty*, Apr. 1969; 'The Industrial Relations Act, 1969,' *Liberty*, Aug. 1969.

31. ITGWU, Annual Report for 1961 and Proceedings of Annual Conference, 1962, p. 25–8, 106–8; Annual Report for 1962 and Proceedings of Annual Conference, 1963, p. 97–9; Annual Report for 1968 and Proceedings of Annual Conference, 1969, p. 227–8; 'A mockery of workers' rights,' *Liberty*, Apr. 1968.

32. ITGWU, Annual Report for 1959 and Proceedings of Annual Conference, 1960, p. 67, 77–8, 80, 93, 102–4, 123–36. The speakers were Donal Nevin (ICTU) and P. Lynch (economist and Chairman of Aer Lingus). Annual Report for 1960 and Proceedings of Annual Conference, 1961, p. 105–14; Annual Report for 1962 and Proceedings of Annual Conference, 1963, p. 93–7; Annual Report for 1963 and Proceedings of Annual Conference, 1964, p. 156; Annual Report for 1964 and Proceedings of Annual Conference, Kilkee, 1965, p. 157–8; Annual Report for 1965 and Proceedings of Annual Conference, 1966, p. 162–6; Annual Report for 1968 and Proceedings of Annual Conference, 1969, p. 226–7; *Liberty*, Feb. 1961; *Liberty*, Nov. 1963. The ITGWU was represented on the NIEC by Conroy. 'This new year of 1964,' *Liberty*, Jan. 1964; 'Economic planning and trade unions,' *Liberty*, Mar. 1965; *Liberty*, June 1967, for full report; 'The living dead,' *Liberty*, July 1968.

33. ITGWU, Annual Report for 1961 and Proceedings of Annual Conference, 1962, p. 12–16, 98–100; Annual Report for 1966 and Proceedings of Annual Conference, 1967, p. 208–213; 'Sharp impact of Common Market veto,' *Liberty*, Feb. 1963.

34. ITGWU, Annual Report for 1959 and Proceedings of Annual Conference, Buncrana, 7–10 June 1960, p. 80–81, 105–10; Annual Report for 1961 and Proceedings of Annual Conference, Killarney, 5–8 June 1962, p. 115–20; Annual Report for 1962 and Proceedings of Annual Conference, 1963, p. 66; Annual Report for 1965 and Proceedings of Annual Conference, 1966, p. 180–83; 'Cherishing all the children of the nation equally . . .' *Liberty*, Feb. 1968; *Liberty*, Jan. 1969.

35. ITGWU, Annual Report for 1959 and Proceedings of Annual Conference, 1960, p. 114; Annual Report for 1960 and Proceedings of Annual Conference, 1961, p. 26–8, 99; Annual Report for 1961, p. 28–32; Annual Report for 1963 and Proceedings of Annual Conference, 1964, p. 173–6; Annual Report for 1964 and Proceedings of Annual Conference, 1965, p. 42–3, 141; 'Accent on safety,' *Liberty*, Mar. 1960; *Liberty*, June 1960; Barry Desmond, 'Job safety and welfare,' *Liberty*, May and June 1962; 'NISO,' *Liberty*, Jan. 1963; 'Reducing toll of industrial accidents,' *Liberty*, Feb. 1963; 'Alcoholism in industry,' *Liberty*, Jan. 1965.

36. ITGWU, Annual Report for 1966 and Proceedings of Annual Conference, 1967, p. 226–32; Annual Report for 1968 and Proceedings of Annual Conference, 1969, p. 326–27, 336–8; Annual Report for 1969 and Proceedings of Annual Conference, 1970, p. 297–300; 'Need to develop safety consciousness,' *Liberty,* Mar. 1967; 'Your hands are your real wage-earners,' *Liberty,* Aug. 1968; Derek Humphry, 'The cancer that is spread by shyness,' *Liberty,* Mar. 1969.

37. ITGWU, Annual Report for 1965 and Proceedings of Annual Conference, 1966, p. 72, 183–4; *Liberty,* Sep.–Nov. 1963; 'Mise Éire,' *Liberty,* Mar. 1966; 'James Connolly: A biography: Part 1, The early years,' *Liberty,* Mar. 1966; 'James Connolly: A biography: Part 2, The search for roots,' *Liberty,* Apr. 1966; 'James Connolly: A biography: Part 3, The return of the Wild Geese,' *Liberty,* May 1966; 'James Connolly: A biography: Part 4, Belfast: Early battles and consolidation,' *Liberty,* June 1966; 'James Connolly: A biography: Part 5, 1913: The General Strike,' *Liberty,* July 1966; James Connolly: A biography: Part 6, We serve neither king nor kaiser, but Ireland,' *Liberty,* Aug. 1966; 'James Connolly: A biography: Part 7, Final preparations,' *Liberty,* Sep. 1966; 'James Connolly: A biography: Part 8: A full life and a good end,' *Liberty,* Oct. 1966; 'Historic items returned to Liberty Hall,' *Liberty,* May 1966. An unnamed British officer's brother had handed the items to Edward P. Carey in London, who had forwarded them to the Taoiseach, Éamon de Valera, and they had been kept in the National Museum. 'Connolly commemoration in Edinburgh' and 'Belfast ceremony,' *Liberty,* July 1966. The Edinburgh plaque read: *To the memory of James Connolly. Born 5 June, 1869 at 107 Cowgate. Renowned International Trade Union and working class Leader; founder of the Irish Socialist Republican Party; member of Provisional Government of Irish Republic. Executed 12 May, 1916 at Kilmainham Jail, Dublin.*

38. Annual Report for 1959 and Proceedings of Annual Conference, 1960, p. 76, 97–8, 120–21; Annual Report for 1960 and Proceedings of Annual Conference, 1961, p. 28–30, 35, 62–5, 81–3, 115. Walter Carpenter, John Cassidy and Leo Crawford were the others. Members attended a weekend school at Whitehead and the Social Study Summer School, Gormanston; Annual Report for 1961, p. 8–10; 'Gael-Linn Chairman thanks trades unions,' *Liberty,* Mar. 1961.

39. ITGWU, Annual Report for 1961 and Proceedings of Annual Conference, 1962, p. 85–92; Annual Report for 1962 and Proceedings of Annual Conference, 1963, p. 7–8, 85–8; Annual Report for 1963 and Proceedings of Annual Conference, 1964, p. 6, 111. See *Liberty,* May 1962, for Ballina event. 'Enthusiastic support for No. 3 Branch Education Committee,' *Liberty,* Jan. 1963; 'The CWC, SJ: "These are our aims",' *Liberty,* Feb. 1963; 'Education Committees seminar' and 'A membership thinking for itself,' *Liberty,* Mar. 1963; 'This concerns you,' *Liberty,* Apr.–May 1963; 'Education drive by Liberty Study Group,' *Liberty,* Oct. 1963; 'This new year of 1964,' *Liberty,* Jan. 1964; 'Reports from Branch Education Committees,' *Liberty,* June 1964; 'A year of steady growth and progress,' *Liberty,* Aug. 1964. Attendance at the trade courses showed a slight fall, from 861 to 776. The magazine published the name of every successful candidate—no doubt a big factor in the minds of students and their families. A further promotion of the Catholic Workers' College appeared in *Liberty* in September 1964, with a two-page outline of courses offered.

40. ITGWU, Annual Report for 1966 and Proceedings of Annual Conference, 1967, p. 10–11, 160–62; Annual Report for 1967 and Proceedings of Annual Conference, 1968,

p. 256–8; Annual Report for 1968 and Proceedings of Annual Conference, 1969, p. 10–11, 15–16, 204–5; Annual Report for 1969, p. 18–20; 'Trade union information,' *Liberty,* July 1966; 'Union holiday camp suggestion,' *Liberty,* Nov. 1967; 'Need for education and training in industry' and 'Diplomas conferred on Cork Officials and members,' *Liberty,* Nov. 1967.

41. ITGWU, Annual Report for 1962 and Proceedings of Annual Conference, Waterford, 4–7 June 1963, p. 85; Annual Report for 1964 and Proceedings of Annual Conference, Kilkee, 8–11 June 1965, p. 128–30; Annual Report for 1966 and Proceedings of Annual Conference, Limerick, 2–5 May 1967, p. 235; 'The G.P. page,' *Liberty,* Feb. 1965; 'Ideas and suggestions on Liberty,' *Liberty,* Nov. 1966. The ideas, proposed by May O'Brien, came from two meetings held by Michael Callanan, Eva Carey, Seán Connolly, Tony Kelly and May and Michael O'Connor. *Liberty,* Aug. 1967.

42. ITGWU, Annual Report for 1959 and Proceedings of Annual Conference, Buncrana, 7–10 June 1960, p. 92; ITGWU, Annual Report for 1960 and Proceedings of Annual Conference, Salthill, 13–16 June 1961, p. 81; Annual Report for 1963 and Proceedings of Annual Conference, Cork, 9–12 June 1964, p. 186; Annual Report for 1964 and Proceedings of Annual Conference, Kilkee, 8–11 June 1965, p. 107, 151–2; Annual Report for 1965 and Proceedings of Annual Conference, Liberty Hall, 7–10 June 1966, p. 117–18; *Liberty,* Oct. 1960; 'The new Liberty Hall,' *Liberty,* Dec. 1960; 'Impressive Liberty Hall ceremony,' *Liberty,* June 1962; *Liberty,* Sep. 1963; *Liberty,* Oct. 1964; 'The message of the new Liberty Hall' and 'Liberty Hall: A "living" building,' *Liberty,* Feb. 1965; *Liberty,* Special Commemorative Issue, May 1965.

43. ITGWU, Annual Report for 1962 and Proceedings of Annual Conference, Waterford, 4–7 June 1963, p. 75.

44. 'The International Musical Olympiad,' *Liberty,* Sep. 1966; 'Further triumphs for the union Band,' *Liberty,* Christmas 1967; 'Praise for Liberty Choir,' *Liberty,* Jan. 1968. 'Golden Jubilee concert,' *Liberty,* Oct. 1969.

45. ITGWU, Annual Report for 1961 and Proceedings of Annual Conference, Killarney, 5–8 June 1962, p. 115; 'Apartheid and trade unionism in South Africa,' *Liberty,* Apr. 1960; 'American transport workers' debt to Connolly and the ITGWU,' *Liberty,* Oct. 1964; *Liberty,* Aug. 1967; 'Employment of young people in developing countries,' *Liberty,* Apr. 1969; 'Race, politics, unions, sport and news,' *Liberty,* Christmas 1969.

46. ITGWU, Annual Report for 1959 and Proceedings of Annual Conference, 1960, p. 70, 78–9; Annual Report for 1960 and Proceedings of Annual Conference, 1961, p. 71; Annual Report for 1961 and Proceedings of Annual Conference, 1962, p. 119; Annual Report for 1962 and Proceedings of Annual Conference, 1963, p. 66; *Liberty,* July 1961.

47. ITGWU, Annual Report for 1965 and Proceedings of Annual Conference, 1966, p. 116; Annual Report for 1968 and Proceedings of Annual Conference, 1969, p. 176–8. For example see 'The social role of management,' *Liberty,* May 1963; 'Honorary members of Belfast Branch,' *Liberty,* Oct. 1966; 'The 1970s,' 'A recent visit to Russia' and 'The Church and trade unionism,' *Liberty,* June 1967.

48. ITGWU, Annual Report for 1959 and Proceedings of Annual Conference, Buncrana, 7–10 June 1960, p. 118–19; *Liberty,* Feb. 1960; 'Youth and vigour now at the helm,' *Liberty,* Apr. 1960; 'Vote for your union representative in the local elections,' *Liberty,* June and Aug. 1960.

49. ITGWU, Annual Report for 1960 and Proceedings of Annual Conference, Salthill, 13–16 June 1961, p. 84; Annual Report for 1961 and Proceedings of Annual Conference, Killarney, 5–8 June 1962, p. 64–5, 112–15; Annual Report for 1962 and Proceedings of Annual Conference, Waterford, 4–7 June 1963, p. 112–13; Annual Report for 1964 and Proceedings of Annual Conference, Kilkee, 8–11 June 1965, p. 132–3, 158–9; Annual Report for 1965 and Proceedings of Annual Conference, Liberty Hall, 7–10 June 1966, p. 151–2; Annual Report for 1966 and Proceedings of Annual Conference, Limerick, 2–5 May 1967, p. 195–208; *Liberty*, Oct. 1961; 'Tribute to James Everett TD,' *Liberty*, Apr. 1963; Why affiliate?' *Liberty*, Feb. 1967; 'The union's political dimension,' *Liberty News*, summer, 1985. The seven TDs were Brendan Corish (Wexford), James Everett (Wicklow), Paddy McAuliffe (Cork North-East), Michael Mullen (Dublin North-West), Séamus Pattison (Carlow-Kilkenny), Dan Spring (Kerry North) and Paddy Tierney (Tipperary North).

50. Brendan Corish (Wexford), Stephen Coughlan (Limerick East), Barry Desmond (Dún Laoghaire-Rathdown), Seán Dunne (Dublin South-West), Liam Kavanagh (Wicklow), Conor Cruise O'Brien (Dublin North-East), John O'Connell (Dublin South-West), John O'Donovan (Dublin South-Central), Michael O'Leary (Dublin North-Central), Séamus Pattison (Carlow-Kilkenny), Dan Spring (Kerry North), and David Thornley (Dublin North-West).

51. ITGWU, Annual Report for 1967 and Proceedings of Annual Conference, Arklow, 14–17 May 1968, p. 188–9; Annual Report for 1968 and Proceedings of Annual Conference, Wexford, 14–17 Apr. 1969, p. 16–17, 213–14. The vote on retaining PR was 657,898 for, 423,500 against; on multiple single-seat constituencies the vote was 656,803 against, 424,185 for. 'Most significant development in Irish politics,' *Liberty*, June 1967; 'The local Government elections,' *Liberty*, July 1967; 'Labour Party Annual Conference, 1967,' *Liberty*, Oct. 1967; 'General Election,' *Liberty*, June 1969; 'Unsuccessful compound interest,' *Liberty*, July 1969. The candidates were Thomas Brennan (Waterford), Michael Gannon (Dublin North County), Thomas Higgins and P. V. O'Rourke (Sligo-Leitrim), Flan Honan and Terry Higgins (Clare), George Hunter (Donegal-Leitrim), Kevin Hurley (Cork City South-East), Patrick Kerrigan (Cork City North-West), Michael Lipper (Limerick East), Michael McEvoy (Dublin North-West), Flor O'Mahony (Dún Laoghaire-Rathdown), Dónal O'Sullivan, Thomas O'Brien and Seán Fitzpatrick (Dublin South County), Thomas Shanahan (Tipperary North) and Thomas Tierney (Galway West). Fintan Kennedy joined the Labour Party as an individual member in 1969 when nominated by Congress for Seanad Éireann.

Chapter 27 (p. 551–84)

1. WUI, Report of General Executive Committee for 1959–1960, p. 7–8; 1959–1960, p. 25–6; Report of General Executive Council, 1960–1961, p. 10–13, 28–9, 33–4; minutes of General Executive Council, 15 July 1960, 19 Aug. 1960, 21 Sep. 1960. Byrne was given a lump sum of £100 or a year's salary, whichever was the greater.

2. WUI, Report of Annual Delegate Conference, 28–29 May 1960, p. 51–6; 92–5; Report of General Executive Council, 1960–1961 and Report of Annual Delegate Conference, 27–28 May 1961, p. 10–13, 18–20, 69–71, 92–5.

3. WUI, Report of Annual Delegate Conference, 27–28 May 1961, p. 58–60, 96–8; Report

of General Executive Council, 1961–1962, and Annual Delegate Conference, 26–27 May 1962, p. 17–18, 48–51; Irish Trades Union Congress, Report of 63rd Congress, Galway, 27–29 July 1957, p. 287–9.

4. WUI, Report of Annual Delegate Conference, 26–27 May 1962, p. 45–8, 63–5; Report of Annual Delegate Conference, 25–26 May 1963, p. 31–3; minutes of General Executive Council, 11 Jan. 963, 29 Mar. 1963, 17 May 1963, 15 Nov. 1963. O'Reilly was given three months' notice from 1 June to try to turn matters around.

5. WUI, Report of Annual Delegate Conference, 29–30 May 1965, p. 83–4; minutes of General Executive Council, 20 Mar. 1964. No. 1, general, 3,880; No. 2, public services, 1,800; No. 3, miscellaneous, 1,000; No. 4, food, 2,663; No. 5, butchers' porters, 335; No. 6, engineering and CIÉ, 1,800; No. 7, tobacco, 840; No. 8, building, 950; No. 9, Guinness, 2,380; No. 11, pork butchers, 989; No. 12, aviation, 2,000; No. 13, gas, 1,088; No. 14, operative butchers, 1,015; No. 15, clerical, 1,682; and national hospitals, 1,800. Affiliated were the Irish Airline Pilots' Association (1951), Assistance Officers' and Superintendent Assistance Officers' Association (1953), Irish Liver Agents' Union (1956), John Player Clerical Staff Association (1960), Medical Laboratory Technologists' Association (1961), Vocational Educational Clerks' Association (1962), Institute of Industrial Research and Standards Staff Association (1964), Irish Airlines Executive Staffs' Association (1964) Irish Pharmaceutical and Medical Representatives' Association (1964), Voluntary Hospitals Clerical and Administrative Staffs' Association (1964), Agricultural Institute [Foras Talúntais] Technical Officers' Staff Association (1965), Association of Irish Radiographers (1965), Dublin Institute of Higher Studies Staff Association (1965) and Irish Marine Officers' Association (1966).

6. WUI, Report of Annual Delegate Conference, 29–30 May 1965, p. 88–91; Report of General Executive Council, 1965–1966, p. 16–18; Report of Annual Delegate Conference, 13–14 May 1967, p. 30, 45–51; Report of General Executive Council, 1968–1969, and Annual Delegate Conference, 7–8 June 1969, p. i, 23–34, 93–8; minutes of General Executive Council, 22 Jan. 1965.

7. WUI, Report of General Executive Council, 1968–1969, and Annual Delegate Conference, 7–8 June 1969, p. 2–3, 18–20, 74–6, 121–22; minutes of General Executive Council, 18 Dec. 1968, 22 Jan. 1969, 5 Feb. 1969. Cardiff received 117 votes, Cluskey 83 and Watt 2. Burke, 4, was eliminated in the 1st count; J. Dorgan, 10 (2nd); Canavan, 12–13 (3rd); O'Dea, 20 (4th); Gibson, 22–26 (5th); Watt, 25–27 (6th); Harte, 26–37 (7th); Cardiff, 48, 48, 56, 63, 68, 92, 93, 101; Foster, 44, 46, 46, 47, 54, 55, 68, 109.

8. WUI, Report of Annual Delegate Conference, 28–29 May 1960, p. 113–14; Report of Annual Delegate Conference, 27–28 May 1961, p. 116–17; Report of Annual Delegate Conference, 25–26 May 1963, p. 49; Report of Annual Delegate Conference, 23–24 May 1964, p. 56–8; Report of Annual Delegate Conference, 13–14 May 1967, p. 47–51; minutes of General Executive Council, 9 July 1965, 27 Aug. 1965, 5 Nov. 1965, 2 Sep. 1965.

9. WUI, Report of General Executive Council, 1959–1960, p. 13–14; Report of Annual Delegate Conference, 27–28 May 1961, p. 78–82; Report of Annual Delegate Conference, 26–27 May 1962, p. 67–8; Report of General Executive Council, 1963–1964, p. 31; Report of General Executive Council, 1964–1965, and Annual Delegate Conference, 29–30 May 1965, p. 18–19, 31, 81–2; 29–33, 81–2; Report of General

Executive Council, 1965–1966, p. 15–16, 22–3; Report of General Executive Council, 1967–1968, p. 3–5. £500 was given. The MPGWU loan was quickly repaid. Minutes of General Executive Council, 12 Jan. 1968.

10. WUI, Report of Annual Delegate Conference, 28–29 May 1960, p. 43, 109–110; Report of General Executive Council, 1960–1961, and Annual Delegate Conference, 27–28 May 1961, p. 27–9, 53–61; Report of Annual Delegate Conference, 14–15 May 1966, p. 50–52; Report of General Executive Council, 1966–1967, p. 10–13; minutes of General Executive Council, 27 Nov. 1964, 19 Feb. 1965, 6 Jan. 1967, 3 Feb. 1967, 3 Mar. 1967.

11. WUI, Report of Annual Delegate Conference, 13–14 May 1967, p. 51–7; minutes of General Executive Council, 27 Oct. 1967, 12 Jan. 1967, 2 Aug. 1968; Report of General Executive Council, 1967–1968, p. 5–7; minutes of General Executive Council, 26 Jan. 1968, 17 May 1968, 30 Oct. 1968, 27 Nov. 1968, 18 Dec. 1968. The WUI Delegates were: General Officers: John Smithers, James Larkin, Denis Larkin; GEC members: Séamus Bleakley, Joseph Butler, Brian Carney, Edward Cassidy, Michael Collins, William Cumiskey, Edward Conlon, Thomas Duffy, William Gibson, John Harte, Thomas Kavanagh, Paul Matthews, Vincent O'Hara, Ambrose O'Rourke, Peter Purcell and Thomas Quinn. The ITGWU Delegates were: General Officers: John Conroy, Edward Browne and Fintan Kennedy; NEC members: James Blake, Nicholas Boran, John Brady, Patrick Clancy, Peter Cullen, Joseph McBrinn, James McSweeney, Michael Moynihan, Patrick O'Brien, Frank O'Toole, Patrick Powell and Laurence White. Report of General Executive Council, 1968–1969, p. 16. The WUI Delegates were John Foster, Denis Larkin, Leo Gibson, William Gibson, Jack Harte, Vincent O'Hara and Ambrose O'Rourke, while Fintan Kennedy, John Carroll, John Brady, James Cullen, Paddy Clancy, James Blake and Laurence White represented the ITGWU. Report of Annual Delegate Conference, 7–8 June 1969, p. 86–9.

12. WUI, Report of General Executive Council, 1969–1970, p. 10–11; minutes of General Executive Council, 10 and 17 Dec. 1969.

13. *Bulletin,* Jan. 1960, cited by O'Riordan in *The Voice of a Thinking Intelligent Movement,* p. 53–68.

14. WUI, Report of General Executive Council, 1959–1960, and Annual Delegate Conference, 28–29 May 1960, p. 16–18, 67–72; Report of General Executive Council, 1961–1962, p. 18–19; Report of General Executive Council, 1962–1963, and Report of Annual Delegate Conference, 25–26 May 1963, p. 3–4, 22–4, 63–5; Report of General Executive Council, 1963–1964, p. 15–22; Report of General Executive Council, 1964–1965, and Annual Delegate Conference, 29–30 May 1965, p. 4, 14–16, 58–68; Report of General Executive Council, 1965–1966, p. 1–8; Report of Annual Delegate Conference, 13–14 May 1967, p. 41–43; Report of General Executive Council, 1967–1968, p. 1; Report of Annual Delegate Conference, 7–8 June 1969, p. 22–3, 38; minutes of General Executive Council, 10 Jan. 1964.

15. WUI, Report of General Executive Council, 1959–1960, p. 22–3, 27–8; Report of General Executive Council, 1960–1961, p. 17–18, 24–5; minutes of General Executive Council, 8 Apr. 1960, 13 May 1960.

16. WUI, Report of Annual Delegate Conference, 28–29 May 1960, p. 95–7; Report of Annual Delegate Conference, 27–28 May 1961, p. 94, 105–08; Report of General Executive Council, 1961–1962, and Annual Delegate Conference, 26–27 May 1962, p. 19–21, 62. The minutes of the General Executive Council for 9 June 1961 record

another lengthy stoppage. Others included Henshaw's, £325; Brushmakers, £455; ESB, £824; Liffey Dockyard, £266; and Torc £473. Minutes of General Executive Council, 1 Sep. 1961, 7 Feb. 1964.

17. WUI, Report of General Executive Council, 1962–1963, p. 26; Report of General Executive Council, 1964–1965, p. 25–6, 87; Report of General Executive Council, 1965–1966, p. 16–18, 19–22, 36; minutes of General Executive Council, 18 and 28 Sep. 1964, 9 Oct. 1964, 15 Apr. 1966, 24 June 1066, 30 Sep. 1966, 13 Oct. 1966. I am grateful to John P. Swift for his observations on the bakery trade.

18. WUI, Report of General Executive Council, 1965–1966, p. 24; Report of General Executive Council, 1966–1967, and Annual Delegate Conference, 13–14 May 1967, p. 9–11, 23–4, 63–74; Report of General Executive Council, 1967–1968, p. 22–3; minutes of General Executive Council, 7 May 1965.

19. WUI, Report of General Executive Council, 1968–1969, and Annual Delegate Conference, 7–8 June 1969, p. 10, 80–81; minutes of General Executive Council, 23 Aug. 1968, 4 Sep. 1968.

20. WUI, Report of Annual Delegate Conference, 7–8 June 1969, p. 91–3; minutes of General Executive Council, 23 Apr. 1969.

21. WUI, Report of General Executive Council, 1960–1961, p. 25–7; Report of General Executive Council, 1965–1966, p. 22–3.

22. WUI, WUI, Report of General Executive Council, 1960–1961, p. 32–6; Report of General Executive Council, 1964–1965, p. 27; Report of General Executive Council, 1965–1966, p. 24–6; minutes of General Executive Council, 11 Mar. 1960, 3 Feb. 1961, 17 May 1966, 10 and 24 June 1966, 25 Nov. 1966, 6 Aug. 1969, 1 Oct. 1969. Three months' salary was given as a parting gift. Minutes of General Executive Council, 9 June 1967, 11 Aug. 1967, 24 Nov. 1967, 1 Dec. 1967.

23. WUI, minutes of General Executive Council, 3 Feb. 1961, 17 May, 1966, 10 and 24 June 1966, 9 June 1967, 11 Aug. 1967, 24 Nov. 1967, 1 Dec. 1967.

24. WUI, Report of General Executive Council, 1967–1968, p. 23–5; Report of Annual Delegate Conference, 7–8 June 1969, p. 76–8; minutes of Finance Committee, 22 Jan. 1965; minutes of General Executive Council, 7 and 21 July 1967, 6 and 27 Oct. 1967.

25. WUI, Report of General Executive Council, 1962–1963, p. 25; Report of General Executive Council, 1965–1966, p. 22; Report of General Executive Council, 1966–1967, p. 18; minutes of General Executive Council, 12 Jan. 1968, 9 July 1969.

26. WUI, Report of General Executive Council, 1959–1960, and Annual Delegate Conference, 28–29 May 1960, p. 15, 89–90; Report of Annual Delegate Conference, 27–28 May 1961, p. 65, 119; Report of General Executive Council, 1964–1965, and Annual Delegate Conference, 29–30 May 1965, p. 23–5, 54–6; Report of General Executive Council, 1966–1967, p. 22–3; minutes of General Executive Council, 20 May 1964, 12 and 24 June 1964. The newspapers were the *Irish Independent, Irish Press* and *Irish Times,* 9 and 30 July 1965.

27. Correspondence with Barry Desmond, Apr. 2008; Con Murphy, *Dispute Between FUE and Maintenance Craft Unions: Report of Inquiry Presented to the Minister for Labour* (Dublin: Stationery Office, 1969).

28. WUI, minutes of General Executive Council, 22 Jan. 1969, 5 and 26 Feb. 1969, 5 and 26 Mar. 1969, 9 and 16 Apr. 1969. All of Dublin No. 4 Branch; No. 1: 855; No. 15: 81;

No. 3: 101; Athy: 200; Athlone: 700; Meat Federation: 700. Report of General Executive Council, 1968–1969, and Annual Delegate Conference, 7–8 June 1969, p. 9, 20–22, 29–42, 73–4.

29. WUI, Report of Annual Delegate Conference, 28–29 May 1960, p. 56–62, 100–104; Report of Annual Delegate Conference, 25–26 May 1963, p. 98; Report of Annual Delegate Conference, 29–30 May 1965, p. 93–4.

30. WUI, Report of Annual Delegate Conference, 27–28 May 1961, p. 47–53, 66–8; Report of General Executive Council, 1961–1962, and Annual Delegate Conference, 26–27 May 1962, p. 1–12, 29–42; Report of General Executive Council, 1962–1963, and Annual Delegate Conference, 25–26 May 1963, p. 1–2, 5–12, 52–69; Report of General Executive Council, 1963–1964, p. 14–15; Report of General Executive Council, 1966–1967, and Annual Delegate Conference, 13–14 May 1967, p. 1–2, 7, 35–41.

31. WUI, Report of Annual Delegate Conference, 29–30 May 1965, p. 42–6; Report of General Executive Council, 1966–1967, and Annual Delegate Conference, 13–14 May 1967, p. 18, 71–3.

32. WUI, Report of Annual Delegate Conference, 28–29 May 1960, p. 110–11; Report of Annual Delegate Conference, 13–14 May 1967, p. 55, 79; Report of General Executive Council, 7–8 June 1969, p. 121; minutes of General Executive Council, 28 June 1963.

33. WUI, Report of General Executive Council, 1959–1960, and Annual Delegate Conference, 27–28 May 1961, p. 21, 113–15; Report of General Executive Council, 1962–1963, p. 24–5; Report of General Executive Council, 1963–1964, p. 30; minutes of General Executive Council, 13 Oct. 1961, 2 Nov. 1962 (when the figure was given).

34. WUI, Report of Annual Delegate Conference, 25–26 May 1963, p. 28–30, 88; Report of Annual Delegate Conference, 23–24 May 1964, p. 43; Report of Annual Delegate Conference, 29–30 May 1965, p. 76–7. Expenses were £1,012 9s and sales a mere £130 6s 8d. £190 was secured in advertisements, and at 2s each a sale of 1,000 would bring in £100. The quote was £250 for 1,000. Minutes of General Executive Council, 12 July 1963. The costs declared on 13 May 1964 at the General Executive Council were £930. Minutes of General Executive Council, 1 June 1962. The members of the WUI Committee were Paddy Cardiff, J. Fitzsimons, Peter Purcell, Thomas Quinn and Christy Troy. Minutes of General Executive Council, 14 June 1963, 22 Aug. 1963, 15 Nov. 1963. The WUI gave the Dublin Trades Council £25.

35. WUI, Report of Annual Delegate Conference, 14–15 May 1966, p. 29–31; minutes of General Executive Council, 15 Oct. 1969.

36. WUI, Report of Annual Delegate Conference, 27–28 May 1961, p. 117–18; Report of Annual Delegate Conference, 7–8 June 1969, p. 59–60; minutes of General Executive Council, 8 Dec. 1961, 21 Feb. 1964, 6 Mar. 1984, 9 Oct. 1964.

37. WUI, Report of General Executive Council, 1959–1960, p. 11, 65–7; Report of General Executive Council, 1960–1961, p. 15; Report of Annual Delegate Conference, Dublin, 25–26 May 1963, p. 75; Report of Annual Delegate Conference, Dublin, 29–30 May 1965, p. 76–7; Report of General Executive Council, 1965–1966, p. 15–16; minutes of General Executive Council, 1 June 1962. Both were given a bonus of £30.

38. WUI, Report of General Executive Council, 1959–1960, and Annual Delegate Conference, Dublin, 29–30 May 1960, p. 10, 41–2. Smithers said that Forde died in October, but the General Executive Council report stated August. Brack had been a member of the Brass and Reed Band. Report of General Executive Council, 1960–

1961, and Annual Delegate Conference, 27–28 May 1961, p. 14–17, 68–9. Matthew Lamb, a carpenter in Head Office and a member of the ASW, also retired. Lamb was a 'devoted and unselfish stalwart' and 'one of the most intimate and closest friends' of Larkin in Ireland and the United States. Report of General Executive Council, 1965–1966, and Annual Delegate Conference, 14–15 May 1966, p. 14, 53–5. The 'price' was £55,000, and the premises had been brought for £3,500.

39. WUI, Report of General Executive Council, 1961–1962, p. 14–15; Report of General Executive Council, 1962–1963, and Annual Delegate Conference, 25–26 May 1963, p. 19, 34, 93–6. J. Duffy and Joseph O'Connor were asked to leave, while Paddy Moran left for Cork County Council. Report of General Executive Council, 1963–1964, p. 30; minutes of General Executive Council, 13 Apr. 1962, 4 and 18 May 1962, 12 Oct. 1062, 16 Nov. 1962, 7 Feb. 1964, 24 July 1964, 30 July 1965, 5 Nov. 1965. The purchasers were the Provincial Bank. The deal was completed only in April 1966. Minutes of General Executive Council, 15 Apr. 1966.

40. WUI, Report of General Executive Council, 1964–1965, and Annual Delegate Conference, 29–30 May 1965, p. 21, 33.

41. WUI, Report of General Executive Council, 1966–1967, p. 15–17; Report of General Executive Council, 1968–1969, and Annual Delegate Conference, 7–8 June 1969, p. 2, 99–108; minutes of General Executive Council, 6 Aug. 1969.

42. WUI, Report of Annual Delegate Conference, 26–27 May 1962, p. 25–6; Report of Annual Delegate Conference, 25–26 May 1963, p. 34–5; Report of Annual Delegate Conference, 7–8 June 1969, p. 100; minutes of General Executive Council, 12 and 26 Feb. 1960, 11 and 24 Mar. 1960.

43. WUI, Report of General Executive Council, 1959–1960, and Annual Delegate Conference, 28–29 May 1960, p. 19, 77–8; minutes of General Executive Council, 29 Jan. 1960.

44. WUI, Report of General Executive Council, 1963–1964, p. 31–2; Report of Annual Delegate Conference, 13–14 May 1967, p. 57–63; minutes of General Executive Council, 25 Nov. 1966, 12 Jan. 1968, 21 July 1967, 23 Aug. 1968.

45. WUI, Report of General Executive Council, 1960–1961, and Annual Delegate Conference, 27–28 May 1961, p. 20–21, 71–8; Report of Annual Delegate Conference, 26–27 May 1962, p. 44–5, 69–72; minutes of General Executive Council, 24 Mar. 1960.

46. WUI, Report of Annual Delegate Conference, 25–26 May 1963, p. 83; Report of General Executive Council, 1963–1964, p. 24–5, 37–8.

47. WUI, Report of Annual Delegate Conference, 23–24 May 1964, p. 61–71; Report of General Executive Council, 1964–1965, and Annual Delegate Conference, 29–30 May 1965, p. 17, 77–81; Report of General Executive Council, 1965–1966, and Annual Delegate Conference, 14–15 May 1966, p. 10–11, 66–72; Report of General Executive Council, 1969–1970, and Annual Delegate Conference, 7–8 June 1969, p. 15–17, 89–90; minutes of General Executive Council, 26 June 1969. Other WUI candidates were William Cumiskey and James Quinn (Dublin North-Central), Thomas Duffy and Patrick Dunne (Dublin North-East), T. D. Watt (Dublin North-West), Dermot O'Rourke (Dublin South-Central), George Butler (Dublin South-West) and Joseph Bermingham (Kildare). Minutes of General Executive Council, 22 Jan. 1965. The WUI paid £472 for 25,000 members.

48. WUI, minutes of General Executive Council, 20 Aug. 1969.

Chapter 28 (585–8)

1. McCarthy, *The Decade of Upheaval.*

Chapter 29 (589–646)

1. ITGWU, Annual Report for 1969 and Proceedings of Annual Conference, 1970, p. 215–16, 225–78. Note: Class 1, 1970, 3s 6d; 1972, 25p; Class 2, 3s (20p); Class 3, 2s 6d (18p); Class 4, 2s (15p); Class 5, 1s 6d (10p); Class 6, 1s (10p); Class 7, 9d (8p); Class 8, 1d (½p).

2. ITGWU, Annual Report for 1971 and Proceedings of Annual Conference, 1972, p. 124–30; Annual Report for 1972 and Proceedings of Annual Conference, 1973, p. 11, 192–215; minutes of National Executive Council, 20–22 Nov. 1971.

3. ITGWU, Annual Report for 1973 and Proceedings of Annual Conference, 1974, p. 11, 186–205; Annual Report for 1975, p. 12, 123–4; minutes of National Executive Council, 19–21 May 1973, 19–21 1974, 23–25 Jan. 1974, 23–25 Mar. 1974, 23–25 Nov. 1974, 22–24 Feb. 1975. Kevin Duffy recalls the Limerick incident as an important factor for the ISWM. 'First Gaeltacht Branch established,' *Liberty,* Aug. 1973; 'An féidir an Ghaelig a shábháil?' *Liberty,* Sep. 1973; 'A huge success,' *Liberty,* July 1975; 'Professional organisation,' *Liberty,* Oct. 1975.

4. ITGWU, Annual Report for 1975 and Proceedings of Annual Conference, 1976, p. 229–41. Other contribution rates were: £25–£60 per week, 40p; £20–£25, 35p; £15–£20, 25p; up to £15, 20p. Annual Report for 1976, p. 8, 12, 110–11; Annual Report for 1977, p. 123–4. Éamonn O'Brien, 'A touch of gold,' *Liberty,* May 1976. 'ISLWU amalgamates with ITGWU,' *Liberty,* Sep. 1977. This merger was long in the making. After initial discussions with the WUI, the ITGWU began talking to the ISLWU in 1971. See minutes of National Executive Council, 22–24 May and 24–26 July 1971, in which the ISLWU is continually referred to as the 'Boot and Shoe Operatives' or National Union of Boot and Shoe Operatives, the British union from which it had amicably seceded in 1953! It seems that the proposed legislation was what held matters up, as Paddy Clancy reported to the NEC in June 1973 that the merger with the 'Boot and Shoe Union' was 'on' but 'was awaiting Ministerial action to enable a smooth amalgamation of both unions.' Minutes of National Executive Council, 23–25 June 1973.

5. ITGWU, Annual Report for 1977, p. 12; Annual Report for 1978, p. 13; minutes of National Executive Council, 20–22 Jan. 1977, 19–21 Feb. 1977, 23–25 Apr. 1977, 20–22 Mar. 1978, 24–26 June 1978, 22–24 July 1978. Dan McCarthy led the National Land League. Séamus Lynch, a Workers' Party activist, was Secretary of Belfast No. 2 Branch.

6. ITGWU, Annual Report for 1978 and Proceedings of Annual Conference, 1979, p. 275; Annual Report for 1979, p. 13–15; minutes of National Executive Council, 28–30 Apr. 1979. They played an open-air concert in Eyre Square, Galway, for example. Minutes of National Executive Council, 19–21 May 1979, 17–19 Nov. 1979.

7. ITGWU, Annual Report. for 1969 and Proceedings of Annual Conference, 1970, p. 309–10; Annual Report for 1970 and Proceedings of Annual Conference, 1971, p. 190; Annual Report for 1972, p. 52–3, citing Employer-Labour Conference, National Agreement, 1972, clauses 5–16.

8. ITGWU, Annual Report for 1972 and Proceedings of Annual Conference, 1973, p. 284–5, 316–17; Annual Report for 1974 and Proceedings of Annual Conference, 1975,

p. 235–6; minutes of National Executive Council, 14–16 Apr. 1973. 'Woman Worker,' *Liberty*, Jan. 1973; Rosheen Callender, 'Some progress on equal pay,' *Liberty*, Sep. 1974.

9. ITGWU, Annual Report for 1974 and Proceedings of Annual Conference, Wexford, 3–6 June 1975, p. 320–39; 'International Women's Year,' *Liberty*, Feb. 1975; Pauline Larkin, 'Women on the march,' *Liberty*, Apr. 1975; 'Women's Year ends,' *Liberty*, Jan. 1976.

10. ITGWU, Annual Report for 1977 and Proceedings of Annual Conference, 1978, p. 267; *Liberty*, Jan. 1976; 'Massive support for equal pay,' *Liberty*, Feb. 1976. The speakers included Monica Barnes, Senator Mary Robinson, Evelyn Owens, Donal Nevin, Dan Murphy and Sylvia Meehan. 'Political diary,' *Liberty*, March 1976; Rosheen Callender, 'How fare they now?' *Liberty*, May 1977; 'Equal pay hopes hit by Court,' *Liberty*, Sep. 1977. See Women's Representative Committee, 'Progress Report on the Implementation of the Recommendations in the Report of the Commission on the Status of Women' (December 1976).

11. ITGWU, Annual Report for 1978 and Proceedings of Annual Conference, 1979, p. 369–91; *Liberty*, Feb. 1978; 'We lose out on maternity leave,' *Liberty*, Oct. 1978.

12. ITGWU, Annual Report for 1969 and Proceedings of Annual Conference, 1970, p. 346–56; Annual Report for 1970 and Proceedings of Annual Conference, 1971, p. 202–8, 218–24.

13. ITGWU, Annual Report for 1971, p. 11, 86–90; Stephen McGonagle, 'How is peace to be achieved?' *Liberty*, Sep. 1972.

14. ITGWU, Annual Report for 1971 and Proceedings of Annual Conference, 1972, p. 119, 180–190. An exhibition of items made by interned ITGWU members was displayed at the Conference. Minutes of National Executive Council, 1971–1972; McBrinn was welcomed home by the General President, Fintan Kennedy, and General Secretary, Michael Mullen. *Liberty*, Jan. 1972. 'Vindicating a Belfast trade Unionist,' 'Editorial' and 'Workers take part in national mourning,' *Liberty*, Feb. 1972; 'ITGWU campaign against internment,' *Liberty*, Mar. 1972; 'Letter of thanks from Derry Bloody Sunday Appeal Fund' and 'Unionists planning UDI for Northern Ireland,' *Liberty*, June 1972; 'Bloody Sunday Fund,' *Liberty*, Aug. 1972.

15. ITGWU, Annual Report for 1972, p. 141–5; minutes of National Executive Council, 19–21 Feb. 1972, 23–25 Sep. 1972; 'Bomb blasts Bill into law,' *Liberty*, Dec. 1972. £1,200 was raised by February 1973.

16. ITGWU, Annual Report for 1973 and Proceedings of Annual Conference, 1974, p. 179–81, 228–31, 287–306; Annual Report for 1974 and Proceedings of Annual Conference, 1975, p. 173–82, 230–32; two pages were in Irish. 'Na Sé Chontae' and 'Bombings,' *Liberty*, Dec. 1974.

17. ITGWU, Annual Report for 1975 and Report of Proceedings of Annual Conference, Killarney, 8–11 June 1976, p. 176–9, 221–3; Annual Report for 1976 and Proceedings of Annual Conference, 1977, p. 167–, 262; Annual Report for 1977, p. 203; 'No trade union division,' *Liberty*, Sep. 1974. See Workers' Association for the Democratic Settlement of the National Conflict in Ireland, *What's Wrong with Ulster Trade Unionism?* The Workers' Association was associated with the 'two-nationist' British and Irish Communist Organisation. 'Better Life for All,' *Liberty*, Jan. 1977; 'Dispute is not an inter-union one' and 'History at Ballycastle,' *Liberty*, Dec. 1977. Siobhán Bonner was Branch Secretary, Máire McQuilliken was president and Mary Lynn was Vice-President.

18. ITGWU, Annual Report for 1975 and Proceedings of Annual Conference, 1976, p. 427–69; Annual Report for 1977 and Report of Proceedings of Annual Conference, Sligo, 30 May to 2 June 1978, p. 203–8, 272–93, 449, 453; Annual Report for 1979, p. 221–5; *Liberty*, July 1978. The Boilermen's Branch Secretary was Peter Jackson, Newry, and most worked in the health service. ITGWU, minutes of National Executive Council, 24–26 June 1978.

19. ITGWU, Annual Report for 1969 and Proceedings of Annual Conference, 1970, p. 212–14, 225–7; Annual Report for 1972 and Proceedings of Annual Conference, 1973, p. 237–8, 250–52; minutes of National Executive Council, 25–27 Sep. 1971, 6 Jan. 1973, 16–18 Feb. 1974, 7–9 Sep. 1974.

20. ITGWU, Annual Report for 1977 and Proceedings of Annual Conference, 1978, p. 260; Annual Report for 1978 and Proceedings of Annual Conference, 1979, p. 276; minutes of National Executive Council, 21–24 Sep. 1974, 22–24 Jan. 1977, 21–23 May 1977, 19–21 May 1979, 22–24 Sep. 1979.

21. ITGWU, Annual Report for 1969 and Proceedings of Annual Conference, 1970, p. 201–2. The two were John Mulhall, General Secretary of the Irish Painters' and Decorators' Trade Union, and Frank O'Connor, General Secretary of the Irish Building Workers' Trade Union. ITGWU, Annual Report for 1970, p. 9–10; *Irish Times*, 18 May 1971.

22. ITGWU, Annual Report for 1969 and Proceedings of Annual Conference, 1970, p. 330–33; Annual Report for 1970 and Proceedings of Annual Conference, 1971, p. 143–4; Annual Report for 1971 and Proceedings of Annual Conference, 1972, p. 122; Annual Report for 1972 and Proceedings of Annual Conference, 1974, p. 292; minutes of National Executive Council, 22–24 May 1975; *Liberty*, Sep.–Dec. 197; 'Larkin's address,' *Liberty*, July 1974.

23. ITGWU, minutes of National Executive Council, 16–18 Oct. 1971, 23–25 Sep. 1972, 21–23 Oct. 1972, 17–19 Nov. 1972, 14–16 Apr. 1973, 20–22 Oct. 1973, 16–18 Feb. 1974.

24. ITGWU, minutes of National Executive Council, 20–22 July 1974, 22–24 May 1975, 24–26 Apr. 1976, 27–29 Nov. 1976, 15–17 Oct. 1977, 19–21 Nov. 1977. NATE finally merged with the FWUI in 1987.

25. Francis Devine, 'Jim Larkin, 1976–1947,' *Liberty*, Jan. 1976; 'Call for unity,' *Liberty*, Nov. 1977; 'Social and economic progress,' *Liberty*, June 1979; ITGWU, Annual Report for 1978 and Proceedings of Annual Conference, 1979, p. 269–70.

26. ITGWU, Annual Report for 1969 and Proceedings of Annual Conference, 1970, p. 283–7, 353–7; Annual Report for 1970 and Proceedings of Annual Conference, 1971, p. 25–32, 172–4.

27. ITGWU, Annual Report for 1970, p. 22–3; Annual Report for 1971 and Proceedings of Annual Conference, 1972, p. 45–7, 119–20, 155–9; 'Editorial,' *Liberty*, July 1972. The rejections were 'decisive and unequivocal'; 'Unions accept principle of pay talks without commitment,' *Liberty*, Mar. 1972.

28. ITGWU, Annual Report for 1972 and Report of Proceedings of Annual Conference, 1973, p. 40–44, 224, 258–64, 259–321.

29. ITGWU, Annual Report for 1972 and Proceedings of Annual Conference, 1974, p. 44, 241–4; Annual Report for 1974 and Proceedings of Annual Conference, 1975, p. 49, 233–4, 246–8; minutes of National Executive Council, 7–9 Sep. 1974, 15 Nov. 1974; 'ITGWU support talks,' *Liberty*, Oct. 1973; 'Union rejects Agreement,' *Liberty*, Feb.

1974; 'Conference votes yes,' *Liberty,* Mar. 1974. The ICTU vote was 295 to 103. The ITGWU ballot was 95,628, with 65,722 in favour and 29,438 against, a majority in favour of 36,284.

30. ITGWU, Annual Report for 1975, p. 57–63, 119–20; minutes of National Executive Council, 22–24 May 1975; *Liberty,* Feb. 1975; 'Sit-in ends strike,' *Liberty,* Apr. 1975; *Proposed 16th Round National Agreement, 1975: ITGWU Explanatory Guide;* 'ICTU Conference votes for 16th Round,' *Liberty,* May 1975; 'Unions set the limit,' *Liberty,* Aug. 1975. The ICTU vote for acceptance was 258 to 106.

31. ITGWU, Annual Report for 1975 and Proceedings of Annual Conference, 1976, p. 308–; 'No commitment,' *Liberty,* Mar. 1976; 'A most vicious strike,' *Liberty,* May 1976; 'A close vote by ICTU for rejection of terms,' *Liberty,* July 1976; 'Ballot,' *Liberty,* Aug. 1976; this issue contained a four-page pull-out supplement. 'NEC recommends acceptance of interim Agreement,' *Liberty,* Sep. 1976; 'ICTU yes to interim Agreement,' *Liberty,* Oct. 1976. 100,000 had voted by 3½ to 1 in favour. Annual Report for 1976, p. 56–60.

32. The ITGWU ballot was: for, 56,483; against, 34,858, a majority of 21,625. ITGWU, Annual Report for 1976 and Proceedings of Annual Conference, 1977, p. 414–24; Annual Report for 1977, p. 118–19; ITGWU, minutes of National Executive Council, 29 Jan. 1977, 19–21 Feb. 1977; 'NEC recommends NWA acceptance,' *Liberty,* Feb. 1977; 'Conference says "Yes",' *Liberty,* Mar. 1977; 'Kilmartin's,' *Liberty,* Oct. and Dec. 1977.

33. ITGWU, Annual Report for 1978, p. 59–60; minutes of National Executive Council, 24–26 June 1978, 22–24 July 1978; 'A new Agreement,' *Liberty,* Apr. 1977; 'National Wage Agreement or free-for-all?' *Liberty,* Aug. 1978; 'Reject this Agreement,' *Liberty,* Mar. 1978; 'HELP campaign outlined,' *Liberty,* June 1978; 'HELP,' *Liberty,* July 1978.

34. ITGWU, Annual Report for 1977 and Proceedings of Annual Conference, 1978, p. 336–60; Annual Report for 1978, p. 83, 96, 185–190; *Liberty,* Oct. 1978; 'No talks on show of hands' and 'NEC's policy on wages and related matters,' *Liberty,* Nov. 1978.

35. ITGWU, minutes of National Executive Council, 28–30 Apr. 1979. Andy Burke, Seán Roche and Fergal Costello were the main voices against acceptance. See statement by the NEC on the 'National Understanding for Economic and Social Development.' The voting was 24,430 in favour, 85,500 against. Annual Report for 1979, p. 46–52; Annual Report for 1978 and Proceedings of Annual Conference, 1979, p. 292, 24–305. The valid poll was 107,930; for: 24, 430; against: 83, 500. 'No complacency,' *Liberty,* Jan. 1979; 'It must be flat rate' and 'Trade union policy proposals,' *Liberty,* Mar. 1979; 'War against privilege, injustice,' *Liberty,* Apr. 1979; 'National Understanding: Problem for low paid' and 'Vote No!' *Liberty,* May 1979; '1909 to 1979,' *Liberty,* June 1979; 'It's a deal' and 'Our comment,' *Liberty,* July 1979; 'Progress to report . . .' *Liberty,* Aug. 1979 ; 'We are serious,' *Liberty,* Oct. 1979; 'Dockers got their rights—not a bonanza,' *Liberty,* Jan. 1980.

36. ITGWU, Annual Report for 1969, p. 43–9; Annual Report for 1970, p. 21–3; ICTU, 'Proposals on Picketing Endorsed by the Annual Delegate Conference,' 1970; 'RTÉ strike,' *Liberty,* June 1976; 'The picket,' *Liberty,* Oct. 1977.

37. ITGWU, Annual Report for 1969 and Proceedings of Annual Conference, 1970, p. 256–8, 287–96; Annual Report for 1970, p. 61–6. LCR 2482 and all other documents were reproduced in full. The members of the Committee were Diarmaid Mac Diarmada (Chairman), Tom Reynolds and J. Jennings (CIF), John Mulhall (INPDTU) and P. Ferris (Plumbing Trade Union).

38. ITGWU, Annual Report for 1969, p. 43–9.

39. ITGWU, Annual Report for 1971, p. 53–7.

40. ITGWU, Annual Report for 1971, p. 62–5; 'ITGWU call for public inquiry into CIÉ management,' *Liberty,* Jan. 1973; 'Breakthrough for busmen' and 'On the buses,' *Liberty,* Oct. 1976; 'Bad management main cause for bus strike,' *Liberty,* Dec. 1976; 'Keeping violence off the buses,' *Liberty,* Mar. 1978.

41. ITGWU, Annual Report for 1976, p. 116–19.

42. ITGWU, Annual Report for 1976, p. 110, 153; minutes of National Executive Council, 19–21 Feb. 1977; 'Ferenka—what a blow,' *Liberty,* Mar. 1975.

43. ITGWU, minutes of National Executive Council, 15–17 Oct. 1977; 'The Ferenka case,' *Liberty,* Oct. 1977; 'Gains at Ferenka,' *Liberty,* Nov. 1977. Vincent Moran, who had laboured long and hard, was now the man under pressure, fairly or unfairly.

44. ITGWU, Annual Report for 1977, p. 176–7; minutes of National Executive Council, 19–21 Nov. 1977, 17–19 Dec. 1977, 22–24 Mar. 1978, 21–23 Mar. 1981; 'Reply to FUE on Ferenka statement,' *Liberty,* Dec. 1977; 'Important precedent,' *Liberty,* Sep. 1978.

45. *Liberty* Construction Supplement, Jan. 1978; 'Direct Labour Unit for Dublin,' *Liberty,* Aug. 1978.

46. ITGWU, Annual Report for 1979, p. 13, 203–4; 'Dublin members fight for recognition,' *Liberty,* Apr. 1979; 'The story of Big Mac,' *Liberty,* May 1979, a review of Max Boas and Steve Chain, *Big Mac: The Unauthorised Story of McDonald's* (London: Mentor, 1979); 'McDonald's fight for union rights,' *Liberty,* July 1979.

47. ITGWU, minutes of National Executive Council, 19–21 Feb. 1977; Rosheen Callender, 'The Labour Court: Prospect of change?' *Liberty,* July 1978; 'Information disclosure and early days of the Labour Court in 1946,' *Liberty,* Nov. 1979.

48. ITGWU, Annual Report for 1977 and Proceedings of Annual Conference, 1978, p. 373–5; 'No repressive law' and 'Towards a broadcasting policy,' *Liberty,* July 1975; 'GP on banks dispute,' *Liberty,* Aug. 1976.

49. ITGWU, Annual Report for 1969 and Proceedings of Annual Conference, 1970, p. 221–3, 285; Annual Report for 1970 and Proceedings of Annual Conference, 1971, p. 218–19; Annual Report for 1972 and Proceedings of Annual Conference, 1973, p. 227–37, 253–4, 330–34; Annual Report for 1973 and Proceedings of Annual Conference, 1974, p. 247–8; Annual Report for 1974 and Proceedings of Annual Conference, 1975, p. 298–306, 353–4; Annual Report for 1976 and Proceedings of Annual Conference, 1977, p. 245; Annual Report for 1978, p. 23–4; minutes of National Executive Council, 22–24 Mar. 1975.

50. ITGWU, Annual Report for 1969 and Proceedings of Annual Conference, 1970, p. 285; Annual Report for 1972 and Proceedings of Annual Conference, 1973, p. 227–37, 263–6; Annual Report for 1974 and Proceedings of Annual Conference, 1975, p. 295–8, 351–2; Annual Report for 1975 and Proceedings of Annual Conference, 1976, p. 371–5; minutes of National Executive Council, 23–25 Mar. 1974, 20–22 Apr. 1974, 20–22 May 1978; 'Semperit workers may get decision-making role,' *Liberty,* Oct. 1972; 'Workers' participation in Europe,' *Liberty,* June 1973; 'Disclosure of company information,' *Liberty,* Feb. 1979; 'Open the books,' *Liberty,* July 1979.

51. ITGWU, Annual Report for 1969 and Proceedings of Annual Conference, 1970, p. 301–2; Annual Report for 1970 and Proceedings of Annual Conference, 1971, p. 172–202; Annual Report for 1971 and Report of Proceedings of Annual Conference, 1972,

p. 134–43, 145–7, 153–4; 'Long-term development of Dublin Port,' *Liberty*, Sep. 1972.

52. ITGWU, Annual Report for 1972 and Proceedings of Annual Conference, 1973, p. 227–53, 265–8; Annual Report for 1973 and Proceedings of Annual Conference, 1974, p. 213–28; 'Wanted: An economic and social plan,' *Liberty*, June 1973; 'TU movement's views on natural resources outlined by VP,' *Liberty*, Nov. 1974; 'Save Irish jobs,' full-page notice, *Liberty*, Dec. 1974.

53. ITGWU, Annual Report for 1974 and Proceedings of Annual Conference, 1975, p. 266–95; Annual Report for 1975 and Proceedings of Annual Conference, 1976, p. 242–61, 261–76. Motions from Waterford on similar themes were also adopted. Annual Report for 1976 and Proceedings of Annual Conference, 1977, p. 275–317; 'Guaranteed Irish is about jobs,' *Liberty*, Dec. 1975; 'Tackling unemployment,' *Liberty*, Apr. 1977.

54. ITGWU, Annual Report for 1977 and Proceedings of Annual Conference, 1978, p. 295–304; Annual Report for 1978 and Proceedings of Annual Conference, 1979, p. 309–36; Annual Report for 1979, p. 36–41; minutes of National Executive Council, 24–26 June 1978; 'Nothing to discuss in Green Paper,' *Liberty*, July 1978; 'Gorey fights,' *Liberty*, Feb. 1979.

55. ITGWU, Annual Report for 1977 and Proceedings of Annual Conference, 1978, p. 321–3; Annual Report for 1978 and Proceedings of Annual Conference, 1979, p. 337–44; 'Mr Chip Levinson comes to town' and 'Capital inflation and the multinationals,' *Liberty*, Jan. 1972. See Charles Levinson, *Capital, Inflation and the Multinationals* (London: Macmillan, 1971), and ITGWU, *Multi-National Companies and Conglomerates*. Levinson died in 1997 in Geneva.

56. ITGWU, Annual Report for 1970 and Proceedings of Annual Conference, 1971, p. 15–17, 143–4, 183–6. Apology must be made to any Halifax Town supporters. ITGWU, *The Question Posed* (Dublin, 1971); 'Union opposes EEC entry' and 'Congress opposes EEC entry,' *Liberty*, Feb. 1972; Editorial, *Liberty*, Mar. 1972, Apr. 1972.

57. ITGWU, Annual Report for 1972 and Proceedings of Annual Conference, 1973, p. 221–4; 'Textile industry faces massive redundancies,' *Liberty*, Nov. 1972; 'Irish trade union movement to fight for social policy,' *Liberty*, Jan. 1973; 'EEC reconsidered,' *Liberty*, Aug. 1974. Other speakers included Brendan Harkin (Northern Ireland Civil Service Association) and Paddy Murphy (Federation of Rural Workers).

58. ITGWU, Annual Report for 1974 and Proceedings of Annual Conference, 1975, p. 244–8, 252–6; Annual Report for 1976 and Proceedings of Annual Conference, 1977, p. 246. The motion was moved again by Cork No. 3 Branch in 1979 but was referred back. Annual Report for 1978 and Proceedings of Annual Conference, 1979, p. 309–11; 'ITGWU EEC survey of members,' *Liberty*, May 1975; 'Whither the EEC?' *Liberty*, July 1975; 'Fight for a better future' and 'We were promised more jobs,' *Liberty*, Dec. 1979.

59. ITGWU, Annual Report for 1969 and Proceedings of Annual Conference, 1970, p. 303–6, 357–66; Annual Report for 1972 and Proceedings of Annual Conference, 1973, p. 274–80, 360–70; Annual Report for 1977, p. 58–62; Annual Report for 1979, p. 41–5; 'Housing Conference,' *Liberty*, Jan. 1973; 'Health care,' *Liberty*, Aug. 1979.

60. ITGWU, Annual Report for 1972 and Proceedings of Annual Conference, 1973, p. 372–3; ITGWU, Annual Report for 1976 and Proceedings of Annual Conference, 1977, p. 246, 318–20, 363–4, 366–82; 'Tax the farmers call by ITGWU,' *Liberty*, Feb. 1973; 'Cut tax evasion,' *Liberty*, Jan. 1978.

61. ITGWU, Annual Report for 1978 and Proceedings of Annual Conference, 1979, p. 276–81; 'PAYE march,' *Liberty*, Mar. 1979; 'Unity-of-action,' *Liberty*, Apr. 1979; 'PAYE tax revolt' and 'Total review on PAYE,' *Liberty*, May 1979; 'ICTU plans future action,' *Liberty*, Sep. 1979; 'PAYE tax rebate,' *Liberty*, Nov. 1979. See ITGWU, Statement by the National Executive Council on the National Understanding for Economic and Social Development. ITGWU, minutes of National Executive Council, 28–30 Apr. 1979. Rallies led by the ITGWU were held in Ballina, Ballinasloe, Bray, Carlow, Cavan, Clonmel, Cóbh, Cork, Derry, Dublin, Dundalk, Galway, Killarney, Kilkenny, Limerick, Longford, Mallow, Midleton, Mitchelstown, Mullingar, Naas, Navan, Nenagh, Port Laoise, Sligo, Thurles, Tralee, Tuam, Waterford, Wexford and Youghal.

62. 'Women worse off: pension survey' and *Liberty* Equal Pay and Pensions Supplement, *Liberty*, Feb. 1978.

63. ITGWU, Annual Report for 1969 and Proceedings of Annual Conference, 1970, p. 306–7; Annual Report for 1971 and Proceedings of Annual Conference, 1972, p. 162–4; Annual Report for 1972 and Proceedings of Annual Conference, 1973, p. 226; Annual Report for 1974, p. 21–22; Eileen King, 'Industrial accidents don't happen: they are caused,' *Liberty*, May 1975.

64. ITGWU, Annual Report for 1976 and Proceedings of Annual Conference, 1977, p. 349–52; 'ITGWU Industrial Environment Service launched,' *Liberty*, June 1975; 'Safety guidelines in the EEC,' *Liberty*, July 1975; Damien Daly, 'Hazards of workers,' *Liberty*, Nov. 1976; *Liberty*, Mar. 1977; 'RDS death leads to safety Agreement,' *Liberty*, Aug. 1977; 'Human brucellosis: A serious occupational disease,' *Liberty*, July 1979; *Guidelines for Meat Factories on Precautions to Be Taken for the Prevention of Occupational Brucellosis and Precautions to Be Taken for the Prevention of Occupational Brucellosis* (Dublin: Department of Labour, 1979). The eight were to encourage concerted action between member-states on regulations and monitoring procedures; improve the co-ordination of research action; improve statistics on industrial accidents and occupational diseases; develop training, education and informative programmes; promote participation by employers and workers to prevent accidents; promote pictorial signage of hazards; and develop codes of best practice for accident prevention, safe handling and hygiene standards.

65. ITGWU, Annual Report for 1978 and Proceedings of Annual Conference, 1979, p. 356–89; minutes of National Executive Council, 19–21 Jan. 1980; 'VP on environment,' *Liberty*, Nov. 1976; *Liberty*, Sep.-Oct. 1978. See John F. Carroll and Petra Kelly (eds.), *A Nuclear Ireland?* (Dublin: ITGWU, 1979).

66. ITGWU, Annual Report for 1969 and Report of Proceedings of Annual Conference, 1970, p. 201, 217, 220, 279–82, 336–71; Annual Report for 1970 and Proceedings of Annual Conference, 1971, p. 11–12, 150–51, 154.

67. ITGWU, Annual Report for 1971 and Proceedings of Annual Conference, 1972, p. 9–14, 127–34; ITGWU, Annual Report for 1932 and Proceedings of Annual Conference, 1974, p. 12–15, 281.

68. ITGWU, Annual Report for 1976, p. 14; Annual Report for 1977, p. 17; minutes of National Executive Council, 20–22 Apr. 1974, 22–24 June 1974; 'Union commences tutor training courses,' *Liberty*, Apr. 1973. Geraghty, then aged twenty-nine, entered employment in Dublin No. 1 Branch in 1969 from the RTÉ Section Committee;

Lehane (forty-eight) was Secretary of Cork No. 4 Branch, having joined the union in 1943 when a bread salesman (his father had founded the Cork Bakery Section in 1919) and became an Official in 1950. Mahon (thirty-one) had joined the Finance Department in 1961. 'Money for education' and 'Union education plans,' *Liberty*, Sep. 1973. Newcomers were Pádraig Canny, Western Area Secretary, WUI; Francis Devine, socialist trade unionist and economist from Hull; and Naomi Wayne, academic lawyer from London. 'Education,' *Liberty*, Apr. 1976; Eileen King, 'You can read this, but thousands cannot!' *Liberty*, Feb. 1977; 'Account for yourself,' *Liberty*, Dec. 1977. The recipient of the fellowship was Hugh M. Pollock. See ITGWU, *Guide to EEC Transport Regulations* (Dublin: ITGWU, 1979).

69. ITGWU, Annual Report for 1978, p. 14–21; Annual Report for 1979, p. 16–18, 20–22; minutes of National Executive Council, 31 May 1977, 20–22 May 1978, 23–25 Sep. 1978, 21–23 June 1980. A profit of £100,000 was made. See Jer O'Leary, *Jer O'Leary's Banners of Unity: Hand-Crafted Banners of the Labour and Progressive Movement* (Dublin: North Inner City Folklore Project, 1994). Apart from appearing regularly as Jim Larkin in Plunkett's *The Risen People*, O'Leary had parts in the films *Michael Collins, My Left Foot, In the Name of the Father* and *The Field*.

70. ITGWU, Annual Report for 1975 and Proceedings of Annual Conference, 1976, p. 287–9; Proceedings of Annual Conference, 1978, p. 304–11; Annual Report for 1979, p. 17–18; 'Dublin No. 2 forms a Youth Committee,' *Liberty*, Mar. 1976. The members were Mick Wall (Chairman), Martin King (Secretary), Mick Gogarty (Treasurer), Peter Brady, Mary Graham, Dominic McCauley, Terry McDermott, Brendan Morrissey and Helen Traynor.

71. ITGWU, minutes of National Executive Council, 16–18 Dec. 1972; 'Offences against the state,' 'Bombs blast Bill into law' and 'ITGWU to launch fund,' *Liberty*, Dec. 1972.

72. ITGWU, Annual Report for 1970, p. 9; Annual Report for 1971, p. 9; 'New Newry union premises opened,' *Liberty*, Apr. 1973; 'New Connolly Hall opened by GP' and 'Cork's new premises,' Liberty, Oct. 1976. It had been announced in August 1972. 'New Union premises to be erected in Cork,' *Liberty*, Sep. 1972. See *Cork Examiner* supplement, 'Official Opening of New Connolly Hall on September 25 1976.'

73. ITGWU, minutes of National Executive Council, 17–19 Nov. 1973; 'ITGWU Dublin District Council Sports and Social Club,' *Liberty*, Nov. 1972; 'Judo Section,' 'Films' and 'Dress dance,' *Liberty*, Dec. 1973; 'The Eddie Lawless story,' *Liberty*, Jan. 1973.

74. ITGWU, Annual Report for 1970 and Proceedings of Annual Conference, 1971, p. 224; Annual Report for 1973, p. 27; 'ITGWU hosts USSR group,' *Liberty*, Nov. 1972; Annual Report for 1977 and Proceedings of Annual Conference, 1978, p. 329, 442–8; 'Amilcar Cabral,' *Liberty*, Feb. 1973; 'The unions in South Africa,' 'Ireland and the Third World' and 'Lions tour,' *Liberty*, Apr. 1973; 'SA workers take up the struggle,' *Liberty*, Dec. 1973; 'TU seminar on South Africa,' *Liberty*, Oct. 1976; Kader Asmal and Austin Flannery, 'Help A-A Year,' *Liberty*, Apr. 1978; 'Apartheid motion passed,' *Liberty*, July 1979; 'Tug-of-war at Dundalk,' *Liberty*, Aug. 1979; 'Ban the Barbarians,' *Liberty*, Sep. 1979.

75. ITGWU, Annual Report for 1978 and Proceedings of Annual Conference, 1979, p. 281–92; 'The Irish trade union movement and the October Revolution,' *Liberty*, Oct.-Nov. 1977; 'Don't scrap Connolly Day parade,' *Liberty*, Apr. 1978; '5,000 on Dublin May Day march,' *Liberty*, May 1978.

76. ITGWU, minutes of National Executive Council, 27–29 Nov. 1976, 23–25 Sep. 1978, 17–19 Feb. 1979, 21 Sep. 1979.

77. ITGWU, Annual Report for 1970 and Proceedings of Annual Conference, 1971, p. 151–2, 155–61; Annual Report for 1971 and Proceedings of Annual Conference, 1972, p. 164–80; minutes of National Executive Council, 20–22 Mar. 1972.

78. ITGWU, Annual Report for 1972 and Proceedings of Annual Conference, 1973, p. 186–8, 224, 335–7; minutes of National Executive Council, 12 Jan. 1973; *Liberty*, Feb. 1973; 'At last! A huge triumph for the people,' *Liberty*, Mar. 1973.

79. ITGWU, Annual Report for 1973 and Proceedings of Annual Conference, 1974, p. 323–37; Annual Report for 1975 and Proceedings of Annual Conference, 1976, p. 416–46; minutes of National Executive Council, 23–25 Apr. 1977, 15–17 Oct. 1977; 'Union unhappy with Conference,' *Liberty*, Nov. 1974; 'VP: No commitment to FF proposals,' *Liberty*, July 1977; 'Political diary,' *Liberty*, Nov. 1977.

80. ITGWU, Annual Report for 1977 and Proceedings of Annual Conference, 1978, p. 270–93; Annual Report for 1979, p. 30–32; minutes of National Executive Council, 20–22 Oct. 1979; 'Close vote on Labour and Coalition question,' *Liberty*, July 1978.

Chapter 30 (p. 647–83)

1. WUI, Report of General Executive Committee, 1969–1970, and Report of Annual Delegate Conference, 9–10 May 1970, p. 11–12, 20–21, 54–60, 97–107; WUI, Report of General Executive Council, 1970–1971, p. 13–14.

2. WUI, Report of Annual Delegate Conference, Dún Laoghaire, 23–24 Oct. 1971, p. 87–92, 112–14; Report of General Executive Council, 1971–1972, and Annual Delegate Conference, Wexford, 27–28 May 1972, p. 32–6, 49–51, 129–31. On affiliates, the Irish Airline Pilots' Association had 282 members and paid £650 p.a., receiving advisory and negotiation services but no benefits; Assistance Officers' and Superintendent Assistance Officers' Association: 209 members, 10p per member per week, negotiation and advisory services, entitled to all benefits except strike pay (although none claimed); Irish Pharmacists' Association: 134 members, £400 p.a., advisory and negotiation services, no benefits; Irish Airlines Executive Staff Association: 232 members, £3.50 per member p.a., negotiation and secretarial services, no benefits; Association of Irish Radiographers: 147 members, 10p per week, negotiation and secretarial services, no benefits; Vocational Education Clerks' Association: 48 members, £100 p.a., negotiation and secretarial service, no benefits; Agricultural Institute [Foras Talúntais] Technical Staff Association: 321 members, 7½p per member per week, negotiation and secretarial services, no benefits; Medical Laboratory Technologists' Association: 420 members, £500 p.a. plus costs, secretarial and negotiation services, no benefits; Association of Chief Administrative Officers of Hospitals: 20 members, £10.40 per quarter, negotiation and secretarial services, no benefits; National Rehabilitation Placement Officers: 16 members, 12p per member per week, negotiation and secretarial services, no benefits; Racing Staffs Association: 80 members, £50 per quarter, negotiation and secretarial services, no benefits; Irish Liver Employees' Union: 498 members, 10p per member per week, negotiation and secretarial services, all benefits except funeral and marriage.

3. WUI, Report of General Executive Council, 1972–1973, and Annual Delegate Conference, Athlone, 26–27 May 1973, p. 21–6, 135–6; Report of Annual Delegate

Conference, Dublin, 20–22 Sep. 1974, p. 38–45, 171–5, 199–201.

4. WUI, Report of Annual Delegate Conference, Galway, 24–25 May 1975, p. 164–81. The rates and Dispute Pay were: A: up to £15, 15p, £7; B: £15–20, 20p, £9; C: £20–25, 25p, £10; D: £25–30, 30p, £11; E: £30–35, 35p, £12.50; F: over £35, 40p. Report of General Executive Council, 1975–1976, p. 17–19, 32; Report of General Executive Council, 1976–1977, and Annual Delegate Conference, Dublin, 11–12 June 1977, p. 28–31, 112, 143–59.

5. WUI, Report of Annual Delegate Conference, Dún Laoghaire, 7–8 Oct. 1978, p. 217–18, 278–300.

6. FWUI, Report of General Executive Council, 1978–1979, and Annual Delegate Conference, Dublin, 16–17 June 1979, p. 19–20; 171–9, 278–301; minutes of General Executive Council, 9 and 30 May 1979.

7. WUI, Report of Adjourned Annual Delegate Conference, Dublin, 23 Apr. 1977, p. 127–34; Report of Annual Delegate Conference, Dublin, 11–12 June 1977, p. 111–12, 262–7. Attley, with 138 votes, defeated Peter Keating (43), Paul Boushell (31) and John (Seán) Breslin (31) on the first count.

8. WUI, Report of General Executive Council, 1977–1978, and Annual Delegate Conference, Dún Laoghaire, 7–8 Oct. 1978, p. 99–102, 139–79, 318–32; FWUI, Report of General Executive Council, 1978–1979, p. 107–19. The minutes of the General Executive Council, 8 Feb. 1979, give the FRW vote as 4,248 for merger, 205 against, and 54 spoiled votes, a ratio of 20 to 1.

9. WUI, Report of Annual Delegate Conference, 9–10 May 1970, p. 37–43, 106–7, 117–19; minutes of General Executive Council, 8 and 30 Apr. 1970, 6 May 1970, 6 June 1970, 29 July 1970, 9 and 23 Sep. 1970, 26 Nov. 1970. Jack Harte was later to comment on the close collaboration between himself and Fintan Kennedy in the recent Seanad election.

10. WUI, Report of Annual Delegate Conference, 9–10 May 1970, p. 52–3; Report of General Executive Council, 1970–1971, and Annual Delegate Conference, Dún Laoghaire, 23–24 Oct. 1971, p. 17–18, 77–9, 105–6, 120–24; Report of Annual Delegate Conference, 23–24 Oct. 1971, p. 101–5; minutes of General Executive Council, 29 Apr. 1971, 17 Nov. 1971.

11. WUI, Report of Annual Delegate Conference, Athlone, 26–27 May 1973, p. 62–4; Report of Annual Delegate Conference, Dublin, 20–22 Sep. 1974, p. 49; Report of Adjourned Annual Delegate Conference, Dublin, 23 Apr. 1977, p. 64–9; FWUI, Report of Annual Delegate Conference, Dublin, 16–17 June 1979, p. 242–5; minutes of General Executive Council, 14 Nov. 1979, 5 Dec. 1979. The unsuccessful poaching gamekeeper was Bríd Horan.

12. WUI, Report of Annual Delegate Conference, Dún Laoghaire, 9–10 May 1970, p. 77–81.

13. WUI, Report of Annual Delegate Conference, Dún Laoghaire, 9–10 May 1970, p. 44–52, 108; Report of Annual Delegate Conference, Wexford, 27–28 May 1972, p. 166–9; Report of General Executive Council, 1972–1973, and Report of Annual Delegate Conference, Athlone, 26–27 May 1973, p. 27–8, 136–7; Report of Annual Delegate Conference, Galway, 24–25 May 1975, p. 212–16; Report of Annual Delegate Conference, Dún Laoghaire, 30–31 Oct. 1976, p. 8, 63–6; Report of General Executive Council, 1976–1977, and Report of Annual Delegate Conference, Dublin, 11–12 June

1977, p. 106–7, 143, 195–8; Report of Annual Delegate Conference, Dún Laoghaire, 7–8 Oct. 1978, p. 302–10; FWUI, Report of Annual Delegate Conference, Dublin, 16–17 June 1979, p. 245–9.

14. WUI, Report of General Executive Council, 1969–1970, and Annual Delegate Conference, 9–10 May 1970, p. 3–4, 26–7; Report of General Executive Council, 1970–1971, and Annual Delegate Conference, Dún Laoghaire, 23–24 Oct. 1971, p. 3–5, 15–17, 33–8.

15. WUI, Report of Annual Delegate Conference, Dún Laoghaire, 23–24 Oct. 1971, p. 56–69, 70–73, 76. Tellers were called for after the initial show of hands, suggesting that the voting was close enough.

16. WUI, Report of General Executive Council, 1971–1972, p. 3–6; Report of Annual Delegate Conference, Athlone, 26–27 May 1973, p. 82–104; Report of General Executive Council, 1973–74; Report of Annual Delegate Conference, Dublin, 20–22 Sep. 1974, p. 14–16, 77–91.

17. WUI, Report of General Executive Council, 1974–1975, p. 23–7; Report of General Executive Council, 1975–1976, and Annual Delegate Conference, Dún Laoghaire, 30–31 Oct. 1976, p. 4–6, 117–18; Report of Annual Delegate Conference, Dublin, 11–12 June 1977, p. 169–93; Report of Annual Delegate Conference, Dún Laoghaire, 7–8 Oct. 1978, p. 222–38; FWUI, Report of Annual Delegate Conference, Dublin, 16–17 June 1979, p. 172–, 217–24; Report of General Executive Council, 1979–1980, p. 32–4. The WUI had approved the first terms, by 59 to 41%, while Congress rejected them, 119 to 318. Minutes of General Executive Council, 23 Apr. 1979, 30 May 1979. The WUI vote was 10,472 for, 7,147 against, or 59 to 40, with 1% spoiled.

18. WUI, Report of General Executive Council, 1969–1970, p. 21–4; Report of Annual Delegate Conference, Dún Laoghaire, 23–24 Oct. 1971, p. 132–5; Report of Adjourned Annual Delegate Conference, Dublin, 23 Apr. 1977, p. 74–5; Report of Annual Delegate Conference, Dublin, 16–17 June 1979, p. 278–309; minutes of General Executive Council, 9 May 1979.

19. WUI, Report of General Executive Council, 1976–1977, p. 62–9.

20. WUI, Report of Annual Delegate Conference, Wexford, 27–28 May 1972, p. 159–61; Report of Annual Delegate Conference, Athlone, 26–27 May 1973, p. 153–63; Report of Annual Delegate Conference, Galway, 24–25 May 1975, p. 196–8.

21. WUI, Report of General Executive Council, 1974–1975, p. 36; Report of Annual Delegate Conference, Dún Laoghaire, 30–31 Oct. 1976, p. 110–13; Report of General Executive Council, 1976–1977, and Annual Delegate Conference, Dublin, 11–12 June 1977, p. 74, 205–6, 262, 267–8. The Beef Tribunal was eventually established in 1991.

22. WUI, Report of General Executive Council, 1977–1978, and Annual Delegate Conference, Dún Laoghaire, 7–8 Oct. 1978, p. 82–4, 315–18; minutes of General Executive Council, 8 Sep. 1971, 15 Dec. 1971, 28 Feb. 1979.

23. FWUI, Report of General Executive Council, 1978–1979, and Annual Delegate Conference, Dublin, 16–17 June 1979, p. 94–7, 270–77, 289–92; minutes of General Executive Council, 17 Jan. 1979, 8 and 28 Feb. 1979. Other signatories were Joe Larragy (No. 15 Branch), J. Farrelly (No. 13 Branch), Bernadette Berry and Patricia McCarthy (No. 16 Branch), Colette Fallon (AUEW-TASS), P. Bolger (IPOEU), Christina Carney (Local Government and Public Services Union), Andy Johnston (Galway Trades Council), Catherine McGillan (National Union of Public

Employees and Belfast Trades Council), Paddy Behan (ITGWU); and Ned Cahill (IPOEU and Navan Trades Council). The GEC dismissed suggestions of disciplinary action against WUI signatories.

24. WUI, Report of General Executive Council, 1970–1971, p. 10–12; Report of Annual Delegate Conference, Dublin, 20–22 Sep. 1974, p. 150–52; Report of Annual Delegate Conference, Dublin, 11–12 June 1977, p. 204–7.

25. FWUI, Report of Annual Delegate Conference, Dublin, 11–12 June 1977, p. 200–201; Report of General Executive Council, 1977–1978, p. 64–5; Report of General Executive Council, 1978–1979, p. 51–5.

26. WUI, Report of Annual Delegate Conference, 9–10 May 1970, p. 129–32; Report of General Executive Council, 1970–1971, and Annual Delegate Conference, Dún Laoghaire, 23–24 Oct. 1971, p. 18–20, 42–6, 115–30; Report of Special Delegate Conference on the European Economic Community, Dún Laoghaire, 15 Jan. 1972, p. 169–222; Report of General Executive Council, 1971–1972, p. 25–31.

27. WUI, Report of Annual Delegate Conference, Wexford, 27–28 May 1972, p. 60–77; Report of Annual Delegate Conference, Athlone, 26–27 May 1973, p. 65–78; Report of Annual Delegate Conference, Dublin, 20–22 Sep. 1974, p. 61–8, 128–31, 188–9; Report of Annual Delegate Conference, Galway, 24–25 May 1975, p. 181–97, 114–15, 123–38, 217–20; Report of General Executive Council, 1975–1976, and Annual Delegate Conference, Dún Laoghaire, 30–31 Oct. 1976, p. 6–8, 15–19, 32–52, 124–35, 194–213, 238–56; FWUI, Report of Annual Delegate Conference, Dublin, 16–17 June 1979, p. 174–214, 256–70; Report of General Executive Council, 1979–1980, p. 109.

28. WUI, Report of Annual Delegate Conference, Dún Laoghaire, 23–24 Oct. 1971, p. 73–5, 148–52; Report of Annual Delegate Conference, Wexford, 27–28 May 1972, p. 148–52, 171–2; Report of Annual Delegate Conference, Wexford, 27–28 May 1972, p. 165; Report of Annual Delegate Conference, Athlone, 26–27 May 1973, p. 148–53; Report of Annual Delegate Conference, Dublin, 20–22 Sep. 1974, p. 200–204; Report of Annual Delegate Conference, Dún Laoghaire, 30–31 Oct. 1976, p. 155–7; Report of Annual Delegate Conference, Dublin, 10–11 June 1977, p. 228–44; Report of Annual Delegate Conference, Dún Laoghaire, 7–8 Oct. 1978, p. 251–5. Matters were complicated by a further amendment to the effect that the union affiliate to the Irish Civil Rights Association. FWUI, Report of Annual Delegate Conference, Dublin, 16–17 June 1979, p. 234–42; minutes of General Executive Council, 3 Oct. 1979.

29. WUI, Report of Annual Delegate Conference, Dún Laoghaire, 30–31 Oct. 1976, p. 23–32; Report of General Executive Council, 1976–1977, and Annual Delegate Conference, Dublin, 10–11 June 1977, p. 89–97, 122–6; Report of Annual Delegate Conference, Dún Laoghaire, 7–8 Oct. 1978, p. 188–94; FWUI, Report of General Executive Council, 1978–1979, and Annual Delegate Conference, Dublin, 16–17 June 1979, p. 119–20, 173–96; minutes of General Executive Council, 12 Mar. 1979, 12, 23 and 28 Apr. 1979.

30. WUI, Report of Annual Delegate Conference, Dublin, 10–11 June 1977, p. 293–5.

31. WUI, Report of Annual Delegate Conference, Galway, 24–25 May 1975, p. 208–12; Report of Annual Delegate Conference, Dublin, 10–11 June 1977, p. 281–3.

32. WUI, Report of General Executive Council, 1969–1970, and Annual Delegate Conference, 9–10 May 1970, p. 16–, 133–6; Report of General Executive Council, 1970–1971, and Annual Delegate Conference, Dún Laoghaire, 23–24 Oct. 1971, p. 25–8,

136–7. The Central Education Committee consisted of Peter Purcell (Chairman), Michael Cassidy (Secretary), Mick Canavan, Jim Larkin, Walter Hammond (No. 15 Branch), Sylvester Currin and William Cumiskey (General Executive Council) and Tom Garry (Guinness). Report of General Executive Council, 1971–1972, p. 39; Report of Annual Delegate Conference, Athlone, 26–27 May 1973, p. 137–45; Report of General Executive Council, 1973–1974, p. 26–31. The members of the Committee were Paddy Cardiff, Ross Connolly and Tom Garry, while the new Central Education Committee were Peter Purcell, Paddy Cardiff, Thomas Hayes, James Larkin, Pádraigín Ní Mhurchú, Sylvester Currin, Liam Cumiskey and Tom Garry. Report of General Executive Council, 1974–1975, p. 6–7, 12–19; Report of General Executive Council, 1976–1977, and Annual Delegate Conference, Dublin, 11–12 June 1977, p. 31–51, 159–69, 295–8.

33. WUI, Report of Annual Delegate Conference, Wexford, 27–28 May 1972, p. 80–90; Report of General Executive Council, 1975–1976, p. 28–31; minutes of General Executive Council, 21 Mar. 1979.

34. WUI, Report of Annual Delegate Conference, Dublin, 20–22 Sep. 1974, p. 100–104; Report of Annual Delegate Conference, Dublin, 11–12 June 1977, p. 283–9.

35. WUI, Report of General Executive Council, 1974–1975, p. 60–62; Report of Annual Delegate Conference, Dún Laoghaire, 30–31 Oct. 1976, p. 4; Report of General Executive Council, 1976–1977, p. 20; Report of General Executive Council, 1977–1978, p. 16–17. The Trustees of the subscription fund were Brian Carney, Michael Frank Cluskey TD, Michael Collins, Denis Larkin and Donal Nevin (Assistant General Secretary, ICTU). FWUI, Report of Annual Delegate Conference, Dublin, 16–17 June 1979, p. 345–7; minutes of General Executive Council, 23 Sep. 1970. The speakers were Eric Taplin (Liverpool Polytechnic), Bill Moran (University of Warwick), Henry Patterson (Ulster Polytechnic), Terry McCarthy (National Museum of Labour History, London), Manus O'Riordan (ITGWU), Miriam Daly (Queen's University, Belfast), Donal Nevin (ICTU), Charles McCarthy (Trinity College, Dublin) and James Plunkett Kelly (WUI). WUI, Report of General Executive Council, 1975–1976, p. 38–9. See Saothar, 4 (1978).

36. WUI, Report of General Executive Council, 1969–1970, and Annual Delegate Conference, 9–10 May 1970, p. 14–15, 107–9; Report of General Executive Council, 1970–1971, p. 21–4; Report of Annual Delegate Conference, Wexford, 27–28 May 1972, p. 95–7, 107–11; Report of General Executive Council, 1972–1973, p. 27–9; Report of Annual Delegate Conference, Galway, 24–25 May 1975, p. 169; Report of General Executive Council, 1975–1976, p. 33–8; Report of Adjourned Annual Delegate Conference, Dublin, 23 Apr. 1977, p. 139–43; minutes of General Executive Council, 23 June 1970, 17 Jan. 1979.

37. WUI, Report of Annual Delegate Conference, 9–10 May 1970, p. 109–13, 138–40; Report of General Executive Council, 1975–1976, p. 29–32; Report of Annual Delegate Conference, Dublin, 16–17 June 1979, p. 177–8; minutes of General Executive Council, 7 Jan. 1970, 17 Jan. 1979.

38. WUI, Report of Annual Delegate Conference, 9–10 May 1970, p. 112–16; Report of General Executive Council, 1970–1971, p. 29–32; Report of Annual Delegate Conference, Dublin, 20–22 Sep. 1974, p. 131–4; Report of Annual Delegate Conference, Galway, 24–25 May 1975, p. 198–207; Report of Annual Delegate

Conference, Dún Laoghaire, 30–31 Oct. 1976, p. 75–90; Report of Adjourned Annual Delegate Conference, Dublin, 23 Apr. 1977, p. 61–3, 78–127, 135–81.

39. WUI, Report of Annual Delegate Conference, 9–10 May 1970, p. 122–7; Report of Annual Delegate Conference, Dún Laoghaire, 23–24 Oct. 1971, p. 140–45; Report of General Executive Council, 1971–1972, and Annual Delegate Conference, Wexford, 27–28 May 1972, p. 23–4, 162–5, 169–70; Report of Annual Delegate Conference, Dublin, 20–22 Sep. 1974, p. 136–7; Report of Annual Delegate Conference, Dún Laoghaire, 30–31 Oct. 1976, p. 146–52; Report of Annual Delegate Conference, Dublin, 11–12 June 1977, p. 109–10, 244–53, 328–56; WUI, minutes of General Executive Council, 3 Oct. 1979.

Chapter 31 (p. 684–8)

1. See James Wickham, 'The new Irish working class?' *Saothar,* 6 (1980), p. 81–8, and Francis Devine, 'A start to Irish labour's forward march?' in Pollock, *Reform of Industrial Relations,* p. 66–81.

Chapter 32 (p. 689–748)

1. ITGWU, Annual Report for 1979 and Report of Proceedings of Annual Conference, Wexford, 27–30 May 1980, p. 279–80; 'Into the 1980s,' *Liberty,* Dec. 1979; 'A new horizon for writers, performers and artists,' *Liberty,* Jan. 1980; 'Engineers agree to transfer' and 'Final tribute to Séamus B. Kelly,' *Liberty,* Mar. 1980. Kelly was buried in Duleek, Co. Meath, on 26 February. See also ITGWU, minutes of National Executive Council, 1 Mar. 1980; 'Footballers sign up with ITGWU' and 'Low pay, little glamour in Irish League,' *Liberty,* Aug. 1980; 'Navan is filled with music for opening ceremony,' *Liberty,* Jan. 1981.

2. ITGWU, Annual Report for 1980 and Proceedings of Annual Conference, 1981, p. 14–15, 161–73, 308; Annual Report for 1981, p. 3–4; minutes of National Executive Council, 12 Oct. 1980, 17–19 Jan 1981, 16–18 May 1981, 25–27 July 1981, 27 Sep. 1981, 21–23 Nov. 1981. John P. Swift was Secretary of Dublin No. 19 Branch and Pat Brady was Nursing Officer. The valid poll was 653 and the voting was 46 for remaining in Castlebar No. 1 Branch and 607 for transfer to Mayo County Branch, a victory for Dave Mullis (who later left for personnel management) over Michael Kilcoyne (still on SIPTU's staff). 'New Union Appeals Body,' *Liberty,* July 1981.

3. ITGWU, Annual Report for 1981 and Proceedings of Annual Conference, 1982, p. 294; Annual Report for 1982, p. 3, 108–9; Annual Report for 1982 and Proceedings of Annual Conference, 1983, p. 4–5, 299–300; 'Insurance workers join the union,' *Liberty,* Feb. 1982; 'We demand justice!' *Liberty,* Sep. 1982; 'Union denies "poaching",' *Liberty,* Aug. 1983.

4. ITGWU, Annual Report for 1984, p. 4; Annual Report for 1985, p. 4–12 (emphasis in the original); *Liberty,* Feb. 1984. The new Group Secretaries were Des Geraghty, Pat Rabbitte, Jimmy Somers and Tom Walsh. 'Recruitment blitz planned,' *Liberty News,* summer 1985. 2,300 jobs were to go in 1985 at Burlington Industries, Clover Meats, Atari, Travenol, Koss and Cooney Jennings, and there had been 7,796 redundancies in 1984.

5. 'ITGWU, Annual Report for 1986 and Proceedings of Annual Conference, 1986, 26–29 May 1987, p. 17–; Annual Report for 1987, p. 3–7; 'Union survey reveals £1 an hour,' *Liberty News,* Spring 1987.

6. ITGWU, Report of Proceedings of Annual Conference, 1988, p. 22–6, 31–46, 268; Report of Proceedings of Annual Conference, 1989, p. 29–30; 'Take the financial headache out of a stay in hospital!' *Liberty News*, autumn 1987.

7. ITGWU, Report of Proceedings of Annual Conference, 1988, p. 16–17; Annual Report for 1988 and Proceedings of Annual Conference, 1989, p. 3–8, 12–25; William A. Attley, 'Denis Larkin,' *Liberty News*, summer 1987 (reprinted from *Irish Times*); 'PNR negotiations concluded,' *Liberty News*, autumn 1987 and *Unity*, n.d.; 'Jim Larkin returns to Dublin' and '1913: 75 years after the Lock Out: What does it mean today?' *Liberty News*, Mar.–Apr. 1988; 'May Day in Dublin, 1988' and 'One Big Union: A beginning,' *Liberty News*, May-Aug. 1988; 'Remembering the lock out,' *Liberty News*, Sep.-Oct. 1988.

8. ITGWU, Report of Proceedings of Annual Conference, 1989, p. 26–8, 33–4; 'SIPTU: The union of the future,' *Liberty News*, Special Supplement, Mar. 1989; 'Think positive: Vote "Yes",' *Liberty News*, Mar.-Apr. 1989; 'Yes!' and 'New horizon,' *Liberty News*, May-Aug. 1989; 'Trade unions and change,' *Liberty News*, Sep.-Oct. 1989; 'A message from the General President,' *Liberty News*, Nov.–Dec. 1989.

9. ITGWU, Annual Report for 1979 and Proceedings of Annual Conference, 1980, p. 504–8; Annual Report for 1981, p. xiv; minutes of National Executive Council, 21–23 Nov. 1981. Kirwan defeated Des Geraghty on the fifth count, 192 to 158. 'Farewell, Fintan …' *Liberty*, Feb. 1981. May O'Brien defeated Eddie Browne, John Dwan, Mick Gannon, Des Geraghty and Chris Kirwan. 'Michael Mullen, 1919–1982,' *Liberty*, Nov. 1982; 'General Secretary elected,' *Liberty*, Mar. 1983; 'Browne wins union election,' July 1983. The vote was 222 to 134. 'Fintan Kennedy: One of nature's greatest and gentlest' and Mattie O'Neill, 'A personal memoir,' *Liberty*, Apr. 1984.

10. ITGWU, Annual Report for 1983 and Proceedings of Annual Conference, 1984, p. 247–53; Proceedings of Annual Conference, 1988, p. 15–16, 19–20, 37; 'One Big Union: Seventy-five years of the ITGWU,' *Liberty*, Jan. 1984. Three hundred schools participated.

11. ITGWU, Annual Report for 1979 and Proceedings of Annual Conference, 1980, p. 393–430; 'ICTU want 20% increase in benefits' and 'TUWF argue their case,' *Liberty*, Feb. 1980; 'ICTU demand workplace nurseries' and 'Paid leave is now a major bargaining issue,' *Liberty*, Apr. 1980; 'Whatever happened to equal pay?' *Liberty*, May 1980; 'Time for positive action?' *Liberty*, June 1980. See 'Equality for Women! A Discussion Paper Presented to Annual Conference, 1980'.

12. The speakers were Kader Asmal, Liam Cassidy (Dublin No. 7 Branch), Fergal Costello (National Executive Council), Willie John Curran (Midleton), Irene Dunne (Dublin No. 6 Branch), John Dwan (Waterford No. 1 Branch), Bríd Farrell (Clare), Mary Fitzmaurice (Galway), Arthur Kelly (Dublin No. 14 Branch), Mary Kerrigan (Shannon Airport), Eleanor Laffan (Midleton), Jack Nash (Derry), Martin Naughton (Mullingar), Pat Rabbitte (Dublin District Council), John Scott (Cork No. 3 Branch), Tony Tobin (Dublin District Council), Paddy Wade (Dublin No. 15 Branch) and Anne Wilkinson (Letterkenny). Charlie Taggart (Belfast) spoke in favour but also asked, If reserved NEC places for women, why not a reserved place for Northern members? The author of the paper, Rosheen Callender, as an observer, played no formal part in the debate.

13. ITGWU, minutes of National Executive Council, 21–23 Mar. 1981; 'The Labour Court and equal pay,' *Liberty*, Sep. 1980; 'Delegates call for major changes,' *Liberty*, Jan.

1981; 'Union moves on equality,' *Liberty*, Oct. 1981. The members of the Working Party were Mary Burke (Clonmel), Anne Eagar (Branch Assistant, Cork No. 2 Branch), Nóirín Greene (Dublin No. 2 Branch), Eleanor Laffan (Midleton), Patricia McCarthy (Shannon), Derry McDermott (Branch Assistant, Dublin No. 2 Branch), Mai O'Brien (Branch Assistant, Dublin No. 6/8 Branch), Jean Roche (Dublin No. 6/8 Branch), Patricia Walsh (UCG) and Rosheen Callender (Research), secretary.

14. ITGWU, Annual Report for 1980 and Report of Proceedings of Annual Conference, Killarney, 26–29 May 1981, p. 427–31, 491–448; Annual Report for 1981, p. 30–32; Rosheen Callender, 'At long last . . . Maternity leave,' *Liberty*, Mar. 1981.

15. ITGWU, Annual Report for 1981 and Proceedings of Annual Conference, 1982, p. 423–33; Annual Report for 1982 and Proceedings of Annual Conference, 1983, p. 19–27, 455–67. Exchanges between Nóirín Greene and the platform were tetchy, reflecting tensions between women's expectations and the speed of the NEC's implementation of agreed equality policies. ITGWU, Annual Report for 1983, p. 12–19; Annual Report for 1984, p. 15–24; 'A first for the union!' *Liberty*, July 1982; *Liberty*, Oct. 1982; 'Time for positive action,' *Liberty*, Nov. 1983.

16. ITGWU, Annual Report for 1984 and Report of Proceedings of Annual Conference, 1985, p. 236–54; Annual Report for 1985, p. 20–26; Annual Report for 1986 and Proceedings of Annual Conference, 1987, p. 12–20, 40–56. The vote was 63 to 36% with a turn-out of 63%. 'Weekend school in Derry on low pay, health for women' and 'More Delegates than ever before for new format Conference,' *Liberty News*, autumn 1986; 'New workplace health service for women' and 'Lifting of night work ban on women a step back,' *Liberty*, spring 1987.

17. ITGWU, Report of Proceedings of Annual Conference, 1988, p. 168–90; 'Equal pay successes in Cork,' *Liberty News*, Jan.–Feb. 1988; 'Women, trade unions and society,' *Liberty News*, Nov. 1988; 'Conference report,' *Liberty News*, May–Aug. 1989.

18. ITGWU, Annual Report for 1979 and Proceedings of Annual Conference, 1980, p. 483–96; Annual Report for 1980 and Proceedings of Annual Conference, 1981, p. 296–8, 499–509; minutes of National Executive Council, 18–20 July 1980, 23–25 Apr. 1981, 16–18 May 1981; 'Failure to help lower paid,' *Liberty*, Feb. 1980. Devlin actively engaged with the Low Pay Unit. 'NI equal pay victory for ITGWU,' *Liberty*, Aug. 1980; 'Cuts continue in North,' *Liberty*, Jan. 1981. The bodies were the Advisory Committee on Health Education, Northern Ireland Training Council, Youth Careers and Youth Opportunities Committees, Agricultural Training Committee, Extra-Statutory Compensation Tribunal, Employment Services Management Committee, Northern Ireland Consumer Council, Electricity Consumers' Council and Transport Users' Committee, Northern Ireland Council for Nurses and Midwives, Northern Ireland Construction Advisory Council, and Northern Ireland Agricultural Trust. 'Bobby Sands,' *Liberty*, May 1981; 'Union calls on H-block impasse,' *Liberty*, Aug. 1981. The union's Counsel was Carmel O'Reilly, who resigned from the Fair Employment Agency in 1979 because of its inactivity on equal pay. Trade union representatives had resigned from the agency for the same reason. See also ITGWU, Annual Report for 1980, p. 238–41.

19. ITGWU, Annual Report for 1981, p. 201–2, 223–4; 'Facing the long hot winter,' *Liberty*, Jan. 1980; 'Breakthrough for NI Branch,' *Liberty*, Jan. 1982. 'Tory Bill threatens the right to strike,' *Liberty*, Apr. 1982; 'Norbrook appeal,' *Liberty*, Jan. 1984.

20. ITGWU, Annual Report for 1985, p. 217–29; Annual Report for 1986, p. 190; Annual Report for 1987, p. 71–5; Annual Report for 1988, p. 67–70; 'Congress campaigns against intimidation, sectarianism in North,' *Liberty News,* autumn 1986; 'Blind only to the truth' and 'The Guildford Four: Innocent victims,' *Liberty,* May–Aug. 1988; 'Major equality breakthrough in North,' May–Aug. 1989. Technical advice was provided by May O'Brien and Eugene Kearney.

21. ITGWU, Annual Report for 1980, p. 14–15; minutes of National Executive Council, 16–18 Feb. 1980, 17–19 May 1980, 19–21 July 1980, 15–17 Nov. 1980, 21–23 Mar. 1981. Problems had arisen in Centronics, Drogheda, and Cork Regional Hospital. FWUI, minutes of General Executive Council, 21 Jan. 1981. The FWUI's recorded position was one of neutrality.

22. ITGWU, Annual Report for 1979 and Proceedings of Annual Conference, 1980, p. 278–9; Annual Report for 1980 and Proceedings of Annual Conference, 1981, p. 307; minutes of National Executive Council, 20–22 Dec. 1980; 17–19 Jan. 1981, 21–23 Feb. 1981, 16–18 May 1981, 25–27 July 1981. ITGWU affiliations were to the International Transport Workers' Federation for 10,001 members; the International Metal Workers' Federation, 8,000; the International Textile, Garment and Leather Workers' Federation, 10,000; the International Union of Food Workers, 10,000; the International Federation of Building and Woodworkers' Unions, 7,000; the International Chemical, Energy and General Workers' Unions, 10,000; EEC Transport Workers, 10,001; European Metalworkers, 10,000; the Contact Office of Metalworkers in the EEC, 4,000; European Food and Allied Workers, 10,000; European Building and Woodworkers, 7,000; the Co-ordinating Committee of Chemical and General Workers in the EEC, 10,000; and the European Federation of Agricultural Workers, 2,000.

23. ITGWU, Annual Report for 1984 and Proceedings of Annual Conference, 1985, p. 254–64; Annual Report for 1985 and Proceedings of Annual Conference, 1986, p. 21, 28. Motions came from Dublin No. 14 Branch and Cóbh. Annual Report for 1986 and Proceedings of Annual Conference, 1987, p. 12; 'Two unions sign pact,' *Liberty,* Mar. 1984; photograph, *Liberty,* Apr. 1984.

24. ITGWU, minutes of National Executive Council, 20–22 Sep. 1980; 'Priorities,' *Liberty,* Mar. 1980; 'Beyond wages,' *Liberty,* Sep. 1980. See ITGWU, 'Economic and Social Policy: A Review Paper Presented to Annual Delegate Conference, 1980.'

25. ITGWU, Annual Report for 1979 and Proceedings of Annual Conference, 1980, p. 279–80, 299–310; 'Make it work,' *Liberty,* Nov. 1980. The ITGWU ballot was 92,712 in favour and 27,304 against. ITGWU, Annual Report for 1980, p. 50–54; 'ICTU accepts,' *Liberty,* Nov. 1980; 'Employers resist increases and demand new disputes law,' *Liberty,* Dec. 1980; Manus O'Riordan, 'Safety net . . . or snare?' *Liberty,* Mar. 1981.

26. 'Wages policy,' *Liberty,* Nov. 1981.

27. ITGWU, Annual Report for 1980 and Proceedings of Annual Conference, 1981, p. 431–46; Annual Report for 1981 and Proceedings of Annual Conference, 1982, p. 3–4, 356–72, 404–14; 'Jobs, money and madness,' *Liberty,* Dec. 1981.

28. ITGWU, Annual Report for 1982, p. 48–51, 88–9, 125–35; 'Is the ice breaking on the pay freeze?' *Liberty,* Sep. 1982.

29. ITGWU, Annual Report for 1983, p. 33–39; Paul Sweeney, 'Survey reveals sharp drop in take-home pay,' *Liberty,* Jan. 1983; 'Clondalkin,' *Liberty,* Nov. 1983.

30. 'Union takes on Condrons,' 'Union wins Blarney dispute' and 'Pizzaland: UK bosses

try to break union,' *Liberty*, May 1983; 'Strike ends in Pizzaland,' *Liberty*, June 1983; 'Condrons: The strike continues,' *Liberty*, Aug. 1983; 'Strike now in seventh month,' *Liberty*, Sep. 1983; 'Dunlop: The fight for justice' and 'Strike fund appeal,' *Liberty*, Oct. 1983; 'Ford shock,' *Liberty*, Feb. 1984; 'Legacy of Condron's dispute,' *Liberty*, May 1984.

31. ITGWU, Annual Report for 1984 and Proceedings of Annual Conference, 1985, p. 224–35, 434–7; 'A recipe for disaster' and 'No to Govt. meddling in wage bargaining,' *Liberty*, Apr. 1984.

32. ITGWU, Annual Report for 1985 and Proceedings of Annual Conference, 1986, p. 26–7; Annual Report for 1986, p. 158, 188; 'Veha: An issue of principle,' *Liberty News*, summer 1986. All this was assisted by the new 'desktop publishing' equipment in the Communications Department. The innovative menu was circulated throughout the world by the International Federation of Food and Allied Workers' Unions. See ITGWU, Annual Report for 1986, p. 73, 23; 'Hotel Lock-Out,' *Liberty*, Sep. 1983; 'Hotel to re-open,' *Liberty*, Nov. 1983; 'The most distinguished pickets in Ireland,' *Liberty News*, autumn 1986; 'Substantial pay increases follow end of Shelbourne Hotel strike,' *Liberty News*, spring 1987.

33. ITGWU, Annual Report for 1986 and Proceedings of Annual Conference, 1987, p. 12–13; Annual Report for 1987, p. 30–31, 34–7. The valid vote was 74,009: the result was 38,068 for, 35,941 against. 'ICTU seeks National Understanding,' *Liberty News*, spring 1987; 'Vote Yes!—National Agreement "best deal available," says National Executive Council' and a supplement, 'Talks on Plan for National Recovery concluded,' *Liberty News*, autumn 1987; 'It's agreed,' *Liberty News*, winter 1987.

34. ITGWU, Annual Report for 1987 and Proceedings of Annual Conference, 1988, p. 11–12, 76–83, 134–7, 105–8. Motions from Cork District Council and Wexford wanted withdrawal from the Plan for National Recovery if the £4 floor was denied.

35. ITGWU, Annual Report for 1988, p. 70–75; 'Naas women join union to fight poverty line wages,' *Liberty News*, Sep.–Oct. 1988; 'Premier Disposables strike ends in success' and 'Return to work formula agreed at Memorex,' *Liberty News*, Nov.–Dec. 1988; 'Sharing the benefits,' *Liberty News*, Nov.–Dec. 1989.

36. 'Statement issued by National Nursing Council,' *Liberty*, May 1980, signed by Dick McGuinness, Psychiatric Nurses, and John Boland, General Nurses; 'Union holds nursing seminar,' *Liberty*, Jan. 198'; 'Nurses threaten to strike for better patient care,' *Liberty News*, spring 1987.

37. ITGWU, Annual Report for 1980, p. 128–9; 'Alcan: Union record defended,' *Liberty*, June 1980; 'A major test for the unions,' *Liberty*, July 1980.

38. ITGWU, Annual Report for 1980 and Proceedings of Annual Conference, 1981, p. 175–84, 522–7. The full vote was: Arklow, 11 to 2; Castlebar, 2 to 5; Athlone, 6 to 3; Dundalk, 4 to 0; Galway, 36 to 1; Shannon, 24 to 10; Waterford, 11 to 0; New Ross, 15 to 4; Limerick, 60 to 65; Cork, 92 to 19; Dublin, 77 to 334. Voting on the second occasion was: Arklow, 10 to 3; Athlone, 10 to 2; Castlebar, 7 to 0; Dundalk, 4 to 0; Galway, 35 to 1; Shannon, 31 to 5; Waterford, 12 to 0; New Ross, 19 to 2; Limerick, 51 to 18; Cork, 116 to 5; Dublin, 273 to 158. ITGWU, minutes of National Executive Council, 18–20 Oct. 1980, 19–21 Dec. 1981; 'Major implications of oil crisis,' *Liberty*, Oct. 1980; 'Union to hold inquiry' and 'Media horror . . . no shock!' *Liberty*, Nov. 1980. The inquiry team were Andy Burke (Dublin No. 4 Branch), Tom Colgan

(Laois), Paddy Mooney (Dublin No. 2 Branch), Seán Roche (Waterford) and Paddy Clancy (Development Services Division) (Chairperson). See FWUI, minutes of General Executive Council, 1 Oct. 1980; Pádraig Yeates, 'A dispute that should never have happened,' *Sunday Tribune,* 8 Aug. 1982.

39. ITGWU, Annual Report for 1980, p. 150–61; Annual Report for 1983, p. 132–49; Annual Report for 1985, p. 189–91; Annual Report for 1986, p. 166–8; 'McKinsey or Charlie Haughey?' *Liberty,* Feb. 1981; Bill McCamley, 'Stress on the buses,' *Liberty,* Sep. 1981; 'Getting back on the right track,' *Liberty,* Dec. 1981.

40. ITGWU, Annual Report for 1986, p. 131–2.

41. ITGWU, Annual Report for 1981, p. 134–5; Annual Report for 1987, p. 193–6. Annual Report for 1988, p. 194–6; 'Company rejects Labour Court recommendation,' *Liberty News,* summer 1987. The Minister for Industry and Commerce—a friend of Hanlon's—used Dáil privilege to make an 'irresponsible and insensitive intervention' in the dispute. 'Settlement at Hanlon's?' *Liberty News,* autumn 1987; 'New strike at Hanlon's,' *Liberty,* Mar.–Apr. 1988; 'Withdrawal of capital at Hanlon's' and 'Managerial suicide,' *Liberty,* May–Aug. 1988; 'Hanlon's workers secure redundancy compensation,' *Liberty,* Jan.–Feb. 1989.

42. 'Why we are back on the streets,' 'Renewed effort in campaign,' 'What we want in Charlie's Budget' and 'A need for political courage,' *Liberty,* Jan. 1980; 'The day we took to the streets' and 'Budget, 1980,' *Liberty,* Feb. 1980; '1980 priorities,' Mar. 1980.

43. ITGWU, Annual Report for 1979 and Report of Proceedings of Annual Conference, 1980, p. 278–9, 448–58; minutes of National Executive Council, 25–27 Apr. 1981, 16–18 May 1981; 'The Budget was a beginning but did not meet ICTU demands,' *Liberty,* Mar. 1980; 'Supreme Court ruling: More discrimination against PAYE workers,' *Liberty,* May 1980; 'Workers pay more tax,' *Liberty,* Jan. 1981.

44. ITGWU, Annual Report for 1981 and Proceedings of Annual Conference, 1982, p. 465–70; Annual Report for 1982 and Proceedings of Annual Conference, 1983, p. 343–7, 419–39; 'We pay highest taxes in EEC,' *Liberty,* Jan. 1982. Ireland was at 39%, Denmark 28%, France 27%, Italy 26%, Belgium 22%, Britain 21%, Netherlands and Germany 20% and Luxembourg 16%. Paul Sweeney, 'The Commission reports' and 'Public sector must not be made the scapegoat,' *Liberty,* Aug. 1982; *Liberty,* Mar. 1983, front-page picture; 'The Finance Bill: Union launches major campaign,' *Liberty,* May 1983; 'Let the members decide!' *Liberty News,* autumn 1986.

45. ITGWU, Annual Report for 1985 and Proceedings of Annual Conference, 1986, p. 86–139; Report of Proceedings of Annual Conference, 1989, p. 106–9; 'Union puts politicians on the spot over jobs, tax,' *Liberty News,* winter 1986. 5,859 (10%) voted for a national half-day stoppage, 8,050 (14%) for a full day's stoppage; 8,029 (13%) voted for up to five or six one-day stoppages, and 7,481 (13%) for a week-long stoppage. After the elimination of option B, option A carried the day, with 30,431 (53%) of the total. The full figures for each March were: 1979, 19%; 1980, 21%; 1981, 20%; 1982, 21%; 1983, 23%; 1984, 26%; 1985, 27%; 1986, 27%; 1987, 27%. 'Behind the Budget' and 'The alternative Budget,' *Liberty,* Jan.–Feb. 1989.

46. ITGWU, Annual Report for 1978 and Proceedings of Annual Conference, 1979, p. 365–90; Annual Report for 1979 and Proceedings of Annual Conference, 1980, p. 26–7, 330–38, 345–75; Annual Report for 1981, p. 20–23; 'The law will solve nothing,' *Liberty,* Jan. 1980.

47. ITGWU, Annual Report for 1981 and Proceedings of Annual Conference, 1982, p. 377–83; Annual Report for 1985 and Proceedings of Annual Conference, 1986, p. 20–21; Annual Report for 1986 and Proceedings of Annual Conference, 1987, p. 10–12; 'Cash or cheque: What's the difference?' *Liberty*, Feb. 1980; 'At last! A guide to workers' rights,' *Liberty*, June 1980; Rosheen Callender, 'Part-time workers, full-time victims,' *Liberty*, Dec. 1980; 'The Minister's blueprint,' *Liberty News*, summer 1985; 'Changes in industrial disputes law unlikely to benefit unions,' *Liberty News*, winter 1986. See Wayne, *Labour Law in Ireland*.

48. ITGWU, Report of Proceedings of Annual Conference, 1989, p. 168–90. The NEC motion incorrectly referred to the Trade Union Act (1906). ITGWU, Report of Proceedings of Annual Conference, 1988, p. 18–19, 124–8. 'Labour Court slates clause 4,' *Liberty*, Aug. 1980.

49. ITGWU, Annual Report for 1979 and Proceedings of Annual Conference, 1980, p. 318–30; 'Economic and Social Policy: A Review Paper presented to Annual Delegate Conference, 1980'; Annual Report for 1980 and Proceedings of Annual Conference, 1981, p. 83–4, 346–408; Annual Report for 1981 and Proceedings of Annual Conference, 1982, p. 323–56, 365–9; Annual Report for 1982 and Proceedings of Annual Conference, 1983, p. 34–8, 321–408; Annual Report for 1983 and Proceedings of Annual Conference, 1984, p. 281–332; Annual Report for 1984 and Proceedings of Annual Conference, 1985, p. 32–4, 283–322; Annual Report for 1985 and Proceedings of Annual Conference, 1986, p. 17–18, 29–83; Annual Report for 1986 and Proceedings of Annual Conference, 1987, p. 20, 32–42, 56–66; Report of Proceedings of Annual Conference, 1988, p. 71–96, 135–8; Annual Report for 1988 and Proceedings of Annual Conference, 1989, p. 31–40, 52–86; 'Creeping Thatcherism,' *Liberty*, Feb. 1980; 'A radical new jobs initiative,' *Liberty*, Apr. 1980; Manus O'Riordan, 'Telesis nails Government failures,' *Liberty*, Sep. 1980; 'Tuam's future: The fight continues,' *Liberty*, Oct. 1980. 'Thousands march in jobs protest' and 'Clothing trade crisis,' *Liberty*, Aug. 1980; 'No time for pessimism!' *Liberty*, Sep. 1980; 'As the crisis deepens . . .' *Liberty*, Jan. 1980; 'There is an alternative,' *Liberty*, Oct. 1981; 'Blizzards and blizzards' and 'Dublin: Deprivation and decay,' *Liberty*, Jan. 1982; 'The union, the Budget and the election,' *Liberty*, Feb. 1980; 'The real national interest,' *Liberty*, Mar. 1980; 'Union acts on Arklow jobs crisis' and 'Labour costs myth exposed,' *Liberty*, May 1980; 'You can do something,' *Liberty*, Dec. 1980; 'Avoca miners win in the end,' *Liberty*, Jan. 1983; 'Finglas Centre: A New Union approach to unemployment,' *Liberty*, June 1984. Des Geraghty (Group Secretary) and Eric Fleming (Secretary, Dublin No. 5 Branch) were central to the campaign. 'Building workers demand action' and 'Arklow—Down but not out,' *Liberty*, July 1984; 'Is public enterprise alive and well?' *Liberty*, Sep. 1984; 'Co-op wears well,' *Liberty*, Jan. 1984; 'Not a plan—just more propaganda' and 'NEC condemns Planning Board's proposals,' *Liberty*, May 1984; *Liberty News*, autumn 1985; 'RTÉ refuses union ad campaign,' *Liberty News*, spring 1986; 'Budget special,' *Liberty News*, spring 1987. Among the authors were Rosheen Callender and Paul Sweeney (ITGWU Research staff). A report by the National Economic and Social Council, *An Analysis of Job Losses in Irish Manufacturing Industry*, essentially concurred with the union's analysis of competitiveness; 'Budget Special: Unemployment: No hope for the jobless,' *Liberty News*, n.d. [Jan. 1986?]; 'Budget Special,' *Liberty News*, spring 1986; 'OK, Ray,

but where are the jobs?' *Liberty News,* Jan.–Feb. 1988; 'Job creation still below expectations,' *Liberty,* Sep.–Oct. See Kilmurray, *Fight, Starve or Emigrate.*

50. ITGWU, Annual Report for 1986 and Proceedings of Annual Conference, 1987, p. 114–18, 184–8; Annual Report for 1987 and Proceedings of Annual Conference, 1988, p. 63–70, 158–61, 113–20, 176–9; Annual Report for 1988 and Proceedings of Annual Conference, 1989, p. 86–9, 108–9.

51. ITGWU, Annual Report for 1983 and Proceedings of Annual Conference, 1984, p. 262–79; Annual Report for 1987 and Proceedings of Annual Conference, 1988, p. 14–15, 20–22, 115–21; 'Dublin EEC summit: A failure,' *Liberty,* Jan. 1980; 'For jobs' sake—vote No!' *Liberty News,* spring 1987; Single Euro Act Referendum Special Edition, summer 1987, and 'Confronting the challenge of 1992,' *Liberty News,* Sep.–Oct. 1988.

52. ITGWU, Annual Report for 1978 and Proceedings of Annual Conference, 1979, p. 365–90; Annual Report for 1980 and Proceedings of Annual Conference, 1981, p. 408–14; Annual Report for 1984 and Proceedings of Annual Conference, 1985, p. 273–83; Annual Report for 1986 and Proceedings of Annual Conference, 1987, p. 128–30; minutes of National Executive Council, 17–19 Jan. 1981.

53. ITGWU, Annual Report for 1979 and Proceedings of Annual Conference, 1980, p. 432–41; Annual Report for 1982, p. 38–48; ITGWU, 'Economic and Social Policy: A Review Paper Presented to Annual Delegate Conference, 1980'; 'Priorities,' *Liberty,* Mar. 1980; 'Please don't leave me alone,' *Liberty,* Apr. 1980; 'Strikers: Get your credits,' *Liberty,* Nov. 1980; 'The system that degrades,' *Liberty,* Apr. 1981; Rosheen Callender, 'Social welfare victory for Comer Yarns workers,' and Dee McGarry, 'Social welfare appeals, a very rough justice,' *Liberty,* Jan. 1983; 'Savage attacks on social welfare,' *Liberty,* Feb. 1983. The two ICTU members of the Social Welfare Appeals Tribunal were Tom McGrath (ICTU) and Paddy Murphy (FWUI), while the FUE representatives were Ralph de Zaayer (Pretty Polly) and John Doherty (PMPA). Bill Farrell (former Rights Commissioner) was Chairperson.

54. ITGWU, Annual Report for 1982 and Proceedings of Annual Conference, 1983, p. 489–95; Annual Report for 1984, p. 39–46; Annual Report for 1985 and Proceedings of Annual Conference, 1986, p. 152–68, 50–155; Annual Report for 1986 and Proceedings of Annual Conference, 1987, p. 42–50, 106–8, 142–56; Annual Report for 1987, p. 42–59; Report of Proceedings of Annual Conference, 1989, p. 23, 86–167; 'Social welfare: The system must change!' *Liberty,* Mar. 1984; 'Health cuts: the fight goes on' and 'Welfare Tribunal backs Rooskey bacon factory workers' claim in Lock-Out,' *Liberty News,* summer 1987; 'The poverty line' and 'More caught in poverty trap,' *Liberty,* Sep.–Oct. 1988.

55. ITGWU, Annual Report for 1980 and Proceedings of Annual Conference, 1981, p. 33–5, 300–302 (Worker Participation: A Discussion Paper); Report of Proceedings of Annual Conference, 1988, p. 218–22; 'Beyond wages,' *Liberty,* Sep. 1980; 'Union men win CIÉ elections,' *Liberty,* Oct. 1980. John Loughlin (TSSA) and Dick O'Donovan (NBU) were others.

56. ITGWU, Annual Report for 1979 and Proceedings of Annual Conference, 1980, p. 376–92; Annual Report for 1980 and Proceedings of Annual Conference, 1981, p. 512–16; Annual Report for 1981, p. 7, 242–4; Annual Report for 1982 and Proceedings of Annual Conference, 1983, p. 467–72; Report of Proceedings of Annual

Conference, 1984, p. 256–8; minutes of National Executive Council, 18 July 1981, 21–23 Nov. 1981. The NISO was asked for as many posters as possible. 'New Safety Act' and 'The chemicals that maim and deform,' *Liberty*, June 1980; 'The cancer threat,' *Liberty*, Sep. 1980; 'Workers must act on new safety law,' *Liberty*, Jan. 1981; Eileen King, 'Danger in the office,' *Liberty*, June 1981, a review of R. Marianne Craig, *Office Workers' Survival Handbook: A Guide to Fighting Health Hazards in the Office* (London: BSSR Publications, 1981); 'Lethal labs?' *Liberty*, Aug. 1981; 'Good design saves lives,' *Liberty*, Sep. 1981; 'The dust that kills,' *Liberty*, Oct. 1981; *Liberty*, Mar. 1984.

57. ITGWU, Annual Report for 1985 and Proceedings of Annual Conference, 1986, p. 187–97; Annual Report for 1987, p. 13–14; 'Union launches major safety report,' *Liberty News*, autumn 1986; Dónal O'Sullivan and Eugene Kearney, *How Safe is Irish Industry?: A Report of a National Survey of Safety Committees* (Dublin: ITGWU, 1986); 'Union launches new health and safety computer "dial-o-fax": A new environment for health and safety,' *Liberty*, May–Aug. 1989; *Liberty*, Sep.–Oct. 1989.

58. ITGWU, Annual Report for 1979 and Proceedings of Annual Conference, 1980, p. 282–5, 288; Annual Report for 1980 and Proceedings of Annual Conference, 1981, p. 15–25, 424–5; Annual Report for 1981 and Proceedings of Annual Conference, 1982, p. 7, 242–4, 295; Annual Report for 1984, p. 5–11; Annual Report for 1985, p. 12–19; Annual Report for 1986 and Proceedings of Annual Conference, 1987, p. 7–13, 21–22, 26–40; Annual Report for 1987, p. 9–12; 'Direction of our march,' *Liberty*, June 1982; 'The ITGWU Educational Scholarships, 1987,' *Liberty News*, winter 1987. The first winners of the higher education scholarship for members' children were Paul Harrington (Association of Nursing Officers), Patricia Harrington (Association of Nursing Officers), Michael Hussey (Local Authority Professional Officers) and David Wheatley (Dublin No. 2 Branch), while the successful members were Séamus Buggle (Kildare) and Kieran O'Brien (Dublin No. 17 Branch). See Pollock, *Case Studies in Industrial Relations*.

59. ITGWU, Annual Report for 1979 and Proceedings of Annual Conference, 1980, p. 430–32, 485–486; Annual Report for 1980, p. 25–28; Annual Report for 1981 and Proceedings of Annual Conference, 1982, p. 213–19, 300–303, 401–3; Annual Report for 1982 and Proceedings of Annual Conference, 1983, p. 300–301, 413–17; Annual Report for 1983, p. 203–6. Robert Carrickford, Dermot Doolan and Maurice Taylor represented Actors' Equity; Noel Coade and Jack Flahive, IFM; Séamus Mac Amhlaoibh, John Keenan, Críostóir Ó Cearnaigh and Tomás Ó Glaccuss (ITM); Harry Hamilton and Malcolm Neale, NIMA; and Louis Rolston, Joe McPartland and Alex Clark, British Equity. ITGWU, minutes of National Executive Council, 17 June 1981, 7 Nov. 1981, 23 Jan. 1982; 'A new horizon for writers, performers and artists,' *Liberty*, Jan. 1980; 'Equity group opposes RTÉ cuts' and 'Bringing live theatre to the people,' *Liberty*, Apr. 1980; 'Union supports public control of local radio' and 'A very important issue,' *Liberty*, Aug. 1981; 'Portrait of the artist—as a union member,' *Liberty*, Oct. 1982; 'Government threatens the future of RTÉ,' *Liberty*, Nov. 1982. See Devine, *Acting for the Actors*.

60. ITGWU, Annual Report for 1979 and Proceedings of Annual Conference, 1980, p. 441–7; Annual Report for 1980 and Proceedings of Annual Conference, 1981, p. 305–6; 'Disabled people have the right to work,' *Liberty*, Mar. 1981.

61. ITGWU, Annual Report for 1984 and Proceedings of Annual Conference, 1985, p. 230–34; Annual Report for 1985 and Proceedings of Annual Conference, 1986, p. 27–8.

62. ITGWU, Annual Report for 1979 and Proceedings of Annual Conference, 1980, p. 292–3; Annual Report for 1983 and Proceedings of Annual Conference, 1984, p. 350–63; Annual Report for 1984 and Proceedings of Annual Conference, 1985, p. 288–95; Annual Report for 1985, p. 36–9; Annual Report for 1986 and Proceedings of Annual Conference, 1987, p. 20–21; Report of Proceedings of Annual Conference, 1988, p. 27–32; minutes of National Executive Council, 19–21 Jan. 1980; 'Young workers, don't be ripped off.' *Liberty*, July 1981; 'Labour Party's "poor performance" criticised' and 'Drug abuse and glue sniffing,' *Liberty*, July 1982; 'Youth Employment Levy: A cynical con job,' *Liberty*, Oct. 1983; *Liberty News*, winter 1985.

63. ITGWU, Annual Report for 1979 and Proceedings of Annual Conference, 1980, p. 293–301; Annual Report for 1980 and Proceedings of Annual Conference, 1981, p. 327–42. Other speakers included Michael Mullen (ITGWU), Denis Larkin (WUI), Frank Cluskey TD (Labour Party), Garret FitzGerald (Fine Gael), David Andrews (Fianna Fáil), Seán MacBride, and Kader Asmal. Annual Report for 1981 and Proceedings of Annual Conference, 1982, p. 314–17; Annual Report for 1985 and Proceedings of Annual Conference, 1986, p. 157; minutes of National Executive Council, 17–19 Jan. 1981; 'Call for peace and security,' *Liberty*, Feb. 1980; Jan Hanlon and Ann Riordan, 'The Third World,' *Liberty*, Sep. 1980; 'Union opposes rugby tour,' *Liberty*, Jan. 1981; 'Stop tour,' *Liberty*, Mar. 1981; 'Summer of shame,' *Liberty*, Apr. 1981. Honourable mention was made of Tony Ward's opposition in his *Sunday Tribune* column and to Donald Woods's eye-witness account of the horrors of apartheid: Donald Woods, *Black and White* (Dublin: Ward River Press, 1981). 'Repression in Philippines,' *Liberty*, Oct. 1982. Martin King and Séamus Sheils were important activists in this area. 'Mullen Trust to aid South African workers,' *Liberty*, Dec. 1982. The Trustees were John Carroll, Donal Nevin and Austin Flannery. *Liberty News*, autumn 1985, winter 1985; 'Wapping: Nine months at the front line,' *Liberty News*, autumn 1986; 'The coffee brigadier,' *Liberty*, Jan.–Feb. 1988.

64. ITGWU, Annual Report for 1983 and Proceedings of Annual Conference, 1984, p. 346–7; 'Steel strikers' thanks,' *Liberty*, Apr. 1980; Jack Gannon, 'Welsh miners face serious redundancy,' *Liberty*, May 1980; Francis Devine, 'Miners' choir's Irish tour' and 'Scab,' *Liberty News*, spring 1986. See Jonathan Saunders, *Across Frontiers: International Support for the Miners' Strike* (London: Canary, 1989).

65. ITGWU, Annual Report for 1979 and Proceedings of Annual Conference, 1980, p. 289–97: Annual Report for 1980 and Proceedings of Annual Conference, 1981, p. 322–42; Annual Report for 1981, p. 16–18; minutes of National Executive Council, 17–19 Jan. 1981; 'The union, the Budget and the election,' *Liberty*, Feb. 1982. In addition to the Labour Party TDs Brendan Corish, Barry Desmond, Liam Kavanagh, Michael Moynihan, Michael O'Leary, Séamus Pattison and Dick Spring, Joe Sherlock represented the Workers' Party, and John Carroll, Tim Conway, Mick Ferris and Mary Robinson served in the Seanad.

66. ITGWU, Annual Report for 1981 and Proceedings of Annual Conference, 1982, p. 303–14; Annual Report for 1982, p. 30–32; 'Labour Party's "poor performance" criticised,' *Liberty*, July 1982.

67. ITGWU, Annual Report for 1982 and Proceedings of Annual Conference, 1983, p. 302–20; Annual Report for 1983, p. 20–22; 'Hopeless Budget,' *Liberty*, Feb. 1983; 'Throwing down the gauntlet!' *Liberty*, May 1983; *Liberty*, Jan. 1984; 'No-hope Budget—NEC,' *Liberty*, Feb. 1984.

68. ITGWU, Annual Report for 1984 and Proceedings of Annual Conference, 1985, p. 385–425; Annual Report for 1985 and Proceedings of Annual Conference, 1986, p. 83–5; Annual Report for 1986 and Proceedings of Annual Conference, 1987, p. 9–; Report of Proceedings of Annual Conference, 1988, p. 39–40; 'Union keeps Labour link but seeks Coalition break,' *Liberty News*, autumn 1985; 'The Labour Party Conference: Fighting for your future,' *Liberty News*, autumn 1987; *Liberty*, Mar.–Apr. 1989; Barry Desmond, 'There is an alternative,' *Liberty*, Jan.–Feb. 1988.

Chapter 33 (p. 749–91)

1. FWUI, Report of Annual Delegate Conference, 1980, p. 356–69, 399–408; Report of General Executive Council, 1980–1981, and Annual Delegate Conference, 1981, p. 399–429, 187–223; Report of General Executive Council, 1982–1983, p. 261; minutes of General Executive Council, 16 Jan. 1980, 16 Apr. 1980, 7 May 1980. The Branches in 1980 were: No. 1, general; No. 2, Dublin Corporation, ESB, marine; No. 3, manufacturing; No. 4, food, sugar and confectionery, and Meat Federation; No. 7, tobacco; No. 6, engineering; No. 8, construction; No. 9, Guinness; No. 12, civil aviation; No. 13, gas; No. 16, shipping and insurance; No. 17, clerical; No. 18, hospitals and health; Central Area (Tullamore), Bray, Dún Laoghaire, South-East Area (Athy), Trim, Western Area (Galway) and Rural Workers' Group. The new Branches settled down as: No. 20: Cos. Cavan, Donegal, Leitrim, Sligo, NWHB (Paul Clarke); No. 21: Cos. Louth, Monaghan, NEHB (Paul Clarke); No. 22: Cos. Carlow, Kilkenny, Laois, Limerick, Waterford, Wexford (Tony Dunne); No. 23: Bord na Móna West, Cos. Longford and Roscommon (Kevin McMahon); No. 24: Bord na Móna East, Co. Kildare (Ned O'Rourke); No. 25: Cos. Dublin, Meath and Wicklow and School Bus Drivers (Jack O'Connor). 'National' was a pejorative term, as the WUI had no members in the Six Counties.

2. FWUI, Report of General Executive Council, 1981–1982, and Annual Delegate Conference, 1982, p. 8, 325–8; Report of General Executive Council, 1982–1983, p. 38–9; minutes of General Executive Council, 9 July 1980, 17 Dec. 1980; 20 May 1981, 17 June 1981, 7 and 28 Nov. 1981, 17 Dec. 1981, 13 Feb. 1982. Callan became an instructor in the new AnCO Training Centre. FWUI, minutes of General Executive Council, 26 June 1982, 24 July 1982, 28 Aug. 1982, 25 Sep. 1982, 6 Nov. 1982.

3. FWUI, Report of Annual Delegate Conference, Dublin, 21–22 May 1983, p. 397–5, 496–504; Report of General Executive Council, 1983–1984, and Annual Delegate Conference, 1984, p. 40, 454–68, 1984, 580–96; minutes of General Executive Council, 16 Apr. 1983, 11 June 1983; 'Dignity, rights and work' and 'Merger between the FWUI and the IWWU,' *Unity*, winter 1984.

4. FWUI, Report of Annual Delegate Conference, 1985, p. 564–80; Report of Annual Delegate Conference, 1986, p. 522–38; Report of General Executive Council, 1986–1987, p. 8–9; 'NATE/FWUI merger,' *Unity*, summer 1988.

5. FWUI, Report of Annual Delegate Conference, 1986, p. 602–3; Report of Reconvened Annual Delegate Conference, 1986, p. 702–24. Attracta Dorrigan was the staff member dismissed. Report of General Executive Council, 1986–1987, p. 32.

6. FWUI, Report of General Executive Council, 1986–1987, and Annual Delegate Conference, 1987 p. 9, 34–40, 428–41, 570–86, 586–99. Previous figures were 1985, 91%; 1984, 82%; 1983, 91%; 1982, 93%.

7. FWUI, Report of General Executive Council, 1987–1988, and Annual Delegate Conference, 1988, p. 6–7, 47, 530–39; Report of General Executive Council, 1988–1989, p. 39–41, 219–38. 'Financial services' and 'Union re-organisation,' *Unity*, Summer 1988.

8. FWUI, minutes of General Executive Council, 27 Feb. 1980, 17 Dec. 1980; 21 Jan. 1981, 18 Feb. 1981, 22 July 1981.

9. FWUI, Report of General Executive Council, 1987–1988, and Annual Delegate Conference, 1988, p. 11, 415–23; Report of General Executive Council, 1988–1989, p. 10–13; 'Talks on PNR concluded,' *Unity*, n.d., and *Liberty News*, autumn 1987; '1913 joint commemorative concert,' *Unity*, summer 1988.

10. FWUI, Report of General Executive Council, 1988–1989, p. 14–15, 381–8; Report of Special Delegate Conference, 1989. The motion was moved by Pat Bolger and Peter Masterson. Most speakers who queried matters were from No. 15 Branch, but the Aer Lingus Clerical Branch was one of the few to have a mandate to vote against. Jim Monaghan (No. 19 Branch), although mandated to vote in favour, expressed personal reservations harking back to the Ferenka dispute (and erroneously citing the ATGWU rather than MPGWU as the 'other union' on that occasion). Final Report of General Executive Council, May-Dec. 1989, p. 5–6; 'SIPTU: The union of the future,' *Unity*, special issue, spring 1989.

11. FWUI, Report of Annual Delegate Conference, 1982, p. 486–90. Garry polled 216, Geraghty 90 and O'Malley 31. Report of General Executive Council, 1982–1983, p. 38–9; minutes of General Executive Council, 15 Jan. 1983, 7 May 1983. McCarthy retired on 31 May 1988, Wynter on 31 October 1988 and Keating in April 1989. See Devine, *Understanding Social Justice.*

12. FWUI, Report of Annual Delegate Conference, 1981, p. 333–41; minutes of General Executive Council, 6 and 27 Feb. 1979. John Caden, John McAdam and Tom Redmond did their best to gain assistance for the TUWF. Minutes of General Executive Council, 19 Nov. 1980, 20 May 1981, 6 Nov. 1982.

13. FWUI, Report of Annual Delegate Conference, 1981, p. 346–57. For the 'Report on Women's Participation within the FWUI' see p. 473–9. Minutes of General Executive Council, 20 May 1981. Hayes was elected in 1974–8 and 1979–80.

14. FWUI, Report of General Executive Council, 1982–1983, p. 328–59 ('Status of Women'); Report of General Executive Council, 1983–1984, p. 366–413; minutes of General Executive Council, 24 July 1982; FWUI Submission to Dáil Committee on Women's Affairs, Report of General Executive Council, 1983–1984, p. 426–9. See also ICTU, 'Submission to the Oireachtas Joint Committee on Marriage Breakdown,' which the FWUI supported, p. 430–37.

15. FWUI, Report of Annual Delegate Conference, Malahide, 19–20 May 1984, p. 561–6, 622–34; Report of General Executive Council, 1984–1985, and Annual Delegate Conference, 1985, p. 400–424, 438–43, 621–35. The speakers were Maureen Bray (No. 18 Branch), Clare Bulman (Women Workers), Jane Foreman (No. 19 Branch), Kay Garvey (No. 12 Branch), Kay Geraghty (No. 3 Branch), Máire Higgins (No. 17 Branch), Jacqueline Johnson (No. 19 Branch), Kate Kirwan (No. 17 Branch), Caroline McCamley (No. 15 Branch), Ann O'Brien (No. 2 Branch), Maura

O'Donovan (No. 19 Branch) and Jo Walsh (No. 12 Branch). Seán Atkins (No. 12 Branch), Michael D. Higgins and Tom Murphy also spoke. Report of General Executive Council, 1985–1986, and Annual Delegate Conference, 1986, p. 408–32, 626–46. 'Status of women,' *Unity*, winter 1984.

16. FWUI, Report of General Executive Council, 1985–1986, p. 12; Report of General Executive Council, 1987–1988, p. 350–94. The speakers were Seán Ruth, 'Men and Equality'; Catherine McGuinness, 'Women and Politics' and Ruth Tansey, 'Women and the European Dimension.' Report of General Executive Council, 1988–1989, p. 9–10; 'Equal pay win in Europe,' *Unity*, summer 1988. See Francis Devine, 'Mai Clifford,' *Liberty News*, spring 1986; ITGWU, Annual Report, 1986, p. viii.

17. FWUI, Report of General Executive Council, 1988–1989, p. 8–9, 272–82; minutes of General Executive Council, 1988–1989, p. 370–.

18. FWUI, Report of Annual Delegate Conference, 1984, p. 481–90; minutes of General Executive Council, 7 Mar. 1982, 15 May 1982. This bust is now in the Irish Labour History Society Museum. It cost £2,500 plus £750 VAT. Minutes of General Executive Council, 11 June 1983. Whilst this claim may be true, certainly in the modern era, Young Jim confided that the WUI regularly had to go heavily into overdraft and debt in the 1950s in order to do so. Correspondence with Barry Desmond, 25 Apr. 2008.

19. FWUI, Report of Annual Delegate Conference, Dublin, 20–21 June 1981, p. 397–8; Report of General Executive Council, 1981–1982, p. 292–4; Report of General Executive Council, 1988–1989, p. 368–70; minutes of General Executive Council, 16 Jan. 1980, 10 Oct. 1091, 7 Nov. 1981 (to which the Inter-Union Relations Agreement is attached).

20. FWUI, Report of Annual Delegate Conference, 1980, p. 270–80; Report of Annual Delegate Conference, 1981, p. 379–95; minutes of General Executive Council, 20 Sep. 1980, 29 Oct. 1980. Those against were P. Daly, John McAdam, Jim Quinn and Tom Redmond.

21. FWUI, Report of General Executive Council, 1981–1982, p. 7–8, 44–51; Report of General Executive Council, 1982–1983, p. 49–58, 79; minutes of General Executive Council, 28 Nov. 1982, 17 Dec. 1981, 23 Jan. 1982.

22. FWUI, Report of General Executive Council, 1987–1988, p. 7–10; Report of General Executive Council, 1988–1989, p. 5–8; minutes of General Executive Council, 28 Aug. 1982, 25 Sep. 1982, 16 Oct. 1982. 'Talks on PNR concluded,' *Unity*, n.d., and *Liberty News*, autumn 1987.

23. FWUI, Report of General Executive Council, 1981–1982, p. 81–3; Report of General Executive Council, 1982–1983, and Annual Delegate Conference, 1983, p. 79–80, 474; minutes of General Executive Council, 22 Jan. 1983, 5 Mar. 1983. The first ballot on this issue had been held in 1981. Minutes of General Executive Council, 7 Nov. 1981. The vote was 170 to 35. An unfortunate by-product was the Branch's need to expel some members for strike-breaking. Minutes of General Executive Council, 16 Apr. 1983, 2 July 1983. Report of General Executive Council, 1984–1985, p. 177–8; minutes of General Executive Council, 19 May 1982. The FWUI ballot was 220 in favour to 28, representing about 80% of the membership. The ITGWU poll was 479 to 78. FWUI, minutes of General Executive Council, 17 Dec. 1984.

24. FWUI, Report of General Executive Council, 1986–1987, p. 5–8; Report of General Executive Council, 1986–1987, and Annual Delegate Conference, 1987, p. 149–50,

161–7, 471; Report of Annual Delegate Conference, 1988, p. 512–13; 'Around the Branches,' *Unity*, summer 1985.

25. FWUI, Report of General Executive Council, 1981–1982, p. 83–5, 170–71; Report of General Executive Council, 1982–1983, p. 80–84; Report of General Executive Council, 1983–1984, and Annual Delegate Conference, 1984, p. 81–2, 241, 555–6; Report of General Executive Council, 1984–1985, p. 197; Report of General Executive Council, 1985–1986, p. 37, 89, 104–5; Report of General Executive Council, 1988–1989, p. 82; minutes of General Executive Council, 29 Apr. 1982, 15 and 19 May 1982; minutes of General Executive Council, 12 Feb. 1983, 5 and 26 Mar. 1983, 17 Sep. 1983, 8 Oct. 1983, 5, 15 and 26 Nov. 1983; Peter Keating, 'Leinster Paper Mills,' *Unity*, summer 1988.

26. FWUI, Report of General Executive Council, 1984–1985, p. 91–2; Report of Annual Delegate Conference, Salthill, 1986, p. 612–13; Report of General Executive Council, 1986–1987, p. 96; Report of General Executive Council, 1987–1988, p. 109–; minutes of General Executive Council, 10 Sep. 1981, 10 Oct. 1981. Membership was 'between 700 and 800' and the vote was 306 to 123; Minutes of General Executive Council, Jan. 1982, p. 389–165. Ruairí Quinn, in *Straight Left: A Journey in Politics* (Dublin: Hodder Headline, 2005), gives the dispute no mention.

27. FWUI, Report of General Executive Council, 1984–1985, p. 159–62; 'Smokescreen lifts after Gas Company settlement,' *Unity*, winter 1984.

28. FWUI, Report of General Executive Council, 1984–1985, and Annual Delegate Conference, 1985, p. 175–7, 185–96, 474–5, 594–601; Report of General Executive Council, 1985–1986, and Annual Delegate Conference, 1986, p. 481; Report of General Executive Council, 1986–1987, p. 187–8; Report of General Executive Council, 1987–1988, p. 5–6, 193–6, 1988–1989, p. 201; 'Irish Shipping: The fight goes on' and 'Mitchell cop-out on Irish Shipping workers,' *Unity*, winter 1984; 'The continuing scandal of Irish Shipping,' *Unity*, spring 1986; 'B&I Line,' *Unity*, summer 1988.

29. FWUI, Report of General Executive Council, 1985–1986, p. 36–44, 128; Report of 1986–1987 and Annual Delegate Conference, 1987, p. 118, 568–9; Report of General Executive Council, 1988–1989, p. 112.

30. FWUI, Report of General Executive Council, 1987–1988, and Annual Delegate Conference, 1988, p. 8–9, 111–14, 523–4; 'Branch reports,' *Unity*, summer 1988; FWUI, Report of General Executive Council, 1988–1989, p. 89–99. Three members of the FBU—Aubrey Crawford (Derry), Robert Clarke and Jim Hughes (Belfast)—led tremendous solidarity in Northern Ireland.

31. FWUI, Report of General Executive Council, 1987–1988, and Annual Delegate Conference, 1988, p. 189–91, 521–22, 553–62; Report of General Executive Council, 1988–1989, p. 8; minutes of General Executive Council, 16 and 30 Apr. 1980, 7 and 28 May 1980, 4 June 1980, 9 July 1980, 29 Oct. 1980, 7 Nov. 1981, 17 Dec. 1981, 23 Jan. 1982. The result was 254 to 114 out of 600 entitled to vote. 'RTÉ management to blame for unnecessary strike,' *Union News*, 9 July 1982.

32. FWUI, Report of Annual Delegate Conference, Salthill, 23–25 May 1986, p. 552–62.

33. FWUI, Report of Annual Delegate Conference, 1980, p. 313–16; Report of Annual Delegate Conference, 1983, p. 490; Report of Annual Delegate Conference, 1987, p. 473–4; 'FWUI amends labour law,' *Unity*, summer 1988.

34. FWUI, Report of Annual Delegate Conference, 1980, p. 232–, 337–80; Report of General Executive Council, 1980–1981, p. 16–21; 'Economic and social planning,' Report of General Executive Council, 1980–1981, p. 238–43.

35. FWUI, Report of Annual Delegate Conference, 1981, p. 304–12, 328–33, 429–36; Report of Annual Delegate Conference, 1982, p. 359–68, 373–90; Report of General Executive Council, 1984–1985, p. 48–9; Report of Annual Delegate Conference, 1985, p. 9, 502–8; 'Unreality,' *Unity*, winter 1984.

36. FWUI, Report of Annual Delegate Conference, 1986, p. 517–20, 574–626; Report of General Executive Council, 1986–1987, and Annual Delegate Conference, 1987, p. 8, 52–, 538–53, 600–618; Report of Annual Delegate Conference, 1988, p. 458–61, 497–507. The quotation is from ICTU, *Confronting the Jobs Crisis*, published in September 1984, eighteen months before the formation of the Progressive Democrats.

37. FWUI, Report of General Executive Council, 1979–1980, and Annual Delegate Conference, 1980, p. 158–9, 244–52; Report of Annual Delegate Conference, 1981, p. 312–16; minutes of General Executive Council, 19 Mar. 1980. The views are those of John Caden and Tom Geraghty.

38. FWUI, Report of General Executive Council, 1981–1982, and Annual Delegate Conference, 1982, p. 289–91, 338–51; Report of General Executive Council, 1982–1983, and Annual Delegate Conference, 1983, p. 9, 410–16, 489–508; Report of Annual Delegate Conference, 1985, p. 9, 485–8; minutes of General Executive Council, 21 May 1981, where they asserted 'it was essential [that] we ensure that this motion be defeated.' Minutes of General Executive Council, 23 Apr. 1982, 15 and 19 May 1982, 22 Jan. 1983, 11 June 1983, 7 May 1983.

39. FWUI, Report of Annual Delegate Conference, 1986, p. 9, 494–501; Report of Annual Delegate Conference, 1987, p. 471–96.

40. FWUI, Report of Annual Delegate Conference, 1980, p. 383–95; Report of Annual Delegate Conference, 1981, p. 316–28, 452–65; Report of Annual Delegate Conference, 1983, p. 416–30; Report of Annual Delegate Conference, 1984, p. 509–31; Report of Annual Delegate Conference, 1986, p. 500–506; Report of Annual Delegate Conference, 1987, p. 471–97, 515–28, 533–8. See 'Economic and Social Planning,' Report of General Executive Council, 1980–1981, p. 238–43.

41. FWUI, Report of Annual Delegate Conference, 1980, p. 322–5, 468–9; Report of Annual Delegate Conference, 1983, p. 427–9; Report of General Executive Council, 1983–1984, and Annual Delegate Conference, 1984, p. 9, 496–7; Report of General Executive Council, 1985–1986, p. 29–30; Report of General Executive Council, 1986–1987, p. 27; minutes of General Executive Council, 6 Nov. 1982, 17 Sep. 1983; 'Facilities for the disabled,' *Unity*, summer 1987. See Peter Moore, *Rebel on Wheels* (Dublin: Poolbeg, 1990).

42. FWUI, Report of Annual Delegate Conference, 1980, p. 346–8, 395–8; Report of General Executive Council, 1980–1981, p. 278–94; Report of Annual Delegate Conference, 1983, p. 433–41. 428 members attended briefing days. Report of General Executive Council, 1985–1985, p. 149–52; Report of Annual Delegate Conference, 1988, p. 515–18.

43. FWUI, Report of Annual Delegate Conference, 1980, p. 414–19; Report of Annual Delegate Conference, 1981, p. 370–79; Report of General Executive Council, 1983–1984, p. 41–2; Report of Annual Delegate Conference, 1985, p. 533–7; minutes of

General Executive Council, 8 Apr. 1981; 'Labour history survey,' *Unity,* spring 1986; Ward-Perkins, *Select Guide to Trade Union Records in Dublin.*

44. FWUI, Report of Annual Delegate Conference, 1981, p. 341–3; Report of Annual Delegate Conference, 1982, p. 390–96; Report of Annual Delegate Conference, 1985, p. 473; Report of Annual Delegate Conference, 1986, p. 540–50; Report of General Executive Council, 1988–1989, p. 55–6.

45. FWUI, Report of General Executive Council, 1981–1982, p. 30–31; Report of General Executive Council, 1985–1986, p. 28–30; Report of General Executive Council, 1986–1987, p. 27–8; Report of General Executive Council, 1987–1988, p. 38–9; minutes of General Executive Council, 16 Apr. 1983, 5 Nov. 1983; 'Larkin Hall officially opened,' *Union News,* Nov.–Dec. 1983; 'Kilkenny office,' *Unity,* spring 1986.

46. FWUI, Report of Annual Delegate Conference, 1985, p. 513–24; Report of General Executive Council, 1985–1986, p. 31–3; Report of General Executive Council, 1986–1987, and Annual Delegate Conference, 1987, p. 10, 29–31, 555–62; Report of General Executive Council, 1987–1988, p. 40–43. The co-ops were Winstanley Footwear, Aonad Computer Services, Athy Foundry, Larkin Co-op Café, Organic Food Growing, Cotech Building Services, Childsplay Creche, and Ballymun East-Side Clothing. Report of General Executive Council, 1988–1989, p. 36–8. Brian Bórú Café, Clogs Music Venue and Bar, Galway, Cló Mná Print Finishing and Bread and Roses Restaurant and Coffee Shop were new. 'A new future for Winstanley,' *Unity,* spring 1986; 'WUT: Co-ops on the move,' *Unity,* summer 1988.

47. FWUI, Report of Annual Delegate Conference, 1981, p. 298–9; Report of Annual Delegate Conference, 1983, p. 398–9, 525–8; Report of Annual Delegate Conference, 1984, p. 599, 612–14, moved by Caroline McCamley and Tom Redmond. The FWUI gave £1,000 to the South African Congress of Trade Unions. Minutes of General Executive Council, 1 Oct. 1980, proposed by Tom Geraghty and Paul Boushell; minutes of General Executive Council, 19 Mar. 1980, 16 Apr. 1980. The money was actually given to the Iron and Steel Trades Confederation. Minutes of General Executive Council, 26 Jan. 1981, 10 Oct. 1981, 26 Mar. 1983; Tom Murphy, 'British miners' strike,' and Paul Clarke, 'Holiday for miners' children in Monaghan,' *Unity,* winter 1984. A Delegation from Dublin Trades Council, consisting of Tom Murphy (Deputy General Secretary), Matt Merrigan Junior and Paddy Trehy (Branch Secretaries), and Ben Kearney (DCTU) and Francis Devine (ITGWU) accompanied a container-load of food to Gorseinnon, near Swansea.

48. FWUI, Report of Annual Delegate Conference, 1980, p. 282–8, 297–9; minutes of General Executive Council, 23 Jan. 1981. The beneficiaries were Cluskey, £900; Higgins, £700; Quinn and O'Halloran, £600; Taylor and Bermingham, £500; and Desmond, £400. Minutes of General Executive Council, 18 Mar. 1981, 17 June 1981. The candidates were: Dublin South-Central: Frank Cluskey, Michael Collins and Séamus Ashe; Dublin North-West: Brendan Halligan and Paddy Dunn; Dublin North-Central: Mick O'Halloran; Dublin South-West: Mervyn Taylor; Dublin South-East: Ruairí Quinn; Dublin North-West: Joe Holohan; Kildare: Joe Bermingham and Emmet Stagg; Dún Laoghaire: Frank Smyth; Meath: James Tully and Frank McLoughlin; Cork South-Central: Eileen Flynn; Galway West: Michael D. Higgins. Minutes of General Executive Council, 6 Mar. 1982.

49. FWUI, Report of Annual Delegate Conference, 1982, p. 411–25, 440–48; minutes of

General Executive Council, 10 Sep. 1981, 6 Mar. 1982, 15 and 22 Nov. 1983.

50. FWUI, Report of Annual Delegate Conference, 1983, p. 443–69, 568–71; Report of General Executive Council, 1983–1984, and Annual Delegate Conference, 1984, p. 365, 488–9; minutes of General Executive Council, 23 Jan. 1983, 15 and 22 Nov. 1983, 17 Dec. 1983. The beneficiaries were Cluskey, £900; Higgins, £700; Quinn and O'Halloran, £600; Taylor and Bermingham, £500; and Desmond, £400. Minutes of General Executive Council, 18 Mar. 1981 and 17 June 1981. The candidates were: Dublin South-Central: Frank Cluskey, Michael Collins and Séamus Ashe; Dublin North-West: Brendan Halligan and Paddy Dunne; Dublin North-Central: Mick O'Halloran; Dublin South-West: Mervyn Taylor; Dublin South-East: Ruairí Quinn; Dublin North-West: Joe Holohan; Kildare: Joe Bermingham and Emmet Stagg; Dún Laoghaire: Frank Smyth; Meath: James Tully and Frank McLoughlin; Cork South-Central: Eileen Flynn; Galway West: Michael D. Higgins. Minutes of General Executive Council, 14 May 1983. Some suggest that FWUI leaders thought that Cluskey's resignation would cause the collapse of the Government, Spring would be ousted and Cluskey would resume the Party leadership. They underestimated Spring.

51. FWUI, Report of General Executive Council, 1984–1985, and Annual Delegate Conference, 1985, p. 49, 534–62; minutes of General Executive Council, 21 Jan. 1984.

52. FWUI, Report of General Executive Council, 1985–1986, p. 52–3; Report of Annual Delegate Conference, 1987, p. 496–508; Report of General Executive Council, 1987–1988, and Annual Delegate Conference, 1988, p. 12, 425, 552, 629–37. Flor O'Mahony, 'The Labour Party Trade Union Group,' *Unity*, summer 1988.

53. FWUI, Report of Annual Delegate Conference, 1980, p. 288–97; minutes of General Executive Council, 19 and 26 Nov. 1980.

54. FWUI, Report of Annual Delegate Conference, Malahide, 28–29, 1988, p. 422–4; 576–82.

Part 5 (p. 797–801)

1. For a discussion of the 'Celtic Tiger' see Kieran Allen, *The Celtic Tiger?: The Myth of Social Partnership* (Manchester: Manchester University Press, 2000) and *The Corporate Takeover of Ireland* (Dublin: Irish Academic Press, 2007), Paul Sweeney, *The Celtic Tiger: Ireland's Economic Miracle Explained* (Dublin: Oak Tree Press, 1998) and *Ireland's Economic Success: Reasons and Lessons* (Dublin: New Island Books, 2008) and Tim Hastings, Brian Sheehan and Pádraig Yeates, *Saving the Future: How Social Partnership Shaped Ireland's Economic Success* (Dublin: Blackhall Publishing, 2007).

2. The European Foundation for the Improvement of Living and Working Conditions (at www.eurofound.europe.eu/eiro/2005/10/feature/ie0510201f.htm) suggests figures ranging from 23% to 10–15%.

Chapter 35 (p. 802–37)

1. SIPTU, Report of National Executive Council, 1990, p. 10–11; Report of National Executive Council, 1992, p. 108–11; Report of National Executive Council, 1991, p. 106–7; *Newsline*, May 1990. Other stalwarts who passed on were Michael Collins, once Lord Mayor of Dublin; Willie John Curran, a popular and tough Branch

Secretary in Midleton; Maura Doolan, WUI stalwart in Irish Hospitals Trust; Willie Flanagan, Mountmellick, much-loved Laois-Offaly ITGWU Secretary; Mary Kearns, WUI No. 2 Branch stalwart; Conor O'Brien, long-time secretary of ITGWU No. 3 Branch; Mattie O'Neill, tutor and previously a members of the National Executive Council of the ITGWU and Secretary of No. 4 Branch; and Jimmy Tully, Labour TD and Minister, former General Secretary of the Federation of Rural Workers, 1954–1973. 'Fired up with commitment' and 'Paddy McKenna bows out,' *Newsline*, July 1991. He had started in the post room in Feb. 1950. 'Painters and decorators say 'Yes' to SIPTU,' *Newsline*, autumn 1991. It should be noted that the INPDTU transferred assets of £337,306 to SIPTU: premises, £41,737; investments, £154,428; bank deposit, £74,407; and other assets (net), £66,734. SIPTU, Report of National Executive Council, 1992, p. 34; *Newsline*, winter 1992. Ken Cameron, General Secretary, FBU, and Tom Geraghty, SIPTU, were the inspiration for the event.

2. SIPTU, Report of National Executive Council, 1993–1994, p. 6, 10–13. Conferences were held in Jury's Hotel, Dublin (Region 1), Liberty Hall (Region 2), Waterford (Region 3), Cork (Region 4), NUI, Maynooth (Region 5), Ennis (Region 6), Letterkenny (Region 7) and Magee College, Derry (Region 8).

3. SIPTU, Report of National Executive Council, 1993–1994, p. 30–31; 'Writers' Union to join Cultural Division,' *Newsline*, Mar. 1993, May 1994. The result was: Somers, 37,022; Kane, 19,633; Walsh, 11,092; Croke, 9,113.

4. SIPTU, Report of National Executive Council, 1995, p. 3–6, 12. Discount schemes operated with Advance Tyre; the Association of Optometrists in Ireland; Bord na Móna; Bus Átha Cliath; Doyle Hotels; Energy Conservation Enterprises; First National Building Society; Flood, Maguire and Robertson; Jury's Hotels; Newbridge Silverware; Swan Car Hire; Tower Hotels; and VHI.

5. SIPTU, Report of National Executive Council, 1995, p. 9; Annual Report, 1997, p. 4–5, 68; 'Union contributions,' *Newsline*, Sep. 1996; 'Choosing a General President,' *Newsline*, Feb. 1997; 'Thanks, Eddie,' *Newsline*, May 1997; 'AGEMOU members say "yes" to unity with SIPTU,' *Newsline*, June 1997. Croke had been a candidate for General President but withdrew. Geraghty won on the first count, with 51,554: others were Norman Croke (Hotels, Restaurants and Catering), 3,829; Carolann Duggan, 21,074; Nóirín Greene (Waterford), 11,610; and George Hunter (Donegal), 14,810. 'Geraghty romps to victory,' *Newsline*, Sep. 1997.

6. SIPTU, Annual Report, 1997, p. 4–6; 1998, p. 4–7; 'McDonnell's victory is decisive,' *Newsline*, Feb. 1998; 'Union protection for security staff,' *Newsline*, July; 'Printers join up' and 'MPGWU on board,' *Newsline*, Nov. 1998; 'Organising SIPTU people,' *Newsline*, Sep. 1999. The vote was: McDonnell, 46,014; Brendan Hayes, 36,707; Carolann Duggan, 24,842. Kevin McMahon and Gerry Flanagan were Branch Secretary and President, respectively.

7. SIPTU, Report of National Executive Council, 1996, p. 3–4; SIPTU 96 Annual Report, p. 9–10; 'Renewing the union,' *Newsline*, Jan. 1995; 'Renewing the union,' *Newsline*, Dec. 1995.

8. SIPTU, Annual Report, 1997, p. 11–12; Annual Report, 1998, p. 11–12; 1999, p. 13; 'SIPTU 2000,' *Newsline*, Mar. 1996; 'Your union at work,' *Newsline*, Dec. In 1997 the following companies and organisations participated in the SIPTU bonus scheme: Abbey and Peacock Theatres; Advance Tyre; Association of Optometrists; Bus Átha Cliath;

Doyle Hotels; Energy Conservation Enterprises; First National Building Society; Flood, Maguire and Robertson; Jury's Hotels; Newbridge Silverware; OPW Visitor Centres; Swan Car Rental; Taxcheck; Tower Hotels; VHI.

9. SIPTU, Report of National Executive Council, 1990, p. 7–8; *Newsline*, Regional Executive Election Supplement, Aug. 1994.

10. SIPTU, Report of National Executive Council, 1990, p. 27–30; Report of National Executive Council, 1991, p. 38–47, 105; *Newsline*, Sep. 1998. Boushell was Branch Chairperson, 1975–85, and a member of the General Executive Council of the FWUI. He championed worker democracy and was elected as a worker-director. Report of National Executive Council, 1992, p. 26, 36–42.

11. SIPTU, Report of National Executive Council, 1990, p. 31–6, 1991, p. 48–55; 1992, p. 43–53; SIPTU 96 Annual Report, p. 18; 'Union campaign on hotel industry,' *Newsline*, winter 1991; Norman Croke, 'A tradition of service,' *Newsline*, June 1993, July–Aug. 1993; 'The rights stuff for hotel workers,' *Newsline*, July 1998.

12. SIPTU, Report of National Executive Council, 1990, p. 37–40; Report of National Executive Council, 1991, p. 56–61; Report of National Executive Council, 1992, 54–61; 'Part-time fire-fighters ballot on national strike,' *Newsline*, Aug. 1995; 'Organising is key to strong union,' *Newsline*, Dec. 1998. A rally was addressed by Mick Wall (Branch Secretary) and Mick Roche, with national speakers from SIPTU and the FBU.

13. SIPTU, Report of National Executive Council, 1990, p. 41–4; 1991, p. 62–7; 1992, 62–8; Annual Report, 1997, p. 38–9; 'Survival through co-operation,' *Newsline*, Winter 1992; 'Incomprehensible and appalling,' May 1997; 'Five-month-old strike at Killarney hotel settled,' Sep.; 'Apple job cuts leave sour taste,' Feb. 1999.

14. SIPTU, Report of National Executive Council, 1990, p. 45–9; Report of National Executive Council, 1992, p. 69–73; *Newsline*, May 1999.

15. SIPTU, Report of National Executive Council, 1990, p. 50–53; Report of National Executive Council, 1991, p. 72–3; Report of National Executive Council, 1992, p. 74–8; 'Shannon: The gateway to job opportunities in the west,' *Newsline*, winter 1991, winter 1992; 'SIPTU and development,' *Newsline*, Mar. 1995; 'Privatisation drive halted by picket line unity,' *Newsline*, Sep. 1996; 'Janet Hughes is new Rights Commissioner,' *Newsline*, Aug. 1997.

16. SIPTU, Report of National Executive Council, 1990, p. 54–6; Report of National Executive Council, 1992, p. 79–81; Report of National Executive Council, 1997, p. 39; 'Brady bows out,' *Newsline*, May 1998; 'McCarren's dispute,' *Newsline*, July 1988; 'Little Christmas cheer in Donegal,' *Newsline*, Dec. 1988.

17. SIPTU, Report of National Executive Council, 1990; p. 57–9; Report of National Executive Council, 1991, p. 83–4, 107; Report of National Executive Council, 1992, p. 82–4, 96–9. Bobby Dickey held the doors firm. Obituaries for Jim Brown, James Cameron and Mark Rodgers, Report of National Executive Council, 1992, p. 103–4. 'Peace,' *Newsline*, Dec. 1993; 'Building the peace,' *Newsline*, Nov. 1994.

18. SIPTU, Report of National Executive Council, 1995, p. 36; SIPTU 96 Annual Report, p. 35–6; 'Give peace a chance,' *Newsline*, Mar. 1996. Other venues were Carrickmacross (3,000), Cóbh (1,000), Derry (10,000), Fermoy (3,000), Gorey (2,000), Limerick (5,000), Sligo (7,000), Tralee (5,000), Waterford (8,000) and Wexford (3,000). The Lord Mayor of Cork was a SIPTU Official, Joe O'Callaghan.

Report of National Executive Council, 1997, p. 46, 49. The factories were City Factory, Courtauld's Lingerie, Desmond's, Fruit of the Loom, Graham Hunter Shirts and Ben Shermon.

19. SIPTU, Annual Report, 1998, p. 4, 52–3; Annual Report, 1999, p. 61; 'Ballotline,' *Newsline*, May 1998.

20. SIPTU, Report of National Executive Council, 1990, p. 69; Report of National Executive Council, 1991, p. 97–9; Report of National Executive Council, 1992, p. 97–8; 'Cervical cancer,' *Newsline*, May 1990; 'The equalisers,' *Newsline*, Nov. 1992; 'May's days,' *Newsline*, summer 1992. Nóirín Greene, born in Belfast in 1947, joined the ITGWU when a librarian in the *Irish Press* and became the second woman elected to the National Executive Council, 1982–87. A member of the Executive Council of the ICTU, 1985–88, she became Branch Assistant in Clare, 1987, Waterford, 1988, and Branch Secretary, Waterford, 1990. May O'Brien, *Clouds on My Window: A Dublin Memoir* (Dingle: Brandon, 2004).

21. SIPTU, Report of National Executive Council, 1991, p. 64–5; Report of National Executive Council, 1992, p. 15, 45; Report of National Executive Council, 1993–1994, p. 91–5; Report of National Executive Council, 1995, p. 18, 33–4; SIPTU 96 Annual Report, p. 30, 38; Report of National Executive Council, 1997, p. 44–5; Report of National Executive Council, 1998, p. 7, 47–8; Report of National Executive Council, 1999, p. 55–7; 'Just desserts,' *Newsline*, Sep. 1997; 'Harassers are not welcome,' *Newsline*, Nov. 1998; 'Remembering Hanna,' *Newsline*, Feb. 1998; 'A new equality force,' *Newsline*, May 1998; 'Bronwyn bids for big breakthrough,' *Newsline*, July 1998.

22. SIPTU, Annual Report, 1999, p. 57–8; 'Women on the verge of the 21st century,' *Newsline*, May 1999. Rosheen Callender was born in Karachi in 1948 but lived in her mother's home city, Dublin, from 1959. After graduating from the University of Dublin (Trinity College) she worked in Belfast, 1969–1973, before joining the ITGWU Research Department. She published texts on reading company accounts (1977) and equality law (1994), was a member of the Expert Working Group on Tax and Social Welfare that reported in 1996, and was Irish representative on the EU Commission's Network of Experts on the Implementation of Equality Directives. From January 1995 to June 1997 she took leave of absence to work as an adviser to the Minister for Social Welfare, Proinsias de Rossa. In August 1998 she became National Equality Secretary of SIPTU. She was a member of the Executive Council of the ICTU, of the National Action Plan Against Racism's Special Initiative on Migration and Interculturalism, the Pensions Board, the Foundation of Fiscal Studies and the Basic Income Working Group under 'Partnership 2000'.

23. 'Congress to celebrate Centenary in style,' *Newsline*, Feb. 1994.

24. SIPTU, Report of National Executive Council, 1990, p. 7–8. Craft workers received £43.70 on 1 Sep. 1991, 1 Sep. 1992 and 1 Apr. 1993; general operatives got £15. Report of National Executive Council, 1990, p. 20–21. 'The Programme continues,' *Newsline*, May 1990; 'Shaping our future,' Sep. 1990.

25. SIPTU, Report of National Executive Council, 1991, p. 10–13; Report of National Executive Council, 1992, p. 13–14, 16–18; 'The PESP,' *Newsline*, Special Supplement, Jan. 1991; 'PESP to continue,' *Newsline*, Feb. 1993. Concessions included payment by non-cash means; co-operation with change and new technology; new work practices and higher productivity; rationalisation and new job contents; multi-skilling;

co-operation with security searches; job evaluation; the introduction of contractors; and changed hours.

26. SIPTU, Report of National Executive Council, 1993–1994, p. 50–56; 'Bertie's progress,'
Newsline, winter 1991; 'No new deal unless 1% levy axed . . . and all the Dirty Dozen
too!' *Newsline,* May 1993; 'Progress reports,' *Newsline,* Sep. 1993; 'Life after PESP,'
Newsline, Oct.-Nov. 1993; 'PESP 2 talks on again,' *Newsline,* Jan. 1994; 'The
Programme in context,' *Newsline,* Feb. 1994.

27. SIPTU, Report of National Executive Council, 1995, p. 15–18; SIPTU 96 Annual
Report, p. 13–16; SIPTU 96 Annual Report, p. 33; Report of National Executive
Council, 1997, p. 13–26; 'Consensus objections,' *Newsline,* Dec. 1995; 'Hanging in the
balance,' *Newsline,* July 1996; 'Partnership 2000 ratified,' *Newsline,* Feb. 1997.

28. SIPTU Annual Report, 1998, p. 16–24; Annual Report, 1999, p. 17–32; Annual Report,
1999, p. 50–53; 'Looking to the future' and 'Yes to talks!' *Newsline,* Nov. 1999.

29. SIPTU, Report of National Executive Council, 1992, p. 23; Annual Report, 1997, p. 38–
9. The rates were: grade 1, 91%; grade 2, 88%; grade 3, 85%; grade 4, 80%. Report of
National Executive Council, 1993–1994, p. 59–65; 'RTÉ has become a political football,' *Newsline,* Sep. 1990.

30. SIPTU, Annual Report, 1997, p. 31–2, 38–9; Annual Report, 1998, p. 24–6, 33–4;
Annual Report, 1999, p. 33–6; 'Shaping the future,' *Newsline,* Oct. 1995; 'Partners in
progress,' *Newsline,* Sep. 1998. The project manager was Ron Kelly and the partici-
pating firms were: Allergan (Westport), Ezy Koter (Virginia), Flair International
(Bailieborough), Glen Electric (Newry), Hawksbay (Ardee), Jury's Hotel (Dublin),
Langan's (Dublin), Lund International (Athlone), Mohawk (Shannon), NEC
(Ballivor) and Smurfit Corrugated Cases (Cork).

31. SIPTU, Report of National Executive Council, 1993–1994, p. 56–8; Annual Report,
1997, p. 42; Annual Report, 1998, p. 46; Annual Report, 1999, p. 53; 'Enough really is
enough,' *Newsline,* May 1995; Audrey Healy, 'Move over, Florence!' *Newsline,* Feb.
1999. Noel Dowling was National Nursing Officer. 'Nurses set for strike ballot,'
Newsline, Sep. 1999.

32. SIPTU, Annual Report, 1996, p. 23; Annual Report, 1997, p. 34–5; Annual Report, 1998,
p. 37–40; Annual Report, 1999, p. 46–7; Report of National Executive Council, 1993–
1994, p. 64–5, 75–6 ('Labour legislation'); Report of National Executive Council, 1995,
p. 25–6; 'Courts lack appeal,' a report of the Conference Workshop, Nov. 1995. Success
was achieved, as the Harbour Police finally won the right to join a trade union; but
Donegal Parian China and Nena Models denied their workers this right. 'Savages:
Picketers threatened with iron bars and hammer,' *Newsline,* Mar. 1993; 'New Ross
pickets defy intimidation,' *Newsline,* May 1993; 'Supreme Court challenge,' *Newsline,*
Feb. 1995; 'Promises on industrial law broken,' *Newsline,* Aug. 1995; 'Labour Bill aims
to break recognition crux,' *Newsline,* Feb. 1998; 'Somers' vow,' *Newsline,* Nov. 1997.

33. SIPTU, Annual Report, 1998, p. 37–40; 'Hearts of lions' and 'Ryanair: Big profits, low
pay,' *Newsline,* Feb. 1998; 'Solidarity in action' and 'End of Round one,' *Newsline,*
Apr. 1998; 'Ryanair report backs union's claim of low pay,' *Newsline,* July 1998.

34. SIPTU, Report of National Executive Council, 1990, p. 14–16; Report of National
Executive Council, 1991, p. 25; Report of National Executive Council, 1993–1994, p.
68–9; 'Massive job cuts in Aer Lingus plan,' *Newsline,* June–July 1993; 'No change
without agreement,' *Newsline,* July-Aug. 1993.

35. SIPTU, Report of National Executive Council, 1990, p. 16–17; Report of National Executive Council, 1991, p. 16–20.

36. SIPTU, Annual Report, 1998, p. 32–3; Report of National Executive Council, 1991, p. 12–13, 96; Report of National Executive Council, 1992, p. 5–6; Report of National Executive Council, 1995, p. 13–23; SIPTU 96 Annual Report, p. 13–14; 1997, p. 16–; 'The jobs crisis: Employers fail to deliver', 'NEC urges Yes vote' and 'Maastricht: The SIPTU briefing,' Newsline, spring 1992; 'Buy Irish—buy jobs,' Newsline, winter 1992; 'Steeled for survival,' Newsline, Mar. 1994; 'Fighting back,' Newsline, Apr. 1994; 'Woman of steel,' Newsline, Sep. 1994 (a profile of Ann Egar); 'Back from the brink . . . again,' Newsline, Oct. 1994; 'Save our duty-free,' Newsline, Feb. 1998; 'The Amsterdam Treaty,' Newsline, May 1998; 'Celtic Tiger—jungle law,' Newsline, Sep. 1998.

37. SIPTU, Annual Report, 1998, p. 44–5; Report of National Executive Council, 1992, p. 7–8; Report of National Executive Council, 1993–1994, p. 81–5; 'The double standard,' Newsline, June–July 1993; 'The tax facts,' Newsline, July 1996; 'The "Dirty Dozen" and the taxation of social welfare benefits' and 'Now you C45 and now you don't!' Newsline, July 1994; 'Time to deliver,' Newsline, Jan. 1995; Ronald Kelly, 'Anger at welfare cuts,' Newsline, Nov. 1995; 'Far from a fair share,' Newsline, Feb. 1996; 'So far, so good,' Newsline, Feb. 1997; 'That's rich' and 'The rich get richer,' Newsline, Nov. 1997; 'Voluntary bodies, SIPTU checking up on Charlie,' Newsline, Nov. 1998; 'Charlie finally meets P2K tax commitments,' Newsline, Dec. 1998; 'Celtic Tiger roars,' Newsline, Feb. 1999; 'House prices still going through the roof,' Newsline, July 1999; 'Golden circle must be ended,' Newsline, Aug. 1999; 'D'unbelievable' and 'The poorest of the poor,' Newsline, Sep. 1999. The document was 'Affordable Accommodation'.

38. 'Campaign aims to eliminate low pay,' Newsline, Nov. 1997.

39. SIPTU, Report of National Executive Council, 1992, p. 68, 90, 99; 'The tragedy of Ballycotton,' Newsline, Sep. 1990. Michael Fanning survived the incident. Newsline, spring and July 1991. See Health and Safety at Work (Dublin: SIPTU, 1992). Other members of the Band were Raphy Doyle (guitar and vocals), Porky Murphy (fiddle) and Leo Rickard (uilleann pipes). They issued the CD and tape Step by Step, with a cover design by Robert Ballagh (Association of Artists in Ireland).

40. SIPTU, Report of National Executive Council, 1993–1994, p. 37, 57–8; Report of National Executive Council, 1995, p. 24. A three-day workshop was held in Cork in association with the pharmaceuticals and chemicals Section of IBEC and the Health and Safety Authority. SIPTU 96 Annual Report, p. 22. 'Violence in the workplace,' Newsline, Oct. 1994; '300 workplace deaths since 1990,' Newsline, Mar. 1995; 'Working to death,' Newsline, June 1995; 'Task force on violence' (a demand for protection for bus workers), Newsline, Dec. 1995; 'Fighting back together,' Newsline, Feb. 1996; 'Sites for sore eyes,' Newsline, Mar. 1996; 'Building on very sound foundations,' Newsline, July 1996; 'Life and death on the building site,' Newsline, Dec. 1997; 'Death trap!' Newsline, July 1998. Dónal O'Sullivan retired in March 1993. A seaman, he had worked in Australia, trained as a work study adviser and worked for the ICTU before being appointed Head of Management Services at the School of Management Studies, Rathmines, Dublin. He joined the ITGWU Development Services Division in 1971 as Head of Industrial Engineering. He was a former Treasurer of the Labour Party. Newsline, May 1993.

41. SIPTU, Annual Report, 1997, p. 33–4; Annual Report, 1998, p. 34–7; Annual Report, 1999, p. 43–5; 'Dedicated to safety,' *Newsline,* July 1998; 'Deadly fibres still a major hazard,' *Newsline,* May 1999; 'Building workers seek action on site safety,' *Newsline,* Sep. 1999. The members of the Committee were Cecily Canning and Sylvester Cronin (SIPTU College), Tom Kelly (Navan), Michael O'Toole (Aviation), Chris Rowland (Dublin Health Services) and Dónal Tobin (Tralee).

42. SIPTU, Report of National Executive Council, 1995, p. 38; SIPTU 96 Annual Report, p. 38; Report of National Executive Council, 1998, p. 55; Report of National Executive Council, 1999, p. 63; 'The vicious circle,' *Newsline,* Aug. 1995; 'Partners against drug abuse,' *Newsline,* Mar. 1996. The Dublin Region reaffirmed this policy in 2007 and held a seminar on drug and alcohol abuse in the work-place on 11 April 2008.

43. SIPTU, Report of National Executive Council, 1990, p. 63–4; Report of National Executive Council, 1991, p. 93–4; Report of National Executive Council, 1992, p. 93–6; 'Tom McCarthy retires,' *Newsline,* July 1990; 'The right to read,' *Newsline,* Sep. 1990. McCarthy had joined the union in 1971, having been senior psychologist and adviser to the City of Dublin Vocational Education Committee. He had been a central behind-the-scenes figure in the talks leading to the creation of SIPTU. The speakers included Eric Hobsbawm, Claud Cockburn and Dick Spring.

44. SIPTU, Report of National Executive Council, 1993–1994, p. 30–31, 80. The Convention was held in Dublin Castle, 11–23 Oct. 1993. For 1993 scholarship awards see p. 46–7. Report of National Executive Council, 1995, p. 29; 'National Education seminar,' *Newsline,* Dec. 1995.

45. SIPTU, Report of National Executive Council, 1995, p. 10; SIPTU 96 Annual Report, p. 10–11; Report of National Executive Council, 1997, p. 8, 12–13; Report of National Executive Council, 1998, p. 12–13; Report of National Executive Council, 1999, p. 12–14; 'The graduates,' *Newsline,* Nov. 1997; 'SIPTU College,' *Newsline,* Apr. 1998. The teams were in Jury's Hotel (Dublin), Smurfit Corrugated Cases (Cork), Lund (Athlone), NEC (Ballivor), Allergan (Westport), Mohawk (Shannon), Ezy Koter (Virginia), Flair International (Bailieborough) and Glen Electric (Newry).

46. SIPTU, Report of National Executive Council, 1992, p. 87–92; Report of National Executive Council, 1993–1994, p. 39, 45; Report of National Executive Council, 1997, p. 9.

47. SIPTU, Report of National Executive Council, 1990, p. 38, 85–6, 91; Report of National Executive Council, 1992, p. 86; Report of National Executive Council, 1993–1994, p. 88–90. Other events sponsored by SIPTU were the *Sea Sanctuary* Sculpture Garden Project at St James's Hospital, Dublin; Calypso, a theatre company dealing with development and human rights issues; a Woman's Place Project; a union museum in Connolly Hall, Cork; and the James Larkin Memorial Lecture. 'Striking a chord: RTÉ musicians fight back in concert,' *Newsline,* spring 1991; 'May Day celebrated with music and song,' *Newsline,* May 1993; Francis Devine, '1913: The story of the lock out,' *Newsline,* Sep. 1993; 'Donegal marks O'Donnell Centenary,' *Newsline,* Dec. 1993; *Newsline,* Jan. 1994.

48. SIPTU 96 Annual Report, p. 34; Annual Report, 1997, p. 48. Those performing were Paul Bennett, Emmet Bergin, Brendan Cauldwell, Francis Devine, Des Geraghty, Nóirín Greene, Marie Jones, Jimmy Kelly, Ian McElhinney, Mary Maher, Brenda

Ní Ríordáin, Sam Nolan, Kevin O'Connor, Jer O'Leary, Manus O'Riordan, Noel Pocock, Eileen Webster and Macdara Woods; Annual Report, 1998, p. 51; 'Bread and roses' and 'Honouring Connolly,' *Newsline*, Mar. 1996; 'Larkin 50,' *Newsline*, Feb. 1997; 'Honouring Big Jim,' *Newsline*, Sep. 1997; 'Author of "Red Flag" commemorated in Meath village,' *Newsline*, May 1998. See Devine, *Acting for the Actors*.

49. SIPTU, Report of National Executive Council, 1991, p. 103–4; Report of National Executive Council, 1992, p. 105–7; Report of National Executive Council, 1993–1994, p. 41–4; Executive Review, 1995–1996, p. 9; SIPTU 96 Annual Report, p. 31; Report of National Executive Council, 1997, p. 45–6; Report of National Executive Council, 1998, p. 48–9; 'ITUT: Practical help for the unemployed' and 'ICTU launches Bill of Rights for Disabled,' *Newsline*, July 1990; 'Solidarity becomes reality: ITUT launched,' *Newsline*, Dec. 1990'; 'Area-based strategies,' *Newsline*, spring 1992; 'In jobs we Trust,' *Newsline*, Jan. 1995; 'An injury to one is the concern of all: The politics of disability,' *Newsline*, May 1998; 'Power to the people . . . with disabilities,' *Newsline*, Nov. 1998. Ross Connolly had been Office Administrator. He had joined the Federation of Rural Workers in 1948, serving as Organiser. After working in Irish Hospitals Trust he joined the Bray Branch of the WUI and served two lengthy terms on the General Executive Council. He was Secretary of Bray Trades Council, 1952–1968.

50. SIPTU 96 Annual Report, p. 5, 20–21; Annual Report, 1997, p. 15, 32–3; Annual Report, 1998, p. 15; Annual Report, 1999, p. 16; '"Grey Panthers" get organised,' *Newsline*, Sep. 1996; 'In jobs we Trust,' *Newsline*, June 1997; 'Solidarity forever!' *Newsline*, May 1998; 'Redundancy: The union fights back,' *Newsline*, July 1999.

51. SIPTU, Report of National Executive Council, 1993–1994, p. 32; SIPTU 96 Annual Report, p. 7; Report of National Executive Council, 1999, p. 9; 'New offices opened in Limerick,' *Newsline*, Dec. 1990; 'Longford's proud history recalled,' *Newsline*, Apr. 1994; 'Moving house: End of an era in Parnell Square,' *Newsline*, Feb. 1995; '"Gentleman Fintan" honoured in Limerick,' *Newsline*, May 1995.

52. 'Union staff salaries,' *Newsline*, Nov. 1995; 'Partnership forum in SIPTU,' *Newsline*, July 1999. The scale, with its public-sector equivalents published alongside, ran from £10,879 to £15,718 for porters, £10,049 to £18,688 for clerical and administrative staff, £19,423 to £23,493 for Branch Assistants, £27,764 to £31,737 for Branch Secretaries, £34,422 to £58,016 for regional secretaries and ANEOS and £73,891 for General Officers.

53. *Newsline*, Mar. 1996, May 1997; 'To Belarus with love,' *Newsline*, Nov. 1998; 'McDonnell, Geraghty take the pledge,' *Newsline*, Nov. 1998; 'Holidays: Key to kids' health for Sheila,' *Newsline*, Feb. 1999; 'Kevin's drive to aid Kosovo war victims,' *Newsline*, May 1999; 'Sheila's children,' *Newsline*, July 1999.

54. SIPTU, Report of National Executive Council, 1990, p. 9; Report of National Executive Council, 1992, 9–12; 'Politics is too important to be left to politicians,' *Newsline*, Sep. 1990; 'President Robinson,' *Newsline*, Nov. 1990, autumn 1992. She had been a member since 1978.

55. SIPTU, Report of National Executive Council, 1993–1994, p. 86–7; Report of National Executive Council, 1995, p. 7; Annual Report, 1997, p. 10; Annual Report, 1999, p. 12; 'Budget of mixed blessings' and 'Framework document,' *Newsline*, Feb. 1995; 'Axe the tax,' *Newsline*, May 1995; 'Removing the re-marriage ban,' *Newsline*, Nov. 1995; 'What a let down,' *Newsline*, Feb. 1996; 'So far, so good,' *Newsline*, Feb. 1997; 'Uniting the left,' *Newsline*, July 1998. £80,000 to Labour Party central funds; £1,750 to

Michael Bell (Louth), Niamh Bhreatnach (Dún Laoghaire), Michael Ferris (Tipperary South), Eithne FitzGerald (Dublin South), Marian Gaffney (Longford-Roscommon), Pat Gallagher (Laois-Offaly), Michael D. Higgins (Galway West), Breda Moynihan Cronin (Kerry South), Séamus Pattison (Carlow-Kilkenny), Ruairí Quinn (Dublin South-East), Dick Spring (Kerry North), Pat Upton (Dublin South Central); and £1,500 to Declan Bree (Sligo-Leitrim), Brian Fitzgerald (Meath), Brendan Howlin (Wexford), Seán Maloney (Donegal North-East and Seanad), John Mulvihill (Cork East), Sheila O'Sullivan (Cork North-Central), Willie Penrose (Westmeath) and Emmet Stagg (Kildare North).

Chapter 36 (p. 838–79)

1. SIPTU, Annual Report, 2000, p. 4–6, 12, 42; Annual Report, 2001, p. 4–7, 8; Annual Report, 2002, p. 4–5; 'Four join vote race,' Newsline, Jan. 2000; 'Jack high' and 'From a Jack to a king,' Newsline, May 2000; 'No satisfaction for taxi drivers,' Liberty, Jan. 2004. O'Connor polled 54,444, Carolann Duggan 16,278, Jack Nash 12,758 and Nuala Keher 6,059.

2. SIPTU, Annual Report, 2003, p. 4; 'SIPTU, TEEU agree to closer co-operation,' Liberty, Jan. 2002; 'O'Flynn victor in close contest,' Liberty, Dec. 2002; 'Solidarity' and 'Overture to organising,' Liberty, Mar. 2003. O'Flynn polled 55,327, Dowling 48,036 and Derwin 7,512. After Derwin's elimination O'Flynn was elected by 57,592 to 52,293.

3. SIPTU, Annual Report, 2004, p. 4–5, 42; Annual Report, 2005, p. 4–8, 44; 'Two bid for Vice President's post,' Liberty, Jan. 2004; 'Election victory for Hayes' and 'Brendan's voyage to top union post,' Liberty, Mar. 2004; 'John Fay retires,' Liberty, Feb. 2005; 'Two largest unions to sign co-operation pact,' Liberty, Mar. 2005; 'SIPTU and IM Proceedings of Annual Conference in co-operation pact,' Liberty, Dec. 2007.

4. 'Organising for progress: Building a stronger union,' Liberty, Dec. 2003; 'Rising to the challenge,' Liberty, Mar. 2005.

5. SIPTU, Annual Report, 2006, p. 3–7; 'Organise, organise, organise,' Liberty, Sep. 2003; 'Home helps take a stand,' Liberty, Apr. 2004; 'Slave wage scandal,' Liberty, July 2006. The leaflets were 'SIPTU and You,' 'Here's What to Expect from Management,' 'SIPTU for Schools,' 'Code of Practice on Grievance and Discipline,' 'Code of Practice on Facilities for Employee Representatives' and 'Bullying and Harassment in the Workplace'.

6. The members of the Commission were Brian Byrd, Noel Clune, David Johnston, Jack Kelly, Jack McGinley and Mary O'Rourke (National Executive Council), Tom Costello, Jim Lyng, Bill McCamley and Maurice O'Donoghue (Resident Executive Committee), Joe Fagan, Ger Malone, Mags O'Brien and Gráinne O'Neill (staff), Rose O'Reilly (Women's Committee), Seán Roche (Retired Members), Joe Cunningham (Regional Secretary and Department Head), Martin Naughton (Head of Administration and Finance) and Sallyanne Kinahan (ICTU).

7. SIPTU, Dublin Region Executive Review, 2000–01; 2002–03. 'Labour backs union demands for improved statutory redundancy payments,' Liberty, May 2002; 'Glass workers shattered,' Liberty, Sep. 2002; 'Campaign for improvement in redundancy compensation,' Liberty, Dec. 2002.

8. SIPTU, Annual Report, 2001, p. 33; Annual Report, 2003; Region 2 Executive Review, 2001–02, 2003–04, 2004–05; 'Two new Regional Secretaries,' Newsline, Sep. 2000;

'New Immigrant Workers' Rights Unit demanded,' *Newsline*, Feb. 2001; 'IFI workers contest closure,' *Liberty*, Dec. 2002; 'Betrayed!' *Liberty*, Feb. 2005; 'Jennings heads to IFUT,' *Liberty*, Apr. 2007. McQuillan was Branch Assistant, Meath, 1978–1982, Branch Secretary, Meath, 1982–2001, and Branch Secretary, Aer Lingus, 2001–05, before his appointment as Sectoral Organiser.

9. SIPTU, Annual Report, 2003, p. 32; Region 3 West Executive Reviews, 2000–05, 'Unfair and square,' *Liberty*, Mar. 2003; 'Uniting to tackle site exploitation,' *Liberty*, Mar. 2005.

10. SIPTU, Region 4 (South-West), Executive Reports, 2000–05; 'Two new Regional Secretaries,' *Newsline*, Sep. 2000; 'Major jobs schemes rises out of ashes of Krups,' *Liberty*, Jan. 2002.

11. SIPTU, Annual Report, 2000, p. 44; Annual Report, 2001, p. 40–41; Annual Report, 2002, p. 33–4; Annual Report, 2003, p. 40–41; Annual Report, 2004, p. 45–7; Annual Report, 2005, p. 42–3; Region 5 (Northern) Executive Review, 2004–05; 'No new jeans deal,' *Newsline*, Jan. 2000; 'Loud and clear: End the violence,' *Newsline*, Jan. 2002; 'Richardson's gets results—but not for employees,' *Newsline*, June 2003; 'Man of peace,' *Newsline*, Nov. 2004; 'Concrete commitment,' *Newsline*, July 2005; 'Sudden death of union stalwart,' *Newsline*, Sep. 2006.

12. SIPTU, Annual Report, 2000, p. 37–8; Annual Report, 2001, p. 5, 34–7; Annual Report, 2002, p. 36–7; Annual Report, 2003, p. 33–5; Annual Report, 2004, p. 24, 36–8; Annual Report, 2005, p. 32; 'Linking the levellers,' *Newsline*, Mar. 2000; 'SIPTU co-sponsors equality statue in Galway,' *Newsline*, May 2000; 'West awake as equality emerges,' *Liberty*, Jan. 2002; 'Gender pay gap,' *Liberty*, Mar. 2003; 'Violence against women,' *Liberty*, Jan. 2004; 'More women to take seats on ICTU Executive,' *Liberty*, Sep. 2004; 'Reggie backs campaign against domestic violence,' *Liberty*, Mar. 2005. The statue of *Equality Emerging*, based on an idea of Eddie Higgins and Nuala Keher, has an inscription in three languages: *Briseadh na héagóra—Equality emerging—Hacia la igualdad.*

13. SIPTU, Annual Report, 2005, p. 35–7; Annual Report, 2006, p. 18, 53. Francis Devine, 'Equality How?: SIPTU Guide to Taking Cases under the Employment Equality Acts, 1998–2004,' and 'Equal Status Acts, 2000–2004.'

14. SIPTU, Annual Report, 2000, p. 41; Annual Report, 2001, p. 36–7; Annual Report, 2002, p. 36–7; 'Welfare unfair,' *Newsline*, May 2000; 'Anton's anti-racism acclaimed in award,' *Liberty*, 2002. McCabe was also recognised by Metro Media Éireann and Multicultural Awards in 2003.

15. SIPTU, Annual Report, 2002, p. 9–10; Annual Report, 2003, p. 34; Annual Report, 2004, p. 37–8; Annual Report, 2005, p. 10; Annual Report, 2006, p. 50; 'Migrant workers grossly exploited,' *Liberty*, Mar. 2004. It is interesting to note that Nolan Transport, New Ross, were subject to official complaint from the Polish Embassy over their employment of five Polish drivers.

16. SIPTU, Annual Report, 2000, p. 15–22; 'New deal on offer?' *Newsline*, Jan. 2000; 'It's a deal,' *Newsline*, Mar. 2000.

17. SIPTU, Annual Report, 2001, p. 11–22; Annual Report, 2002, p. 11–22; 'SIPTU stance yields positive outcome,' *Newsline*, Feb. 2001; 'Average take-home pay to rise by 35% under PPF deal,' *Liberty*, May 2002; 'Will McCreevy's Budget sink pay talks?' and 'McCreevy's latest DIRT dozen,' *Liberty*, Sep. 2002; 'Sustaining Progress,' *Liberty*, Mar.

2002; 'Priorities for the Minister for Finance,' *Liberty*, Dec. 2003.

18. SIPTU, Annual Report, 2004, p. 10–14, 18; 'New Agreement must protect workers' rights,' *Liberty*, Apr. 2004; 'Back into talks,' *Liberty*, June 2004; 'Statement from the NE Officers and Council,' *Liberty*, July 2004; 'Unions back national deal,' *Liberty*, Sep. 2004; 'SIPTU's 10-point pre-Budget demands,' *Liberty*, Nov. 2004.

19. SIPTU, Annual Report, 2005, p. 12–13.

20. SIPTU, Annual Report, 2005, p. 25–31; *Liberty*, Special Supplement, July 2006; 'National Agreement ratified,' *Liberty*, Sep. 2006; 'A Budget with mixed blessings,' *Liberty*, Dec. 2006; 'He promised little . . . and that's just what he delivered,' *Liberty*, Dec. 2007.

21. SIPTU, Annual Report, 2000, p. 34; Annual Report, 2001, p. 29–30; 'Lockout,' *Newsline*, May 2000; 'High rise' and 'The track record,' *Newsline*, Sep. 2000.

22. SIPTU, Annual Report, 2002, p. 30–31; 'Head to head on beef crisis,' *Newsline*, Feb. 2001.

23. SIPTU, Annual Report, 2003, p. 24–5; Annual Report, 2004, p. 27–31; 'Refuse staff reject bribe,' *Liberty*, Dec. 2003; 'No to Big Brother,' *Liberty*, July 2004; 'Security with safety,' *Liberty*, Sep. 2004.

24. SIPTU, Annual Report, 2005, p. 30; Annual Report, 2006, p. 38–9.

25. SIPTU, Annual Report, 2000, p. 35–6; Annual Report, 2001, p. 31–3; 'Breakthrough for home helps,' *Newsline*, Sep. 2000.

26. SIPTU, Annual Report, 2002, p. 31–4; Annual Report, 2003, p. 27–8, 30–31; Annual Report, 2004, p. 31–6; Annual Report, 2005, p. 31; Annual Report, 2006, 40–47; 'Bin the charge,' *Liberty*, Sep. 2003; 'Foot in mouth outbreak,' *Liberty*, Jan. 2004; 'No go!' *Liberty*, July 2004; 'Condition critical,' *Liberty*, Sep. 2004; 'What is to be done about the crisis in health care?' *Liberty*, Nov. 2004; 'The "left-wing" approach to health care is European norm,' *Liberty*, Dec. 2004; 'Freelance workers not entitled to collective bargaining says Competition Authority,' *Liberty*, Dec. 2005; 'Union opposes sale of hotels,' *Liberty*, Feb. 2006; 'We shall not be moved,' *Liberty*, Feb. 2007; 'Health service workers back "fighting fund" and "equal rights for agency workers",' *Liberty*, Dec. 2007.

27. SIPTU, Annual Report, 2001, p. 29; Annual Report, 2002, p. 30; Annual Report, 2003, p. 26–7; Annual Report, 2004, p. 31–4; Annual Report, 2005, p. 32–4; Annual Report, 2006, p. 24, 44–5; 'Servisair staff bag better wage terms,' *Newsline*, Jan. 2000; 'How low can you get!' *Liberty*, Jan. 2002; 'Airport dispute may escalate,' *Liberty*, Dec. 2003; 'Aer Lingus is vital state asset: No to sale—McQuillan,' *Liberty*, Jan. 2004; 'Shannon under siege,' *Liberty*, Mar. 2004; 'Newslib,' *Liberty*, July 2004. See Sweeney, *Selling Out?*

28. SIPTU, Annual Report, 2004, p. 28–9; Annual Report, 2005, p. 28–9; Annual Report, 2006, p. 13, 25–6; 'Rough waters ahead,' *Liberty*, Mar. 2004; 'Ferry action halted to allow for new talks,' *Liberty*, Dec. 2004; 'Standing up for Salvacion,' *Liberty*, Mar. 2005; 'Unfair sailing' and 'Time to call halt,' *Liberty*, Sep. 2005; 'Tackling race to bottom is union's bottom line' and 'Ferry angry,' *Liberty*, Nov. 2005; 'Standing up for decency,' 'United for justice' and 'Not just another industrial dispute,' *Liberty*, Dec. 2005; 'Union takes funds out of Bank of Ireland,' *Liberty*, Dec. 2006. See 'National Employment Rights Authority' at www.employmentrights.ie.

29. SIPTU, Annual Report, 2005, p. 26–7.

30. SIPTU, Annual Report, 2000, p. 33; Annual Report, 2001, p. 28; Annual Report, 2002, p. 28; 'No accommodation—without representation,' *Liberty*, Dec. 2002.

31. SIPTU, Annual Report, 2003, p. 23; Annual Report, 2004, p. 26; Annual Report, 2006, p. 37; *Liberty*, Apr. 2004.

32. SIPTU, Annual Report, 2000, p. 29–30; Annual Report, 2001, p. 20–25; Annual Report, 2002, p. 14–15, 26; Annual Report, 2003, p. 16–19.

33. SIPTU, Annual Report, 2006, p. 55; 'Brennan's strange idea of partnership,' *Liberty*, Jan. 2004.

34. SIPTU, Annual Report, 2001, p. 42; 'Union strengthens international links to protect seafarers, dockers,' *Newsline*, Sep. 2000; 'Union halts "slave ship" terror,' *Liberty*, Sep. 2002; 'Sweatships,' *Liberty*, Dec. 2002; 'ITF Inspectors expose sweat ships on Irish Sea,' *Liberty*, Nov. 2004; 'EU Ports Directive sunk,' *Liberty*, Feb. 2006. It was moved by Peter Lahay (ILWU, Canada) and Roberto Alarcón (CCUD, Argentina).

35. SIPTU, Annual Report, 2002, p. 41–2; Annual Report, 2003, p. 28–9, 43; 'Comrades in alms,' *Liberty*, May 2002; 'No to war,' *Liberty*, Mar. 2003; 'Tsunami crisis' and 'Time for Asia,' *Liberty*, Feb. 2005; 'Make poverty history,' *Liberty*, July 2005; 'To Shell or Connacht?' *Liberty*, Feb. 2006; ' Solidarność—z Solidarności,' *Liberty*, Dec. 2006.

36. SIPTU, Annual Report, 2000, p. 27; Annual Report, 2001, 11–19, 32; Annual Report, 2002, p. 16–, 33; Annual Report, 2005, p. 34; Annual Report, 2006, p. 41–2. Fruit of the Loom shed jobs in Dunglow (53), Milford (158), Malin (120), Raphoe (372) and Buncrana (640)—a huge impact on Co. Donegal. 'Offaly hit by major jobs blows,' *Newsline*, Feb. 2001; David Begg, 'The case for' and Roger Cole, 'The case against,' *Newsline*, Sep. 2002; 'Frankenstein buried,' *Newsline*, Mar. 2005; 'The Frankenstein Directive,' *Newsline*, Dec. 2005; 'Surgery for Frankenstein,' *Newsline*, Dec. 2006; SIPTU, 'The Lisbon Treaty: Issues for Workers' (2008), and 'The Lisbon Treaty: What Next?: Issues for Workers' (2008).

37. SIPTU, Annual Report, 2000, p. 36; Annual Report, 2001, p. 11; Annual Report, 2001, p. 11, 16–19; Annual Report, 2002, p. 17–19; Annual Report, 2003, p. 14–16, 31; Annual Report, 2004, p. 14–17; Annual Report, 2005, p. 15–18; Annual Report, 2006, p. 26–9; 'SIPTU donates site for housing co-op,' *Newsline*, May 2000; 'Pensions report "a mixed bag",' *Newsline*, Feb. 2001; 'Massive pensions rip-off,' *Liberty*, Dec. 2003; 'Breakthrough on pensions,' *Liberty*, Jan. 2004.

38. SIPTU, Annual Report, 2002, p. 32; Annual Report, 2003, p. 20–21, 30; Annual Report, 2004, p. 19–23; 'Campaign for improvements in redundancy compensation,' *Liberty*, Dec. 2002; 'Welcome for increased statutory redundancy,' *Liberty*, June 2003; 'Resisting the race to the bottom,' *Liberty*, June 2004. See Irish Trade Union Federation, *The TUF Guide to Labour Law for Union Representatives*.

39. SIPTU, Annual Report, 2005, p. 30–31; Annual Report, 2006, p. 25–6; 'New Department of Labour needed' and 'Strengthening the Labour Inspectorate,' *Liberty*, Mar. 2005. See Devine, *Enforcement of Employment Rights*.

40. SIPTU, Annual Report, 2000, p. 31–2; Annual Report, 2001, p. 25–7; Annual Report, 2002, p. 27–8; Annual Report, 2003, p. 22–3; Annual Report, 2004, p. 25; Annual Report, 2005, p. 23–4; Annual Report, 2006, p. 35–6; 'Plan for safer building sites,' *Newsline*, Mar. 2000; 'Stop death traps,' *Liberty*, Mar. 2003; 'Safety shocker,' *Liberty*, June 2003; 'New laws proposed,' *Liberty*, July 2004; 'A guide to the Safety, Health and Welfare at Work Act, 2005,' *Liberty*, Sep. 2005; 'Organised workplaces are safer

workplaces,' *Liberty*, Dec. 2006; 'Fire heroes mourned in Bray,' *Liberty*, Dec. 2007. Francis Devine, a tutor, was a member of the Committee. The codes were *Code of Practice on the Prevention of Workplace Bullying under the Safety, Health and Welfare at Work Act (1989)*, issued by the Health and Safety Authority, *Code of Practice Detailing Procedures for Addressing Bullying in the Workplace Made under the Industrial Relations Act (1990)*, issued by the Labour Relations Commission and *Code of Practice on Guidance on Prevention and Procedures for Dealing with Sexual Harassment and Harassment at Work Made under the Employment Equality Act (1998)*, issued by the Equality Authority. The HSA code was revised in 2005.

41. SIPTU, Annual Report, 2000, p. 12–13; Annual Report, 2001, p. 9; Annual Report, 2005, p. 8–10; Annual Report, 2006, p. 15–17; 'Click onto college,' *Liberty*, Nov. 2004; 'WIELD,' *Liberty*, July 2006. See 'SIPTU College' at www.siptucollege.ie.

42. SIPTU, Annual Report, 2001, p. 9–10; Annual Report, 2006, p. 10. The authors were David Jacobson, Terrence McDonough and Keith Warnock.

43. SIPTU, Annual Report, 2000, p. 43; Annual Report, 2002, p. 9; Annual Report, 2002, p. 38–9; Annual Report, 2003, p. 31, 39; Annual Report, 2005, p. 41; Annual Report, 2006, p. 63–5; 'Buncrana trade union pioneer remembered,' *Newsline*, Sep. 2000; 'Tressell's gable,' *Liberty*, May 2002; 'Opening night' and 'Remembering "Big Jim"', *Liberty*, Sep. 2002; 'Equity hits 50' and 'O'Donnell launches Clé Club,' *Liberty*, Dec. 2002; 'O'Casey comes home,' *Liberty*, Mar. 2003; Francis Devine, 'Remembering 1913,' *Liberty*, Sep. 2003; 'Tressell remembered,' *Liberty*, Dec. 2003; 'Connolly: More than a movie,' *Liberty*, Mar. 2005; 'Union to back Connolly film' and 'Slane poet commemorated in SIPTU's Meath offices,' *Liberty*, July 2006; 'Courage of 1907 strikers praised in Belfast,' *Liberty*, Dec. 2007. The speakers at the Tressell Festival included Jack O'Connor, Paddy Coughlan, Charles Callan and Francis Devine (SIPTU), Stan Newens (former British Labour MP) and John Nettleton (Liverpool Trades Council). The Larkin musical was written by Brian Gallagher and Shaun Purcell and produced by Brian Merriman. See Gray, *City in Revolt*, and Nevin, *Between Comrades*.

44. SIPTU, Annual Report, 2000, p. 39–4, 430; Annual Report, 2001, p. 37, 43; Annual Report, 2002, p. 36–7; Annual Report, 2003, p. 10, 35; Annual Report, 2004, p. 38–9; Annual Report, 2005, p. 39; Annual Report, 2006, p. 51; 'Older persons' charter seeks fairer society,' *Newsline*, May 2000; 'People with disabilities still lose out on jobs,' *Newsline*, Feb. 2001; 'Be at the heart of it,' *Liberty*, May 2002; 'Making a difference,' *Liberty*, Dec. 2003; 'A very similar kind of union,' *Liberty*, Sep. 2004; 'Who cares?' *Liberty*, July 2005; 'Caring for older people,' *Liberty*, July 2006. See, for example, Equality Authority, *Code of Practice for the Employment of People with Disabilities*.

45. SIPTU, Annual Report, 2001, p. 7; Annual Report, 2002, p. 6–7; Annual Report, 2004, p. 7; Annual Report, 2006, p. 10; 'Growing stronger' and 'Honouring Ledwidge,' *Liberty*, July 2004.

46. SIPTU, Annual Report, 2006, p. 11, 19, 63; 'Liberty Hall at 40,' *Liberty*, Mar. 2005; 'Building for the future,' *Liberty*, Nov. 2005; 'Remembering the labour movement in 1916,' *Liberty*,' July 2006; 'The rebuilding of Liberty Hall,' *Liberty*, Dec. 2006; 'Tall order,' *Liberty*, Dec. 2007. Devine and O'Riordan, *James Connolly, Liberty Hall and the Rising*.

47. SIPTU, Annual Report, 2002, p. 32–3; 'We're sick waiting' and 'Parties' positions on key workplace issues,' *Liberty,* May 2002; Fergal Bowers. 'The commitments,' *Liberty,* Mar. 2003.

48. SIPTU, Annual Report, 2003, p. 36–7; Annual Report, 2004, p. 40–41; 'New Leader aims to re-energise Labour,' *Liberty,* Dec. 2002; 'Yes to link with Labour but no to blank cheques!' *Liberty,* Sep. 2003.

49. SIPTU, Annual Report, 2005, p. 41; 'Up and running' and 'Labour for Europe,' *Liberty,* June 2004; *Liberty,* July 2006; *Liberty* General Election Special, May 2007.

Appendix 1 (p. 888–97)

1. Greaves, *The Irish Transport and General Workers' Union,* p. 327–41.

Appendix 6 (p. 997–1004)

1. De Rossa was a member of Democratic Left.

2. Morrissey was expelled with R. S. Anthony in 1931 and was Minister for Industry and Commerce (Fine Gael), 1948–51.

3. A TD who may have been a member of the ITGWU but whose membership cannot be verified is James Shannon, Wexford, 1927.

4. Butler left the Labour Party in 1927, ran as an independent, then joined Fine Gael, sitting in Seanad Éireann, 1938–57 and 1961–5.

5. Lipper was elected as Independent Labour.

6. Lyons defected from the ITGWU and was returned as an independent, moving to the right.

7. Morrissey sat as Independent Labour in 1932 and defected to Fine Gael in 1933, being re-elected until 1957.

8. O'Connell was elected as non-party, 1981, was Ceann Comhairle 1981–82, and was elected for Fianna Fáil, 1987–97.

9. O'Leary resigned as Party Leader in 1982 and was elected for Fine Gael, 1982–87.

10. Sherlock was elected for Sinn Féin the Workers' Party in 1981, for the Workers' Party in 1987 and for the Labour Party in 2002.

11. Treacy was a member of the Irish Shoe and Leather Workers until their merger with the ITGWU in 1977.

12. Maureen O'Carroll, Dublin North-Central, 1954–7, had been a teacher but is thought to have been a member of the WUI when subsequently working in Irish Hospitals Trust.

13. Desmond was sponsored by the WUI after 1969.

14. Dunne was returned as Independent Labour in 1961 but rejoined the Labour Party. He was a member of the ITGWU from 1967.

15. Pat Upton, TD for Dublin South-Central, 1992–97 and 1997–99, and Mary Upton, TD for Dublin South-Central, 1999–, were both members of the WUI (later FWUI) but were not sponsored by the FWUI or SIPTU.

16. Gilmore was elected for the Workers' Party in 1989, for Democratic Left in 1992 and for the Labour Party from 2002.

17. Lynch was elected for Democratic Left in 1992 and for the Labour Party from 2002.

18. McManus was elected for Democratic Left in 1992 and for the Labour Party in 2002. She is a member of the Irish Writers' Union, affiliated to SIPTU.

19. Rabbitte was elected for the Workers' Party in 1989, for Democratic Left in 1992 and for the Labour Party in 2002.
20. It has been suggested that the following were also members of the union, but it cannot be determined for certain: Eleanor Butler, 1948–51; John Gaffney, 1936–8; Ann Gallagher, 1993–7; and Patrick Tierney, 1954–7.
21. Burke was refused sponsorship by the National Executive Council of the ITGWU but must have been a member in order to have applied.
22. Foran is listed as an independent, 1922–34.
23. Kirwan sat as an independent.
24. Fitt was the only member of the ITGWU after the SDLP was formed with Cooper, Currie, Devlin and Hume.
25. Desmond was appointed to the European Court of Auditors, 1994–2000.
26. Geraghty substituted for de Rossa, Democratic Left.

BIBLIOGRAPHY

— Boyd, Andrew, *The Rise of the Irish Trade Unions, 1729–1970,* Tralee: Anvil Books, 1972.

— Bradley, Daniel G., *Farm Labourers' Irish Struggle, 1900–1976,* Belfast: Athol Books, 1988.

— Clarkson, J. Dunsmore, *Labour and Nationalism in Ireland,* New York: Columbia University Press, 1925; revised 1970.

— Cody, Séamus, O'Dowd, John, and Rigney, Peter, *The Parliament of Labour:* 100 *Years of the Dublin Council of Trade Unions,* Dublin: DCTU, 1986.

— Congress of Irish Unions, *A History of the Foundation of Comhar Ceárd Éireann,* Dublin: CIU, 1945.

— Croke, Norman, and Devine, Francis, *James Connolly Labour College, 1919–1921,* Dublin: Irish Labour History Society, 2007.

— Cunningham, John, *Labour in the West of Ireland: Working Life and Struggle, 1890–1914,* Belfast: Athol Books, 1995.

— Curran, Owen, *Two Hundred Years of Trade Unionism, 1809–2009,* Dublin: Irish Print Group, SIPTU, 2009.

— Devine, Francis, *Acting for the Actors: Dermot Doolan and the Organisation of Irish Actors and Performing Artists, 1947–1985* (Studies in Irish Labour History, 3), Dublin: Irish Labour History Society, 1997.

— Devine, Francis, *An Eccentric Chemistry: Michael Moynihan and Labour in Kerry, 1917–2001* (Studies in Irish Labour History, 10), Dublin: Irish Labour History Society, 2004.

— Devine, Francis, *Enforcement of Employment Rights: A Discussion,* Dublin: SIPTU, 2005.

— Devine, Francis, *Organising the Union: A Centenary of SIPTU, 1909–2009,* Dublin: SIPTU, 2009.

— Devine, Francis, Lane, Fintan, and Puirséil, Niamh (eds.), *Essays in Labour History: A Festschrift for Elizabeth and J. W. Boyle,* Dublin: Irish Academic Press, 2008.

— Devine, Francis, and O'Riordan, Manus, *James Connolly, Liberty Hall and the* 1916 *Rising* (Studies in Irish Labour History, 11), Dublin: SIPTU, 2006.

— Devlin, Paddy, *'Yes, We Have No Bananas': Outdoor Relief in Belfast, 1920–39,* Belfast: Blackstaff Press, 1981.

— Fleming, N. C., and O'Day, Alan, *The Longman Handbook of Modern Irish History since* 1800, Harlow (Middx): Longman, 2005, p. 489–515.

— Fox, R. M., *Jim Larkin: The Rise of the Underman,* London: Lawrence and Wishart, 1957.

— Gaughan, J. Anthony (ed.), *Memoirs of Senator James G. Douglas, 1887–1954: Concerned Citizen* (Dublin: UCD Press, 1998).

— Gaughan, J. Anthony, *Thomas Johnson, 1872–1963: First Leader of the Labour Party in Dáil Éireann,* Dublin: Kingdom Books, 1980.

— Geraghty, Hugh, *William Patrick Partridge and his Times, 1874–1917*, Dublin: Curlew Books, 2003.
— Gray, John, *City in Revolt: James Larkin and the Belfast Dock Strike of 1907* (second edition), Belfast: Linen Hall Library, and Dublin: SIPTU, 2007.
— Greaves, C. Desmond, *The Irish Transport and General Workers' Union: The Formative Years, 1909–1923*, Dublin: Gill & Macmillan, 1982.
— Hyman, Richard, *The Workers' Union, 1898–1925*, Oxford: Oxford University Press, 1971.
— Irish Transport and General Workers' Union, *Multi-National Companies and Conglomerates: The Problems for Trade Unions* (Proceedings of a Seminar held in Dún Laoghaire, 14–16 November 1969), Dublin: ITGWU, 1969.
— Irish Transport and General Workers' Union, *The Attempt to Smash the Irish Transport and General Workers' Union*, Dublin: National Executive, ITGWU, 1924.
— Irish Transport and General Workers' Union, *The Question Posed*, Dublin: ITGWU, 1971.
— Jones, Mary, *These Obstreperous Lassies: A History of the Irish Women Workers' Union*, Dublin: Gill & Macmillan, 1988.
— Keogh, Dermot, *The Rise of the Irish Working Class: The Dublin Trade Union Movement and Labour Leadership, 1890–1914*, Belfast: Appletree Press, 1982.
— Kilmurray, Evanne, *Fight, Starve or Emigrate: A History of the Unemployed Associations in the 1950s*, Dublin: Larkin Unemployed Centre, 1989.
— Larkin, Emmet, *James Larkin, 1976–1947: Irish Labour Leader*, London: Routledge and Kegan Paul, 1965.
— Larkin, James, *In the Footsteps of Big Jim: A Family History*, Dublin: Blackwater Press, 1996.
— Lee, J. J., *Ireland, 1912–1985: Politics and Society*, Cambridge: Cambridge University Press, 1985.
— Lynch, David, *Radical Politics in Modern Ireland: The Irish Socialist Republican Party, 1896–1904*, Dublin: Irish Academic Press, 2005.
— McCabe, Anton, and Devine, Francis, *'Navigating a Lone Channel': Stephen McGonagle and Labour Politics in Derry, 1914–1997*, Dublin: SIPTU, 2000 (reprinted from *Saothar*, 22 (1997), p. 139–52).
— McCamley, Bill, *Dublin's Tram Workers, 1872–1945: A History of the Dublin United Tramways Company (DUTC)*, Dublin: published by the author, 2008.
— McCamley, Bill, *The Third James: James Fearon, 1874–1924: An Unsung Hero of Our Struggle*, Dublin: SIPTU, 2000.
— McCarthy, Charles, *The Decade of Upheaval: Irish Trade Unions in the 1960s*, Dublin: Institute of Public Administration, 1973.
— Morgan, Austen, *Labour and Partition: The Belfast Working Class, 1905–23*, London: Pluto Press, 1991.
— Morrissey, Thomas, *William Martin Murphy*, Dundalk: Dundalgan Press, 1997.
— Morrissey, Thomas J., *William O'Brien, 1881–1968: Socialist, Republican, Dáil Deputy, Editor and Trade Union Leader*, Dublin: Four Courts Press, 2007.
— Murphy, Patrick, *The Federation of Rural Workers, 1946–1979: A Selection of Pages from the History of the FRW, 1946–1979: The Twilight Years, 1943–1946; The Early Years, 1946–1951*, Dublin: FWUI, 1988.

— Nevin, Donal (ed.), *Between Comrades: James Connolly: Letters and Correspondence*, 1889–1916, Dublin: Gill & Macmillan, 2007.

— Nevin, Donal, *James Connolly: A Full Life*, Dublin: Gill & Macmillan, 2005.

— Nevin, Donal (ed.), *James Larkin: Lion of the Fold*, Dublin: Gill & Macmillan, 1998.

— Nevin, Donal (ed.), 1913, *Jim Larkin and the Dublin Lock-Out*, Dublin: Workers' Union of Ireland, 1964.

— Nevin, Donal (ed.), *Trade Union Century*, Cork and Dublin: Mercier Press, for RTÉ, 1994.

— Newby, Andrew G., *The Life and Times of Edward McHugh (1853–1915): Land Reformer, Trade Unionist and Labour Activist*, Lampeter (Ceredigion): Edwin Mellen Press, 2004.

— Newsinger, John, *Rebel City: Larkin, Connolly and the Dublin Labour Movement*, London: Merlin Press, 2004.

— O'Brien, William (as told to Edward MacLysaght), *Forth the Banners Go: Reminiscences of William O'Brien*, Dublin: Three Candles, 1969.

— Ó Cathasaigh, P. [Seán O'Casey], *The Story of the Irish Citizen Army*, Dublin: Maunsel, 1919.

— O'Connor, Emmet, *A Labour History of Ireland*, 1824–1960, Dublin: Gill & Macmillan, 1992.

— O'Riordan, Manus, *Next to the Revolution, The Greatest Event of 1916: Liberty Hall as a Cultural Centre: The Early Years*, Dublin: SIPTU, 2002.

— O'Riordan, Manus, *The Voice of a Thinking, Intelligent Movement: James Larkin Junior and the Ideological Modernisation of Irish Trade Unionism* (second edition), Dublin: Irish Labour History Society, 2001. (Originally published as 'James Larkin Junior and the forging of a thinking, intelligent movement,' *Saothar*, 19 (1994), p. 53–68.)

— O'Shannon, Cathal (ed.), *Fifty Years of Liberty Hall: The Golden Jubilee of the ITGWU*, 1909–1959, Dublin: Three Candles, 1959.

— Patterson, Henry, *Class Conflict and Sectarianism in Belfast: The Protestant Working Class and the Belfast Labour Movement*, 1868–1920, Belfast: Blackstaff Press, 1980.

— Pollock, Hugh M., *Case Studies in Industrial Relations*, Dublin: School and College Publishing, 1983.

— Pollock, Hugh M., *Reform of Industrial Relations*, Dublin: O'Brien Press, 1982.

— Puirséil, Niamh, *The Irish Labour Party*, 1922–73, Dublin: UCD Press, 2007.

— Redmond, Seán, The Irish Municipal Employees' Trade Union, 1883–1983, Dublin: IMETU, 1983.

— Robbins, Frank, *Under the Starry Plough: Recollections of the Irish Citizen Army*, Dublin: Academy Press, 1977.

— Roberts, Ruaidhrí, and Clarke, Dardis, *The Story of the People's College*, Dublin: O'Brien Press, 1986.

— Sexton, James, *Sir James Sexton, Agitator: The Life of the Dockers' MP: An Autobiography*, London: Faber and Faber, 1936.

— Sheehy Skeffington, Andrée, *Skeff: A Life of Owen Sheehy Skeffington*, 1909-1970, Dublin: Lilliput Press, 1991.

— Sweeney, Paul, *Selling Out?: Privatisation in Ireland*, Dublin: New Island Publications, 2004.

— Swift, John P., *John Swift: An Irish Dissident*, Dublin: Gill & Macmillan, 1991.

— Taplin, Eric, *The Dockers' Union: A History of the National Union of Dock Labourers, 1889–1922*, Leicester: Leicester University Press, 1984.

— Trade Union Federation, *The TUF Guide to Labour Law for Union Representatives*, Dublin: ITUF, 2003.

— Walker, Brian M., *Parliamentary Election Results in Ireland, 1918–92: Irish Elections to Parliaments and Parliamentary Assemblies at Westminster, Belfast, Dublin, Strasbourg*, Belfast and Dublin: Royal Irish Academy, 1992.

— Ward-Perkins, Sarah (ed.), *Select Guide to Trade Union Records in Dublin, with Details of Unions Operating in Ireland to 1970*, Dublin: Irish Manuscripts Commission, 1996.

— Wayne, Naomi, *Labour Law in Ireland: A Guide to Workers' Rights*, Dublin: Kincora Press, in association with ITGWU, 1980.

— White, Jack Robert, *Misfit: An Autobiography*, London: Jonathan Cape, 1930; reprinted Dublin: Livewire Publications, 2005.

— Yeates, Pádraig, *Lockout: Dublin, 1913*, Dublin: Gill & Macmillan, 2000.

INDEX